KT-469-643

# WOMEN IN
# AMERICAN HISTORY

# Clio Bibliography Series No. 5

*Abstracts from the periodicals data base of the*
**American Bibliographical Center**

**Eric H. Boehm, Editor**
**Joyce Duncan Falk, Executive Editor**
**Pamela R. Byrne, Managing Editor**

*Users of the Clio Bibliography Series may refer to current issues of*
America: History and Life *and* Historical Abstracts
*for continuous bibliographic coverage of the subject areas*
*treated by each individual volume in the series.*

# WOMEN
## in American History
## A BIBLIOGRAPHY

FCH LEARNING CENTRE
UNIVERSITY OF GLOUCESTERSHIRE
Swindon Road
Cheltenham GL50 4AZ
Tel: 01242 532913

**Cynthia E. Harrison**

Editor

**Anne Firor Scott**

Introduction

**Pamela R. Byrne**

Managing Editor

Santa Barbara, California
Oxford, England

**Library of Congress Cataloging in Publication Data**

Harrison, Cynthia.
    Women in American history.

    (Clio bibliography series; 5)
    Includes indexes.
    1. Women—United States—History—Periodicals—
Indexes. 2. Women—Canada—History—Periodicals—
Indexes. I. Title.
Z7962.H37  [HQ1410]  016.30141'2'0973  78-26194
ISBN 0-87436-260-1

Ref 016 305420973

67930

© 1979 by ABC-Clio, Inc.

All rights reserved.
This book or any part thereof may not be reproduced in any form
without the written permission of the publishers.

American Bibliographical Center—Clio Press, Inc.
2040 Alameda Padre Serra, Box 4397
Santa Barbara, California

European Bibliographical Center—Clio Press
Woodside House, Hinksey Hill
Oxford OXI 5BE, England

Design by Don French
Printed and bound in the United States of America

# Table of Contents

# PREFACE

*Women in American History* contains 3395 abstracts and is the fifth volume in the Clio Bibliography Series. Although the abstracts come primarily from volumes one through fourteen (1964-1977) of *America: History and Life* (AHL), more than 350 abstracts not yet published in AHL have also been included. This work may be updated by consulting subsequent volumes of AHL. The American Bibliographical Center also plans periodic supplements to *Women in American History*.

The abstracts in this volume are of articles in some 550 periodicals and five collections published from 1963 to 1976. Every effort was made to ensure complete coverage of each title on the list of peridocals, but this was not always possible. Gaps, ranging from single issues to several volumes of a few obscure or peripheral journals, may have occurred. Because of the varying time lags between publication of a journal and receipt of abstracts, the inclusion of 1976 material is especially uneven. The list of periodicals indicates the year AHL began covering each journal.

In selecting the abstracts from the volumes of AHL, I tried to include any article that might be of value to an historian of women in the United States or Canada. Had I interpreted this criterion too broadly, however, I would have finished by reproducing the original volumes of AHL. Therefore, I limited my selection to certain categories of articles. I chose all those abstracts that dealt explicitly with women: women's organizations, woman suffrage, their image, ideology, education, politics, legal status, sex roles, religion, employment, and social problems. I also selected those abstracts that concerned marriage and the family, but not articles that dealt exclusively with children, and I included abstracts on consumerism, works by and about individual women (including eyewitness accounts and travel memoirs, but not, obviously, every abstract of an article written by a woman), abstracts of articles about women novelists and fiction that dealt markedly with the subject of women's lives, and abstracts of works concerning fertility of certain groups, but not those about population control as a national policy.

The abstracts presented many problems peculiar to the subject of women. For example, until recently, historians who should have included material on women in their work did not; furthermore, it seems likely that even when the historian did, the abstracter for one reason or another neglected to mention this facet of the article. Therefore, no doubt, articles which should be included in this bibliography are not. A subsidiary problem concerns abstracts of articles about certain groups in which women played a large part, but where they are not mentioned in the abstract. In some cases, for instance articles on the profession of the teaching of children, nursing, settlement work, and social work in the Progressive Era, the abstract is included, whether women were mentioned or not, under the premise that the participation of women was critical. I did not include discussions of teaching or social work as professions in the post-1945 period unless they dealt with women as professionals. Although I attempted to be consistent, I cannot pretend that I succeeded in every instance. In any case, the abstracts that appear touch on the full range of women's experience in the United States and Canada.

The subject matter and chronology of the abstract determines its location in this bibliography. Abstracts that cover two or more chronological sections are located under the heading United States General. The subsections labelled General contain abstracts that span two or more of the subject sections without clearly emphasizing one or the other. For example, an abstract on the sex roles of women on the frontier during 1800-1850 would appear in the General section under the main heading Social Sphere. The regional sections contain material of a strictly local or regional scope, including memoirs, eyewitness accounts, biographies of individual women, travel descriptions, and demographics.

The reader can gain additional access to the abstracts, which are arranged topically and chronologically, by using the subject and author indexes which follow the text. In the Subject Profile Index (SPIndex), a complete profile of each abstract appears an average of four times, listed by subject, geographic, or biographic descriptors, followed by the date of the period covered by the article. The list of periodicals and list of abstracters follow the indexes.

We are fortunate that Anne Firor Scott, professor of history at Duke University, noted for her important work on the history of women and her activism on behalf of equal opportunity, has written the introduction. Her discussion of the field of women's history provides a valuable context for the use of this volume.

I would like to acknowldege the contributions of the principal editorial staff in the production of this book. Pamela R. Byrne, the managing editor of the Clio Bibliography Series, contributed an enormous amount to this volume while maintaining an unfailingly cooperative and cheerful disposition. She edited, classified, and indexed the entries, coordinated the work with the Data Processing Services Department, and managed the production aspects throughout; she was assisted in the editing, classifying, and indexing by Ann Wiederrecht, a doctoral candidate in American History at the University of California at Santa Barbara. Joyce Duncan Falk, the director of the American Bibliographical Center and executive editor of the Clio Bibliography Series, who holds general responsibility for the series, consulted on classification, indexing, and the selection of abstracts not yet published in AHL. Together, they did a major portion of the work, and so this book represents a cooperative effort in the truest sense. The technical services were provided by the Data Processing Services Department under the supervision of Kenneth H. Baser, Director, and Cheryl Wittenauer, Production Supervisor. A special acknowledgement goes to the abstracters whose initial work enabled this volume to be produced. Finally, I offer yet one more note of appreciation to my husband, Richard J. Peppin, who provided encouragement and assistance of every kind.

CYNTHIA E. HARRISON

*Columbia University and*
*Institute for Research in History*

*Cynthia Harrison is a fellow in Governmental Studies at the Brookings Institute for one year beginning August 1979 and is a member of the Institute for Research in History. A doctoral candidate in history at Columbia University, she is completing a dissertation on "Federal Policy Concerning Women from 1945-1966" under the direction of William E. Leuchtenburg. Ms. Harrison is the editor of* Women's Movement Media *(1975) and currently chairs the National NOW Credit Task Force.*

# INTRODUCTION

From time to time over the years it has occurred to people, historians and others, that women have a history which is somewhat different from that of men, that life experience is shaped as much by sex as by race or class, and that the past is bound to be misunderstood if it is described only through the records created by men. Only in the past decade, however, has "women's history" attained the dignity of a field of study in American historiography, with all the attendant paraphernalia of courses, departmental slots, learned journals, national conferences, dissertations, fellowships and the like. The number of practicing historians of women has risen exponentially in the past fifteen years, and most of these, quite logically, are young.

Both the causes and the consequences of this extremely rapid development of a new field of study are of more than passing interest to those who like to reflect upon the sociology of knowledge. Doubtless the reasons for this sudden burgeoning are more complex than we yet know, but at least two are clear. First, the resurgent feminist movement, like its predecessor, stimulated widespread curiosity among its followers about the women who had gone before: how had they lived? how did they feel about their place in the society? did they suffer from imputations of inferiority? did they fight or submit? what work did they do? what part did they play in the creation of the communities which made up American society? It was at once exhilarating and discouraging to discover that nearly every feminist issue of the 1960's had already been discussed in the 1850's.

Much of the impetus for the study of women's past thus came initially from outside the historical fraternity, and understandably this made many of its members uneasy. Was this after all "real history" or a political movement masquerading as scholarship? Did women, who played so small a part in politics and diplomacy in time past, truly have a history worth studying? Further, many male historians found feminism a hundred years ago no more appealing than the feminism that was just then upsetting the complacency of the white male club which had dominated the American historical profession since its beginning. In time the male historians divided into three groups. A few found this new field of study challenging and joined the research effort with enthusiasm, or at least began to read and incorporate the work of women's historians into their thinking. A large middle group viewed the whole thing as a necessary evil which they could accept so long as no one made them really think about it or read the research as it was published. A few labelled the whole movement a fad and condemned what they could not or would not try to understand.

It was fortunate, therefore, that the second impetus to the study of women's history came from inside the profession. Beginning in the 1930's, and slowly gaining strength, there was developing what has been called cultural history, the effort to apply some of the tools of the anthropologist to the past. (The introduction to Caroline F. Ware, ed., *The Cultural Approach to History*, New York: Columbia U. Pr., 1940 is as good a statement of the nature of cultural history as I have ever found. It should be pondered by historians of women.) Then, after the second World War, French and English demographic studies reenvigorated social history and reshaped the study of family history. Both these trends fed into the development of women's history, for the effort to analyze cultures with anthropological tools led inevitably to questions about sex roles, and the study of the part women played in the formation and maintenance of cultures. Demographic studies and family studies also required close attention to women.

As we move forward into the 1980's, it is clear that women's history is in process of achieving a firm scholarly base and is moving toward greater conceptual clarity and sophistication. A new field that has developed rapidly is bound to be uneven, and there is plenty of chaff but, more important, there is an ever-growing amount of wheat in the scholarly productions of this field. The future is promising, and the boldest scholars of women's past are asserting that much of our social history will have to be rewritten to accommodate what we are learning about the way social movements have developed and the way women have shaped community life.

If this fundamental reassessment is in fact to happen, certain prerequisites are necessary: the existence and accessibility of primary data, tools with which to collect and analyze that data, standards by which research can be evaluated, opportunities for scholars to exchange ideas, and the encouragement and interest of historians in related fields. All these necessities, in varying degree, are coming into being.

In a rapidly developing field, periodical literature is of the first importance, since it is there that new ideas first appear, there that the fully developed monographs are first foreshadowed, there that promising talents first appear. It is often from periodicals that skeptics are exposed to new ideas and new data. It is a piece of very good fortune, therefore, that the American Bibliographical Center, which has established itself as the leading provider of historical abstracts in this country, has chosen to publish a specialized collection of 3395 abstracts of articles dealing with women, drawn from the more than 64,000 abstracts published in *America: History and Life*, Volumes 1-14.

In order to make sure that nothing relevant to women's history was overlooked, a wide net was cast into the sea of abstracts. It brought in every article even remotely touching upon the subjects of women, family, or sex. These come from dozens of fields: sociology, anthropology, literature, demography, religion, economics, statistics, comparative studies, medicine, psychology, politics—to list a few. Their subject matter covers a broad spectrum, ranging from bibliography to spiritualism, from prostitution to utopia. There are review articles, archival articles, primary documents, autobiographies, biographies, theoretical constructs, polemics, and interpretation. Since relationships between the sexes have always presented and perhaps always will present a complex social problem, contemporary materials on that issue have been included.

Leafing through this mass one touches old subjects and new ones: women's work in all its manifold aspects, including the largely unstudied question of nineteenth-century professional women; women in the churches; women as institution builders; as reformers; Socialists; Populists; labor organizers; scholars; community workers; teachers. There are articles about the family, about the Civil War, about the perennial question of how domesticity came to be a major value in nineteenth-century America, as well as articles which delineate alternatives to "traditional" family life. There are particularly interesting materials dealing with the almost untouched subject of women in agriculture, and many dealing with women in the westward movement. Useful primary sources are identified, and the rich (and often overlooked) resources of local history journals are made available.

These abstracts are drawn from an international body of periodicals dealing with the history and interdisciplinary study of American culture. In addition to the basic list of history journals covering the United States and Canada, *America: History and Life* (AHL) also covers scholarly journals in the related social sciences and humanities. Beginning with volume 11 of AHL two kinds of abstracts began to appear, one a precis of the article in question, the other a simple annotative sentence for articles drawn from journals less central to the study of history. The abstracts are intended to be descriptive rather than evaluative, though inevitably in some cases evaluation is implied.

No scholar embarking on a new study dealing with women, or working on an old subject, should fail to examine this reference, and no teacher in search of fresh materials should overlook its potential value. The young scholar in search of a topic will find ideas here that need further investigation, and some aspiring sociologist could do a fine study of the patterns of subject matter appearing here, associated with the date of publication.

This bibliography documents the development of scholarship in women's history over the past fifteen years. Predictably the largest number of articles are from the recent past, and taken together they reflect both what has been done and what has not yet been undertaken.

Close study of the subject breakdown of articles in each chronological period will reveal a good deal about the direction of scholarly interest and will suggest to the alert some important lacunae. The subject breakdown does not bear out the often repeated assertion that most historical attention has concentrated on women's right and feminism. Articles dealing with the frontier, the Civil War, religion, sex roles, and employment together make up a much larger body of the periodical literature noted here than women's rights. There is an astonishing neglect, relatively speaking, of women's organizations and of women as institution builders. Southern women are also relatively less thoroughly studied than those from the Northeast and the West, and in Canadian materials Quebec seems to have attracted a disproportionate amount of attention.

Given the catholicity which governed the choice of abstracts, only a rigorous system of classification could make such variety useful. Fortunately such a system is provided. Within a broad chronological framework, subject areas are carefully defined, and the system of numbering is such that abstracts on any subject are easily tracked. Once found, the abstracts are usually adequate for a judgment as to whether one wishes to seek the original article. Some have a particularly helpful notation as to whether the article in question is based upon primary sources. The index is excellent. The publication of this volume should stimulate a great leap forward in the study of women, past and present.

ANNE FIROR SCOTT

*Duke University*

*Anne Firor Scott, Professor of History at Duke University, is the author of* Women in American Life *(1970),* The Southern Lady *(1970), and* One Half the People *(1974) and the editor of* The American Woman: Who Was She? *(1971). Professor Scott has been a senior fellow at the Institute for Southern History at Johns Hopkins University and has held two National Endowment for the Humanities fellowships.*

# List of Abbreviations

| | |
|---|---|
| A | Author-prepared Abstract |
| Acad | Academy, Académie, Academia |
| Agric | Agriculture, Agricultural |
| AIA | Abstracts in Anthropology |
| Akad | Akademie |
| Am | America, American |
| Ann | Annals, Annales, Annual, Annali |
| Anthrop | Anthropology, Anthropological |
| Arch | Archives |
| Archaeol | Archaeology, Archaeological |
| Art | Article |
| Assoc | Association, Associate |
| Biblio | Bibliography, Bibliographical |
| Biog | Biography, Biographical |
| Bol | Boletim, Boletín |
| Bull | Bulletin |
| c | century (in index) |
| ca | circa |
| Can | Canada, Canadian, Canadien |
| Cent | Century |
| Coll | College |
| Com | Committee |
| Comm | Commission |
| Comp | Compiler |
| DAI | Dissertation Abstracts International |
| Dept | Department |
| Dir | Director, Direktor |
| Econ | Economy, Econom-. |
| Ed | Editor, Edition |
| Educ | Education, Educational |
| Geneal | Genealogy, Genealogical, Généalogique |
| Grad | Graduate |
| Hist | History, Hist-. |
| IHE | Indice Histórico Español |

| | |
|---|---|
| Illus | Illustrated, Illustration |
| Inst | Institute, Institut-. |
| Int | International, Internacional, Internationaal, Internationaux, Internazionale |
| J | Journal, Journal-prepared Abstract |
| Lib | Library, Libraries |
| Mag | Magazine |
| Mus | Museum, Musée, Museo |
| Nac | Nacional |
| Natl | National, Nationale |
| Naz | Nazionale |
| Phil | Philosophy, Philosophical |
| Photo | Photograph |
| Pol | Politics, Political, Politique, Político |
| Pr | Press |
| Pres | President |
| Pro | Proceedings |
| Publ | Publishing, Publication |
| Q | Quarterly |
| Rev | Review, Revue, Revista, Revised |
| Riv | Rivista |
| Res | Research |
| S | Staff-prepared Abstract |
| Sci | Science, Scientific |
| Secy | Secretary |
| Soc | Society, Société, Sociedad, Società |
| Sociol | Sociology, Sociological |
| Tr | Transactions |
| Transl | Translator, Translation |
| U | University, Universi-. |
| US | United States |
| Vol | Volume |
| Y | Yearbook |

Abbreviations also apply to feminine and plural forms.
Abbreviations not noted above are based on *Webster's Third New International Dictionary*
and the *United States Government Printing Office Style Manual.*

# 1. Research and Teaching

## General

*(including historiography, meetings, and women's history curricula)*

1. Banner, Lois W. ON WRITING WOMEN'S HISTORY. *J. of Interdisciplinary Hist. 1971 2(2): 347-358.* Reviews recent studies and reprints and discusses various approaches to the study of women's history; studies of male attitudes; studies of women's influence upon male-directed power; and studies of extra-legal, conventional modes of female action and response. What is needed are definitions and analyses of women's roles and the ways in which they have acted out these roles in particular periods and cultures. This must be done from a perspective which avoids the male prejudice found in so much writing on the subject. 2 notes.                                                         E. J. Hundert

2. Baxter, Annette K. WOMEN'S STUDIES AND AMERICAN STUDIES: THE USES OF THE INTERDISCIPLINARY. *Am. Q. 1974 26(4): 433-439.* Review essay of two works which have adopted the interdisciplinary approach toward Women's and American Studies: Alice Crozier, *The Novels of Harriet Beecher Stowe* (New York: Oxford U. Press, 1973), and Gail Thain Parker, *The Oven Birds: American Women on Womanhood, 1820-1920* (Garden City: Doubleday Anchor Books, 1972).                                                         C. W. Olson

3. Benson, Ruth Crego. WOMEN'S STUDIES: THEORY AND PRACTICE. *AAUP Bull. 1972 58(3): 283-286.* Women's studies attempts to counteract the absence of women in traditional curriculum and to correct the distorted view of women presented by society at large and by college courses reflecting that view. Most women's studies courses are multidisciplinary and taught by women. There is disagreement about whether women's studies should constitute a separate department or be integrated with other departments. Classroom experience suggests that an important by-product is the training of female students to deal with the chauvinism and sexism of most of their teachers and fellow students.                                                         J. M. McCarthy

4. Blewett, Mary. WOMEN IN HISTORY: A HISTORY THROUGH FILM APPROACH. *Film and Hist. 1974 4(4): 12-15, 20.* Discusses the portrayal of women in films.                                                         S

5. Brown, Richard Maxwell. THE FORTIETH ANNUAL MEETING. *J. of Southern Hist. 1975 41(1): 59-88.* Summary of the meeting of the Southern Historical Association held in Dallas, Texas, 6-9 November 1974. Describes subject matter, speakers, audience responses, and anecdotes from the 47 regular sessions, 27 of which focused on Southern history, including the antebellum South, the Civil War and its aftermath, aspects of the New South, slavery, black history and racism, and women in the South.                                                         S

6. Burki, Mary Ann Mason. WOMEN IN THE NINETEENTH CENTURY AS SEEN THROUGH HISTORY AND LITERATURE. *Hist. Teacher 1975 8(2): 193-198.* Discusses a course at San Francisco State University which draws upon history and the novel to probe 19th-century middle-class attitudes about women in the United States and Great Britain. This approach provides an opportunity to understand that century in broad social context, and to appreciate the survival of attitudes into the present. Note.                                                         P. W. Kennedy

7. Burnham, John C. AMERICAN HISTORIANS AND THE SUBJECT OF SEX. *Societas—A R. of Social Hist. 1972 2(4): 307-316.* Most US history on the subject of sex deals with the family, temperance, and other reform movements such as women's suffrage. William L. O'Neill's *Divorce in the Progressive Era* (Yale U. Pr., 1967) is an exception. David Pivar has shown "how the mainstream of the American reform impulse after the Civil War went into the crusade against prostitution and social impurity of all sorts." 27 notes.                                                         E. P. Stickney

8. Carroll, Berenice A. MARY BEARD'S "WOMAN AS FORCE IN HISTORY": A CRITIQUE. *Massachusetts R. 1972 13(1/2): 125-143.* Mary Ritter Beard's (1876-1958) *Woman as Force in History* (New York: Macmillan, Collier Books, 1962) was first published in 1946 and received sympathetic treatment from lay critics, but was coldly received by professional historians. After a decade and a half of oblivion, the book was reissued in paperback in 1962 and is now enjoying a revival of interest. Mary Beard denied that women had been subjugated throughout history and condemned the feminists who propagated the myth of female subjection. She portrayed women in an active and dynamic role, contending that they were a civilizing force in the history of civilization. The book, with all its conceptual defects, is an important work of historiography that blazed the trail for the writing and development of women's history as a separate historical discipline. Based on secondary sources; 16 notes.                                                         G. Kurland

9. Daniels, Arlene Kaplan. FEMINIST PERSPECTIVES IN SOCIOLOGICAL RESEARCH. *Sociol. Inquiry 1975 45(2-3): 340-380.* Discusses current trends in sociology and the ways in which a feminist perspective contributes to the sociology of knowledge.

10. Degler, Carl N. *WOMAN AS FORCE IN HISTORY* BY MARY BEARD. *Daedalus 1974 103(1): 67-73. Woman as Force in History* (New York, 1946) never caught on, even during the current period of interest in women's history. Not a traditional feminist, Mary R. Beard did not accept conventional feminist interpretations of history. Rejecting the notion that women were subjected in the past, Beard preferred to emphasize the achievements of women. Primary and secondary sources; 6 notes.                                                         E. McCarthy

11. Ehrlich, Carol. THE WOMAN BOOK INDUSTRY. *Am. J. of Sociol. 1973 78(4): 1030-1044.* "This article reviews and evaluates 17 recent products of the woman book industry. The books are all either by female authors or, if coedited or coauthored, by at least one female. The products include monographs, edited readers, works for general audiences, and textbooks. All 17 were issued for the first time in 1971 or 1972."                                                         J

12. Eichler, Margrit. A REVIEW OF SELECTED RECENT LITERATURE ON WOMEN. *Can. R. of Sociol. and Anthrop. 1972 9(1): 86-96.* A descriptive and critical review article covering 14 books on women published in 1970-71. Examines three groups: books for the general public written or edited by sociologists, books for the general public by non-sociologists, and books for sociologists by sociologists. The second group includes analyses of the Women's Liberation Movement, Movement members on the Movement, and books on specialized subjects. The books indicate the underdeveloped nature of the subject, are prone to over-generalizations, have too narrow an outlook, harp constantly on the inferiority of women, and endlessly repeat already disproved arguments. There is need for a good, comprehensive reader covering sociological materials and a more general evaluation of ideas considered important in the past. Biblio.                                                         R. V. Ritter

13. Farley, Jennie. FACULTY REACTION TO WOMEN'S STUDIES. *Women's Studies 1974 2(1): 115-119.* Experiences establishing Women's Studies at Cornell University show substantial barriers to innovative programs at traditional institutions. These barriers can be overcome if the proponents of such programs are persistent, systematic, and thick-skinned. The effort to establish Women's Studies at Cornell began in 1970, received little faculty support, and met with ridicule. By 1972, more faculty support and less hostility were evident. Once faculty members accepted and supported the program, it was taken seriously. The experience at Cornell suggests that those who wish to establish interdisciplinary, innovative, or problem-oriented programs must place high priority on obtaining faculty support if the program is to succeed.                                                         A. E. Wiederrecht

14. Fireman, Janet R. REFLECTIONS ON TEACHING WOMEN'S HISTORY: FIRST DOWN AND GOAL TO GO! *J. of the West*

*1973 12(2): 197-211.* "The subject of women has generally been neglected by historians." There has been little historical literature about women except from the feminist viewpoint. "Though incomplete and naive, the work of the feminist writers is important today as a catalog of the women's rights movement." Notes various libraries and research centers on women's history. Today more than 1000 women's studies courses are taught in Canada and the United States. 26 notes.

E. P. Stickney

15.   Ginger, Ray and Ginger, Victoria.   FEMINIST AND FAMILY HISTORY: SOME PITFALLS.   *Labor Hist. 1971 12(4): 614-618.* A critical essay-review of Aileen S. Kraditor's *Up From the Pedestal* (Chicago, Ill.: Quadrangle Books, 1970) and William L. O'Neill's *Everyone was Brave* (Chicago, Ill.: Quadrangle Books, 1969) and *Divorce in the Progressive Era* (New Haven, Conn.: Yale U. Press, 1967). Needed is study of the daily life of women, to achieve better understanding. Undocumented.

L. L. Athey

16.   Gordon, Linda; Hunt, Persis; Peck, Elizabeth; Ruthchild, Rochelle Goldberg; and Scott, Marcia.   HISTORICAL PHALLACIES: SEXISM IN AMERICAN HISTORICAL WRITING.   Carroll, Berenice A., ed. Liberating Women's History (Chicago: U. of Illinois Pr., 1976): 55-74. Identifies and analyzes sexism in contemporary historical books and articles on American women. Explores why sexism, the belief of men's superiority over women, must lead to distorted historical interpretations of women's oppression. An examination of works by Robert Riegel, William O'Neill, Christopher Lasch, James R. McGovern, Carl Degler, David Potter and Page Smith reveals that their historical writings on women are badly skewed because of sexist bias. 51 notes.

B. Sussman

17.   Gordon, Linda et al.   A REVIEW OF SEXISM IN AMERICAN HISTORICAL WRITING.   *Women's Studies 1972 1(1): 133-158.* Survey and review prominent books and articles, written by male historians, about women in the United States. The male historians, whose works were published during 1963-71, include: Robert Riegel, William O'Neill, Christopher Lasch, James McGovern, Carl Degler, Page Smith, David Potter, and Andrew Sinclair. Authors argue that these male historians write sexist history, discuss the various aspects of this sexism, and give evidence of it from the writings of each of the male historians. Based on primary materials; 64 notes, biblio.

A. E. Wiederrecht

18.   Graham, Patricia Albjerg.   SO MUCH TO DO: GUIDES FOR HISTORICAL RESEARCH ON WOMEN IN HIGHER EDUCATION.   *Teachers Coll. Record 1975 76(3): 421-429.* Reviews the literature on women in higher education and proposes a number of areas and questions that deserve exploration by historians, both those interested in the history of women and those interested in the history of higher education.

W. H. Mulligan, Jr.

19.   Grahl, Christine; Kennedy, Elizabeth; Robinson, Lillian S.; and Zimmerman, Bonnie.   WOMEN'S STUDIES: A CASE IN POINT.   *Feminist Studies 1972 1(2): 109-120.* Describes the founding, governance, curriculum, and current problems of the Women's Studies College of the State University of New York at Buffalo. Its organization is based on "the principle that women are not passive objects to be studied, analyzed and categorized, but active subjects in the historical process."

J. D. Falk

20.   Grantham, Dewey W.   THE SIXTY-SIXTH ANNUAL MEETING OF THE ORGANIZATION OF AMERICAN HISTORIANS.   *J. of Am. Hist. 1973 60(3): 714-751.* The meeting attracted about 3,000 persons to Chicago 11-14 April, for 56 sessions with 279 participating scholars. It reflected continuing interest in minority studies including women, 20th-century reform movements, and social and cultural history, and considerable concern for sources and research tools, psychohistorical methods, and improved history courses in universities and high schools. 60 notes.

K. B. West

21.   Hackett, Amy and Pomeroy, Sarah.   MAKING HISTORY: *THE FIRST SEX.*   *Feminist Studies 1972 1(2): 97-108.* Reviews Elizabeth Gould Davis' *The First Sex* (New York: Penguin Books, 1971) and challenges her use of history as an ally for feminists. Davis demonstrates through myth, archaeology, anthropology, biology, and history that

females once ruled males and credits woman with all culture and invention. She uncritically accepts J. J. Bachofen's assumption of the universality of matriarchy in prehistory (*Myth, Religion and Mother Right,* 1861) and depicts Christianity as almost the sole historical agent of women's degradation. Neither historiography nor feminism is well served by Davis' speculations and polemics. 18 notes.

J. D. Falk

22.   Hareven, Tamara K.   THE HISTORY OF THE FAMILY AS AN INTERDISCIPLINARY FIELD.   *J. of Interdisciplinary Hist. 1971 2(2): 399-414.* Reviews recent literature and claims that until recently histories of the family have been haphazardly done. Recent work is more sophisticated, derives from a renewed interest in the field and the recent conflicts of the generations, and has an interdisciplinary orientation. Reviews the strengths and weaknesses of the tools of demography and the conceptual models of anthropology, psychology, and sociology as they have been applied to the history of the family. The fundamental unanswered question arising from all these approaches is the problem of the interaction between the family and social change. This must be pursued by historians interested in macrodevelopments while studies of particular families go on. Future work should be both interdisciplinary and comparative. Based on secondary sources; 46 notes.

E. J. Hundert

23.   Holman, Dorothy Riggs.   TEACHING ABOUT WOMEN IN SECONDARY SCHOOLS: SPRINGBOARD FOR INQUIRY.   *Social Educ. 1975 39(3): 140-143.* Discusses courses about women currently being taught in San Diego, California, area high schools, lists names and addresses of the teachers, and presents a bibliography of materials useful for the courses.

24.   Hudson, Gossie Harold.   WOMEN, TOO, IN AMERICAN HISTORY.   *Crisis 1974 81(7): 229-231.* Mentions women's history, including their part in the anti-slavery struggles of the 19th century.

S

25.   Hutson, James H.   WOMEN IN THE ERA OF THE AMERICAN REVOLUTION: THE HISTORIAN AS SUFFRAGIST.   *Q. J. of the Lib. of Congress 1975 32(4): 290-303.* More than 50 years after the passage of the 19th amendment, the women's suffrage movement is still shaping the character of present-day writing about women during the era of the American Revolution. The first comprehensive work was *The Women of the American Revolution,* by Elizabeth F. Ellet, 1848-1850. This work was second in importance only to the *History of Woman Suffrage,* by Elizabeth Cady Stanton, Susan B. Anthony, and others. The new field of women's history is largely controlled by the propagandistic work written nearly a century ago. More attention should be given to traditional information. Illus., 44 notes.

E. P. Stickney

26.   Kirschner, Betty Frankle.   INTRODUCING STUDENTS TO WOMEN'S PLACE IN SOCIETY.   *Am. J. of Sociol. 1973 78(4): 1051-1054.* "An examination of a random selection of recent introductory sociology texts shows that we seldom expose introductory students to a systematic analysis of the role of women in this society."

J

27.   Kruppa, Patricia S.   THE AMERICAN WOMAN AND THE MALE HISTORIAN.   *Social Sci. Q. 1974 55(3): 605-614.* Examines the respective roles of men and women as they have been portrayed traditionally in American history and history theory, and discusses hero and cultism concepts.

S

28.   Lerner, Gerda   WOMEN'S RIGHTS AND AMERICAN FEMINISM.   *Am. Scholar 1971 40(2): 235-248.* Only recently have American historians given any serious concern to the history of women. However, even this recent work has been preoccupied with the women's rights movement in its legal and political aspects. Basically, the questions of how women fit into human history, how one is to conceptualize their role, and how one is to evaluate their contributions, remain to be solved. To clarify some of the basic assumptions with which historians approach the history of women, the author formulates two fundamental definitions. The first is women's rights. Essentially they are civil rights. They legally open justice and equity to women in terms of voting, officeholding, and property. The second term is American feminism. It embraces all aspects of the emancipation of the American woman. American feminism is an expansive term, defined in the most pervasive cultural institutions. It includes all social institutions, whether economic, familial, religious, ethical, or moral. Evolving technology and changing values are helping to free

"both men and women from a sex-dominated archaic division of labor and from the values that sustain it."          F. F. Harling

29.    Lofland, Lyn H.   THE "THERENESS" OF WOMEN: A SELECTIVE REVIEW OF URBAN SOCIOLOGY.   *Sociol. Inquiry 1975 45(2-3): 144-170.* Surveys the literature of urban sociology in which women usually have been treated as irrelevant figures.

30.    Mabbutt, Fred R.   THE MYTH OF THE AMERICAN WOMAN.   *Colorado Q. 1973 21(3): 293-305.* Discusses the misinterpretation of the place and importance of women in American history by American historians. Women received their first real opportunity when urbanization began, but women in only one segment of society gained. Includes a brief history of women's struggle for equality and mentions radical organizations such as NOW (National Organization for Women), WITCH (Women's International Terrorist Conspiracy from Hell), and SCUM (Society for Cutting Up Men). 10 notes.          B. A. Storey

31.    Martin, Wendy.   WHY WOMEN'S STUDIES.   *Women's Studies 1972 1(1): 1-2.* Discusses feminist scholarship, the relation of feminism to academia, and the objectives of the journal, *Women's Studies.*

32.    Matthews, Jean.   ADAM'S RIB.   *Can. R. of Am. Studies 1971 2(2): 114-124.* An essay-review prompted by three recent publications on women in American history: Anne Firor Scott's *The Southern Lady: From Pedestal to Politics, 1830-1930* (Chicago: U. of Chicago Press, 1970), Emily Jane Putnam's *The Lady: Studies of Certain Significant Phases of Her History* (Chicago: U. of Chicago Press, 1970; first edition, 1910), and Carrie Chapman Catt and Nettie Rogers Shuler's *Woman Suffrage and Politics: The Inner Story of the Suffrage Movement* (Seattle: U. of Washington Press, 1969; first edition, 1923). The first part of Scott's book focuses on the realities of plantation life for the wife of the plantation owner. Before the Civil War, the women's movement in the North had little impact on the South because it was tied up with abolitionism. But the war and its impact created conditions in which a limited women's movement could begin in the South. *The Lady* is "an exploration of differing difficulties in various periods of Western history of 'what a woman of the upper classes should be and how she should behave." The purpose of the book was to show that through history human culture had provided many different roles for women and that 19th-century middle-class ideals were not unchangeable. The third book, Catt and Shuler's *Woman Suffrage and Politics,* illustrates not only the history of the woman suffrage movement but also its racist and nativist tendencies. Catt and Shuler's work shows that woman suffrage did not lead to a dramatic new social order, but Scott shows that it was important in the movements for progressive reform in the South in the 1920's. 20 notes.          J. M. Hawes

33.    Miller, Roberta Balstad.   WOMEN AND AMERICAN HISTORY.   *Women's Studies 1974 2(1): 105-113.* Reviews the emergence of women's history as a field of inquiry within the discipline of history. Three areas in which teaching women's history differs from teaching other American history courses are: 1) special problems inherent in defining the content of women's history courses; 2) the presence of many non-history majors with needs and expectations different from those found in most history courses; and 3) the ideological nature of women's history. Unlike most history courses, women's history attracts dedicated feminists. Students also may wish to use women's history as a means of radicalization or consciousness-raising or may wish to narrowly focus on the contemporary women's movement. A teacher of women's history must deal with different constituencies and carefully handle the relation between an academic discipline and feminist principles. 10 notes.          A. E. Wiederrecht

34.    Rich, Adrienne.   WOMEN'S STUDIES—RENAISSANCE OR REVOLUTION?   *Women's Studies 1976 3(2): 121-126.* It is a fallacy to assume that traditional major turning points in history have the same significance for women that they have for men. Historically, men have determined what are the major events. Men's power to describe the world is the ultimate power because it determines options. Women's studies resist this male attempt to make the world in his image. Women's studies involves the dissemination of knowledge about and the activities of women in the world-at-large. Within the university, women's studies can provide a false illusion of power because, while it may help discover

women's past and present culture, it becomes institutionalized outside the mainstream of androcentric classes. Women must redefine themselves and work to end the patriarchy. This is painful, dangerous work in a world in which women are the victims of psychological and physical violence. Authentic feminist culture must be in rebellion and must sustain a collective female vision. Reprint of a paper read at the University of Pennsylvania Women's Studies Conference, 15 November 1974. 3 notes.          A. E. Wiederrecht

35.    Rosenberg, Jean.   A REVIEW OF THE ROLE OF WOMEN IN MODERN ECONOMIC LIFE AND POLITICAL ECONOMY OF WOMEN: COURSE SYLLABI AND BIBLIOGRAPHIES.   *Rev. of Radical Pol. Econ. 1972 4(3): 124-154.* Poses questions about women's role from a radical viewpoint and suggests that a course on the subject must avoid being either "a rather unexciting course on labor statistics or an exciting but confused course on women's liberation." Seven course syllabi and bibliographies for college courses are appended.          C. P. de Young

36.    Rothman, David J.   DOCUMENTS IN SEARCH OF A HISTORIAN: TOWARD A HISTORY OF CHILDREN AND YOUTH IN AMERICA.   *J. of Interdisciplinary Hist. 1971 2(2): 367-377.* In reviewing Robert H. Bremner, *Childhood and Youth in America: A Documentary History* (Cambridge, Mass.: Harvard U. Press, 1970-71), discusses the field of the history of children and notes the main contributions. This field is still underdeveloped, the family for too long has been taken for granted by historians, and the historical relationship between the young and the community is still unknown. These issues must be explored if we are to have a history of American childhood and youth. Based on secondary sources; 8 notes.          E. J. Hundert

37.    Saveth, Edward N.   THE PROBLEM OF AMERICAN FAMILY HISTORY.   *Am. Q. 1969 21(2, pt. 2): 311-329.* Addresses the paucity of historical scholarship on the American family. Inadequate conceptualization and the lack of representative source materials have contributed to a low yield of sound historical studies and the continued proliferation of unsubstantiated "grand theory." Although studies of historical family life have been particularly susceptible to subjectivism and sentiment, recent scholarship is finally beginning to challenge time-honored assumptions such as the existence of "the traditional family." Historians may continue to lament the problems inherent in the examination of the "microconcept of the family," but such examination remains a necessary and fruitful approach to analysis of larger constructs such as culture and social class. 83 notes.          R. S. Pickett

38.    Schmidt, Dolores Barracano and Schmidt, Earl Robert.   THE INVISIBLE WOMAN: THE HISTORIAN AS PROFESSIONAL MAGICIAN.   Carroll, Berenice A., Ed. Liberating Women's History (Chicago: U. of Illinois Pr., 1976): 42-54. The textbook publishing industry and the historical profession, both male dominated, must consider the damaging social and psychological implications of American history textbooks for women college students. A study of 27 texts used in most American history survey courses, shows references to females varied from a high of 2 percent to a low of .05 percent. Female intellectual and political contributions were characterized by sexual stereotyping. Women's accomplishments are erased from history, leaving a historical "truth" that denies women their vital role models. Table.          B. Sussman

39.    Secor, Cynthia.   "THE ANDROGYNY PAPERS."   *Women's Studies 1974 2(2): 139-141.* Introduces a 1974 issue of *Women's Studies* (vol. 2 no. 2), which focuses on androgyny. The collection of writings in the journal grew out of the 1973 Modern Language Association's annual meeting at which a forum titled "Androgyny: Fact or Fiction" was held. The collection also reflects the effects of the feminist movement and the renewed scholarly interest in women. The major ideas presented in the various articles are summarized.          A. E. Wiederrecht

40.    Shanley, Mary L. and Schuck, Victoria.   IN SEARCH OF POLITICAL WOMEN.   *Social Sci. Q. 1974 55(3): 632-644.* Examines how American political science has dealt with women as an object of study and discusses possible reasons why this discipline evolved as it did.          S

41.    Smith, Catherine F.   PUBLISHERS ON BOOKS IN WOMEN'S STUDIES.   *Women's Studies 1975 3(1): 111-116.* Presents the results of

a 1974 survey examining whether there are publishing opportunities for scholars and programs in women's studies. The survey profile is based on 16 commercial presses and 13 university presses. Most publishers exhibited a small commitment to women's studies publications; showed some interest in women's studies works, particularly if they were generalist or interdisciplinary approaches; indicated a book must be self-supporting; viewed the women's studies market as a growing one which may level off in the near future; and wanted books of high quality. 3 notes.

A. E. Wiederrecht

42. Smith, Dorothy E. WOMEN'S PERSPECTIVE AS A RADICAL CRITIQUE OF SOCIOLOGY. *Sociol. Inquiry [Canada] 1974 44(1): 7-13.* Explores possible differences in sociology if constructed from a woman's experience and perspective.                        S

43. Stimpson, Catharine R. THE NEW FEMINISM AND WOMEN'S STUDIES. *Change 1973 5(7): 43-48.* Largely the result of efforts of the new feminists, the emergent women's studies cover a range of curricular options from elective courses to master's-degree programs. It grew out of a variety of movements in the 1960's for more vital education, for a fair share in American life for minorities, and for an end to the warrior ethos that traditional masculinity has sanctioned. Vulnerable to internal quarrels and to hostility from without, the discipline may nevertheless succeed in advancing the intellectual, psychological, and political changes it supports.                        J

44. Stimpson, Catharine R. WHAT MATTER MIND: A THEORY ABOUT THE PRACTICE OF WOMEN'S STUDIES. *Women's Studies 1973 1(3): 293-314.* Discusses the present status and future existence of Women's Studies programs. Believing that impulses within the Women's Studies movement may lead to its destruction, author examines these impulses. Internal disruptions within the movement include internecine quarrels based on distrust, suspicion, and fears about elitism, activism, and success; ideological, political, and tactical differences; and problems of interdisciplinary work. External dangers to the movement include institutional conservatism; women's own fears about changing definitions of sexuality; racial tensions between black and white women; and problems sustaining sisterhood. The strongest external threat comes from younger, male faculty members who fear women as colleagues. Deep cultural bias against the intelligent woman also persists. For the movement to survive such problems, the author offers a political strategy that includes learning more about students' needs, bringing women of different backgrounds and ages together, forming flexible coalitions, and establishing a national organization. 14 notes.                        A. E. Wiederrecht

45. Tobias, Sheila. TEACHING FEMALE STUDIES: LOOKING BACK OVER THREE YEARS. *Liberal Educ. 1972 58(2): 258-264.* Discusses the development of women's studies courses in which the author participated. Each course provided a critique of the American experience and its male-dominated culture. The multidisciplinary approach and team teaching gave strength to the courses. Author comments on the responses to the courses by both men and women and insists that such courses should remain permanent undergraduate programs and be required for degrees in human services. 3 notes.                        W. H. Ahern

46. Trecker, Janice Law. WOMEN IN U.S. HISTORY HIGH SCHOOL TEXTBOOKS. *Social Educ. 1971 35(3): 249-260, 338.* America's societal bias toward women relegates females to virtual second-class citizenship. Argues that women's sparse share of college degrees, high governmental offices, and executive positions reflects the nation's cultural stereotypes of women. One of the largest transmitters of cultural bias toward women is the high school history textbook. Women are usually treated, if at all, as supplemental material. Because most textbooks dwell on political, military, and diplomatic affairs, many outstanding American women go unmentioned. "Most works are marred by sins of omission and commission." Most of the females mentioned in the 13 textbooks consulted are homogenized to fit the cultural stereotypes or are included for comic relief - e.g., Carry Nation and her hatchet. The tragedy of all this is that it reinforces the poor self-image and low aspirations of many American women. Undocumented; 32 photos.                        G. D. Doyle

47. Weinstein, Allen. THE SIXTY-FIFTH ANNUAL MEETING OF THE ORGANIZATION OF AMERICAN HISTORIANS. *J. of Am. History 1973 60(2): 373-408.* The OAH meeting was held in Washington, D.C., 5-8 April 1972. Some 232 individuals participated in 56 sessions which reflected a cross section of significant work on women's history, black history, social and cultural history, interdisciplinary programs, and historiography with an emphasis on materials for women's history, quantification, and audiovisual materials. The future focus of post-World War II political history would appear to be the Eisenhower era.                        K. B. West

# Methods

48. Austin, Judith. NEW HORIZONS IN ORAL HISTORY: THE NINTH ANNUAL COLLOQUIUM OF THE ORAL HISTORY ASSOCIATION. *Oral Hist. R. 1975: 82-94.* Reports the sessions of the Oral History Association Colloquium at Jackson Lake Lodge, Grand Teton National Park, Wyoming, on 13-15 September 1974, attended by 190 persons. Includes 1) Alice Hoffman and Karen Budd on the value of oral interviewing in supplementing written records, using the Memorial Day Massacre of 1937 at the South Chicago Mill of the Republican Steel Corporation; 2) keynote address of Alden Whitman on the use of oral history in preparing advance obituaries for the *New York Times*; 3) use of oral history in feminine studies with Gwendolyn Safier on women in nursing and Clara Shirpser on women in politics; 4) exploitation of subjects by oral historians with comments by Horace M. Albright, Bill Moss, and Charles Morrissey; 5) a 1974 survey on oral history in teaching; 6) panel sessions on the exploitation of interviewees, Oral History Association publications, and video-taping; 7) panel on prospects in western conservation, Alaska and the energy crisis, and technology in California; 8) sessions on oral history projects of the Mormons; 9) gold mining; 10) oral history among contemporary commune groups; 11) psychological aspects of oral history; and 12) sessions on Asian studies and ethnic groups.                        D. A. Yanchisin

49. Bell, Susan Groag. DISCOVERING WOMEN'S HISTORY THROUGH ART IN THE CLASSROOM. *Hist. Teacher 1973 6(4): 503-510.* Proposes teaching women's history through the use of slides. For centuries art has depicted attitudes toward women and their activities, dress, and life-style. Based on primary and secondary sources; notes, biblio.                        P. W. Kennedy

50. Epstein, Cynthia Fuchs. A DIFFERENT ANGLE OF VISION: NOTES ON THE SELECTIVE EYE OF SOCIOLOGY. *Social Sci. Q. 1974 55(3): 645-656.* Explores the deficiencies of American sociology in dealing meaningfully with the place of women in society.                        S

51. Gordon, Ann D.; Buhle, Mari Jo; and Dye, Nancy Schrom. THE PROBLEM OF WOMEN'S HISTORY. Carroll, Berenice A., ed. Liberating Women's History (Chicago: U. of Illinois Pr., 1976): 75-92. Historians have traditionally looked upon women's spheres as monolithic, passive, and isolated from social change; and current historiography reflects these beliefs. In the study of women's history, present categories of historical methodology are bound by the traditional notion that only public and political spheres are of historical significance, areas in which women are not highly visible. Feminists, opposed to this line of inquiry, seek to develop categories to fit women into history and to redefine significant events to encompass personal and subjective experiences. 31 notes.                        B. Sussman

52. Hochschild, Arlie Russell. A REVIEW OF SEX ROLE RESEARCH. *Am. J. of Sociol. 1973 78(4): 1011-1029.* "This article describes four types of research on sex roles done in the last decade. The first type deals with sex differences, notably those reflected in measures of cognitive and emotional traits. Its theoretical focus is on the nature-nurture debate. The second type deals with sex roles as reflected in behavior and norms and draws on role theory. The third deals with women as a minority group and draws on minority group theory. The fourth, the politics of caste, looks at the sexes from the perspective of power. The article examines the different intellectual roots, questions, and data involved in each type and discusses the possible implications for sociology."                        J

53. Hochstrasser, Donald L.; Arthur, Gerry; and Lewis, Michael. FERTILITY DECLINE IN SOUTHERN APPALACHIA: AN AN-

THROPOLOGICAL PERSPECTIVE. *Human Organization 1973 32(4): 331-336.* Reviews the demographic literature on the fertility decline in Southern Appalachia, and makes a case for the anthropological community study approach to explain it. 2 notes, biblio.

E. S. Johnson

54. Jensen, Richard and Campbell, Barbara HOW TO HANDLE A LIBERATED WOMAN. *Hist. Methods Newsletter 1972 5(3): 109-113.* Describes the method of analyzing the questionnaires returned by nine thousand American women for the 1914 edition of *Women's Who's Who in America.* The method devised is designed to gauge what the American woman regarded as the criteria of a successful life, and to measure her attitudes on social and political issues without distorting those attitudes by subjecting them to current ideological tests or male-imposed standards of social success. Based on primary and secondary sources; table, 3 notes.

G. Kurland

55. Johannson, Sheila Ryan. "HERSTORY" AS HISTORY: A NEW FIELD OR ANOTHER FAD? Carroll, Berenice A., ed. Liberating Women's History (Chicago: U. of Illinois Pr., 1976): 400-430. Discusses methodological changes necessary if women's historical experience is to become more than a series of interesting facts unrelated to the mainstream of historical concerns. Suggests this can be accomplished by developing the relationship between the lives and social roles of women and the nature of social change. To this end various aspects of women's history must be explored: the complex problem of status; attitudes and values of men toward females; the importance of production, reproduction, sexuality, and socialization; and, most important, how women have been instrumental in changing the structure and function of their societies. 55 notes.

B. Sussman

56. Kelly-Gadol, Joan. THE SOCIAL RELATION OF THE SEXES: METHODOLOGICAL IMPLICATIONS OF WOMEN'S HISTORY. *Signs 1976 1(4): 809-823.* Women's history has moved beyond compensatory history to focus on women's place and power. Because the history of women is not the same as the history of men, three areas of historical methodology require re-examination, periodization, categories of social analysis, and theories of social change. Present periodization may be retained to refer to major structural societal changes, but these changes should be evaluated to consider the effects on women as distinct from men. Sex is a category of social thought as legitimate as race and class, and the study of the relationship between sexes, the range in sex roles and sexual symbolism helps clarify women's situation as "other." Especially important to historical analysis is the relationship of familial and public activities. Women's status is high when they coincide and low when clearly distinguished. Based on recent feminist studies; 26 notes.

J. Gammage

57. Lerner, Gerda. NEW APPROACHES TO THE STUDY OF WOMEN IN AMERICAN HISTORY. *J. of Social Hist. 1969 3(1): 53-62.* Rejects the traditional framework for studying women in American history and suggests a new conceptual model incorporating psychology, role playing, status differentiation, and societal expectations counterpointed against reality. The feminist writers of the Progressive years, with few exceptions, saw American women as an oppressed group struggling for equality of rights; however, they ignored women's accomplishments outside the suffrage movement. In retrospect their framework was too middle-class, nativist, and moralistic to be of use to scholars any longer. Suggests a new approach which provides a wider framework, yet permits a narrower focus on specific groups of women or individuals in America's past. Based on secondary sources, feminist literature, and biographies, 13 notes.

J. P. Harahan

58. Lerner, Gerda. PLACING WOMEN IN HISTORY: A 1975 PERSPECTIVE. Carroll, Berenice A., ed. Liberating Women's History (Chicago: U. of Illinois Pr., 1976): 357-367. No single methodology and conceptual framework can organize the historical experience of all types of women. Methods are only tools for analysis, to be used when needed and then replaced by new tools when necessary. A new history is essential, a universal history that is equally concerned with men, women, and the establishment and passing of patriarchy. To achieve this goal historians must become aware of the sexist bias that pervades the culture and recognize that women have always been an essential part of history. 14 notes.

B. Sussman

59. Lightfoot, Sara Lawrence. SOCIOLOGY OF EDUCATION: PERSPECTIVES ON WOMEN. *Sociol. Inquiry 1975 45(2-3): 106-143.* Discusses the nature of the sociology of education, focuses on the role of teachers and classroom structure, and analyzes how educational sociologists have perceived women as teachers and as significant figures in the classroom.

60. Lorber, Judith. WOMEN AND MEDICAL SOCIOLOGY: INVISIBLE PROFESSIONALS AND UBIQUITOUS PATIENTS. *Sociol. Inquiry 1975 45(2-3): 75-105.* Studies of training, career tracking, and work situations of medical professionals have excluded women except as nurses while studies of patients have included women and depicted them as deviants who are sick because of their reproductive functions and who poorly manage their emotions.

61. Martin, Wendy and Briscoe, Mary Louise. WOMEN'S STUDIES: PROBLEMS IN RESEARCH. *Women's Studies 1974 2(2): 249-259.* Outlines trends in the literature of feminist criticism. Discusses these trends in the fields of literary criticism, literary history, linguistics, psychology, biological sciences, kinesthesiology, anthropology, history, and economics. Most feminist criticism deals with sex roles and stereotypes, woman as protagonist, works by women writers, and bibliography. The strengths, limitations, and possibilities of feminist criticism in all these categories are discussed.

A. E. Wiederrecht

62. McCormack, Thelma. TOWARD A NONSEXIST PERSPECTIVE ON SOCIAL AND POLITICAL CHANGE. *Sociol. Inquiry 1975 45(2-3): 1-33.* Analyzes the concept of social change, discusses the nature of political sociology and its biases about women, and suggests a nonsexist perspective for understanding political and social changes.

63. Millman, Marcia. SHE DID IT ALL FOR LOVE: A FEMINIST VIEW OF THE SOCIOLOGY OF DEVIANCE. *Sociol. Inquiry 1975 45(2-3): 251-279.* Discusses the relationship among social deviance, popular stereotypes of deviant and conventional behavior, and sociological theories of deviance.

64. Smith, Hilda. FEMINISM AND THE METHODOLOGY OF WOMEN'S HISTORY. Carroll, Berenice A., ed. Liberating Women's History (Chicago: U. of Illinois Pr., 1976): 369-384. Women's history must be viewed from the feminist perspective of women as a distinct sociological group. Sexual division has created a separate past for men and women. Regardless of individual differences among women, they are distinguished from all other groups because of this division. In reassessing women's role, women must not be isolated from historical experiences. Because women were always a part of society, absorbed its values, and in turn affected life through their own peculiar experiences, a comparison between male and female life styles and value systems is essential if we are to uncover the realities of women's past. 14 notes.

B. Sussman

65. Stanley, Judith M. A SOUND RENDERING OF WOMEN'S HISTORY. *Hist. Teacher 1973 6(4): 511-522.* Discusses the use of tapes in teaching women's history. Several tapes are recommended, and two are discussed in detail, one depicting a pioneer woman in Oregon and the other a frontier woman in early 20th-century Wyoming. Notes.

P. W. Kennedy

66. Tresemer, David. ASSUMPTIONS MADE ABOUT GENDER ROLES. *Sociol. Inquiry 1975 45(2-3): 308-339.* Distinguishes between "sex" and "gender," discusses the assumptions social scientists make about gender roles, and suggests ways to overcome the biases which social scientists bring to their research about gender roles and sex roles.

67. Wood, Elizabeth B. POTS AND PANS HISTORY: RELATING MANUSCRIPTS AND PRINTED SOURCES TO THE STUDY OF DOMESTIC ART OBJECTS. *Am. Archivist 1967 30(3): 431-442.* Examines the study of American domestic culture, which is beginning to find acceptance in university curricula. Professional historians - salaried staff members of museums, historical societies, and historical homes and parks - are making many contributions. Discusses some research approaches used by the cultural historians. The author says that her purpose is to explain to archivists and librarians what the "pots and pans" historians are trying to do, and why, with the hope of improving cooperation.

Illustrates the interplay between objects and documents, and the ingenuity and patience needed for successful interpretation, by the story of a research on the 19th-century engraved trade label, eventually attributed to Thomas Fletcher and Sidney Gardiner. Archivists and librarians can help by preserving, describing, evaluating, and interpreting documents.

D. E. Horn

68. Zangrando, Joanna Schneider　WOMEN IN ARCHIVES: AN HISTORIAN'S VIEW ON THE LIBERATION OF CLIO. *Am. Archivist 1973 36(2): 203-214.* Asks why women have not been given more consideration in the historical treatment of men and women. Explains the role of the Coordinating Committee of Women in the History Profession, part of the American Historical Association (AHA), and describes the impact of the women's rights movement on the AHA. More research on women is necessary to increase information and to help women understand their roles. Discusses methods of research in women's history and suggests that archivists can promulgate information about sources. Table, 17 notes.

D. E. Horn

# Bibliography

69. Bazin, Nancy Topping.　THE CONCEPT OF ANDROGYNY: A WORKING BIBLIOGRAPHY. *Women's Studies 1974 2(2): 217-235.* A brief introduction discusses the term "androgyny" and explains the organization and intent of the bibliography which follows. The bibliographic material is interdisciplinary and grouped under topical headings. The topics are: background reading; misogyny/fear of women; the history of androgyny; the Dionysian and the Appolonian; the myth of feminity; masculine and feminine principles; androgyny and the body; the androgynous moment; need for the "feminization" of society; the androgynous ideal and literature; feminist consciousness/marxist consciousness; the androgynous ideal and teaching; and androgyny related to contemporary life.

A. E. Wiederrecht

70. Cheda, Sherrill.　WOMEN AND MANAGEMENT: A SELECTIVE BIBLIOGRAPHY 1970-73. *Can. Lib. J. 1974 31(1): 18-19, 22, 24, 26-27.* Lists eight books, three essays, 26 articles, and two bibliographies that deal with the subject.

S

71. Horne, Grenda.　THE LIBERATION OF BRITISH AND AMERICAN WOMEN'S HISTORY. *Bull. of the Soc. for the Study of Labour Hist. [Great Britain] 1973 (26): 28-39.* A bibliographic essay noting the main areas of research in women's history. Biblio.

L. L. Athey

72. Huddleston, Eugene L.　FEMINIST VERSE SATIRE IN AMERICA: A CHECKLIST, 1700-1800. *Bull. of Biblio. and Mag. Notes 1975 32(3): 115-122.*

73. Lankford, John.　THE WRITING OF AMERICAN HISTORY IN THE 1960S: A CRITICAL BIBLIOGRAPHY OF MATERIALS OF INTEREST TO SOCIOLOGISTS. *Sociol. Q. 1973 14(1): 99-126.* "This essay is not a contribution to the theoretical literature on the relationships between sociology and history. Rather it is directed at those who have an active commitment to interdisciplinary investigations and who are at work on the common problems and frontiers shared by sociology and history." The series of categories which reflect patterns of sociological concern are as follows: stratification and mobility; politics and power; family; violence; immigration; urbanization; racial, sexual, and cultural minorities; professions; religion; education; economic growth and development; and large scale analysis of American society. 24 notes.

D. D. Cameron

74. Litoff, Judy Barrett and Litoff, Hal.　WORKING WOMEN IN MAINE: A NOTE ON SOURCES. *Labor Hist. 1976 17(1): 88-95.* Surveys sources for the study of working women in Maine, including published works, articles, dissertations and theses, government publications, and unpublished papers. 5 notes.

L. L. Athey

75. Rothstein, Pauline Marcus.　WOMEN: A SELECTED BIBLIOGRAPHY OF BOOKS. *Bull. of Bibliography and Mag. Notes 1975 32(2): 45-54, 76.* Covers the Women's Movement in America during 1848-1975.

S

76. Sive, Mary Robinson.　HELEN E. HAINES, 1872-1961 AN ANNOTATED BIBLIOGRAPHY. *J. of Lib. Hist., Philosophy and Comparative Librarianship 1970 5(2): 146-164.* Helen Haines, author of *Living With Books,* was an active force in the concern for intellectual freedom, in library education, and in both national and state professional library organizations. The 169 references include her own books, pamphlets, articles, and book reviews, as well as publications about her—biography, obituaries, and criticisms of her books.

D. M. Hedrick

# Archives, Libraries, Museums

77. Beck, Leonard N.　THE LIBRARY OF SUSAN B. ANTHONY. *Q. J. of the Lib. of Congress 1975 32(4): 324-336.* In 1903 Susan B. Anthony gave her personal library along with her manuscripts to the Library of Congress. Numbering less than 400 items, it has no pretensions to rarity; its interest lies in the glimpses it affords of the private person generally overshadowed by the feminist movement symbol. Anthony read primarily for "immediately practical information." She annotated several volumes of poetry, the one which meant most to her being Elizabeth Barrett Browning's *Aurora Leigh.* Of John Stuart Mill's *The Subjugation of Women,* she wrote: "This book has been the law for me since 1869." Illus., 7 notes.

E. P. Stickney

78. Bowers, Beth.　DAUGHTERS OF THE AMERICAN REVOLUTION MUSEUM. *Texana 1973 11(4): 362-373.* Describes the exhibits of first ladies of Texas in the Daughters of the American Revolution museum which was given to Texas Women's University in 1940.

79. Carbery, Michael C.　A HELEN KELLER "SCRAPBOOK." *Manuscripts 1972 24(4): 242-249.* Describes the contents and care provided the Helen Keller Papers at the Hadley School for the Blind in Winnetka, Illinois. The Hadley-Keller scrapbook, comprised of 38 letters in 89 items, appears insignificant when contrasted to the Keller papers at the University of Southern California, but the scrapbook represents a selective sample of Keller's writing. A brief biography and description of Keller's handicaps introduces some tentative comments regarding creativity, genius, experience, and sense perception, particularly in relation to this remarkable woman.

D. A. Yanchisin

80. Foote, Edward.　A REPORT ON MARY FOOTE. *Yale U. Lib. Gazette 1974 49(2): 225-230.* Presents a brief biographical sketch of Mary Foote (1872-1968), portraitist, student, and friend of Dr. Carl G. Jung, who became the editor and guardian of the Jung English language seminars. Her papers, donated by the family to Yale, contain "a very large portion of the still unpublished work of Dr. Jung in English," and are supplemented by a group of Jung's German first editions and Foote's correspondence with the English-speaking members of the Jung circle. Note.

D. A. Yanchisin

81. James, Janet Wilson.　HISTORY AND WOMEN AT HARVARD: THE SCHLESINGER LIBRARY. *Harvard Lib. Bull. 1968 16(4): 385-399.* Maud Wood Park, who lobbied the Woman Suffrage Amendment through Congress and became the first President of the League of Women Voters, gave her collection of correspondence and other papers to Radcliffe in 1943. Gifts by Mary Beard, Mary Putnam Jacobi, and Arthur M. Schlesinger, Sr., established a major women's archives. "In recent years the library has made a special effort to gather materials documenting woman's life at home and in her volunteer services."

E. P. Stickney

82. Kenney, Alice P.　WOMEN, HISTORY AND THE MUSEUM. *Hist. Teacher 1974 7(4): 511-523.* Suggests using museum materials in teaching feminist history. Local museums, historical societies, and historic houses contain useful teaching materials, as do major museums and restorations. Objects made by and useful to women can be used to explore feminist history in the colonies, on the frontier, and in the industrial period. 4 illus.

P. W. Kennedy

83. Kohn, John S. Van E.　GIVING EMILY DICKINSON TO THE WORLD. *Princeton U. Lib. Chronicle 1969 31(1): 47-54.* Mrs. John Pershing of Richmond, Virginia, presented her Emily Dickinson Collec-

tion to the Princeton University Library on 7 June 1969. The collection shows the persons responsible for publishing the poetry of Emily Dickinson and describes the history of the poems.                    D. Brockway

84.   Laura X; Hill, Vicki Lynn; Moe, Louisa; and Snowden, Elizabeth. WOMEN'S HISTORY RESEARCH CENTER: THE ANNOTATED REVOLUTION OR FOOTNOTES TO THE REVOLUTION. *California Librarian 1976 37(1): 22-31.* Discusses various aspects of the American Revolution Bicentennial Administration Task Force on the National Women's History Center, including the Women's History Library, the International Women's Art Festival, and Women's History Research Center Collections.

85.   Lemisch, Jesse.   THE PAPERS OF A FEW GREAT BLACK MEN AND A FEW GREAT WHITE WOMEN.   *Maryland Historian 1975 6(1): 60-66.*                                            G. O. Gagnon

86.   Manning, Josephine Asaro.   THE MARY MARTIN REBOW LETTERS, 1778-1779 (PART II).   *Record 1972 33: 5-25.* The love letters written by Mary Martin Rebow to her fiancé Isaac Martin Rebow, in Great Britain during 1778-79, are located at the Washington State University Library in Pullman, Washington. .

87.   Moseley, Eva   WOMEN IN ARCHIVES: DOCUMENTING THE HISTORY OF WOMEN IN AMERICA.   *Am. Archivist 1973 36(2): 215-222.* Presents methods and problems, especially in manuscripts, of research in the history of women in the United States. Recounts the formation of the Women's Archives, now the Arthur and Elizabeth Schlesinger Library on the History of Women in America, at Radcliffe College and describes the holdings in suffrage, reform, medicine, politics, government service, and volunteer organizations. Describes other collections at Smith College, the Library of Congress, the University of Illinois (Chicago Circle), the Women's History Research Center (Berkeley), and other places. Some modern organizations are maintaining their own archives. Some guides to this material are available, but others are needed. Based on secondary works sources; 6 notes.                    D. E. Horn

88.   Nolen, Anita Lonnes.   THE FEMININE PRESENCE: WOMEN'S PAPERS IN THE MANUSCRIPT DIVISION.   *Q. J. of the Lib. of Congress 1975 32(4): 348-365.* The struggle for suffrage occupies a primary place in the papers of women in the Library of Congress. The records of the National Association for the Advancement of Colored People includes many by and relating to women. The papers of other women are important because they were keen observers of life in Washington. Also significant are the papers of women who served as mistresses of the White House. Illus.                                    E. P. Stickney

89.   Norman, Dorothy.   THE DOROTHY NORMAN PAPERS. *Yale U. Lib. Gazette 1968 42(3): 131-139.* Explains the origin of the documents presented by Dorothy Norman to the Yale Library, most of which span the period from the 1930's to the early 1950's.

90.   Triesch, Manfred.   THE LILLIAN HELLMAN COLLECTION. *Lib. Chronicle of the U. of Texas 1965 8(1): 17-20.* The University of Texas contains a collection of the playwright's notebooks and drafts of her dramas, 1934-63.                                            S

91.   Wright, Eugene Patrick.   A CATALOGUE OF THE JOANNA SOUTHCOTT COLLECTION AT THE UNIVERSITY OF TEXAS AT AUSTIN.   *Tex. Q. 1969 12(1): 145 ff.* A catalog of the numerous items connected with the writings of this religious fanatic of the late 18th and early 19th century. The items range from short newspaper clippings to the published works of Joanna Southcott, in addition to paintings, pamphlets, miscellaneous seals, etc., of Southcott and her followers. The collection is housed in the Library of the University of Texas. Joanna Southcott was an evangelist whose preachings and writings attracted more than one hundred thousand followers in Europe and America. The Southcottian movement goes on today, mainly in England. In the United States the sect is better known as the House of David.

R. W. Delaney

92.   —.   FLOODGATES AND WATERGATE: RECENT ACQUISITIONS OF THE MANUSCRIPT DIVISION.   *Q. J. of the Lib. of Congress 1975 32(3): 172-206.* The Tax Reform Act (1969) has inhibited gifts of literary manuscripts by their creators. Among the most important papers acquired by the Library of Congress in 1974 were those of Hugo L. Black, Frederick Douglass, the John W. Draper family, Lillian Gish, Henry R. Luce, and Agnes E. Meyer, the records of the Brotherhood of Sleeping Car Porters, and substantial additions to the Reid family and Roosevelt-Willard family papers and those of Charles Phelps Taft II. Among archives and records a notable addition is the gift of the Leadership Conference on Civil Rights. 5 notes, appendix.

E. P. Stickney

93.   —.   RECENT ACQUISITIONS OF THE MANUSCRIPT DIVISION.   *Q. J. of the Lib. of Congress 1968 25(4): 328-361.* The staff of the Manuscript Division highlight a number of important additions, beginning with the Marsh letter on Lincoln as a village postmaster. Among the most important collections on recent history are the Felix Frankfurter and the James M. Landis Papers. In the field of literary and cultural history, the Edna St. Vincent Millay Papers are important as are those of Truman Capote and John Toland. Particularly noteworthy are the David C. Mearns Papers. Two collections relating to scientific history have been selected for extended description: the J. Robert Oppenheimer Papers and those of Vannevar Bush. The Manuscript Division also added during 1967 more than 750 reels of manuscripts on microfilm, the research value of which is high. Presents a classified list of principal manuscript acquisitions added during 1967. 3 notes.                    E. P. Stickney

# 2. United States General

*(including articles on United States and Canada)*

## General

94. Bell, Patricia. MARY TODD LINCOLN: A PERSONALITY PORTRAIT. *Civil War Times Illus. 1968 7(7): 4-11.* Pictures Mary Todd Lincoln (1818-82) as a woman whose emotional and mental instability prohibited self-control and sound judgment. Her poor reputation is attributed to William Hearndon who began his lectures about Abraham Lincoln in 1886. Her stormy marriage to Lincoln is described, as well as her money troubles and travels after his death.                    R. N. Alvis

95. Benjamin, Theodosia. A THANK-YOU NOTE FROM MISS AUDUBON. *Pacific Historian 1969 13(3): 42-44.* John Audubon's daughter, Maria, sent a note in 1904 to Mrs. Alice Walsh Tone, thanking her for the help she gave in recalling names and dates for a biographical memoir Miss Audubon attached to *Audubon's Western Journal.* Both Mrs. Tone's father, Nicholas Walsh, and her husband, John H. Tone, had been members of a party which Audubon led to California in 1849. 2 illus., 4 notes.                    F. I. Murphy

96. Bernard, Jessie. THE STATUS OF WOMEN IN MODERN PATTERNS OF CULTURE. *Ann. of the Am. Acad. of Pol. and Social Sci. 1968 375: 3-14.* "Modern industrialism makes equality of the sexes possible, but such equality is not likely to be achieved. Two roadblocks, according to W. J. Goode, stand in the way: the domestic and maternal obligations assigned to women and the lack of interest of women in assuming equal responsibilities. Care of the house need not be serious. Nor need motherhood be a serious obstacle if the number of children is small and if aids are supplied by community agencies. The lack of interest in high-level positions suggests that women are settling for jobs rather than careers. As contrasted with the past, the issues which concern the modern generation have to do with personal, private, even sexual, rights rather than legal, political, and economic rights. Whereas some women seem to have succumbed to the glamour ideal, others move toward the de-emphasis of sex. There is beginning to be recognition of the fact that the change in the status of women may have a deleterious effect on men."                    J

97. Bianchini, Angela. DOROTHY DAY E IL MOVIMENTO CATTOLICO AMERICANO [Dorothy Day and the American Catholic movement]. *Nuova Antologia [Italy] 1971 512(2045): 76-80.* Describes the origins and activities of Dorothy Day (1917-67), a progressive member of the Catholic Church and an accomplished social worker.                    M. T. Wilson

98. Blake, Judith. INCOME AND REPRODUCTIVE MOTIVATION. *Population Studies [Great Britain] 1967 21(3): 185-206.* "It is often assumed that family size and income would be positively related if unwanted births among the less advantaged were prevented. But this assumption rests on a prior expectation that family size *preferences* bear a direct relation to income in modern societies. Data on such reproductive preferences in relation to economic status from thirteen studies in the United States dating between 1936 and 1966 do not support the notion of a positive association between reproductive preferences and income. Only when Catholics are considered is there even a U-shaped relation between family-size desires and income. These results cast doubts on the notion that the economic theory of demand for consumer durables is relevant to reproductive motivation. Rather, the data lend credence to the idea that significant non-economic influences associated with prosperity depress family-size desires among the well-to-do. Only if these influences are specifically weakened by a counter-force (such as Catholicism) do wealthier people show a preference for somewhat larger families. In no case, however, are the Catholic/non-Catholic differences in reproductive preference large. Moreover, no economic group, even among non-Catholics, prefers very small families." 22 notes.                    J

99. Bryan, Robert. THE STORY OF ARIEL AND WILL DURANT. *Westways 1975 67(8): 43-47.* Relates incidents in the personal lives of the historians Ariel Durant and William Durant, 1910's-70's.                    S

100. Chafetz, Janet Saltzman and Polk, Barbara Bovee. ROOM AT THE TOP: SOCIAL RECOGNITION OF BRITISH AND AMERICAN FEMALES OVER TIME. *Social Sci. Q. 1974 54(4): 843-853.* "The relative proportions of females to males, the bases for social recognition, educational and marital data are compared to examine the effects of changes in the formal opportunity structure and the early Women's Rights Movement . . . Data from both Britain and the United States show predicted changes in education and bases of fame but that marital data suggest a lack of concomitant value changes regarding the female role."                    J

101. Colie, Fosalie PORTRAIT..."O QUAM TE MEMOREM," MARJORIE HOPE NICOLSON. *Am. Scholar 1965 34(3): 463-470.* Pays tribute to Dr. Marjorie Hope Nicolson (quondam dean at Smith College and later a greatly respected administrator in the Graduate School at Columbia University) as a research scholar, teacher, and administrator. "After Miss Nicolson's work, no seventeenth-century scholar could afford to ignore the effect upon thought of the new science of the Renaissance, although before she published there was little enough to consult on that subject....She related, of all things, the science of geology to the aesthetic theory subsequently called 'romantic'; she outlined classical, medieval and renaissance tradition of space fiction so that, to us, modern space machines seem curiously simple and derivative....An extraordinary woman: frightening, commanding, admirable, irrevocably lovable (if one dares to love), larger than life, for whom one must adjust the proportion of one's thoughts." Undocumented.

D. D. Cameron

102. Douglas, Ann. INTRODUCTION TO *RITES OF PASSAGE FOR AMERICAN WOMEN.* *Women's Studies 1976 4(1): 1-2.* Introduces a 1976 issue of *Women's Studies* (vol. 4 no. 1) which focuses on critical periods and times of change in the lives of American women. Contributions to the issue include poetry, history, biography, short stories, and photography, and concern the 17th to the 20th centuries. All the contributions deal with the importance and precariousness of female identity, women's maturation, and the necessity for communication and support among women.                    A. E. Wiederrecht

103. Goldstücker, Eduard. YOUTH SEPARATED BY THIRTY YEARS: AN AUTOBIOGRAPHICAL ACCOUNT OF THE SIMILARITIES AND DIFFERENCES BETWEEN THE YOUNG PEOPLE OF THE NINETEEN-THIRTIES AND THOSE OF THE NINETEEN-SIXTIES. *Center Mag. 1973 6(4): 37-46.*

104. Gordon, Ann D. and Buhle, Mari Jo. SEX AND CLASS IN COLONIAL AND NINETEENTH-CENTURY AMERICA. Carroll, Berenice A., ed. Liberating Women's History (Chicago: U. of Illinois Pr., 1976): pp. 278-300. Examines how changing economic conditions over three centuries altered feminist consciousness. Pre-industrial colonial society concentrated a variety of essential economic activities in the family and women participated fully. In the transitional 19th century industrial economy, individual wage earners replaced families as the productive unit and sexual polarization was established. Because of their class position, wives of merchant capitalists gained control over female cultural patterns; and old traditions of women's usefulness were set aside for subjugation to domesticity. This repressive femininity placed working-class women outside the pale of respectability, and it is where women stayed until they confronted their own class interests toward the close of the century. 46 notes.                    B. Sussman

105. Herrera, Mary Armstrong. THE FIREBALL. *North Carolina Folklore 1972 20(3): 115-118.* Discusses the tale of a mysterious fireball that was supposed to have been seen by a poor, young hillbilly girl in the mountain country of North Carolina many years ago.

R. N. Lokken

106. Hoskins, Janina W. THE IMAGE OF AMERICA IN AC-COUNTS OF POLISH TRAVELERS OF THE 18TH AND 19TH CENTURIES. *Q. J. of the Lib. of Congress 1965 22(3): 226-245.* Reviews and analyzes writings and reactions of leading Polish visitors to the United States, 1783-1870's. Poets, novelists, journalists, military- and women-travelers are included; dates, distinguished persons and areas visited are given, and the bibliography precisely covers manuscript as well as printed sources in both the United States and Poland. Illus.

H. J. Graham

107. Johnson, Sheila K. A LOOK AT MARGARET MEAD. *Commentary 1973 55(3): 70-72.* A short biography of Margaret Mead.

S

108. Kammen, Michael. PERSONAE AS PASTIME: THE SENSE OF SELF IN TIME PAST. *New York Hist. 1973 54(4): 448-463.* Comparative review of Bruce Catton, *Waiting for the Morning Train: An American Boyhood* (Garden City, New York: Doubleday, 1972), and Margaret Mead, *Blackberry Winter: My Earlier Years* (New York: William Morrow, 1972). Noting the upsurge in the number of autobiographies being written (in consequence of the current search for one's identity), Kammen suggests that autobiographies are an excellent source by which the historian can gauge the reaction of individuals and social groups to social change and flux. Secondary works; 3 illus., 14 notes.

G. Kurland

109. Karp, Walter. THE FEMININE UTOPIA. *Horizon 1971 13(2): 4-14.* Examines the women's liberation movement and points out that universal male ascendancy was made possible by mankind's fundamental social organization: the institution of the family. Sees the present women's movement as successful only when the family is abolished as a primary unit of human life. Feels the price is too high for this kind of victory and suggests instead that women only do as they please until they have children, then accept their social responsibility to rear those children. States that women should engage in local politics and seek power and fulfillment by political means.

R. N. Alvis

110. Keniston, Ellen and Keniston, Kenneth. THE AMERICAN ANACHRONISM: THE IMAGE OF WOMEN AND WORK. *Am. Scholar 1964 33(3): 355-375.* "Conceptions of womanliness and images of work left over from an era when they were necessary for social survival and congruent with family function have persisted into an era in which they are no longer viable." The result of this cultural lag is the "problem" of American women. We need to emphasize with both young men and young women that most women *will* work and that society has so changed as to make fulfillment within the family impossible. We need to provide adolescent girls with more viable models of womanhood.

E. P. Stickney

111. Kessler-Harris, Alice. WOMEN, WORK, AND THE SOCIAL ORDER. Carroll, Berenice A., ed. Liberating Women's History (Chicago: U. of Illinois Pr., 1976): 330-343. Explores women's work outside the home in the context of the interaction between the fluctuations of the economy and the need for social order contingent upon the family. Traces women's participation in the labor force from colonial New England to the present and contends that varying needs of the labor market determine changes in family structure and women's roles. Because the ideology of the family has always been considered crucial to the social order, the enormous number of women presently employed prompts questions about whether working women undermine family structure, and, even more importantly, whether the role of the family is to maintain the social order. 46 notes.

B. Sussman

112. Massey, Mary Elizabeth. MARY TODD LINCOLN. *Am. Hist. Illus. 1975 10(2): 4-9, 44-48.* Discusses Mary Todd Lincoln's life of neurotic behavior (1819-82) and evaluates contemporary media criticism of her.

113. McCullough, David G. THE UNEXPECTED MRS. STOWE. *Am. Heritage 1973 24(5): 4-9, 76-80.* Biographical sketch of the author, painter, and abolitionist, Harriet Beecher Stowe (1811-96).

S

114. McNeil, W. K. MARY HENDERSON EASTMAN, PIONEER COLLECTOR OF AMERICAN FOLKLORE. *Southern Folklore Q. 1975 39(3): 271-289.* Discusses the life and work of 19th-century author Mary Henderson Eastman, the first American woman to publish volumes of folklore.

115. Neale, Robert E. SEE THE DIRT. *Religion in Life 1972 41(4): 497-508.* Discusses dirt as dirty, dirt as mother, dirt as damned, and dirt as mud. Written from the mythical and psychiatric points of view. Includes a discussion of witches and alchemy. 15 notes.

E. P. Stickney

116. Paltiel, Freda L. INTERNATIONAL PERSPECTIVE ON EQUAL OPPORTUNITY. *Can. Labour 1975 20(2): 19-22.* Presents the efforts of national (including US and Canadian) and international organizations against sex discrimination since the 1960's.

117. Raeithel, Get. DER ANATOMISCHE SHICKSALGLAUBE UND DIE AMERIKANISCHE FRAU [Belief in anatomical fate and the American woman]. *Frankfurter Hefte [West Germany] 1976 31(1): 25-34.* Discusses the current status of women in the United States (with a single reference to contemporary Canada), tracing that status through its historical development from colonial times. Emphasizes such topics as the lack of women's rights under the English common law, the slow development of female suffrage, the double standard for sexual behavior, and the Kinsey Report. Also discusses changes in sexual mores (especially those instituted by utopian religious experiments), black-white sexual relations, and the changing familial configurations of recent decades. The conclusion is that American women today are, through hard struggles, defining their new and different roles in American life. 20 notes.

J. L. Colwell

118. Redon, Royana Bailey. MRS. SUSAN WHEELER DECATUR. *Historic Preservation 1967 19(3/4): 48-52.* A biographical sketch of the wife of Commodore Stephen Decatur, Jr., which emphasizes her efforts to recover the prize money owed to her husband (who was killed in a duel in 1820) for his capture of the *Philadelphia.* Illus. J. M. Hawes

119. Reed, Evelyn. IS BIOLOGY WOMAN'S DESTINY? *Int. Socialist Rev. 1971 32(11): 6-11, 35-39.* Discusses the ideology of the biological inferiority of women in patriarchal societies and anthropology in the 20th century, emphasizing cultural stereotypes of family structure and sexual division of labor.

120. Rosenbaum, Bella W. IN MY LIFETIME. *Am. Jewish Arch. 1967 19(1): 3-33.* The author was born in Kamenets Podolsk, on the Russo-Polish border, and spent her childhood in Winnipeg, Manitoba. She describes the life of Jewish immigrants in the western prairie lands during the 1880's, and later in Seattle, Washington. These reminiscences include personal observations of Indians in Manitoba and the Pacific Northwest, as well as the commercial growth of Seattle stimulated by the Klondike gold rush. Mrs. Rosenbaum was the first woman to practice law in the State of Washington. By 1914, she moved to New York, where she was impressed with the congestion and suffering within the ghettos of East European immigrants. She comments on their willingness to work arduously under difficult circumstances, describing the sweatshops, small stores, and airless tenements. Illus. J. Brandes

121. Shakow, David. GRACE HELEN KENT. *J. of the Hist. of the Behavioral Sci. 1974 10(3): 275-280.* Discusses the career, accomplishments, and influence of clinical psychologist Grace Helen Kent (1875-1973).

S

122. Silver, Morris. BIRTHS, MARRIAGES, AND BUSINESS CY-CLES IN THE UNITED STATES. *J. of Pol. Economy 1965 73(3): 237-255.* Attempts to analyze the effects of business cycles on births and marriages. The analysis is confined to data on the United States. The following questions are considered: 1) Do business cycles affect births and marriages?; 2) If they do, in what direction and with what strength? Have there been trends in cyclical responses? Two major conclusions emerge

from the study. Births and marriages conform positively to business cycles, and there have been no clear trends in the strengths of the cyclical responses of births and marriages.                                    H. Proschansky

123.   Smith, Page.   FROM MASSES TO PEOPLEHOOD.   *Hist. Reflections [Canada] 1974 1(1): 113-138.* Subordinate groups in a society "assert their humanity" or move from the "masses" to the "people" through self-definition and self-consciousness, not through any efforts of members of the dominant culture. Women and Negroes, the primary examples of this process, are compared to various immigrant and ethnic groups. Subordinate groups seeking to escape from the "masses" have common traits: passionate speech, eccentric and symbolic costume, discipline, violence, and pronounced sexual elements. Secondary sources; 20 notes, French summary.                                    C. G. Eiel

124.   Steiner, Ruth Heller.   "THE GIRLS" IN CHICAGO.   *Am. Jewish Arch. 1974 26(1): 5-22.* "Aunt Ernestine and Aunt Louise would have summed up their lives as 'a combination of luck and nerve,' but their niece, Mrs. Steiner, reflected that the word she would have chosen 'would be *character.'* "                                    J

125.   Stevenson, Janet.   A WOMAN'S PLACE.   *Am. Heritage 1968 19(3): 6-11, 96-102.* Frances Anne (Fanny) Kemble (1809-93), a remarkably gifted actress, was a member of an outstanding English theatrical family. She hated acting, however, and while on tour in the United States she married the wealthy Philadelphian, Pierce Butler. Describes the consequences of her marriage, the ensuing quarrels with Butler, and the subsequent divorce in 1849. The marriage suffered not only because of unique interpersonal relations but because the Butler fortune was predicated upon cotton profits derived from Southern slavery. Fanny was an outspoken abolitionist who published *The Journal of a Residence on a Georgia Plantation 1838-1839* which became a best seller on the eve of the Civil War. Details Fanny's life after divorce, relationships with her daughters, and her influence on Owen Wister, Fanny's gifted grandson who became an outstanding American novelist. Photos.
                                    J. D. Born, Jr.

126.   Stockwell, Edward G.   SOME NOTES ON THE CHANGING AGE COMPOSITION OF THE POPULATION OF THE UNITED STATES.   *Rural Sociol. 1964 29(1): 67-74.* Knowledge of age structure of population is necessary in planning for the future needs of a society. Up until 1950, median age in the United States was increasing; a decline was noticed in 1960. Population is analyzed by three major phases: "youth" (under 15 years), "adulthood" (15 to 64 years), and "old age" (65 years and over). Only the latter phase exhibits an unbroken increase between 1900 and 1960 and this is attributed to decline in the birth rate. The dependency ratio (persons under 15 and over 65) reached an all-time high in 1960 - 67.6 dependents per 100 active persons. There is also a narrowing of the gap between urban and rural populations. Between 1950 and 1960 there was an increase in youth dependency in urban areas and aged dependency in rural areas. The major characteristic of U.S. population is the large number of young people resulting from the baby boom of World War II and the continuation of high levels of fertility.
                                    A. S. Freedman

127.   Taeuber, Irene B. and Taeuber, Conrad.   PEOPLE OF THE UNITED STATES IN THE TWENTIETH CENTURY: CONTINUITY, DIVERSITY AND CHANGE.   *Social Sci. Res. Council Items 1971 25(2): 13-18.* Discusses demographic and fertility changes in the United States, especially internal migratory patterns, urbanization, levels of education, and economic and ethnic differences. Comparative statistics with each of these factors demonstrate effects on rates of fertility since 1900. Future demographic studies will require this more integrated type of approach to analyze changes within regions and subregions, within rural areas and cities, and inside and outside metropolitan areas.
                                    D. P. Peltier

128.   Taylor, Lloyd C.   HARRIET LANE - MIRROR OF AN AGE.   *Pennsylvania Hist. 1963 30(2): 231-225.* Describes briefly the personal life, political interests, and cultural contributions of Harriet Lane, James Buchanan's vivacious niece who accompanied him to England, served as first lady of the land, and was prominent in social welfare work in the period after the Civil War.                                    W. B. Miller

129.   Turner, Victor R.   HARMAN BLENNERHASSETT: HIS RISE AND FALL.   *Filson Club Hist. Q. 1964 38(4): 316-322.* Traces the lives of Harman Blennerhassett and his wife, Margaret Agnew Blennerhassett. Deals primarily with their misfortune stemming from their involvement in the conspiracy of Aaron Burr. Based largely on letters and documents in the possession of the Filson Club.                                    S. Frank

130.   Uhlenberg, P. R.   A STUDY OF COHORT LIFE CYCLES: COHORTS OF NATIVE-BORN MASSACHUSETTS WOMEN, 1830-1920.   *Population Studies [Great Britain] 1969 23(3): 407-420.* "This paper expands the conceptual apparatus of family life cycle analysis and illustrates its usefulness by applying it to a population. There is a normatively sanctioned life cycle that a female born into American society is expected to follow as she moves from birth to death: she is expected to survive through childhood, marry, bear and rear children, and survive jointly with her husband until her children leave the home. Paul Gliok, in several articles, has calculated mean ages at which these various events are experienced. The life cycle analysis proposed here, however, [is] on the distribution of women according to type of life cycle experienced. Starting with a cohort of 100,000 females, six alternative life cycle possibilities are differentiated and the number who follow each of the types is calculated. The six types are: 1) *abbreviated,* the female dies before she is exposed to the risk of marriage; 2) *spinster,* the woman is exposed to the risk of marriage but does not marry; 3) *barren,* the woman marries but remains childless; 4) *dying mother,* the woman has children but dies before the last one leaves home; 5) *widowed mother,* the woman has children and survives until they leave home, but her husband dies before that event; and 6) *typical,* the woman marries, has children, and survives jointly with her husband until the last one leaves home. Applying this approach to several cohorts of native-born Massachusetts women born at different times some striking changes appear. For example, the number of women from a birth cohort of 100,000 who follow the *typical* life cycle increases from 21,000 for the cohort born in 1830 to 57,000 for the cohort born in 1920. The demographic social and economic implications of a change of this magnitude are of considerable consequence." 5 tables, 11 notes, appendix.                                    J

131.   Wildavsky, Aaron.   THE SEARCH FOR THE OPPRESSED.   *Freedom at Issue 1972 (16): 5-6, 12, 14-16.* Discusses the growth of oppressed minorities, 1930-70, including consumers, women, ethnic groups, and racial minorities. There is loss of meaning for those who remain socially, culturally, politically, and economically deprived.

132.   —.   [WOMEN AND THE COMMUNITY].   *Radical Am. 1972 6(1): 62-102.*
James, Selma.   INTRODUCTION TO THE ENGLISH TRANSLATION (OF FOLLOWING ARTICLE),   *pp. 62-66.*
Costa, Mariarosa Dalla.   WOMEN AND THE SUBVERSION OF THE COMMUNITY,   *pp. 67-102.*
Discusses women's role in the family, the Catholic Church, and the labor force.                                    S

# Economic Sphere
### (including domestic labor)

133.   Arbogast, Kate A.   WOMEN IN THE ARMED FORCES: A REDISCOVERED RESOURCE.   *Military R. 1973 53(11): 9-19.* The lesson from the past for women in the American military has been one of acceptance only as a last resort. With the end of the draft, however, women could prove to be the answer to the military's qualitative and quantitative personnel problems. Based on primary and secondary sources; 2 illus., 4 figs., 18 notes.                                    J. K. Ohl

134.   Baker, Gladys L.   WOMEN IN THE U.S. DEPARTMENT OF AGRICULTURE.   *Agric. Hist. 1976 50(1): 190-201.* In its first decades the US Department of Agriculture hired only a few women, mainly as clerks, librarians, and assistant microscopists. Gradually in the early 20th century a few women made their mark as scientists and in the Office of Home Economics. Since then several women have advanced to important positions, although their percentage in the Department workforce remains small. 48 notes.                                    D. E. Bowers

135. Bartol, Kathryn M. and Bartol, Robert A. WOMEN IN MANA-GERIAL AND PROFESSIONAL POSITIONS: THE UNITED STATES AND THE SOVIET UNION. *Industrial & Labor Relations R. 1975 28(4): 524-534.* This study compares the employment of women in professional and managerial positions in the Soviet Union and the United States. The results indicate that women in the Soviet Union have made considerably greater progress than American women in the attainment of professional positions, but differences are less dramatic in managerial occupations. The data also suggest that many employment problems persist for Soviet women workers and that the USSR perhaps has been overrated as a model of employment equality.                      J

136. Boyd, Monica. OCCUPATIONS OF FEMALE IMMI-GRANTS AND NORTH AMERICAN IMMIGRATION STATIS-TICS. *Internat. Migration R. 1976 10(1): 73-80.* Discusses labor force potential and occupations of women immigrants to the United States and Canada, 1964-71.

137. Brugh, Anne E. and Beede, Benjamin R. AMERICAN LI-BRARIANSHIP. *Signs 1976 1(4): 943-955.* As in other woman domi-nated fields, library jobs are sex-typed according to the "harem" model. Men advance further and faster, earn higher salaries, and dominate the prestigious large academic libraries. The history of the feminization of library work illustrates how the high moral position of women, the cul-tural atmosphere of the public library movement, and library work's origin as a service to children combined to attract women to the occupa-tion. Their professionalization was discouraged in the 19th century by the social norm that once they married they retired from paid work. Today many women librarians are working for equitable treatment through a task force in the American Library Association, the Women Library Workers, trade unions, affirmative action programs, and consciousness-raising activities. Based on research reports and secondary works; 53 notes.                                                                          J. Gammage

138. Carnegie, Mary Elizabeth. THE IMPACT OF INTEGRATION ON THE NURSING PROFESSION: AN HISTORICAL SKETCH. *Negro Hist. Bull. 1965 28(7): 154-155, 168.* The Negro nurses in 1908 banded together into the National Association of Colored Graduate Nurses. Its archives contain invaluable information on the history of its struggle for integration. The Association was dissolved in 1951 after the American Nurses' Association agreed to admit Negroes. The author details the ways in which "prejudice in nursing is being exposed, identi-fied, and dealt with," as well as the extent to which Negro nurses are achieving recognition by holding important positions in a profession "fur-ther along the road to complete integration than any other profession" in the United States. Illus., 9 notes.                                     Edith P. Stickney

139. Cleverdon, Stephanie. ON THE BRINK: THREE ATTEMPTS TO LIBERATE WOMEN. *Working Papers For a New Soc. 1975 3(1): 28-36.* A survey of labor markets in Israel, Sweden, and the USSR shows that conditions in sex-segregated job markets must be equalized in the United States before equal employment opportunity will exist for women.                                                                                     S

140. Cowan, Ruth Schwartz. A CASE STUDY OF TECHNOLOGI-CAL AND SOCIAL CHANGE: THE WASHING MACHINE AND THE WORKING WIFE. Hartman, Mary and Banner, Lois W., eds. *Clio's Consciousness Raised: New Perspectives on the History of Women* (New York: Harper Torchbooks, 1974): 245-252. The industrial revolu-tion supposedly gave married women a new independence by freeing them from household duties and by creating factory and service jobs for them outside the home. Preliminary studies, however, do not substantiate this direct correlation between technological and social change. "Housewives used labor-saving devices to raise their standard of household care, thereby maintaining or even increasing the burden of their chores." Wom-en's occupations were low-paid and subservient and did not necessarily encourage a spirit of independence. Suggests areas for further research. 13 notes.                                                                          S

141. Ehrenreich, Barbara. THE HEALTH CARE INDUSTRY: A THEORY OF INDUSTRIAL MEDICINE. *Social Policy 1975 6(3): 4-11.* Discusses the respective roles of men and women in medicine from 1848 to the present, speculating on possible sex discrimination in the occupations of doctors and nurses.

142. Ehrenreich, Barbara and English, Dierdre. WITCHES, MID-WIVES, AND NURSES. *Monthly R. 1973 25(5): 25-40.* Describes witch suppression in medieval Europe and the rise of the medical profes-sion in 19th-century America as a means whereby men relegated women to a subservient role in health care.                                        S

143. Epstein, Cynthia. WOMEN AND THE PROFESSIONS. *New Generation 1969 51(4): 16-22.* Despite changes in the social status of women throughout the world, American women's participation in the professions has remained constant during the past 70 years.

144. Fletcher, Max E. HARRIET MARTINEAU AND AYN RAND: ECONOMICS IN THE GUISE OF FICTION. *Am. J. of Econ. and Sociol. 1974 33(4): 367-379.* The economic philosophies of Harriet Martineau and Ayn Rand are examined in their fiction. Their belief in the free-enterprise system is highlighted. Secondary sources; 31 notes.                                                                          W. L. Marr

145. Goldstein, Jinny M. AFFIRMATIVE ACTION: EQUAL EM-PLOYMENT RIGHTS FOR WOMEN IN ACADEMIA. *Teachers Coll. Record 1973 74(3): 395-422.* Analyzes evolving relationship be-tween the federal government and colleges in the field of sex discrimina-tion.                                                                          S

146. Haber, Sheldon. TRENDS IN WORK RATES OF WHITE FEMALES, 1890 TO 1950. *Industrial and Labor Relations R. 1973 26(4): 1122-1134.* "The dramatic increase over the years in the labor force participation rate of women has been the subject of considerable specula-tion and research, with most analysts stressing the effect on this rate of changes that have occurred on the supply side of the market. Using census data for 1890, 1920, and 1950, this study tests the relationship between the participation rates of white females and a major demand variable— the industrial structure of the economy—as well as supply variables such as educational attainment. The author concludes that changes in indus-trial structure have been far more significant than previously realized as a determinant of the increase in the work rates of women."            J

147. Henderson, James D. MEALS BY FRED HARVEY. *Arizona and the West 1966 8(4): 305-322.* In 1850, Frederick Henry Harvey, an English lad of 15, arrived in New York with two pounds cash. Securing a two-dollar-a-week dishwashing job he began to accumulate restaurant business knowledge. By 1859 he had become an American citizen and had saved enough money to establish his own restaurant in St. Louis. Because a partner absconded with the restaurant funds, Harvey found employ-ment in a variety of other occupations and gained valuable experience in railroading, ranching, and journalism. These forced him to travel about the country considerably. Impressed with the miserable facilities or even lack of them for travelers, he experimented briefly with two eating houses on the Kansas Pacific Railroad. In 1876 he sold the Atchison, Topeka and Santa Fe on his ideas and was soon revamping their two-year-old food service. The first Fred Harvey House was opened in Topeka, Kansas, and and was an immediate success. His first restaurant-hotel was opened in Florence, Kansas, in mid-1878. Others followed, and with his high stan-dards and the surprise-inspection visit device Harvey was able to maintain near perfection. A fortunate move was the replacement of all male waiters by the "Harvey girls" who were uniformly dressed, well-trained and the essence of proficiency and politeness. Fred Harvey built America's first restaurant chain, with his 75 Harvey Houses placed at regular meal stops along the 12,000-mile Santa Fe system. Santa Fe officials pampered Har-vey, to their mutual benefit. 5 illus., map.                              D. L. Smith

148. Kriegel, Leonard. SILENT IN THE SUPERMARKET. *Dissent 1972 19(1): 91-98.* An interview with a retired organizer for the Fur Workers who gives vignettes of the history of the International Ladies' Garment Workers' Union.                                            S

149. Leal, Ronald. RUB A DUB DUB: A SHORT HISTORY OF HOME LAUNDRY. *Mankind 1968 1(10): 50-54.* Traces laundry methods from about 1184 B.C. to the invention of the mechanical washer in the late 19th century.                                                    S

150. Madden, Janice. THE DEVELOPMENT OF ECONOMIC THOUGHT ON THE "WOMAN PROBLEM." *Rev. of Radical Pol. Econ. 1972 4(3): 21-39.* Writings about the economic role of women

commonly are found outside economic journals. Reviews British and American theories of discrimination and wonders if their assumptions about the market are valid. Notes effects of different definitions. Early feminist literature, Marxist contributions, and more recent theories are considered. Based on statistical data and secondary sources; 3 figs., 41 notes.                                        C. P. de Young

151.  Markoff, Helene S.  THE FEDERAL WOMEN'S PROGRAM. *Public Administration Rev. 1972 32(2): 144-151.* In spite of the fact that women were employed in public service before the Constitution was signed; in spite of the fact that the Civil Service Act of 1883 encouraged women to compete in civil service examinations on the same basis as men; and in spite of the fact that the Classification Act of 1923 established the concept of "equal pay for equal work," it took other actions to move toward equal opportunity for women in the federal service. In 1965, an 1870 law that permitted agencies to select men or women for vacancies was repealed by Congress; in 1967, an Executive Order added sex to other prohibited forms of discrimination (race, color, religion, and national origin); and subsequently, in 1967, the Federal Women's Program was established to enhance the employment and advancement of women in the federal government. Further, President Nixon's Executive Order 11478 of August 8, 1969, raised the level of attention on the Federal Women's Program by integrating it into the overall Equal Employment Opportunity Program. Equal opportunity for women is public policy. The Federal Women's Program is designed to insure that this policy becomes practice.                                                        J

152.  McKelvey, Blake.  ORGANIZED LABOR IN ROCHESTER BEFORE 1914. *Rochester Hist. 1963 25(1): 1-24.* Traces, from the early 1800's, the emergence and activities of organized labor in Rochester, New York. Old journeymen's associations, dating from colonial times, became aggressively interested in working conditions, wages, and hours. Coopers, masons, garment workers (who organized the Women's Protection Union in 1848), cigar makers, etc., formed the first central-trades council in America in 1863. Strikes and increasing membership are recorded as they occurred in Rochester up to the beginning of World War I. Based on local and city records.                        M. W. Machan

153.  Moore, R. Laurence.  THE SPIRITUALIST MEDIUM: A STUDY OF FEMALE PROFESSIONALISM IN VICTORIAN AMERICA. *Am. Q. 1975 27(2): 200-221.* Female spiritualists in the 19th century gained upward social mobility, self-esteem, and a feeling of helping others through the practice of their profession. Many times physically weak and sickly before engaging in spiritualism, these women were able to endure extensive travel and arduous road conditions in the practice of their work and often were able to achieve financial independence, respect from males, and a sense of sexual freedom.          N. Lederer

154.  Oppenheimer, Valerie.  THE INTERACTION OF DEMAND AND SUPPLY AND ITS EFFECT ON THE FEMALE LABOUR FORCE IN THE UNITED STATES. *Population Studies [Great Britain] 1967 21(3): 239-259.* "In both 1900 and 1940 young women and unmarried women formed the most component of the female labour force. By 1960 however older women and married women had replaced them. An explanation for this shift is sought in divergent trends in the demand for female labour and in the supply of the kind of female workers typical of the 1900-1940 period. Three series of estimates of the demand for female labour are compared to six series of estimates for the supply of different types women. It was found that all three series of estimates of demand showed a rising demand for female workers in the 1900 to 1960 period. However, the number of young women (those aged 18-34) and of unmarried women, aged 18-64, was actually declining in the 1940 to 1960 period. As a consequence, the supply of such women was well below our estimates of demand in 1960. The maintenance and continued expansion of the female labour force in the 1940 to 1960 period rested, therefore, on the greater utilization of married women and women over the age of 35. As a consequence, the age and marital-status composition of the female labour force has undergone considerable changes in the 1940 to 1960 period." 21 notes.                                          J

155.  Plischke, Elmer.  UNITED STATES DIPLOMATS SINCE 1778: BICENTENNIAL REVIEW AND FUTURE PROJECTION. *World Affairs 1975-76 138(3): 205-218.* Reviews US diplomats since 1778 in terms of age, sex, assignments, and careers.

156.  Rabinowitz, Dorothy.  THE CASE OF THE ILGWU. *Dissent 1972 19(1): 83-90.* Depicts rational and nonrational racial and ethnic conflicts in the International Ladies' Garment Workers' Union.          S

157.  Robinson, Dwight E.  THE IMPORTANCE OF FASHIONS IN TASTE TO BUSINESS HISTORY: AN INTRODUCTORY ESSAY. *Business Hist. R. 1963 37(1/2): 5-36.* Concludes that the relationship of consumer tastes to marketing of standardized products is of interest to both the historian of style and the business historian. The author states that "volume production of standardized commodities has been essential to Western civilization's great gains in productivity, but, equally well, that standardization or conformity of consumer tastes has been essential to volume marketing of standardized products."              J. H. Krenkel

158.  Rohrlich, Laura T. and Vatter, Ethel L.  WOMEN IN THE WORLD OF WORK: PAST, PRESENT AND FUTURE. *Women's Studies 1973 1(3): 263-277.* Provides historical analysis of changes responsible for women's entry and participation in the American labor market. Four main aspects to these social and technological changes are: women have always worked but the site of economic activity has changed; the economy has shifted from one demanding brawn to one demanding brains; improved health, contraception and longevity have affected job tenure; and the possibility for several careers in one lifetime has altered people's aspirations. Author predicts that the recent surge of women's participation in the labor market will continue if the utilization of women workers is essential to maintain the prevailing level of economic activity and if women use political power to work for equal opportunity. Future labor force requirements, trends in demographic, educational, and technological developments, and the implications of these for women's future participation in the labor force also are discussed. Based on primary and secondary materials; table, 20 notes.              A. E. Wiederrecht

159.  Sandell, Steven H.  DISCUSSION. *Amer. Econ. Rev. 1972 62(2): 175-176.* Discusses employment discrimination against women in the labor market and in the home in the 20th century.

160.  Sassower, Doris L.  WOMEN IN THE LAW: THE SECOND HUNDRED YEARS. *Am. Bar Assoc. J. 1971 57(4): 329-332.* "The first woman was admitted to a state Bar in the United States in 1869. But the 'progress' of women in the law since then has been little short of dismal. What does the next hundred years hold in store? The Professional Women's Caucus, a new group, hopes that its activities will make the second hundred brighter than the first."                            J

161.  Sharpsteen, Bernice T.  THE CALLUSTRO COMPANY. *California Historian 1967 13(4): 119-120, 134.* Relates the efforts of Emma P. Eels, widow of a Congregational minister and several of her women friends to organize and operate a company which would market "Callustro," a product to clean and polish metal surfaces. The product was accepted as efficient, but the quantities sold were small and expenses were heavy. Foreclosure of mortgages brought an end to the Callustro Company.                                        O. L. Miller

162.  Sorkin, Alan L.  ON THE OCCUPATIONAL STATUS OF WOMEN, 1870-1970. *Am. J. of Econ. and Sociol. 1973 32(3): 235-243.* Constructs an occupational-earnings index comparing males and females in the United States, 1870-1970. Explores the reasons for females doing relatively better before 1920 and worse after 1920. Secondary sources; 2 tables, 23 notes.                                        W. L. Marr

163.  Spengler, Joseph J.  SERVICES AND THE FUTURE OF THE AMERICAN ECONOMY. *South Atlantic Q. 1967 66(1): 105-115.* The United States is mankind's first "service economy," where less than half the labor force produces tangible goods. The shift to services became pronounced after World War I, and the "ability of most Americans to find employment in the next twenty to twenty-five years depends mainly on the degree to which services are expanded." The service sector differs from the goods sector in that women, older workers, and part-time workers find it easier to get jobs. Moreover, the service sector is less subject to cyclical fluctuation, is less highly unionized, and olfers more scope for small-scale enterprise and self-employment. But there are many problems inherent in a service economy in economic terms, and in educational ones as well. 11 notes.                                    J. M. Bumsted

164. Stover, Ed. INFLATION AND THE FEMALE LABOR FORCE. *Monthly R. 1975 26(8): 50-58.* Inflation has increased the number of women in the labor force and diminished family production while increasing family consumption and turning the housewife into a person directly exploited by capitalism.

165. Sumner, Helen L. THE HISTORICAL DEVELOPMENT OF WOMEN'S WORK IN THE UNITED STATES. *Pro. of the Acad. of Pol. Sci. 1971 30(3): 101-113.* One of 22 articles in this issue on "Control or Fate in Economic Affairs"; previously published in the October 1910 issue.                                                          S

166. —. [HISTORICAL STUDIES OF THE AMERICAN PUBLIC LIBRARY]. *J. of Lib. Hist., Philosophy, and Comparative Librarianship 1975 10(2): 99-116.*
Fain, Elaine. MANNERS AND MORALS IN THE PUBLIC LIBRARY: A GLANCE AT SOME NEW HISTORY, pp. 99-105. A comparison and critique of Michael H. Harris' "The Purpose of the American Public Library: A Revisionist Interpretation of History" (*Library Journal* 1973 98: 2509-2514) and Dee Garrison's "The Tender Technicians: The Feminization of Public Librarianship, 1876-1905" (Journal of Social History 1973 6(2): 131-159; see abstract 12A:). While there is a need for new historical studies of the American public library, these two authors demonstrate "a kind of single-minded pursuit of a thesis which prevents them from examining evidence as carefully as they might," and draw virtually unfounded, sweeping conclusions. Secondary sources; 15 notes.
Garrison, Dee. REJOINDER, pp. 111-116. A rejoinder to Fain's critique, claiming that Fain misinterpreted Garrison's article. Early women librarians did not really lack authority, but were simply believers in the antifeminist ideology of the time. Primary and secondary sources; 4 notes.
Harris, Michael H. EXTERNALIST OR INTERNALIST FRAMEWORKS FOR THE INTERPRETATION OF AMERICAN LIBRARY HISTORY—THE CONTINUING DEBATE, pp. 106-110. An apologia to Fain's critique of the articles by Harris and Garrison. Explains the differences in his and Garrison's approaches as a result of their different backgrounds and career emphases and defends his position that librarians have really had very little control over their professional destinies. Primary sources; 7 notes.                                                          A. C. Dewees

167. —. LOOM, BROOM AND WOMB: PRODUCERS, MAINTAINERS AND REPRODUCERS. *Radical Am. 1976 10(2): 29-45.* Women's work under capitalism can be examined in the historical phases of precapitalism (before 1820), competitive capitalism (1820-90), and monopoly capitalism (from 1890 to the present). Housework has contradictory demands placed on it under capitalism and can be understood in its contradictions only in relation to the capitalist sphere. The long-term increase in the numbers and percentages of women working for wages and salaries has been accompanied by an increase in women permanently employed. However, women are still used as a source of cheap and temporary or seasonal labor. A study by the Women's Work Study Group.                                                          N. Lederer

# Social Sphere

168. Andrews, William D. and Andrews, Deborah C. TECHNOLOGY AND THE HOUSEWIFE IN NINETEENTH-CENTURY AMERICA. *Women's Studies 1974 2(3): 309-328.* Analyzes the complex relationship between technology and the housewife within the social context of the 19th century United States. Technology stimulated a perception of the home as a moral center with woman the divinely appointed ruler and provided bases for woman's role as professional housekeeper. For people such as Catherine Beecher, who lauded woman's domestic role and protested her subordinate position, the professionalization of housekeeping raised woman's status and increased her power. The advocates of domestic science, in contrast to the feminists, believed women's problems and wrongs could be solved in domestic terms when women had a profession, housekeeping, equal in status and power to the professions of men. Artifacts of technology, such as the Rumford stove, put women in the kitchen, the core of the home, rather than removing them from

household activities. Domestic science emphasized order, economy, system, efficiency, and time expenditure which reflected the values and assumptions of professional disciplines such as engineering. The Woman's Building at the Centennial Exhibition of 1876, in Philadelphia, gave symbolic expression to the relation between technology and woman's status as professional housekeeper. Based on primary and secondary materials; 6 illus., 10 notes.                                                          A. E. Wiederrecht

169. Bardis, Panos D. CHANGES IN THE COLONIAL AND MODERN AMERICAN FAMILY SYSTEMS. *Social Sci. 1963 38(2): 103-114.* Contrasts American family systems in the colonial and modern periods by analyzing the salient features during each era. Major changes which have taken place include: choosing a mate on the basis of romantic love; a decline in parental authority; the emancipation of women; reduction in the size of families; greater emphasis on child welfare; the decline in economic, educational, religious, recreational, and protective functions of the family; and an increase in various forms of family disorganization. Drawn from standard publications about the family.                                                          M. Small

170. Barker-Benfield, Ben. THE SPERMATIC ECONOMY: A NINETEENTH CENTURY VIEW OF SEXUALITY. *Feminist Studies 1972 1(1): 45-74.* "Explores the sexual anxieties of men in 19th-century America, and describes their expression in masturbation phobia and in the phenomenal development of gynecology . . . ," which is associated with democracy. Reverend John Todd (1800-73), whose views of male psychology were typical of American writers, wrote the most popular of the self-help books, *The Student's Manual* (1835), which is pervaded explicitly and implicitly with masturbation phobia. Drastic gynecological surgery and the rise of eugenics were coterminous expressions of a "desperate attempt to control and shape procreative powers as if the American body politic were literally a body." The aims of the gynecologists were those of society: retaliation against and control of women. Their methods were clitoridectomy, banishment of midwives, and female castration. Gynecologists and writers identified the mastery of woman's body with man's exploitation of nature's body and used the same metaphors to describe man's conquest of self, of woman, and of nature. The 19th-century male concept of woman in rhetoric and practice was fraught with ironies, contradictions, and psychic ambiguities. 166 notes.                                                          J. D. Falk

171. Barrett, Wayne. GEORGE AND BETSY AND POLLY AND PATSY AND SALLY . . . AND SALLY . . . AND SALLY. *Smithsonian 1973 4(8): 90-99.* Discusses George Washington's romances (1750's-99) and his love for Sally Cary Fairfax, a married woman.                                                          S

172. Bartlett, Irving H. and Cambor, C. Glenn. THE HISTORY AND PSYCHODYNAMICS OF SOUTHERN WOMANHOOD. *Women's Studies 1974 2(1): 9-24.* Using the perspectives of history and of psychoanalysis, the authors depict and analyze the 19th century stereotype of the southern lady. Although the stereotype reflected the ideal, feminine image of womanhood common throughout the United States, the southern feminine stereotype of the lady was significantly different from the national norm. The stereotype of the southern, white lady grew out of the close, personal relationships among black and white persons under the conditions of slavery. In the eyes of the South, the existence of black slave women permitted southern white women to be pure and kept white prostitutes out of the region. Southern childrearing practices, in which black women raised white men, shaped the psycho-sexual development of the white male child, and help explain the sexual attraction of black women for white men, why the white men compensatorily overevaluated white women, and why southern white womanhood became identified as the preserver of purity, the perpetuator of white superiority, and the symbol of the South itself. Any attack on the South and its culture became an attack on southern white womanhood. Based on primary and secondary materials; 38 notes.                                                          A. E. Wiederrecht

173. Bazin, Nancy Topping and Freeman, Alma. THE ANDROGYNOUS VISION. *Women's Studies 1974 2(2): 185-215.* Suggests a vision of androgyny essential for the eradication of sex roles and the elimination of male structures and values. In an androgynous society, there are no sex roles and no economic, racial, or sexual inequalities. There is a social unity and a psychic unity in which everyone has a new sense of wholeness. Discusses the historical meaning of androgyny and examines the significance of the Masculine and Feminine principles as traditional symbolic

concepts by analyzing pertinent writings particularly from Taoist philosophy, Western literature, and psychology. Examines the nature of the patriarchal, capitalistic society which exalts male values, assesses the danger and costs such a society poses for individuals and human relationships, and suggests the radical change required by the androgynous ideal. Based on primary materials; 52 notes.                    A. E. Wiederrecht

174. Berghorn, Forrest and Steere, Geoffrey H. ARE AMERICAN VALUES CHANGING? THE PROBLEM OF INNER - OR OTHER - DIRECTION. *Am. Q. 1966 18(1): 52-62.* Examines David Riesman's concepts of inner and other direction to determine their "applicability to empirical research." Procedures for a validation study are described and findings are related. Riesman's typology breaks down in that respondents do not consistently reveal either inner or other direction. Instead, values of respondents tended to become composites of inner plus other direction. A historical study of American child-rearing values in the 19th and 20th centuries also reveals that the Riesman categories failed to materialize. Neither did a historical shift in child-rearing values from one century to the next appear as Riesman had theorized. The only apparent shift occurred in the *sources* of child-rearing authority. Increasingly, secular authorities, e.g., psychoanalysts, came to replace religious authorities, e.g., ministers. Although values no doubt changed, Riesman's categories do not appear to be viable instruments for interpreting the shift. 17 notes.                    R. S. Pickett

175. Bien, Bettina. THE LIBERATION OF WOMEN: THOUGHTS ON READING SOME OLD COOKBOOKS. *Freeman 1971 21(2): 87-92.* Recent decades have witnessed an unprecedented expansion in the professional and economic opportunities available to women as well as in guaranteed legal equality. This emancipation is due in large part to the successful operation of the capitalist system, which has liberated women from their once most onerous task and full-time occupation, the care of family and home. For example, simply contrast the exhausting nature of homemaking in the 19th century, as suggested in such housekeeping manuals as Lydia Maria Francis Child's *The American Frugal Housewife* (12th ed., 1832) and Mrs. M. H. Cornelius' *The Young Housekeeper's Friend* (1859), with that of the push-button ease of 1970. Illus., note.                    D. A. Yanchisin

176. Brogan, Catherine Lee. CHANGING PERSPECTIVES ON THE ROLE OF WOMEN. *Smith Coll. Studies in Social Work 1972 42(2): 155-173.* A theoretical analysis of changing views of female psychology and woman's role in society. Evaluates the ideas of Sigmund Freud, Alfred Adler, Helene Deutsch, Karen Horney, and others. Reviews anthropological and sociological approaches to the problem. "The traditional view emphasizes innate biological factors and the alternatives emphasize the influence of a patriarchal culture, the socialization process, and the importance of economics, law and politics in shaping the prescribed social role for woman and ultimately the individual woman's attitude toward herself." 71 notes.                    M. A. Kaufman

177. Brown, Carol. SEXISM AND THE RUSSELL SAGE FOUNDATION. *Feminist Studies 1972 1(1): 25-44.* Examines the permeation of sexism in a major social research foundation which, founded by a woman, at first emphasized women. The financial crisis of 1947 resulted in a reorganization of the foundation, modification of goals and programs, and a change in the proportion and status of women personnel. The foundation shifted its emphasis from amelioration of social problems to research, with decreased concern for the social and living conditions of human beings and especially for women. Concludes with specific suggestions for redefining the foundation, presently run by and in the interests of the managerial elite white males, so it could benefit social science and society. 50 notes.                    J. D. Falk

178. Buhle, Mari Jo; Gordon, Ann D.; and Schrom, Nancy. WOMEN IN AMERICAN SOCIETY: AN HISTORICAL CONTRIBUTION. *Radical Am. 1971 5(4): 3-66.* Discusses the historical role of women in the 19th and 20th centuries and how in spite of economic, technological, and social changes, the ideological assumptions regarding women have remained the same.

179. Bullough, Vern L. AN EARLY AMERICAN SEX MANUAL, OR, ARISTOTLE WHO? *Early Am. Literature 1973 7(3): 236-246.* A pseudonymous sex manual, usually identified as *Aristotle's Master-piece* or *The Complete Works of Aristotle,* was probably the most widely reprinted "medical" book in the 18th and early 19th centuries. It presented a hard core of sexual information and misinformation to English and American readers. Medically the work was based on the Hippocratic humoral pathology and included numerous potions and antidotes that would cause the modern physician to shudder, but from a cultural and psychological point of view it promoted a healthier view of sex and was much more accurate than many "scientific" treatises on sex in the late 19th century and early 20th century. Based on primary and secondary sources; illus., 10 notes.                    D. P. Wharton

180. Bullough, Vern L. and Voght, Martha. HOMOSEXUALITY AND ITS CONFUSION WITH THE "SECRET SIN" IN PRE-FREUDIAN AMERICA. *J. of the Hist. of Medicine and Allied Sci. 1973 28(2): 143-155.* Describes American medical views of masturbation and homosexuality in the 19th century, based on a few such examples and the effect of the confusion of the two in creating a general fear of sex. Homosexuality was often classified under the term onanism or masturbation. In effect everything except heterosexual intercourse undertaken as part of procreation was abuse, and abuse in much of the 19th century was equated with onanism. Inevitably masturbation became the term which American physicians used, even when they were aware of the variety of human sexual activities. Though physicians finally began to have a better understanding of sex, the misconceptions under which they labored became the dominant theme of American sex manuals until fairly late into the 20th century. Based on primary and secondary sources; 36 notes.                    J. L. Susskind

181. Bullough, Vern and Voght, Martha. WOMEN, MENSTRUATION, AND NINETEENTH-CENTURY MEDICINE. *Bull. of the Hist. of Medicine 1973 47(1): 66-82.* Examines the misconceptions of 19th-century physicians concerning the consequences of menstruation. Paper read at the 45th annual meeting of the American Association for the History of Medicine in Montreal, Canada, 4 May 1972.                    S

182. Burke, Armand F. THE CHANGING FAMILY IN AMERICAN FICTION. *Contemporary R. [Great Britain] 1966 208(1202): 151-159.* The American family has been critically portrayed in fiction for over a century. In the 19th century only serious novels of manners are a valid source, and the example quoted stresses the destructive impact of a changing world on the family unit. In the early part of this century the city and materialism continued as causes of family disruption, but after 1920 the moral, spiritual, and emotional failure of America was seen as manifesting itself at the family level. The best fiction in the 1930's dealing with family life was found in the proletarian novel, while some of the most interesting fiction of the past decade has dealt with Jewish-American families and their search for happiness in an affluent society. Portrayal of the family in the novel reflects the "old American see-saw between idealism and pragmatism." Undocumented but extensive reference to novels in the text.                    D. H. Murdoch

183. Butz, Pauline. THE FASHION CYCLE OF COSTUME. *Northwest Ohio Q. 1966 38(1): 10-14.* Using an exhibition of 19th-century fashions at the Wolcott House Museum of Maumee, Ohio in October 1965 as a background, the author traces the major trends in feminine fashions from 1827 to 1895. Women's skirts are identified as tubular, bell, and with back fullness. Since the early 1700's fashion cycles have followed an orderly succession with approximately three changes per century. Styles are shown to have been influenced greatly by such things as the invention of the sewing machine, the Civil War, the bicycle-riding craze, a mounting concern over the influence of dress on health, and an interest in designing clothing that granted the body greater freedom and "no longer swept up the dust and microbes on the pavement."                    W. F. Zornow

184. Cable, Mary. S*X EDUCATION. *Am. Heritage 1974 25(6): 41-47, 73.* Victorian moralist sex education for children.                    S

185. Calhoun, Daniel. THE CITY AS TEACHER: HISTORICAL PROBLEMS. *Hist. of Educ. Q. 1969 9(3): 312-325.* Effects of an urban environment filter down to individuals through family and child-rearing attitudes and are more educative than is the school as an institution. The author asks that we investigate more closely these environmental influences and their relationship to intelligence. How did urbanization serve

to heighten the mental performance of children? What were the historical forms in which were cast the conflict between inward personal forces and environmental influences? The author points to the tension that has existed between an evangelical revivalism and an urban culture, between grace (Antinomianism) and environment (Arminianism), and between child-rearing fads in an indulgent, maternal household.   J. Herbst

186. Carson, Gerald. THE PIANO IN THE PARLOR. *Am. Heritage 1965 17(1): 54-58, 91.* Traces the rise and decline in popularity of the piano in the parlor. "The pianoforte made the transit to America in the eighteenth century. Thomas Jefferson saw a *forte piano* in 1771 and was charmed with it. In 1788, a French journalist recorded that he saw an occasional piano in Boston drawing rooms. All were London-made. By 1840 the 'American piano girl' was a recognizable type . . . In 1905, before the bathroom emerged as the shrine of the American home, there were more pianos and organs in this country than bathtubs." By the 1930's the era of the piano as a social symbol had ended. Illus.
D. D. Cameron

187. Cervantes, Lucius F. WOMAN'S CHANGING ROLE IN SOCIETY. *Thought 1965 40(158): 325-368.* Surveys woman's changing position in society, opening with a short discussion of woman's differences from man, physically and psychically, and then takes up the history of woman's social position from primitive societies to the present. The importance of Christianity in the changes that have taken place, particularly the influence of the Roman Catholic Church, is stressed. Biblio.
W. S. Reid

188. Christensen, Harold T. and Cannon, Kenneth L. TEMPLE "VERSUS" NONTEMPLE MARRIAGE IN UTAH: SOME DEMOGRAPHIC CONSIDERATIONS. *Social Sci. 1964 39(1): 26-33.* Compares temple marriage, the most valued type in Mormon culture, with nontemple marriage in two Utah counties. The temple group had fewer teenage marriages, vastly fewer premarital pregnancies, and a considerably lower eventual divorce rate. Temple marriages showed a greater tendency toward beginning a family soon after the wedding - consistent with the higher-than-average birth rate in Utah. Study is based on marriages in Utah County during 1939-41 and 1949-51, and in Salt Lake County during 1950.
M. Small

189. Coy, Edna. MARRIAGE. *Midwest Q. 1969 10(3): 247-260.* A study of the institution of marriage among our cultural ancestors and contemporary peoples including primitives, inferring neither decadence nor decline but examining an interesting variety of customs, many of which have been and still are changing. Probably the oldest human institution, marriage would seem to be universal and essential for the care of the young and the regulation of the sex drive. Some of the aspects discussed are incest, religious elements, dowry, bride price, plural marriages, illegitimacy, and divorce. In each culture changes within the structure and influences from outside cultures are the two modes of departure from the only true and proper pattern. Undocumented.
G. H. G. Jones

190. Curtis, James. VOLUNTARY ASSOCIATION JOINING: A CROSS-NATIONAL COMPARATIVE NOTE. *Am. Sociol. R. 1971 36(5): 872-880.* "Secondary analysis of data from national surveys of Americans, Canadians and adults in four other countries are offered in order to provide perspective on the observation that Americans are a nation of joiners and related propositions in the literature. The broad hypotheses considered are that: (1) the uniqueness and scope of the American pattern of association joining have been overemphasized; and (2) previous American findings on correlates of association membership should obtain in other democracies as well. For each nation, findings on the relationship of membership to social class, sex, age level and marital status are in essential agreement with earlier American findings. Results on affiliation by community size indicate no consistent direct relationships. Subgroups of Canadians and Americans have similar, comparatively high, proportions of memberships. Analysis of membership by sex shows that the uniqueness of the affiliation patterns in these two countries may be, in large part, a result of national differences in the participatory roles of women."
J

191. DeMille, Agnes. WHATEVER HAS BECOME OF MOMMY? *Horizon 1966 8(3): 4-15.* Examines the dress of both sexes in the 19th and 20th centuries and finds recurring patterns: wild extravagance, followed by an abrupt return to romanticism, then revolution or war. Today "Mama imitates her daughter, who imitates big brother, who is revolting against Papa in the strongest form he can find to express disapproval, namely, un-masculinity....He goes fancy and feminine, i.e., toward Mama." Exaggerations in the differentiation of sex, as well as confusions, are symptomatic of social reconstruction. Illus.
E. P. Stickney

192. Demos, John. THE AMERICAN FAMILY IN PAST TIME. *Am. Scholar 1974 43(3): 422-446.* Traces the history of the family in the United States from colonial times to the 20th century, discussing the tremendous changes in life and culture which have put great pressures on the family. Examines authority relations in the family, the role of children, women, sex, and the impact made upon the family by immigration and Negroes. Denies there is a continuous decline and decay in the family as both conservatives and counterculturists claim.
C. W. Olson

193. Dixon, Ruth B. HALLELUJAH THE PILL? *Trans-Action 1970 8(1/2): 44-49, 92.* Examines the use of oral contraceptives and the effect which they have had on women's choice in reproduction. Maintains that freedom of choice in these areas is not enough. Freedom in the choice of careers and life-styles through change in societal values must also be accomplished before true liberation is reached, 1930-70.
G. A. Hewlett

194. Edmands, John B. THE PATTERNS, THE COMMUNITY, AND THE PEOPLE. *Pacific Historian 1965 9(2): 69-72.* Text of the keynote address delivered to the California History Institute at its 1965 meeting, dealing primarily with the impact of social change on the family and other institutions.
S

195. Farley, Reynolds and Hermalin, Albert I. FAMILY STABILITY: A COMPARISON OF TRENDS BETWEEN BLACKS AND WHITES. *Am. Sociol. R. 1971 36(1): 1-17.* "From the 1890s to the present, writers have commented upon the instability of Negro family life. Most have observed that discrimination in the job and housing markets have made it difficult for black men to support their wives and children. As a result, desertion occurs commonly. Family stability has been of interest because of the belief that children who grow up apart from their parents will be adversely affected. Indeed, some investigations imply that being raised in a home which did not have both parents is linked to lower rates of achievement in school, higher rates of delinquency and lower occupational status. While commentators have discussed family stability, there has been little consensus as to how this concept should be measured. Moreover, there are only a few demographic indicators available for operationalizing this concept, particularly if one desires to study long-term trends or to compare blacks and whites. The major portion of this paper examines Negro and white trends on a number of indicators related to a specific definition of family stability. This study concludes that (1) the majority of both blacks and whites are in the statuses indicative of family stability. Contrary to the images which are sometimes portrayed, most black families are husband-wife families, and the majority of black children live with both parents. (2) In every comparison, the proportion of people in the status indicative of family stability is greater among whites than among blacks. (3) In recent years there have been changes in family status, although most of them have been small. Some changes suggest a trend toward greater stability while others indicate a trend in the opposite direction."
J

196. Ferrarotti, Franco. LA FAMIGLIA IN USA [The family in the United States]. *I Problemi di Ulisse [Italy] 1963 8(51): 70-77.* The status of the family in one of the most highly industrialized societies may harbinger a problem in countries of lesser technological development. During the past 60 years the American family has changed in structure and in function. The father has ceased to represent the apex of authority and responsibility; the mother is often economically independent and consequently she and the children take their own places in the family on a par with the father. The old familial functions of care and education are being transferred to organizations outside the home. At the same time new values and roles are gradually forming that may possibly furnish the basis for the family ties of tomorrow. Documented.
M. P. Trauth

197.  Festy, P.  CANADA, UNITED STATES, AUSTRALIA AND NEW ZEALAND: NUPTIALITY TRENDS.  *Population Studies [Great Britain] 1973 27(3): 479-492.* "Nuptiality, which is generally supposed to be stable in the long run, has undergone important changes in the last 100 birth cohorts (1830 to 1940 approximately). There was, first, a convergence of nuptiality levels among the four countries, then a general increase of proportions ever-married in the 30 generations 1900 to 1930. Moreover, the decline in the age at first marriage has greatly accelerated in the last 15 cohorts. Some other movements resulted from sex imbalance on the marriage market and economic fluctuations. Over the 1950-1970 period, some correlation has been shown to exist between short-term changes in nuptiality and economic activity, but the continuing decline in age at marriage resulted in a high level of nuptiality during most of the period."                                                      J

198.  Freedman, Alex S.  THE PASSING OF THE ARKANSAS GRANNY MIDWIFE.  *Kentucky Folklore Record 1974 20(4): 101-103.*

199.  Furstenberg, Frank F., Jr.  INDUSTRIALIZATION AND THE AMERICAN FAMILY: A LOOK BACKWARD.  *Am. Sociol. R. 1966 31(3): 326-337.* "It is frequently assumed that the American family has undergone considerable change since industrialization. By referring to the accounts of European travelers visiting the United States during the first half of the nineteenth century, it is possible to bring together a large number of detailed observations on the American family prior to industrialization. Great similarities are apparent between the modern family and the family of a century ago. Certain strains, often thought to be associated with the advent of industrialization, are evident in the pre-industrial family. Tensions resulting from free mate selection, stress on early marriage, permissive childrearing, and the woman's role were observed. Changes in family problems that have occurred in the past century are noted."                                                      J

200.  Gelpi, Barbara Charlesworth.  THE POLITICS OF ANDROGYNY.  *Women's Studies 1974 2(2): 151-160.* Discusses the meaning of androgyny and examines the different theories of androgyny historically put forth in Western society. There are two sorts of androgynes: the feminine personality which is fulfilled and completed by the masculine and the masculine personality which is fulfilled and completed by the feminine. Analysis of Greek myths, Judaeo-Christian writings, 17th and 19th century theories shows their patriarchal nature and their assumptions of women's inferiority. The visions of androgyny are always of the masculine personality fulfilled and completed by the feminine. It is necessary for women to begin speculating on what it means to have the reintegration of the masculine principles into the feminine personality. Based on primary materials; 17 notes.                   A. E. Wiederrecht

201.  Giele, Janet Zollinger.  CENTURIES OF WOMANHOOD: AN EVOLUTIONARY PERSPECTIVE ON THE FEMININE ROLE.  *Women's Studies 1972 1(1): 97-110.* Proposes a cross-cultural and historical theoretical formulation of sex roles adapted from Robert Bellah's schema of religious evolution. The major states of evolution are primitive, archaic, historic, early modern, and modern. Each successive state entails greater complexity of imagery for masculinity and feminity, greater range of individual behavior, and greater individual autonomy relative to reproductive differentiation. Only in the early modern stage of evolution, particularly in the 19th century, is woman's consciousness of inequality with men possible because it is only at this stage that women and men share enough experiences in common to be able to compare their situations. Based on primary sources; 27 notes.                   A. E. Wiederrecht

202.  Gordon, Linda.  THE POLITICS OF POPULATION: BIRTH CONTROL AND THE EUGENICS MOVEMENT.  *Radical America 1974 8(4): 61-98.*

203.  Graebner, Alan.  BIRTH CONTROL AND THE LUTHERANS: THE MISSOURI SYNOD AS A CASE STUDY.  *J. of Social Hist. [Great Britain] 1969 2(4): 303-332.* Traces the reversal of Missouri Synod Lutheran attitudes on birth control from the 19th century to the 1960's. Through the 1930's the church was flatly opposed to all forms of contraception because family limitation was at odds with the ordained natural order. Defections among the clergy of other Protestant denominations on the issue of birth control and public opinion in general, influenced by the hardships of the depression, left the Missouri Synod increasingly isolated. The next 30 years witnessed a change of clerical views. The reversal resulted from changes within and pressures outside the Synod, the lack of Biblical authority on the subject, the secular context, individual conscience, and the lack of a rigid church hierarchy to uphold the old views. 2 figs., 77 notes.                   C. W. Olson

204.  Greer, Richard A.  COLLARBONE AND THE SOCIAL EVIL.  *Hawaiian J. of Hist. 1973 7: 3-17.* "Collarbone" refers to the Iwilei district of Honolulu, which was the old prostitution district. Traces the laws and the social attitude toward prostitution from 1835 to 1917, when the final raid was made and the district closed. Photos, map.                   R. N. Alvis

205.  Hareven, Tamara K.  THE FAMILY PROCESS: THE HISTORICAL STUDY OF THE FAMILY CYCLE.  *J. of Social Hist. [Great Britain] 1974 7(3): 322-329.* Proposes a new mode of analysis of family patterns in 19th-century society. The family is viewed as a process over time rather than as a static unit within certain time periods. This model "assumes fluidity, change and transition in family structure . . . that individuals live through a variety of patterns of family structure and household organization during different stages of their life cycle, and that families and households evolve different types of organization, structure and relationships which are generally obscured in cross-sectional analysis." Supports the validity of this approach by data from a study of family structure in 19th-century Boston. 15 notes.                   R. V. Ritter

206.  Hareven, Tamara K.  INTRODUCTION: THE HISTORICAL STUDY OF THE FAMILY IN URBAN SOCIETY.  *J. of Urban Hist. 1975 1(3): 259-267.* Considers "the family . . . a critical variable" shedding "light on . . . migration . . . patterns which determine population change." This overview covers ca. 1750-1975 and introduces five papers in the same issue. 17 notes.                   S. S. Sprague

207.  Harris, Daniel A.  ANDROGYNY: THE SEXIST MYTH IN DISGUISE.  *Women's Studies 1974 2(2): 171-184.* Analyzes the concept of androgyny. Finds that it reflects the sexist power relations of the dominant patriarchal culture. The history of the idea of androgyny illustrates its heterosexual bias and the tradition of negative attitudes towards both men and women. This tradition is traced from the writings of Herodotus and Plato to those of C. G. Jung. Particular attention is given to Jung's ideas about *anima* and the androgynous psyche. Argues that the myth of androgyny must be rejected because it perpetuates the oppression of women, alienates men from themselves, and thwarts examination of problems of self-identity. Based on primary and secondary materials; 18 notes.                   A. E. Wiederrecht

208.  Heer, David M.  ECONOMIC DEVELOPMENT AND THE FERTILITY TRANSITION.  *Daedalus 1968 97(2): 447-462.* Discusses two differing views on fertility. One view states that increased per capita income (i.e., greater economic development) inhibits fertility. The second view holds that economic development increases fertility (i.e., labor demand causes more people to marry at an earlier age, thus increasing the birth rate). Mentions other factors in this connection, such as the level of infant mortality and population density. Emphasizes the United States between 1800 and 1965, concerning the effects of child mortality levels on the parents' decision whether to have more children and the value parents obtain from the productive labor of their children. 32 notes.                   A. Krichmar

209.  Hubbell, Thelma Lee and Lothrop, Gloria R.  THE FRIDAY MORNING CLUB, A LOS ANGELES LEGACY.  *Southern California Q. 1968 50(1): 59-90.* A narrative history of the Los Angeles Friday Morning Club, a women's organization founded by Caroline M. Severance in 1891. Mrs. Severance, a pioneer in the women's rights movement, started the club as a means of working for female equality and also to give women an opportunity to involve themselves in civic and educational activities. Beginning with only a few women and a modest program in 1891, the club has grown to thousands with a broad program of social, philanthropic, and educational activities. Based on material from the archives of the Los Angeles Friday Morning Club. Undocumented, 2 illus.                   W. L. Bowers

210. Jeffrey, Kirk. MARRIAGE, CAREER, AND FEMININE IDEOLOGY IN NINETEENTH-CENTURY AMERICA: RECONSTRUCTING THE MARITAL EXPERIENCE OF LYDIA MARIA CHILD, 1828-1874. *Feminist Studies 1975 2(2/3): 113-130.* Calls for a more objective analysis of Victorian women's attitudes, exploring the life and writings of Lydia Maria Francis Child (1802-80). Child was not covertly protesting her subordination and expressing hostility to men in her sentimental, didactic stories and novels; nor did she consider herself deprived and oppressed. Rather, she wrote and lived a feminine ideology of homebuilding, acting as wife, mother, and moral guardian, which was for many women too important to be given up for the integration advocated by the feminists. Based on Child's letters, manuscripts, and published writings, and secondary works; 58 notes. J. D. Falk

211. Johnson, Claudia D. THAT GUILTY THIRD TIER: PROSTITUTION IN NINETEENTH-CENTURY AMERICAN THEATERS. *Am. Q. 1975 27(5): 575-584.* The assignment of prostitutes to the third tier in 19th-century theaters was a serious problem to those working for the survival of the theatrical institution. Not only was the issue one of continual controversy between moralists and artists; but it also had an impact on theater design, theatrical economics, and the acceptance and support of the theater in American life. The theater gradually achieved respectability only through a dissociation from prostitution. Based on primary and secondary sources. N. Lederer

212. Kidwell, Claudia B. YOU CAN JUDGE US BY WHAT WE WEAR. *Smithsonian 1974 5(6): 84-86.* A Smithsonian exhibit shows the democratization of American dress since the 18th century when anyone could easily distinguish country folk from prosperous townsmen by the striking differences in their clothing. The exhibit shows the influence of the Industrial Revolution. Ready-made clothing for men before 1860 already showed a wide range of styles at the same time women's silk dresses were still custom-made by dressmakers. Store clothes for men as well as women assumed an acceptable character by 1920. 3 illus., 3 photos. E. P. Stickney

213. Knowles, Sally. EARLY AMERICAN KITCHEN UTENSILS AND THE ART OF BREADMAKING. *Daughters of Am. Revolution Mag. 1975 109(7): 784-789.* Presents an old American breadmaking recipe and outlines a history of American kitchen utensils since 1727. S

214. Kreidberg, Marjorie CORN BREAD, PORTABLE SOUP, AND WRINKLE CURES. *Minnesota Hist. 1968 41(3): 105-116.* A comparative and sometimes humorous study of the many 19th-century cook books in the archives of the Minnesota Historical Society. Most of them were concerned primarily with the "what" and "how to" of cooking but several also included advice on table manners and social habits in general. These books underscore problems that the modern housewife does not face, e.g., lack of constant oven temperature, uniform measures (not just a "pinch"), and variations in pan and utensil size and composition. The books are a valuable contemporary record of cooking and domestic life. P. L. Simon

215. Lane, Ann J. HIM/HER/SELF EXPOSED. *R. in Am. Hist. 1975 3(4): 438-442.* Peter Gabriel Filene in *Him/Her/Self: Sex Roles in Modern America* (New York: Harcourt Brace Jovanovich, 1974) discusses sex roles and feminist movements of the middle class, 1890's-1970's.

216. Louis, James P. THE ROOTS OF FEMINISM: A REVIEW ESSAY. *Civil War Hist. 1971 17(2): 162-170.* A critical study of three recent works that "deal at least in part" with feminism in the 19th century. William L. O'Neill's *Everyone Was Brave* (Chicago, Ill.: Quadrangle Books, 1969) focuses too narrowly on feminist ideology. Louis R. Noun's *Strong-Minded Women: The Emergence of the Woman-Suffrage Movement in Iowa* (Ames: Iowa State U. Press, 1969) lacks perspective and interpretive qualities, and will be of use only to specialists. Anne Firor Scott's *The Southern Lady: From Pedestal to Politics, 1830-1930* (Chicago, Ill.: U. of Chicago Press, 1970) is "the most perceptive, illuminating, and rewarding single work on the American feminist movement." E. C. Murdock

217. Luckey, Eleanore B. and Nass, Gilbert D. A COMPARISON OF SEXUAL ATTITUDES AND BEHAVIOR IN AN INTERNATIONAL SAMPLE. *J. of Marriage and the Family 1969 31(2): 364-379.* "Survey data regarding attitudes and behavior in the areas of sex role and courtship were obtained from 2,230 male and female college students in five countries, including the United States. Comparisons by country indicate Canada and United States students have more conservative views than European. England and Norway students were the most liberal. In each country, women held more conservative views. Rates of reported sexual behavior were also lowest among North American students." J

218. Lyman, Stanford M. MARRIAGE AND THE FAMILY AMONG CHINESE IMMIGRANTS TO AMERICA, 1850-1960. *Phylon 1968 29(4): 321-330.* "Whether or not an immigrant group established families in America had a profound effect on its subsequent community organization and acculturation." Applying this generalization to a study of Chinese immigrants to America during the period 1850-1960, the author finds that the virtual lack of family life among the Chinese had a crucial influence on their communities and acculturation. Chinese women immigrated in very small numbers; in 1920 there were 695 men for every 100 women, and by 1960 there were 135,430 males to 100,654 females in the United States. Leaving their families behind in China meant that Chinese men were "congregated in congested ghettos, [where] prostitution and concubinage were carried on as a business under the ownership or control of secret societies." Much of the social behavior of the Chinese immigrants can be explained by an understanding of their lack of family life. Based on primary and secondary sources; 36 notes. R. D. Cohen

219. Matras, Judah. SOCIAL STRATEGIES OF FAMILY FORMATION: SOME COMPARATIVE DATA FOR SCANDINAVIA, THE BRITISH ISLES, AND NORTH AMERICA. *Internat. Social Sci. J. [France] 1965 17(2): 260-275.* Using census-type data on women classified by age at marriage and number of children born, the author estimates the numbers or percentages controlling or attempting to control fertility. For the United States, the tables show earlier marriage among rural groups than among urban, while in Canada urban-rural differences are nonexistent. In the 1940 U.S. Census data, Negroes married much earlier than whites with considerably less frequent practice of fertility control by Negroes, though over a period of years the Negro-white differences diminished. Some comparisons are given with field studies in the United States. 3 tables. E. P. Stickney

220. Mechling, Jay E. ADVICE TO HISTORIANS ON ADVICE TO MOTHERS. *J. of Social Hist. 1975 9(1): 44-63.* Advises historians that 19th-century manuals on child-rearing are an index of the values of the writers of the manuals and not those of the readers, much less of actual practices. 42 notes. M. Hough

221. Monro, D. H. GODWIN, OAKESHOTT, AND MRS. BLOOMER. *J. of the Hist. of Ideas 1974 35(4): 611-624.* Examines the opposition between rationalism, represented by William Godwin, and the traditionalism of Michael Oakeshott. Focuses on Oakeshott's use of the Victorian "rational dress" movement, associated with Amelia Jenks Bloomer, as an instance of simplistic rationalism. Concludes that Oakeshott misjudged the dress reformers, who really confirmed "his thesis about the only way in which reform is possible," while Oakeshott himself abridged complex experience in just the way he accused the reformers of having done. Based on published primary and secondary sources; 16 notes. D. B. Marti

222. Morantz, Regina. THE LADY AND HER PHYSICIAN. Hartman, Mary and Banner, Lois W., eds. *Clio's Consciousness Raised: New Perspectives on the History of Women* (New York: Harper Torchbooks, 1974): 38-53. Examines the hypotheses of historians such as Ben Barker-Benfield and Ann Douglas Wood that 19th-century "American physicians were hostile to their female patients and that their animosity was expressed in the painful and ineffective therapy they administered." Both men and women were subjected to the primitive cures of the "heroic" school of medicine and the "rest cures" of S. Weir Mitchell. Many male physicians, however, were sympathetic to women's problems. Some advocated training women to treat women patients, seeing medicine as a natural extension of woman's domestic sphere and as a means of dealing with patients' "female modesty." S

223. O'Neill, William L. DIVORCE AS A MORAL ISSUE: A HUNDRED YEARS OF CONTROVERSY. George, Carol V. R., ed. "Remember the Ladies": New Perspectives on Women in American History: Essays in Honor of Nelson Manfred Blake (Syracuse: Syracuse U. Pr., 1975): 127-143. The increase in the divorce rate remained relatively constant from 1860 to the 1970's. Divorce provided a safety valve for those who wed badly or could not adjust to marital demands. The legal facilities and rationale for divorce existed in 1860 before there was a need for mass divorce. After the Civil War, in an age with many pressures, high demands, affluence, mobility, declining religious authority, and self-indulgence, divorce became essential to the survival of marriage and family. After 1880, divorce became a major moral and social issue. Religious, historical, political, and social views all entered the debate. The destruction of the family as the keystone of civilization was the strongest argument against divorce. A legitimizing ideology for divorce was worked out before World War I. But following the war, the flood of divorces and changing social values brought about the modern attitude toward divorce, as an unpleasant but necessary natural right, with which Americans in the 1970's are accustomed. Based on primary and secondary materials; 17 notes.       P. R. Byrne

224. Paul, J. POPULATION "QUALITY" AND "FITNESS FOR PARENTHOOD" IN THE LIGHT OF STATE EUGENIC STERILIZATION EXPERIENCES, 1907-66. Population Studies [Great Britain] 1967 21(3): 295-299. "Although the use of state eugenic sterilization laws has declined sharply since the end of World War II, the primitive views of the earlier extreme hereditarians are returning in the new guise of legislative attempts to pass laws that would sterilize mothers of illegitimate children receiving welfare assistance. The author urges a closer examination of the 'right' of procreation, the use of so-called 'consent' procedures in states having sterilization laws, and especially the probable impact of new scientific breakthroughs in medicine, genetics, biochemistry and other fields on individual liberty in America. He believes that the relation between science and public policy will be even more complex and agonizing in the years ahead." 8 notes.       J

225. Pavalko, Ronald M. and Nager, Norma. CONTINGENCIES OF MARRIAGE TO HIGH STATUS MEN. Social Forces 1968 46(4): 523-531. The problem of how women gain access to higher status males for matrimony is explored. The following variables are discussed: socioeconomic background, educational attainment, occupational attainment, and community size. Data were obtained from Wisconsin high school seniors in 1957 and 1964. Since this was a mail-out questionnaire, there was little control exercised despite the high returns indicated. Those girls who selected "nursing" as a career were followed up from the original sample. Those variables which were considered most valuable were occupational attainment followed by educational attainment and community size. Those females who became nurses were significantly more likely to marry high-status men than were those who did not become nurses. Thus, occupational attainment may be as important as going to college from the point of view of meeting higher status marriageable males. 7 tables, 13 notes.       A. S. Freedman

226. Petersen, William J. ROMANCING IN PIONEER DAYS. Palimpsest 1969 50(11): 613-629. Discusses 19th-century attitudes and advice about love and romance as portrayed by Iowa newspapers.       S

227. Pickens, Donald K. THE STERILIZATION MOVEMENT: THE SEARCH FOR PURITY IN MIND AND STATE. Phylon 1967 28(1): 78-94. Traces the history of the sterilization movement in the United States during the 20th century. The author concludes that it was a logical and organic development of 19th-century naturalistic, nationalistic, and nativistic thought as it contributed to the progressive reform movement of the 20th century. Conservatives within the progressive crusade believed that the state had a responsibility to stop the reproduction of the mentally inadequate. After World War I, more than 20 states passed sterilization legislation, but a decision of the Supreme Court declaring the Oklahoma Habitual Criminal Sterilization Act of 1935 to be unconstitutional severely damaged the punitive aspect of sterilization. Despite a decline in public and scientific interest in eugenic sterilization, the movement continues, with its advocates urging voluntary sterilization for socioeconomic and psychological reasons. Documented from published sources, 88 notes.       D. N. Brown

228. Reynolds, Bertha C. THE SOCIAL CASE WORK OF AN UNCHARTERED JOURNEY. Social Work 1964 9(4): 13-17. Mary Richmond's pioneer concepts in the field of social case work such as the privileged giving aid to the underprivileged and building bridges of understanding between the two through volunteer "friendly visitors," was radically changed because of our experiences during the period of two world wars and the depression. The concept of social case work has become fluid: what criteria should mark situations appropriate for social case work, and are mass programs of welfare services able to supply a setting for it? Today one must think in terms of adjustment rather than maladjustment, health instead of pathology. Social workers must help the individual to find conditions of normal living, e.g., to encourage each person to achieve his own best balance.       W. L. Willigan

229. Riegel, Robert E. CHANGING AMERICAN ATTITUDES TOWARD PROSTITUTION (1800-1920). J. of the Hist. of Ideas 1968 29(3): 437-452. "The attitude of XIXth-century America toward prostitution was rather self-contradictory. One side of the picture was a generally resigned acceptance of the institution as inevitable. Everyone knew of its existence, even though Victorian manners excluded it from polite conversation. . . . Both the reformation of the prostitute and the elimination of prostitution seemed very remote through the XIXth century. . . . Explanation of why women became prostitutes changed gradually during the years after the Civil War. . . . The attitude toward prostitution steadily changed during the 1890's and 1900's. The stress on individual responsibility in both causation and reform lost ground, though the change was one of emphasis rather than of replacement. . . . The newer point of view was that prostitution was the product of a multitude of factors, connected particularly with the growing cities, and that it could be handled only by a whole battery of reforms."       W. H. Coates

230. Robacker, Earl F. THE SHAPE OF FOOD THAT WAS. Pennsylvania Folklife 1964 14(2): 10-15. During the 18th and 19th centuries, when women cooked over an open flame, much paraphernalia evolved to make food look prettier. With the passing of the fireplace for cooking, two things occurred. Heavy, cumbersome cooking utensils gradually gave way to lighter ones, and "the fanciful, decorative, creative touch diminished in corresponding degree." Discusses several of the cooking aids, how they were used, and what they have evolved into today, such as: waffle irons, pudding molds, cast-iron quick bread molds, candy molds, cookie cutters, and cake molds. The butter mold was a particularly important and decorative utensil of the day and is surrounded by folk motifs in Pennsylvania. Based on primary sources; 15 photos.       M. J. McBaine

231. Rosenberg, Charles and Smith-Rosenberg, Carroll. THE FEMALE ANIMAL: MEDICAL AND BIOLOGICAL VIEWS OF WOMAN AND HER ROLE IN NINETEENTH CENTURY AMERICA. J. of Am. Hist. 1973 60(2): 332-356. In the 19th century economic and social change created opportunities for women outside of the home and enabled them to envision the real possibility of family limitation. At the same time, however, male gynecologists provided an allegedly scientific "proof" that a woman's place was in the home, and that refusal to bear and raise children was unhealthy for women and would lead to the "race suicide" of native Americans when one noted the higher birth rate of the foreign-born. Woman's role was defined by her reproductive system, and nearly all of her illnesses were attributed to some breakdown of that system. Education was believed to misdirect women's nervous energy from their proper nurturant role and to weaken them and their offspring. 51 notes.       K. B. West

232. Rosenberg, Charles E. SEXUALITY, CLASS AND ROLE IN 19TH-CENTURY AMERICA. Am. Q. 1973 25(2): 131-153. Considers the relationship between 19th-century medical literature and the existing social classes and sex roles. Medical tracts after 1830 adopted a tone of increasing repressiveness, including an obsession with masturbation, inconsistently connected to an archaically aggressive male-oriented behavioral ethos. The ideological sanctions for sexual self-control were interrelated to the middle-class social realities of later marriages, smaller families, and required male achievement. Primary and secondary sources; 50 notes.       W. D. Piersen

233. Rossi, Alice S. NAMING CHILDREN IN MIDDLE-CLASS FAMILIES. Am. Sociol. R. 1965 30(4): 499-513. Data on who the

relatives' children were named after are analyzed as an empirical index to the subjectively salient inner core of kin in a sample of 347 urban middle-class mothers. Kins are the major source of the personal names chosen for the 951 children of these women. Boys are more apt to be named for kin than girls, and kin-naming declines sharply and uniformly with each higher order of birth. The kin for whom children were named consist largely of consanguineal lineal kin, one or two generations removed from the child. Analysis shows a trend over the past 40 years away from naming sons for their paternal kin and daughters for their maternal kin, suggesting that while a structural symmetry has long existed between the nuclear family's two families of origin, an affective social symmetry between them is only now in the making. 27 notes.                    J

234. Rothman, Sheila M.   OTHER PEOPLE'S CHILDREN: THE DAY CARE EXPERIENCE IN AMERICA.   *Public Interest 1973 (30): 11-27.* The history of day care centers during 1854-1973 indicates that the centers may be poor institutions for promoting social reform, particularly with respect to the women's liberation movement.      S

235. Rudikoff, Sonya.   MARRIAGE AND HOUSEHOLD.   *Commentary 1973 55(6): 56-64.* Discusses spectrum of attitudes on marriage.
S

236. Sauer, R.   ATTITUDES TO ABORTION IN AMERICA, 1800-1973.   *Population Studies [Great Britain] 1974 28(1): 53-68.* "A survey of popular and professional literature indicates that there have been significant changes both in the popular and legal attitudes to abortion in America since 1800. The evolution of these attitudes may be broken into four periods: (1) the early nineteenth-century period, in which women apparently only infrequently sought abortions, even though legal norms proscribing most abortions were non-existent; (2) the mid-nineteenth-century period, in which women were seen to resort to abortion increasingly while at the same time more restrictive abortion laws were passed; (3) the late nineteenth and early twentieth-century period, in which abortion became more common even though the prevailing anti-abortion norms still went publicly unchallenged; (4) the 1930-73 period, in which there developed, at first slowly, and then in the 1960s rapidly, an overt rejection of anti-abortion norms which was then reflected in corresponding changes of the law. Several possible factors in the liberalization of abortion attitudes are briefly presented, perhaps the most important being the development of low-fertility values evoked by the emergence of a modern industrial society."                                     J

237. Schlesinger, Benjamin.   THE WIDOWED AS A ONE-PARENT FAMILY UNIT.   *Social Sci. 1971 46(1): 26-32.* "North American family sociologists, in the main, have paid little attention to the one-parent family which comprises about 13 percent of families in America and 9 percent of families in Canada. Widows constitute the largest group among one-parent families. Some of the results of the first Canadian study of one-parent families are presented in relation to widowhood, and are illustrated by case material obtained through personal interviews. Further studies are urgently needed to understand and attempt to meet the special needs of the evergrowing numbers of one-parent families in North America."                                                               J

238. Schneider, Kathleen.   SOCIAL ASPECTS OF STYLE WITH PARTICULAR FOCUS ON NINETEENTH CENTURY WOMEN'S DRESS.   *Staten Island Historian 1973 31(15): 126, 128-131.* Chronicles the change in women's dress style throughout the 19th century and the social strata reflected therein.                                         S

239. Seagle, William.   THE TWILIGHT OF THE MANN ACT. *Am. Bar Assoc. J. 1969 55(7): 641-647.* Sexual immorality was not the "soul-harrowing horror" at which the Mann Act was aimed, yet many will imagine themselves liberated when the act reaches its demise.   J

240. Sears, Hal D.   THE SEX RADICALS IN HIGH VICTORIAN AMERICA.   *Virginia Q. R. 1972 48(3): 377-392.* Describes the varying attitudes of 19th-century groups - Mormons, Shakers, Oneidans, Spiritualists, anarchists, and others - toward marriage and sex. The year 1871 saw the end of "serious and widespread discussion of sexual alternatives in nineteenth-century America." Some "sex radicals" nevertheless continued the discussion. Thus, they raised "questions of government censorship and individual self-ownership." Numerous publications appeared,

such as *Lucifer the Light Bearer* which was edited and published 1883-1907 by Moses Harman (1830-1910). Their advocacy of free love and their use of blunt language resulted in suppression in Comstockian America.                                                                 O. H. Zabel

241. Sennett, Richard.   THE BRUTALITY OF MODERN FAMILIES.   *Trans-action 1970 7(11): 29-37.* Brutalization of social relations among members of nuclear middle-class families in Chicago, Illinois.
S

242. Smigel, Erwin O. and Seiden, Rita.   THE DECLINE AND FALL OF THE DOUBLE STANDARD.   *Ann. of the Am. Acad. of Pol. and Social Sci. 1968 376: 6-17.* "The limited available information on premarital, heterosexual behavior of young people in the United States reveals that the changes in sexual behavior which took place in the 1920's have changed only slightly in the 1960's and that this slow change is continuing. The belief that a gradual transformation is taking place (except in overtness) rests on a comparison of the early studies on sexual behavior, the data from attitudinal studies, researched from 1940 to 1963, and observations of the current scene. Conclusion: the double standard is declining but has not yet fallen."                               J

243. Smith-Rosenberg, Carroll.   PUBERTY TO MENOPAUSE: THE CYCLE OF FEMININITY IN NINETEENTH-CENTURY AMERICA.   Hartman, Mary and Banner, Lois W., eds. *Clio's Consciousness Raised: New Perspectives on the History of Women* (New York: Harper Torchbooks, 1974): 23-37. Describes attitudes of Victorian male physicians and of women toward puberty and menopause. Medical descriptions of and prescriptions for these "crisis periods" served to perpetuate woman's passive social role, helped physicians function in their role as healer, and expressed the Victorian ambivalence toward sexuality. 45 notes.                                                                 S

244. Somerville, James K.   FAMILY DEMOGRAPHY AND THE PUBLISHED RECORDS: AN ANALYSIS OF THE VITAL STATISTICS OF SALEM, MASSACHUSETTS.   *Essex Inst. Hist. Collections 1970 106(4): 243-51.* Studies the demography of the colonial family that has recently become an item of historical interest, as reflected in the works of scholars such as Greven and Demos. Examines one set of representative statistics, the *Vital Records of Salem, Mass. to the End of the Year 1849*, to evaluate their role and importance in the overall task of family re-creation. In six volumes the Salem statistics list marriages, births, and deaths. These are drawn from church and court records, gravestone markings, family manuscripts and bibles, personal diaries, and obituaries. Outlines the problems inherent in using these records and concludes that these obviously couldn't supply all needed information for recreating Salem families. Children's marriages and deaths are listed infrequently with slight linking evidence. 17 notes.                         H. M. Rosen

245. Soule, Ethel V.   FIREPLACE AND OVEN UTENSILS FOR COOKING IN THE EARLY AMERICAN KITCHEN.   *North Jersey Highlander 1971 7(4): 21-28.* Discusses the development and use of cooking utensils in America. Many utensils were brought from Europe or adopted in the United States, although the crane (used to swing pots out from over the fire) was invented in America in 1720. Examines the use of popcorn, an Indian food served at the first Thanksgiving, grease pans, essential in open fire cooking to control the fire and to collect fat for candles, soap and lighting, and the development of matches. Based on secondary sources and original articles; 11 illus., biblio.
A. C. Aimone

246. Stage, Sarah J.   OUT OF THE ATTIC: STUDIES OF VICTORIAN SEXUALITY.   *Am. Q. 1975 27(4): 480-485.* A review essay prompted by recent works on Victorian sexual attitudes in America by Carl N. Degler, Robin and Mark Haller, and Ronald G. Walters. Despite the indicated significance of sex as a factor in history in these works, a full determination of the relationship between sexual ideology and behavior cannot be achieved unless sexual advice literature, such as that used as source material in these studies, is balanced against actual sexual behavior and demographic, economic, social and legal factors.
N. Lederer

247. Stimpson, Catharine R.   THE ANDROGYNE AND THE HOMOSEXUAL.   *Women's Studies 1974 2(2): 237-247.* Assesses the an-

drogyne and the homosexual as models of human behavior. Discusses the meanings of "androgyne" and "homosexual." The androgyne and the homosexual offer values and promises which include a belief that people are able to create their own character structure, a belief that freedom is necessary for self-creation, and the promise that the androgyne and the homosexual embody the potential for creativity. To society, the homosexual is a threatening figure while the androgyne is an idea. The nature of the homosexual threat, the nature of the androgynous idea, the social and psycho-sexual implications of both, and the relation among androgyny, homosexuality, and social change are discussed. Based on primary materials; 14 notes.                                           A. E. Wiederrecht

248.   Stokes, C. Shannon and Ritchey, P. Neal.  SOME FURTHER OBSERVATIONS ON CHILDLESSNESS AND COLOR.  *J. of Black Studies 1974 5(2): 203-209.* Studies show that older nonwhite women are more often childless than older white women. This study shows that young white women have a greater rate of childlessness than young black women. White and black women at ages 30-39 have a similar rate of childlessness. It seems that white and black women will probably have equal rates of childlessness throughout the 70's. Biblio.
                                                        K. Butcher

249.   Sweezy, A.  THE ECONOMIC EXPLANATION OF FERTILITY CHANGES IN THE UNITED STATES.  *Population Studies [Great Britain] 1971 25(2): 255-268.* "It is widely assumed that fertility varies positively with economic conditions. Actually this assumption receives little support from the historical record. For a century before 1930 fertility declined while the economy expanded and real incomes rose. Then for nearly three decades fertility and incomes fell and rose together. Since 1960 they have again moved in opposite directions. Clearly, no simple generalization about their relation will hold water. More sophisticated explanations are based on relative rather than absolute incomes. Banks suggested that the downturn in English fertility in the 1870's might have occurred because standards of middle-class consumption rose faster than middle-class incomes, but he found the evidence inconclusive. To reconcile the post-war baby boom in the United States with earlier experience, Easterlin has argued that fertility is determined by the relationship between the income of couples in their twenties and the income of their parents ten to fifteen years earlier. Among the weaknesses of this theory as applied to U.S. experience are its failure to explain the sharp drop in fertility, including that of native white urban women, in the 1920's; the fact that fertility rose most in the baby boom at the higher socio-economic levels where incomes rose least; and the sharp decline of fertility after 1962 in spite of the favourable trend of incomes, including those of younger people. The broad conclusion is that while couples no doubt do consider income, employment opportunities, etc. in deciding how many children to have, such considerations have had a relatively minor influence on *changes* in fertility, which for the most part have been the result of changes in attitudes. Even the post-war baby boom was a result not only of higher incomes and full employment but also of a shift in attitudes toward family size, particularly among the better-educated, economically better-off sections of society."                                        J

250.   Symanski, Richard.  PROSTITUTION IN NEVADA.  *Ann. of the Assoc. of Am. Geographers 1974 64(3): 357-377.* "Thirty-three brothels in rural and small-town Nevada, which contain between 225 and 250 prostitutes, are legal or openly tolerated and strictly controlled by state statute, city and county ordinances, and local rules. Twenty-two of the brothels are in places with populations between 500 and 8,000, and the remaining eleven are in rural areas. The legal and quasi-legal restrictions placed on prostitutes severely limit their activities outside brothels. These restrictions in conjunction with historical inertia, perceived benefits of crime and venereal disease control, and the good image of madams contribute to widespread positive local attitudes toward brothel prostitution. Interactions between clients and prostitutes in brothel parlors are also restricted and limited to a few basic types which are largely determined by entrepreneurial philosophy."                                         J

251.   Travis, Anthony R.  THE ORIGIN OF MOTHERS' PENSIONS IN ILLINOIS.  *J. of the Illinois State Hist. Soc. 1975 68(5): 421-428.* The Illinois mothers' pensions program that began in Cook County in October 1911 served as a model for other state programs and also for the present federal program of Aid to Families with Dependent Children, which arose out of the New Deal. Despite criticism that the

Illinois program violated family privacy and placed too much power in the hands of bureaucrats, investigation revealed that the program was financially superior to any other available form of charity.
                                                        N. Lederer

252.   Van Ness, James S.  ON UNTIEING THE KNOT: THE MARYLAND LEGISLATURE AND DIVORCE PETITIONS.  *Maryland Hist. Mag. 1972 67(2): 171-175.* The only recourse for unhappily married couples in colonial Maryland to obtain a divorce was applying for a special act of the legislature, since no formal procedure for divorce existed. No divorce bill petition, however, reached the voting stage in either house of the Maryland legislature for the first 140 years of the colony's existence. The landmark act involved the case of John Sewell of Talbot County in 1790. The legislature passed an act annulling his marriage to Eve Sewell, who pleaded guilty to bearing a mulatto bastard child. This set a precedent which expanded for half a century. At first confining itself to annulments, the house gradually accepted other petitions and causes other than adultery. Ultimately it granted outright divorce decrees. The question was resolved by the state constitutional convention of 1851, which prohibited the General Assembly from granting divorces. Based on primary sources; 25 notes.
                                                        G. J. Bobango

253.   Verbrugge, Martha H.  WOMEN AND MEDICINE IN NINETEENTH-CENTURY AMERICA.  *Signs 1976 1(4): 957-972.* The history of women in medicine in 19th-century America has evolved from general histories of gynecology, obstetrics, and contraception, to women as practitioners and women as objects, tracing the ways medicine has conceptualized and treated women. Ann D. Wood characterizes the medical treatment of 19th-century American women as "condemnation disguised as diagnosis and punishment offered as cure." Carroll Smith-Rosenberg and Charles E. Rosenberg relate the structure of medical ideas, personal roles, and society in a given period. Linda Gordon's history of birth control in America presents a political conception of medical history and views it as part of a whole system of social control. Based on secondary sources; 49 notes.
                                                        J. Gammage

254.   Wells, Robert V.  DEMOGRAPHIC CHANGE AND THE LIFE CYCLE OF AMERICAN FAMILIES.  *J. of Interdisciplinary Hist. 1971 2(2): 273-282.* Massive decline in the birth rate and increase in life expectancy have altered the life cycle of the American family since the American Revolution. The 20th-century family spends less of its life rearing children and is more stable, and the marriage partners remain together for a longer period of time. Longer marriages combined with a continuing decline in fertility mean that couples now expect a life together after their children are gone. Children are thus less important in 20th-century families and the phenomenon of old age with no children is a peculiarly modern one. These changes have contributed to a more complex family cycle in the 20th century than was the case in the 18th. Based on a study of 18th-century Quaker families and recent demographic sources on the later period; 2 tables, 19 notes.      E. J. Hundert

255.   Word, S. Buford.  THE FATHER OF GYNECOLOGY.  *Alabama J. of Medical Sci. 1972 9(1): 33-39.* Biographical sketch of James Marion Sims, focusing on his medical interests and insights which led to the founding of the first hospital for women (Women's Hospital, New York City) in 1855, and the development of gynecology as a medical speciality.                                          S

256.   Yates, Wilson.  BIRTH CONTROL LITERATURE AND THE MEDICAL PROFESSION IN NINETEENTH CENTURY AMERICA.  *J. of the Hist. of Medicine & Allied Sci. 1976 31(1): 42-54.* Describes and analyzes literature on birth control in the 19th century, beginning with Robert Dale Owen's *Moral Physiology* (1831). The medical and popular works of Frederick Hollick helped to popularize contraceptive information in the decades of the 1850's, 1860's, and 1870's. Edward Bliss Foote's *Medical Common Sense* (1858 and numerous subsequent editions) was the second most widely circulated book on birth control, after Hollick's *The Marriage Guide* (1850). Some physicians opposed birth control, and their works are described. The latter decades of the 19th century saw an interest in birth control and contraceptives, and medical writers debated the merits of specific preventives. 55 notes.
                                                        M. Kaufman

257. Zimet, Sara Goodman. LITTLE BOY LOST. *Teachers Coll. Record 1970 72(1): 31-40.* Examines "the sex role models portrayed in primary reading . . . from 1600 to 1966." S

258. —. [BONNIE AND CLYDE].
Rich, Carroll Y. CLYDE BARROW'S LAST FORD. *J. of Popular Culture 1973 6(4): 631-641.* Describes the fortunes of the Ford automobile in which Bonnie Parker and Clyde Barrow were killed, from its purchase by Jesse Warren in 1934 to the Bonnie and Clyde revival of 1967.
Wollheim, Peter. THE CASE OF BONNIE AND CLYDE. *J. of Popular Culture 1973 7(3): 602-605.* Criticizes Rich's article for its lack of penetration of the psychological level of the fascination with Barrow's Ford automobile, and begins an analysis of the gangster myth in American culture. S

259. —. [FARM POPULATION IN THE NORTHERN UNITED STATES]. *J. of Econ. Hist. 1976 36(1): 45-83.*
Easterlin, Richard A. POPULATION CHANGE AND FARM SETTLEMENT IN THE NORTHERN UNITED STATES, *pp. 45-75.* As farm settlement spread westward, area after area exhibited remarkably similar economic and demographic changes, among them, the establishment of a virtually zero growth rate of farm population. At bottom this was due to a shift in farm family fertility from very high to replacement levels, a trend apparent in older areas as early as the beginning of the nineteenth century despite the abundance of good farm land to the west. The principal source of this wholly voluntary adjustment of fertility was the increasing difficulty encountered by farm parents in providing for their children the kind of start in life they would like them to have. Similar pressures may account for other rural fertility declines in the historical past or today's LDC's.
Bogue, Allan G. and Easterlin, Richard A. DISCUSSION, *pp. 76-83.* J

260. —. PROGRESS IN FAMILY LAW. *Ann. of the Am. Acad. of Pol. and Social Sci. 1969 383: 1-144.*
Infausto, Felix PERSPECTIVE ON ADOPTION, *pp. 1-12.* "Adoption law in the United States traces its origin to early Roman law. Although Roman law Provided for adoption, its singular purpose was to provide the adopter with an heir. European civil law carried on the Roman tradition providing that only persons over twenty-one could be adopted and only those over fifty could adopt. Late in the nineteenth century, the United States formalized its adoption law, basing its procedural aspects on Roman law, but originating the social-conscience aspect of adoption which mandated that the adoption be in the best interests of the child. The cause of social-conscience adoption was a public opinion which had been outraged by the processes of indenture and the binding out of children. Gradually, the states enacted legislation providing for judicial inquiry and social inverstigation to ensure that the child's interests would be furthered as well as the interests of the adoptive and natural parents. Today, enlightened state and federal statutes, along with the assistance of private and public child-care agencies, have eliminated many of the gross abuses and uncertainties that were the companions of the adoptions of yesterday."
Ploscowe, Morris. ALIMONY, *pp. 13-22.* "Money and property are weapons in the matrimonial war. A woman usually drives a hard bargain as the price for a divorce. There are limiting factors in the battleground over alimony, even where agreeable to the husband and wife. Most husbands and wives cannot afford divorces, but the wife makes the best bargain possible. In court, the judge has to decide how much money should be paid by the husband to the wife. Awards of alimony vary with individual cases and also with the philosophy of the judge. Alimony is a perquisite of wives legally married. Traditionally, it cannot be granted to a woman who has not been married, or if the marriage has been annulled. But even in annulments, the legislature frequently makes provision for the wife. Frequently, the husband and wife enter into a separation agreement which aids the court. The factors to be taken into account are many and varied. There are sharp disputes as to how much income and property the husband has. Alimony awards are not fixed and permanent. A court order may be changed if circumstances change, but generally there is no certainty in alimony ar-

rangements. If the husband refuses to pay the alimony, the law provides the wife with many legal weapons. Is it desirable to continue the alimony system? Should alimony be granted for a specific period, for example three years? Should the basis of alimony be the wife's net need, consistent with income and assets of the husband? Should not all divorce courts employ techniques to reduce the areas of disputes in awarding or modifying alimony?" J

# Political Sphere

261. Alley, Rewi. SOME MEMORIES OF ANNA LOUISE STRONG. *Eastern Horizon [Hong Kong] 1970 9(2): 7-19, (3): 45-55.* Part I. Reviews the early life and works of American Communist Anna Louise Strong. The Russian Revolution of 1917 altered her political conceptions forever. A dedicated journalist, she patrolled the world, striving always to get the facts behind often-manufactured headlines, and she soon became a fierce and indomitable figure in world affairs. Her reporting of the Chinese Revolution in the 1920's was one of the few accurate accounts available at the time. She spent many years in the United States and the Soviet Union, but China remained her first love. In 1958, she returned to Peking to stay. Part II. After settling permanently in China in 1958, she continued to write and to lecture. Death came in 1970 when she was 85. Anna Louise Strong's career remains unique for its devotion and intensity. Her efforts on their behalf will never be forgotten by the humble peoples of the world. 2 photos. V. L. Human

262. Banner, Lois W. TWO WOMEN. *R. in Am. Hist. 1975 3(2): 164-169.* The techniques of psychohistory are used in Hannah Josephson's *Jeannette Rankin, First Lady in Congress: A Biography* (Indianapolis, Indiana: Bobbs-Merrill, 1974) which covers the reform politics, feminism, and pacifism of Jeannette Rankin in the 20th century, and in Katharine Du Pre Lumpkin's *The Emancipation of Angelina Grimké* (Chapel Hill: U. of North Carolina Press, 1974) which studies the antislavery sentiments of Angelina Grimké in the 19th century.

263. Bauman, Mary Kay. MADISON ORGANIZATION FOR INTERNATIONAL PEACE AND FREEDOM. *Wisconsin Then and Now 1965 12(2): 1-3.* In celebration of the 50th anniversary of the Women's International League for Peace and Freedom, organized in 1915, the Madison branch donated its files and papers to the State Historical Society of Wisconsin. The Madison chapter, begun in 1922, tried to influence legislators to vote for disarmament measures, treaties, and cuts in military expenditures. After being relatively inactive during World War II, the branch revived in the 1950's, promoting such issues as the ban on nuclear weapons. More recently it has taken a stand against the escalation of the Vietnam conflict. The papers include business correspondence, telegrams, pamphlets, plays, and songs. 3 illus. B. J. Paul

264. Benson, Lucy Wilson. WOMAN SUFFRAGE. *Nat. Civic R. 1970 59(5): 252-255.* The year 1970 marks the 50th anniversary of woman suffrage and the League of Women Voters. For these 50 years the league has worked to develop the vote as an instrument of change, for the vote is still the individual's tool of participation in government. Therefore, in 1970 the league members decided in favor of the direct election of the President and Vice President and the abolition of the present Electoral College system. The challenges of the 1970's allow no time to relax our efforts. If we are to maintain our system of self-government, full citizen participation is essential. H. S. Marks

265. Board, John C. THE LADY FROM MONTANA. *Montana: Mag. of Western Hist. 1967 17(3): 2-17.* Jeannette Rankin's decision to run for Congress in 1916 grew out of her campaign experience in the suffragist movement. Victory placed her in the House of Representatives in time to vote against declaring war on Germany. As the first woman elected to Congress, she became widely acquainted in official Washington, and in this interview relates many incidents and anecdotes of those years. Today, still vigorous at 86, Miss Rankin is building a "cooperative homestead for unemployed homemakers" on her farm. Illus. S. R. Davison

266. Boyd, Rosamonde Ramsay. WOMEN AND POLITICS IN THE UNITED STATES AND CANADA. *Ann. of the Am. Acad. of Pol. and Social Sci. 1968 375: 52-57.* "Since 1920 the women of the United States and Canada have steadily increased their responsibilites as voters. They have, however, been slow to assume policy-making positions at the state and federal levels. Many of them accept political responsibilites on boards and municipal councils, thereby functioning in areas of local education, welfare, and budgeting. Thus, they permit their interests and activities continually to revolve around the time-honored role of women. In both countries, there are a few women who have held Cabinet positions, and women are representatives in the Congress of the United States and the Canadian parliament. These women continue an interest in health, education, and welfare, but most of their committee appointments are in areas of male specialization, such as armed services, transportation, banking, atomic energy, aeronautics, and flood control. This fact supports recent findings that the political behavior of men and women is similar at the higher educational levels. The lag between the voting habits of women and their acceptance of responsible public office may be attributable to traditional roles, ethnic and regional differentials, sporadic interest in politics, localized political activity, and woman's underestimation of her political potential."                                    J

267. Boyman, Elsa. NOUVELLE VAGUE DE FEMINISME EN AMERIQUE [The new wave of feminism in America]. *Synthéses [Belgium] 1965 (225): 52-59.* This provides some background on the feminist movement which resulted from the Industrial Revolution. It is pointed out that woman has four dimensions. Three of these are traditional - marriage, a home and children. The fourth is permitting a woman to realize her full potential. The factors which contribute to and against this new feminism are discussed at length.                    H. L. Calkin

268. Childs, Marjorie M. THE WOMEN LAWYERS CENTENNIAL. *Am. Bar Assoc. J. 1970 56(1): 68-70.* Last year was the centennial of the admission of the first woman to a state bar, but that century did not bring women full equality "in the law and under the law."    J

269. Delp, Robert W. AMERICAN SPIRITUALISM AND SOCIAL REFORM, 1847-1900. *Northwest Ohio Q. 1972 44(4): 85-99.* American Spiritualism began in 1844 with a belief that communication could be established with departed spirits. While many Spiritualists clung to this narrow concept of their movement, others moved quickly to a literary attack on the evils of the day and to joint movements with other reform groups. The author offers examples from the literary output of Andrew Jackson Davis, Samuel Brittan, William Fishbough, Thomas Lake Harris, and Warren Chase and provides illustrations of the roles played by Spiritualists in the campaigns for abolition, women's rights, temperance, regulation of industry, protection of the rights of labor, and the abolition of capital punishment. Based on primary and secondary sources; 95 notes.                               W. F. Zornow

270. Dixon, Marlene. WOMEN'S LIBERATION: OPENING CHAPTER TWO. *Can. Dimension 1975 10(8): 56-69.* The problems before the women's movement in North America are that since the 1960's it has come to be dominated by a middle-class leadership and has become "a politically and ideologically co-opted reformist movement."    S

271. Flynn, James R. THE U.S. PEACE MOVEMENT: ITS ELECTORAL PROSPECTS. *Pol. Sci. [New Zealand] 1964 16(1): 60-80.* Discusses whether or not the present American peace movement, which includes various Quaker groups, SANE, and the Women's Strike for Peace, have any sort of political potential. Flynn surveys 19th-century American peace movements and suggests specific steps the United States might take to solve the "psychological problem" or over-reaction to limited Soviet imperialism, as well as specific targets for negotiation. He foresees only limited successes for peace candidates unless the movement develops broadened appeal and its own mass media. Documented.                                    H. Schalck

272. Gallagher, Robert S. "I WAS ARRESTED, OF COURSE." *Am. Heritage 1974 25(2): 16-24, 92-94.* Interview with Alice Paul (b. 1885) on her role in the women's suffrage movement, the ratification of the 21st amendment, and the early beginnings of the Equal Rights Amendment.                                    S

273. Hall, Jacqueline. REMINISCENCES OF JESSIE DANIEL AMES: "I REALLY DO LIKE A GOOD FIGHT." *New South 1972 27(2): 31-41.* Transcriptions of an interview with Jessie Daniel Ames, a white woman in the South, who describes her efforts (ca. 1900-72) for Negro rights and women's rights, and especially her fight against lynching.

274. Hargreaves, Reginald. THE INTRUDERS. *Military R. 1964 44(12): 83-91.* Notes the role of women in military affairs since the Crusades of the 11th century.                                    S

275. Hill, Nellie H. HISTORICAL ROLE OF WOMEN IN THE UNITED STATES ARMED FORCES. *Daughters of the Am. Revolution Mag. 1975 109(5): 438-441.*

276. Jaffe, Philip. THE STRANGE CASE OF ANNA LOUISE STRONG. *Survey [Great Britain] 1964 (53): 129-139.* An account of the American journalist, whose life "has been closely intertwined with the communist revolution in China" for 40 years. She was reared in Seattle, where she witnessed the general strike of February 1919 which became a turning point in her life. "Beginning with a sort of Christian-Social worker type of humanitarianism, she developed into a militant pacifist during the First World War, and then drifted into an emotional socialism - and the emotionalism has remained with her to this day." She went to Russia in 1921, beginning a long association which led her to involvement with the Russian effort to aid Communists in China in 1927. She spent the next 10 years mostly in the Soviet Union, publishing *Moscow News* and generally writing about the USSR in English for foreign consumption. In 1946 she settled in China, becoming a propagandist for Maoist communism. She wrote a book about Mao and his accomplishments, taking it to the USSR and eastern Europe in 1947 and 1948, and causing quite a stir because of Mao's definite trend away from Communist orthodoxy. In 1949 she was arrested in Moscow. All the European and other Western Communists dutifully joined in attacking her as a spy. After being deported to Poland she traveled to the United States where she lived for 10 years, somewhat bewildered at the treatment she had received. In 1955 she was rehabilitated in the USSR but never returned there, going instead to China in 1959 to be welcomed warmly by Mao. 9 notes.                                    A. K. Main

277. Jensen, Amy LaFollette. THE PRESIDENT'S LADY. *Am. Heritage 1964 15(5): 54-61.* Portraits of first ladies from Abigail Adams to Eleanor Roosevelt. Undocumented, illus.
                                    H. F. Bedford

278. Koontz, Elizabeth Duncan. THE WOMEN'S BUREAU LOOKS TO THE FUTURE. *Monthly Labor R. 1970 93(6): 3-9.* History of the Labor Department's Women's Bureau in enforcing equal employment opportunity and ending discrimination against women in the labor force, 1920-70.                                    S

279. Lansing, Marjorie. POLITICAL CHANGE FOR THE AMERICAN WOMAN. Iglitzin, Lynne B. and Ross, Ruth, eds. *Women in the World* (Santa Barbara, Ca.: Clio Books, 1976): 175-181. The 19th-century feminist movement was begun by women abolitionists who wanted equality with men "in the state, the church and the home." After the passage of the 15th Amendment, which granted the vote to black men but not to women, the feminist movement directed its energies toward securing the vote for women. After the franchise was extended to women in 1920, the feminist movement remained largely inactive until the 1960's. Although there was no organized movement, the status of women changed dramatically during World War II when they entered the work force in large numbers. Concomitant to the rise in employment for women was a rise in the number of female voters. Moreover, the number of women voters increased as they became more educated. In recent years, women politicians have been increasingly accepted by the public. Secondary sources; 13 notes.                                    J. Holzinger

280. Lebedum, Jean. HARRIET BEECHER STOWE'S INTEREST IN SOJOURNER TRUTH, BLACK FEMINIST. *Am. Literature 1973 46(3): 359-363.* Mrs. Stowe, contrary to previous opinion, was interested in feminism. This interest was sparked by feminist Sojourner Truth's work during the 1850's-60's. Stowe's attack on feminism in *My Wife and I* was directed solely at a personal enemy in the movement. In

her *The Minister's Wooing* (1859) she presents a character much like Truth, and in her magazine articles there is strong support for feminism. Based on Mrs. Stowe's works and letters.                         M. Stockstill

281. Levitt, Morris.   THE POLITICAL ROLE OF AMERICAN WOMEN.   *J. of Human Relations 1967 15(1): 23-35.* Surveys the scholarly literature on the relative failure of American women to vote and participate in politics since winning the right to vote in 1920. The psychological, social, and economic variables determining political involvement are discussed. Women do not participate in the electoral process to a high degree because it is out of keeping with their social role in a "man's world," and they hold political attitudes "which contribute to their withdrawal." The author's own research, based on surveys conducted shortly after the presidential elections of 1956, 1960, and 1964, reveals "that the working experience is a primary factor in affecting the political role of" American women and that educational experience is a secondary factor. 23 notes.                                                    D. J. Abramoske

282. Lockwood, Maren.   THE EXPERIMENTAL UTOPIA IN AMERICA.   *Daedalus 1965 94(2): 401-418.* A survey and analysis of the various utopian communities established in the United States between the second half of the 19th century and the first half of the 20th century. Details the community founded by John Humphrey Noyes (1811-86) in Oneida, New York, in 1848. "Accommodated in the great rambling Mansion House, which was set in spacious, tastefully landscaped grounds, the three hundred Perfectionists supplemented the regular creature-comforts with elaborate theatrical properties, musical instruments, a library of at least one thousand volumes, and even a Swedish bath." Their ideas of Perfection were expressed in new interpretations of Christianity, educational reform, varied work routines, joint decisionmaking, dietary experiments, faith healing, complex marriage, and the stirpiculture (selective breeding) experiment. In 1899, Pierrepont Burt Noyes, one of the Oneida founder's stirpiculture children, introduced a new utopian vision to the original organization in an attempt to extend its objectives beyond mere economic cooperation. "Under his guidance, Oneida continued this process of the dissolution of utopia as it resigns its functions to experts, as it joins the affairs and assumes the ways of the outside society." The new idealism, however, began to fade in the 1940's. 33 notes.
                                                           D. D. Cameron

283. Mabee, Carleton.   WOMEN AND NEGROES MARCH.   *Midwest Q. 1966 6(2): 163-174.* Compares the early struggles of women's rights advocates with the demonstrations of Negro civil rights workers today. The author cites examples of similar newspaper statements on the inferiority of women and Negroes. He describes attacks on suffragist demonstrations, refusal of police protection, jailing, fines for obstructing traffic, and notes their similarities to incidents which have occurred in the integrationists' marches. The author conjectures that alarm and antagonism may be necessary before results can be obtained by the less shocking channels of discussion, press, and politics. Largely based on newspaper reports of the time.                                            G. H. G. Jones

284. Marcuse, Herbert.   MARXISM AND FEMINISM.   *Women's Studies 1974 2(3): 279-288.* In this lecture given at Stanford University, 7 March 1974, the author analyzes the women's liberation movement and its relation to capitalism and to Marxist socialism. The movement originates and operates within a patriarchal, class society in which women have been repressed and directed in specific channels. The goals of the movement cannot be reached within a capitalist framework nor within a class society. Feminist socialism requires modification of Marxian socialism. New values and new social institutions are necessary for the realization of feminist goals. The first countertrend to the aggressive and repressive values and needs of male-dominated Western culture appeared in the 12th and 13th centuries as part of the radical and heretical movements of the Cathars and Albigensians which protested hierarchical relations, asserted the autonomy of love, and declared the autonomy of women. Over time, changes in capitalism increased women's exploitation and provided the woman's movement with the bases for a radical, revolutionary movement which is now politically significant.
                                                           A. E. Wiederrecht

285. Meltzer, Milton.   FOUR WHO LOCKED HORNS WITH THE CENSORS.   *Wilson Lib. Bull. 1969 44(3): 278-286.* Examines the writings of four American authors (Mark Twain, Margaret Sanger, Lydia Maria Child, and Langston Hughes) and their battles with censorship.
                                                                        S

286. Mitchell, Bonnie.   LEAGUE OF WOMEN VOTERS MARKS 50 YEARS.   *Wisconsin Then and Now 1969 16(2): 1-3.* Gives a brief review of the history of the national League of Women Voters, founded 50 years ago by two Wisconsin women, Carrie Chapman Catt and Jessie Jack Hooper. In 1921 Wisconsin became the first state to have a "Bill of Rights" for women through the support of the league and other women's organizations. The league, however, opposed a blanket amendment for women's equal rights brought before the national Senate in 1921. It has consistently followed its own dictum throughout the years of working for specific legislation in such areas as education, employment, and housing.
                                                           D. P. Peltier

287. Normand-Auclair, Nicole.   UN ASPECT MORAL DE LA PROMOTION DE LA FEMME [The moral aspect in the liberation of women]. *L'Action Nationale [Canada] 1972 61(10): 787-795.* The rise of the feminist movement has unfortunately resulted in the rejection of the moral relationship between woman and child in the eyes of numerous feminist militants, which is unacceptable since it negates the possibility of the woman fully developing herself. Problems exist from the time of conception, to birth, to the education of the offspring, but the liberated woman can face up to the moral imperatives while achieving her own fulfillment.                                              A. E. LeBlanc

288. Plessner, Monika.   DIE WEISSE DAME UND DER SCHWARZE MANN [The white lady and the black man]. *Frankfurter Hefte [West Germany] 1972 27(3): 201-210.* Reflects on Harriet Beecher Stowe's *Uncle Tom's Cabin* and concludes that white women and black men were natural allies in their common struggle, women for emancipation, blacks for freedom.

289. Sassower, Doris L.   WOMEN AND THE JUDICIARY: UNDOING "THE LAW OF THE CREATOR."   *Judicature 1974 57(7): 282-288.*

290. Secor, Cynthia.   ANDROGYNY: AN EARLY REAPPRAISAL.   *Women's Studies 1974 2(2): 161-169.* Explores the meaning of androgyny and its relevance to the feminist movement. Finds androgyny an exciting, intriguing concept which is gaining popularity and pertinence. It is widely discussed, part of the counterculture, and particularly appealing to women of humanistic values who live and work closely with men. Author is apprehensive about the concept because it perpetuates the categories of masculine and feminine, continues to define women in relation to men, and undermines the sense of selfhood and independence which ought be encouraged. Rather than increasingly using the image of the androgyne, author suggests women ought adopt the strategy Margaret Fuller articulated in the 1840's. This means women must rid themselves of the influence of other minds, think for themselves, and help each other.
                                                           A. E. Wiederrecht

291. Semonche, John E.   COMMON-LAW MARRIAGE IN NORTH CAROLINA: A STUDY IN LEGAL HISTORY.   *Am. J. of Legal Hist. 1965 9(4): 320-349.* Presents evidence that common-law marriage was regarded as valid in North Carolina despite legal prescriptions requiring the formalities of marriage.       N. C. Brockman

292. Shaffer, Ellen.   GLIMPSES OF FIVE FIRST LADIES.   *Manuscripts 1970 22(2): 88-95.* Comments on five domestic letters by Abigail Amelia Smith Adams, Jane Means Appleton Pierce, Florence Kling Harding, Grace Anna Goodhue Coolidge, and Anna Eleanor Roosevelt (neé Roosevelt) from the private collection of Norman H. Strouse placed on display in 1969 at the Free Library of Philadelphia as part of an exhibit entitled "Ladies in My Library."
                                                           D. A. Yanchisin

293. Shuck, Victoria.   SEXISM AND SCHOLARSHIP: A BRIEF OVERVIEW OF WOMEN, ACADEMIA, AND THE DISCIPLINES.   *Social Sci. Q. 1974 55(3): 563-585.* Examines traditional and current issues, assumptions, and techniques in American feminism.       S

294. Sterling, Suzan.   LE NOUVEAU FÉMINISME AMÉRICAIN [The new American feminism]. *Études [France] 1971 335(11): 537-559.*

Surveys the women's movements and their leaders in the United States from suffragism in the 1920's, through the new feminism of the New Left and the National Organization for Women (NOW) in the 1960's, to Women's Liberation in the 1970's. Their organizations, racism, and political and legal objectives are discussed. They have been moderately successful and "women comprise the largest revolutionary force in today's America." Based on primary and secondary sources; 26 notes.

R. K. Adams

295. Waters, Mary-Alice. FEMINISM AND THE MARXIST MOVEMENT. *Int. Socialist Rev. 1972 33(9): 8-23.* Examines the historical relationship between feminism and Marxism during 1848-1970's, including the role of women in the *Communist Manifesto,* the class struggle, and socialist and revolutionary ideology.

296. Weaver, Robert C. ELEANOR AND L. B. J. AND BLACK AMERICA. *Crisis 1972 79(6): 186-193.* Discusses relations between Eleanor Roosevelt, Lyndon Baines Johnson, and Negroes, 1930's-70's, and reviews *Eleanor and Franklin* (New York: Norton, 1972) by Joseph P. Lash and *The Vantage Point* (New York: Holt, Rinehart and Winston, 1972) by Johnson.

S

297. Werner, Emmy E. WOMEN IN CONGRESS: 1917-1964. *Western Pol. Q. 1966 19(1): 16-30.* Deals with the 70 women who have served in Congress (both House and Senate) between 1916 and 1964. Participation of women in U.S. legislatures has been low; only two percent are in Congress. Of the 50 states, 36 have sent women to Congress. Relative to population, the Western States have sent a significantly larger proportion than any other region. Party affiliation follows national trends; 40 of the 70 have been Democrats, the remainder Republicans. During the first two decades after women were enfranchised, the majority of women reached Congress via the "widow's succession"; since World War II this is no longer true. About 90 percent of the women have been married; the modal age of these women, when elected, is 52. Their educational level is rather high, with four-fifths having gone beyond high school. Of the 70, 10 were in the Senate (seven appointed); of the 60 in the House, two-thirds were elected. About 65 percent of the women held responsible positions after Congressional service. Fluctuation has been high; there were four women in Congress in 1921 and 13 in 1963, but the latter figure is lower than the total from 1953 through 1961. The number of women serving in State legislatures has steadily increased, from 29 in 1920 to 351 in 1963. An appendix gives the names of all 70 women and the Congresses in which they served. 12 tables, 15 notes.

H. Aptheker

298. Werner, Emmy E. WOMEN IN THE STATE LEGISLATURES. *Western Pol. Q. 1968 21(1): 40-50.* Discusses trends in women's representation in State legislatures and Congress from 1920 to 1964, the effects of geography on such representation, and background experience and reasons for officeholding by women in 1963-64. Women's political success follows the economic and political trends of the Nation, as does their party affiliation. More women are elected to the legislature in numerically small States with less rapid population and urban growth. The majority of women in the 1963-64 State legislatures had college degrees and considerable training and experience, were married, and felt strong moral commitments. More women need to and will enter politics to help meet the needs of society. 3 tables, 15 notes.

J. L. Rasmussen

299. Woodroofe, Debby. AMERICAN FEMINISM, 1848-1920: FIRST ROUND IN THE FIGHT FOR LIBERATION. *Int. Socialist Rev. 1971 32(3): 20-31, 41-42.* Traces feminism from its inception at the 1848 Woman's Rights Convention at Seneca Falls, New York, and discusses strikes of female workers, attempts to reform the institution of marriage, the relation between the abolition movement and the women's movement, and the battle for suffrage which succeeded in the 19th Constitutional Amendment in 1920.

# Religion and Ethnicity

300. Andres, Faith. THE SHAKER MANNER OF DRESS AS PRESCRIBED FOR MOTHER ANN'S CHILDREN. *New-England Galaxy 1965 6(4): 40-48.* The Shakers, or "Mother Ann's children," embraced a fundamental precept of simplicity; in rejecting all "superfluities" they achieved a pure and lasting beauty in worship, architecture, and craftsmanship. As the 19th century advanced, the Shakers bought cloth from the "world." While still attempting to achieve uniformity, this practice resulted in a certain "variety in uniformity." Pictures and descriptions are given of a series of dolls dressed to represent Shakers of different ages and occupations. Illus.

E. P. Stickney

301. Arrington, Leonard J. BLESSED DAMOZELS: WOMEN IN MORMON HISTORY. *Dialogue: A J. of Mormon Thought 1971 6(2): 22-31.*

302. Arrington, Leonard J. and Haupt, Jon. INTOLERABLE ZION: THE IMAGE OF MORMONISM IN NINETEENTH CENTURY AMERICAN LITERATURE. *Western Humanities R. 1968 22(3): 243-260.* Statements made in America about Mormons have tended in recent years to be favorable. Quite the contrary was true in the 19th century. Fifty novels and tales of adventure about Mormons published in the second half of that century (listed at the conclusion of this essay) advance seven stereotypes or images which contributed to the public opinion of Mormons: the drunken, abusive husband; the white slave procurer; the seducer; the sinister secret society; the sinful, fallen city; the lustful Turk; and the cruel, lustful Southern slaveholder. Four of the earliest novels, published by women authors in 1855 and 1856, are analyzed in detail. 28 notes.

A. Turner

303. Bair, JoAnn Woodruff. BELLE SPAFFORD: A SKETCH. *Dialogue: A J. of Mormon Thought 1971 6(2): 71-73.* The life of Belle Spafford, president of the Mormon Relief Society.

S

304. Barnes, Robert. GENEALOGICA MARYLANDIA: SOMERSET PARISH RECORDS. *Maryland Hist. Mag. 1974 69(4): 418-425.* Somerset Parish was one of the original parishes established in 1692 in Maryland, its first church probably built during 1694-97 on the Elzy estate known as Almodington. The parish register is one of the few not already transcribed by Lucy H. Harrison. The church register records births, marriages, baptisms, according to surnames, alphabetically during 1696-1805. Includes comments such as "negro slave girl" or "Eligitimate child of . . . " and occasionally a death date. Entries range from 1696 through 1805. Based on the original register; note.

G. J. Bobango

305. Barrett, Ellen M. VALIDITY AND REGULARITY: A HISTORICAL PERSPECTIVE. *Anglican Theological R. 1976 58(3): 307-329.* Takes a historical perspective on the definitions of the concepts validity and regularity, giving traditional Catholic definitions dating back as far as 44 A.D., and tracing these definitions through the American Anglican experience, including the 1974 ordination of the Philadelphia Eleven, the ceremony in which women were ordained to the Anglican priesthood.

306. Bednarowski, Mary Farrell. SPIRITUALISM IN WISCONSIN IN THE NINETEENTH CENTURY. *Wisconsin Mag. of Hist. 1975 59(1): 2-19.* Three major groups comprised Wisconsin Spiritualism: 1) followers of Mary Hayes Chynoweth in the Madison-Lake Mills-Whitewater area, 2) the Fox River Valley group, including Warren Chase, Nathaniel P. Tallmadge, and R. T. Mason, and 3) those led by Mrs. Julia Severance and Dr. H. S. Brown in the Milwaukee area. All three groups had "a liberal spirit in regard to politics, religion, and social relationships, and a conviction that Spiritualism, as a radical belief untainted by the fears and superstitions fostered by traditional religions, could provide humanity with certain knowledge not only of the nature of laws of this world, but of the next as well." 7 illus., 48 notes.

N. C. Burckel

307. Bennett, David H. WOMEN AND THE NATIVIST MOVEMENT. George, Carol V. R., ed. *"Remember the Ladies": New Perspectives on Women in American History: Essays in Honor of Nelson Manfred Blake* (Syracuse: Syracuse U. Pr., 1975): 71-89. From the 1830's

to the 1920's, nativist movements provided men with fraternal organizations offering security in times of social upheaval. Designed to protect traditional American values, the organizations promoted exclusionary politics, particularly exclusion of Roman Catholic immigrants because of their alien customs. Part of the nativist mission was to protect pure American womanhood from foreign degradation. During the 1830's-50's, Know Nothing literature depicted women's terrorization by lustful, brutal, Catholic clergy. This propaganda encouraged anti-Catholic militancy and may have served latent psycho-sexual needs of nativist men by providing outlets for their angers and frustrations in a competitive, sexually-repressed society in which sex roles were being challenged. Nativist organizations gave these men an opportunity to demonstrate their concept of manhood and virtue by defending endangered womanhood. The American Protective Association, in the 1890's, and the Ku Klux Klan, in the 1920's, exhibited similar behavior and produced comparable propaganda literature. These movements rejected sexual equality and clung to the older ideal of the morally superior, vulnerable woman who must be protected. Based on primary and secondary sources; 30 notes.

P. R. Byrne

308. Bevins, Ann B. SISTERS OF THE VISITATION: 100 YEARS IN SCOTT COUNTY, MT. ADMIRABILIS AND CARDOME. *Register of the Kentucky Hist. Soc. 1976 74(1): 30-39.* Surveys the origins and development of the educational efforts of the Sisters of the Visitation in Scott County, Kentucky. The first academy, Mount Admirabilis, opened in 1875. In 1896, the nuns moved to Cardome, the Georgetown home of former governor James Fisher Robinson. Based on primary and secondary sources; 30 notes.

J. F. Paul

309. Billingsley, Andrew and Billingsley, Amy Tate. NEGRO FAMILY LIFE IN AMERICA. *Social Service R. 1965 39(3): 310-319.* The authors maintain that both the problems and the creative potential of Negroes are highly related to the economic, social, and psychological stability of Negro family life. Six crises for the Negro family have influenced its historical development: 1) from Africa to America, 2) from slavery to emancipation, 3) from rural to urban areas, 4) from the South to the North and West, 5) from negative to positive social status, and 6) from negative to positive self-image. Three patterns of Negro family life have emerged: patriarchal, equalitarian, and matriarchal. 15 notes.

D. H. Swift

310. Boyd, Monica. ORIENTAL IMMIGRATION: THE EXPERIENCE OF THE CHINESE, JAPANESE, AND FILIPINO POPULATIONS IN THE UNITED STATES. *Internat. Migration R. 1971 5(1): 48-61.* A demographic narrative designed to describe the patterns of immigration of Chinese, Filipinos, and Japanese. Reversal of the trend toward predominantly male immigration was hampered by anti-Oriental American laws; since World War II, more women and children are immigrating and immigrants tend toward higher socioeconomic niches. Resumé in French, Spanish, and German. Based on U.S. Census reports and demographic studies; 4 tables, 27 notes.

G. O. Gagnon

311. Brackenridge, R. Douglas; Garcia-Treto, Francisco O.; and Stover, John. PRESBYTERIAN MISSIONS TO MEXICAN AMERICANS IN TEXAS IN THE NINETEENTH CENTURY. *J. of Presbyterian Hist. 1971 49(2): 105-132.* Presbyterian missionary work among the Mexicans in Texas was most active during 1830-60. The first Presbyterian to make contact with the Spanish authorities in Texas in 1793 was expelled for being a Protestant. Sumner Bacon, commissioned by the American Bible Society in 1830, was the first of several Presbyterian missionaries to work with the Mexicans in Texas. Bacon distributed Spanish language Bibles and religious tracts, but his efforts received little outside support. Melinda Rankin, after the Mexican-American War, established a school for Mexican girls in Brownsville. Most of the missionaries in Texas, with the exception of Miss Rankin, were sponsored by some group outside the state. The missionaries, all with a severe dislike for Catholicism, sought to convert the Mexicans to Protestantism. They also sought to anglicize the Mexican culture, equating the Hispanic culture with Catholicism. The missionaries viewed their efforts in Texas as a preliminary step toward missionary work in Mexico. When Mexico was opened to Protestant missionaries in 1860, many abandoned their efforts in Texas to work there and missionary activity among the Mexicans in Texas declined until the 1880's. A small group of Protestant Mexican Americans retained their new faith. With little outside assistance they formed the Mexican Pres-

byterian Church of San Marcos in 1887 and an autonomous Texas-Mexican Presbytery in 1908. Primary and secondary sources; 91 notes.

S. C. Pearson, Jr.

312. Brain, Jeffrey P. THE NATCHEZ "PARADOX." *Ethnology 1971 10(2): 215-222.* "The concern of many scholars with the interpretation of the Natchez social system proposed by Swanton may be valid, but the controversy has become greatly complicated by extrinsic approaches and by a lack of historic perspective. This paper has a twofold objective. First, it adds to the discussion a historical dimension drawn from archeological and ethnological data which suggests how and why the class systems might have come to operate among the Natchez. Second, it proposes an explanation for the operation of the system in the form described by Swanton. It is proposed that the reported exogamous, hierarchical class system was a logical transformation from a pre-existing endogamous caste system (which was probably operating under matrilineal descent rules) subjected to outside pressures and faced with the alternative of assimilating new peoples into the social fabric or surrendering to chaos. The system at time of contact was serving two functions, the integration of diverse groups into a new social solidarity, and the maintenance of the old aristocratic core." AIA(2:1:4) J

313. Brauer, Ruth. TRACING WOMEN'S SERVICES IN THE MISSOURI SYNOD. *Concordia Hist. Inst. Q. 1963 36(1): 5-13.*

314. Breeze, Lawrence E. THE INSKIPS: UNION IN HOLINESS. *Methodist Hist. 1975 13(4): 25-45.* John S. Inskip (1816-84) and his wife, Martha Jane Inskip (1819-90), were leaders in the Holiness Movement within the Methodist Church. In their joint ministerial career they carried their message of Christian perfection throughout the United States and into other lands through evangelism, revivals, class and camp meetings, publications, and preaching. Based largely on a biography of John Inskip by William McDonald and John E. Searles and an unpublished diary of Mrs. Inskip; 88 notes. H. L. Calkin

315. Brown, Earl Kent. ARCHETYPES AND STEREOTYPES: CHURCH WOMEN IN THE NINETEENTH CENTURY. *Religion in Life 1974 43(3): 325-337.* The contributions of Barbara Heck, Lois Stiles Parker, Sarah Dickey, Frances Willard, and Anna Howard Shaw as leaders in the Methodist Church disprove stereotypes about church women in the 19th century. S

316. Brown, Judith K. ECONOMIC ORGANIZATION AND THE POSITION OF WOMEN AMONG THE IROQUOIS. *Ethnohist. 1970 17(3/4): 151-167.* "The relationship between the position of women and their economic role is examined by comparing ethnohistoric and ethnographic data relating to the Iroquois of North America and the Bemba of Northern Rhodesia. It is concluded that the high status of Iroquois women reflected their control of their tribe's economic organization." J

317. Brown, Minnie Miller. BLACK WOMEN IN AMERICAN AGRICULTURE. *Agric. Hist. 1976 50(1): 202-212.* Black women have had agricultural roles similar to black men with the additional responsibilities of rearing children and running a household. The plantation system and the difficulty Negroes have had in obtaining land after freedom have made it hard for them to become independent farmers. 18 notes. D. E. Bowers

318. Browne, Joseph. THE GREENING OF AMERICA: IRISH-AMERICAN WRITERS. *J. of Ethnic Studies 1975 2(4): 71-76.* Irish Americans, only eight percent of the population, have supplied America with a high number of significant and talented writers. Discusses the experiences and conditions that have created writers out of a large number of Irish Americans: first, because of the father-son relationship in the Irish family, and second, the "strong Manicheistic element in the Irish culture," combined with a large dose of Jansenism. The former produces a strong matriarchal tendency compensating for a world which has downtrodden and debased the Irish male, an Oedipal milieu attested to by the frequency and manner of the alienated son theme. The latter, the endless war between good and evil in which the forces of evil always prevail, results in one of two possible reactions to life: that of being "a stoical purveyor of doom," or one who can "laugh at it or blow it up into sudden drama." Thus the Irish "way of joking is to tell the truth." All this is

further prompted by the *Seanachie* tradition, the love of words and storytelling carefully and deliberately cultivated for centuries. 11 notes.

G. J. Bobango

319. Butler, William B.   TWO INITIAL MIDDLE MISSOURI TRADITION TOOL KITS. *Plains Anthropologist 1975 20(67): 53-59.* Stone and bone tools contained in the remains of two charred baskets from an Initial Middle Missouri site, Fay Tolton, House 1, are interpreted as two different tool kits associated with different aspects of animal skin processing. Spatulate-shaped bone tools previously described as "quill flatteners" are interpreted here as skin burnishers. The ethnographic association of women with skin working activities suggests that these two skin working tool kits were the property of a woman of the household.

J

320. Calvo, Janis.   QUAKER WOMEN MINISTERS IN NINE-TEENTH CENTURY AMERICA. *Quaker Hist. 1974 63(2): 75-93.* The Quietist-prophetic view that God speaks through pure, obedient, empty vessels enabled the traveling woman Friend to fulfill the conventional image of pure, submissive female, reluctantly accepting God's will to preach. She also accepted her conventional domestic role in everything else. We know little about child care during the mother-minister's absence. 58 notes.

T. D. S. Bassett

321. Chu, Yung-Deh Richard.   CHINESE SECRET SOCIETIES IN AMERICA: A HISTORICAL SURVEY. *Asian Profile [Hong Kong] 1973 1(1): 21-38.* Examines the history of Chinese tong societies in the United States. These organizations had their origins in the Hung-men societies organized in China to overthrow the Manchu rulers. The first wave of Chinese immigration to America came in the 1850's and the 1860's during the Gold Rush and the building of the transcontinental railroad, and following the defeat of the Taiping rebels. The great majority of these Chinese were men who had virtually no family life and who turned to gambling, opium, and prostitution. When Irish mobs burned their residences and all levels of government imposed prejudicial laws against them, these Chinese immigrants turned to their secret societies. In the decades following 1870 many Chinese moved from California to the metropolitan areas of America and organized new tongs. Their identification with the anti-Manchu organizations in China continued, although their activities centered on local issues in America. In the years following World War II immigration and other restrictive laws have been amended and Chinese immigration has markedly increased. In New York City the Chinese population increased from 6,000 in the pre-World War II period to 12,000 in 1954, 30,000 in 1967, and 60,000 by 1972, with more than 100,000 in the greater New York metropolitan area. This new immigration has been not of single individuals but of urban families. Tongs have continued to provide assistance and protection for numbers of newly arrived Chinese. Based on interviews and secondary sources; 70 notes.

S. H. Frank

322. Clark, A. J.   CATHOLIC EDUCATION IN TRANSITION. *Catholic Educ. R. 1966 64(5): 289-315.* Historical and religious factors responsible for the three types of Catholic schools - parish, private and diocesan - point to a Catholic school "pattern" in the United States but not a genuine "system." Authority is divided among diocesan officials, parish pastors and leaders of the religious orders. "Historically...Catholic schools were set up with a view to saving the faith and morals of Catholic boys and girls." The middle-class Catholic parent today wants academic excellence in Catholic education, a costly enterprise, particularly in the light of a steadily climbing enrollment (double the total of 1940). Related educational projects (Confraternity of Christian Doctrine which "flourishes as never before" and Newman Club Federation "now very much in flux") serve Catholic students attending non-Catholic schools. Higher education, the role of the lay teacher, teacher preparation (especially the Sister Formation Conference), and Montessorian methods are stressed. Sources cited in text.

D. H. Broderick

323. Clark, Laverne Harrell.   EARLY HORSE TRAPPINGS OF THE NAVAJO AND APACHE INDIANS. *Arizona and the West 1963 5(3): 233-248.* Navajo and Apache Indians were proud horsemen. From the early 17th century, when they began to acquire their horses in raids from Spaniards, Mexicans, Anglo-Americans, and other Indians, they began to work with their own resources to provide trappings for the horses by blending imitation and ingenuity. Ropes were made of rawhide,

buckskin, horsehair, wool, or yucca leaves. Bridles were fashioned from animal skins. Metal bits came later. Silversmithing developed as an ancillary skill for decorative purposes. The saddles were closely patterned after the popular Spanish and Mexican ones in use in the Southwest. Saddle blankets were either woven by Navajo women or serapes acquired in Mexico were used. Saddlebags were made from skins and were frequently decorated with beadwork. Boots were fashioned from hides to protect the hoofs. Not until late in the prereservation period did the Indians learn to work metal to copy the horseshoes used by whites. Even today a splendid set of trappings is a prestige factor for a Navajo or Apache. Based on monographic studies and published source material; illus., 60 notes.

D. L. Smith

324. Cole, Johnnetta.   BLACK WOMEN IN AMERICA: AN ANNOTATED BIBLIOGRAPHY. *Black Scholar 1971 3(4): 42-53.* A selective, topical bibliography focusing on black women in America but also including works pertinent to black women's experiences in Africa and the Caribbean.

325. Corbett, Beatrice.   SUSAN MOULTON FRASER MC MASTER. *Inland Seas 1975 31(3): 192-200.* Born in Rhode Island in 1819, Susan Moulton married James Fraser, a Bay City, Michigan, lumberman and Indian agent, in 1851. After Fraser's death in 1866 she built a Baptist church in his memory in Bay City. She married the Toronto banker Senator William McMaster in 1871 and continued to be an active Baptist. She convinced her husband to establish McMaster Hall as a theological college. Based on family information.

K. J. Bauer

326. Davies, Vernon.   FERTILITY VERSUS WELFARE: THE NEGRO AMERICAN DILEMMA. *Phylon 1966 27(3): 226-232.* Traces fertility trends among Negro Americans since about 1850 and compares them with trends among Caucasian Americans. A 1900 fertility ratio differential of Negroes and whites virtually disappeared by 1920 with a rapid decline in white mortality rates. From 1920 to 1935 crude birth rates of Negroes dropped 9.2 points, but from 1935 to 1955 they rose nine points. The fertility ratio acceleration from 1935 to 1955 was about 50 percent faster than for whites, in part because of a rapidly declining Negro mortality rate. Birth rates declined again after 1958, and by 1962 the birth rate for whites stood at 21.4 and for nonwhites at 30.5. The major contribution to the high fertility of Negroes derives from the rural South. Considering high fertility a major element in the etiology of poverty, the author recommends a population control program among rural Negroes of the South. Based on the U.S. Census of Population, 12 notes.

S. C. Pearson, Jr.

327. Dayton, Lucille Sider and Dayton, Donald W.   "YOUR DAUGHTERS SHALL PROPHESY": FEMINISM IN THE HOLINESS MOVEMENT. *Methodist Hist. 1976 14(2): 67-92.* The feminist theme permeates the literature of the Holiness Movement in America. It varied in intensity over two centuries from reserved openness, to acceptance of religious activity by women, to favoring the ordination of women. The role of women in holiness traditions was foreshadowed by Susanna Wesley's activities in the 1730's. The Holiness Movement intensified in America as early as 1827, with Phoebe Palmer later having a great impact both evangelically and as a feminist. By 1973 there was considerably less emphasis on feminism in the movement. 116 notes.

H. L. Calkin

328. Dodge, Bayard.   AMERICAN EDUCATIONAL AND MISSIONARY EFFORTS IN THE NINETEENTH AND EARLY TWENTIETH CENTURIES. *Ann. of the Am. Acad. of Pol. and Social Sci. 1972 (401): 15-22.* "In 1810 the American Board Mission was founded. Nine years later two missionaries were sent to the Middle East. They were followed by many men and women who devoted themselves to evangelism in the Ottoman Empire and later in Iran. Because the Ottoman government did not permit them to proselytize Muslims, and the Catholics objected to any form of interference, their work was principally with the Greek Orthodox, Armenians, and Nestorians. In 1850 the Ottoman government authorized the establishment of an evangelical 'millet,' or sect; so Protestant churches were built and congregations organized. During the middle of the nineteenth century, the missionaries also established many high schools, as well as ten or a dozen colleges. Because of the war and political disturbances, some of the colleges have been obliged to transfer to new localities, or else to close down. Robert College

and the Constantinople Woman's College at Istanbul, the American University of Beirut, and the American University in Cairo have grown to be large institutions, still active and useful. These schools, colleges, and universities have been influential in creating constructive contacts between the peoples of the Middle East and of America." J

329. Edwards, O. C., Jr. and Holmes, Urban T., III. MARRIAGE AND MATING: CREATION, SOCIETY, AND JESUS. *Anglican Theological R. Supplementary Series 1973 (2): 4-27.*

330. Engo, Paul B. ON AFRICAN LIBERATION AND THE ROLE OF THE BLACK WOMAN IN AMERICA. *Pan-African J. [Kenya] 1971 4(2): 151-157.* Reprints a speech delivered at African Liberation Day ceremonies, 24 May 1970, in Harlem, New York City. Important factors in black awareness include the idea that man's freedom is not negotiable and black people must safeguard their earned liberties. Women in America have a vital role. In Africa and America women had more freedom than enslaved men, and are ahead of men in economic development and political awareness.                      H. G. Soff

331. Ergood, Bruce. THE FEMALE PROTECTION AND THE SUN LIGHT: TWO CONTEMPORARY NEGRO MUTUAL AID SOCIETIES. *Florida Hist. Q. 1971 50(1): 25-38.* Mutual aid societies, early associations of free Negroes begun in Philadelphia, New York City, and Charleston (South Carolina) in the 18th century, had become commonplace by the mid-19th century. The combined membership of six statewide Negro mutual aid societies in Florida in 1968 was 41,000. One of the local burial societies, the Female Protective Society of Alachua County, founded in 1903, requires membership for more than two years for reception of benefits in the form of burial payments. Membership numbers between 150 and 200. The Sun Light, a mutual benefit sick and burial society, is a splinter group from the statewide Sun Light Pall Bearers Charitable Society. A full year's membership or payment of three quarterly contributions is required for reception of the full death benefit from the organization. Although blacks make up the total membership of the Sun Light, no whites have been refused membership. 18 notes.
R. V. Calvert

332. Eyman, Frances. THE TESHOA, A SHOSHONEAN WOMAN'S KNIFE: A STUDY OF AMERICAN INDIAN CHOPPER INDUSTRIES. *Wyoming Archaeologist 1970 13(3): 1-63.* "The evidence for, the nature of, as well as the circumstances surrounding a simple stone tool type called the Teshoa are reviewed. Various aspects are explored in some detail including: distribution through time and space, possible relationships and derivations from comparable materials in the Old World, uses and contexts (both ethnographic and archaeological) throughout North America, methods whereby this kind of tool can be manufactured, classification of choppers and teshoa, other kinds of tools similar to Teshoa, as well as the opinions and errors of others on the general subject of Teshoa. In presenting these facets of 'the Teshoa problems', the intent, as a whole, is to increase our comprehension of the antiquity, the hows and whys of Teshoa."                      AIA(2:1:20) J

333. Falls, Helen E. THE VOCATION OF HOME MISSIONS 1845-1970. *Baptist Hist. and Heritage 1972 7(1): 25-32.* There were five critical periods in the creation of the Baptist Home Mission Board. Organized at New Orleans in 1845, the board appointed six missionaries to preach and establish churches for minority groups. Within 15 years some 900 missionaries worked to establish 179 churches. During the Civil War work was hindered, but by 1885 work among Negroes, Indians, and C.S.A. veterans was initiated in a haphazard way. Effort among the "New Immigrants" was spearheaded by Marie Buhlmaier at Baltimore in 1886. Sporadic efforts were made to evangelize the West, and by 1903 a specific strategy was outlined for missionary work. Five years later language training was incorporated into ministerial training. During World War I the Board provided "camp pastors." Primary efforts of the missions in the 1920's were directed toward immigrants. The first real attempt to coordinate activities was in 1927 with the creation of the Department of Independent and Direct Missions. From 1930 to 1945 economic pressures hampered the program. After World War II home missions were reorganized with four priorities - Negroes, cities, rural areas, and evangelism. Special programs were inaugurated by the board as it laid more stress on qualifications of ministerial candidates. Professionalization ensued. The Baptist Mission Board has continued its ministry since the war. Based on primary and secondary sources; 32 notes.                      J. D. Born, Jr.

334. Frost, Jerry W. AS THE TWIG IS BENT: QUAKER IDEAS OF CHILDHOOD. *Quaker Hist. 1971 60(2): 67-87.* In the colonial period, Friends and non-Friends were more alike than different in raising children. Friends shared attitudes most fully with other groups growing out of Puritanism. The meeting had responsibility for the training and support of children if misfortune befell the parents. Quakers were vague about what spiritual state their children were in, but were clear in rejecting both original sin and imputed grace. They seemed to feel that children were innocent until they could distinguish right from wrong - perhaps between the ages of five and 12. Friends originally limited membership to "saints" but slipped into birthright membership without the half-way covenant compromise of the Congregationalists. This registration of Friends' children provided the equivalent of baptismal or birth certification. They lowered their missionary sights to their children as the main body of potential converts. Unlike the first generation Friends, they segregated children from "the world," maintaining plainness in dress and speech, family devotions, Bible reading, and avoidance of the arts. Father was boss, Mother his deputy. Children must learn to keep quiet and fear God. After 1760 the focus shifted to Mother, play, and sentimentality. As roads and postal service improved, more personal letters were written, with evidence of the new attitudes. Based mainly on correspondence and textbooks; 88 notes.                      T. D. S. Bassett

335. Fryer, Judith. AMERICAN EVES IN AMERICAN EDENS. *Am. Scholar 1974/75 44(1): 78-99.* Between the 1840's and the 1880's communitarians were searching for alternative modes of living that would break down the sex roles of traditional American society and create a new role for the American woman. There were two strands in the utopian experimentation, the religious and the secular. Examines the three foremost religious communities: the Shakers, the Mormons, and the Oneida Perfectionists. Most secular communities were implementations of the philosophies of Robert Owen or Charles Fourier. As illustrations, examines the community at New Harmony, Indiana and the Brook Farm experiment.                      R. V. Ritter

336. Gayle, Addison, Jr. STRANGERS IN A STRANGE LAND. *Southern Exposure 1975 3(1): 4-7.* The mass migration of Negroes to the North after the American Civil War was a cultural loss. Black authors, cut off from their roots in the South and their source of creative inspiration, wrote distorted views of Black life. Whites and middle-class blacks demanded that "the reality of the racial problem be fictionalized," but overlooked black writers such as Jean Toomer (1894-1967) and Zora Hurston (1901-60) who portrayed the strength, endurance, and survival of their people. Primary sources; illus.                      G. A. Bolton

337. Gill, George W. THE GLENDO SKELETON AND ITS MEANING IN LIGHT OF POST-CONTACT RACIAL DYNAMICS IN THE GREAT PLAINS. *Plains Anthropologist 1976 21(72): 81-88.* A protohistoric burial from the Glendo Site in eastern Wyoming produced a nearly complete human skeleton of a young adult female. Osteological analysis of the specimen reveals predominantly Caucasoid physical characteristics. A skeleton exhibiting such an anatomical pattern, and coming from a grave clearly exhibiting Plains Indian cultural affinities, raises interesting but somewhat difficult questions for interpretation.                      J

338. Gingerich, Melvin. CHANGE AND UNIFORMITY IN MENNONITE ATTIRE. *Mennonite Q. R. 1966 40(4): 243-259.* Historically Anabaptist-Mennonite teaching and regulation of dress has consisted primarily of proscription of ostentation and display, with prescription of specific forms playing a secondary role, often nonexistent. From pictorial material it is evident that Mennonites of northern Europe 300 years ago did not dress like those of Switzerland. The Dutch during the first four centuries of their history maintained simplicity in their clothing but not uniformity. The costumes brought to colonial Pennsylvania by Mennonite immigrants of central Europe were those of the Swiss and Palatine. In this country in the first half of the 20th century a vigorous program tried to enforce a garb for both men and women - a bonnet and capedress for women, a "plain coat" without lapels for men. "When the self-identity of the group was threatened the recourse seemed to be an enforced, simple garb." Based on the author's forthcoming book, *A History of Mennonite Costume.*                      E. P. Stickney

339. Gittelsohn, Roland B. WOMEN'S LIB AND JUDAISM. *Midstream 1971 17(8): 51-58.* Discusses the historical treatment of the Jewish woman from ancient times to the present. Concludes that "Judaism never pretended to extend complete equality to its women. But it consistently expressed far more understanding and acceptance of them as persons than did other civilizations of the time. And - properly, fairly understood - it contains an openness to the rights and needs of women which bodes well for tomorrow." Note.     R. J. Wechman

340. Goranson, Greta K. IN SEARCH OF MY HERITAGE. *Swedish Pioneer Hist. Q. 1976 27(1): 26-43.* The author had a genealogical account left by her great-great-grandfather, Gustaf Göransson (b. 1832), and wanted to discover why and how he had left Sweden. She went to Sweden as a student and discovered relatives at a house near the parish church of her ancestor. She visited the isolated and enclosed farm her ancestor had owned. They had been the only family to emigrate from the parish. 5 photos.     K. J. Puffer

341. Green, Rayna D. THE POCAHONTAS PERPLEX: THE IMAGE OF INDIAN WOMEN IN AMERICAN CULTURE. *Massachusetts R. 1975 16(4): 698-714.* The American Indian woman has been a symbolic paradox. Depending on man's needs, she has been continually viewed as either the civilized princess or the destructive squaw. It is now time to revaluate her—bereft of myths—as a human being. Based on primary and secondary sources; 9 illus., 8 notes.     M. J. Barach

342. Griessman, B. Eugene and Henson, Curtis T., Jr. THE HISTORY AND SOCIAL TOPOGRAPHY OF AN ETHNIC ISLAND IN ALABAMA. *Phylon 1975 36(2): 97-112.* An "ethnic island" has emerged during the past century-and-a-half along the west bank of the Tombigbee River, 35 miles north of Mobile, in present-day Washington County. The inhabitants, who are often referred to as Cajans or Cajuns, are a mixture of red, black, and white. Probably the first settlers in the area were Daniel Reed and his wife Rose, who moved there early in the 19th century. The authors trace the background of the settlement, and its growth, and discuss how demographic and social topographic characteristics such as the roads and transportation networks, the schools, the churches, the land tenure, and economic conditions helped keep the settlement isolated. Recently, the members of the community have been merging with the society that surrounds them. Primary and secondary sources; 5 tables, 28 notes.     B. A. Glasrud

343. Gude, George J., Jr. WOMEN TEACHERS IN THE MISSOURI SYNOD. *Concordia Hist. Inst. Q. 1971 44(4): 163-170.* The record, while not clear, does indicate that some women were teaching in the Missouri Synod districts before 1872. Since then several voices have been raised for and against women teachers in the Lutheran schools. From George Stoeckhardt's support in 1897 to John Eiselmeier's criticism in 1925 the debate has continued. In 1929 the Synod decreed that in emergency situations women could be employed in place of men. The Depression, however, caused a reduction of the number of women teachers. Since then the number has steadily grown. "At this time the official position of [the] Synod is that the woman teacher is to be regarded as called in the same sense as the man, even though this is not practiced very widely." Based on primary and secondary sources; 32 notes.     A. M. Brescia

344. Hansen, Chadwick. THE METAMORPHOSIS OF TITUBA, OR WHY AMERICAN INTELLECTUALS CAN'T TELL AN INDIAN WITCH FROM A NEGRO. *New England Q. 1974 47(1): 3-12.* Tituba, a Carib Indian woman, was the first confessor in the Salem witchcraft trials. She was a slave brought from the Barbados. The magic she had practiced was English, not Indian as suggested by an historian in 1831. Later historians preferred to consider her half-Indian, or half-Negro to Indian, or Negro to half-Indian and half-Negro. This racial metamorphosis began after the Civil War. The Tituba of Arthur Miller's *The Crucible* (1971) shows racism is still a part of present society. 27 notes.     E. P. Stickney

345. Harkness, Georgia PIONEER WOMEN IN THE MINISTRY. *Religion in Life 1970 39(2): 261-271.* The earliest women preachers were Quakers. The first to be ordained was a Congregationalist, Antoinette Louisa Brown, on 15 September 1853 in South Butler, New York. Brief outlines are given of the lives of Olympia Brown, Lucretia Coffin Mott (1793-1880), Sybil Jones (1808-73), Sarah Frances Smiley (b. 1830), Phebe Hanaford, Anna Oliver, and Maggie Newton Van Cott. 13 notes.     D. Brockway

346. Harwood, Edwin and Hodge, Claire C. JOBS AND THE NEGRO FAMILY: A REAPPRAISAL. *Public Interest 1971 23: 125-131.* The authors describe as false the stereotype that Negro women have an advantage in the urban labor market, thus keeping the black man at an even greater disadvantage, in contrast to the situation in the white labor market. Analysis of the labor market since 1890 shows that black men have enjoyed a greater diversification of jobs than black women. This follows the pattern of white employment. It is the handicaps endured by the Negro woman in the job market, not by the male, which have often contributed to economic and social problems for Negroes.     E. C. Hyslop

347. Hastings, Donald W., Reynolds, C. H., and Canning, R. R. MORMONISM AND BIRTH PLANNING: THE DISCREPANCY BETWEEN CHURCH AUTHORITIES' TEACHINGS AND LAY ATTITUDES. *Population Studies [Great Britain] 1972 26(1, pt. 1): 19-28.* "This paper examines the traditional stance taken by Mormon Church authorities regarding birth control. Special attention is given to the theological context used as a justification for pro-natalist benefits. Previous research which treats Mormons as a special sub-group in KAP studies is reviewed. We find that while the stance of Church leaders has been consistent historically, the college-educated Mormon is more accepting of family planning to-day than previously."     J

348. Henderson, Edwin B. THE NEGRO AS ATHLETE. *Crisis 1970 77(2): 51-56.* In less than 50 years the numbers and abilities of black athletes have changed race relations in professional sports. The first professional black athletes were boxers. Jack Johnson and Joe Louis were the popular heavyweights in the 20th century. The color barrier fell easiest in track and field, now almost dominated by blacks. Baseball, football, and basketball include blacks in the highest paying categories of players. Black participation is least in tennis, golf, bowling, wrestling, and swimming. Black superiority in sports may be inherited from the days slave traders selected only the strongest and healthiest Africans for the middle passage; and then only the strongest of those survived. Black women are also proving their abilities in athletics. 13 photos.     A. G. Belles

349. Hitchings, Catherine F. UNIVERSALIST AND UNITARIAN WOMEN MINISTERS. *J. of the Universalist Hist. Soc. 1975 10: 3-165.* The entire issue is a biographical dictionary of 163 deceased Universalist and Unitarian women ministers, limited to those who were ordained into the ministry and who served within the United States. Several sketches indicate discrimination endured by these women. Many of them also pursued careers in writing, lecturing, law, medicine, and particularly social welfare. Based on primary and secondary sources, especially archival materials in the Universalist Historical Society, the Unitarian Universalist Association, and two unpublished biographical manuscripts of women ministers compiled by Unitarian minister Clara Cook Helvie (1876-1969). 13 photos, notes, 2 appendixes.     P. A. Beaber

350. Holway, Hope. THE AMERICAN INDIAN AND HIS NAME. *Chronicles of Oklahoma 1965 43(3): 340-344.* The origins of our names are very similar to those of Indians. In primitive society there was little need for names. Sometimes an individual would acquire a name related to a happening. Often not until puberty did a boy know his name, then he often changed it to indicate his prowess. Names were changed when the owners became ill to assure recovery. There were "nikie" names referring to some remote ancestor. "Great Walker," for example, might refer to an individual or to an ancestor. "Small Boiler" was a name for an Omaha woman who gave a feast but did not have enough food for her guests. There were dream names, color names, animal names, nature names, number names. Names presented a problem in signing legal papers, and names were a problem to census takers. Teachers sought to give children names of which they could be proud. Under the agency system an effort was made to introduce our own practical and useable name system. Wives and children had to be known by the husband's name. The preservation of dignified and easily handled Indian names is a custom to be followed. Note on sources.     I. W. Van Noppen

351. Horvitz, Eleanor F.  THE YEARS OF THE JEWISH WOMAN. *Rhode Island Jewish Hist. Notes 1975 7(1): 152-170.* Discusses the various benevolent organizations in Rhode Island established by Jewish women, ca. 1877-1975.

352. Hottenstein, Mary Deturk.  TRADITIONAL PENNSYLVANIA GERMAN CHRISTMAS COOKIES. *Hist. Rev. of Berks County 1970-71 36(1): 14-16.* Relates the Pennsylvania Dutch customs of cookie making at Christmas time. Preparations started in mid-October and continued for six to eight weeks. It took time to gather spices as well as season cookies. Corn and wheat sometimes were taken from Berks County to Philadelphia and exchanged for ingredients. Homegrown hickory nuts and black walnuts were used extensively. Mothers taught daughters how to prepare the goodies. They passed recipes and cookie cutters on to their children. Mrs. Hottenstein's receipts for Springerle and Reichardt Platzchen and pictures of her wooden and tin cookie cutters are included. Illus.
H. B. Powell

353. Houchens, Mariam S.  SHAKERTOWN AT PLEASANT HILL, KENTUCKY. *Filson Club Hist. Q. 1971 45(3): 264-285.* Discusses the life of the founder of the Shakers, Mother Ann Lee, the development of the Shaker organization, and the unique social institution of sexual segregation. Traces the history of Pleasant Hill from the emotional religious revival of 1799-1805, to the end of the community in the early 20th century. Notes the industriousness of the Shakers and the excellent reputation their furniture and simple architecture enjoyed. Extensive quotations from the journals kept by the community provide insights into the daily life of the Shakers. Based on secondary sources and the Filson Club Shaker journals; 55 notes.
G. B. McKinney

354. Huff, Archie V., Jr.  THE BLACK HERO IN SOUTH CAROLINA HISTORY. *South Carolina Rev. 1972 4(2): 20-28.* Integration of black and white histories into a single narrative is difficult for a white-dominated society because the aims of the two racial groups are diametrically opposed. The careers of four black heroes in South Carolina history—Denmark Vesey, Robert Smalls, Mary McLeod Bethune, and Benjamin Mays—illustrate how black leaders achieved fame in spite of the prevailing white culture. Making the plight of their race a major concern of their lives, these black heroes stand in judgment against the white society and the American dream. Based on biographical and autobiographical sources; 19 notes.
A. V. Huff, Jr.

355. Inglis, Gordon B.  NORTHWEST AMERICAN MATRILINY: THE PROBLEM OF ORIGINS. *Ethnology 1970 9(2): 149-159.* "A scientific historical hypothesis is proposed regarding the emergence of matriliny among the peoples of the northern northwest coast of North America and the adjacent interior, integrating historical data and reconstruction with theory. It is suggested that: (1) when the Na-Dene-speaking ancestors of the Eyak, Tlingit, and Haida moved to the coast, the men became sea-mammal hunters and deep-sea fishermen, while the women learned to gather coastal foods; (2) they became matrilocal and matrilineal as a result of the peculiar distribution of those gathered foods, since the gathering activities of the women included features analogous to those postulated as conducive to the emergence of matrilocality and matriliny among horticulturalists; (3) river-fishing techniques for taking salmon and oolichan were developed or acquired as man's activity after matriliny had become established, thus leading to avunculocal residence and the social structures reported for historic times. It is also suggested that Murdock's statement to the effect that traits of social structure are borrowed only in circumstances favoring their independent development, merely presents a special case of the more general principle that cultural traits of any kind may be borrowed when they work to the advantage of the borrowers. Therefore, it is postulated that the Athabaskans of the interior and the Northern Kwakiutl adopted matrilineal institutions through association with the wealthy and powerful people controlling the rich resources of the lower Skeena and Nass rivers. Archaeological data will test the hypothesis and it will be supported or refuted by evidence regarding the historical priority of deep-sea hunting and fishing over the river fishery. (amended abstract)"
AIA(2:2/3:408)

356. Jacob, John.  NORTH AMERICAN INDIAN BAND ENDOGAMY: OPPOSITION TO A MODULAR CONCEPT. *Masterkey 1972 46(3): 101-107.* Discusses dominant marriage patterns of hunting and gathering Indian tribes indigenous to North America, centering on endogamy and exogamy.

357. Jadin, Louis.  LES SOEURS DE NOTRE-DAME ET LES SOEURS DE SAINTE-MARIE DE NAMUR AUX U.S.A., AU GUATEMALA ET EN ANGLETERRE SOUS LEOPOLD IER [The Sisters of Notre Dame and the Sisters of Saint Mary of Namur go to the United States, Guatemala, and England under Leopold I]. *Bull. des Séances de l'Acad. Royale des Sci. d'Outre Mer [Belgium] 1965 11(3): 662-670.* Tells of Julie Billiart, foundress of the Sisters of Notre Dame de Namur, and the arrival of the order in the United States. The activities of the order in Cincinnati are given attention. The author also relates a history of the Sisters of Sainte-Marie de Namur in America after their invitation by Father Pierre de Smet and Bishop John Timon of Buffalo. Based on published sources and on MSS preserved in the archives at Namur.
A. J. Hamilton

358. Johnston, Jean.  ANCESTRY AND DESCENDANTS OF MOLLY BRANT. *Ontario Hist. [Canada] 1971 63(2): 87ff.* Presents a genealogical analysis of the children of the sister of the Loyalist Mohawk leader, Joseph Brant, from the late 1750's to the third quarter of the 19th century. Table, 16 notes.
W. R. Whitham

359. Jones, Faustine C.  THE LOFTY ROLE OF THE BLACK GRANDMOTHER. *Crisis 1973 80(1): 19-21.* Tells of the importance of the grandmother to the black family in the 19th and 20th centuries.
S

360. Ladner, Joyce A.  RACISM AND TRADITION: BLACK WOMANHOOD IN HISTORICAL PERSPECTIVE. Carroll, Berenice A., ed. Liberating Women's History (Chicago: U. of Illinois Press, 1976): 179-193. Past historiography generally has compared the black family to middle class whites, a method which emphasizes the weaknesses of the blacks and overlooks their positive features. To comprehend the position of black women in today's society, family life in pre-colonial African cultures, the structural effects of slavery, and the modern oppression of blacks must be analyzed. Only then can a true assessment of the strengths of the black personality be made. 39 notes.
B. Sussman

361. Lindsey, David.  MINISTERING ANGELS IN ALIEN LANDS. *Am. Hist. Illus. 1975 9(10): 19-27.* Discusses the involvement of women in the American overseas missionary movement in the 19th century. Various women's missionary societies, over 700 by mid-century, were formed to promote and support missionary efforts, financing a great portion of the overseas mission crusade. Many women went overseas as missionaries' wives and evangelists. Missionary women were most notably involved in education and medicine, and worked to emancipate non-Christian women from oppression. 10 illus., 2 photos.
N. J. Street

362. Lundsgaarde, Henry P.  A STRUCTURAL ANALYSIS OF NEZ PERCE KINSHIP. *Res. Studies 1967 35(1): 48-77.* Studies the interpersonal relations of the Nez Percé Indians of Idaho centering on an analysis of marriage and kinship group alliance. The author outlines some of the influences of acculturative agents on traditional Nez Percé culture, the kinship terminology of which appears to have persisted from precontact times to the present in only slightly modified form. From data on Nez Percé kinship terminology and social behavior the contemporary reservation population largely follows customary modes of behavior, but changes of custom can be expected in the next generation. There is a strong emphasis on status allocation on the basis of advanced age and male sex evidenced in the kinship nomenclature in use today. By analyzing separate kin classes for major structural principles, it is possible to point to an area of field investigation which can aid in amplifying weaknesses in the data and predicting where subsequent investigation of related subsystems is likely to lead. Based on secondary sources and field investigation; 5 tables, biblio.
D. R. Picht

363. MacPeek, Gertrude A.  "TALL OAKS FROM LITTLE ACORNS GROW": THE STORY OF ST. MARY'S EPISCOPAL SCHOOL FOR INDIAN GIRLS. *Daughters of the Am. Revolution Mag. 1973 107(5): 392-398.*

364. Mathur, Mary E. Fleming.  WHO CARES . . . THAT A WOMAN'S WORK IS NEVER DONE . . .? *Indian Historian 1971 4(2): 11-16.* Surveys ethnographic literature on the role of women in non-Euro-American cultures, particularly the Iroquois studied by Joseph François Lafitau in 1724.
S

365. Medicine, Beatrice. THE ROLE OF WOMEN IN NATIVE AMERICAN SOCIETIES, A BIBLIOGRAPHY. *Indian Historian 1975 8(3): 50-54.* This bibliography includes a short introduction, and lists approximately 100 titles including books, periodical articles, government pamphlets, and an occasional thesis. It is neither annotated nor evaluative and is admittedly far from complete.     E. D. Johnson

366. Medlicott, Alexander, Jr. RETURN TO THIS LAND OF LIGHT: A PLEA TO AN UNREDEEMED CAPTIVE. *New England Q. 1965 38(2): 202-216.* An account of the life of Eunice Williams, who was captured at the age of seven when Deerfield, Massachusetts, was destroyed by the Indians. She remained with her captors at Caughnawaga in Canada, near Montreal, married an Indian, reared children, paid visits to her brother Stephen at Longmeadow, Massachusetts, and lived to the age of 88. The account is based on printed sources, manuscript letters, and the manuscript diary kept by Stephen Williams now at the First Church of Christ Congregational, Longmeadow.     A. Turner

367. Micks, Marianne H. EXODUS OR EDEN?: A BATTLE OF IMAGES. *Anglican Theological R. Supplementary Series 1973 (1): 126-139.* Examines the role of women in history, how the Protestant church has supported it, and its contemporary manifestations.     S

368. Mitchell, Norma Taylor. FROM SOCIAL TO RADICAL FEMINISM. *Methodist Hist. 1975 13(3): 21-44.* A survey of the diversity in Methodist women's organizations from the establishment of women's foreign and home missionary societies following the Civil War to the Caucus and the Commission on the Status and Role of Women in the United Methodist Church of the 1970's. Changes in the nature of feminism during this period, the accomplishments of the movement, and the problems still to be solved are discussed. 47 notes.     H. L. Calkin

369. Morsberger, Robert E. THE FURTHER TRANSFORMATION OF TITUBA. *New England Q. 1974 47(3): 456-458.* A review of the continuing racial and moral evolution of Tituba and her husband, John Indian, of Salem witch trials fame. Tituba and John were Carib Indians, but writers first made them half-Indian and half-Negro, and eventually entirely Negro. Ann Petry has now written a children's book describing them as Negro heroes. Tituba is wise, educated, resourceful, hard-working, and polished—in sum, all things good—and saves the fumbling, lazy, racist whites in spite of themselves. Thus has the process come full circle. 2 notes.     V. L. Human

370. Nitkin, Nathaniel. YEAR OF THE PENOBSCOT. *New-England Galaxy 1973 14(4): 8-15.* Describes the hardships of a tribe of Penobscot Indians in Maine, courtship and marriage customs, the family, canoe building, seasonal migration, and hunting and food gathering practices.     S

371. Nitobourg, E. L. K VOPROSU O TAK NAZYAEMOM RASPADE NEGRITYANSKOI SEMIV SSHA [Toward the problem of the so-called breakdown of the Negro family in the U.S.A.]. *Sovetskaia Etnografiia [USSR] 1972 (6): 64-74.* The paper deals with the so-called breakdown of the Negro family in the United States. The author describes the specific situation and the distinctive role of woman and mother as the chief person and the main support in the families of black slaves on the plantations of the American South. In our times the high proportion of matrifocal Negro families, as well as the high percentage of so-called illegitimate births among American Negroes, are due, according to the author, not so much to the peculiar features of the evolution of the family among slaves in the 18th-19th centuries as to racial discrimination and segregation. This has led to the severe social-economic situation of the US Negro population which is undergoing a rapid process of urbanization.     J

372. Officer, James E. THE ROLE OF THE UNITED STATES GOVERNMENT IN INDIAN ACCULTURATION AND ASSIMILATION. *Anuario Indigenista [Mexico] 1965 25: 73-86.* A survey of the successes and failures of Federal policies toward the American Indian from 1776 to 1965, highlighting the legislative milestones and their effects on various aspects of Indian culture, e.g., family structure, language, religion, social and legal status. The author suggests that careful study of the Indian question in the United States can be of great value to Latin American leaders who are facing much greater problems of cultural unification. 11 notes, biblio.     R. L. Utt

373. Passi, Michael M. MYTH AS HISTORY, HISTORY AS MYTH: FAMILY AND CHURCH AMONG ITALO-AMERICANS. *J. of Ethnic Studies 1975 3(2): 97-103.* Reviews Silvano Tomasi's *Piety and Power: The Role of the Italian Parishes in the New York Metropolitan Area, 1880-1930* (1975), Richard Gambino's *Blood of My Blood: The Dilemma of the Italian Americans* (1974), and Carla Bianco's *The Two Rosetos* (1974). All three attempt to explain the nature of Italian-American society. Tomasi finds the core to be the Catholic Church and its ethnic parishes, Gambino sees the family system as the central element, and Bianco tackles the issue by comparing Rosetos, Italy, with its namesake in Pennsylvania. Of these three finds Bianco's to be the most illuminating and promising. 14 notes.     T. W. Smith

374. Radzialowski, Thaddeus C. REFLECTIONS ON THE HISTORY OF THE FELICIANS IN AMERICA. *Polish Am. Studies 1975 32(1): 19-28.* Stresses the importance of this sisterhood in Polish American history. Though originating in Poland in 1855, the order spread to the United States in 1874 and soon became a predominantly American order, with 82 percent of its membership residing on this side of the Atlantic. Throughout its history it provided social mobility for immigrant women. Although the congregation was involved in the care of orphans, the aged, and the sick, teaching remained its primary concern. Only after the decline and almost total disappearance of the Polish language from parochial schools did the order accept other responsibilities. As a result of their dedication and hard work, the Felicians were able to draw capital and invest it in schools, orphanages, hospitals, and retirement homes. Based on primary and secondary sources; 21 notes.     S. R. Pliska

375. Render, Sylvia Lyons. AFRO-AMERICAN WOMEN: THE OUTSTANDING AND THE OBSCURE. *Q. J. of the Lib. of Congress 1975 32(4): 306-321.* Discusses the lives of three Afro-American women residents of the District of Columbia. The first was Anna Murry Douglass, relatively obscure, but whose influence upon her husband, Frederick Douglass, should not be minimized. The second woman was the outstanding Mary Church Terrell, 1863-1954. She represented Negro women abroad on a number of occasions, and was a pioneer in attacking segregation in Washington. The third woman, the obscure Ruth Anna Fisher, 1886-1975, spent most of her life copying foreign documents for the Library of Congress. Illus., 24 notes.     E. P. Stickney

376. Ricciardelli, Alex F. THE ADOPTION OF WHITE AGRICULTURE BY THE ONEIDA INDIANS. *Ethnohistory 1963 10(4): 309-328.* Re-examines Oneida society and culture through three stages, in three environments (New York, Wisconsin, Ontario), stressing five factors that made farming the prevailing mode of life by 1860: necessity, tribal ideals, a strong horticultural tradition among women, precept and example of helpful Indian and white neighbors, relocation.     H. J. Graham

377. Robbins, Russell Hope. THE ROCHESTER RAPPINGS. *Dalhousie R. [Canada] 1965 45(2): 153-164.* Two children of mid-19th-century America began an international movement that claimed to be revealed religion-spiritualism. Catherine (1839-92) and Margaretta Fox (1836-93) began communicating with spirits through knockings in 1848 at Hydesville, New York. They attracted much enthusiasm and frequent exposure, finally confessing publicly in 1888 that the spirit knockings had been made by cracking the toe and ankle bones.     L. F. S. Upton

378. Russell, C. Allyn. THE RISE AND DECLINE OF THE SHAKERS. *N. Y. Hist. 1968 49(1): 29-55.* Shakerism was founded by Ann Lee (1736-84) who came to America from Manchester, England, in 1774. The Shakers constituted one of the more colorful of the many utopian communities founded in the early years of the American Republic. Stressing communal ownership of property, absolute celibacy, public confession of sins, and separation from the world, the Shakers sought a community where man would not knowingly sin. Establishing colonies throughout the Northeast, their main community was centered at New Lebanon, New York. On the eve of the Civil War the Shakers had some six thousand followers. With the end of the war, however, their religious zeal declined, their extreme asceticism was not conducive to the gaining of converts, and the optimistic society proved an infertile field for the propagation of Shaker doctrine. As a result the Shakers underwent a rapid decline and,

as of 1968, the Shaker community consisted of 19 elderly "sisters." Based on Shaker literature and on primary and secondary sources; 3 illus., 83 notes. G. Kurland

379. Scruggs, Otey. THE MEANING OF HARRIET TUBMAN. George, Carol V. R., ed. *"Remember the Ladies": New Perspectives on Women in American History: Essays in Honor of Nelson Manfred Blake* (Syracuse: Syracuse U. Pr., 1975): 110-121. Born a slave, Harriet Tubman (ca. 1820-1913) valued freedom and dedicated her life to freeing herself and others. The strongest influences in her life were her family and religious faith. During the 1850's, she was the most successful underground railroad conductor, and she became the symbol of abolitionism. Tubman participated in the Port Royal "experiment," worked in freedmen's hospitals, and engaged in reconnaissance and military intelligence activities during the Civil War. Subsequently, her career reflected the declining fortunes of blacks. Her wartime service went monetarily uncompensated until 1899. She wed, eked out a living in Auburn, New York, raised money for black schools, established a home for the aged and indigent, and participated in the feminist movement. Her entire life was a quest for human dignity. It negated the myth of the improvident, child-like Negro and symbolized the strength of moral individuals. Based on primary and secondary materials; 25 notes. P. R. Byrne

380. Sherer, Lorraine M. THE CLAN SYSTEM OF THE FORT MOJAVE INDIANS: A CONTEMPORARY SURVEY. *Southern Calif. Q. 1965 47(1): 1-72.* Between 1859 and 1890 the Mojave lived under military occupation, but retained their clan names, ancient stories, and songs through oral communication. From 1890 to 1931 boarding schools, intermarriage, and the assigning of English names by the Department of Interior broke down tribal ties and caused confusion. The shattering of the Mojave social system fragmented stories and songs and almost destroyed their oral tradition. With the aid of Mojave consultants and printed documents, the author gathered for the first time complete records of the old Mojave family clan names. J. Jensen

381. Sister Mary Eileen. MOTHER MARY ANN, FOUNDRESS OF THE SISTERS OF SAINT ANN: HER CONTRIBUTION TO THE CHURCH IN BRITISH COLUMBIA, ALASKA AND THE YUKON. *Can. Catholic Hist. Assoc. Annual Report 1965 32: 47-62.* Marie Esther Sureau (1809-90) founded the Daughters of Saint Ann in 1848 to educate children of both sexes in Quebec. The community, after several struggling decades, has spread across Canada and into the United States, devoting its efforts to teaching, nursing, and social service. This work in the Provinces of British Columbia, the Yukon, and Alaska is studied in detail. Documented, 66 notes. C. Thibault

382. Smith, David G. MODERNIZATION, POPULATION, DISPERSION AND PAPAGO GENETIC INTEGRITY. *Human Organization 1972 31(2): 187-199.* Examines Papago Indian childbearing patterns through time. Finds the Papago less closely related in the 19th century than during recent times. Notes and explains differences between modern and traditional villages. Concludes that the Papago have favored dispersed mating patterns when threatened and encouraged kin group consolidation during periods of security. 7 tables, 4 notes, biblio. E. S. Johnson

383. Smylie, James H. NOTABLE PRESBYTERIAN WOMEN. *J. of Presbyterian Hist. 1974 52(2): 99-121.* Biographic sketches of 25 prominent black and white Presbyterian women from Jane Aitken (1764-1832), a Bible printer and bookbinder, to Lois Harkrider Stair (b. 1923), the first woman moderator of the general assembly of the Presbyterian Church. They include a mother and wives of presidents, missionaries, educators, journalists, philanthropists, authors, businesswomen, humanitarian reformers, social workers, and an industrialist. 9 illus., 6 notes. D. L. Smith

384. Spain, Johnny. THE BLACK FAMILY AND THE PRISONS. *Black Scholar 1972 4(2): 18-34.* Examines the basis for the black family and the difficulty which it has had historically because of slavery, the myth of matriarchy, and the competitive economic system of the US economy; places the black family in the context of modern society and examines the effects of the penal code and prison populations, which are overwhelmingly black.

385. Stroupe, Henry S. "CITE THEM BOTH TO ATTEND THE NEXT CHURCH CONFERENCE": SOCIAL CONTROL BY NORTH CAROLINA BAPTIST CHURCHES, 1772-1908. *North Carolina Hist. R. 1975 52(2): 156-170.* Baptist church congregations in North Carolina have exercised direct control over the personal conduct of members since the 18th century. Until the early 20th century transgressors were made to fear for their souls and their social standing in the community. Churches excommunicated or suspended white and black congregants for adultery, drunkenness, thievery, lying, swearing, quarreling, etc. Following World War I the church began employing indirect methods for social control, such as the temperance movement and blue laws. Based on manuscript church records, and published primary and secondary sources; 4 illus., table, 37 notes. T. L. Savitt

386. Tooker, Elisabeth. NATCHEZ SOCIAL ORGANIZATION: FACT OR ANTHROPOLOGICAL FOLKLORE? *Ethnohistory 1963 10(4): 358-372.* Questions the now accepted yet inherently incongruous view of Natchez society as one which combined caste and exogamy; shows from analysis that John R. Swanton possibly misread once-scanty documentary evidence relating to this extinct tribe. H. J. Graham

387. Tucker, Norma. NANCY WARD, GHIGHAU OF THE CHEROKEES. *Ga. Hist. Q. 1969 53(2): 192-200.* A biography of a woman leader of the Cherokee during the Revolutionary and national periods who received the honored title of Ghighau, meaning "beloved woman." When her Cherokee husband died in a 1755 battle with the Creek, Nancy Ward joined the fight with his weapon. She later married a British Indian trader named Brian Ward. She helped promote peaceful relations with Americans during the Revolution and after, encouraged agricultural improvements among her people, and fought against Indian removal. R. A. Mohl

388. Wagner, William. THE SISTERS OF SS. CYRIL AND METHODIUS AND THE PRESERVATION OF SLOVAK CULTURE IN AMERICA. *Slovakia 1974 24(47): 132-155.* Discusses the work of the sisters of St. Cyril Academy (1909-73) to preserve Slovak culture in Danville, Pennsylvania. S

389. White, John. WHATEVER HAPPENED TO THE SLAVE FAMILY IN THE OLD SOUTH? *J. of Am. Studies [Great Britain] 1974 8(3): 383-390.* Reviews a wide range of literature on Negro slavery, beginning with Abolitionist writings of the 1850's and concluding with the revisionist and Marxist studies published in the 1960's and 1970's. Slavery was inimical to the Negro family, but the actions of slave masters and the personal resilience of the slaves ensured the perpetuation of family life among the slaves. Economic and cultural forces following the Civil War produced more familial deterioration among American Negroes than did pre-Civil War slavery. Based on secondary sources; 38 notes. H. T. Lovin

390. Whyte, J. Bruce. THE PUBLICK UNIVERSAL FRIEND. *Rhode Island Hist. 1967 26(4): 103-112.* A biographical sketch of the mystic Jemima Wilkinson, the founder of the United Friends. Based on secondary material, journals, and government documents. To be continued. P. J. Coleman

391. Wisbey, Herbert A., Jr. JEMIMA WILKINSON: HISTORICAL FIGURE AND FOLK CHARACTER. *New York Folklore Q. 1964 20(1): 5-13.* Discusses the life, thought, and personality of religious society founder Jemima Wilkinson in New England from 1752-1819, emphasizing her belief in Quaker theology.

392. —. THE UPPER SKAGIT INDIANS OF WESTERN WASHINGTON: TWO REVIEWS. *J. of Ethnic Studies 1976 3(4): 74-79.* Amoss, Pamela T. AN ANTHROPOLOGIST'S VIEWPOINT, pp. 74-77. Reviews June McCormick Collins' *Valley of the Spirits: The Upper Skagit Indians of Western Washington* (1974). Praises the book for preserving information, but criticizes the awkward writing, careless recording of native terms, and lack of an attempt to apply the material to contemporary issues in anthropology. Among the most valuable parts of the book are her sensitive insights into Indian women's feelings about marriage, family, and the kinship system, and her interviews with the shaman John Fornsby.

Hilbert, V. AN INDIAN'S VIEWPOINT, *pp. 77-79*. Criticizes Collins' book for its lack of scope and dullness of presentation, "a colorless account of a vibrant people." Suggests that the book would have been improved by fewer spelling errors of Indian names, photographs of locations discussed, and the use of genealogies instead of scientific kinship terminology.

# Image and Self-Image

393. Deming, Barbara. TWO PERSPECTIVES ON WOMEN'S STRUGGLE. *Liberation 1973 17(10): 30-37*. Discusses the image of women in 19th- and 20th-century novels by women, and the concept of androgyny as it relates to the women's liberation movement.

394. Fife, Austin and Fife, Alta. PUG-NOSED LIL AND THE GIRL WITH THE BLUE VELVET BAND: A BRIEF MEDLEY OF WOMEN IN WESTERN SONGS. *Am. West 1970 7(2): 32-37*. Camp followers and other women of easy virtue made dramatic early appearances in cow towns, army posts, mining towns, and railroad junctions. They were celebrated in ballads and songs such as: "No Use for the Women," "Belle Starr: Queen of the Desperadoes," "Pug-Nosed Lil," and "The Girl with the Blue Velvet Band." Included is the score for one song and the lyrics for all four. Derived from a forthcoming book. 4 illus.
D. L. Smith

395. Gecas, Viktor. MOTIVES AND AGGRESSIVE ACTS IN POPULAR FICTION: SEX AND CLASS DIFFERENCES. *Am. J. of Sociol. 1972 77(4): 680-696*. "The present study examines the depictions of aggressive acts and their motives for different social classes and sexes as these groups have been portrayed in popular magazine fiction. A random selection of short stories in *Argosy, Esquire, True Confessions*, and *McCall's*, for the time period 1925-65, was content analyzed for descriptions of aggressive behavior and the characters associated with it. Women were found to be more frequently portrayed as expressing verbal aggression and in utilizing affective and ethical motives for it. Men were much more likely to aggress physically and to do it for utilitarian or normatively required reasons. Lower-class characters were more frequently portrayed as aggressing physically and in using affective motives. Verbal aggression and utilitarian as well as ethical motives were more characteristic of middle- and upper- class characters. This general pattern of associations did not change appreciably over the 40-year period covered. What did change noticeably was the magnitude of the difference between the stereotypes of male and female aggressive behavior. Reasons for this fluctuation as well as the association of gender with different motives for aggression are explored and some explanations offered."
J

396. Henry, Lyell D. THE SIGNIFICANCE OF "MOTHER" PILLOWS IN AMERICAN HISTORY AND CULTURE. *J. of Popular Culture 1971 5(1): 1-9*. Sketches features of pillows with characterizations of mother and notes the relationship of their popularity to wars since 1812.
S

397. Hoffman, Frank A. PROLEGOMENA TO A STUDY OF TRADITIONAL ELEMENTS IN THE EROTIC FILM. *J. of Am. Folklore 1965 78(308): 143-148*. Discusses the "thoroughly illegal pornographic" film, and suggests that "we must go on in our research to determine its extent, meaning, and function in ours and other cultures." Many such films use variations on simple, repeating themes. Traces the evolution of the erotic film over the last century, mentioning areas in which production techniques have improved. Discusses plot development (if any) of several films, considering actors, setting, and subject matter. 7 notes.
W. H. Crossley

398. Jones, Archie H. COPS, ROBBERS, HEROES AND ANTIHEROINES: THE AMERICAN NEED TO CREATE. *J. of Popular Culture 1967 1(2): 114-127*. Explores the rise of the Buffalo Bill hero myth, which dates from the 1872 performance of *The Scouts of the Prairie; or Red Deviltry As It Is* in Chicago, starring William F. (Buffalo Bill) Cody. Also considers the effects of Frederick Jackson Turner's frontier thesis, television heroes, and the mother myth.
S

399. Jones, James P. NANCY DREW, WASP SUPER GIRL OF THE 1930'S. *J. of Popular Culture 1973 6(4): 707-717*. Nancy Drew books, juvenile formula fiction, abounded in racial and national stereotypes and avoided direct political comment, but opposed New Deal welfare policies. Many titles have been rewritten in the 1960's-70's.
S

400. Petersen, William J. DARLINGS OF THE PRESS. *Palimpsest 1969 50(11): 609-612*. Discusses newspapers of the 19th century and their attitude toward women and traditional womanhood.
S

401. Spilka, Mark. ERICH SEGAL AS LITTLE NELL, OR THE REAL MEANING OF *LOVE STORY*. *J. of Popular Culture 1972 5(4): 782-798*. Compares *Love Story* to *The Old Curiosity Shop* and Jenny, the heroine, is its Little Nell. Jenny's life and death resemble 19th-century myths of women, as moral and spiritual guides for unworthy men, and of young girls as the most virtuous of those guides. Another theme of the book is generational reconciliation.
E. S. Shapiro

# Culture, the Arts, and Recreation

402. Abrahams, Roger D. PATTERNS OF STRUCTURE AND ROLE RELATIONSHIPS IN THE CHILD BALLAD IN THE UNITED STATES. *J. of Am. Folklore 1966 79(313): 448-462*. A study limited to ballads collected from the rural South and Midwest which are found also in Francis James Child's *The English and Scottish Popular Ballads* (1857-58). Most of these American Child ballads fit into two simple structural patterns: morality and romance. In the morality pattern the violations preferred are murder and adultery; the punishments favored, separation from children or death. The Child ballads which fit into the romantic pattern have a separation of lovers and a shared death or a relationship between a comforting mother and a child wounded in love. The narrative tends to be foreshortened with emphasis only on the climax. In many the movement away from action becomes a tendency toward lyric, with dialogue reduced to formula. The American Child ballads rely more on memorization than on improvisation. The rigid style in which they are presented is further evidence of their traditional character. 21 notes.
E. P. Stickney

403. Bandel, Betty THE LITTLE RED SCHOOLHOUSE IN VERMONT. *Vermont Hist. 1972 40(2): 97-104*. The opinions of school administrators should be discounted. Discipline should be evaluated in terms of what society accepts - in those days, moderate corporal punishment. Common schools taught the three R's; apprenticeship taught most skills. Although few teachers were college-trained, many were academy-trained. Teachers were young, so there was no generation gap, and they were low-paid because they were mostly women, soon married. The myth of the common school is the story of something valuable imparted to all, not something false. 2 photos.
T. D. S. Bassett

404. Bascon-Bance, Paulette. LES PROGRES DE L'ENSEIGNEMENT FEMININ DANS LE MONDE [Advances in the education of women throughout the world]. *Information Hist. [France] 1970 32(1): 34-40*. Discusses worldwide progress in women's education since the 19th century. The training of women in research and intellectual programs, especially in the socialist countries, has improved the outlook for women's educational liberation since World War II. Based on statistics mainly supplied by Unesco publications, other primary and secondary sources; illus., 49 notes.
R. K. Adams

405. Blanck, Jacob N. THE JUVENILE READING OF CERTAIN NINETEENTH-CENTURY AMERICAN WORTHIES. *Massachusetts Hist. Soc. Pro. 1967 79: 64-73*. Describes the opposition, mainly religious and clerical, to light reading in the 19th century which resulted in an almost total lack of reading material for adolescents. The more religious the household, the less likely the opportunity for light reading. Some celebrated authors whose reading habits are discussed include James Russell Lowell, Louisa May Alcott, Edward Eggleston, John Greenleaf Whittier, and Charles Dudley Warner.
J. B. Duff

406. Bridges, William E. WARM HEARTH, COLD WORLD: SOCIAL PERSPECTIVES ON THE HOUSEHOLD POETS. *Am. Q. 1969 21(4): 764-779*. Consists of a brief survey of popular poetry of the

19th century, analyzing the complex relationship of literature to contemporary social patterns and values. Suggests that the culture revolved around two foci: the Adamic symbol of independence and self-sustenance, and the American mother. Interlocking and antagonistic, these were used to express the whole range of human potentials and needs. The need for security and caring was expressed in the figure of the loving mother in her home, which was a state of mind, while the Adamic image embodied detachment from others and from the past, and also the means to become whatever one wished. Considers that we have equated the Adamic image with the "real spirit" of American life, relegating literature that celebrates domestic tranquility to a secondary position. Secondary sources; 40 notes.
T. Z. Herman

407.  Bush, Robert.  GRACE KING.  *Am. Literary Realism: 1870-1910 1975 8(1): 43-51.* Bibliographic essay.                                      S

408.  Buxbaum, Katherine.  FROM IOWA STATE NORMAL SCHOOL TO UNIVERSITY OF NORTHERN IOWA.  *Ann. of Iowa 1967 39(1): 50-57.* Reflects upon the changes that the Cedar Falls campus has seen in 91 years. Noting that the institution was one of the best teacher training schools in the midwest, the author wonders how much was gained by calling it State College of Iowa and University of Northern Iowa in an effort to be known as something other than a normal school. Prominent figures in the college's history are discussed, and stages of growth are identified. Undocumented, illus.                        D. C. Swift

409.  Cavin, Susan.  MISSING WOMEN: ON THE VOODOO TRAIL TO JAZZ.  *J. of Jazz Studies 1975 3(1): 4-27.* Discusses the role of voodoo women and black magic cults in the evolution of jazz music in the 19th century, emphasizing the Negro culture of New Orleans.

410.  Chisolm, R. H.  IOWA GIRLS' HIGH SCHOOL ATHLETIC UNION.  *Palimpsest 1968 49(4): 125-132.* The Iowa Girls' High School Athletic Union has been a primary supporter of female participation in sports from its inception in 1923 to the present.                              S

411.  Chisolm, R. H.  STATE TOURNAMENT.  *Palimpsest 1968 49(4): 133-144.* Traces the history of the state basketball tournament sponsored by the Iowa Girls' High School Athletic Union, 1926-68.                                                                       S

412.  Cohen, Sol.  MARIA MONTESSORI: PRIESTESS OR PEDAGOGUE?  *Teachers Coll. Record 1969 71(2): 313-326.* Discusses the life and work of Montessori and recounts her influence in the United States and elsewhere.

413.  Coke, Van Deren.  TAOS AND SANTA FE.  *Art in Am. 1963 51(5): 44-47.* Discussion of art and environment in New Mexico, 1882-1942, emphasizing the work of Marsden Hartley, Georgia O'Keeffe, and others.                                                         W. K. Bottorff

414.  Conway, Jill.  PERSPECTIVES ON THE HISTORY OF WOMEN'S EDUCATION IN THE UNITED STATES.  *Hist. of Educ. Q. 1974 14(1): 1-13.* Traces the history of attitudes about women's education from Puritan times to the present. Sees a historic danger in developing present-day women's studies programs, as they might tend to limit true creativity by channeling it and therefore perpetuate existing patterns of socialization. Based on primary and secondary sources; 11 notes.
L. C. Smith

415.  Corwin, Norman.  AT HOME WITH CAPTAIN BLIGH AND THE BRIDE OF FRANKENSTEIN.  *Westways 1976 68(12): 18-22.* Discusses the social and married life of film actors Charles Laughton and Elsa Lanchester in Hollywood, California.

416.  Cost, Charles C.  EDNA DEAN PROCTOR, POETESS OF THE CONTOOCOOK.  *Hist. New Hampshire 1966 21(2): 2-30.* Biographical and literary notes on Edna Proctor, a genteel spinster who, from the comfortable vantage point of Brooklyn Heights, wrote lovingly of nature in her native New Hampshire or a Zuñi or Tatar village. Her *Russian Journey* sold four editions. She wrote much patriotic verse and was praised by Henry Wadsworth Longfellow and John Greenleaf Whittier. As a member of Henry Ward Beecher's Plymouth Congregational Church, she spread his fame by publishing her notes of his sermons (1858)

and was later touched by the Beecher-Tilton scandal (1875). Five examples from Miss Proctor's *Complete Poetical Works* (Boston: Houghton Mifflin Co., 1925) are reprinted, with an undated portrait. Based on Proctor MSS in the New Hampshire Historical Society and in the Tucker Free Library, Henniker, New Hampshire.               T. D. S. Bassett

417.  Drake, Carlos C.  'MARY HAMILTON' IN TRADITION.  *Southern Folklore Q. 1969 33(1): 39-47.* The beginning of the "Mary Hamilton" ballad (Child No. 173) is unknown; its historical basis, obscure; and its pattern in tradition, uncertain. Discusses the history of "Mary Hamilton" and examines the concept of the "emotional core" or the "basic human reaction to a dramatic situation," which, according to Tristram P. Coffin, has sustained this ballad in oral tradition, and not its plot. 23 notes.                                                 P. McClure

418.  Fabian, Monroe H.  AN ALL-STAR STAGE TROUPE, CAST BY THE PORTRAIT GALLERY.  *Smithsonian 1971 2(6): 18-25.* On 11 September 1971, the National Portrait Gallery opened an exhibition, "Portraits of the American Stage: 1771-1971," which documented the professional careers of approximately 100 actors, singers, dancers, and musicians who contributed to performing arts in America. The chronology of the collection begins with Charles Willson Peale's portrait of actress Nancy Hallam. Portraits include John Durang (1786-1822), first native professional dancer, Jenny Lind, Edwin Forrest, Charlotte Cushman, Edwin Booth, Joseph Jefferson, John Philip Sousa, Arturo Toscanini, Leopold Stokowski, Leonard Bernstein, Enrico Caruso, Adelina Patti, Geraldine Farrar, Isadora Duncan, Tallulah Bankhead, Katharine Cornell, the Lunts, Benny Goodman, Artur Rubinstein, Helen Hayes, Ethel Merman, Joan Baez, and Jimi Hendrix. Includes abbreviated biographical sketches to the partial enumeration of subjects. Illus.
K. A. Harvey

419.  Fishel, Andrew and Pottker, Janice.  SCHOOL BOARDS AND SEX BIAS IN AMERICAN EDUCATION.  *Contemporary Educ. 1974 45(2): 85-89.*

420.  Fletcher, Marie  THE FATE OF WOMEN IN A CHANGING SOUTH: A PERSISTENT THEME IN THE FICTION OF CAROLINE GORDON.  *Mississippi Q. 1968 21(1): 17-28.* Outstanding among the numerous Southern women writers since World War I, Caroline Gordon is concerned with the post-Civil War South and what life does to womankind. Women are the true antagonists in the Gordon novels, while the men are seldom able to measure up to the heroines' ideal of manhood. In chronicling the joys of love, Miss Gordon usually indicates the likelihood of an end in bitter suffering. Attributing much of her homeland's difficulties to intersectional malice, she does not overlook the homegrown causes or universal human failings. For the modern Southern woman of traditional predilections, the novelist pictures four possible responses to male insufficiency or failure: retreat, poor marriage, self-destruction, or being her own person. Miss Gordon's heroines usually have courage and fortitude to endure, although joylessly. Recent Gordon works have indicated hope for Southern women and all the South in the paternalistic Roman Catholic Church—offering order, harmony, and beauty to surpass even that of the old agrarian culture. Based mainly on published Gordon novels and short stories; 14 notes.
R. V. Calvert

421.  Followell, Eleanor.  ROMANCE OF THE QUILT.  *High Country 1971 (18): 44-48.* Quilting is an old craft introduced into the New World by the Dutch and English. The art, particularly the patchwork and applique quilt, has resisted most commercial intrusion. "Patchwork" indicates patches of cloth sewn in a pattern, while "applique" denotes applied tops fit to a background. The Edward-Dean Museum of Decorative Arts in Cheery Valley at Beaumont, California, has held classes under Laura Howard, as well as Carrie Mays in Murrieta Valley and Mrs. Theresa Postley of Sun City—all fascinating places to view quilts and quilt making.                                          K. E. Gilmont

422.  Gordon, Douglas H.  AN ESSAY ON THREE GRACIOUS BALTIMORE HOUSES.  *Maryland Hist. Mag. 1970 65(3): 296-300.* Claims that the three houses on East Mount Vernon Place at St. Paul in Baltimore "have a historic interest which is probably not exceeded by that of any three contiguous buildings in the United States." Originally the property belonged to revolutionary hero John Eager Howard. By 1850,

Baltimore's "Three Graces," the Marchiness of Wellesly, the Baroness Stafford, and the Duchess of Leeds, inherited the property through their grandfather Charles Carroll of Carrollton and his daughter Mary Caton. Other famous Baltimoreans owned or occupied the houses; and finally, in 1962, they passed to the Peabody Institute of Music, perhaps the most famous owners of all.                                                G. T. Sharrer

423. Graham, Eleanor.  NASHVILLE HOME OF ADELICIA ACKLEN. *Tennessee Hist. Q. 1971 30(4): 345-368.* Located two miles south of Nashville, Belmont was designed for Adelicia Acklen as an "Italianate villa with Greek Revival details . . . brilliant white in a setting of trees." A biographical sketch gives the personal background for the development of the estate. Its history is carried to the present as the location of Belmont College. 5 photos, 18 notes.          R. V. Ritter

424. Gray, Cleve.  THE ARTIST IN AMERICA, 1963: ANNIVERSARY ALBUM. *Art in America 1963 51(1): 64-81.* Color and black-and-white reproductions of works by 10 American artists for *Art in America's* 15th anniversary (Richard Lindner, Peter Blume, William Kienbusch, José Guerrero, Barnett, Helen Frankenthaler, Greene, Leon Smith, Rosati, Theodore Stamos), with criticism. Illus.
                                                               W. K. Bottorff

425. Gronowicz, Antoni.  PRELUDE IN AMERICA. *Arizona Q. 1963 19(2): 127-134.* Helena Modjeska was induced to come to San Francisco with her husband and son, in response to letters from Henryk Sienkiewicz begging her to help the Polish immigrants in California found a center of Polish culture. The author describes in detail the events and circumstances leading up to her eventual signing of a two-year contract for a tour of the United States and Canada. Undocumented.
                                                               E. P. Stickney

426. Hall, Peter Nelson  MINIRARA, MINNEAPOLIS' INTERNATIONALLY HISTORIC FALLS. *Historic Preservation 1971 23(3): 36-44.* A sketch of the history of Minirara Falls (the Falls of St. Anthony) in Minneapolis. The first white man to see the falls was Father Louis Hennepin in 1680. An Indian legend tells of a distraught young woman who paddled her canoe over the falls, but who lived in the spray over Spirit Island below the falls. The island was removed by the Corps of Engineers in 1950. American soldiers built a grist mill on the falls in 1823, and the village of St. Anthony grew from this beginning. In 1852 a settlement on the west bank of the Mississippi became Minneapolis. Because of the water power potential a number of flour mills were established there. The most famous of these mills was the Pillsbury A Mill, which in 1881 was the world's largest. This mill is still in operation. Describes efforts to preserve the falls area. In 1971 the St. Anthony Historic District was created. Illus.                    J. M. Hawes

427. Hamblen, Abigail Ann.  EDNA FERBER AND THE AMERICAN DREAM. *J. of Popular Culture 1968 2(3): 404-409.* Discusses the style and importance of the novels of Edna Ferber (1887-1968). Ferber's novels vivify the concept of "the American Dream." Central to each of her works are the "strong central character," "rich and colorful" settings, and "disturbing emphasis on affluence" - all segments of the American dream. Ferber's novels are good but not great, for they tend to ignore the sadness and failure in American life.                      B. A. Lohof

428. Helson, Ravenna.  INNER REALITY OF WOMEN. *Arts in Society 1974 11(1): 24-35.* Examines the conflict between inner and outer reality for women authors. Paper delivered at a conference on Women and the Arts, Racine, Wisconsin, 1973.                        S

429. Hodge, Patt.  THE HISTORY OF HAMMON AND THE RED MOON SCHOOL. *Chronicles of Oklahoma 1966 44(2): 130-139.* In 1892 a post office was established in the home of James and Ida Hammon from whom the town took its name. The Red Moon Boarding School was established in 1897. It became the most modern school in western Oklahoma. The students planted trees, an orchard, built fences, and learned English. The girls learned to knit, sew, cook, and sing. The boys cared for poultry, hogs, cows, and cultivated the soil. All received an academic education. A laundry and a bake house, a chicken house, hog house, two cisterns, a windmill, and a pump were built. By 1912 the boarding aspect of the school was discontinued. Enrollment gradually declined but the school continued until 1925. In 1965 the building burned. 2 illus.,

430. Hodges, Margaret.  PITTSBURGH: SEVEN AUTHORS, SEVEN VIEWS. *Western Pennsylvania Hist. Mag. 1973 56(3): 253-279.* Writings of Hervey Allen, Margaret Deland, Marcia Davenport, Willa Cather, Mary Roberts Rinehart, Gladys Schmitt, and Haniel Long.
                                                               S

431. Hollingsworth, Caroline Cole  EMBROIDERY IN THE SOCIETY'S COLLECTION. *Old-Time New England 1966 56(3): 63-76.* Describes needlework representing the period from the middle of the 18th century to the end of the 19th century, preserved in the Society for the Preservation of New England Antiquities. "The representative embroideries chosen for discussion have been placed in six arbitrary classifications, crewel, flame stitch, memorial pictures, samplers, embroidery on canvas and art squares. For the most part they represent the norm rather than the exceptional and as such illustrate the development of embroidery in this country." 11 illus.                    R. N. Lokken

432. Holstein, Jonathan.  AMERICAN QUILTS AS VISUAL OBJECTS; A PERSONAL VIEW. *Historic Preservation 1972 24(1): 29-33.* Discusses the types and patterns of quilts made in America since colonial times. Early quilts were made of whatever fabric was available and were filled with natural substances such as dried grass or leaves. Later cotton or wool was the filler. Scraps of material would be sewn together to form the top of the quilt - either without pattern or "crazy," or in a great variety of geometrical patterns. A third type of quilt, the top of which was made of a single piece of material and which had as its only design the quilting stitches, is not investigated. Concludes that "quilts are a distinct manifestation of American design. They are highly sophisticated, highly developed, with their own history and styles, reflecting in their changing materials, colors, forms and feelings both the fashions and moods of their times." The author has sponsored exhibitions of American quilts in several major American cities. Photos.          J. M. Hawes

433. Howard, Helen Addison.  LITERARY TRANSLATORS AND INTERPRETERS OF INDIAN SONGS. *J. of the West 1973 12(2): 212-228.* Biographical sketches of women who have done "serious work either as translators of native songs or as interpreters of indigenous subjects and rhythms based on tribal life and rituals," and whose activities were primarily centered in the West. In chronological order they are: Alice C. Fletcher (1828-1923); Frances Densmore (1867-1957); Mary Hunter Austin (1868-1934); Natalie Curtis (Burlin) (1875-1921); Alice Corbin (Henderson) (1881-1949); Eda Lou Walton (1894-1961); and Ruth Murray Underhill (1884- ). 18 notes.          E. P. Stickney

434. Jebb, Marcia and Eddy, Donald D.  MORRIS BISHOP AND ALISON MASON KINGSBURY: A BIBLIOGRAPHY OF THEIR WORKS. *Cornell Lib. J. 1971 (12): 2-63.* A bibliography of original works of Morris Gilbert Bishop (b. 1893), Curator of the Fiske Petrarch Collection at Cornell, who has written extensively in literary biography and history, besides being a poet. Lists paintings and drawings by his wife, Alison Mason Kingsbury (b. 1898). Bishop's bibliography is divided into separate publications and contributions to periodicals. Covers 1904-71. Kingsbury's list includes murals, oils, landscapes, and book illustrations done 1929-71.                              M. M. Williamson

435. Jones, Daryl E.  BLOOD 'N THUNDER: VIRGINS, VILLAINS, AND VIOLENCE IN THE DIME NOVEL WESTERN. *J. of Popular Culture 1970 4(2): 507-517.*

436. Jones, Michael Owen.  "YE MUST CONTRIVE ALLERS TO KEEP JEST THE HAPPY MEDIUM BETWEEN TRUTH AND FALSEHOOD": FOLKLORE AND THE FOLK IN MRS. STOWE'S FICTION. *New York Folklore Q. 1971 27(4): 357-369.* Discusses storytelling techniques, folk dialect, and characters in Harriet Beecher Stowe's *(Oldtown Fireside Stories, The Pearl of Orr's Island,* and *Uncle Tom's Cabin)* from 1852-72.

437. Kendall, Elaine.  BEYOND MOTHER'S KNEE. *Am. Heritage 1973 24(4): 12-16, 73-78.* Overview of early attitudes toward formal education for women in America.                      S

438. Kendall, Elaine.  FOUNDERS FIVE. *Am. Heritage 1975 26(2): 33-48.* Brief biographical sketches of the founders of five of the seven major eastern women's colleges. Sketches include Mary Lyon (Mount

Holyoke), Matthew Vassar (Vassar), Sophia Smith (Smith), Henry Durant (Wellesley), and Elizabeth Agassiz (Radcliffe). Very brief sketches are included of Joseph Taylor (Bryn Mawr) and Annie Nathan Meyer (Barnard). 19 illus. J. F. Paul

439. Klaw, Barbara. QUEEN MOTHER OF TENNIS: AN INTERVIEW WITH HAZEL HOTCHKISS WIGHTMAN. *Am. Heritage 1975 26(5): 16-24, 82-86.* Interviews Hazel Hotchkiss Wightman (1886-1974), founder of the Wightman Cup tennis match and one of the great women tennis stars. Discusses her thoughts on women's tennis. 11 illus. J. F. Paul

440. Lee, Don L. THE ACHIEVEMENT OF GWENDOLYN BROOKS. *Black Scholar 1972 3(10): 32-41.* Examines the evolution in the poetry of Gwendolyn Brooks from that "conditioned to the times and the people" to one of a strong and militant voice for the black experience and personality, 1930's-72.

441. Lewis, Wilber Helen. MANSFIELD FEMALE COLLEGE REUNION—1974. *North Louisiana Hist. Assoc. J. 1974 6(1): 30-32.* Mansfield Female College, the first college for women west of the Mississippi River, was founded in 1844 and closed in 1930. "College spirit has not waned," however, and a large number of alumnae return biennially for a school reunion. The 1974 gathering of 93 alumnae and their friends had representatives from the classes of 1914-30, and the principal speaker was Dr. Walter Lowrey of Centenary College. 3 illus., 5 photos. A. N. Garland

442. McCormack, Mrs. Stewart. ELEGANT ACCOMPLISHMENTS. *Missouri Hist. Soc. Bull. 1965 21(3): 208-215.* Describes the various minor arts and crafts - papyrotamia, mourning pictures, and "hairlooms" - which were an important part of female education and expression in the Victorian era. Illus. R. J. Hanks

443. McDowell, Audrea. "LANDWARD HOUSE," FORMERLY THE STUART ROBINSON—JOSEPH B. MARVIN—BLAKEMORE WHEELER HOME. *Filson Club Hist. Q. 1970 44(2): 117-132.* Landward House was built in Louisville, Kentucky, in 1871 and is an excellent example of a Victorian mansion. While the house was modernized by Mrs. Blakemore Wheeler during her residence from 1913 to 1965, it retained its architectural integrity. It is now owned by a business that rents parts of the house to other enterprises and thereby is able to maintain the building in its original condition. 9 notes. G. B. McKinney

444. McLaughlin, Florence C. MARGARET TOWNSEND SCULLY'S TRUNK: PARTS I-IV. *Western Pennsylvania Hist. Mag. 1970 53(2): 151-180, (3): 255-286, (4): 367-386.* Describes Margaret Scully's ancestry and publishes materials from her novel on her ancestor James O'Hara, Revolutionary War general. Biographical data on O'Hara's career. 70 notes. D. E. Bowers

445. Melder, Keith. MASK OF OPPRESSION: THE FEMALE SEMINARY MOVEMENT IN THE UNITED STATES. *New York Hist. 1974 55(3): 261-279.* Challenges the traditional view that the female seminary movement was an instrument of women's liberation in 19th-century American society. The female seminary movement, by fostering the distinction between education for men and education for women, was actually an oppressive institution perpetuating the dependent status of women in society. Its goal of training teachers, housewives, and mothers was a male centered and sexist definition of woman's social role. Based on primary and secondary works; 4 illus., 40 notes. G. Kurland

446. Nance, William L. KATHERINE ANNE PORTER AND MEXICO. *Southwest R. 1970 55(2): 143-253.* Traces the various ways in which Mexico has played a role in the life and literary career of Katherine Porter (b. 1890). Mexico entered "her earliest work as both motivating force and subject matter." She also found in Mexico something she has called "the atmosphere of the living arts." The author concludes that Mexico initiated Miss Porter's mature work and "provided colorful material for much of it. At the same time it served her as a refuge not only from America and Greenwich Village but from Paris as well." D. F. Henderson

447. Nance, William L. VARIATIONS ON A DREAM: KATHERINE ANNE PORTER AND TRUMAN CAPOTE. *Southern Humanities R. 1969 3(4): 338-345.* Argues that Southern writers, as alienated interpreters of the American dream, look backward to an idealized past. Two prominent Southern writers who have dealt with this theme are Katherine Anne Porter and Truman Capote. In their fiction both writers have attempted to interpret the meaning of the American dream. Secondary sources; 11 notes. N. G. Sapper

448. Nathan, Robert S. MANHATTANVILLE: FROM TRADITION TO INNOVATION. *Change 1972 4(9): 34-41.* Manhattanville, known once as the place "the Kennedy girls went," is breaking with almost every past tradition, boldly carving out an education which is imaginative and open in terms of long-range reform. J

449. Neal, Larry. ZORA NEALE HURSTON: A PROFILE. *Southern Exposure 1974 1(3/4): 160-168.* Zora Neale Hurston (1901-60) was one of the first black writers to explore Afro-American folklore and culture. Her many novels explore the themes of love, personal freedom, spiritual and material aspiration, portraying the black preacher as a poet. Politically conservative, her faith in American justice was destroyed when she was falsely accused on a morals charge. Based on primary sources; 5 illus. G. A. Bolton

450. Nochlin, Linda. HOW FEMINISM IN THE ARTS CAN IMPLEMENT CULTURAL CHANGE. *Arts in Society 1974 11(1): 81-89.* A feminist approach to art history leads to a reevaluation of 19th-century women narrative and genre painters. Paper delivered at a conference on Women and the Arts, Racine, Wisconsin, 1973. S

451. Oxrieder, Julia Woodbridge. ELMIRA HUDSON NEW: FRIEND AND INFORMANT: FOLKLORE FROM ANSON COUNTY, NORTH CAROLINA. *Kentucky Folklore Record 1975 21(1): 3-12.* Gives examples of folklore collected by Elmira Hudson New (1900's to the present) in Anson County, North Carolina, including folk ballads and songs, folk medicines and superstitions.

452. Peiser, Andrew. THE EDUCATION OF WOMEN: A HISTORICAL VIEW. *Social Studies 1976 67(2): 69-72.* Asserts that the neglect of reasonable education for women in the United States has excluded them from significant levels of professional participation, and in many ways they are subjected to a retarded status. 5 notes. L. R. Raife

453. Perry, Sandra. SEX AND SENTIMENT IN AMERICA OR WHAT WAS REALLY GOING ON BETWEEN THE STAVES OF NINETEENTH CENTURY SONGS OF FASHION. *J. of Popular Culture 1972 6(1): 32-48.* Studies the attitudes toward women and the relationship of the sexes expressed in popular songs. S

454. Petersen, William J. BEGINNINGS OF GIRLS' BASKETBALL. *Palimpsest 1968 49(4): 113-124.* Discusses girls' basketball in Iowa and its origins, 1892-1968. S

455. Polak, Felix. LANDING IN LITTLE MAGAZINES - CAPTURING (?) A TREND. *Arizona Q. 1963 19(2): 101-115.* The author, in charge of the Marvin Sukov Collection of little magazines (10,600 issues of 716 titles) at the University of Wisconsin, and currently working on a study of little magazines and their place in our society, quotes T. S. Eliot (*Adam, November 1949*): "It must be the small and obscure... reviews, those that hardly are read by anyone but their own contributors that will keep critical thought alive and encourage authors of original talent." The article proceeds to survey with a wealth of titles and authors' names the development in the United States of the little magazines from the uninhibited ones of the 1910's to the insipid ones of the present. Today very few carry the motto of Margaret Anderson's *Little Review:* "Making No Compromise with Public Taste." E. P. Stickney

456. Presley, Delma Eugene. CARSON MC CULLERS AND THE SOUTH. *Georgia R. 1974 28(1): 19-32.* Presents a biographical sketch of Carson McCullers and an analysis of her relationship with the South as seen in her two most famous novels, *The Heart Is A Lonely Hunter* (1939) and *The Member of the Wedding* (1946). McCullers struggled to displace the burden of being a Southerner. Yet her early success came

when she lived in the South and her later failure can be attributed to her flight northward. Her search was a quest for identity.

M. B. Lucas

457. Pulsifer, Janice Goldsmith.   GAIL HAMILTON 1833-1896. *Essex Inst. Hist. Collections 1968 104(3): 165-216.* Biographical sketch of Gail Hamilton, the pen-name of Mary Abigail Dodge of Hamilton, Massachusetts. Gail Hamilton was an essayist and editor of children's magazines. She was a feminist but not an outspoken one. She was good friends with many noted authors. Based largely on her published works.

J. M. Bumsted

458. Purcell, Mabelle.   A TALE OF TWO FEMALE SEMINARIES. *Daughters of the Am. Revolution Mag. 1972 106(3): 292-295.* History of two church schools in Texas, the Live Oak Female Seminary and the Stuart Female Seminary, considered among the outstanding girls' schools of their time.

S

459. Rather, Lois.   WERE WOMEN FUNNY? SOME 19TH CENTURY HUMORISTS.   *Am. Book Collector 1971 21(5): 5-10.* Most women writers of the 19th century were content with romance in poetry or prose and an occasional character for comic relief, but a few attempted humor. Editors seemed hostile to female wits, and considering the examples of 19th-century female humor their judgments perhaps were sound. 21 notes.

D. A. Yanchisin

460. Robacker, Earl F.   VICTORIAN WALL MOTTOES. *Pennsylvania Folklife 1974 23(3): 2-10.* Needlepoint wall hangings with pithy adages were popular in Victorian Pennsylvania.

S

461. Roby, Pamela.   WOMEN AND AMERICAN HIGHER EDUCATION.   *Ann. of the Am. Acad. of Pol. and Social Sci. 1972 (404): 118-139.* "This article traces the history of the development of higher educational opportunities for women in the United States. The first part shows that the development of higher education for women has been closely related to the economy's need for female workers with particular skills and to the financial needs of colleges and universities. Secondly, it documents that neither the difference between the educational resources offered to men and women, nor the gap between the income going to men and women with the same level of educational attainment, has been significantly reduced. The second half of the article illustrates how institutions of higher education have generally been characterized by the competitive, egotistical, and entrepreneurial culture to which men have been socialized. It then portrays an alternative culture, a culture of cooperation, community, and creativity. The history of women's higher education sketched in this paper suggests that neither educational equality for women nor a cooperative hybrid model of social relations is likely to be realized within the present economic structure. Persons who want academia or any other sphere of life to be characterized by cooperative, egalitarian social relations need to actively concern themselves with questions regarding the nature of the economy and its influence on every aspect of human life and social relations within our society."

J

462. Showalter, Elaine.   KILLING THE ANGEL IN THE HOUSE: THE AUTONOMY OF WOMEN WRITERS.   *Antioch R. 1972 32(3): 339-353.* Previously women authors, such as Virginia Woolf, seldom dealt directly with sexual experience. Women writers eschewed sex because of male disapproval, but today they are no longer willing to be silent about themselves. About a decade ago women writers began to write as women, which launched a "female renaissance," an era of eros and anger. Women writers began to face up to sex, to use it openly, and to exploit it. This creates a dilemma for women writers who either write badly and are patronized, or write well and are attacked.

P. W. Kennedy

463. Simmons, Adele.   EDUCATION AND IDEOLOGY IN NINETEENTH-CENTURY AMERICA: THE RESPONSE OF EDUCATIONAL INSTITUTIONS TO THE CHANGING ROLE OF WOMEN.   Carroll, Berenice A., ed. Liberating Women's History (Chicago: U. of Illinois Press, 1976): 115-126. Establishes the connection between the prevailing ideology toward women and their opportunities for higher education. Female education was deemed important when it prepared a woman for her prescribed role. When it did not, as at the end of the 19th century when there were few jobs for college educated women, societal reaction was not to help women use their abilities but rather to

reject higher education for them. Traces this theme in women's education from the inception of the female seminary through the establishment of women's colleges, coeducational institutions, and coordinate colleges. 46 notes.

B. Sussman

464. Sklar, Robert.   HUMOR IN AMERICA.   *New Zealand J. of Hist. 1970 4(2): 107-119.* Analyzes the main techniques of American humor since the early 19th century. The author stresses the common themes of grotesque imagination, extravagant bragging, sexual competition, and the climactic eruption of violence. Shows how these elements were first used by the genteel middle-class humorists to ridicule popular culture and how the use of the comic mask has gradually evolved through literature, silent and sound films, radio, and television into an authentic expression of American culture liberated from genteel repression and liberal blandness. Biblio.

P. J. Coleman

465. Slout, William L.   *UNCLE TOM'S CABIN* IN AMERICAN FILM HISTORY.   *J. of Popular Film 1973 2(2): 137-151.* Harriet Beecher Stowe's classic has influenced theater and film in the United States for over a century.

S

466. Stansell, Christine.   ELIZABETH STUART PHELPS: A STUDY IN FEMALE REBELLION.   *Massachusetts R. 1972 13(1/2): 239-256.* Analyzes the literary works of Elizabeth Stuart Phelps Ward (1844-1911), whose most famous novel, *The Gates Ajar* (1868), was "a fictional polemic against patriarchal religion." When Elizabeth was eight years old, her mother died. She apparently blamed her father for her mother's death. Her later novels condemned subjugation of women in marriage. Based on primary and secondary works; 48 notes.

G. Kurland

467. Stokes, Maurice S.   A BRIEF SURVEY OF HIGHER EDUCATION FOR NEGROES.   *Social Studies 1964 55(6): 214-220.* A comprehensive, detailed survey of higher education for Negroes in the United States. The period from the establishment of Ashmun Institute in 1854 (now Lincoln University in Pennsylvania) to the year 1960, is covered. Phases of higher education included in the survey are: 1) total enrollment, 2) the type of legal control, whether public or private, 3) enrollment by sex, 4) decennial increases in number of institutions and increases in their enrollments, 5) patterns of curriculum development and organization, 6) types and levels of degrees granted and graduate research, 7) special educational features of curricula, 8) inter-institutional cooperation and 9) business management and finance.

L. Raife

468. Stone, Donald D.   VICTORIAN FEMINISM AND THE NINETEENTH-CENTURY NOVEL.   *Women's Studies 1972 1(1): 65-91.* Analyzes the novels of selected male and female Victorian writers to ascertain their attitudes toward women. Particularly assesses the novels' depictions of women characters, attitudes toward woman's rights, treatment of the 'New Woman,' and analysis of the relation between individual emancipation and the ethic of self-renunciation for the sake of social harmony. The novels of George Eliot, Elizabeth Lynn Linton, Henry James, Grant Allen, Mrs. Humphry Ward, Olive Schreiner, George Moore, Jane Austen, Thomas Hardy, and George Meredith are among those discussed. Author suggests that the Victorian writers were concerned with the place of the individual in society, the idea of self-submission for the sake of society, and the idea of self-assertiveness and fulfillment in the face of society's claims on the individual. The earlier novelists depicted characters who accepted renunciation while the later writers wrote more about individuals fulfilling their own selves. Based on primary and secondary materials; 45 notes.

A. E. Wiederrecht

469. Sugg, Redding S., Jr.   LILLIAN SMITH AND THE CONDITION OF WOMAN.   *South Atlantic Q. 1972 71(2): 155-164.* As a cultural product of the New South, Lillian Smith's views and writings on femininity transcended sectionalism and gender. Her teachings combined a qualified optimism, existential commitment, and Freudian psychoanalysis in her Georgia girls' school. Smith found solutions to racism and sexism in "our mutual willingness to become human beings." Primary and secondary sources.

W. L. Olbrich

470. Swartz, Elizabeth M.   CUSTOMS AND CULTURES IN HISTORIC HANDKERCHIEFS.   *Now and Then 1971 16(12): 695-701.* Discusses printing on handkerchiefs in the 19th century. Briefly notes the

friendship handkerchief quilt, educational handkerchiefs, handkerchiefs of the states, the handkerchief ring, and other facets of handkerchief history. 5 photos. C. A. Newton

471. Tuchman, Gaye. WOMEN AND THE CREATION OF CULTURE. *Sociol. Inquiry 1975 45(2-3): 171-202.* Analyzes women's participation in and influence on the creation of culture, especially in England, France, and the United States since the 17th century.

472. Urcia, Ingeborg. THE GALLOWS AND THE GOLDEN BALL: AN ANALYSIS OF "THE MAID FREED FROM THE GALLOWS" (CHILD 95). *J. of Am. Folklore 1966 79(313): 463-468.* Attempts to uncover the original story of the ballad "The Maid Freed from the Gallows" through a study of the known British and American versions. Francis James Child quotes 12 versions, which all start with an appeal to the judge. This suggests that the ballad once contained a scene in court as well as under the gallows. The Scottish versions are more detailed. The ballad migrated from Yorkshire to Virginia in the 17th century and spread all over the United States. An analysis of various types of this ballad leads to the establishment of the girl's crime as the loss of a golden ball which may originally have symbolized the girl's loss of virginity, "the kind of crime which would possibly turn her family from her" as is the case in all the versions and seems otherwise inexplicable. 21 notes. E. P. Stickney

473. White, William. EMILY ON THE STAGE: CHARACTERIZATIONS OF EMILY DICKINSON IN THE AMERICAN THEATER. *Am. Book Collector 1968 19(3): 13-16.* Four produced plays are considered. The earlier ones (1930, 1949) emphasize biography, especially her love-life. The later ones (1967), the poetry and her personality. D. Brockway

474. Williams, Roger. GWTW: A CIVIC LOVE STORY. *New South 1971 26(1): 70-73.* Examines the impact of Margaret Mitchell's *Gone with the Wind* on the city of Atlanta since 1939.

475. Wilson, Harold. RENDEZVOUS WITH WESLEYAN'S PAST. *Georgia R. 1966 20(3): 270-277.* Interviews R. G. Stephens and J. W. W. Daniel about Wesleyan College, Macon. The first college in the world "chartered to give a diploma to women" (1836), it owed much to Alexander H. Stephens, Confederate Vice President and Stephens' grand-uncle. Describes school and examinations in 1842. Daniel describes life there after 1906. They conclude that there will always be a demand for single-sex education. Note. T. M. Condon

476. Wilson, John B. ELIZABETH PEABODY AND OTHER TRANSCENDENTALISTS ON HISTORY AND HISTORIANS. *Historian 1967 30(1): 72-86.* Theodore Parker, George Ripley, James Freeman Clark, and other Transcendentalists were pioneers in advocating the study of history by adults as well as students, in writing historical treatises and textbooks, in experimenting with different methods of teaching history, and in attempting to formulate a philosophy of history. Elizabeth Palmer Peabody was a leader in all of these activities, beginning with her first class in history in 1834, five years before the appointment of Jared Sparks as first professor of history in the United States, and extending through 50 years filled with studies, reviews, lectures, and conferences, all directed at stressing the important place of history in the curriculum and at producing and refining materials and guides for history teachers. N. W. Moen

477. Wood, Ann Douglas. THE LITERATURE OF IMPOVERISHMENT: THE WOMEN LOCAL COLORISTS IN AMERICA 1865-1914. *Women's Studies 1972 1(1): 3-45.* Compares and contrasts the writings of 10 sentimentalist women writers of the antebellum 19th century with the writings of 10 local colorist women writers of the late 19th and early 20th centuries. Why these women wrote, their socioeconomic backgrounds, and the contents of their writings are analyzed. Emphasizes the writers' depictions of women, women's roles and influences, the circumstances of women's lives, the position of men, and the concept of the home. Suggests that the sentimentalists wrote about the richness of women's lives and the plenitude of women's power and resources while the local colorists mapped the falsities and demise of the sentimental heroine and protested against the male-dominated, technological, urban society which isolated and ignored women and made womanhood obsolescent. Based on primary and secondary materials; 88 notes, 2 appendixes. A. E. Wiederrecht

478. —. UNCLE TOM: THAT ENDURING OLD IMAGE. *Am. Heritage 1971 23(1): 50-57.* The familiar imageries of the characters in Harriet Beecher Stowe's *Uncle Tom's Cabin* have been used for years by political cartoonists to show purity, virtue, and villainy when commenting on politics and society. 15 illus. B. J. Paul

479. —. WINDOWS. *Art in America 1963 51(2): 110-112.* Comparative study of the treatment of windows by such American artists as Anna M. Moses, Andrew Wyeth, Josef Albers, Malvin M. Albright, Georgia O'Keeffe, and Charles Sheeler. Illus. W. K. Bottorff

# 3. Colonial America

## Economic Sphere

480. Bethke, Robert D. CHESTER COUNTY WIDOW WILLS (1714-1800): A FOLKLIFE SOURCE. *Pennsylvania Folklife 1968 18(1): 16-20.* The wills recorded in Will Books A (1714) through J (1800) have been examined to determine the kinds of information they give about Pennsylvania ways. Numerous excerpts from the provisions demonstrate the kinds of property, including slaves, which the widows held. Clothes, beds, and saddles seem to be most important. Discusses funeral arrangements. 60 notes, biblio.                          F. L. Harrold

481. Coon, David L. ELIZA LUCAS PINCKNEY AND THE RE-INTRODUCTION OF INDIGO CULTURE IN SOUTH CAROLINA. *J. of Southern Hist. 1976 42(1): 61-76.* When economic problems led to the decline of rice and the rise of indigo culture, little attention was given to the historical origins of that product into South Carolina. Only when indigo culture began to disappear was there an expressed interest in its introduction into Carolina. Although Eliza Lucas Pinckney is credited with first developing indigo culture in the 1740's, it was the result of various English and French individuals, connections with the indigo growing areas of the Caribbean, and Negro slaves coming from these indigo areas, who brought their skills with them. Based upon primary and secondary sources; 49 notes.          T. D. Schoonover

482. Feiks, Madeleine. NEW ENGLAND AMAZON: THE LIFE AND TIMES OF SARAH KNIGHT, TRAVELER, BUSINESS WOMAN, TEACHER OF BENJAMIN FRANKLIN. *New-England Galaxy 1969 10(4): 16-22.*

483. Tompsett, Christine H. A NOTE ON THE ECONOMIC STATUS OF WOMEN IN COLONIAL NEW YORK. *New York Hist. 1974 55(3): 319-332.* Only in widowhood did colonial women attain independence from male control and supervision. Existing tax and census records can shed light on the economic and social status of a significant portion of the colonial female population. Primary and secondary works; illus., 5 tables, 18 notes.                          G. Kurland

484. Watson, Alan D. ORDINARIES IN COLONIAL EASTERN NORTH CAROLINA. *North Carolina Hist. R. 1968 45(1): 67-83.* Although the terms "ordinary" and "tavern" were used interchangeably in legal documents, most contemporaries thought of a tavern as a first-class establishment (usually urban) and an ordinary as a second-rate country house. In North Carolina, the assembly passed laws regulating ordinaries which were enforced by the county courts. Rejections and revocations of licenses were infrequent. Many keepers were sheriffs, merchants, justices of the peace, schoolmasters, and doctors. A number of women also kept ordinaries, most of which were located on well-traveled routes or ferry stations. Types of liquors served varied, but eating and sleeping accommodations outside the larger towns were abysmal. Nevertheless, ordinaries served a social and commercial purpose and were more numerous in colonial North Carolina than has been generally believed. 74 notes.                          J. M. Bumsted

485. Wilson, Joan Hoff. DANCING DOGS OF THE COLONIAL PERIOD: WOMEN SCIENTISTS. *Early Am. Lit. 1973 7(3): 225-235.* As medical practitioners in an era with few trained physicians, many obscure women practiced "physick and chirurgery" with apparently unlimited freedom because it was thought that they had natural healing abilities. Like male agronomists and botanists before the American Revolution, however, only upper-class women had the opportunity to delve into these sciences. Jane Colden Farquher (1724-66) came from an aristocratic home. Her father, Cadwallader Colden, convinced that women were particularly suited for the study of botany, educated and encouraged his daughter to work in that field. However, even though Jane Colden discovered a new genus, she was unable to communicate her findings directly to the scientific community—that was done by her husband or her father. Few careers related to science were open to women. Horticulturists such as Martha Laurens Ramsay (1759-1811) and Martha Daniell

Logan (1702-79) and even the most noteworthy of all the female agricultural experimenters, agronomist Eliza Lucas Pinckney (1723-93), who perfected the cultivation of indigo, have suffered from neglect in the hands of historians of science. Based on primary and secondary sources; illus., 24 notes.                          D. P. Wharton

## Social Sphere

### General

486. Baldwin, Laura E. TO CRIMP A COD OR SOUSE A MACKEREL. *New-England Galaxy 1969 10(4): 23-30.* Discusses a 1758 cookbook by Hannah Glasse.                          S

487. Blake, John B. *THE COMPLEAT HOUSEWIFE. Bull. of the Hist. of Medicine 1975 49(1): 30-42.* The first cookbook printed in America, *The Compleat Housewife* (Williamsburg, Virginia: 1742), combined cookery with medical remedies, in a fashion typical in England and America during the 17th and 18th centuries, and emphasized charitable treatment for those without access to physicians. Drug recipes combined multiple ingredients, chiefly herbal; and compilers borrowed uncritically from each other. Because of an advancing medical profession after 1750, medicine dropped from cookbooks. Presented as the presidential address of the American Association History of Medicine, Charleston, South Carolina, 3 May 1974. Primary and secondary sources; 37 notes.                          W. B. Bedford

488. Botti, Priscilla Smith. ELIZABETH WHITMORE: MIDWIFE OF MARLBORO. *Vermont Hist. 1971 39(2): 98-100.* From family and D.A.R. sources and the town history, traces the migration of Elizabeth Whitmore (1727-1814), a tinker's wife from Middletown, Connecticut, to Vermont in 1763. She had learned midwifery in Middletown and supported the family on two dollar delivery fees while her husband traveled, cleared the farm, fought in the Revolution, and represented the town at political conventions.                          T. D. S. Bassett

489. Faragher, John. OLD WOMEN AND OLD MEN IN SEVENTEENTH-CENTURY WETHERSFIELD, CONNECTICUT. *Women's Studies 1976 4(1): 11-31.* Uses demographic methodology and literary materials to examine the old age and sex roles of men and women in the colonial community of Wethersfield, Connecticut during 1640-1700. The community had a growing population based on a high fertility rate and a low mortality rate. This lessened the proportional importance of the relatively small population of aged. Remarriage patterns of widows and widowers showed important differences between the sexes in terms of rate of remarriage, age at remarriage, and economic conditions. Failure to remarry, for men, was not attractive because their old age was defined by loss of patriarchal functions and productivity in the community. Women had greater flexibility when dealing with the crises of remarriage and old age. Women's dower rights were protected. When there was an insufficient estate for a widow, the church had a special obligation to provide for her. In addition, women continued to fill important social roles, such as ministering to the sick and poor. Based on primary and secondary materials; 5 tables, 33 notes.                          A. E. Wiederrecht

490. Hartdagen, Gerald E. THE VESTRIES AND MORALS IN COLONIAL MARYLAND. *Maryland Hist. Mag. 1968 63(4): 360-378.* In colonial Maryland, the Vestries of the Established Anglican Church were responsible for the regulation of morals of the Maryland parishes. Discusses morals in terms of indentured servants, slaves, illegitimate children, marriages, adultery, fornication, drunkenness, profanity, and other offenses during 1690-1775.                          G. A. Hewlett

491. Higgs, Robert and Stettler, H. Louis, III. COLONIAL NEW ENGLAND DEMOGRAPHY: A SAMPLING APPROACH. *William and Mary Q. 1970 27(2): 282-294.* Attempts to give a broader base to statistical data on New England population than has been ac-

quired from single towns. The author corrects some stereotype's about New England population - particularly that marriages occurred at a later age than had been thought the case. However, ages for marriage and birth rates varied sharply from town to town. The author argues that samplings of selected families from various towns offer more accurate information on trends than do definitive statistics on a single town. Includes seven tables on a cross-section of New England towns, listing age of marriages, births per thousand, births per families affected by epidemics, births according to marriage date, towns' populations, total recorded births, and total recorded deaths; 12 notes.                                    H. M. Ward

492. Knight, Russell W.  TOM BOWEN'S CHURCH.  *Essex Inst. Hist. Collections 1963 99(1): 58-63.* A historical sketch of the "renowned tippling house" run by Tom Bowen in 17th-century Marblehead, Massachusetts. From 1640 to 1673 husbands of church-going women escorted their wives, headed for church, to a small ferry and then repaired to the grogshop. The barkeep spent a good deal of time before the magistrates answering questions about wrongdoing in his community, but only in his last years was he convicted of labor on the Sabbath.
                                                                    J. M. Bumsted

493. Leighton, Ann.  "TAKE A HANDFUL OF BUGLOSSE." *Am. Heritage 1966 17(6): 66-71.* Discusses the Puritans' cooking.    S

494. Potter, Gail M.  MAID OF MARBLEHEAD.  *New-England Galaxy 1975 16(3): 34-40.* Describes the "rags to riches" life of Agnes Surriage, the daughter of a Marblehead fisherman, who became the protégée of Charles Henry Frankland, royal Collector of the Port of Boston. When Agnes moved into Frankland's house in 1746, she was no longer accepted in polite society and was snubbed by members of the Frankland family in England. Frankland, who was almost killed in the Lisbon earthquake (1755), vowed to marry her if he survived. After the marriage they were accepted by society. Briefly describes Agnes' activities as a Loyalist in the American Revolution.                                   P. C. Marshall

495. Scheick, William J.  THE WIDOWER NARRATOR IN NATHANIEL WARD'S *THE SIMPLE COBLER OF AGGAWAM IN AMERICA.  New England Q. 1974 47(1): 87-96.* Called the pleasantest book ever written by a New England Puritan, Nathaniel Ward's *The Simple Cobler of Aggawam in America* (1647) is of interest not only for the attack on religious toleration, but for its satire and "sheer exuberance of language." The *Cobler* is composed of references to marriage, adultery, prostitution, and parturition. "The mate he would have each of us find, is truth." 18 notes.                                  E. P. Stickney

496. Somerville, James K.  THE SALEM (MASS.) WOMAN IN THE HOME, 1660-1770.  *Eighteenth-Cent. Life 1974 1(1): 11-14.* Uses wills to explore the way the position of women in the home changed through generations.                                                            S

497. Tharp, Louise Hall.  NEW ENGLAND UNDER OBSERVATION.  *New-England Galaxy 1964 6(2): 3-9.* Based upon accounts of German soldiers of the British army in colonial America. Most of the observations are from letters describing the people, with many descriptions of women and their social role. Illus.                            S

498. Ulrich, Laurel Thatcher.  VIRTUOUS WOMEN FOUND: NEW ENGLAND MINISTERIAL LITERATURE, 1668-1735. *Am. Q. 1976 28(1): 20-40.* Examines 17th- and 18th-century New England ministerial elegies, memorials, funeral sermons, and works of practical piety concerning women indicating a tension existing in male minds between a view of the private worth and the public position of women. Ministers' genuine concern for sex equality eventually generated discrete and ultimately confining notions of femininity. The common historiographical view of Puritan women being regarded as inferior by their male counterparts must be reexamined in the light of the evidence presented.
                                                                    N. Lederer

## Marriage and the Family

499. Beales, Ross W., Jr.  IN SEARCH OF THE HISTORICAL CHILD: MINIATURE ADULTHOOD AND YOUTH IN COLONIAL NEW ENGLAND.  *Am. Q. 1975 27(4): 379-398.* Interpretations of colonial treatment of children as "miniature adults" and assertions that adolescence was absent as a stage of growth in colonial New England are at best exaggerations. The Aries paradigm of French parent-children relationships is not applicable to America. In colonial New England childhood was succeeded by a lengthy and closely supervised stage of "youth" rather than by "miniature adulthood."              N. Lederer

500. Coit, Margaret L.  DEAREST FRIENDS.  *Am. Heritage 1968 19(6): 8-13, 102-106.* The relationship between John Adams (1735-1826) and his wife Abigail Smith Adams (1744-1818) was one of deep friendship as well as love.                                                      S

501. Crowson, E. T.  COLONEL JOHN CUSTIS OF ARLINGTON. *Virginia Cavalcade 1970 20(1): 15-19.* An account of the Custis family of Arlington, on Old Plantation Creek, Northampton County on Virginia's Eastern Shore, and particulary of John Custis IV (1678-1749), an active Virginia statesman, and his cantankerous wife, Frances Parke. The widowed daughter-in-law of John Custis, Martha Dandridge Custis, married George Washington on 6 June 1759. Undocumented, illus.
                                                                    N. L. Peterson

502. Demos, John.  FAMILIES IN COLONIAL BRISTOL, RHODE ISLAND: AN EXERCISE IN HISTORICAL DEMOGRAPHY. *William and Mary Q. 1968 25(1): 40-57.* As in an earlier article on Plymouth, the author takes a close look at family life and social mores of the town of Bristol. These conclusions are reached: "nuclear" rather than "extended" families; later marriages; large size of families, though with some qualifications; long life expectancy; mortality rate for infants not as high as in previous estimates; and not so many remarriages. Vital records and census listings are used. 10 tables relating to households, age structure, marriage data, and comparisons with later periods; 20 notes.
                                                                    H. M. Ward

503. Demos, John.  NOTES ON LIFE IN PLYMOUTH COLONY. *William and Mary Q. 1965 22(2): 264-286.* Life in early Plymouth was not a staid existence, but rather one of considerable fluidity - of rapid growth and expansion. The absence of "extended families" - with sons moving out of their parents' households upon marriage - and the fact that one third to one half of the children lived in homes other than those of their parents partially accounted for a rootlessness in Plymouth society. Statistics on family size, life expectancy, marriages, and remarriages are included.                                                        H. M. Ward

504. Fody, Edward S.  JOHN WITHERSPOON: ADVISOR TO THE LOVELORN.  *Pro. of the New Jersey Hist. Soc. 1966 84(4): 239-249.* Analyzes three letters by John Witherspoon, president of Princeton University, to the *Pennsylvania Magazine* (1775-76) on the subject of marriage. They show that the Puritan patriarchal concept of family life was no longer dominant but had given way to the "common sense" philosophy which emanated from Scotland and which satisfied the American urge for the practical. A conclusion discusses sources and modern works on Scottish realism, a topic which appears to have been neglected by American historians.                          E. P. Stickney

505. Greven, Philip J., Jr.  FAMILY STRUCTURE IN SEVENTEENTH-CENTURY ANDOVER, MASSACHUSETTS.  *William and Mary Q. 1966 23(2): 234-256.* Reconstructs family life of early Andover, based on the statistics of genealogies and local records. Stressed are the effects of disease, marriage, mortality, property holding, and paternal authority. Second generation families were combinations of "both the classical extended family and the nuclear family" - a modified extended family, with children dependent on parents but living under separate roofs. Because of the prolonged dependence of the sons, few moved away.
                                                                    H. M. Ward

506. Isaac, Rhys.  ORDER AND GROWTH, AUTHORITY AND MEANING IN COLONIAL NEW ENGLAND.  *Am. Hist. R. 1971 76(3): 728-737.* Reviews the following studies of little communities in

colonial New England: Demos, John, *A Little Commonwealth: Family Life in Plymouth Colony* (New York: Oxford U. Press, 1970), Greven, Philip J., Jr., *Four Generations: Population, Land and Family in Colonial Andover, Massachusetts* (Ithaca, N. Y.: Cornell U. Press, 1969), Lockridge, Kenneth A., *A New England Town: The First Hundred Years Dedham, Massachusetts, 1636-1736* (New York: W. W. Norton and Co., 1970), and Zuckerman, Michael, *Peaceable Kingdoms: New England Towns in the Eighteenth Century* (New York: Alfred A. Knopf, 1970). The attempts of the authors of these books to describe, on the basis of statistical analysis, important aspects of changing community experience, is related to the work of Perry Miller and Bernard Bailyn on articulated ideologies of the 17th and 18th centuries. Stresses the importance of interrelationships between ideology, authority, and social experience and calls special attention to the urgency of closely integrated study of local communities in relationship to the larger society. The study of diversity and contradiction and not the search for aggregate characterizations will advance understanding of 18th-century America. A

507. Kenney, Alice P. PATRICIANS AND PLEBIANS IN COLONIAL ALBANY.

PART III - FAMILY RECONSTITUTION. Halve Maen 1970 45(3): 9-11. Continued from a previous article. Demographic analysis of Albany church records for 1683-1809 shows that Dutch families tended to intermarry, to marry at age 21-25, and to have four children. Gives a reconstitution table for 10 of Albany's leading Dutch families. Based on published church records and on demographic studies; 5 notes.

PART IV - COMMUNITY ANALYSIS. Halve Maen 1971 45(4): 13-14. Statistics of marriage from 1683 to 1809 at Albany show that the 10 politically dominant families had close marriage ties with the 20 largest families. The resultant urban-rural linkage was common to most Dutch communities in the Upper Hudson, but not in the Lower Hudson. Such evidence tends to confirm that there were two Dutch traditions in the region rather than one. Based on published church records; 2 notes.

PART V - THE SILENT TRADITION. Halve Maen 1971 46(1): 13-15. Albany's population, largely Dutch, boomed because of natural increase, during most of the 18th century, and non-Dutch immigration after the Revolution. The leading and largest Dutch families prevailed via intermarriage. Familial interests, especially the accumulation of wealth, were the dominant pursuits of the region's plebians as well as its more familiar patricians. Demographic evidence and artifacts - the silent tradition - rather than personal testimony in literary remains are the best indicators of such tendencies in the Upper Hudson Valley. Based on published records and on secondary sources; 4 notes. G. L. Owen

508. Kenney, Alice P. PRIVATE WORLDS IN THE MIDDLE COLONIES: AN INTRODUCTION TO HUMAN TRADITION IN AMERICAN HISTORY. *New York Hist. 1970 51(1): 5-31.* The English colonists conceived of government as a public institution to be conducted by men of property and standing entirely apart from their private interests. This concept of government was adopted by the American people who sharply differentiated public from private life. American historians have studied the political institutions of the United States without paying much regard to the private institutions of America. However, non-English ethnic groups such as the Dutch of the Hudson Valley and the Germans of Pennsylvania had a much different tradition of government. Their concept of government was medieval; government was the province of the family and consisted of mutual responsibilities and obligations. The family determined the socioeconomic and political structure of the community. Government was a set of private relationships - not public institutional structures. The role of minority groups in American history will never be fully understood unless historians learn to think in terms of these private social arrangements. Based on primary and secondary sources; 12 illus., 24 notes. G. Kurland

509. Keyssar, Alexander. WIDOWHOOD IN EIGHTEENTH-CENTURY MASSACHUSETTS: A PROBLEM IN THE HISTORY OF THE FAMILY. *Perspectives in Am. Hist. 1974 8: 83-119.* This analysis of 60 Woburn, Massachusetts, couples during 1701-10 challenges traditional views about widowhood in colonial Massachusetts. Colonial women married relatively late in life, usually only once, and for long periods of time. Widowhood was terminated by death more often than by

remarriage, and widows could rely on society to fulfill its obligation to care for them if left destitute. 89 notes. W. A. Wiegand

510. Ktorides, Irene. MARRIAGE CUSTOMS IN COLONIAL NEW ENGLAND. *Hist. J. of Western Massachusetts 1973 2(2): 5-21.* Discusses courting and marriage customs and behavior, including matrimonial advertising, courting sticks, bundling, contracts, banns, dowries, punishment for unchaste behavior, disorderly marriages, shift marriages, and wedding ceremonies. Based on secondary sources; 3 illus., 35 notes. S. S. Sprague

511. Lantz, Herman R.; Schmitt, Raymond; Britton, Margaret; and Snyder, Eloise C. PRE-INDUSTRIAL PATTERNS IN THE COLONIAL FAMILY IN AMERICA: A CONTENT ANALYSIS OF COLONIAL MAGAZINES. *Am. Sociol. R. 1968 33(3): 413-426.* "A content analysis of colonial magazines was undertaken in order to examine the extent to which certain pre-industrial patterns of the family may have been present. Power, the existence of the romantic complex, motivations for entering marriage, and the social response to sexual deviance were evaluated. The results indicate that some aspects of the American family structure usually attributed to the effects of industrialization were noted in magazine content. This appears in regard to prevalence of the romantic love complex and the importance placed on personal happiness as a motive in mate choice. The data regarding power confirm the prevalence of male authority, as well as the existence of considerable subtle female power. Although the latter is not inconsistent with patriarchy, there remain unanswered questions regarding the significance and meaning of subtle female power. Data regarding sexual deviance reveal a basically conservative pre-industrial view with the double standard. It is suggested that it is essential to establish base lines in history in order to make meaningful comparisons about the impact of given social phenomena, industrialization, or particular social institutions like the family." J

512. Meehan, Thomas R. "NOT MADE OUT OF LEVITY," EVOLUTION OF DIVORCE IN EARLY PENNSYLVANIA. *Pennsylvania Mag. of Hist. and Biog. 1968 92(4): 441-464.* Traces the history of divorce in the early years of the colony up to the exemplar statute, the Act of 19 September 1785. Several precedent-setting cases came up for adjudication, following the enactment of this statute, and demonstrated that the modern age respecting divorce, implicit in the 1785 act, had indeed arrived. 71 notes. R. V. Ritter

513. Norton, Susan L. POPULATION GROWTH IN COLONIAL AMERICA: A STUDY OF IPSWICH, MASSACHUSETTS. *Population Studies [Great Britain] 1971 25(3): 433-452.* "The population of Ipswich has been studied from the town's vital records, subjected to aggregative analysis for the period from the town's foundation in 1633 to 1790, and to family reconstitution, for families of couples married from 1633 to 1750. The tremendous rate of natural increase seen is attributable to considerably lower mortality rates than those recorded in most contemporaneous European populations; fertility is not significantly higher. Two sources of reduced mortality are discussed: a relatively high level of nutrition, and a notably low incidence of infectious disease." J

514. Parsons, William T. THE BRIEF MARRIED LIFE OF ISAAC AND SARAH NORRIS. *Quaker Hist. 1968 57(2): 67-83.* The son of a leading Philadelphia merchant, shipbuilder, politician, and Quaker, Isaac Norris II ran his widowed mother's estate from 1736 to 1739 and, on 6 June 1739, married Sarah Elizabeth, eldest daughter of James Logan, a prominent merchant-politician. Norris received from his father-in-law a dowry of 500 pounds, which he invested in England, and 500 acres in Bucks County, Pennsylvania. Isaac's journals and accounts record farming activities and much family sickness including his wife's death in childbirth on 13 October 1744. Her two boys died in infancy; two girls survived. T. D. S. Bassett

515. Rothman, David J. A NOTE ON THE STUDY OF THE COLONIAL FAMILY. *William and Mary Q. 1966 23(4): 627-634.* Compares recent historiography on the colonial family, particularly that of Edmund Morgan, Bernard Bailyn, and Philippe Ariès. Generally it is agreed that changes in the family compelled readjustment of social institutions. Poses questions for research about the relationships of family structure, individuality, community, mobility, social status, and occupations. H. M. Ward

516. Shumsky, Neil Larry. PARENTS, CHILDREN, AND THE SELECTION OF MATES IN COLONIAL VIRGINIA. *Eighteenth-Cent. Life 1976 2(4): 83-88.* During the 17th and 18th centuries in Virginia, parents fought for a veto over their children's selection of marriage partners, a situation caused largely by the oversupply of men; by the end of the 18th century Virginians viewed marriage as a contract between two consenting individuals. 39 notes.

517. Slater, James A. and Caulfield, Ernest. THE COLONIAL GRAVESTONE CARVINGS OF OBADIAH WHEELER. *Pro. of the Am. Antiquarian Soc. 1974 84(1): 73-104.* Scholarly interest in colonial gravestones of New England has increased in recent years, as "these stones provide rich source material for studies of religious symbolism, cultural interrelationships, artistic styles, mortality data, family composition, and other aspects of early New England culture." Describes in detail gravestones produced by colonial craftsman Obadiah Wheeler during 1702-49, and maps their location throughout eastern Connecticut. 25 plates, 2 tables, 2 figs., 15 notes.                    B. L. Fenske

518. Vinovskis, Maris. AMERICAN HISTORICAL DEMOGRAPHY: A REVIEW ESSAY. *Hist. Methods Newsletter 1971 4(4): 141-148.* Reviews Philip J. Greven, Jr., *Four Generations: Population, Land and Family in Colonial Andover, Massachusetts* (Ithaca, N.Y.: Cornell U. Press, 1970). Statistically tracing the history of 247 Andover families over four generations, Greven has re-created the socioeconomic history of a New England town. Describes his work as "solid and invaluable." 2 tables, 10 notes.                    G. Kurland

519. Walton, John. GENEALOGICA MARYLANDIA: GERARD'S DAUGHTERS. *Maryland Hist. Mag. 1973 68(4): 443-450.* The daughters of Dr. Thomas Gerard of St. Mary's County were renowned for the number and standing of the husbands they collected. It is claimed that two of them were married, in succession, to John Washington, great-grandfather of the first President. Complex genealogical problems surround the actual number of daughters Gerard had. The best evidence suggests that Jane, Judith, and Anne were not his daughters, although they lived in the same social milieu of interwoven family relationships along the lower Potomac. The tendency of servants to use given names common in their master's family may account for some of the confusion. Primary and secondary sources; 47 notes.
                    G. J. Bobango

520. Waters, John J. THE TRADITIONAL WORLD OF THE NEW ENGLAND PEASANTS: A VIEW FROM SEVENTEENTH-CENTURY BARNSTABLE. *New England Hist. and Genealogical Register 1976 130(1): 3-21.* Explores the values which governed the 17th-century and early 18th-century life of Barnstable County (Cape Cod), Massachusetts. The importance of land, the idea of patrilineage, the reliance on stem families, and the emphasis on religion suggest the Old World background of these immigrants. Property was the most dominant factor affecting dowries, independence of either the eldest or youngest son, ability of sons and daughters to marry, care of the elderly, and wills. The world of the Barnstable inhabitant was the world of the English peasant. Based on primary sources, especially probate and land records, and on published works; 67 notes.                    S. L. Patterson

521. Weisberg, D. Kelly. "UNDER GREET TEMPTATIONS HEER": WOMEN AND DIVORCE IN PURITAN MASSACHUSETTS. *Feminist Studies 1975 2(2/3): 183-193.* Explores the "social conditions affecting women and divorce law in Puritan Massachusetts," 1639-92. Massachusetts departed significantly from English divorce law, as divorces were granted more frequently to women than to men. This was because: 1) the Puritan family was an agency of social control and most divorce petitions were due to a husband's breach of familial duty; 2) Puritans regarded single people as especially susceptible to temptation, and divorce allowed deserted women to remarry; 3) remarriage prevented a woman and her children from draining public welfare funds; and 4) women were scarce and valuable. Divorce was not easy, but Massachusetts women enjoyed a legal status not obtained in England until 200 years later. Secondary sources; 49 notes.                    J. D. Falk

522. Wells, Robert V. FAMILY HISTORY AND THE DEMOGRAPHIC TRANSITION. *J. of Social Hist. 1975 9(1): 1-20.* The study of the family is emerging but still needs tighter integration of its

separate themes: kinship, fertility rates, child-rearing, and women. Attempts a critique and possible revision of the role conventionally attributed to demographic transition. This transition, a sequence conventionally described as a decline in the death rate and then in the birth rate, has been attributed to changed material conditions. Proposes various clues that indicate a more plausible connection with changed motivation. United States examples primarily are from the colonial era. 58 notes.                    M. Hough

523. Wells, Robert V. QUAKER MARRIAGE PATTERNS IN A COLONIAL PERSPECTIVE. *William and Mary Q. 1972 29(3): 415-442.* Examines the marriage patterns of a group of 276 Quaker families from the middle colonies. Subjects for investigation are: age at marriage, duration of marriage, length of survival after death of a spouse, remarriage, proportion of persons not marrying, and size of colonial families. Among the findings: one-half of children born never married, in a majority of cases the husband died first, and there occurred a greater shift in marriage patterns among women. Comments on colonial values on marriage, and makes comparison with European patterns. 10 tables, 44 notes.
                    H. M. Ward

# Witchcraft

524. Allen, Neal W., Jr. A MAINE WITCH. *Old-Time New England 1971 61(3): 75-81.* Describes a witchcraft episode at Kittery, Maine, in 1725-26, as revealed "in a thick packet of papers that rests in a vault at the York County Court House." John Spinney was charged with having abused Sarah Keene, an elderly lady, by publicly accusing her of witchcraft.                    R. N. Lokken

525. Demos, John. UNDERLYING THEMES IN THE WITCHCRAFT OF SEVENTEENTH-CENTURY NEW ENGLAND. *Am. Hist. R. 1970 75(5): 1311-1326.* Witchcraft, an old and over-worked subject in American history, may profitably be studied anew with strategies borrowed from the behavioral sciences. When analyzed from a sociological standpoint, the records of early New England reveal that: 1) alleged witches were mainly middle-aged women of deviant tendencies; 2) their accusers were adolescent girls; and 3) additional testimony against them was frequently supplied by neighbors. These patterns reflect specific points of tension in family and community life. When analyzed from the psychological standpoint, the same records suggest a pervasive concern with the handling of aggressive impulses, and with "orality." This expresses underlying conflicts of personality. Taken altogether, therefore, the study of witchcraft provides a unique opportunity to unravel the irrational "darker side" of colonial New England.                    A

526. Detweiler, Robert. SHIFTING PERSPECTIVES ON THE SALEM WITCHES. *Hist. Teacher 1975 8(4): 596-610.* Reviews the literature concerning witchcraft in Salem Village. Discusses historical interpretations of this phenomenon, and draws attention to studies in anthropology and psychology concerning witchcraft in other societies. Studies by anthropologists show fear of witchcraft to be a form of behavioral control especially in time of stress. Studies in psychology depict witchcraft as a form of revolt by young people against the restraints imposed by an older generation. Recent historians have built upon studies in both these disciplines. Based on primary and secondary sources; 57 notes.                    P. W. Kennedy

527. Drake, Frederick C. WITCHCRAFT IN THE AMERICAN COLONIES, 1647-62. *Am. Q. 1968 20(4): 694-725.* Discusses the historical debate surrounding the treatment of witchcraft in America. The various trials are treated in a table which relates the names of the witches, their accusers and victims, the date and place of the trials, the verdicts, and the final treatment accorded the witches. In probing the causes of the trials, the author examines three factors: the "theological (or ideological) background" of the accusers; the "presence of external stimuli"; and "pressures" existing in Puritan society which would seem to contribute to the fear of witches. 43 notes.                    R. S. Pickett

528. Hansen, Chadwick. SALEM WITCHCRAFT AND DE FOREST'S "WITCHING TIMES." *Essex Inst. Hist. Collections 1968 104(2): 89-108.* Reprints the introduction to a new edition of John W. De

Forest's *Witching Times* (New Haven: Coll. and U. Press, 1967) first published serially in 1856-57, which "with its attention to the physical substance of experience and the force and humor of vernacular speech...is an early and significant document in the history of American realism." The girls in Salem Village, afflicted in February 1691 with what contemporaries called witchcraft, were victims of pathological hysteria; they were not frauds or liars but hysterical; and what they were hysterical about was a belief that they were bewitched. All three degrees of witchcraft - white magic, black magic, and pact - were practiced in late 17th-century New England; and "in a society which believes in witchcraft, witchcraft works." Most of those executed were innocent, but one or two were probably practicing witches. 23 notes.      J. M. Bumsted

529. Langdon, Carolyn S. THE CASE OF LYDIA GILBERT (WITCHCRAFT IN CONNECTICUT). *New-England Galaxy 1964 5(3): 14-23.* Lydia Gilbert (1600-54) was a resident of Windsor, Connecticut, who was executed for witchcraft in 1654. Those charged with witchcraft in Connecticut seem to have been women who were outspoken, disliked by their neighbors, frequently new to a region, and not members of the local church.      T. J. Farnham

530. Proper, David R. SALEM WITCHCRAFT, A BRIEF HISTORY. *Essex Inst. Hist. Collections 1966 102(3): 213-223.* A brief sketch of the witchcraft hysteria of 1692, with a selected bibliography "for the benefit of students."      J. M. Bumsted

531. Robbins, Peggy. THE DEVEL IN SALEM. *Am. Hist. Illus. 1971 6(8): 4-9, 44-48.* In Salem Village, Massachusetts, and its vicinity in 1692, 170 "witches" were imprisoned and 20 of them put to death. Reverend Samuel Parris' daughter and niece were initially "possessed," with girl friends soon joining them, most of the group having been in regular attendance at story tellings by Parris' aging woman slave, Tituba. Accused "witches" appeared in court, the "possessed" girls throwing fits, and the judges and jury agreeing on guilt during June-September, 1692. When the governor's wife publicly called the trials a disgrace, girls cried out against her; and the governor called a halt to the court sessions. Secondary sources; 8 illus.      D. Dodd

532. Thompson, Roger. REVIEW ARTICLE: SALEM REVISITED. *J. of Am. Studies [Great Britain] 1972 6(3): 317-336.* Discusses the historiography of witchcraft (alleged) suppression in Salem, Massachusetts, in 1692, and in England. The psychological aspects and social dynamics of the behavior of many principals in the incidents have proven difficult to explain. Although "temporary and insecure [public] authorities" in each case allowed the "mania" to develop, major differences do exist between the Salem and English experiences. Reexamination of the "connexion between witchcraft and Puritanism" is in order. Based on secondary sources; 22 notes.      H. T. Lovin and S

533. Werking, Richard H. "REFORMATION IS OUR ONLY PRESERVATION": COTTON MATHER AND SALEM WITCHCRAFT. *William and Mary Q. 1972 29(2): 281-290.* Evaluates the historiography of Mather's role in the Salem witchcraft affair (1692). Seeks to explain Mather's interest in the trials. Both curiosity and the need to find new techniques of prayer motivated Mather. Mather's sermon to the court, "The Return of Several Ministers," has been used out of context by historians. Actually Mather pleaded caution and was more concerned, in this document and in other of his expressions, with the renewal of the covenant than the execution of witches. Mather was also in search of a reality of the spiritual world. 37 notes.      H. M. Ward

# Political Sphere

## General

534. Barker-Benfield, Ben. ANNE HUTCHINSON AND THE PURITAN ATTITUDE TOWARD WOMEN. *Feminist Studies 1972 1(2): 65-96.* Anne Hutchinson's antinomianism was a response to the exclusion of women from the priesthood of all believers by Puritan covenant theology and exclusively male control of church membership. Several other women were driven to desperation by theological uncertainties during the same period (1636-38). The radical changes achieved by Puritan men did not leave them secure enough to allow women the same changes in practice (as opposed to theory). The subordination of women made men feel more like God; Christ was to the Puritan man as the man was to his wife. John Winthrop perceived Hutchinson's movement as a sexual threat. He viewed her classes as occasions for the mass reversal of sexual subordination and described unconventional women as masculine or manlike. His virulent reaction to her, expressed in physiological metaphors, further reveals the profound sexual bias of the Puritan concept of grace. Nathaniel Hawthorne's *The Scarlet Letter* presents Puritan history in similar terms. 47 notes.      J. D. Falk

535. Baskett, Sam S. ELIZA LUCAS PINCKNEY: PORTRAIT OF AN EIGHTEENTH CENTURY AMERICAN. *South Carolina Hist. Mag. 1971 72(4): 207-219.* Through her letters, explores the personality, life, and political thought of Pinckney, 1742-93.

536. Carson, Christopher Seberian. THE OLIVER FAMILY IN PEACE AND WAR, 1632-1860. *New England Hist. and Genealogical Register 1976 130(July): 196-205.* Surveys the Oliver family of Massachusetts, beginning with the arrival of Thomas Oliver (1582-1657) and his wife, Anne (d. 1637), in Boston in 1632, and concluding with a summary of the restructured lives of the children and grandchildren of Andrew (1706-74) and Peter Oliver (1713-91) and Thomas Hutchinson (1711-80), their brother-in-law. The family's prominence in Massachusetts was lost when Hutchinson, the royal governor, and Andrew, the lieutenant governor, chose to support King George III and Parliament during the American Revolution. Some family members chose exile, others remained but their influence was severely diminished. Their descendants left politics and turned to colonizing, law, medicine, and history. Based on secondary sources; 2 charts, 7 notes.      S. L. Patterson

537. Etulain, Richard. JOHN COTTON AND THE ANNE HUTCHINSON CONTROVERSY. *Rendezvous 1967 2(2): 9-18.* Discusses the role of John Cotton in the antinomian controversy centering around Anne Hutchinson in the early 17th century. Cotton was a teacher, preacher, and politician in the Massachusetts colony. He expounded the center position between the legalistic, ruling faction and the vocal, radical faction that challenged theology with political and economic overtones. The controversy was so serious that the court disarmed leading antinomians for fear of rebellion. Throughout the turmoil Cotton remained committed to the Puritan oligarchy. He voted to excommunicate and exile some persons on the grounds of physical danger and their untruthfulness on some issues. Cotton did not abandon the antinomians, but they abandoned him. 38 notes.      H. F. Malyon

538. Fisher, Marguerite. EIGHTEENTH-CENTURY THEORISTS OF WOMEN'S LIBERATION. George, Carol V. R., ed. *"Remember the Ladies": New Perspectives on Women in American History: Essays in Honor of Nelson Manfred Blake* (Syracuse: Syracuse U. Pr., 1975): 39-47. During the Enlightenment, European social theorists expressed many of the tenets basic to modern feminism. Rejecting the idea that people were born with an innate character, the theorists believed people were the products of their environments. Thinkers such as Baron Holbach, Thomas Paine, the Marquis de Condorcet, William Godwin, and Mary Wollstonecraft protested prevailing attitudes about women's subordinate roles and subjugation; challenged the accepted political, economic, and social customs; espoused the intrinsic worth of the individual; argued for the right of all to self-development; and advocated a society in which men and women were free and equal. Their ideas provided the philosophical bases for 19th-century American feminism. Based on primary and secondary materials; 17 notes.      P. R. Byrne

539. Fleming, E. McClung THE AMERICAN IMAGE AS INDIAN PRINCESS, 1765-1783. *Winterthur Portfolio 1965 2: 65-81.* Traces the evolution of the allegorical figure used to represent "America" and later the United States. From 1765 to 1783, the symbol was an Indian princess. Portrayed at first as the dependent daughter of Britannia, the princess frees herself from British fetters of taxation and finally gains liberty through the Revolution. Before 1776 the daughter-mother relationship included every kind of affection, alienation, and reconciliation. The American image sought liberty during these years, while England's chief concern was trade. Various artists, both abroad and at home, portrayed the princess in headdress, bow and arrow, and, on occasion, a full robe. The symbol evolved slowly into a Greek goddess, and finally into Uncle Sam in the 19th century. Based on primary and secondary sources; 13 photos, 26 notes.
N. A. Kuntz

540. George, Carol V. R. ANNE HUTCHINSON AND THE "REVOLUTION WHICH NEVER HAPPENED." George, Carol V. R., ed. *"Remember the Ladies": New Perspectives on Women in American History: Essays in Honor of Nelson Manfred Blake* (Syracuse: Syracuse U. Pr., 1975): 13-37. Events in the career and trials of Anne Hutchinson (1591-1643) illumine early 17th-century attitudes and issues related to sexual equality and women's status. Critical of the prevailing order, Hutchinson and her followers forced the people of Massachusetts Bay Colony to re-examine their theological, social, and political values during the 1630's, when the colony already was in political ferment. Hutchinson believed that salvation was a personal experience not needing the assistance of the clergy. This belief contained the seed of an argument for sexual equality and challenged male secular and religious authority. At her civil and religious trials, Hutchinson's gender became an issue. She allegedly behaved in an unwomanly fashion and usurped the customary role of men. Among her followers were many women, including Mary Dyer; and Hutchinson's appeal to women made her appear particularly dangerous to John Winthrop and other colonial authorities. Ultimately the ministers excommunicated her, and the magistrates banished her from the colony as a woman unfit for their society. Based on primary and secondary sources; 30 notes.
P. R. Byrne

541. Koehler, Lyle THE CASE OF THE AMERICAN JEZEBELS: ANNE HUTCHINSON AND FEMALE AGITATION DURING THE YEARS OF ANTINOMIAN TURMOIL, 1636-1640. *William and Mary Q. 1974 31(1): 55-78.* Places the Antinomian controversy into the context of female rebellion, defines the role of women in colonial Massachusetts, and describes some of Anne Hutchinson's followers. Female resistance reached its height when many women sympathized with her. The theological charges stemmed from fear of assertion of women's rights. In the aftermath of the trial, other women became assertive and were involved in cases of legal intimidation. Based on court and church records, and on Puritan writings; 70 notes.
H. M. Ward

542. Morison, Samuel Eliot. THREE GREAT LADIES HELPED ESTABLISH THE UNITED STATES. *Smithsonian 1975 6(7): 96-103.* Presents biographies of Abigail Adams, Mercy Otis Warren, and Martha Washington, focusing on their letters, feminism, and contributions to the American Revolution.

543. Newcomb, Wellington. ANNE HUTCHINSON VERSUS MASSACHUSETTS. *Am. Heritage 1974 25(4): 12-15, 78-81.* Anne Hutchinson's criminal trial in Puritan Boston for her role in the Antinomian controversy.
S

544. Norton, Mary Beth. "MY RESTING REAPING TIMES": SARAH OSBORN'S DEFENSE OF HER "UNFEMININE" ACTIVITIES, 1767. *Signs 1976 2(2): 515-529.* Schoolteacher Sarah Osborn was sharply criticized by her close friend, clergyman Josiah Fish, for assuming a leadership role in the 1766-67 Newport revival. More than 525 colonists, black and white, slave and free, male and female, met weekly at Osborn's. Fish advised her to relinquish her role to a more qualified man so that she could devote her time to feminine pursuits, and complained that her work with blacks was potentially dangerous to the social order. In reply Osborn carefully downplayed her position as a leader of the group, but refused to abandon it. Based on the Osborn-Fish correspondence and secondary works; 27 notes.
J. Gammage

## Legal Status and the Courts

545. Aiken, John R. NEW NETHERLANDS ARBITRATION IN THE 17TH CENTURY. *Arbitration J. 1974 29(3): 145-160.* "Early mercantile arbitration on the American continent is usually assumed to have been derived from English common law and the experience of English merchants and guilds. But there were also Dutch colonies during the 17th century, and their tradition was traceable to Roman law, by way of the Netherlands. In the course of exhaustive research, the author may have found the earliest example of a woman serving as an arbitrator. It appears that in 1662, a dispute arose as to whether a woman had been paid properly for making linen caps. The issue turned on whether she had performed her job without excessive spoilage. A court appointed another women as an expert arbitrator 'to inspect the linen caps' and 'settle the parties' case.' The history of arbitration among Dutch colonies convinces the author that it was superior to that of the English common law."
J

546. DePauw, Linda Grant. LAND OF THE UNFREE: LEGAL LIMITATIONS ON LIBERTY IN PRE-REVOLUTIONARY AMERICA. *Maryland Hist. Mag. 1973 68(4): 355-368.* Contrasts the "life, liberty, and the pursuit of happiness" of the Declaration of Independence with the fact that "no more than 15 percent of the Revolutionary generation was free to enjoy" these things. Negroes, white servants, women, minors, and propertyless white males were excluded from political life and enjoyed no theoretical and little actual equality of economic or personal status. Since the median age in colonial America was 16, and since women made up "almost half of the total population when all age groups are included," with black slaves accounting for about 20 percent, it is wholly wrong to characterize America in 1776 as "democratic." By 18th century standards America was remarkably free, but historians from Bancroft to Becker have overstressed the notion of colonial democracy. Primary and secondary sources; 5 illus., 49 notes.
G. J. Bobango

547. Wyllie, John C., ed. THE SECOND MRS. WAYLAND, AN UNPUBLISHED JEFFERSON OPINION ON A CASE IN EQUITY. *Am. J. of Legal Hist. 1965 9(1): 64-68.* Prints, with brief commentary, a certified copy of an opinion by Thomas Jefferson written for a widow on her rights of inheritance. The original has been lost.
N. C. Brockman

548. —. A BITTER PILL FOR THE WIDOW CENDOYA. *Escribano 1972 9(2): 73-94.* Relates the story of Doña Sebastiana Olazarraga y Aramburu and her three infant children following the death of her husband, Don Manuel de Cendoya, who died while Governor of Florida in 1673. The official attachment of the governor's estate, an inventory, and *residencia* prolonged the settlement, resulted in repeated petitions to the Crown, and complicated litigation. Doña Sebastiana was reduced to subsisting on charity. In 1683, when Crown officials accepted an exonerating *residencia* of the Governor, his wife was granted a portion of the estate. Doña Sebastiana's efforts helped prompt a reform in 1685 so that the wives of deceased Florida governors could return to Spain before completion of the *residencia*. Obscurity shrouded the remainder of her life. Based on Spanish archival materials and secondary sources; 52 notes.
J. F. Vivian

## War for Independence

549. Brush, Ted. SUSSEX COUNTY'S LOYALIST HEROINE. *North Jersey Highlander 1973 9(3): 23-25.* Only one mention of Loyalist Nancy Nevil has come to light. General John Burgoyne's army, after surrendering at Saratoga, was sent to Charlottesville (Virginia) and passed through Sussex County (New Jersey) where Nancy Nevil helped British escapees find their way around the New Jersey militia to New York City. Based on secondary sources; illus., biblio.
A. C. Aimone

550. Carroll, Nan. WOMEN BEHIND THE MEN. *Daughters of the Am. Revolution Mag. 1975 109(1): 22-25.* Wives of the signers of the Declaration of Independence.
S

551. Cole, Adelaide M. WE'VE COME A LONG WAY, BABY? *Daughters of the Am. Revolution Mag. 1976 110(6): 851-855.* Discusses the contributions of women in the American Revolution.

552. Fox, Vicki G. and Stoeckel, Althea L. THE ROLE OF WOMEN IN THE AMERICAN REVOLUTION: AN ANNOTATED BIBLIOGRAPHY. *Indiana Social Studies Q. 1975 28(1): 14-29.*

553. Hortin, Mellie Scott. BICENTENNIAL LADY: FIRST IN THE HEARTS OF HER COUNTRYMEN. *Daughters of the Am. Revolution Mag. 1975 109(2): 100-102.* Brief sketch of Martha Washington and her role in the American Revolution. S

554. Kalinowska, Fryderyka. THREE EARLY HISTORIANS OF THE AMERICAN REVOLUTION. *Am. Studies in Scandinavia [Norway] 1970 (5): 25-46.* Discusses the writing of three historians who lived in the era of the American Revolution and whose writing represents the beginning of American Revolution historiography: Thomas Hutchinson, the loyalist Lieutenant Governor of Massachusetts; Mercy Otis Warren, the fiercely patriotic sister of revolutionary leader James Otis; and David Ramsay, a participant in the Revolution but a more detached and impartial historian than the other two. Secondary sources; 26 notes.
J. E. Findling

555. Matthies, Katharine. BARONESS VON RIEDESEL. *Daughters of the Am. Revolution Mag. 1975 109(9): 984-986.* Describes the life of Baroness Frederika von Riedesel, wife of General Frederich von Riedesel, commander of Hessian troops during the Revolutionary War. S

556. Morgan, Madel Jacobs. SARAH TRULY, A MISSISSIPPI TORY. *J. of Mississippi Hist. 1975 37(1): 87-95.* Sarah Truly was a staunch Tidewater Virginia loyalist who moved in 1773 to the Old Natchez District in West Florida. After the district surrendered to Spain in 1779, Truly aided an unsuccessful loyalist plan to recapture it and later became a farmer and businesswoman. Based chiefly upon published primary sources; 27 notes.
J. W. Hillje

557. Murphy, Orville T. "LA GUERRE ET L'AMOUR": A FOOTNOTE TO THE STORY OF WASHINGTON'S DEFEAT AT LONG ISLAND. *Am. Q. 1966 18(3): 543-547.* Reveals the *cherchez la femme* historical explanation of George Washington's defeat at the Battle of Long Island. The most explicit source, probably a projection of a vivid and sympathetic Gallic imagination, described Washington as the victim of a belle named Gibbon [no given name available] whose British sympathies led her to betray the gallant general. The two sources cited are "Variétés," in *Gazette des Duex Ponts*, 3 March 1777, and Hilliard d'Auberteuil's *Essais Historiques et politiques sur la Revolution de l'Amerique Septentrionale*, II, Part I, 4-24; 2 notes.
R. S. Pickett

558. Norton, Mary Beth. EIGHTEENTH-CENTURY AMERICAN WOMEN IN PEACE AND WAR: THE CASE OF THE LOYALISTS. *William and Mary Q. 1976 33(3): 386-409.* Analyzes the 468 American women loyalists who presented claims (including private letters, loss schedules, and memorials) to the British government. The women form a cross section of society. Examines family relationships, property holdings and knowledge of financial affairs. Deals with the problems facing the women who were uprooted and had to find new homes. The loyalist women had close ties to family and household. Based on loyalist claims records in the Public Record Office in London; 55 notes.
H. M. Ward

559. Pinckney, Elise, ed. LETTERS OF ELIZA LUCAS PINCKNEY, 1768-1782. *South Carolina Hist. Mag. 1975 76(3): 143-170.* Miscellaneous letters held by the South Carolina Historical Society relate family concerns (marriages, births, and illnesses) as well as the hardships of the Revolutionary War on the homefront. Based on primary sources; 54 notes.
R. H. Tomlinson

560. Rogers, George V. WOMAN'S LIBERATION, C. 1781. *New-England Galaxy 1975 16(3): 3-12.* Describes the adventures of Deborah Sampson, who masqueraded as Private Robert Shurtleff of the 4th Massachusetts Regiment of the Continental Army. She served in the Yorktown Campaign in 1781, at Tarrytown, New York, in 1782, where she suffered facial and leg wounds, and in Philadelphia in 1783, where she helped control mutinous Pennsylvania troops. A bout with typhoid in Philadelphia, which nearly killed her, revealed her true identity. Her military career ended with an honorable discharge. 6 illus.
P. C. Marshall

561. Ross, Emily. CAPTAIN MOLLY: FORGOTTEN HEROINE OF THE REVOLUTION. *Daughters of the Am. Revolution Mag. 1972 106(2): 108-111, 186.* Story of Margaret ("Molly") Corbin, first American woman to fight and sustain injuries during the American Revolution. S

562. Slaymaker, Samuel R., II. MRS. FRAZER'S PHILADELPHIA CAMPAIGN. *J. of the Lancaster County Hist. Soc. 1969 73(4): 185-209.* Narrates the activities of Mary Frazer (1745-1830), wife of Col. Persifer Frazer (1736-92), during and after the Philadelphia campaign (1777-78). Persifer Frazer was a wealthy Scotch-Irish merchant-landowner in Chester County (now Delaware County), Pennsylvania. Describes the economic and political antagonisms between Quakers and Presbyterian Scotch-Irish in the area. Follows Mrs. Frazer through her mounted reconnaissances during the Battle of Brandywine, her encounters with British troops plundering her home, and her visits to Philadelphia in the winter of 1777-78 to see her husband, held prisoner by the British. Based on an oral account by Mary Frazer, later transcribed by her granddaughter and currently owned by the author. 7 illus., map.
L. J. Stout

563. Smith, Samuel Stelle. THE SEARCH FOR MOLLY PITCHER. *Daughters of the Am. Revolution Mag. 1975 109(4): 292-295.* Molly Pitcher, a heroine of the 1778 Battle of Monmouth in New Jersey, was an Irish American named Mary Hays McCauly; her maiden name is unknown. S

564. Steedman, Marguerite Couturier. SUSANNAH ELLIOTT'S BLUE FLAG COMES HOME. *South Carolina Hist. Illus. 1970 1(4): 9-14, 68-69.* A blue regimental flag, made by Susannah Elliott for the 2nd South Carolina Regiment in 1776 and captured by the British in 1779 in an assault on Savannah, was located in 1970 and loaned to South Carolina by Queen Elizabeth II for the state's Tricentennial celebration.

565. Stickley, Julia Ward. THE RECORDS OF DEBORAH SAMPSON GANNETT, WOMAN SOLDIER OF THE REVOLUTION. *Prologue 1972 4(4): 233-241.* Photo-essay of documents relating to Deborah Sampson Gannett (d. 1827), who enlisted in 1781 in the Continental army clothed in male garb and under the alias Robert Shurtleff. Traveling from Uxbridge, Massachusetts, to Yorktown and back, she married in 1784 and mothered three children. Documents support her pension applications. Based on primary and secondary sources; illus., 3 notes.
D. G. Davis, Jr.

566. Teunissen, John J. BLOCKHEADISM AND THE PROPAGANDA PLAYS OF THE AMERICAN REVOLUTION. *Early Am. Literature 1972 7(2): 148-162.* American Whigs and Tories met at the blockade of Boston and called each other blockheads for being there. The Tory Jonathan Sewall, the Whig Mercy Otis Warren, and an anonymous author all used the blockhead metaphor in their dramas. Jonathan Sewall's *A Cure for the Spleen. or Amusement for a Winter's Evening; Being the Substance of a Conversation on the Times, over a Friendly Tankard and Pipe* (Boston, 1775; reprinted in New York some months later as *The Americans Roused*) is a philosophical conversation-piece, not a drama. Mercy Warren's *The Blockheads: or the Affrighted Officers. A Farce* (Boston, 1776) is more dramatic and more vitriolic; but there were no theaters in Puritan Boston. The anonymous *The Blockheads; or, Fortunate Contractor* (London, 1782) could be produced as a skillful little musical farce and announced itself, on the title page, as *An Opera, in Two Acts, as it was Performed at New York.* It probably was not performed in London; the New York performance is the contemporary political farce which is the play's subject. Based on primary and secondary sources; 13 notes.
D. P. Wharton

567. Utley, Beverly. BRAVE WOMEN: DISTAFF SIDE OF REVOLUTION. *Am. Hist. Illus. 1968 3(6): 10-18.* During the American War of Independence, women played an important role in helping the colonies gain their freedom. Discusses several of these brave women and the

hardships they endured for their country. Some of the contributions to the cause performed by women included making bullets, sewing clothing for the troops, feeding traveling soldiers, spying on the enemy and reporting information, carrying messages through enemy lines, etc. The women who had the most difficult time during the revolution were those who lived on the frontier, in constant danger from hostile Indians who were often encouraged to attack by the British. Based on secondary sources; 8 illus.                                                        M. J. McBaine

568.    Vernon-Jackson, H. O.    A LOYALIST'S WIFE: LETTERS OF MRS. PHILIP VAN CORTLANDT, 1776-77.    *Hist. Today [Great Britain] 1964 14(8): 574-580.* Extracts from four letters (without commentary) of a wife of a lieutenant-colonel in the New Jersey Brigade, December 1776-February 1777. The letters contain social tid-bits. The author is a descendant.                                      L. Knafla

569.    Wiggins, Florence Roe.    THE LONG VIGIL OF MARY FEAKE ROE.    *Daughters of the Am. Revolution Mag. 1976 110(3): 312-313.* Recounts the life of Mary Feake Roe during the years of her marriage to William Roe, a spy in the service of the American government during 1777-86.

570.    Yeager, Edna H.    LONG ISLAND'S REVOLUTIONARY HEROINES.    *Daughters of the Am. Revolution Mag. 1975 109(8): 908-915.* Discusses the exploits of women on Long Island, New York, during the American Revolution.                                          S

# Religion and Ethnicity

## Religion

571.    Bronner, Edwin B.    AN EARLY ANTISLAVERY STATEMENT: 1676.    *Quaker Hist. 1973 62(1): 47-50.* Alice Curwen (ca. 1619-79) and her husband Thomas (1610-80) were jailed and whipped in Boston, 1676, traveled in New England, Long Island, East Jersey, and Barbados and returned to England. After a 1675 Barbadian slave insurrection, Quakers were not allowed to bring their slaves to meeting or school. Alice Curwen's letter to Martha Tavernor, first printed in 1680, urged the slaveholder to break this law and bring her whole family, including slaves, to worship. 10 notes.                          T. D. S. Bassett

572.    Carroll, Kenneth L.    THE ANATOMY OF A SEPARATION: THE LYNAM CONTROVERSY.    *Quaker Hist. 1966 55(2): 67-78.* John Lynam of Derbyshire and Margaret Ridge of County Antrim had been active and persecuted Friends for several years when they married in 1666. Before they left England in 1681 the writings of this wheelwright and his wife had been published with the imprimatur of Quaker authority. Within the same year a disagreement developed between Quakers who had been in Maryland for 25 years and these newcomers to the Western Shore, who apparently wanted to rule. When John returned to England in 1682, worship was shifted from the Lynam house; but, when he came back, the Lynams started a separate meeting. Negotiation, English visitors, and letters from English leaders got nowhere until one separatist died in 1689. Within a year John Lynam had condemned his former contentiousness. His wife was reconciled before they moved, in 1691, to Pennsylvania, where they lived in harmony with Friends until their deaths in 1698.                                              T. D. S. Bassett

573.    Carroll, Kenneth L.    ELIZABETH HARRIS, THE FOUNDER OF AMERICAN QUAKERISM.    *Quaker Hist. 1968 57(2): 96-111.* When Elizabeth Harris was first in Maryland depends on an estimate of her itinerary and travel time. Because 1656 cash accounts in the Swarthmore MSS, London, show 2 pounds 5 shillings for "books to Virginia," Harris must have started work in Maryland early in 1656. The first Quaker missionaries to Boston arrived in the summer of 1656 and were not allowed to land. Charles Bayly's account of his conversion, written in Bristol Prison in 1663, shows the character of Harris's Maryland mission. Because she converted influential Puritan officials, Maryland Quakers were not persecuted until one of them gave the government back to Baltimore's representatives in 1658. Robert Clarkson's letter of 14 January 1658, printed in full, reached Harris on her return from Italy in

July, and further characterized her mission. She was a demonstrator inclined toward the schismatic followers of John Perrot, who exaggerated the role of individual inspiration. What became of her is not clear, but she was imprisoned in Salisbury (1661), probably at Northampton (1665-72), and may have revisited Maryland in 1662.                        T. D. S. Bassett

574.    Cowing, Cedric B.    SEX AND PREACHING IN THE GREAT AWAKENING.    *Am. Q. 1968 20(3): 624-644.* Notes that a physical cataclysm, the earthquake of 1727, increased the numbers of people accepting communion within New England churches; but it did not alter the sex ratio, normally 5 women to 3 men, in the same fashion as did the Great Awakening. The author refutes the widely held contention that the religious influx of the Great Awakening consisted only of marginal people; the balance of new converts during the early 1740's proved to be middle-aged men. With the notable exception of "Old Light" Boston churches, males were attracted to the "New Light" emphasis on "the Terrors." As opposed to the customary female admissions of fornications, men contributed to a higher percentage of admissions. Little evidence exists to support the contention that the New Lights were any more immoral, in terms of their sexuality, than people in the churches prior to the revival. The author argues that the net effect of Antinomianism was a more open attitude toward religion. Based on primary and secondary sources; 4 tables, 56 notes.                                  R. S. Pickett

575.    Kirkpatrick, Gabriel W.    BUT NOT TO YIELD.    *Daughters of the Am. Revolution Mag. 1973 107(5): 412-413, 496.* Persecution of Quakers in the Massachusetts Bay Colony.                          S

576.    Lumpkin, William L.    THE ROLE OF WOMEN IN 18TH CENTURY VIRGINIA BAPTIST LIFE.    *Baptist Hist. and Heritage 1973 8(3): 158-167.*

577.    Marlin, Charles Lowell.    JEMIMA WILKINSON: ERRANT QUAKER DIVINE.    *Quaker Hist. 1963 52(2): 90-94.* Born in Rhode Island and orphaned at 10, she had little formal education. When delirious with typhoid fever at 24, she had a vision of an indwelling spirit and henceforth called herself "The Public Universal Friend." She developed a personal following through itinerant [errant] preaching and settled her disciples in a western New York enclave called "New Jerusalem" in 1788. She was comely but minimized her sex appeal with mannish garb. Charming in manner, her rhetoric was plain but excelled that of contemporary Quakers.                                                  T. D. S. Bassett

578.    Masson, Margaret W.    THE TYPOLOGY OF THE FEMALE AS A MODEL FOR THE REGENERATE: PURITAN PREACHING, 1690-1730.    *Signs 1976 2(2): 304-315.* Puritan theology used the norms for the female roles of bride and wife to describe the regenerate Christian's relation to God. Since men were required to adopt these subordinate behaviors as church members, the Puritans could not consider such attributes as innately female. Puritan doctrine required a limited egalitarianism, because both sexes were deemed equally capable of conversion and equally in need of it. Although Cotton Mather and others preached that some vices were sex related, such as gossiping and drinking among men, they rejected the idea that women were innately more evil than men. Based on Puritan sermons, secondary works, and dissertations; 49 notes.                                      J. Gammage

579.    Morse, Mary Harrower.    TWO WOMEN OF BOSTON.    *New-England Galaxy 1972 13(3): 27-35.* The persecution of religious dissidents Mary Dyer and Anne Hutchinson in Puritan Boston.          S

580.    Smith, Don Elton.    MARY DYER: CONSCIENTIOUS DISSENTER.    *Mankind 1970 2(7): 38-46.* Mary Dyer, a Quaker, was persecuted by the Puritans of Boston.                              S

581.    Stoever, William R. B.    NATURE, GRACE AND JOHN COTTON: THE THEOLOGICAL DIMENSION IN THE NEW ENGLAND ANTINOMIAN CONTROVERSY.    *Church Hist. 1975 44(1): 22-33.* In 1636, Puritan Massachusetts was confronted with a sectarian outburst which ruined the religious and civil peace of Boston and temporarily threatened the entire colony. Part of the Boston congregation, led by Anne Hutchinson and abetted by John Cotton, charged that many of the Bay clergy were not true ministers of the gospel but a company of unregenerate "legalists" preaching a convenant of "works"

instead of a convenant of grace and hindering the work of redemption. In this re-examination of the so-called Antinomian Controversy, importance is placed on the extent to which the Puritans sought to hold together divine sovereignty and human activity. 48 notes.      M. D. Dibert

## Ethnicity

582. Barnes, Ellis D. LAKE RONKONKOMA'S LOVE STORY. *Long Island Forum 1972 35(4): 76-78.* Retells the Montauk Indian legend of the end of human sacrifice to appease the Great Spirit of Lake Ronkonkoma on Long Island. Some years before the arrival of the white man, Woonanit, Wyandanch's fiance, was selected by the chiefs for sacrifice to keep the waters of the lake from rising. Wyandanch and 50 braves ran off with her. He told the tribe that he and his braves would stand in the lake with the water up to their lips. If the lake rose they would drown and appease the anger of the Great Spirit; but if the water level receded, then that would indicate that the Great Spirit did not wish human sacrifice. Needless to say, the lake waters receded. Undocumented, 2 illus.
     G. Kurland

583. Belig, Harry Baker. MADAME MONTOUR'S INDIAN VILLAGE. *Now and Then 1973 17(9): 393-395.* Madame Montour (ca. 1693-1753) was an interpreter in British-Indian negotiations (1711-53). Mentions the settlement of Montoursville by Indians.      S

584. Billings, Warren M. THE CASES OF FERNANDO AND ELIZABETH KEY: A NOTE ON THE STATUS OF BLACKS IN SEVENTEENTH-CENTURY VIRGINIA. *William and Mary Q. 1973 30(3): 467-474.* Two court cases in early Virginia shed light on the deteriorating status of Christian blacks. Two blacks sued for their freedom. Elizabeth Key won her freedom; Fernando did not. To avert expensive suits and to insure a permanent labor base, the colony subsequently outlawed baptism as an escape from slavery. Based on court and legislative records; 24 notes.      H. M. Ward

585. Brouwer, Merle G. MARRIAGE AND FAMILY LIFE AMONG BLACKS IN COLONIAL PENNSYLVANIA. *Pennsylvania Mag. of Hist. and Biog. 1975 99(3): 368-372.* The moral standards of white society in colonial America were not considered applicable to the black community. Marriage between Negroes had no legal status throughout the period; and, when it did occur, family life was often disrupted since slaves were usually sold individually. 21 notes.
     C. W. Olson

586. Grauman, Melody W. WOMEN AND CULTURE IN RUSSIAN AMERICA. *Am. West 1974 11(3): 24-31.* When the *promyshlenniki,* Russian fur hunters, began to arrive in the Aleutians about 1755, they seized female Aleut hostages demanding ransom in sea otter furs. This introduced the Russians to the native adaptive survival techniques. A Russian-native settlement was established that was more "nativized" than Russian. Russian wives of Russian merchants and officials in Alaska sought "to transplant the superficialities of Russian culture" on the promyshlenniki-native hybrid culture. When the Russian women finally departed in 1867, the "cultural shell" they had established crumbled. Remnants of the promyshlenniki cultural influence persisted. 8 illus., biblio.      D. L. Smith

587. Johnston, Jean. MOLLY BRANT: MOHAWK MATRON. *Ontario Hist. [Canada] 1964 56(2): 105-124.* In 1759 an upper class Mohawk, Molly Brant, became housekeeper for Sir William Johnson, beloved British Indian agent living with the Iroquois. Molly managed Johnson's large household establishment well, and she bore Johnson nine children. When Johnson died in 1774, Molly and her brother Joseph inherited his influence with the Six Nations Indians. Molly proved influential in keeping the confederacy largely on the British side during the American Revolutionary War. In 1796 Molly died with doubts that her people, who had lost their ancestral lands in the war, could rest secure in their cultural identity among the European civilizations.
     G. Emery

588. Lillard, Roy G. THE STORY OF NANCY WARD, 1738-1822. *Daughters of the Am. Revolution Mag. 1976 110(1): 42-43, 158.* Dis-

cusses the role of Tennessee pioneer and Cherokee Indian Nancy Ward in the American Revolution.

589. Mathur, Mary E. Fleming. THE BODY POLITY: IROQUOIS VILLAGE DEMOCRACY. *Indian Hist. 1975 8(1): 31-49.* In an almost literal translation of J. F. Lafitau's *Les Moeurs des Sauvages Ameriquain* (1724), the author excerpts information on the manners and customs of the early 18th-century Iroquois, concentrating on tribal democracy, the role of women in tribal government, crime and punishment, and tribal festivals. The origin and development of the Iroquois Confederation is also briefly examined. 25 notes.      E. D. Johnson

590. Matson, R. Lynn. PHILLIS WHEATLEY: SOUL SISTER? *Phylon 1972 33(3): 222-230.* Contradicts the critical position that Negro poet Phillis Wheatley (1753-84) lacked race consciousness.

591. Riley, Carroll L. BLACKS IN THE EARLY SOUTHWEST. *Ethnohistory 1972 19(3): 247-260.* Beginning with Esteban de Dorantes in 1539, there was a growing number of Blacks—both male and female—who entered the American Southwest during the 16th and 17th centuries. Who these Blacks were and their largely unheralded roles in the history of the Spanish Colonial Southwest are discussed on the basis of a survey of the ethnohistorical literature.      J

592. Smith, Eleanor. PHILLIS WHEATLEY: A BLACK PERSPECTIVE. *J. of Negro Educ. 1974 43(3): 401-407.* Poet of the American Revolution, Phillis Wheatley, was a slave who quasi-integrated with white society but did little for the black cause.

593. Willis, William S., Jr. PATRILINEAL INSTITUTIONS IN SOUTHEASTERN NORTH AMERICA. *Ethnohistory 1963 10(3): 250-269.* Reviews evidence of strong patrilineal institutions among the large tribes (Cherokee, Choctaw, Chickasaw, and Creeks) of the southeast interior during the 18th century. "Heretofore matriliny has been stressed in studies of this area for this century...possibly the entire subject has to be revaluated."      H. J. Graham

594. Wright, Martha R. BIJAH'S LUCE OF GUILFORD, VERMONT. *Negro Hist. Bull. 1965 28(7): 152-153, 159.* Lucy Terry Prince, wife of Obijah Prince of Guilford, Vermont, is credited with being the first American Negro poet. Her poem "Bars Fight" (here given in full) describes an Indian raid on Deerfield in 1746. When she attempted, in vain, to secure the admission of her son to Williams College by appearing before its Board, she was "one of the first American Negroes to attempt to break the color line in higher education." She won a case before the Supreme Court of the United States; her case against a neighbor's claim to some of their farm was handled by Isaac Tichenor who later became governor of Vermont. Lucy herself took over the arguments at length before the court in Vermont. Illus.      E. P. Stickney

## Social Problems

595. Axtell, James. THE VENGEFUL WOMEN OF MARBLEHEAD: ROBERT ROULES'S DEPOSITION OF 1677. *William and Mary Q. 1974 31(4): 647-652.* The hysteria and fear of Indians, generated by guerrilla raids during King Philip's War and Indian wars in Maine, led to murder by mutilation of two Indian captives at Marblehead by the women of the town, 15 July 1677. The deposition by Robert Roules, a mariner, to the General Court recounts the circumstances leading to the capture and murder of the Indians. Comments on the historical significance of the document. Based on Roules's deposition, transcribed from the Edward E. Ayer Collection at the Newberry Library, Chicago; 12 notes.      H. M. Ward

596. Bartlett, Albert L. THE STORY OF HANNAH DUSTON AND MARY NEFF. *Daughters of the Am. Revolution Mag. 1971 105(9): 806-809.* An account of the brave deeds performed by Hannah Duston, wife of Thomas Duston, and the nurse, Mrs. Mary Neff, who were captured, following an attack on the Duston home in Haverhill, Massachusetts, by a band of Indians on 15 March 1697. "With the remembrance of the dreadful things that had happened, the attack on her home, the brutal murder of her helpless infant, the uncertain fate of the

others of her family, the agony of the long march, the sight of other captives murdered on the way, and with the knowledge of the torture and fate that awaited her, Mrs. Duston planned escape." On 30 March 1697, 10 of the Indian captors were scalped and killed on Penacook Island, a few miles above Concord, New Hampshire. On 17 June 1874, a monument was dedicated there to commemorate this event.

D. D. Cameron

597. Bartlett, Albert L. THE STORY OF HANNAH DUSTON AND MARY NEFF. *Daughters of the Am. Revolution Mag. 1971 105(9): 806-809.* Tells the story of Hannah Duston and Mary Neff, two frontier residents who were captured by, and later escaped from, a group of Iroquois Indians.

S

598. Flaherty, David H. LAW AND THE ENFORCEMENT OF MORALS IN EARLY AMERICA. *Perspectives in Am. Hist. 1971 5: 203-253.* An examination of the historical relationship between law and morality enforcement, with particular emphasis on the American sexual code in the 17th and 18th centuries. Colonial Americans equated sin with crime, and colonial legislation reflected this belief. Immorality was punished because of the social problems and disturbances it caused. Yet when enforcement of morals became increasingly difficult, officials charged with law enforcement relaxed their effort. Concludes that the force of public opinion upheld moral law more effectively than the force of secular law and hypothesizes that by the late 18th century America was well on the way to separating criminal law from morality enforcement. 156 notes.

W. A. Wiegand

599. Greenberg, Douglas. PATTERNS OF CRIMINAL PROSECUTION IN EIGHTEENTH-CENTURY NEW YORK. *New York Hist. 1975 56(2): 133-153.* Discusses patterns of criminal prosecution among women, blacks, and descendants of original Dutch settlers living in 18th-century New York. Based on computer-assisted analysis of 5,300 criminal cases reported in court records during 1691-1776; 3 illus., 34 notes.

R. N. Lokken

600. Holdsworth, William K. ADULTERY OR WITCHCRAFT? A NEW NOTE ON AN OLD CASE IN CONNECTICUT. *New England Q. 1975 48(3): 394-409.* Elizabeth Johnson of Hartford, Connecticut, was convicted of a capital crime in 1650. Historians have mistakenly thought that the crime was witchcraft, but new evidence and reexamination of existing evidence indicate that Johnson was convicted, along with Thomas Newton, of adultery. Reviews the history of the case, including Newton's subsequent escape to New York, Johnson's release, and the history of adultery as a capital crime in Connecticut and New England. Based on primary and secondary sources; 45 notes.

B. C. Tharaud

601. Morse, Mary Harrower. MURDERESS OR HEROINE? *New-England Galaxy 1968 9(4): 40-45.* Hannah Dustin, captured in an Indian raid in Haverhill, Massachusetts, murdered her captors and escaped.

S

602. Parramore, Thomas C. THE SAGA OF "THE BEAR" AND THE "EVIL GENIUS." *Bull. of the Hist. of Medicine 1968 42(4): 321-331.* Colonial court records of North Carolina demonstrate the difficulties encountered by physicians in their ministrations to women patients.

S

603. Whitford, Kathryn. HANNAH DUSTIN: THE JUDGMENT OF HISTORY. *Essex Inst. Hist. Collections 1972 108(4): 304-325.* Discusses the captivity of Hannah Dustin in 1697, her subsequent return to her town, and the fact that neither she nor her home were ever attacked by Indians again.

# Culture, the Arts, and Recreation

604. Baker, Muriel L. SOME NEW ENGLAND CREWELWORK BED FURNITURE. *New-England Galaxy 1964 6(1): 29-36.* Describes early New England crewelwork bed hangings which are remarkable pieces of embroidery. The art was one brought from England and was lost during the late colonial period.

T. J. Farnham

605. Chudacoff, Nancy Fisher. WOMAN IN THE NEWS, 1762-1770 —SARAH UPDIKE GODDARD. *Rhode Island Hist. 1973 32(4): 99-105.* Sketches the life of Sarah Updike Goddard (ca 1700-1770), and her association with the weekly *Providence Gazette and Country Journal.* Based on a manuscript in the Providence Public Library, published documents, and secondary accounts.

P. J. Coleman

606. Corey, James R. MISS CHEER: AMERICAN ACTRESS, 1764-1768. *Res. Studies 1971 39(2): 137-143.* Discusses Margaret Cheer, who began acting with the American Company of Comedians in 1764 in Charles-Town, South Carolina, and ended her career in 1768 when she married the Right Honorable Lord Rosehill.

607. Crawford, Richard and McKay, David P. MUSIC IN MANUSCRIPT: A MASSACHUSETTS TUNE-BOOK OF 1782. *Pro. of the Am. Antiquarian Soc. 1974 84(1): 43-64.* "The characteristic musical publication of pre-federal America was the tune collection. . . . Music also circulated in manuscript. . . . The value of most eighteenth-century American manuscript tune collections lies simply in their existence as artifacts from an earlier age." However, Susanna (Sukey) Heath's "Collection from Sundry Authors" (1782) is significant in that its owner and her family history are known; the collection and pieces included are dated; it includes works of William Billings, foremost American composer of the time. Most of the pieces are American in origin, and of those pieces that were published, differences appear between the manuscript and printed versions. Illus., 28 notes.

B. L. Fenske

608. Cummins, Virginia Raymond. HANNAH JONES, HER WORK. *New Jersey Hist. Soc. Pro. 1964 82(1): 47-49.* On samplers. Illus.

S

609. Doggett, Joella. ANOTHER EIGHTEENTH-CENTURY INSTANCE OF ANNE BRADSTREET'S CONTINUING APPEAL. *Essex Inst. Hist. Collections 1975 111(2): 151-154.* Roger Wolcott, a Connecticut businessman, politician, and poet, quoted Bradstreet from memory in his private journal in 1755. Analyzes her influence on him. Based on secondary works, Wolcott's journal, and the poetry of Bradstreet and Wolcott; 7 notes.

R. M. Rollins

610. Hall, Peter Dobkin. WAS LUCINDA FOOTE YALE'S FIRST WOMAN STUDENT—IN 1783? *Yale Alumni Mag. 1975 38(6): 16-18.*

611. Isles, Duncan. THE LENNOX COLLECTION. *Harvard Lib. Bull. 1970 18(4): 317-344; 1971 19(1): 36-60; 19(2): 165-186; 19(4): 416-435.* Charlotte Lennox (ca. 1729-1804) was a London novelist memorable for the reflections in her fiction of her childhood spent in colonial New York. Reprints recently discovered letters to her from David Garrick, Samuel Johnson, Sir Joshua Reynolds, and Samuel Richardson written during 1750-99. Based on manuscripts in the Houghton Library; 233 notes.

L. Smith

612. Miller, Walter V. THE VAN ALEN HOUSE OF KINDERHOOK. *Halve Maen 1963 38(3): 7-8, 14.* Settling in and near Kinderhook (New York) in the late 17th and early 18th centuries, Dutch pioneer families left a permanent imprint upon the life and culture of the region. The area became the locale for some of Washington Irving's finest writings. The Van Alen House was built in 1737 and served as the home of an attractive young maiden. She became the prototype of Katrina Van Tassel, one of the key characters in *The Legend of Sleepy Hollow.*

B. T. Quinten

613. Stanford, Ann. ANNE BRADSTREET: DOGMATIST AND REBEL. *New England Q. 1966 39(3): 373-389.* Examines Anne Bradstreet's writing within the framework of the concurrent existence of con-

flicting tendencies in American life and literature. For example, she accepted the Puritan dogma of male supremacy over the female, but her poems also demonstrate some rebellion toward this concept. The conflict between the temporal and the spiritual is represented as well. In short, she was a harbinger for later American writers who would express what has been called the duplicity of the American literary mind. 13 notes.
W. G. Morgan

614. Terrace, Lisa Cooke. ENGLISH AND NEW ENGLAND EMBROIDERY: SOME RECENT ACCESSIONS. *Mus. of Fine Arts, Boston, Bull. 1964 62(328): 65-80.* A discussion of embroidery practices in the 16th and 17th centuries in England. "Elaborate embroidery patterns were drawn by professional designers and then were worked by the women of the house." There are detailed descriptions of the more recently acquired items, which include: motifs for appliqué work, an embroidered valance, an embroidered curtain, an embroidered chair seat cover, an embroidered picture, and a man's cap. Also included is "the only surviving pattern for needlework known to have existed in New England in the early 18th century." Illus., 19 notes.
J. M. Hawes

615. Waller, Jennifer R. "MY HAND A NEEDLE BETTER FITS": ANNE BRADSTREET AND WOMEN POETS IN THE RENAIS-SANCE. *Dalhousie R. [Canada] 1974 54(3): 436-450.* Argues that the American Anne Bradstreet precedes the Countess of Winchelsea (1666-1720) by 50 years as the first woman to write poetry in English which no man could have written. Despite considerable prejudice against education for women, by 1559 it was possible for William Bercher to list a number of contemporary women who had published both scholarly and popular books. Most prominent women poets of Anne Bradstreet's time did not regard themselves as greater or even as great as men, but did "labor to come in second." 34 notes.
C. Held

616. White, Margaret E. SAMPLER, EXAMPLER, SAM-CLOTH. *New Jersey Hist. Soc. Pro. 1965 83(1): 45-48.* In the 17th century samplers were worked in linen with colored silks and metal threads which had come in from the Levant. The designs recorded were taken from the borders of illuminated missals as well as from pattern books and those handed down from mother to daughter. Smaller size samplers were a task set for childish fingers. Few are found in America before the 18th century, but they are more pictorial than those made in England. Several examples are described and pictured from the collections of the New Jersey Historical Society. Four plates.
E. P. Stickney

# 4. The United States 1783-1865

## Economic Sphere

617. Brigham, Loriman S., ed. AN INDEPENDENT VOICE: A MILL GIRL FROM VERMONT SPEAKS HER MIND. *Vermont Hist. 1973 41(3): 142-146.* A Clinton, Massachusetts, textile operative in 1851 writes her schoolmarm cousin at "the Harbor" about her hard work weaving the cloth around wagon cushions, her reading, and her disdain for church-going hypocrites. Editor's foreword.
T. D. S. Bassett

618. Brown, Frank. NEW LIGHT ON "MOUNTAIN MARY." *Pennsylvania Folklife 1966 15(3): 10-15.* An account of "Mountain Mary" Young, a German farmer and doctor in Pike Township, reprinted from the *Reading Eagle,* 1890.
S

619. Carroll, Rosemary F. MARGARET CLARK GRIFFIS, PLANTATION TEACHER. *Tennessee Hist. Q. 1967 26(3): 295-303.* Margaret Clark Griffis was raised in a prosperous Philadelphia family. She was highly religious and a serious student, but enjoyed social activities. When her family became poor after the 1857 crash, she served a year as a tutor on a West Tennessee plantation. She enjoyed her year of teaching, liked the South, and was sympathetic toward slavery. Based on her diaries and letters; 21 notes.
J. H. Broussard

620. Currie, Mrs. James N. A TEACHER AND HER STUDENTS: MY MOTHER, ELLEN PECK, AND HER ONE-ROOM SCHOOLHOUSE IN EAST MONTPELIER. *Vermont Hist. 1971 39(1): 55-61.* Describes the interior of a one-room schoolhouse, with slate blackboard, disease-spreading gourd cup, the teacher's preference for quill over steel pens, the three R's, corporal punishment, moralism, and the respect engendered, from diaries, letters of Civil War soldiers, and schoolbooks.
T. D. S. Bassett

621. Finley, Linda. NOTES FROM THE DIARY OF SUSAN E. FOREMAN. *Chronicles of Oklahoma 1969/70 47(4): 388-397.* Notations consist primarily of Foreman's life as a school teacher in Webber's Falls, Oklahoma, 1862-63.

622. Gleason, Gene. A MERE WOMAN. *Am. Heritage 1972 24(1): 80-84.* Hannah Adams (1755-1831) was the first American-born woman to publish a book under her own name. She was probably also the first American to become a professional writer. Discusses her various efforts, usually works of history. Illus.
D. L. Smith

623. Kull, Nell W. "I CAN NEVER BE HAPPY THERE IN AMONG SO MANY MOUNTAINS" - THE LETTERS OF SALLY RICE. *Vermont Hist. 1970 38(1): 49-57.* Sarah Rice (b. 1821) was the youngest child of the town clerk and granddaughter of the first settler of Somerset, Vermont. Seven of her letters home between the ages of 17 and 28 reflect her life as a domestic servant in Union Village, New York, Barre and Millbury, Massachusetts, and for part of 1845 as a weaver in a Thompson, Connecticut, cotton mill. Literate though home-taught, frugal, and fond of Methodist meetings, home, and country life, in 1847 she married James M. Alger, 22, engineer on the Boston and Albany Railway, and lived in Worcester.
T. D. S. Bassett

624. Lerner, Gerda. THE LADY AND THE MILL GIRL: CHANGES IN THE STATUS OF WOMEN IN THE AGE OF JACKSON. *MidContinent Am. Studies J. 1969 10(1): 5-15.* Examines the Jacksonian period in America as it affected the status of women, considering factors of environment, frontier conditions, and sex ratio. With industrialization women's political status deteriorated relative to advances made by men. The professionalization of medicine and law eliminated opportunities for women, and fewer opportunities occurred in business and the retail trades. In contrast, the professionalization of teaching and nursing did not result in the elimination of women from these fields, as both were characterized by a shortage of labor and were low paying. The 1830's saw the cult of the lady as advancing prosperity made it possible for middle class women to aspire to a status formerly reserved for upper-class women. Lower-class women joined men in their struggle for economic advancement and protective labor legislation, while wealthier women formed organizations for women's rights.
P. T. Herman

625. Luckingham, Bradford. BENEVOLENCE IN EMERGENT SAN FRANCISCO: A NOTE ON IMMIGRANT LIFE IN THE URBAN FAR WEST. *Southern California Q. 1973 55(4): 431-443.* From almost the inception of San Francisco as a booming urban center of gold rush California, various groups banded together for mutual assistance. Organized along national, religious, or occupational lines, these benevolent associations advised newcomers, provided information about friends and relatives, gave immediate financial aid, maintained clinics, obtained jobs for the unemployed, and provided transportation to the mines or back home. Typical organizations included the French Benevolent Society, Masons, Odd Fellows, Young Men's Christian Association, and the San Francisco Ladies' Protection and Relief Society. The benevolent associations resembled the efforts of groups in older American cities, with the groups attempting to provide for the welfare of their members. Based on primary and secondary sources; 21 notes.
A. Hoffman

626. McDowell, John E. MADAME LA FRAMBOISE. *Michigan Hist. 1972 56(4): 271-286.* Madeline La Framboise, born the daughter of a French trader and an Ottawa girl in 1780, became a prosperous outfitter following her husband's death in 1806. Securing furs from Ottawas in the Grand River Valley each winter and outfitting on Mackinac Island each summer, she proved so successful that the American Fur Company took her into its organization in 1818 in order to eliminate her competition. Benefactor to church and community following her retirement to Mackinac Island in 1821, she became a living legend long before her death in 1846. Based on primary and secondary sources; illus., photo, 76 notes.
D. W. Johnson

627. Melder, Keith E. WOMAN'S HIGH CALLING: THE TEACHING PROFESSION IN AMERICA, 1830-1860. *Am. Studies [Lawrence, KS] 1972 13(2): 19-32.* The influx of women into the teaching profession was part of the educational reform movement and the expansion of educational opportunities of the 1820's-30's. Women and the values of womanhood were associated with the teaching profession. Since women teachers received very low wages, towns and institutions vigorously recruited them. Primary and secondary sources; 40 notes.
J. Andrew

628. Thompson, Agnes L. NEW ENGLAND MILL GIRLS. *New-England Galaxy 1974 16(2): 43-49.* Describes life in the woolen and cotton mills of Lowell, Massachusetts, during the 1840's and 1850's. Farm girls gained economic independence by working for a few years before marriage, but were closely supervised in the mill, boarding house, and community, and had to cope with long hours, low wages, and limited social and educational opportunities. By 1857 competition forced their replacement by a permanent industrial working class of Irish and French Canadians. 6 illus.
P. C. Marshall

629. Wolfe, Allis Rosenberg, ed. LETTERS OF A LOWELL MILL GIRL AND FRIENDS: 1845-1846. *Labor Hist. 1976 17(1): 96-102.* Presents five letters of a Lowell mill girl, Harriet Hanson Robinson, as a reflection of the upbringing, attitudes, and desires of working women in 1845-46. Letters are from the Robinson collection in the Schlesinger Library, Radcliffe College. 3 notes.
L. L. Athey

630. Wright, Helena. THE UNCOMMON MILL GIRLS OF LOWELL. *Hist. Today [Great Britain] 1973 23(1): 10-19.* Describes the life and working conditions of women textile workers at the Boston Manufacturing Company at Lowell, an outgrowth of the Waltham experiment, 1813-50.

# Social Sphere

## General

**631.** Baker, Leonard. THE LOCK OF HAIR. *Am. Hist. Illus. 1971 6(5): 12-21.* Discusses the courtship and marriage of John Marshall and Polly Ambler. Marshall progressed from a successful Richmond lawyer to Chief Justice of the Supreme Court. Letters from John to Polly reveal him to be a warm man whose 50 years of devotion to his wife made one of the "most tender love stories in our history." Primary and secondary sources; 7 illus. 　　　　　　　　　　　D. Dodd

**632.** Chevigny, Bell Gale. THE LONG ARM OF CENSORSHIP: MYTH-MAKING IN MARGARET FULLER'S TIME AND OUR OWN. *Signs 1976 2(2): 450-460.* Margaret Fuller's intellectual colleagues and close personal friends James Freeman Clarke, William Henry Channing, and Ralph Waldo Emerson felt it their duty to protect her reputation as they edited her papers for their *Memoirs of Margaret Fuller Ossoli.* The biggest culprit was Channing, who softened her autonomous spirituality, her clearly-stated sensuality, embellished her role as devoted mother, and clarified her marriage to Ossoli. Later biographers sustained the myth that Fuller's relationship with Ossoli grounded her in the womanly ideal of monogamous devotion by ignoring her attraction to other men, openly expressed in her letters from Italy. Based on letters, manuscripts, and biographies; 20 notes. 　　　　　　　　　　　J. Gammage

**633.** Conner, Paul. PATRIARCHY: OLD WORLD AND NEW. *Am. Q. 1965 17(1): 48-62.* Compares the writings of Sir Robert Filmer, the Kentish codifier of authoritarian familialism (1588-1653), with those of the American George Fitzhugh, an ante bellum barrister from Virginia. "Only time and space separated Filmer and Fitzhugh." If they differed at all it was in Fitzhugh's attempt to gild the patriarch (and Southern society) with benevolent paternalism and a touch of liberalism. Fitzhugh's hedging marked an uneasy surveillance over Negro slaves and Southern women. His defense of paternalism could easily be borrowed in a later day when bureaucracy and organization would call for a multiplication of paternalistic control. Documented, 69 notes. 　　R. S. Pickett

**634.** Cross, Helen Reeder. "I HATE AMERICA": FRANCES TROLLOPE. *Hist. Today [Great Britain] 1970 20(3): 163-173.* "I hate America" was the remark of Mrs. Frances Trollope (1780-1863) in her account of the *Domestic Manners of the Americans,* published in England, in 1832, upon the conclusion of her nearly four-year stay in America. *Domestic Manners* "sets forth the untrimmed truth about this young new nation as an Englishwoman saw it a century and a third ago." The book was one of the most "shocking" of the age. Discusses its author and her travels in America. Recounts the reception of the book in America and Britain, the debates of the critics, and the political reverberations in the English Parliament. Mrs. Trollope was a woman of "intrepid courage, uncompromising honesty, and valiant spirit;" writing her first book at age 52, she went on to write 114 more before she died 33 years later. Illus. 　　　　　　　　　　　L. A. Knafla

**635.** Giffen, Jerena E. MISSOURI WOMEN IN THE 1820'S. *Missouri Hist. Rev. 1971 65(4): 478-504.* Missouri had two divergent family styles - the French and the American. The French placed the mother at the head of the house; the Americans treated the mother as little more than a fellow-worker who often took second place to the men in the family. 　　　　　　　　　　　W. F. Zornow

**636.** Glasco, Laurence A. THE LIFE CYCLES AND HOUSEHOLD STRUCTURE OF AMERICAN ETHNIC GROUPS: IRISH, GERMANS, AND NATIVE-BORN WHITES IN BUFFALO, NEW YORK 1855. *J. of Urban Hist. 1975 1(3): 339-364.* A study of the household structure of different ethnic groups produced evidence that the following trends existed: foreign-born women often became domestics, thus reducing the size of the family living at home; German girls remained domestics for shorter periods of time and married earlier; native-born women were the last to leave home, and German males left home earliest; the Irish were the least apt to be homeowners; and the native-born population most frequently boarded with family. 6 figs., 11 notes. 　　　　　　　　　　　S. S. Sprague

**637.** Griffin, Inez H. MARRIAGE AND DEATH NOTICES FROM THE CITY GAZETTE, 1827. *South Carolina Hist. Mag. 1966 67(1): 46-49.* Continued from a previous article. Short notices, for October through December, of marriages and deaths in Charleston. 　　　　　　　　　　　D. J. Engler

**638.** Heineman, Helen. FRANCES TROLLOPE IN THE NEW WORLD: "DOMESTIC MANNERS OF THE AMERICANS." *Am. Q. 1969 21(3): 544-559.* Regards Mrs. Trollope's account of her nearly four-year stay in antebellum United States as the best analysis of American life and customs. Using the anecdote as her basic foundation, Trollope fashioned a skilled rendering of the daily scenes which she most intimately knew, e.g., western America. *Domestic Manners of the Americans* (1832) is sharpest in its rendering of the specifics of daily life in Cincinnati, Ohio, and of local speech patterns. The further she departed from her Cincinnati observations, the less sure she was of her material and her work degenerated into the standard genre of foreign traveller's account. While Trollope's emphasis on manners was central to the precision of her observations of American society, her fastidiousness prevented her from understanding the egalitarian sources of its strength. Citations from *Domestic Manners of the Americans* plus accounts of Trollope's contemporaries. 　　　　　　　　　　　R. S. Pickett

**639.** Heineman, Helen L. "STARVING IN THAT LAND OF PLENTY": NEW BACKGROUNDS TO FRANCES TROLLOPE'S *DOMESTIC MANNERS OF THE AMERICANS. Am. Q. 1972 24(5): 643-660.* After family financial reverses in England, Frances Milton Trollope (1780-1863) came to America as a recruit for the utopian colony in Nashoba, Tennessee, and to place her son Henry in a good position. After disenchantment with Nashoba and a business failure in Cincinnati, Trollope decided to write a book about her travels. Based on newly discovered letters, other primary and secondary sources; 48 notes. 　　　　　　　　　　　W. D. Piersen

**640.** Hendrix, Mrs. Thomas D. MARRIAGE AND DEATH NOTICES IN THE NEW ORLEANS CHRISTIAN ADVOCATE, 1851-1855. *J. of Mississippi Hist. 1964 26(1): 56-68.* This fourth installment covers the period from 30 September 1854 to 15 April 1855. Continued from parts I-III, 1963 25(2): 139-150, (3): 208-221, and (4): 284-296. Although the materials are from a New Orleans Methodist periodical, persons included are not exclusively Methodists or Louisianians. 　　　　　　　　　　　D. C. James

**641.** Hendrix, Mrs. Thomas D. MARRIAGE AND DEATH NOTICES IN THE NEW ORLEANS CHRISTIAN ADVOCATE, 1851-1855. *J. of Mississippi Hist. 1963 25(2): 139-150, (3): 208-221, and (4): 284-296.* Part I. Lists marriage and death notices as they appeared in the *New Orleans Christian Advocate,* an official Methodist weekly published from 1850 to 1946. This first installment of the 1851-55 material covers the period from 8 Feburary 1851 to 3 July 1852. Marriage and death notices of many persons of faiths other than Methodist and of persons of many areas other than New Orleans are included. The Mississippi Department of Archives and History is microfilming the statistics from the 1851-1946 issues. Part II. Covers the period from 10 July 1852 to 5 November 1853. Part III. Covers the period from 12 November 1853 to 23 September 1854. 　　　　　　　　　　　D. C. James

**642.** Hendrix, Mrs. Thomas D. MARRIAGE AND DEATH NOTICES IN THE NEW ORLEANS CHRISTIAN ADVOCATE, 1851-1855. *J. of Mississippi Hist. 1964 26(2): 158-171.* Continued from 1963 25(2): 139-150, (3): 208-221, and (4): 284-296. Includes marriage and death notices as they appeared in the *New Orleans Christian Advocate,* an official Methodist weekly which was published from 1850 to 1946. This fifth and final installment of the 1851-1855 material covers the period of 21 April 1855 to 29 December 1855. Marriage and death notices of many persons of faiths other than Methodist and of persons from many areas other than the New Orleans vicinity are included. 　　　　　　　　　　　D. C. James

**643.** Horwitz, Richard P. ARCHITECTURE AND CULTURE: THE MEANING OF THE LOWELL BOARDING HOUSE. *Am. Q. 1973 25(1): 64-82.* The early Lowellites' image of home as a rural dwelling of permanence, comfort, and kinship mediated their perceptions of factory boarding houses. The boarding houses of Lowell, Massachusetts, were poor imitations of the rural cottages the mill girls called home. Boasts about the houses' good qualities appear less than sincere. Primary and secondary sources; 41 notes, biblio.     W. D. Piersen

644. Karras, Bill J. TWO CUBANS IN THE UNITED STATES: THE MILANÉS LETTERS: 1848-1849. *Rev. Interamericana Rev. [Puerto Rico] 1972 2(1): 80-89.* José Jacinto Milanés and Federico Milanés, two brothers who occupied an important literary position in Cuba, found the United States an interesting and bewildering country. Predisposed to liking the United States because of their desire to modernize Cuba along the path taken by the northern republic, the two travelers reveal first impressions of American cities, women, and national character. Based on 51 letters; 6 notes.     J. Lewis

645. LaRochefoucaul\, Edmée de. LE VOYAGE AUX ÉTATS-UNIS DE LA ROCHEFOUCAULD-LIANCOURT [La Rochefoucauld-Liancourt's voyage to the United States]. *Nouvelle Rev. des Deux Mondes [France] 1975 (5): 346-355.* Engaging extracts from French philanthropist and émigré duc de La Rochefoucauld-Liancourt's (1747-1827) *Voyage dans les États-Unis d'Amérique* (8 v., 1799), giving his impressions of George Washington, prisons, agriculture and husbandry, Indians, Negroes, and the position of women during his 1794-95 flight from France. Illus.     R. K. Adams

646. Maloney, Mary R. GENERAL REYNOLDS AND "DEAR KATE". *Am. Heritage 1963 15(1): 62-65.* A survey of Catherine Hewitt's relations with the family of General John Reynolds from his death to the last records of her life. After he was killed at Gettysburg, it was learned that General Reynolds, a supposedly confirmed bachelor, had planned to marry her. Undocumented, illus.     C. R. Allen, Jr.

647. McGovern, James R. JOHN PIERCE: YANKEE SOCIAL HISTORIAN. *Old-Time New England 1974 64(3/4): 77-86.* Reverend John Pierce preserved a detailed record of New England men, institutions, social activities, and family economics during 1800-50. Although extensive and available, the Pierce manuscripts have been relatively ignored by scholars. The author offers samples of their value in the study of 19th-century New England social history. 59 notes.     R. N. Lokken

648. Melder, Keith. LADIES BOUNTIFUL: ORGANIZED WOMEN'S BENEVOLENCE IN EARLY 19TH-CENTURY AMERICA. *New York Hist. 1967 48(3): 231-254.* Surveys various women's benevolent associations in the eastern part of the United States, from 1800 to the 1830's, and finds that they represented the female counterpart of the pervasive American desire to form voluntary associations for the accomplishment of a specific social goal. Working for the propagation of evangelical Christianity, for the abolition of prostitution and slavery, and for the amelioration of the condition of the poor, the helpless, and the insane, the women's benevolent movement was an important factor in the reformism of the Jacksonian era. Moreover, by giving women an important role in the struggle for social betterment, the benevolent societies helped spur feminism and the later movement for women's rights. Based on primary and secondary sources; 81 notes.     G. Kurland

649. Steer, Margery W. PARSON BLAKE AND THE FARMER'S WIFE. *Am. Heritage 1965 16(4): 42-45.* From 1850 to 1857 five editions of John Laurus Blake's *The Farmer's Everyday Book* were published. The author notes the great reliance on the book by her great-grandmother during the Civil War. Paging through the well-worn volume of advice to the farmer's wife on social customs, manners, operation of a farm, personal care, and household tasks presents an array of information on 19th-century rural life, emphasizing the comparatively elevated status of women in America.     J. D. Filipiak

650. Taylor, William R. and Lasch, Christopher. TWO "KINDRED SPIRITS": SORORITY AND FAMILY IN NEW ENGLAND, 1839-1846. *New England Q. 1963 36(1): 23-41.* An essay in social history analyzing an early 19th-century New England phenomenon, in which women sought a fulfillment in literature which they could no longer find as wives and mothers. Luella J. B. Case found the "kindred spirit," which her preacher and entrepreneur husband lacked, in a correspondence with Sarah Edgarton, who married in 1846, thereby ending the sense of a "kindred spirit" with Mrs. Case. Analyzes this relationship as an illustration of the beginning of that restlessness which initiated the feminist movement. Compares this situation to the plot of Henry James' *The Bostonians.* 31 notes.     R. V. Ritter

651. Wells, Laurence K., coll. MARRIAGE AND OBITUARY NOTICES FROM *THE PIONEER AND YORKVILLE WEEKLY ADVERTISER,* 1823-1824. *South Carolina Hist. Mag. 1971 72(2): 111-114.*

652. Wells, Laurence K., coll. MARRIAGE AND OBITUARY NOTICES FROM THE *YORKVILLE ENCYCLOPEDIA. South Carolina Hist. Mag. 1971 72(4): 234-235.*

653. Wells, Laurence K., coll. MARRIAGE AND OBITUARY NOTICES FROM THE *YORKVILLE COMPILER,* 1840-41. *South Carolina Hist. Mag. 1971 72(3): 179-183.*

654. Welter, Barbara. THE MERCHANT'S DAUGHTER: A TALE FROM LIFE. *New England Q. 1969 42(1): 3-22.* Caroline Healey's career illustrates several cultural patterns typical of a New England girl in the 19th century. Her father was an importer of moderate fame in Boston. She grew up as a thoughtful, introspective child, became acquainted with Theodore Parker and Margaret Fuller, and became by her own definition a Transcendentalist interested in social reform. Her views on feminine nature made her think of herself as peculiarly sensitive, noble, and self-sacrificing. She believed that her proper sphere was in the home or holding a genteel occupation such as teaching, and that her proper role was to counsel misguided men. Following her father's sudden business failure, Miss Healey was urged by many to make a virtue of her distress and to find nobility of character in adversity, but she instead became embittered. 38 notes.     K. B. West

## Marriage and the Family

655. Blumin, Stuart M. RIP VAN WINKLE'S GRANDCHILDREN: FAMILY AND HOUSEHOLD IN THE HUDSON VALLEY 1800-1860. *J. of Urban Hist. 1975 1(3): 293-315.* Troy, Kingston, and Marlborough represent industrial, commercial, and agricultural towns respectively. Concludes that similarities in family characteristics among the three—household size, boarding houses as a transient experience, and four-fifths of the population living in nuclear families—outweigh the differences. 11 tables, 20 notes.     S. S. Sprague

656. Bridges, William E. FAMILY PATTERNS AND SOCIAL VALUES IN AMERICA, 1825-1875. *Am. Q. 1965 17(1): 3-11.* Notes the absence of sound historical research and the presence of persistent stereotypes. The "closely-knit, stable, patriarchal, self-sustaining, well-disciplined family group" was a nostalgic construction sharply contrasting with the actuality observed by astute 19th-century writers. American parents actually socialized their children for assertive independent roles; such roles did not call for training in self-control and self-denial. The image of the family as a haven from strife also conflicted with the practice of utilizing the family as a training ground for the marketplace. Documented, 27 notes.     R. S. Pickett

657. Goeldner, Paul. THE ARCHITECTURE OF EQUAL COMFORTS: POLYGAMISTS IN UTAH. *Historic Preservation 1972 24(1): 14-17.* Discusses the architecture adopted by polygamous Mormon families in Utah. Examples are few and usually unpretentious. In Midway are two houses built by John Watkins, an English convert and builder who had three wives. The first house contained three apartments, and his first wife continued to live there after the second house was finished. Built about 1868 of soft brick and symmetrical in design, the second house was so admired that Watkins and Moroni Blood, the carpenter who helped him, were commissioned to build several similar houses in Midway. Another example is the house built by Samuel Pierce Hoyt in Hoytsville in 1863. Mentions two of the houses used by Brigham Young and his many wives. They are the Beehive House (1853-55) and the adjoining Lion House (1856). Some houses contained "polygamy pits" - hiding places used to escape US marshals. Photos.     J. M. Hawes

658. Goodman, Paul. ETHICS AND ENTERPRISE: THE VALUES OF A BOSTON ELITE, 1800-1860. *Am. Q. 1966 18(3): 437-451.* Investigates the antebellum Boston aristocratic value system and provides numerous examples of how it operated within a tightly interwoven kinship network. The ideal merchant "prince" possessed wealth plus the personal virtues of the Greek philosopher kings. He also cultivated the arts, supported charities, and assumed the role of community leader. Presumably, the "Good Merchant" transcended countinghouse values; but he often found the thrill of economic success stronger than cultural rewards. The greatest menace to personal achievement within the system was "avarice," and the greatest virtue was "personal responsibility." The total system was buttressed by the strong extended family ties present in Boston society. Family not only served as an economic asset but also as a means of moral restraint against "an excessively acquisitive spirit." Even though threatened by incoming economic and social change, the proper Bostonian continued to hue to a standard of moderation in his various spheres of influence; he shunned the "evils of speculation" and clung to a conservative ethic. 80 notes.                R. S. Pickett

659. Hogeland, Ronald W. CHARLES HODGE, THE ASSOCIATION OF GENTLEMEN AND ORNAMENTAL WOMANHOOD: 1825-1855. *J. of Presbyterian Hist. 1975 53(3): 239-255.* Depicts Princeton University scholar Dr. Charles Hodge's attitude toward women. At a time of considerable fervor for improving the status of the American women, Hodge, as Professor of Theology and editor of *The Biblical Repertory and Princeton Review,* emphasized "ornamental womanhood." Princeton gentlemen of Hodge's time did not take seriously social reforms such as the feminists, particularly Charles G. Finney, offered. For the Association of Gentlemen male relationships were of utmost importance, while women were at best an appendage to the central drama of life. Based on the writings of Hodge; 50 notes.
H. M. Parker, Jr.

660. Holsinger, M. Paul. HENRY M. TELLER AND THE EDMUNDS-TUCKER ACT. *Colorado Mag. 1971 48(1): 1-14.* Anti-Mormonism came to a climax in the Edmunds-Tucker Act (1887). Polygamy was the most important of the many causes of opposition to the Mormons. In 1885 Republican Senator George Franklin Edmunds of Vermont introduced a severe bill into the Senate which provided for dissolution of plural marriages, the forced testimony of wives against their husbands, abrogation of woman suffrage in Utah Territory, and abolition of the corporate structure of the Church of Jesus Christ of Latter Day Saints. One of the few Senators to openly oppose the bill was Henry Moore Teller of Colorado. He did not support polygamy, but felt the Edmunds bill was illegal and unconstitutional. As Teller feared, the Act was followed by persecution and anger. Eventually the Mormons bowed to Federal law and in 1890 "the doctrinal sanction of polygamy officially ended." There is no evidence that Teller ever regretted his stand on the Edmunds-Tucker Act. His stand did not hurt his career because he was returned repeatedly to the Senate. Illus., 47 notes.                O. H. Zabel

661. Ivins, Stanley S. NOTES ON MORMON POLYGAMY. *Utah Hist. Q. 1967 35(4): 309-321.* Concludes that while certain leaders such as Joseph Smith and Brigham Young were enthusiastic protagonists of and participants in plural marriage, the great majority of Mormon men were not and that the experiment was not a satisfactory test of plurality of wives as a social system.                S. L. Jones

662. Lantz, Herman R.; Keyes, Jane; and Schultz, Martin. THE AMERICAN FAMILY IN THE PREINDUSTRIAL PERIOD: FROM BASE LINES IN HISTORY TO CHANGE. *Am. Sociol. R. 1975 40(1): 21-36.* This research parallels two earlier investigations of preindustrial American family patterns during the periods of 1741-1794 and 1794-1825. The present investigation involves a content analysis of magazines for the third period, 1825-1850. Special attention is given to power patterns between husband and wife, romantic love, motivations for marriage, and advocated and actual sanctions implemented toward individuals involved in premarital and extramarital sexual relationships. The results suggest a marked increase in the power of the woman. Romantic love and personal happiness emerge as important criteria in mate selection. It is suggested that during 1825-1850 magazine content indicates a significant move from a traditional to a more emancipated family with new alternatives. The limitations of these findings are discussed and include the problem of identifying the precise period in which industriali-

zation in America emerged and the implications which this difficulty poses for the interpretation of our data. The special problems of causal analysis in understanding family change are also noted.                A

663. Lantz, Herman R.; Schmitt, Raymond L.; and Herman, Richard. THE PREINDUSTRIAL FAMILY IN AMERICA: A FURTHER EXAMINATION OF EARLY MAGAZINES. *Am. J. of Sociol. 1973 79(3): 566-588.* "This research parallels a previous investigation of the authors of preindustrial American family patterns during the 1741-91 period. The present investigation involves a content analysis of colonial magazines for 1794-1825. Special attention is given to power patterns, types of attitudes between the sexes, actions toward premarital and extramarital sex involvement, and motivations for entering the marital relationship. The results concerning overt power among males and females that could be subjected to statistical examination in both studies exhibited an almost identical pattern. There was evidence of general existent and advocated overt male power, although such male power was mediated by other forms of female power as follows: there was evidence of existent overt female power and subtle female power in both courtship and the home. There was also evidence of advocated mutual cooperation between the sexes and extended role activities of the female. This latter trend in the direction of status and power of the women in the 1794-1825 period shows a general change over the period of the earlier study. The evidence regarding romantic love in the fictional material occurred to a greater extent than in our first study. The nonfictional discussions of romantic love and motivations were noticeably less frequent in this study than in the prior study. There were very few direct or indirect discussions of sexual standards. This contrasts with the results of our previous study. It is suggested that the family during the period 1794-1825 was influenced by ongoing internal structural changes, the consequences of the conditions of settlement in America, and humanistic and ideological beliefs which had their roots both in Europe and America. These influences are explored along with their implications for the analysis of changing family structures in historic perspective."                J

664. Laslett, Barbara. HOUSEHOLD STRUCTURE ON AN AMERICAN FRONTIER: LOS ANGELES, CALIFORNIA, IN 1850. *Am. J. of Sociol. 1975 81(1): 109-128.* Based on individual United States federal census schedules, this paper reports on the way in which economic and demographic variables relate to different types of household organization in Los Angeles in 1850. While the findings confirm the results of other recent research that the nuclear family predominated in preindustrial societies, they also emphasize the need to focus on variation rather than on modality in order to understand household organization. Methodological problems of working with this kind of data are discussed, as are the implications of the results for the study of social change.
J

665. Lecompte, Janet. JULES AND ISABELLE DE MUN. *Missouri Hist. Soc. Bull. 1969 26(1): 24-31.* Discusses the marriage of Jules and Isabelle De Mun, their respective families, and the unsuccessful career of Jules De Mun as a fur trader and St. Louis businessman. After 1831 De Mun was a US Commissioner engaged in handling French and Spanish land grant questions. He subsequently became a county official in St. Louis. Reproduces a letter written by De Mun, in 1816, while he was engaged in one of his most disastrous fur-trading ventures. Based on De Mun's journal (previously published), secondary works, and manuscript materials held by the Kansas and Missouri Historical Societies; 28 notes.                H. T. Lovin

666. Leet, Don R. THE DETERMINANTS OF THE FERTILITY TRANSITION IN ANTEBELLUM OHIO. *J. of Econ. Hist. 1976 36(2): 359-378.* The cross-sectional and secular variations in the fertility of the white population in pre-Civil War Ohio are analyzed with special regard to the role of population pressure in conditioning these patterns and trends. Other factors, such as urbanization, education, cultural heritage, and the sex ratio, all of which are often cited as major explanatory variables during the demographic transition are also introduced. Although each of these variables is shown to have some impact, none can account for more than a minor proportion of the variance in human fertility. It appears that the major force affecting both inter-county fertility and the secular trend for the state was the variation in the degree of population pressure as measured by the average assessed value of an acre of non-urban land.                J

667. Mayo, Lida. MISS ADAMS IN LOVE. *Am. Heritage 1965 16(2): 36-39, 80-89.* When John Adams became the first American minister to England, he took his daughter Abigail and Mrs. Adams to London with him. The romances of the charming young lady were ended by her marriage to Colonel William Stephens Smith, the secretary to the legation who married the "boss's daughter." A 10-page portfolio on London accompanies the article.                                    J. D. Filipiak

668. Meyer, Mary K. GENEALOGICA MARYLANDIA: REVEREND LEWIS RICHARDS' MARRIAGE RECORDS, 1784-1790. *Maryland Hist. Mag. 1975 70(3): 311-314.* Manuscript 690 of the Maryland Historical Society is Reverend Lewis Richards' marriage ledger for the First Baptist Church of Baltimore and contains listings of all marriages he performed from 1784 until his retirement in 1818. His successor, Reverend Stephen P. Hill, continued to keep the ledger for 1835-69, the last 15 years of which he spent in Washington. Transcribes only a small portion of these records, December 1784 to 31 December 1789.
G. J. Bobango

669. Modell, John. FAMILY AND FERTILITY ON THE INDIANA FRONTIER, 1820. *Am. Q. 1971 23(5): 615-634.* A statistical study of the relative fertility factor in population growth in relation to both rural and urban environments as reflected in the 1820 census data for the Indiana frontier. Findings: "1) The notion of 'urbanization' has a meaning for the agricultural frontier that extends to quite small places, but its meaning is far from completely understood. 2) While fertility at the state level varied regularly with the frontier, . . . on a lower level it was subject to a variety of factors related complexly to the frontier, notably age at family formation, economic context—both personal and regional—and degree of urbanization. 3) Family structure was overwhelmingly nuclear in all areas on the Indiana frontier. What differences did exist do not seem to have been systematically related to the 'frontier' variables." When the agricultural frontier is viewed as a continuum with the rest of society, great complexity becomes apparent. 5 tables, 19 notes, appendix.                                                    R. V. Ritter

670. Mott, F. L. PORTRAIT OF AN AMERICAN MILL TOWN: DEMOGRAPHIC RESPONSE IN MID-NINETEENTH CENTURY WARREN, RHODE ISLAND. *Population Studies [Great Britain] 1972 26(1): 147-157.* "Utilizing census and vital statistics records, the author demonstrates how low levels of fertility in a nineteenth-century New England mill town are closely interrelated with the economic and social structure of the community. The ready availability of relatively unskilled job opportunities drew large numbers of foreign-born women to this community leading to an imbalance in the sex ratios in the primary marrying ages and a subsequent low percentage of women married. This relative unavailability of marriage partners for the women was further aggravated by a strong unwillingness of men and women to marry outside their own ethnic group. Partly as a result of this unusual marriage pattern, fertility in this nineteenth-century industrial town was well below the level necessary to ensure the long term maintenance of the community. Extremely low levels of marital fertility are also noted for this community and are also attributed to the same economic factors. Thus, a pattern of demographic imbalance is explained within the context of multiphasic response; economic factors affecting migration patterns, sex ratios and marital fertility as well as social norms with regard to marriage limiting an already insufficient supply of men to women of their own ethnic background."                                                        J

671. Petersen, William J. BOYS, KEEP AWAY FROM MUSLIN. *Palimpsest 1969 50(11): 637-648.* Discusses the pros and cons of marriage as parroted by Iowa newspapers, 1830-70.                    S

672. Scanlon, Tom. THE DOMESTICATION OF RIP VAN WINKLE. *Virginia Q. R. 1974 50(1): 51-62.* Joseph Jefferson's popular 19th-century play, "Rip Van Winkle," domesticated Rip and affirmed the importance of both "family structure and freedom from that structure at one and the same time." This concern with family prefigures the 20th-century American drama of O'Neill, Miller, and Williams.
O. H. Zabel

673. Shergold, Peter R. THE WALKER THESIS REVISITED: IMMIGRATION AND WHITE AMERICAN FERTILITY, 1800-60. *Australian Econ. Hist. R. 1974 14(2): 168-189.* Analyzes the thesis presented in the late 19th century by Francis A. Walker, Superintendent of the American Census, that the momentous influx of foreign labor in the United States during 1800-60 caused a reduction in white native fertility, even to the extent that the growth in American population was no greater with immigration than it would have been without it. Based on secondary sources; table, 63 notes.                                R. B. Orr

674. Strickland, Charles. A TRANSCENDENTALIST FATHER: THE CHILD-REARING PRACTICES OF BRONSON ALCOTT. *Perspectives in Am. Hist. 1969 3: 5-73.* On 25 March 1831, shortly after the birth of his first daughter, Amos Bronson Alcott began his "Observations on the Phenomena of Life, as Developed in the Progressive History of an Infant, during the First Year of its Existence," an effort that marks the beginnings of child psychology in America. When Alcott laid down his pen in 1836, he had filled nearly 2,500 manuscript pages with observations on the behavior of his young daughters - Anna, Louisa, and Elizabeth - and with reflections on the significance of the early years of human life. This work actually disclosed much more about Alcott than about his children. "Through a veil of vague mysticisms and philosophic abstractions emerges a rare historic glimpse of a father, and of the way he thought about his children, felt about them, and treated them. Alcott's thinking and feeling about his children were largely a compound of the philosophic idealism, romantic imagery, and native religious sentiment that was to become known as American transcendentalism. . . . The major point of transcendentalist child-rearing, as practised by Alcott, was that gentle means must be used to promote ascetic ends, a view which made the burdens of childhood peculiarly intense." Alcott's worship of the idea of the family reflected an emotion that was gaining force. The family was no longer seen as a mere legal convenience. Neither was it simply a device to protect children. What Alcott had discovered "was that the family should also serve the parent - as a refuge from the world, as a compensation for worldly frustrations, and as a means of renouncing worldliness within one's self. By the agency of Louisa's books, this was the message Alcott left to later generations of American women." Based on the Alcott Family MSS, Houghton Library, Harvard University; 215 notes.
D. J. Abramoske

675. Walters, Ronald G. THE FAMILY AND ANTE-BELLUM REFORM: AN INTERPRETATION. *Societas 1973 3(3): 221-232.* From the 1820's to after the Civil War, an unprecedented flood of nonfiction writing analyzed the family. Conservatives and reformers agreed on the redeeming value of the family and that something was wrong or about to go wrong with the family. All hoped that the family rightly ordered would lead to stability and moral progress. Concern for the family was largely the product of the turbulent economics of Jacksonian America. 16 notes.                                                E. P. Stickney

676. Wreede, Estella H. THE THRIFTY HOUSEWIFE IN 1830. *Northwest Ohio Q. 1966 38(2/3/4): 46-49.* A series of quotations drawn from Lydia Marie Child's *The American Frugal Housewife* (Boston: Carter, Bender and Company, 1833). The quotations are selected with the intention of showing how the housewife of 1830 was advised to practice frugality for the purpose of achieving respectability, prosperity, and peace. The book was reprinted in 1966 as a collector's item. Illus.
W. F. Zornow

677. —. [BRONSON ALCOTT'S CHILD-REARING PRACTICES]. *Hist. of Childhood Q. 1973 1(1): 4-61.*
Strickland, Charles. A TRANSCENDENTALIST FATHER: THE CHILD-REARING PRACTICES OF BRONSON ALCOTT, *pp. 4-51.* A narrative account of the child-rearing practices of Bronson Alcott, educator and father of Louisa May Alcott. The account highlights Alcott's attempts to appeal to love and conscience rather than to use coercion. His practices, adapted from Romantic and Transcendental views of childhood, resulted in an intensification of family identity and isolation. Based primarily on observations that Alcott made of the first years of his daughters' lives. Primary and secondary sources; 175 notes.
Ebel, Henry. COMMENT, *pp. 52-55.* Puts Strickland's essay into a broader historical context, noting the rapidly changing world-view of Western civilization in the early 19th century and the compatibility of child-rearing practices, such as Alcott's, with the changes in ideas concerning hierarchical order and authority. Emphasizes the particularly manipulative psychic domination which came to replace physical domination in child-rearing.

Despert, J. Louise. COMMENT, *pp. 56-57*. Focuses on Alcott, seeking causes for his activity. Finds significance in his constant flirtation with poverty, family rootlessness, conflict with his wife, repressed childhood experiences, and compulsive drive to achieve.

Walzer, John. COMMENT, *pp. 57-61*. Compares Alcott's notions of childhood and training with similar notions of the previous century. Argues that cruelty and neglect have epitomized parental responses to children in earlier ages; the 18th and 19th centuries mark an advance in humane conceptions of childhood.

R. E. Butchart

678. —. [EVANGELICAL CHILD-REARING]. *J. of Social Hist. 1975 9(1): 21-43.*

McLoughlin, William G. EVANGELICAL CHILD-REARING IN THE AGE OF JACKSON: FRANCIS WAYLAND'S VIEW OF WHEN AND HOW TO SUBDUE THE WILLFULNESS OF CHILDREN, *pp. 21-34*. Describes Brown University President Francis Wayland's child-rearing triumph which he submitted anonymously in a letter to the *American Baptist Magazine* in October 1831. 22 notes.

Lipsitt, Lewis P. COMMENT ON "A CASE OF CONVICTION," *pp. 35-43*. Explains the personal and social implications of Wayland's struggle with his son. 5 notes. S

## Sex Roles

679. Angle, Paul M. GEORGE MERRYWEATHER'S UNITED STATES 1861-1862. *Chicago Hist. 1965 7(8): 245-253.* A biographical sketch stressing an English immigrant's impressions of the United States during his first two years. George Merryweather marvelled at midwestern thunderstorms, admired the American people while berating Mrs. Frances Trollope and Charles Dickens for their condemnation, disliked the Canadians, wondered at Niagara, and described American food and the "separation of the sexes." He enlisted in the Union Army, became a sergeant, and was vice-president of the Cross-Creek Coal Company in Chicago at his death in 1924. Based on letters and diaries in the Chicago Historical Society which cover much of his life. Illus.

J. H. Keiser

680. Cirillo, Vincent J. EDWARD FOOTE'S "MEDICAL COMMON SENSE": AN EARLY AMERICAN COMMENT ON BIRTH CONTROL. *J. of the Hist. of Medicine and Allied Sci. 1970 25(3): 341-345.* Deals with the efforts of a New York physician, Edward Bliss Foote (1829-1906), to spread knowledge of birth control through the publication of a small volume written for laymen, *Medical Common Sense*. This work, first published in 1858, was issued again in 1864, with a candid advocacy of birth control. Foote gave reasons for practicing birth control and examined the common methods of contraception of his time. Foote denounced folklore-based contraceptives such as a "prevention pill," douching with water, and *coitus interruptus*. He explained condoms, the cervical diaphragm, and a fraudulent gadget, the "electromagnetic prevention machine." Although he was fined for distributing birth control information through the mails, Foote continued to advocate birth control in his popular writings until death. Based on secondary sources; 28 notes.

J. L. Susskind

681. Cowen, David L. BOYS WILL BE . . . *J. of the Rutgers U. Lib. 1972 35(2): 67-70.* Compares a letter written by Simeon DeWitt (1756-1834) in 1776 with one written by Washington Irving (1783-1859) in 1804. Each letter provides descriptions of chance street encounters by the authors with women who attract by their walk and costume, but prove unattractive when viewed full face. 3 notes. R. Van Benthuysen

682. Hogeland, Ronald W. "THE FEMALE APPENDAGE": FEMININE LIFE-STYLES IN AMERICA, 1820-1860. *Civil War Hist. 1971 17(2): 101-114.* Analyzes the four life-styles imposed upon American women by masculine molders of society, 1820-60. The first two life-styles, "Ornamental Womanhood" and "Romanticized Womanhood," envisaged the female role as strictly domestic. The third, "Evangelical Womanhood," permitted women a limited involvement in antislavery, temperance, educational, and religious crusades, while the fourth, "Radical Womanhood," actually encouraged female participation

in public affairs. The last two forms, however, did not contemplate a fully emancipated woman. For one thing, women were not permitted to hold positions of authority in any organization, and for another, the purpose of such participation was not to liberate women but simply to introduce an elevating influence into a masculine world. Based on secondary sources; 46 notes.

E. C. Murdock

683. Jackson, Donald. A FOOTNOTE TO THE LEWIS AND CLARK EXPEDITION. *Manuscripts 1972 24(1): 2-21.* Reprints a notice for a bill of exchange dated 15 May 1809, signed by Meriwether Lewis, in a dealer's catalog and purchased by the Missouri Historical Society. Comments on the postexpedition careers of Lewis and William Clark, the unhappy fate of Lewis as Governor of the Louisiana Territory, and Clark's attempt to restore their entwined reputations. Illus. Reproduces the bill of exchange, 15 May 1809; lists protested bills prepared by Lewis, August 1809; and reprints a page from Clark's journal of his trip to Washington with Judith (Julia) Clark's instructions on her dress and hair necklace.

D. A. Yanchisin

684. Low, Betty-Bright P. OF MUSLINS AND MERVEILLEUSES: EXCERPTS FROM THE LETTERS OF JOSEPHINE DU PONT AND MARGARET MANIGAULT. *Winterthur Portfolio 1974 (9): 29-75.* The correspondence of Josephine du Pont (Mrs. Victor du Pont, 1770-1837) and Margret Izard Manigault (Mrs. Gabriel Manigault, 1768-1824) gives insight into the fashion of the era of the "merveilleuses." Segments of their correspondence deal with fashion and cultural news of Paris, New York City, and Charleston, South Carolina. Their correspondence 1796-1824 coincides in part with the "decade of undress." Based on primary and secondary sources; 16 photos, 198 notes, appendix.

N. A. Kuntz

685. Richmond, Robert W. "WHEN HOOPS DID TILT AND FALSEHOOD WAS IN FLOWER": WOMEN'S FASHIONS OF THE 1860'S. *Am. Hist. Illus. 1971 6(1): 23-30.* The heyday of the hoopskirt was the 1860's. Male, wolf-like, self-appointed "hoop inspectors" were ever observant of tilt situations such as steep stairs, high winds, or a hoop wearer stepping out of a carriage. The relative merits of exposed calves led to false calves. Before the end of the decade there had been developed artificial bosoms, false lips, cheek plumpers (for round faces), the small "microscopic bonnet," corsets which pulled in and pushed out, and a hairstyle called the "waterfall" - rolled hair in a tight, circular wad behind and below the neck, commonly covered with a net and often false. 10 illus.

D. Dodd

686. Scott, Anne Firor. WOMEN'S PERSPECTIVE ON THE PATRIARCHY IN THE 1850'S. *J. of Am. Hist. 1974 61(1): 52-64.* Analyzes attitudes of southern white women revealing considerable discontent with their assigned role in the patriarchal social system of the antebellum South. They were generally supportive of the plantation system and did not openly rebel, but many showed fear and unhappiness with child-bearing and motherhood, and disgust at the sexual behavior of southern men with slave women, and at the general double standard of morality. Most women upheld slavery, but some doubted the morality of the institution. More women protested the burden of caring for slaves or were motivated by close personal ties with black women. There were a few echoes of the feminism of the North. These feelings reflect a mixture of fear, guilt, and anxiety about southern society. 51 notes.

K. B. West

## Women on the Frontier

687. Atkinson, Betty J. SOME THOUGHTS ON NANCY HANKS LINCOLN. *Lincoln Herald 1971 73(3): 127-137.* On 5 October 1818 Abraham Lincoln's mother, Nancy Hanks Lincoln, was buried. Her 34 years of life were typical for a pioneer wife. Many people have suggested her son was fathered by a famous American statesman, but little is known of the Hanks family. Much material has been written about Nancy Hanks Lincoln. Despite the lack of documentary evidence, she fulfilled her role as wife and mother with all its disappointments and joys. Based on biographies and periodical articles; 46 notes.

A. C. Aimone

688. Bivans, Venola Lewis, ed. THE DIARY OF LUNA E. WARNER, A KANSAS TEENAGER OF THE EARLY 1870'S. *Kansas Hist. Q. 1969 35(3): 276-311; (4): 411-441.* Part I. Luna Warner, her parents, and brother were among a group of 22 settlers who moved from the vicinity of Barre, Massachusetts, to claim homesteads on the Solomon River near Downs, Kansas. Only Walter Warner and his family remained in Kansas when the rest of the settlers later moved to California. Luna Warner remained at the homestead after her marriage in 1881 to Frank Lewis. The editor, Luna Warner Lewis' daughter, presents portions of her mother's diary that were written between 23 February 1871 and 31 March 1872. The entries vary in length from one sentence to a short paragraph. They contain some interesting comments on frontier life as seen through the eyes of a 15-year-old girl. Illus., 9 notes. Part II. This portion of the diary covers the period from 1 April 1872 to 31 December 1874. The entries vary in length from one sentence to a short paragraph. They contain comments on the author's family life and the daily routine on the Kansas frontier.                 W. F. Zornow

689. Blackburn, Forrest R. ARMY FAMILIES IN FRONTIER FORTS. *Military R. 1969 49(10): 17-28.* Discusses the problems encountered by military dependents at frontier forts in the American West in the 1860's. Mentions high food prices, weather hazards, diseases and epidemics, Indians, and dugout homes. 4 photos, 8 notes.
                                                                                      G. E. Snow

690. Brown, D. Alexander. BRIDES BY THE BOATLOAD FOR THE NORTHWEST. *Am. Hist. Illus. 1966 1(1): 40-46.* During the first half of the 19th century there was a tremendous shortage of women in Oregon, Washington, and California. Numerous unsuccessful attempts were made to induce women to travel west, but possibly the most successful promoter was Asa Shinn Mercer. His first attempt to bring eligible young women from the east coast failed when he was able to get only 11 girls to accompany him on the journey in 1864. His second attempt in 1865-66 was far more succesful. After many discouraging experiences he was finally able to obtain financial backing and a vessel for the adventure. Although the local newspapers and journals were uncomplimentary of the trip, Mercer was able to get 100 young women to risk the long trip around South America. The cargo of 100 females safely docked in Seattle on 29 May 1866 under the watchful eyes of hundreds of waiting bachelors. Mercer's later life is reviewed. 3 illus.                 M. J. McBaine

691. Brown, D. Alexander. A GIRL WITH THE DONNER PASS PARTY. *Am. Hist. Illus. 1966 1(6): 42-48.* Virginia Elizabeth Reed, 12 years old, and her family left Illinois in 1846 for California. Virginia wrote letters of her impressions to a cousin, in which she described their daily activities, hardships, and her excitement. Part way through the journey they joined the ill-fated Donner party. Because of killing a man, even though in self-defense, Virginia's father James Reed was banished from the wagon train and sent ahead alone to seek help at Sutter's Fort. The party reached the Sierra Nevada Mountains too late in the winter to cross and was halted by the weather. Although several of the members of the party resorted to cannibalism, Virginia wrote "thank God we have all got thro, and we did not eat human flesh." On 19 February 1847 a relief party from Sutter's Fort arrived. James Reed had made it through the mountains and gotten help. Of the original party of 87, 36 had died in the Sierra snows. Based on the original letters of Virginia Reed; 5 illus., map.
                                                                                      M. J. McBaine

692. Brown, Terry. AN EMIGRANTS' GUIDE FOR WOMEN: MAKING THE NECESSARY PREPARATIONS FOR THE ARDUOUS FIVE-MONTH JOURNEY ALONG THE OREGON TRAIL. *Am. West 1970 7(5): 12-17, 63.* Guidebooks for the Oregon Trail were written "by men for men." They pictured a romantic West and were made more to sell and to attract settlers westward than they were to guide. The present piece is "a fictionalized facsimile of an 1850 guidebook written [in 1970] by a woman for women." In contrast to the half-truth misinformation of the guidebooks contemporary to the trail itself, this one is "accurate and well-researched." It is concerned mainly with questions of interest to wives and mothers, and deals with preparations for the journey, medical supplies, major problems en route, notable sights on the way, the travel train code of conduct, and a typical day on the trail. Illus., map.
                                                                                      D. L. Smith

693. Burke, Yvonne Braithwaite. FEMININE PIONEERS. *Westways 1976 68(7): 53-55.* Discusses women who were pioneers in the West and Pacific Northwest, 1803-1912.

694. Butler, Mann. DETAILS OF FRONTIER LIFE. *Register of the Kentucky Hist. Soc. 1964 62(3): 206-229.* Paints a general picture of the daily life of the settlers living on the frontier of Virginia, Pennsylvania, and Maryland during the Revolutionary period. It briefly describes several aspects of frontier life including: hunting, military duties, mechanic arts, marriages, sports, medicine, religion, and housebuilding. The article is excerpted from *Valley of the Ohio,* a work unfinished when the author died in 1855, and it commemorates the 180th anniversary of the author's birth. Documented. Biblio.                 J. F. Cook

695. Carmony, Donald F., ed. FRONTIER LIFE: LONELINESS AND HOPE. *Indiana Mag. of Hist. 1965 61(1): 53-57.* A reprint of a letter written by Sara Ames Stebbins living in Illinois in 1839 to relatives in Massachusetts. Depicts in a poignant manner life for one pioneer woman - a life of loneliness and unhappiness, yet also one of hope and constant faith in the future.                 J. Findlay

696. Clausen, Clarence A., transl. and ed. A TEXAS MANIFESTO: A LETTER FROM MRS. ELISE WAERENSKJOLD. *Norwegian-Am. Studies and Records 1959 20: 32-45.* Sketches the history of Norwegian immigrants in Texas during the 1840's and early 1850's. Briefly reviews the life of Elise Waerenskjold in Norway and Texas. On 9 July 1851, Waerenskjold wrote a letter to T. A. Gjestvang, the postmaster in Løiten, Hedemark, Norway. This letter, translated and printed as part of the article, responded to earlier letters about Texas, written by a Frenchman named Captain A. Tolmer, which appeared in Norwegian newspapers. Waerenskjold's letter describes life and conditions in Texas and rebuts Tolmer's negative descriptions of Texas. Based on primary and secondary materials; 2 notes.                 A. E. Wiederrecht

697. Clinton, Katherine. PIONEER WOMEN IN CHICAGO, 1833-1837. *J. of the West 1973 12(2): 317-324.* The women pioneers who came to Chicago were a hardy lot. "They played a leading role in civic life through their work in education and reform and through their humanitarian efforts." Unknowingly, they challenged the prevalent 19th-century social attitudes toward femininity—a stereotype which "scarcely fitted the rugged environment of frontier Chicago." 42 notes.
                                                                                      E. P. Stickney

698. Dick, Everett. SUNBONNET AND CALICO, THE HOMESTEADER'S CONSORT. *Nebraska Hist. 1966 47(1): 3-13.* An account of pioneer experience in the second half of the 19th century in the trans-Mississippi prairie and plains area as viewed by the homesteader's consort.                 R. Lowitt

699. Faragher, Johnny and Stansell, Christine. WOMEN AND THEIR FAMILIES ON THE OVERLAND TRAIL TO CALIFORNIA AND OREGON, 1842-1867. *Feminist Studies 1975 2(2/3): 150-166.* Examines the efforts of women to maintain a separate sphere of their own on the Overland Trail. Life on the trail expanded the work roles of women from purely domestic duties to numerous male jobs, but only drastic circumstances forced men to take on traditionally female chores. Rather than use the expanded work roles to free themselves from narrow definitions of "woman's place," women tried to preserve their circumscribed role. Their journals testify to the importance of the female sphere and the tribulations of integration. Based on diaries, journals, memoirs, and secondary works; 75 notes.                 J. D. Falk

700. Guthrie, Blaine A., Jr. CAPTAIN RICHARD CHENOWETH: A FOUNDING FATHER OF LOUISVILLE. *Filson Club Hist. Q. 1972 46(2): 147-160.* Presents a biographical sketch of frontier antihero Richard Chenoweth. One of the earliest settlers in the Louisville, Kentucky, region, his life was distinguished only by constant failure. His service during the Revolutionary War consisted of the construction of Fort Nelson and a series of reprimands from his commanding officers. In 1789, Indians attacked his home, scalped his wife Peggy, and drove Chenoweth off. His wife survived the loss of her hair and became the object of popular curiosity for the remainder of her life. Chenoweth was a poor businessman and died deeply in debt in 1802. Based on local government documents and published manuscripts; 95 notes.
                                                                                      G. B. McKinney

701. Hastings, Homer. PIONEERS OF THE UNCOMPAHGRE PLATEAU. *Colorado Mag. 1964 41(1): 34-38.* Personal reminiscences of Mary Jane Matlock concerning her daily life as a pioneer on the Uncompahgre Plateau of Colorado and the move there from the East, 1870's-80's.

702. Holmes, Jack D. L. ANN WHITE HUTCHINS: ANTHONY'S BETTER HALF? *J. of Mississippi Hist. 1975 37(2): 203-208.* Describes Ann White Hutchins, an indominatable frontier woman, wife of Anthony Hutchins, and mother of nine children, who lived in the Carolinas in the late 1760's and early 1770's and in Mississippi near Natchez from the mid-1770's until her death in 1811. Primary sources; 21 notes.
J. W. Hillje

703. Jackson, Sheldon G. AN ENGLISH QUAKER TOURS CALIFORNIA: THE JOURNAL OF SARAH LINDSEY, 1859-1860, PART III. *Southern Calif. Q. 1969 51(3): 221-246.* Continued from previous article. Reproduces entries from Sarah Lindsey's diary for the period 19 September 1859 through 18 August 1860. During this time the Lindseys again ministered to miners in the San Francisco and Sacramento areas and visited Quakers in the Pacific Northwest and Hawaii. In addition to religious aspects of their California travels, Mrs. Lindsey described the people and their living conditions. The Lindseys departed from California for Australia on 18 August 1860. Based mainly on a manuscript in the Devonshire House Library, London; 21 notes.    W. L. Bowers

704. Jervey, Edward D. and Moss, James E. FROM VIRGINIA TO MISSOURI IN 1846: THE JOURNAL OF ELIZABETH ANN COOLEY. *Missouri Hist. R. 1966 60(2): 162-206.* Elizabeth Ann Cooley kept a diary from 1842 until her death in 1848. The first part of her journal covers the years in Virginia from 1842 to 1846; the second part covers her marriage to James W. McClure and her experiences in Texas and Missouri. The editors summarize the key points covered during the first portion of the journal. They reproduce the entire journal beginning with the entry of 15 March 1846 shortly after her marriage and just before her departure to the West. The diary is kept irregularly, and some of the entries are very brief. The diarist offers many observations on local events. The original journal is in the possession of Elizabeth Cooley McClure's descendants.    W. F. Zornow

705. Johnson, E. Gustav. AN "AMERICA LETTER" IN 1854 FROM A VÄRMLÄNNING. *Swedish Pioneer Hist. Q. 1967 18(2): 93-100.* Translation of a letter written by Christina Lovisa Erix-dotter, a young member of the 1854 Karlskoga and Bjurkärn emigrants, to her relatives back in Sweden. The harsh journey to Quebec and then on to Illinois is described. Cholera left few of the families intact, in good health, or with any support. Christina believes America is a good land and that it is a fortunate person who can make the journey and last through the first year. Particular mention is made of the language difficulty and the necessity of taking the best route for the journey. Illus., 2 notes.
M. K. Kellogg

706. Keen, Elizabeth. WYOMING'S FRONTIER NEWSPAPER. *Ann. of Wyoming 1963 35(1): 88-101.* Discusses the Cheyenne, Laramie, and Douglas newspapers as sources for early Wyoming territorial history. Uses as examples news of opportunities for cattle and sheep raisers, tales of cattle roundups, notices of political meetings, and comments on the first women serving on a trial jury. Includes a checklist of territorial newspapers giving the place of publication, name of the paper, the dates of extant copies, and their depositories. Based primarily on newspapers and published state-local history.    R. L. Nichols

707. Lamar, Howard R. THE NEW OLD WEST. *Yale Alumni Mag. 1972 36(1): 6-15.* Discusses a Western American History course at Yale University, which is taught from the vantage points of minorities (primarily Indians and Chicanos) and women. Their participation in the westward movement, the effects which it had upon these groups, and the prejudices of traditionally taught courses are mentioned.

708. Lecompte, Janet. A LETTER FROM JESSIE TO KIT. *Missouri Hist. Soc. Bull. 1973 29(4, Pt. 1): 260-263.* Reprints an undated letter now in the Newberry Library from Jessie Benton Fremont, wife of explorer John Charles Fremont (1813-90), to Kit Carson (1809-68), the noted western scout and guide. Close relationships had developed between Carson and Fremont.    H. T. Lovin

709. Marks, Bayly Ellen, ed. CORRESPONDENCE OF ANNA BRIGGS BENTLEY FROM COLUMBIANA COUNTY, 1826. *Ohio Hist. 1969 78(1): 38-45.* Presents the text of a letter written by Mrs. Bentley from Columbiana County, Ohio, to friends at her former home in Sandy Springs, Maryland. The letter, written in stages between 17 and 27 August, gives many details about daily life in the pioneer settlement. The Bentleys were Quakers, and in various ways the letter deals with special features of the adjustment of that group to frontier conditions. An introduction and explanatory notes are provided. The letter is one of more than 150 written by Anna Bentley between 1826 and 1884. These letters are now in the Briggs-Stabler Collection of the Maryland Historical Society, Baltimore, Maryland.    S. L. Jones

710. Millbrook, Minnie Dubbs, ed. MRS. GENERAL CUSTER AT FORT RILEY, 1866. *Kansas Hist. Q. 1974 40(1): 63-71.* Elizabeth Bacon Custer, wife of General George Armstrong Custer, accompanied her husband to Fort Riley, Kansas in 1866, when he was assigned to the newly organized Seventh Cavalry. This letter, preserved in the "Elizabeth Bacon Custer Collection" at Custer Battlefield National Monument, was sent from Fort Riley on 6 December 1866 to Mrs. Custer's first cousin, Rebecca Richmond of Grand Rapids, Michigan. The letter supplies information about the Custers' trip to Fort Riley from the east via Detroit and St. Louis; it also provides some illuminating details about their residence at the fort which do not appear in Mrs. Custer's recollections, *Tenting on the Plains.* Primary and secondary sources; 38 notes.
W. F. Zornow

711. Morrissey, Charles T. POSTSCRIPT: DAME SHIRLEY—SHE REJECTED A DIPLOMAT TO MARRY A STUDENT AT CASTLETON MEDICAL COLLEGE AND JOIN THE CALIFORNIA GOLD RUSH. *Vermont Hist. 1974 42(3): 251-255.* The Gold Rush letters of Dame Shirley are famous but only recently has anything been discovered about the woman who wrote them. Rodman Paul, of the California Institute of Technology, has found that her name was Louise Knapp. Wooed by Alexander Everett, diplomat and orator, she rejected his advances and married a medical student named Fayette Clappe. Her marriage to Clappe soon failed and she became a teacher in San Francisco, never to remarry.    V. L. Human

712. Munkres, Robert L. WIVES, MOTHERS, DAUGHTERS: WOMEN'S LIFE ON THE ROAD WEST. *Ann. of Wyoming 1970 42(2): 191-224.* Claims that the usual discussions about opening the West omit half of the story by concentrating entirely on male activities and ignoring the role of women on the frontier. The author describes the travel conditions experienced by female pioneers and their responses to these. Overland travel was physically demanding and the usual difficulties of cooking and related household chores were intensified by the crude or missing facilities on the overland trail. Clothing, diet, health, and constant hardship of travel posed problems. However, healthy, well-prepared travelers might enjoy a wide variety of food and have an interesting, if not enjoyable journey. Based mainly on numerous manuscript and published diaries kept by female pioneers; 158 notes.    R. L. Nichols

713. Myres, Sandra L., ed. EVY ALEXANDER: THE COLONEL'S LADY AT FT. MC DOWELL. *Montana: Mag. of Western Hist. 1974 24(3): 26-38.* Excerpts from letters by an army wife on duty with her husband at Fort McDowell, Arizona, 1868-69. Despite the usual hardships (recorded here in some detail) she remained optimistic and cheerful, sustained by interest in church work and the welfare of Indians in the locality.    S. R. Davison

714. Narell, Irena Penzil. BERNHARD MARKS: RETAILER, MINER, EDUCATOR, AND LAND DEVELOPER. *Western States Jewish Hist. Q. 1975 8(1): 26-38.* In 1852, Bernhard Marks (1832-1913) arrived in California from Providence, Rhode Island. He worked at various jobs and got into gold mining. He became a partner in several mines but met with little success. In 1859, he married Cornelia D. Barlow, a schoolteacher. In 1860, they opened a private school in Columbia. During 1862-72, he was principal of Lincoln Grammar School, San Francisco. In 1874, he established a raisin-growing colony in Fresno County. He failed at ranching, farming, and real estate development. 37 notes.
R. A. Garfinkle

715. Nunn, W. C., ed.   A JOURNAL OF OUR TRIP TO TEXAS, OCT. 6, 1853, BY MARY JAMES EUBANK.   *Texana 1972 10(1): 30-44.* Mary James Eubank was 21 years old when she traveled to Texas from Kentucky with her parents, sisters, and uncle's family. Her journal recounts the daily experiences of the trip that lasted from 6 October to 4 December 1853. Although there were no spectacular events during the journey, the party did experience occasional difficulty finding water and locating suitable land on which to settle in Texas.

J. E. Findling

716.   Paul, Rodman Wilson.   IN SEARCH OF "DAME SHIRLEY." *Pacific Hist. R. 1964 33(2): 127-146.* Identifies the author of the Shirley letters from the Feather River, California mines, 1851-52, as Louisa A. K. S. Clapp, and recounts the methods used to discover her correct name. This frail young lady, born in New Jersey, connected probably with Julia Ward Howe and the New England Lees, came west with her husband, Fayette Clapp, A.B., Brown University. After spending many years in San Francisco as a school teacher and popular literary figure, she returned east and died at the age of 93. The author made use of college records and legal documents, in preparing this account for Radcliffe's forthcoming volume *Notable American Women, 1607-1950.*

J. McCutcheon and S

717.   Peterson, Walter F., ed.   CHRISTMAS ON THE PLAINS: ELIZABETH BACON CUSTER'S NOSTALGIC MEMORIES OF HOLIDAY SEASONS ON THE FRONTIER.   *Am. West 1964 1(4): 53-57.* Elizabeth Bacon Custer traveled with and personally attended General Custer, her husband, during his western campaigns against the Indians in Texas, Kansas, and Dakota Territory. These recollections do not relate specifically to Christmas at any particular army post but range over the whole of her western yuletide experiences. Unpublished manuscript from Milwaukee-Downer College archives. Illus.

D. L. Smith

718.   Robbins, Peggy.   CALAMITY JANE: "HELLCAT IN LEATHER BRITCHES."   *Am. Hist. Illus. 1975 10(3): 12-21.* Discusses Calamity Jane's life in the western states during 1852-1903.

719.   Russell, Helen H.   EARLY PIONEERS OF THE PINE CREEK VALLEY.   *Now and Then 1972 17(5): 189-201.*

720.   Sackett, Marjorie.   KANSAS PIONEER RECIPES.   *Western Folklore 1963 22(2): 103-106.* Collection of folk recipes which demonstrate the conditions of pioneer life.

L. J. White

721.   Shor, Elizabeth N.   PROBLEMS IN THE LAND OF OPPORTUNITY.   *Am. West 1976 13(1): 24-29.* Francis and Sarah Sim and their children moved from Connecticut to southeastern Nebraska Territory in 1856. Their letters reveal the harsh and nearly unbearable circumstances of their first year in the raw frontier area. By spring of the second year their optimism began to return. Hardships continued but the Sim family prospered. 6 illus.

D. L. Smith

722.   Sibbald, John R.   CAMP FOLLOWERS ALL.   *Am. West 1966 3(2): 56-67.* Camp followers are defined to include the three groups of women sanctioned by scattered references in army regulations: wives and daughters of officers, servants, and laundresses. While the females of Soapsuds Row were usually wives of enlisted men, some were civilian wives or single women. Excluded from the present use of the term "camp followers" are the ladies of easy virtue who lived in nearby settlements and were frowned upon by the War Department. The ubiquitous army camp followers managed to string their bloomers on the clotheslines of almost every western American frontier garrison in the four decades following the outbreak of the Civil War. From their letters and diaries, the author determined that their major concerns were the effect of the elements on their complexions, the problems of keeping household goods, the education of their children, the loss of contact with their home churches, and the constant moves which were the lot of army personnel. At least one officer's wife set up housekeeping at 19 different locations. Map, illus., biblio. note.

D. L. Smith

723.   Stansell, Christine.   WOMEN ON THE GREAT PLAINS, 1865-1890.   *Women's Studies 1976 4(1): 87-98.* Discusses the masculine nature of the westward movement, the American West, and, in particular, the Great Plains where masculine interests, occupations, and social structures predominated. Women's experiences on the Great Plains were significantly different from the experiences of men. Men's involvement with occupational success provided a rationale to move West. The responsibilities of women's sphere were best met in settled regions. Women moving to the Great Plains experienced severe cultural disruption. They could not adequately recreate the houses, the networks of supportive female friendships, the feminine social activities, the childrearing practices, and the values of womanhood which they had known and practiced in more settled regions. Plains' society and the patterns of life there did not accommodate women's social, psychological, or emotional needs. Still, women were essential to the settlement of the Plains; their labor was necessary for its agricultural development. Based on primary and secondary materials; 55 notes.

A. E. Wiederrecht

724.   Stevens, Harriet F.   ONE OF THE MERCER GIRLS: A JOURNAL OF LIFE ON THE STEAMER CONTINENTAL.   *Ann. of Wyoming 1963 35(2): 214-228.* The journal of Harriet F. Stevens, one of the "Mercer Girls" - single girls living in the eastern United States whom Asa Shinn Mercer persuaded to emigrate to Washington Territory in 1866. The journal describes living conditions aboard the ship *Continental,* fellow passengers, crossing the equator, several Latin American ports, and coastal scenery. It is now in the collections of the Wyoming State Archives and Historical Department.

R. L. Nichols

725.   Stoeltje, Beverly J.   "A HELPMATE FOR MAN INDEED": THE IMAGE OF THE FRONTIER WOMAN.   *J. Am. Folklore 1975 88(347): 25-41.* On the American frontier three female images predominated: refined lady, helpmate, bad woman. These symbols were associated with the male images of cowboy, settler, and bad man. The celebrated frontier woman was an active and competent helpmate to her husband, while the refined lady was environmentally unsuited and the bad woman socially unacceptable to frontier society. Based on secondary sources; 51 notes.

W. D. Piersen

726.   Strong, Ronald Thomas   YOUNG ADVENTURE BY LUCY ANN HENDERSON.   *Nevada Hist. Soc. Q. 1973 16(2): 66-99.* An account of an overland wagon journey in 1846 from St. Joseph, Missouri, to Oregon. Supplies reminiscences by Lucy Ann Henderson (1835-1923), a member of this emigrant party. The group followed the Oregon Trail as far west as Goose Creek (a tributary of the Snake River) and then decided to travel southwestward through Nevada and to follow the Applegate Cutoff to Oregon. The emigrants' decision later proved ill-advised because of unforeseen hardships along the route. Based on interviews in 1923 with Lucy Henderson, on Henderson family records, and on Jessy Quinn Thornton's *Oregon and California in 1848* (New York: Harper and Brothers, 1855); 4 maps, photo.

H. T. Lovin

727.   Thane, James L., Jr. ed.   LOVE FROM ALL TO ALL: THE GOVERNOR'S LADY WRITES HOME TO OHIO.   *Montana: Mag. of Western Hist. 1974 24(3): 12-25.* Excerpts from letters by Mary Wright Edgerton, the wife of Montana's first territorial Governor, Sidney Edgerton, written at Bannack early in the gold rush. She found management of a household in this mining camp a difficult task, but rarely expressed discouragement. Illus.

S. R. Davison

728.   Thompson, Erwin N.   NARCISSA WHITMAN.   *Montana: Mag. of Western Hist. 1963 13(4): 15-27.* As the recent bride of Dr. Marcus Whitman, missionary and physician, Narcissa was one of the first two white women to cross the plains and mountains to the Oregon country. She lived at the Waiilatpu Mission to the Cayuse Indians from 1836 to 1847, gradually losing both health and hope as mission efforts showed little result in improving the natives. The tragedy culminated in a general massacre of whites at the mission in 1847. Undocumented.

S. R. Davison

729.   Ursenbach, Maureen.   THREE WOMEN AND THE LIFE OF THE MIND.   *Utah Hist. Q. 1975 43(1): 26-40.* Examines the cultural life available for women of intellect in Utah society in the 1850's through the lives of three women: Hannah Tapfield King, Martha Spence Heywood, and Eliza Roxcy Snow. With the barren educational landscape during the early pioneer period, the anti-intellectualism of the church, and the demands of frontier life, there was little more stimulation than private meetings of the mind and occasional gatherings of groups such as

the Polysophical Society. A strong intellectual thrust remained alive, however, reinforced by the lives of these women and others like them. Primary and secondary sources; 4 illus., 21 notes.

J. L. Hazelton

730. Utley, Beverly. THEY MADE THE WEST WORTH WINNING. *Am. Hist. Illus. 1967 2(8): 27-35.* Describes the experiences of American pioneer women. Women trekked westward for love of man, God, and adventure. Mentions vignettes of pleasant times and of hardships such as extremes of weather, lack of food, Indian attacks, disease, etc.

G. H. Skau

731. Walker, Juliette Fish. CROSSING THE PLAINS. *Noticias 1970 16(2): 3-19.* In 1862, Juliette Walker and her family crossed the plains from Howard County, Iowa, to Susanville, California. In 1920, she recounted her experiences on the journey to her grandson, Henry McLaren Brown. Juliette Walker's father first visited Plumas County, California, in 1859. He returned to Iowa to gather his family, and then with the Kennedy wagon train he headed once more for California. On departure the wagon train consisted of 52 wagons and 315 head of cattle. The journey was filled with hardship, some minor—a woman almost lost her entire set of dishes while crossing the Green River—and some major —at Massacre Rock the wagon train was attacked by 200 Indians and 10 lives were lost. Finally, they reached Susanville, California. The Walker family stayed there a short time, then moved to Quincy, California, and then in 1859, to Montecito, California. In 1871, they made their final move to Carpinteria.

K. Butcher

732. Wardle, Ralph M. TERRITORIAL BRIDE. *Nebraska Hist. 1969 50(2): 207-228.* Recounts the career of Emily Greenhow Doane as a young bride in the Territory of Nebraska and as a wife in the State of Nebraska. Stressed are social affairs in a frontier society. Based on Mrs. Doane's reminiscences which were recorded for the *Omaha Daily News* in 1919.

R. Lowitt

733. Welsch, Roger L. "SORRY CHUCK" - PIONEER FOODWAYS. *Nebraska Hist. 1972 53(1): 99-113.* Examines the homesteader's menu and investigates his home life, literature, and folklore. Though social pressure, for example, forced the abandonment of European foodways, it also prevented the borrowing of foods from the Plains Indians.

R. Lowitt

734. White, Lonnie J. WHITE WOMEN CAPTIVES OF THE SOUTHERN PLAINS INDIANS, 1866-1875. *J. of the West 1969 8(3): 327-354.* Tells of the experiences of several women captured by the Indians during raids in Kansas. The stories are related in detail and transcripts and newspaper stories are included. All of the experiences are similar. Men in the party were killed immediately and the younger women were carried off. If the Indian camp was attacked, the prisoners were killed. When the women were returned, they told of cruel treatment and were often pregnant.

R. N. Alvis

735. Whitman, Clifford Dale, ed. PRIVATE JOURNAL OF MARY ANN OWEN SIMS. *Arkansas Hist. Q. 1976 35(2): 142-187, (3): 261-291.* Part I. Mary Anne Owen Sims (1830-61?), a Tennessean who moved to Arkansas in 1838, kept a diary between June 1855 (the death of her physician husband, Dr. John D. Sims) and her own death sometime in 1861. The diary describes frontier family life, especially frequent illnesses and remedies, religious and social activities, and personal affairs. Based on primary and secondary sources; 4 illus., 59 notes. Part II. Covers 1865-61 and deals with giving up the farm, hiring out the slaves, and the start of the Civil War.

T. L. Savitt

736. Wiederaenders, Roland P. THE IMMIGRATION AND SETTLEMENT OF THE WIEDERAENDERS FAMILY. *Concordia Hist. Inst. Q. 1969 42(3): 113-118.* The Wiederaenders family stems from Annaberg, Saxony. Carl Gottlob Wiederaenders, born in 1790, was a master cooper. In 1854 he migrated with his family to Round Top, Texas. His eldest son, also named Carl Gottlob (1825-90) and also a cooper, worked for two plantation owners and then bought a small farm for 50 cents an acre in the Rabbs Creek Community near Serbin, Texas, in 1856. Carl Gottlob's young family had much work to do on the new farm: "land to clear, a crop to plant, and fences to build; in fact little thought was given to providing even the simplest of comforts." Not till the winter of

1857 was a log cabin built. Life was nonetheless easier than it had been in Germany. This one branch of the Wiederaenders family was destined to serve the Lutheran churches in America with 21 ministers and 19 parochial school teachers. Undocumented.

D. J. Abramoske

# Political Sphere

## General

737. Adams, D. K. THE ADAMS PAPERS. *Am. Q. 1962 14(4): 624-626.* Reviews L. H. Butterfield's four-volume work, *The Adams Papers, Series I, Diaries* (Belknap Press of Harvard University, 1961), which features the diaries of John Adams, 1755-81, part of Adams' autobiography, and segments of the diary of Abigail Adams through 1804.

738. Alberts, Robert C. THE NOTORIOUS AFFAIR OF MRS. REYNOLDS. *Am. Heritage 1973 24(2): 8-11, 89-93.* Alexander Hamilton's alleged adultery in 1791 with Maria Lewis Reynolds led to blackmail, which in turn led to a quarrel, a near duel, an incident in Federalist and Anti-Federalist politics, and charges of dishonesty against Hamilton, the secretary of the treasury. In 1971 Julian Boyd reexamined the Hamilton-Reynolds incident and called for a reassessment of Hamilton's character and of his services to the early republic. Illus.

D. L. Smith

739. Argo, Brenda S. MADAME OCTAVIA LEVERT'S TRIBUTE TO HENRY CLAY. *Louisiana Studies 1973 12(4): 631-638.* Explains the circumstances of Octavia Walton Levert's 1856 tribute to Henry Clay.

S

740. Bailey, Howard. MILLARD FILLMORE: THE FORGOTTEN PRESIDENT. *Am. Hist. Illus. 1971 6(3): 26-35.* Millard Fillmore, the 13th President, was born in western New York's Cayuga County on 7 January 1800 and died in Buffalo on 7 March 1874. His first wife, Abigail Powers, educated him (she was his school teacher before becoming his wife), and his second wife, Mrs. Caroline C. McIntosh, a wealthy widow of Troy, York, supported him after his political career ended as an unsuccessful presidential candidate of the Know-Nothings in 1856. After successful local political efforts in New York under the tutelage of Buffalo newspaperman Thurlow Weed, he became the running mate of Whig presidential nominee Zachary Taylor in 1848. He was selected because of his connection with Weed, his voter appeal in New York, and his impressive appearance (to balance the unkempt, slovenly appearance of Taylor). Taylor died on 9 July 1850, and Fillmore became President. His main achievement in his term as President was the signing of the "Compromise of 1850." Secondary sources; 12 illus.

D. Dodd

741. Bell, Patricia. DOLLY MADISON: A PERSONALITY PROFILE. *Am. Hist. Illus. 1969 4(1): 12-19.* Many historians have dismissed Dolly Madison as a "shallow, empty-headed party-giver;" but she was in fact a product of her training, her century, and her position as the wife of the President, utterly feminine and with no interest in the affairs of men. During her years as first lady (1809-17), she is best remembered for her bravery in saving George Washington's portrait and many other important items of historical value from the Presidential mansion before it was burned by the British in 1814. Secondary sources; 8 illus.

R. V. McBaine

742. Beloff, Max. THE SALLY HEMINGS AFFAIR: A "FOUNDING FATHER." *Encounter [Great Britain] 1974 43(3): 52-56.* Three recent books on Thomas Jefferson [Leonard W. Levy's *Jefferson and Civil Liberties: The Darker Side* (Harvard U. Pr., 1963), Dumas Malone's *Jefferson the President: Second Term* (Little, Brown, 1974), and Fawn M. Brodie's *Thomas Jefferson, An Intimate History* (Norton)], taken together, give a more personal view of Jefferson as a human being. Discusses the relationship of Jefferson and Hemings.

743. Burrus, Vivian R. JEAN ASHLEY'S CONFISCATED PROPERTY, 1795-1796. *Escribano 1975 12(4):134-142.* Discusses the Spanish government's confiscation of the property and belongings of East Florida settler Mrs. Jean Ashley during the Patriot War of 1795-96.

744. Butterfield, L. H. TENDING A DRAGON-KILLER: NOTES FOR THE BIOGRAPHER OF MRS. JOHN QUINCY ADAMS. *Pro. of the Am. Phil. Soc. 1974 118(2): 165-178.* A sketch intended for the eventual biographer of Louisa Catherine Johnson Adams (1775-1852), married for "more than five decades to one of the most trying of men," John Quincy Adams, and the grandmother of Henry Adams. Born in London to a family of Maryland background, she lived an extraordinarily varied life. No biography of her has been written because her papers have been closed to the public. 7 figs., 50 notes.

C. W. Olson

745. Cadenhead, J. W., Jr. THE CORRESPONDENCE OF CONGRESSMAN AND MRS. ROLAND JONES, BETWEEN SHREVEPORT, LOUISIANA AND WASHINGTON, D.C. (DECEMBER 1853-SEPTEMBER 1854). *North Louisiana Hist. Assoc. J. 1975 6(2): 45-51.* Roland Jones was elected to the US House of Representatives to represent Louisiana's Fourth District and took his seat on 22 December 1853. His family—his wife, a son, and two daughters—remained in Shreveport. The congressman and his wife immediately began corresponding with each other. Her letters were filled with items of local interest, the health of the family, and her financial affairs. Jones's letters also mentioned financial matters. While he did occasionally write about political matters, Jones' letters "also are sprinkled with . . . endearments." Jones seems to have been "fairly representative of Southern Congressmen of the decade before the Civil War" in that he "was primarily concerned with land questions, the interests of his constituents as well as the protection of the institution of slavery." 38 notes.

A. N. Garland

746. Crawford, Charles W., ed. THE SUBJECT IS A PAINFUL ONE TO ME. *Tennessee Hist. Q. 1967 26(1): 59-63.* Presents, with comments, a letter from Andrew Jackson to his grandniece Mary Eastin. The young lady had accompanied her aunt Emily Donelson to Washington when the latter had served as White House hostess. The ladies had broken with the President over receiving Peggy O'Neale Eaton and he had sent them home to Tennessee. The letter expresses sadness that the situation arose, his hopes that they may return soon, and disappointment with their conduct. He blames the trouble on gossip and politics and expresses a willingness to make peace if his opponents take the initiative. 5 notes.

C. F. Ogilvie

747. Cullen, Joseph P. THE MADAME POMPADOUR OF AMERICA. *Am. Hist. Illus. 1966 1(6): 20-29.* In 1829, the presidency and government of Andrew Jackson were a mockery due to Peggy O'Neale Eaton. Peggy was the wife of Secretary of War John H. Eaton. She was the symbol of the transition in Washington of government controlled "by the Eastern gentlemen in their wigs, ruffles, and knee breeches" and the Western frontiersmen with their coonskin caps and buckskin pants. Peggy had been a barmaid, and all of Washington society cringed at the thought of having to associate with her. The result was clashes between the President and several of his cabinet members. The author suggests that John C. Calhoun's future bid for the presidency was doomed because he refused to cater to Peggy. Because Van Buren sided with the President concerning Mrs. Eaton, he became Jackson's choice for the presidency. Finally, Jackson was forced to dismiss the Cabinet. Thus, one woman was the direct cause of the complete disruption of the US government. 9 illus.

M. J. McBaine

748. Cunningham, Nobel E., Jr., ed. THE DIARY OF FRANCES FEW, 1808-1809. *J. of Southern Hist. 1963 29(3): 345-361.* From October 1808 to March 1809, Frances Few, daughter of William Few, a Georgia signer of the Constitution, visited in Washington with her aunt, Mrs. Albert Gallatin, wife of the Secretary of the Treasury. She dined with President Thomas Jefferson, attended the New Year's reception at the White House, and attended a Dolly Madison party and the inauguration of President James Madison, as well as debates in Congress. She kept a diary of her observations, of which the main portion is published.

S. E. Humphreys

749. Dahl, Curtis. THE CLERGYMAN, THE HUSSY, AND OLD HICKORY: EZRA STILES ELY AND THE PEGGY EATON AFFAIR. *J. of Presbyterian Hist. 1974 52(2): 137-155.* The Peggy Eaton affair had considerable effect on the Democratic Party, the presidency of Andrew Jackson, and the ambitions of prominent politicians. Explain the role of Presbyterian clergyman Reverend Dr. Ezra Stiles Ely in the scandal. 64 notes.

D. L. Smith

750. Evans, William B. JOHN ADAMS' OPINION OF BENJAMIN FRANKLIN. *Pennsylvania Mag. of Hist. and Biog. 1968 92(2): 220-238.* Traces John Adams' animosity toward Benjamin Franklin in 10 1807 letters to Mercy Otis Warren questioning her favorable treatment of Franklin in *History of the Rise, Progress, and Termination of the American Revolution.* Differences between the two revolutionary giants began in 1776, when Franklin supported a unicameral legislature in Pennsylvania, and continued in Paris (1778-79) until their joint presence on the peace commission in 1780 brought an open breach when Adams opposed Franklin's supposedly pro-French policy. Not only differences on policy but Adams' envy and pride may have colored his view of Franklin. Based primarily on the papers of John Adams; 67 notes.

R. G. Mitchell

751. Forbes-Robertson, Diana. "LADY" KNOX. *Am. Heritage 1966 17(3): 46-47, 74-79.* Short biography of Henry Knox's wife, Lucy Knox.

S

752. Gatewood, Joanne L. RICHMOND DURING THE VIRGINIA CONSTITUTIONAL CONVENTION OF 1829-1830: AN EXTRACT FROM THE DIARY OF THOMAS GREEN, OCTOBER 1, 1829, TO JANUARY 31, 1830. *Virginia Mag. of Hist. and Biog. 1976 84(3): 287-332.* Thomas Green (1798-1883), a Richmond attorney, frequently attended the sessions of the Virginia Constitutional Convention of 1829-30. He and his wife knew and entertained many of the delegates, and his diary records his impressions of the convention and the men who participated in it. Edited from the diary in the Virginia Historical Society; 4 illus., 175 notes.

R. F. Oaks

753. Gifford, James M. EMILY TUBMAN AND THE AFRICAN COLONIZATION MOVEMENT IN GEORGIA. *Georgia Hist. Q. 1975 59(1): 10-24.* Discusses the works and projects of Georgia philanthropist Emily Tubman, 1816-57, emphasizing the emancipation of her slaves and their colonization in Liberia through the African Colonization Movement.

754. Hackensmith, C. W. FAMILY BACKGROUND AND EDUCATION OF MARY TODD. *Register of the Kentucky Hist. Soc. 1971 69(3): 187-196.* Traces the genealogy and early education of Mary Todd, wife of Abraham Lincoln. Her father, Robert S. Todd, and his first wife, Eliza Ann Parker, had six children, including Mary who was born 13 December 1818. After her mother's death, Mary's father remarried and fathered eight more children. Mary entered a private academy in Lexington at about eight years of age. At 14, she entered a select boarding school where she "spent four happy years." During the summer of 1837, Mary spent three months visiting two of her sisters in Springfield, Illinois, where she heard of the exploits of her cousin John T. Stuart's new law partner, Abraham Lincoln, but did not meet him during this visit. Primary and secondary sources; illus., 25 notes.

J. F. Paul

755. Herbert, Eugenia W. A NOTE ON RICHARD BACHE (1737-1811). *Pennsylvania Mag. of Hist. and Biog. 1976 100(1): 97-103.* After arriving in Philadelphia from Yorkshire, England, in 1761, Richard Bache, the future son-in-law of Benjamin Franklin, prospered as a marine insurance underwriter and importer. In 1767, misfortune struck; debts contracted by him were repudiated by his London associate, Edward Green. Because of his impecunious state and reputation as a fortune hunter, Franklin objected to Bache's proposal to marry his daughter, Deborah. Although Franklin never formally approved, he acquiesced to the marriage, and after returning to America installed Bache as head of the US Post Office. Bache quit the post a few years after Franklin's death (1790) and lived off Franklin's inheritance on a country estate. Based on primary and secondary sources; 19 notes.

E. W. Carp

756. Ketcham, Ralph. THE PURITAN ETHIC IN THE REVOLUTIONARY ERA: ABIGAIL ADAMS AND THOMAS JEFFERSON. George, Carol V. R., ed. *"Remember the Ladies": New Perspectives on Women in American History: Essays in Honor of Nelson Manfred Blake* (Syracuse: Syracuse U. Pr., 1975): 49-65. The lives of Thomas Jefferson and Abigail Adams and the relationship between them reveal much about the relationship between Puritanism and the Enlightenment. Abigail

Adams, the Puritan, and Thomas Jefferson, the Enlightenment man, shared many values about morality, family matters, child rearing, personal relationships, and women's education. They exchanged views on American politics, European society, and economic affairs. They discussed the nature of the good society and how best to work for the public good. While Adams worried about abuses to the new Republic by the governed, Jefferson fretted about abuses by the governors. Despite differences in emphases and arguments about the Alien and Sedition Acts and the radical Republicans, both individuals valued rational discourse, stable government, and public morality because both shared, in different degrees, the legacy of Puritan habits and Enlightenment thought. Based on primary sources; 11 notes.                    P. R. Byrne

757. Koch, Adrienne.  THE SIGNIFICANCE OF THE GRIMKE FAMILY.  *Maryland Hist. 1972 3(1): 59-84.* Examines the Grimké family of Charleston, South Carolina. The family provided three generations of members who were in the forefront of reform: John Faucheraud Grimké, a Revolutionary War leader; the sisters, Sarah and Angelina, who were the first southern women abolitionists and leaders in the cause for women's rights; and Thomas Grimké, a leader in the moral reform movements of peace, temperance, and colonization, and an inveterate Unionist. A study of this family is an intimate study of the dominant themes of American History: Revolution, Rights of Man, Sectionalism, the Abolitionist Movement, and the Civil War.                    G. O. Gagnon

758. Koch, Adrienne.  A VERY AMERICAN TALE.  *Maryland Hist. 1972 3(1): 51-58.* Outlines the author's evolving conception of the role of the Grimké sisters in American history and contains an autobiographical sketch.                    G. O. Gagnon

759. Malone, Dumas.  MR. JEFFERSON'S PRIVATE LIFE.  *Pro. of the Am. Antiquarian Soc. 1974 84(1): 65-72.* Reprints a letter written by Ellen Randolph Coolidge in 1858 to her husband concerning the personal life of her grandfather, Thomas Jefferson and countering certain allegations made against his character, particularly the story initially circulated by journalist James Thomson Callender, that Jefferson had fathered children by one of his slaves, Sally Hemings. 14 notes.                    B. L. Fenske

760. Martin, Wendy.  EDITORIAL: CORRESPONDENCE OF JOHN AND ABIGAIL ADAMS: CONSIDERATIONS FOR THE BICENTENNIAL.  *Women's Studies 1975 3(1): 1-3.* The correspondence between John and Abigail Adams reveals Abigail as a representative American woman who, in a time of revolution, wants woman's role to be redefined. John Adams reflects the 18th-century patriarchal attitude which accepts the Pauline proscriptions on female behavior. Women's participation in public affairs would undermine the well-being and harmony of the social order which John valued. Undocumented.                    A. E. Wiederrecht

761. Munroe, John A., ed.  MRS. MC LANE'S COLORED BOY AND PEGGY O'NEALE.  *Delaware Hist. 1963 10(4): 361-366.* Publishes an 1836 letter of Francis Hillery, Negro servant of Louis McLane, to Mrs. McLane describing Hillery's stops in London and Spain. Of particular interest is Hillery's uncomplimentary observation concerning Margaret (Peggy) O'Neale Eaton (1796-1879): "She is the most compleat Peaice of deception that ever god made, and as a mistres: it would be Cruelty to put a dumb brute, under her Command. . . . " 14 notes.                    R. M. Miller

762. Nelson, Anna Kasten.  MISSION TO MEXICO—MOSES Y. BEACH, SECRET AGENT.  *New York Hist. Soc. Q. 1975 59(3): 226-245.* Moses Y. Beach served as a secret agent for President James K. Polk in Mexico for a brief time during the Mexican War. In this capacity, accompanied by the remarkable Jane McManus Storms, who had been an editorial writer for Beach's newspaper, the New York *Sun,* he spent considerable time in contact with the Mexican authorities in an attempt to bring about a peace. Polk said in his diary that Beach had given him valuable information. Primary sources; 5 illus., 38 notes.                    C. L. Grant

763. Nunn, Leona Day.  ABE LINCOLN AND HIS SISTER.  *Daughters of the Am. Revolution Mag. 1972 106(2): 120-122, 157, 177.* Story of Sarah ("Sally") Lincoln and her relationship with her brother, Abraham Lincoln.                    S

764. Pulley, Judith.  THE BITTERSWEET FRIENDSHIP OF THOMAS JEFFERSON AND ABIGAIL ADAMS.  *Essex Inst. Hist. Collections 1972 108(3): 193-216.* Discusses the friendship between the two, its breakup (over the political beliefs of Adams' husband), and its renewal in 1811.

765. Reninger, Marion Wallace.  HARRIET LANE.  *J. of the Lancaster County Hist. Soc. 1963 67(3): 145-148.* Harriet Lane Johnston resided with her uncle James Buchanan in Pennsylvania and in Washington, D.C.                    S

766. Rosenberger, Homer T.  TO WHAT EXTENT DID HARRIET LANE INFLUENCE THE PUBLIC POLICIES OF JAMES BUCHANAN?  *J. of the Lancaster County Hist. Soc. 1970 74(1): 1-22.* Describes Harriet Lane, niece and First Lady of James Buchanan, as a cosmopolitan woman, well versed in the politics of the day. Letters from Buchanan to Lane show that the President regarded her as a confidante, and contemporary writers asserted that she could change the President's mind with ease. The demands for her intercession with the President for jobs in Washington are well documented, and the author surmises that she was a person of strong character who had the power to influence Buchanan for conciliatory policies regarding slavery and other issues. Based on contemporary accounts and manuscript materials in the Library of Congress and Dickinson College Library; 3 illus.                    L. J. Stout

767. Sifton, Paul G.  "WHAT A DREAD PROSPECT. . . . ": DOLLEY MADISON'S PLAGUE YEAR.  *Pennsylvania Mag. of Hist. and Biog. 1963 87(2): 182-188.* Attempts to clarify the statement that Dolley Payne Todd (later Madison) was left a wealthy widow when her husband died in 1793. After her husband's death Dolley was unable to take possession of her husband's effects, which had been taken over by her brother-in-law, James Todd. It was not until 1795, 14 months after her husband's death, that Dolley received her inheritance. Based on letters written by Dolley, James Madison, and members of the Todd family (8 of which are reproduced); 19 notes.                    M. J. McBaine

768. Sinclair, Marjorie.  THE SACRED WIFE OF KAMEHAMEHA I.  *Hawaiian J. of Hist. 1971 5: 3-23.* Keopuolani, the sacred wife of Kamehameha I, was born with divine rank, which gave her a special power in the reigns of Kamehameha I and II. She took the lead in breaking the power of the kapus, saw the implication of Hawaii's early contact with Western culture, realized the importance of reading and writing, and embraced Christianity. Opposes overemphasis on Queen Kaahumanu who became premier.                    R. N. Alvis

769. Squires, J. Duane.  LINCOLN'S TODD IN-LAWS.  *Lincoln Herald 1967 69(3): 121-128.* Analyzes the various ways in which Mary Lincoln's family affected her marriage with Lincoln and how it influenced his administration.                    S. L. Jones

770. Swick, Ronald.  THEODOSIA BURR ALSTON.  *South Atlantic Q. 1975 74(4): 495-506.* Reviews the life of Theodosia Burr Alston (1783-1813), daughter of Aaron Burr. Contrary to the expectations of the time, Burr educated his daughter almost to the point of fanaticism. Theodosia grew up a beautiful, witty, and accomplished woman, closely tied to her father emotionally and intellectually. She married Joseph Alston, who later became governor of South Carolina. Their only child was sickly and soon died. Suffering from cancer, Theodosia wished to see her father one last time, but the boat on which she sailed disappeared and was never seen again. 24 notes.                    V. L. Human

771. Trickey, Katharine Shelburne.  YOUNG HICKORY AND SARAH.  *Daughters of the Am. Revolution Mag. 1974 108(5): 430-434.* Describes the presidential term of James K. Polk.                    S

# Civil War

772. Ashcraft, Allan C., ed.  MRS. RUSSELL AND THE BATTLE OF RAYMOND, MISSISSIPPI.  *J. of Mississippi Hist. 1963 25(1): 38-40.* Includes a letter written by Mrs. J. W. Russell, who lived on a plantation near Raymond, Mississippi, to her husband, who was in the Confederate ranks in Tennessee. The letter, dated 13 May 1863, one day

after Ulysses S. Grant's victory at the battle of Raymond, does not describe the fighting, but rather the confiscatory actions by Union troops passing the plantation and the reactions of the slaves, some of whom left to follow the Union forces but quickly returned, "saying they were tired of Yankees" already. The context of the letter is described in Ashcraft's brief introductory remarks.                                    D. C. James

773.  Blackburn, George M.  LETTERS TO THE FRONT: A DISTAFF VIEW OF THE CIVIL WAR.  *Michigan Hist. 1965 49(1): 53-67.* Seeks to determine what the Civil War meant to a contemporary, Sophia Buchanan, on the basis of letters written to her husband, Captain John C. Buchanan of the 8th Michigan Infantry. She was perceptive and articulate, and the more than 60 letters written between 1862 and 1865, which are now part of the Bingham Papers in the Clarke Historical Library at Central Michigan University, reveal "the anxieties and trials suffered by women left behind as men fought the war." Moreover, they indicate that throughout the struggle she remained intensely idealistic and loyal to the Union.                                                    J. K. Flack

774.  Bratcher, James T., ed.  AN 1866 LETTER ON THE WAR AND RECONSTRUCTION.  *Tennessee Hist. Q. 1963 22(1): 83-86.* Presents a letter written by Nancy Cox, Readyville, Tennessee, 27 May 1866 to her children, and cites the privations of the period. Chiefly of local and genealogical interest. 12 notes of genealogy.           W. A. Klutts

775.  Brav, Stanley R.  THE JEWISH WOMAN, 1861-1865. *Am. Jewish Arch. 1965 17(1): 34-75.* From contemporary journals and books describes the homelife, war activities, and attitudes of Jewish women both North and South.                                 A. B. Rollins

776.  Brown, D. Alexander.  A CIVIL WAR LOVE STORY. *Civil War Times Illus. 1967 5(9): 28-39.* Describes the meeting, courtship, and marriage of a young Illinois couple. Included are descriptions of the 12th Illinois Volunteer Infantry's actions in the Atlanta campaign and the march to the sea. Based on the principals' correspondence. Illus.
W. R. Boedecker

777.  Bryan, T. Conn, ed.  A GEORGIA WOMAN'S CIVIL WAR DIARY: THE JOURNAL OF MINERVA LEAH ROWLES MC CLATCHEY, 1864-65.  *Georgia Hist. Q. 1967 51(2): 197-216.* The diary of a plantation wife in Northwest Georgia during the final years of the Confederacy, this document is an illuminating contribution to the social history of the Civil War period. Part of Sherman's army passed over the McClatchey plantation on its march through Georgia. The diarist records her impressions of the evacuation of the area by civilians and Confederate soldiers and of the swarms of Union troops that soon followed. She also describes the confusion, uncertainty, and despair of the last days of the Confederacy.                                R. A. Mohl

778.  Buni, Andrew, ed.  RECONSTRUCTION IN ORANGE COUNTY, VIRGINIA: A LETTER FROM HANNAH GARLICK RAWLINGS TO HER SISTER, CLARISSA LAWRENCE RAWLINGS, AUGUST 9, 1865.  *Virginia Mag. of Hist. and Biog. 1967 75(4): 459-465.* Reprints, with an introduction and eight explanatory notes, a 28-year-old Virginian's letter to her sister in Pennsylvania recounting her reactions to the collapse of the Confederacy.           K. J. Bauer

779.  Bynum, Hartwell T.  SHERMAN'S EXPULSION OF THE ROSWELL WOMEN IN 1864.  *Georgia Hist. Q. 1970 54(2): 169-182.* Concerns General Sherman's capture and destruction of the Roswell Factory textile mills in Georgia and the disposition of approximately 400 female workers. In accordance with Sherman's policy of dispersing Confederate sympathizers to protect his supply line, most of the women were taken to Marietta (Georgia) and Nashville (Tennessee). The author favors the opinion that the women were unnecessarily scattered widely and few ever returned. Based on research in letters, newspapers, official correspondence, and local histories; 4 photos, 35 notes.         R. A. Mohl

780.  Carson, William G. B.  "SECESH."  *Missouri Hist. Soc. Bull. 1967 23(2): 119-145.* Excerpts from letters written between 1861 and 1863 reveal the impact of the Civil War on a "rebel" family of St. Louis - Dr. William Carr Lane (the first Mayor of St. Louis), his wife (the former Mary Ewing), their two daughters (Anne, 42 when she wrote the first letter quoted in 1861, and Sarah, wife of William Glasgow, who was

a loyal Unionist). All four Lanes were rabid secessionists, or "Sesesh" as they were called. Because of Sarah's ill health, her husband decided to take her and five of their eldest children to Wiesbaden, Germany, where it was hoped that Sarah would find relief in the mineral springs. Whenever Anne sat down to write to her sister in Germany, her resentments boiled up, and she poured forth her troubles without restraint, dwelling always upon her unhappy situation. In 1863, Glasgow brought his family back to St. Louis, and Anne left for Europe. "With her departure, her mournful letters came to an end, and so does this chronicle." 97 notes.
D. D. Cameron

781.  Case, Richard G.  MRS. REDFIELD'S SOCKS.  *New York Folklore Q. 1967 23(2): 136-139.* Relates the story of a painting of a pair of socks owned by Mrs. Amy Redfield of Syracuse, New York, during the Civil War, and currently owned by the Onondaga Historical Association in Syracuse.

782.  Chancellor, Sue M.  PERSONAL RECOLLECTIONS OF THE BATTLE OF CHANCELLORSVILLE.  *Register of the Kentucky Hist. Soc. 1968 66(2): 137-146.* "Chancellorsville was not a village but a large country home." A personal account of the Battle of Chancellorsville in May 1863, by a Southern lady whose home was in the middle of the fighting, describes the use of the house as a hospital and the treatment the family received from Union officers. The house was burned to the ground. 4 notes.                                         B. Wilkins

783.  Coleman, Kenneth.  MARY ANN COBB IN CONFEDERATE ATHENS.  *Georgia R. 1968 22(3): 360-369.* Plantation life during the Civil War in Athens, Georgia.                                   S

784.  Cullen, J. P.  KATE CHASE: PETTICOAT POLITICIAN. *Civil War Times Illus. 1963 2(2): 14-20.* Kate Chase was the daughter of Salmon P. Chase.                                             S

785.  Daniel, W. Harrison.  THE EFFECTS OF THE CIVIL WAR ON SOUTHERN PROTESTANTISM.  *Maryland Hist. Mag. 1974 69(1): 44-63.* All branches of Protestantism were scarred and afflicted by the Civil War. All denominations carried on extensive activities to care for the wounded, orphans, and widows of the Southern armies. Northern troops committed many unjustifiable outrages on Southern churches, while inflation brought serious financial problems to the clergy, many of whom took secular employment. Southern Presbyterians, Lutherans, and Episcopalians all split from their Northern brethren and formed separate organizations, but war brought no revival enthusiasm to the Southern churches as it did in the camps. Federal treatment of Southern clergymen was largely moderate and tolerant, but those who persisted in "political preaching" were punished. All denominations "faced a major rebuilding task in the spring of 1865." Primary and secondary sources; 6 illus., 79 notes.                                           G. J. Bobango

786.  Dannet, Sylvia G. L.  REBECCA WRIGHT - TRAITOR OR PATRIOT?  *Lincoln Herald 1963 65(3): 103-112.* Relates how Rebecca Wright provided General Philip H. Sheridan with information about the disposition of Confederate troops in the Shenandoah Valley which enabled Sheridan to capture Winchester, Virginia, in September 1864. The article also traces Miss Wright's life (she later married William C. Bonsal) to her death in 1914.                                          S. L. Jones

787.  Darst, Maury.  SIX WEEKS TO TEXAS.  *Texana 1968 6(2): 140-152.* Presents the 1861 diary kept by Mrs. George Marchmann during a trip from New York to LaGrange, Texas, with her daughter Anna. The two women traveled by train through the North to Louisville, across Kentucky and Tennessee to Memphis, down the Mississippi River to New Orleans, and finally across Louisiana by coach to Texas. Encounters with both Union and Confederate troops are described as well as various difficulties in transportation due to war conditions. 5 notes.
J. E. Findling

788.  Davis, Curtis Carroll.  EFFIE GOLDSBOROUGH: CONFEDERATE COURIER.  *Civil War Times Illus. 1968 7(1): 29-31.* Describes some episodes in the career of this courier. Included are photographs of her writing desk showing a secret compartment. Arrested in 1863, she was banished from the United States until the end of the war. She spent these years in Richmond working in the Confederate Treasury.
R. N. Alvis

789. Deutrich, Bernice M. PROPRIETY AND PAY. *Prologue 1971 3(2): 67-72.* The first widespread employment of women in the federal government occurred during the Civil War and was based on the need for cheap labor to handle increased demands—rather than on altruistic concern for equal opportunities for women. These women primarily filled low-paying positions or received less compensation than men when they held important appointments. Based on primary sources, including correspondence of Quartermaster General Montgomery C. Meigs, and other National Archives materials; illus., 12 notes.

D. G. Davis, Jr.

790. Fladeland, Betty. NEW LIGHT ON SARAH EMMA ED-MONDS ALIAS FRANKLIN THOMPSON. *Michigan Hist. 1963 47(4): 357-362.* Corroborates the story that Franklin Thompson of the 2nd Michigan Infantry Regiment during the Civil War was actually a woman, Sarah Emma Edmonds. Provides evidence from a diary recently acquired by the Michigan Historical Collection of the University of Michigan.

J. K. Flack

791. Hammett, Evelyn Allen. WITH PEN IN HAND: LETTERS OF MALACHI AND AVLINE GROVES (1860-1867). *J. of Mississippi Hist. 1971 33(3): 219-229.* Several letters written by the author's grandfather and grandmother (a cousin of Ulysses S. Grant) in Mississippi to his family in Pennsylvania, 1860-67. The letters include information regarding the 1860 election, wages and prices in Port Gibson, criticism of the South, the early confidence of Southern military success, and, regarding Reconstruction, antiblack statements and information regarding hardships and economic problems.

J. W. Hillje

792. Hass, Paul H., ed. A VOLUNTEER NURSE IN THE CIVIL WAR: THE LETTERS OF HARRIET DOUGLAS WHETTEN. *Wisconsin Mag. of Hist. 1964 48(2): 131-151.* The letters provide information about the day-to-day activities of a Sanitary Commission nurse in the hospital transport service, during the spring and summer of 1862, in the Chesapeake Bay-James River area of the Civil War campaigns. Whetten's duty was to nurse and care for the wounded aboard ship as they were transported from battlefields to land-based hospitals or from one hospital to another. Included are details concerning the weather, the areas through which she passed, the war, the wounded men, and the persons with whom she came in contact. The letters give a "woman's-eye," on-the-spot report of the effects of the campaigning in that area. Illus., map, 23 notes. Article to be continued.

H. A. Negaard

793. Hass, Paul H., ed. A VOLUNTEER NURSE IN THE CIVIL WAR: THE DIARY OF HARRIET DOUGLAS WHETTEN. *Wisconsin Mag. of Hist. 1965 48(3): 205-221.* Continued from previous article. The author was assigned to the hospital transport service of the US Sanitary Commission as a volunteer nurse. She kept the portion of the diary printed during July and August 1862 and; like her letters, it presents a vivid and diverse account of the "last days of the Peninsular campaign." Personnel, manners and morals, weather, women, nursing, the war, hospital and ship conditions, and the soldiers brought in for care are all discussed. The damage caused by the war is illustrated by her eyewitness description of the burning of Edmund Ruffin's home. 6 photos, engraving, 17 notes.

H. A. Negaard

794. Hunter, Kate. NEWPORT: MID-NINETEENTH CENTURY. *Newport Hist. 1972 45(1): 7-11.* Short descriptions of Newport social and recreational activities as written by 15-year-old Kate Hunter, daughter of Captain Charles and Mary Hunter, in 1863-64. She was especially taken by the men of the US Naval Academy who were temporarily stationed in Newport during the war. Some of the favorite recreational activities were parties, musicals, gala balls, and drives or walks along the shore.

D. P. Peltier

795. Kemper, Mary Lee, ed. CIVIL WAR REMINISCENCES AT DANVILLE FEMALE ACADEMY. *Missouri Hist. R. 1968 62(3): 314-320.* Presents recollections of the author's mother, Mary Robinson, of a Confederate raid on Danville, Missouri, 14 October 1864. The girls and the five buildings on the campus of the academy were saved from the men by an unnamed captain. Many years after the war the same captain was tried for murdering a man during the raid, but the girls were able to clear him by showing that he was at the seminary when the murder occurred. Illus., 5 notes.

W. F. Zornow

796. King, Spencer B., Jr. A POOR WIDOW ASKS FOR FOOD: 1865. *Georgia Hist. Q. 1968 52(4): 449-450.* Focuses upon the poverty and desolation of the post-Civil War South, particularly the area ravaged by General Sherman. The author reproduces a letter written by a Milledgeville widow in 1865 to Union General James H. Wilson, begging food for her family. Such petitions were referred to local authorities for disposition.

R. A. Mohl

797. Kondert, Nancy T. THE ROMANCE AND REALITY OF DEFEAT: SOUTHERN WOMEN IN 1865. *J. of Mississippi Hist. 1973 35(2): 141-152.* Describes the attitudes of southern women toward the defeat of the Confederacy in 1865. Some refused to accept defeat, but "the poor, backwoods Southern women were generally glad to see the end of the war." There was despondency, hopelessness, and anxiety. Southern women feared northern oppression and expressed hatred and contempt for the North. They generally felt sympathy for the freedmen but also "apprehension and distrust of what the freedmen might do." Based on published primary sources; 36 notes.

J. W. Hillje

798. Lander, Ernest M., Jr. A CONFEDERATE GIRL VISITS PENNSYLVANIA, JULY-SEPTEMBER 1863. *Western Pennsylvania Hist. Mag. 1966 49(2): 111-126, (3): 197-211.* Letters of Floride Clemson offer descriptions of the physical geography and the social customs of Pennsylvania during the Civil War.

S

799. Leland, Isabella Middleton. MIDDLETON CORRESPONDENCE, 1861-1865. *South Carolina Hist. Mag. 1964 65(1): 33-44, (2): 98-109.* Continued from previous articles. Further correspondence of Harriott Middleton of Flat Rock, North Carolina and Susan Middleton, of Columbia, South Carolina, concerning the Civil War, society, personalities, and prices.

V. O. Bardsley

800. Leland, Isabella Middleton. MIDDLETON CORRESPONDENCE, 1861-1865. *South Carolina Hist. Mag. 1963 64(1): 28-38, (2): 95-104, and (3): 158-168.* In a continuation of letters beginning 3 January 1863, sent between Flat Rock, North Carolina and Columbia, South Carolina, the Middleton women, Susan and Harriott, exchange gossip of neighbors and discuss the abilities of the Union and Confederate fighting men, forms of dances, sales of houses, General Beauregard, an "infernal machine" designed to sink monitors, and scarcities. Continuing in April, they review the assault on Sumter and excoriate Mrs. Henry Duncan for Union sympathies. They mention the death of Jackson, the assassination of Van Dorn, the Davis postage stamps, the decline in the tone of society, the scarcity of food, and the gallantry of Lee. Beginning again in July, they speak of the course of the war, family affairs, and the sinking of the *Ironsides.*

V. E. Bardsley

801. Leland, Isabella Middleton. MIDDLETON CORRESPONDENCE, 1861-1865. *South Carolina Hist. Mag. 1963 64(4): 212-220.* Correspondence between Harriott Middleton and Susan Middleton, Flat Rock, North Carolina, and Columbia, South Carolina, gives an account of notable personages, scarcities, suffering and privation, the course of the war, warm love for the Low Country, Jefferson Davis, gossip, society.

V. E. Bardsley

802. Long, E. B. ANNA ELLA CARROLL: EXAGGERATED HEROINE? *Civil War Times Illus. 1975 14(4): 28-35.* A biography of Anna Ella Carroll, arguing that her part in the Civil War was greatly exaggerated, and tracing some of the controversy among historians over her career.

S

803. McMillan, Edward, ed. ALICE FARMER: A YANKEE IN THE CIVIL WAR SOUTH. *Louisiana Studies 1968 7(4): 321-328.* The autobiography of Alice Farmer (1847-1942) written in 1903 for her son for the purpose of preserving the fascinating details of her life. Her manuscript relates why the family came to Louisiana in 1850, and her account of life in Louisiana from 1850 to 1872 is especially revealing. Illus., 10 notes.

G. W. McGinty

804. Murray, Robert B. MRS. ALEXANDER'S COTTON. *Louisiana Hist. 1965 6(4): 393-400.* The story of the capture of cotton bales from Mrs. Elizabeth Alexander's plantation on the Red River in Louisiana by Federal forces on one of Rear Admiral David D. Porter's gunboats is unique in that the Supreme Court "treated Mrs. Alexander

as a party to an action in the United States court system when as a matter of physical fact she was a citizen of the Confederacy." The Supreme Court dismissed the original decision declaring the cotton a maritime prize but held the money in trust in the US Treasury until Mrs. Alexander should be in a position after the war to file another suit to prove that she had been loyal.                                                    E. P. Stickney

805. Naisawald, L. VanLoan. FANNY RICKETTS, NURSE, DIARIST, DEVOTED WIFE. *Virginia Cavalcade 1972 21(3): 14-21.* Frances Lawrence Ricketts was the wife of Captain James B. Ricketts of the Union Army. Captain Ricketts was wounded severely at the First Battle of Manassas and was captured on 21 July 1861. Mrs. Ricketts journeyed to Manassas to care for her husband and then went on to Richmond to tend him during his long recovery. She kept a diary of the period. The diary describes the conditions of captivity and other incidents surrounding life in a southern hospital during the Civil War. 12 photos.
E. P. Costello

806. O'Brien, Jean Getman and Hoffsommer, Robert D. DOROTHEA DIX. *Civil War Times Illus. 1965 4(5): 39-44.* Outlines Dorothea L. Dix's contributions to the Union war effort. Undocumented, illus.
W. R. Boedecker

807. Partin, Robert. THE WARTIME EXPERIENCES OF MARGARET MC CALLA: CONFEDERATE REFUGEE FROM EAST TENNESSEE. *Tennessee Hist. Q. 1965 24(1): 39-53.* Quotes from 28 letters to her husband, a Confederate soldier. The letters were written chiefly after she fled Morristown, Tennessee, about 1 September 1863, settling in Chester District, South Carolina. The comments in the letters reflect economic conditions and morale. Based on family papers; 19 notes.
W. A. Klutts

808. Pye, Carol Benson, ed. LETTERS FROM AN ILLINOIS FARM; 1864-1865. *J. of the Illinois State Hist. Soc. 1973 66(4): 387-403.* Louisa Jane Phifer's letters to her husband, George Brown Phifer, a corporal in the 32nd Illinois Infantry, describe the daily life of a family headed by a woman during the Civil War. The resourceful woman optimistically managed seven young children and a farm near Vandalia in Fayette County, Illinois. George's letters and other family papers are cited as they elucidate Louisa's narrative. Based on 10 letters; illus., 3 photos, 41 notes.                                          A. C. Aimone

809. Richman, Irwin PAULINE CUSHMAN: A PERSONALITY PROFILE. *Civil War Times Illus. 1969 7(10): 38-44.* Relates the brief career of "the lady spy of the Cumberland." Offered 300 dollars to give a Southern toast on the stage in Louisville, the actress reported the offer to the provost marshall. At his suggestion she gave the toast and became a spy for the North, from March until June 1863. Traces her subsequent career until her suicide in San Francisco in 1893.          R. N. Alvis

810. Robertson, James I., Jr., ed. AN INDIANA SOLDIER IN LOVE AND WAR: THE CIVIL WAR LETTERS OF JOHN V. HADLEY. *Indiana Mag. of Hist. 1963 59(3): 189-288.* Describes the wartime career of a Hoosier soldier who gained recognition after the war as a justice of the Indiana Supreme Court. The article includes descriptions of the battles of Port Republic, Second Manassas, Fredericksburg, and Chancellorsville, provides commentaries on leading military commanders, and sheds new light on social life both in and out of the wartime military camps.                                              J. Findlay

811. Sabine, David B. CAPTAIN SALLY TOMPKINS. *Civil War Times Illus. 1965 4(7): 36-39.* "The founder and supervisor of one of the best-run hospitals in Richmond, this energetic little woman was the only person of her sex to hold a Confederate Army commission." Undocumented, illus.                                          W. R. Boedecker

812. Sabine, David B. THE MIDNIGHT RIDE OF MOLLIE TYNES. *Civil War Times Illus. 1964 3(5): 36-38.* A Virginia girl rode many miles to save a vital salt works from Yankee raiders. Illus.    S

813. Schnell, Christopher J. MARY LIVERMORE AND THE GREAT NORTHWESTERN FAIR. *Chicago Hist. 1975 4(1): 34-43.* Biography of Mary Livermore, Chicago feminist, emphasizing her fundraising efforts during the Civil War for the US Sanitary Commission and Chicago's Great Northwestern Fair.                         S

814. Shattuck, George C. SARAH CABOT WHEELWRIGHT'S ACCOUNT OF THE WIDOW BIXBY. *Massachusetts Hist. Soc. Pro. 1963 75: 107-108.* Doubts whether the Widow Bixby deserved the famous letter of condolences she received from President Lincoln on the loss of five sons killed in action. Mrs. Wheelwright, who had employed Mrs. Bixby, discovered that the latter was "perfectly untrustworthy," operated a house of ill-fame, and had probably not more than two sons in the Union Army. Mrs. Wheelwright's full account and Lincoln's letter are reproduced.                                                   J. B. Duff

815. Sigaud, Louis A. WILLIAM BOYD COMPTON: BELLE BOYD'S COUSIN. *Lincoln Herald 1965 67(1): 22-33.* Relates Compton's activities as Confederate recruiter and spy behind the Union lines in West Virginia, his capture, Lincoln's suspension of his sentence of execution, and his escape in May 1864. Emphasis is given to his association with Belle Boyd and his courtship of and marriage to Kate Kerr. Based on the *Official Records of the Union and Confederate Armies,* the Confederate records in the National Archives, and letters from Compton and his family now in the possession of Mrs. George Evans, Bruceton Mills, West Virginia.                                       S. L. Jones

816. Smith, Maria MacGregor. "IT WAS A VERY SERIOUS UNDERTAKING." *Civil War Times Illus. 1974 13(5): 18-22.* Personal narrative by Maria MacGregor Smith (Mrs. Charles Henry), of her return to the Union to visit her dying father at the close of the Civil War.
S

817. Snyder, Charles McCool. ANNA ELLA CARROLL, POLITICAL STRATEGIST AND GADFLY OF PRESIDENT FILLMORE. *Maryland Hist. Mag. 1973 68(1): 36-63.* Anna Ella Carroll never received Congressional payment for her claim of being the architect of the Union's western strategy in the Civil War. The discovery of more than 50 of her letters written to Millard Fillmore during 1852-73 characterizes her as "a woman at war with Victorian conventions," striving for recognition as a pamphleteer, propagandist, and politician. Her books, such as *The Star of the West* (1856), and numerous pamphlets and sycophantic correspondence with political figures made her New York hotel a nerve center of the American Party movement. Full of self-importance, her letters are "judicious mixtures of extravagant praise and requests for favors." Carroll's defenders have since developed a full martyr image of her life as one of an unappreciated heroine. Based on primary and secondary sources; 8 illus., 71 notes.                                         G. J. Bobango

818. Stanfield, Elizabeth P. SELECTED SOCIAL CORRESPONDENCE OF MISS ELEANOR HARDIN JACKSON OF RUTHERFORD COUNTY (1860-1865). *Tennessee Folklore Soc. Bull. 1975 41(1): 9-18.*                                              S

819. Stinson, Byron T. PIN-UPS OF THE CIVIL WAR. *Civil War Times Illus. 1969 8(5): 38-41.* Gives eight examples of Civil War pin-ups, two of them nudes. "The usual source of pinups in the Civil War was *Frank Leslie's Family Magazine.*" These were ripped out and tacked to the walls of living quarters. Few examples of Civil War pin-up art remain today.                                                  R. N. Alvis

820. Temple, Wayne C. LINCOLN AND W. H. W. CUSHMAN. *Lincoln Herald 1966 68(2): 81-88.* Raises a question as to why Lincoln virtually ordered the Secretary of War to commission Illinois Democrat Cushman as a colonel of an Illinois regiment and concludes that the action derived from a friendship between the two men growing out of an intimacy which existed between their wives. The text and a photographic copy of a newly discovered note by Lincoln endorsing Cushman's application for the appointment are printed here.                  S. L. Jones

821. Thomas, Charles E., ed. THE DIARY OF ANNA HASELL THOMAS (JULY 1864-MAY 1865). *South Carolina Hist. Mag. 1973 74(3): 128-143.* South Carolinian Anna Hasell Thomas (1828-1908), who lived in New York, was granted presidential permission to visit South Carolina during the Civil War. Reproduces entries 26 December 1864 to 31 May 1865 describing the hardships of the closing days of the war. 11 notes.                                                   D. L. Smith

822. Tompkins, Ellen Wilkins, ed. THE COLONEL'S LADY: SOME LETTERS OF ELLEN WILKINS TOMPKINS, JULY-DECEMBER

1861. *Virginia Mag. of Hist. and Biog. 1961 69(4): 387-419.* Presents letters dealing with the Civil War written to, and by, Ellen Wilkins Tompkins in Fayette County, West Virginia, in 1861.

823. Turney, Catherine. CRAZY BETTY. *Mankind 1971 3(3): 58-64.* Living in her family's Richmond mansion, genteel Elizabeth Van Lew spied for the Union during the Civil War.                                      S

824. Viener, Saul. ROSENA HUTZLER LEVY RECALLS THE CIVIL WAR. *Am. Jewish Hist. Q. 1973 62(3): 306-313.* A letter written in 1907 by Rosena Hutzler Levy (1840-1914) to her children recalled the Civil War service of their father, Richard Levy (1828-97). The hitherto unpublished letter is a telling record of the catastrophe which altered so many southern families.                                      F. Rosenthal

825. Weathers, Willie T. JUDITH W. MC GUIRE: *A LADY OF VIRGINIA.* *Virginia Mag. of Hist. and Biog. 1974 82(1): 100-113.* Biographical account of the author of *Diary of a Southern Refugee During the War* (1865). Also contains genealogical information. Based on newspaper and secondary sources; 50 notes.                                      R. F. Oaks

826. Werlich, Robert. MARY WALKER: FROM UNION ARMY SURGEON TO SIDESHOW FREAK. *Civil War Times Illus. 1967 6(3): 46-49.* During a considerable part of the Civil War Mary Walker, one of the few female practitioners of the day, served the Union Army as a contract surgeon. Although she failed in an effort to be commissioned, at the close of the war she was awarded the Medal of Honor. The award was canceled by Congress in 1917 when the requirements for the medal were upgraded. Mary spent the later years of her life lecturing on her wartime experiences. Evidently bad tempered, she did not get on well in the predominantly male world she chose to live in.
R. N. Alvis

827. Wiley, Bell I. WOMEN OF THE LOST CAUSE. *Am. Hist. Illus. 1973 8(8): 10-23.* Activities of Confederate women during the Civil War as spies, nurses and social leaders.                                      S

828. Williams, Marjorie Logan, ed. CECILIA LABADIE: DIARY FRAGMENT, JANUARY 29, 1863-FEBRUARY 5, 1863. *Texana 1972 10(3): 273-283.* Contains a brief history of Galveston and a sketch of the life of Cecilia Labadie (1839-1873), who lived in Galveston. Describes the shelling of the town by the *Brooklyn,* a Union frigate, and three gunboats, as well as a poem probably written to Major Philip Crosby Tucker, whom Labadie later married. Based on primary and secondary sources; 58 notes.                                      J. E. Findling

829. Williams, Ora G. MUSKETS AND MAGNOLIAS: FOUR CIVIL WAR DIARIES BY LOUISIANA GIRLS. *Louisiana Studies 1965 4(3): 187-197.* States the main contents of each diary; the period each covers; and compares them as to author, message, philosophy, and factual content.                                      G. W. McGinty

830. Wong, Celia. TWO POLISH WOMEN IN THE CONFEDERACY. *Polish Am. Studies 1966 23(2): 97-101.* An account of the role played by Sophie Sosnowski and Apolonia Jagiello Tochman in service to the Confederacy. Both accounts merely identify the service with no mention of influence or exact participation. Activities of each woman before and after the war are mentioned.                                      S. R. Pliska

831. Wood, Ann Douglas. THE WAR WITHIN A WAR: WOMEN NURSES IN THE UNION ARMY. *Civil War Hist. 1972 18(3): 197-212.* With American medicine in a rather primitive state during the Civil War, it is not surprising that there was no nurses' corps. A small body of courageous women, untrained professionally yet possessing skill, devotion, and perseverance, brought aid to the battlefield. They supplied an element absent from the Army Medical Corps' crude operations. Such persons as Dorothea Dix, Clara Barton, Mary Ann Bickerdyke, and Annie Wittenmyer cut through reams of red tape and walls of opposition from the all-male profession to bring aid and comfort to wounded men at the front. Unpaid and abused by doctors who believed a woman's place was in the home, these pioneers paved the way for the formal nurses' training schools which appeared after the war.                                      E. C. Murdock

# Feminism

832. Allen, Margaret V. THE POLITICAL AND SOCIAL CRITICISM OF MARGARET FULLER. *South Atlantic Q. 1973 72(4): 560-578.* Margaret Fuller's early life was a sheltered one. She abhorred politicians and political philosophy, with the exception of that of Thomas Jefferson; and it took time for her to develop a social conscience and an awareness of injustice. She gradually developed humanist and feminist sympathies which culminated in her book, *Woman in the Nineteenth Century,* in 1843. After becoming a reviewer-critic for Horace Greeley's *New York Daily Tribune,* she was exposed to poverty and exploitation and became a political leftist. After an assignment to Italy during the Roman revolution of 1848-49, she became a political radical. 39 notes.
E. P. Stickney

833. Deiss, Joseph Jay. MEN, WOMEN, AND MARGARET FULLER. *Am. Heritage 1972 23(5): 42-47, 94-97.* Margaret Fuller (1810-50) was possibly the first liberated female in America, editor of the Transcendentalist periodical *Dial,* columnist for the New York *Tribune,* and a strong advocate of women's rights.                                      S

834. Douglas, Ann. MARGARET FULLER AND THE SEARCH FOR HISTORY: A BIOGRAPHICAL STUDY. *Women's Studies 1976 4(1): 37-86.* Analyzes the life and thought of Margaret Fuller, who challenged the sexual, political, and cultural assumptions of early 19th century American society. Fuller's development as a person fell into 3 major parts: 1) intellectual and scholarly training under her father, Timothy Fuller; 2) relationship with Ralph Waldo Emerson; and 3) experiences in New York and Italy. Lacking adequate feminine models and striving to find her "sovereign self," Fuller struggled against cultural assumptions and strived for a life of activity. Ultimately, she rejected the life of feminine fantasy, literature, and conversation and moved to journalism, history, cultural analysis, and an active role of political and personal participation in the events around her. Based on primary and secondary materials; 168 notes.                                      A. E. Wiederrecht

835. Gambone, Joseph G., ed. THE FORGOTTEN FEMINIST OF KANSAS: THE PAPERS OF CLARINA I. H. NICHOLS, 1854-1885. *Kansas Hist. Q. 1973 39(1): 12-57, (2): 220-261.* Part I. After an active career in controversy about temperance, slavery, and women's rights that began in Vermont in 1839, Mrs. Nichols moved to Kansas in 1854 "to work for a Government of equality, liberty, [and] fraternity." She spent most of her time in Kansas until poor health forced her to move to California in 1871. She helped to amend the Kansas constitution to grant women liberal property rights, equal guardianship of their children, and the right to vote. 2 illus., 140 notes. Part II. In this series of letters to prominent editors and personal friends from stopping-places between Kansas and the east coast (1855-56), Mrs. Nichols discussed her reaction to the territorial strife in Kansas and to antifeminism. Many of the letters were to Thaddeus Hyatt, a supporter of the Kansas Free-State party who in 1856 made Mrs. Nichols a relief agent in New York. 2 photos, 81 notes. Article to be continued.                                      W. F. Zornow

836. Kaye, Frances W. THE LADIES' DEPARTMENT OF THE *OHIO CULTIVATOR,* 1845-1855: A FEMINIST FORUM. *Agric. Hist. 1976 50(2): 414-423.* Between 1845 and 1855 a number of profeminist articles appeared in the Ladies' Department of the *Ohio Cultivator,* a leading Midwestern agricultural journal. Under the leadership of Hannah Maria Tracy-Cutler and Frances Dana Gage, the Department printed articles on the role of women in the home, education, suffrage, and jobs for women. It was a grass-roots forum for feminism. 23 notes.
D. E. Bowers

837. Kendall, Kathleen Edgerton and Fisher, Jeanne Y. FRANCES WRIGHT ON WOMEN'S RIGHTS: ELOQUENCE VERSUS ETHOS. *Q. J. of Speech 1974 60(1): 58-68.* "Frances Wright, a Scotswoman and first woman public speaker in America, failed to persuade 1828-1830 audiences of the importance of women's rights becuase of her low extrinsic ethos. She met all the criteria for 'eloquence' defined by Longinus, and contemporary audiences granted her high intrinsic ethos; however, her radical behavior and ideas such as the invasion of the male lecture platform, association with free love practices, and attacks on organized religion violated societal norms and thereby mitigated her effectiveness."
J

838. Martin, Wendy. PROFILE: FRANCES WRIGHT, 1795-1852. *Women's Studies 1974 2(3): 273-278.* Surveys the life and thought of Frances Wright, emphasizing her activities in the United States. Born in Scotland, in 1795, Wright wrote, spoke, and worked for women's rights, the emancipation of slaves, civil rights, and socialist principles. She protested the power of the church, capital punishment, and imprisonment for debt. Her career as a public lecturer, the hostility of the American public and press, the Nashoba community, Robert Owen and his New Harmony colony, the *Free Enquirer,* and the New York Workingman's Party are discussed. Wright married Phiquepal D'Arusmont and returned to Europe a number of times. She lived her final years in Cincinnati where she died on 13 December 1852.                         A. E. Wiederrecht

839. Melder, Keith E. FORERUNNERS OF FREEDOM: THE GRIMKE SISTERS IN MASSACHUSETTS, 1837-1838. *Essex Inst. Hist. Collections 1967 103(3): 223-249.* The arrival of the Grimké sisters - Angelina and Sarah - in Massachusetts in 1837 in the cause of antislavery soon changed into a much broader movement for female emancipation. The sisters were well-received by many in the State, especially women active in the growing lyceum movement of these years. But criticism, largely from clergymen, of women publicly preaching (even in opposition to slavery) forced the sisters to defend a woman's right to speak in public by extending the concept of equality to women. Several leading abolitionists supported them, and Angelina spoke before a special legislative subcommittee on behalf of antislavery and in defense of women's participation in the movement. In 1838, Angelina left Boston to marry Theodore Weld, and the sisters dropped from public view. But they left a legacy of division among reformers over the question of women's rights and awakened a previously dormant issue. Based mostly on unpublished manuscripts.                                    J. M. Bumsted

840. Pease, William H. and Pease, Jane H. SAMUEL J. MAY: CIVIL LIBERTARIAN. *Cornell Lib. J. 1967 3: 7-25.* Discusses Samuel Joseph May, the Unitarian clergyman and civil libertarian whose library provided the foundation for Cornell University's Antislavery Collection. Covering the years from 1832 to 1861, the authors examine May's belief in spiritual freedom as the basis of civil liberty. The minister's convictions led him to champion unpopular causes of his day, such as pacifism, women's rights, and abolitionism. May defended Prudence Crandall whose school for young ladies in Canterbury, Connecticut, was attacked by local citizenry when she accepted a student who was part Negro. From 1835, when May was General Agent for the Massachusetts Anti-Slavery Society, until the Rochester Convention of 1861, when antiabolitionists seized the hall reserved by him for the antislavery groups, May often faced angry and violent mobs. At times, he had doubts about the wisdom of provocation in emotional times. The authors found, however, that May never wavered in defending the principle of civil rights. Based on primary and secondary sources; 32 notes.                    M. M. Williamson

841. Porter, Lorle Anne. AMELIA BLOOMER: AN EARLY IOWA FEMINIST'S SOJOURN ON THE WAY WEST. *Ann. of Iowa 1973 41(8): 1242-1257.* The 1853 lecture tour of Iowa feminist Amelia Jenks Bloomer led to a one-year stay in Mt. Vernon, Ohio.            S

842. Rao, Adapa Ramakrishna. EMERSON AND THE FEMINISTS. *Indian J. of Am. Studies [India] 1974 4(1/2): 13-20.* Traces the stages through which Ralph Waldo Emerson came by the end of the American Civil War to sympathize publicly with the feminist movement. His philosophy of self-reliant individualism prompted him to recognize the general validity of the feminist position. Because he always affirmed the right of individuals to decide for themselves whatever is good for their individual growth, he logically had no choice but to agree that women unquestionably had the right to own property and to engage in politics. Yet his view of woman as civilizer kept Emerson from accepting the activist position that women should engage in public agitation in order to win their property and voting rights. 15 notes.            L. Eid

843. Sokolow, Jayme A. HENRY CLARKE WRIGHT: ANTEBELLUM CRUSADER. *Essex Inst. Hist. Collections 1975 111(2): 122-137.* Examines the origin of Wright's ideas on reform. Evangelical revivalism led to his interest in and advocacy of temperance, immediate abolition of slavery, women's suffrage, pacifism, and humanitarian education. Based on historical essays, newspapers, letters, journals, and Wright's work; 41 notes.                                     R. M. Rollins

844. Stern, Madeleine B. WILLIAM HENRY CHANNING'S LETTERS ON "WOMAN IN HER SOCIAL RELATIONS." *Cornell Lib. J. 1968 6: 54-62.* Concerns a report entitled "Woman in Her Social Relations," given by William Henry Channing, Unitarian clergyman and social reformer, at the Second National Woman's Rights Convention held at Worcester, Massachusetts, on 15-16 October 1851. This report was not published with the convention's proceedings and was only briefly abstracted in a newspaper article. The author discovered three of Channing's letters, reproduced in this article, which were sent to Charlotte Fowler Wells, the phrenologist-publisher, before Channing gave his address. The first letter mentions the four questions he discussed: 1) How could single women have happy, independent, and dignified lives? 2) How could unhappy marriages be prevented? 3) How could unsuccessful marriages be dissolved? 4) How could "Licentiousness" be stopped? Channing suggested that an association of women could establish a country home to teach single women such subjects as horticulture and the fine arts. Affiliated unions would offer assistance to distressed women in cities and towns. The author concludes that these letters give some indication of the contents of Channing's never-published report. The three letters are part of the Fowler-Wells Papers in Cornell University Library's Collection of Regional History and University Archives. Based on primary and secondary sources; 12 notes.                     M. M. Williamson

845. Swidler, Arlene. BROWNSON AND THE "WOMAN QUESTION." *Am. Benedictine R. 1968 19(2): 211-219.* After his conversion to Roman Catholicism in 1844 following a career in the Protestant ministry, Orestes A. Brownson used his fame as a writer and editor to propagate his new faith. Brownson emerged quite early as an antifeminist and expressed his view that suffrage was a civil right. This argument was largely nullified in 1870 with the passage of the 15th amendment giving suffrage to all Negro males. After this, Brownson based his arguments largely on religious grounds and, in his last years, saw the Catholic Church as the one bulwark against the "shameful" women's rights movement. By this time, his views were too rigid to adjust to changing social conditions and his opinions on suffrage became irrelevant. 40 notes.
                                                  E. J. O'Brien

# Abolitionism

846. Davis, J. Treadwell. NASHOBA: FRANCES WRIGHT'S EXPERIMENT IN SELF-EMANCIPATION. *Southern Q. 1972 11(1): 63-90.* Studies Frances Wright's influence on slavery during the 19th century. Wright's attitudes toward slavery included a plan for the gradual freeing of slaves along with an accompanying educational program to prepare the slave for the duties and responsibilities of citizenship. Many of her ideas came from a German Pietist colony established by George Rapp at Harmonic, Indiana. In 1825, Miss Wright purchased land near Memphis, Tennessee, and established a plantation, which was named Nashoba. She then acquired slaves and set her plan for self-emancipation into action. The experiment ended in failure. 76 notes.
                                                  R. W. Dubay

847. Friedman, Lawrence J. RACISM AND SEXISM IN ANTEBELLUM AMERICA: THE PRUDENCE CRANDALL EPISODE RECONSIDERED. *Societas 1974 4(3): 211-227.* In 1830 Prudence Crandall (1803-90) opened a school for black girls in Canterbury, Connecticut, which caused a storm of protest. The author reexamines the incident not only as an example of northern racism, but also as an example of the problems white male abolitionists had in dealing with strong-willed women and sexuality. Discusses William Lloyd Garrison's personal and professional relationship with Crandall. 53 notes.
                                                  W. H. Mulligan, Jr.

848. Hornick, Nancy Slocum. THE LAST APPEAL: LYDIA CHILD'S ANTISLAVERY LETTERS TO JOHN C. UNDERWOOD. *Virginia Mag. of Hist. and Biog. 1971 79(1): 45-54.* Brief biographical sketches of Lydia Maria Francis Child (1802-80) and John Curtiss Underwood (1809-73), a Virginian, precede reproduction of four letters from Child, in 1860, on the mutually obsessive theme of abolition without Southern secession.                       C. A. Newton

849. Kearns, Francis E.   MARGARET FULLER AND THE ABO-
LITION MOVEMENT.   *J. of the Hist. of Ideas 1964 25(1): 120-127.*
"Margaret Fuller's aloofness towards the anti-slavery movement has been
thoroughly exaggerated. Her cautious attitude towards partisans of that
movement was caused not by her refusal to come to grips with the
problems facing American democracy, . . . but resulted from the fact that
her equalitarian principles, embracing the desire to liberate not only the
Negro but also woman, were far more radical than those embraced by the
more conservative reformers constituting the Abolition group."
W. H. Coates

850. Lerner, Gerda.   THE GRIMKE SISTERS AND THE STRUG-
GLE AGAINST RACE PREJUDICE.   *J. of Negro Hist. 1963 48(4):
277-291.* Describes the efforts of Sarah and Angelina Grimké in combat-
ting prejudice against Negroes in the slave states of the South and later
in the North. The Grimké sisters frequently spoke at public meetings on
behalf of the colored people, wrote a number of tracts and pamphlets, and
consistently acted upon their principles in their personal lives. As the only
Southern white women active in the antislavery movement, their example
was influential. Documented with manuscript material.   L. Gara

851. Pease, Jane H. and Pease, William H.   THE ROLE OF WOMEN
IN THE ANTISLAVERY MOVEMENT.   *Can. Hist. Assoc. Annual
Report 1967: 167-183.* A study of four women who do not fit the stereotypes used to explain the activities of antislavery leaders. While different
in character and background, Lydia Maria Francis Child, Maria Weston
Chapman, Abigail Kelly Foster, and Sallie Holley did have in common
assured financial position, education above the average, and mothers who
were not dominant in early life. All rebelled against the role expected of
them, exercised rights denied them by society, and were morally committed to antislavery activity which was to free both slaves and women. Based
on papers at Boston Public Library, Radcliffe College, the Library of
Congress, on reports of antislavery societies, and on secondary sources;
33 notes.   G. E. Panting

852. Riegel, Robert E.   ABBY KELLEY.   *New-England Galaxy
1965 6(4): 21-26.* Despite her abilities and good looks, Abby Kelley
suffered as an extreme and doctrinaire abolitionist in a New England that
was still marked by strong proslavery sentiment. In 1837 she decided to
desert the comparative safety of teaching in order to devote all her efforts
to freedom for the American Negro. After her marriage in 1841 to Stephen Symonds Foster, a coworker for the cause, their home was a well-
known station on the underground railroad. Abby was typical of the New
England intellectuals who worked for reforms that would benefit others.
On this basis she was an important factor in the ultimate success of the
movement to free the slave. Illus.   E. P. Stickney

853. Rivera, Betty.   MILITANT MARTHA.   *New-England Galaxy
1968 9(4): 53-58.* Martha Turner Hudson, of Torringford, was one of the
first northern women involved in the antislavery movement.   S

854. Stevenson, Janet.   A FAMILY DIVIDED.   *Am. Heritage 1967
18(3): 4-8, 84-91.* The history of Sarah Grimké and Angelina Grimké
Weld's antislavery sentiments and their contribution to the abolition
movement.   S

855. Turner, Wallace B.   ABOLITIONISM IN KENTUCKY.
*Register of the Kentucky Hist. Soc. 1971 69(4): 319-338.* Abolitionism
began in Kentucky before statehood and continued until the Civil War.
A Kentucky Abolition Society was founded in 1810 but died from lack
of funds in 1827. In 1833, James G. Birney organized the Kentucky
Anti-Slavery Society, affiliated with William Lloyd Garrison's organization, but soon moved to Ohio under pressure. Cassius Marcellus Clay
began publication of *The True American,* in 1845, but bowed to an
injunction to cease publishing. A mob dismantled his press and he became
the popular leader of the antislavery forces in Kentucky. Abolitionists
failed to get their plank into a new constitution in 1849. Other abolitionist
efforts were made by Calvin Fairbank and Delia Webster, both of whom
served prison sentences for their work. The writing of Harriet Beecher
Stowe influenced others, including John G. Fee, who established the
community of Berea, where, with the aid of the American Missionary
Society, a college was established in 1858, with one avowed goal of
opposition to slavery. Efforts to establish abolition newspapers were uniformly unsuccessful; and, in 1859, the legislature made it a criminal
offense to even try. Primary and secondary sources; 46 notes.
J. F. Paul

856. Walters, Ronald G.   THE EROTIC SOUTH: CIVILIZATION
AND SEXUALITY IN AMERICAN ABOLITIONISM.   *Am. Q. 1973
25(2): 177-201.* The growth of the antislavery movement after 1830 was
based on northern fears of the unrestrained power of the South. Criticism
of the unbridled lasciviousness between masters and slaves was activated
by northern middle-class insecurities over the expansion of the franchise
to the lower-class majority. Concern for southern reform mirrored a
growing reformist belief that civilization depended on controlling man's
animal nature to achieve social progress. Primary and secondary sources;
47 notes.   W. D. Piersen

857. Williman, William H.   THE GRIMKE SISTERS: PROPHETIC
PARIAHS.   *South Carolina Hist. Illus. 1970 1(2): 15-17, 56-58.* Angelina and Sarah M. Grimké were the daughters of one of Charleston's
most affluent and influential families. Their father, John F. Grimké, was
a Revolutionary War officer, state supreme court justice, author, and
planter. A conservative in both racial and social spheres, he rejected
Sarah's request to study Latin as unbecoming to a proper Charleston
female. Although denied formal education, she read widely and became
well informed on a variety of issues. Her religious pilgrimage carried her
from Anglicanism to Presbyterianism to Quakerism. She also became a
devoted abolitionist. The lonely, discontented woman converted her
younger sister Angelina to her views; and both left hostile Charleston for
a Quaker community in Philadelphia. Here they became activists in the
Abolition movement, speaking to 40,000 people in 67 New England towns
during one 23-week period. Basing their opposition to slavery on religious
grounds, they became extremely influential. Before their deaths in the
1870's, they also became prominent advocates of women's rights.
A. W. Flynt

## Utopianism

858. Arndt, Karl John Richard.   THE INDIANA DECADE OF
GEORGE RAPP'S HARMONY SOCIETY, 1814-1824.   *Pro. of the
Am. Antiquarian Soc. 1970 80(2): 299-323.* George Rapp (1757-1847) -
lauded by the Pittsburgh press, after his death, as the "greatest communist of his age" - founded Rapp's Harmony Society, the most successful
American communist group. The Harmony Society attempted to carry
out its interpretation of the prophecy concerning the Sunwoman according to the Book of Revelation. Needing more space, the Harmony Society
left its first American settlement (Harmony, Pennsylvania) and settled in
Indiana Territory, where the society began its second decade in America.
Establishment of the efficient commonwealth influenced the political
development of Indiana; politicians seeking office considered it wise to
take the Harmony Society into consideration. The State borrowed money
from the society on occasion. Many persons from all over the world wrote
to inquire about the remarkable success of the communal society. Evidently the answer lay in its unselfish industry and religious zeal. Without
the religious impulse, Robert Owen's New Harmony failed in two years,
while the Harmony Society moved on to its third new start and further
great accomplishments. Based on unpublished letters and documents; 6
illus., 3 notes.   R. V. Calvert

859. Bishop, Morris.   THE GREAT ONEIDA LOVE-IN.   *Am. Heritage 1969 20(2): 14-17, 86-92.* Discusses John Humphrey Noyes, (1811-
86), founder of the Oneida Colony; emphasizes his philosophy and views
on marriage, sex, and child rearing.   S

860. Bronner, Edwin B.   QUAKERS LABOR WITH JEMIMA WIL-
KINSON - 1794.   *Quaker Hist. 1969 58(1): 41-47.* During Indian nego-
tiations with the Six Nations at Canandiagua, New York, two ministers
(William Savery and John Parrish) and two elders (David Bacon and
James Emlen) had time to visit nearby Jerusalem, founded in 1788 by a
woman of Quaker upbringing, Jemima Wilkinson. She called herself "The
Publick Universal Friend," and the community included former Friends.
Hitherto unpublished comments are selected from the journals of Savery
and Bacon at Haverford College and from the journal of Emlen at the
New York State Library.   T. D. S. Bassett

861. Coffey, David M.   THE HOPEDALE COMMUNITY.   *Hist. J.
of Western Massachusetts 1975 4(1): 16-26.* Adin Ballou established
Hopedale, a utopian community, (1841) so that moral and religious ele-

ments would predominate over family and material considerations. This proved unrealistic. Joint-stock industries were established; and, by 1846, private investors took control. Antislavery and women's rights were among the causes espoused in the community. E. D. Draper's withdrawal of investment in 1856 ended the community. Based on Heywood's and Ballou's works; 3 illus., 49 notes.                                    S. S. Sprague

862. Francis, Richard. CIRCUMSTANCES AND SALVATION: THE IDEOLOGY OF THE FRUITLANDS UTOPIA. *Am. Q. 1973 25(2): 202-234.* Describes the failure in 1843 of the six-month old Fruitlands community of central Massachusetts, resulting from a misunderstanding between Amos Bronson Alcott (1799-1888) and the English transcendentalist Charles Lane (d. 1870). Lane, who believed social reform could be accelerated by gathering like-minded individuals in a "consociate family," rejected the narrowness of the biological family celebrated by Alcott—a familialism Lane had not expected when Alcott invited him to Massachusetts. 103 notes.                          W. D. Piersen

863. Jones, Arnita Ament. FROM UTOPIA TO REFORM. *Hist. Today [Great Britain] 1976 26(6): 393-401.* Discusses the work of Frances Wright and Robert Dale Owen in reform movements and Utopias, includes their philosophy on religion, social order, marriage, politics, and communal living, 1826-32.

864. Payne-Gaposchkin, Cecilia Helena. THE NASHOBA PLAN FOR REMOVING THE EVIL OF SLAVERY: LETTERS OF FRANCES AND CAMILLA WRIGHT, 1820-1829. *Harvard Lib. Bull. 1975 23(3): 221-251, (4): 429-461.* Supplies background to the establishment and abandonment of Nashoba, the west Tennessee community the Wright sisters founded to provide a self-sufficient, cooperative agricultural operation through which chosen slaves could, by amassing a surplus fund, purchase their own emancipation. Indicates the relationship of Robert Dale Owen to Nashoba and gives insight into conditions of frontier travel. Based on correspondence in the Houghton Library; 103 notes.                                               L. D. Smith

865. Sandeen, Ernest R. JOHN HUMPHREY NOYES AS THE NEW ADAM. *Church Hist. 1971 40(1): 82-90.* Studies the early career of Noyes (1811-86), the American communitarian, from the perspective of ideas of an American Adam. R. W. B. Lewis and Leo Marx have suggested that the Edenic image dominated American thought in the early 19th century, and the author suggests that Noyes cast himself as the new Adam. Noyes early espoused perfectionism and antinomianism which led him to experimentation with communitarianism and with complex marriage. In his paper, the *Perfectionist,* Noyes advocated these views. In his community at Putney, Vermont, he believed that the Kingdom of God had been established and a victory over death achieved. Many of Noyes' views may be traced to unresolved psychological conflicts. Noyes was neurotic, occupied with sexual fantasies, frightened of meaningful relationships with women, intimidated by his mother, the victim of frequent nervous breakdowns, and incapable of normal societal relationships. In his inability to accept the death of Mary Cragin, the "Eve of his Eden," Noyes experienced the final shattering of his utopian vision. Based on secondary sources; 21 notes.                  S. C. Pearson, Jr.

866. Stern, Madeleine B. STEPHEN PEARL ANDREWS AND MODERN TIMES, LONG ISLAND. *J. of Long Island Hist. 1964 4(4): 1-15.* Discusses the founding of the Utopian community of Modern Times, located in the township of Islip, Suffolk County, New York, by Stephen P. Andrews in March 1851. Andrews attempted to establish the haven according to an economic theory of "Cost the Limit of Price," and to the social concept of "Free Love." Public animosity, the Panic of 1857, and the oncoming Civil War combined to destroy Modern Times.
                                                                    J. Judd

867. Wyatt, Philip R. JOHN HUMPHREY NOYES AND THE STIRPICULTURAL EXPERIMENT. *J. of the Hist. of Medicine & Allied Sci. 1976 31(1): 55-66.* The Oneida Community, established by John Humphrey Noyes (1811-86) emphasized the desire for perfection. Noyes developed four unique concepts to achieve this goal. These were male continence, complex marriage, community child care, and the stirpicultural experiment. The success of male continence freed women from unwanted pregnancies and permitted the practice of complex marriage. To assure that children were as perfect as possible, Noyes developed the

policy of stirpiculture, the culture of a new race, produced by carefully controlled selective breeding. During 1869-79, 58 live births occurred in the Oneida community as a result of the experiments in scientific breeding. There was a low infant mortality rate, indicating that the combination of selective breeding and community child care had good results. Noyes demonstrated that the nature of man could be improved by controlling the environment and man's biological inheritance. The children became exceptionally successful later in life. 26 notes.       M. Kaufman

868. —. [WILLIAM MACLURE AND EDUCATION]. *Hist. of Educ. Q. 1963 3(2): 58-80.*
Burgess, Charles. WILLIAM MACLURE AND EDUCATION FOR A GOOD SOCIETY, *pp. 58-76.*
Boram, William A. WILLIAM MACLURE: RESPONSE, *pp. 77-80.* Evaluates the program of social reform through education, advocated by William Maclure. Particular emphasis is placed on the individualistic and distinctly American features of Maclure's works at New Harmony, Indiana, on his attacks on social inequality which he regarded as a consequence of ignorance, on his preference for factual science, on his opposition to politicians and clergymen, and on his view on education as euthenics.            J. Herbst

# Religion and Ethnicity

## Religion

869. Anderson, Richard Lloyd. THE RELIABILITY OF THE EARLY HISTORY OF LUCY AND JOSEPH SMITH. *Dialogue: A J. of Mormon Thought 1969 4(2): 12-28.* Examines sources concerning early career of Joseph Smith and his family in the area of western New York. The material gathered by Philastus Hurlbut, published in 1834 by E. D. Howe in *Mormonism Unvailed* (sic), is contrasted with the writings of Joseph Smith and his mother, Lucy. The Smiths' writings in every case where vital or legal records permit a contrast are basically more accurate than Howe's work. Based on primary and secondary sources; illus., 57 notes.                                                    W. J. McNiff

870. Balderston, Marion. RACHEL PATTERSON, PRIMITIVE QUAKER. *Quaker Hist. 1970 59(1): 44-48.* Summarizes the 350-page journal of a Wilburite (from 1860 called Primitive) minister, with notes of sermons and copies of letters, in the Huntington Library. Born Rachel Edgerton in Belmont County in 1810, she married a Quaker minister in 1829 and lived in Somerton until the Civil War, then in Iowa. One letter tells of her uncle Joseph's 2,300-mile journey to Nova Scotia in 1839.
                                                                T. D. S. Bassett

871. Davidson, Carlisle G. A PROFILE OF HICKSITE QUAKERISM IN MICHIGAN, 1830-1860. *Quaker Hist. 1970 59(2): 106-112.* "Michigan Fever" reached western New York Quakers in the early 1830's. A Hicksite congregation was organized near Detroit in 1834, and those in western Michigan had gathered into three meetings by 1840. John Mott of Parma, Elizabeth Margaret Chandler of Adrian, and Erastus Hussey, mayor of Battle Creek and Free Soil and Republican legislator, were active abolitionists. Hussey became the leader of Progressive Friends ("Friends of Universal Human Progress"), some of whom became spiritualists. Both kinds of Michigan Hicksite "had all but disappeared by the end of the Civil War."            T. D. S. Bassett

872. Drury, Clifford M. THE SPOKANE INDIAN MISSION AT TSHIMAKAIN, 1838-1848. *Pacific Northwest Q. 1976 67(1): 1-9.* At the urging of Old Chief of the Spokane Indians, the American Board of Commissioners for Foreign Missions launched mission activities at Tshimakain in September 1838. Despite protestations from William Gray that he be given the appointment due to his earlier contact with the tribe, the assignment went to Elkanah Walker and Cushing Eells. The Indians provided labor in constructing the mission; but due to the isolation of the post, life remained hard for the two men and their families. Attempts to convert Old Chief's band to an agricultural lifestyle produced only limited success because unpredictable weather played havoc with crops. Monotony and day-to-day survival instincts characterized the small settlement's history. Yet Walker prepared a small pamphlet of the Spokane language and cultivated good will, which paved the way for later mission-

aries. The mission was closed in 1848, but the lengthy diaries of Mary and Elkanah Walker remain today as works of historical significance. Primary and secondary sources; 4 photos, 15 notes. M. L. Tate

873. Edward, C. ELIZABETH ANN SETON: MOTHER, FOUNDER, SAINT. *Am. Hist. Illus. 1975 10(8): 12-21.* Describes the life of Elizabeth Ann Seton (1774-1821), founder of The White House, the first Catholic parochial school in the United States.

874. Foster, Lawrence. A LITTLE-KNOWN DEFENSE OF PO- LYGAMY FROM THE MORMON PRESS IN 1842. *Dialogue: A J. of Mormon Thought 1974 9(4): 21-34.* An 1842 Mormon pamphlet (ap- parently authorized by church leaders) which justified polygamy reveals the social and theological rationalization for the practice. Ostensibly, social ills reflected female assumption of male authority; the only solution was restoration of male dominance in the family on the basis of marriage as practiced by the ancient Patriarchs. Since only women alienated from husbands could seek divorce, husbands alienated from wives could rees- tablish family harmony only by taking another wife. Based on Mormon published sources and manuscripts; illus., 24 notes. D. L. Rowe

875. Hansen, Klaus J. THE METAMORPHOSIS OF THE KING- DOM OF GOD: TOWARD A REINTERPRETATION OF MOR- MON HISTORY. *Dialogue: A J. of Mormon Thought 1966 1(3): 63-83.* Historians for generations have believed that the key to the "Mormon question" was the understanding of the theory and practice of polygamy. The author suggests that though the doctrine of polygamy is important, he would direct attention to the concept of a political kingdom of God as "promulgated by a secret Council of Fifty." Further, he suggests that Mormon leaders may have "subtly invited assaults" on the institution of polygamy "in order to shield an institution of greater significance for Mormon history, the political Kingdom of God." The metamorphosis of this concept from a purely political to an ecclesiastical concept and the "cessation of the centralized control over Mormon politics" can be at- tributed to two points: the decline in the expectancy of the Second Com- ing and loyalty to the Constitution of the United States as a "point of doctrine." L. P. Hofeling

876. Healy, Kathleen. THE EARLY HISTORY OF THE SISTERS OF MERCY IN WESTERN PENNSYLVANIA. *Western Pennsylva- nia Hist. Mag. 1972 55(2): 159-170.* Religious history (covering 1843-51) of the convent of the Congregation of Sisters of Mercy in Pennsylvania, and especially the role of Frances Warde in founding the Mount St. Vincent Academy, a school for women. S

877. Howell, Erle. CHLOE AURELIA CLARKE WILLSON. *Pacific Historian 1970 14(3): 50-62.* Willson, a missionary, was the first teacher on Puget Sound, 1838-49.

878. Jackson, Hermione Dannelly. WIFE NUMBER TWO: ELIZA G. SEXTON SHUCK, THE FIRST BAPTIST FOREIGN MISSION- ARY FROM ALABAMA. *Baptist Hist. and Heritage 1973 8(2): 69-78.* Church history of a Baptist missionary to China. S

879. Kaganoff, Nathan M. ORGANIZED JEWISH WELFARE AC- TIVITY IN NEW YORK CITY (1848-1860). *Am. Jewish Hist. Q. 1966 56(1): 27-61.* Although the Jewish population of New York was less than five percent of the total population, activities in the area of social welfare equaled in number if not in size those of the entire community. The documents preserved indicate most of these societies - *landsman- shaften* compatriot society, widows and orphans societies, and women's aid groups - were fashioned by the Jewish immigrant group to fill specific needs in times of emergency. Ninety-three Jewish benevolent societies are listed and the characteristics of their incorporation papers are analyzed. F. Rosenthal

880. McVay, Georgianne. YANKEE FANATICS UNMASKED: CARTOONS ON THE BURNING OF A CONVENT. *Records of the Am. Catholic Hist. Soc. of Philadelphia 1972 83(3-4): 159-168.* A series of pro-Catholic caricatures done by David Claypool Johnston in the wake of the burning of the Charlestown convent in 1834 are presented and commented upon. 11 figs., 36 notes. J. M. McCarthy

881. Murphy, Carol. TWO DESEGREGATED HEARTS. *Quaker Hist. 1964 53(2): 87-92.* Sarah Moore Grimké (1792-1873) and Angelina Emily Grimké (1805-79) were daughters of John Faucheraud Grimké, a Charleston, South Carolina slaveholder, revolutionary veteran, and judge. Raised Episcopalians, they became Friends soon after 1819. Years of inner conflict continued, for many Quakers were too rigid to accept these bright, energetic, and articulate women. Angelina first published her abolitionist views in 1835 [article misprints, 1853]; and soon both sisters were writing and lecturing against slavery (a role new to women). Because Angelina married the non-Friend Theodore D. Weld "out of meeting" in 1838 (and Sarah attended the wedding), both were disowned and remained unaffiliated thereafter. Derived from Catherine H. Birney, *The Grimké Sisters* (1885). T. D. S. Bassett

882. Shively, Frances. NARCISSA WHITMAN. *Am. Hist. Illus. 1968 3(3): 28-34.* Narcissa Whitman, with her husband Marcus, became a missionary to the Cayuse Indians in Oregon. S

883. Sieber, Robert; Paterson, Keith; and Searl, Marjorie, eds. THE FOX SISTERS IN ACTION: A CLERGYMAN'S ACCOUNT. *New York Hist. 1974 55(3): 301-318.* In 1848, Margaretta and Katie Fox (15 and 12 years old respectively) created a sensation by claiming that they had communicated with the dead. Forty years later, they admitted that the whole incident had been a fraud. The Fox sisters claimed to communicate with the spirit of Rev. Lemuel Clark's daughter, who had died two years previously. Starting out as a skeptic, Clark became a convert and believed that the Fox sisters had the powers they claimed. Reproduces text of Clark's letter. 2 illus., 3 notes. G. Kurland

884. Surratt, Jerry L. THE ROLE OF DISSENT IN COMMUNITY EVOLUTION AMONG MORAVIANS IN SALEM, 1772-1860. *North Carolina Hist. R. 1975 52(3): 235-255.* Alterations in the nature of the Salem Moravian theocracy, from *gemeinschaft* to *gesellschaft,* can be traced through the effects of rising dissent on military involvement, relationships between the sexes, and the rise of economic individualism. Salem Brethren were forced, between 1820 and 1850, to permit residents to join the militia, ease the strict rules regarding courting and marriage, abandon the community landholding system, and allow residents to en- gage in the slave trade. Based primarily on manuscript and printed records at the Moravian Archives, as well as on secondary materials; 7 illus., 74 notes. T. L. Savitt

885. Thorp, Willard. CATHOLIC NOVELISTS IN DEFENSE OF THEIR FAITH, 1829-1865. *Pro. of the Am. Antiquarian Soc. 1968 78(1): 25-117.* In the three decades preceding the Civil War, in which propaganda novels were flourishing, religious novels (produced in consid- erable numbers by Baptists, Methodists, and Episcopalians) often at- tacked sects that were disliked. Most absurd and vicious were the anti-Catholic novels. Catholic writers coming to the defense of their faith responded with nearly 50 pro-Catholic novels on American themes be- tween 1829 and 1865. Using the affirmative approach, Catholic novelists contrived plots allowing occasions for someone speaking with authority to explain doctrines and mysteries of the Catholic religion and providing young Catholic champions to do battle with acquaintances or employers, so that Protestant bigotry and theological ignorance could be exposed. Priest-novelists of note were Charles Constantine Pise, John Boyce, John T. Roddan, and Hugh Quigley. Five professional authors stand out by reason of the amazing quantity of fiction they produced: Charles James Cannon, George Henry Miles, Jedidiah Vincent Huntington, Mrs. Ann Hanson McKenney Dorsey, and Mrs. Mary Anne Madden Sadlier. Hav- ing reviewed many Catholic novels and given instructions in the theory of Catholic fiction, Orestes Brownson also wrote a Catholic novel, *The Spirit-Rapper: An Autobiography* (Boston: Little, Brown & Company, 1854). Based mainly on the subject novelists' works; 86 notes. R. V. Calvert

886. Welter, Barbara. THE FEMINIZATION OF AMERICAN RE- LIGION: 1800-1860. Hartman, Mary and Banner, Lois W., eds. *Clio's Consciousness Raised: New Perspectives on the History of Women* (New York: Harper Torchbooks, 1974): 137-157. After the American Revolu- tion, religion declined as a male activity. Humility, submission, and weak- ness were incompatible with the "male" activities of politics and economics and were relegated to women and religion. Religion, like the family and popular culture, "entered a process of change whereby it

became more domesticated, more emotional, more soft and accommodating—in a word, more 'feminine.' " Women made up a large percent of congregations and participated in missionary and volunteer church activities. These women gained experience in organizing and a sense of self-worth valuable for women's independence. 65 notes.                           S

887.   Wood, Raymund F.   EAST AND WEST MEET IN CALIFORNIA IN 1806.  *Pacific Historian 1976 20(1): 22-33.* Recounts meeting of Catholicism and Orthodoxy in California, after each set out in opposite directions from Jerusalem several centuries earlier. The first meeting was at San Francisco when Russian Nikolai Rezanov arrived in 1806 seeking to trade for foodstuffs. His betrothal to the daughter of the Spanish Comandante, Maria de la Concepcion Arguello, marked the formal meeting of the two branches of the Church. Based on secondary sources; biblio.
G. L. Olson

# Ethnicity

## Blacks

888.   Andrew, John A., III.   BETSEY STOCKTON: STRANGER IN A STRANGE LAND.  *J. of Presbyterian Hist. 1974 52(2): 157-166.* Betsey Stockton (d. 1865) was born in slavery, raised in a clergyman's home, freed at age 20, and self-educated. In 1822 she went to Hawaii with missionaries. Relates her missionary activities, return to New Jersey, and other biographic details. 30 notes.                                    D. L. Smith

889.   Basler, Roy P.   AND FOR HIS WIDOW AND HIS ORPHAN.  *Q. J. of the Lib. of Congress 1970 27(4): 291-294.* Reproduces the remarkable letter of Abraham Lincoln to Senator Charles Sumner on 19 May 1864. Lincoln stated that the widow of Major Booth had asked that "widows and children in *fact* of colored soldiers who fall in our service, be placed in law, the same as if their marriages were legal, so that they can have the benefits of the provisions made the widows and children of white soldiers." Congress finally adopted the bill, adding the proviso that such widows and children be free persons. Illus., 7 notes.
E. P. Stickney

890.   Bogin, Ruth.   SARA PARKER REMOND: BLACK ABOLITIONIST FROM SALEM.  *Essex Inst. Hist. Collections 1974 110(2): 120-150.* Recounts career of this woman as an antislavery lecturer in Great Britain and the United States, 1856-87.                           S

891.   Eblen, J. E.   GROWTH OF THE BLACK POPULATION IN "ANTE BELLUM" AMERICA 1820-1860.  *Population Studies [Great Britain] 1972 26(2): 273-290.* "Although the data from the decennial censuses of 1820 to 1860 are serviceable for an analysis of the *ante bellum* black population, they require some reorganisation and correction before they can be made to yield acceptable estimates of its parameters. In this study four separate analyses were used, but all of them ultimately rested upon the use of the model life tables developed by Coale and Demeny. Three of the approaches produced unacceptably extreme results (fitting Model West at Level 4), and even those derived from the most refined model (adapted from Valaoras) seem in some respects to be excessive. This fit in Model West was at Level 5 - the level around which the results of the annual continuous growth rates ranging from 2.40 to 1.75 [percent] fit points to crude birth rates of 54 to 62, a crude death rate of about 37 or 38, gross reproduction rates of 3.29 to 3.88, and an infant mortality rate of 368 for males and 307 for females. An analysis of the suitability of the Coale and Demeny model life tables suggests that they exaggerate the severity of infant mortality, but the precise degree of distortion is as yet uncertain, so a definitive adjustment of the parameters for the black population at Level 5 cannot be made at this time. Nevertheless, the model life table expectations of life at birth and age 20 (for males respectively, 28 and 32 years; for females, 30 and 34) may be considered firm. Those for older ages may have to be increased by a year or two. The black crude birth rates probably did not exceed 58, and gross reproduction rates somewhat closer to 3.00 are indicated by the likelihood that infant mortality rates for males and females were nearer 275 and 225 than the figures in the model life tables. Definitive mortality rates for ages one to nine, on the other hand, would probably be higher than in the model life tables. If this reconstruction of the black population is somewhat less than

perfect, it nevertheless comes close enough to affirm five generalisations of fundamental historical significance: (1) the free blacks, who constituted only 10 [percent] of the total in 1860, were - with an optimum fit at Level 6 in Model West - only slightly better off than the slaves; (2) maximum fertility among slaves was *generally* encouraged, which is to say that a slave-breeding psychology clearly permeated the South, even if the most modest estimates derived from this study are used as the measure; (3) slavery was even more profitable than estimated by Conrad and Meyer; (4) the number of slaves imported illegally during the *ante bellum* period was probably under 40,000 and could hardly have exceeded the concurrent losses sustained by the whole black population; and, (5) if Roberts's life table for British Guiana - which is based on data that will also fit Model West at Level 5 - can be taken as a guide, the mortality conditions of different slave systems in the nineteenth century were much more similar than different."                                              J

892.   Edwards, Frances.   CONNECTICUT'S BLACK LAW.  *New-England Galaxy 1963 5(2): 34-42.* Discusses the attempt of Prudence Crandall (1803-89) to establish a school for Negro girls in Canterbury, Connecticut. Local opposition eventually forced the closing of the school, and Miss Crandall went to jail for violating a law of the State of Connecticut which forbade schools such as hers.           T. J. Farnham

893.   Elusche, Michael.   ANTISLAVERY AND SPIRITUALISM: MYRTILLA MINER AND HER SCHOOL.  *New York Hist. Soc. Q. 1975 59(2): 149-172.* Founded in 1851, the Miner School for Negro Girls in Washington D.C., offered one of the few opportunities in the nation to young black girls seeking an education. Miss Miner, a sickly, intense, pious native of upstate New York, was able to establish and continue the school despite limited resources and much opposition. For a decade the school limped along until she left suddenly in 1861 for California where she became absorbed in spiritualism. Three years later she died, still hoping for the millennium. The school she founded eventually (1955) became part of the District of Columbia Teachers College, while her name is preserved on a District of Columbia elementary school. Primary and secondary sources; 4 illus., 45 notes.                            C. L. Grant

894.   Hartvik, Allen.   CATHERINE FERGUSON, BLACK FOUNDER OF A SUNDAY-SCHOOL.  *Negro Hist. Bull. 1972 35(8): 176-177.* Sketches the life of Catherine Ferguson (1779-1854), who was born a slave in New York City and, in 1814, founded a Sunday school in that city to provide an education for poor children.           S

895.   Mills, Gary B.   COINCOIN: AN EIGHTEENTH-CENTURY "LIBERATED" WOMAN.  *J. of Southern Hist. 1976 42(2): 205-222.* Documents the Louisiana legend of the exceptional black woman Coincoin. Freed when she was 46 years old and given about 80 acres of unimproved land, she managed to increase her estate to about 1000 acres, owned 16 slaves, and had purchased freedom for all of her children and grandchildren before dying at 75. Within a generation after her death, the family estate in Metoyer, Louisiana had increased to some 15,000 acres with over 400 slaves. This was an exceptionally impressive record for a black woman and her descendants in the antebellum South. Based on primary and secondary sources; 62 notes.           T. D. Schoonover

896.   Porter, Dorothy, ed.   SOJOURNER TRUTH CALLS UPON THE PRESIDENT: AN 1864 LETTER.  *Massachusetts R. 1972 13(1/2): 297-299.* Reproduces a letter by Truth (ca. 1797-1883) in which she described her interview with Abraham Lincoln on 25 October 1864. She thanked him for the Emancipation Proclamation and he autographed her autograph book. 5 notes.                            G. Kurland

897.   Reinders, Robert C.   THE FREE NEGRO IN THE NEW ORLEANS ECONOMY, 1850-1860.  *Louisiana Hist. 1965 6(3): 273-285.* The free Negro in the 1850's in New Orleans held his own in the skilled trades, and the demand for common labor was great enough to prevent large-scale Negro unemployment. Negro businessmen had declined in number and prosperity since the 1830's. The one hope of security was land. Free Negro women owned real estate to a far greater extent than their white sisters. The 1850's was generally a period of white hostility, restrictive laws, and declining economic opportunities. Consequently most local free Negroes, rich and poor alike, were extremely pleased when the "Bluecoats" arrived in 1862. 52 notes.           E. P. Stickney

898. Ripley, C. Peter. THE BLACK FAMILY IN TRANSITION: LOUISIANA, 1860-1865. *J. of Southern Hist. 1975 41(3): 369-380.* Slave owners generally supported slave marriages. The Civil War shattered the marital stability of slaves. Planters fled the approaching armies, often taking male slaves with them. The Union Army conscripted male Negroes for soldiering and work with little regard for their families. The majority of Negro refugees were women who had nowhere else to go. The end of the war saw great efforts by former slaves to reunite with their families. The slave family was a strong, cohesive unit which adequately survived the massive dislocations of war. Table, 33 notes.

V. L. Human

899. Shafer, Elizabeth. SOJOURNER TRUTH: "A SELF-MADE WOMAN." *Am. Hist. Illus. 1974 8(9): 34-39.* Biography of former slave Sojourner Truth, who was a powerful speaker against slavery and for women's rights in mid-19th century America.

S

900. Smith, Grace Ferguson. SOJOURNER TRUTH—LISTENER TO THE VOICE. *Negro Hist. Bull. 1973 36(3): 63-65.* Discusses Isabella Baumfree, who later took the name of Sojourner Truth, and her work for black civil rights, 1825-60.

S

901. Vacha, John E. THE CASE OF SARA LUCY BAGBY. *Ohio Hist. 1967 76(4): 222-231.* Describes reactions in Cleveland and elsewhere in the Western Reserve to the arrest and trial of Sara Lucy Bagby, escaped slave from Virginia, under the Fugitive Slave Act. The return of Sara Lucy Bagby to prison in Virginia without violent intervention in Cleveland was viewed as evidence of the extent to which Republicans were willing to uphold the Fugitive Slave Act in order to preserve the Union. Based on contemporary newspaper accounts.

S. L. Jones

902. Woodward, Carl R. A PROFILE IN DEDICATION, SARAH HARRIS AND THE FAYERWEATHER FAMILY. *New-England Galaxy 1973 15(1): 3-14.* A biography of Sarah Harris (1812-79), a mulatto, who crusaded with Prudence Crandall for equal educational opportunities for minority youth.

S

903. Zelnik, M. FERTILITY OF THE AMERICAN NEGRO IN 1830 AND 1850. *Population Studies [Great Britain] 1966 20(1): 77-83.* "A comparison of the proportionate age distributions for negroes enumerated in the decennial censuses of the United States: the first half of the 19th cent. indicates that by 1850, negro fertility had apparently been declining for at least 20 years. This paper develops the relationship of the age distribution of a declining fertility population, where the decline has persisted for less than 25 years, to the stable population with the same current schedules of fertility and mortality. This relationship is used to estimate the negro birth rate and total fertility as of 1850. In turn, these estimates and the relationship of the age distributions of two stable populations with different fertility are used to estimate the negro birth rate and total fertility as of 1850." Based mainly on secondary sources; 20 notes.

J

## Indians

904. Anderson, Irving W. PROBING THE RIDDLE OF THE BIRD WOMAN. *Montana: Mag. of Western Hist. 1973 23(4): 2-17.* Presents evidence that Sacagawea, of the Lewis and Clark Expedition, died at Fort Manuel, South Dakota, in 1812. Denies that she lived until 1884 and was buried in Wyoming. Responsibility for the error is charged to early 20th-century feminists, who sought to exploit this Indian heroine to the utmost.

S. R. Davison

905. Barry, Louise. THE KANSA INDIANS AND THE CENSUS OF 1843. *Kansas Hist. Q. 1973 39(4): 478-490.* Summarizes some 18th- and early 19th-century references to the Kansa Indians that shed light on the tribes' size and condition, including an 1843 census taken by Agent Richard W. Cummins and now preserved in the records of the Office of Indian Affairs held by the National Archives. The census groups the 1,588 Indians into 245 households, showing members' names, age, and sex. Notes.

W. F. Zornow

906. Blankenburg, William B. THE ROLE OF THE PRESS IN AN INDIAN MASSACRE, 1871. *Journalism Q. 1968 45(1): 61-70.* Examines press treatment of the Camp Grant Massacre in which 100 Indians, mostly women and children, were slaughtered.

907. Chandler, M. G. SIDELIGHTS ON SACAJAWEA. *Masterkey 1969 43(2): 58-66.* With the vast amount of territory obtained by the Louisiana Purchase, it became necessary to explore and occupy this new land. The author describes the advance preparations made by the explorers chosen by President Jefferson to lead the first expedition into the Far West - Meriwether Lewis and William Clark. After outfitting the group in St. Louis, they made their way up the Missouri to a Minitaree village where they took on Toussaint Charbonneau and his pregnant 14-year-old Shoshone slave girl, named Sacajawea (Bird Woman) by the Minitaree. As the Shoshone were a hostile tribe, Sacajawea was not only a godsend as a guide, but also insured the expedition's safe conduct through Shoshone territory. In later life Sacajawea left Charbonneau and married a Comanche warrior. The son she bore while on the expedition, Jean Baptiste, and a nephew she adopted while in Shoshone country, Bazil, were educated in Europe at Clark's expense. Both boys returned to the Wind River Shoshone Reservation to be joined later by the widowed Sacajawea, who died on 9 April 1884 in her mid-90's. Based primarily on discussions with C. A. Eastman, noted Sioux Indian authority.

C. N. Warren

908. Chuinard, E. G. THE ACTUAL ROLE OF THE BIRD WOMAN. *Montana: Mag. of Western Hist. 1976 26(3): 18-29.* The Lewis and Clark Expedition engaged Sacagawea and her French husband primarily as interpreters. Controversy exists over her probably minimal value as a guide, but her service in obtaining help for the explorers from her Shoshoni tribesmen in Idaho entitles her to respected status as a member of the corps of discovery. Derived from standard printed sources on Lewis and Clark. Illus.

S. R. Davison

909. Howard, Helen Addison. THE MYSTERY OF SACAGAWEA'S DEATH. *Pacific Northwest Q. 1967 58(1): 1-6.* Summarizes some of the controversial assumptions, books, and articles relating to the role and life span of the young Indian woman Sacagawea who accompanied Lewis and Clark as an interpreter on their expedition through the regions of the Rocky Mountains in 1805. Documented.

C. C. Gorchels

910. Jones, Dorothy V. JOHN DOUGHERTY AND THE PAWNEE RITE OF HUMAN SACRIFICE: APRIL, 1827. *Missouri Hist. R. 1969 63(3): 291-316.* The Skidi Pawnee had been pressured into giving up their custom of making human sacrifices to the Morning Star, but in 1827 hunger or personal rivalry may have prodded them into capturing a Cheyenne squaw for sacrifice. This is an account of the sacrificial ritual as a religious custom of the Skidi Pawnee and the efforts of John Dougherty, the acting Indian agent for the Upper Missouri Agency, to arrange her ransom. Although the tribe hacked her to pieces as she was being led to safety, Dougherty consoled himself with the thought that she had been spared the torture that accompanied the sacrificial ritual. The incident demonstrated the width of the gulf that lay between Indian and white cultures on the frontier in 1827. Based on books, articles, newspapers, the Dougherty Papers in the State Historical Society of Missouri, and the William Clark Papers in the Kansas State Historical Society; illus., 32 notes.

W. F. Zornow

911. McLoughlin, William G. THE CHOCTAW SLAVE BURNING: A CRISIS IN MISSION WORK AMONG THE INDIANS. *J. of the West 1974 13(1): 113-127.* On 28 December 1858 a black slave killed his Choctaw master, Richard Harkins. He claimed he had been instigated by another slave, a woman. After he escaped and killed himself the woman, despite protestations of innocence, was burned at the stake by the widow of the murdered man. The victim was a member, along with the Harkinses, of the Congregational mission church of the Reverend Cyrus Byington. When the incident was revealed a year later it precipitated a crisis over slavery and the relation of the church to slavery among a slave-holding people like the Choctaw Indians. 34 notes.

R. V. Ritter

912. Reynolds, Sam. A DAKOTA TIPI. *North Dakota Hist. 1975 40(4): 20-29.* The Dakota tipi presently in the Oklahoma Historical Soci-

ety Museum was captured by General Alfred Sully in his campaign through North Teton and Yanktonai Dakota territory in 1864. The tipi is covered with 125 paintings which give a picture of family customs, social and economic organization, religious beliefs, and warfare practices of the Dakota Indians. 28 figs., 40 notes.

913. Russell, Taylor. KENDALL LEWIS. *Texana 1971 9(1): 17-32.* Provides a biography of Kendall Lewis, a white member of the Creek Nation who married a Creek Indian woman and was the first white to settle in Titus County, Texas, in 1835 with the intention of beginning farming operations; covers his life 1781-1846 as well as those of his children through 1917.

914. Schaeffer, Claude E. THE KUTENAI FEMALE BERDACHE: COURIER, GUIDE, PROPHETESS, AND WARRIOR. *Ethnohistory 1965 12(3): 193-236.* Describes the assumption of male role and status by a woman of the Kutenai in the early 19th century. Her social and sexual deviancy was infrequent; more often, the homosexuality or intersexuality involved a shift from male to female role. 22 notes, biblio.
R. S. Burns

915. Snyder, Gerald S. THE GIRL OF HISTORY WHO BECAME A WOMAN OF FABLE. *Westways 1974 66(3): 36-39, 71, 73, 74.* Reappraisal of Shoshone Indian woman Sacagawea's contributions to the Lewis and Clark Expedition.
S

916. Stewart, Kenneth M. A BRIEF HISTORY OF THE MOHAVE INDIANS SINCE 1850. *Kiva 1969 34(4): 219-236.* "Descriptions of Mohave culture in the middle of the nineteenth century are contained in such writings as [R. B.] Stratton's account of the captivity of the Oatman girls *The Captivity of the Oatman Girls,* 1857, the reports of railroad surveyors [(Lorenzo) Sitgreaves and [Amiel Weeks] Whipple) and accounts of the steamboat captains [(Joseph C.] Ives). The long period of intertribal warfare was ending, but the apprehensive Mohave fought the White intruders on several occasions before they were finally subdued. Reservations were established, but the Mohave had to undergo many hardships before making a better adjustment to changing times." J

917. Wilson, Gilbert L. WAHEENEE: AN INDIAN GIRL'S STORY. *North Dakota Hist. 1971 28(1/2): 3-188.* A facsimile reprint of the children's book, *Waheenee,* written by Dr. Gilbert L. Wilson and published by Webb Publishing Company, St. Paul, in 1921. Designed for young teens, the book is based on the reminiscences of Waheenee-wea or "Buffalo Bird Woman," a member of the Hidatsa Sioux tribe. *Waheenee* includes descriptive passages of Indian life on the upper Great Plains during the mid-19th century. Frederick N. Wilson, the author's brother, drew more than 100 illustrations.
H. R. Grant

918. Wilson, William E. FRANCES SLOCUM: "THE LOST SISTER." *Am. Hist. Illus. 1968 3(5): 42-48.* In 1778 Jonathan Slocum and his family, who had a farm in Pennsylvania's Wyoming Valley, were attacked by Delaware Indians, and five-year-old Frances Slocum was abducted. The family searched for 60 years to find Frances. She was finally located at Deaf Man's Village, Ohio, by Colonel George W. Ewing, an Indian trader. Frances had lived as an Indian named Ma-con-a-qua and refused to leave her Indian way of life. She died 9 March 1847. Secondary sources; 7 illus., photo, map.
M. J. McBaine

# Social Problems

## General

919. Baker, Leonard. THE SCANDAL OF GLENLYVAR. *Am. Hist. Illus. 1971 5(10): 20-29.* On 1 October 1792, Richard Randolph, his homely wife Judith, and her attractive sister Nancy Randolph visited a cousin, Randolph Harrison, at his home, Glenlyvar. During the night screams were heard and the next morning bloodstains were on Nancy's bed. Rumors were that Nancy had given birth to Richard's baby and that Richard had killed it. To dispel the rumors Richard demanded that he be charged with murder in a public trial. He was, and with John Marshall and Patrick Henry to defend him, he was found not guilty.

Nancy was happily married to Gouverneur Morris 23 years later when John Randolph, a younger brother of Richard, repeated the charges against her. In a public reply, Nancy related that a child was born - dead - at Glenlyvar but that the father was Richard's brother Theodorick, to whom she was engaged but who died almost eight months earlier - and before their marriage. Based on primary sources; 8 illus.
D. B. Dodd

920. Baradel, Louise M. THE ONLY OFFICIAL HANGING IN CORTLAND COUNTY: THE CRIME AND PUNISHMENT OF PATRICK O'DONOUGH. *New York Folklore Q. 1968 24(3): 203-211.* Discusses the 1853 hanging of Patrick O'Donough in Truxton, Cortland County, New York, for the murder of two women in 1852.

921. Blodgett, Geoffrey JOHN MERCER LANGSTON AND THE CASE OF EDMONIA LEWIS: OBERLIN, 1862. *J. of Negro Hist. 1968 53(3): 201-218.* Describes the events of 1862 when two Oberlin College coeds became seriously ill during a sleigh ride, presumably because of poison given them in spiced wine by their fellow-student Edmonia Lewis, a black girl. Most likely the poison was cantharides, or "Spanish Fly," a traditional aphrodisiac and also an irritant, which had been added to the girls' drinks to stimulate them sexually. Vigilantes brutally beat Edmonia Lewis, who was arrested but never brought to trial. At a preliminary hearing her lawyer John Mercer Langston demolished the case against her on the grounds of insufficient evidence. In Oberlin little was said publicly about the case; and, until Langston's autobiography appeared in 1894, none of the participants published an account of the incident. Edmonia Lewis later gained temporary renown as an artist and sculptor whose works were based on Indian and Negro themes. Based on primary and secondary sources; 32 notes.
L. Gara

922. Delly, Lillian. EPISODE AT CORNWALL. *Chronicles of Oklahoma 1973/74 51(4): 444-450.* Recounts the events of (1824-39) of the marriage of Cherokee Indian Elias Boudinot, and Harriet Gold, whose native town of Cornwall, Connecticut, produced a public demonstration against the marriage.
S

923. Kaser, David. NASHVILLE'S WOMEN OF PLEASURE IN 1860. *Tennessee Hist. Q. 1964 23(4): 379-382.* Summarizes census data on 207 women whom Nashville's census takers of 1860, for reasons unknown, took pains to designate as prostitutes - a quirk shedding light on "an otherwise beclouded chapter of the past." Note.
W. A. Klutts

924. Luchetts, Valya. THE FATE OF JULIA BULETTE. *Westways 1976 68(9): 31-33, 69-70.* Examines the life of Julia Bulette, a young prostitute in Virginia City, 1862-64; highlights her friendship with the town sheriff, Tom Peasley, and her murder, allegedly at the hands of a local resident, John Millain.

925. Siegel, Adrienne. BROTHELS, BETS, AND BARS: POPULAR LITERATURE AS GUIDEBOOK TO THE URBAN UNDERGROUND, 1840-1870. *North Dakota Q. 1976 44(2): 4-22.*

926. Smith-Rosenberg, Carroll. BEAUTY, THE BEAST AND THE MILITANT WOMAN: A CASE STUDY IN SEX ROLES AND SOCIAL STRESS IN JACKSONIAN AMERICA. *Am. Q. 1971 23(4): 562-584.* A study of women and women's role in antebellum America through an analysis of the philosophy, methods, and activities of the New York Moral Reform Society organized in 1834 as a self-consciously female voluntary association dedicated to the eradication of sexual immorality whether among prostitutes or as expressed in the double standard regularly condoned among man. A women's universe was bounded by her home and the career of father or husband; within the home it was woman's duty to be submissive and patient. The inner frustration and anger at such a role were expressed in the Reform Society and its implicit assertion of the right to control the mores of men permitted an expression of anti-male sentiments. Publication of a weekly, *The Advocate of Moral Reform,* gave opportunity for education in the principles of the movement and news of its progress. They stopped short, however, of becoming fully feminist with a complete woman's rights program. 75 notes.
R. V. Ritter

927. Trulio, Beverly. ANGLO-AMERICAN ATTITUDES TO-WARD NEW MEXICAN WOMEN. *J. of the West 1973 12(2): 229-239.* Diaries and journals of the first half of the 19th century show that Anglo-Americans held the Mexican women of New Mexico in relatively high esteem, admiring them for "their physical attractiveness, alluring dress, and immorality." Yet the women of this period failed to escape the stigma of racial bias. 62 notes.                                E. P. Stickney

928. —. THE WITCH OF CLARKSTOWN. *York State Tradition 1974 28(2): 28-30.* Discusses Jane Kanniff, a Rockland County woman suspected of witchcraft in 1816.                                S

## Illness and Medical Treatment

929. Carlson, Eric T. and Simpson, Meribeth M. TARANTISM OR HYSTERIA? AN AMERICAN CASE OF 1801. *J. of the Hist. of Medicine and Allied Sci. 1971 26(3): 293-302.* Relates a case of Nancy Hazard, a girl of 15 from North Kingston, Rhode Island, who in 1801 was bitten by a spider and afterward displayed unusual nervous affections. Dr. Joseph Comstock's accounts of her case show her heightened percep-tual sensitivity, which included smell and hearing. She had fits which were treated with a music therapy. Comstock raised several issues in his account of the case: witchcraft, the differentiation between tarantism and hysteria, and the use of music therapy. The suspicion of witchcraft was aroused in the public by Nancy's case, but her doctors entertained no such idea. In this case, Comstock made his working diagnosis tarantism and hysteria. The use of music as the principal therapy for Nancy came at a time when music therapy was undergoing a revival, as it found a natural place in the moral treatment rationale of the late 18th and early 19th centuries. Based on secondary and primary sources; 19 notes.
J. L. Susskind

930. Donegan, Jane B. MAN-MIDWIFERY AND THE DELICACY OF THE SEXES. George, Carol V. R., ed. *"Remember the Ladies": New Perspectives on Women in American History: Essays in Honor of Nelson Manfred Blake* (Syracuse: Syracuse U. Pr., 1975): 90-109. Between 1760 and 1860 midwifery changed from a traditional skill practiced by untrained women to a branch of medicine practiced by trained male physicians. Although not lucrative in itself, midwifery in-creased a doctor's practice. Consequently, doctors wanted midwife cases and encouraged their own presence at parturition by stressing the need for safety and the dangers of childbirth which only male doctors trained in obstetrics could offset. Such doctors were potential disasters. Many had little, if any, clinical experience in obstetrics and used obstetrical instru-ments indiscriminately. These incompetencies were not common knowl-edge, and the doctors extended their practices to other women's diseases. The most formidable obstacles to male medical dominance were increas-ingly prudish cultural mores stressing female modesty and virtue. Doctors publicly campaigned against false modesty, but propriety made vaginal examinations and other gynecological procedures awkward for patient and doctor. Some people began demanding female midwives and female physicians; but medical colleges, hospitals, and medical societies re-mained closed to all but a few women. Based on primary and secondary sources; 32 notes.                                P. R. Byrne

931. King, Arthur G. JOHN LAMBERT RICHMOND, M.D. "THE FIRST CAESARIAN SECTION IN AMERICA." *Cincinnati Hist. Soc. Bull. 1971 29(1): 58-65.* On 22 April 1827, Richmond performed the first Caesarian operation in America, seven miles from the village of Newtown, Ohio. This operation was courageously performed by a back-woods doctor without assistance, under the most difficult circumstances imaginable in the field of obstetrics. The mother recovered and was able to walk a mile and back by her fifth week of convalescence. Based largely on medical journals; 3 illus., 16 notes.                                H. S. Marks

932. Legan, Marshall Scott. HYDROPATHY IN AMERICA: A NINETEENTH-CENTURY PANACEA. *Bull. of the Hist. of Medi-cine 1971 45(3): 267-280.* Hydropathy in 19th-century America became a medical cult, "quite outside the limits of regular medicine."       S

933. Stinson, Byron. 19TH CENTURY TREATMENT OF THE MENTALLY ILL. *Am. Hist. Illus. 1969 4(1): 36-41.* At the beginning

of the 19th century the mentally ill lived in squalid isolation, treatment consisting of purging and bleeding. The mid-19th century saw the rise of social reformers and the birth of American psychiatry. The reformers, particularly Dorothea Dix, stimulated the building of new mental hospi-tals with better facilities. Psychiatrists urged a new system of "moral treatment;" and discipline consisted of isolation, a straightjacket, or a spare diet, not whips and chains. The result was a cure rate of about one-third. Discusses the advancements in the fields of psychiatry and neurology during the latter half of the 19th century. Secondary sources; 2 illus., 2 photos.                                R. V. McBaine

934. Valle, Rosemary Keupper. THE CESAREAN OPERATION IN ALTA CALIFORNIA DURING THE FRANCISCAN MISSION PERIOD (1769-1833). *Bull. of the Hist. of Medicine 1974 48(2): 265-275.*

## Slavery

935. Alford, Terry L. LETTER FROM LIBERIA, 1848. *Missis-sippi Q. 1969 22(2): 150-151.* After conversion to Methodism in 1832, Edward Brett Randolph of Columbus, Mississippi, decided to free his 21 slaves, valued at approximately 10,000 dollars. They sailed for Africa on the cargo vessel *Swift* in 1836. One manumittee Elisa Thilman wrote to her former owner from Greenville, Liberia, on 11 May 1848. Randolph apparently had also provided his slaves with education in Christian fun-damentalism, since the writer consoles herself with her belief in God despite her difficulties. Describing her recovery from grave illness and declaring that her sister and her sister's children have all died, the letter writer feels isolated in the new African nation and requests that her former owner get a message to her mother, her father, and her sisters who are still in the United States to let them know that she is alive and to ask them to write to her. Elisa also sends her love to Virginia, the daughter of her former owner and closes by declaring "I remain Your Friend." The letter is in the Randolph-Sherman Papers (1813-1947) at the Mississippi State University; 6 notes.                                R. V. Calvert

936. Black, Frederick R. BIBLIOGRAPHICAL ESSAY: BENJA-MIN DREW'S *REFUGEE* AND THE BLACK FAMILY. *J. of Ne-gro Hist. 1972 57(3): 284-289.* Ex-slave accounts constitute a large body of literature reflecting a black view of the family in bondage. In 1855, Benjamin Drew, a white journalist from Boston, interviewed more than one hundred blacks who had fled from bondage in the United States to Canada. This testimony was incorporated into *The Refugee: A North-Side View of Slavery,* a work published in 1856 which still provides a useable record of ante-bellum black family life. Hopefully a more system-atic study of this literature will yield answers to several central questions about the slave family. Secondary sources; 14 notes.
N. G. Sapper

937. Blassingame, John W. THE SLAVE FAMILY IN AMERICA. *Am. Hist. Illus. 1972 7(6): 10-17.* Analysis of the functions and difficul-ties of the monogamous slave family from 1836 to 1860.              S

938. Bridner, Elwood L., Jr. THE FUGITIVE SLAVES OF MARY-LAND. *Maryland Hist. Mag. 1971 66(1): 33-50.* The underground railroad carried a number of slaves out of Maryland. Others made it to freedom on their own. The closeness of Pennsylvania, a free state, alerted Maryland slaves to the possibilities of running away. At the same time, slaveowners were relentless in trying to prevent escapes. Baltimore was "one of the most difficult places in the South for even free colored people to get away from, much more for slaves." Yet some slaves were able to overcome the hunger, disorientation, and fear in fleeing Maryland. Fred-erick Douglass and Harriet Tubman were the most famous. Unfortu-nately, too few others followed. The hardships fugitive slaves faced also are discussed.                                G. T. Sharrer

939. Davis, Angela. REFLECTIONS ON THE BLACK WOMAN'S ROLE IN THE COMMUNITY OF SLAVES. *Black Scholar 1971 3(4): 2-15.* Examines the role of black women in the slave system and critiques the myth of the black matriarch. American slavery tried to disorganize family life and to prevent all social structures within which black people could form a collective consciousness. Black women, as

domestic slaves, were indispensable to the white oppressors, were the center of the slave community, and were essential to that community's survival. The women promoted resistance to oppression by open participation in rebellion and in their less noticeable sabotage of the master's household. The sexual abuse of black women by white men was a basic form of terrorism by which white men asserted their power over the blacks. Black women's continued resistance to sexual assault also was a form of insurgency. Together, black men and women suffered oppression, rebelled, and left a legacy of a persistent and heroic struggle for freedom. Based on primary and secondary materials; 45 notes.

A. E. Wiederrecht

940. Dowty, Alan. URBAN SLAVERY IN PRO-SOUTHERN FIC-TION OF THE 1850'S. *J. of Southern Hist. 1966 32(1): 25-41.* The numerous novels written to answer *Uncle Tom's Cabin* by defending the institution of slavery might have been expected to mention the virtues of the Negro's life in urban centers of the South, as contrasted to the picture painted by Harriet Beecher Stowe of slavery on the plantations; but they did so scarcely at all. Whether the city provided contentment or provocation for the slave, it provided no scope for the talents of the proslavery propagandist. It meant a loosening of the slavery system and the offering of new horizons to the Negro. The city was part of a civilization the defenders of slavery were fighting. Documented.

S. E. Humphreys

941. Duvall, Severn. *UNCLE TOM'S CABIN:* THE SINISTER SIDE OF THE PATRIARCHY. *New England Q. 1963 36(1): 3-22.* A study of the southern response to Harriet Beecher Stowe's *Uncle Tom's Cabin.* Demonstrates the way in which she dramatized the essential torture of southern life and isolates the basic contradictions and issues: the estate as a patriarchy with the slaves viewed in a benevolent familial relationship vs. the legal definition which saw them as "things," without personal identity or rights; miscegenation and the fundamental challenge to the slaveholder's wife posed by the institution; and the assumption of racial inferiority. 39 notes.

R. V. Ritter

942. Glazier, Lyle. POINTING UPWARD. *Hacettepe Bull. of Social Sci. and Humanities [Turkey] 1971 3(1): 34-39.* Analyzes *Uncle Tom's Cabin* (1852). Contends that Mrs. Stowe had a strong conviction that slavery was wrong and should be eliminated, yet she seemed also to be suspicious that blackness was evidence of sin. Therefore, the book contains a double standard—what is good for whites is not necessarily good for Negroes. There is also a double standard with respect to sex—all men are either black or sinful and must be purified, while all women are virtuous, unless they are black. Moreover, the author feels that Mrs. Stowe did not really understand the social and economic forces that affected slavery, so that much of the conversation in the book tends to be unreal. The result is that *Uncle Tom's Cabin* is a frustrating book.

J. V. Groves

943. Haught, James A. INSTITUTE: IT SPRINGS FROM EPIC LOVE STORY. *West Virginia Hist. 1971 32(2): 101-107.* The largest Negro town in West Virginia owes its origin to the union of a white planter, Samuel I. Cabell, with his slave Mary Barnes. At his death in 1865 he willed his estate to Mary Barnes and their children. Despite attempts by his relatives to break his wills, the county commissioner declared them valid. When in 1891 the state found it necessary to create the West Virginia Colored Institute, it purchased portions of the estate, giving rise to the name "Institute" for the community that shortly thereafter sprang up. Based on county records; 2 photos.         C. A. Newton

944. Hayne, Barrie. YANKEE IN THE PATRIARCHY: T. B. THORPE'S REPLY TO "UNCLE TOM'S CABIN." *Am. Q. 1968 20(2, pt. 1): 180-195.* Discusses 16 proslavery literary rebuttals, appearing around 1852-54, to Harriet Beecher Stowe's novel. Six of them were written by Northerners, six by "native Southerners," one by a Southerner who lived in the North, and three by Northerners "who had become Southerners by adoption." The author remarks that the principal motivations behind these works seems to have been either a fear of national disunity or regional sensitivity. Thomas B. Thorpe's *The Master's House* (1853) is one of the most high-minded and complex of these books. Of all the authors, only Thorpe depicts the slave master as a conscience-stricken character and expresses doubts concerning the virtues of slavery. The novel's "chaotic social breakdown" at the end reveals Thorpe's pessimism and perception of impending national disaster. 22 notes.

R. S. Pickett

945. Jones, J. Ralph and Landess, Tom, ed. PORTRAITS OF GEORGIA SLAVES. *Georgia R. 1967 21(1): 126-132, (2): 268-273, (3): 407-411, (4): 521-525; 1968 22(1): 125-127, (2): 254-257.* Part I. Interviews ex-slaves in Georgia, 1936. Comments on their credibility, as the interviewer (Jones) was trying to find out about Negro life, and not trying to test a hypothesis. The first subject, Mary Gladdy (born about 1853), had experienced "visitations of the spirit" for over 20 years. She described slave religion and life during the Civil War. Ella Hawkins (born about 1856) described the Civil War years and how her brothers hid their owners' silverware and "treasures" from looting "Yankees." Note. Part II. Includes two 1937 interviews with the Reverend W. B. Allen (born about 1850). Covers slave traders, plantation life, the slaves' religious nature, patrols, and runaway slaves. Mentions the hours worked, "Yankees," overseers ("the regular run of them were trash"), punishment, and tortures. Part III. A portrait of "Uncle" Rias Body, a Georgia slave who was the property of Ben Body, a Harris County planter and an owner of some 80 slaves. Part IV. Interviews Robert Kimbrough and Frances Kimbrough, ex-slaves (1936). Robert's mother was auctioned in Broad Street, Richmond, in 1835, and he was born on a plantation in 1837. Discusses the war, "Yankee" thievery, foot-propelled cotton gins, and the lack of cruel punishment by owners. Frances Kimbrough remembered her owners with near-reverence and had a strong superstitious bent. Part V. The story of "Mammy Dink" (Dink Walton Young, ca. 1840-1936) touches on the familiar antebellum relationships between white and black children, the weekly slave diet on the Walton plantation, and the clothing and general treatment of the blacks by an apparently humane and compassionate white family. Part VI. Harriet Benton, of Columbus, tells how her father was sold into slavery and tells of her childhood days. Mary Carpenter, of Columbus, says that her owner protected her from a whipping by another planter and details ravages by the "Yankee" soldiers.

T. M. Condon, D. D. Cameron, and J. S. Pula

946. Labinjoh, Justin. THE SEXUAL LIFE OF THE OPPRESSED: AN EXAMINATION OF THE FAMILY LIFE OF ANTE-BELLUM SLAVES. *Phylon 1974 35(4): 375-397.* Antebellum black slaves had fairly stable families. Although slavery in its abstraction and in its practice was unconducive to the stability of black social institutions, the paternalism of the slaveholders, the indestructible human desires of the slaves, and the mature economic considerations of the society conspired to sustain family cohesion. Amidst the chaos of slavery there existed stability, though only on the large plantations which contained 25 per cent of the slaves did everything conspire to give them cohesion. Slave narratives especially revealed the respect of black family members for each other and for the institution of marriage. Yet, the main function of slave family life was to provide emotional gratification. Based on primary and secondary sources, including plantation records and slave narratives; 61 notes.

B. A. Glasrud

947. Liedel, Donald E. THE PUFFING OF *IDA MAY*: PUBLISH-ERS EXPLOIT THE ANTISLAVERY NOVEL. *J. of Popular Culture 1969 3(2): 287-306. Ida May: The Story of Things Actual and Possible* (1854) by Mrs. Mary Hayden Green Pike was the fourth most popular antislavery novel of the 1850's because of its sensational content and the intensive and skillful advertising campaign by the publisher; it was more influential on the antislavery novels than was *Uncle Tom's Cabin.*         S

948. Schweninger, Loren. A SLAVE FAMILY IN THE ANTE BEL-LUM SOUTH. *J. of Negro Hist. 1975 60(1): 29-44.* Recognizing the modern controversy concerning the effect of slavery upon the black family, this family history serves to shed some light on the family experiences of many slaves in the antebellum South. The Thomas-Rapier slave family experienced legal restrictions, separation, miscegenation, and sexual exploitation, but these forces served to promote feelings of family loyalty, unity, and love. Based on primary sources in the Moorland-Spingarn Research Center and secondary sources; 53 notes.         N. G. Sapper

949. Scott, Virginia. AN EARLY EPISODE OF BLACK RESIS-TANCE. *Pan-African J. [Kenya] 1970 3(3): 203-208.* There has been a century-long struggle by oppressed peoples to free themselves of Western control. An early instance of black resistance to slavery in the United States is presented in Harriet Beecher Stowe's novel *Dred* (1856). At the time of publication this book was almost as popular as *Uncle Tom's Cabin,* but it has since been relegated to obscurity by racist whites. The black rebel Dred is the most forceful figure in the abolitionist fiction of

the 1850's. Mrs. Beecher authenticated her portrayal of Dred by invoking *The Confessions of Nat Turner,* in which he reveals that one of his chief followers was named Dred. Dred was the son of Denmark Vesey and an enslaved Mandingo woman. Early in youth he escaped from slavery to dwell in swamps along the southeast Atlantic shore where he led armed maroons until he was cut down in South Carolina's Great Dismal Swamp. Undocumented.                                 E. E. Beauregard

950. Sides, Sudie Duncan. SLAVE WEDDINGS AND RELIGION. *Hist. Today [Great Britain] 1974 24(2): 77-87.* Describes religious practices and celebrations of Negroes on plantations in the South.

951. Sides, Sudie Duncan SOUTHERN WOMEN AND SLAVERY. *Hist. Today [Great Britain] 1970 20(1): 54-60, 20(2): 124-130.* Part I. Studies the attitudes of Southern women toward slavery from 1810 to 1860. Reveals a picture "of squalor, discontent, annoyance, frustration, bitterness, self-pity." Women were continually wrapped in racial problems they did not understand and did not want. Slavery was a white male policy foisted and imposed on an unwilling white female sex. Women, however, made little attempt to examine the deeper issues. Based on selected published letters and diaries; illus. Part II. The opinions of Southern women toward slavery changed strongly after the Civil War. Slavery was thought a positive good for Negroes and often a great hardship to white women. Slavery symbolized all the beauties of the past, the romantic past of the patriarchal society that was characterized by trust, tender affection, and providence. White woman had come to reject the facts and reality of life, and a simple racist mentality permeated her attitudes and beliefs. Based on contemporary diaries, chronicles, memorials, and recollections; illus.                              L. A. Knafla

952. Vinovskis, Maris A. THE DEMOGRAPHY OF THE SLAVE POPULATION IN ANTEBELLUM AMERICA. *J. of Interdisciplinary Hist. 1975 5(3): 459-467.* Review and analysis of Robert William Fogel and Stanley L. Engerman, *Time on the Cross* (Boston, 1974) with particular respect to the demographic issues involved in the study. Life expectancy and fertility receive major attention. Argues that both the methodology and the conclusions of the book raise questions that can only be resolved by further research. Table, 16 notes.     R. Howell

953. Wernick, Robert. GLAMOROUS ACTRESS FOUND NO GLAMOR IN GEORGIA SLAVERY. *Smithsonian 1974 5(8): 74-81.* Presents Fanny Kemble's views on slavery. Fanny Kemble was an English actress who found herself marooned in a United States which she considered beneath her. She promptly married a wealthy Philadelphian, who took her to his plantation in Georgia. Fanny hated the South even more than she hated the North. She reviled slavery, although "she was not sentimental about the slaves who waited on her." She kept a diary which was published in England during the Civil War. It caused a stir which may have prevented Great Britain from allying with the Confederacy. 18 photos.                           V. L. Human

954. Zanger, Jules. THE "TRAGIC OCTOROON" IN PRE-CIVIL WAR FICTION. *Am. Q. 1966 18(1): 63-70.* Describes the central role of the "tragic octoroon" as a fictional stereotype in antebellum abolitionist fiction. From R. Hildreth's *The Slave* (1836) to Harriet Beecher Stowe's *Uncle Tom's Cabin* (1852) and Dion Boucicault's *The Octoroon* (1859) over a dozen works featured the "tragic octoroon," a "beautiful young girl who possesses only the slightest evidences of Negro blood" and who is raised by and descended from white aristocracy on her father's side. In the standard account, the girl learns of her fate only upon her father's sudden death. She is then sold into slavery, victimized by an evil Yankee slave dealer, and, if she manages to survive, rescued by a handsome young white aristocrat from the North. Southern apologists have regarded the octoroon plot as a means to gain support for abolitionism by appealing to "white sensibilities" and pro-Negro commentators have regarded it as "racial snobbery." Such charges fail to acknowledge the propaganda value and wide appeal of the plot. It appealed to northern notions of superiority and self-righteousness and showed the southerner's sin. The nightmarish reversal of the octoroon's situation resembled, for some young middle-class women, the precariousness of their own existence. In order to illustrate contempt for Yankees who condoned slavery, the most evil beings in the books are Yankee overseers. As potential exploiters of the octoroon, these lowly creatures indicate the irrelevance of the "kindly master" myth. The shrewd, hard-driving overseer also had

qualities about him which many would recognize as emerging cultural values in the North. Relevant novels are fully cited in the initial note. Critical works on American Negro fiction are cited thereafter. 5 notes.                                         R. S. Pickett

# Image and Self-Image

955. Baym, Nina. THE WOMEN OF COOPER'S *LEATHERSTOCKING TALES. Am. Q. 1971 23(5): 696-709.* James Fenimore Cooper has often been charged with a denigration of womanhood. However, on the contrary, though women as persons in the romantic or existential sense do not rise very high, they are to Cooper of central social significance, being the "nexus of social interaction." It is the group which is the chief "existent," and for Cooper society is patriarchal. Analysis of the women in the Leatherstocking Tales illustrates this thesis. "Order is achieved only at the cost of a social submission that falls with particular completeness and severity on the women." 9 notes.                    R. V. Ritter

956. Bunkle, Phillida. SENTIMENTAL WOMANHOOD AND DOMESTIC EDUCATION, 1830-1870. *Hist. of Educ. Q. 1974 14(1): 13-31.* Attacks the thesis that industrialization and its displacement of the household and family farm as productive centers alone caused the antifeminist ideal of sentimental womanhood to develop. Argues instead that the new domestic education of the 1830's-70's had strong religious influences coming from the second Great Awakening that helped to foster the ideas of morality, motherhood, and domesticity. Based on primary and secondary sources; 43 notes.                    L. C. Smith

957. Hayne, Barrie. STANDING ON NEUTRAL GROUND: CHARLES JACOBS PETERSON OF PETERSON'S. *Pennsylvania Mag. of Hist. and Biog. 1969 93(4): 510-526.* Charles Jacobs Peterson of Philadelphia emerges "as almost the representative writer of his day, a barometer of the changes and tensions which exercised American life between 1840 and 1860." His writings in *Graham's* and especially *Peterson's,* two Philadelphia magazines, offer an insight into the thinking of the average man and woman of the day. A moderate on major issues of the day, Peterson wrote a reply to *Uncle Tom's Cabin* entitled *The Cabin and Parlor.* He also worked briefly with Edgar Allan Poe in the early forties. He is described as "a patriot, (or jingoist), racial moderate (or stereotypist), and patron (or patronizer) of American womanhood, who above all gave the American public for nearly fifty years what it wanted to read." Primary and secondary sources; 39 notes.                  R. G. Mitchell

958. Kellner, Robert. "NO VIRTUE IN WOMEN": A STUDY OF THE PSYCHOLOGICAL THEMES IN *THE SCARLET LETTER. North Dakota Q. 1974 42(2): 28-39.*

959. McAlexander, Patricia Jewell. THE CREATION OF THE AMERICAN EVE: THE CULTURAL DIALOGUE ON THE NATURE AND ROLE OF WOMEN IN LATE EIGHTEENTH-CENTURY AMERICA. *Early Am. Literature 1975 9(3): 252-266.* The evolution of the perceived role of women in American literature from sexual, sufficient, and active partners of their husbands in the 17th century to the sexless, helpless, restricted "lady" of the 18th and 19th centuries occurred not as the result of economic development but as the result of a cultural debate over the proper relation of passion and reason—the basic conflict of the age. The socially and culturally conservative position on the issue ultimately defined the role of women in the 19th century, but only after considerable debate with liberal and radical alternatives. Based on primary and secondary sources; 54 notes.                D. P. Wharton

960. Ricciotti, Dominic. POPULAR ART IN "GODEY'S LADY'S BOOK": AN IMAGE OF THE AMERICAN WOMAN, 1830-1860. *Hist. New Hampshire 1972 27(1): 3-26.* Under Louis Antoine Godey's management (1830-77) and Sarah Josepha Buell Hale's editorship (1837-77), *Godey's,* the most widely circulated American magazine, reflected American opinion about women and educated the public "to accept a partial modification of woman's role." Aimed at nonagricultural, middle-to-upper-income families, *Godey's* promoted woman as the arbiter of taste and patron of arts. It set the tone for many Victorian interiors. Its

ideas of the pure and beautiful implied repression of most emotions except grief for a husband or child, but even its iconography of mourning was restrained. Although boasting of Americanism, *Godey's* derived its style from British gift books and annuals. Its best prints were by second-rate artists: H. S. Sadd, A. L. Dick, G. H. Cushman, W. E. Tucker, W. H. Ellis, and J. N. Gimbrede. Durand, Darley, and Sartain did little work for *Godey's*. Often the image carried the message, with the text built around it. Reproduces 13 illustrations, clustering around 1849, which portray the American woman "as the faithful wife, devoted mother, constant companion; the embodiment of virtue; and a purveyor of established culture." 28 notes.                                    T. D. S. Bassett

961.  Riley, Glenda Gates.  THE SUBTLE SUBVERSION: CHANGES IN THE TRADITIONALIST IMAGE OF THE AMERICAN WOMAN.  *Historian 1970 32(2): 210-227.* Shows how the view of the woman as the moral guardian of society gradually undermined the traditional concept of woman as passive, subordinate, and fulfilled only through family life. The author traces the views and writings of such leaders as Sarah Josepha Hale (who became co-editor of *Godey's Lady's Book* in 1837), Caroline Lee Whiting Hentz, Emma Dorothy Eliza Nevitte Southworth, Lydia Howard Huntley Sigourney, and others. Points out that the moral guardian argument proved to be a preliminary step in the emergence of an organized and effective women's rights movement in America.                                               N. W. Moen

962.  Ruoff, John C.  FRIVOLITY TO CONSUMPTION: OR, SOUTHERN WOMANHOOD IN ANTEBELLUM LITERATURE.  *Civil War Hist. 1972 18(3): 213-229.* Studies southern fiction in the antebellum era in order to discover if the "typical southern woman" of historical legend conformed to reality. This typical woman was generally a planter's wife who was supposed to live a life of relative leisure, bear children, and manage the household, but stay out of politics and her husband's business affairs. According to the literature of the period, very few female characters resembled the "typical southern woman;" and author concedes that his effort to find such a creature was a "fruitless search."                                              E. C. Murdock

963.  Welter, Barbara.  ANTI-INTELLECTUALISM AND THE AMERICAN WOMAN: 1800-1860.  *Mid-Am. 1966 48(4): 258-270.* Womanhood as defined by contemporary science, religion, literature, and many of the leading citizens of the period was untouched by human intellect. Within this definition the American woman could not be truly womanly if she were truly intellectual. She was faced with this dilemma during her striving for new knowledge and opportunities.
L. D. Silveri

964.  Welter, Barbara.  THE CULT OF TRUE WOMANHOOD: 1820-1860.  *Am. Q. 1966 18(2, pt. 1): 151-174.* Women's periodicals and religious polemics contributed a means of supporting the confinement of women to their homes. According to 19th-century canons, the ideal woman should be pious, chaste, submissive, and domestic. Female education reinforced the cultural edict by emphasizing religious training and sharply delineating between men and women. Numerous authors advised women to be pure and asensual. At the same time, man was described as a creature of few scruples and many desires. By withstanding his assaults upon her, the virtuous woman demonstrated superiority and power. Efforts to introduce social and cultural change often became equated with attacks on feminine virtue. In keeping with their request that women be docile and domestic, writers insisted that they engage in "morally uplifting tasks" such as nursing, cooking, comforting the menfolk, needlework, and flower growing. Reading matter was judged by its presumed moral impact on young women. Women's advisers preferred the art and "gentle science of homemaking" to the cultivation of intellectuality. They did not wish to punish "old maids," but writers did feel that "unselfish" marriage and motherhood contributed the highest order for womenkind. Women who sought honor through other means were reproved. Ultimately, "True Womanhood," by its unreasonable inflexibility, contributed to its own demise as a code for social behavior. With the forces of social and economic change abetting their work, women who thought the standard phony or unrealistic helped one another to tear it down. 117 notes.
R. S. Pickett

# Culture, the Arts, and Recreation

## General

965.  Anderson, John Q.  LOUISIANA ROMEOS OF THE 1840'S.  *Louisiana Studies 1963 2(3): 151-156.* Two examples of frontier humor as reported in *Spirit of the Times,* a New York weekly, in 1842 and 1848. While typical humor usually concerned the masculine sports and amusements of hunting, fishing, fighting, drinking, and practical joking, these deal with courtship and marriage in Louisiana.           G. W. McGinty

966.  Carey, George G.  FOLKLORE FROM THE PRINTED SOURCES OF ESSEX COUNTY, MASSACHUSETTS.  *Southern Folklore Q. 1968 32(1): 17-43.* Discusses folklore and legends of witchcraft in Essex County, Massachusetts, as reported in local newspapers from 1812-60.

967.  Clark, James W., Jr.  WASHINGTON IRVING AND NEW ENGLAND WITCHLORE.  *New York Folklore Q. 1973 29(4): 304-313.*

968.  Jones, James P.  "I HAVE BEEN READING": A LITERARY JOURNAL, 1861.  *Georgia R. 1963 17(2): 173-180.* A study of the reading habits of Aeneas R. Armstrong, a young Georgia planter and naval officer, and his wife, Henriette Vickers Armstrong, during the first year of the Civil War. Reading to each other and alone was done by this young couple for enjoyment and relaxation, and to obtain the latest news. Reading material included novels, poems, newspapers, histories, and magazines. This study points out what has been common knowledge, that intelligent southerners were influenced during the antebellum period by British romantic writers and their description of medieval chivalry. Frequently read were the works of Dickens, Cooper, Charlotte Brontë, Byron, and Scott.                                        H. G. Earnhart

969.  Myerson, Joel.  CAROLINE DALL'S REMINISCENCES OF MARGARET FULLER.  *Harvard Lib. Bull. 1974 22(4): 414-428.* Transcript of Caroline Dall's journal describing the 1841 Conversations on Greek Mythology. Gives interpolated reflections on Margaret Fuller, Elizabeth Peabody, and others of the Transcendentalist circle. Based chiefly on manuscript in the Schlesinger Library of Radcliffe College; 34 notes.                                            L. D. Smith

970.  Salomone, A. William.  THE NINETEENTH-CENTURY DISCOVERY OF ITALY: AN ESSAY IN AMERICAN CULTURAL HISTORY. PROLEGOMENA TO A HISTORIOGRAPHICAL PROBLEM.  *Am. Hist. R. 1968 73(3): 1359-1391.* Reinterprets the 19th-century cultural and intellectual premises of 20th-century American historiography on modern Italy. The study is a prehistory of American historical thought and writing on the *Risorgimento.* Through an analysis of original sources—epistolary, diaristic, and novelistic—as well as of the most important literature on the subject, the author retraces the origins and expressions of modes of consciousness and of thought and feeling on the part of an influential sector of 19th-century American intelligentsia —particularly the New England "passionate pilgrims" to Italy—in the quest for self-recognition and historical and ethical self-definition by "emergent" American civilization vis-à-vis the "classic" Italian world. A subtle cultural dialectic is shown to have occurred which tended to pit a vision of a fixed cultural entity—"timeless Italy" and "eternal Rome"— against a series of moving, changing realities in contemporary Italian, European, and American life. The reactions to Italy by James Fenimore Cooper, George Ticknor, Margaret Fuller, and Charles Eliot Norton are used as major points of reference. Through the two generations (1830-90) with the revolutions of 1848-49 and the European crisis of 1870-71 as focal points, the American "idea" of Italy went full circle between idyll and mythos, flight and escape. These constituted a kind of nonrational, if not subconscious, basis for views of modern Italy but also a burden of antinomies which was inherited by practically all varieties of 20th-century American historiography on the *Risorgimento.*                            A

971.  Wilson, John B.  GRIMM'S LAW AND THE BRAHMINS.  *New England Q. 1965 38(2): 234-239.* Elizabeth Peabody is taken as representative of her contemporaries in Boston who followed the German

philosophers in attempting to relate all languages to a postulated primitive, universal tongue. One result of their attempt was the assertion of erroneous etymologies. Sources are Elizabeth Peabody's *Aesthetic Papers,* 1849, and other contemporary publications.          A. Turner

# Education

972. Atwood, Barbara P.   MISS PIERCE OF LITCHFIELD. *New-England Galaxy 1967 9(1): 32-40.* Life and teachings of Sarah Pierce (d. 1852), founder of the Litchfield Female Seminary and a pioneer in education for women.          S

973.   Blake, John B.   WOMEN AND MEDICINE IN ANTE-BELLUM AMERICA.   *Bull. of the Hist. of Medicine 1965 39(2): 99-123.* On 23 January 1849, Elizabeth Blackwell received, at Geneva Medical College, "the first M.D. degree ever conferred on a woman by an American medical school." Other women, including Elizabeth's sister Emily, Dr. Marie E. Zakrewska, and Dr. Harriot K. Hunt, "the first woman practitioner of note in 19th century America," followed shortly the path blazed by Dr. Blackwell. "The demand for woman's rights and job opportunities was not the sole motive for the entrance of women into medicine. During the years before the Civil War, a belief was widespread that American women were generally unhealthy.... This was commonly attributed to their ignorance of hygiene, even though physicians for centuries had been writing books giving precepts for health." So health reform was a stimulus to the establishment of medical education for women. "By 1861, enough had been accomplished to show that women could become fully qualified physicians, given the opportunity."          W. L. Fox

974.   Burstyn, Joan N.   CATHARINE BEECHER AND THE EDUCATION OF AMERICAN WOMEN.   *New England Q. 1974 47(3): 386-403.* Catharine Beecher perceived that men had professionalized their occupations, whereas women had not. Beecher did not propose to mix the sexes in all work, nor did she argue that women should be permitted employment in all occupations; each sex had a sphere reserved to it. Education was the medium of professionalization; she established schools and trained teachers for work throughout the nation. She wrote textbooks which expounded her views. Beecher was always an experimenter with new methods, but she never swerved from her view that the sexes are equal but separate. 38 notes.          V. L. Human

975.   Carson, Gerald.   CATHERINE BEECHER.   *New-England Galaxy 1964 5(4): 3-10.* Catherine Esther Beecher (1800-78) decided that the salvation of American women depended upon education; specifically, a program of rigorous training for their special role as cook, healthkeeper, and housekeeper for the American home. For her writings in this area, she occupies first place among the founders of the homemaking movement in the United States.          T. J. Farnham

976.   Coleman, Kenneth, ed.   AN 1861 VIEW OF WESLEYAN COLLEGE, MACON, GEORGIA.   *Georgia Hist. Q. 1967 51(4): 488-491.* Represents one student's view of Wesleyan Female College in 1861, as set forth in a letter to a friend and former student. The letter deals mainly with typical college grievances (food and professors) and typical coed interests (men). No reference is made, however, to secession and the impending sectional conflict. 6 notes.          R. A. Mohl

977.   Crighton, John.   THE COLUMBIA FEMALE ACADEMY: A PIONEER IN EDUCATION FOR WOMEN.   *Missouri Hist. R. 1970 64(2): 177-196.* In 1833 some citizens of Columbia started a school for girls. The original charter, which was granted in 1837, was amended in 1851 to provide collegiate as well as elementary and secondary education. The author discusses the curriculum, finances, teachers, and administrators of the school. Although the academy lasted only until 1855, it served to make Columbia an educational center and paved the way for the establishment of famous, lasting schools. A number of women who achieved prominence in Missouri during the late 19th century graduated from the academy. Based on books, local histories, newspapers, and state records; illus., 77 notes.          W. F. Zornow

978.   Durnin, Richard Gerry.   MARBLEHEAD ACADEMY, 1788-1865.   *Essex Inst. Hist. Collections 1964 100(3): 145-154.* Unlike its predecessors, Essex County's third academy - Marblehead Academy, founded 1788 - was a local project supported largely by the townspeople. Like other academies, that at Marblehead was intended to be a secondary school of broader range and scope than the grammar school. Marblehead Academy was coeducational. Before its demise and absorption by Marblehead High School in 1865, the Academy met the needs of its mercantile community admirably. 24 notes, illus.          J. M. Bumsted

979.   Estill, Mary S.   THE EDUCATION OF ANNA KAUFMAN. *Texana 1966 4(3): 247-257.* Shows how different the education of a girl from eastern Texas was in the days of the 1850's from a young woman's schooling of the 1960's. Anna was the daughter of a prominent Texas politician. In 1855, when she was 11, she was sent to the Salem Female Academy in North Carolina. After Salem, she spent two years at the Nashville Female Academy, a famous and popular school for genteel young ladies. Much is recounted about the fashions and mode of travel of that day. Based on contemporary records.          R. J. Roske

980.   Grant, H. Roger.   VIOLA OLERICH, "THE FAMOUS BABY SCHOLAR": AN EXPERIMENT IN EDUCATION.   *Palimpsest 1975 56(3): 88-95.* The utopian novelist and social reformer Henry Olerich began his experiment in progressive education in 1897 when he and his wife adopted a baby girl. Olerich believed that a voluntary process which utilized educational toys and other paraphernalia was more likely to guarantee the acquisition of advanced academic skills than were the orthodox pedagogical methods then in fashion. He methodically recorded his daughter's physical and mental growth, paying particular attention to verbal skills, reasoning ability, and emotional development. An early proponent of behavior modification, Olerich established a system of learning rewards. His desire for order resembled the Montessori method. Olerich had disdain for those who criticized his approach and finally ended his experiments out of discouragement. Based chiefly on an interview with Mrs. Viola Olerich Storms; 5 photos, note.

D. W. Johnson

981.   Griffin, Richard W.   WESLEYAN COLLEGE: ITS GENESIS, 1835-1840.   *Georgia Hist. Q. 1966 50(1): 54-73.* Discusses the founding and early years of Georgia Female College, rechartered in 1842 as Wesleyan Female College. Relates the financial difficulties and controversies of the college to prevailing national, state, and local conditions.

R. Lowitt

982.   Hites, Margaret Ann.   PETER DOUB, 1796-1869, HIS CONTRIBUTION TO THE RELIGIOUS AND EDUCATIONAL DEVELOPMENT OF NORTH CAROLINA.   *Methodist Hist. 1973 11(4): 19-45.* Doub, a Methodist Episcopal preacher in North Carolina, was active in expanding the work of the church, in developing educational facilities for women, and in the church controversy over slavery. Based on Doub's autobiography, journal, and letters in the Perkins Library, Duke University; 71 notes.          H. L. Calkin

983.   Hogeland, Ronald W.   COEDUCATION OF THE SEXES AT OBERLIN COLLEGE: A STUDY OF SOCIAL IDEAS IN MID-NINETEENTH-CENTURY AMERICA.   *J. of Social Hist. [Great Britain] 1972-73 6(2): 160-176.* The introduction of coeducation at Oberlin College was not equally directed toward men and women. It was conceived of and implemented with masculine priorities in mind and reflected mid-19th century American society in general and the Church in particular. At Oberlin women were used to achieve a greater good; they were expected to be catalysts for cultivation, reservoirs for wifedom, and redemptive agents for male sensuality.... they were to give unselfishly of themselves in order to assist the mission of the Church which ultimately was dependent upon the "leading sex." 50 notes.

L. E. Ziewacz

984.   Norse, Clifford C.   SCHOOL LIFE OF AMANDA WORTHINGTON OF WASHINGTON COUNTY, 1857-1862.   *J. of Mississippi Hist. 1972 34(2): 107-116.* Describes some aspects of the school life of Amanda Worthington, daughter of a wealthy cotton planter in Washington County, during 1857-62. Beginning in 1862, Miss Worthington, then 16 years old, kept a journal which today provides valuable information regarding one of the private old field schools in Mississippi. Based chiefly on the Worthington family papers, a microfilm copy of which is in the University of North Carolina Library; 10 notes.

J. W. Hillje

985. Patton, James W. SERIOUS READING IN HALIFAX COUNTY 1860-1865. *North Carolina Hist. R. 1965 42(2): 169-179.* Contemporaries recorded that North Carolina in the middle of the 19th century was very backward in education and literary interest. There were special restrictions on the reading of women, who were not to encounter impure thoughts. One exception to these conditions was Mrs. Catherine Anne (Devereux) Edmonston of Halifax County, whose diary records a wide acquaintance with books and periodicals. Shakespeare, Scott, and the Bible were read most purposefully by Mrs. Edmonston; but they constituted only a small segment of her reading, which included a wide range of fiction, nonfiction, and newspapers. Based on an unpublished diary in the State Department of Archives and History, Raleigh, North Carolina; 82 notes. J. M. Bumsted

986. Rees, John O. ELIZABETH PEABODY AND "THE VERY A B C": A NOTE ON "THE HOUSE OF THE SEVEN GABLES." *Am. Literature 1967 38(4): 537-540.* In Chapter II of Nathaniel Hawthorne's *The House of the Seven Gables,* Hepzibah Pyncheon gives up the idea of becoming a schoolmistress because "in our day, the very A B C has become a science greatly too abstruse to be any longer taught by pointing a pin from letter to letter." When Hawthorne made this dry comment in the fall of 1850, Elizabeth Peabody, his sister-in-law, was nearing the end of a long, spirited effort to popularize a "scientific" way of looking at the alphabet. In 1846 she had published Charles Kraitsir's *The Significance of the Alphabet* and soon became an ardent convert to Kraitsir's theory. In October or early November 1850, Elizabeth Peabody visited the Hawthornes at Lenox, Massachusetts. It seems possible that this visit prompted the reference to "the very A B C." It is apparent, however, that Hawthorne mistrusted the Kraitsir-Peabody theory of language. 10 notes. D. D. Cameron

987. Rembert, Sarah H. "BARHAMVILLE: A COLUMBIA ANTEBELLUM GIRLS' SCHOOL." *South Carolina Hist. Illus. 1970 1(1): 44-48.* The South Carolina Female Collegiate Institute was founded in 1826 at Barhamville, near Columbia, South Carolina. A pioneer in higher education for women, the school was established by Dr. Elias Marks, whose first and second wives—Jane Barham and Julia Warne— were both feminist educators. Some 160 girls usually attended, paying tuition of $200 per year. The four-year curriculum emphasized "thinking rather than memory;" and the faculty included many Europeans, especially in the fine arts and languages. The school continued until 1869 when the main building burned. Undocumented; 4 photos. J. W. Flynt

988. Riley, Glenda ORIGINS OF THE ARGUMENT FOR IMPROVED FEMALE EDUCATION. *Hist. of Educ. Q. 1969 9(4): 455-470.* It was the middle-class woman who, in the 1830's and 1840's, lost function and focus of her life, who became increasingly dependent financially on her husband, and who was regarded as the guardian of American morality. To fulfill this latter role, the argument for the necessity of female education was developed by Sarah Josepha Buell Hale, editor of *Ladies' Magazine* (1828) and *Godey's Lady's Book* (1838). The woman's role as mother was seen as that of teacher of reason, virtue, and spirituality. An educated woman, too, would be a better housekeeper and her husband's intellectual companion. This change of attitude toward women and education found its concrete expression in the growing number of women who became teachers during the 1830's and 1840's. Based on magazines, novels, and other printed sources; 69 notes. J. Herbst

989. Rogers, Tommy Wayne. THE SCHOOLS OF HIGHER LEARNING AT SHARON: MISSISSIPPI. *J. of Mississippi Hist. 1966 28(1): 40-55.* Traces the history of two schools in the village of Sharon in Madison County, Mississippi. In 1837 Sharon College and Sharon Female Academy were established as interdenominational schools. In 1842 the male college was discontinued, the academy was renamed Sharon Female College, and, at its request, was taken over by the Mississippi Conference of the Methodist Church. In 1851 Madison College, a nondenominational school, was established. Both schools prospered during the 1850's, suspended operation during the Civil War, and reopened in 1865-66. Declining population and the growing dominance of Canton, the county seat, were among the factors which led both schools to cease operation in the early 1870's. Based on school catalogs, published state documents, and secondary works. J. W. Hillje

990. Stokes, Allen EDUCATION IN YOUNG ARKANSAS: SPRING HILL FEMALE ACADEMY. *Arkansas Hist. Q. 968 27(2): 105-112.* This academy was one of many which had a brief existence in the early years following statehood. A description of courses of studies and activities is given. Based largely on newspaper advertisements; illus., 19 notes. B. A. Drummond

991. Straub, Jean S. BENJAMIN RUSH'S VIEW ON WOMEN'S EDUCATION. *Pennsylvania Hist. 1967 34(2): 147-157.* In the years following the revolution, Benjamin Rush argued for an educational program for women that would include a knowledge of the English language, vocal music, dancing, certain sciences, bookkeeping, history, and moral philosophy. A utilitarian in his educational philosophy, Rush saw little need for training women in metaphysics, logic, mathematics, or the higher reaches of the physical sciences. Emphasis should be laid on guiding women toward reading moral essays, poetry, history, and religious writings because women are especially suited to uplifting the nation's morals and manners. Rush also argued that women could perform a vital service in instructing the young in the obligations of patriotism and the blessings of liberty. These goals necessitate separate instruction of women. In educating both sexes, Rush held the most important task to be that of instructing youth in the Christian religion. This instructional task could be most easily accomplished by segregating students by denomination. Based on Rush's writings; 32 notes. D. C. Swift

992. White, Mary H. MADAME SOPHIE SOSNOWSKI, EDUCATOR OF YOUNG LADIES. *Georgia Hist. Q. 1966 50(3): 283-287.* A biographical sketch of Sophie Sosnowski, who was associated with various schools and notable American educators and who conducted successful schools for girls in South Carolina and Georgia. R. Lowitt

## Literature
### *(including journalism)*

993. Allaback, Steven. MRS. CLEMM AND HENRY WADSWORTH LONGFELLOW. *Harvard Lib. Bull. 1970 18(1): 32-42.* Transcript of, and commentary on, 15 letters from Poe's aunt and mother-in-law, Mrs. Clemm, to Henry Wadsworth Longfellow. Mrs. Clemm had been the object of Poe's intense devotion. The correspondence reveals the pride and faith of this enigmatic woman, reduced in her old age to living on charity. Longfellow is reflected as charitable and long-suffering, but Mrs. Clemm's claims to their close friendship are unsubstantiated. Based on letters in the Houghton Library, Harvard, the Ingram Poe Collection at the U. of Virginia, and other primary and secondary sources; 36 notes. L. Smith

994. Allen, Margaret V. "THIS IMPASSIONED YANKEE": MARGARET FULLER'S WRITING REVISITED. *Southwest R. 1973 58(2): 162-171.* Although there has been a resurgence of interest recently in Margaret Fuller (1810-50)—New England transcendentalist, social and literary critic, and European traveller—one wonders why her writings have remained "virtually forgotten for more than a hundred years?" There are three possible answers: 1) some of her contemporaries felt that her writings had little merit, 2) her reputation as a conversationalist far outweighed her reputation as a writer, and 3) she was her own severest critic. Defends Fuller's writings from both her contemporaries and current critics. D. F. Henderson

995. Anderson, Carl L. FREDERIKA BREMER'S "SPIRIT OF THE NEW WORLD." *New England Q. 1965 38(2): 187-201.* The Swedish novelist Frederika Bremer visited America in 1849. She wrote of her visit in a book published in 1853, *Homes of the New World.* She wrote also a thesis novel *Hertha* (1856) in which she embodied her interpretation of concern for greater rights for women. To her mind, the greatness of America's future was bound up with the glowing future it offered women. A. Turner

996. Anderson, Hilton AMERICANS IN EUROPE BEFORE THE CIVIL WAR. *Southern Q. 1967 5(3): 273-294.* In between the American Revolution and the Civil War, most Americans in Europe felt bound to defend the American way of life and its lack of things European. "Before the Civil War, most of the literature concerning Europe written

by Americans was in the form of travel or guide books. It is true that Americans had written novels set in Europe long before the Civil War, and some of Cooper's novels actually concerned Americans in Europe and their experiences. However, with the exception of Hawthorne there was practically no American fiction dealing with the expatriate or international theme before Henry James entered the scene." Among the American writers and artists who lived in Europe and commented on life there were James Fenimore Cooper (1789-1851), Margaret Fuller (1810-50), William Wetmore Story (1819-95), and Nathaniel Hawthorne (1804-64). "When Henry James wrote his first novel of Americans abroad, *Roderick Hudson* (1875), he was merely following closely in the footsteps of those who had preceded him." 41 notes.                    D. D. Cameron

997. Ashby, Clifford. FANNY KEMBLE'S "VULGAR" JOURNAL. *Pennsylvania Mag. of Hist. and Biog. 1974 98(1): 58-66.* Even before publication of Fanny Kemble's daily record of her 1832-34 tour of the United States, rumors hinted at its scandalous content. After publication of the *Journal* (1835), reviewers denounced its language as "vulgar" and unladylike, articles appeared refuting it, and two satires held it up to ridicule. As late as 1840 Kemble's *Journal* was influencing literary publications. Based on primary sources; 31 notes.
E. W. Carp

998. Behr, Robert von. THE LIFE OF MARY MEHITABLE CHASE. *Quaker Hist. 1964 53(1): 27-36.* Mary Chase, Quaker poetess, grew up on her father's "Hillside Farm" near Chatham, New York. At 21 she attended Albany Female Academy, whose *Monthly Rose* she edited after graduation. She sent a collection of 300 wildflowers to the London Crystal Palace Exhibition of 1851. She taught composition at Brooklyn Female Academy, and died, unmarried, of tuberculosis. Her letters and poems were romantic, nature-loving.
T. D. S. Bassett

999. Brandstadter, Evan. UNCLE TOM AND ARCHY MOORE: THE ANTISLAVERY NOVEL AS IDEOLOGICAL SYMBOL. *Am. Q. 1974 26(2): 160-175.* Compares and contrasts the literary and subject quality of the little known fictional account by Richard Hildreth, *The Slave or Memoirs of Archy Moore* (1836), with Harriet Beecher Stowe's *Uncle Tom's Cabin* (1852). Hildreth was involved with the temperance movement and abolitionism. His novel was ahead of its time and undoubtedly influenced Mrs. Stowe, but it never achieved the popular appeal of *Uncle Tom's Cabin*. Abolitionists such as William Lloyd Garrison may have preferred Hildreth's realistic portrayal of Negro slavery, but most Americans were not ready for that even in 1852. 30 notes.
C. W. Olson

1000. Davis, Curtis Carroll. DR. CARUTHERS AIDS A LADY. *Georgia Hist. Q. 1972 56(4): 583-587.* William Alexander Caruthers produced some literary works which received frequent attention in the southern press. Mrs. Benjamin (Sarah Lawrence Drew) Griffin was attempting to begin a new southern magazine in Georgia and wanted contributions from Caruthers. Through a series of letters (1841), she finally prevailed upon him to write. Primary and secondary sources; 12 notes.
M. R. Gillam

1001. Diehl, Gertrude Barrowclough. THE ACE OF HEARTS. *New-England Galaxy 1971 13(1): 14-21.* An account of the courtship of Henry Wadsworth Longfellow and Fanny Appleton.                    S

1002. Downey, Jean. WHITTIER AND COOKE: UNPUBLISHED LETTERS. *Quaker Hist. 1963 52(1): 33-36.* The literary friendship between Whittier and Rose Terry Cooke, Connecticut local colorist, may have started in the 1850's when both were contributors to the *Atlantic Monthly*. Seven letters, 11 notes.                    E. P. Stickney

1003. Duncan, Janice K. *RUTH ROVER:* VINDICTIVE FALSEHOOD OR HISTORICAL TRUTH? *J. of the West 1973 12(2): 240-253.* The suppressed *The Grains, or Passages in the Life of Ruth Rover,* written by Margaret Jewett Bailey, clearly documents that Methodist missionaries were more interested in exploiting agricultural and manufacturing opportunities than in spreading Christianity in mid-19th-century Oregon. 48 notes.                    E. P. Stickney

1004. Hamblen, Abigail Ann. THE BELLE OF TRANSCENDENTALISM. *J. of Popular Culture 1973 7(1): 172-178.* Discusses Margaret Fuller, her interaction with Horace Greeley and Ralph Waldo Emerson, and her attitude toward love and the men in her life.                    S

1005. Harding, Walter. THOREAU AND KATE BRADY. *Am. Literature 1964 36(3): 347-349.* Bronson Alcott's assertion that Thoreau was once in love with an Irish girl is overstated; the girl was Kate Brady whose love of nature impressed Thoreau, but who was 20 years his junior. 3 notes.                    R. S. Burns

1006. Hepler, John C. A PROPOSED QUAKER POEM. *Quaker Hist. 1968 57(1): 42-48.* Printed here, with an introduction, is a letter from Elizabeth Lloyd of Philadelphia to John Greenleaf Whittier who was living in Amesbury, Massachusetts. Dated 3 August 1840, the letter expands her proposal that Whittier write an "epic" poem about Quakerism. Four other letters on this theme from Miss Lloyd to Whittier were published in a book by Thomas F. Currier, *Elizabeth Lloyd and the Whittiers* (Cambridge, 1939).                    T. D. S. Bassett

1007. Hirsch, Lester M. THE SWEET SINGER OF HARTFORD. *New-England Galaxy 1974 16(2): 28-33.* Evaluates the writings of Lydia Howard Huntley Sigourney (1791-1865), whose saccharine, sentimental style and preoccupation with the theme of death characterize most of the 67 books she wrote. She held conservative attitudes about the role of women in society; but her condemnation of war, her abolitionist stance, and support of conservation efforts reflect an otherwise liberal political orientation. Illus.                    P. C. Marshall

1008. Huddleston, Eugene L. DEPICTIONS OF NEW YORK IN EARLY AMERICAN POETRY. *New York Folklore Q. 1968 24(4): 275-293.* Discusses the poetic portrayal of New York during 1783-1812, in the works of John D. McKinnon, Margaretta V. Faugeres, and Alexander Wilson.

1009. Hudson, Benjamin F. ANOTHER VIEW OF "UNCLE TOM." *Phylon 1963 24(1): 79-87.* "Uncle Tom" has come to connote a cowardly and contemptible character. A French critic, in 1854 reviewing a play based on Mrs. Stowe's novel, saw him as a stoic philosopher, and likened him to Epictetus, who was patient, courageous, and resigned. The author of this article agrees, noting that goodness was a basic Stoic quality, and that the Uncle Tom of the novel was distinguished by goodness. His absolute Christian faith protected him, and distinguished him from the Stoics. Although shoddy play productions helped demean Uncle Tom, his character merits appreciation.                    L. Filler

1010. Kearns, Francis E. MARGARET FULLER AS A MODEL FOR HESTER PRYNNE. *Jahrbuch für Amerikastudien [West Germany] 1965 10: 191-197.* Argues that Hawthorne had Margaret Fuller in mind in creating Hester Prynne, the heroine of *The Scarlet Letter* (1850). Documented.                    G. Bassler

1011. Kirkham, E. Bruce THE FIRST EDITION OF "UNCLE TOM'S CABIN": A BIBLIOGRAPHICAL STUDY. *Papers of the Biblio. Soc. of Am. 1971 65(4): 365-382.* Notes and documents eight variants which separate the first run of the first edition (John B. Jewett and Co., Boston) from later runs of *Uncle Tom's Cabin*. Attributes these variants to authorial changes. An appendix lists 288 of the earliest copies of the novel. Based on primary and secondary sources; 2 illus., 11 notes.
C. A. Newton

1012. Martin, Wendy. PROFILE: SUSANNA ROWSON, EARLY AMERICAN NOVELIST. *Women's Studies 1974 2(1): 1-8.* Sketches the publishing history of the first American bestseller, *Tale of Truth* (1791) and the life of its author, Susanna Haswell Rowson (1762-1824). Rowson, born in England, spent most of her life in the United States. She worked as an actress, established and administered a young ladies' academy, and wrote novels, poetry, plays, and grammar school texts. Rowson wrote sentimental novels in an age critical of false sentiment and fiction. She insisted that her books taught moral principles and cultivated the minds of the young; but it is doubtful that people read Rowson's novels solely for moral instruction. The books were popular and sensational; they were filled with incidents of seduction, infidelity, poverty, suicide, and rape. Economic and social factors contributed to the books' popularity in England and the United States where a growing middle class and its bourgeois housewife had the time and money to buy and read domestic novels which taught women to accept their economically dependent lives and the polarization of sex roles. Rowson's novels helped establish the fictional stereotype of American women and define the cult of true womanhood. Based on primary and secondary materials; biblio.

A. E. Wiederrecht

1013. Matlack, James H. THE *ALTA CALIFORNIA'S* LADY CORRESPONDENT. *New York Hist. Soc. Q. 1974 58(4): 280-303.* For over three years, beginning in October 1854, Elizabeth Barstow Stoddard (1823-1902) wrote semimonthly newsletters "From Our Lady Correspondent" for the San Francisco *Daily Alta California.* Although she wrote several novels, her best known work was the newsletters. In addition to her views and the picture of society she presents, she should be remembered as the first New York woman to write on a regular basis for an out-of-town newspaper. 6 illus., 15 notes. C. L. Grant

1014. Medlicott, Alexander, Jr. THE LEGEND OF LUCY BREWER: AN EARLY AMERICAN NOVEL. *New England Q. 1966 39(4): 461-473.* Discusses *The Female Marine,* or *The Adventures of Miss Lucy Brewer,* a pseudoautobiography, as an example in the emerging of the American novel from British domination in the period from about 1789 until 1818, the year *The Female Marine* was printed for the final time. Though not entirely different from the English novel pattern, this book, published first in 1814, embodies an American patriotic thrust that differentiates it from the British form. The story centers around the fictitious Miss Brewer's early career as a prostitute in Boston and her subsequent activities as an American marine for nearly three years on the USS *Constitution.* After leaving the service (never having been discovered to be a woman), Lucy lives a more acceptable moral life replete with sermons for wayward youths. Thus *The Female Marine* also served as a satire on the didactic novel of sentiment which abounded in early 19th-century America. 11 notes. W. G. Morgan

1015. Moore, Robert. HAWTHORNE'S FOLK-MOTIFS AND *THE HOUSE OF THE SEVEN GABLES. New York Folklore Q. 1972 28(3): 221-233.* Discusses the theme of witchcraft and New England folklore in Nathaniel Hawthorne's *The House of the Seven Gables* in 1851.

1016. Myerson, Joel. MARGARET FULLER'S 1842 JOURNAL: AT CONCORD WITH THE EMERSONS. *Harvard Lib. Bull. 1973 21(3): 320-340.* Discusses the relationship between writer Margaret Fuller and Ralph Waldo Emerson, 1836-42, based on Fuller's journal fragments. S

1017. O'Donnell, Thomas F. THE RETURN OF THE WIDOW BEDOTT: MRS. F. M. WHITCHER OF WHITESBORO AND ELMIRA. *New York Hist. 1974 55(1): 5-34.* The *Widow Bedott Papers* (first published in book form in 1855) is today unread and forgotten, but it was an American best-seller, as late as the mid-1890's, and exemplifies the dialect literature so popular in 19th-century America. The *Widow Bedott Papers* was a forerunner of literary realism and "one of the most incisive pieces of social criticism to surface in antebellum America." Written by Frances Miriam Berry Whitcher (1811-52), the work portrayed hypocrisy and viciousness in Yankee small-town life in upstate New York. The sketches were drawn from Mrs. Whitcher's personal experience and observation. After marrying the Reverend Benjamin W. Whitcher in 1847, she began writing the papers, which appeared in *Godey's Lady's Book* and other journals, in order to supplement her husband's meager salary. The sketches so outraged the Reverend Whitcher's Elmira congregation that he was forced to resign his pulpit, in June 1849, and move back to his wife's home town of Whitesboro. Primary and secondary sources; 10 illus., 42 notes. G. Kurland

1018. Patterson, Rebecca. THE CARDINAL POINTS SYMBOLISM OF EMILY DICKINSON. PART II. *Midwest Q. 1973 15(1): 31-60.* Discusses the symbolism in Emily Dickinson's poetry.

1019. Pulsifer, Janice Goldsmith. ALICE AND PHOEBE CARY, WHITTIER'S SWEET SINGERS OF THE WEST. *Essex Inst. Hist. Collections 1973 109(1): 9-59.* Discusses the lives and writings of the Ohio-born Cary sisters in the 19th century, emphasizing their poetic contributions to the cultural life of New England and New York. S

1020. Reilly, John E. MRS. OSGOOD AND THE BROADWAY JOURNAL. *Duquesne R. 1967 12(2): 131-146.* Examines Edgar Allan Poe's relationship with the poetess, Frances Sargent Osgood. The two wrote love poetry to each other in the pages of *The Broadway Journal,* a New York weekly with which Poe was associated. 20 notes.

L. V. Eid

1021. Ross, Emily. MADONNA IN BUSTLES. *Daughters of the Am. Revolution Mag. 1971 105(8): 708-711.* Biographical sketch of Sarah Josepha Hale, editor of *Godey's Lady's Book* and moderate campaigner for women's rights in America in the mid-19th century. Gives details on her New Hampshire upbringing, her marriage to lawyer David Hale, and her early widowhood. Hale's first contact with literature as a profession came through her editing of the Boston publication, *The Ladies' Magazine.* In the 1830's she organized the Seaman's Aid Society, then joined Louis A. Godey of Philadelphia as literary editor of his magazine, a partnership that lasted for 40 years. Discusses Hale's quiet advocacy of a wide range of reforms in the area of women's rights through the pages of the magazine. Illus., biblio. D. A. Sloan

1022. Schlesinger, Elizabeth Bancroft. TWO EARLY HARVARD WIVES: ELIZA FARRAR AND ELIZA FOLLEN. *New England Q. 1965 38(2): 147-167.* Biographies of two women of the 19th century, whose chief interest lies, as the title indicates, in the fact that they married professors at a great university. Mrs. Farrar published a manners book, *The Young Lady's Friend* (1836) and an abolitionist work *Congo in Search of His Master* (1854). Mrs. Follen wrote voluminously for children, in both verse and prose. She, too, wrote abolitionist works.

A. Turner

1023. Smith, C. N. EMMA MARSHALL AND LONGFELLOW: SOME ADDITIONS TO HILEN'S *LETTERS. J. of Am. Studies* [Great Britain] *1974 8(1): 81-90.* Reprints and comments on portions of seven letters from Henry Wadsworth Longfellow (1807-82), written 1851-62. Contains brief comments on several other letters written by Longfellow in the 1870's. H. T. Lovin

1024. Sweetser, Mary Chisholm. THE LEGEND OF APPLEDORE. *New-England Galaxy 1966 7(4): 22-28.* The life of Celia Thaxter, the poet of Appledore Island, Maine is reviewed in this selection. Emphasis is placed upon the many important personages who visited Appledore Island during the mid-19th century. Hawthorne and Whittier and their acquaintance with the island are covered at length. Photos of Celia Thaxter and scenes of Appledore Island are included (pp. 23-27).

A. B. Lampe

1025. Tucker, Louis L. THE SEMICOLON CLUB OF CINCINNATI. *Ohio Hist. 1964 73(1): 13-26.* Evaluates the influence of a literary and social organization, the Semi-Colon Club, which existed in Cincinnati roughly between 1829 and 1846. Though its general influence is difficult to assess, the club did provide an outlet for the first literary efforts of Harriet Beecher Stowe. Based on papers of the club and papers of several members of the club, now on deposit in the Cincinnati Historical Society. S. L. Jones

1026. Walsh, Peggy M. POETRY AS A HISTORICAL SOURCE: ROMANTIC SYMBOLOGY AND SOCIAL ATTITUDES TOWARD WOMEN IN THE ANTE-BELLUM SOUTH. *Montclair J. of Social Sci. and Humanities 1974 3(1): 14-19.*

1027. Wisbey, Herbert A., Jr. THE WIDOW BEDOTT. *York State Tradition 1972 26(4): 15-21.* Discusses the nature of Frances Berry Whitcher's (b. 1811-d. 1852) social satire and its impact on her life during the late 1840's. Her satire was modeled after her life as the wife of an Elmira, New York, minister. Based on primary and secondary sources. D. A. Franz

1028. Wood, Ann Douglas. MRS. SIGOURNEY AND THE SENSIBILITY OF THE INNER SPACE. *New England Q. 1972 45(2): 163-181.* Discusses the life and works of the popular American poetess Lydia Huntley Sigourney (1791-1865). She used poetry to reflect the role of women and to move herself upward on the social scale. Women were passive, docile creatures of the home. Men were disruptive and terrifying. Her poetry involved sexual sublimation to the point of reveling in blindness and death, where perfect tranquility is achieved. 44 notes.

V. L. Human

# Arts and Music

## (including Folk Art)

1029. Cavanah, Frances. JENNY LIND FEVER. *Historic Preservation 1970 22(4): 15-24.* Discusses the nationwide tour (1850-52) of Lind (1821-87), the famous European opera singer. Phineas T. Barnum sponsored her tour, although Americans were not generally a music-loving people. The tour was a great success. "Jenny Lind" became an advertising label for many different items of merchandise. Relates the trip, including Lind's marriage (1852) to Otto Goldschmidt (1829-1907) in Boston. Illus.
J. M. Hawes

1030. Cole, Glyndon. JENNY LIND, THE SWEDISH NIGHTINGALE. *York State Tradition 1971 25(1): 2-6.* Describes the US tour (1850-51) of Jenny Lind, emphasizing public response to the tour and Phineas T. Barnum's role as its promoter. The Lind tour marked the commencement "of the development of female talent in the performing arts in America." Secondary sources.
D. A. Franz

1031. Krich, John F. THE AMIABLE LADY CHARMS THE IRON CITY: ADAH ISAACS MENKEN CHARMS PITTSBURGH. *Western Pennsylvania Hist. Mag. 1968 51(3): 259-278.* Adah Isaacs Menken (ca. 1835-68) was a popular actress who visited Pittsburgh's Old Drury Theater several times between 1859 and 1862. Although she was adept at acting, singing, and dancing, her popularity in large part was due to her "scandalous" life, including four marriages, one to American boxer John Carmel Heenan. After leaving Pittsburgh in 1862 she embarked on a successful European career. Based on primary and secondary sources; illus., 2 photos, 44 notes, appendixes.
D. E. Bowers

1032. McCormack, Mrs. Stewart. ELEGANT ACCOMPLISHMENTS, PART II. *Missouri Hist. Soc. Bull. 1965 21(4, pt. 1): 308-314.* Continued from a previous article. Pictures 11 art-craft pieces ("elegant accomplishments") produced by young American women between 1792 and 1876 and now owned by the Missouri Historical Society. The collection includes two samplers in fine cross-stitch, art works created from natural materials (seeds, pods, grains, nuts, sea shells, and seaweed), embroidery work, and wax reproductions of flowers and fruit. 11 illus.
D. D. Cameron

1033. Pearce, John N. MISS PORTER'S HOUSES: A SCHOOL PRESERVES ITS SURROUNDINGS. *Historic Preservation 1971 23(4): 18-25.* Discusses the architecture of the buildings of Miss [Sarah] Porter's School in Farmington, Connecticut. The buildings date from the mid-18th century and provide a "remarkable record of American Architecture." With the exception of the earliest examples of the English manor house, "virtually every major trend in American architecture is represented by a building at Miss Porter's School." The doorway and keystone of the Deming-Lewis House (1740) represents the addition of Italian Renaissance details to English manor houses. The next phase of American architecture, neoclassicism, is represented by two buildings, Colony (1799) and Humphrey (1800). The largest single collection of structures in one style illustrates the mid-19th-century villa introduced by Alexander Jackson Davis and made popular by Andrew Jackson Downing. Undocumented, photos.
J. M. Hawes

1034. Smither, Nelle. "THE BRIGHT PARTICULAR STAR": CHARLOTTE CUSHMAN IN ALBANY. *Bull. of the New York Public Lib. 1967 71(9): 563-572.* Discusses actress Charlotte Cushman's engagement at the Albany Theater, Albany, New York, during 1836 and 1837. Going there after a fire destroyed the Bowery Theater where she was performing in New York City, she received valuable experience playing a variety of roles, both female and male, in tragedies, comedies, melodramas, operas, farces, and musical entertainments. Miss Cushman played 42 roles at Albany, most for the first time. Her reviews indicate that she was highly successful in her performances, and it was predicted that she would become the best tragic actress in the United States. Not long after leaving Albany, she signed a three-year contract with the Park, New York's foremost theater, which took her one step further along the path to becoming "the most magnificent actress America has ever produced." The article contains a day-to-day record of Miss Cushman's roles while in Albany. Based on letters in the Harvard Theater Collection, contemporary newspaper accounts, and biographies of Charlotte Cushman; 2 illus., 28 notes.
W. L. Bowers

1035. Smither, Nelle. "A NEW LADY-ACTOR OF GENTLEMEN": CHARLOTTE CUSHMAN'S SECOND NEW YORK ENGAGEMENT. *Bull. of the New York Public Lib. 1970 74(6): 391-395.* An account of American actress Charlotte Saunders Cushman's (1816-76) second theatrical engagement in New York City (April-May 1837). Several of her roles were male parts. Describes the reception of her talent by theater-goers and critics. As with her earlier one-week engagement during the previous fall, Miss Cushman was enthusiastically received and acclaimed by New Yorkers. Based mainly on contemporary newspaper articles; illus., 15 notes.
W. L. Bowers

1036. Smither, Nelle. "THE SOVEREIGN IN THE ASCENDANT": CHARLOTTE CUSHMAN'S FIRST NEW YORK ENGAGEMENT. *Bull. of the New York Public Lib. 1966 70(7): 419-424.* Concerns actress Charlotte Cushman's 1836 engagement at the Bowery Theater in New York City. The writer contends that Miss Cushman's preparation for her New York debut and the reception she received have been consistently misrepresented. Contrary to what Charlotte and her biographers wrote, she was not poorly prepared for the engagement nor was she unfavorably received by the New York critics and public. Neither had she turned to drama out of desperation after losing her voice while aspiring to become an opera singer. She had appeared in opera in New Orleans in 1835 but her voice displeased the audience, and she therefore began doing dramatic roles although still continuing to sing. She won praise for her acting and had appeared in at least nine tragic parts before her opening in New York. At the Bowery, she predictably triumphed in her role as Lady Macbeth; and critics declared her an actress of great promise at the age of 20. Based on primary sources; illus., 15 notes.
W. L. Bowers

1037. Tamburro, Francis. A TALE OF A SONG: "THE LOWELL FACTORY GIRL." *Southern Exposure 1974 2(1): 42-51.* Analyzes this folk song, circulated in Lowell, Massachusetts, during the 1840's, and its spread throughout the country.
S

1038. Tanselle, G. Thomas. ROYALL TYLER, JUDITH SARGENT MURRAY, AND "THE MEDIUM." *New England Q. 1968 41(1): 115-117.* Until 1923 Royall Tyler was popularly supposed to be the author of the play, "The Medium, or Happy Tea-Party," performed in the Federal Street Theatre in Boston only once, 2 March 1795. Then, in 1923, Arthur Holeson Quinn, the drama historian, positively identified Judith Sargent Stevens Murray (1751-1820) as the author. However, a poem by Murray praised Tyler's play, "The Contrast," showing that Tyler, while not the author of "The Medium," was an inspiration for it. 7 notes.
K. B. West

1039. Theodore, Terry. LAURA KEENE AND MR. LINCOLN. *Lincoln Herald 1971 73(4): 199-204.* Laura Keene was the first performer at Ford's Theater to recognize John Wilkes Booth as the assassin of President Abraham Lincoln. A review of Laura Keene's life clears up distorted details about this leading actress in America. She became the first woman to successfully manage her own theater in America, trained her own actors, adapted most of her scripts, designed costumes, and did publicity. Some particulars of the Lincoln assassination are analyzed. Based on secondary works and contemporary printed sources; 20 notes.
A. C. Aimone

# 5. The United States 1865-1945

## General

1040. Adickes, Sandra. MIND AMONG THE SPINDLES: AN EXAMINATION OF SOME OF THE JOURNALS, NEWSPAPERS, AND MEMOIRS OF THE LOWELL FEMALE OPERATIVES. *Women's Studies 1973 1(3): 279-287.* Discusses the lives and attitudes of Lowell mill operatives toward their work and work experiences. During the 1830's, the New England-born women who worked in the mills found a sense of dignity in receiving pay for producing goods and also found a common bond of sisterhood. Many viewed their Lowell work as temporary occupations and perceived the work to be a character-building experience and an opportunity for self-improvement. By 1840, conditions in Lowell changed. With increased industrial competition and a depression, the operatives received lower wages and tended more machines. Turnouts, labor agitation, and labor organizing became common. By the late 1840's, other jobs offered New England women wages competitive with those the mills paid; many women joined the westward movement; and the influx of European immigrants provided the mills with a cheaper labor force. Changes within the industry and in the labor force effectively broke down the paternal system of the early Lowell mills. Based on primary and secondary materials; 25 notes. A. E. Wiederrecht

## Economic Sphere

### General

1041. Bailey, Hugh C. ETHEL ARMES AND "THE STORY OF COAL AND IRON IN ALABAMA." *Alabama R. 1969 22(3): 188-199.* One of two major works by Ethel Armes, *The Story of Coal and Iron in Alabama* (Massachusetts: Cambridge U. Press, 1910) is a primary source book on the development of industrial Alabama. She not only consulted the ordinary records but also conducted hundreds of interviews with industrial pioneers. The work has come under some criticism for failing to condemn convict labor and child labor, and for failing to deal more fully with the labor union movement. 20 notes. D. F. Henderson

1042. Carson, Gerald. SWEET EXTRACT OF HOKUM. *Am. Heritage 1971 22(4): 18-27, 108-110.* Patent medicines of the late 19th and early 20th centuries, among them Lydia Pinkham's Vegetable Compound. S

1043. Early, Eleanor. SING A SONG OF LYDIA PINKHAM. *New-England Galaxy 1964 5(3): 34-40.* Tells the story of Lydia Estes Pinkham's Vegetable Compound. The origin of the compound, the founding of the Pinkham Company, and the advertising techniques of the company are discussed. T. J. Farnham

1044. Hall, Linda. NEIMAN-MARCUS: THE BEGINNING. *Western States Jewish Hist. Q. 1975 7(2): 138-150.* On 10 September 1907 in Dallas, Texas, Herbert Marcus and Al and Carrie Neiman opened their first store, which specialized in fine clothes for women. They had operated a store in Atlanta for two years, but sold it to open their new store in Dallas. They developed new methods of merchandising ready-to-wear clothing. In 1913, the store was destroyed by a fire, after which it moved to larger quarters and continued to grow. The Neiman-Marcus Co. contributed greatly to the development of Dallas as the major fashion market in the Southwest. 36 notes. R. A. Garfinkle

1045. Kerr, Thomas J., IV THE NEW YORK FACTORY INVESTIGATING COMMISSION AND THE MINIMUM WAGE MOVEMENT. *Labor Hist. 1971 12(3): 373-391.* Analyzes the New York State Factory Investigating Commission reports and their influence upon the minimum wage movement in the United States from 1910 to 1938. The commission, formed as a result of the 1911 Triangle Shirtwaist Company fire, made a detailed investigation of wages of women and children and their relationship to the cost of living. Exploding several myths, the report became the basis for a drive for a New York minimum wage law which failed to pass the legislature, but the data included in the survey remained the basis for much of the minimum wage movement in the 1920's and early 1930's. The report was used in defense of the passage of minimum wage legislation in New York in 1933 and was influential on the development of the N.I.R.A. and the F.L.S.A. of the New Deal. Based on the reports of the commission, and records of the American Association for Labor Legislation and the Consumers' League; 69 notes. L. L. Athey

1046. Leff, Mark H. CONSENSUS FOR REFORM: THE MOTHERS' PENSION MOVEMENT IN THE PROGRESSIVE ERA. *Social Service R. 1973 47(3): 397-429.* The United States, alone among the major industrialized nations of the world, showed a great concern for ameliorating the effects of poverty on fatherless children and an utter fear of giving help to indigent men. This study of the 1911-21 legislative career of the drive for mothers' pensions details the unrivaled support for this progressive enactment; it also points to the greater difficulties of enacting its successor in the 1930's. 63 notes. M. Hough

1047. Patterson, James T. MARY DEWSON AND THE AMERICAN MINIMUM WAGE MOVEMENT. *Labor Hist. 1964 5(2): 134-152.* Describes the role played by Mary Williams Dewson in the American minimum wage movement. After graduating from Wellesley College in 1897, Miss Dewson followed the career of social welfare work until her death in 1962. Her activities included campaigning for a women's minimum wage law in Massachusetts (1911-12), working for a bill to regulate hours of work in New York (1928-30), and in compiling statistics which contributed to the draft of the Social Security Act. She served as a member of the Social Security Board from 1935 to 1940. J. H. Krenkel

1048. Price, Beaulah M. D'Olive. THE SILK ENTERPRISES AT CORINTH IN THE 1880'S. *J. of Mississippi Hist. 1965 27(3): 249-258.* Describes the silk farms of Mrs. Marie Louise Combs Doche and of L. S. Crozier in Corinth, Mississippi. The enterprises were discontinued about 1889 for reasons which are not clear. Based on personal correspondence, newspapers, and county records. J. W. Hillje

1049. Underhill, Lonnie E. and Littlefield, Daniel F., Jr. WOMEN HOMESEEKERS IN OKLAHOMA TERRITORY, 1889-1901. *Pacific Historian 1973 17(3): 36-47.*

## Employment Outside the Home

1050. Atwood, Barbara P. CONNECTICUT'S LADY HISTORIANS. *New-England Galaxy 1971 12(3): 32-41.* Biographical sketches of Frances Manwaring Caulkins and Ellen Douglas Larned. S

1051. Aurand, Harold W. DIVERSIFYING THE ECONOMY OF THE ANTHRACITE REGIONS, 1880-1900. *Pennsylvania Mag. of Hist. and Biog. 1970 94(1): 54-61.* Studies late 19th-century attempts to broaden the industrial base of the anthracite mining regions of Pennsylvania. It was not an attempt to replace the mining industry, but a search to provide employment opportunities for women and thereby add supplementary income to families of mine workers as a buffer to the mining industry's sporadic employment practices. They did not anticipate a decline in the coal-mining industry; hence the approach was different from later attempts at diversification. 40 notes. R. V. Ritter

1052. Barney, Robert K. ADELE PAROT: BEACON OF THE DIOCLESIAN LEWIS SCHOOL OF GYMNASTIC EXPRESSION IN THE AMERICAN WEST. *Canadian J. of Hist. of Sport and Physical Educ. 1974 5(2): 63-73.* The impact of Dioclesius Lewis gymnastics reached the Pacific Coast through Adele Parot when she began teaching at the State Normal School in San Francisco in 1862. Suggests her influence on the first state law requiring physical education instruction in California 1866. Based on 16 primary and secondary sources. R. A. Smith

1053. Bartlett, Harriett M. IDA M. CANNON: PIONEER IN MEDICAL SOCIAL WORK. *Social Service R. 1975 49(2): 208-229.* Relates the story and the contributions to social work of early pioneer Ida M. Cannon (1877-1960) at Massachusetts General Hospital.    S

1054. Bassett, Preston R. AERIAL ADVENTURES OF CARLOTTA, THE LADY AERONAUT, OR SKY-LARKING IN CLOUDLAND; BEING HAP-HAZARD ACCOUNTS OF THE PERILS AND PLEASURES OF AERIAL NAVIGATION. *Am. Heritage 1966 17(5): 64-67.* Describes the aeronautical career of Mary Breed Hawley (known as Carlotta), a woman balloonist, who by the time of her retirement in 1891 had "made more ascensions than all other women combined throughout the world, and more than any man living in America."    S

1055. Benjamin, Ludy T., Jr. THE PIONEERING WORK OF LETA HOLLINGSWORTH IN THE PSYCHOLOGY OF WOMEN. *Nebraska Hist. 1975 56(4): 493-507.* Examines the early work of Leta Hollingsworth, wife of Harry L. Hollingsworth, who in her early career as a psychologist destroyed the claims for the inferiority of women propounded by leading psychologists early in the 20th century. Her work clearly showed there were no differences in variability between males and females. When she received her Ph.D. in 1916 she had published one book and nine papers, all concerned with the psychology of women. Thereafter she shifted her research interests to the psychology of the exceptional child.    R. Lowitt

1056. Bernstein, A. A. QUEEN OF THE BOWERY. *New York Folklore Q. 1967 23(3): 196-201.* Discusses the occupation of Millie Hull, a tattoo artist in the Bowery of New York City in 1939.

1057. Bixler, Miriam E. ELLEN A. BRUBAKER, PIONEER FREE KINDERGARTENER. *J. of the Lancaster County Hist. Soc. 1967 71(3): 165-175.* The first Free Kindergarten Association of Lancaster County came into existence in 1897 as a private institution. The first teacher the association hired was Ellen A. Brubaker (1870-1954). Largely through her efforts the kindergarten concept became an accepted principle of child education in Pennsylvania. The article sketches the life and interests of Ellen Brubaker, and the formation of the private and public kindergartens in Lancaster County. 2 photos, 29 notes.    J. S. Pula

1058. Bogardus, Emory S. DR. BESSIE A. MC CLENAHAN AS SOCIOLOGIST. *Sociol. and Social Res. 1969 53(4): 523-529.* McClenahan was born in Des Moines, Iowa, in 1885, graduated with a bachelor's degree from Drake University in 1910, and accepted a research fellowship in sociology at the University of Southern California in 1926. She taught undergraduate classes and conducted graduate seminars on specialized social and community problems at the University of Southern California until her retirement in 1951. "The essence of Dr. McClenahan's methods of sociological research was basically the study of one example after another of behavior in a given area of human life until she found a definite behavior tendency. She would describe and explain the tendency and then present one or more illustrations of the repeated behavior patterns. Hers was essentially the interview method of research." Biblio.    D. D. Cameron

1059. Brisley, Melissa Ann. CORNELIA MARVIN PIERCE: PIONEER IN LIBRARY EXTENSION. *Lib. Q. 968 38(2): 125-153.* Reviews highlights and goals of the career of Cornelia Marvin Pierce. A graduate of the library school of Armour Institute of Technology, Mrs. Pierce served her apprentice years as a librarian in Illinois and nearby, served next (1897-1905) on the Wisconsin Library Commission, and finally removed to Oregon where she headed the Oregon State Library until 1928. Solicitous and ambitious to a fault, she argued that library services were active, aggressive educational agents. Special reference facilities, traveling libraries, mail-order loans, county systems of libraries, and bulletins evaluating books for both homes and libraries were among her ideas (not all of them successful) designed to realize her concept of library service to the community. Documented.    C. A. Newton

1060. Carlson, William H. IDA ANGELINE KIDDER: PIONEER WESTERN LAND-GRANT LIBRARIAN. *Coll. and Res. Lib. 1968 29(3): 217-223.* Discusses the professional career of Ida Angeline Kidder (1855-1920) as Librarian of Oregon State Agricultural College, 1908-20. Based upon secondary sources.    E. R. McKinstry

1061. Carroll, Gladys Hasty. SUMMER OF 1921. *New-England Galaxy 1963 5(1): 37-41.* Memoir of a college girl's summer employment at the Pacific Mills, Dover, New Hampshire.    T. J. Farnham

1062. Coffey, Marie Butler. COUNTRY SCHOOLTEACHER. *New-England Galaxy 1974 16(1): 51-57.* Autobiographical memoir of a teacher.    S

1063. Corwin, Margaret Ann. AN INVESTIGATION OF FEMALE LEADERSHIP IN REGIONAL, STATE, AND LOCAL LIBRARY ASSOCIATIONS, 1876-1923. *Lib. Q. 1974 44(2): 133-144.* "This study was undertaken to extend the thesis of Sharon B. Wells on 'The Feminization of the American Library Profession, 1876-1923,' which concluded that women never dominated the top positions in the profession nationally. This study tested the hypothesis that female librarians did provide leadership in state organizations, local associations, and state positions during the years 1876-1923. The method employed was to list all persons who held the executive positions in particular national associations and to compare the sex distribution with that of the persons who held executive positions in state library associations, library commissions, and local library associations. The data are derived from a sample of such listings for every third year during the period. The data indicate that women made up 31 percent of the officers in national library associations for the years 1890-1923; they also show that women tended to be better represented when the office was not a governmental position; only 20 percent of the state librarians were women. However, during the same period, 56 percent of the officers in library commissions, 60 percent of those in state associations, and 68 percent in local associations were women. Thus, the hypothesis—that women were more active in leadership roles on the local and state scene than at the national level—is supported by the data. While the proportion of women in such leadership roles never equaled their proportion in the profession overall, they were probably more active than might have been predicted considering the cultural climate of the period covered by the study."    J

1064. Currier, Mary Hyland. MONTANA SCHOOL TEACHER. *Montana: Mag. of Western Hist. 1975 25(1): 22-31.* Mary McLaughlin Hyland (ca. 1881-1962) taught in rural schools in Montana from 1916 until 1939, when illness caused her to retire. Hardships of isolation and primitive housing were offset by the friendliness of neighbors and school patrons. Illus.    S. R. Davison

1065. Dale, Doris Cruger. AN AMERICAN IN GENEVA: FLORENCE WILSON AND THE LEAGUE OF NATIONS. *J. of Lib. Hist., Philosophy, and Comparative Librarianship 1972 7(2): 109-129.* Florence Wilson was appointed to the League of Nations Library as Assistant Librarian on 1 October 1919, and became Chief Librarian approximately a year later. With no specific mandate from the secretariat to guide her in the development of the library, Wilson drafted technical procedures to perfect the library operation. She also prepared an important publication of the documentary history of the drafting of the League of Nations Covenant. She hoped to make the library truly international using American methods. Her attempts met with strong opposition, and her basic weakness was the inability to obtain funds. After a five-year contract and two-year extension, she was not reappointed. Based on interviews with Miss Wilson, documents from the archives of the League of Nations in Geneva, ALA Archives, primary and secondary works; 76 notes.    L. G. Will

1066. Delgado, Jeanne Hunnicutt, ed. NELLIE KEDZIE JONES' ADVICE TO FARM WOMEN: LETTERS FROM WISCONSIN, 1912-1916. *Wisconsin Mag. of Hist. 1973 57(1): 2-27.* Nellie Sawyer, the first woman professor at Kansas State College, founded and taught all courses in the new department of domestic economy. After 15 years at Kansas State and five at Bradley Polytechnic Institute, she married for a second time and moved to Michigan with her minister husband, moving to a Wisconsin farm in 1911. From her experiences there Nellie Kedzie Jones wrote a series of articles in the national farm magazine, *The Country Gentleman*, in the form of letters to an imaginary niece with no practical farm experience. These articles, excerpted here, appeared regularly during 1912-16, giving advice to the rural wife on how to organize and lighten housework, and providing a colorful glimpse into midwestern farm life in the first two decades of the century. 12 illus., 10 notes.

N. C. Burckel

1067. Downes, Randolph C. A NEWSPAPER'S CHILDHOOD - THE MARION STAR FROM HUME TO HARDING. *Northwest Ohio Q. 1964 36(3): 134-145.* Samuel Hume, his two sons, and wife operated the Marion *Star,* 1877-84. He offered Marion a brand of personal journalism. Several examples and instances are cited to support Warren Harding's assertion that Hume was a benefactor to Marion. The next owner ruined himself by becoming involved in politics, a step that Hume had avoided by keeping his paper independent. The paper passed to Warren Harding. It was rumored that the local weekly, the *Mirror,* tried to put the *Star* out of business; but by 1888 Harding had built the *Star* into a formidable rival of the *Mirror.*          W. F. Zornow

1068. Fry, Alice. RECOLLECTIONS OF A FLORIDA SCHOOL-TEACHER. *Florida Hist. Q. 1965 43(3): 270-275.* Hard but interesting experiences of a young school teacher, Alice Fry, in a rural Florida school, 1909-10.          G. L. Lycan

1069. Fuller, Wayne E. COUNTRY SCHOOLTEACHING ON THE SOD-HOUSE FRONTIER. *Arizona and the West 1975 17(2): 121-140.* The one-room country school remained the backbone of the educational systems of Kansas and Nebraska until World War I. The teachers, mostly young girls from rural areas, boosted the literacy rates of their states to the highest in the nation at the turn of the century. 5 illus., 41 notes.          D. L. Smith

1070. Garrison, Dee. THE TENDER TECHNICIANS: THE FEMINIZATION OF PUBLIC LIBRARIANSHIP, 1876-1905. *J. of Social Hist. [Great Britain] 1972/73 6(2): 131-159.* "The feminization of public librarianship did much to shape and stunt the development of an important American cultural institution." Although more job opportunities were made available to women, the lack of professional commitment and the desire to serve readers (rather than to lead and educate them) have stunted librarianship. Until the librarian deals "with the implications of feminization with its varied inhibitory effects on intellectual excellence and leadership—progress towards professionalization will be limited." 77 notes.          L. E. Ziewacz

1071. Garrison, Dee. THE TENDER TECHNICIANS: THE FEMINIZATION OF PUBLIC LIBRARIANSHIP, 1876-1905. Hartman, Mary and Banner, Lois W., eds. *Clio's Consciousness Raised: New Perspectives on the History of Women* (New York: Harper Torchbooks, 1974): 158-178. The feminization of librarianship paralleled the rapid growth of public libraries. The newly abundant, low-paying librarianships fit the narrow sphere of domestic and cultural activity deemed acceptable for educated women. "By 1910 78 [and one half] percent of library workers in the United States were women; only teaching surpassed librarianship as the most feminized 'profession.' " The preponderance of women with their passive feminine virtues inhibited the aggressive, professional development of librarianships, perpetuated the low status of women workers, and stunted the libraries' growth as important cultural institutions. 77 notes.          S

1072. Gosling, Glen. THE PORTRAIT OF A TEACHER. *Michigan Q. Rev. 1965 4(3): 163-165.* A former student recalls the teaching methods of Mary Louise Hinsdale, 1925-36.

1073. Grotzinger, Laurel. THE PROTO-FEMINIST LIBRARIAN AT THE TURN OF THE CENTURY: TWO STUDIES. *J. of Lib. Hist., Philosophy, and Comparative Librarianship 1975 10(3): 195-213.* Biographies of Katharine Lucinda Sharp (1865-1914) and Margaret Mann (1873-1960), with comparative descriptions of their backgrounds, lives, careers, and personalities. Both were striking, poised, dynamic, immaculately-groomed ladies of Victorian principles (as opposed to Dee Garrison's stereotype of women who sought librarianship only as a refuge); yet neither were advocates of a feminist society. Based on primary and secondary sources; 45 notes.          A. C. Dewees

1074. Hareven, Tamara K. FAMILY TIME AND INDUSTRIAL TIME: FAMILY AND WORK IN A PLANNED CORPORATION TOWN 1900-1924. *J. of Urban Hist. 1975 1(3): 365-389.* Cumulative

individual employee files 1910-36 of the Amoskeag Manufacturing Company of Manchester, New Hampshire, coupled with marriage and insurance records and oral histories, reveal a pervasive family influence in working. Vacancies were discovered via word-of-mouth, family members substituted for each other, family finances postponed marriages and caused babies to be dropped off so women could return to work. Young children found summer jobs in the mills, and many met their future spouses there. 45 notes.          S. S. Sprague

1075. Heidbreder, Edna. MARY WHITON CALKINS: A DISCUSSION. *J. of the Hist. of the Behavioral Sci. 1972 8(1): 56-68.* Calkins (1863-1930) believed that psychology should be considered the science of the self, or person, as related to its environment, physical and social. "In psychology her concern for the empirical was most characteristically present in her determination to face and cope with the complex contents of ordinary experience as they are recognized in what for lack of a better name we may call our common-sense knowledge; in her insistence that a satisfactory conceptual framework for psychology must maintain active and effective contact with such knowledge." Like Darwin, she did not take as a model a conceptual scheme which was effective in another science but produced one that took into account what she regarded as the specific and distinguishing features of the subject-matter of her own field. "She did not solve her problem. But her way of perceiving it and the manner in which she worked on it, are instructive partly in negative ways, but also for their important positive significance." 26 notes.

D. D. Cameron

1076. Heiges, George L. LANCASTER 1870: CELEBRATED PEOPLE LECTURED IN THE CITY ONE HUNDRED YEARS AGO. *J. of the Lancaster County Hist. Soc. 1970 74(3): 81-93.* Presents a compilation of newspaper commentaries on 14 notable lecturers who spoke in Lancaster, Pennsylvania, in 1870. Includes Wendell Phillips (1811-84), Frederick Douglass (1817-95), John Wanamaker (1832-1922), Anna E. Dickinson (1842-1932), and Ulysses S. Grant (1822-85). Based on newspaper accounts; 2 illus.          L. J. Stout

1077. Heller, Elizabeth Wright. A YOUNG WOMAN IN IOWA. *Palimpsest 1973 54(2): 18-31.* Excerpts from an autobiography, concerning the period 1880-81 when the author was a milliner, printer, and teacher.          S

1078. Hill, Burton S. A GIRL CALLED NETTIE. *Ann. of Wyoming 1965 37(2): 147-156.* Discusses the activities of Nettie Wright in Buffalo, Wyoming. Includes biographical material on Mrs. Wright prior to her arrival in Buffalo and describes her business activities as a saloon keeper and dance-hall operator in that community. Based on Johnson County Court House records and personal reminiscences of pioneer settlers. Illus.          R. L. Nichols

1079. Hinckley, Ted C. SHELDON JACKSON COLLEGE: HISTORIC NUCLEUS OF THE PRESBYTERIAN ENTERPRISE IN ALASKA. *J. of Presbyterian Hist. 1971 49(1): 59-79.* Dr. Sheldon Jackson, prominent Presbyterian clergyman, organized Protestant missionary and educational efforts for Alaskan native children at Sitka after the Army closed its temporary school there in 1877. Jackson persuaded a young Yale graduate, Reverend John Green Brady, to establish a ministry at Sitka, at that time a rough, isolated trading and mining boom-town. Jackson was rivaled in his efforts by Dr. Aaron Lindsley, a Presbyterian leader from Portland, Oregon. Lindsley sent his niece, Fannie Kellogg, to Sitka where she established a school for the Indians in 1878. With the help of the Navy from 1879 to 1881, compulsory education legislation was enforced. Jackson was successful in 1884 in obtaining a grant from Congress for training Alaskan native children. The school at Sitka, later known as Sheldon Jackson Institute, taught practical trade skills and Christian moral values. Jackson insisted that Alaskan Indians could be assimilated into western society. The school became the largest in the Territory and was later expanded to junior college status. In 1945, Caucasians were admitted for the first time. Recently Sitka and Sheldon Jackson College have been overshadowed by Anchorage and the new Alaskan Methodist University. The continuing prestige of Jackson's school among Alaskans is in doubt. Based on primary and secondary sources; 78 notes.

S. C. Pearson, Jr.

1080. Holbrook, Francis X.　AMELIA EARHART'S FINAL FLIGHT. *U.S. Naval Inst. Pro. 1971 97(2): 48-55.* The sole reason behind Amelia Earhart's ill-fated flight in 1937 was publicity and financial gain. She also wanted to show the world that women could do things as well as, if not better than, men. All in all - the contract with Harcourt, Brace and Company to write a story of the flight; a position as special correspondent for the New York *Herald Tribune,* reporting on the progress of her flight; a cargo of stamp covers; radio commitments in Honolulu and California - there can be little doubt that the Earhart mission was designed to increase the prestige of the Putnams (Amelia and her husband, George Palmer Putnam) and to use the resultant publicity to enhance the new commercial venture they planned to participate in at the end of the flight. Disputes the claims that Earhart acted as a spy for the US Government, or that she was on a scientific mission. 4 photos.
　　　　　　　　　　　　　　　　　　　　　A. N. Garland

1081. Husband, Michael B., ed.　THE RECOLLECTIONS OF A SCHOOLTEACHER IN THE DISAPPOINTMENT CREEK VALLEY. *Colorado Mag. 1974 51(2): 141-156.* Edited reminiscence describes Nellie Carnahan Robinson's experiences as a schoolteacher in a one-room school near Lavender, in southwestern Colorado. In search of health, she accepted a teaching position in an isolated ranching community, where she observed the mores of a cattleman's frontier society and found a husband. 5 illus., 19 notes.
　　　　　　　　　　　　　　　　　　　　　O. H. Zabel

1082. Isaac, Rael Jean.　AMERICAN WOMEN IN THE GREAT SOCIETY. *Colorado Q. 1967 16(1): 83-95.* The greatest surge of women into professional work took place not in the 1920's, but in the period 1880-1910. Asks why that period, fraught with restrictions against women, was full of achievement, while the 1920's, when many restrictions had been removed, saw a relative retrogression. Discusses the changes which must be made in modern society before women may once again begin an upward surge in professional jobholding.　B. A. Storey

1083. Johnson, Anna.　RECOLLECTIONS OF A COUNTRY SCHOOL TEACHER. *Ann. of Iowa 1975 42(7): 485-505.* Traces the beginnings of the author's 37-year teaching career in Iowa rural schools. Takes issue with the argument that one-room schools were of inferior educational quality, believing instead that students had the advantage of personal attention and developed a sense of self-reliance. 2 photos.
　　　　　　　　　　　　　　　　　　　　　C. W. Olson

1084. Kammen, Carol, ed.　THE PROBLEM OF PROFESSIONAL CAREERS FOR WOMEN: LETTERS OF JUANITA BRECKENRIDGE, 1872-1893. *New York Hist. 1974 55(3): 281-300.* Juanita Breckenridge (1860-1946) represents 19th century women "whose aspirations were lofty but whose public achievement was limited." Born in Illinois, the daughter of a Methodist minister, she graduated from Wheaton College in 1885. After the death of her father in 1887, she entered Oberlin Theological Seminary, becoming its first female graduate in 1891. Ordained as a minister by the Congregational Church of Brookton, New York, in 1892, she left the pulpit upon her marriage to Fred E. Bates in September, 1893. Settling in Ithaca, she bore two children but never resumed her ministerial career. Reproduces letters sent and received by Juanita Breckenridge 1872-93. Based on primary and secondary works; 4 illus., 18 notes.　　　　　　　　　　　　　G. Kurland

1085. Kingsbury, Mary E.　"TO SHINE IN USE": THE LIBRARY AND WAR SERVICE OF OREGON'S PIONEER LIBRARIAN, MARY FRANCIS ISOM. *J. of Lib. Hist., Philosophy, and Comparative Librarianship 1975 10(1): 22-34.* A biography of Mary Frances Isom who at the age of 34 went into library service and devoted her life to the Multnomah County Library and the Oregon Library Association. Includes a description of her experiences in Europe during World War I in the American Library Association's program of "A book for every man." Based on primary and secondary sources; 40 notes.
　　　　　　　　　　　　　　　　　　　　　A. C. Dewees

1086. Kobrin, Francis E.　THE AMERICAN MIDWIFE CONTROVERSY: A CRISIS OF PROFESSIONALIZATION. *Bull. of the Hist. of Medicine 1966 40(4): 350-363.* Discusses the growth of obstetrical specialists and their conflicts with midwives. From 1910 to 1919 obstetricians were seeking to find a place for themselves as a part of the American medical establishment. The author examines the methods and procedures

through which they sought to win the support of the public and to lessen the influence of midwives. Based on medical periodicals of the period, 51 notes.
　　　　　　　　　　　　　　　　　　　　　P. D. Thomas

1087. Lind, Anna M.　WOMEN IN EARLY LOGGING CAMPS: A PERSONAL REMINISCENCE. *J. of Forest Hist. 1975 19(3): 128-135.* Firsthand account of women at work in logging camps of the Pacific Northwest during 1920-40. 5 illus.　　　L. F. Johnson

1088. Lurie, Nancy Oestreich.　LADY FROM BOSTON AND THE OMAHA INDIANS. *Am. West 1966 3(4): 31-33, 80-85.* Alice Cunningham Fletcher was a pioneer anthropologist of widely recognized scholarly achievements. Little known is her role as an activist for Indian reform, resulting, in particular, in Federal legislation that established the earliest experiment in applied anthropology. In 1881, on her first field trip, she visited Indian reservations in Nebraska and South Dakota. At once Miss Fletcher became an outspoken critic of Indian policy and the injustices done to the Indians. She was the architect and moving spirit behind the Omaha Allotment Act of 1882 which became the model for the 1887 Dawes Severalty Act. By it, tribally held reservations were allotted into individually owned tracts. Unallotted lands were sold on the assumption that Indian population would continue to decrease. Within a decade, however, Indian disdain for the responsibilities of farming, depleted resources, increase in population, and other problems negated much of the hoped for reform from the allotment program. The author analyzes and evaluates the reasons for Miss Fletcher's misguided efforts. Based on a forthcoming essay on female American anthropologists, note, illus., biblio.　　　　　　　　　　　　　　D. L. Smith

1089. Monroe, Margaret Towers.　A SHORT SKETCH OF MRS. ANNA CALHOUN SMITH'S VERNON SCHOOL, 1885-1901. *North Louisiana Hist. Assoc. J. 1976 7(3): 104-109.* Anna Calhoun Smith's school, established at Vernon in 1885, was "the primary instrument of education for the children of the entire community." Among her students were "future ministers, teachers, presidents of three Louisiana colleges, and a United States Senator." Prior to her marriage to Judge Newton McKay Smith in 1885, Anna Calhoun had been "presiding teacher of Minden Female College at Minden." Descended from "a long line of Presbyterian teachers and preachers," she had been "largely educated by her mother." She started her school in Vernon primarily to instruct her stepchildren and emphasized reading, writing, arithmetic, and Latin. The school was closed before Judge and Mrs. Smith moved to Ruston in 1901. Condensed from a more detailed article in the Prescott Memorial Library at Louisiana Tech University. Contains a list of students who attended Mrs. Smith's Vernon school. Photo, 9 notes.
　　　　　　　　　　　　　　　　　　　　　A. N. Garland

1090. Mulvay, Jill.　THE TWO MISS COOKS: PIONEER PROFESSIONALS FOR UTAH SCHOOLS. *Utah Hist. Q. 1975 43(4): 396-409.* Mary Elizabeth Cook and Ida Ione Cook made significant contributions to Utah education 1870-96. M. E. Cook's Graded School in Salt Lake City served as a preparatory school for the university. Ida was principal of a high school in Logan and of Brigham Young College. By 1892 she was the general coordinator of Logan's schools. The Cooks' schools served as models, and their experience in curriculum and methodology exposed many new teachers to training otherwise unavailable. Based on primary and secondary sources; 4 illus., 36 notes.　　　J. L. Hazelton

1091. Myers, John B.　THE EDUCATION OF ALABAMA FREEDMEN DURING PRESIDENTIAL RECONSTRUCTION 1865-1867. *J. of Negro Educ. 1971 30(2): 163-176.* After emancipation, ex-slaves eagerly sought education. The Freedmen's Bureau conducted schools, kindergarten through college. White leaders used violence against the schools and teachers, especially women, and sought control, but they failed to set up a public education system. Freedmen supported educational measures, building schools, raising money, self-learning, and training teachers. Nevertheless, many counties had no schools. Freedmen with educational opportunities were the exception, not the rule. Based on correspondence in the American Missionary Association Archives, Fisk University; papers in the Alabama Department of Archives and History; U.S. Bureau of Refugees Reports; 48 notes.　　G. M. Fishman

1092. Nottingham, Zera Pendleton.　MASTER-TEACHER - MASTER-BUILDER. *Georgia R. 1966 20(2): 188-197.* Reviews the life of

Florence Bernd, Macon schoolteacher. "Her subject was Ancient History; her intent, to mold boys into men." "Miss Florence" taught for 51 years, seeing all the while that her boys were well-fed and well-clothed. She founded a materials bureau in Bibb County two years before her death in 1942. A grade school is named after her.　　　T. M. Condon

1093. Ostendorf, Lloyd. ELIZABETH KECKLEY'S LOST LINCOLN RELICS. *Lincoln Herald 1969 71(1): 14-18.* Describes a search for Lincoln relics possessed at Lincoln's death by Elizabeth Keckley, White House seamstress for Mrs. Lincoln. In 1868 Mrs. Keckley gave the Lincoln items to Wilberforce University, where she later taught domestic arts. In a recent visit to Wilberforce, the author was unable to find the items or to locate anyone who had any recollection of them.
　　　S. L. Jones

1094. Palcos, Alberto. EDUCADORAS NORTEAMERICANAS EN LA ARGENTINA: LA EXPERIENCIA DE D. F. SARMIENTO [US women educators in Argentina: the experience of D. F. Sarmiento]. *Cahiers d'Hist. Mondiale [France] 1966 11(1): 139-158.* Domingo Faustino Sarmiento (1811-88), president of Argentina, 1868-74, devoted his life to educational reform and school organization. He established the first nomal school based on US educational principles in Paranà with George A. Stearns as director. Grammar, husbandry, and forestry schools were founded and staffed during the 1870's and 1880's by numbers of women teachers from the United States. Primary and secondary sources; 22 notes, biblio.　　　R. K. Adams

1095. Papanikolas, Helen Zeese. MAGEROU: THE GREEK MIDWIFE. *Utah Hist. Q. 1970 38(1): 50-60.* The life story of a Greek woman, Georgia Lathouris (Mrs. Nicholas Mageras, 1867-1950), how she became a midwife in Greece, and how she continued that profession when she migrated to a mining community near Magna, Utah.
　　　S. L. Jones

1096. Powell, Paul. MARGARET CROSS NORTON, ARCHIVIST EMERITA. *Am. Archivist 1966 29(4): 489-492.* Appointed 20 June 1934, traces Miss Norton's contribution as the first archivist of the Archives Division of the Illinois State Library. A historian and librarian, she gathered records from the Capitol until there was no room for expansion. The State Arsenal burned 18 February 1934, and the loss of many military and bonus records led to an appropriation for the State Archives Building, commenced in 1936. A leader in experimentation, she helped lay the foundations for records management and the use of microfilm. She compiled indexes of legislative records and a history of Illinois State agencies, taught summer courses for archivists at the American University at Washington, D.C., and served the Society of American Archivists, of which she became president. Much of her career was served under the late Edward J. Hughes, Secretary of State. Based on an address delivered at a convocation honoring Margaret Cross Norton, on 18 July 1966, at the Illinois State Archives Building, Springfield, Illinois, at which Governor Otto Kerner of Illinois invested her with the title of Archivist Emerita for the State; illus.　　　D. C. Duniway

1097. Reninger, Marion Wallace. ALICE OF KOREA. *J. of the Lancaster County Hist. Soc. 1970 74(3): 109-123.* Presents a chronicle and personal memoir of the life of Alice Appenzeller (1885-1950) by a girlhood friend. Alice, daughter of Henry Gerhart Appenzeller (1858-1902), pioneer missionary to Korea, was raised in Korea and returned there as a missionary educator after graduation from Wellesley College. She served as President of Ewha College for Girls from 1922 to 1938. Based on secondary and primary sources; photo.　　　L. J. Stout

1098. Rochlin, Harriet. THE AMAZING ADVENTURES OF A GOOD WOMAN. *J. of the West 1973 12(2): 281-295.* Nellie Cashman's name was widely known at the turn of the 20th century. Newspapers printed feature stories about "the West's only girl mining expert" and accounts of the altruistic undertakings that earned her the appellation of the "Angel of Tombstone." Some of her work was in Dawson, Alaska, the rest in Southern California and Arizona. Besides mining, her activities included restaurant-keeping, child-rearing, and town-building. Her adventures sometimes "led through uncharted, inhospitable terrain, and to close calls with disaster." Illus., 51 notes.　　　E. P. Stickney

1099. Sharkey, Eugene G. THE DIARY OF FLORENCE ATKINSON, 1883-1886. *J. of the Rutgers U. Lib. 1970 34(1): 23-27.* In the 1880's Domingo Sarmiento of Argentina invited North Americans to teach in his country, in order to reform the Argentine educational system along the lines of that in the United States. In July 1883, Florence Atkinson and 16 other young women accepted the invitation. Miss Atkinson kept a diary which begins on the ship from New York and continues until her return three years later. The diary includes material on education, politics, religion, and economics, as well as descriptions and interpretations of her life in San Juan and her travels. Based on examination of these diaries in the Special Collections Department, Rutgers University Library.　　　M. J. Kroeger

1100. Simister, Florence Parker. IDA LEWIS: KEEPER OF THE LIGHT. *New-England Galaxy 1968 10(2): 51-55.* Ida Lewis (1842-1911) was keeper of the Lime Rock Lighthouse in Newport, 1858-1911.
　　　S

1101. Spector, Robert M. WOMAN AGAINST THE LAW: MYRA BRADWELL'S STRUGGLE FOR ADMISSION TO THE ILLINOIS BAR. *J. of the Illinois State Hist. Soc. 1975 68(3): 228-242.* The unsuccessful effort of Myra Bradwell to gain admission to the Illinois bar led to her appeal to the US Supreme Court in 1873. The Court ruled that her case was not justified under the Fourteenth Amendment or the privileges and immunities clause of Section IV of the United States Constitution. Bradwell's case, however, did prepare the way for other women to be admitted to law practice in Illinois and in other states. She successfully edited the *Chicago Legal News* until her death in 1894, making this legal publication one of the most respected in the country.　　　N. Lederer

1102. Stevens, M. James. BILOXI'S LADY LIGHTHOUSE KEEPER. *J. of Mississippi Hist. 1974 36(1): 39-41.* A brief note and letter regarding three women who served as Biloxi's lighthouse keepers, 1854-61 and 1867-1929.　　　J. W. Hillje

1103. Stewart, John Hall. BEATRICE FRY HYSLOP: A TRIBUTE. *French Hist. Studies 1972 7(4): 473-478.* Writes in tribute to Hyslop, citing personal reminiscences, giving brief biographical data, and noting her most important published works. Of the titles mentioned, her *Répertoire critique des cahiers de doléances pour les Etats-généraux de 1789* (Paris, E. Leroux, 1933) established her as an authority on the cahiers. Considers her *Guide to the Central Cahiers of 1789* (New York, Columbia University Press, 1936) to be her greatest work. Her greatest contributions to the study of French history have been made in connection with the society of which she was cofounder: the Society for French Historical Studies.　　　L. Pouncey

1104. Stroud, Jessie Ruth. MA OF THE FIERCE JONES GANG - OR, TEACHING COUNTRY SCHOOL IN THE GANGSTER REGION. *J. of the Illinois State Hist. Soc. 1969 62(1): 65-71.* Recalls the writer's experience teaching a country school in southern Illinois in 1918 and 1919.　　　S. L. Jones

1105. Strunk, Orlo, Jr. THE SELF-PSYCHOLOGY OF MARY WHITON CALKINS. *J. of the Hist. of the Behavioral Sci. 1972 8(2): 196-203.* Mary Whiton Calkins, a student of William James and later president of the American Psychological Association, endeavored from about 1900 to 1930 to make self-psychology into a system which could comprehend structuralist, functionalist, and (to some extent) psychoanalytic theories. Based on primary and secondary sources; 4 notes, biblio.　　　R. Glen

1106. Templeton, Ronald K. THE NEW HISTORY? *Social Educ. 1968 32(8): 800-803.* Notes that the "new" emphasis in history teaching of using a primary sources curriculum was encouraged first by Mary Sheldon Barnes in the 1880's.　　　S

1107. Thoresen, Timothy H. H. PAYING THE PIPER AND CALLING THE TUNE: THE BEGINNINGS OF ACADEMIC ANTHROPOLOGY IN CALIFORNIA. *J. of the Hist. of the Behavioral Sci. 1975 11(3): 257-275.* Discusses the development of anthropology and archeological expeditions at the University of California during 1890-1908, emphasizing the contributions of Phoebe Apperson Hearst.

1108. Townley, Carrie Miller. HELEN J. STEWART: FIRST LADY OF LAS VEGAS. *Nevada Hist. Soc. Q.* 1973 16(4): 214-244, 1974 17(1): 2-32. Part I. Recounts ranching, land speculation, and mining in Nevada, 1879-94. Widowed by the murder of her husband, Helen Stewart (1854-1926) undertook the management of extensive properties near Pioche and Las Vegas which her deceased husband had acquired earlier. Based on newspaper and manuscript sources; 3 photos, 158 notes. Part II. Mrs. Stewart continued ranching in the Las Vegas Valley until 1903. Subsequently, her historical studies and many civic activities contributed notably to her reputation as "First Lady of Las Vegas." Based on primary sources; 3 photos, 159 notes. 　　　　　H. T. Lovin

1109. Warren, Claude N. TIME AND TOPOGRAPHY. *Masterkey* 1970 44(1): 5-14. Defends Elizabeth W. Crozer Campbell's archaeological work in the Lake Mojave area of California in the 1930's and 1940's. "The fact that her approach and the questions she asked are still valid, while those of others have fallen by the way, stands as a tribute to the fertile mind and honest scholarship from which they originated." Biblio. 　　　　　V. D. Anness and S

1110. Weigley, Emma Seifrit. THE PHILADELPHIA CHEF: MASTERING THE ART OF PHILADELPHIA COOKERY. *Pennsylvania Mag. of Hist. and Biog.* 1972 96(2): 229-240. Describes the lecture-demonstrations of Sarah Tyson Rorer (1849-1937), popular Philadelphia cookery expert. She founded the Philadelphia Cooking School, published the *Philadelphia Cook Book* in 1886, and contributed monthly articles to various periodicals. Rorer was a principal lecturer at the Retail Grocers', Manufacturers' and Pure Food Expositions. Based on contemporary newspapers and journals; 40 notes. 　　　　　J. B. Street

1111. —. THE CHICAGO BAR: 1872. *Chicago Hist.* 1965 7(10): 302-314. Discusses a book published by Franc B. Wilkie in 1872, *The Chicago Bar,* a compendium of biographical sketches of leading Chicago lawyers. Several of Wilkie's character studies are summarized or quoted, including that of Robert T. Lincoln, William K. McAllister, Samuel W. Fuller, Leonard Sweet, Corydon Beckwith, Sidney Smith, Thomas Dent, and Mrs. Myra Bradwell, who, in 1885, was the first woman to be admitted to the Illinois bar. Illus. 　　　　　D. J. Abramoske

## Domestic Labor

1112. Chay, Marie. EVERYTHING IN SEASON. *Modern Age* 1968 12(2): 169-172. Author describes the time in the 1890's when her grandmother ran a boardinghouse for Piedmontese only in a mining camp in the southern Colorado Rockies. 　　　　　M. J. Barach

1113. Cowan, Ruth Schwartz. THE "INDUSTRIAL REVOLUTION" IN THE HOME: HOUSEHOLD TECHNOLOGY AND SOCIAL CHANGE IN THE 20TH CENTURY. *Technology and Culture* 1976 17(1): 1-23. Contrary to "the standard sociological model for the impact of modern technology on family life," the advent in the 1920's-30's of labor-saving devices in the middle-class household did not decrease the housewife's work. Her duties in the home, possibly because of the new ideology of the perfectly happy and healthy family purveyed by women's magazines, "expanded to fill the time available." Based partly on surveys of women's periodicals; 4 illus., 46 notes. 　　　　　C. O. Smith

1114. Cram, Ralph W. DAVENPORT WOMAN IN THE WHITE HOUSE. *Ann. of Iowa* 1966 38(7): 558-560. A reprint of an article that appeared in the *Davenport Democrat* in 1938, gleaned from the magazine publication of reminiscences of a onetime Davenport, Iowa, resident Mrs. Elizabeth Jaffray. As White House housekeeper, she served Presidents Taft, Wilson, Harding, and Coolidge. Undocumented. 　　　　　D. C. Swift

1115. Kleinberg, Susan J. TECHNOLOGY AND WOMEN'S WORK: THE LIVES OF WORKING CLASS WOMEN IN PITTSBURGH, 1870-1900. *Labor Hist.* 1976 17(1): 58-72. Pittsburgh's economic structure relied primarily on male labor which prevented working-class women from an industrial role, thus reinforcing the traditional segregation of men and women. Working-class women continued time-consuming housework without technological advantages well into the 20th century, because of the political priorities of the city. For example, the decision to lay only small water pipes in working-class neighborhoods meant that only the middle and upper classes and heavy industry got enough water and sewage facilities. Working-class women were forced to perform all their household cleaning chores without adequate water. Domestic, technological inventions such as washing machines and gas stoves were also beyond the means of the working class. Based upon Pittsburgh government publications and secondary sources; 35 notes. 　　　　　L. L. Athey

1116. Weigley, Emma. IT MIGHT HAVE BEEN EUTHENICS: THE LAKE PLACID CONFERENCES AND THE HOME ECONOMICS MOVEMENT. *Am. Q.* 1974 26(1): 79-96. The 10 conferences of home economists held at Lake Placid, New York, during 1898-1908, coordinated efforts leading to the founding of the American Home Economics Association in 1908. The goals of professional legitimacy and academic respectability greatly concerned the participants, men and women in educational and social service positions. The influence of women, especially Catharine Beecher, in the home economics field from its beginnings made this area of study unique among contemporary male-dominated academic pursuits. 　　　　　N. Lederer

## Labor Relations and Reform

1117. Brown, Richard C. THE LADY MUCKRAKERS. *Am. Hist. Illus.* 1973 8(7): 32-37. Women journalists Marie and Bessie Van Vorst exposed working conditions endured by women factory workers. 　　S

1118. Buhle, Mari Jo. SOCIALIST WOMEN AND THE "GIRL STRIKERS," CHICAGO, 1910. *Signs* 1976 1(4): 1039-1051. The 1910 Chicago garment workers' strike showed a new determined spirit in the American labor movement. The "new immigrants," especially young women, militantly opposed the United Garment Workers' conciliations with factory owners. Contemporary newspaper articles by Nellie M. Zeh and Mary O'Reilly represented Socialist women's responses to the strike and their efforts to publicize the implications of the struggle. Their perspective was rooted in their interpretation of the historic position of women workers. They themselves had given their girlhood to commodity production and felt a sisterhood with the young strikers. They saw the actions of the "girl strikers" as a symbol of the larger tendency in the industrial working class to determine their own destiny. Based on newspaper articles; 11 notes. 　　　　　J. Gammage

1119. Davis, Allen F. THE WOMEN'S TRADE UNION LEAGUE: ORIGINS AND ORGANIZATION. *Labor Hist.* 1964 5(1): 3-17. Describes the organization and activities of the Women's Trade Union League. The League, which had its prototype in Great Britain, was established in New York at a series of meetings held during November 1930. The constitution announced that the purpose of the League was "to assist in the organization of women wage workers into trade unions." Branches were established at Boston and Chicago. The author concludes that "the League's operation and organization is a prime example of the cooperation that existed between reformers and labor leaders . . . in the progressive era." 　　　　　J. H. Krenkel

1120. Elazar, Daniel J., ed. WORKING CONDITIONS IN CHICAGO IN THE EARLY 20TH CENTURY - TESTIMONY BEFORE THE ILLINOIS SENATORIAL VICE COMMITTEE, 1913. *Am. Jewish Arch.* 1969 21(2): 149-171. Presents part of the testimony of Jewish female employees and Jewish factory owners in Chicago's garment industry before a special committee investigating the connections between prostitution and poor working conditions during the Progressive era. Details wage rates of labor and profits of management in the Near West Side sweatshops. Undocumented. 　　　　　E. S. Shapiro

1121. Hobby, Daniel T., ed. "WE HAVE GOT RESULTS": A DOCUMENT ON THE ORGANIZATION OF DOMESTICS IN THE PROGRESSIVE ERA. *Labor Hist.* 1976 17(1): 103-108. Presents a 1917 letter from Jane Street, Industrial Workers of the World organizer of domestics, as a reflection of philosophy and tactics of organizing unskilled workers. The letter, intercepted by the Post Office and sent to the Justice Department, was found in the National Archives. 　　　　　L. L. Athey

1122. Johnson, Allen. MOTHER JONES. *J. of Hist. Studies 1968 1(2): 154-158.* An anecdotal account of methods employed in 1910 by pioneer labor organizers.                    N. W. Moen

1123. Keiser, John H. THE UNION MINERS CEMETERY AT MOUNT OLIVE, ILLINOIS - A SPIRIT-THREAD OF LABOR HISTORY. *J. of the Ill. State Hist. Soc. 1969 62(3): 229-266.* Established due to the refusal of other cemeteries to accept the bodies of miners killed in the Virden riots in 1898, the Union Miners Cemetery was first owned by the United Mine Workers of America and by the Progressive Mine Workers of America after 1932. It became a national symbol of the struggle of organized labor in the face of opposing management forces. The author recapitulates the events of the Virden riots, emphasizing the role of union leader "General" Alexander Bradley, and reviews the career of "Mother" Mary Harris Jones, who was buried in the cemetery. In 1936 a monument was erected in the cemetery to honor "Mother" Jones. Based partly on interviews with union leaders and mine workers in Mount Olive, on the John E. Fenwick Papers in the author's possession, and on contemporary newspaper accounts.                    S. L. Jones

1124. Kenneally, James J. WOMEN AND TRADE UNIONS 1870-1920: THE QUANDARY OF THE REFORMER. *Labor Hist. 1973 14(1): 42-55.* Surveys the changing role of women in the trade union movement 1870-1920, focusing primarily upon the Women's Trade Union League's struggle with the A.F.L. Trade unionists believed that women should be organized, but at the same time held that women belonged at home. Based on publications of the A.F.L. and W.T.U.L., manuscripts, and the Gompers Letterbooks; 60 notes.
                    L. L. Athey

1125. Kessler-Harris, Alice. THE AUTOBIOGRAPHY OF ANN WASHINGTON CRATON. *Signs 1976 1(4): 1019-1037.* Glimpses the fears, sensibilities, hurts, and joys of an organizer for the socialist dominated Amalgamated Clothing Workers Union. Ann Washington Craton, a college graduate schooled in social work, considered herself a born crusader and reformer. In the 1920's she organized factory women in the rural northeast, where mill owners had retreated with their factories to escape urban unions and take advantage of the cheap labor of coal miners' wives. Craton's autobiography reveals that the Jewish constituency in the union resented a gentile being hired as an organizer, but her background stood her in good stead when she was sent to organize the "new immigrant." Based on excerpts from Craton's autobiography; note.                    J. Gammage

1126. Kessler-Harris, Alice. ORGANIZING THE UNORGANIZABLE: THREE JEWISH WOMEN AND THEIR UNION. *Labor Hist. 1976 17(1): 5-23.* Surveys the lives and work of Pauline Newman, Fannia Cohn, and Rose Pesotta of the International Ladies' Garment Workers' Union. Their experience as women and their tasks as union officers persistently conflicted, but their class consciousness took precedence over their identification as women. Based upon the Pesotta, Schneiderman, and Cohn papers; 84 notes.                    L. L. Athey

1127. Kizer, Benjamin H. ELIZABETH GURLEY FLYNN. *Pacific Northwest Q. 1966 57(3): 110-112.* Biographical sketch of Elizabeth Gurley Flynn who was an eloquent advocate of human rights for unskilled laborers, 1909-64. A major part of the article is devoted to her activities on behalf of the Industrial Workers of the World and her subsequent court trial in Spokane, Washington in 1909.
                    C. C. Gorchels

1128. Lemons, J. Stanley. SOCIAL FEMINISM IN THE 1920S: PROGRESSIVE WOMEN AND INDUSTRIAL LEGISLATION. *Labor Hist. 1973 14(1): 83-91.* Surveys the continuing struggle for industrial legislation in the 1920's. A group of women's organizations pressed for many reforms including the elimination of child labor, maternity and infant care, nightwork laws, and labor legislation. Although attacked bitterly, the groups kept alive the hope for industrial legislation which was finally realized under the impetus of the Depression. Based on periodicals, proceedings of organizations, and a doctoral dissertation; 21 notes.
                    L. L. Athey

1129. McFarland, C. K. CRUSADE FOR CHILD LABORERS: "MOTHER" JONES AND THE MARCH OF THE MILL CHILDREN. *Pennsylvania Hist. 1971 38(3): 283-296.* Mary Harris ("Mother") Jones was an Irish-born seamstress and widow who had lived in a number of places in the United States. After the Chicago fire of 1871 destroyed the dressmaking establishment where she worked, Mother Jones devoted her life to working for organized labor. The United Mine Workers dubbed her the "Joan of Arc of American labor." In 1903 she visited Philadelphia to assist 100 thousand textile workers who were on strike. Noticing many children in their ranks, Mother Jones organized a march from Philadelphia to New York in order to call attention to the need for better child labor legislation. The march began with about two hundred children and adults; about two dozen finished the three-week march. Mother Jones, then 73, often traveled ahead of the group to make arrangements and obtain supplies. During the march, she announced her intention to visit President Theodore Roosevelt at Oyster Bay as a means of dramatizing her cause and attracting financial support. For a time the President refused to answer her letter, and preparations were made to bar the advance of the "army." Eventually, Mother Jones and two others were permitted to speak to his secretary, Benjamin F. Barnes. The march produced no immediate legislative gains, but it did dramatize the need for stronger child labor laws. Based on newspapers; 43 notes.
                    D. C. Swift

1130. Powell, Allan Kent. THE "FOREIGN ELEMENT" AND THE 1903-4 CARBON COUNTY COAL MINERS' STRIKE. *Utah Hist. Q. 1975 43(2): 125-154.* Finnish, Slavic, and Italian miners provided the strength behind a serious labor confrontation in Carbon County, Utah, in 1903. The Utah Fuel Company refused union recognition. The Utah National Guard was called out. Charles DeMolli, Con Kelliner, Mother Mary Jones, and Samuel H. Gilson involved themselves in the strike. The strike failed because the union lacked internal and external support and the company played on antiforeign sentiments in defending its position. Based on primary and secondary sources; 9 illus., 65 notes.                    J. L. Hazelton

1131. Scharnau, Ralph. ELIZABETH MORGAN, CRUSADER FOR LABOR REFORM. *Labor Hist. 1973 14(3): 340-351.* Elizabeth Chambers Morgan (b. 1850), Chicago trade unionist and social reformer, rose from unskilled labor to prominence in Chicago reform and union circles. With a power base in the Ladies' Federal Labor Union and the Illinois Women's Alliance, Mrs. Morgan was partly instrumental in extending compulsory education for children, updating child labor laws, and the attack on sweatshops which resulted in the Factory and Workshop Inspection Act of 1893 in Illinois. Working with Hull House reformers and others, Mrs. Morgan helped explore detrimental health and labor conditions—for which exploration she has not received due credit. Based on the Thomas J. Morgan collection, Chicago newspapers, government reports, and secondary sources; 63 notes.                    L. L. Athey

1132. Smith, Russell E. THE MARCH OF THE MILL CHILDREN. *Social Service R. 1967 41(3): 298-303.* In the summer of 1903 a group of children, led by United Mine Workers of America organizer Mary Harris (Mother) Jones, marched from Philadelphia to New York to dramatize the need for federal protection of women and children in factories and the right of children to an education and free childhood.

1133. Steel, Edward M. MOTHER JONES IN THE FAIRMONT FIELD, 1902. *J. of Am. Hist. 1970 57(2): 290-307.* In 1901, 10 years after its organization, the United Mine Workers of America had successfully concluded an annual agreement on basic bargaining points with coal operators in Illinois, Indiana, Ohio, and western Pennsylvania, and was on the brink of victory in the anthracite mines of eastern Pennsylvania. However, the U.M.W.A. failed to organize the bituminous workers in the fields of West Virginia, an effort undertaken by Mary Harris "Mother" Jones. This failure threatened the welfare of miners in the central coal fields, and was due to a number of factors: tight family control of the Fairmont fields by the James Otis Watson family, which owned many of the towns; hostile local law enforcement agencies and grand juries; injunctions from the Federal bench of Judge John Jay Jackson, an old conservative upholder of property and Federal authority; and the unwillingness of the union leadership to assign priority to the strike. One important result was a tighter control of coal operators in the State. 65 notes.
                    K. B. West

1134. Walkowitz, Daniel J. WORKING-CLASS WOMEN IN THE GILDED AGE: FACTORY, COMMUNITY AND FAMILY LIFE

AMONG COHOES, NEW YORK COTTON WORKERS. *J. of Social Hist. [Great Britain] 1972 5(4): 464-490.* The experience of working class women in Cohoes, New York, during the Gilded Age indicates that studies of working class mobility must not be narrowly examined within industrial and economic terms. The perception of the workers' mobility by themselves and the nature of their cultural experience must be also considered. Such considerations explain why Cohoes' workers remained passive during the strike-ridden 1870's but engaged in labor violence during the 1880's. Since most of the workers were adolescent Irish and French girls, the factory and its wage meant social mobility and a position of some social prestige. Labor violence in the 1880's, therefore, was "defensive—an attempt to protect their modest social position." 7 tables, 31 notes.
L. E. Ziewacz

# Social Sphere

## General

1135. Alcorn, Rowena L. and Alcorn, Gordon D. TACOMA SEAMEN'S REST: WATERFRONT MISSION, 1897-1903. *Oregon Hist. Q. 1965 66(2): 101-131.* Collection of diary entries, letters, and descriptive material pertaining to a Tacoma waterfront mission for seafaring men. The role of Mrs. Brigitte Funnemark and daughter, Christine, and experiences of sailors are included.
C. C. Gorchels

1136. Coben, Stanley. THE ASSAULT ON VICTORIANISM IN THE TWENTIETH CENTURY. *Am. Q. 1975 27(5): 604-625.* During the 1920's confidence in Victorianism primarily declined because of academic and literary intellectual attacks on its conceptual foundations. Social scientists, historians, literary critics, ethnic minority representatives, and feminists attacked various aspects of Victorian culture. The Ku Klux Klan and its upper class counterparts tried unsuccessfully to protect it. They failed because of the strength of the opposition and their own lack of complete confidence in their beliefs. Based on primary and secondary sources.
N. Lederer

1137. Cook, Margaret. NEW JERSEY'S CHARITABLE COOKS: A CHECKLIST OF FUND-RAISING COOK BOOKS PUBLISHED IN NEW JERSEY (1879-1915). *J. of the Rutgers U. Lib. 1971 35(1): 15-26.* The recipes in early locally published cookbooks are often amateurish, but they reflect the cooking fashions of the period in various parts of the United States more accurately than do the standard works by professional authors. Excerpted from the author's *America's Charitable Cooks: A Bibliography of Fund-Raising Cook Books Published in the United States (1861-1915)* (Kent, Ohio, 1971). City index, 67 works cited with locations; biblio.
R. Van Benthuysen

1138. Critoph, Gerald E. THE FLAPPER AND HER CRITICS. George, Carol V. R., ed. *"Remember the Ladies": New Perspectives on Women in American History: Essays in Honor of Nelson Manfred Blake* (Syracuse: Syracuse U. Pr., 1975): 145-160. After World War I, young women termed Flappers became a social phenomenon. They and their male counterparts rebelled against Victorian values which assumed women's moral superiority, propriety, physical inferiority, domesticity, emotionality, and dependence on men. Even before the war, women's increased job opportunities and the affluence afforded by industrialization had weakened the Victorian code. Relations between the sexes had changed as the Victorian woman's modesty and innocence gave way to the comraderie of the Flapper who engaged in sports, rough-housing, and petting parties with men. Popular literature in the 1920's reflected and debated the significance of the Flapper with her cosmetics, short hair, drinking, swearing, and pre-marital sex. Critics viewed the changes as outrageous and subversive to the family and society; but the Flapper's defenders increased. She became a symbol of vigor, sensible attire, excitement, independence, and self-assertion. By 1928, the outward signs and popular image waned with the disappearance of the short hair and skirts. Yet the Flapper left an important legacy for women. She breached the wall of tradition, freed women from constricting dress styles, established women's equal claim to such male prerogatives as sexual aggressiveness, and undercut the strength of Victorian social values. Based on primary sources; 11 notes.
P. R. Byrne

1139. Davis, Ronald L. SOILED DOVES & ORNAMENTAL CULTURE: KANSAS COWTOWN ENTERTAINMENTS. *Am. West 1967 4(4): 19-25, 69-70.* The drama of the shoot-out and the pathos of the wages of sin have occupied most of the attention of pulp writers and historians of the West over the years. In striking contrast was the endemic yearning for respectability and refinement. A prime example of this was in the Kansas cowtowns where respectability versus moral anarchy was quite apparent. Abilene, Ellsworth, Newton, Wichita, and Dodge City all contained considerable numbers of solid citizens who were "moral to the point of prudery." Depravity usually flourished, despite efforts to control it, south of the railroad tracks and during nights of the summer months when the Texas cowboys were in town. The "soiled doves" of the title was one of the names given to the prostitutes who flourished on the south side of the tracks. Home-owned books, subscriptions to eastern magazines and newspapers, pianos in homes, and theaters (opera houses) that supported traveling performers as well as local amateurs were some of the more self-evident symbols of refinement. There was an intermingling from both sides of the tracks and a pragmatic mutual tolerance. 5 illus., biblio. note.
D. L. Smith

1140. Elder, Glen H., Jr. APPEARANCE AND EDUCATION IN MARRIAGE MOBILITY. *Am. Sociol. R. 1969 34(4): 519-533.* "The relative influence of attractiveness and educational attainment in mobility was investigated in a longitudinal sample of women from middle- and working-class families. The women were born in the early 1920s, were intensively studied during the 1930s, and most of them participated in at least one adult follow-up. During adolescence, middle-class girls were significantly higher on physical attractiveness, groomed appearance, and IQ than girls from the working class. The two groups did not differ on status aspiration or academic aptitude. In the total sample, girls who became upwardly mobile through marriage were characterized by physical attractiveness, a desire to impress and control others, high aspirations for the future, and an avoidance of steady dating. Intelligence and academic aptitude were not directly predictive of marriage mobility, although both factors influenced the adult status of the women through their educational attainment. Among women from the working class, physical attractiveness was more predictive of marriage to a high-status man than educational attainment, while the relative effects of these factors were reversed among women of middle-class origin. Social ascent from the working class was also related to sexual restraint and a well-groomed appearance."
J

1141. Haller, John S., Jr. FROM MAIDENHOOD TO MENOPAUSE: SEX EDUCATION FOR WOMEN IN VICTORIAN AMERICA. *J. of Popular Culture 1972 6(1): 49-69.* Hygiene manuals, religious and ethics pamphlets, medical articles, and etiquette books were caricatures of middle-class values; they romanticized family and marriage to explain the incongruity between middle-class principles and reality.
S

1142. Keetz, Frank. NOSTALGIA, HISTORY, AND POSTCARDS. *Social Educ. 1976 40(1): 19-25.* Discusses current interest in collecting 1890's-1915 illustrated postcards, emphasizing themes pictorializing politics, humor, family life, and social conditions and issues.

1143. Roemer, Kenneth. SEX ROLES, UTOPIA AND CHANGE: THE FAMILY IN LATE NINETEENTH-CENTURY UTOPIAN LITERATURE. *Am. Studies [Lawrence, KS] 1972 13(2): 33-47.* Authors of utopian novels in the late 19th century sugarcoated their radical ideas with sentimental love stories. Torn between a longing for and a fear of change, basic reforms often appeared as a return to traditional values. The family remained central to American life, and the woman central to the family. Based on Edward Bellamy's *Looking Backward* and other utopian novels; 49 notes.
J. Andrew

1144. Samuels, Ernest. HENRY ADAMS AND THE GOSSIP MILLS. *Northwestern Report 1968 3(4): 20-25.* The author replies to an English critic who accused him of suppressing evidence from his three-volume biography of Henry Brooks Adams (*The Young Henry Adams, The Middle Years, The Major Phase,* Cambridge, Massachusetts: Harvard U. Press) that Adams kept a mistress. The woman in question - Elizabeth Sherman Cameron (wife of Pennsylvania Senator James Donald Cameron) - was an old family friend, and after the suicide of his wife Adams turned to her for consolation. The sympathetic Mrs.

Cameron gave Adams some much-needed "mothering," and he did fall in love with her. There is no evidence, however, that their relationship was anything more than platonic. Adams strongly disapproved of adultery, and was, in his sixties, "past the age of passion." The author concludes that Adams' relationship with Mrs. Cameron was that of an "uncle," but admits that he erred in not discussing it in his biography. Undocumented, illus.                                                                            G. Kurland

1145.  Sargent, Shirley.  HOW TO PLEASE A SENATOR.  *Pacific Historian 1971 15(1): 39-42.* Discusses the cooking of Jessie Benton Frémont, the wife of John C. Frémont.

1146.  Warren, Dale.  RECORD OF FESTIVE DAYS.  *New-England Galaxy 1965 7(2): 38-45.* An account of life in the Henry Gordon Taft household at Uxbridge, Massachusetts between 1886 and the turn of the century as portrayed by entries in a guest book, thereby putting stress on festive occasions.                                         A. B. Lampe

1147.  —.  SOCIAL NOTES FROM THE 1880'S.  *Ann. of Iowa 1965 37(8): 574-578.* Several Iowa newspapers in the late 19th century were founded to cover social affairs. The *Saturday Evening Mail Car* of Des Moines was devoted exclusively to society matters. Several excerpts from this publication are provided. The author concludes with a piece from the *Saturday Evening Flat Car,* a publication issued to spoof the *Mail Car.* Undocumented, illus.                                                    D. C. Swift

# Marriage and the Family

1148.  Apostle, C. N. and Schmidt, Joan C.  MARRIAGE: A TWENTIETH CENTURY SOCIAL PROBLEM.  *Indian Sociological Bull. [India] 1967 5(1): 39-47.* A summary contrast of the marital interactional difference from 1850 to 1950 under the following headings: pace of life; frequency and variety of interaction between the sexes; mobility patterns; sex roles; age discrepancy in marriage; life expectancy and death rates; duration of marital interaction; and divorce. "Until someone seriously comes up with an alternative to the 'eternity' principle as the dominant theme in the 20th Century marital interaction, the problems . . . will not only remain with us but increase." Undocumented.
D. D. Cameron

1149.  Bloomberg, Susan E.; Fox, Mary Frank; Warner, Robert M.; and Warner, Sam Bass, Jr.  A CENSUS PROBE INTO NINETEENTH-CENTURY FAMILY HISTORY: SOUTHERN MICHIGAN, 1850-1880.  *J. of Social Hist. 1971 5(1): 26-45.* Presents a case study to determine factors leading to changes in family structure as the United States moved from a rural to an urban nation. Discusses the decline in family size and the closer spacing of children. The pattern is confused by the large influx of immigrants into Detroit. Migration, changing occupational profiles, and the end of the frontier era in Michigan were contributing factors. Based on national census data; 10 tables, 20 notes.
V. L. Human

1150.  Cable, Mary.  SHE WHO SHALL BE NAMELESS.  *Am. Heritage 1965 16(2): 50-55.* Relates the discovery that the author's great, great grandmother was the fifth wife of Brigham Young. Augusta Adams left her husband in Boston to marry Young after she heard him give a lecture. She lived until 1886 and was credited with being "the first woman in New England" to become a Latter-day Saint. Some explanation of the Mormon beliefs regarding plural marriage is given.
J. D. Filipiak

1151.  Cumbler, John T.  THREE GENERATIONS OF POVERTY: A NOTE ON THE LIFE OF AN UNSKILLED WORKER'S FAMILY.  *Labor Hist. 1974 15(1): 78-85.* Reviews the need for more information and new methods of approach to the study of the life of the everyday laborer. The remnants of a case history of a family in Lynn from 1915-40 are published as an example of the types of material needed to understand poverty. Based on a case history from the files of the Associated Charities of Lynn, Massachusetts. 4 notes.         L. L. Athey

1152.  Driggs, Nevada W.  HOW COME NEVADA?  *Nevada Hist. Soc. Q. 1973 16(3): 180-185.* A memoir of the author's family. Emily

Crane and Lorenzo Dow Watson, the author's parents, were parties to a polygamous marriage in Utah when polygamy enjoyed legal and social sanction. When polygamy was outlawed in Utah, polygamists were harassed. Emily Watson and her children fled to Panaca, Nevada, where the author and a younger sister were born. For two years, Lorenzo Watson maintained one family at Panaca and another in Utah, but the problems of keeping two houses so far apart forced him to relocate Emily and their children in Utah. 2 photos.                                         H. T. Lovin

1153.  Duck, Edward Walker.  MEMORIES OF FAMILY LIFE IN WEST TENNESSEE FROM AROUND 1890 TO 1910.  *West Tennessee Hist. Soc. Papers 1971 (25): 26-46.* Presents a nostalgic view of southern family life. Author's father was a teacher in West Tennessee and his mother operated the family farm. All but one of the children spent at least some time teaching. The family grew up on a farm near Cedar Grove, Carroll County, Tennessee. Depicts a warm family life, how a farm family whose father was able to work together, numerous "ancient industries rarely encountered today," children's schooling in this period, home remedies, childhood pranks, and pets.
H. M. Parker, Jr.

1154.  Hardy, B. Carmon.  THE AMERICAN SIBERIA: MORMON PRISONERS IN DETROIT IN THE 1880'S.  *Michigan Hist. 1966 50(3): 197-210.* Deals with the imprisonment of four Arizona Mormons in the Detroit House of Correction from December 1884 until October 1886. They had been found guilty of violating the Edmunds Law (1882) which prohibited polygamy in the territories; and their experiences, as reported in the church-owned *Desert News,* hastened the exodus of Mormons into Mexico to avoid arrest. Utilizes many primary and secondary sources, including manuscript collections at Brigham Young University and the Church Historian's Office, Salt Lake City, Utah.
J. K. Flack

1155.  Hastings, Donald W. and Robinson, J. Gregory.  A RE-EXAMINATION OF HERNES' MODEL ON THE PROCESS OF ENTRY INTO FIRST MARRIAGE FOR UNITED STATES WOMEN, COHORTS 1891-1945.  *Am. Sociol. R. 1973 38(1): 138-142.* "Hernes' mathematical model for the process of entry into first marriage is applied to US women, cohorts 1891-1945. Selected cohorts with incomplete data proportions on age-specific first marriage were estimated following a modification of a technique suggested by Ryder. Hernes' model was found applicable across successive cohorts and estimated parameters of his model depicted historical shifts in the nuptial tempo."         J

1156.  Heath, Mary.  MARRIAGES: ZELDA AND SCOTT, ELEANOR AND FRANKLIN.  *Massachusetts R. 1972 13(1/2): 281-288.* Reviews Sara Mayfield's *Exiles from Paradise: Zelda and Scott Fitzgerald* (New York: Delacorte, 1971), and Joseph P. Lash's *Eleanor and Franklin* (New York: W. W. Norton, 1971). Both Zelda Sayre Fitzgerald and Anna Eleanor Roosevelt (née Roosevelt) subordinated their own careers and development as individuals to serve their husbands in their careers. 2 notes.                                                         G. Kurland

1157.  Heller, Mary Belle Stahr.  COLLEGE HILL IN THE 80'S AND 90'S: MEMOIRS OF A FRANKLIN AND MARSHALL FACULTY DAUGHTER.  *J. of the Lancaster County Hist. Soc. 1971 75(1): 19-37.*

1158.  Herman, Sondra R.  LOVING COURTSHIP OR THE MARRIAGE MARKET? THE IDEAL AND ITS CRITICS 1871-1911.  *Am. Q. 1973 25(2): 235-252.* During 1871-1911 a debate arose about whether courtship was a love-seeking or a marriage market. Critics of marriage argued that women's economic dependence made marriage an economic transaction. Defenders responded that increased adherence to the ideals of female domesticity, submissiveness, and purity would insure happy marriages. Both groups were responding to strains fostered by new urban social conditions. Primary and secondary sources; 50 notes.
W. D. Piersen

1159.  Kenney, Alice P.  STAR-CROSSED LOVERS.  *New-England Galaxy 1970 12(2): 13-24.* Economic obstacles to marriage in Cape Cod during the 1880's and 1890's as reflected in the writings of Joseph C. Lincoln.                                                                S

1160. Larson, Gustive O. AN INDUSTRIAL HOME FOR POLYG-AMOUS WIVES. *Utah Hist. Q. 1970 38(3): 263-275.* Describes the antipolygamy crusade of Mrs. Angie F. Newman, the foundation of the Anti-Polygamy Society, and the establishment of an institution designed to train and shelter homeless women and children during the anticipated breakup of the Mormon polygamy system. The Industrial Home was opposed by Mormons and became a political issue. Republicans supported the home, and Democrats opposed it. The building was completed in Salt Lake City in 1889 but the project failed because few persons availed themselves of its benefits. In 1893 it was turned over to the Utah Commission and later was used for state administration offices. Primary and secondary sources; 2 illus., 40 notes.      P. Taylorson

1161. Littlefield, Daniel F., Jr. and Underhill, Lonnie E. DIVORCE SEEKER'S PARADISE: OKLAHOMA TERRITORY, 1890-1897. *Arizona and the West 1975 17(1): 21-34.* Soon after Oklahoma gained territorial status in 1890, the "divorce mill" came into being. A short residency requirement, confusion as to which court had jurisdiction in matters of divorce, and the publicity furnished by lawyers and hotel and boarding house owners made Oklahoma the "divorce center" of the nation. Many lawyers became wealthy; and Oklahoma towns prospered from the spending of temporary, divorce-seeking residents. The campaign of a territorial judge, the veto of legislation by the governor, a federal law lengthening residency requirements for divorce in territories, and a 1906 US Supreme Court decision ended Oklahoma's notorious divorce business. 4 illus., 25 notes.      D. L. Smith

1162. Maccraken, Brooks W. ALTHEA AND THE JUDGES. *Am. Heritage 1967 18(4): 60-63, 75-79.* Divorce trial of Sarah Althea Hill and Senator William Sharon preceded the ambush of Supreme Court Justice Stephen J. Field and killing of lawyer David S. Terry in 1889.      S

1163. Miller, Florence Lowden. THE PULLMANS OF PRAIRIE AVENUE: A DOMESTIC PORTRAIT FROM LETTERS AND DIARIES. *Chicago Hist. 1971 1(3): 142-155.* George Mortimer Pullman (1831-97) married Harriet Amelia Sanger in 1867, the year he organized the Pullman Palace Car Company. The Pullmans survived the Great Chicago Fire in 1871 to become one of Chicago's leading families. Although normally portrayed as a cold and impersonal businessman, Pullman was a different person, as his letters and his wife's diary show. His letters reveal a hardworking businessman, but one of warmth and sentimentality. The letters explain the development of the town of Pullman and his daily activities. Though the Panic of 1893 and the Pullman Strike (1894) greatly damaged the family business, Pullman maintained his many philanthropies. Based on the Pullman letters; 10 photos, 3 notes.      N. A. Kuntz

1164. Newmark, Rosa. A LETTER FROM MOTHER TO DAUGH-TER—LOS ANGELES TO NEW YORK, 1867. *Western States Jewish Hist. Q. 1973 5(4): 274-284.* Mrs. Joseph Newmark, née Rosa Levy, describes the Jewish marriage celebration, and attendant social customs, of her daughter, Harriet, to Eugene Meyer in Los Angeles.

1165. O'Neill, William L. DIVORCE IN THE PROGRESSIVE ERA. *Am. Q. 1965 17(2, Part 1): 203-217.* Despite the attempts of conservative critics to prevent or control divorce, it became accepted as a natural consequence of a more complex society. Sociologists, feminists, and liberal churchmen banded together to defeat opposition to divorce. Between 1906 and 1917, while the drive against divorce collapsed, even the press, formerly a wall of opposition, swung toward moral relativism. The failure of conservatives to hold the line against divorce signalled the onset of the moral and sexual revolution which was to characterize the 1920's. 59 notes.      R. S. Pickett

1166. O'Neill, William L. SAMUEL W. DIKE AND THE HAZ-ARDS OF MORAL REFORM. *Vermont Hist. 1967 35(3): 160-168.* A Congregational minister in Randolph, Vermont (1866-77) refused to marry a divorced man, lost his job, and found a career in divorce reform. During his Royalton, Vermont, pastorate, 1878-82, Samuel Dike came to know "more about divorce than any man in America." A "modest, charitable, reasonably open-minded, and studious" man, as corresponding secretary (1881-1912) for the New England Divorce Reform League, later the National League for the Protection of the Family, he came too

late to battle "Evil" with mere sensationalism, too soon for statistics. He died in Massachusetts in 1913.      T. D. S. Bassett

1167. Schlossman, Steven L. BEFORE HOME START: NOTES TO-WARD A HISTORY OF PARENT EDUCATION IN AMERICA, 1897-1929. *Harvard Educ. R. 1976 46(3): 436-467.* Discusses parent education to upgrade child care practices in the home 1897-1929, emphasizing the role of behavioral science.

1168. Smith, Daniel Scott. FAMILY LIMITATION, SEXUAL CONTROL AND DOMESTIC FEMINISM IN VICTORIAN AMER-ICA. *Feminist Studies 1973 1(3/4): 40-57.* "Suggests the hypothesis that over the course of the 19th century the average woman experienced a great increase in power and autonomy *within* the family . . ." which is shown by the "important contribution women made to the radical decline in . . . marital fertility."      T. Simmerman

1169. Smith, Suzanne. THE CHILDREN'S HOUR. *Am. Heritage 1975 26(4): 42-51.* Childhood photographs of the James A. Drake daughters taken in the 1880's and 1890's depicting family life. 29 illus.      B. J. Paul

1170. Smythe, Donald. YOU DEAR OLD JACK PERSHING. *Am. Hist. Illus. 1972 7(6): 18-24.* The courtship and married life of John J. Pershing and Frances Warren.      S

1171. Steere, Geoffrey H. FREUDIANISM AND CHILD-REAR-ING IN THE TWENTIES. *Am. Q. 1968 20(4): 759-767.* Analyzes child-rearing and socialization advice written for the public during the 1920's and finds that the authorities incorporated relatively little of the Freudian approach in their works. Using categories representing ortho-dox Freudian thought supplied by Calvin S. Hall's *A Primer of Freudian Psychology* (New York: New American Library, 1954), the author finds that only 16 out of 42 works analyzed contain reference which could be associated with Freudianism. Although the authors of the manuals do not seem hostile to Freud's ideas, they seem to bypass his ideas in favor of competing schools of thought. The most important book of the period seems to have been Emmett Holt's mildly behavioristic *The Care and Feeding of Children* (1894). Considerable extracting from representative books under analysis occurs within the text. 22 notes. Appendix containing complete citations of the 42 books analyzed.      R. S. Pickett

1172. Stewart, Edgar I. THE CUSTER BATTLE AND WIDOW'S WEEDS. *Montana: Mag. of Western Hist. 1972 22(1): 52-59.* The families of the men killed in the Battle of the Little Big Horn in 1876 were left destitute. Since the 7th Cavalry had been nearly wiped out, little help could come from the customary source of donations from within the regiment. A month after the battle, the *Army and Navy Journal* started a drive for funds to provide emergency support. Men throughout the Army responded generously, as did some Navy personnel and a number of civilians; several corporate donations were for major amounts. Yet the total of 14 thousand dollars was small in terms of the need. A count showed 24 widows and twice as many children, about 15 of the families being those of enlisted men. There is evidence that Mrs. Custer and two other widows whose officer husbands had carried insurance offered to forego their shares of the fund in favor of soldiers' survivors. Based on files of the *Army and Navy Journal.*      S. R. Davison

1173. Twombly, Robert C. SAVING THE FAMILY: MIDDLE CLASS ATTRACTION TO WRIGHT'S PRAIRIE HOUSE 1901-1909. *Am. Q. 1975 27(1): 57-72.* Despite the widely accepted view that Frank Lloyd Wright's prairie houses were unpopular, the upper middle class provided the architect with many commissions. The house appealed to conventional suburbanites owing to its harkening back to their rural origins, its close association with nature, and its emphasis on securing the family from the real and alleged dangers of a rapidly changing urban environment. The house stressed shelter, internal intimacy, and together-ness with motifs of strength, security, and durability.      N. Lederer

1174. Watson, Ora V. FERTILITY OF NORTHWESTERN STATE COLLEGE GRADUATES: 1920-1950. *Louisiana Studies 1963 2(1): 44-51.* A study of the fertility of the graduates for the 30 years, 1920-50, based on reproduction rates. Data based on 202 married graduates responding, of whom 96 were male and 106 were female.      G. W. McGinty

# Sex Roles

1175. Burstyn, Joan N. AMERICAN SOCIETY DURING THE EIGHTEEN-NINETIES: "THE WOMAN QUESTION." *Studies in Hist. and Soc. 1973 4(2): 34-40.* Deals with the great debate over the role of women during the last decade of the 19th century with emphasis on the impact of industrialization. Railroad expansion and the development of machinery helped liberate women from the drudgery of domestic life.
J. O. Baylen

1176. Cannon, Charles A. THE AWESOME POWER OF SEX: THE POLEMICAL CAMPAIGN AGAINST MORMON POLYGAMY. *Pacific Hist. R. 1974 43(1): 61-82.* A study of the content and methods of the polemics against Mormon polygamy, concentrating on morality. Polygamy was viewed by its critics as unrestrained sexuality legitimized by religion. Closer examination suggests considerable ambience in regard to sex on the part of the authors and their readers. "The campaign allowed Americans to express vicariously their repressed desires at the same time that they reinforced the rigid sexual values of the existing order." 60 notes.
R. V. Ritter

1177. Cirillo, Vincent J. EDWARD BLISS FOOTE: PIONEER AMERICAN ADVOCATE OF BIRTH CONTROL. *Bull. of the Hist. of Medicine 1973 47(5): 471-479.* Edward Bliss Foote, a New York physician, entered this controversy in 1858 with the first edition of his *Medical Common Sense.*
S

1178. Contosta, David R. HENRY ADAMS ON THE ROLE OF WOMEN. *New Scholar 1974 4(2): 181-190.* Adams wanted women to accept their traditional nuptial and maternal identities; women must maintain their natural dignity. Like other Gilded Age intellectuals, Adams believed that middle-class family structure was the cornerstone of American civilization. Regarding the suicide of Adams' wife, Marian, maintains that Adams believed it resulted from her rejection of traditional female piety.
D. K. Pickens

1179. Degler, Carl N. WHAT OUGHT TO BE AND WHAT WAS: WOMEN'S SEXUALITY IN THE NINETEENTH CENTURY. *Am. Hist. R. 1974 79(5): 1467-1490.* The article argues against the view that women in the 19th century United States were thought to be without sexual feeling and that their actual behavior tended to follow that ideal. Evidence is presented from a variety of published medical sources to show that women were advised, by both popular and professional medical writers, to give expression to their sexuality. Some of the data show that the sexuality of women was often assumed by writers as well as being advocated by them. The existence of the more usual view of women's sexuality in the 19th century is explained by the fact that previous writers on the subject have mistaken prescriptive views of sexual behavior for women for descriptive ones. The traditional view is shown to be prescriptive in intent and therefore untrustworthy as a description of behavior. The article concludes with a detailed description and analysis of a hitherto unknown survey of the sexual habits of 45 married women, made in the 1890's and after by Dr. Clelia D. Mosher, of Stanford University. Seventy percent of the women surveyed were born before 1870. Among the conclusions drawn from the survey is that women of the 19th century not only had sexual feelings but that they satisfied them. For example, the women in the Mosher survey experienced orgasm in a proportion equal to that reported by Kinsey for women born in the 20th century.
A

1180. Evans, Walter. MONSTER MOVIES: A SEXUAL THEORY. *J. of Popular Film 1973 2(4): 253-265.* Describes the continued public interest in the horror films of the 1930's-40's, arguing that their power is related to the sexual traumas of adolescence.
S

1181. Gordon, Linda. VOLUNTARY MOTHERHOOD: THE BEGINNINGS OF FEMINIST BIRTH CONTROL IDEAS IN THE UNITED STATES. *Feminist Studies 1973 1(3/4): 5-22.* Discusses the motives and aims of the three feminist groups—the suffragists, the moral reformers, and the Free Love movement—advocating birth control during the 1870's-80's. The groups failed to challenge traditional sex roles while motherhood "remained almost exclusively a tool for women to strengthen their positions within conventional marriages and families...."
T. Simmerman

1182. Hall, Linda B. FASHION AND STYLE IN THE TWENTIES: THE CHANGE. *Historian 1972 34(3): 485-497.* Influences stemming from World War I (French modes, deprivation of consumer goods, and postwar prosperity) made the 1920's a new era in American fashion. Draws upon contemporary editions of such periodicals as *Good Housekeeping, Literary Digest, Vogue,* and the Sears-Roebuck catalog to show how styles changed, undeterred by an accompanying moral uproar. The new clothes created problems for manufacturers and reflected a new self-image for American women. 47 notes.
N. W. Moen

1183. Harmond, Richard. PROGRESS AND FLIGHT: AN INTERPRETATION OF THE AMERICAN CYCLE CRAZE OF 1890'S. *J. of Social Hist. [Great Britain] 1971/72 5(2): 235-257.* The popularity of the bicycle during the 1890's fulfilled, for a short time, the American desire for a "vehicle of flight." The bicycle represented another advance in American technology and aided clothing reform and female equality. By the end of World War I the automobile had replaced the bicycle as the progressive vehicle of transportation, yet the bicycle had " 'whetted' the public appetite for wheeled contrivances." 68 notes.
L. Ziewacz

1184. Jeansonne, Glen. THE AUTOMOBILE AND AMERICAN MORALITY. *J. of Popular Culture 1974 8(1): 125-131.* The automobile was viewed in the 1920's as a threat to traditional morality. The car displaced the parlor in courtship and emancipated youth by allowing them to escape from parental supervision. It also facilitated bank robberies and bootlegging. The automobile industry fostered installment buying and this moderated traditional hostility to indebtedness. Primary and secondary sources; 30 notes.
E. S. Shapiro

1185. McGovern, James R. THE AMERICAN WOMAN'S PRE-WORLD WAR I FREEDOM IN MANNERS AND MORALS. *J. of Am. Hist. 1968 55(2): 315-333.* The period of the 1920's, often depicted as a period unique unto itself, has been shown in politics and ideas to have had important continuities with the prewar Progressive era. However, the view of the "flapper era" of the twenties as a time that inaugurated a revolutionary change in sexual manners and morals still constitutes an enduring stereotype. A study of newspapers, novels, and periodicals (often focusing on advertising) indicates that this "new freedom" for the American girl developed from around 1910 and was consequent on changes in working and living conditions in the city, the increasing use of the automobile, and advances in household techniques. Most of the characteristics associated with the American woman in the twenties in fact go back to 1910.
K. B. West

1186. Shideler, James H. FLAPPERS AND PHILOSOPHERS, AND FARMERS: RURAL-URBAN TENSIONS OF THE TWENTIES. *Agric. Hist. 1973 47(4): 283-299.* Census bureau statistics of 1920 indicate that for the first time the urban population outnumbered that of rural areas. Spokesmen for both sides were apprehensive about changing life-styles in America. To rural dwellers the city was a lair for gunmen, bootleggers, killers like Leopold and Loeb, jazz bands, aimless wastrels, and gum-chewing flapper stenographers of easy virtue. Urban residents scorned farmers as a rabble army of defectives holding clusters of civilized intellectuals under siege in a few walled towns. In the competition between polarized rural and urban worlds, the rural was fated to lose because it was economically and socially disadvantaged. Based on primary and secondary sources; 48 notes.
R. T. Fulton

1187. Simms, L. Moody, Jr., ed. A HORROR OF HOOPS. *Southwestern Hist. Q. 1968 72(1): 88-92.* Rebelling against hoopskirt fashions, the ladies of Brenham, Texas, organized the Anti-Crinoline League in 1893. The members of the short-lived organization condemned the contemporary fashions and published the "Chaldean Manuscript," a satire on women's dress, in the local newspaper; but they continued to wear hoopskirts and crinolines. 8 notes.
D. L. Smith

1188. Strong, Bryan. IDEAS OF THE EARLY SEX EDUCATION MOVEMENT IN AMERICA, 1890-1920. *Hist. of Educ. Q. 1972 12(2): 129-162.* Details how sex education manuals attempted to explain the change in sexual attitudes of the era. They changed from the early dominant one of "a sexual ideology of sex as restraint" to the radical one of "sex as pleasure." Shows that the manuals tried to reinforce the older threatened morality because "sexual repression was the basis of civilization." Based on primary and secondary sources; 51 notes.
L. C. Smith

1189. Yellis, Kenneth A. PROSPERITY'S CHILD: SOME THOUGHTS ON THE FLAPPER. *Am. Q. 1969 21(1): 44-64.* Contends that the Flapper symbolized the antithesis of her predecessor, the late Victorian Gibson Girl. Where the costume of the Gibson Girl emphasized sexuality via coy concealment and strategic emphasis, the Flapper's attire deemphasized it. Straight lines and "motion" characterized the Flapper; she typified the approach of the 1920's. Her very being assaulted Victorian morality with its masculine bias and heralded the rise of the modern, liberated women. Although the term "Flapper" originated in England, it became post-World War I America's aesthetic ideal. Emphasis shifted away from the trunk to the limbs and toward youth and efficiency. Working women, for the first time, set the fashion pattern and the parisian couturiers found it difficult to control the clothing market. Simplicity and uniformity, as well as variety, were made possible by mass production and distribution. The American women did not return to a "more feminine" attire until 1929-30. But by then, the message had been broadcast that a new American woman existed. 40 notes.
　　　　　　　　　　　　　　　　　　　　　　　R. S. Pickett

1190. —. DREAM WORLD OF ADVERTISING. *Am. Heritage 1965 16(5): 70-75.* Pictorial essay on advertising in the 1920's. Modern advertising took advantage of the revolution in morals and was openly hedonistic. 6 illus.
　　　　　　　　　　　　　　　　　　　　　　　J. F. Paul

1191. —. FASHIONS OF 101 YEARS AGO. *York State Tradition 1972 26(2): 6-10.* Reproduces illustrations from *Peterson's Magazine* (1871) of women's and children's fashions. Five illustrated pages.
　　　　　　　　　　　　　　　　　　　　　　　D. A. Franz

1192. —. THE LOOK OF THE 20's. *Am. Heritage 1965 16(5): 41-55.* From the American Heritage picture file come these black-and-white photographs representative of the 1920's. Subjects include: woman getting her hair bobbed; arrested for indecency - wearing the "new" one-piece bathing suit; listening to the radio with ear phones; traffic jam on a country road; Darrow and Bryan at the Scopes trial; a gangster funeral; Gertrude Ederle; and New York's reception for Lindbergh.
　　　　　　　　　　　　　　　　　　　　　　　J. D. Filipiak

## Women's Organizations

1193. Ables, L. Robert. THE SECOND BATTLE FOR THE ALAMO. *Southwestern Hist. Q. 1967 70(3): 372-413.* Describes the 1903-13 factional dispute within the Daughters of the Republic of Texas for custody of the Alamo. Adina De Zavala (1861-1955) and Clara Driscoll (1881-1945) were the principal protagonists. Vestiges of the dispute continued to their deaths. 5 illus., 166 notes.
　　　　　　　　　　　　　　　　　　　　　　　D. L. Smith

1194. Grinder, Robert Dale. THE WAR AGAINST ST. LOUIS'S SMOKE 1891-1924. *Missouri Hist. R. 1975 69(2): 191-205.* After 1891 St. Louis initiated a series of "smoke abatement crusades." The movement contained professional and bureaucratic elements. The first considered smoke an engineering problem to be solved by educating businessmen; the second felt it was a problem to be solved with time and a large staff of inspectors. The movement contained a third element composed of public-minded citizens concerned about the harmful effects of smoke. They worked through such groups as the Civic League, the Business Men's Club, the women's Wednesday Club, and the Socialist Party. Based on primary and secondary sources; 65 notes.
　　　　　　　　　　　　　　　　　　　　　　　W. F. Zornow

1195. Hook, Alice P. THE YWCA IN CINCINNATI: A CENTURY OF SERVICE, 1868-1968. *Cincinnati Hist. Soc. Bull. 1968 26(2): 119-136.* The Civil War provided impetus to the development of women's work, resulting in the creation of Women's Christian Associations. The Women's Association of Cincinnati, the fifth such to be established in the United States, was founded 6 June 1868. The Cincinnati YWCA was the first to create classes in sewing, to institute vocational training in clerical fields, to establish an employment bureau exclusively for women, and to organize a program for Negro women. 27 notes.
　　　　　　　　　　　　　　　　　　　　　　　H. S. Marks

1196. Rauch, Julia B. WOMEN IN SOCIAL WORK: FRIENDLY VISITORS IN PHILADELPHIA, 1880. *Social Service R. 1975 49(2): 241-259.* Examines the characteristics of the women involved in the Philadelphia Society for Organizing Charitable Relief and Repressing Mendicancy during the years 1864-1909, using data obtained from schedules of the 1880 US Census.
　　　　　　　　　　　　　　　　　　　　　　　S

1197. Reishtein, Eleanor Fein. MINUTES OF THE WEST GROVE HOUSEKEEPERS ASSOCIATION AS SOURCE MATERIAL FOR FOLKLIFE STUDIES. *Pennsylvania Folklife 1971 21(1): 16-25.* Uses the minutes of the West Grove Housekeepers Association, 1860-69, for insights into Pennsylvania family life, domestic concerns, and customs.
　　　　　　　　　　　　　　　　　　　　　　　S

1198. Saum, Lewis O. "THE BROOM BRIGADE, COLONEL DONAN AND 'CLEMENTINE.'" *Missouri Hist. Soc. Bull. 1969 25(3): 192-200.* In 1882 several groups of young women in Saint Louis gave mock military demonstrations to raise money for a new armory. One group was dubbed the "Broom Brigade" because its drills were performed with brooms, instead of rifles. Flamboyant Colonel Peter Donan, a journalist and promoter, conceived the idea of a tour to the resort area of Minnesota and talked the railroads into sponsorship and transportation. Banquets, receptions, performances, and publicity attended the tour. Other broom brigades began to appear elsewhere in "epidemic" proportions. A permanent legacy of the tour was "the company anthem," the ballad "Clementine." 41 notes.
　　　　　　　　　　　　　　　　　　　　　　　D. L. Smith

1199. Sutherland, John F. THE ORIGINS OF PHILADELPHIA'S OCTAVIA HILL ASSOCIATION: SOCIAL REFORM IN THE "CONTENTED" CITY. *Pennsylvania Mag. of Hist. and Biog. 1975 99(1): 20-44.* An analysis of the philosophy, works, and influence of the Octavia Hill Association, a private reform group in Philadelphia dedicated to the improvement of the lot of the urban poor. The association purchased and improved homes, introduced strict sanitation measures, and meticulously avoided disrupting established neighborhoods. Its members lived in the affected neighborhoods but were socially not part of them. Their efforts were handicapped by the philosophy of the time but eventually led to governmental reform programs which enjoyed some success. 46 notes.
　　　　　　　　　　　　　　　　　　　　　　　V. L. Human

# Political Sphere

## General

1200. Auchincloss, Louis. "NEVER LEAVE ME, NEVER LEAVE ME." *Am. Heritage 1970 21(2): 20-22, 69-70.* Discusses the daily life of and the relationship between Henry Adams and his secretary-companion Aileen Tone during the final years of Adams' life, 1913-18.　　S

1201. Bakken, Douglas A., ed. LUNA E. KELLIE AND THE FARMERS' ALLIANCE. *Nebraska Hist. 1969 50(2): 185-205.* An account written in 1926 by Luna E. Kellie recalling her experiences as Secretary of the Farmers' Alliance in Nebraska from 1894 to 1900. Photos, 30 notes.
　　　　　　　　　　　　　　　　　　　　　　　R. Lowitt

1202. Barnard, Kate. "STUMP" ASHBY SAVES THE DAY. *J. of the West 1973 12(2): 296-306.* Kate Barnard of Oklahoma visited the World's Fair in St. Louis in 1904 where, moved by the need for child labor laws, she began her career as a reformer. In 1908 at the annual meeting of the National Child Labor Committee she lectured to a national audience. The following year the Child Labor Law was passed in Oklahoma, and she was subsequently elected first vice-president of the newly formed Southern Conference on Woman and Child Labor. 47 notes.
　　　　　　　　　　　　　　　　　　　　　　　E. P. Stickney

1203. Baxandall, Rosalynn Fraad. ELIZABETH GURLEY FLYNN: THE EARLY YEARS. *Radical Am. 1975 9(1): 97-115.* Discusses the early life of Elizabeth Gurley Flynn (1890-1964), a feminist and Communist, based on her unpublished writings and containing new evidence about her personal and political development.

1204. Beezer, Bruce G. ARTHURDALE: AN EXPERIMENT IN COMMUNITY EDUCATION. *West Virginia Hist. 1974 36(1): 17-36.* The Arthurdale community was a New Deal experiment in rural homesteading which resettled 200 poor West Virginia coal mining families. Run by a succession of government agencies in the 1930's and with the heavy unofficial involvement of Eleanor Roosevelt, Arthurdale cost far more than expected and failed chiefly because there was no industry located there to provide permanent jobs. The Arthurdale school, run by Elsie Ripley Clapp, tried with some limited success to apply John Dewey's educational ideas about community-oriented schooling. Based on Clapp's own account and contemporary articles; 76 notes.
J. H. Broussard

1205. Brooks, Carol F. THE EARLY HISTORY OF THE ANTI-CONTRACEPTIVE LAWS IN MASSACHUSETTS AND CONNECTICUT. *Am. Q. 1966 18(1): 3-23.* The so-called "Comstock laws" adhered to prevailing views of love and sex in the late 19th century. In Massachusetts and Connecticut, provisions relative to conception prevention were hidden away in the midst of obscenity prohibitions. When aroused liberals challenged the statutes, they did so on the grounds that the laws limited freedom of the press. With the exception of a very small minority, opponents of the bills did not notice abridgement of personal liberties. Restriction of birth control information thus became law. Substantial use of newspapers, the Annual Reports of the New York and New England Societies for the Suppression of Vice, and State assembly and senate documents; 70 notes.
R. S. Pickett

1206. Buroker, Robert L. FROM VOLUNTARY ASSOCIATION TO WELFARE STATE: THE ILLINOIS IMMIGRANTS' PROTECTIVE LEAGUE, 1908-1926. *J. of Am. Hist. 1971 58(3): 643-660.* Historians have often asked how it was that many members of the middle classes joined reform efforts at the turn of the century. Some have answered by pointing to a general reaction against the evils of an industrial society, while others have focused on an alleged concern for the declining status of the "old rich" and the intelligentsia. The reform effort was in part the natural result of the growth of professional people in numbers and in organizations, and of their intuition that they had a stake in the stability of society. The teachers, journalists, lawyers, corporation executives, and women social workers who staffed the Immigrants' Protective League saw their particular function as safeguarding the rights of immigrants in employment, education, legal matters, and their general adjustment to society. Their efforts paved the way for the establishment of a State agency, the Immigrants' Commission. 53 notes.
K. B. West

1207. Cannon, Helen. FIRST LADIES OF COLORADO: MARY GOODELL GRANT. *Colorado Mag. 1964 41(1): 27-33.* Presents a short biography of Mary Matteson Goodell Grant, 1857-1941, the wife of Colorado governor, James Benton Grant.

1208. Cannon, Helen. FIRST LADIES OF COLORADO: CELIA O. CRANE WAITE. *Colorado Mag. 1969 46(2): 120-130.* Widowed Celia O. Crane (1845-1937) was the second wife of Davis Hanson Waite, Colorado's Populist governor (1893-95). She was not a conventional First Lady. Instead of tending to "women's interests," sharing her husband's reform ideas, she gave her time and energy to aiding and protecting him. After her husband's defeat for a second term, she spoke out bitterly against women who, voting for the first time in Colorado, opposed the party which enfranchised them. The Waites retired to Aspen where he died in 1901. She lived until 1937. Illus., 27 notes.
O. H. Zabel

1209. Cannon, Helen. FIRST LADIES OF COLORADO: EMMA FLETCHER THOMAS. *Colorado Mag. 1972 49(2): 163-170.* A brief biography of Mrs. Thomas (1853-1940), wife of Charles S. Thomas, Governor of Colorado (1899-1901) and US Senator from Colorado (1913-21). Based on documents in the State Historical Society of Colorado Library, and on secondary sources; 3 illus., 23 notes.
O. H. Zabel

1210. Carrigan, D. Owen. MARTHA MOORE AVERY: CRUSADER FOR SOCIAL JUSTICE. *Catholic Hist. R. 1968 54(1): 17-38.* Mrs. Avery was one of the most active lay apologists and social actionists in the Catholic Church in America. Before converting to Catholicism, in 1904, she had been prominent in the Bellamy Nationalist movement, the Socialist Labor Party, and the Socialist Party of America. After her conversion her work was sponsored by the National Civic Federation and

the Catholic Church. She was a lecturer, author, and the player of a leading role in such organizations as the Boston School of Political Economy, the Catholic Truth Guild, and the Common Cause Society. She died in 1929.
A

1211. Carson, Ruth. INDIANS CALLED HER "THE MEASURING WOMAN": ALICE FLETCHER AND THE APPORTIONMENT OF RESERVATION LANDS. *Am. West 1975 12(4): 12-15.* Committing her interests, energies, and resources to the betterment of the Indians, Alice Cunningham Fletcher (1838-1923) was one of the driving forces behind the drafting and passage of the Dawes Act (1882). During the 1880's and 1890's she personally directed the survey and allotment of lands for the Omaha, Winnebago, and Nez Percé. She also gathered anthropological data and artifacts and convinced American classical archaeologists of the importance of the study of prehistory. 2 illus.
D. L. Smith

1212. Clanton, O. Gene INTOLERANT POPULIST? THE DISAFFECTION OF MARY ELIZABETH LEASE. *Kansas Hist. Q. 1968 34(2): 189-200.* A biographical sketch of a distinguished Populist orator with a major emphasis on the period from 1890 to 1894. She became estranged from the Populists when they began to think of fusing with the Democrats. She accused the Populist administration of being allied with gambling interests. Efforts to remove her as a member of the Board of Charities sparked a lively court battle over the governor's removal power. The keys to Mrs. Lease's actions during this period are to be found in her exaggerated sense of self-importance, her hatred for any thought of fusing with the Democrats, and her failure to understand the problems of her times. Based on articles, newspapers, and a manuscript biography in the Kansas State Historical Society; illus., 35 notes.
W. F. Zornow

1213. Coode, Thomas H. and Fabbri, Dennis E. THE NEW DEAL'S ARTHURDALE PROJECT IN WEST VIRGINIA. *West Virginia Hist. 1975 36(4): 291-308.* Arthurdale was the first self-help project funded under the National Industrial Recovery Act's Subsistence Homesteads Program to resettle unemployed miners on subsistence farms. Families were selected only after thorough investigation, and only native whites were allowed. From the beginning, Arthurdale suffered from mismanagement, delays, and cost overruns. Mrs. Eleanor Roosevelt and Louis Howe, though having no official connection with the project, intervened continually. Plans to attract industry never worked out, and cooperative farming failed also. Arthurdale was the most publicized project in the country and was extremely controversial. Finally, the government sold off the houses during World War II at a great loss. Based on Bushrod Grimes MSS and other primary sources; 49 notes.
J. H. Broussard

1214. Costin, Lela B. GRACE ABBOTT OF NEBRASKA. *Nebraska Hist. 1975 56(2): 165-191.* A biographical sketch of Grace Abbott (1878-1939), stressing her Nebraskan background and her work in the Children's Bureau, 1916-34.
R. Lowitt

1215. Cutler, Charles L., Jr. "MY DEAR MRS. PECK." *Am. Hist. Illus. 1971 6(3): 4-9, 46-48.* Woodrow Wilson, president of Princeton University, met Mary Hulbert Peck, the wife of Thomas D. Peck, a Pittsfield, Massachusetts manufacturer, during a vacation to Bermuda in 1907. Mr. Wilson and Mrs. Peck developed a friendship which continued through Wilson's subsequent visits to Bermuda and Mrs. Peck's visits with the Wilsons, including two visits to the White House, but their basic contact was through a correspondence of more than 200 letters. With Wilson's remarriage in 1915 to the former Edith Bolling Galt, the correspondence ended, as the second Mrs. Wilson was not as generous towards Wilson's friendships as the first Mrs. Wilson had been. Although Wilson sometimes discussed politics in his letters, he most frequently wrote of social matters. The letters were a political issue in the presidential election of 1912 and a source of potential embarrassment thereafter, but the author seems to agree with Theodore Roosevelt's jeer that: "You can't cast a man as Romeo who looks and acts so much like an apothecary's clerk." Primary and secondary sources; 5 illus.
D. Dodd

1216. Davis, Allen F. SETTLEMENT WORKERS IN POLITICS, 1890-1914. *R. of Pol. 1964 26(4): 505-517.* Proposes that "settlement workers during the Progressive era were probably more committed to political action than any other group of welfare workers before or since."

The author shows how, though they could not always agree among themselves, settlement workers became involved one way or another in politics, first in the ward, then in the city, the state, and the nation. Based on mss., on an interview with J. G. Phelps Stokes, 22 January 1959, and on extensive published sources.                                    Sr. Mary McAuley

1217.   Davis, Allen F.   WELFARE, REFORM AND WORLD WAR I.  *Am. Q. 1967 19(3): 516-533.* Much progressivism survived into the 1920's. The economic and social planning of World War I was an important model for the New Deal. During the war, progressives continued to promote social welfare legislation (Seaman's bill, child labor law) and applauded the Wilson administration for taking over the railroads and mobilizing industry and agriculture. They contemplated the "social possibilities of war" and continued their crusade for social justice, including improved urban housing and health insurance. The presence of women in the war led eventually to the establishment of the Women's Bureau in the Department of Labor. The war also improved Negroes' lot. After the war, the Wilson administration quickly abandoned public housing and social insurance. 64 notes.                         E. P. Stickney

1218.   Davis, Kenneth S.   MISS ELEANOR ROOSEVELT.   *Am. Heritage 1971 22(6): 49-59.* Covers the years 1886-1905.        S

1219.   Davison, Kenneth E.   PRESIDENT HAYES AND THE REFORM OF AMERICAN INDIAN POLICY.   *Ohio Hist. 1973 82(3/4): 205-214.* The conclusion of the last major Indian war, the defeat of the movement to return the Indian Bureau to the Department of War, and the appointment of reform-minded Carl Schurz as Secretary of the Interior all led to a new turn in Indian policy. An investigation led to firings and reform. All Indian traders had to be bonded and licensed, and Indian education improved. Despite bad publicity from mismanagement of the removal of the Poncas and the issuance of Helen Hunt Jackson's *A Century of Dishonor*, conditions for the Indians improved under the administration of President Hayes. Based on primary and secondary sources; 3 illus., 25 notes.                         S. S. Sprague

1220.   DeWhitt, Bennie L.   A WIDER SPHERE OF USEFULNESS: MARILLA RICKER'S QUEST FOR A DIPLOMATIC POST. *Prologue 1973 5(4): 203-207.* Biographical sketch of Marilla Marks Ricker, first woman to seek a major diplomatic post in the US foreign service, and her unsuccessful pursuit for the post of minister to Colombia during the administration of President William McKinley. Primary and secondary sources; 2 illus., 21 notes.                         R. W. Tissing, Jr.

1221.   Dratch, Howard.   THE POLITICS OF CHILD CARE IN THE 1940'S.  *Sci. and Soc. 1974 38(2): 167-204.*

1222.   Duckett, Kenneth W. and Russell, Francis.   THE HARDING PAPERS: HOW SOME WERE BURNED...AND SOME WERE SAVED.  *Am. Heritage 1965 16(2): 24-31, 102-110.* The public and private papers of former President Warren G. Harding are the subject of these two articles, published side-by-side. The first is devoted to the Harding Papers that are now at the Ohio Historical Society. The many diversions of the papers before their deposit in that archival source and the destruction of most of the material that origianlly accompanied them are covered. The author says the destruction process began the night of Harding's funeral and continued for the next few years. The second article is devoted to those now-famous Harding love letters to Mrs. Carrie Phillips, the wife of a close friend in Marion, Ohio. The author regards their contents as having greater significance than the scandal treatment given them in the newspapers. He also relates how they were discovered and their status at the time of writing the article.             J. D. Filipiak

1223.   Fenberg, Matilda.   I REMEMBER CLARENCE DARROW. *Chicago Hist. 1973 2(4): 216-223.* Clarence Darrow (1857-1938) began his career in Ohio as city solicitor before moving to Chicago. There he quickly established himself as a rising lawyer and as an engaging intellectual. Before gaining legal fame he became close friends with Jane Addams and John and Emma Altgeld. Darrow proved to be a great humanitarian with a special interest in intellectual women. Based on primary sources; 7 photos.                                    N. A. Kuntz

1224.   Fischer, Louis   LETTERS FROM MRS. ROOSEVELT. *J. of Hist. Studies 1967 1(1): 24-30.* Provides four letters written to the author, hitherto unpublished, which add to our knowledge of Anna Eleanor Roosevelt's attitudes during the Spanish Civil War and to our appreciation of the character of a busy public personage willing to take time and trouble in a private matter.                         N. W. Moen

1225.   Foster, Laura.   HONEYMOON IN HETCH HETCHY: A 1914 GLIMPSE OF A YOSEMITE VALLEY —FOCAL POINT OF AMERICA'S FIRST MAJOR CONSERVATION CRUSADE. *Am. West 1971 8(3): 10-15.* Hetch Hetchy Valley of the Tuolumne River in the Sierra Nevada of California was said to have rivaled Yosemite Valley a few miles to its southeast. In the 1910's a dam created a reservoir which provides most of the water supply for San Francisco. Hetch Hetchy represents the absolute defeat of one of America's first conservation crusades. In 1914, in the midst of the controversy, two young people, Dorothy Stillman and Robert Duryea, whose families were on opposite sides of the question, married and then spent their two-week honeymoon on a mule-packing trip to the floor of the valley. Their conclusion was a qualified affirmative in favor of construction of the dam. 10 illus.
                                        D. L. Smith

1226.   Gatewood, Willard B.   THEODORE ROOSEVELT AND THE CASE OF MRS. MINOR MORRIS.   *Mid-Am. 1966 48(1): 3-18.* The forcible expulsion of Laura Hull Morris from The White House in January 1906 triggered an outburst of anti-Roosevelt sentiment at a critical juncture in his administration. Ultimately, the Morris affair became involved either directly or indirectly with such issues as Federal patronage, protection of the president's person, Roosevelt's legislative program, his relationship with the press, and his long-standing feud with Senator Benjamin Tillman of South Carolina.                         L. D. Silveri

1227.   Geer, Emily Apt.   LUCY WEBB HAYES AND HER FAMILY.   *Ohio Hist. 1968 77(1): 33-57.* Relates the story of the Hayes's courtship and marriage from the point of view of Lucy Webb Hayes and suggests that her interest in politics was a significant factor in drawing Hayes into political activity and in his subsequent decision to remain in politics.                                    S. L. Jones

1228.   Gladwin, Lee A.   ARTHURDALE: ADVENTURE INTO UTOPIA.   *West Virginia Hist. 1967 28(4): 305-317.* Arthurdale was a New Deal project near Morgantown. It was conceived by Mrs. Eleanor Roosevelt as an experiment in social planning which, if successful, might be applied in other depressed communities. The plan was to provide homesteads for people who would earn their living from employment in the construction of homes and then in such cooperative enterprises as farming, processing, and commercial activities. Mrs. Roosevelt proposed a plant for the production of mailboxes. Arthurdale quickly became the symbol of the Government's attempt to produce for itself as a competitor of private industry. Congressional opposition was so intense that first plans for the factory were abandoned. Houses were built but small contractors complained that the awarding of contracts was unfair. The first settlers arrived in July 1934 and the first factory was operative in 1936. It was a failure as were its successors. At huge cost the Government built a planned community but pump priming could not create an industrial center artificially. By 1947 all of the factories and houses had been sold. Based on government reports and letter, 52 notes.             D. N. Brown

1229.   Hackensmith, C. W.   THE MUCH MALIGNED MARY TODD LINCOLN.   *Filson Club Hist. Q. 1970 44(3): 282-292.* A highly sympathetic review of the life of Abraham Lincoln's wife. Dwells on the tremendous personal tragedies that Mary Todd Lincoln had to endure— the death of three sons and her husband. Her legendary spending sprees were necessary for someone in her position, and she was very aware of the family's financial troubles. The stories of William H. Herndon caused her continual suffering. Concludes with the sanity trial instituted by her son Robert Lincoln. Documentation includes letters from the Chicago Historical Society and the University of Chicago and secondary works. 24 notes.                                    G. B. McKinney

1230.   Head, Faye E.   THE THEATRICAL SYNDICATE VS. THE CHILD LABOR LAW OF LOUISIANA.   *Louisiana Studies 1974 13(4): 365-374.* The Theatrical Syndicate's monopoly was opposed by the Child Labor Law (Louisiana, 1908), which had a costly though not immediate effect upon New Orleans theaters. In 1912, after a battle by Jean Gordon and a small group of women, the theatrical interests were the victors: the Child Labor Law was amended by the pressure of New York interests to permit children under 16 to act on the stages of Louisiana. Note.                                                                                              E. P. Stickney

1231. Hirsch, Eleanor G. GRANDMA FELTON AND THE U.S. SENATE. *Mankind 1974 4(6): 52-57.* The story of one of the most active women reformers of the 19th and early 20th centuries.                    S

1232. Holsinger, M. Paul. J. C. BURROWS AND THE FIGHT AGAINST MORMONISM: 1903-1907. *Mich. Hist. 1968 52(3): 181-195.* Traces the abortive four-year effort of Michigan Senator Julius Caesar Burrows to expel from Congress his fellow Republican Reed Smoot of Utah. Smoot was an apostle of the Mormon Church and one of the denomination's most conspicuous officials. Burrows had been a persistent critic of Mormonism in Congress for over two decades and the "Smoot Case" provided him with ammunition for a major assault against Mormon hierarchy and doctrine. Directing the fight from his position as chairman of the Senate Committee on Privileges and Elections, Burrows conducted lengthy hearings designed to enrage passions against polygamy —even though Smoot neither believed in nor practiced plural marriage. In 1904 as the issue reached a climax, the Michigan Legislature affirmed its support of Burrow's crusade by reelecting him unanimously. He did not fare as well in the Senate, however, when his motion to bar Smoot was finally defeated in 1907. Three years later, in Michigan's first direct senatorial election, he was retired from office, having served nearly 40 years in Congress. Based on manuscript sources, newspapers, the *Congressional Record,* and other public documents; 5 illus., 55 notes.
                                                                                                           J. K. Flack

1233. Horowitz, Helen L. VARIETIES OF CULTURAL EXPERIENCE OF JANE ADDAM'S CHICAGO. *Hist. of Educ. Q. 1974 14(1): 69-86.* Analyzes the attitudes toward and the definitions of art in Chicago and compares them with Jane Addams' ideas. Discusses the roots of her ideas first in Ruskinian idealism and elitism. Later Addams differed with her art patron supporters over politics and reform and her belief that the establishment of city-wide cultural institutions could be achieved in the political arena. Based on primary and secondary sources; 69 notes.                                                             L. C. Smith

1234. Howard, Mary K. AN EXAMPLE OF WOMEN IN POLITICS. *Utah Hist. Q. 1970 38(1): 61-64.* Reprint of article first published in *The Improvement Era* (July, 1914). The author was chairman of the board and mayor of Kanab, Utah, 1912-14, when the town board was composed entirely of women. Lists the achievements of the board.
                                                                                                           S. L. Jones

1235. Jensen, Joan M. AFTER SLAVERY: CAROLINE SEVERENCE IN LOS ANGELES. *Southern California Q. 1966 48(2): 175-186.* The later career of a New England abolitionist and woman suffrage advocate, who brought the kindergarten and the Unitarian Church to Los Angeles. 25 notes.                                                        H. Kelsey

1236. Johnson, James. THE ROLE OF WOMEN IN THE FOUNDING OF THE UNITED STATES CHILDREN'S BUREAU. George, Carol V. R., ed. *"Remember the Ladies": New Perspectives on Women in American History: Essays in Honor of Nelson Manfred Blake* (Syracuse: Syracuse U. Pr., 1975): 179-196. Florence Kelley, Grace Abbott, Julia Lathrop, and Lillian Wald were social reformers who tirelessly worked for child welfare legislation and institutions. Their work in the first half of the 20th century focused on minimal standards of decency in child welfare, the problems of child labor, the child labor amendment, the establishment and development of the Children's Bureau, and the passage of the Sheppard-Towner Act. They appealed to and used the support of women's groups for their political agitation. Their public activities subjected them to personal abuse, and their demands were met with charges of socialism, feminism, and Bolshevism. In 1935, with the passage of the Social Security Act, both the Children's Bureau and the health care provisions of the Sheppard-Towner Act finally were secured. This ended 30 years of agitation in which women played the central role to secure legislation designed to protect children's rights and interests. Based on primary and secondary materials; 42 notes.                           P. R. Byrne

1237. Jones, Alton DuMar. THE CHILD LABOR REFORM MOVEMENT IN GEORGIA. *Georgia Hist. Q. 1965 49(4): 396-417.*

A discussion of the movement for child labor reform from 1870 to the enactment of a relatively strong bill in 1925. Opposition to the movement is analyzed as are the arguments in favor of it. The focus is largely, but not exclusively, on conditions in the textile industry.                  R. Lowitt

1238. Kersey, Harry A., Jr. THE "FRIENDS OF THE FLORIDA SEMINOLES" SOCIETY: 1899-1926. *Tequesta 1974 (34): 3-20.* In 1891 an Indian mission was established on land purchased at Immokalee, in Collier County. In 1899 the Friends of the Florida Seminoles was organized in Kissimmee. Jim Willson was secretary of the charitable organization from its founding until it became defunct in 1926. His wife, Minnie Moore Willson, is known in Florida history as the "mother of the Seminole Land Bill," enacted into law in 1915. This organization helped to protect Seminoles until the Bureau of Indian Affairs assumed the burden. Based on primary and secondary sources; 55 notes.
                                                                                                           H. S. Marks

1239. Kintrea, Frank. LARCENOUS MRS. CODY VS. PIOUS MISS GOULD. *Am. Heritage 1975 26(4): 73-77.* Recounts the trials of Margaret E. Cody, an elderly widow from Denver, who attempted to challenge the will of financier Jay Gould on behalf of a woman who believed herself to be a daughter of Gould. As no verdict was reached in the first trial, a second was held and the evidence against Cody found conclusive. When the judge ordered the sentence suspended, Gould's daughter, Helen, lashed out and turned public sympathy to Mrs. Cody. 4 illus.                                                                           J. F. Paul

1240. Kirby, Luella M. and Lenz, Carolyn B. WIFE OF CLEMENCEAU WAS WISCONSIN GIRL. *Wis. Then and Now 1969 16(4): 6-7.* Briefly reviews the life of Wisconsin-reared Mary Plummer, wife of Georges Clemenceau, premier of France during World War I. Mary was born in Springfield, Massachusetts, in 1849, but came with her family to Skinner Prairie and later Durand, Wisconsin, in 1857. At age 15 she was sent by a wealthy uncle to the exclusive Catherine Aiken Seminary in Stamford, Connecticut. Here she met Clemenceau, a young French instructor at the seminary. At the time, Clemenceau was a political exile from his native country. In 1869 the two were married in New York City Hall. The next year, Clemenceau took his wife to his ancestral castle L'Aubray Vendee, in the west of France. It was here that their daughters Madeline and Theresa Juliette, and a son Michel, were born. In the 1870's Clemenceau became estranged from his American-born wife. Until her death in 1923, Mary Plummer Clemenceau remained a fond, if distant, admirer of her husband, and she was buried in France.
                                                                                                           D. P. Peltier

1241. Kogan, Herman. MYRA BRADWELL: CRUSADER AT LAW. *Chicago Hist. 1974/75 3(3): 132-140.* Myra Bradwell fought for law reforms in Chicago, particularly in the areas of women's rights, taxation and penalties for crimes.                                             S

1242. Lash, Joseph P. THE ROOSEVELTS AND ARTHURDALE. *Washington Monthly 1971 3(9): 22-37.* Discusses the New Deal attempt at rural resettlement, focusing on the Arthurdale experiment in West Virginia. Eleanor Roosevelt was in charge of the project from the beginning, seeing it as a way to combat the poverty of the unemployed miners and as a way to forestall the spread of communism. Chronicles her troubles with Congress over money and with administrators such as Harold Ickes and Rexford Tugwell. The project was attacked from the Right as a threat to free enterprise and from the Left as a mechanism to decentralize poverty. The population of Arthurdale remained on relief throughout the 1930's until the war, when a defense plant was located there. In 1946 Arthurdale and the other resettlement communities were sold by the government. An excerpt from the author's *Eleanor and Franklin Roosevelt* (New York: W. W. Norton and Co., 1971).
                                                                                                           S. R. Duguid

1243. Lillard, Richard G. WHOSE RIGHT OF WAY? *Westways 1976 68(6): 18-19, 21-22, 64-65, 72-73.* Discusses the Rancho Topanga Malibu Sequit, 13,300 acres of beachfront property in southern California, and the attempts of its owner May Knight Rindge to keep county and eventually state roads from traversing the land through Topanga Canyon, 1905-25.

1244. Lutz, Paul V. HARDING'S LOVE LETTERS PRESERVED: WHEN SHOULD "PROPERTY RIGHTS" IN LETTERS PASS INTO THE PUBLIC DOMAIN. *Manuscripts 1972 24(2): 97-99.* Reviews the case of the unearthed Warren G. Harding letters to Carrie Phillips (1910-1920) with a plea for a revision of the copyright law.                                        D.A. Yanchisin

1245. Maddox, Robert J. MRS. WILSON AND THE PRESIDENCY. *Am. Hist. Illus. 1973 7(10): 36-44.* Edith Bolling Galt Wilson, wife of Woodrow Wilson, became the surrogate President during her husband's illness.                                         S

1246. Mallach, Stanley. RED KATE O'HARE COMES TO MADISON: THE POLITICS OF FREE SPEECH. *Wisconsin Mag. of Hist. 1970 53(3): 204-222.* A vigorous Socialist, Kate Richards O'Hare's controversial appearance at the University of Wisconsin in the early 20th century stimulated right-wing protest.                      S

1247. Martin, George. HOW MISS PERKINS LEARNED TO LOBBY. *Am. Heritage 1976 27(3): 64-71.* Frances Perkins, FDR's Secretary of Labor for 12 years, learned much about lobbying when she represented the Consumers League of New York before the New York state legislature in 1911. The experience in getting a bill passed in Albany served her well in Washington. Excerpted from *Madam Secretary: Frances Perkins* (Houghton Mifflin, 1976). 5 illus.        B. J. Paul

1248. Morris, Cheryl Haun. ALICE M. ROBERTSON: FRIEND OR FOE OF THE AMERICAN SOLDIER? *J. of the West 1973 12(2): 307-316.* Alice M. Robertson was America's only woman member of Congress during 1921-23. After her election to Congress she promised to support veterans' benefits. "Yet, when the bonus bill for soldiers of World War I was proposed, Miss Robertson openly opposed it," refusing to be swayed by pressure groups. Although she helped build a veterans' hospital in Muskogee, Oklahoma, her stand against the bonus bill hurt her reelection campaign, and she lost her congressional seat. Illus., 37 notes.
E. P. Stickney

1249. Nichols, Irby C. and Nichols, Margaret I. LILLIAN GUNTER AND TEXAS COUNTY LEGISLATION 1914-1919. *J. of Lib. Hist., Phil. and Comparative Librarianship 1973 8(1): 11-17.* Lillian Gunter played an important role (1914-19) in the attempt to produce an effective county library law for Texas. She faced many disappointments—but with the help of certain legislators, the Texas Library Association, and others she instigated the amended County Library Law of Texas (1919). Based on primary and secondary sources; 40 notes.        D. G. Williams

1250. Phifer, Gregg. EDITH BOLLING WILSON: GATEKEEPER EXTRAORDINARY. *Speech Monographs 1971 38(4): 277-289.* President Woodrow Wilson's illness, which began in October 1919, is "a case study in what happens to communication between a nation and its President when he is unable to function normally." In her *Memoir* Mrs. Wilson details the crucial decisionmaking process. Every letter or document directed to the president was passed to Mrs. Wilson who digested the messages she selected before presenting them. Opinions differ as to when the "regency" ended and as to what effect Mrs. Wilson's stewardship had on affairs of state, especially on the fate of the League of Nations. President Wilson decided it "would be better to go down with flags flying than surrender to the League's enemies." 61 notes.
E. P. Stickney

1251. Pryor, Helen B. HOMEMAKER IN MANY LANDS. *Palimpsest 1971 52(7): 369-376.* Lou Henry and Herbert C. Hoover, after their marriage in 1899, traveled to several countries and had two sons. Covers Lou Henry Hoover's life through the presidential inauguration, 1928.

1252. Pryor, Helen B. LOU HOOVER: GALLANT FIRST LADY. *Palimpsest 1971 52(7): 377-387.* Discusses Lou Henry Hoover's life as the first lady during Herbert's presidency, 1929-32.

1253. Pryor, Helen B. THE YEARS FOLLOWING 1933. *Palimpsest 1971 52(7): 388-400.* Discusses Lou Henry Hoover's life in California and her work with the Hoover War Library at Stanford University, the Girl Scouts, and the Finnish Relief Fund until her death in 1944.

1254. Reeves, Thomas C. THE DIARIES OF MALVINA ARTHUR: WINDOWS INTO THE PAST OF OUR 21ST PRESIDENT. *Vermont Hist. 1970 38(3): 177-188.* Chester Alan Arthur is partly responsible for his own obscurity, having burned most of his private papers. Since George F. Howe's 1934 biography many sources have turned up which have not been utilized by historians. The diaries of Arthur's sister Malvina (1832-1916), at Cohoes, New York, in 1853 and Albany, New York, in 1869, show that she loathed her self-righteous father, adored her long-suffering mother, and enjoyed her siblings, especially Chester. During the winter of 1853 Malvina, uneasily betrothed, taught in Chester's Cohoes academy. After studying for another term in Albany, she returned for a hypochondriac summer with her parents in West Troy, New York, and them resumed teaching in Cohoes. Chester, sociable and attractive, frequented the library and table-tipped for amusement. In 1854 Malvina went South; then she married Henry Haynesworth, an Albany merchant. Fifteen years later, childless and brooding over her mother's impending death, she again kept a diary.                          T. D. S. Bassett

1255. Reeves, Thomas C. THE PRESIDENT'S DWARF: THE LETTERS OF JULIA SAND TO CHESTER A. ARTHUR. *New York Hist. 1971 52(1): 73-83.* Between 27 August 1881 and 15 September 1883, Julia Sand, a self-described New York City invalid, wrote 23 letters to President Chester Alan Arthur. While Arthur never replied to her letters, he carefully preserved all of them and visited the Sand home on 20 August 1882. Sand urged Arthur to repudiate the Stalwarts, champion civil service reform, and become "a great President." The nature and importance of their relationship, however, remains a mystery. Sand died in 1933, aged 83. Based on primary and secondary sources; 5 illus., 26 notes.
G. Kurland

1256. Scott, Anne Firor. HEROINES AND HEROINE WORSHIP. *R. in Am. Hist. 1974 2(3): 413-418.* Allen F. Davis' *American Heroine: The Life and Legend of Jane Addams* (New York: Oxford U. Pr., 1973) misunderstands the meaning of Jane Addams' life, allowing a mistaken version of an overly ambitious, egocentric woman to overshadow her achievements in social reform from the 1880's to the 1930's.

1257. Taylor, Paul S. MIGRANT MOTHER: 1936. *Am. West 1970 7(3): 41-47.* Dorothea Lange was put on the payroll of a California State relief bureau as a typist. She was really a photographer with an assignment to document a research report the bureau was conducting on rural rehabilitation. A set of poignant photographs which she made in 1936 of starving migrant pea pickers is credited with State action for the construction of camps for migratory laborers. Lange's own account is appended as "The Assignment I'll Never Forget." 7 illus.        D. L. Smith

1258. Thompson, Arthur W. THE RECEPTION OF RUSSIAN REVOLUTIONARY LEADERS IN AMERICA, 1904-06. *Am. Q. 1966 18(3): 452-476.* Describes an influx of foreign revolutionary visitors. Numerous "Russian parties and factions," operating in the van of a series of internal Russian crises, sent most of the visitors to secure financial, moral, and material support from sympathetic Americans. Although early visitors received wide acclaim and support, later luminaries found growing antipathy. The Russian Bund, a socialist unit bent on mobilizing American Jewish support over the Russian pogroms, and the Social Revolutionary Party, which spread the word of Russian atrocities through leaders such as the immensely popular Catherine Breshkovsky, were at the forefront. A third group, the Social Democrats, sent the literary hero Maxim Gorki. A widespread moralistic condemnation of Gorki's private life underscored a growing alienation of Russian and American radicals from the respectable American majority who remained more concerned about sexual orthodoxy than social justice. Despite the efforts of American supporters, favorable sentiments and support for the Russian revolutionaries remained concentrated in small intellectualist enclaves and in urban immigrant areas. American socialism gained impetus as a result of the visitations, but the cause of the Russian revolutionaries made little headway. Most of the European radicals left the United States with a profound distaste for all things American. 58 notes.
R. S. Pickett

1259. Venn, George W. THE WOBBLIES AND MONTANA'S GARDEN CITY. *Montana: Mag. of Western Hist. 1971 21(4): 18-30.* Traces the struggle by leaders of the Industrial Workers of the World to disrupt civic life in Missoula briefly in 1909. The immediate object was to organize support for the IWW and to attack local employment agencies accused of defrauding clients. The indirect goal seems to have been the testing and perfecting of tactics such as street speaking and clogging of courts and jails with agitators assembled from other towns. The episode marked the rise to prominence of Elizabeth Gurley Flynn (1890-1964), who went on to a lifetime career in radical politics. Flynn chaired the Communist Party U.S.A. in 1961.

S. R. Davison

1260.   White, Jean Bickmore.   GENTLE PERSUADERS: UTAH'S FIRST WOMEN LEGISLATORS.   *Utah Hist. Q. 1970 38(1): 31-49.* Evaluates the careers of the first three women to be elected to the state legislature of Utah, in 1896. Some contemporary observers concluded that their contributions were trivial, but the conclusion here is that the results of their work differed little from those of their male colleagues'.

S. L. Jones

1261.   White, Mary.   MARY WHITE: AUTOBIOGRAPHY OF AN OHIO FIRST LADY.   *Ohio Hist. 1973 82(1/2): 63-87.* Widower George White became governor of Ohio in 1931 and his 24-year-old daughter Mary served as first lady. In 1958 she wrote a 58-page reminiscence about those years. The result was a personal view of the White administration. Mentions anecdotes about Coolidge and characterizations of Will Rogers, Eleanor Roosevelt, and other prominent figures. 9 illus.

S. S. Sprague

1262.   Wilson, William H.   "MORE ALMOST THAN THE MEN": MIRA LLOYD DOCK AND THE BEAUTIFICATION OF HARRISBURG.   *Pennsylvania Mag. of Hist. and Biog. 1975 99(4): 490-499.* Discusses the campaign for city beautification in Harrisburg, Pennsylvania, and the role of Mira Lloyd Dock, one of the founders of the Civic Club of Harrisburg. Miss Dock lectured successfully to inspire the city's leaders to begin a 40-year improvement program. 23 notes.

C. W. Olson

1263.   Winestine, Belle Fligelman.   MOTHER WAS SHOCKED. *Montana: Mag. of Western Hist. 1974 24(3): 70-78.* Prominent in the woman suffrage movement in Montana was Jeannette Rankin, first woman elected to Congress, whose story is recalled by her first-term secretary and campaign assistant. Political activity, especially making public speeches, was considered unladylike and distressed some families concerned. Illus.

S. R. Davison

1264.   —.   [THE BEALE FAMILY AND DECATUR HOUSE.] *Historic Preservation 1967 19(3,4): 69-90.*
Morton, Mrs. Terry B.   GEN. EDWARD FITZGERALD BEALE OF TEJON RANCHO AND LAFAYETTE SQUARE,   *pp. 69-81.* A biographical sketch of General Beale and an account of his remodeling of Decatur House (formerly the residence of Commodore Stephen Decatur, Jr.) on Lafayette Square in Washington after 1872. Illus.
Detwiler, Hazel Scaife.   THE TRUXTUN BEALE YEARS, *pp. 82-86.* Discusses early life of Truxtun Beale, son of General Edward F. Beale, and the parties given in Decatur House by Mrs. Truxtun Beale. Illus.
Krock, Arthur.   MRS. MARIE BEALE ENTERTAINS, *pp. 87-90.* An impression of the famous parties given in the 30 years before World War II by Mrs. Truxtun Beale in Decatur House, across Lafayette Square from the White House. Most of the parties were for the diplomatic corps in Washington. Illus.

J. M. Hawes

## Political Behavior

### General

1265.   Arndt, Karl J. R.   BISMARCK'S SOCIALIST LAWS OF 1878 AND THE HARMONISTS.   *Western Pennsylvania Hist. Mag. 1976 59(1): 55-70.* Following Otto von Bismarck's socialist laws of 1878, German socialist Clara Pittman applied for membership in George Rapp's Harmony Society (1879), an organization of Christian communists, headquartered in Economy, Pennsylvania.

1266.   Blumberg, Dorothy Rose.   DEAR "MR. ENGELS," UNPUBLISHED LETTERS, 1884-1894, OF FLORENCE KELLEY (-WISCHNEWETZKY) TO FRIEDRICH ENGELS.   *Labor Hist. 1964 5(2): 103-133.* Presents quotations from 40 letters written by Florence Kelley (-Wischnewetzky) to Friedrich Engels. Miss Kelley was an active member of the socialist movement in the United States. In 1884 she married a Russian socialist, Lazare Wischnewetzky, a medical student, whom she met at the University of Zurich. The letters quoted are in possession of the Archives of the Marx-Engels Institute in Moscow.

J. H. Krenkel

1267.   Bryant, Keith L., Jr.   KATE BARNARD, ORGANIZED LABOR, AND SOCIAL JUSTICE IN OKLAHOMA DURING THE PROGRESSIVE ERA.   *J. of Southern Hist. 1969 35(2): 145-164.* Anger over "low prices of farm commodities, the high railroad and interest rates, the presence of territorial officials appointed by the federal government, and the unregulated growth of business" made Oklahoma "ripe for reform" in the early 1900's. The potential "became effective through the unique ability and energy of Kate Barnard," who spearheaded a coalition of humanitarians and representatives of organized labor. These Oklahoma progressives, who do "not fit the stereotyped pattern" espoused reforms advocated by social workers, unionists, and the lower classes, and transmitted them into legislative enactments. 83 notes.

I. M. Leonard

1268.   Levine, Daniel.   JANE ADDAMS: ROMANTIC RADICAL 1889-1912.   *Mid-Am. 1962 44(4): 195-210.* Jane Addams' social outlook was based on a romantic faith in the natural goodness of man, in the instinctive wisdom of the meek and poor, and on a conviction that men were more healthy in every way as they lived closer to nature. Deep within every human soul, obscured by urban industrialism, was a kind and benevolent nature, thirsting for fundamental communication with the rest of humanity. Miss Addams believed that government should help these people fulfill their destiny, and called for a welfare state more inclusive than anything that was to appear for over half a century.

L. D. Silveri

1269.   LeWarne, Charles P.   EQUALITY COLONY: THE PLAN TO SOCIALIZE WASHINGTON.   *Pacific Northwest Q. 1968 59(3): 137-146.* The rise and fall of the colony of Equality founded in the State of Washington under the auspices of the National Union of the Brotherhood of the Co-operative Commonwealth, 1897-1907. This colony was one of a number of utopian socialistic settlements which sprang up in the State and across the Nation especially in the 19th century. After an industrious beginning, the Equality Colony declined because of disagreements and the latter-day activities of members who allegedly included anarchists, spiritualists, and free lovers.

C. C. Gorchels

1270.   Miller, David Humphreys.   SITTING BULL'S WHITE SQUAW.   *Montana 1964 14(2): 55-71.* In 1889 an eccentric Brooklyn artist, Mrs. Catherine Weldon, joined Sitting Bull's household and influenced his negotiations with government authorities until his death in December 1890.

S. R. Davison

1271.   Platt, Anthony.   THE RISE OF THE CHILD-SAVING MOVEMENT: A STUDY IN SOCIAL POLICY AND CORRECTIONAL REFORM.   *Ann. of the Am. Acad. of Pol. and Social Sci. 1969 381: 21-38.* "Contemporary programs of delinquency-control can be traced to the enterprising reforms of the child-savers who, at the end of the nineteenth century, helped to create special judicial and correctional instititutons for the labeling, processing, and management of troublesome youth. Child-saving was a conservative and romantic movement, designed to impose sanctions on conduct unbecoming youth and to disqualify youth from enjoying adult privileges. The child-savers were prohibitionists, in a general sense, who believed in close supervision of adolescents' recreation and leisure. The movement brought attention to, and thus invented, new categories of youthful misbehavior which had been previously unappreciated or had been dealt with on an informal basis. Child-saving was heavily influenced by middle-class women who extended their housewifely roles into public service and emphasized the dependence of the social order on the proper socialization of children. This analysis of the child-savers offers an opportunity to examine more general issues in correctional research: What are the dynamics of the popular and legislative drive to bring undesirable behavior within the ambit of the criminal law? What problems are caused by 'agency-determined' research? What are the practical and policy implications of research on politically sensitive institutions?"  J

1272.  Pratt, William C.  WOMEN AND AMERICAN SOCIALISM: THE READING EXPERIENCE.  *Pennsylvania Mag. of Hist. and Biog. 1975 99(1): 72-91.*  Reviews the role of women in building the Socialist Party in Reading, Pennsylvania. The party enjoyed considerable local electoral success during 1927-36, and much of this success depended on the women's vote. Women played a larger role in Socialist Party affairs than was the case with either of the majority parties, but this role was subordinate and supportive, as the Party was neither willing nor able to break through the prevailing philosophy of male dominance. 61 notes.
V. L. Human

1273.  Stanley, Ruth Moore.  ALICE M. ROBERTSON, OKLAHOMA'S FIRST CONGRESSWOMAN.  *Chronicles of Okla. 1967 45(3): 259-289.*  Miss Robertson, a Republican, was elected Oklahoma's first congresswoman in 1921 over a veteran Indian-Democrat in a Democratic State. Her widely known efforts, going back to the Spanish-American War, to supply soldiers with canteen-type comforts and her unique classified advertising newspaper campaign were prominent factors in the success. Ironically, her opposition to a World War I bonus bill was a principal reason for defeat in her bid for reelection in 1923. 6 illus., 75 notes.
D. L. Smith

1274.  Trattner, Walter I.  THEODORE ROOSEVELT, SOCIAL WORKERS, AND THE ELECTION OF 1912: A NOTE.  *Mid-Am. 1968 50(1): 64-69.*  Shows the divisions and mixed emotions within the social work community occasioned by Theodore Roosevelt's candidacy and the Progressive Party platform in 1912 in an hitherto unpublished correspondence between two prominent social workers - Homer Folks and Gertrude Stevens Rice. The seven letters quoted show Folks' support of Roosevelt while Gertrude Rice was unalterably opposed to having the social workers support the Bull Mooser because of distrust. 14 notes.
L. D. Silveri

1275.  —.  [WOMEN REFORMERS].  *J. of Social Hist. [Great Britain] 1971/72 5(2): 164-182.*
Conway, Jill.  WOMEN REFORMERS AND AMERICAN CULTURE, 1870-1930,  *pp. 164-177.*  Post-Civil War female reformers were one of two social types: a sage or prophetess possessed of feminine insights, or the professional expert. The former type was preferred and accepted by American society and the latter type rejected. Women reformers such as Jane Addams and Lillian Wald could not perceive that their type of reform (which accepted the concept of the morally superior woman) only helped to reinforce the traditional middle-class stereotyped image of women as passive and irrational creatures. 16 notes.
O'Neill, William L.  COMMENT,  *pp. 178-182.*  Analyzes Robert H. McNeal's "Women in the Russian Radical Movement" as well as Conway's article [both accompanying this article in *Journal of Social History* 1971/72 5(2)]. McNeal's study is an interesting indication that "women's status in liberal and left-wing movements correlates with social position" and is a model study worthy of emulation. Finds Conway's categories of "sage" and "expert" useful but notes that women became sages "not only from calculation and inadvertence, but out of deep emotional ties and experiences that militated against less self-defeating alternatives." Both studies raise questions which need further investigation. 9 notes.
L. Ziewacz

## Women's Organizations

1276.  Barber, Henry E.  THE ASSOCIATION OF SOUTHERN WOMEN FOR THE PREVENTION OF LYNCHING, 1930-1942.  *Phylon 1973 34(4): 378-389.*  Studies the effects of the Association of Southern Women for the Prevention of Lynching, 1930-42.  S

1277.  Carlson, Mrs. Harry.  THE FIRST DECADE OF THE ST. LOUIS LEAGUE OF WOMEN VOTERS.  *Missouri Hist. Soc. Bull. 1969 26(1): 32-52.*  The St. Louis League of Women Voters, founded in 1919 at the urging of nationally known suffragettes, especially Carrie Chapman Catt, replaced the Missouri Suffrage Association when Missouri allowed female suffrage. The St. Louis league and several groups organized in other Missouri cities by Edna Gellhorn and Marie Ames, predated the national organization of the League of Women Voters. Between 1919 and 1929 the Missouri groups pioneered by operating citizenship schools, performing nonpartisan work with voters, overcoming hostility of politicians, and lobbying for legislation in eight areas that the local leagues decided on. Based on secondary sources and oral history recordings held by the Missouri Historical Society; photos, 20 notes.
H. T. Lovin

1278.  Dye, Nancy Schrom.  CREATING A FEMINIST ALLIANCE: SISTERHOOD AND CLASS CONFLICT IN THE NEW YORK WOMEN'S TRADE UNION LEAGUE, 1903-1914.  *Feminist Studies 1975 2(2/3): 24-38.*  In 1903 a "coalition of women workers and wealthy women disenchanted with conventional philanthropic and social reform activities" formed the Women's Trade Union League of New York. There was personal, cultural, and political strife among the members, but they were not divided between trade unionists and social workers as Pauline Newman claimed in 1914. A major source of discord was the conflict between commitment to organized labor and commitment to the women's movement, although during 1903-14 the League chose to emphasize the labor movement. Based on personal papers and periodical literature, League papers, and government reports; 37 notes.
J. D. Falk

1279.  Fullerton, Eula.  THE OKLAHOMA STATE FLAG.  *Chronicles of Oklahoma 1975 53(2): 270-273.*  Examines the evolution of a state flag for Oklahoma to replace the one created in 1911. By 1924 the Oklahoma Historical Society and the State Chapter of the Daughters of the American Revolution created enough sentiment for a new flag that a design campaign was launched. The design offered by Mrs. George Fluke was accepted by the state legislature in March 1925. The pattern remained unchanged until 1941 when the word "Oklahoma" was added along the bottom border. Photo.
M. L. Tate

1280.  Jacoby, Robin Miller.  FEMINISM AND CLASS CONSCIOUSNESS IN THE BRITISH AND AMERICAN WOMEN'S TRADE UNION LEAGUE, 1890-1925.  Carroll, Berenice A., ed. Liberating Women's History (Chicago: U. of Illinois Pr., 1976): pp. 137-160.  Discusses the influence of class consciousness on British and American trade union women when their goals for women conflicted with an ideology of class loyalty. Analyzes the different relationships of both leagues to the women's suffrage movement, and the effect these differences had on the International Federation of Working Women. Concludes that despite the priority given by the British to class based contexts and by the Americans to interaction between women of all classes, the British and American women were essentially participants in the same struggle. 64 notes.
B. Sussman

1281.  Johnson, Dorothy E.  ORGANIZED WOMEN AS LOBBYISTS IN THE 1920'S.  *Capitol Studies 1972 1(1): 41-58.*  With the ratification of the 19th Amendment in 1920, 21 women's organizations unified under the Women's Joint Congressional Committee, which served as a clearing house for the legislative efforts of its members.  S

1282.  Lemons, J. Stanley  THE SHEPPARD-TOWNER ACT: PROGRESSIVISM IN THE 1920'S.  *J. of Am. Hist. 1969 55(4): 776-786.*  The Sheppard-Towner Act (1921) provided Federal matching money to States developing programs of assistance for maternal and infant care. Congressional concern for relatively high rates of infant and maternal mortality motivated passage of the act largely because of the fear of alienating women's votes which had been recently granted. The act was supported by the League of Women Voters and the National Consumers League, but was opposed by the American Medical Association, Daughters of the American Revolution, and antisuffrage groups who denounced it as "a step toward Sovietism" and as inimical to States rights. It was allowed to die in 1929, but did good work in the interim. The Sheppard-Towner Act reveals the continuation of Progressive impulses in the 1920's and is a link between Progressivism and the New Deal Social Security measures. 30 notes.
K. B. West

1283. Pivar, Donald J. THEOCRATIC BUSINESSMEN AND PHILADELPHIA MUNICIPAL REFORM, 1870-1900. *Pennsylvania Hist. 1966 33(3): 289-307.* Examines the role of religion (which could almost be taken to mean the moral impulse) in educational, social, and political reform in late 19th-century Philadelphia. The author attempts to answer the question "Was the Phildelphia reform movement more the business man's answer to socialism than an outgrowth of the moral precepts of those involved in the movement?" Both elements were so interrelated that the primacy of one cannot be established. The Episcopalians, Unitarians, and Friends responded to the movement more readily than other denominations. At base the religious reform movement was nondenominational and stressed internalization of the values central to all religions. Particular attention is given to the Philadelphia Social Science Association, the Municipal League, and several groups in which women were active. Based on a variety of primary and secondary sources; 76 notes.                                                         D. C. Swift

1284. Romanofsky, Peter. "THE PUBLIC IS AROUSED": THE MISSOURI CHILDREN'S CODE COMMISSION, 1915-1919. *Missouri Hist. R. 1974 68(2): 204-222.* Discusses the origins and history of the Missouri Children's Code Commission, a Progressive reform movement which involved prominent educators and social workers and a coalition of citizens' groups. The first commission was appointed in 1915 to protect children from adverse conditions in labor and from delinquency, neglect, welfare and other problems, but its proposals were a failure because the more significant measures were rejected by the legislature. Appointed in 1917, the second commission revised the earlier proposals and actively engaged in an educational promotional campaign, gaining the support of various organizations such as the Woman's Christian Temperance Union, The Red Cross, women's clubs, suffrage groups, and others. The Missouri Children's Code was finally passed in 1919. Based on contemporary newspaper reports, primary and secondary sources; 3 illus., 5 photos, 64 notes.                         N. J. Street

1285. Scott, Anne Firor. AFTER SUFFRAGE: SOUTHERN WOMEN IN THE TWENTIES. *J. of Southern Hist. 1963 30(3): 298-318.* Although Southern women have an impressive record of accomplishment since the effective date of the 19th Amendment, the high expectations of those who led the suffrage movement did not come to pass. The number of women in public life is probably no greater today than in 1925. There has been a strong reluctance upon the part of political leaders to give the women any real voice in party decisions or any real places on the tickets. Women have worked effectively in party organizational work and can possibly lay claim to having decided the outcome of some elections. Even more real are their achievements, through such organizations as the League of Women Voters and the Young Women's Christian Association, in influencing public policy on such subjects as female and child labor, unionization and racial matters. Documented.
                                                         S. E. Humphreys

1286. Searle, Newell. MINNESOTA NATIONAL FOREST: THE POLITICS OF COMPROMISE, 1898-1908. *Minnesota Hist. 1971 42(7): 243-257.* Explains how state conservation groups compromised on legislative proposals that led to the creation of the Minnesota National Forest in 1908. Controversy over timber harvesting on ceded Chippewa Indian land prompted the Minnesota Federation of Women's Clubs to propose that Congress make the area into a national park in 1899. After other groups and individuals offered conflicting proposals, the women adopted the forest reserve plan of Herman Haupt Chapman, a University of Minnesota forester. The united conservationists encountered stiff opposition from northern Minnesota middle-class farmers and entrepreneuers who hoped to exploit local land and timber resources to the fullest, but Chapman and Gifford Pinchot, chief of the US Forestry Bureau, persuaded the state congressional delegation to co-sponsor a bill creating the Minnesota Forest Reserve. Congress passed this measure in 1902 and approved the Minnesota National Forest Act six years later. Based on primary and secondary sources; illus., 7 photos, map, 48 notes.
                                                         G. R. Adams

1287. Thorpe, Elizabeth J. THE OWLS OF NEWCASTLE. *Montana: Mag. of Western Hist. 1969 19(2): 71-73.* A score of women in a frontier town attempted to offset their isolation by forming a club to encourage cultural and educational interests. On becoming one of the first federated clubs in Wyoming in 1909 its name was changed from the "Owls" to the "Twentieth Century Club." Undocumented, illus.
                                                         S. R. Davison

1288. Wolfe, Allis Rosenberg. WOMEN, CONSUMERISM, AND THE NATIONAL CONSUMERS' LEAGUE IN THE PROGRESSIVE ERA, 1900-1923. *Labor Hist. 1976 16(3): 378-392.* Contends that a growing consciousness about women's roles as consumers provided a base from which the National Consumers' League arose. Activities of the League were primarily in protective legislation for women and the ethical control of consumption. Never a mass organization, the League declined by 1923. Based on dissertations, records of the Massachusetts Consumers' League, and secondary sources; 29 notes.                    L. L. Athey

# World War I

1289. Brommel, Bernard J. KATE RICHARDS O'HARE: A MIDWESTERN PACIFIST'S FIGHT FOR FREE SPEECH. *North Dakota Q. 1976 44(1): 5-19.* Describes events leading up to the arrest, trial and conviction (1900-25) of major Socialist Party and leftist movement figure, Kate Richards O'Hare, in North Dakota for violating the Espionage Act of 1917 by speaking out against World War I.

1290. Corcoran, Theresa. VIDA DUTTON SCUDDER: THE IMPACT OF WORLD WAR I ON THE RADICAL WOMAN PROFESSOR. *Anglican Theological R. 1975 57(2): 164-180.*

1291. Greenwald, Maureen. WOMEN WORKERS AND WORLD WAR I: THE AMERICAN RAILROAD INDUSTRY, A CASE STUDY. *J. of Social Hist. 1975 9(2): 154-177.* World War I records of the railroad industry shows women moved into jobs already identified as women's jobs. During 1917-30 the number of women workers increased 42%. 55 notes.                                            M. Hough

1292. Malan, Nancy E. HOW 'YA GONNA KEEP 'EM DOWN?': WOMEN AND WORLD WAR I. *Prologue 1973 5(4): 209-239.* Brief narrative and pictorial essay of the American woman and her varied and comprehensive service in World War I. Primary and secondary sources; 26 illus.                                            R. W. Tissing, Jr.

1293. Maurer, Maurer. THE COURT-MARTIALING OF CAMP FOLLOWERS, WORLD WAR I. *Am. J. of Legal Hist. 1965 9(3): 203-215.* Using case reports and opinions of the judge advocate general, studies the treatment of civilians connected with the U.S. armed forces in World War I who were subject to military law and discipline. The courts upheld the military jurisdiction and it was later expanded by Congress.                                            N. Brockman

1294. Pope, Theodate. ". . . AND THEN THE WATER CLOSED OVER ME . . ." *Am. Heritage 1975 26(3): 98-101.* A letter written by Miss Pope describing her survival of the sinking of the *Lusitania* on 7 May 1915. 2 illus.                                            B. J. Paul

1295. Pownall, Dorothy Ashby. A GIRL REPORTER AT CAMP DODGE. *Palimpsest 1966 47(6): 225-256.* The author has recorded some of her experiences as a young cub reporter assigned to cover the human interest side of the 88th Division of the National Army stationed at Camp Dodge, Iowa, from 1917 to its demobilization in 1919. Of particular interest are her descriptions of visits to the camp and her interviews of people like Theodore Roosevelt, William Howard Taft, General Pershing, and Madame Schumann-Heink who asked to be called "Mamma Heink." Illus.                                        D. W. Curl

1296. Sterrett, Grace Dubois. THEY HELD DANCES FOR THE "DOUGHBOYS." *Long Island Forum 1973 36(7): 130-133.* Discusses the female members of the Jamaica Masonic Lodge and the dances they held for soldiers during World War I.                                 S

1297. Talmadge, John E. CORRA HARRIS GOES TO WAR. *Georgia R. 1964 18(2): 150-156.* A consideration of the European wartime experiences of the *Saturday Evening Post* fiction writer, Corra Harris. Undocumented.                                        H. G. Earnhart

1298. Watts, Phyllis Atwood. CASEWORK ABOVE THE POVERTY LINE: THE INFLUENCE OF HOME SERVICE IN WORLD WAR I ON SOCIAL WORK. *Social Service R. 1964 38(3): 303-315.*

Traces the creation and development of Home Service in the United States, which began in 1918 in collaboration with the American Red Cross to provide casework services for uprooted soldiers and their families. "Home Service casework 'above the poverty line' tested and expanded theory and practice and facilitated social work's shift from a socioeconomic to a psychological base....The Home Service manuals make clear that the goals were to protect, preserve, and enhance the serviceman's family in all crises and to maintain or improve their living standards....If social workers had retained consciousness of their experience with, and focus on, families above the poverty line who were coping with stress, the integration of psychoanalytic theory of the individual might have been more orderly...without minimizing the greatly deepened understanding achieved in the forty-year interval. As a multifunction agency, Home Service was available to a whole community." 49 notes.

D. D. Cameron

## World War II

1299. Johnson, Ann R. THE WASP IN WORLD WAR II. *Aerospace Hist. 1970 17(2-3): 76-82.* Presents a brief history of the Women's Air Force Service Pilots (WASP). The use of women aircrew members for noncombat flying operations was considered by General H. H. (Hap) Arnold in early 1941, but the program was not begun until late 1942. First using women who had extensive flying experience, the WASP training program was developed at Sweetwater, Texas, to train less-experienced women. The program lasted 30 weeks and included 210 hours of flying time. The ground school was similar to that of aviation cadets, and 1,102 WASPs were graduated and assigned to operational duties, flying all types of aircraft in noncombat roles. The women were considered Civil Service employees and not military. The WASP program officially disbanded in December 1944 when there were enough male pilots to fill the requirements. Details the program as to statistics for training, accidents, medical, etc., and compares the female and male counterparts. 4 photos.

C. W. Ohrvall

1300. McLaughlin, Florence C. DOWN TO THE SEA IN SLIPS. *Western Pennsylvania Hist. Mag. 1968 51(4): 377-387.* The Pittsburgh office of the Navy WAVES (Women Accepted for Volunteer Emergency Service) during World War II was responsible for recruiting women from western Pennsylvania. By the end of its third year in 1945, the office had 3,200 women on active duty. WAVES underwent strict discipline and were trained in a number of technical capacities to relieve men for the battlefront. WAVE recruiters were responsible for going from town to town, making speeches, and signing up enlistees. The Pittsburgh recruiting office was headed by Captain Mildred H. McAfee [later, Horton]. Based on primary and secondary sources; 21 notes.

D. E. Bowers

1301. Quick, Paddy. ROSIE THE RIVETER: MYTHS AND REALITIES. *Radical Am. 1975 9(4-5): 115-132.* Tells of the participation of women in World War II war work.

S

1302. Scargle, Russ. MUSIC AND MEN'S MINDS: A WORLD WAR II VIGNETTE. *Pacific Historian 1972 16(1): 28-35.* A group of Bay Area women entertained hospitalized soldiers with music, 1943-45.

1303. Straub, Eleanor F. UNITED STATES GOVERNMENT POLICY TOWARD CIVILIAN WOMEN DURING WORLD WAR II. *Prologue 1973 5(4): 240-254.* Detailed analysis of the actions and inactions of federal programs concerning civilian women during World War II. Total war created mobilization of women workers for war production, but a combination of elements limited their participation in manpower policies and lessened the war's impact on women's status in American society. Primary and secondary sources; 5 illus., 46 notes.

R. W. Tissing, Jr.

1304. Thompson, Susan Otis. THE AMERICAN LIBRARY IN PARIS: AN INTERNATIONAL DEVELOPMENT IN THE AMERICAN LIBRARY MOVEMENT. *Lib. Q. 1964 34(2): 179-190.* A chronological survey of the organization, services, and contributions of the American Library in Paris since its founding in 1918 to serve American troops. Expansion of its operation prevailed until the depression of the

1930's when only occasional grants and donations enabled the library to maintain minimal service. During World War II the library remained open because of the continued intercession of Dorothy Reeder, Countess of Chambrun. Renewed French interest in America and adequate financial support have enabled the library since 1945 to extend services, enlarge holdings, and play a significant role in teaching American library methods. Sources: printed English-language articles and books.

C. A. Newton

1305. Trey, Joan Ellen. WOMEN IN THE WAR ECONOMY. *Rev. of Radical Pol. Econ. 1972 4(3): 40-57.* Women's experience working in a war economy led to significant change. The war work was popular not only because Hitler was clearly an enemy of women, but also because women were not satisfied at home and wanted work away from it. The same factors work today. Based on contemporary and secondary sources; 49 notes, biblio.

C. P. de Young

1306. —. WORKING WOMEN AND THE WAR: FOUR NARRATIVES. *Radical Am. 1975 9(4-5): 133-162.*
—. INTRODUCTION, *pp. 133-134.*
Clawson, Augusta. SHIPYARD DIARY OF A WOMAN WELDER, *pp. 134-138.*
Archibald, Katherine. WOMEN IN THE SHIPYARD, *pp. 139-144.*
Sonnenberg, Mary. TWO EPISODES, *pp. 145-155.*
Stein, Anne. POST-WAR CONSUMER BOYCOTTS, *pp. 156-162.*
Personal narratives include examples of sex discrimination, betrayals by labor unions, and the 1946 meat boycott in Washington, D.C.

S

## Feminism

### General

1307. Abernathy, Mollie C. SOUTHERN WOMEN, SOCIAL RECONSTRUCTION, AND THE CHURCH IN THE 1920'S. *Louisiana Studies 1974 13(4): 289-312.* Southern radical social feminists comprised a special group of southern women who combined extreme or hard-core feminism and a social reconstructionist program. Despite significant changes in the decades before World War I, the evolution of women's organizations in the South was a decade behind that of their northern sisters, though many southern women served in the Y.W.C.A. "Without the radical social feminists spurring on ordinary southern club and church-women to action little progress pertaining to women would have been accomplished during the reactionary decade of the 1920's." 60 notes.

E. P. Stickney

1308. Boydston, Jo Ann. JOHN DEWEY AND THE NEW FEMINISM. *Teachers Coll. Record 1975 76(3): 441-448.* John Dewey, long known as a leading educational reformer, was also a "forerunner" on the "woman question." His views are clearly expressed in his correspondence with Scudder Klyce. In public he restricted his comments to the issues of coeducation and suffrage, but he wrote on a broad spectrum of concerns in this correspondence.

W. H. Mulligan, Jr.

1309. Brown, Ira V. THE WOMAN'S RIGHTS MOVEMENT IN PENNSYLVANIA, 1848-1873. *Pa. Hist. 1965 32(2): 153-165.* On 19 and 20 July 1848 some three hundred people attended the Seneca Falls Convention for women's rights, led by Lucretia Mott of Philadelphia. This convention was the beginning of an organized women's reform movement that extended across the States. "The immediate matrix of organized feminism was the anti-slavery movement." Early gains for women were made in the area of education where several colleges were opened to women. However, women made no great gains in the area of politics during this period. The 14th and the 15th ammendments were a crushing blow to the feminist movement. In 1869 the feminists at last formed national organizations - the National Woman Suffrage Association and the American Woman Suffrage Association. Pennsylvania's development of feminist organizations paralleled the national trend as local suffrage groups developed. The culmination of the early women's reform movement in Pennsylvania occurred with the Constitutional Convention of 1872-73. This convention voted down a proposal to refer the question of women's suffrage to a popular referendum. Although the feminist movement made some headway between 1848 and 1873, it did not succeed in the area of politics until 1920.                          M. J. McBaine

1310. Eaton, Clement. BREAKING A PATH FOR THE LIBERATION OF WOMEN IN THE SOUTH. *Georgia R. 1974 28(2): 187-199.* With chivalry and the Bible as its guide, the South placed enormous restraints on the rights of women. Neverless, a small group of women spoke out against the double standard applied to southern females. Leading the struggle for equal rights for women were Rebecca L. Felton, Ellen Glasgow, Gertrude T. Clanton, Belle Kearney, Kate Gordon, Laura Clay, and Kate Chopin, all of whom had a part in the liberation of women.                                                    M. B. Lucas

1311. Ek, Richard A. VICTORIA WOODHULL AND THE PHARISEES. *Journalism Q. 1972 49(3): 453-459.* Women's liberation champion Victoria Woodhull's fiery speeches (1873) forced the press to speak more openly of 19th-century social ills.                      S

1312. Foner, Philip S. A PENNSYLVANIA STATE SENATOR ON WOMEN'S RIGHTS IN 1868. *Pennsylvania Hist. 1974 41(4): 423-426.* Presents a letter written in 1868 by State Senator Morrow B. Lowry of Meadville endorsing the equal right of women to higher education. The letter was written to a resident of Smethport, Pennsylvania. Lowry, a forgotten figure in Pennsylvania history, was a philanthropist and radical abolitionist. The letter is in the Frederick Douglass papers; illus., 3 notes.
                                                            D. C. Swift

1313. Freedman, Estelle B. THE NEW WOMAN: CHANGING VIEWS OF WOMEN IN THE 1920'S. *J. of Am. Hist. 1974 61(2): 372-393.* Historians have not been consistent in their evaluation of the women's movement in the 1920's. They have differed in their evaluation of the uses to which women put the newly acquired economic parity with men, and in their attitudes toward reality of the sexual revolution of the 20's. Most recent works by William O'Neill and William Chafe see women as having made little progress in either the political or nonpolitical realms in the period, though they differ in whether this failure should be attributed to splits within the feminist movement or to social barriers to full emancipation. Common to nearly all studies is a tendency toward broad and unsubstantiated generalizations about women without fully recognizing class, race, region, and ethnicity. 63 notes.
                                                            K. B. West

1314. Glazer, Penina Migdal ORGANIZING FOR FREEDOM. *Massachusetts R. 1972 13(1/2): 29-44.* The women's suffrage movement was the largest, most well-organized, and effective feminist movement in the history of women's rights. However, it was not a unified, one-dimensional movement. Analyzes the radical wing of the women's suffrage movement as it expressed itself in the Settlement House and Women's Trade Union League movement. Unlike the moderates and conservatives who merely wanted equal rights for women within the existing sociopolitical system, the radicals wanted to secure women's rights as a springboard to radical social reform throughout society. Based on primary and secondary sources; 23 notes, biblio.                          G. Kurland

1315. Gordon, Linda. ARE THE INTERESTS OF MEN AND WOMEN INDENTICAL? *Signs 1976 1(4): 1011-1018.* During the early 20th century the Socialist Party organized women's branches in 156 party locals. At that time it was the only political party to allow women's participation and endorse equal rights and woman suffrage. The attempt to create a socialist feminism anchored in the working-class experience failed, in part due to the reluctance of socialist men to incorporate feminism into their program, and partly due to the legalistic middle-class women's rights movement which could not offer much to working class or radical women. The attempt to create a mass movement, however, advanced the analysis of women's situation. Based on three newspaper articles; 6 notes.                                        J. Gammage

1316. Israel, Jerry. THE MISSIONARY CATALYST: BISHOP JAMES W. BASHFORD AND THE SOCIAL GOSPEL IN CHINA. *Methodist Hist. 1975 14(1): 24-43.* James W. Bashford, bishop of the Methodist Episcopal Church and missionary to China, saw commercial dominance of the Pacific Ocean by the United States as the final stage in the development of civilization. He also thought the United States had the

ability to export its domestic success, particularly in dealing with social problems, including educational reform and women's rights. 85 notes.
                                                            H. L. Calkin

1317. McGovern, James R. ANNA HOWARD SHAW: NEW APPROACHES TO FEMINISM. *J. of Social Hist. 1969/70 3(2): 135-154.* Anna Howard Shaw (1847-1919), ordained minister, suffrage leader, and vice-president and later president of Susan B. Anthony's National Woman's Organization, had a personal psychology typical among those who led the women's movement. She had an unhappy childhood, pitied but did not respect her mother, competed with her domineering father, and finally left home to become a minister. Shaw's activities within the feminist movement had deep psychological roots separate from the movement's ideology. Susan B. Anthony, Charlotte Gilman, Margaret Sanger, Lucy Anthony, and others had similar drives and behavioral experiences and, like Shaw, devoted their lives to the feminist cause. Based on archival collections, biographical, and autobiographical works, and secondary sources; 101 notes.                                    J. P. Harahan

1318. Oneal, Marion Sherrard. NEW ORLEANS SCENES. *Louisiana Hist. 1965 6(2): 189-209.* Includes reminiscences of an orphans' picnic and a Mardi Gras, both in the 1890's, and of a rights for women meeting in 1903. At this meeting Mrs. Carrie Chapman Catt "urged us to fight, and if necessary to bleed, for freedom"; Doctor Anna Shaw was present, looking "motherly and sympathetic"; and Charlotte Perkins Gilman "filled the air with cries of how badly we were treated, and how we should rise up and fight for our down-trodden sex."
                                                            E. P. Stickney

1319. Preston, L. E. SPEAKERS FOR WOMEN'S RIGHTS IN PENNSYLVANIA. *Western Pennsylvania Hist. Mag. 1971 54(3): 245-263.* Profiles the careers and achievements (1837-1920) of pro-feminists in Pennsylvania, culminating in the ratification of the 19th Amendment.
                                                            S

1320. Riegel, Robert E. WOMEN'S CLOTHES AND WOMEN'S RIGHTS. *Am. Q. 1963 15(3): 390-401.* The dress reform movement, strong in the 1850's, disappeared during the Civil War but revived vigorously in the 1870's. During World War I it disappeared but failed to revive in the 1920's when feminism itself had lost its impetus. And yet dress became lighter and skimpier and skirts shorter, providing great freedom of movement. In this way the prophecy of the *Woman's Journal* in 1870 that reformed dress "is dependent upon and must come after suffrage," was borne out. "Improved clothes had in fact played no part in feminine emancipation, but feminine emancipation had brought greater dress reform than the most visionary of the early feminists had advocated." Based largely on contemporary newspapers and magazines.
                                                            E. P. Stickney

1321. Scott, Clifford H. A NATURALISTIC RATIONALE FOR WOMEN'S REFORM: LESTER FRANK WARD ON THE EVOLUTION OF SEXUAL RELATIONS. *Historian 1970 33(1): 54-67.* Trained in biology and paleontology and a member of the scientific bureaucracy in Washington, Ward (1841-1913) became a late 19th-century advocate of women's rights. He was convinced that the female sex was then in economic, political, and intellectual bondage to males because of belief in an outdated biological theory that man is primary and woman secondary in the organic scheme. The inequality imposed on women in the past, Ward argued, had become so institutionalized that they had come to glory in their subjugation. His attempt to provide evolutionary and scientific ammunition in the cause of popular reform was noticed and capitalized on by only a few feminist leaders of his day. Based primarily on Ward's books and articles; 31 notes.                          N. W. Moen

1322. Shimda, Noriko et al. UME TSUDA AND MOTOKO HANI: ECHOES OF AMERICAN CULTURAL FEMINISM IN JAPAN. George, Carol V. R., ed. *"Remember the Ladies": New Perspectives on Women in American History: Essays in Honor of Nelson Manfred Blake* (Syracuse: Syracuse U. Pr., 1975): 161-178. Ume Tsuda (1864-1929) and Motoko Hani (1873-1957) were "new women" who promoted cultural feminism in Japan during 1900-30. Their work to free women from discriminatory practices rested on education not political action. Born in Japan, Tsuda lived and attended school in the United States. Returning to Japan, she was struck by the power men held over women and set out to rid the women of their inferior position. Borrowing from her American experiences, Tsuda established a school for upper-class women. It combined traditional Japanese manners and etiquette with liberal arts education and teacher training to produce well-rounded, liberated women capable of being more than ladylike, obedient wives. Hani confronted the task of liberating middle- and lower-class housewives. Educated in Tokyo, she absorbed egalitarian principles from Christianity, and attended the most liberal schools in the 1890's. Subsequently, she embarked upon an unconventional career as a journalist and published a magazine for the "new woman." She stressed the importance of the home as the basic social unit and as an agent for social change in which the housewife played the key role. She also advocated vocational training for women's economic independence. In 1921, she established a school for girls to perpetuate her ideas. Based on primary and secondary sources; 26 notes.

P. R. Byrne

1323. Sklar, Kathryn Kish. "ALL HAIL TO PURE COLD WATER!" *Am. Heritage 1974 26(1): 64-69, 100-101.* In the second half of the 19th century the water cure, or hydropathy, was popularized by women who were also involved in promoting dress reform, temperance, women's rights, and medical reform. The water cure consisted of numerous baths, exercise, simple food, and extended stays at a sanitarium. Victorian women received sympathy and understanding from water-cure physicians. 3 illus.

B. J. Paul

1324. Sochen, June. HENRIETTA RODMAN AND THE FEMINIST ALLIANCE: 1914-1917. *J. of Popular Culture 1970 4(1): 57-65.* One of the main projects of the Feminist Alliance was a modern housing structure for professional women to be built in Washington Square, a collective venture including child care and delivery of prepared food to the individual apartments.

S

## Suffrage

1325. Alexander, Thomas G. AN EXPERIMENT IN PROGRESSIVE LEGISLATION: THE GRANTING OF WOMAN SUFFRAGE IN UTAH IN 1870. *Utah Hist. Q. 1970 38(1): 20-30.* The granting of woman suffrage in Utah Territory in 1870 reflected a general sentiment favoring reform and humane progressive action. Nationally the act was viewed as strengthening rather than weakening polygamy and in the Edmunds-Tucker Act (1887), Congress disfranchised all women in the territory.

S. L. Jones

1326. Blocker, Jack S., Jr. THE POLITICS OF REFORM: POPULISTS, PROHIBITION, AND WOMAN SUFFRAGE, 1891-1892. *Historian 1972 34(4): 614-632.* Analyzes deliberations and arguments about goals and platforms of Populism at its formative conventions in Cincinnati and St. Louis. Argues that the Populist movement was primarily political; when confronted with the need to win elections, interest in reform—especially causes then categorized as "moral reform"— became subordinate to practical politics. Based on the contemporary press and the national organs of such groups as the Prohibition party, Farmers' Alliance, and the Knights of Labor. 81 notes.

N. W. Moen

1327. Bosmajian, Haig A. THE ABROGATION OF THE SUFFRAGISTS' FIRST AMENDMENT RIGHTS. *Western Speech 1974 38(4): 218-232.* Covers the period 1912-19; mentions the National Women's Party.

S

1328. Buenker, John D. THE URBAN POLITICAL MACHINE AND WOMAN SUFFRAGE: A STUDY IN POLITICAL ADAPTABILITY. *Historian 1971 33(2): 264-279.* A State-by-State analysis of the operation of what Richard Hofstadter in 1955 called the "boss-immigrant-machine complex" in *Age of Reform* (New York: Random House). Examination of the Northeastern industrial section of the United States shows that although these complexes tended to be reactionary during much of the 19th century, they became responsive to many of the reforms advocated during the Progressive era. Uses the contemporary press, journals of State legislatures, and accounts of the movement to show how and why machines in cities such as Chicago, Boston, Cleveland, Philadelphia, and New York reversed initial opposition to become solid if not enthusiastic supporters of woman suffrage. 51 notes.

N. W. Moen

1329. Cheney, Lynne. HOW ALICE PAUL BECAME THE MOST MILITANT FEMINIST OF THEM ALL. *Smithsonian 1972 3(8): 94-100.* Alice Paul, despite her petite size, became the most militant leader of the woman suffrage movement, 1914-23.

1330. Cheney, Lynne. IT ALL BEGAN IN WYOMING. *Am. Heritage 1973 24(3): 62-66, 97.* Details the fight for the first woman suffrage law led by Esther Morris, and its passage in Wyoming in 1869. S

1331. Chittenden, Elizabeth F. "BY NO MEANS EXCLUDING WOMEN"; ABIGAIL SCOTT DUNIWAY, WESTERN PIONEER IN THE STRUGGLE FOR EQUAL VOTING RIGHTS. *Am. West 1975 12(2): 24-27.* A biographical sketch of suffragette Abigail Scott Duniway (b. 1834) who spearheaded the movement which culminated in the Equal Suffrage Amendment to the constitution of Oregon in 1912. She was also active in the national movement. 2 illus., bibliographic note.

D. L. Smith

1332. Drake, St. Clair. URBAN VIOLENCE AND AMERICAN SOCIAL MOVEMENTS. *Pro. of the Acad. of Pol. Sci. 1968 29(1): 13-24.* "Violence in the cities . . . is nothing new," although "the involvement of Negroes in urban violence is of increasingly serious concern to the nation, for members of this particular ethnic group are now concentrated at the nerve centers of American life." Believes that some consideration of the past can increase our understanding "and place contemporary problems in a perspective that renders decision making less hasty and improvised." Three past social movements which involved some amount of urban violence are discussed: the abolition movement, the labor movement, and the woman suffrage movement. Discusses various black views on the use of violence to gain desired ends. The problem for the blacks is that at some point "violence is likely to become counterproductive," bringing about "severe repression, with the locus of the backlash being in the white working-class strata."

A. N. Garland

1333. Fry, Amelia. ALONG THE SUFFRAGE TRAIL: FROM WEST TO EAST FOR FREEDOM NOW! *Am. West 1969 6(1): 16-25.* A half century of agitation enfranchised women in a dozen western states. The activist suffragist Congressional Union was impatient for this reform to be written into the Federal Constitution. A freedom booth at the Panama Pacific International Exposition in San Francisco in 1915 resulted in a petition on an 18-thousand-foot roll of paper that boasted a half-million signatures. A five-day Women Voters' Convention whipped up enthusiasm for a cross-country mission to add names to the petition, garner public statements of support from local congressmen, and to stage parades and rallies. Although transcontinental automobile travel was still a rigorous pioneering venture, grass widow Sara Bard Field accepted the challenge to take the cause and the suffrage petition to President Woodrow Wilson himself and to the Congress for its opening of the 1915-16 session. Two ladies had just bought an Overland and wanted to drive it to Rhode Island. They offered to take Sara Field on the jaunt from San Francisco to Washington by way of New England. No detail was overlooked; a female press agent preceded her, by train, to round up autocades, bands, mayors, congressmen, and governors, thus assuring fitting receptions in each city on the way. Not without considerable hardship and opposition, the mission was completed. The 19th amendment was not proposed and ratified into the Constitution, however, until after the war, in 1920. Based partly on Sara Bard Field's oral history manuscript; 11 illus., biblio. note.

D. L. Smith

1334. Furer, Howard B. THE AMERICAN CITY: A CATALYST FOR THE WOMEN'S RIGHTS MOVEMENT. *Wisconsin Mag. of Hist. 1969 52(4): 285-305.* Increasing industrialization and urbanization in late 19th-century America influenced and quickened the coming of woman suffrage.

S

1335. Hall, Robert F. WOMEN HAVE BEEN VOTING EVER SINCE. *Adirondack Life 1971 2(1): 46-49.* Inez Milholland Boissevain (1886-1916) was an activist in the feminist movement. She enrolled two-thirds of her Vassar classmates in the feminist movement. Later she led the 1913 inauguration day parade to force Congress into action on the suffrage amendment. When Woodrow Wilson favored State action on women's rights in 1916, Boissevain campaigned for Charles Evans Hughes. She died shortly after the election, probably of leukemia. Based on interviews; 13 illus.

D. R. Jamieson

1336. Jensen, Billie Barnes. COLORADO WOMAN SUFFRAGE CAMPAIGNS OF THE 1870'S. *J. of the West 1973 12(2): 254-271.* Colorado did not achieve woman suffrage until 1893, but the campaign of the 1870's paved the way to victory. Although the issue was widely discussed in the legislature, the newspapers provided the best forum for public opinion. The constitutional convention of 1876 denied women the right to vote in general elections but gave them the right of franchise and office-holding in school districts, provided for a referendum process, and occasioned the organization of a woman suffrage association. 91 notes.
E. P. Stickney

1337. Jensen, Billie Barnes. LET THE WOMEN VOTE. *Colorado Mag. 1964 41(1): 13-26.* Examines the successful drive for woman suffrage in Colorado, 1893.

1338. Johnson, Kenneth R. FLORIDA WOMEN GET THE VOTE. *Fla. Hist. Q. 1970 48(3): 299-312.* Beginning in 1912 with the organization of the Florida Equal Franchise League, a few women worked long and hard to secure woman suffrage in Florida. Organized in 1913, the Florida Equal Suffrage Association carried on the main fight. Unsuccessful attempts by the Florida suffragists to obtain passage of a constitutional amendment by the legislature in 1913, 1915, and 1917, and a better organized request in 1919, made it evident that action for woman suffrage in Florida would depend on the national Congress. The woman suffrage amendment, passed by Congress in June 1919, became law in August 1920 when Tennessee became the 36th State to ratify it, while Florida won the unique honor of being the last State to take action. Despite concern of Democratic leaders in Florida that Florida women might become Republican, their economic interests and social preferences were the same as those of their husbands and fathers; they voted in the Democratic column. Apparently, two-thirds of potential women voters in Florida in 1920 did not vote; therefore, it would appear that no widespread need was satisfied by the 19th amendment. Based on unpublished letters, dissertations, newspapers, and secondary material; 54 notes.
R. V. Calvert

1339. Johnson, Kenneth R. KATE GORDON AND THE WOMAN-SUFFRAGE MOVEMENT IN THE SOUTH. *J. of Southern Hist. 1972 38(3): 365-392.* Kate M. Gordon of New Orleans and other "states' rightists without hesitation joined the forces which had consistently opposed women suffrage and worked to prevent ratification in Louisiana and Mississippi." Any federal control of the elective process seemed to pose a threat to states' rights and white supremacy. "They were successful in these states, but by August 1920, 36 states had ratified the federal amendment. Ms. Gordon and her cohorts were thus enfranchised by federal action despite their best efforts." 94 notes.
I. M. Leonard

1340. Kenneally, James J. CATHOLICISM AND WOMAN SUFFRAGE IN MASSACHUSETTS. *Catholic Hist. R. 1967 53(1): 43-57.* The leadership of the Catholic community in late 19th-century Massachusetts opposed woman suffrage, not only as contrary to natural law but also due to its association with other "reforms" - particularly nativism. But with a change in political and social conditions, many Catholics began to support woman suffrage with the result that a rather reluctant clergy substituted a public profession of "neutrality" for their outspoken opposition, and thus removed the question from the sphere of religion.
A

1341. Kenneally, James J. WOMAN SUFFRAGE AND THE MASSACHUSETTS "REFERENDUM" OF 1895. *Historian 1968 30(4): 617-633.* After the Civil War, feminists believed that women's rights would march hand in hand with Negro freedom because the objectives of each group rested on the common denominator of equality before the law without distinction as to sex or color. When the 14th amendment proved to contain the word "male," movements were founded to secure votes for women in State elections. The author tells of suffrage agitation in Massachusetts, culminating in a referendum on the question, the only one in a large Eastern State before 1915. Based on newspapers and the papers of various Massachusetts suffrage organizations held in the Houghton Library at Harvard University and the Massachusetts Historical Society in Boston.
N. W. Moen

1342. Kolmer, Elizabeth. NINETEENTH CENTURY WOMAN'S RIGHTS MOVEMENT. *Negro Hist. Bull. 1972 35(8): 179-180.* Examines the racial attitudes of the leaders of the woman's suffrage movement and the reasons for Negroes organizing separate woman's groups in the 1890's.
S

1343. Kraditor, Aileen S. TACTICAL PROBLEMS OF THE WOMAN-SUFFRAGE MOVEMENT IN THE SOUTH. *Louisiana Studies 1966 5(4): 289-305.* A discourse on the women's suffrage movement in the South that begins with a statement of conditions that delayed the movement a generation after it appeared in the Northeast. Five reasons that Clement Eaton suggested in his *The Freedom-of-Thought Struggle in the Old South* (New York: Harper, 1964) for the weakness of the women's rights movement in the middle of the 19th century are given. Then the observation is made that the rise of a women's rights movement is dependent on "a group of educated, capable women who need outlets for their energies" and "a lack of such outlets that are socially acceptable." Southern women had special problems caused by four circumstances peculiar to their region. These were: 1) the South was the most conservative region with regard to the woman's role, 2) the South was a one-party section, 3) the states' rights shibboleth created special problems for a movement to amend the Federal Constitution, and 4) the Negro question. Each of the four circumstances is discussed. 28 notes.
G. W. McGinty

1344. Larson, T. A. DOLLS, VASSALS, AND DRUDGES - PIONEER WOMEN IN THE WEST. *Western Hist. Q. 1972 3(1): 4-16.* Population in the Territory of Wyoming plummeted after the completion of the transcontinental railroad. In 1869 the half-bachelor territorial legislature passed a woman suffrage law. The most effective arguments in favor of this precedent were assurances that the Territory would thereby receive much free publicity and advertising and that it would promote immigration, including significant numbers of women. For varying reasons enough momentum developed so that the Western States, except New Mexico, had all granted the franchise to women by 1914. Kansas was the only State outside the western third of the country to enact such legislation. No simple explanation explains the West's priority in the matter of woman suffrage. One suffragette insisted that to deprive women the right to vote kept them from self-development. Keeping this opportunity from them made "dolls of society women, vassals of most wives, and hopeless drudges of the rest." Illus., 13 notes.
D. L. Smith

1345. Larson, T. A. EMANCIPATING THE WEST'S DOLLS, VASSALS AND HOPELESS DRUDGES: THE ORIGINS OF WOMAN SUFFRAGE IN THE WEST. *U. of Wyoming Pub. 1971 37: 1-16.* Examines the reasons the Territories of Wyoming and Utah adopted woman suffrage in 1869. Expediency rather than liberal democratic attitudes moved both governments. Wyoming legislators wanted to gain free publicity, to attract a female population to their territory, to immortalize themselves, and to embarrass the Governor. In Utah the major reasons were a desire for equal justice for women and an attempt to counteract the campaign against polygamy. Older reasons such as chivalry, strengthening the home against transients and bachelors, and rewarding helpmates cannot be substantiated by facts. In every western State, different factors worked for woman suffrage. 85 notes.
H. B. Powell

1346. Larson, T. A. IDAHO'S ROLE IN AMERICA'S WOMEN SUFFRAGE CRUSADE. *Idaho Yesterdays 1974 18(1): 2-15.*

1347. Larson, T. A. MONTANA WOMEN AND THE BATTLE OF THE BALLOT. *Montana: Mag. of Western Hist. 1973 23(1): 24-41.* Efforts to write woman suffrage into Montana's 1889 constitution failed. Montana women, especially "society women," did not strongly support the suffragists. Help from national leaders and from Jeannette Rankin (b. 1880), soon to be the nation's first congresswoman, led to success in 1914 when voters ratified a suffrage amendment passed by the legislature the previous year. Based on contemporary periodicals and correspondence; 46 notes.
S. R. Davison

1348. Larson, T. A. WOMAN SUFFRAGE IN WYOMING. *Pacific Northwest Q. 1965 56(2): 57-66.* Evidence on why woman suffrage came to Wyoming first, with the history of events and people contributing to the successful enfranchising of women. One section gives the reasons for women enjoying voting rights without other political power in early days.　　　　　　C. C. Gorchels

1349. Larson, T. A. WOMAN SUFFRAGE IN WESTERN AMERICA. *Utah Hist. Q. 1970 38(1): 7-19.* Suggests that, although the spirit of the frontier may have been a significant factor in producing woman suffrage in Western states and territories in some instances, and particularly in Wyoming and Utah, mere chance turned the trick.
　　　　　　S. L. Jones

1350. Larson, T. A. THE WOMEN'S RIGHTS MOVEMENT IN IDAHO. *Idaho Yesterdays 1972 16(1): 2-15, 18-19.* In Idaho the first territorial legislative vote on women's suffrage failed by a tie vote in 1871. Although women like Abigail S. Duniway and Carrie C. Catt, along with the Woman's Christian Temperance Union and National American Woman Suffrage Association kept the issue alive, it wasn't until 1896 that a state constitutional amendment was passed. Primary sources; 3 illus., 77 notes.　　　　　　B. Paul

1351. Larson, T. A. WYOMING STATEHOOD. *Ann. of Wyoming 1965 37(1): 4-29.* Discusses the movement for statehood in Wyoming, particularly during the 1880's, and shows that the Republican territorial governor and territorial delegate led their party in this movement. Wyoming Democrats either opposed statehood or wanted to wait until they controlled the territorial government. Describes the state constitutional convention and lists the major disputes as: size of counties, organization of the state judiciary system, woman suffrage, legislative apportionment, taxes on mining corporations, and the location of permanent state institutions. Illus., 10 notes.　　　　　　R. L. Nichols

1352. Loewy, Jean. KATHERINE PHILIPS EDSON AND THE CALIFORNIA SUFFRAGETTE MOVEMENT, 1919-1920. *Calif. Hist. Soc. Q. 1968 47(4): 343-350.* In one decade (1911-21) Katherine Philips Edson moved from a suffragette to a Presidential appointee as a member of an international conference (Washington Conference on the Limitations of Armaments, 1921). The author details her political career in California including her membership in and chairmanship of the State Industrial Welfare Commission from 1913 to 1931. She played an important part in the passage of the state's equal suffrage referendum in 1911. When woman suffrage again became important to California, she was a delegate to the 50th Anniversary Jubilee Convention of the National American Woman Suffrage Association in March 1919 which led to the passage of the 19th amendment and the formation of the League of Women Voters. The California Legislature did not meet in special session for the exclusive purpose of ratifying the amendment until 1 November 1919. This paper was presented at the regional meeting of the Southern California branch of the national history honorary society Phi Alpha Theta in 1963. 35 notes.　　　　　　E. P. Stickney

1353. Louis, James P. SUE SHELTON WHITE AND THE WOMAN SUFFRAGE MOVEMENT IN TENNESSEE, 1913-20. *Tennessee Hist. Q. 1963 22(2): 170-190.* Explores her role in national agitation leading to the 19th Amendment to the Constitution. State work with the American Woman Suffrage Association and after 1917 with the National Woman's Party helped the amendment's decisive ratification in Tennessee by a bare minimum of votes. Her bent as a feminist and not merely a woman suffragist is emphasized. 58 notes, few from published sources, drawn largely from the White Papers at Radcliffe College, and letters.　　　　　　W. A. Klutts

1354. Mahoney, Joseph F. WOMAN SUFFRAGE AND THE URBAN MASSES. *New Jersey Hist. 1969 87(3): 151-172.* Discusses the woman suffrage movement in metropolitan areas of New Jersey, including the activities of the Women's Political Union, the New Jersey Woman Suffrage Movement, and the Men's League for Woman Suffrage, 1915. 10 photos, 5 graphs.

1355. Mansfield, Dorothy M. ABIGAIL S. DUNIWAY: SUFFRAGETTE WITH NOT-SO-COMMON SENSE. *Western Speech 1971 35(1): 24-29.* Examines reasons for the disassociation of the woman suffrage movement from the prohibition movement. Suggests that while the lack of women's freedom created some dishonesty in the home, Abigail S. Duniway's argument that women's rights would lead to a moral community lacked any basis. 13 notes.　　　　　　L. Russell

1356. McFarland, Charles K. and Neal, Nevin E. THE RELUCTANT REFORMER: WOODROW WILSON AND WOMAN SUFFRAGE, 1913-1920. *Rocky Mountain Social Sci. J. 1974 11(2): 33-43.*

1357. McKenna, Jeanne. "WITH THE HELP OF GOD AND LUCY STONE." *Kan. Hist. Q. 1970 36(1): 13-26.* An account of the election of 1867 in Kansas with special emphasis on the unsuccessful effort to secure the ratification of two amendments enfranchising Negroes and women. Samuel Newitt Wood (1825-91), the leading personality in the State legislature, is shown to have played a key role in the campaign. He made his major effort in support of woman suffrage by organizing a Kansas Impartial Suffrage Association and bypassing the local Republicans to work directly with powerful suffrage interests in the East. His motives were mixed. He may have wished to build a national political following or to sell land to eastern suffragists. Whether his motives were personal gain or lofty idealism, Wood gave himself unstintingly to the campaign. Based on local newspapers and manuscripts in the Kansas State Historical Society and the Library of Congress; illus., 46 notes.　　　　　　W. F. Zornow

1358. McPherson, James M. ABOLITIONISTS, WOMAN SUFFRAGE, AND THE NEGRO, 1865-1869. *Mid-America 1965 47(1): 40-47.* When the Civil War ended, many feminists wanted to unite the cause of the woman and the Negro, and to work for the simultaneous elevation of both classes to civil and political equality. But because of the political exigencies of Reconstruction, most abolitionists desired to concentrate on the attainment of Negro suffrage while the opportunity was favorable, and to postpone the drive for woman suffrage. The result was the schism of 1869 in the woman suffrage movement.
　　　　　　L. D. Silveri

1359. Morris, John R. THE WOMEN AND GOVERNOR WAITE. *Colorado Mag. 1967 44(1): 11-19.* It was during the term of Davis Waite as governor of Colorado that women gained voting rights in that state. Such an act was his greatest legislative accomplishment; but, strangely enough, the next year Waite turned against suffrage and toured the country speaking in opposition. In this monograph the most dramatic episode in the story of equal rights in Colorado is outlined. Because of the approval of Colorado males, their female counterparts were given the right to vote in 1893. After this success Waite commented that women should be allowed to vote because there should be no taxation without representation, and the right to vote should be based on intelligence, not sex. If women paid taxes and possessed enough intelligence to protest unfair laws they should vote. However, after Waite was defeated in 1894, he changed his mind and came to believe that the majority of the women had voted against him. Despite this change of heart, he gave Colorado women the vote. Illus.　　　　　　R. Sexauer

1360. Nugent, Walter T. K. HOW THE POPULISTS LOST IN 1894. *Kansas Hist. Q. 1965 31(3): 245-255.* During the two years that followed their successes in the 1892 election, the Populists in Kansas were weakened by a series of national and local misfortunes. The depression of 1893 and the Pullman strike of 1894 were events that cast a long shadow. The inexperienced Populists of Kansas were further hurt by their inability to carry out a local reform program in 1893. Republican leader Cyrus Leland may have played an astute game by using his own influence and that of dissident Populists to get the Populist Party to take a position on prohibition and woman's suffrage totally unacceptable to the Democrats. Failing to get Democratic support and arguing among themselves, the Populists were easy targets in 1894. Based on local newspapers.
　　　　　　W. F. Zornow

1361. Petersen, William J. EQUAL RIGHTS FOR ALL! *Palimpsest 1970 51(1): 27-37.* Discusses and reprints Iowa newspaper opinion on Negro rights, women's suffrage, and Indian rights, 1869-70.

1362. Porter, Melba Dean. MADELINE MC DOWELL BRECKINRIDGE: HER ROLE IN THE KENTUCKY WOMAN SUFFRAGE MOVEMENT, 1908-1920. *Register of the Kentucky Hist. Soc. 1974 72(4): 342-363.* Mrs. Breckinridge was a major force in Kentucky's ratification of the 19th amendment. Working through the Federation of Women's Clubs and, after 1912, the Kentucky Equal Rights Association, she devoted her life to many reforms, but primarily to the cause of woman suffrage on both state and national levels. Replacing Laura Clay as head of the KERA in 1912, she lived to see Kentucky become the 24th state to ratify in 1920. Based on primary and secondary sources; 101 notes.                                                               J. F. Paul

1363. Prescott, Grace Elizabeth. THE WOMAN SUFFRAGE MOVEMENT IN MEMPHIS: ITS PLACE IN THE STATE, SECTIONAL AND NATIONAL MOVEMENTS. *West Tennessee Hist. Soc. Papers 1964 18: 87-106.* Describes the movement from the days of Mrs. Elizabeth Avery Meriwether, first Southerner who lectured for woman suffrage, in 1876, to the struggle for the ratification of the 19th Amendment in which Tennessee's vote was decisive. 98 notes from published sources, newspapers, and personal interviews.

W. A. Klutts

1364. Reichard, Gary W. THE DEFEAT OF GOVERNOR ROBERTS. *Tennessee Hist. Q. 1971 30(1): 94-109.* The gubernatorial election of 1920 is one of only two Republican victories in Tennessee in the 20th century. The simple answer to the defeat of an incumbent Governor by a Republican is to attribute the victory to the Harding landslide. Such an interpretation ignores a number of issues in Tennessee politics which were primarily responsible for Roberts' defeat. These issues were: the unpopularity of Roberts' tax reform scheme, a brutally divisive Democratic primary, and the drama surrounding the Governor's support of the enfranchisement of women. Primary and secondary sources; 54 notes.

M. B. Lucas

1365. Richey, Elinor. THE UNSINKABLE ABIGAIL. *Am. Heritage 1975 26(2): 72-75, 86-89.* Abigail Scott Duniway (1835-1915) was a leader in the women's suffrage movement in the Pacific Northwest for over four decades. Editing her own paper, she spread her cause through writing, lecturing, and lobbying. Her efforts led to the passage of suffrage legislation in Idaho, Washington, and Oregon. 6 illus.     J. F. Paul

1366. Robbins, Peggy. SUSAN B. ANTHONY. *Am. Hist. Illus. 1971 6(5): 36-43.* Susan Brownell Anthony (1820-1906) was born in Adams, Massachusetts, of Quaker parents. In the late 1840's, she became active in temperance, antislavery movements, and women's rights, devoting her full time after 1849 to "social action." Although the years 1855-65 were devoted to the American Antislavery Society in New York, Susan also led the fight which resulted in an 1860 New York law granting property rights to married women. After the Civil War, she concentrated on winning woman suffrage, and 14 years after she died the 19th Amendment was ratified, 26 August 1920, often called the "Susan Anthony Amendment." Secondary sources; 5 illus.                   D. Dodd

1367. Schaffer, Ronald. THE MONTANA WOMAN SUFFRAGE CAMPAIGN; 1911-14. *Pacific Northwest Q. 1964 55(1): 9-15.* Describes the role of Jeannette Rankin and others in gaining equal voting rights for women in Montana. Contemporary arguments for and against suffrage are given. Colorful campaign methods, including fund-raising methods, are described.                                     C. C. Gorchels

1368. Sheldon, Richard N. RICHMOND PEARSON HOBSON AS A PROGRESSIVE REFORMER. *Alabama R. 1972 25(4): 243-261.* Congressman Richmond Pearson Hobson was a typical Southern Progressive on most contemporary issues during his incumbency, 1907-15. He supported the principle of federal economic regulation, a large navy, tariff reform, and federal aid to education. He voted for the Mann-Elkins Act, the Underwood Tariff Act, the income tax amendment, creation of a Labor Department, direct election of senators, abolition of the electoral college, and prohibition. Hobson wrongly believed his Progressive record could win him a seat in the Senate in 1914, and he failed to retain his Congressional seat after the 1916 primary elections because of his "soft" attitude toward white supremacy and his support of woman suffrage.

Hobson continued to work for prohibition and woman suffrage during his retirement until his death in 1937. Based on primary and secondary sources, including Hobson's personal papers and newspaper files; 47 notes.

J. F. Vivian

1370. Snapp, Meredith A. DEFEAT THE DEMOCRATS: THE CONGRESSIONAL UNION FOR WOMAN SUFFRAGE IN ARIZONA, 1914 AND 1916. *J. of the West 1975 14(4): 131-139.* Discusses an attempt in 1914 and 1916 by the Congressional Union for Woman Suffrage organizers to convince women voters in Arizona (one of nine states which enfranchised women) to vote against Democratic Party candidates—the party they held responsible for inaction on the woman suffrage question. 34 notes.

1371. Taber, Ronald W. SACAGAWEA AND THE SUFFRAGETTES. *Pacific Northwest Q. 1967 58(1): 7-13.* Sacagawea, the Indian woman who accompanied her husband as guide and interpreter on the Lewis and Clark expedition, was hailed as a heroine by the women's suffrage movement, especially in Oregon and Wyoming from 1902 to 1921. Activities of some of the women who led the struggle for equal suffrage are related, including their efforts in fund raising and political campaigns.                                      C. C. Gorchels

1372. Taylor, A. Elizabeth. THE WOMAN SUFFRAGE MOVEMENT IN MISSISSIPPI, 1890-1920. *J. of Miss. Hist. 1968 30(1): 1-34.* Describes the woman suffrage movement in Mississippi from 1890, when a State constitutional convention considered the subject, until 1920 when the Federal amendment for woman suffrage was ratified. The author focuses primarily upon the activities of the Mississippi Woman Suffrage Association, organized in 1897 and which throughout its history was affiliated with the National American Woman Suffrage Association. The State organization engaged in various pressure group activities but achieved limited political success. The Mississippi Legislature several times defeated proposals for woman suffrage, as in 1920 when it rejected the proposed Federal amendment. In 1920, however, the legislature approved a resolution to give women the right to vote by amending the State constitution. Although this plan received more favorable than unfavorable votes in the November 1920 elections, it failed because it did not receive a majority of all votes cast. Opponents of woman suffrage often argued that it would be dangerous because it would give Negro women the right to vote. Based on various primary sources including newspapers; 143 notes.                                      J. W. Hillje

1373. Trecker, Janice Law. A GENTEEL TRADITION. *New-England Galaxy 1974 16(2): 19-27.* Describes the growing involvement of Isabella Beecher Hooker (1822-1907), wife of Joseph Hooker of Hartford, in the suffrage movement from 1861 until her death in 1907. Originally conservative, she finally embraced the ideas of radical suffragettes Susan B. Anthony (1820-1906), Elizabeth Cady Stanton (1815-1902), and Victoria Woodhull (1838-1927). 4 illus.                P. C. Marshall

1374. Trecker, Janice Law. THE SUFFRAGE PRISONERS. *Am. Scholar 1972 41(3): 409-423.* Describes interaction between woman suffrage leaders and the Wilson administration in 1917. Concludes, "ironically, the pickets became the victims, not only of the contradictions in American democracy, but of the very success of the long suffrage campaign and of the long-awaited 'conversion' of the Wilson administration."                                                       F. F. Harling

1375. White, Jean Bickmore. WOMAN'S PLACE IS IN THE CONSTITUTION: THE STRUGGLE FOR EQUAL RIGHTS IN UTAH IN 1895. *Utah Hist. Q. 1974 42(4): 344-369.* Reviews Utah women's struggle to acquire voting rights when the territory became a state in 1895. Initially, both political parties supported universal suffrage, but opposition soon developed. Militancy was wholly absent, and the women won because their leaders were respected members of the Mormon Church. 5 photos, 58 notes.                                V. L. Human

1376. Wiggins, Sarah W. A PROPOSAL FOR WOMEN''S SUF-FRAGE IN ALABAMA IN 1867. *Alabama Hist. Q. 1970 32(3/4): 181-185.* Reprints an article from the Livingston *Journal* of 14 October 1870, originally written in 1867 by Pierce Burton and published in the Demopolis *New Era* on 20 March 1867, proposing women's suffrage. Discusses Burton's reason for the proposal and for its revival in 1870. 5 notes.
                                                                E. E. Eminhizer

1377. Wilhite, Ann L. Wiegman. SIXTY-FIVE YEARS TILL VIC-TORY: A HISTORY OF WOMAN SUFFRAGE IN NEBRASKA. *Nebraska Hist. 1968 49(2): 149-163.* Surveys the struggle for woman suffrage in Nebraska from 1855 when Amelia Bloomer spoke in Omaha until 1920 when the Nebraska Woman Suffrage Association reorganized as the Nebraska League of Woman Voters and the women prepared to exercise their first voting privileges.
                                                                R. Lowitt

1378. Willis, Gwendolen B. OLYMPIA BROWN. *Universalist Hist. Soc. J. 1963 4: 1-76.* This autobiography of Mrs. John Henry Willis, née Olympia Brown (1835-1926), was edited and completed by her daughter and published in Racine, Wisconsin in 1960. Olympia Brown was the first woman to graduate from an established theological school (Universalist Divinity School of Saint Lawrence University) in 1860 and, as far as is known, in 1863 was the first woman to be ordained (by the Northern Universalist Association at Malone, New York). The autobiography also includes a historical account of the campaign in the United States for Women's Suffrage from 1867 until women were granted suffrage by Congress in 1920. Olympia Brown was president of the Wisconsin Woman Suffrage Association from 1884 to 1912. In 1912 she published *Acquaintances, Old and New, Among Reformers.* Her papers and books have recently been deposited in the Woman's Archives of Radcliffe College. She believed that "freedom of religious thought and a liberal church would supply the groundwork for all other freedoms. Her difficulties and disillusionments in this field were numerous. That she could rise superior to such difficulties and disillusionments was the consequence of the hopefulness and courage with which she was richly endowed." 3 photos.
                                                                D. D. Cameron

1379. Wright, James R., Jr. THE ASSIDUOUS WEDGE: WOMAN SUFFRAGE AND THE OKLAHOMA CONSTITUTIONAL CON-VENTION. *Chronicles of Oklahoma 1973/74 51(4): 421-443.* Traces the Oklahoma Territory's Woman Suffrage Movement from 1870 to the Oklahoma Constitutional Convention in 1907, where it was defeated by the Southern Democrats.
                                                                S

1380. Yellin, Jean Fagan. DUBOIS' *CRISIS* AND WOMEN'S SUF-FRAGE. *Massachusetts R. 1973 14(2): 365-375.* William Edward Burghardt DuBois' attitudes toward women's rights were expressed in *Crisis,* the magazine of the National Association for the Advancement of Colored People (NAACP) which he edited 1910-34. DuBois consistently sided with suffragettes, even after exposing the racism predominant in the feminist movement. He hoped to unite the women's movement with the black movement, because both groups were traditionally victims in American society. As the 19th Amendment neared ratification, DuBois urged black women to exercise their future voter's rights to the best interests of black people in general. While the amendment brought white women the franchise, it did little to uplift the status of black women. Because feminist groups continued to ignore this glaring inequity throughout the 1920's, DuBois realized that there could be no "women-Negro" alliance. 11 notes.
                                                                W. A. Wiegand

1381. Zacharis, John C. EMMELINE PANKHURST: AN EN-GLISH SUFFRAGETTE INFLUENCES AMERICA. *Speech Mono-graphs 1971 38(3): 198-206.* Discusses Emmeline Pankhurst's impact on woman suffrage during three lecture tours in the United States. The tours, each lasting three months, were made in the autumns of 1909, 1911, and 1913. Pankhurst visited sizable metropolitan areas where she drew large crowds. Both her supporters and her opposition agreed that her speaking tours significantly aided the progress of the American suffrage movement. Evidence indicates that she may have influenced political action to the point that, by 1914, the issue was being discussed in the House of Representatives for the first time. 70 notes.
                                                                D. R. Richardson

1382. Ziebarth, Marilyn. WOMAN'S RIGHTS MOVEMENT. *Minnesota Hist. 1971 42(6): 225-230.* Briefly summarizes the national and Minnesota woman's rights movements from 1848 to 1920. Following the lead of feminists who attended the Seneca Falls Convention of 1848 and subsequently founded the National Woman Suffrage Association, Minnesota women organized state suffrage groups, self-improvement societies, and a woman's employment service during the second half of the 19th century. In 1875, Minnesota feminists won the right to vote in school elections, and in 1897, a state constitutional amendment enabled them to participate in public library affairs. Minnesota refused to enact full woman's suffrage until 1919, when increased female participation in America's wartime economy spurred Congress to pass the 19th Amendment. The states ratified this voting rights measure in 1920. Based partly on Minnesota Historical Society photograph collections; 12 photos.
                                                                G. R. Adams

## Progressivism

1383. Brown, Alan S. CAROLINE BARTLETT CRANE AND UR-BAN REFORM. *Michigan Hist. 1972 56(4): 287-301.* The career of Caroline Bartlett Crane, who became a municipal sanitarian during the Progressive period, exemplifies the nonpolitical state and local projects in which many reformers of that era engaged. Tenements, schools, jails, drainage and sewer systems, water and food supplies, and impure air fell under Mrs. Crane's perceptive eye. Relentless, candid, and thoughtful criticism characterized the more than 60 sanitary surveys in 14 states which the Kalamazoo reformer eventually made as a nationally famous paid consultant. Based largely on primary sources; 4 photos, 46 notes.
                                                                D. W. Johnson

1384. Candeloro, Dominic. THE CHICAGO SCHOOL BOARD CRISIS OF 1907. *J. of the Illinois State Hist. Soc. 1975 68(5): 396-406.* The election of reform Democrat Edward F. Dunne as mayor of Chicago in 1905 led to the appointment of Progressives such as Louis F. Post and Jane Addams to the School Board. The Board's reform element endeavored to implement staff and curriculum reforms in the school system and also to raise revenue through renegotiating private leases on downtown school land. Intense criticism from newspapers and business interests and the defeat for reelection of Dunne led to the removal of the reformers from the Board. Many of their reforms were implemented, however, following the appointment of Ella Flagg Young as school superintendent in 1910.
                                                                N. Lederer

1385. Davis, Allen F. THE CAMPAIGN FOR THE INDUSTRIAL RELATIONS COMMISSION, 1911-1913. *Mid-Am. 1963 45(4): 211-228.* More than most progressives, social workers combined an almost naive faith in progress and reform with a realistic understanding of the workings of the American political system. The campaign for the federal industrial relations commission is an illustration of their realistic reform tactics, while the failure of the commission to live up to the social workers' expectations, and their own disillusionment with reform in the face of World War I, help to define some of the limitations and frustrations of reform in the progressive era.
                                                                L. D. Silveri

1386. Davis, Allen F. THE SOCIAL WORKERS AND THE PRO-GRESSIVE PARTY, 1912-1916. *Am. Hist. R. 1964 69(3): 671-688.* "To many social workers, the Progressive party, made possible by Roosevelt's bolt from the Republican convention in June 1912, seemed to be the climax to 20 years of struggle for social justice; it seemed to be the great cause they had been seeking, and they played a major role in making the new party stand for social reform. They supported the party not because of Roosevelt, nor because of the New Nationalism, but because of the social and industrial planks of the Progressive Party platform, which they played a large part in drafting."
                                                                M. Berman

1387. Feldman, Egal. PROSTITUTION, THE ALIEN WOMAN AND THE PROGRESSIVE IMAGINATION, 1910-15. *Am. Q. 1967 19(2, pt. 1): 192-206.* Describes two divergent groups which became concerned over the relationship between prostitution and immigration. One school of thought was the largely agrarian-oriented nativist, eager to condemn the city, Europe, and American Jews as the sources of prostitution. A group of militant social reformers, many female, comprised the second group. Eager to refute the nativists, they concentrated on clearing the name of the immigrant woman at the same time they attacked the system which so often ensnared her. Women such as Jane Addams, Grace Abbott, Kate Waller Barrett, Frances A. Kellor, Hannah Greenbaum Solomon, and Lillian D. Wald investigated the situation, led the onslaught against immigration procedures, and simultaneously founded protective associations for young women. The presence of so many female activists in the crusade against vice testified to the emergence of the "new woman" of 20th-century America. Based mainly on Progressive journals and reports; 51 notes.                          R. S. Pickett

1388. McGovern, James R.   DAVID GRAHAM PHILLIPS AND THE VIRILITY IMPULSE OF PROGRESSIVES.   New England Q. 1966 39(3): 334-355.  Psychologically analyzes the Progressive movement in terms of its members' impulse toward virility (i.e., manliness, power, and activity) as seen in David Graham Phillips as a representative of the group. Biographical data about Phillips is evaluated with regard to his virility drive, and this material shows he viewed dependency and weakness with contempt, which explains why psychological rather than economic motivation lay behind his dismay that organizations were encroaching upon the individual. Phillips' heroes were dynamically independent and active males. Interestingly enough, his novels spoke loudly in favor of woman's social liberation, and this suggests he wished to appear to women to be a supermale but actually wanted to be "submissive to a powerful, asexual woman." These virility views developed largely in response to the challenges to numerous fundamental values during the period. The Progressive movement was ultimately the result of psychological elements, socioeconomic ideas, and abstract considerations all combined into a decidedly virile mixture. Based on Phillips' works and secondary materials; 126 notes.                          W. G. Morgan

1389. Osofsky, Gilbert.   PROGRESSIVISM AND THE NEGRO: NEW YORK, 1900-1915.   Am. Q. 1964 16(2, part 1): 153-168.  Negro migration to northern cities from the 1890's to World War I did more than arouse racial antagonism; it also motivated nonpolitical progressives such as Mrs. Victoria Earle Matthews, Francis A. Kellor and Mary White Ovington to spearhead labor and housing reforms. Ovington and labor reformer Dr. William Lewis Buckley also helped to found the NAACP, and in 1906 Buckley and others created the Committee for Improving the Industrial Condition of the Negro in New York. This organization later merged with others to form the National Urban League.

R. S. Pickett

1390. Semonche, John E.   THE "AMERICAN MAGAZINE" OF 1906-15: PRINCIPLE VS. PROFIT.   Journalism Q. 1963 40(1): 36-44.  The American Magazine was founded by John S. Phillips, Ida M. Tarbell, Ray Stannard Baker, Lincoln Steffens, William Allen White, Finley Peter Dunne, John M. Siddall and others of the muckraker tradition after a break with McClure's Magazine in 1906. It had financial help from William Kent, millionaire reformer from California, had an outstanding series on the Negro and a controversial one on the Mexico of Porfirio Diaz, and took part in the opposition to President William Howard Taft. Financial difficulties, particularly lack of capital, plagued the group, and it finally sold out to the Crowell Company, which began to moderate the muckraking slightly. Most of the original group resigned in 1915 and the Crowell management created a different kind of magazine under Siddall.

S. E. Humphreys

1391. Tobin, Eugene M.   THE PROGRESSIVE AS HUMANITARIAN: JERSEY CITY'S SEARCH FOR SOCIAL JUSTICE, 1890-1917.   New Jersey Hist. 1975 93(3-4): 77-98.  Social reformers in Jersey City are classified into three groups: private, religious, and public. The Whittier House social settlement tackled problems associated with tenement slums, crime, infant mortality, and juvenile delinquency. Protestants campaigned for broad social welfare reform, while less affluent Catholics opted for assistance on an individual basis for its immigrant communicants. A separate juvenile court was established. World War I changed the priorities of reformers. A typical Jersey City reformer was "a native-stock, middle-class Protestant who resided in the Eighth or Ninth Ward and had some college training." Based on primary and secondary sources; 7 illus., 44 notes.                          E. R. McKinstry

## Temperance

1392. Caldwell, Dorothy J.   CARRY NATION, A MISSOURI WOMAN, WON FAME IN KANSAS.   Mo. Hist. R. 1969 63(4): 461-488.  A brief biographical sketch of the famous prohibition leader Carry Nation (1846-1911) who won national prominence by smashing Kansas saloons in Medicine Lodge, Kiowa, Wichita, and Topeka. Her family background and youth are described briefly. The author gives a detailed description of her visit to Saint Louis, Kansas City, and other Missouri towns in 1901. Based on local newspapers, biographies, articles, local histories, and biographical directories; illus., 105 notes.

W. F. Zornow

1393. Carter, Paul A.   PROHIBITION AND DEMOCRACY: THE NOBLE EXPERIMENT REASSESSED.   Wisconsin Mag. of Hist. 1973 56(3): 189-201.  Challenges the traditional view of prohibition as a battle of liberal wets fighting for democratic principles against a conservative and well organized fanatic minority that imposed the 18th Amendment on an unsuspecting public. Examines prohibitionists' literature, leaders, and opponents, and argues that the prohibition movement used many of the arguments of future New Dealers and radicals. Explores the role of women's organizations in the prohibition controversy. 8 illus., 45 notes.                          N. C. Burckel

1394. Fitzgerald, Louis.   CARRIE [SIC] NATION IN IOWA, 1901.   Ann. of Iowa 1967 39(1): 62-74.  Carry Nation's appearances in Iowa in 1901 were part of a lecture tour. In 1899, the "Kansas Cyclone" began her career of wrecking saloons and denouncing smoking and secret fraternal orders. Mrs. Nation spoke from the back of her train in several places in Iowa and gave two lectures in Des Moines and Muscatine. Everywhere she proclaimed that God had appointed her to stamp out evils. She sold 25-cent souvenir hatchets, but did not do physical harm to saloons in Iowa. Her two lectures were not financial successes and the Iowa antisaloon league gave her a less than enthusiastic welcome. Undocumented, illus.                          D. C. Swift

1395. Franklin, J. L.   THE FIGHT FOR PROHIBITION IN OKLAHOMA TERRITORY.   Social Sci. Q. 1969 49(4): 876-885.  Through the efforts of the Woman's Christian Temperance Union and the Anti-Saloon League, the well-entrenched liquor interests were defeated in 1907 when prohibition was included in the first Oklahoma constitution. The struggle began in 1888. Local option grew to the point that, by 1906, statewide prohibition seemed possible. By the Oklahoma Enabling Act (1907), Congress linked Indian Territory and Oklahoma Territory and required continuation of prohibition in the Indian portion as a condition of statehood for the whole. Based chiefly on newspapers and public documents; 45 notes.                          M. Hough

1396. Franklin, Jimmie L.   THAT NOBLE EXPERIMENT: A NOTE ON PROHIBITION IN OKLAHOMA.   Chronicles of Oklahoma 1965 43(1): 19-34.  The Enabling Act which provided for statehood for Oklahoma prohibited the sale of alcoholic beverages in Indian Territory. The constitutional convention faced the necessity of deciding whether such sale would be legal in the western part of the State. The Anti-Saloon League and the Woman's Christian Temperance Union campaigned for complete prohibition and these forces won. The first legislature enacted a law providing for State dispensaries in which liquors would be sold upon doctors' prescriptions, such sales to be registered with the names of the purchasers. Such dispensaries were to be located only in towns of over two thousand population. As some counties had no such towns, an effort was made to amend the law in the next session of the legislature to allow every county to have at least one such dispensary. This amendment failed to pass. After much agitation, in 1911 a new law was passed abolishing the dispensaries. Thus prohibition continued for more than another half century in Oklahoma. 65 notes.

I. W. Van Noppen

1397. Graybar, Lloyd J., ed.   THE WHISKEY WAR AT PADDY'S RUN: EXCERPTS FROM A DIARY OF ALBERT SHAW.   Ohio Hist. 1966 75(1): 48-54.  Uses a sequence of entries dated 2 March to 24 April 1874 in the diary of Albert Shaw (then 17 years old; later the editor of the American Review of Reviews) to chronicle an abortive temperance drive by the ladies of New London (called Paddy's Run), Ohio. Shaw's mother was a leader in the fight. The diary is one item in a large collection of Shaw manuscripts in the New York Public Library. (See also abstract 2:1680).              S. L. Jones

1398. Hohner, Robert A. PROHIBITION COMES TO VIRGINIA: THE REFERENDUM OF 1914. *Virginia Mag. of Hist. and Biog. 1967 75(4): 473-488.* The Anti-Saloon League forced a reluctant General Assembly to authorize a referendum on statewide prohibiton in 1914. The league with its allies in the Woman's Christian Temperance Union and the Methodist and Baptist Churches organized carefully and effectively for the referendum which they won handily in a spirited campaign against the belatedly organized wets. Based on manuscripts and printed sources, 84 notes.              K. J. Bauer

1399. Ross, Irwin. CARRY NATION - SALOON'S NEMESIS. *Am. Hist. Illus. 1968 2(10): 13-17.* Discusses Carry Amelia Moore Nation (1846-1911), who was six feet tall and weighed 180 pounds. In the early 1900's she was an active militant for Prohibition. She called herself a servant of God, and with her hatchet she did God the service of destroying and closing saloons. Most of the time Carry Nation did her work unopposed - "when she walked in, saloonkeepers either froze or fled." Newspapers made her name a household word from coast to coast. People offered her money and support, both moral and physical, if only she would come and do some smashing. "She tried to go everywhere she was invited, and everywhere she went she did some smashing." Mentions some of the monuments erected in her memory. "But the greatest monument of all to her zeal, her will, her faith in her mission - the 18th Amendment - has toppled and fallen." 6 illus.      R. V. McBaine

1400. Smith, Becky. PROHIBITION IN ALASKA. *Alaska J. 1973 3(3): 170-179.* Discusses eras of alcoholic prohibition in Alaska 1842-1917, emphasizing the activities of the Woman's Christian Temperance Union.

1401. Whitaker, F. M. OHIO WCTU AND THE PROHIBITION AMENDMENT CAMPAIGN OF 1883. *Ohio Hist. 1974 83(2): 84-102.* Describes the founding of the Woman's Christian Temperance Union of Ohio in 1874 and its activities through the prohibition amendment campaign of 1883. In its first years the Union struggled with the liquor licensing issue and tried to avoid partisan politics. After a few years of reduced activity, the Union joined the prohibition campaign, which ended in defeat of the amendment. After the campaign of 1883 the Union became more closely associated with the Prohibition Party, and its independent influence declined. Based on minutes of the Ohio WCTU meetings, newspapers, the author's dissertation, and secondary works; 3 photos, 70 notes.      J. B. Street

## Movement to Outlaw Prostitution

1402. Betts, Peter J. THE LAW AND ORDER SOCIETY OF LANCASTER. *J. of the Lancaster County Hist. Soc. 1965 69(4): 216-239.* An account of the establishment of a civic reform group to suppress vice conditions in a "wide open" city and the methods of attacking the problem. Difficulties in securing governmental and church cooperation are described. Different classes of prostitution are analyzed. The history ends with the triumph of morality over vice without the use of oppressive measures or narrow evangelistic zeal. Documented.      J (J. W. W. Loose)

1403. Burnham, John C. THE PROGRESSIVE ERA REVOLUTION IN AMERICAN ATTITUDES TOWARD SEX. *J. of Am. Hist. 1973 59(4): 885-908.* The "revolution" in attitudes toward sex led to an attack on the double standard of morality through antiprostitution campaigns, the abolition of red-light districts, a franker discussion of sex in literature and on the stage, and sex education in the public schools. The impetus came from feminists, "purity" reformers, and physicians such as Prince Albert Morrow (1846-1913), who were concerned about venereal disease. Morrow and others formed organizations to combat prostitution and to educate about venereal disease and sex. To some the consequence was an embarrassing flood of "Sexology" literature, but the campaign represented Progressive efforts toward moral improvement through education. 77 notes.      K. B. West

1404. Burnham, John C. THE SOCIAL EVIL ORDINANCE - A SOCIAL EXPERIMENT IN NINETEENTH CENTURY ST. LOUIS. *Missouri Hist. Soc. Bull. 1971 27(3): 203-217.* From 1870 to 1874, the St. Louis city government tried to enforce a system of compulsory medical inspection and treatment of prostitutes in order to control venereal infection. Proponents of the system held that society, unable to banish prostitution, must regulate it. Mayor Joseph Brown directed the system and defended it from its many critics. The opponents - led by William Greenleaf Eliot - crusaded and finally persuaded the Missouri Legislatures to nullify the "social evil" ordinance. The St. Louis experiment, meanwhile, inspired similar ones in San Francisco, Cincinnati, and Chicago. Based on newspaper accounts, governmental reports and documents, and medical literature; 49 notes.      H. T. Lovin

## Settlement Houses

1405. Gans, Herbert J. REDEFINING THE SETTLEMENT'S FUNCTION FOR THE WAR ON POVERTY. *Social Work 1964 9(4): 3-12.* A hundred years ago the settlement house movement was established for the purpose of removing the deprivations of urban poverty. The European immigrant population has been replaced by Negroes, Puerto Ricans, and white Appalachians. The early success of the settlement house movement was due to the predominance of Jewish clients. The old settlement house movement wanted to change the slum-dwellers, not understand them, and to establish neighborhood democracy in the slums. Today, the settlement house must discover how socially mobile people can be helped in their efforts to become middle class. To achieve this goal, incomes have to be raised among the poor and racial discrimination has to be dealt with more forcefully than is now the case.      W. L. Willigan

1406. Hess, Jeffrey A. BLACK SETTLEMENT HOUSE, EAST GREENWICH, 1902-1914. *Rhode Island Hist. 1970 29(3/4): 113-127.* Traces the history of a Rhode Island welfare agency against the background of the national settlement house movement. The East Greenwich Neighborhood Cottage at Scolloptown, Rhode Island, failed to become more than a charity organization devoted in the end to abolishing the very community it purported to serve, because its leaders despised existing social patterns in the Negro community. Based on newspapers, periodicals, census records, and secondary sources.      P. J. Coleman

1407. Kogut, Alvin. THE SETTLEMENTS AND ETHNICITY: 1890-1914. *Social Work 1972 17(3): 22-31.* Studies settlement houses in Chicago, Boston, and New York City before World War I. Examines 1) the theories of ethnic minorities and races, 2) advocacy of a specific structural relationship such as assimilation, melting-pot, cultural pluralism, separation, 3) positions on migration restriction, 4) interest in ethnic minorities, and 5) the nature of programs and practices. 24 notes.      W. L. Willigan

1408. Leonard, Henry B. THE IMMIGRANTS' PROTECTIVE LEAGUE OF CHICAGO, 1908-1921. *J. of the Illinois State Hist. Soc. 1973 66(3): 271-284.* The unprecedented numbers of immigrants from southern and eastern Europe were called racially inferior by people descended from northwestern Europeans. The Immigrants' Protective League, founded in Chicago in 1908 by Jane Addams and other reformers, helped the new immigrants in urban-industrial American life. The league sought broad government intervention to protect the immigrants in employment, education, and the courts. Despite some failures, the league guided immigrants in an imaginative, enlightened, and humane way that acquainted the public with their problems. Based on the league's annual reports and papers in the manuscript division of the Library of the University of Illinois, Chicago Circle; 2 photos, 34 notes.      A. C. Aimone

1409. McCree, Mary Lynn. THE FIRST YEAR OF HULL-HOUSE, 1889-1890, IN LETTERS BY JANE ADDAMS AND ELLEN GATES STARR. *Chicago Hist. 1970 1(2): 101-114.* Discusses the early history of Hull-House, the Chicago settlement house founded by Jane Addams and Ellen Gates Starr in 1889. These two young women, impressed by the example of London's Toynbee Hall, were anxious to find some useful activity for themselves and other educated women who were bored by their lack of usefulness. Several long letters, published here for the first time, describe the methods Addams and Starr used in gaining support for their "scheme," the acquisition and remodeling of Hull-House, and the early programs - kindergarten classes, clubs for children of all ages, art classes, lectures and discussions, and college extension courses. "Both women minded children, listened to problems, cooked and washed, acted as midwives, and helped prepare the dead for burial. No task was too great or too small." Among the most popular events were the social receptions held three nights a week, one each for the French, Germans, and Italians. Based on manuscript collections at Indiana University, University of Illinois at Chicago Circle, Smith College, and Swarthmore College; illus. D. J. Abramoske

1410. Mohl, Raymond and Betten, Neil. PATERNALISM AND PLURALISM: IMMIGRANTS AND SOCIAL WELFARE IN GARY, INDIANA, 1906-1940. *Am. Studies [Lawrence, KS] 1974 15(1): 5-30.* Examines social welfare in Gary and substantiates the theme that public welfare programs manipulate the poor, keep them under social control, and drive them into low income, menial jobs. Settlement house work served "the interests of American society more than those of the immigrants themselves." The houses exhibited a nativist paternalism, and tried to Americanize all immigrants. A few exceptions, such as the International Institute, fostered a sense of ethnic identification. Based on primary and secondary sources; 56 notes. J. Andrew

1411. Phillips, J. O. C. THE EDUCATION OF JANE ADDAMS. *Hist. of Educ. Q. 1974 14(1): 49-67.* Analyzes the three determining forces in Jane Addams's life: the ideology of domestic piety, the influence of her Quaker father, and the changing mood in women's education during the 1870's. Follows these themes in her adult life, and shows how Addams' work at Hull House resulted from these early forces. Finds that Addams did not challenge "the basic assumptions of the ideology, nor the doctrines of a separate woman's sphere and a distinct female nature." Based on primary and secondary sources; 38 notes. L. C. Smith

1412. Rousmaniere, John P. CULTURAL HYBRID IN THE SLUMS: THE COLLEGE WOMAN AND THE SETTLEMENT HOUSE, 1889-1894. *Am. Q. 1970 22(1): 45-66.* A case study of the first five years of the College Settlement Association (CSA) and the residents who staffed its settlement house activities. Examines the goals of the settlement founders, the self-conceptions and recruitment patterns of the early residents, and four ascriptive characteristics of the CSA settlements: as charity, as social movement, as "colony," and as voluntary association, in order to understand their attractiveness to college women. Sees the settlement as the product of a cultural rather than of a purely moral or ideological conflict, a conclusion which is not to denigrate its role in social and political reform. 2 tables; 46 notes. R. V. Ritter

1413. Scott, Anne Firor. JANE ADDAMS AND THE CITY. *Virginia Q. R. 1967 43(1): 53-62.* Emphasizes Jane Addams' position not only as one living and working with the immigrant population of Chicago but also as an urban pioneer attempting to understand and explain the effects of urbanism on American society. Later sociologists were to document her perceptive insights into such areas as the need for governmental social action, the role of political bosses, and the effect of the city upon family life. From her center at Hull House "she delineated a field of study and offered enough provocative ideas to keep rafts of researchers going for years. She was clearly one of the seminal philosophers of the new urban world." O. H. Zabel

1414. Speizman, Milton D. THE MOVEMENT OF THE SETTLEMENT HOUSE IDEA INTO THE SOUTH. *Southwestern Social Sci. Q. 1963 44(3): 237-246.* While the South has large elements of population which could benefit from the settlement house type of establishment, little has been done in this field. The first Southern settlement house was established in New Orleans in 1899. Some effort has been made to work with the Negro and Latin American elements in the South, but much remains to be done. The author does point out that the "story of settlement work in the South is yet to be told." Perhaps with the unveiling of the full story more credit can be given to the Southern settlement work. D. F. Henderson

# Religion and Ethnicity

## Religion

1415. Agnew, Theodore L. REFLECTIONS ON THE WOMAN'S FOREIGN MISSIONARY MOVEMENT IN LATE 19TH CENTURY AMERICAN METHODISM. *Methodist Hist. 1968 6(2): 3-16.* Discusses women's movements in the Methodist Church during the latter part of the 19th century. Described are the backgrounds and activities of some of the leading women, including Frances Willard, in the movement; the background, establishment, and early activities of the Woman's Foreign Missionary Society and the Woman's Home Missionary Society; and the relationship of the Methodists to American society. Based largely on *Heathen Woman's Friend* and *The Ladies' Repository.* 76 notes. H. L. Calkin

1416. Berge, Dennis E. REMINISCENCES OF LOMALAND: MADAME TINGLEY AND THE THEOSOPHICAL INSTITUTE IN SAN DIEGO. *J. of San Diego Hist. 1975 20(3): 1-32.* Describes the Theosophical movement and the development and history of the Theosophical Institute at Point Loma, 1897-1940, and its founder, Katherine Augusta Tingley. S

1417. Bergmark, Matts. MARY BAKER EDDY OCH CHRISTIAN SCIENCE [Mary Baker Eddy and Christian Science]. *Medicinhistorisk Årsbok [Sweden] 1963: 1-12, 39.* Discusses the life of the American religious leader, Mary Baker Eddy (1821-1910), and her doctrine of Christian Science. Mrs. Eddy early showed a drive to dominate others, along with extreme selfishness. She learned the techniques of hypnotism from Phineas Parkhurst Quimby (1802-66) in 1862, then repudiated him and developed her own version of faith healing, publishing in 1875 her book *Science and Health.* This formed the basis for her religious sect, centered at Boston, Massachusetts, and her own power and wealth. Although there is medical value in the denial of illness, Mrs. Eddy's success was due mainly to her ruthless administrative techniques. In her last years she was sick in body and mind. Undocumented, 4 illus., English summary of the yearbook introduction. R. G. Selleck

1418. Berry, Hannah Shwayder. A COLORADO FAMILY HISTORY. *Western States Jewish Hist. Q. 1973 5(3): 158-165.* Chronicles the history of the Isaac and Rachel Shwayder family, from their emigration from Poland in 1865, to their successful business activities in Denver in 1916.

1419. Black, Margie. "OUR OWN LOTTIE MOON": THE STORY OF LOTTIE MOON AND HER RELATIONSHIP WITH CARTERSVILLE BAPTIST CHURCH. *Viewpoints: Georgia Baptist Hist. 1974 4: 5-16.*

1420. Borzo, Henry. OUR LADY IN PEKING. *Ann. of Iowa 1968 39(6): 401-413.* Sarah J. Pike Conger was the wife of the United States minister to China from 1898 to 1905. Differing with many of her contemporaries, Mrs. Conger was convinced that China was not doomed to extinction. The facets of China's character were enduring. They were the soil in which Christianity could flourish. Had Christianity prevailed in the Western penetration of China instead of economic and political exploitation, China would not have resented the Western world. 2 illus., 47 notes. D. L. Smith

1421. Brudnoy, David. A DECADE IN ZION: THEODORE SCHROEDER'S INITIAL ASSAULT ON THE MORMONS. *Historian 1975 37(2): 241-256.* Free-thinking Theodore Schroeder (1864-1953) began as a lawyer practicing in Salt Lake City (1889-1900) at a time when national controversies about Mormon polygamy delayed statehood for Utah Territory. Schroeder became a strident critic of Mormonism. His pamphlets and short-lived journal *Lucifer's Lantern* focused on plural marriage, and he campaigned successfully to deny polygamous Brigham Roberts the seat in Congress to which he had been elected. In the years after 1900 when he moved to New York, Schroeder became a prolific contributor to First Amendment studies and a leading advocate of free speech and press causes. The Free Speech League, which he helped form, is one of the forebears of the American Civil Liberties Union. Based on the Schroeder papers at the State Historical Society of Wisconsin, and the library of Southern Illinois University; 31 notes.                N. W. Moen

1422. Coleman, Michael C. CHRISTIANIZING AND AMERICANIZING THE NEZ PERCE: SUE L. MC BETH AND HER ATTITUDES TO THE INDIANS. *J. of Presbyterian Hist. 1975 53(4): 339-361.* Discusses the personal attitudes of Sue L. McBeth, a Scotland-born American Presbyterian missionary to the Nez Percé Indians, as well as those of the Mission Board of the Presbyterian Church in the last quarter of the 19th century. Her attitude to the Indian culture was one of sustained and relentless hostility. Christianity was equated with Americanism. The only "good" Indian was the converted one. Conversion embraced the totality of life—religion, eating habits, dress, family living, agriculture. The Indian was urged to forsake his old customs and enter the mainstream of American life. Miss McBeth gave a score of years to the training of Nez Percé Christians so that they would become leaders in their church. Based on documents in the Presbyterian Historical Society (American Indian Correspondence Collection) and secondary works; illus., 85 notes.                H. M. Parker, Jr.

1423. Cunningham, R. J. THE IMPACT OF CHRISTIAN SCIENCE ON THE AMERICAN CHURCHES 1880-1910. *Am. Hist. R. 1967 72(3): 885-905.* Examines the influence of Christian Science on the historic churches and their reactions. While Christian Science influence was felt by Catholicism and Judaism, its principal impact was on Protestant denominations. Reaction ranged from rejection to cautious approval. Although a number of liberal clergy found value in the cult, the majority took a hostile attitude which became sharper as Christian Science made large gains in membership. By 1900 Christian Science had become an issue of national interest. Clergymen were joined by physicians, psychologists, and others in efforts to evaluate and deal with it. Criticism focused on four main areas: the relation of the cult and its founder to historic Christianity, the moral tendency of its teachings, its bearing on the Christian social ethic, and its hygienic implications. By 1910, the year of Mrs. Eddy's death, most of the excitement was over, due in large measure to advances in psychotherapy and the emergence of pastoral counseling which curtailed the appeal of irregular religious healers.                A

1424. Daniel, W. Harrison. VIRGINIA BAPTISTS AND THE MYTH OF THE SOUTHERN MIND, 1865-1900. *South Atlantic Q. 1974 73(1): 85-98.* Virginia Baptists in the late 19th century strongly supported the racist prejudices prevalent in the nation at the time. Their sentiments relative to the expansionist activities of the United States were in close harmony with the opinions of religious groups in other areas. They echoed the arguments of the opponents of women's rights. Their views were a part of the mainstream of American social and intellectual development rather than a mirror of a distinctive southern mind. The concept of the southern mind is a myth. 54 notes.

E. P. Stickney

1425. Deen, Maurine Benson. MY GRANDMOTHER, ALDINE WURSTEN MOSER. *Pacific Historian 1965 9(2): 73-78.* Describes author's grandmother's conversion to Mormonism and her subsequent immigration to Utah.                S

1426. Gingerich, Melvin. THE MENNONITE WOMAN'S MISSIONARY SOCIETY. *Mennonite Q. R. 1963 37(3): 213-233.* A study of this society from 1914 to 1929, with names, dates, and quotes. The society came in conflict with the traditional male Mennonite leadership, but succeeded in doing its share of missionary work.

C. G. Hamilton

1427. Gingerich, Melvin. THE MENNONITE WOMAN'S MISSIONARY SOCIETY. *Mennonite Q. R. 1963 37(2): 113-125, and (3): 214-233.* The Woman's Union Missionary Society was established in 1861, and by 1912 nearly all the major denominations had national women's missionary societies. By the early 1890's many sewing circles were formed to provide clothing for those in mission stations and the poor in their own communities. The first public general meeting of the sewing circle women was held in 1915 near Wauseon, Ohio at the time of the session of Mennonite General Conference. Despite some opposition, by 1921 there were 12 branches of the Woman's Missionary Society with 3,721 members in 131 societies. In 1929 the Women's Missionary Committee of five elected members replaced the society, and in 1947 and 1955 it was again reorganized. The lack of confidence between conservative leaders of the church and the society reflected the rift in the Mennonite Church. 24 notes.                E. P. Stickney

1428. Glanz, Rudolf. THE RISE OF THE JEWISH CLUB IN AMERICA. *Jewish Social Studies 1969 31(2): 82-99.* Post-Civil War affluence encouraged German Jews to seek social relations with Gentiles. But Gentile clubs stressed "heredity" and "refinement," blackballing Jews from all but political and professional associations. Desiring social distinctions which mirrored economic status, Jews turned to German clubs for cultural-linguistic and shared immigrant experience. Gradually Jewish mercantile leaders created exclusive clubs but retained Germanic features. Jewish women attacked clubs as frivolous and dangerous to traditional communal and family life. Moreover, clubs enticed bachelors from hitherto arranged courtships. Assimilationists criticized clubs for their clannishness; they recommended Gentile membership. Later influxes of East European Jews to America raised problems that left social clubs peripheral in Jewish community life. Based on contemporary Jewish newspapers, magazines, and club handbooks.                K. Goldstein

1429. Gradwohl, Rebecca J. THE JEWESS IN SAN FRANCISCO —1896. *Western States Jewish Hist. Q. 1974 6(4): 273-276.* The Jewish woman of San Francisco in 1896 was not only concerned with running her household but was also active in charities and other societies. A few of the outstanding Jewish women in the city were: Dr. Adele Solomons Jaffa, Natalie Selling, and Amelia Levinson in medicine; writers Emma Wolf and her sister, Alice Wolf; teacher Mary Prag; Rabbi Ray Frank; and musicians Meta Asher and Mrs. Noah Brandt. Reprinted from *The American Jewess,* New York, October 1896.                R. A. Garfinkle

1430. Gripe, Elizabeth Howell. WOMEN, RESTRUCTURING AND UNREST IN THE 1920'S. *J. of Presbyterian Hist. 1974 52(2): 188-189.* Women gradually increased their participation and position within the structure of the Presbyterian Church throughout the 19th century. Restructuring in 1923, however, removed their principal power base. The church lost some of its support, but "set the stage for the next . . . struggle . . . to achieve ecclesiastical equality in . . . ordination as elders and ministers." 29 notes.                D. L. Smith

1431. Hiller, Harry H. THE SLEEPING PREACHERS: AN HISTORICAL STUDY OF THE ROLE OF CHARISMA IN AMISH SOCIETY. *Pennsylvania Folklife 1968 18(2): 19-31.* Studies two Midwestern Amish men who preached while unconscious. After relating the careers of Noah Troyer (1831-86) and John D. Kaufman (1847-1913), discusses their theological concepts, methodology, charisma (using the methods of Max Weber), and credibility. Offers a tentative psychological explanation of the phenomena. Reprints the deathbed prophecy of Barbara Stutzman that defended Preacher Kaufman. 11 notes, biblio.

F. L. Harrold

1432. James, Eleanor. THE SANCTIFICATIONISTS OF BELTON. *Am. West 1965 2(3): 65-73.* In 1866, Martha White McWhirter, a devout Methodist, had a religious experience out of which she considered herself "sanctified" for a special purpose. Her weekly afternoon prayer meetings gained other sanctified female converts and strained relations with the churches of Belton, Texas. The enforced celibacy and other preachments of this self-styled prophetess brought troubles with the unsanctified husbands of her followers. By taking in washings, nursing, and other activities the Sanctified Sisters built up an independent income. The dream of financial security led to a smoothly-run hotel venture. Inheritance netted the sisters real estate and other property. For no apparent reason the flourishing female communistic enterprise disposed of its community properties in Texas in 1899 and moved to Washington, D.C. The accumulated funds were sufficient to keep the founding sisters reasonably comfortable in their declining years. Men were not barred but the few who joined the group stayed for only a short time. Biblio. note, illus.

D. L. Smith

1433. Jentsch, Theodore W. OLD ORDER MENNONITE FAMILY LIFE IN THE EAST PENN VALLEY. *Pennsylvania Folklife 1974 24(1): 18-27.* Surveys present-day aspects of Old Order Mennonite family life: courtship and marriage, the home, recreation, sickness and death.                S

1434. Johnson, Kenneth M. THE IMPEACHMENT OF JUDGE CARLOS S. HARDY. *J. of the West 1971 10(4): 726-733.* Los Angeles Superior Court Judge Carlos S. Hardy was a friend and advisor of evangelist Aimee Semple McPherson. After a grand jury investigation of the alleged kidnapping of McPherson, Judge Hardy's association with her brought him under criticism for breach of ethics. The California State Assembly impeached him for judicial misconduct. Although acquitted by majority vote on each article of impeachment, the trial ended Hardy's judicial career. Note.                                              B. S. Porter

1435. Marty, Martin E. IN THE MAINSTREAM. *R. in Am. Hist. 1974 2(3): 408-413.* Stephen Gottschalk's *The Emergence of Christian Science in American Religious Life* (Berkeley: U. of California Pr., 1973) examines the tenets of Christian Science as propounded by its founder Mary Baker Eddy, the spiritual climate in which the movement grew and passed from "the charismatic to the bureaucratic stage," and its critics and followers, 1885-1910.

1436. McLoughlin, William G. AIMEE SEMPLE MC PHERSON: "YOUR SISTER IN THE KING'S GLAD SERVICE." *J. of Popular Culture 1967 1(3): 193-217.* Evaluates the career of evangelist Aimee Semple McPherson (1890-1944), founder of the International Church of the Foursquare Gospel.

1437. Morrill, Allen and Morrill, Eleanor. KATE MC BETH'S "PICNIC." *Idaho Yesterdays 1970 14(2): 23-28.* Discusses the events of a Fourth of July picnic in Kamiah, Idaho, in 1885 among Nez Percé Indians which resulted in an attempted arrest by tribal police and the death of two Indians, and the removal of the two Presbyterian missionaries in charge, Sue and Kate McBeth.

1438. Morrill, Allen and Morrill, Eleanor. OLD CHURCH MADE NEW. *Idaho Yesterdays 1972 16(2): 16-25.* In 1890 the generosity of Mary Copley Thaw restored the Presbyterian Church at Kamiah, Idaho, on the Nez Percé Indian Reservation. The project was initiated by two of her friends, Alice C. Fletcher, special government agent, and her companion, Jane Gay. Kate and Sue McBeth, missionaries to the Nez Percé, also benefited from Mrs. Thaw's concern. Primary and secondary sources; 8 illus., 33 notes.                               B. J. Paul

1439. Nolan, Charles E. RECOLLECTIONS OF TULSA, INDIAN TERRITORY, FROM SISTER MARY AGNES NEWCHURCH, O. CARM. *Chronicles of Oklahoma 1971 49(1): 92-99.* Records anecdotes and customs at the Carmelite mission school in Indian Territory, 1902-03.                                                          S

1440. Noon, Rozanne E. THE BISHOP'S CHILDREN. *Hist. Mag. of the Protestant Episcopal Church 1974 43(1): 5-20.* Reviews the life, works, and theological philosophies of Frederick Huntington, Episcopal Bishop of Central New York during 1869-1904, and his children. His daughters, Arria and Ruth, shared the Bishop's zeal and energy for good works, but not his view of woman's place as being in the home. His son James also leaned toward a religious life, but deplored the money-raising, good works aspects of the Church, causing conflict with his father; another son, George, was undecided. The death of the Bishop left James to turn to the quiet life he so much desired. 28 notes.     V. L. Human

1441. Potvin, Raymond H. and Lee, Che-Fu. CATHOLIC COLLEGE WOMEN AND FAMILY-SIZE PREFERENCES: A REANALYSIS. *Sociol. Analysis 1974 35(1): 24-34.* "Data on family-size preferences of a 1964-67 cohort of Catholic college women are reanalyzed using standardized matrices and analysis of covariance. The earlier Westoff and Potvin conclusion that the higher fertility preferences of these women educated in Catholic colleges was in part a function of selectivity is sustained, but the conclusion that the Catholic college also maintained high levels is to be modified somewhat. Different types of college affected the general decline in family-size preferences over the four years in different ways depending on the type of high school attended. Though the data are somewhat dated, their reanalysis suggests that changes in preferences should be studied with a model that differentiates individual probabilities of change from group effects, especially if selectivity is a factor."          J

1442. Sawyer, Donald J. A CHURCH FROM DEVIL'S MONEY. *New York Folklore Q. 1964 20(1): 20-26.* Describes how the church of Perth, Fulton County, New York, was financed by gambling winnings of two women in Monte Carlo, France, near the end of the 19th century.

1443. Schmidt, Sarah. THE *PARUSHIM*: A SECRET EPISODE IN AMERICAN ZIONIST HISTORY. *Am. Jewish Hist. Q. 1975 65(2): 121-139.* Horace M. Kallen, best known in American intellectual history for his theory of cultural pluralism, became a Zionist in 1903 as a means to retain Jewish identity. Ten years later he founded a secret Zionist society which he called *Parushim* (separate ones) to realize his ideas on Zionism and to bring about statehood in Palestine. Even though the *Parushim* failed in these endeavors, their activities stirred and directed an unwieldy organizational structure, bedevilled by clashes of strong personalities, such as Rabbi Wise, Justice Brandeis, and Henrietta Szold. Contains excerpts of letters written in 1914.         F. Rosenthal

1444. Searcey, Mildred. THE LITTLE BROWN JUG. *Hist. Mag. of the Protestant Episcopal Church 1974 43(1): 57-64.* A brief history of the establishment of the Episcopal Church in Pendleton, Oregon. The town was too small to attract clergymen during the 19th century, but eventually a determined group of women succeeded in having a small church built. Informally named "The Little Brown Jug," the building and operation of the church attracted a colorful congregation. Note.                                                          V. L. Human

1445. Somerlott, Robert. THE MEDIUM HAD THE MESSAGE: MRS. PIPER AND THE PROFESSORS. *Am. Heritage 1971 22(2): 33-37, 94-95.* Career of Leonora E. Piper, a 19th-century psychic medium from Boston, taken from Somerlott's book on the occult, *"Here, Mr. Splitfoot"* (New York; Viking Press, 1971).                            S

1446. Spencer, Ralph W. ANNA HOWARD SHAW. *Methodist Hist. 1975 13(2): 33-51.* Anna Howard Shaw (1847-1919) was the first woman ordained in the Methodist Protestant Church, but she is best known for her work on behalf of the woman suffrage movement. Discusses her efforts to get theological and medical training, her service in the ministry, and as an exponent of the Social Gospel Movement. 41 notes.                                                    H. L. Calkin

1447. Szajkowski, Zosa. THE *YAHUDI* AND THE IMMIGRANT: A REAPPRAISAL. *Am. Jewish Hist. Q. 1973 53(1): 13-44.* Recent research has shown that the American Jews of German origin—called the *yahudim* by their East-European brethren—undertook positive and meaningful action to assure mass immigration of Russian Jews into the United States in the period before World War I. Distribution of immigrants away from New York, care of women and children, appeals to prevent unjust deportations, and ultimately strenuous efforts to prevent limiting legislation were some of the efforts of the established Jewish organizations and of leaders such as Jacob Schiff, Abram I. Elkus, Max James Kohler, Louis Marschall, and Simon Wolf. Based on contemporary newspapers, archives, and collections of papers; 72 notes.                                                       F. Rosenthal

1448. Voth, M. Agnes. MOTHER M. BEATRICE RENGGLI, O.S.B.[:] FOUNDRESS OF THE AMERICAN OLIVETAN BENEDICTINE SISTERS[,] JONESBORO, ARKANSAS. *Am. Benedictine R. 1974 25(3): 389-409.* Presents a brief biography of Rose Renggli, foundress of the American Olivetan Benedictine Sisters, and a history of Roman Catholic missionary work in Arkansas during the late 19th and early 20th centuries. 15 notes.                          J. H. Pragman

1449. Wolfinger, Henry J. A REEXAMINATION OF THE WOODRUFF MANIFESTO IN THE LIGHT OF UTAH CONSTITUTIONAL HISTORY. *Utah Hist. Q. 1971 39(4): 328-349.* Deals with federal attempts to outlaw polygamy and the alleged capitulation to superior authority in the Woodruff Manifesto of 1890. Church President Woodruff's manifesto suggests that the end of plural marriage was a sudden event, but it was a drawn-out process that involved years of struggle and argument. Discusses the political climate in Utah and elsewhere that prompted the 1890 move and traces the various Congressional moves, bills, and debates that culminated in the Church's acceptance of the federal ban on polygamy. Details debates within the Church and concludes that the Manifesto, when it came, was the last of a series of painful steps in retreat. Based on primary sources; 6 illus., 35 notes.                                                         N. E. Tutorow

## Ethnicity

### General

1450. Griswold del Castillo, Richard. A PRELIMINARY COMPARISON OF CHICANO, IMMIGRANT AND NATIVE BORN FAMILY STRUCTURES 1850-1880. *Aztlan 1975 6(1): 87-95.* Compares European immigrants and native born Anglo Americans in Detroit, Michigan, with Mexican Americans in Los Angeles during 1850-80. The urban Chicano family was more drastically affected by economic changes, and economic opportunities were more restricted for Chicano household heads. Chicano family structure resembled that of the native born Anglo American. 14 notes.                                              A

1451. Hareven, Tamara K. THE LABORERS OF MANCHESTER, NEW HAMPSHIRE, 1912-1922: THE ROLE OF FAMILY AND ETHNICITY IN ADJUSTMENT TO INDUSTRIAL LIFE. *Labor Hist. 1975 16(2): 249-265.* A case study of the Amoskeag Mills in Manchester, New Hampshire, which demonstrates the effect of ethnocentrism and family ties upon the modernization process. When the corporation introduced an efficiency and welfare system, the workers responded with attempts to control job mobility and hiring through their own ethnic and family affiliations. This was largely successful until the nine-month strike of 1922. Based on statistical family research, government reports and the *Amoskeag Bulletin*. Table; 25 notes.                         L. L. Athey

1452. Hareven, Tamara K. and Vinovskis, Maris A. MARITAL FERTILITY, ETHNICITY, AND OCCUPATION IN URBAN FAMILIES: AN ANALYSIS OF SOUTH BOSTON AND THE SOUTH END IN 1880. *J. of Social Hist. 1975 8(3): 69-93.* Quantitative study of fertility in South Boston and the South End in 1880 suggests that "ethnicity was a major determinant of fertility differentials at the household levels." Occupation and location in the city also had an impact on fertility ratios. More work is needed on the relationship of fertility and women's work and also on evaluating the importance of the "level of education, religion, and income." 7 tables, 6 graphs, 29 notes, appendix.                                              L. Ziewacz

1453. Klaczynska, Barbara. WHY WOMEN WORK: A COMPARISON OF VARIOUS GROUPS—PHILADELPHIA, 1910-1930. *Labor Hist. 1976 17(1): 73-87.* Analyzes the reasons for women working by comparing patterns of Italian, Polish, Irish, Jewish, black, and native-born white women. Central determinants were strong ethnic familial traditions, the lack of strong familial ties, and class consciousness. Italian and Polish women worked least often, and blacks, native-born whites, and Irish most often. Jewish women tended to move from a work tradition to a nonwork position as they moved into the middle class. Based on government publications and periodicals; 20 notes.                   L. L. Athey

### Blacks

1454. Aptheker, Bettina. W. E. B. DU BOIS AND THE STRUGGLE FOR WOMEN'S RIGHTS: 1910-1920. *San Jose Studies 1975 1(2): 7-16.* Discusses the achievements of William Edward Burghardt Du Bois (1868-1963), especially in the area of human rights, and notes that a dominant theme in much of his work is the subjugation of women, especially black women, within the social, cultural, and personal milieu of contemporary America.                                         S

1455. Athey, Louis L. FLORENCE KELLEY AND THE QUEST FOR NEGRO EQUALITY. *J. of Negro Hist. 1971 54(4): 249-261.* Florence Kelley (1859-1932) was a founding member of the NAACP (National Association for the Advancement of Colored People), but more emphasis has been traditionally given to her work as an early American socialist reformer and crusader. Recounts her efforts to obtain total equality for the Negro, and emphasizes her work and occasional disagreements with the NAACP. Her greatest concern, though, was for the discrimination and injustice society placed upon women, and in this regard she was willing to allow legislated protection for women and children to take precedence over that on racial equality. 40 notes.       R. S. Melamed

1456. Batchelder, Alan B. DECLINE IN THE RELATIVE INCOME OF NEGRO MEN. *Q. J. of Econ. 1964 78(4): 525-548.* Based on decennial census data, between 1949 and 1959 the income of Negro men advanced more slowly than the income of white men in the North, in the West, and in the South. In contrast, the income of Negro women increased more rapidly than the income of white women.
T. Hočevar

1457. Blake, Emma L. ZORA NEALE HURSTON: AUTHOR AND FOLKLORIST. *Negro Hist. Bull. 1966 29(7): 149-150, 165.* Hurston was born in Eatonville, Florida, on 7 January 1901, entered Howard University in 1919, transferred to Barnard College, and in 1929 received a bachelor's degree in anthropology. She was the first Negro woman to be awarded a Guggenheim Fellowship, which enabled her to gather material in the West Indies for future publications. "That Miss Hurston was a most versatile writer may be seen in the fact that in addition to her novels, definitive studies in anthropology, and autobiography, she wrote a number of short stories, a one-act play, two librettos, and many magazine articles. During the last years of her life she earned a precarious living as a substitute teacher at Lincoln Park Academy in Fort Pierce, Florida. She contributed to the local Negro paper, *The Chronicle*, and began work on a new novel which she never completed." She died on 3 February 1960. 2 photos.                            D. D. Cameron

1458. Chaffin, Glenn. AUNT TISH: BELOVED GOURMET OF THE BITTER ROOT. *Montana: Mag. of Western Hist. 1971 21(4): 67-69.* Appreciative account of Tish Nevins, born a slave in 1862, who went to Montana's Bitter Root Valley in 1899 as housekeeper for a motherless family. In later years she operated a boarding house in Hamilton, serving food whose fame extended beyond the State. Stresses the high character and lovable personality of a humble lady who recognized her limitations but refused to regard herself as "disadvantaged." Illus.
S. R. Davison

1459. Chittenden, Elizabeth F. AS WE CLIMB: MARY CHURCH TERRELL. *Negro Hist. Bull. 1975 38(2): 351-354.* In 1892 Mary Church Terrell began the Colored Women's League of Washington, D.C., which spread to other cities and became the National Association of Colored Women. Their motto, "lifting as we climb," characterized her life as an educator, suffragist, and reformer. Biblio.
M. J. Wentworth

1460. Cooney, Charles F. WALTER WHITE AND THE HARLEM RENAISSANCE. *J. of Negro Hist. 1972 57(3): 231-240.* Walter White contributed materially to the flowering of black literary efforts in the 1920's. The Negro writers aided by Walter White in gaining the attention of white publishers and editors included: Countee Cullen, Claude McKay, Rudolph Fisher, Nella Larsen Imes, Georgia Douglas Johnson, and Langston Hughes. Based on the NAACP papers in the Manuscript Division of the Library of Congress; 36 notes.               N. G. Sapper

1461. Dunnigan, Alice E. EARLY HISTORY OF NEGRO WOMEN IN JOURNALISM. *Negro Hist. Bull. 1965 28(8): 178-179, 193, 197.* The first Negro newspaper was *Freedom's Journal*, New York City, 1827, while the first Negro paper to be published in the South was the *Colored American* started in Augusta, Georgia in 1865. Frederick Douglass started the *New National Era* in Washington, D.C. soon after the Civil War. With the upsurge of Negro papers throughout the nation in the 1870's came an increased number of new journalists, including many Negro women writers. The names and achievements of 19 such Negro women are given in some detail. Many wrote for religious papers.
E. P. Stickney

1462. Everly, Elaine C. MARRIAGE REGISTERS OF FREEDMEN. *Prologue 1973 5(3): 150-154.* Brief explanation of marriage certificates and registers of Reconstruction freed slaves found in the records of the Bureau of Refugees, Freedmen, and Abandoned Lands in the National Archives. These records are fragmentary and were not uniformly recorded, but do contain valuable information about slave families after the Civil War. Based on primary material from National Archives and secondary sources; 3 illus., 8 notes.           R. W. Tissing, Jr.

1463. Gatewood, Willard B. THEODORE ROOSEVELT AND THE INDIANOLA AFFAIR. *J. of Negro Hist. 1968 53(1): 48-69.* Discusses the political repercussions of the "Indianola Affair," which grew out of Theodore Roosevelt's defense of a Negro, Minnie M. Cox, longtime postmistress of Indianola, Mississippi. Anti-Negro sentiment revolving around Cox became a major issue in the State political campaigns of 1903, and, when whites demanded the removal of Cox, Roosevelt moved to close down the post office instead. In 1904 he reopened the office with a white postmaster. Victory for the whites, however, was not complete, for the new postmaster was a longtime defender of Cox and the postal facility was reopened as a fourth-class office rather than a third-class one as it had been previously. Based on manuscript and newspaper sources; 44 notes.                                                                    L. Gara

1464. Hornsby, Alton, Jr. THE HOPE PAPERS PROJECT: PROBLEMS AND PROSPECTS. *Maryland Historian 1975 6(1): 51-54.* Summarizes the author's perspective of his editorship of the John and Lugenia Burns Hope Papers Project. John Hope, a contemporary of Booker T. Washington, was an outstanding black educator. Mrs. Lugenia Burns Hope was a leading civic affairs champion.                             G. O. Gagnon

1465. Lerner, Gerda. EARLY COMMUNITY WORK OF BLACK CLUB WOMEN. *J. of Negro Hist. 1972 59(2): 158-167.* The contribution of the black women's club movement to the survival of the black community has escaped the attention of students of the modern black experience in the United States. From the 1890's to the 1930's, black club women provided assistance to the poor, working mothers, and tenant farm wives. Their emphasis upon racial pride and racial advancement bridged the class barrier that marked their white counterparts. Primary and secondary sources; 14 notes.                             N. G. Sapper

1466. Massa, Ann. BLACK WOMEN IN THE "WHITE CITY." *J. of Am. Studies [Great Britain] 1974 8(3): 319-337.* Describes efforts by Negro womens' groups in Chicago to participate in the World's Columbian Exposition (1893). Despite protests from Negro groups, the exhibits in the pavilions and the proceedings of the meetings at the fair extended only token recognition to Negro achievements in America.
                                                                H. T. Lovin

1467. Peoples, Morgan D. "KANSAS FEVER" IN NORTH LOUISIANA. *Louisiana Hist. 1970 11(2): 121-135.* A short, but lively, migration of freed Negroes from the lower Mississippi Valley to Kansas occurred in 1879-80. A U.S. Senate committee investigated the mass migration, but its conclusions simply reflected party-line positions. The Democrats blamed Republicans for luring the Negroes to States where they were fighting for continuance of Republican strength. The Republicans accused Southern white Democrats of imposing intolerable hardships upon the freedmen, forcing them to flee. The reasons for the exodus were several: blacks were ill treated, although their condition was better than in much of the rest of the South; white political domination had been achieved in 1878 by much terrorism of the blacks; a yellow fever epidemic in 1878 had added to the turmoil; blacks complained of sexual outrages against their women by the whites; educational facilities for the blacks were nonexistent or inadequate; propaganda encouraging the immigration was effective in Louisiana, sponsored by civil rights groups, the railroads, and Kansas land interests. Negroes found Kansas as difficult as the South, and no more than a third of the immigrants remained there. A majority of those leaving returned to their old homes in the lower Mississippi Valley. Based principally on *Senate Reports* and Louisiana newspapers; 6 photos, 72 notes.                   R. L. Woodward

1468. Robbins, Gerald. ROSSA B. COOLEY AND PENN SCHOOL: SOCIAL DYNAMO IN A NEGRO RURAL SUBCULTURE, 1901-1930. *J. of Negro Educ. 1964 33(1): 43-51.* The author traces the impact of Miss Cooley's educational philosophy on Penn School, an institution founded on St. Helena Island, South Carolina, in 1862. Miss Cooley came to Penn School from Hampton Institute with an interest in "education for life" and in improving social conditions in the community. Based on published materials.
                                                          S. C. Pearson, Jr.

1469. Ross, B. Joyce. MARY MC LEOD BETHUNE AND THE NATIONAL YOUTH ADMINISTRATION: A CASE STUDY OF POWER RELATIONSHIPS IN THE BLACK CABINET OF FRANKLIN D. ROOSEVELT. *J. of Negro Hist. 1975 60(1): 1-28.* Argues that the 1930's rather than the 1960's should be termed the

beginning of the "Second Reconstruction" because of the revival of federal support for racial equality. The existence of a so-called New Deal "Black Cabinet" was illustrated by the career of Mary McLeod Bethune with the National Youth Administration (NYA). As Director of the NYA's Division of Negro Affairs, Bethune was a symbol of black aspiration in the earliest years of the "Second Reconstruction." Based on primary sources in the records of the NYA in the National Archives; 39 notes.
                                                              N. G. Sapper

1470. Schwartz, Henry. THE MARY WALKER INCIDENT: BLACK PREJUDICE IN SAN DIEGO, 1866. *J. of San Diego Hist. 1973 19(2): 14-20.* This incident of racial discrimination resulted in the attempted firing of schoolmarm Mary Chase Walker.            S

1471. Shockley, Ann Allen. PAULINE ELIZABETH HOPKINS: A BIOGRAPHICAL EXCURSION INTO OBSCURITY. *Phylon 1972 33(1): 22-26.* A short biographical investigation of the Negro poet Pauline Elizabeth Hopkins (1859-1930).

1472. Simmons, Charles W. MAGGIE LENA WALKER AND THE CONSOLIDATED BANK & TRUST COMPANY. *Negro Hist. Bull. 1975 38(2): 345-349.* Maggie Lena Walker, Grand Secretary of the United Order of St. Luke, a Richmond, Virginia, black mutual-aid organization, urged the Order to establish a savings bank. In 1903 the Order opened the St. Luke's Penny Savings Bank, which flourished under Mrs. Walker's financial leadership, merging with two other banks in 1930. 56 notes, biblio.                                          M. J. Wentworth

1473. Tucker, David M. MISS IDA B. WELLS AND MEMPHIS LYNCHING. *Phylon 1971 32(2): 112-122.* As a newspaperwoman and lecturer, Ida B. Wells decried violence against Negroes in Memphis. The pressure on authorities, resulting from the unfavorable publicity Wells gave Memphis, may have contributed to the indictment of 13 white men after an 1894 lynching. Based on newspaper sources; 43 notes.
                                                              C. K. Piehl

1474. Walling, William and Shatzkin, Roger. IT AIN'T THE BLUES: BILLIE HOLIDAY, SIDNEY FURIE AND KITSCH. *J. of Jazz Studies 1973 1(1): 21-33.* Discusses the music of Billie Holiday in the 1930's and the rendition of her life and jazz style in the 1972 film by Sidney Furie, *Lady Sings the Blues.*                              S

1475. Windham, Wyolene. HUDDIE "LEADBELLY" LEDBETTER: SOME REMINISCENCES OF HIS COUSIN, BLANCHE LOVE. *North Louisiana Hist. Assoc. J. 1976 7(3): 96-100.* The author recounts the conversation she had recently with Blanche Love, a cousin of Huddie "Leadbelly" Ledbetter, the black folk and blues singer-composer who died in 1949 and who is buried in Shiloh Cemetery near Longwood, where he was born on the Jeter place in the 1880's. She remembers that "Huddie always had music—'it was born in him' "; that he was not a regular church-goer; and that, despite his prison record, "he never meddled nobody, he never stole anything, and he never started no fuss. He just wouldn't take nothing off nobody, so if anybody tried to start something with him, he lit right into them; it didn't make no difference if they was black or white." 2 photos, 4 notes.           A. N. Garland

## Indians

1476. Briggs, Jean L. KAPLUNA DAUGHTER: LIVING WITH ESKIMOS. *Trans-action 1970 7(8): 12-24.*

1477. Clough, Wilson O. MINI-AKU, DAUGHTER OF SPOTTED TAIL. *Ann. of Wyoming 1967 39(2): 187-216.* Examines the sources from which the story of the death and burial of Spotted Tail's daughter Mini-Aku at Fort Laramie, Wyoming, in 1866 has developed. The author discusses the original accounts of the incident, traces the additions, and shows the sources for later secondary descriptions. He concludes that Mini-Aku was one of Spotted Tail's elder daughters, that she was about 18 when she died and was buried at Fort Laramie, and that she probably helped persuade her father to remain at peace. Based on Indian Office records, military reminiscences, and secondary material; illus., 30 notes, biblio.                                              R. L. Nichols

**1478.** Davisson, Lori. THE APACHES AT HOME: A PHOTO-GRAPHIC ESSAY. *J. of Arizona Hist. 1973 14(2): 113-132.* Their environment and religious beliefs shaped the daily lives of the Apache before the arrival of Europeans. Contact with the Spanish and the Anglo-Americans brought irreversible destruction or modification of the old patterns of life and introduced new ones. The transition can be documented from the 1880's when photographers began making pictorial records. 25 illustrations with accompanying textual comment show some of the changes in the Arizona Apache, especially the women.

D. L. Smith

**1479.** Ewers, John C. DEADLIER THAN THE MALE. *Am. Heritage 1965 16(4): 10-13.* Among the Indians the female could also be deadly. Related are the following stories of Indian women: 1) Elk Hollering in the Water, a Blackfoot, who often accompanied Blackfeet war and horse-stealing parties; 2) The Other Magpie, a Crow, who went with the Crow scouts that assisted General George Crook against the Sioux in 1876, and who returned with one of the 11 scalps taken from Sioux by the Crow at the Battle of the Rosebud 17 June 1876; 3) Woman Chief, a Gros Ventre who grew up with the Crow and who even became a member of their council of chiefs; and, perhaps, the most noted of all, 4) Running Eagle, a Blackfoot woman warrior who led many raids on enemy tribes.

J. D. Filipiak

**1480.** Gilles, Albert S., Sr. POLYGAMY IN COMANCHE COUNTRY. *Southwest R. 1966 51(3): 286-297.* In defense of the Comanche practice of having several wives, the author contends that the loss of men in war, the numerous tasks necessary to keep a camp functioning properly, and the necessity for a woman to become a wife once she left her father's house, forced the Comanches to adopt the practice of polygamy which proved, at least for most, to be successful.

D. F. Henderson

**1481.** Green, Norma Kidd. FOUR SISTERS: DAUGHTERS OF JOSEPH LA FLESCHE. *Nebraska Hist. 1964 45(2): 165-176.* Briefly relates through the life stories of four daughters of Joseph La Flesche, the last recognized chief of the Omaha tribe, how they made their place in a new culture and became competent and accepted citizens in the white man's society.

R. Lowitt

**1482.** Haygood, William C. RED CHILD, WHITE CHILD: THE STRANGE DISAPPEARANCE OF CASPAR PARTRIDGE. *Wisconsin Mag. of Hist. 1975 58(4): 258-312.* A narrative of the Alvin and Lucia Partridge family and the controversy surrounding the disappearance of their six-year-old son Caspar. The Partridges came from Ohio and settled in Wisconsin's Winnebago County in the 1840's just as the Menominee Indians were vacating their lands. In the spring of 1852, Caspar disappeared. After a few days of searches involving 1,000 volunteers, the Partridges began to believe rumors that their son must have been stolen by the Indians. Later, one of the Menominee boys who looked and acted like a white child was thought to be Caspar. The boy, whose Indian name was Oakaha, was taken from his mother, Nahkom, and given to the Partridges who at first were unsure he was their child. Describes Nahkom's attempt to win her son's return and the flight of the Partridges to escape court jurisdiction. The Indian boy, raised as a white man and renamed Joseph, led a profligate life and died in 1916. 44 illus., 122 notes.

N. C. Burckel

**1483.** Jensen, Joan M. THE INDIAN LEGENDS OF MARIA ALTO. *Western Explorer 1965 3(3): 25-28.* Legends performed the function for the Indian that history performs for more civilized peoples. Thus, they give valuable insight into the world view of the Indian. Mary Elizabeth Johnson published 12 legends of the San Diego Indians in her book, *Indian Legends of the Wyomaca Mountains* (San Diego: Frye and Smith, 1914). The legends were told to her by Mary Alto, a member of that declining tribe. To Mary Johnson, these stories were "a revelation of the poetic instinct, the dramatic impulse, and the nobility of character hidden beneath the social mask of our primitive people," and they allowed a glimpse of the "inner shrine of their lives." The author of the article reproduces one of the legends, "The Old Woman's Whip" which explains how the birds and beasts received their major distinguishable physical characteristics.

W. L. Bowers

**1484.** Kehoe, Alice B. THE FUNCTION OF CEREMONIAL SEXUAL INTERCOURSE AMONG THE NORTHERN PLAINS INDIANS. *Plains Anthropologist 1970 15(48): 99-103.* "Sexual intimacy as a means of transferring spiritual power appears to have been a Mandan-Hidatsa ceremonial trait borrowed by three Algonkian Plains tribes as part of the graded men's societies complex. The Algonkian tribes modified the rite, which in the village tribes emphasized the role of father's clan. The Arapaho emphasized the cosmic symbolism of the rite, the Atsina made it a test of self-discipline, and the Blackfoot stressed the dangerous power commanded by those who performed it. These modifications parallel the differences in kinship structure between village and nomadic Plains tribes discussed by [Fred] Eggan."

J

**1485.** McAnulty, Sarah D. ANGEL DE CORA: AMERICAN ARTIST AND EDUCATOR. *Nebraska Hist. 1976 57(2): 143-199.* Examines the career of Angel DeCora (1871-1919), Winnebago artist and educator. Focuses on her contribution as an American Indian artist and her role as an educator, primarily at the Indian school in Carlisle, Pennsylvania.

R. Lowitt

**1486.** McWilliams, K. Richard and Jones, William K. THE POAF-PYBITTY SITE: A LATE NINETEENTH CENTURY KIOWA BURIAL FROM SOUTHWESTERN OKLAHOMA. *Plains Anthropologist 1976 21(71): 13-28.* This report concerns the excavation of two Plains Indian burials in southwestern Oklahoma, six miles north of Fort Sill. The landowner, herself a Comanche, had been told by her father that the burials were of Kiowas killed near that place by soldiers from the fort in the latter 1800's. Removal of the grave fill revealed the skeletons of a middle-aged female and a teenaged boy, plus a large inventory of grave goods acquired both by trade and indigenous manufacture. The grave goods confirm that the burials were Kiowas, buried between 1872 and 1875. The burials from this site are compared to other documented Plains Indian burials.

J

**1487.** Richey, Elinor. SAGEBRUSH PRINCESS WITH A CAUSE: SARAH WINNEMUCCA. *Am. West 1975 12(6): 30-33, 57-63.* Paiute Princess Sarah Winnemucca (1843?-91) attended a white school, adopted white customs, and twice married white men. When she became disillusioned with the belief, inherited from a tribal myth, that whites worked in the best interest of Indians, she began to protest. She took her protests to the highest officials, went on the lecture platform, and wrote a widely discussed book on injustices. Adapted from a forthcoming volume. 2 illus.

D. L. Smith

**1488.** Stewart, Patricia. SARAH WINNEMUCCA. *Nevada Hist. Soc. Q. 1971 14(4): 23-38.* A biographical sketch of Sarah Winnemucca Hopkins, a Paiute Indian. Sarah Winnemucca, as she is most commonly known, would have been well-known and respected in the white world if only she had adhered to the stereotype of the noble savage. Instead, she fought for her people against the depredations of the whites. Her particular enemy was the Indian Agent. She carried her fight for justice for the Indian to the highest levels of government, winning some battles but losing the war. Her flamboyant behavior could not be overcome by her sharp intelligence in the eyes of the white men, and as a result most of her efforts were doomed to failure. Based on primary and secondary sources; 56 notes.

E. P. Costello

**1489.** —. SITTING BULL COLLECTION. *South Dakota Hist. 1975 5(3): 245-265.* Reproduces the Sitting Bull Collection, 23 photographs possibly taken by Stanley J. Morrow, of the Sioux Indians imprisoned at Fort Randall, Dakota Territory. The photos, several of Sitting Bull and his wives and children, depict the Indians' daily life at Fort Randall. Some shots are of Army personnel inspecting the camp, issuing rations, and drilling. The collection, believed to have been taken between 1869-83 and copyrighted in 1882 by the firm of Bailey, Dix, and Mead, is now the property of the South Dakota State Historical Society.

A. J. Larson and S

## Other

**1490.** Barton, H. Arnold. SCANDINAVIAN IMMIGRANT WOMEN'S ENCOUNTER WITH AMERICA. *Swedish Pioneer Hist. Q.*

*1974 25(1): 37-42.* The Swedish immigrants' response to the position of women in America (ca. 1850-90) depended upon social background, age, and marital status. Young, unmarried women adopted American conventions of gentility. Men were impressed by the consideration shown women, whom they found spoiled and pretentious. Only a few upper-class women found a "Woman Problem" in America. Originally a paper for the Society for the Advancement of Scandinavian Study in May 1973. Based on primary and secondary sources; 8 notes.                  K. J. Puffer

1491. Bodnar, John E. SOCIALIZATION AND ADAPTATION: IMMIGRANT FAMILIES IN SCRANTON, 1880-1890. *Pennsylvania Hist. 1976 43(2): 147-162.* Studies the social mobility of the Irish and Welsh in Scranton during 1880-90 in order to test hypotheses advanced by Talcott Parsons, Philippe Aries, and Richard Sennett regarding the role of family structure in preparing children for adulthood in industrial society. Children from Irish and Welsh nuclear families enjoyed greater economic success than those reared in extended families. The sons of Welsh parents were more successful than those of Irish background because they were exposed to industrial life at an earlier age. The Welsh were somewhat more inclined to live in nuclear families than were the Irish. Based on census data and other sources; illus., 7 tables, 30 notes.
                                                        D. C. Swift

1492. Carter, Gregg Lee. SOCIAL DEMOGRAPHY OF THE CHINESE IN NEVADA: 1870-1880. *Nevada Hist. Soc. Q. 1975 18(2): 72-89.* The first Chinese immigrants to Nevada were miners and railroad laborers. Most were males because strong cultural pressure in China discouraged the emigration of women from China. The immigrants generally drifted into unskilled occupations, with only a few, the merchant elite in Nevada "Chinatowns," ever rising above menial labor. Based on Census Bureau documents and secondary sources; photo, 9 tables, 30 notes.
                                                        H. T. Lovin

1493. Folkedahl, Beulah, transl. and ed. ELIZABETH FEDDE'S DIARY, 1883-88. *Norwegian-Am. Studies and Records 1959 20: 170-196.* Gives a biographical sketch of Elizabeth Fedde from her birth, in 1850, in Norway until her death in 1921. Fedde came to the United States, in 1883, to do social work among Norwegian immigrants in New York City; and she played a major role in founding the Norwegian Lutheran Deaconesses' Home and Hospital in Brooklyn. The article focuses on Fedde's life and work in New York City during the 1880's and 1890's. Excerpts from Fedde's diary, April 1883 to May 1888, reveal her work and the conditions among Norwegian immigrants, faced with the complexity and economic uncertainty of a different culture in urban America. Primary sources; 43 notes.                              A. E. Wiederrecht

1494. Griswold del Castillo, Richard. LA FAMILIA CHICANA: SOCIAL CHANGE IN THE CHICANO FAMILY IN LOS ANGELES, 1850-1880. *J. of Ethnic Studies 1975 3(1): 41-58.* Examines the reaction of Mexican American families in light of the impact of modernization (urbanization and industrialization) during the period 1850-80. The pre-modern family is found to be paternalistic and extended. Modernization led to a decline in the proportion of extended families, a rise in the proportion of female headed families, and an increase in common law marriages. Rather than being functional adjustments to industrialization, these are interpreted as dysfunctional since both literacy and social mobility were associated with the declining extended family structure. Based largely on manuscript censuses and other primary sources; 27 notes.                                            T. W. Smith

1495. Kaups, Matti. A FINNISH SAVUSAUNA IN MINNESOTA. *Minnesota Hist. 1976 45(1): 11-20.* The Finnish Savusauna was a cultural transplant with several different traditions. It chiefly provided a place to bathe and perspire, but it also served as summer sleeping quarters, a place for wet cupping, a maternity ward, and a laundry. Construction techniques are described in detail. Based on interviews, inspections of the remains of savusauna, and published sources; 12 illus., 26 notes.
                                                        S. S. Sprague

1496. Lindquist, Emory. A SWEDISH IMMIGRANT WOMAN VIEWS HER HOME IN KANSAS, 1870-1881: THE LETTERS AND DIARY OF IDA NIBELIUS LINDGREN. *Swedish Pioneer Hist. Q. 1965 16(1): 3-17.* Lindgren's privately printed diary and letters to her mother and sister in Sweden are excellent source materials. They reveal

homesickness and the difficulties and insecurities of pioneer life as well as joyous holiday celebrations with other Swedes. Many aspects of pioneer life in Kansas are minutely detailed in the letters and diary, especially the solace found in regular religious activities. The Lindgren family returned to Sweden in 1881, in part because of isolation from other Swedes in Kansas. Based on primary and secondary sources; 5 notes.
                                                        A. Boehm

1497. McLaughlin, Virginia Yans. PATTERNS OF WORK AND FAMILY ORGANIZATION: BUFFALO'S ITALIANS. *J. of Interdisciplinary Hist. 1971 2(2): 299-314.* Examines the relationship between female occupational patterns and family organization among south Italians in Buffalo, ca. 1900-30. The female assumption of new economic functions did not alter family power arrangements or disrupt the traditional family as many social scientists have suggested. Male authority did not depend entirely upon fulfillment of economic obligations, and the seasonal, sporadic or part-time work of women coincided with the demands of a developing capitalist economy. The traditional, conservative, working-class south Italian family remained coherent. Based on primary and secondary sources; 29 notes.                    E. J. Hundert

1498. Millgård, Per-Olof. LETTERS FROM NEW SWEDEN, MAINE. *Swedish Pioneer Hist. Q. 1975 26(2): 104-111.* Selections from the letters of Swedish immigrant families in Maine, 1873-88. Things went badly at first, the new settlers feeling homesick and many household items hard to find. By 1879, food became plentiful and work for wages available. The selection from 1888 is by a widow informing her mother-in-law of her husband's death from pneumonia. Primary sources; illus.
                                                        K. J. Puffer

1499. Nagorka, Suzanne. THE LIFE OF FELICIA NAGORKA. *New York Folklore Q. 1972 28(4): 286-292.* Discusses the life of Polish-American immigrant Felicia Pawlowski Nagorka in Schenectady, New York, in the early 20th century, emphasizing her religion and marriage.

1500. O'Connell, Lucille. TRAVELERS' AID FOR POLISH IMMIGRANT WOMEN. *Polish Am. Studies 1974 31(1): 15-19.* The Travelers' Aid Society was formed in 1907 to protect rural American and immigrant girls who came to New York City alone. After immigration had peaked, and during the depression of the 1930's, the Society took care primarily of native American girls, eventually evolving into an organization to help all travelers in all major cities of the United States. Gives examples of assistance rendered Polish immigrant girls. 15 notes.
                                                        S. R. Pliska

1501. Peterson, Martin. THE SWEDES OF YAMHILL. *Oregon Hist. Q. 1975 76(1): 5-27.* Presents the history and personal memoirs of the Swedish American community in the vicinity of Carlton, Oregon, and the Yamhill River Valley. In the late 19th century John Wennerberg helped many of his fellow Swedes to settle in western Oregon. The immigrants labored as farmhands and housekeepers, and purchased farms with the aid of Wennerberg. Describes the Swedish folkways, expressions, agricultural methods, and recreational activities established in the immigrants' new environment. Based on remembrances of 14 persons and letters to the author; 14 photos, 5 notes.              J. D. Smith

1502. Rossi, Jean. EVDOKIA GREGOVNA ZAHAROFF (HER LIFE AND FLIGHT FROM RUSSIA). *Pacific Historian 1970 14(1): 41-48.* Discusses a Russian Baptist family's emigration from Tsarist Russia to Hawaii via Manchuria and Japan to escape persecution. 4 photos, map, 4 notes.                                  F. I. Murphy

1503. Zebrowski, Walter. POLES IN GLADYS HASTY CARROLL'S "AS THE EARTH TURNS." *Polish Am. Studies 1963 20(1): 17-20.* Reviews the plot of *As the Earth Turns* and then comments on the fact that the Janowskis are not depicted as a true Polish family. Some of the first names given to them in the novel are not true Polish. Also, the family seems to assimilate much too rapidly for first-generation Polish immigrants.                                          S. R. Pliska

# Social Problems

## General

### *(including race relations)*

**1504.** Andrist, Ralph K. PALADIN OF PURITY. *Am. Heritage 1973 24(6): 4-7, 84-89.* Discusses Anthony Comstock's (1844-1915) Victorian morality and his efforts to eliminate vice, pornography, and birth control.
S

**1505.** Becker, Dorothy G. EXIT LADY BOUNTIFUL: THE VOLUNTEER AND THE PROFESSIONAL SOCIAL WORKER. *Social Service R. 1964 38(1): 57-72.* Concerns the place of the volunteer social worker in service. "Lady Bountiful" was a "friendly visitor," who visited the homes of the poor to try, "by means of personal influence and practical suggestion, to improve their condition." From the middle of the 19th century, social service agencies depended on women volunteers. Societies were founded by them to further their "charity work." The goals were often higher than could be reached, yet the women continued for decades to instruct and assist the poor. The stereotype of the do-gooder has caused the demise of Lady Bountiful, together with the increased professionalism of the field and growing bureaucratization. 60 notes.
M. W. Machan

**1506.** Bordin, Ruth B. EMMA HALL AND THE REFORMATORY PRINCIPLE. *Michigan Hist. 1964 48(4): 315-332.* Traces Emma Amelia Hall's career as a penal reformer during the latter part of the 19th century. Miss Hall, while serving as the first superintendent of the Girls' Training School at Adrian, Michigan, between 1881 and 1884, was one of several prison administrators who stressed the correctional principles of labor, education, and religion.
J. K. Flack

**1507.** Cheever, L. O. IOWA ANNIE WITTENMYER HOME. *Palimpsest 1967 48(6): 249-288.* Annie Wittenmyer was a well-to-do widow living in Keokuk, Iowa, at the time of the Civil War. As president of a group whose object was the founding of a home for soldiers' orphans she organized a statewide campaign and opened her first home in Farmington in June 1864. Her second home was opened in Cedar Falls in 1865. As both proved too small for the growing demands made upon them, Mrs. Wittenmyer secured from the War Department title to the abandoned Camp Kinsman army barrack in Davenport and moved her Farmington children to the new location in late 1865. In the next 10 years the main home and the Cedar Falls and new Glenwood branches had an average enrollment of over 700 children. It was also during this period that the State of Iowa assumed direction in the institution. As the orphans of soldiers from the Civil War grew older, the homes were open to other destitute children. Ultimately consolidated at the Davenport location, it was officially named the Iowa Annie Wittenmyer Home in 1949. Illus.
D. W. Curl

**1508.** Curti, Merle; Green, Judith; and Nash, Roderick. ANATOMY OF GIVING: MILLIONAIRES IN THE LATE 19TH CENTURY. *Am. Q. 1963 15(3): 416-435.* The validity of the American reputation for generosity is one of the concerns of the University of Wisconsin Project on the History of American Philanthropy. Tables show that almost all giving was directed toward the local community. Other tables show allocation of gifts and bequests in relation to sex, to philanthropic categories, to residence, to religion, while another indicates allocation to categories compared with the extent of education of the donors. Apparently the most significant differences in philanthropic habits existed - contrary to expectations - between the possessors of self-made and inherited wealth, the former being distinctly more generous. Based on newspapers and periodicals of the period.
E. P. Stickney

**1509.** Gettleman, Marvin E. CHARITY AND SOCIAL CLASSES IN THE UNITED STATES, 1874-1900. *Am. J. of Econ. and Sociol. 1963 22(2): 313-329, and (3): 417-426.* Attempts to show how the "Simultaneous recognition and evasion of the problem of social classes were...the dominant characteristics of the formulative years of the American profession and institution of social work." Part I: The author examines the program and ideology of the Charity Organization movement and its relationship to 19th century business enterprise and social Darwinism.

Part II: The author concludes that the 19th century charity movement failed in its attempt to engage in interclass communication. The COS (Charity Organization Society) program had ill-formulated goals and great duplication.
B. E. Swanson

**1510.** Gilmore, Al-Tony. JACK JOHNSON AND WHITE WOMEN: THE NATIONAL IMPACT, 1912-1913. *J. of Negro Hist. 1973 58(1): 18-38.* The national reaction to Jack Johnson and his personal relationships with white women vastly reduced his popularity, not only among whites but also among blacks. Based on secondary sources; 75 notes.
N. G. Sapper

**1511.** Goodman, Abram Vossem. ADOLPHUS S. SOLOMONS AND CLARA BARTON: A FORGOTTEN CHAPTER IN THE EARLY YEARS OF THE AMERICAN RED CROSS. *Am. Jewish Hist. Q. 1970 59(3): 331-356.* The exchange of letters between Adolphus S. Solomons (1826-1910) and Clara Barton, the American founder of the Red Cross, highlight the early achievements of the Red Cross in the years between its official establishment in 1881 and 1893 (when the organization received its second charter of incorporation). Based on the voluminous Clara Barton Papers, now presented to the Library of Congress, and the Solomons documents in the collections of the American Jewish Historical Society which include the letters he received from Miss Barton; photo., 67 notes.
F. Rosenthal

**1512.** Kusmer, Kenneth L. THE FUNCTIONS OF ORGANIZED CHARITY IN THE PROGRESSIVE ERA: CHICAGO AS A CASE STUDY. *J. of Am. Hist. 1973 60(3): 657-678.* A study of the Charities Organization Society Movement in Chicago in the 1880's and 1890's demonstrates that in the beginning the society was concerned with transmitting the values of small-town rural America to the urban context. Values of community, country life, and the middle class were stressed by upwardly mobile charity workers from small midwestern towns whose cultural values were threatened by the many immigrant poor. The movement employed as "friendly visitors" middle-class women who applied values of the "home" to the city, and was financed by wealthy merchants, bankers, and lawyers who thought broadly of the need to avoid growing social conflict. Increasing economic dislocation and unemployment after 1890 led toward a more modern welfare system. Table, 90 notes.
K. B. West

**1513.** Roberts, Randy. HEAVYWEIGHT CHAMPION JACK JOHNSON: HIS OMAHA IMAGE, A PUBLIC RELATIONS STUDY. *Nebraska Hist. 1976 57(2): 226-241.* An examination of the Omaha press during 1908-15, when Jack Johnson held the heavyweight title. Press reaction tended to reflect the social and cultural values of an overwhelmingly white community. It was only toward the end of this period, and primarily because of Johnson's relationship with a white woman, that the press in Omaha became hostile toward him. Yet the Omaha press was more moderate in its views towards the black champion than that in most cities.
R. Lowitt

**1514.** Turner, Frederick W., III. THE CENTURY AFTER A CENTURY OF DISHONOR: AMERICAN CONSCIENCE AND CONSCIOUSNESS. *Massachusetts R. 1975 16(4): 715-731.* America "needs to be saved from the conscience it has developed," partially reflected in 1881 in Helen Hunt Jackson's *A Century of Dishonor.* The book, urging justice for the Ponca, was the first pro-Indian book to have a serious impact. Bicentennial events should be used to reexamine past events so that a truly responsive culture can emerge. Based on primary and secondary sources.
M. J. Barach

**1515.** Wynes, Charles E. THE RACE QUESTION IN THE SOUTH AS VIEWED BY BRITISH TRAVELERS, 1865-1914. *Louisiana Studies 1974 13(3): 223-240.* Surveys the opinions of British visitors to America regarding American race relations in the South. The effectiveness of black labor and the shift to white labor for the more skilled jobs and trades were noted. Segregation was rather general though not universal, but it was often indicated that the crux of the problem lay in the fear of intermarriage and assimilation. As time passed, the accounts of the Negro became more and more stereotyped, thereby reducing their significance, including as sophisticated an observer as James Bryce. 65 notes.
R. V. Ritter

# Crime

## (by and against women)

1516. Biddick, William, Jr. THE CELEBRATED EMMA LE DOUX CASE. *Pacific Historian 1967 11(4): 37-54.* An account of a trunk murder discovered on 24 March 1906 in Stockton, California, in the baggage room of the Southern Pacific Railway. Soon after, the police apprehended Emma Le Doux for the murder of A. N. McVicar. Newspapers made a carnival of gore from the impending trial. The author follows the details of the relationship between the two principals, establishing Emma's reputation as an "oddity." Then in great detail the narrative exposes the story of the trial and its subsequent conclusion of a verdict of guilty in the first degree. After a number of appeal procedures, Emma Le Doux was paroled in the custody of her sister in 1920, but a year later was returned to custody when her sister complained that she had been running a house of prostitution. Paroled again in 1925, she broke parole with a conviction for theft and returned to prison at Tehachapi where she died in 1941. The article is offered as a look into legal and judicial practices in Stockton in the early 1900's. Documented from court records, interviews, and newspapers; illus., 56 notes.　　　T. R. Cripps

1517. Carver, Carolyn. A DAY WITH BONNIE AND CLYDE. *North Louisiana Hist. Assoc. J. 1971 2(2): 59-62.* Recounts the experiences of H. Dillard Darby and Sophia Stone of Ruston, Louisiana, on 27 April 1933, when they were held for 12 hours by Clyde and Buck Barrow and Bonnie Parker. Darby, a mortician, was eating lunch at his boarding house when he saw a youth enter his car and drive it off. He and Miss Stone pursued in the latter's car. They were flagged down by a man who turned out to be Clyde Barrow, put into the back seat of the Barrow car, and for the next half-day continually threatened with death. Eventually, Darby and Stone were released near Walde, Arkansas. Describes the last days of the gang, and points out that Darby later was called on "to identify the bodies of Bonnie and Clyde and did embalm them." 9 notes.　　　A. N. Garland

1518. Case, Richard G. THE DRUSE CASE: MURDER BALLAD FRAGMENTS. *New York Folklore Q. 1969 25(2): 93-99.* Discusses popular folk songs about Roxalana Druse, a Herkimer County, New York, farm wife who was hanged for the murder of her husband in the 1880's.

1519. Freedman, Estelle B. THEIR SISTERS' KEEPERS: AN HISTORICAL PERSPECTIVE ON FEMALE CORRECTIONAL INSTITUTIONS IN THE UNITED STATES: 1870-1900. *Feminist Studies 1974 2(1): 77-95.* The attack of 19th-century women prison reformers on the patriarchal prison system and the substitution of a matriarchal one was a "necessary intermediate route to sexual equality." In the 1820's a number of American women began efforts to reform the prisons and several states enacted reforms such as hiring female matrons and providing separate quarters for women. The post-Civil War women's prison reform movement grew out of four factors: 1) the increase in female prison population, 2) women's Civil War social service experience, 3) the charities organization movement and prison reform movement, and 4) an "embryonic feminist analysis of women's place in American society" which led to a separatist approach to female correction. Reformers argued for female superiority in correctional work and structured their reformatory programs on the traditional female virtues of domesticity and purity, which contradicted the concept of equal rights and limited their work to traditional women's roles. Today's reintegration of the correctional system should aim at equal rights, the integration of the "achievements of women's reforms into co-educational institutions" and the end to the "treatment of women as morally superior domestics." 70 notes.　　　J. D. Falk

1520. Hunter, Charles H. MURDER, RAPE, AND CARPETBAGGERS. *Pacific Northwest Q. 1967 58(3): 151-154.* Analysis of three controversial books written about the alleged rape of the wife of Lieutenant Thomas Massie of the U.S. Navy in 1931 on the island of Oahu. The case became famous because of incidents involving race relations, inept police work, and sensational journalism.　　　C. C. Gorchels

1521. Jenista, Frank L. PROBLEMS OF THE COLONIAL CIVIL SERVICE: AN ILLUSTRATION FROM THE CAREER OF MAN-

UEL L. QUEZON. *Southeast Asia 1974 3(3): 809-829.* As a young man Manuel Quezon served for 13 months as a prosecuting attorney for the American Insular Civil Service in Calapan, Mindoro. The results of his experiences were mixed. While he ended some corrupt practices in his district, he was involved in criminal activities that resulted in his resignation. In 1904, he reportedly kidnapped and raped Tomasa Alcalá, a young girl from the village of Silonay. An official inquiry into the incident and other criminal complaints showed Quezon to be probably guilty of six criminal actions ranging from rape to malfeasance of office. In later life Quezon sought to impose upon other civil servants the modern sense of responsibility which he himself had lacked in 1904. Based mainly on US government sources; 36 notes.　　　R. H. Detrick

1522. Levy, Eugene. "IS THE JEW A WHITE MAN?": PRESS RE-ACTION TO THE LEO FRANK CASE, 1913-1915. *Phylon 1974 35(2): 212-222.* An analysis of white, black, and Jewish press reactions to the trial, conviction, and appeal of Leo Frank, a Jew, for the murder of a young Gentile girl in Atlanta, Georgia, in 1913. Frank's conviction depended on the testimony of James Conley, a black. The big city, white newspapers questioned the character of Conley, an ex-convict. The Jewish press perceived a shift in prejudices from Negroes to Jews. During the appeals processes, the black newspapers decried the attempt to substitute a black man for the Jew as perpetrator of the crime. 50 notes.　　　V. L. Human

1523. Muller, Howard W. THE MOONLIGHT MURDERS ON THE ISLES OF SHOALS. *New-England Galaxy 1976 17(3): 8-16.* Describes the brutal, money-motivated murders of Karen Christensen (sister of Maren Hontvet) and Anethe Christensen (bride of Ivan Christensen) on the isolated island of Smutty Nose off the New Hampshire coast on the night of 5-6 March 1873 by a German immigrant, Louis Wagner, a friend of the Hontvets. 6 illus.　　　P. C. Marshall

1524. Murray, Hugh T., Jr. THE NAACP VERSUS THE COMMUNIST PARTY: THE SCOTTSBORO RAPE CASES, 1931-1932. *Phylon 1967 28(3): 276-287.* Examines the charge that the Communist Party sought to sacrifice the nine young Negroes who allegedly raped two white prostitutes near Scottsboro, Alabama, in 1931 in order to make martyrs for the cause of Communist propaganda. Eight of the boys were quickly found guilty and all but the youngest were sentenced to die in the electric chair. Before this case, the International Labor Defense, a Communist front organization, had been inactive in the defense of Negroes, but it won out in its struggle with the National Association for the Advancement of Colored People in the fight to represent the youths' appeals. The ILD promoted mass public appeals for justice as well as engaging in the legal efforts to secure a reversal of the convictions. The author notes that this was the first time such widespread mass efforts had been staged on behalf of Negro rights, and the NAACP opposed them. The author concludes that the Communists did not attempt to make martyrs of the Scottsboro boys, but instead saved them from a bungling defense and initiated a mass movement on behalf of the Negroes. Based largely on published sources; 68 notes.　　　D. N. Brown

1525. Rich, Carroll Y. THE AUTOPSY OF BONNIE AND CLYDE. *Western Folklore 1970 29(1): 27-33.* Corrects some of the misconceptions and myths that have arisen from the recent romanticization of Bonnie Parker Thornton and Clyde Champion Barrow. Discusses the transformation of these two "poor-white" robbers and killers into folk heroes. Points out some of the realities that have been overlooked (such as their appearance, romantic life, etc.). States that the true story of their ambush death in Louisiana in 1934 is available from many primary sources. Emphasizes a reconstruction of events after they were killed. Reproduces the coroner's reports and several other pieces of testimony. Based on original documents and photos, as well as on recent writings; 7 notes.　　　R. A. Trennert

# Illness and Medical Treatment

1526. Duffy, John. ANGLO-AMERICAN REACTION TO OB-STETRICAL ANESTHESIA. *Bull. of the Hist. of Medicine 1964 38(1): 32-44.* "Although the main battle for obstetrical anesthesia had been won by 1860, the wide lag between medical developments and medical practices in the nineteenth century meant that the use of anesthesia was not nearly as universal as might have been expected." Many doctors did not read medical journals, and many others were opposed to anesthesia in principle. "...by the outbreak of World War I some type of anesthesia was available for any parturient woman under a physician's care."

W. L. Fox

1527. Fox, V. and Lowe, G. D., II. DAY-HOSPITAL TREATMENT OF THE ALCOHOLIC PATIENT. *Q. J. of Studies on Alcohol 1968 29(3): 634-641.* "Since 1956 the Georgian Clinic in Atlanta has been operating a day hospital for alcoholics. An average of 92 patients take part in the hospital's program every day of the week; about 78 [percent] are first admissions, 77 [percent] are men, 89 [percent] are White, 60 [percent] married, 66 [percent] aged 35 to 54, 53 [percent] clerical, sales or skilled workers; 46 [percent] of the men are unemployed but 81 [percent] of the professionals-managers were still working at their occupations. Treatment is primarily group therapy, conducted by physicians, clergymen and psychologists; in addition, patients take part in cinema and discussion, orientation, recreation, and vocational-rehabilitation groups. The hospital is open from 9 AM to 9 PM and patients spend an average of 8 to 10 hours a day at the hospital. Family members are also involved in the treatment. The day-hospital program allows the patient to maintain continuous contact with the same therapeutic reference groups as he moves back into community life. It provides daily testing in responsibility; fosters a view of treatment, by the patient and his family, as 'work'; enables the patient to pace his own progress through the stages of treatment; encourages continuous discharge planning from the beginning of treatment; and facilitates the involvement of the patient's family in therapy. The costs of day-hospital programs may be almost as high as residential hospitals and, under some circumstances, more difficult to justify. Also, the day-hospital program poses some threat to traditional professional modes of operation. Consequently, staff recruitment and training are likely to be major and continuing problems."

J

1528. Halvorsen, Helen Olson. 19TH CENTURY MIDWIFE: SOME RECOLLECTIONS. *Ore. Hist. Q. 1969 70(1): 39-49.* Recollections of a woman who was born in Wisconsin in 1863, the daughter of Norwegian immigrants, dealing with domestic incidents of her life in Wisconsin, Minnesota, and Oregon. Emphasis is on her experiences as a midwife and as a mother of eight children of her own.

C. C. Gorchels

1529. Labarbera, Michael. AN OUNCE OF PREVENTION, AND GRANDMA TRIED THEM ALL. *New York Folklore Q. 1964 20(2): 126-129.* Discusses superstitions about diseases and folk medicine in New York in the mid-to-late 19th century.

1530. MacGaffey, Edward A PATTERN FOR PROGRESS: THE MINNESOTA CHILDREN'S CODE. *Minnesota Hist. 1969 41(5): 229-236.* Discusses the enactment of the Minnesota Children's Code, 35 laws passed in 1917. Emphasizes preceding State child welfare legislation, the work of the semiofficial Minnesota Child Welfare Commission in making specific proposals for the code, editorial support rendered by the *Minneapolis Journal,* and the special need for the implementation of sections of the code regarding maternity hospitals, infant homes, and child care and placement agencies. In addition to providing for State licensing and supervision of these agencies, the code made the State the guardian of all children committed to State institutions, juveniles entrusted to State by the courts, and all feebleminded persons. Although it met resistance in the legislature in 1913 and 1915 and required some legislative clarification in 1919, the code is perhaps Minnesota's greatest achievement in social legislation. Based primarily on State documents, the report of the Child Welfare Commission, and the papers of a commission member; illus., 19 notes.

G. R. Adams

1531. Ross, Rodney A. MARY TODD LINCOLN, PATIENT AT BELLEVUE PLACE, BATAVIA. *J. of the Ill. State Hist. Soc. 1970 63(1): 5-34.* Reviews the question of Mrs. Lincoln's sanity, focusing on the events associated with her residence at Bellevue Place. Included in the article is a transcript of the entries made regarding Mrs. Lincoln in a journal in which reports of her activities were entered virtually every day between 20 May and 19 August 1875. Based on Patient Progress Reports for Bellevue Place and the Letter Book of Richard J. Patterson in possession of the author, the David Davis Papers at the Illinois State Historical

Society Library at Springfield, the Robert Todd Lincoln Collection at the Chicago Historical Society, and contemporary newspapers.

S. L. Jones

1532. Sawyer, Donald J. THE LADY WITH THE SNAKE IN HER. *New York Folklore Q. 1969 25(4): 299-305.* Relates the story of a woman in Broadalbin, New York, who reputedly swallowed a snake; emphasizes the medical treatment she received for it, 1870's-80's.

1533. Sufrin, Mark. THE CASE OF THE DISAPPEARING COOK. *Am. Heritage 1970 21(5): 37-43.* Relates the story of Mary Mallon, Typhoid Mary, a cook whose personal habits led to the spread of typhoid wherever she worked. As the result of the investigations by a New York City sanitary engineer, Mary was arrested and confined to hospitals for nearly half of her seventy years. 4 illus.

J. F. Paul

1534. Wood, Ann Douglas "THE FASHIONABLE DISEASES": WOMEN'S COMPLAINTS AND THEIR TREATMENT IN NINETEENTH-CENTURY AMERICA. *J. of Interdisciplinary Hist. 1973 4(1): 25-52.* Analyzes 19th-century diagnosis and treatment of American women's nervous and sexual diseases as revealed in the health books and medical manuals of that time. Because medical analysis of women focused on the womb, "medical reactions to female nervous complaints are indicative of nineteenth-century American attitudes not only toward disease and sexuality in general but, more significantly, toward feminine sexual identity in particular." Discusses the writings of Elizabeth Blackwell, Harriot Kezia Hunt, and Elizabeth Stuart Phelps Ward. 73 notes.

D. D. Cameron

# Prostitution

1535. Anderson, Eric. PROSTITUTION AND SOCIAL JUSTICE: CHICAGO, 1910-15. *Social Service R. 1974 48(2): 203-228.*

1536. Betten, Neil. NATIVISM AND THE KLAN IN TOWN AND CITY: VALPARAISO AND GARY, INDIANA. *Studies in Hist. and Soc. 1973 4(2): 3-16.* A study of the Ku Klux Klan during the 1920's in two urban centers. Indicates that "The Klan grew in Gary and Valparaiso by fashioning its appeal to the concerns of its white Protestant citizens . . ." and focused on such "myriad enemies" as corrupt politicians, bootleggers, prostitutes, imagined radicals, and immigrants who would not or could not instantly assimilate.

J. O. Baylen

1537. Brier, Warren J. TILTING SKIRTS AND HURDY-GURDIES: A COMMENTARY ON GOLD CAMP WOMEN. *Montana: Mag. of Western Hist 1969 19(4): 58-67.* A gathering of anecdotes and editorial comments about wild women on the Montana frontier, particularly in Virginia City. Reform campaigns by editors and townspeople did not appear to succeed in closing the notorious hurdy-gurdy houses of the community. Interspersed with quotes from the Virginia City *Post.*

S. R. Davison

1538. Goldman, Marion. PROSTITUTION AND VIRTUE IN NEVADA. *Society 1972 10(1): 32-38.*

1539. Lasswell, David. CHICAGO BEFORE THE FIRE: SOME PEOPLE, PLACES, AND THINGS. *Chicago Hist. 1971 1(4): 196-203.* Prior to the fire (8-10 October 1871), Michigan Avenue already had the smell of richness; Terrace Row contained a block of 11 elegantly matched four-story houses, faced with carved Joliet limestone. The north side of the city was "the city in the garden" with its fine homes and bucolic way of life. Along with the recognized modes of business, the downtown area was known for prostitution, gambling, and other vices. At the time, many citizens thought the fire was caused by "desperadoes." There was never any proven incendiarism or large-scale civil disorder. 5 photos.

N. A. Kuntz

1540. MacPhail, Elizabeth C. WHEN THE RED LIGHTS WENT OUT IN SAN DIEGO: THE LITTLE KNOWN STORY OF SAN DIEGO'S "RESTRICTED" DISTRICT. *J. of San Diego Hist. 1975 20(2): 1-28.* Describes San Diego's Stingaree and Redlight Districts, 1870's-1917, and the efforts of Walter Bellon, City Health Inspector, to clean up the waterfront slums.

S

1541. Mayfield, John S. THE EASIEST WAY, OR "I AM A BAD GIRL NOW," A PROBLEM RELATING TO THE ETHICS OF RESEARCH. *Manuscripts 1974 26(2): 96-104.* Tells of delicate research in tracing two "bad" people of 19th-century mid-America from an autograph letter, 25 February 1881, purchased from the shop of Walter R. Benjamin. Relates inquiries about two natives of Ada, Ohio—Annie Brown (1865-1939), who operated two brothels in Cincinnati before dying in a state mental hospital, and her correspondent, Samuel W. Shockley (1858-1941), who in the words of his own daughter "turned out to be a really bad man, drunkard, gambler, and adulterer."
D. A. Yanchisin

1542. McGovern, James R. "SPORTING LIFE ON THE LINE": PROSTITUTION IN PROGRESSIVE ERA PENSACOLA. *Florida Hist. Q. 1975 54(2): 131-144.* In the first few decades of the 20th century Pensacola, Florida's police and city officials succeeded in confining prostitution and saloons to a restricted area of the city rather than trying to eliminate the problems entirely. Confining prostitution to a specific area afforded both safety and economy to the rest of the city. In addition, the city received revenue in fines from occasional crackdowns. Changing morals and attitudes brought an end to the district of brothels by the beginning of World War II. Based on primary and secondary works; illus., 73 notes.
P. A. Beaber

# Image and Self-Image

1543. Burstyn, Joan N. and Corrigan, Ruth R. IMAGES OF WOMEN IN TEXTBOOKS 1880-1920. *Teachers Coll. Record 1975 76(3): 431-440.* Studies geography, physiology, and arithmetic texts published between 1880 and 1920 to see how they reflected changes in the images of American women. Except for those books written by women, the texts made almost no mention of the great changes in the lives of women during the time chosen for study.
W. H. Mulligan, Jr.

1544. Cowan, Ruth Schwartz. TWO WASHES IN THE MORNING AND A BRIDGE PARTY AT NIGHT: THE AMERICAN HOUSEWIFE BETWEEN THE WARS. *Women's Studies 1976 3(2): 147-171.* Locates the emergence of the feminine mystique in the 1920's rather than in the 1940's and 50's as suggested by Betty Friedan. The advertisements, advice columns, and informative articles found in popular women's magazines, during the 1920's-30's, disseminated the mystique's basic tenets that women were purely domestic beings whose goals in life were to have a husband, family, and home and that women who worked outside the home did so because they were odd or had to work. In the popular literature, servants disappeared from domestic scenes and housework became an extension of the housewife's personality. The housewife became a consumer instead of a producer. She became more slender, elegant, and manicured than her predecessors and her most important task in life was child rearing. Technology altered the housewife's responsibilities. Shaped in the 1920's, the social ideology of the feminine mystique was solidified during the 1930's. Based on primary and secondary sources; 78 notes.
A. E. Wiederrecht

1545. Hasbany, Richard. BROMIDIC PARABLES: THE AMERICAN MUSICAL THEATRE DURING THE SECOND WORLD WAR. *J. of Popular Culture 1973 6(4): 642-665.* Oklahoma! (1943) represented a revolution in musical theater. Along with *Porgy and Bess*, *Carousel*, and *On the Town*, Broadway musicals began to take serious works of literature and music as their subjects. The most successful shows after the war dealt with Americana. Local color and the ideas of national unity, freedom, and America as a land of reform were important elements in the plays. The use of cultural archetypes such as the peculiarly American reformer and the chaste maiden and wife made the shows, especially *Oklahoma!*, cultural parables of the American myth, and were an oblique response to the war. 26 notes.
J. D. Falk

1546. Haverstock, Mary Sayre. A HALCYON SUMMER THAT LINGERED ON AND ON ... IN PAINTING. *Smithsonian 1972 3(4): 32-39.* Discusses the group of painters, 1885-1920, who came to be labeled as the Summer School for their paintings of women in blissful summer scenes.

1547. Koch, Robert. GIBSON GIRL REVISITED. *Art in Am. 1965 53(1): 70-73.* Reviews the *fin de siécle*, idealized image of the American Girl created by Charles Dana Gibson. Illus.
W. K. Bottorff

1548. Meldrum, Barbara. IMAGES OF WOMEN IN WESTERN AMERICAN LITERATURE. *Midwest Q. 1976 17(3): 252-267.* More attention should be given to the important role played by women in western literature. Three possible approaches to the subject are: 1) a thematic approach, such as the portrayal of women as the civilizing force in an uncivilized environment, 2) the archetypal approach, providing tension through the conflict of masculine versus feminine ideals, and 3) the historical role approach, the most typical of which is the pioneer woman. One stereotype which seems to be missing from this literature is the image of the submissive wife. These approaches are discussed in the context of various literary works by such authors as Owen Wister, Bret Harte, Mari Sandoz, Willa Cather, and others.
S. J. Quinlan

1549. Purcell, L. Edward. COLORFUL GREETINGS. *Palimpsest 1974 55(3): 78-83.* Reprints early postcards displaying stone lithography and discusses attitudes toward women revealed in postcard art.
S

1550. Seller, Maxine S. BEYOND THE STEREOTYPE: A NEW LOOK AT THE IMMIGRANT WOMAN, 1880-1924. *J. of Ethnic Studies 1975 3(1): 59-70.* Questions the standard stereotypes of immigrant women as ignorant seamstresses or subservient, simplistic wives and mothers. Studies of Antonietta Pisanelli Alessandro (founder of professional Italian theater in the United States), Josephine Humpel Zeman (Bohemian journalist), and Rose Pesotta (Russian Jewish trade unionist), show that immigrant women often led movements for cultural, intellectual, and economic improvement. Sources exist to further examine the contributions of the neglected half of the immigrant population. Secondary and autobiographical sources; 38 notes.
T. W. Smith

1551. Smith, Gene. A LITTLE VISIT TO THE LOWER DEPTHS VIA THE POLICE GAZETTE. *Am. Heritage 1972 23(6): 65-73.* The *Police Gazette* began publishing in 1845. Taken over by Richard Kyle Fox in the 1870's, the *Gazette* became widely known for its entertainment, raciness, and readability. With emphasis upon sports, theater, and women, it became standard reading fare in barbershops and saloons. Fox died a multimillionaire in 1922. 12 illus.
J. F. Paul

1552. —. THE GIBSON GIRL. *York State Tradition 1973 27(3): 2-7, 9.* Discusses the popular pin-up Gibson Girls created by Charles Dana Gibson.
S

# Culture, the Arts, and Recreation

## General

1554. Caldwell, Dorothy. MISSOURIANS AND THE SPIRIT OF '76. *Missouri Hist. Rev. 1972 67(1): 31-51.* Describes the difficulties experienced by Missourians to provide a building and suitable exhibits at the Centennial Exposition of 1876. Discusses the Missouri exhibition and reports public reaction to it. A women's ways and means committee was more effective in providing exhibits than a men's ways and means committee that had been assigned the task of raising money. The Missouri exhibit fell short of the original ambitious goals, but the enthusiasm generated throughout the state remained alive and provided a spark for the Louisiana Purchase Exposition of 1904. Based on books, articles, newspapers, state and federal publications; 10 illus., 89 notes.
W. F. Zornow

1555. Chambliss, Amy. THE FRIENDSHIP OF HELEN KELLER AND MARK TWAIN. *Georgia R. 1970 24(3): 305-310.* Helen Keller and Mark Twain were close friends for 16 years before his death. Twain was concerned with Keller's education, obtained financial support for her, and was a constant friend. Their influence on each other is noted in excerpts from their notes and letters.                                        J. S. Pula

1556.   Coulter, E. Merton.   LULU HURST, "GEORGIA WON-DER."   *Georgia Hist. Q. 1971 55(1): 26-61.* Describes the stage career of Lulu Hurst, born in 1869 in Cedar Valley, Georgia. At 14 she began to exhibit unusual powers inexplicable to family and friends. Her first public performance was in her home town. In chair, billiard cue, and umbrella acts, volunteers were tossed about the stage by some irresistible force. Describes her tours, scientific tests of the acts, and her sensational reception on the stage 1883-85. After that she retired permanently and married her manager, Paul M. Atkinson. She lived quietly in Madison, Georgia, until her death at age 81 in 1950. In her autobiography she claimed that all acts were done through physical force. Photos, 116 notes.
R. V. Ritter

1557.   Day, Louise.   MY CHAUTAUQUA.   *Idaho Yesterdays 1969 13(3): 2-5.* The author participated in Chautauqua in 1919-20.

1558.   Gravitz, Maybelle.   CHAUTAUQUA: THE MOST AMERI-CAN THING IN AMERICA.   *Wisconsin Then And Now 1972 18(11): 4-5, 8.* The author relates her experiences at a Chautauqua session in 1920. Provides a brief history of the Chautauqua circuit from its origin in 1874 by the Reverend John H. Vincent, and names many Chautauqua speakers and entertainment acts.                                        D. P. Peltier

1559.   Jackson, Carl T.   THE NEW THOUGHT MOVEMENT AND THE NINETEENTH-CENTURY DISCOVERY OF ORIENTAL PHILOSOPHY.   *J. of Popular Culture 1975 9(3): 523-548.* Examines the New Thought movement's discovery of ancient Indian philosophy as one example of the late 19th-century Oriental vogue. It developed from Phineas Parkhurst Quimby's discoveries of mental-healing in the 1850's. His disciple Warren Felt Evans then directed attention to the Orient and India; the Vedanta became commonplace in New Thought periodicals. Three of the foremost leaders of the movement, Elizabeth Towne, William Walker Atkinson, and Horatio Dresser reacted to Indian thought in different ways. 91 notes.                                        J. D. Falk

1560.   Myers, Carmel.   FILM INDUSTRY RECOLLECTIONS. *Western States Jewish Hist. Q. 1976 8(2): 126-135.* An early movie star tells how she got started in films. Her father was Rabbi Isidore Myers (1856-1922). Rabbi Myers was asked by film director David Wark Griffith to be a consultant for his film *Intolerance.* As payment for his services, Rabbi Myers' daughter was allowed to try out for a movie part in Griffith's next film. She got a part and that started her career in which she played leading roles opposite such male stars as Rudolph Valentino, Douglas Fairbanks, Jr., John Gilbert, Lew Cody, and William Haines. She was also very active in Jewish community affairs in Los Angeles. Based on personal recollection; 4 photos, 12 notes.
R. A. Garfinkle

1561.   Russell, Don.   CODY, KINGS, AND CORONETS: A SPRIGHTLY ACCOUNT OF BUFFALO BILL'S WILD WEST SHOW AT HOME AND ABROAD.   *Am. West 1970 7(4): 4-10, 62.* Stage melodramatist William Frederick Cody was asked to get together an appropriate Fourth of July celebration in his home town of North Platte, Nebraska, in 1882. The unprecedented and unexpected success of the occasion inspired "Buffalo Bill's Wild West," not a "circus" or a "show" according to its promoters, but an "exhibition." Annie Oakley, Sitting Bull, and other famous names added luster to the exhibition. Cody's insistence on realism with Indians, wild animals, and all the other appropriate personnel and gadgetry he could employ gave his audiences vicarious thrills. European royalty and other assorted luminaries were his avid fans, adding their own luster to his performances. His European seasons were hard acts to follow, and his Canadian and American tours were successful. The 1893 season, near the entrance but not a part of the World's Columbian Exposition in Chicago, with profits near one million dollars, was the best year for Cody's extravaganza. Cody was copied and imitated by competitors, but he was never equaled. Adapted from a recent book; 8 illus.                                        D. L. Smith

1562.   —.   [BOREIN DRAWINGS AND VERSE].   *Noticias 1967 Occasional Papers (7): 1-29.* Drawings and verse by Edward (1872-1947) and Lucile Borein, mostly from Christmas cards the couple sent. The

subjects are the West and California and include cowboys, burros, the de la Guerra *Casa Grande* in Santa Barbara, California, cattle drives, and wagon trains. Includes an etching made for the Rough Riders' reunion on Long Island in July, 1910. 26 illus.                                        T. M. Condon

# Education

1563.   Beeler, Kent D. and Chamberlain, Philip C.   "GIVE A BUCK TO SAVE A COLLEGE": THE DEMISE OF CENTRAL NORMAL COLLEGE.   *Indiana Mag. of Hist. 1971 67(2): 117-128.* Discusses the efforts in 1951 to save Canterbury College, the successor to Central Normal College, from bankruptcy and dissolution. A parade was held with the theme "Give a Buck To Save a College." Traces the academic contributions of the school, particularly the careers of its more illustrious graduates, and details its history from 1900 to 1951. Canterbury College in 1951 succumbed to the stronger purposes of Central Normal College, purposes which five years earlier were considered outdated. Canterbury retained to a high degree the teacher training program of Central Normal. The parade was in a sense a eulogy for an institution which had played so important a role in the life of the community but which was an anachronism whose death was inevitable. Based on primary and secondary sources; 5 illus., 40 notes.                                        N. E. Tutorow

1564.   Benedict, Sarah Bryan; Cannon, Ophelia Colley; and Cayce, Mary Elizabeth.   THE BELLS OF WARD-BELMONT: A REMINIS-CENCE.   *Tennessee Hist. Q. 1971 30(4): 379-382.* Three alumnae of Ward-Belmont, a finishing school for young ladies on the Belmont Estate near Nashville, recall their experiences and way of life as students. The school functioned from 1912 until 1935.                                        R. V. Ritter

1565.   Bruce, Robert V.   A CONQUEST OF SOLITUDE.   *Am. Heritage 1973 24(3): 28-31, 96.* Alexander Graham Bell's (1847-1922) interest in the education of deaf people led to a long friendship with Helen Keller (1880-1968) and her tutor Anne Sullivan Macy.                                        S

1566.   Daniel, W. Harrison.   SOUTHERN BAPTISTS AND EDU-CATION, 1865-1900: A CASE STUDY.   *Maryland Hist. Mag. 1969 64(3): 218-247.* An historical investigation of the post-Civil War educational projects of Virginia Southern Baptists, covering efforts at educating children of Confederate soldiers, the re-opening of Richmond College in 1865, and its subsequent growth. Interest in women's education prompted the founding of the Southwest Virginia Institute and the Woman's College of Richmond, both of which transferred to the supervision of the Baptist General Association of Virginia. By 1900 all Baptist schools had been brought under the aegis of the Virginia Baptist Education Commission. Despite some Baptist criticism of the public school system and its universal tax support, there was strong support of the system, especially for the University of Virginia. Based on primary sources; 80 notes, 4 prints.                                        R. V. Ritter

1567.   Divett, Robert T.   UTAH'S FIRST MEDICAL COLLEGE. *Utah Hist. Q. 1963 31(1): 51-59.* Provides detailed information on the history of the Medical College of Utah, which was founded at Morgan, Utah, in 1880, graduated a class in 1882, and closed in 1883. The central figure in the history of the college was Dr. Frederick S. Kohler, a native of Pennsylvania. A woman of considerable importance in Utah's history, Emeline Grover Rich was a member of the graduating class of 1882. An attack on the college by the Salt Lake *Daily Herald* and hostile community sentiment forced the college to close.                                        S. L. Jones

1568.   Freeman, Anne Hobson.   MARY MUNFORD'S FIGHT FOR A COLLEGE FOR WOMEN CO-ORDINATE WITH THE UNIVER-SITY OF VIRGINIA.   *Virginia Mag. of Hist. and Biog. 1970 78(4): 481-491.* Reviews the narrow defeat in the Virginia Legislature in 1916 of Mary-Cooke Branch Munford's attempt (begun in 1910) to persuade the State to create a woman's college along the coordinate lines of the Radcliffe, Barnard, and Sophie Newcombe colleges. Intense emotions and fear of financial deficit contributed to the defeat of an enabling bill in March by a vote of 48 to 46. 42 notes.                                        C. A. Newton

1569.   Friend, Neita Oviatt.   ELLEN CLARA SABIN AND MY YEARS AT DOWNER.   *Wisconsin Mag. of Hist. 1976 59(3): 178-191.*

Reminisces about the author's years as a student at Milwaukee-Downer Seminary and College during 1905-09. Although the article focuses primarily on Ellen Sabin, first president of Downer (1899-1921), the author relates several episodes about seminary life that illuminate what formal education at the turn of the century was like for women in Wisconsin. She writes less about academic affairs, except for a discussion of home economics, than about social events and school traditions, including a "hat hunt" and Tennyson Pageant. 8 illus.                    N. C. Burckel

1570.  Gaines, William H., Jr. STUART HALL. *Virginia Cavalcade 1969 18(3): 34-40.* An account of a 125-year-old Episcopalian school for young ladies, located in Staunton, Virginia, and originally known as the Virginia Female Institute. Mrs. J. E. B. Stuart served as principal from 1880 to 1898. Interesting aspects of the development of education in Virginia are included. Undocumented, illus.                    N. L. Peterson

1571.  Griffin, Richard W. ATHENS COLLEGE: THE MIDDLE YEARS, 1873-1914. *Methodist Hist. 1965 4(1): 46-58.* Athens College of Athens, Alabama, was chartered as a college in 1842. The college's middle years were characterized by change - a change that was often damaging to progress and support. No fewer than 13 presidents served during this period. The author discusses financial problems, attempts to increase enrollment, curriculum changes, faculty and administrative problems, and other situations confronting an academic institution having difficulty in achieving and maintaining a position of importance. By 1914, Athens College had grown from a poor boarding school to one of the fine colleges for women in the South.                    H. L. Calkin

1572.  Grotzinger, Laurel. THE UNIVERSITY OF ILLINOIS LIBRARY SCHOOL, 1893-1942. *J. of Lib. Hist., Philosophy, and Comparative Librarianship 1967 2(2): 129-141.* Traces the school's development from 1893, when it was established as a Department of Library Economy at Armour Institute, through its move (with Katharine Sharp as director) to the University of Illinois where the B.L.S. Degree was instituted, to the establishment of librarianship as a professional discipline. Mentions the leadership of Phineas Windsor and Frances Simpson. Primary and secondary sources; 33 notes.
                    A. C. Dewees

1573.  House, R. Morton. THE CLASS OF 1903 AT A. AND M. COLLEGE. *Chronicles of Oklahoma 1966 44(4): 391-408.* The first classes of Oklahoma Agricultural and Mechanical College were held in the Congregational Church in December 1891. Old Central, the oldest college building, was dedicated in 1894. In September 1899 46 girls and 49 boys enrolled in the class of 1903 in the college. In 1900 the Athletic Association was organized. The first Territorial Field Meet was held on 4 May 1900. The girls had a basketball team in 1901. In 1903, of the 95 entering freshmen 23 were graduated. Illus., 2 notes.
                    I. W. Van Noppen

1574.  Lazerson, Marvin. URBAN REFORM AND THE SCHOOLS: KINDERGARTENS IN MASSACHUSETTS, 1870-1915. *Hist. of Educ. Q. 1971 11(2): 115-142.* Discusses the evolution of the motives behind the kindergarten movement which was popularized by Elizabeth Palmer Peabody (1804-94) in the United States. This idea was first seen as a movement for the affluent in the Boston area to promote a child's creativity. Later, under the leadership of Pauline Agassiz Shaw (1841-1917), the kindergarten became a charity institution and an instrument of social reform whereby sound moral and health attitudes inculcated in the child could help change a bad home environment. After a struggle over costs and the proper role of the kindergarten in the educational process, it became part of the public school system. But the aims had changed: creative play and expression and the humanization of early childhood were deemphasized and order, discipline, and preparation for the primary grades became the principal purposes of the kindergarten. Also, the educational reformers were using the kindergarten in the early years of the 20th century to inculcate their American values on the immigrant children of the slum. Based on primary and secondary sources; 39 notes.                    L. C. Smith

1575.  Lovejoy, Esther C. P. and Hallam, Bertha. MY MEDICAL SCHOOL (1890-1894). *Oregon Hist. Q. 1974 75(1): 7-36.* A biographical sketch introduces Esther Clayson Pohl Lovejoy's (1869-1967) account of her five years at the University of Oregon Medical School from

which she received the M.D. degree in 1894. She was the second woman graduate and the first to devote a lifetime to medicine. She gives a brief account of her earlier life in Washington and Portland, and her decision to prepare for a career in medicine. Many anecdotes throw interesting sidelights on the medical education of the period. 6 photos.
                    R. V. Ritter

1576.  McCants, Dorothea Olga. ST. VINCENT'S ACADEMY: THE FIRST CENTURY, 1866-1971. *North Louisiana Hist. Assoc. J. 1972 3(3): 73-79.* In May 1866, the Daughters of the Cross, a French religious teaching order, purchased the 100-acre plantation of Captain Leroy Nutt on Fairfield Hill near Shreveport, Louisiana, to establish a school for girls. The nuns planned to transform the complex of buildings then on the plantation "into a motherhouse, a novitiate, a boarding and a day school." St. Vincent's Academy was ready for occupancy by the fall of 1868. Lists the names of the first faculty members and the names of several of the students from the early classes. Tells of the course of studies, the increase in enrollments, the first graduation exercises held in June 1869, the effects of the yellow fever epidemic of 1873, and the coming of better days after 1883. Discusses the major happenings at the Academy from that time, and concludes with a brief mention of the Academy's standing today. Photo, 10 notes.                    A. N. Garland

1577.  McLemore, Richard A. THE ROOTS OF HIGHER EDUCATION IN MISSISSIPPI. *J. of Mississippi Hist. 1964 26(3): 207-218.* Discusses the founding and development of Mississippi's various colleges and universities from 1802 to the present. Particular attention is given to Jefferson College, the first college chartered; Mississippi College, a Baptist school; the University of Mississippi; and the Mississippi Industrial Institute and College, 1884 (now Mississippi State College for Women), "the first public tax-supported institution of higher education for women in the United States." McLemore concludes: "The only live question in higher education in Mississippi today is our admission policies....On the whole, the biggest problems today seem to be the tasks of doing the old jobs better." Based mainly on secondary works.                    D. C. James

1578.  Nelms, Willie E., Jr. CORA WILSON STEWART AND THE CRUSADE AGAINST ILLITERACY IN KENTUCKY. *Register of the Kentucky Hist. Soc. 1976 74(1): 10-29.* Cora Wilson Stewart (b. 1875) began a campaign to teach illiterates in Rowan County, Kentucky, in September, 1911. A school teacher and administrator, Stewart was most concerned with the problem of illiteracy. By 1914, she had attracted nationwide attention. One of the high points of her career came in 1914 when the legislature established the Kentucky Illiteracy Commission and she was appointed to it. She continued her work until the Commission expired in 1920. Based on primary and secondary sources; 68 notes.
                    J. F. Paul

1579.  Peterson, Sue and Kleinmaier, Judith. MOTHER'S DREAM, HISTORIANS' DELIGHT. *Wisconsin Then and Now 1971 18(5): 4-5, 8.* Gives a brief account of college days at Carroll College in Waukesha by Thomas Scott Johnson while an undergraduate there in 1859-60. Some of the educational methods and campus scenes were described by Johnson in his letters home. Johnson later became a chaplain during the Civil War and a Presbyterian minister after the war. He helped to found several schools for soldiers in 1866 and became president of the College for Girls at Fox Lake during the late 19th century.                    D. P. Peltier

1580.  Rottier, Catherine M. ELLEN SPENCER MUSSEY AND THE WASHINGTON COLLEGE OF LAW. *Maryland Hist. Mag. 1974 69(4): 361-382.* The path to legal education for women was a slow and difficult one until 1898, "when the Washington College of Law, a school established 'primarily for women,' was founded by two pioneer female attorneys, Ellen Spencer Mussey and Emma M. Gillett." Surveys women's attempts to remove restrictive charter provisions of law schools and gain bar recognition. The school's early years and progress under various deans are described until 1949 when it merged with American University. Mrs. Mussey's extensive involvement in the women's rights movement and the work of the Red Cross, the Grand Army of the Republic, and temperance groups is also detailed, and the College's graduates are traced in their careers. Primary and secondary works; 11 illus., 47 notes.                    G. J. Bobango

1581. Sawyer, R. McLaran  NO TEACHER FOR THE SCHOOL: THE NEBRASKA JUNIOR NORMAL SCHOOL MOVEMENT. *Nebraska Hist. 1971 52(2): 191-203.* Tells of the unique effort to improve rural teaching in Nebraska during 1903-14, when summer programs were conducted throughout the State to prepare new teachers for rural elementary schools and to improve the skills of those practitioners with little professional training. After 1914 other educational institutions in the State absorbed the program. The program resulted from the educational frontier that still existed in western Nebraska.　　　　R. Lowitt

1582. Smith, Victoria Ann.  A SOCIAL HISTORY OF MARSHALL UNIVERSITY DURING THE PERIOD AS THE STATE NORMAL SCHOOL 1867-1900. *West Virginia Hist. 1963 25(1): 32-41.* Founded as an academy in 1837, for more than a decade before the Civil War Marshall College was run under the auspices of the Methodist Episcopal Church South. In 1867 the new state acquired the property, which became the first of a group of state normal schools established to train teachers for the common schools. The author covers all aspects of student life. Based on college catalogues, student publications, newspapers.　　　　E. P. Stickney

1583. Trecker, Janice Law.  SEX, SCIENCE AND EDUCATION. *Am. Q. 1974 26(4): 352-366.* "Despite their confidence in their complete objectivity, the 19th century scientists' analysis of the Woman Problem forms a striking case study of the ways in which nonscientific ideas and social needs shape scientific thinking." Discusses this thinking as it relates to women in education. Conservative scientists believed a woman's health could not stand up to the rigors of higher education. They insisted that if a woman's brain was overstimulated, the body deteriorated and hysteria or neuralgia resulted, with the reproductive system also being affected. Ultimately scientists were unsuccessful in preventing higher education for women, but many of the problems of female education today have simply reappeared in a different form. 34 notes.　　　　C. W. Olson

1584. Vance, W. Silas.  THE TEACHER OF HELEN KELLER. *Alabama R. 1971 24(1): 51-62.* Sketches the life of Anne Sullivan, an unskilled, meagerly schooled orphan who became the teacher of Helen Keller. Nearly blind herself, Anne Sullivan was rescued from an almshouse at 14 and taken to the Perkins Institution for the Blind. Nothing in her background appeared to prepare her for her later phenomenal success as a teacher. "Acting apparently from instinct, but certainly making full use of her limited education, her insight into human motivation and the springs of character, and particularly her remarkable understanding of the psychology of children and the learning process, she put into practice theories that were later to be developed by Maria Montessori and John Dewey." 37 notes.　　　　D. F. Henderson

1585. Wein, Roberta.  WOMEN'S COLLEGES AND DOMESTICITY, 1875-1918. *Hist. of Educ. Q. 1974 14(1): 31-47.* Compares Bryn Mawr College and Wellesley College. Also analyzes the educational ideas of two important presidents of these institutions, Alice Freeman Palmer and M. Carey Thomas. Finds that Bryn Mawr graduates were more feminist and career-oriented than the Wellesley graduates, who tended to look at education as supplementary to the traditional sex roles of wife and mother. Based on primary and secondary sources; 36 notes.　　　　L. C. Smith

1586. —.  A SCHOOLGIRL'S ALBUM. *Am. Heritage 1971 23(1): 72-79.* In 1883 Jay Cooke offered his Philadelphia mansion, Ogontz, rent-free to the Chestnut Street Female Seminary. The school changed its name to the Ogontz School for Young Ladies and was a very fashionable finishing school for many years. The photographs are from the album of Elizabeth Granger Rust Heinz, class of 1900. 7 illus.　　　　B. J. Paul

## Literature

*(including journalism)*

1587. Abbott, Moreton.  "ALONG SHORE" DAYS. *New-England Galaxy 1971 13(2): 20-25.* Traces Sarah Orne Jewett's writing career during the second half of the 19th century.　　　　S

1588. Aldrich, Bess Streeter.  THE STORY BEHIND *A LANTERN IN HER HAND. Nebraska Hist. 1975 56(2): 237-241.* Reprint of an article first published in the *Christian Herald* (March 1952) in which Bess Streeter Aldrich (1881-1954) tells the story behind her famous novel by reviewing her family history in pioneer Nebraska.　　　　R. Lowitt

1589. Amaral, Anthony.  IDAH MEACHAM STROBRIDGE: FIRST WOMAN OF NEVADA LETTERS. *Nev. Hist. Soc. Q. 1967 10(3): 3-28.* The three books by Idah Meacham Strobridge, written between 1904 and 1909, have been forgotten. They were privately printed in limited editions and are seldom listed in catalogs of booksellers. She is, nevertheless, one of the few writers who has ever presented graphic and vivid impressions of the northern Nevada country. Her subject matter was reporting of what she had seen by living in the desert from the late 1860's to the end of the century. Appended is a facsimile reprint of "The Quail's Cañon," from *The Land of Purple Shadows* (1909).　　　　D. L. Smith

1590. Anderson, Hilton.  EDITH WHARTON AND THE VULGAR AMERICAN. *Southern Q. 1968 7(1): 17-22.* An examination of the role of American characters in Edith Wharton's novels. The vulgar aspect of her characters receives considerable attention because critics have neglected it and because she personally found these kinds of individuals to be more numerous and interesting as literary types. Concludes that Wharton is highly critical of vulgar Americans who travel in Europe. 8 notes.　　　　R. W. Dubay

1591. Anderson, Hilton.  EDITH WHARTON AS FICTIONAL HEROINE. *South Atlantic Q. 1970 69(1): 118-123.* A study of four Edith Wharton (1862-1937) novels about "proper" American women living in Europe, especially their marital problems and frustrations. They are a key to understanding the frustrations Edith Wharton felt in her relationships with Edward Wharton, whom she divorced in 1913 after 25 years of marriage, and with Walter Berry, a distant cousin, close friend, and literary confidant, in whom she became interested in a more romantic way about 1908. 10 notes.　　　　R. V. Ritter

1592. Anderson, John Q.  LOUISIANA AND MISSISSIPPI LORE IN THE FICTION OF SARAH ANNE DORSEY 1829-1879. *Louisiana Studies 1972 11(3): 230-239.* The four novels of Sarah Ann Dorsey, written between 1863 and 1877, are scrutinized with the intention of showing the origin of each character, and disclosing the contents. Characters are compared with events in Dorsey's life to indicate the extent to which each novel corresponded to her life. 15 notes.　　　　G. W. McGinty

1593. Arms, George.  KATE CHOPIN'S "THE AWAKENING" IN THE PERSPECTIVE OF HER LITERARY CAREER. *Essays on American Literature in Honor of Jay B. Hubbell* (Durham: Duke U. Pr., 1967): 215-228. Kate Chopin "principally presents her material with a sense of constant contrast, partly in the whole social situation, partly in Edna, but essentially in the author's way of looking at life." Characters are moved by "'the dual life - that outward existence which conforms, the inward life which questions!'" Contrasts of "purpose and aimlessness, of romance and realism, and of sleep and awakening" move throughout the novel, but Chopin "is unwilling to extract a final truth. Rather she sees truth as constantly re-forming itself and as so much a part of the context of what happens that it can never be final or for that matter abstractly stated." 11 notes.　　　　C. L. Eichelberger

1594. Arner, Robert D.  LANDSCAPE SYMBOLISM IN KATE CHOPIN'S "AT FAULT." *Louisiana Studies 1970 9(3): 142-153.* A diagnosis of Kate O'Flaherty Chopin's *At Fault* (1890). Analyzes and compares its contents with her other writings, in order to get a clearer understanding of her story. 7 notes.　　　　G. W. McGinty

1595. Arner, Robert D.  PRIDE AND PREJUDICE: KATE CHOPIN'S *DESIREE'S BABY. Mississippi Q. 1972 25(2): 131-140.* Heralding this as a highly successful literary work, examines the racial, romantic, and psychological elements in Kate Chopin's (1851-1904) "Désirée's Baby." 9 notes.　　　　S

1596. Avery, Christine.  SCIENCE, TECHNOLOGY, AND EMILY DICKINSON. *British Assoc. for Am. Studies Bull. [Great Britain] 1964 (9): 47-55.* Examines the poetry of Emily Dickinson and concludes that although "she was out of sympathy with most of the basic assumptions of science," some of its methods did appeal to her; and "she was uniquely sensitive to the incisive quality of scientific terms." Unlike Walt Whitman, with whom she is compared, she "is the free spirit which most delicately and effectively registers whatever exists, but maintains its own values within itself." Undocumented.

D. J. Abramoske

1597. Baetzhold, Howard G. FOUND: MARK TWAIN'S "LOST SWEETHEART." *Am. Literature 1972 44(3): 414-429.* Examines the evidence that Mark Twain's brief acquaintance with Laura Wright during his piloting days on the Mississippi provided the stimulus for his dream of a "lost Sweetheart" and inspired a number of episodes and details in his fiction.

H. M. Burns.

1598. Baker, Bruce, II. NEBRASKA REGIONALISM IN SELECTED WORKS OF WILLA CATHER. *Western Am. Literature 1968 3(1): 19-35.*

1599. Baumann, Gustave. CONCERNING A SMALL UNTROUBLED WORLD. *Palacio 1971 78(1): 15-33.* Recounts experiences in and impressions of New Mexico. Reflects on encounters with other cultural figures: Mary Austin, Julius Rolshoven, B. J. O. Nordfeldt, and Aaron Copland. Cites anecdotes about the early traveling situation in New Mexico and community projects such as the development of the Art Museum and Community Theatre in Santa Fe. 13 illus. of Baumann's woodcuts.

N. E. Ramirez

1600. Bellman, Samuel Irving. MARJORIE KINNAN RAWLINGS: A SOLITARY SOJOURNER IN THE FLORIDA BACKWOODS. *Kansas Q. 1970 2(2): 78-87.* Rawlings (1896-1953) was a regional writer though she did not approve of regionalism for its own sake. She felt that regionalism was acceptable only if it was the result of the setting one used to outline one's theme. She saw life as a constant struggle and her works contended that one area was as good as another; i.e., permanence of residence was not particularly important. Based largely on Rawling's works.

B. A. Storey

1601. Beltz, Lynda. NEVER TOO OLD FOR NEW VENTURES: IDA M. TARBELL'S "SECOND PROFESSION." *Pennsylvania Mag. of Hist. and Biog. 1975 99(4): 476-489.* When the *American Magazine* changed owners and editorial policy in 1915, Ida M. Tarbell, the famous journalist and author of *History of the Standard Oil Company* had to look for another source of income. Describes her public speaking career with the Chautauqua Circuit and lyceum tours during 1916-32. Her subjects were outgrowths of her personal interests and works. 33 notes.

C. W. Olson

1602. Bennett, Mildred. WHAT HAPPENED TO THE REST OF THE CHARLES CATHER FAMILY? *Nebraska Hist. 1973 54(4): 619-624.* Biographical sketches of Willa Cather's (1873-1947) brothers and sisters, relying heavily upon quotes from their children. All were successful, though only Willa Cather had a literary career.

R. Lowitt

1603. Bennett, Mildred R. WILLA CATHER AND THE PRAIRIE. *Nebraska Hist. 1975 56(2): 231-235.* Reprint of an article from the *Nature Conservancy News,* (Winter 1975), describing the influence of the Nebraska prairie on the life and writings of Willa Cather. In August 1974, the *Nature Conservancy* purchased 610 acres of native grassland in Webster County, Nebraska, and set it aside as a memorial to Willa Cather.

R. Lowitt

1604. Bennett, S. M. ORNAMENT AND ENVIRONMENT: USES OF FOLKLORE IN WILLA CATHER'S FICTION. *Tennessee Folklore Soc. Bull. 1974 40(3): 95-102.*

1605. Berry, Wilkes. MARY AUSTIN: SIBYLIC GOURMET OF THE SOUTHWEST. *Western R. 1972 9(2): 3-8.* Mary Hunter Austin (1868-1934) wrote extensively about the Southwest, exhibiting insight which earned her a reputation as a prophet. She took pride in her reputation as a seer, but she was equally proud of her talents as a cook. She regarded cooking as a complement to her literary art, and believed that much could be learned about the shepherds, Indians, and Spanish-speaking peoples of the Southwest by an awareness of their cookery. Her writings contained many recipes and references to their culinary practices. 4 notes.

W. J. Furdell

1606. Blom, T. E. ANITA LOOS AND SEXUAL ECONOMICS: "*GENTLEMEN PREFER BLONDES.*" *Can. R. of Am. Studies 1976 7(1): 39-47.* Analyzes the devastating satire with which Anita Loos (b. 1893) attacked American middle-class culture and social values in "*Gentlemen Prefer Blondes*": *The Illuminating Diary of a Professional Lady* (New York, 1925). Since 1925, the book has passed through 45 printings and been translated into 13 languages. It has also been repeatedly presented on the stage and in motion pictures. 12 notes.

H. T. Lovin

1607. Bloom, Ellen F. THREE STEINS. A VERY PERSONAL RECITAL. *Texas Q. 1970 13(2): 15-22.* Select vignettes of Gertrude Stein (1874-1946) and her two brothers by a relative. The author remembers Miss Stein as an imperious lady with a mustache who never finished her work toward a degree in psychology because she hated the abnormal. When asked why she chose to live in France rather than America, she replied that only in Paris was her privacy respected. Nevertheless, she was an ebullient person of great personal magnetism. In spite of the many critics who felt that she was hoodwinking the public, she had great faith in her own writing and its important place in literature.

B. Newman

1608. Bluestein, Gene. CONSTANCE ROURKE AND THE FOLK SOURCES OF AMERICAN LITERATURE. *Western Folklore 1967 26(2): 77-87.* An analysis of the method and approach of Constance Rourke is made in this review of her *American Humor, A Study of the National Character* (1931, reprinted in 1953 by Anchor Books). Her focus is on the folk sources of an American literary tradition and the role of humor in its development. She is preoccupied in offsetting the assertion that American civilization has little to offer in the fine arts. Her "characterological" studies identify the Yankee, the backwoodsman, and the Negro in the steady accretion of national characteristics of the emerging portrait of the American. After establishing these sources she turns to environmental and institutional forces. 9 notes.

D. L. Smith

1609. Brown, Charles B. A WOMAN'S ODYSSEY: THE WAR CORRESPONDENCE OF ANNA BENJAMIN. *Journalism Q. 1969 46(3): 522-530.* The advent of the female war correspondent was when the New York *World* and New York *Journal* sent Anna Northend Benjamin (1874-1902) to write about the Cuban revolt against Spain. Unsmitten with the glamor of war, she worked hard, reporting with unsentimentality and directness. With the outbreak of fighting in the Philippines, she obtained a commission from the New York *Tribune* and San Francisco *Chronicle.* She visited the battlefront and lived among the natives and Spaniards. After about six months in the Philippines, she set out around the world. During the trip she wrote about 12 articles. In the fall of 1901 she returned to Europe, studying peasant life in Russia. In 1902 her death (from a tumor) was reported. Based on primary sources; 20 notes, biblio.

K. J. Puffer

1610. Bush, Robert. GRACE KING AND MARK TWAIN. *Am. Literature 1972 44(1): 29-51.* Considers observations made by New Orleans author Grace King regarding Mark Twain, his family, and the social atmosphere in Hartford. Assesses differences in background and the influence of the post-Civil War southern environment upon Miss King's viewpoint.

H. M. Burns

1611. Bush, Sargent, Jr. "SHADOWS ON THE ROCK" AND WILLA CATHER'S VIEW OF THE PAST. *Queen's Q. 1969 76(2): 269-285.* Argues that in *Shadows on the Rock* (1931), unlike her novels with a Nebraskan setting, Willa Cather indicates that she has become reconciled to the acceptance of change. Yet she also realizes the importance of utilizing our sense and memory of the past to construct a better present and future. *Shadows on the Rock,* one of Cather's late novels, is set in 17th-century Quebec. In the story, the St. Lawrence River serves as a symbol of the relationship between the past and present. The work epitomizes Cather's sense of history in that it shows that continuity from the past constitutes an essential ingredient of the present. 14 notes.

J. A. Casada

**1612.** Byrne, Kathleen Derrigan. WILLA CATHER'S PITTS-BURGH YEARS 1896-1906. *Western Pennsylvania Hist. Mag. 1968 51(1): 1-15.* Cather came to Pittsburgh from Wisconsin in 1896 as a young woman just beginning her career as a writer. In her 10 years in the city she worked as a reporter and editor, contributed to a number of magazines, taught school for several years, and published *April Twilights,* a collection of poems. Cather's four years as drama critic for the Pittsburgh *Leader* and her friendships with other writers helped widen her experience and prepare her to be a full-time creative writer. 5 illus.
D. E. Bowers

**1613.** Carleton, Reese M. MARY NOAILLES MURFREE (1850-1922): AN ANNOTATED BIBLIOGRAPHY. *Am. Literary Realism, 1870-1910 1974 7(4): 293-378.* An annotated bibliography of the works of Mary Noailles Murfree, late 19th- early 20th-century writer (known as "Charles Egbert Craddock") of Tennessee mountain stories.                    S

**1614.** Cary, Richard, ed. "YOURS ALWAYS LOVINGLY": SARAH ORNE JEWETT TO JOHN GREENLEAF WHITTIER. *Essex Inst. Hist. Collections 1971 107(4): 412-450.* Presents 28 extant letters of Sarah Orne Jewett (1849-1909) to John Greenleaf Whittier (1807-1892) written between 1877 and 1890. There also are a brief critical introduction and explanatory notes.                    R. V. Ritter

**1615.** Cather, Willa. WILLA CATHER, "THE MEATAX GIRL." *Horizon 1967 9(2): 116-119.* Gives selections from the book *The Kingdom of Art: Willa Cather's First Principles and Critical Statements, 1893-96* edited by Bernice Sloth (U. of Nebraska Press, 1967). These selections include reviews of plays, Shakespeare's "Cleopatra," a Rusco and Swift production of "Uncle Tom's Cabin," and critiques of Shakespeare and Walt Whitman as writers.                    R. N. Alvis

**1616.** Chametzky, Jules. OUR DECENTRALIZED LIT-ERATURE: A CONSIDERATION OF REGIONAL, ETHNIC, RACIAL AND SEXUAL FACTORS. *Jahrbuch für Amerikastudien [West Germany] 1972 17: 56-72.* Examines the careers and some of the works of four writers who were accepted as regional or local color writers of considerable achievement but who were misunderstood, misrepresented, or totally denied in their significant concerns. They are: George Washington Cable, Abraham Cahan, Charles Waddell Chesnutt, and Kate Chopin. Their real concerns were, respectively: the racial grounds of the Southern tragedy, the stakes involved in the acculturation of immigrant populations, the assertion of a black ethos, and the terms of women's entrapment within our cultural assumptions.                    G. Bassler

**1617.** Cheney, Lynne Vincent. MRS. FRANK LESLIE'S ILLUSTRATED NEWSPAPER. *Am. Heritage 1975 26(6): 42-48, 90-91.* Miriam Florence Follin Leslie (1836-1914) gained publishing experience while working for Frank Leslie. She later married him and inherited his publishing house after he died. Her business success led to a large fortune, the bulk of which she left to Carrie Chapman Catt to use for woman suffrage. 9 illus.                    B. J. Paul

**1618.** Ciklamini, Marlene SIGRID UNDSET'S LETTERS TO HOPE EMILY ALLEN. *J. of the Rutgers U. Lib. 1969 33(1): 20-27.* Discusses letters from Sigrid Undset (1882-1949), the Norwegian novelist, to Hope Emily Allen (1883-1960), a medievalist. These letters date from February 1941 to December 1948. They contain few remarks on modern works or authors, but are concerned with Undset and Allen's mutual interest in medieval Scandinavian literature. Daily activities are reported but few truly personal comments are made in these letters, which are now in the Special Collections of the Rutgers University Library. 7 notes.                    M. Kroeger

**1619.** Clark, Laverne Harrell. THE VIEW FROM INDIAN HILL: CHILDHOOD YEARS OF MARI SANDOZ. *Bits and Pieces 1972 8(6): 5-13.* Mari Sandoz's writings reflect her early experiences with the Plains Indians of Nebraska.                    S

**1620.** Cohn, Jan THE NEGRO CHARACTER IN NORTHERN MAGAZINE FICTION OF THE 1860'S. *New England Q. 1970 43(4): 572-592.* In the 1860's American fiction writers had their first opportunity to deal realistically with black people, free of the stereotype of northern abolitionists and southern slaveholders. A study of stories by writers such as Louisa May Alcott, Helen W. Pierson, Mary Elizabeth Mapes Dodge, John William DeForest, and others demonstrates the survival of some of these stereotypes: an increased adoption of southern views of Negroes as childlike, potentially brutal, and generally inferior to whites in the finer qualities of humanity. However, one also observes somewhat more complexity and realism, a willingness to treat themes such as miscegenation, and, among some, a realization of the difficulties involved with a white author treating black characters. Overall, one notices the survival of a complacent racism.                    K. B. West

**1621.** Corrigan, R. A. SOMEWHERE WEST OF LARAMIE, ON THE ROAD TO WEST EGG: AUTOMOBILES, FILLIES, AND THE WEST IN *THE GREAT GATSBY. J. of Popular Culture 1973 7(1): 152-158.* Discusses the automobile as a symbol of personal and sexual liberation in literature of the 1920's (specifically in F. Scott Fitzgerald's *The Great Gatsby*) and the image which eastern writers attached to the American West.                    S

**1622.** Cox, James M. AUTOBIOGRAPHY AND AMERICA. *Virginia Q. R. 1971 47(2): 252-277.* Autobiography makes up a large proportion of American classics. Autobiography is the history of a person's life written by himself, and differs from both memoirs and confessions. Benjamin Franklin's "Memoirs" *(Autobiography)* "almost exactly coincides with the birth of America" and is the "history of a self-made life written by the man who made it." It presents somewhat a model life. Henry David Thoreau, in *Walden* (on the eve of the Civil War), "sees freedom not as Franklin's self-making but as self-possession." Walt Whitman, while not primarily an autobiographer, did write "Song of Myself," in which he fuses the "I" and the "You" so that it becomes "the song of ourselves." Henry Brooks Adams' *Education* is written in the third person and leaves a gap of some 20 years in the middle. Adams presents an ironic vision of history. Adams' poles of past and future - the Virgin and the dynamo - are also poles of energy and "make possible his dynamic theory and act of history." His "'Education' is the heroic act of the imagination unifying history and science in an act of mind and art." Gertrude Stein extended the American autobiographical tradition by striving to make "the words everything and the life nothing." She is "both the fact and the mystery at the end of American autobiography."
O. H. Zabel

**1623.** Curry, Jane. SAMANTHA "RASTLES" THE WOMAN QUESTION OR "IF GOD HAD MEANT WIMMEN SHOULD BE NOTHIN' BUT MEN'S SHADDERS, HE WOULD HAVE MADE GOSTS AND FANTOMS OF 'EM AT ONCE." *J. of Popular Culture 1974 8(4): 805-824.* Discusses the feminist and humorous writings of Marietta Holley, 1870-1926, centering on *My Opinions and Betsy Bobbet's* (1873).

**1624.** Davis, Richard Beale. MRS. STOWE'S CHARACTERS-IN-SITUATIONS AND A SOUTHERN LITERARY TRADITION. *Essays on American Literature in Honor of Jay B. Hubbell* (Durham: Duke U. Pr., 1967): 108-125. Harriet Beecher Stowe, in her two antislavery novels *Uncle Tom's Cabin* (1851) and *Dred* (1856), more than presenting "a peculiar variety of characters and their unusual tragic situations," actually marked "the definite beginnings of a literary tradition" by establishing varying patterns of characters-in-situations. George Washington Cable, Mark Twain, Robert Penn Warren, and William Faulkner, like Mrs. Stowe, "knew of their Southern situations partly by hearsay," but more than she, "they knew by experience." They followed her in "the writing of a story of their own land that moved them, a story told by placing human beings in situations." 10 notes.
C. L. Eichelberger

**1625.** Davison, Stanley R. THE AUTHOR WAS A LADY. *Montana: Mag. of Western Hist. 1973 23(2): 2-15.* Bertha Muzzy Bower Sinclair Cowan (1871-1940), best known for her "Flying U" stories, authored 67 novels and numerous short stories under the name "B. M. Bower." Her style was light and pleasant, with realistic characterizations. Based on reviews and readers' responses; illus., 10 notes.                    A

**1626.** Day, Douglas T. ELLEN GLASGOW'S LETTERS TO THE SAXTONS. *Am. Literature 1963 35(2): 230-236.* Discusses five letters written by Ellen Glasgow to Eugene F. Saxton and his wife between 1925 and 1937. Of the letters presented in full, two reveal her impressions of

contemporary fiction. Saxton had chosen her to be a judge for the Harper Prize Novel Competition, and in these two letters she discusses the merits and demerits of several of the competing novels. In another of the letters she displays her unwillingness to be categorized as a "Southern" writer: "I have always written, or tried to write, not of Southern characteristics, but of human beings." Based on primary and secondary sources; 13 notes.
M. J. McBaine

1627. Delaney, Caldwell. MARY MC NEIL FENOLLOSA, AN ALABAMA WOMAN OF LETTERS. *Alabama R. 1963 16(3): 163-173.* Brief biography of Mary McNeil Fenollosa, who wrote under the pseudonym Sidney McCall. *Out of the Nest* (1899), *Truth Dexter* (rev. ed. 1912), *The Breath of Gods* (1905), *The Dragon Painter* (1906), *Red Horse Hill* (1899) are among the better known of her works. She was co-author with her husband Ernest Fenollosa of *Epochs of Chinese and Japanese Art* (1912). Undocumented.
D. F. Henderson

1628. Durham, Frank THE REPUTED DEMISES OF UNCLE TOM: OR, THE TREATMENT OF THE NEGRO IN FICTION BY WHITE SOUTHERN AUTHORS IN THE 1920'S. *Southern Literary J. 1970 2(2): 26-50.* Discusses the "New Negro" as portrayed in the 1920's by authors from a region whose inhabitants "have rather loudly proclaimed that they alone 'know' the Negro and hence are best fitted to deal with him in both life and letters." Traces the background of 19th-century literary racial stereotypes and illustrates "a serious and conscious attempt on the part of Southern writers to present the Negro in new ways....." Draws on Thomas Sigismund Stribling's *Birthright* (1922), Hubert Anthony Shands' *White and Black* (1922), DuBose Heyward's *Porgy* (1925), and Julia Mood Peterkin's *Scarlet Sister Mary* (1928). 31 notes.
J. L. Colwell

1629. Eakin, Paul John. SARAH ORNE JEWETT AND THE MEANING OF COUNTRY LIFE. *Am. Literature 1967 38(4): 508-531.* Because of her limited novelistic ability, Miss Jewett's conservative view of village life was best expressed by the technique of "the visit" in *The Country of the Pointed Firs* (1896). A perceptive observer enters the subsurface world of the village via her relationship with a village woman; the interaction of personalities reveals Miss Jewett's complex opinions. 41 notes.
R. S. Burns

1630. Eby, Cecil D. "I TASTE A LIQUOR NEVER BREWED": A VARIANT READING. *Am. Literature 1965 36(4): 516-518.* The first person in the poem is traditionally assumed to be the poet Emily Dickinson "intoxicated" by the warm air and flowers of her garden. However, it is really a hummingbird which the poet imagines to be telling about its drunken spree. 7 notes.
R. S. Burns

1631. Edwards, C. H. THE EARLY LITERARY CRITICISM OF CORRA HARRIS. *Georgia R. 1963 17(4): 449-455.* Surveys the attitude of Corra Harris toward American fiction in the early 20th century. Her romantic and moral approach to literature hindered her literary judgment of authors writing in terms of realism and literalism. She was especially critical of Southern writers for glorifying the antebellum past. Undocumented.
H. G. Earnhart

1632. Erisman, Fred R. TRANSCENDENTALISM FOR AMERICAN YOUTH: THE CHILDREN'S BOOKS OF KATE DOUGLAS WIGGIN. *New England Q. 1968 41(2): 238-247.* As a young lady, Kate was exposed to the nature idealism of German and English romanticism through a study of Friedrick Froebel's educational theories and attendance at Bronson Alcott's Concord School of Philosophy in 1879. At this school she met William Ellery Channing and Ralph Waldo Emerson. Three doctrines were important to her: the law of compensation which allowed her to see some good in every evil; individualism, which made all her characters paragons of self-reliance; and a belief in the ethical power of unfettered nature which led her to extol the pastoral as a source of peace, hope, and self-understanding. Conversely, she condemned the city as ugly and sordid. Her views were put forward to Americans in the years between 1890 and 1910. They were unrealistic, but seemed to appeal to many. Through reading her books, Kate Wiggin hoped her little readers might, when grown to adulthood, translate these ideals into a transcendentalist utopia. 29 notes.
K. B. West

1633. Etulain, Richard. MARY HALLOCK FOOTE: A CHECKLIST. *Western Am. Literature 1975 10(1): 59-65.* During the last quarter of the 19th century, Mary Hallock Foote (1847-1948) attained a notable literary reputation for her novels dealing with the Far West. Her reputation had waned until recently when there has been renewed interest in her work.
M. Genung

1634. Fendelman, Earl. HAPPY BIRTHDAY, GERTRUDE STEIN. *Am. Q. 1975 27(1): 99-107.* Review essay of Richard Bridgman's *Gertrude Stein in Pieces* (1970); Margaret Potter, ed., *Four Americans in Paris: The Collections of Gertrude Stein and Her Family* (1970); Norman Weinstein's *Gertrude Stein and the Literature of the Modern Consciousness* (1970); Edward Burns, ed., *Staying on Alone: Letters of Alice B. Toklas* (1973); and James R. Mellow's *Charmed Circle: Gertrude Stein & Company* (1974). Illustrates the manner in which Stein chose art as a life as well as an occupation, reflecting her concern with the manner in which the immediacy of experience can be recreated in art, the expression of one's inner nature given the distortions of modern publicity, and the struggle to free oneself from the constrictions of meaningless interpretations.
N. Lederer

1635. Fitch, Noel. SYLVIA BEACH'S SHAKESPEARE AND COMPANY: PORT OF CALL FOR AMERICAN EXPATRIATES. *Res. Studies 1965 33(4): 197-207.* Sylvia Beach's Shakespeare and Company Bookshop in Paris, France, was a meeting place for expatriate American writers and artists during 1920's-30's.

1636. Fletcher, Marie. GRACE ELIZABETH KING. *Louisiana Studies 1966 5(1): 50-60.* In 1888 Grace King of New Orleans, in her writing, began to help change the fictional picture of the southern heroine. Hers were among "the first steps in the shift from the glorification of the traditional aristocratic lady who dominated the literary scene in the 1850's and 1860's to admiration of and for the more democratic woman" who gradually replaced most of the "born ladies" in southern fiction by the end of the 19th century. Miss King's books are no longer in print. 27 notes.
R. S. Burke

1637. Fletcher, Marie. THE SOUTHERN WOMAN IN THE FICTION OF KATE CHOPIN. *Louisiana Hist. 1966 7(2): 117-132.* Sketches the career of Kate O'Flaherty Chopin, representative of the local color movement among American writers of the postbellum period and of the transition from romantic sentimentality to realism. She lived in Louisiana from 1870 to 1882, after which she returned to her native Saint Louis where she did all of her writing. The women in Mrs. Chopin's works, although drawn from a lower strata of Louisiana society, display many of the same characteristics of plantation belles of antebellum literature. Although more robust and natural, "they still represent the ideal of the fragile and lovely girl who is pure of character." Based on biographical studies of Mrs. Chopin and on her works; 43 notes.
R. L. Woodward

1638. Forman, Henry James. KATE DOUGLAS WIGGIN: A WOMAN OF LETTERS. *Southern California Q. 1962 44(4): 273-285.* Kate Douglas Wiggin's stories are novels - novels, however, different from the usual run. They are "fairy tales for children from six to ninety-six." Mrs. Wiggin was deeply involved in the kindergarten movement in San Francisco in the 1870's. *Timothy's Quest* (1890) and *The Bird's Christmas Carol* (1888) were highly successful in America and England. Beyond any doubt *Rebecca of Sunnybrook Farm* (1908) stands out as her masterpiece of fiction. Jack London praised the character Rebecca and wrote how alive she was in the story. Mrs. Wiggin states that her best stories were "just innocent escapades, indulged in to vary the monotony that might creep into a literary life."
D. H. Swift

1639. Forrey, Carolyn. THE NEW WOMAN REVISITED. *Women's Studies 1974 2(1): 37-56.* Examines eight novels written by eight different women who depicted the character of the New Woman during the 1880's and 90's. The novels show that profound changes were occurring among women and that the New Woman was part of an emerging wave of women's self-assertion. The novelists and novels examined are Louisa May Alcott's *Jo's Boys* (1886), Sarah Orne Jewitt's *A Country Doctor* (1884), Constance Cary Harrison's *A Bachelor Maid* (1894), Olive Schreiner's *The Story of an African Farm* (1883), Mona Caird's *A Romance of the Moors* (1891), Ellen Glasgow's *The Descendant*

(1897), Amelia Barr's *Between Two Loves* (1886), and Kate Chopin's *The Awakening* (1899). All the novels deal with the social roles and alternatives open and closed to women. The novelists generally were unable to imagine satisfactory new roles for their New Woman characters. This reflected reality where there was no satisfactory place for the New Woman in American society. Based on primary and secondary materials; 20 notes.          A. E. Wiederrecht

1640.  Freis, Susan.   EMILY DICKINSON: A CHECK LIST OF CRITICISM, 1930-1966.   *Papers of the Biblio. Soc. of Am. 1967 61(4): 359-385.* This checklist of 456 entries is a first attempt at a bibliography of criticism of Emily Dickinson since her centenary year of 1930. It is in four parts: books, periodical articles, parts of books, and dissertations.          C. A. Newton

1641.  Giannone, Richard.   THE SOUTHWEST'S ETERNAL ECHO: MUSIC IN "DEATH COMES FOR THE ARCHBISHOP." *Arizona Q. 1966 22(1): 5-18.* An interpretation of the symbolic use of music "for the spontaneous, direct, and universal expression of feeling which blends ethnic variety into spiritual unity" in Willa Cather's *Death Comes for the Archbishop* (New York: Alfred A. Knopf, 1927). Documented.          J. D. Filipiak

1642.  Gleason, Gene.   WHATEVER HAPPENED TO OLIVER OPTIC?   *Wilson Lib. Bull. 1975 49(9): 647-650.* Describes the moral attack in Louisa May Alcott's *Eight Cousins* (1875) on the writings of William T. Adams ("Oliver Optic") and Horatio Alger, Jr., in a sketch of the literary careers of these three popular children's writers from the Boston area.          S

1643.  Godbold, E. Stanly, Jr.   A BATTLEGROUND REVISITED: RECONSTRUCTION IN SOUTHERN FICTION, 1895-1905. *South Atlantic Q. 1974 73(1): 99-116.* The six southern novelists who wrote about Reconstruction during 1895-1905 had a variety of attitudes which contributed far more to the knowledge of Reconstruction than they might have if they had been of one mind. Discusses the work of Geroge W. Cable, Ellen Glasgow, Thomas Nelson Page, Thomas Dixon, Jr., Joel Chandler Harris, and John S. Wise. 32 notes.          E. P. Stickney

1644.  Going, William T.   TWO ALABAMA WRITERS: ZELDA SAYRE FITZGERALD AND SARA HAARDT MENCKEN. *Alabama R. 1970 23(1): 3-29.* Describes the literary careers of two Montgomery girls, Sara Powell Haardt, wife of H. L. Mencken, and Zelda Sayre, wife of F. Scott Fitzgerald. Although they were easily eclipsed by their more famous husbands, each wrote numerous articles, several short stories, and a novel.          D. F. Henderson

1645.  Gordan, John D.   A LEGEND REVISITED: ELINOR WYLIE.   *Am. Scholar 1969 38(3): 459-468.* A brief survey of the life-as-legend of the poetess-novelist, Elinor Hoyt Wylie (d. 1928). The account is drawn exclusively from a wide range of *literati* who knew her, of which all but one were touching, personal, and loving. Based on anecdotes taken from copiously quoted unpublished letters.          T. R. Cripps

1646.  Graham, Ina Agnes.   MY AUNT, INA COOLBRITH. *Pacific Hist. 1973 17(3): 12-19.* A biographical sketch of Ina Coolbrith, focusing on her family relationships and the influences they had on her poetry.

1647.  Greenwell, Scott L.   THE LITERARY APPRENTICESHIP OF MARI SANDOZ.   *Nebraska Hist. 1976 57(2): 249-272.* Examines the arduous literary apprenticeship of Mari Sandoz. At age 11 her first story was published on the "junior page" of the Omaha *Daily News*. She was nearly 40 when in 1935 the publication of *Old Jules* launched her career. The years in between were discouraging, but throughout she continued to write despite a lack of success and under trying circumstances.          R. Lowitt

1648.  Groover, Robert L.   MARGARET MITCHELL, THE LADY FROM ATLANTA.   *Georgia Hist. Q. 1968 52(1): 53-69.* A popular, undocumented biographical account of Margaret Mitchell and the circumstances behind the writing of *Gone with the Wind*—"the most successful novel ever written about the South and the Civil War." The author shows that Margaret Mitchell's Atlanta upbringing provided the back-

ground for her only novel. After a year at Smith College, she became a writer for the *Atlanta Journal Magazine.* Meanwhile, she began researching and writing her fictional classic. The book was published in 1936, became an immediate best seller, won the Pulitzer Prize, and was made into a highly successful motion picture.          R. A. Mohl

1649.  Grossman, Edward.   HENRY JAMES & THE SEXUAL-MILITARY COMPLEX.   *Commentary 1972 53(4): 37-50.* The author blends some experiences of his youth into a discussion of the thought and values of Henry James, exemplified principally in *The Bostonians* (New York, 1886).          S

1650.  Gumina, Deanna.   KATHLEEN NORRIS: THE PHILOSOPHY OF A WOMAN.   *Pacific Historian 1974 18(4): 68-74.* Reviews the fiction of Kathleen Norris and her attitudes toward women, marriage, and society. Her stories and magazine articles "categorized her as a romantic sentimentalist whose basic theme was that love triumphs over all." Biblio.          S

1651.  Gunday, H. Pearson.   FLOURISHES AND CADENCES: LETTERS OF BLISS CARMAN AND LOUISE IMOGEN GUINEY. *Dalhousie R. [Canada] 1975 55(2): 205-226.* Contains background information on the Canadian poet William Bliss Carman's early years, especially in Boston, and mentions a number of acquaintances in his circle including Josiah Royce, Charles Eliot Norton, Bernard Berenson and Louise Imogen Guiney. Special attention is paid to his relationship with Guiney and includes 22 letters in whole or part in the text. The correspondence began in 1887 and continued into 1898.          C. Held

1652.  Halliday, E. M.   SCOTT & ZELDA.   *Am. Heritage 1974 25(6): 4-13.* Pictorial autobiography of F. Scott Fitzgerald and Zelda Sayre Fitzgerald, an excerpt from *The Romantic Egoists,* Scottie Fitzgerald Smith, Matthew J. Bruccoli, and Joan P. Kerr, eds. (New York: Charles Scribner's Sons, 1974).          S

1653.  Hamblen, Abigail Ann.   EDITH WHARTON IN NEW ENGLAND.   *New England Q. 1965 38(2): 239-244.* States that, although Edith Wharton asserts in *A Backward Glance* (1934) that she knew New England well, she knew it only from summer residences and as an outsider. As a consequence *Ethan Frome* (1911) and *Summer* (1917) picture the region as one producing deprived and sordid lives.          A. Turner

1654.  Hamilton, Virginia Van Der Veer.   THE GENTLEWOMAN AND THE ROBBER BARON.   *Am. Heritage 1970 21(3): 78-86.* Relates Ida M. Tarbell's (1857-1944) probes into John D. Rockefeller's (1839-1937) Standard Oil trust for *McClure's Magazine.*          S

1655.  Haugen, Einar.   IBSEN IN AMERICA.   *Norwegian-Am. Studies and Records 1959 20: 1-23.* Discusses the history of Henrik Ibsen's works in America. Reviews the American literature about Ibsen, his plays, their style, symbolism, and social commentary. Since 1900, a critical tradition developed in the US which gave serious consideration to Ibsen. Outlines and assesses the growth of this tradition, emphasizing the work of Eva Le Gallienne as a translator and interpreter of Ibsen's works. Concludes that Ibsen's influence in America is significant and that his plays have become a part of American cultural life and been accepted as classics of the theater. Based on primary and secondary materials; 21 notes.          A. E. Wiederrecht

1656.  Heald, William F.   ELLEN GLASGOW AND THE GROTESQUE.   *Mississippi Q. 1965 18(1): 7-11.* Approaching Ellen Glasgow through some of her well-drawn minor characters serves to help in understanding her art and her relationship to the 20th-century milieu. Among her grotesque minor characters are Mrs. Jane Dudley Webb and Aunt Griselda Grigsby in *The Voice of the People* (1900) and Mrs. Burden in *They Stooped to Folly* (1929), while such major characters as Judge Gamaliel Bland Honeywell in *The Romantic Comedians* (1926), Mary Victoria Littlepage in *They Stopped to Folly,* and Dorinda Oakley in *Barren Ground* (1925) are representative of grotesque tendencies in major characters. Revealing in her minor characters a view of life similar to the pessimistic outlook of important writers of the past 20 years, Ellen Glasgow failed to do as well with her major characterizations or with integration of humor with plot and situations. Miss Glasgow's grotesqueness embodies a "bizarre combination of the somber, the gay, the sublime, and the absurd."          R. V. Calvert

1657. Healey, Claire. AMY LOWELL VISITS LONDON. *New England Q. 1973 46(3): 439-453.* Amy Lowell met most of the Imagist coterie, including Ezra Pound, in 1913. Before her trip to London in 1914 she had been arranging to sponsor the publication of several anthologies of Imagist poetry. During the London visit, Pound threatened to copyright the term "Imagist." However, "time softened the memory of the rancour and distrust which accompanied the misunderstandings, charges, and countercharges in the evolution of the Imagist movement." 36 notes.
E. P. Stickney

1658. Helmick, Evelyn Thomas. MYTH IN THE WORKS OF WILLA CATHER. *MidContinent Am. Studies J. 1968 9(2): 63-69.* Analyzes the works of Willa Cather (1873-1947) in terms of her reliance on a classical literary approach to the American novel. Her adoption of the heroic epic to dramatize the Western frontier is shown by the prominence of Nature, as in the cycle of the seasons and the grandeur of the western landscape. Through the use of the myth, Willa Cather conveyed the enduring custom of human thought and feeling and thus enriched her writing with archetypal figures complemented by the universality of man's experience. Based on primary and secondary sources; 18 notes.
B. M. Morrison

1659. Higgins, David J. M. TWENTY-FIVE POEMS BY EMILY DICKINSON: UNPUBLISHED VARIANT VERSIONS. *Am. Literature 1966 38(1): 1-21.* Presents 25 poems not included in the variorum edition, *The Poems of Emily Dickinson* (Cambridge: Harvard U. Press, 1955). Sources are manuscripts, transcripts by Mabel Loomis Todd, transcripts by Frances Norcross, and one unidentified transcript. Eleven notes correct the 1955 edition of Dickinson's works.          R. S. Burns

1660. Jenkins, R. B. A NEW LOOK AT AN OLD TOMBSTONE. *New England Q. 1972 45(3): 417-421.* Studies the last sentence of Nathaniel Hawthorne's *The Scarlet Letter:* "On a Field, Sable, the Letter A, Gules." Argues that the tombstone contained only an "A," implying Angel, was first on Dimmesdale's tomb. Only secondarily did it symbolize adultery. Hester was not buried beside him until years later.
R. V. Ritter

1661. Jones, Douglas C. TERESA DEAN: LADY CORRESPONDENT AMONG THE SIOUX INDIANS. *Journalism Q. 1972 49(4): 656-662.* Following her stay at the Sioux Indians' reservation at Wounded Knee, South Dakota, in 1891, news correspondent Teresa Dean disclosed the bad living conditions of the Sioux in her articles.          S

1662. Joost, Nicholas. CULTURE VS. POWER: RANDOLPH BOURNE, JOHN DEWEY, AND "THE DIAL." *Midwest Q. 1968 9(3): 245-259.* Concerns *The Dial's* history during World War I, particularly with the pacifist dissent of one of its contributing editors Randolph Bourne, and the near foundering of the magazine torn between dedication to culture and the lure of power. In its early days in Chicago *The Dial* was opposed to the American jingoism of its time, standing aside from politics and remaining constant to its aim of being "an intelligent guide and agreeable companion to the book lover and book buyer." At the outbreak of World War I, Bourne became the most ardent proponent of American noninvolvement, and continued to advocate pacifist transnationalism throughout the war. His chief opponent, writing in *The New Republic, Seven Arts,* and *The Dial,* was John Dewey who advocated the powerful and popular policy of rallying to the Wilson administration. The later history of *The Dial* is touched on, mentioning contributors Thorstein Veblen, Louis Mumford, Marianne Moore, and Schofield Thayer. Biblio.          G. H. G. Jones

1663. Josephson, Matthew. DAWN POWELL: A WOMAN OF ESPRIT. *Southern R. 1973 9(1): 18-52.* The ironic humorist and novelist Dawn Powell was not widely read by the public, but her admirers and friends included John Dos Passos, Malcolm Cowley, Edmund Wilson, and Ernest Hemingway. Her works were usually light, but because they underscore changing American social behavior they have historical and literary value. Among her most discussed works are *The Happy Island, The Golden Spur,* and *The Locusts Have No King.*
R. W. Dubay

1664. Keeler, Clinton. NARRATIVE WITHOUT ACCENT: WILLA CATHER AND PUVIS DE CHAVANNES. *Am. Q. 1965*

*17(1): 119-126.* Argues with critics who accuse Willa S. Cather of withdrawing from life in her *Death Comes for the Archbishop* (1927). Instead, he maintains that her work is a fictional replica of Pierre Puvis de Chavannes' mural "L'Enfance de Sainte Geneviève." Stylistically, both works depict a charged immobility. Intense feeling is definitely present even though the dominant mood appears to be calm and detachment. Cather and de Chavannes thus reverse contemporary aesthetic trends by creating a world where light is action and where distance and space create a sustained impact of order and monumentalism. Illustrated with a detail from "Ste. Geneviève en Prière" by de Chavannes (p. 121); 16 notes.
R. S. Pickett

1665. Kenney, Alice P. MARY L. D. FERRIS AND THE DUTCH TRADITION: I. *Halve Maen 1973 47(4): 7-8, 14.* A descendant of early settlers, Mary L. D. Ferris collected and recorded their history in poetry and prose throughout the late Victorian era. Much of her work was published in the *Albany Argus* or presented at Holland Society affairs. Based on Mrs. Ferris' writings, from a private collection; 13 notes.
G. L. Owen

1666. Kirk, Clara M. and Kirk, Rudolf. EDITH WYATT: THE JANE AUSTEN OF CHICAGO? *Chicago Hist. 1971 1(3): 172-178.* Discusses the role played by William Dean Howells (1837-1920) informing the public of Edith Franklin Wyatt (1873-1958), a young Chicago writer. Normally Howells' stamp of approval meant literary fame, but not in this case. Although Howells used every opportunity to promote Wyatt, he failed. In 1903 Wyatt published her first novel, followed by another in 1907. Howells ranked her at the head of the "Chicago School," which included George Ade. Despite Howells' attempt to establish her in the top literary circles, Edith Wyatt still remains unknown. Based on the Edith Wyatt Papers in the Newberry Library; 3 photos, appendix.
N. A. Kuntz

1667. Kissane, Leedice. D. H. LAWRENCE, RUTH SUCKOW, AND "MODERN MARRIAGE." *Rendezvous 1969 4(1): 39-45.* Discusses the portrayal of marriage and women in the literature of Ruth Suckow (*Country People, The Bonney Family*) and D. H. Lawrence (*Sons and Lovers, Lady Chatterley's Lover*) in the 1920's and 30's.

1668. Knox, George. THE GREAT AMERICAN NOVEL: FINAL CHAPTER. *Am. Q. 1969 21(4): 667-682.* Considers why and how the idea of literary nationalism, the opposition between universalist and localist, European and American, nationalist and separatist emphasis, has been abandoned or debunked in the 20th century. Discusses Frank Norris's protests at the triteness of the notion in *The Octopus.* The internationalist Edith Wharton remarked on the narrowing of the concept of the "greatest American Novel." H. L. Mencken and George Jean Nathan ridiculed American provincialism and Theodore Dreiser stated that the so-called American realistic writers were narrow and thinly class-conscious. Considers the work of Clyde Brion Davis, Dos Passos, A. S. M. Hutchinson, Thomas Wolfe, and Gertrude Stein and states that the American novel is neither more nor less local or universal, retrospective or futuristic than in the 19th century, and that American fiction no longer has to call attention to itself with nationalist labels. Secondary sources; 24 notes.          P. T. Herman

1669. Lampson, Robin. BOOK REVIEW: INA COOLBRITH LIBRARIAN AND LAUREATE OF CALIFORNIA. *Pacific Hist. 1973 17(3): 32-34.* Discusses the San Francisco poet and librarian, Ina Coolbrith, 1841-1928.          S

1670. Landess, Thomas H. THE ACHIEVEMENT OF JULIA PETERKIN. *Mississippi Q. 1976 29(2): 221-232.* Discusses the fiction of Julia Peterkin, a Pulitzer Prize-winning southern author during the 1920's-30's.

1671. Lanier, Doris, ed. MARY NOAILLES MURFREE: AN INTERVIEW. *Tennessee Hist. Q. 1972 31(3): 276-278.* Reprints an interview, first published in Macon, Georgia (1885), in which author Mary Noailles Murfree's activities at Montvale Springs, Tennessee, are discussed by a friend.          S

1672. Lau, Joseph S. M. TWO EMANCIPATED PHAEDRAS: CHOU FAN-YI AND ABBIE PUTNAM AS SOCIAL REBELS.

*J. of Asian Studies 1966 25(4): 699-711.* Compares the character of "Chou Fan-yi" in Ts'ao Yu's *Thunderstorm* (Lei-yü), published in 1933, and "Abbie Putnam" in Eugene O'Neill's *Desire Under the Elms* (1925). "By design, Fan-yi is modelled upon Abbie Putnam in her defiance of traditional morals. But Abbie, though refusing to be judged by the rigidity of religious standards, has not slighted her responsibility toward society. And, insofar as love is regarded as the highest ordering reality in the human scheme, Abbie's adultery, the consequences of which she accepts with as much agony as exhilaration, can be viewed as a self-justifying affirmation of a personal faith - a faith that is socially frowned upon but for the lovers at least, has a sanctity of its own....Adhering to no values, abiding by no law, and honoring no commitment of a mother, what else could Fan-yi's 'defiance' point to if not moral anarchy? She is, typically, the sum product of an age of transition in China in which iconoclasm was one of the most fashionable occupations, in which the mere murmur of the word 'modern' would evoke apocalyptical joy. However courageous, passionate, and even sacrosanct she might have appeared to her creator, to us she cannot be more than a glossy abstraction of inordinate intellectual pretensions, strutting in the dark, her face all ablur." Summarizes the plot of *Thunderstorm.* 49 notes.                    D. D. Cameron

1673.  Lederer, Francis L., II.  NORA MARKS, INVESTIGATIVE REPORTER.  *J. of the Illinois State Hist. Soc. 1975 68(4): 306-318.* Eleanora Stackhouse, writing under the pen name of Nora Marks, published 80 pieces of investigative reporting in the Chicago *Daily Tribune* during August 1888-July 1890. Her exposés included coverage of the domestic servant situation, divorce mills, the Salvation Army, work conditions of peddlers and stockyard workers, Chicago's charity agencies, and delinquent and poor children's custodial care. Little is known of her life and career. Based on primary sources.                    N. Lederer

1674.  Lentricchia, Frank, Jr.  HARRIET BEECHER STOWE AND THE BYRON WHIRLWIND.  *Bull. of the New York Public Lib. 1966 70(4): 218-228.* In September 1869 Harriet Beecher Stowe published an article in the *Atlantic Monthly* magazine which discussed Lord Byron's alleged incestuous relationship with his half sister. The article was meant to destroy Byron's already declining reputation in America, but it misfired. Instead of tarnishing Byron's name, a series of events sparked by the writing caused Mrs. Stowe's reputation to plummet and a new interest in Byron to generate. Literary figures such as William Dean Howells, Oliver Wendell Holmes, and James Russell Lowell, and newspapers and magazines such as the *Nation* and the *New York Times* rejected Mrs. Stowe's work because it flaunted propriety and was based only on the word of Byron's divorced wife. Besides, it tended to revive Byron's otherwise moribund literary reputation. Mrs. Stowe had very few defenders although among her supporters were such respected names as *Harper's Magazine* and Mark Twain. As a result of the incident, Mrs. Stowe's reputation suffered, the sale of Byron's works increased, and the *Atlantic Monthly* lost 15,000 subscribers. Based on primary and secondary sources, 45 notes.                    W. L. Bowers

1675.  Lewis, R. W. B.  EDITH WHARTON: THE BECKONING QUARRY.  *Am. Heritage 1975 26(6): 53-56, 73.* The author spent several years pursuing the life of Edith Wharton, following tantalizing bits of evidence, interviewing contemporaries, and searching through papers in an effort to discover the real Wharton. Lewis slowly realized that she was much more passionate, sensual, and erotic than most people believed. 2 illus.                    B. J. Paul

1676.  Lind, Sidney E.  EMILY DICKINSON'S "FURTHER IN SUMMER THAN THE BIRDS" AND NATHANIEL HAWTHORNE'S "THE OLD MANSE."  *Am. Literature 1967 39(2): 163-169.* Hawthorne's essay "The Old Manse" (1846) is a parallel to Miss Dickinson's poem "Further in Summer than the Birds" (1866). 12 notes.                    R. S. Burns

1677.  Litz, Joyce H.  LILLIAN'S MONTANA SCENE.  *Montana: Mag. of Western Hist. 1974 24(3): 58-69.* Lillian W. Hazen (1864-1949), daughter of the professional pedestrian Edward Payson Weston (1839-1929), spent much of her life as a housewife in Gilt Edge, a mining camp in central Montana, and on a homestead nearby. Attendant hardships were not enough to deprive her of a career in journalism and poetry. Illus.                    S. R. Davison

1678.  Loftin, Bernadette K.  A WOMAN LIBERATED: LILLIAN C. WEST, EDITOR.  *Florida Hist. Q. 1974 52(4): 396-410.* Lillian Carlisle West (1884-1970) was editor of the weekly Panama City (Florida) *Pilot* during 1917-37. She also managed two other newspapers during this time and operated a land company and a publishing house. Her professional involvement gave her a position of community leadership equalled by few women of her time. West succeeded her husband in these positions but, once on her own, staked out strongly independent editorial positions until she sold her newspaper and retired from public life in 1937. Based on interviews, newspaper, census, and secondary sources; 73 notes.                    J. E. Findling

1679.  Long, Robert Emmet.  A SOURCE FOR DR. MARY PRANCE IN "THE BOSTONIANS."  *Nineteenth-Cent. Fiction 1964 19(1): 87-88.* Dr. Mary Walker, a suffragette who practiced medicine during and following the Civil War, may have been the model for Dr. Mary Prance in Henry James' *The Bostonians* (1886).                    C. L. Eichelberger

1680.  Loyd, Dennis.  TENNESSEE'S MYSTERY WOMAN NOVELIST.  *Tennessee Hist. Q. 1970 29(3): 272-277.* One of the best-kept literary secrets of the late 19th and early 20th centuries was that Mary Noailles Murfree was Charles Egbert Craddock. "Miss Mary," as she was known in Murfreesboro, Tennessee, wrote for the *Atlantic Monthly* and produced numerous novels in the dialect of the Tennessee Mountain people. For several years, neither her Boston publisher nor her Murfreesboro neighbors knew that "Craddock" was her pen-name. With the loss of her sight in later years, anonymity returned; at her death in 1922 few of the younger generation were aware of her identity or of her contribution to literature. Based on secondary sources. 7 notes.                    M. B. Lucas

1681.  MacDonald, Edgar E.  THE GLASGOW-CABELL ENTENTE.  *Am. Literature 1969 41(1): 76-91.* Letters between Ellen Glasgow and James Branch Cabell reveal the limited artistic usefulness of the writers to each other in an aesthetically arid Richmond.                    R. S. Burns

1682.  Mathews, James W.  THE CIVIL WAR OF 1936: "GONE WITH THE WIND" AND "ABSALOM! ABSALOM!"  *Georgia R. 1967 21(4): 462-469.* Discusses the different reception by critics of Margaret Mitchell's *Gone With The Wind* (New York: Macmillan Co.) and William Faulkner's *Absalom! Absalom!* (New York: Random House). Both were published in 1936, but while the former was accepted by nearly all as a masterpiece, the latter was generally rejected. Quotes national and Georgia reviews. Concludes, "both have become classics, the one the most successful historical romance ever written, and the other a masterpiece in psychological realism." 29 notes.                    T. M. Condon

1683.  McClure, Charlotte S.  A CHECKLIST OF THE WRITINGS OF AND ABOUT GERTRUDE ATHERTON.  *Am. Literary Realism 1870 1910 1976 9(2): 103-162.* Furnishes an indexed checklist of primary and secondary materials relating to the work of early 20th-century American novelist Gertrude Atherton.

1684.  McClure, Charlotte S.  GERTRUDE ATHERTON (1857-1948).  *Am. Literary Realism 1870-1910 1976 9(2): 95-101.* A description of the writings of the American author Gertrude Atherton in terms of their style, content, editions, and critical reception.

1685.  Meier, A. Mabel  BESS STREETER ALDRICH: A LITERARY PORTRAIT.  *Nebraska Hist. 1969 50(1): 67-100.* A careful examination of the literary career of a distinguished Nebraska novelist (1881-1954) whose seven novels and more than 160 short stories attracted attention by stressing the more positive aspects of small town life.                    R. Lowitt Surveys and

1686.  Merideth, Robert.  EMILY DICKINSON AND THE ACQUISITIVE SOCIETY.  *New England Q. 1964 37(4): 435-452.* In view of the familiar account of Emily Dickinson's withdrawal from life, she seems almost unbelievable in the role of critic of the acquisitive society. Miss Dickinson was, however, not only seeking permanent truths but also attacking counterfeit values of her time. Her continuing concern with the relation of the self to the cosmos often depended for its meaning and effect on the contrast to the businessmen of the "Age of Enterprise" in which she lived. In over 150 of her poems, or about 10 percent of them, she appropriated the language of economics to criticize by implication of diction and imagery the values of her society. Her "merchant poems," for example, usually serve to contrast what may be bought with what may not. The poem, "I never saw a Moor," if understood in the irony of the use of the word "checks" becomes, rather than a statement of religious certainty, a critique of the values of her time. In a limited sense, then, Emily Dickinson was not a private poet at all, since her concerns were in part public and critical. She belongs to the American Romantic tradition of both withdrawal from society into self and of Romantic opposition. Based on the Dickinson poems and letters and secondary works; 14 notes.                R. V. Calvert

1687. Michaelson, L. W.   THE WORST AMERICAN NOVEL. *North Dakota Q. 1964 32(4): 101-103.* Nominates Julia A. Moore's *Sunshine and Shadow* (1915) as the worst American novel.
J. F. Mahoney

1688. Miller, F. De Wolf.   EMILY DICKINSON: SELF-PORTRAIT IN THE THIRD PERSON.   *New England Q. 1973 46(1): 119-124.* Anthologists and editors have missed the poem J283, which is a self-portrait of Emily Dickinson. In her first-person statements about herself she is deprecatory or at least modest, but in this poem she speaks of "the qualities which she is willing privately to acclaim." Reprints the poem in its entirety. 11 notes.                E. P. Stickney

1689. Molson, Francis J.   EMILY DICKINSON'S REJECTION OF THE HEAVENLY FATHER.   *New England Q. 1974 47(3): 404-426.* Reviews Emily Dickinson's philosophy of religion. Contrary to some opinion, Dickinson did not reject the God of orthodox Protestantism. She strongly believed in a personal God, but insisted that He prove his existence. When her most cherished prayers were not answered, especially her prayers for love, Dickinson turned instead to a God of love, or love itself, within her own heart. She was never content to sacrifice her life for possible future rewards; rather she wished to be rewarded first and then work as payment for the reward. 14 notes.                V. L. Human

1690. Moore, Rayburn S.   SHERWOOD BONNER'S CONTRIBUTIONS TO LIPPINCOTT'S MAGAZINE AND HARPER'S NEW MONTHLY.   *Mississippi Q. 1964 17(4): 226-230.* Katharine Sherwood Bonner McDowell, a Mississippi native who had left husband and home for a literary career in Boston, contributed six stories, a serial novelette, and an autobiographical sketch to Lippincott's in the 1870's and 1880's. Disregarding Longfellow's advice, she drew on her Southern background for most of those contributions. Although appearing in her novelette to be an advocate of the "New South," she was actually another "unreconstructed" Southerner. Of four stories contributed to *Harper's New Monthly Magazine,* all but one are based on Southern material. Considered together, Mrs. McDowell's contributions to *Harper's* are less significant in scope and originality than those appearing in *Lippincott's.* Based on an unpublished doctoral dissertation; 4 notes.                R. V. Calvert

1691. Murphy, John J.   ELIZABETH MADOX ROBERTS AND THE CIVILIZING CONSCIOUSNESS.   *Register of the Kentucky Hist. Soc. 1966 64(2): 110-120.* Analyzes the style of Elizabeth Madox Roberts as depicted in two of her novels, *The Great Meadow* (New York, 1930) and *The Time of Man* (New York, 1926).                J. F. Cook

1692. Nichols, William W.   A CHANGING ATTITUDE TOWARD POVERTY IN THE "LADIES' HOME JOURNAL": 1895-1919. *Midcontinent Am. Studies J. 1964 5(1): 3-16.* Describes the changing attitude toward poverty when Edward Bok was editor of the *Ladies' Home Journal.* Despite a predictable cultural lag there was a genuine awakening to poverty, a growing unwillingness to identify poverty with moral evil. Illus., 10 notes.                E. P. Stickney

1693. O'Neill, Kate.   SCHOOLMARM IN THE CITY ROOM. *Michigan Q. Rev. 1964 3(1): 18-22.* Ellen Browning Scripps joined her brother James in 1873 to found *The Detroit News.*

1694. Parker, Gail Thain.   SEX, SENTIMENT, AND OLIVER WENDELL HOLMES.   *Women's Studies 1972 1(1): 47-63.* Examines the concept of sexual spheres in the 19th century. Discusses the ideas

about women's sphere held by Lydia Howard Sigourney and Catharine Beecher and briefly contrasts Oliver Wendell Holmes' ideas about women with those of Nathaniel Hawthorne. Focuses on the contents of Holmes' novels, essays, and medical treatises in order to investigate what the 19th century's concept of sexual spheres meant to one American male. Discusses Holmes' ideas about women's spiritual superiority, male and female physical sexuality, and the characteristics of male and female temperaments. Also assesses Holmes' personal difficulties in dealing with separate sexual spheres for men and women. Based on primary sources; 38 notes.                A. E. Wiederrecht

1695. Patten, Irene M.   THE CIVIL WAR AS ROMANCE: OF NOBLE WARRIORS AND MAIDENS CHASTE.   *Am. Heritage 1971 22(3): 48-53. 109.* Civil War romantic novels, such as George Ward Nichols' *The Sanctuary* and John Esten Cooke's *Surry of Eagle's Nest.*
S

1696. Patterson, Rebecca.   EMILY DICKINSON'S PALETTE (PART I).   *Midwest Q. 1964 5(4): 271-291.* The first half of what is probably the most detailed color analysis yet written about a poet. It contains a table of color incidence in all Emily Dickinson's letters and poems year by year, and another table comparing color incidence in some specific works of Elizabeth Barrett Browning, Robert Browning, Emerson, Keats, and Shakespeare. One of the principal elements of romanticism is a deliberate cultivation of color for both descriptive and symbolic intent, and this study indicates that Emily Dickinson in her extreme use of color words makes a kaleidoscopic impression on the mind of the reader. After a lengthy discussion of the chronological phases of the use of color, there is one section on the use of greens and one section on the use of blues. Note, biblio. To be continued.                G. H. G. Jones

1697. Patterson, Rebecca.   EMILY DICKINSON'S PALETTE (II). *Midwest Q. 1964 6(1): 97-117.* Continued from a previous article. This last half of a detailed color analysis of the poet dwells on her preoccupation with the color yellow and its shades of gold and amber. Purple and its derivatives are used as symbols rather than epithets. "Red is Emily Dickinson's color. Outwardly she may wear the white of martyred renunciation, but inwardly she is red, scarlet, carmine, vermilion, whether in ecstatic happiness or in the violence of loss and suffering - until...the vitality drains away and the white so gains upon the red that the latter pales to pink."                R. S. Burke

1698. Pauly, Thomas H.   *RAGGED DICK* AND *LITTLE WOMEN*: IDEALIZED HOMES AND UNWANTED MARRIAGES.   *J. of Popular Culture 1975 9(3): 583-592.* Horatio Alger's *Ragged Dick* (1867) and Louisa May Alcott's *Little Women* (1868) addressed audiences almost exclusively of either boys or girls, thus reflecting society's sharp differentiation of the sexes. Both celebrated marriage but unwittingly undermined it: protagonists of both novels were fatherless and both avoided, even resisted, marriage. 16 notes.                J. D. Falk

1699. Pearsall, Robert Brainard.   ELIZABETH BARRETT MEETS WOLF LARSEN.   *Western Am. Literature 1969 4(1): 3-13.* The source of Jack London's character Maud Brewster in *The Sea Wolf* (1904) is Elizabeth Barrett, not Anna Strunsky.                S

1700. Plante, Patricia R.   EDITH WHARTON AND THE INVADING GOTHS.   *Midcontinent Am. Studies J. 1964 5(2): 18-23.* A discussion of recent and contemporary interpretations regarding Edith Wharton's novels of World War I and their effects on French and American society.                B. M. Morrison

1701. Powell, Lawrence C.   A DEDICATION TO THE MEMORY OF MARY HUNTER AUSTIN, 1868-1934.   *Arizona and the West 1968 10(1): 1-4.* Illinois-born Mary Hunter developed a passion for the early history and lore of California when her family homesteaded there after she had completed her college education. An unsuccessful marriage to a rancher, a career as a school teacher, and membership in an informal literary colony, along with her domineering personality and Bohemian proclivities, affected her writings which she had been producing since college days. From 1892 on, her stories, plays, novels, and essays earned her substantial sums from Western and national magazines. After a stay abroad and in the East where she was identified with feminist and Fabian movements she settled down in New Mexico where she became "a local sage and regional spokeswoman." Her 35 volumes and numerous other writings on the Southwest deal with history, travel, Indian lore, and related subjects. She could produce beautiful, lasting prose "when she forgot her own ego...and this happened all too rarely." Much of her later work was marred by egocentricity, mysticism and social zeal. Appended with a selected list of her works relating to the American Southwest and biographical studies of her life; illus.　　　　　　D. L. Smith

1702. Price, Robert MARY HARTWELL CATHERWOOD AND CINCINNATI. *Cincinnati Hist. Soc. Bull. 1964 22(3): 162-169.* An account of the life and literary activities of Mary Hartwell Catherwood (1847-1902), "the first American woman novelist of any significance to be born of the Appalachians" and "the first woman in America to acquire a college education." She was also "the first woman writer from the West to succeed in supporting herself independently...by her efforts as a full-time writer." In the 1880's and 1890's she produced "first, a long series of children's books, then the fine regional short stories from the old corn belt and from French Canada for two decades in the *Atlantic, Harper's Bazaar* and *Harper's Monthly,* and finally...the historical romances that began with *The Romance of Dollard* in 1889 and concluded with *Lazarre* in 1901." Documented from published biographies by M. L. Wilson and Robert Price. Photo, 18 notes.　　　　　　D. D. Cameron

1703. Rice, Howard C., Jr. THE SYLVIA BEACH COLLECTION. *Princeton U. Lib. Chronicle 1964 26(1): 7-13.* The papers and books of Sylvia Beach (1887-1962), proprietor of Shakespeare and Company, are located in the Princeton University Library. Included are letters and other materials related to French, English, Irish, and American writers of the 1920's and 1930's.　　　　　　D. Brockway

1704. Richey, Elinor. THE FLAPPERS WERE HER DAUGHTERS: THE LIBERATED, LITERARY WORLD OF GERTRUDE ATHERTON. *Am. West 1974 11(4): 4-10, 60-63.* Conditioned by her childhood in a broken home in California and by an unhappy marriage, Gertrude Atherton (1857-1948) turned to writing as a means of independence and fame. After anonymous brief articles and essays in a San Francisco weekly, she produced a six-installment novel based on a scandal that had rocked San Francisco a few years earlier. Unacceptable to critics and readers, she sought exile in New York, and then moved on to England. Her novels about young women who were uninhibited by Victorian mores and who were involved in lechery, suicide, alcohol, and adultery brought London to her feet. Changing her theme somewhat, she produced an anonymous novel that earned favorable American reviews. A fictionalized biography (a new literary form created by Gertrude Atherton) based on Alexander Hamilton firmly established her reputation in the United States. Despite the triumph of her literary production, 56 books, she was largely "an observer in human relations." From a forthcoming book; 5 illus.　　　　　　D. L. Smith

1705. Riggio, Thomas P. UNCLE TOM RECONSTRUCTED: A NEGLECTED CHAPTER IN THE HISTORY OF A BOOK. *Am. Q. 1976 28(1): 56-70.* An important link in the history of the reception and impact of *Uncle Tom's Cabin* is found in its role in Southern Reconstruction fiction, especially in the novels of Thomas Dixon. In *The Leopard's Spots,* he achieved a direct and complete metamorphosis of Stowe's books through his characterizations. Dixon replaced Stowe's language of evangelical humanism with a rhetoric of white manifest destiny in which all except Negroes would be united in a new bond.　　　　　　N. Lederer

1706. Ringler, Donald P. MARY AUSTIN: KERN COUNTY DAYS, 1888-1892. *Southern California Q. 1963 45(1): 25-63.* Mary Austin (1868-1934) followed in the footsteps of several other famous American writers in writing about the California frontier. She lived in Kern County with her family from 1888 to 1892. Material drawn from her Kern County experience was used in about one-third of her published works. The author describes her life in the area, showing how much of it was used in her writing. 36 notes.　　　　　　A. K. Main

1707. Sargent, Shirley. LITERARY LADIES. *Pacific Historian 1965 9(2): 97-101, (3): 129-132.* Describes and quotes the writings of early women settlers in and around Yosemite Valley.　　　　　　S

1708. Schmitt, Peter. WILDERNESS NOVELS IN THE PROGRESSIVE ERA. *J. of Popular Culture 1969 3(1): 72-90.* Discusses the nature theme as it appeared in various popular books published during the era of Progressivism. Mentions the fictional works of Jack London, James Oliver Curwood, Harold Bell Wright, Mary Waller, and Gene Stratton Porter. While much of popular fiction during the Progressive era was wilderness-oriented, the wilderness portrayed by this fiction was benign and arcadian. Based on primary and secondary sources; 66 notes.　　　　　　B. A. Lohof

1709. Schneider, Lucy. "LAND" RELEVANCE IN "NEIGHBOUR ROSICKY." *Kansas Q. 1968 1(1): 105-110.* A discussion of Willa Cather's symbolic and specific use of "land" in her writings, with special emphasis on land symbolism in her story "Neighbour Rosicky." 4 notes.　　　　　　B. A. Storey

1710. Scura, Dorothy M. HOMAGE TO CONSTANCE CARY HARRISON. *Southern Humanities R. 1976 (Special Issue): 35-46.* Discusses the themes of plantation life and the Civil War in the novels of Constance Cary Harrison, 1863-1911.

1711. Self, Robert T. THE CORRESPONDENCE OF AMY LOWELL AND BARRETT WENDELL, 1915-1919. *New England Q. 1974 47(1): 65-86.* Reprints 22 letters between Amy Lowell and Barrett Wendell discussing poetry and literature during the years 1915-19. These letters reveal "that the lines of communication between the old guard and the new radicals were not so sharply severed as literary history has led us to believe." But they illustrate Wendell's older, more critical standards, and Lowell's concern for her poetry of "unrhymed cadence." 34 notes.　　　　　　E. P. Stickney

1712. Seyersted, Per E. KATE CHOPIN: AN IMPORTANT ST. LOUIS WRITER RECONSIDERED. *Missouri Hist. Soc. Bull. 1963 19(2): 89-114.* Traces the life of Kate O'Flaherty Chopin and analyzes her writings and literary style. Lists four short stories which deal with the early history of Illinois and Missouri. Chopin was unique because she accepted men and women as they are and transformed human foibles into poetic truth.　　　　　　D. H. Swift

1713. Shanahan, William. ROBERT BENCHLEY AND DOROTHY PARKER: PUNCH AND JUDY IN FORMAL DRESS. *Rendezvous 1968 3(1): 23-34.* Discusses the years (1919-26) when Benchley and Parker wrote, talked, and shared basic ideas of American society for their comments and criticism. Their main themes were literary freedom, sex, economic justice, ghetto justice, humor, style, technical merits, and insights necessary to a humorist. Quotations from their works are included. 48 notes.　　　　　　H. Malyon

1714. Simms, L. Moody, Jr. CORRA HARRIS ON SOUTHERN AND NORTHERN FICTION. *Mississippi Q. 1974 27(4): 475-482.* Reprints an essay of the southern critic Corra Harris on northern and southern fiction, 1903.　　　　　　S

1715. Simms, L. Moody, Jr. CORRA HARRIS ON PATRIOTIC LITERARY CRITICISM IN THE POST-CIVIL WAR SOUTH. *Mississippi Q. 1972 25(4): 459-466.* Discusses literary critic Corra Harris, including a reprint of her essay "Patriotic Criticism in the South," as published in the June 1904 issue of *The Critic.*　　　　　　S

1716. Slote, Bernice. WILLA CATHER AS A REGIONAL WRITER. *Kansas Q. 1970 2(2): 7-15.* Willa Cather obviously used regional materials in her writing, and these materials were heavily drawn from northwestern Nebraska to which her family had moved in the 1880's. However, while she used regional materials, she treated universal themes. Because she had seen difficult times, she often described these and, as a result, some Nebraskans criticized her work. Other critics considered her work realistic because of this treatment of hard times. Based largely on Cather's works.　　　　　　B. A. Storey

1717. Smith, Henry Ladd. THE BEAUTEOUS JENNIE JUNE: PIONEER WOMAN JOURNALIST. *Journalism Q. 1963 40(2): 169-174.* Jane Cunningham Croly (1829-1901) was one of the first women to be employed by a major US newspaper (first the *New York Herald,* then the *New York World*). She was the first to write a national newspaper column for women and in doing so pioneered the "duplicate exchange agreement" that became a basis for syndicate development, founded the oldest existing women's club (Sorosis), the first women's press club, and led in the formation of the General Federation of Women's Clubs. She was the first woman to teach a course in journalism. Her husband, David Croly, was an editor and her son, Herbert Croly, was founder of the *New Republic*. Based on published sources.

S. E. Humphreys

1718. Smith, Jo Reinhard. NEW TROY IN THE BLUEGRASS: VERGILIAN METAPHOR AND "THE GREAT MEADOW." *Mississippi Q. 1969 22(1): 39-46.* Proper understanding of Elizabeth Madox Roberts' novel *The Great Meadow* (New York, 1930) requires reference to the Vergilian image which is its backbone. The narrative of westward expansion is wrapped neatly in the conservative favorite, the Aeneas myth; but, like other Southern writers, Mrs. Roberts interprets the myth in a way contrary to the modern view. She never suggests that her people are in search of or are building a holy city. Using the same pattern followed by several writers of the Southern Renaissance, she emphasizes man's desire to transplant and establish his inherited culture in a new country. Her Kentuckians have the necessary stamina and courage, but no wandering Ulysses spirit as their guiding light. The Aeneas myth gives concreteness to the idealist philosophy and makes it possible to understand, in the fullest historical context, what was realized in Kentucky in the 1790's. Based on published works; 10 notes.

R. V. Calvert

1719. Soderbergh, Peter A. FLORIDA'S IMAGE IN JUVENILE FICTION, 1909-1914. *Florida Hist. Q. 1972 51(2): 153-165.* Analyzes the image of Florida in juvenile fiction popular around World War I. Such series as *The Motor Boys, The Outdoor Girls, The Automobile Girls, The Motion Picture Girls,* and the *Boy Scouts* featured provincial, wealthy, mobile, and liberated central characters who eventually discovered Florida, usually with considerable enthusiasm. Most often, heroes or heroines went to the Everglades, struggled with alligators, endured hurricanes, and ate strange fruits. They were enchanted by Florida's natural beauty but eventually tired of it and went off to another adventure elsewhere. In general, authors wrote superficially of Florida, doing the state an injustice, but inflicting no permanent damage to the image. 18 notes.

1720. Stewart, Janice S. CONTENT AND READERSHIP OF TEEN MAGAZINES. *Journalism Q. 1964 41(4): 580-583.* Questionnaire study of 259 boys and 173 girls in the seventh through the 12th grades of a junior-senior high school in an advantaged area of Madison, Wisconsin, sought to learn reading habits in respect to so-called "teenage" magazines. The survey showed that in this group the teenage magazines were of far less importance than adult magazines. Content study showed that, with one or two exceptions, the teen magazines were not particularly harmful.

S. E. Humphreys

1721. Stinson, Byron. THE FRANK LESLIES. *Am. Hist. Illus. 1970 5(4): 12-21.* History of Frank and Miriam Leslie's publishing empire, built on *Frank Leslie's Illustrated Newspaper.*          S

1722. Strong, Leah A., ed. THE DAUGHTER OF THE CONFEDERACY. *Mississippi Q. 1967 20(4): 234-239.* A publication of nine letters from Jefferson Davis' daughter, Varina Anne ("Winnie"), and her mother, Varina Howell Davis, to the writer Charles Dudley Warner whom they met during a visit to New Orleans. Following her father's death, Winnie and her mother lived for some time in New York, where Winnie's writing contributed to their support. A correspondence was begun with Warner following his sending a copy of his *Roundabout Journey* (1883) to Winnie, and her mother continued writing to him after the daughter's death. Letters from manuscripts in the Charles Dudley Warner Collection, Trinity College, Connecticut; note.

R. V. Calvert

1723. Suderman, Elmer F. ELIZABETH STUART PHELPS [WARD] AND THE GATES AJAR NOVELS. *J. of Popular Culture 1969 3(1): 91-106.* Analyzes the literary content and social impact of a "school" of novels which appeared between 1868 and 1900. These novels, which the author collectively calls the "Gates-Ajar" novels, were all set in heaven and shared a plot line which explained life after death. As such, the novels represented a popular eschatology. Contends that the image of

everyday life as seen in the novels is merely a perfected counterpart of life on earth in the late 19th century. The novels "offer no insight into the...feelings of men when they contemplate the nameless feelings men experience when they consider death and eternity." 30 notes.

B. A. Lohof

1724. Sutherland,, Raymond Carter. THE KENTUCKY GIRL IN TWO LITERARY CLASSICS. *Register of the Kentucky Hist. Soc. 1967 65(2): 134-143.* Describes the character of the Kentucky girl as she is presented in Willa Cather's *Death Comes for the Archbishop* (New York: Knopf, 1926) and Meredith Nicholson's *The House of a Thousand Candles* (Indianapolis: Bobbs-Merrill, 1905). Both books give the Kentucky girl an unfavorable character. She is portrayed in the "moonlight and magnolia" tradition with a broad Southern accent and an extreme self-centeredness, although, as Sutherland points out, another type exists: the charming, capable, and intelligent aristocrat. It is the former image that the North has adopted and transferred to the whole South. Drawn from the author's experience. 3 notes.          B. Wilkins

1725. Sweeney, Ben. JACK LONDON'S NOBLE LADY. *Pacific Hist. 1973 17(3): 20-31.*

1726. Thomas, Owen. FATHER AND DAUGHTER: EDWARD AND EMILY DICKINSON. *Am. Literature 1969 40(4): 510-523.* Traces the long-lasting spiritual influence on Emily Dickinson by her father, Edward. Patterns of imagery and diction in Emily's poetry were drawn from her father's legal and financial interests. 9 notes.

R. S. Burns

1727. Toth, Emily. ST. LOUIS AND THE FICTION OF KATE CHOPIN. *Missouri Hist. Soc. Bull. 1975 32(1): 33-50.* Analyzes the fiction of Kate Chopin (1851-1904). In numerous short stories and two novels, *At Fault* (1891) and *The Awakening* (1899), her descriptions of the sordid side of life and social criticism of the city enraged most of her St. Louis readers. Based on Chopin's writings and secondary sources; 61 notes.          H. T. Lovin

1728. Toth, Susan Allen. DEFIANT LIGHT: A POSITIVE VIEW OF MARY WILKINS FREEMAN. *New England Q. 1973 46(1): 82-93.* Literary historians have viewed Mary Wilkins Freeman (1852-1930) as a pessimistic recorder of New England's decline. "Many of her characters suffer, but they also fight their way to significant victories." "A Village Singer" is typical of her best stories. The positive force in her stories is vastly underestimated. "The struggles she depicts of individual and community glow with an intense and modern light." 27 notes.

E. P. Stickney

1729. Trautmann, Fredrick. HARRIET BEECHER STOWE'S PUBLIC READINGS IN NEW ENGLAND. *New England Q. 1974 47(2): 279-289.* In the autumn of 1872 Harriet Beecher Stowe read in public from her works in all but one of the New England states and in New York City. Encouraged by James T. Fields to face audiences because of her need of money, Harriet Beecher Stowe chose an excellent repertory from the serious to the comic which represented her best qualities as a storyteller. Her local color was brilliant, and she was very successful with both Negro and Yankee dialects. 35 notes.          E. P. Stickney

1730. Tufte, Virginia J. GERTRUDE STEIN'S PROTHALAMIUM: A UNIQUE POEM IN A CLASSICAL MODE. *Yale U. Lib. Gazette 1968 43(1): 17-23.* Discusses a poem written in 1939 by the American poet Gertrude Stein to celebrate the engagement of Robert Bartlett Haas and his bride-to-be, Louise Antoinette Krause, variously titled: "Prothalamium for Bobolink and His Louise," "Very Well I Thank You," and "Love Like Anything."

1731. Tyler, William R. PERSONAL MEMORIES OF EDITH WHARTON. *Massachusetts Hist. Soc. Pro. 1973 85: 91-104.* Comments on the generally accepted view of Edith Wharton as a brilliant but cold and inaccessible woman. The author describes his more than 20-year relationship with her and portrays a kind and generous woman. Based on correspondence between the author and Mrs. Wharton.

J. B. Duff

1732. Vaughan, Alma F. PIONEER WOMEN OF THE MISSOURI PRESS. *Missouri Hist. R. 1970 64(3): 289-305.* The importance of women in 20th-century Missouri's journalism is shown to have been grounded on years of apprenticeship between 1876 and 1900. Many women helped their husbands operate papers before 1876, but it was only in that year that women began to attend the Missouri Press Association's meetings. The first women played a minor role in the State association and on the papers by which they were employed. These pioneers constantly improved their position. By 1896 the women formed their own press association, and at the end of the century women were editing or publishing 25 newspapers in Missouri. Based on local newspapers, articles, the records of the Missouri Editors' and Publishers' Association, and the Missouri Press Association; illus., 80 notes.                W. F. Zornow

1733. Vigil, Ralph H. WILLA CATHER AND HISTORICAL REALITY. *New Mexico Hist. R. 1975 50(2): 123-139.* Willa Cather's *Death Comes for the Archbishop* (New York: Vintage Books, 1971) is representative of fictional history and literature dealing with New Mexico. Author deals with Cather's portrayal of Father Antonio Jose Martinez (1793-1867), the parish priest of Taos who favored annexation of New Mexico by the United States. 45 notes.                J. H. Krenkel

1734. Walker, Don D. THE WESTERN HUMANISM OF WILLA CATHER. *Western Am. Literature 1966 1(2): 75-90.* Discusses humanism in Willa Cather's writing. Though unlike her naturalistic contemporaries, she was aware of and influenced by them. For example, the biological determinism of Jack London and Frank Norris were in conflict with her view of the free human spirit. Miss Cather's focus was not on the natural world but on human passion. Her humanism was western because her novels were set in the Western American States where her characters humanized the landscape and found a happy relationship with the wild land. The author concludes with a discussion of Miss Cather's insight into human relationships. Although every human needs to relate to other humans, no relationship is ever totally satisfying, and so man finds himself seeking more humans while simultaneously pulling away from them. 68 notes.                S. L. McNeel

1735. Wegelin, Christof. EDITH WHARTON AND THE TWILIGHT OF THE INTERNATIONAL NOVEL. *Southern R. 1969 5(2): 398-418.* Analyzes Edith Wharton's novels, of which *The Custom of the Country* (New York: Scribner, 1956) is considered the most significant. The author compares and contrasts Wharton's writings with those of Henry James. Major themes examined include manners, love, social ambitions, and social relations. Her works reflect the social history and the impact of historical events on the author. The major themes found in Wharton's writings are the contrast between the 19th and 20th centuries and the differentiation of social relations and ideals between the New World and the Old.                R. W. Dubay

1736. Weir, Sybil. GERTRUDE ATHERTON: THE LIMITS OF FEMINISM IN THE 1890'S. *San Jose Studies 1975 1(1): 24-31.* The popularity during the 1890's of Gertrude Atherton's novels, which portray sexually-vital heroines actively seeking their own identities, suggests the need to alter our notions about the attitudes of the 19th-century reading public.                S

1737. West, John Foster. MRS. MOREHOUSE'S *RAIN ON THE JUST. North Carolina Folklore 1971 19(2): 47-54.* Analyzes Kathleen Morehouse's use of the folklore of the Brushy Mountains area in Wilkes County, North Carolina, in her novel *Rain on the Just* (1936). Morehouse lived in the Brushy Mountains less than seven years, collecting material for her novel. She was attacked in the Wilkes County area newspapers because of her criticisms in the novel of the morals and culture of Brushy Mountains natives. Specifically discussed are her uses of dialect, folk speech patterns, superstitions, folk humor, folk maxims, and folk tales.                R. N. Lokken

1738. Weston, James J. SHARLOT HALL: ARIZONA'S PIONEER LADY OF LITERATURE. *J. of the West 1965 4(4): 539-552.* Sharlot Mabridth Hall was born in Kansas on 27 October 1870. When she was 11 her family moved to Arizona Territory where her father was to engage in ranching and mining. During the move she was thrown from a horse and suffered a spinal injury. The injury never fully healed and in 1890 she was confined to bed for an entire year. During her convalescence she

began to write poems and articles. Some of these were published in western newspapers. Recovering her health, she improved her 160-acre claim, but still found time to continue writing. In 1897 she wrote a historical article for *Land of Sunshine,* a California magazine edited by Charles F. Lummis. His interest brought her out of obscurity. In 1901 Lummis hired her for his staff of *Out West,* a position she held until 1909 when she resigned to accept a political appointment. Despite some ups and downs her influence as a writer and poet and her influence as a historian and politican continued until her death in 1943. Based on materials in the Sharlot Hall Museum; 53 notes.                D. N. Brown

1739. White, Helen and Sugg, Redding S., Jr. LADY INTO ARTIST: THE LITERARY ACHIEVEMENT OF ANNE GOODWIN WINSLOW. *Mississippi Q. 1969 22(4): 289-302.* Between the ages of 65 and 84, Winslow published six books, a collection of stories, four novels, and nine stories in periodicals. A volume of poetry, *The Long Gallery* (1925), review articles, critical essays, and poems in periodicals appeared during her brief period of literary activity following World War I. During the next 15 years, however, she published very little. Not until the deaths of family, husband, and son, and the marriage of her daughter did she turn attention to becoming a serious writer. Her point of view is that of the southern gentlewoman who must - in order to maintain decorum - evade any potentially dishevelling experience. At her best, the southern lady is represented by Winslow not as innocent, repressed, or evasive, but rather as discriminating and knowing. The first and the last of her novels, respectively, *Cloudy Trophies* (1946) and *It Was Like This* (1949), are her best novels, although the novellas and short stories are superior to the novels. Based partly on unpublished Winslow Papers at Memphis State University; 25 notes.                R. V. Calvert

1740. White, Ray Lewis. THE ORIGINAL FOR SHERWOOD ANDERSON'S "KIT BRANDON." *Newberry Lib. Bull. 1965 6(6): 196-199.* Reprints items from the Marion (Virginia) *Democrat* and *Smyth County News,* August-October 1928, purporting to show that the idea for the main character of the novel *Kit Brandon* (1936) came to Anderson from these stories which he had written about Mamie Palmer, a tuberculous "bootleg queen" who died soon after her arrest as a liquor runner.                H. J. Graham

1741. Williams, Ellen. HARRIET MONROE AND *POETRY* MAGAZINE. *Chicago Hist. 1975/76 4(4): 204-213.* Retraces the life and career of art critic, writer, and editor of *Poetry* magazine Harriet Monroe, and her ties with various literary personalities in Chicago in the late 19th and early 20th centuries.

1742. Wilson, Suzanne M. [EMILY DICKINSON.] *Am. Literature.*
STRUCTURAL PATTERNS IN THE POETRY OF EMILY DICKINSON. 1963 35(1): 53-59. In the canon of Emily Dickinson's works, one major pattern predominates, with several variations revealing experiment and sophisticated development. The sermon form - statement or introduction of topic, elaboration, conclusion - is the major structural pattern. Variations are three: initial statement without a figure, initial statement with a figure, repetition and elaboration of statement. Note.
EMILY DICKINSON AND TWENTIETH-CENTURY POETRY OF SENSIBILITY. 1964 36(3): 349-358. Emily Dickinson's imagery is expository and its major form is the sermon. The imagery often relies on associations suggested to the reader's mind rather than on a comparison or analogy. This effect on the reader's intuition is akin to the meaning of the 20th-century term "sensibility" and is also found in T. S. Eliot and Ezra Pound. 7 notes.                R. S. Burns

1743. Woodress, James. "UNCLE TOM'S CABIN" IN ITALY. *Essays on American Literature in Honor of Jay B. Hubbell* (Durham: Duke U. Pr., 1967): 126-140. *Uncle Tom's Cabin* has been more continuously popular in Italy than elsewhere and has been constantly in print since 1852. "Three periods of maximum popularity...coincide with the emergence of major political crises" in Italy: during the Risorgimento in the early 1860's, during the Fascist era, and "after World War II, when liberty returned to Italy." A bibliographic listing of 67 Italian editions of *Uncle Tom's Cabin* is included.                C. L. Eichelberger

1744. Wortham, Thomas. LOWELL'S "AGASSIZ" AND MRS. AL-EXANDER. *Yale U. Lib. Gazette 1971 45(3): 118-122.* Reproduces a letter from James Russell Lowell to Mrs. Francis Alexander (Lucia Gray Swett) respecting Lowell's "Agassiz," found with a manuscript copy of the poem. Provides background of the friendship between these two Americans during Lowell's visit to Florence in the winter of 1873-74. 8 notes.
D. A. Yanchisin

1745. —. [THE FORGOTTEN DECADES OF SOUTHERN WRITING, 1890-1920]. *Mississippi Q. 1968 21(4): 277-290.*
Adams, Richard P. SOUTHERN LITERATURE IN THE 1890'S, *pp. 277-281.* In this decade the South was culturally and economically underdeveloped. Despite a brain drain of the best writers and a vassalage of Southern writers to Northern publishers, reviewers, and readers, out of the chaotic 1890's came significant foundations. Thomas Nelson Page so successfully popularized the sentimental myth of the South that everyone writing about the South since Page has had to do so with reference to his mythical values. Page anticipated William Faulkner in portrayal of his aristocrats as not only proud and brave but also narrow, inflexible, and pigheaded to the point of idiocy. Another predecessor to Faulkner in his representation of the ideal of chivalry is James Lane Allen. George Washington Cable was more realistic than Page in his handling of the weaknesses of the aristocratic character such as its tendency to ill-considered violence and susceptibility to corruption. Also, Cable apparently understood, as Page did not, the fact that the Yankees oppressed the aristocrats no more than the aristocrats oppressed the Negroes and poor whites. Mark Twain attacked the prewar Southern ideal of chivalry and the institution of slavery in relation to the aristocracy as well as the effects of miscegenation on individual personality and on social relations, thus anticipating a Faulkner theme. *The Awakening* (1899) by Kate Chopin is ahead of its time in its sympathetic treatment of a woman's sensuality, and ahead of Faulkner in sensitive exploration of cultural contrast between the Protestant morality of the rural mid-South and the relatively sophisticated mores of the Louisiana Creoles. The Southern renaissance was partly based on an intense feeling of cultural disharmony and strain produced by the realization by sensitive Southerners that their traditional way of life had been condemned by the world and by these Southerners' need to communicate for the sake of understanding.
Turner, Darwin T. SOUTHERN FICTION, 1900-1910, *pp. 281-285.* Only here and there in Southern fiction from 1900 through 1909 is there a source of influence on later writers. The decade produced no masterpiece or landmark. The most artistic novelists, James Branch Cabell and Ellen Glasgow, did not produce their best work during this particular period. Southern fiction suffered from melodrama, idealized characterization, provincial thought, and didactic moralizing. An economically impoverished, militarily conquered society had discouraged literary effort so that no new group of maturing young writers emerged in the 1900's, and older writers continued to offer themes and characters dependent on a mythic agrarian, aristocratic society. Objectivity was not yet possible.
Reeves, Paschal. FROM HALLEY'S COMET TO PROHIBITION, *pp. 285-290.* Careful research in the period from 1910 to 1920 eventually leads to agreement with the conclusion of J. B. Hubbell that, except for Ellen Glasgow and James Branch Cabell, "It was a slack time in Southern literature." Naturalism, permeating American fiction elsewhere, did not get a foothold in the South at this time. Continuing prevalent themes were local color, historical romance, and sentimental fiction. The two most significant writers of the decade, however, rejected traditionalism - James Branch Cabell satirizing the romantic idealism of the South, and Ellen Glasgow (most consequential writer of the decade) becoming the bridge between 19th-century romanticism and realism for the South. Not one important Southern poet appeared during the decade, and the case was much the same with drama. No new literary magazine was begun, no important critic appeared, and no history, biography, or autobiography of high literary quality was written. With the exclusion of Glasgow and Cabell, Southern literature from 1910 to 1920 is negligible before the great burst of creativity that soon followed.
R. V. Calvert

# Arts and Music
## (including Folk Art)

1746. Batman, Richard Dale. THE FOUNDING OF THE HOLLYWOOD MOTION PICTURE INDUSTRY. *J. of the West 1971 10(4): 609-623.* In 1909 a motion picture touring company from William Selig's Polyscope Company of Chicago established a permanent studio in Los Angeles. The weather and scenery in Southern California proved ideal for making movies and other motion picture companies followed suit. The Biograph Company sent Director David Wark Griffith and actors Mack Sennett and Mary Pickford in 1910. The first Hollywood studio was established by Nestor Pictures in 1911. By 1915 the fast growing motion picture industry had developed its elaborate studios, "million-dollar" stars, and "blockbuster" pictures. Based on documents in Academy of Motion Picture Arts and Sciences Library and secondary sources; 68 notes.
B. S. Porter

1747. Cole, Glyndon. WAY DOWN EAST. *York State Tradition 1971 25(2): 2-5.* Discusses the history of Charlotte Blair Parker's melodramatic play "Way Down East" from its presentation in New York City, through its filming by David Wark Griffith in 1920, to its second filming in 1935. Based on secondary sources; 9 notes.
D. A. Franz

1748. Coleman, Marion Moore. MODJESKA AND NEW ORLEANS. *Polish Am. Studies 1967 24(1): 1-14.* Deals with seven visits of Helena Modjeska (nee Opid), the Polish actress, to New Orleans. The first occurred in 1879, the last in 1901. Includes accounts of the artist's performances, interviews, and descriptive glimpses of the city in the latter part of the 19th century.
S. R. Pliska

1749. Coleman, Marion Moore. A POLISH PLAY FOR MODJESKA. *Polish Am. Studies 1965 22(1): 1-9, 64.* Traces the attempts made to produce a Polish play in English on the American stage for Helen Modjeska. This is one dream the great Polish actress never realized. Some "possible" Polish plays were too idiomatic; others were too exclusively Polish, not understandable without a full knowledge of Polish history. Then, after some 30 years of trying, it was sadly learned that Modjeska would be too old for the heroine parts of other plays. Thus the great Modjeska was to pass away with two unrealized dreams: no play in English for the glory of the homeland, and no return to her native land, forbidden by the czar.
S. R. Pliska

1750. Cone, Edward T. THE MISS ETTA CONES, THE STEINS, AND M'SIEU MATISSE: A MEMOIR. *Am. Scholar 1973 42(3): 441-460.* Recalls the author's association with his aunts, Claribel and Etta Cone of Baltimore, famous art collectors. Describes the Cone collection and recounts experiences in Europe with Aunt Etta in 1933. Describes Etta's relationships with Gertrude Stein and her brothers, and with the painter Henri Matisse.
J. B. Street

1751. Cox, Richard W. WANDA GÁG: THE BITE OF THE PICTURE BOOK. *Minnesota Hist. 1975 44(7): Cover, 238-254. Millions of Cats* is the best known work of book illustrator Wanda Gág. After a New Ulm childhood and training in the Twin Cities, she left for New York City where she did illustrations for *The Masses.* Her lithographs of the 1920's were urban in content. Her penchant for spoof and irony, realism and stylism, and her interest in folklore and fairy tales made her work unique. Based on her books and other sources; 21 illus., 64 notes.
S. S. Sprague

1752. Emlen, Robert P. RAISED, RAZED, AND RAISED AGAIN: THE SHAKER MEETINGHOUSE AT ENFIELD, NEW HAMPSHIRE, 1793-1902. *Hist. New Hampshire 1975 30(3): 133-146.* The Shaker meetinghouse at Enfield, New Hampshire, was "the eighth of ten remarkable meetinghouses." Designed and framed by Brother Moses Johnson, master builder, it was altered in 1815 to provide more space. When membership in the community declined after the 1850's the old church became less important, and from 1889 ceased to be used on a regular basis. In 1902 Annetta and Louis Saint-Gaudens purchased the structure, dismantled it, and had it erected, with modifications, at Cornish, New Hampshire, where it still stands, as the Saint-Gaudens' National Historic Site. 6 illus., 31 notes.
D. F. Chard

1753. Fletcher, Richard D. "OUR OWN" MARY GARDEN. *Chicago Hist. 1972 2(1): 34-46.* Garden (1874-1967) had strong connections with Chicago. She arrived in Chicago in 1887 and received her first vocal training there. Later, after study in Paris, she returned to Chicago, first as an operatic artist and later as manager of the Chicago Opera Association (1921-22). Upon her return in 1910 she performed four great roles in one month and revealed her great range of acting and singing gifts. Her career shows supreme artistic technique, and, more importantly, intellectual genius. Based on primary and secondary sources; 12 photos.          N. A. Kuntz

1754. Geselbracht, Raymond H. TRANSCENDENTAL RENAISSANCE IN THE ARTS: 1890-1920. *New England Q. 1975 48(4): 463-486.* The religious Transcendentalists were in their graves by 1890, their concept of immediate products of pure reason replaced by the inexorable laws of Darwinian evolution. The demise seemed final, but Transcendentalism suddenly sprang up again in the arts, led by architect Frank Lloyd Wright, composer Charles Ives, and dancer Isadora Duncan. All three turned from the slow pedestrianism of evolution and the cultural dictates of Europe to seek inspiration in nature and sudden insight. They did not fundamentally alter the course of American culture, but they served notice that alternatives were possible. 64 notes.          V. L. Human

1755. Goodrich, Lloyd. PAST, PRESENT, AND FUTURE. *Art in Am. 1966 54(5): 30-31.* Relates the development of the Whitney Museum from 1914, when Gertrude Vanderbilt Whitney converted an old house at West Eighth Street into a gallery called the Whitney Studio. In January 1930 Mrs. Whitney's collection of about 500 American paintings and sculptures was exhibited in three remodeled houses at 8, 10, and 12 Eighth Street. In 1954, a new building opened on West Fifty-fourth Street. "Today, our new building on Madison Avenue and Seventy-fifth Street gives us about three times our former space as well as many new features....It is a genuinely functional building, using space to the utmost, and providing the flexibility needed for an active exhibition program." 3 photos.          D. D. Cameron

1756. Gottlieb, Lois C. THE DOUBLE STANDARD DEBATE IN EARLY 20TH CENTURY AMERICAN DRAMA. *Michigan Academician 1975 7(4): 441-452.* Discusses the influence of the Woman's Rights Movement in the development of 20th-century American drama as portrayed in three plays concerned with woman's place in society.          S

1757. Gottlieb, Lois C. THE PERILS OF FREEDOM: THE NEW WOMAN IN THREE AMERICAN PLAYS OF THE 1900'S. *Can. R. of Am. Studies 1975 6(1): 84-98.* Comments on three dramas, *The Easiest Way* (1908) by Eugene Walter, *The City* (1909) by Clyde Fitch, and *The Faith Healer* (1910) by William Vaughn Moody. These playwrights treated the early 20th-century feminist movement with very little sympathy. Based on secondary sources; 42 notes.          H. T. Lovin

1758. Grant, H. Roger. LUCIA A. GRIFFIN: PLATFORM SPEAKER OF THE LATE NINETEENTH CENTURY. *Ann. of Iowa 1974 42(6): 462-467.* Traces the life and speaking career of Lucia B. Griffin (1865-1940). "Never involved in the women's rights movement, she instead sought to earn a decent living as a platform entertainer during the closing years of the nineteenth century. Her professional career not only reveals the activities of one of the few nationally known women elocutionists of the period but provides useful insights into American popular culture." She was best known as a recitationist and impersonator whose extensive repertoire reflected her Iowa Protestant background and ethics. Griffin performed her largely nonpolitical programs before women's lodges, clubs, and church meetings throughout the country; but her career was cut short by a railroad accident in 1902 which permanently affected her mind. Illus., 18 notes.          C. W. Olson

1759. Graves, John. AUNT CLARA'S LUMINOUS WORLD. *Am. Heritage 1970 21(5): 46-56.* Presents a pictorial record of the paintings of "Aunt Clara," Clara McDonald Williamson, whose paintings depict the "pretty and true, but not sad" life in Iredell, Texas, in the late 19th and early 20th centuries. 12 illus.          J. F. Paul

1760. Grimsted, David. *UNCLE TOM* FROM PAGE TO STAGE: LIMITATIONS OF NINETEENTH-CENTURY DRAMA. *Q. J. of Speech 1970 56(3): 235-244.* Discusses shortcomings in theatrical adaptations of Harriet Beecher Stowe's novel *Uncle Tom's Cabin* in the 1870's, emphasizing a production by actor George L. Aiken.

1761. Hall, Linda. LILLIE LANGTRY AND THE AMERICAN WEST. *J. of Popular Culture 1974 7(4): 873-881.* Describes the British actress Lillie Langtry's trips to the West, 1884-1913, including her stop at Langtry, Texas, and her purchase of a ranch in California.          S

1762. Holman, Harriet R. INTERLUDE: SCENES FROM JOHN FOX'S COURTSHIP OF FRITZI SCHEFF, AS REPORTED BY RICHARD HARDING DAVIS. *Southern Literary J. 1975 7(2): 77-87.* The courtship of opera singer Fritzi Scheff by novelist John Fox in 1908 was reported in Europe and America by Davis.          S

1763. Karr, Kathleen. THE LONG SQUARE-UP: EXPLOITATION TRENDS IN THE SILENT FILM. *J. of Popular Film 1974 3(2): 107-128.* Discusses the early use of sex, gambling, and drugs as themes in silent films.          S

1764. King, C. Richard. SARAH BERNHARDT IN TEXAS. *Southwestern Hist. Q. 1964 68(2): 196-206.* Describes the performances, hospitality, and sponsorship of French actress Sarah Bernhardt on tours in Texas in 1892 and 1906. 31 notes.          D. L. Smith

1765. Maiden, Lewis. THREE THEATRICAL STARS IN NASHVILLE, 1876-1906. *Southern Speech J. 1966 31(4): 388-347.* Describes the impact of appearances by Edwin Booth, Joseph Jefferson, and Sarah Bernhardt on the Nashville stage and community. 44 notes.          H. G. Stelzner

1766. Marberry, M. M. "THE NAKED LADY", OR DONT TAKE YOUR SISTER TO ASTLEY'S. *Horizon 1964 6(1): 112-118.* The Victorian actress, Adah Isaacs Menken, became the toast of two continents for her daring act in "Mazeppa or the Wild Horse of Tartary" (written in 1830 by Henry M. Milner), when, dressed in flesh-colored tights, she was strapped to the wild horse of Tartary. In San Francisco she was the favorite of the literary group headed by Artemus Ward and Bret Harte. In London Mazeppa was a *succès de scandale*. Finally in Paris she "rid herself of the chore of playing nothing but Mazeppa." She was a friend of Dumas *(père)* and of Swinburne. Illus.          E. P. Stickney

1767. Marberry, M. M. THE OVERLOVED ONE. *Am. Heritage 1965 16(5): 84-87, 107-109.* Describes the mourning over the death of Rudolph Valentino in 1926 at the age of 31. Publicity seekers abounded, particularly Polish actress Pola Negri, who used Valentino's death to announce that they had been engaged. 6 illus.          J. F. Paul

1768. Merrill, Richard. MARY CASSATT: AMERICA'S FIRST LADY OF ART. *Mankind 1969 1(12): 62-65.*

1769. Overstreet, Robert. SARAH BERNHARDT IN SAVANNAH. *Western Speech 1975 39(1): 20-25.* Sarah Bernhardt gave two performances in Savannah: *Camille* and *La Tosca* in 1892 and *Camille* again in 1906.          S

1770. Payne, Elizabeth Rogers. ANNE WHITNEY: ART AND SOCIAL JUSTICE. *Massachusetts Rev. 1971 12(2): 245-260.* Surveys the life of Anne Whitney (1821-1915) both as sculptor and active champion of social justice. She integrated these passions by making most of her sculpture portray either champions of freedom or those oppressed by its lack. For a woman of her time, a career as a sculptor was a challenge to convention; at one point she lost a prize in a competition when the judges discovered her sex. Describes her main pieces and the causes she espoused: women's rights, abolition, and various socialist causes. 9 plates.          R. V. Ritter

1771. Price, Raye. UTAH'S LEADING LADIES OF THE ARTS. *Utah Hist. Q. 1970 38(1): 65-85.* Reviews contributions to the arts made by five women whose lives were related to Utah in some significant way. Two (Maude Adams and Maud May Babcock) were in theater, one

(Emma Lucy Gates Bowen) had an international success as a singer, one (Mary Teasdel) was a painter, and the fifth (Alice Merrill Horne) was a patron of the arts. The central theme of the essay is the frontier environment in which these careers developed.

S. L. Jones

1772. Prideaux, Tom. ELLEN TERRY WOWED THE NEW WORLD ONSTAGE—AND OFF. *Smithsonian 1975 6(8): 52-61.* Follows the dramatic careers of Ellen Terry and her acting partner, Henry Irving, both of Great Britain, as they captured American audiences, 1883-1915.

1773. Remley, Mary Lou. THE WISCONSIN IDEA OF DANCE: A DECADE OF PROGRESS 1917-1926. *Wisconsin Mag. of Hist. 1975 58(3): 178-195.* Describes Margaret N. H'Doubler's early efforts at legitimizing dance as part of the physical education curriculum at the University of Wisconsin. Invited to remain at the university as an assistant with primary responsibilities for basketball and baseball, Miss H'Doubler was encouraged to take a year of graduate study. At the studio of Alys E. Bently, H'Doubler began her career-long interest in dance, developing her theoretical ideas about time-space-force into what is now known as modern interpretative dancing. After her return to Wisconsin she worked successfully to establish the first dance major at an institution of higher learning, continuing to exercise dominant influence through her teaching and publications. 17 illus., 50 notes.

N. C. Burckel

1774. Rigby, Chris. ADA DWYER: BRIGHT LIGHTS AND LILACS. *Utah Hist. Q. 1975 43(1): 41-51.* Prominent Utah actress Ada Dwyer (1863-1952) was the daughter of a bookstore owner whose shop and home were cultural centers for Salt Lake City society. Her early contacts with notable people of every profession influenced her interest in acting. She was successful on the New York stage and on foreign tours. She married Harold Russell. They separated after the birth of a daughter, but she retained his name. Closely associated with Amy Lowell (d. 1925) since 1912, she was instrumental in publication of her poetry and was her secretary, nurse, and critic. Dwyer obtained fame as an actress, but her lasting gift to the arts was the contribution she made to Amy Lowell's life. Primary and secondary sources; 3 illus., 36 notes.

J. L. Hazelton

1775. Ripley, John W. A TEAR-JERKING ILLUSTRATED SONG OF 1897, "THE LETTER EDGED IN BLACK." *Kansas Hist. Q. 1963 29(4): 369-371.* In 1895 photographic song-slides were introduced to encourage the sale of sheet music. Robert B. Hansford, a popular, professional photographer in Kansas City, Kansas, was asked by music publisher Frank Woodbury to make some slides to illustrate "The Letter Edged in Black," a song composed shortly before by the publisher's wife. Illustrated with the eight slides Hansford made to sell this song.

W. F. Zornow

1776. Rochlin, Harriet. DESIGNED BY JULIA MORGAN. *Westways 1976 68(3): 26-29, 75-76, 80.* Describes the career of California architect Julia Morgan (1872-1957), who designed more than 700 buildings, including William Randolph Hearst's estate, La Cuesta Encantada, at San Simeon.

1777. Rowell, Adelaide. EMMA BELL MILES, ARTIST, AUTHOR, AND POET OF THE TENNESSEE MOUNTAINS. *Tennessee Hist. Q. 1966 25(1): 77-89.* A brief descriptive biography of Emma Bell Miles (1880-1919). A promising young artist, Miles studied art for two years in St. Louis. A young mountain woman, she was homesick for the hills of Tennessee, returned to the mountains, and refused to accept her friends' plans to send her to Europe for additional study. Shortly after her return, at the age of 24, she married Frank Miles, "a typically shiftless" mountain man. Her bright future turned into 15 years of drudgery and ill health. Pregnancy followed pregnancy and tuberculosis and poverty caused her death at the age of 32. Excerpts from her diary show how the years were filled with despair, humility, and complete disillusionment.

B. B. Swift

1778. Sharf, Frederic A. FIDELIA BRIDGES (1835-1923) PAINTER OF BIRDS AND FLOWERS. *Essex Inst. Hist. Collections 1968 104(3): 217-234.* The first biographical sketch of a noted female artist, best remembered for her studies of birds and flowers which were principally done in water colors. In addition to her artwork, Fidelia

Bridges worked at many jobs (especially as a female companion) since she was not wealthy. Her production was thus limited and usually sold privately. She had few public exhibitions. Included is a list of her known works. Illus., biblio.

J. M. Bumsted

1779. Smith, Elizabeth H. THE STORY OF EMMA WIXOM, THE GREAT OPERATIC DIVA FROM THE MOTHER LODE. *California Historian 1967 13(3): 85-88.* Discusses the life of Emma Wixom who took the stage name of Emma Nevada and became an outstanding concert and opera singer. Emma's early life was spent in the mining towns of California and Nevada. Emma "began to sing as soon as she could talk." After training in San Francisco and Paris, she was showered with acclaim in concerts and opera in Europe and the United States. Following her marriage to Raymond Palmer, her career continued as a teacher. She died in 1940.

O. L. Miller

1780. Stathis, Stephen W. and Roderick, Lee. MALLET, CHISEL, AND CURLS. *Am. Heritage 1976 27(2): 44-47, 94-96.* Vinnie Ream Hoxie (1847-1914), who had been sculpting a bust of President Abraham Lincoln before his death, received a commission from Congress in 1866 to do a full-length statue of him. Although caught up in the impeachment of President Johnson, she finished the statue in 1871. 6 illus.

B. J. Paul

1781. Stearns, Marshall and Stearns, Jean. AMERICAN VERNACULAR DANCE: THE WHITMAN SISTERS. *Southwest R. 1966 51(4): 350-358.* The Whitman sisters - Mabel, Essie, Alberta, and Alice - trouped the country from 1903 to 1943. Consisting of from 20 to 30 performers, their troupe was the highest paid act on the Theater Owners Booking Association circuit, and perhaps the greatest incubator of dancing talent for Negro shows in the country.

D. F. Henderson

1782. Tees, Arthur T. MAXWELL ANDERSON'S LIBERATED WOMEN. *North Dakota Q. 1974 42(2): 53-59.* Several of Anderson's plays used women in the leading roles.

S

1783. Wark, Robert R. ARABELLA HUNTINGTON AND THE BEGINNING OF THE ART COLLECTION. *Huntington Lib. Q. 1969 32(4): 309-331.* A truly great collector, Mrs. Huntington bought extensively for several decades and in "an incredible spending spree" from 1900 to 1910 during her widowhood. It was her partnership with H. E. Huntington (whom she married in 1913) which was responsible for the gallery in their former dwelling at San Marino. His contribution was especially to concentrate development in the field of 18th-century British portraiture.

H. D. Jordan

1784. Winter, Robert W. AMERICAN SHEAVES FROM "C.R.A." AND JANET ASHBEE. *J. of the Soc. of Architectural Historians 1971 30(4): 317-322.* Excerpts from Charles Robert Ashbee's *Memoirs* describing his American travels with his wife, Janet, and the British Arts and Crafts movement.

S

1785. Woodbury, David O. SUSY OAKES—THE GIRL WHO COULDN'T PAINT. *New-England Galaxy 1967 8(3): 2-12.* The author's mother, Marcia Oakes Woodbury, was a New England painter.

S

1786. —. [JOHN STEUART CURRY]. *Kansas Q. 1970 2(4): 6-18.*
Waller, Bret. AN INTERVIEW WITH MRS. JOHN STEUART CURRY, *pp. 6-12.*
Waller, Bret. AN INTERVIEW WITH MRS. DANIEL SCHUSTER, *pp. 13-18.*
An entire issue devoted to American regionalist painter John Steuart Curry, including a reminiscence by one of Curry's assistants and interviews with Curry's wife and daughter. Additional articles consider critics' views of Curry, Curry's use of the Negro as a subject, and the controversy concerning Curry's proposed murals for the Kansas state capitol in Topeka.

B. A. Storey

1787. —. THE ONDERDONKS . . . A FAMILY OF TEXAS PAINTERS. *Southwestern Art 1976 5(1): 32-43.* Discusses the painting of the members of the Onderdonk family, Robert Jenkins (1852-1917), Robert Julian (1882-1922), and Eleanor Rogers (1884-1964).

1788. —. THE SMALL BRIGHT WORLD OF ANNA LINDNER. *Am. Heritage 1975 27(1): 4-10.* Illustrations of the work of Anna Lindner (1845-1922), a self-taught artist who, though crippled by polio, began painting at the age of 18. Her work, showing scenes from her daily life, were recently given to the New Jersey Historical Society in Newark. 11 illus. J. F. Paul

1789. —. THE STORY OF A STATUE. *Wisconsin Then and Now 1963 9(8): 1-3.* "Miss Forward," the statue that tops the dome of the Wisconsin State capitol, was quite a controversial figure in 1911. Helen Farnsworth Mears was the first sculptress whose design was considered. After several months and considerable dissatisfaction, the Capitol Commission paid Miss Mears 1,500 dollars for her work and voted to retain Daniel Chester French as sculptor. In 1914 French's statue was hoisted to the roof. Though popularly known as "Miss Forward," it is properly called simply "Wisconsin." Illus. E. P. Stickney

## Athletics
### *(including physical education)*

1790. Gerber, Ellen. THE CONTROLLED DEVELOPMENT OF COLLEGIATE SPORT FOR WOMEN, 1923-1936. *J. of Sport Hist. 1975 2(1): 1-28.* Traces the development of collegiate sports for women, 1890-1936. In 1923 a national philosophy was articulated as a result of the attempt by the Amateur Athletic Union to take over women's track and field. Women physical educators asserting their own authority outlined the educational, moral, and social implications of the union and influenced the final decision. The play day form of competition was invented to implement the philosophy and by 1936 nearly all colleges engaged in intercollegiate competition. 2 illus., 89 notes. M. Kaufman

1791. Halliday, E. M. SPHAIRISTIKÉ, ANYONE? *Am. Heritage 1971 22(4): 48-59.* Traces the history of tennis, introduced in America in 1874 by Mary Ewing Outerbridge. 16 photos.

1792. Remley, Mary Lou. WOMEN AND COMPETITIVE ATHLETICS. *Maryland Historian 1973 4(2): 89-94.* Briefly describes the ambivalent attitudes which restricted female participation in competitive sports during the early 20th century. Based on contemporary sources; 14 notes. G. O. Gagnon

1793. Robicheaux, Laura. AN ANALYSIS OF ATTITUDES TOWARDS WOMEN'S ATHLETICS IN THE U.S. IN THE EARLY TWENTIETH CENTURY. *Can. J. of Hist. of Sport and Physical Educ. 1975 6(1): 12-22.*

1794. Struna, Nancy and Remley, Mary L. PHYSICAL EDUCATION FOR WOMEN AT THE UNIVERSITY OF WISCONSIN, 1863-1913: A HALF CENTURY OF PROGRESS. *Can. J. of Hist. of Sport and Physical Educ. 1973 4(1): 8-26.* Concern for the health and physical welfare of women at the University of Wisconsin existed in 1863 when they were first admitted, but few provisions were made for them in the next 25 years. When women agitated for physical education, the university built facilities and hired instructors. By the 1890's a program had been established based on the Swedish and Delsarte systems of gymnastics, and women were pursuing many sports. By the early 1900's a women's athletic association was formed and a physical education major was initiated with 11 women enrolled. Based on primary sources including newspapers, university catalogues, and regents' reports; 66 notes. R. A. Smith

1795. Wilke, Phyllis Kay. PHYSICAL EDUCATION FOR WOMEN AT NEBRASKA UNIVERSITY, 1879-1923. *Nebraska Hist. 1975 56(2): 193-220.* Examines the development of a program of physical education for women at the University of Nebraska, including the women and students involved. R. Lowitt

## Recreation

1796. Buxbaum, Katherine. AND ALL PROMENADE. *Ann. of Iowa 1968 39(4): 282-286.* Describes the "play-parties" she witnessed as a girl in late 19th-century Iowa. The folk dances—though the latter word was studiously avoided—were often performed to the music of a mouth harp. The violin was never used because it was considered the devil's instrument. The verses of a number of songs used in these party games are given. Undocumented. D. C. Swift

1797. Moore, Austin L., ed. THE LAST EDEN. THE DIARY OF ALICE MOORE AT THE XX RANCH. *Ann. of Wyoming 1969 41(1): 63-81.* In addition to giving an account of a teen-age girl's camping on the XX Ranch in southeastern Wyoming during 1912, the editor discusses the ranch and the William R. Williams family which founded it. The diary describes a summer camping vacation of the Frank Moore family of five. It includes comments on the tents, weather, food, hiking, fishing, reading, and general remarks about the bird and animal life then abounding in the Laramie Mountains. The editor participated in the vacation as a boy of eleven and thus uses no annotations. Illus. R. L. Nichols

1798. Nye, Russel B. SATURDAY NIGHT AT THE PARADISE BALLROOM: OR, DANCE HALLS IN THE TWENTIES. *J. of Popular Culture 1973 7(1): 14-22.* Discusses background, music, and atmosphere of dance halls, particularly in major cities during 1910-29. S

1799. Thompson, Sally. PLYMOUTH OLD-TIME DANCE ORCHESTRA. *Vermont Hist. 1972 40(3): 185-189.* Miss Florence L. Cilley, former schoolteacher and postmistress, organized Saturday night round and square dances in the hall over her general store. The local orchestra (piano, drums, clarinet, violins) toured Loew's movie theaters in 13 states, performing with a set of four couples in the fall of 1926. 3 illus. T. D. S. Bassett

# 6. The United States Since 1945

## General

1800. Bell, Carolyn Shaw. ECONOMICS, SEX, AND GENDER. *Social Sci. Q. 1974 55(3): 615-631.* Discusses the way economic analysis shapes political policy and how this analysis has been traditionally performed by men.                                                                S

1801. Miller, Bernice J. INNER CITY WOMEN IN WHITE SCHOOLS. *J. of Negro Educ. 1973 42(3): 392-413.* Examines career training within continuing education programs in terms of the vocational needs of mature black women studying in white colleges and universities.                                                                S

## Economic Sphere

### General

1802. Ackerman, Frank; Birnbaum, Howard; Wetzler, James; and Zimbalist, Andrew. INCOME DISTRIBUTION IN THE UNITED STATES. *R. of Radical Pol. Econ. 1971 3(3): 20-43.* Persistent inequality of income distribution is commonly accepted as necessary to promote growth, despite causing political embarrassment in a democracy. Authors reject this acceptance, since ecological costs and developing nations will limit growth, incentives leading to inequality are unnecessary, and inequality has harmful human consequences. Besides income, wealth is also surveyed and is found to be very unequally distributed, while poverty is found to be declining but at too slow a rate. Inequal income distribution is related to class, race, sex, and parental occupation, with education being an ineffective vehicle for social mobility. Based on government documents and secondary works; 15 tables, 35 notes.

C. P. de Young

1803. Barnett, Larry D. ACHIEVEMENT VALUES AND ANO-MIE AMONG WOMEN IN A LOW-INCOME HOUSING PROJECT. *Social Forces 1970 49(1): 127-133.* "Rosen's achievement values scale and Srole's anomie scale were administered to adult women residents of a low-income family housing project. The data analysis indicated that religion was an antecedent condition for achievement values only, with Catholics characterized by higher achievement values than Protestants, and that education was an antecedent condition for both achievement values and anomie, with those possessing a post-high school education characterized by higher achievement values and lower anomie than those possessing no more than a high school diploma. Income was not related to either scale. The data also indicated that in general no intrinsic relationship exists between anomie and achievement values."                                                                J

1804. Bell, Carolyn Shaw. AGE, SEX, MARRIAGE, AND JOBS. *Public Interest 1973 (30): 76-87.* Discusses whether unemployment during 1950-72 was related to the entrance of more women and teenage youths into the labor market.                                                                S

1805. Boyenton, William H. ENTER THE LADIES - 86 PROOF: A STUDY IN ADVERTISING ETHICS. *Journalism Q. 1967 44(3): 445-453.* Women first appeared in advertising for distilled spirits in 1958. Increasing boldness in appeals to women and youth subsequent to that year is traced. 19 notes.                                                S. E. Humphreys

1806. Bradshaw, T. F. and Stinson, J. F. TRENDS IN WEEKLY EARNINGS: AN ANALYSIS. *Monthly Labor R. 1975 98(8): 22-32.* Discusses existing weekly wage gaps between whites and Negroes and between men and women.                                                                S

1807. Burma, John H.; Cretser, Gary A.; and Seacrest, Ted. A COMPARISON OF THE OCCUPATIONAL STATUS OF INTRAMAR-RYING AND INTERMARRYING COUPLES: A RESEARCH NOTE. *Sociol. and Social Res. 1970 54(4): 508-519.* "Six hypotheses

differentially relating occupational status to intramarrying and intermarrying couples in Los Angeles County are suggested and tested. The results indicate little difference exists between intramarrying and intermarrying couples with regard to occupational status."                                                                J

1808. Davies, David G. UNEMPLOYMENT, INFLATION, AND PUBLIC POLICY. *South Atlantic Q. 1974 73(4): 460-474.* Analyzes the causes and potential cures of the present unemployment and inflation. Economic theory in vogue is not convincing. Unemployment is caused by minimum wages, unemployment benefits, working women, and monopoly power, as well as by lesser factors. No cure will be effected until these causes are attacked. The major problem is lack of knowledge: no one understands the American economy. Table, 46 notes.

V. L. Human

1809. Dernberg, Thomas F. and Strand, Kenneth T. HIDDEN UN-EMPLOYMENT 1953-62: A QUANTITATIVE ANALYSIS BY AGE AND SEX. *Am. Econ. R. 1966 56(1): 71-95.* Reports the results of an attempt to answer six questions: 1) Who are the discouraged workers who leave the labor force when employment declines? 2) Who are the additional workers who enter the labor force under the pressure of economic adversity? 3) What is the quantitative relationship between employment and labor force participation in these respective groups? 4) What are the additional employment requirements, both in the aggregate and for each group, that would achieve a 4 percent overall unemployment rate? 5) What unemployment rates, for the individual groups, would be associated with overall full employment? 6) Has there been a structural shift in the composition of the labor force of a sort that might render the attainment of full employment more difficult? "The attainment of a 4 per cent unemployment rate for 1962 would have necessitated the creation of over three million additional jobs. Had this additional employment been forthcoming, the remaining unemployment would have been split about evenly between males and females. This contrasts with a split of 66 per cent to 34 per cent for 1954." Documented from the monthly Bureau of Labor Statistics; 11 tables, 7 notes, biblio.                                                D. D. Cameron

1810. Dresser, Norine. "IS IT FRESH?" AN EXAMINATION OF JEWISH-AMERICAN SHOPPING HABITS. *New York Folklore Q. 1971 27(1): 153-160.* Discusses the shopping habits of Jewish-American women in Los Angeles, California, in 1969, emphasizing the purchasing of kosher food.

1811. Fallows, James. THE GOLD IN THE GARBAGE: WHAT THE LEFT CAN LEARN FROM AYN RAND. *Washington Monthly 1975 7(3): 54-59.* Ayn Rand's *Atlas Shrugged* can teach liberals about basic economic competence and productivity.

1812. Fuchs, Victor R. RECENT TRENDS AND LONG-RUN PROSPECTS FOR FEMALE EARNINGS. *Am. Econ. R. 1974 64(2): 236-242.* Discusses the trends in income earned by women during 1960-70, and predicts future trends.

1813. Goldberg, Philip. ARE WOMEN PREJUDICED AGAINST WOMEN? *Trans-action 1968 5(5): 28-30.* Women consider their own sex inferior, according to a survey of 140 college girls taken by the author. This is even so when the facts do not support such a belief. It is true when the subjects evaluated the intellectual and professional competence of other females. This bias by women against themselves occurs not only in traditionally masculine fields but also extends to traditionally feminine fields, such as education. Women even think that men are better at dietetics. As far as sex is concerned, the intellectual double standard is neither dead nor dying. Table.                                                A. Erlebacher

1814. Gottlieb, David and Bell, Mary Lou. WORK EXPECTA-TIONS AND WORK REALITIES: A STUDY OF GRADUATING COLLEGE SENIORS. *Youth and Soc. 1975 7(1): 69-83.* Women experience less career fulfillment than do men. Both men and women, after some experience, tend to emphasize personal satisfaction over security or stability in job goals, and to realize that hard work is not necessarily a way of reaching those goals. Based on a study of five Pennsylvania colleges and universities in 1972 and 1973; 6 tables, 1 note.

J. H. Sweetland

1815. Hedges, Janice Neipert. WOMEN WORKERS AND MANPOWER DEMANDS IN THE 1970'S. *Monthly Labor R. 1970 93(6): 19-29.*

1816. Johnston, Denis F. THE UNITED STATES ECONOMY IN 1985: POPULATION AND LABOR FORCE PROJECTIONS. *Monthly Labor R. 1973 96(12): 8-17.* Discusses 1960-72 Bureau of Labor Statistics projections for size of labor force and population distribution by age and sex for 1980 and 1985.

1817. Kahne, Hilda and Kohen, Andrew I. ECONOMIC PERSPECTIVES ON THE ROLES OF WOMEN IN THE AMERICAN ECONOMY. *J. of Econ. Literature 1975 13(4): 1249-1292.* Bibliographical survey of recent economic literature on the economic role of women since 1940.

1818. Keefe, Dennia R. and Burk, Marguerite C. INTERDISCIPLINARY ANALYSIS OF FARM-HOME INTERRELATIONSHIPS IN DECISION-MAKING AND ACTION ON THE FAMILY FARM. *Am. J. of Econ. and Sociology 1967 26(1): 33-46.* Reviews and evaluates extension and research activities in farm and home interrelationships and introduces some literature in the other social sciences which may make economic research on the events of farm-home decision-making more useful. 2 notes.

D. F. Rossi

1819. Lewis, Deborah A. INSURING WOMEN'S HEALTH. *Social Policy 1976 7(1): 19-25.* Considers the three approaches to national health insurance embodied in 1975 bills before Congress, noting which one would best counter the sex discrimination now practiced by private insurance companies.

1820. MacRae, C. Duncan and Yezer, Anthony M. J. THE PERSONAL INCOME TAX AND FAMILY LABOR SUPPLY. *Southern Econ. J. 1976 43(1): 783-792.* Discusses labor supply functions in families in the presence of a progressive income tax in the 1970's, including the influence of wages.

1821. Niemi, A. W. THE IMPACT OF RECENT CIVIL RIGHTS LAWS. *Am. J. of Econ. and Sociol. 1974 33(2): 137-144.* Presents employment and income data on southern and northern white and nonwhite labor forces for the period 1960-70. Concludes that only for northern Negro women has occupational and income structure moved toward equality with whites over this decade in the United States. Secondary sources; 7 tables, 9 notes.

W. L. Marr

1822. North, Gary THE FEMININE MISTAKE: THE ECONOMICS OF WOMEN'S LIBERATION. *Freeman 1971 21(1): 3-14.* Comments on the rise of the Women's Liberation Front since 1969. The organization's success is accountable to its seizure of the popular but misleading slogan of "Equal pay for equal work." That principle lends respectability to an otherwise ludicrous movement because it places the organization within the framework of a wage laws fallacy popularized by an interfering and anticapitalistic government. Both deny such economic realities as employment levels and labor payments balanced by actual production costs. The front's principle is suicidal for women and ignores the true problem for women in business - male hostility grounded in a desire for security.

D. A. Yanchisin

1823. North, Gary. A NOTE ON THE OPPORTUNITY COST OF MARRIAGE. *J. of Pol. Econ. 1968 76(2): 321-323.* Examines the financial burden caused by marrying an educated woman.      S

1824. Owen, John D. WORKWEEKS AND LEISURE: AN ANALYSIS OF TRENDS, 1948-75. *Monthly Labor R. 1976 99(8): 3-8.* Discusses trends since the end of World War II in the American labor market, showing that the postwar period marked a shift in the composition of the working class, with larger proportions of women and students in the working force, and offering a hypothesis for the postwar leveling-off of working hours.

1825. Penrod, James H. FOLK BELIEFS ABOUT WORK, TRADES, AND PROFESSIONS FROM NEW MEXICO. *Western Folklore 1968 27(3): 180-183.* The 57 folk beliefs are classified as: general beliefs, sailors, actors, women in industry, prostitutes, airplane pilots, automobile racers or drivers, and rodeo performers.      D. L. Smith

1826. Quick, Paddy. WOMEN'S WORK. *Rev. of Radical Pol. Econ. 1972 4(3): 2-19.* Surveys women's work. Deals with the institution of marriage and work done in the home under the marriage contract, including housework, child-rearing, and ego-building for the spouse. Outside the home discrimination based on sexual roles within the home is women's lot. Based on secondary sources.      C. P. de Young

1827. Rascoe, Judith. "YOU CAN TELL IT'S MATTEL, IT'S SWELL." *Audience 1972 2(1): 4-10.* Presents a wry view of the Mattel Toy Corporation. Discusses its history, products such as the Barbie Doll, and the production of toys at the factory.      J. Coberly

1828. Roby, Pamela. SOCIOLOGY AND WOMEN IN WORKING-CLASS JOBS. *Sociol. Inquiry 1975 45(2-3): 203-239.* Surveys the literature of research on women in blue collar, industrial, and service jobs. Discusses the direction such research should take in the future, and describes the changes in public policy which are needed to improve the living and working conditions of blue collar women.

1829. Rowbotham, Sheila. THE CARROT, THE STICK, AND THE MOVEMENT. *Radical Am. 1973 7(4/5): 73-79.* Deals with Women's Liberation and the search for adequate jobs and pay in a capitalistic society in the 1950's-60's.      S

1830. Smith, James D. VARIABILITY OF ECONOMIC WELL-BEING AND ITS DETERMINANTS. *Am. Econ. R. 1970 60(2): 286-295.* An analysis of family movement up or down the income scale over short time periods. A surprising degree of movement does take place, caused by job loss, retirement, wife employment, and family break-up. A few families moved out of the poverty bracket, but almost as many dropped into it. Upper income families experience considerable movement because of business or farm reverses and children leaving home. Based on a study of selected families, 1967-69; 5 tables, 3 figs., 8 notes.

V. L. Human

1831. Suter, Larry E. and Miller, Herman P. INCOME DIFFERENCES BETWEEN MEN AND CAREER WOMEN. *Am. J. of Sociol. 1973 78(4): 962-974.* "It is often alleged that one of the reasons women earn less than men is because of their intermittent labor force behavior during their prime working years. This analysis of wage or salary income in 1966 for a national sample of men and women 30-44 years old attempts to estimate that part of the difference between the incomes of men and women which is due to age, lifetime career experience, education, occupational status, and extent of employment during 1966. The average earnings of women in this sample was 39 percent of that received by men. The results of a regression analysis show that, if women had the same occupational status as men, had worked all their lives, and had the same education and year-round full-time employment in 1966, their income would be increased to 62 percent of that received by men. The coefficient of determination ($R^2$) between wage and salary income and the other factors selected for study is .49 for women and .29 for men, indicating that the income level of women is more dependent on these few factors than is the income of men. The analysis suggests that fewer women than men are able to break away from only average-paying jobs into those with higher incomes.      J

1832. Velarde, Albert J. and Warlick, Mark. MASSAGE PARLORS: THE SENSUALITY BUSINESS. *Society 1973 11(1): 63-74.*

1833. Waldman, Elizabeth. MARITAL AND FAMILY CHARACTERISTICS OF THE U.S. LABOR FORCE. *Monthly Labor R. 1970 93(5): 18-27.*

1834. Weir, Angela and Wilson, Elisabeth. WOMEN'S LABOR, WOMEN'S DISCONTENT. *Radical Am. 1973 7(4/5): 80-94.* A discussion of Selma James' pamphlet *Women, the Unions and Work, or What is Not to be Done* involves an analysis of the "social formations which produce the conditions of capitalism" at a particular time (1972-73), and the "particular contradictions of capitalism."      S

1835. Wise, Gordon L. DIFFERENTIAL PRICING AND TREATMENT BY NEW-CAR SALESMEN: THE EFFECT OF THE PROSPECT'S RACE, SEX, AND DRESS. *J. of Business 1974 47(2): 218-230.* Discusses 19 automobile dealerships in Dayton, Ohio, at which, during 1970, shabbily-dressed black males paid a higher new-car price than did white counterparts, although both received poor treatment. Well-dressed white and black males obtained equal treatment and prices. A well-dressed Oriental male received good treatment but paid the highest price. Women gained better treatment than men but realized no pricing advantage. Primary sources; 10 tables, 9 notes.

J. W. Williams

1836. —. [FAMILY INVESTMENTS IN HUMAN CAPITAL: EARNINGS OF WOMEN]. *J. of Pol. Econ. 1974 82(2, part II): 76-110.*
Mincer, Jacob and Polachek, Solomon. FAMILY INVESTMENTS IN HUMAN CAPITAL: EARNINGS OF WOMEN, *pp. 76-108.*
Duncan, Otis Dudley. COMMENT, *pp. 109-110.*
Proceedings of a conference on marriage, family, human capital, and fertility on 4-5 June, 1973.

S

1837. —. [HOUSEHOLD AND ECONOMY: TOWARD A NEW THEORY OF POPULATION AND ECONOMIC GROWTH]. *J. of Pol. Econ. 1974 82(2, part II): 200-221.*
Nerlove, Marc. HOUSEHOLD AND ECONOMY: TOWARD A NEW THEORY OF POPULATION AND ECONOMIC GROWTH, *pp. 200-218.*
Griliches, Zvi. COMMENT, *pp. 219-221.*
Proceedings of a conference on marriage, family, human capital, and fertility on 4-5 June 1973.

S

## Employment Outside the Home

### General

1838. Agassi, Judith Buber. WOMEN WHO WORK IN FACTORIES. *Dissent 1972 19(1): 233-239.*

1839. Bass, Bernard M. Krusell, Judith and Alexander, Ralph A. MALE MANAGERS' ATTITUDES TOWARD WORKING WOMEN. *Am. Behavioral Scientist 1971 15(2): 221-236.* The authors report findings of a survey of attitudes administered to 174 males in managerial positions in the Rochester, New York, area. Statistical analysis of seven discriminating factors and other variables revealed that the subjects felt most strongly about attitudes of deference (interaction between men and women determined by norms) and dependability of women. The solution for integrating the sexes in the work force is not necessarily the employment of more women but involvement of managers in examination of their own attitudes toward women in the work situation, evaluation of actual performance data, and provision of opportunities for the sexes to interact as equals. 2 notes, biblio.

D. G. Davis, Jr.

1840. Bell, Carolyn Shaw. SHOULD EVERY JOB SUPPORT A FAMILY? *Public Interest 1975 (40): 109-118.* Considers public welfare and the relationship of employment to family support.

S

1841. Benham, Lee. THE LABOR MARKET FOR REGISTERED NURSES: A THREE EQUATION MODEL. *Rev. of Econ. and Statistics 1971 53(3): 246-252.* Constructs a model relating nurses' wages, participation, and numbers to demand for nurses, attendants' wages, per capita income, husbands' income, number of children, and the number of nursing graduates lagged by ten years. Concludes that the model characterizes some features of the labor market for registered nurses, and has possibilities for application to other professions. 2 tables, 13 notes.

E. S. Johnson

1842. Bergmann, Barbara R. and Maxfield, Myles, Jr. HOW TO ANALYZE THE FAIRNESS OF FACULTY WOMEN'S SALARIES ON YOUR OWN CAMPUS. *AAUP Bull. 1975 61(3): 262-265.*

1843. Bergmann, Barbara R. and Adelman, Irma. THE 1973 REPORT OF THE PRESIDENT'S COUNCIL OF ECONOMIC ADVISERS: THE ECONOMIC ROLE OF WOMEN. *Am. Econ. R. 1973 63(4): 509-514.* Considers Chapter 4 of the 1973 Economic Report of the President as giving "creditable coverage" to the economic role of women in the United States. There is not only sex discrimination in employment but also job segregation; the authors' own tabulations based on the 1960-70 censuses show that more than 70% of women workers were employed in occupations in which women were overrepresented. Quit rates, layoff rates, and unemployment are all higher for women. The bleak picture of economic facts painted in the report still "tends to underestimate the possibilities and need for social change." Table, 8 notes.

C. W. Olson

1844. Billings, Gloria. NEEDED: 850,000 NURSES BY 1970. *Am. Educ. 1968 4(2): 8-10.* Describes the development of an expanding program of intensive refresher training designed to permit inactive professional nurses to reenter nursing. This program may in part reduce the growing shortage of trained nurses. The author contrasts the rocketing cost of medical care with the relatively low salaries for nurses. Apparently based on a variety of government documents.

W. R. Boedecker

1845. Blitz, Rudolph C. AN INTERNATIONAL COMPARISON OF WOMEN'S PARTICIPATION IN THE PROFESSIONS. *J. of Developing Areas 1975 9(4): 499-510.* Analyzes the role of women in the professions and the labor market in 49 countries in various stages of economic development. Historically the percentage of women in the professions has increased just as per capita income has increased. Using equally weighted indicators of per capita energy consumption and percentage of male labor force in non-agricultural pursuits, it was discovered that female labor force participation increases with advancing economic development. In the early stages of development where conservative values predominate, women were employed primarily in the lower skill strata. Based on 1950-67 censuses of 49 nations; 3 tables, 24 notes.

O. W. Eads, Jr.

1846. Bogan, Forrest A. WORK EXPERIENCE OF THE POPULATION: SPOTLIGHT ON WOMEN AND YOUTH. *Monthly Labor R. 1969 92(6): 44-50.* Study of 1967 figures reveals that women and youth made gains as year-round, full-time workers in a tight labor market, marking a shift from the predominantly prime-age male work force.

S

1847. Bogan, Forrest A. and O'Boyle, Edward J. WORK EXPERIENCE OF THE POPULATION. *Monthly Labor R. 1968 91(1): 35-45.* Examines the following components of the labor force: part-time, unemployed, nonworker, Negro worker, and teenager. For the first time, the number of persons working full-time for an entire year (1966) reached 50 million. Forty-seven percent of the advance was among women, who constituted only 40 percent of the annual labor force. During 1966, part-time employment expanded to 16 million persons, an increase of 600 thousand over the previous year, and unemployment was reduced, with the greatest improvement observed among those who had been jobless for more than 15 weeks. Negro unemployment remained stable at 22 percent. 3 tables, 4 charts, 9 notes.

A. P. Young

1848. Boskin, Michael J. THE EFFECTS OF GOVERNMENT EXPENDITURES AND TAXES ON FEMALE LABOR. *Am. Econ. R. 1974 64(2): 251-256.*

1849. Boyd, Julian P. ADRIENNE KOCH: HISTORIAN. *Maryland Hist. 1972 3(1): 9-14.* Describes Professor Koch's scholarship of the American Enlightenment period. Her *The Philosophy of Thomas Jefferson* (New York: Columbia U. Press, 1943) and *Jefferson and Madison: The Great Collaboration* (New York: Alfred A. Knopf, 1950) are definitive studies.

G. O. Gagnon

1850. Cahill, Jane P. THE EDUCATION OF WOMEN AND THE NATIONAL ECONOMY. *Liberal Educ. 1974 60(supplement): 74-80.* Calls for a greater influx of educated women into the higher paying job market.

S

1851. Chafetz, Janet Saltzman. WOMEN IN SOCIAL WORK. *Social Work 1972 17(5): 12-18.* Examines the status of women in social work. Considers: 1) the comparative status of male and female social workers; 2) possible role conflicts experienced by married female workers; and 3) the ramifications on the profession of the large number of female workers. "From one vantage point professionalization is an effort to 'defeminize' social work, i.e., make it more intellectual, rational, scientific, and administrative—in short, to give it 'male' qualities . . . . Certainly, a substantial number of women who are or have been married have lost at least a few years of their professional careers . . . . such time loss has far-reaching consequences for the professional status of all career women, including social workers." 29 notes.       D. D. Cameron

1852. Chang, Won H. CHARACTERISTICS AND SELF PERCEPTIONS OF WOMEN'S PAGE EDITORS. *Journalism Q. 1975 52(1): 61-65.* Studies women's page editors, a position traditionally assigned to women. Male editors had higher salaries and more education. Most editors had some college education, and the mean journalism experience was 12.5 years. The editors felt qualifications should be the only consideration in employment and that opportunities for women were improving. Women did not feel they were tokens or that they were lucky to have their jobs. Primary sources; 4 notes.       K. J. Puffer

1853. Cohen, Malcolm. MARRIED WOMEN IN THE LABOR FORCE: AN ANALYSIS OF PARTICIPATION RATES. *Monthly Labor R. 1969 92(10): 31-35.* Uses a study of married women to illustrate the value of a "micro labor supply model," developed to assess effects of complex characteristics, such as age and education, on a subject's behavior.       S

1854. Collins, D. Jean. HIGHLIGHTING THE ARTS IN COMMUNITY RECREATION: INTERVIEW WITH RAYMOND FORSBERG AND ANN DAY. *Arts in Soc. 1975 12(1): 32-37.* Raymond Forsberg and Ann Day work in recreation in Waterloo, Iowa (1970's).       S

1855. Cotton, Frank E., Jr. RECENT TRENDS IN MANUFACTURING EMPLOYMENT IN MISSISSIPPI, 1940-1960. *J. of Mississippi Hist. 1967 29(1): 28-42.* A statistical analysis which shows that the most significant developments in manufacturing employment in Mississippi between 1940 and 1960 were 1) a considerable decline in "the degree of underspecialization in manufacturing relative to other industry groups"; 2) a 275 percent increase in employment in textile manufacturing; 3) substantial rates of increase of employment in several types of durable goods manufacturing; 4) an especially sharp increase in female employment "although a majority of the additional jobs employed males"; and 5) an increase in nonwhite employment during the 1940's but a decline in it during the 1950's. Also studied are the chief factors responsible for the establishment of 140 new plants since 1951 in northeastern Mississippi counties served by TVA electric power. The author concludes that industry was "very strongly attracted" by sizable quantities of cheap, nonunion labor. Based on Census Bureau publications and secondary works; 8 notes.       J. W. Hillje

1856. Crawford, Miriam I. WOMEN IN ARCHIVES: A PROGRAM FOR ACTION. *Am. Archivist 1973 36(2): 223-232.* The movement for women's rights can aid the archival profession and the Society of American Archivists (SAA). The movement has a wide base, is identified with other rights movements, and is primarily concerned with equal employment opportunities. Women have been no more successful in archives work than in other fields; they have not reached top positions. Women archivists should improve their self-images, publish more, and pursue advanced degrees. After statistics on women in archival agencies are obtained, the pattern used in other professional organizations should be followed. Lists several suggestions for the SAA, for archivists, and for increased availability of information on women's history studies. 8 notes.       D. E. Horn

1857. Darian, Jean C. FACTORS INFLUENCING THE RISING LABOR FORCE PARTICIPATION RATES OF MARRIED WOMEN WITH PRE-SCHOOL CHILDREN. *Social Sci. Q. 1976 56(4): 614-630.* Investigates factors influencing the rising labor force participation rates of married women with pre-school children.       J

1858. Degnam, James P. MISS MITFORD AT SAN JOSE STATE: JESSICA THUMBS HER TOES. *Change 1974/75 6(10): 38-41.* Jessica Mitford was a Distinguished Professor until the "Great Finger Flap" changed her status to Extinguished Professor in three short weeks. She was fired for refusing to be fingerprinted.       J and S

1859. Deischer, Claude K. EVA VIVIAN ARMSTRONG, 1877-1962: HISTORIAN AND FRIEND OF HISTORIANS. *Isis 1962 53, 4(174): 500-501.* This obituary notes the work done by Armstrong as "curator of the Edgar Fahs Smith Memorial Collection in the History of Chemistry at the University of Pennsylvania, and one of the founders of *Chymia,*" a journal of chemistry history.       S

1860. DeRoche, Edward F. OCCUPATIONAL VALUES OF PUBLIC AND PRIVATE HIGH SCHOOL SENIORS. *Catholic Educ. R. 1969 66(13): 838-843.* A study of 613 males and 831 females in public and private high schools in a large metropolitan school system indicates that differences exist between public and private high school seniors in job value selection. The assumption needs further study, and the consistency of such choice throughout adolescent and early adult years also needs further study. 9 notes.       J. M. McCarthy

1861. Deutrich, Mabel E. WOMEN IN ARCHIVES: MS. VS. MR. ARCHIVIST. *Am. Archivist 1973 36(2): 171-181.* Gives salient facts about archival service by men and women members of the Society of American Archivists (SAA). Archivists are analyzed by education, positions held, type of work performed, type of position (administrative, professional, technical), publications, and participation in convention programs. Women now head fewer state archival agencies than formerly, publish less, and have received no awards from the SAA. Advances some reasons for the conditions and urges women archivists to organize and to work for improved status. Based on SAA records, including membership questionnaires; 8 tables, 21 notes.       D. E. Horn

1862. Diamond, Irma. THE LIBERATION OF WOMEN IN A FULL EMPLOYMENT SOCIETY. *Ann. of Am. Acad. of Pol. and Soc. Sci. 1975 418: 138-146.* After 10 years of struggle for the right to full participation in public life, American women, along with the rest of the country, are facing a national economic crisis. Economic issues like equal work and access to educational opportunity, bolstered by support services needed by women, can be clearly identified as the major public policy issues in 1975 for women. Equal employment increases the probability of women's participating in responsible, decision making jobs. However, this will not be possible unless adequate support services are provided on a large scale. The need for these services is urgent. In the recent past, we have witnessed increased labor and higher education participation by women. We have also witnessed an increase in the status of women. These two facts are interdependent. Therefore, in order to arrive at a high status for women, a full employment society is a necessity. In addition to this, a women's policy bureau is needed to speak to the specific issues raised by increased participation in public life of half of the citizens of this country—women.       J

1863. Dixon, Elizabeth I. SOMETHING NEW HAS BEEN ADDED. *J. of Lib. Hist., Philosophy and Comparative Librarianship 1967 2(1): 68-72.* Interviews Miss Frances Richardson, Librarian of Twentieth Century Fox Studios, dealing with her entry into the field of librarianship. Primary sources.       A. C. Dewees

1864. Dowdall, Jean A. STRUCTURAL AND ATTITUDINAL FACTORS ASSOCIATED WITH FEMALE LABOR FORCE PARTICIPATION. *Social Sci. Q. 1974 55(1): 121-130.* "Finds that for a sample of married women with children, the prediction of employment status is improved by the inclusion of the attitude measure. Moreover, the strength of the attitude measure is greater at higher income levels."       J

1865. Eckert, Ruth E. ACADEMIC WOMAN REVISITED. *Liberal Educ. 1971 57(4): 479-487.* Today only 19 percent of full-time academic staff are women, a lower percentage than in the mid-1950's. A recent study, supported by one completed in 1956, showed that fewer women than men academics were married, that women academics were six years older than their male counterparts, had received fewer financial aids in graduate school, and frequently had only a master's degree. Women as a group were shown to spend less time on research, had less outside funding, and had produced many fewer publications than the men. 4 notes.       E. M. Gersman

1866.   Epstein, Cynthia Fuchs.   SEX ROLE STEREOTYPING, OC-CUPATIONS AND SOCIAL EXCHANGE.   *Women's Studies 1976 3(2): 185-194.* The female sex-role and beliefs about women's roles have been integrated into the structure of professional occupations. Trained, talented, intelligent women form a pool of eligible workers serving elite structures. There is a large disparity between the number of women eligible to enter professional elites and the number who actually attain positions of high rank. Women's talents are exploited and their contributions remain unidentified and uncredited. Women holding occupational status are paid off in rewards related to sex-status not occupation. Their roles are institutionalized as helpers, supporters, and adjuncts to professional men. 5 notes, biblio.                    A. E. Wiederrecht

1867.   Falk, William W. and Cosby, Arthur G.   WOMEN AND THE STATUS ATTAINMENT PROCESS.   *Social Sci. Q. 1975 56(2): 307-314.* [The authors] review the major occupational choice theories and show them to be biased toward males and thus inadequate in their handling of factors which influence the occupational choices of women. A leading status attainment model, the Wisconsin model, is revised and extended to incorporate contigencies for women.                    J

1868.   Fenner, Mildred Sandison.   WOMEN IN EDUCATIONAL JOURNALISM.   *Contemporary Educ. 1972 43(4): 209-213.* Describes difficulty of women editors in educational and business journalism.                    S

1869.   Franzwa, Helen H.   WORKING WOMEN IN FACT AND FICTION.   *J. of Communication 1974 24(2): 104-109.* Discusses the attitude that "a woman's place is in the home," citing figures on working women, 1940-67, and seeking to show social conditions which lead to this attitude.

1870.   Fullerton, H. N., Jr. and Byrne, J. J.   LENGTH OF WORK-ING LIFE FOR MEN AND WOMEN, 1970.   *Monthly Labor R. 1976 99(2): 31-35.* Worklife expectancy increased for women, especially married women with children, and decreased slightly for men.

1871.   Fusfeld, Daniel R.   A LIVING WAGE.   *Ann. of the Am. Acad. of Pol. and Social Sci. 1973 (409): 34-41.* "The only effective way to eliminate poverty in the United States is to pay all workers a living wage, defined as one that would enable a worker to maintain an urban family of four in health and decency. In 1972 that implied a minimum wage of 3.50 dollars per hour. Such a minimum wage would have important repercussions on the low wage industries and the workers they employ. The impact on business firms can be eased by special tax and loan programs. The most important problems will arise from loss of jobs as the low wage industries adapt to the high minimum wage. A three-pronged program is called for: (1) full employment, (2) public service employment and (3) education and training. A sharply accelerated equal opportunity employment program will also be needed, because many low wage workers are Blacks, Latins and women. This program implies a redistribution of income in favor of the low wage worker that could be negated by wage increases for other workers, triggering price increases throughout the economy. Reduced income taxes for workers with annual incomes above 7,000 dollars and up to perhaps 15,000 dollars will be needed to overcome that effect. The net result would be an end to poverty and to many of its social evils."                    J

1872.   Harrison, Evelyn.   THE WORKING WOMAN'S BARRIERS IN EMPLOYMENT.   *Public Administration R. 1964 24(2): 78-85.* The author, who received the Federal Woman's Award in 1962 and who served on President Johnson's Commission on the Status of Women, identifies and debunks some of the conventional assumptions concerning comparative employment characteristics of men and women workers. This study covered a broad sample of nearly 30 thousand career employees. All occupations were included except several such as nurses and investigators which do not include large enough groups of one of the sexes to afford a basis for comparison. "In summary, these data strongly suggest that on the job, as in other social relationships, the acceptance of one group by another is related to the extent to which the groups have been associated. One way of gaining greater male acceptance in higher grade jobs is to provide more men with the opportunity to share their work experience with women at least at a colleague level." Information as to employment practices in the public service in 43 States and 32 cities of

500 thousand or more population was obtained through a special survey of the Public Personnel Association in 1962 for the President's Commission on the Status of Women. 2 tables, 9 notes.                    D. D. Cameron

1873.   Hassinger, Edward W. and Grubb, Charles E.   THE LINKING ROLE OF THE LOCAL PUBLIC HEALTH NURSE IN MISSOURI.   *Rural Sociology 1965 30(3): 299-310.* Shows how public health nurses are linked to a central system of bureaucratically organized health services. This system functions at several levels via the county court house, local health boards, local physicians, and the general populace. The authors hypothesize that the nurses' norms are intermediate to those of the central position and the local positions. Thirty items were tested including writing articles about health for local newspapers, spending time in self-improvement, and attending public health meetings. Findings indicate that norms of the local public health nurse were usually between those of the local and central positions. 2 figs., 3 tables, 17 notes.

A. S. Freedman

1874.   Havens, Elizabeth M.   WOMEN, WORK, AND WEDLOCK: A NOTE ON FEMALE MARITAL PATTERNS IN THE UNITED STATES.   *Am. J. of Sociol. 1973 78(4): 975-981.* "The marital patterns of economically active females in the United States do not appear to fit the general pattern previously described as characteristic of 'the American population.' Census data indicate diverse marital patterns for females by occupational and income categories. Moreover, the findings of this study are the reverse of those usually suggested. The findings suggest a strong *direct* relationship between economic attainment and unmarried status among females in the United States. Attempting to interpret these findings, the author explores the possibility that female marital status can be considered a dependent variable with economic attainment the independent variable. This 'rejecting marriage' interpretation is antithetical to the traditional view which takes female marital status as the independent variable, that is, females who are 'marital rejects' turn to occupational pursuits."                    J

1875.   Havighurst, Robert J.   INDIVIDUAL AND GROUP RIGHTS IN A DEMOCRACY.   *Society 1976 13(2): 13, 25-28.* Discusses the federal government's current policy of requiring institutions to offer jobs to women and ethnic minorities in order to receive federal grants.

1876.   Helson, Ravenna.   THE CHANGING IMAGE OF THE CAREER WOMAN.   *J. of Social Issues 1972 28(2): 33-46.* Discusses changes in attitudes toward working women during the 1950's-1970's.

1877.   Hook, Sidney.   ADRIENNE KOCH: STUDENT AND COLLEAGUE.   *Maryland Hist. 1972 3(1): 5-8.* Professor Koch was a paragon of scholarly qualities and an unmatched colleague.

G. O. Gagnon

1878.   Hosmer, Charles B.   REFLECTIONS—AN INTERVIEW WITH HELEN DUPREY BULLOCK, WALTER MUIR WHITE-HILL AND CHARLES B. HOSMER, JR.   *Historic Preservation 1974 26(4): 18-28.* Hosmer interviews Bullock and Whitehill on the history and future of the National Trust for Historic Preservation and the preservation movement. Discussed are Frederick L. Rath, Jr., Louise du Pont Crowninshield, H. Alexander Smith, Jr., Robert N. S. Whitelaw, John Codman, and Bainbridge Bunting. 12 photos.                    R. M. Frame III

1879.   Hughes, Helen MacGill.   MAID OF ALL WORK OR DEPARTMENTAL SISTER-IN-LAW? THE FACULTY WIFE EMPLOYED ON CAMPUS.   *Am. J. of Sociol. 1973 78(4): 767-772.* "Three propositions issue from an analysis of protracted personal experience in the editorial office of the *American Journal of Sociology*: a possible effect of employing a faculty wife in a position on campus where her superiors include her husband's colleagues may be a downward transfer of responsibility, initiated by them or by herself; with such a change in relationships a job which had been defined as temporary and amateur may become permanent and professionalized; the change may manifest itself in standards and working practices and in the quality of the product.                    J

1880.   Hunt, Chester L.   FEMALE OCCUPATIONAL ROLES AND URBAN SEX RATIOS IN THE UNITED STATES, JAPAN, AND THE PHILIPPINES.   *Social Forces 1965 43(3): 407-417.* "In the United States a low urban sex ratio has been attributed to industrialization and the consequent demand for female labor in urban centers. Japanese cities, however, have not attracted a disproportionately female population in spite of heavy industrialization. On the other hand, Philippine cities now show a sex ratio similar to the United States although industrialization is in the beginning stages. Japanese cultural patterns have maintained female subordination in spite of a potential industrial demand for female labor. Socioeconomic forces in the United States have directed women workers into supplementary rather than fully equal occupational roles. Filipino culture has favored occupational participation by women on a basis equal or superior to the male with the result that a slight movement toward industrialization stimulates a heavy migration to the cities."                                                                                J

1881.  James, Selma.  WOMEN, THE UNIONS AND WORK, OR . . . WHAT IS NOT TO BE DONE.  *Radical Am. 1973 7(4/5): 51-72.* Examines women's liberation and the struggle for adequate employment and wages for qualified women.                                      S

1882.  Jenness, Linda.  FEMINISM AND THE WOMAN WORKER.  *Internat. Socialist R. 1974 35(3): 4-7.* Statistical analysis of working women.                                                                           S

1883.  Johnson, Dorothy M.  NUMBER PLEASE! TRUE CONFESSIONS OF A TEEN-AGED "CENTRAL."  *Montana: Mag. of Western Hist. 1973 23(4): 54-60.* Reminiscences, in a humorous vein, of a telephone operator in Whitefish, Montana, ca. 1922. The switchboard was entirely hand-operated, and the woman on duty had responsibility for handling all calls, from the desperately important to the utterly frivolous.
                                                                                S. R. Davison

1884.  Johnson, George E. and Stafford, Frank P.  THE EARNINGS AND PROMOTION OF WOMEN FACULTY.  *Am. Econ. R. 1974 64(6): 888-903.* A comparison of male-female salary and promotion performances by Ph.D.'s in academic employment. Available data demonstrate that differences exist, but they are not large, and are explainable by phenomena other than sex discrimination, specifically the more rapid turnover of female personnel and breaks for pregnancy. Women permanently and regularly employed experience little difference in salary or promotional treatment. Based on National Science Foundation statistics; 11 tables, fig., 34 notes, biblio.                          V. L. Human

1885.  Jones, H. G.  MARY GIVENS BRYAN.  *Am. Archivist 1964 27(4): 505-507.* An obituary of the state archivist of Georgia whose whole working career was devoted to the Department of Archives and History, from clerk to director. As chairman of the Committee on State Records of the Society of American Archivists, 1954-57, she published major studies of the archives of the states, and later served as president of the society, 1959. Her major monument was the nearly six million dollar Archives Building completed shortly after her untimely death.
                                                                                D. C. Duniway

1886.  Kelsey, Harry.  A DEDICATION TO THE MEMORY OF ANNIE HELOISE ABEL-HENDERSON, 1873-1947.  *Arizona and the West 1973 15(1): 1-4.* Born in England, Annie Heloise Abel alternated teaching in Kansas high schools with her own education at the University of Kansas, Cornell, and Yale. Her doctoral dissertation on American Indians earned her the Justin Winsor Prize in 1906 in a field to which she made notable contributions. After teaching at Wells College, Goucher College, Johns Hopkins University, and Smith College, and serving as Official Historian of the Bureau of Indian Affairs, she researched in Australia, England, Canada, and the United States toward a never-completed comparative study of British and American native policy. Her most important service was the editing and publication of many original documents. Illus., biblio.                                        D. L. Smith

1887.  Klemmack, David L. and Edwards, John N.  WOMEN'S ACQUISITION OF STEREOTYPED OCCUPATIONAL ASPIRATIONS.  *Sociol. and Social Res. 1973 57(4): 510-525.* "Assuming that type of work desired by women is increasingly problematic, a multivariate model is developed to account for the degree to which women select stereotypically feminine work roles. The model indicates that the degree of feminity of occupational aspirations is an indirect function of family background. Marriage and family plans serve a critical mediational function in determining the type of occupation desired."                     J

1888.  Lasswell, Thomas E. and Benbrook, Sandra L.  SOCIAL STRATIFICATION: 1969-1973.  *Ann. of the Am. Acad. of Pol. and Social Sci. 1974 (414): 105-137.* "This article has been organized around contemporary concepts, theory, research procedures and research findings reported in the sociological literature on social stratification, social class and social mobility." Findings include: women are generally more mobile than men, social welfare and service professions will become more prestigious, and the increasing emphasis on status achievement rather than educational attainment will result in a decreased emphasis on social origin. 202 notes.                                           E. P. Stickney

1889.  Leininger, Madeleine.  TWO STRANGE HEALTH TRIBES: THE GNISRUN AND ENICIDEM IN THE UNITED STATES.  *Human Organization 1976 35(3): 253-261.* Presents an allegorical analysis of medicine, physicians, nurses, and hospital social stratification in the 1970's.

1890.  Lodahl, Thomas M.  PATTERNS OF JOB ATTITUDES IN TWO ASSEMBLY TECHNOLOGIES.  *Administrative Sci. Q. 1964 8(4): 482-519.* Presents results of a highly statistical comparative study of job attitudes of male assembly line workers in an automobile plant and female tube assemblers in an electronics plant. The data were obtained by duplicated personal interviews of workers in their homes. Twenty attitude variables grouped into six classes were obtained and studied by factor analysis and correlation techniques to determine how motivation can be managed. In both groups two technological factors and three attitude factors which could be termed "satisfiers" and "motivators" were found. The responsibility of management to create conditions leading to job satisfaction is emphasized and suggestions are made for improving job satisfaction on the assembly line. 2 tables, 53 notes, appendix: definitions of variables.                                             R. Strain

1891.  Lumpkin, Ben Gray.  MARJORIE M. KIMMERLE (1906-1963).  *Western Folklore 1963 22(3): 191.* Obituary of Marjorie M. Kimmerle, a prominent American folklorist.              L. J. White

1892.  McKay, Roberta V.  COMMUTING PATTERNS OF INNER-CITY RESIDENTS.  *Monthly Labor R. 1973 96(11): 43-48.* A statistical survey of sex, ethnic, and occupational characteristics of inner-city commuters to the suburbs does not clarify the role of transportation in job choice.                                                          S

1893.  Mennerick, Lewis A.  ORGANIZATIONAL STRUCTURING OF SEX ROLES IN A NONSTEREOTYPED INDUSTRY.  *Administrative Sci. Q. 1975 20(4): 570-586.* Analyzes the sex structuring which occurs in the travel agency industry in New York City based on industry data for 1974, indicating that male agents tend to hold management positions and female agents tend to hold sales positions.

1894.  Mitchell, Joyce M. and Starr, Rachel R.  A REGIONAL APPROACH FOR ANALYZING THE RECRUITMENT OF ACADEMIC WOMEN.  *Am. Behavioral Scientist 1971 15(2): 183-205.* The authors report the findings and significance of a study of graduate students involved in academic departments related to the Western Political Science Association. Surveying sex differences in factors such as enrollment and degrees conferred, faculty members within departments, and enrollment and degree conferrals, the authors relate their findings to other nationwide studies indicating male dominance in political science graduate programs. Based on primary and secondary sources; 11 notes, biblio.                                               D. G. Davis, Jr.

1895.  Mitchell, Memory F.  PUBLISHING IN STATE HISTORICAL JOURNALS.  *Wisconsin Mag. of Hist. 1975-76 59(2): 135-142.* Originally presented as a paper before the Organization of American Historians in Boston in April, 1975, this article outlines the process of publishing articles in state historical journals. In particular, the author discusses the relationship between the editors and their contributors, citing examples from her own editorial experience, and from responses to her questionnaire by 35 other journal editors. Her suggestions and illustrations deal with submission of the manuscript by an author, criteria for review by an editorial staff and outside readers, the process of revision, use of illustrations, compensation to authors, and the amount of time between submission by a contributor and publication of the article. 3 notes.                                                 N. C. Burckel

1896. Morse, Dean W. THE PERIPHERAL WORKER IN THE AFFLUENT SOCIETY. *Monthly Labor R. 1968 91(2): 17-20.* Most peripheral workers, less than full-time, full-year employees, are nonwhite males between 25 and 54 years old. Originally made up of immigrants, the category now includes nonwhites and women. Although they need and deserve help, they have not had protection from government or labor unions. J. E. Brinley

1897. Mount, R. I. and Bennett, R. E. ECONOMIC AND SOCIAL FACTORS IN INCOME INEQUALITY. *Am. J. of Econ. and Sociol. 1975 34(2): 161-174.* The economic and social factors in wage differentials are examined for US data in 1969. Possession of an academic degree, and a person's sex, are important determinants of these differentials. Based on secondary sources; 4 tables, 6 notes. W. L. Marr

1898. Oppenheimer, Valerie Kincade. DEMOGRAPHIC INFLUENCE ON FEMALE EMPLOYMENT AND THE STATUS OF WOMEN. *Am. J. of Sociol. 1973 78(4): 946-961.* "This paper is concerned with one example of demographically related social change—women's changing work roles. The argument is that continued economic development in our society has led to increases in the demand for female labor which, combined with demographically induced shifts in the supply of unmarried and young women, have resulted in the considerable post-World War II rise in the labor-force participation of married women. The evidence is that these changes are irreversible and will not be greatly affected by the entry of the baby-boom cohorts into the labor market. Nevertheless, women's increasing dissatisfaction with job opportunities can be expected because several of the higher-level traditional female occupations will probably not expand greatly in the near future. J

1899. Orden, Susan R. and Bradburn, Norman M. WORKING WIVES AND MARRIAGE HAPPINESS. *Am. J. of Sociol. 1969 74(4): 392-407.* "A woman's freedom to choose among alternative life styles is an important predictor of happiness in marriage. Both partners are lower in marriage happiness if the wife participates in the labor market out of economic necessity than if she participates by choice. This finding holds across educational levels, stages in the life cycle, and part-time and full-time employment. Among the less educated, the strain comes from an increase in tensions for husbands and a decline in sociability for wives; while among the better educated, husbands and wives both experience an increase in tensions and a decrease in sociability. A woman's choice of the labor market over the home market strains the marriage only when there are preschool children in the family. At other stages in the life cycle, the choice between the labor market and the home market makes little difference in an individual's assessment of his own marriage happiness. However, the labor market choice is generally associated with a higher balance between satisfactions and tensions for both husbands and wives." J

1900. Papanek, Hanna. MEN, WOMEN, AND WORK: REFLECTIONS ON THE TWO-PERSON CAREER. *Am. J. of Sociol. 1973 78(4): 852-872.* "Women adapt in different ways to the demands of their husbands' occupations. In the United States, the 'two-person single career' is a special combination of roles whereby wives are inducted by the institutions employing their husbands into a pattern of vicarious achievement. The two-person career pattern serves as a social control mechanism which derails the occupational aspirations of the highly educated woman into a subsidiary role determined by her husband's career. It is a very American solution to a common American dilemma, in which an explicit ideology of equal opportunity in education conflicts with inequalities in occupational opportunities. Some reflections on the two-person career serve to illustrate the necessity for more determined efforts to include studies of women's lives in modern sociology and anthropology. Some areas are indicated where such studies would contribute to the development of methods and theory. Particular emphasis is placed on the kinds of education women receive: training for women's work in Pakistan, Bangladesh, and India is used to point out particular contrasts with the U.S. setting, indicating also some of the features of highly sex-segregated *purdah* societies." J

1901. Pavalko, Ronald M. RECRUITMENT TO TEACHING: PATTERNS OF SELECTIONS AND RETENTION. *Sociol. of Educ. 1970 43(3): 340-353.* "Utilizing data from a seven-year longitudinal study of high school graduates, this paper focuses on the careers of girls who planned to become and/or eventually became elementary and secondary school teachers. The concern of the paper is the way in which factors such as socioeconomic status background, rural-urban residence, measured intelligence, time of occupational choice, level of education, marital status, and husbands' occupational status are related to recruitment to teaching and to retention in the teaching profession." J

1902. Perrella, Vera C. WOMEN AND THE LABOR FORCE. *Monthly Labor R. 1968 91(2): 1-12.* Describes increased participation of married women in the labor force. Discusses education level, husband's income, unemployment rates and the shift from operative to clerical occupations. Married women have traditionally been the most important element in the elasticity of the labor supply because of the large number of part-time workers. Earnings did not improve in relation to men's. Black women were more likely to work and at lower wages. The percentage of women in the labor force will continue to grow and their earnings will improve. 7 tables, chart, 12 notes. J. E. Brinley

1903. Poston, Dudley L., Jr. and Johnson, Gordon C. INDUSTRIALIZATION AND PROFESSIONAL DIFFERENTIATION BY SEX IN THE METROPOLITAN SOUTHWEST. *Social Sci. Q. 1971 52(2): 331-348.* "*Industrialization and Professional Differentiation by Sex in the Metropolitan Southwest* are hypothesized to be inversely related by Dudley L. Poston, Jr., and Gordon C. Johnson. Arguments are presented suggesting that the more industrialized SMSAs should be more characterized by achievement than ascription and should thus show low professional differentiation by sex. Data presented confirm the hypothesis and their ecological model of industrialization is then evaluated with a forward stepwise regression analysis." J

1904. Prather, Jane. WHY CAN'T WOMEN BE MORE LIKE MEN: A SUMMARY OF THE SOCIOPSYCHOLOGICAL FACTORS HINDERING WOMEN'S ADVANCEMENT IN THE PROFESSIONS. *Am. Behavioral Scientist 1971 15(2): 172-182.* In American society women have images of being primarily sexual objects and servants. These conceptions emphasize behavior that is "dependent, other-oriented, passive and nonassertive" and thus result in a self-fulfilling prophecy. Since in American society work is defined in masculine terms, women are not viewed as "serious participants in the labor force who can command responsible positions and demand high salaries." This mythology inhibits women from achieving equality with men in the labor force. Biblio. D. G. Davis, Jr.

1905. Psathas, George. TOWARD A THEORY OF OCCUPATIONAL CHOICE FOR WOMEN. *Sociol. and Social Res. 1968 52(2): 253-268.* "Development of a general theory of occupational choice requires attention to factors which operate in special ways for women. Several approaches are evaluated and a number of factors are elaborated, such as marriage, mobility, and family finances, which indicate that the setting within which choices are made needs to be explicated." J

1906. Read, Allen Walker. MARGARET M. BRYANT'S WORK IN LINGUISTICS. *Names 1974 22(3): 82-84.*

1907. Remmert, James E. EXECUTIVE ORDER 11,246: EXECUTIVE ENCROACHMENT. *Am. Bar Assoc. J. 1969 55(11): 1037-1040.* Executive Order 11,246 has furthered equal employment opportunity, but it also sets a precedent for use of the President's contract power to bypass the Congress. J

1908. Ritter, Kathleen V. and Hargens, Lowell L. OCCUPATIONAL POSITIONS AND CLASS IDENTIFICATIONS OF MARRIED WORKING WOMEN: A TEST OF THE ASYMMETRY HYPOTHESIS. *Am. J. of Sociol. 1975 80(4): 934-948.* Data for 566 married working women from the 1960, 1964, 1968, and 1970 Survey Research Center election studies . . . suggests that traditional assumptions that wives derive their class positions and identifications exclusively or predominantly from the occupational positions of their husbands do not hold for working wives. S

1909. Rosenblatt, Aaron; Turner, Eileen M.; Patterson, Adalene R.; and Rollosson, Clare K. PREDOMINANCE OF MALE AUTHORS IN SOCIAL WORK PUBLICATIONS. *Social Casework 1970 51(7): 421-430.* A study of leading social work journals indicates that males, although a minority in the social work profession, are greatly overrepre-

sented in publication activities. In spite of the fact that feminine qualities are needed for excellence in social work practice, and in spite of the fact that most of the founding "fathers" of social work were women, men hold the majority of major positions in the profession. Men are twice as likely to hold administrative positions, and in 1969 the top executive officer of eight major national social work organizations was a man. The authors explain the predominance of male authors, and of males generally in the profession, in terms of sex typing in society, which expects less aggression and dominance from women, and which emphasizes child rearing rather than professional competence in women graduates. This inequality may be difficult to eliminate; for many men and women, the typical arrangement is preferred because it limits competition between the sexes. 35 notes.
M. A. Kaufman

1910. Schiller, Anita R. ACADEMIC LIBRARIANS' SALARIES. *Coll. and Res. Lib. 1969 30(2): 101-111.* Compares men's and women's salaries according to type of institution, position, length of contract, faculty rank, number of years experience, and educational level. Based on primary and secondary sources; 11 tables, 13 notes.
E. R. McKinstry

1911. Sigelman, Lee. THE CURIOUS CASE OF WOMEN IN STATE AND LOCAL GOVERNMENT. *Social Sci. Q. 1976 56(4): 591-604.* Examines the quantity and quality of female employment in state and local government.
J

1912. Simpson, Elizabeth J. MOVE OVER, GENTS. *Am. Education 1970 6(10): 3-6.* Describes a research project funded by the US Office of Education currently under way at Cornell University, Purdue University, and Ohio State University concerned with American women's dual roles as homemakers and wage earners. Notice is taken of improved opportunities in what were once male-oriented professions and educational institutions. Predicts that the trend toward women entering the professions will rapidly increase in the next decade. Illus.
V. Shapiro

1913. Stoker, Myra. WOMEN ECONOMISTS: CAREER ASPIRATIONS, EDUCATION. *Am. Econ. R. 1975 65(2): 92-99.* Draws three major conclusions about women economists: the high school years are important to a woman's future career; women become economists because they like the subject matter; and supporting their families is the major reason why most women interrupt their studies at the Ph.D. level.
D. K. Pickens

1914. Sudman, Seymour. TIME ALLOCATION IN SURVEY INTERVIEWING AND IN OTHER FIELD OCCUPATIONS. *Public Opinion Q. 1965 29(4): 638-648.* Time study in which interviewers and salesmen spent one-third of their time in contact with people and two-thirds of their time at other duties. Public health nurses spend more than one-half of their time in direct contact. The reason for less time spent was that the tension was so great and people needed time to recuperate.
S. L. Banks

1915. Suelzle, Marijean. WOMEN IN LABOR. *Trans-Action 1970 8(1/2): 50-58.* Examines changing profiles of the American working woman. Declines in birth, marriage, and death rates have allowed more women to join the working classes at all levels, but primarily in low-paying jobs. Readily available educational opportunities, more extensive experience in job markets during and after World War II, desegregation of work situations as well as professions have added females to the labor force. Examines myths concerning female employment including women's desire for jobs, not careers; interest in personal development rather than career development; higher absenteeism and turnover among female employees; employment as a method of gaining pin money rather than living wages; female control of national wealth; disruption of work situation when women and men work together; and the belief that women function better in human-oriented or tedious jobs and are less mechanically minded than men.
G. A. Hewlett

1916. Sweet, James A. THE EMPLOYMENT OF RURAL FARM WIVES. *Rural Sociol. 1972 37(4): 553-577.* "The employment patterns of rural farm wives [are] examined by use of data from the 1960 census 1/1000 sample and published census reports. Multivariate analysis of both the probability of being currently employed in a nonfarm job and the probability of having received wage and salary income during 1959 are presented, and the employment differentials among rural farm wives are compared with those among urban wives. Some speculation is offered on the reasons for the observed regional, racial, and educational differentials in employment and for the lack of an effect of other family income on employment. An attempt is made to differentiate the farm population according to husband's occupation, tenure of housing, and source of income (self-employment *vs.* wage and salary), and to examine differential patterns of wife's employment."
J

1917. Tangri, Sandra Schwartz. DETERMINANTS OF OCCUPATIONAL ROLE INNOVATION AMONG COLLEGE WOMEN. *J. of Social Issues 1972 28(2): 177-200.*

1918. Tinker, Irene. NONACADEMIC PROFESSIONAL POLITICAL SCIENTISTS. *Am. Behavioral Scientist 1971 15(2): 206-212.* Reports findings of a study of 60 women responding to a sample drawn from lists of nonacademic professionals in fields related to political science, such as government agencies and departments, foreign service, and service organizations. While most respondents perceived discrimination, they did not think it had affected them personally. This "invidious socialization" is reinforced by relatively successful women comparing themselves to their peers who failed, rather than to their male counterparts. Biblio.
D. G. Davis, Jr.

1919. Waite, Linda J. WORKING WIVES: 1940-1960. *Am. Sociol. R. 1976 41(1): 65-80.* Changes since 1940 in the rates and patterns of labor force participation of married women are examined using retrospective work histories of wives taken from the 1960 Growth of American Families Study. The effects of certain predictor variables, such as income of the husband, wage potential of the wife and number of children under six, on the probability of a woman working are determined for life cycle stages. Changes since 1940 in the effects of these predictors are examined using a single-equation, additive linear model and analysis of covariance techniques. The major hypothesis tested in this research is that significant changes have occurred since 1940 in the effects of the factors influencing working by wives. The reseach supports this hypothesis for the early stages of marriage and childbearing only. No changes in either probability of work activity between births or the effects of all predictors when these are considered together on this activity are found for wives with three or more children. When each causal variable is considered separately, a significant decrease is noted in the effects of those factors which tend to inhibit wives' working. Among these are the presence of children under six, the age of the wife and her educational level. The factors which tend to facilitate working, past labor force activity and wife's earning power, have tended to increase in effect or have remained strongly positive influences.
J

1920. Waldman, Elizabeth. CHANGES IN THE LABOR FORCE ACTIVITIES OF WOMEN. *Monthly Labor R. 1970 93(6): 10-18.*

1921. Weissbrodt, Sylvia. CHANGES IN STATE LABOR LAWS IN 1972. *Monthly Labor R. 1973 96(1): 27-36.* Discusses issues in occupational safety, employment discrimination, wages, child labor, and agricultural labor.

1922. Weisskoff, Francine Blau. "WOMEN'S PLACE" IN THE LABOR MARKET. *Am. Econ. Rev. 1972 62(2): 161-166.*

1923. Willacy, Hazel M. and Hilaski, Harvey J. WORKING WOMEN IN URBAN POVERTY NEIGHBORHOODS. *Monthly Labor R. 1970 93(6): 35-38.*

1924. Wilson, Victoria AN ANALYSIS OF FEMININITY IN NURSING. *Am. Behavioral Scientist 1971 15(2): 213-220.* Analyzes the changing roles of women with respect to the evolution of the nursing profession. Shaped by "militaristic," "Christianic," and "feminist" influences, the profession of nursing has reflected the problems of women in general - the expectation of intuition more than intellect, nurturance rather than productivity, and dependency more than independence. Better health care systems will result as the emergent nursing profession begins an affirmative relationship with the medical establishment. Biblio.
D. G. Davis, Jr.

1925. Wright, Benjamin D. and Tuska, Shirley A.  CAREER DREAMS OF TEACHERS.  *Trans-action 1968 6(10): 43-47.* A study of the reasons why women chose teaching and of the level of teaching they chose. The authors examine the quality of influence that mothers, fathers, and teachers had on these women, and conclude that: 1) high school teachers had been strongly influenced by their teachers and had a loving but no longer stimulating relationship with their mothers; 2) grade school teachers had a strong relationship with their fathers, frustration by teachers, and poor relationship with mothers; 3) junior high school teachers admired their teachers and were not strongly influenced by their feelings about either parent. The authors feel that teachers will seek to re-create in their own teaching the kind of emotional situation which stimulated them into education. 4 tables.                              A. Erlebacher

1926. Zeisel, Rose N.  TECHNOLOGY AND LABOR IN THE TEXTILE INDUSTRY.  *Monthly Labor R. 1968 91(2): 49-55.* Describes large-scale changes in the textile industry stimulated by foreign competition, high profits beginning in 1962, and corporate mergers and purchases leading to larger, vertically integrated companies. Unit labor costs declined drastically because of technological changes. Employment in the industry declined after World War II until 1962, and then made a slight recovery. The mills continued to be overwhelmingly nonunion and the workers, who were still generally women, worked for low wages and negligible fringe benefits. 4 tables, chart, 10 notes.
                                                                          J. E. Brinley

1927. —.  [EFFECTS OF CHILD-CARE PROGRAMS ON WOMEN'S WORK EFFORT].  *J. of Pol. Econ. 1974 82(2, part II): 136-169.*
Heckman, James J.  EFFECTS OF CHILD-CARE PROGRAMS ON WOMEN'S WORK EFFORT,  *pp. 136-163.*
Rosen, Sherwin.  COMMENT,  *pp. 164-169.*
Proceedings of a conference on marriage, family, human capital, and fertility held on 4-5 June 1973.                                              S

1928. —.  PEGGY HOWARD.  *R. of Radical Pol. Econ. 1973 5(2): 103-105.*
—.  PEGGY HOWARD: OCTOBER 27, 1944 - OCTOBER 9, 1972,  *p. 103.*
Howard, Peggy.  THERE AREN'T MANY WOMEN ECONOMISTS ARE THERE?,  *pp. 104-105.*
A notice of this radical economist's death and an autobiographical account of her life.

## Discrimination

1929. Baker, Joan E.  EMPLOYMENT DISCRIMINATION AGAINST WOMEN LAWYERS.  *Am. Bar Assoc. J. 1973 59(9): 1029-1032.* Law firms and law schools should take note that amendments have strengthened the equal employment opportunity law.                        S

1930. Baker, Sally Hillsman and Levenson, Bernard.  JOB OPPORTUNITIES OF BLACK AND WHITE WORKING-CLASS WOMEN.  *Social Problems 1975 22(4): 510-533.* Examines entry employment of black, Puerto Rican, and white female graduates of a New York City vocational school—High School of Fashion Industry—and shows that job referral and placement depend more on race than on vocational training. Minority women have restricted access to white-collar jobs and are channeled into industries characterized by minimum advancement opportunities. Also, women in general are prepared for low-level, sex-typed occupations. Training alone is not the answer for economic inequality, but job search networks must be broadened for all groups that suffer discrimination. Notes, biblio.                                         A. M. Osur

1931. Bayles, Michael D.  COMPENSATORY REVERSE DISCRIMINATION IN HIRING.  *Social Theory and Practice 1973 2(3): 301-312.* Discusses ethical questions posed by the problem of reverse discrimination, the preferential hiring of minorities and women in the 1970's.

1932. Blumrosen, Alfred W.  LABOR ARBITRATION AND DISCRIMINATION: THE SITUATION AFTER GRIGGS AND RIOS.  *Arbitration J. 1973 28(3): 145-158.* "To the proverbial man on the street,

race discrimination is a matter of evil intent. But the Supreme Court has made it clear in the Griggs case that the target of the Civil Rights Act of 1964 is not the deliberate wrongdoer or racist alone, but the whole body of attitudes and practices that even well-intentioned individuals may exhibit. Thus, 'the law has focused over the years on reforming systems which discriminate,' the author points out. On the basis of his study of published awards three years ago, he concluded that arbitrators have dealt effectively with discriminatory practices which also constituted contractual violations. But where the contract was inherently discriminatory, arbitrators had felt obliged to uphold the agreement, at whatever cost to the statutory rights of employees. Now, three years later, he finds some improvement, based upon 'consciousness raising experience,' particularly in cases involving discrimination against women. But if arbitration awards are to be deferred to, in the manner anticipated by the Fifth Circuit decision in the Rios case, it might become advisable for parties to broaden the scope of arbitral authority so as to permit them to strike down provisions that are clearly repugnant to the purpose of the Civil Rights Act."                                                                    J

1933. Blumrosen, Alfred W.  LABOR ARBITRATION, EEOC CONCILIATION, AND DISCRIMINATION IN EMPLOYMENT.  *Arbitration J. 1969 24(2): 88-105.* "When a job applicant or an employee claims that he has been discriminated against because of his race, age, or sex, the matter may fall within the jurisdiction of any one of several public agencies as well as within the scope of a private arbitrator's authority. From the vantage point of one whose experience has brought him in contact with all forums of such determinations, the author believes that none have dealt adequately with the problem of job discrimination. The reason for this failure, he says, is that the courts have not yet spoken 'forcefully,' giving guidance to the industrial relations community. When that is done, 'the techniques of negotiation, settlement, and informal decision will be more valuable than they have been in the past.'"      J

1934. Bridges, Amy and Hartman, Heidi.  PEDAGOGY BY THE OPPRESSED.  *R. of Radical Pol. Econ. 1975 6(4): 75-79.* Discusses the problems of sexism faced by radical women teachers in colleges and universities, 1974.

1935. Cary, Eve.  PREGNANCY WITHOUT PENALTY.  *Civil Liberties R. 1973 1(1): 31-48.* Even after the Supreme Court's abortion decision, women still suffer discrimination if they want to become or remain pregnant. Eve Cary describes the current battle against employers, banks, insurance companies, and welfare agencies which levy a wide range of penalties on the right to be pregnant.                             J

1936. Clement, Mary Lynn.  JOB DISCRIMINATION IN A SEXIST SOCIETY.  *New Scholar 1970 2(2): 217-223.* Citing government documents and statistics, concludes that women are underpaid compared to men in similar jobs and that the situation is even worse for black women. The end to this form of sex discrimination will come when women are free from housework, which must be industrialized. This industrialization is unlikely, however, unless women leave the house for jobs.                                                                   D. K. Pickens

1937. Cook, Alice H.  SEX DISCRIMINATION AT UNIVERSITIES: AN OMBUDSMAN'S VIEW.  *AAUP Bull. 1972 58(3): 279-282.* If colleges do not in effect insist that the academic woman remain childless, or that she carry a load so heavy that only the extraordinary person can manage the burden, they must consider the matters of maternity leave, part-time employment at nontenured and tenured levels with appropriately extended probationary periods and intervals between tenure promotions, and late arrival in the academic market. Not only must nepotism rules be rescinded, but universities also must look at "incest" rules.                                                                 J. M. McCarthy

1938. Corfman, Eunice.  VIEWS OF THE PRESS: THE BIGOTRY OF LIBERAL MAGAZINES.  *Washington Monthly 1972 4(4): 53-60.* Examines charges of racism and sex discrimination leveled at eight of the national liberal magazines, and suggests ways the editors of these journals can increase the contributions from women and blacks, 1971.         S

1939. Davies, Margery.  WOMAN'S PLACE IS AT THE TYPEWRITER: THE FEMINIZATION OF THE CLERICAL WORK FORCE.  *Radical America 1974 8(4): 1-28.*

1940. Deckard, Barbara and Sherman, Howard. MONOPOLY POWER AND SEX DISCRIMINATION. *Pol. and Soc. 1974 4(4): 475-482.* Criticizes conservative and liberal explanations of the dilemma presented by capitalist maximizing-of-profits theory and the reality of sex discrimination against female workers. Presents an outline of an interdisciplinary model which shows the dilemma to be more apparent than real. Based on secondary sources; 16 notes.                    D. G. Nielson

1941. Deutrich, Mabel E. WOMEN IN ARCHIVES: A SUMMARY REPORT OF THE COMMITTEE ON THE STATUS OF WOMEN IN THE ARCHIVAL PROFESSION. *Am. Archivist 1975 38(1): 43-46.* A survey conducted by the Committee on the Status of Women in the Archival Profession revealed that men receive higher salaries than women even where educational levels and assigned duties are similar. Male archivists are generally better educated, publish more than female archivists, and hold more high level administrative positions. 34% of the male and 58% of the female respondents indicated that sex discrimination exists in their institutions.                    J. A. Benson

1942. Dinerman, Beatrice. SEX DISCRIMINATION IN ACADEMIA. *J. of Higher Educ. 1971 42(4): 253-264.* Discusses discrimination against women in higher education. Examines the arguments of critics of women in high ranking university teaching positions, especially those that claim that the female faculty member is deficient in credibility, originality, and productivity. Based on secondary sources; 34 notes.                    R. B. Orr

1943. Dinerman, Beatrice. SEX DISCRIMINATION IN THE LEGAL PROFESSION. *Am. Bar Assoc. J. 1969 55(10): 951-954.* Are women lawyers members of an inherently masculine profession in which they are discriminated against on good grounds, or do they have reason to fight back?                    J

1944. Eastwood, Mary. FIGHTING JOB DISCRIMINATION: THREE FEDERAL APPROACHES. *Feminist Studies 1972 1(1): 75-103.* Reviews the history and present status of federal government efforts at equal employment opportunity for women in private employment, government contract work, and federal employment. Compares the nondiscrimination program for federal employment with private employment covered by the Civil Rights Act, Title VII (1964). Outlines affirmative action, complaint procedures, sanctions, sex discrimination still allowed by law, and special restrictions on women workers. Perhaps the worst injustice is employment discrimination based on women's heavier home responsibilities as mothers and housekeepers. 191 notes.                    S

1945. Epstein, Cynthia Fuchs. SEPARATE AND UNEQUAL: NOTES ON WOMEN'S ACHIEVEMENT. *Social Policy 1976 6(5): 17-23.* Discusses sociological factors in employment discrimination against women in the 1970's.

1946. Fasman, Zachary D. and Clark, R. Theodore, Jr. NON-DISCRIMINATORY DISCRIMINATION: AN OVERVIEW OF THE DISCRIMINATION PROBLEM. *J. of Intergroup Relations 1974 3(2): 25-44.* Reviews the problems of the goals and achievements of the Civil Rights Act of 1964 (Title VII) concerning employment discrimination.                    S

1947. Ferber, Marianne A. and Loeb, Jane W. PERFORMANCE, REWARDS, AND PERCEPTIONS OF SEX DISCRIMINATION AMONG MALE AND FEMALE FACULTY. *Am. J. of Sociol. 1973 78(4): 995-1002.* "Data from male and female faculty at the Urbana-Champaign campus of the University of Illinois, matched by department and rank, reveal that 1) rewards are influenced by marital status but in opposite directions for men and women, 2) rewards are not higher in fields with a smaller proportion of women, and 3) perception of sex discrimination is more realistic among women than men."                    J

1948. Fishel, Andrew and Pottker, Janice. WOMEN TEACHERS AND TEACHER POWER. *Urban Rev. 1972 6(2): 40-44.* Discusses sex discrimination toward women teachers in public schools and teacher organizations from 1956-72, emphasizing inequities in income and maternity policies.

1949. Flanders, Dwight P. and Anderson, Peggy Engelhardt. SEX DISCRIMINATION IN EMPLOYMENT: THEORY AND PRACTICE. *Industrial and Labor Relations R. 1973 26(3): 938-955.* "The authors of this study first employ microeconomic theory to illustrate the choices an employer faces in deciding on the male-female mix of his labor force. They then test several hypotheses suggested by economic theory, using a sample of 337 males and 106 females employed in four managerial levels within the personnel departments of sixty-one firms. Variations in the male-female employment mix are measured against variations in salary, education work experience, age, size of firm, and the sex mix of each firm's total labor force."                    J

1950. Flora, Cornelia B. WOMEN IN RURAL SOCIOLOGY. *Rural Sociol. 1972 37(3): 454-462.* Since 1940, the ratio of students to total membership in the Rural Sociological Society has increased markedly and the percentage of women who are student members has increased from 0 in 1940 to 14.8 percent in 1970. This increase suggests growing interest in the field by women, although the lack of change between 1950 and 1970 means that women are not now gaining in the student category as quickly as they might. "From the data examined, it can be concluded that there is a dearth of women in the field of rural sociology. Underrepresentation of women is due not so much to overt discrimination against them on the part of rural sociologists as to a covert kind of sexism which 'cools out' the prospective female in the field by systematically not including her in the semiformal networks that are the source of professional socialization, employment, and rewards." 7 tables, biblio.                    D. D. Cameron

1951. Formby, John. THE EXTENT OF WAGE AND SALARY DISCRIMINATION AGAINST NON-WHITE LABOR. *Southern Econ. J. 1968 35(2): 140-150.* The cost of discrimination in economic terms is the net value of output to the whole economy which is foregone because of the resultant misallocation of resources. Market discrimination against nonwhites is measured by the net wage and salary income differentials between perfectly substitutable white and nonwhite labor. Basing his analysis on the U.S. census data for 1950 and 1960, the author concludes that the extent of wage and salary discrimination adjusted for price changes increased from 4 billion dollars in 1949 to 6.6 billion dollars in 1959, i.e. an almost 20 percent increase in per capita income (from 750 to 896 dollars). The extent of discrimination in absolute terms rose in the South far more than in the North, although it decreased for females in the North and West.                    A. W. Coats

1952. Freivogel, Elsie Freeman. WOMEN IN ARCHIVES: THE STATUS OF WOMEN IN THE ACADEMIC PROFESSIONS. *Am. Archivist 1973 36(2): 183-201.* Reviews the activities of women's caucuses in professional societies and examines the career status of women in the archival profession. Seeking to dispel popular notions about women and work, discusses women's importance in the work force, performance in graduate schools, absence from top university positions, typical duties on first job, salary, relationship with colleagues, and attitudes. Describes the work of Alice Rossi in the American Sociological Association and mentions similar activity in other professional societies such as the American Association of University Professors' work against antinepotism laws and restrictions on part-time workers. Examines the Society of American Archivists and recommends changes in employment practices in the archival profession. Based on published reports and private correspondence; 17 notes.                    D. E. Horn

1953. Glacel, Barbara Pate. THE STATUS OF EQUAL EMPLOYMENT OPPORTUNITY FOR WOMEN IN THE FEDERAL GOVERNMENT. *J. of Intergroup Relations 1976 5(1): 15-30.* Discusses sex discrimination against women in federal employment in the 1970's.

1954. Grooms, Sally. WHO IS YOUR FATHER? *Foreign Service J. 1974 51(2): 4-8.* Personal account of sex discrimination in the Foreign Service Corps in New Delhi, India, in 1971.                    S

1955. Hamilton, Mary Townsend. SEX AND INCOME INEQUALITY AMONG THE EMPLOYED. *Ann. of the Am. Acad. of Pol. and Social Sci. 1973 (409): 42-52.* "Discrimination in the labor market has received considerable attention in the last two decades. Racial aspects have been a primary concern, but the question of discrimination against females has assumed an increasing importance. Despite statements of alleged discrimination against women, there is a paucity of empirical evidence. For the most part, the evidence cited— including that in governmental studies—is based upon comparisons of gross earnings by sex obtained from census studies or studies of particular industries. The purpose of this study is to isolate pure measures of wage discrimination on the basis of sex, within narrowly defined occupations. The measures are pure in that factors other than sex, to which wage differentials might be attributed, are taken into account. The results of the analysis of wages in four narrowly defined occupations clearly suggest that wage discrimination has a sex dimension. A sex variable is consistently powerful in explaining wage dispersion. Moreover, the estimated sex differentials generally exceed those related to color, often by considerable amounts. This finding poses obvious theoretical questions. If the wage for labor is determined under free market conditions, the continued existence of discrimination seems implausible in the absence of real differences in productivity among sex and color groups. This suggests that there are differences in the supply and demand curves relating to different groups of labor which arise out of subjective, rather than objective, factors." J

1956. Hamovitch, William and Morgenstern, Richard D. THE COST OF BEING A WOMAN IN ACADEMIA. *New York Affairs 1974 2(2): 84-89.* "Comparing the qualifications of male and female professors at a 'liberal' New York City college reveals the persistence of apparently unfair salary differentials." J

1957. Harris, Ann Sutherland. THE SECOND SEX IN ACADEME. *AAUP Bull. 1970 56(3): 283-295.* Bias against women in higher education takes a variety of forms, including the discouraging of female students and discrimination in hiring, paying, and promoting female employees. Such bias encompasses both de jure and de facto discrimination. 23 notes. J. M. McCarthy

1958. Hopkins, Elaine B. UNEMPLOYED! AN ACADEMIC WOMAN'S SAGA. *Change 1973/74 5(10): 49-53.* "The experience of losing her university teaching position because she did not possess a doctorate led this teacher to a more thorough study of women in academe and policies she believes discriminate against them. 'Allowing women permanent places in the ivory tower will require revolutionary changes,' she concludes, but such changes could humanize the university." J

1959. Ingram, Timothy H. FAIR EMPLOYMENT: THE MACHINERY CONTINUES TO RUST. *Washington Monthly 1972 4(10): 37-45.* In 1972 the federal government is doing little to end employment discrimination against women and Negroes; cites the examples of Bethlehem Steel (1970) and American Telephone and Telegraph's Bell System (1971). S

1960. Kendrigan, G. M. THE LADY AND THE ROUSTABOUTS. *Am. Bar Assoc. J. 1973 59(4): 399-401.* Judicial astigmatism and outright discrimination plague women who seek equality and opportunity in the job market. S

1961. LaSorte, Michael A. ACADEMIC WOMEN'S SALARIES: EQUAL PAY FOR EQUAL WORK? *J. of Higher Educ. 1971 42(4): 265-278.* Compares the median salaries by sex and academic rank for the 1967-68 academic year with samples of academic teachers from four prior academic years in order to determine if the salary gap between the sexes has decreased during the past decade. The attributes of academic degree, second work activity, geographic region, years of professional experience, profession, and age are examined in order to detect if a salary gap persists between the sexes. Based on primary and secondary sources; 3 tables, 14 notes. R. B. Orr

1962. Levinson, Richard M. SEX DISCRIMINATION AND EMPLOYMENT PRACTICES: AN EXPERIMENT WITH UNCONVENTIONAL JOB INQUIRIES. *Social Problems 1975 22(4): 533-543.* Examines discriminatory acts in occupational recruitment based on job inquiries in response to 256 different classified advertisements in Atlanta, Georgia. Discrimination by sex was found in more than one-third of the inquiries, with men experiencing greater discrimination. The sex of an individual is very important for jobs associated with women, and male callers are seen as deviant or abnormal for applying for such jobs. Notes, biblio. A. M. Osur

1963. Levitin, Teresa; Quinn, Robert P.; and Staines, Graham L. SEX DISCRIMINATION AGAINST THE AMERICAN WORKING WOMAN. *Am. Behavioral Scientist 1971 15(2): 237-254.* The authors report the findings of a study of 351 women and 695 men, from data collected at the Survey Research Center, University of Michigan. The subjects were surveyed for occupational rewards (income and quality of work), objective discrimination (difference between real and expected reward), perceived discrimination (direct query regarding personal discrimination), and job satisfaction (five independent dimensions). Statistical correlations aid in providing answers to four research questions. Besides noting the discrepancies in equal income for equal work for women, the study notes the greater problem of women in higher status occupations and the difference between observable and reported discrimination. Biblio. D. G. Davis, Jr.

1964. Lublin, Joann S. DISCRIMINATION AGAINST WOMEN IN NEWSROOMS: FACT OR FANTASY? *Journalism Q. 1972 49(2): 357-361.* Discusses the validity of charges of discrimination against women journalists in American newspapers; based on 1971 data.

1965. Malkiel, Burton G. and Malkiel, Judith A. MALE-FEMALE PAY DIFFERENTIALS IN PROFESSIONAL EMPLOYMENT. *Am. Econ. R. 1973 63(4): 693-705.* Analyzes salary differentials of professional employees of a single corporation to determine 1) if education, experience, and productivity explain the salary structure, and 2) if there is discrimination against women. Education, experience, and productivity variables do explain over three-fourths of the salary variance for both men and women. And, at equal job levels, with the same characteristics, men and women do get equal pay. But the answer is "No" to the question, "Do men and women, with equal characteristics, get equal pay?" The difference is explained by the fact that "women with the same training, experience, etc. as men tend to be assigned to lower job levels." There is no absence of discrimination, merely a different method by which it occurs. 7 tables, 12 notes. C. W. Olson

1966. Martin, Walter T. and Poston, Dudley L., Jr. THE OCCUPATIONAL COMPOSITION OF WHITE FEMALES: SEXISM, RACISM AND OCCUPATIONAL DIFFERENTIATION. *Social Forces 1972 50(3): 349-355.* "This discussion focuses on the degree of occupational differentiation when white females are compared with white males and nonwhite females. The index of dissimilarity provides a measure of occupational differentiation applied to data from 66 SMSAs for 1960. The results show major variations among SMSAs in the degree of occupational differentiation. Differences between white females and nonwhite females (presumably reflecting racial discrimination) and differences between white females and white males (presumably reflecting sexual discrimination) show roughly the same maximum and minimum values but are only loosely correlated. It is speculated that physiological factors will be more important in reducing the degree of occupational differentiation in the latter case than in the former." J

1967. Medsgar, Betty. MEDIA STEREOTYPES OF WOMEN AND ONE MODEST ATTEMPT AT ERASING SOME OF THEM. *California Librarian 1976 37(2): 11-15.* Discusses stereotypes of women in the field of library science, including discriminatory practices in hiring, promotion, and salaries, ca. 1950-75.

1968. Mills, Kay. FIGHTING SEXISM ON THE AIRWAVES. *J. of Communication 1974 24(2): 150-155.* Discusses sexism in public broadcasting, both in content and in employment practices, citing statistics and suggesting strategies for women to persuade the FCC and the National Association of Broadcasters to change their sexist policies.

1969. Moran, Robert D. REDUCING DISCRIMINATION: ROLE OF THE EQUAL PAY ACT. *Monthly Labor R. 1970 93(6): 30-34.* Discusses the Act (1963) vis-à-vis sex discrimination. S

1970. Munts, Raymond and Rice, David C. WOMEN WORKERS: PROTECTION OR EQUALITY? *Industrial and Labor Relations Rev. 1970 24(1): 3-13.* "In banning sex discrimination in employment, Title VII of the Civil Rights Act of 1964 poses a serious threat to state legislation designed to protect women workers against long hours and conditions endangering their health and safety. This article examines the issues involved in the position taken by the Equal Employment Opportunities

Commission that laws prohibiting women from certain occupations or limiting their hours of work tend to discriminate rather than protect. The authors suggest that the advocates of equal rights are unaware of the risks involved in leaving determination of employment conditions to the free market."                                                                    J

1971. Niemi, Beth and Lloyd, Cynthia. SEX DIFFERENTIALS IN EARNINGS AND UNEMPLOYMENT RATES. *Feminist Studies 1975 2(2/3): 194-201.* Discusses the ways sex discrimination affects wage and unemployment differentials between women and men. "As female labor-force participation rises, the occupational segregation of women both depresses their relative wages and raises their unemployment rate." Table, 13 notes.                                                    J. D. Falk

1972. Oster, Sharon M. INDUSTRY DIFFERENCES IN THE LEVEL OF DISCRIMINATION AGAINST WOMEN. *Q. J. of Econ. 1975 89(2): 215-229.* Data from the early 1960's indicate that discrimination against professional women is not produced by employers but by employee behavior.                                                                   S

1973. Pierre-Noel, Lois Jones. CHANGING THE VALUES AND PRACTICES OF CULTURAL INSTITUTIONS. *Arts in Society 1974 11(1): 70-74.* Panel of women artists discuss how they can gain the power to force equal representation in museums and universities. Part of a conference on Women and the Arts, Racine, Wisconsin, 1973.        S

1974. Pietrofesa, John J. WOMEN AND THE WORLD OF WORK. *Catholic Educ. R. 1968 66(4): 256-259.* The number of women at work has expanded to a point where they represent more than one-third of the work force, yet they do not enjoy equal opportunity. Counselors have a major role to play in achieving equal opportunities for women and for directing women into satisfying occupations. 7 notes.

J. M. McCarthy

1975. Reagan, Barbara B. and Maynard, Betty J. SEX DISCRIMINATION IN UNIVERSITIES: AN APPROACH THROUGH INTERNAL LABOR MARKET ANALYSIS. *AAUP Bull. 1974 60(1): 13-21.*

1976. Roberts, Sylvia. EQUALITY OF OPPORTUNITY IN HIGHER EDUCATION: IMPACT OF CONTRACT COMPLIANCE AND THE EQUAL RIGHTS AMENDMENT. *Liberal Educ. 1973 59(2): 202-217.* Summarizes evidence of discrimination against women, especially in hiring, by institutions of higher education, the development of legal precedents and legislation, and the constitutional amendment aimed at correcting these abuses. Argues the advantages for institutions and plaintiffs alike in reform through voluntary compliance. Primary and secondary sources; 19 notes.                                        W. H. Ahern

1977. Safier, Gwendolyn. "I SENSED THE CHALLENGES" LEADERS AMONG CONTEMPORARY U.S. NURSES. *Oral Hist. R. 1975: 30-58.* Examines the changes in American nursing since World War II through interviews with 16 recognized leaders in the profession. Their comments expose the sexist basis of American life and the problems encountered by professional women before the feminist drive for equal rights. Illus., 43 notes.                                          D. A. Yanchisin

1978. Scotch, C. B. SEX STATUS IN SOCIAL WORK: GRIST FOR WOMEN'S LIBERATION. *Social Work 1971 16(3): 5-11.* Calls for the development of a sound social policy within the social work profession so that social workers may more actively engage in the women's liberation movement. Contends that female social workers are discriminated against in the areas of salary and upward mobility in the profession. 17 notes.                                             W. L. Willigan

1979. Sigworth, Heather. THE LEGAL STATUS OF ANTINEPOTISM REGULATIONS. *AAUP Bull. 1972 58(1): 31-34.* Institutions that persist in enforcing antinepotism rules will be subject to negotiating pressure from the Health, Education and Welfare Department and to legal suits by faculty wives whose careers have been affected by sex discrimination. 39 notes.                                         J. M. McCarthy

1980. Simpson, Richard L. SEX STEREOTYPES OF SECONDARY SCHOOL TEACHING SUBJECTS: MALE AND FEMALE STATUS GAINS AND LOSSES. *Sociol. of Educ. 1974 47(3): 388-398.* Describes a 1969 survey of sex discrimination in the choice of teachers for certain subjects.                                                     S

1981. Smith, Arthur B., Jr. THE IMPACT ON COLLECTIVE BARGAINING OF EQUAL EMPLOYMENT OPPORTUNITY REMEDIES. *Industrial and Labor Relations R. 1975 28(3): 376-394.* Discusses the impact of Title VII of the Civil Rights Act of 1964 and Executive Order 11246 on employment discrimination.          S

1982. Soule, Bradley and Standley, Kay. PERCEPTIONS OF SEX DISCRIMINATION IN LAW. *Am. Bar Assoc. J. 1973 59(10): 1144-1147.* "In a study of several professional groups, sex discrimination was reported most often in the legal profession. Both male and female lawyers perceived substantial barriers to women practitioners, a circumstance most surprising in a profession that has sought to diminish discrimination in other areas of society."                                           J

1983. Stevenson, Mary. WOMEN'S WAGES AND JOB SEGREGATION. *Pol. and Soc. 1973 4(1): 83-96.* Charges that economic discrimination may be the direct product of sex discrimination in the occupational structure and asserts that economists have been remiss in examining the female worker in her economic role. Central to the examination of this charge are the ambiguities that exist in the division of labor by sex which have been further confounded by technological advancements. Suggests an alternative way of classifying occupations that avoids prior shortcomings and which provides an index of discrimination on the basis of sex. Secondary sources; table, 28 notes.                            D. G. Nielson

1984. Szymanski, Albert. RACISM AND SEXISM AS FUNCTIONAL SUBSTITUTES IN THE LABOR MARKET. *Sociol. Q. 1976 17(1): 65-73.* The returns from the 1970 U.S. census are used to examine whether racial and sexual discrimination tend to vary together or whether they are functional substitutes for one another in the labor market, i.e., whether they operate in the same manner to produce the same results. The impact of racial discrimination is measured by both the percentage of the population of a state that is of third world origin and the ratio of black to white male annual earnings. Sexual discrimination is measured by the ratio of white female to white male earnings and urban female to urban male earnings. The values of each of these indicators is compared for the 50 U.S. states. The effect of the percentage of the population that is urban, the percentage of the economically active population in manufacturing, the level of personal income, region, and percentage of the population that is third world is controlled for. The results show that sexual discrimination can be seen as a functional substitute for racial discrimination in the labor market. Where racial discrimination is the most significant, sexual discrimination is the least. This supports the argument that the capitalist economic system needs a specially oppressed group of menial laborers to perform its most menial and low-paying tasks. Either white women or third world people (men and women) can fill these jobs. When third world people are available, white working women do not have to be pressed into them to the same extent. However, when third world people are not present, or are not especially discriminated against, then white working women tend more to perform the "dirty work" jobs and are consequently less likely to be found in the "better" jobs.       J

1985. Williams, Gregory. A RESEARCH NOTE ON TRENDS IN OCCUPATIONAL DIFFERENTIATION BY SEX. *Social Problems 1975 22(4): 543-547.* Replicates and extends the research of Edward Gross on the measurement of long-term trends in occupational differentiation by sex in the US labor force, taking into account methodological problems that Gross faced. The result is a substantial and consistent decline in differentiation as opposed to Gross' findings of little or no decline during 1900-60. The data suggest some but not rapid progress toward reducing segregation of women in occupations. Notes, biblio.

A. M. Osur

1986. Yokopenic, Patricia A.; Bourque, Linda Brookover; and Brogan, Donna. PROFESSIONAL COMMUNICATION NETWORKS: A CASE STUDY OF WOMEN IN THE AMERICAN PUBLIC HEALTH ASSOCIATION. *Social Problems 1975 22(4): 493-509.* Analyzes the underlying process of occupational discrimination against women in the professions by providing information about the level of official participation by women in the American Public Health Association (APHA). One structural barrier to women—access to communication networks—plays a crucial role in the career development process. Women are underrepresented except for those areas traditionally defined as "female." Notes, biblio.                                A. M. Osur

1987.  Zellner, Harriet.  DISCRIMINATION AGAINST WOMEN, OCCUPATIONAL SEGREGATION, AND THE RELATIVE WAGE,  *Am. Econ. Rev. 1972 62(2): 157-160.*

## Affirmative Action

1988.  Amsden, Alice H. and Moser, Collette.  JOB SEARCH AND AFFIRMATIVE ACTION.  *Am. Econ. R. 1975 65(2): 83-91.* Deals with the hiring of men and women economists during 1973-74, and measures the effect of affirmative action. Concludes that, even with affirmative action programs, improvements for women economists seem to be marginal. 4 tables.                                D. K. Pickens

1989.  Blackstone, William T.  REVERSE DISCRIMINATION AND COMPENSATORY JUSTICE.  *Social Theory and Practice 1975 3(3): 253-288.* Discusses legal and ethical aspects of reverse discrimination in preferential treatment for women and ethnic minorities in the 1970's, emphasizing the Supreme Court's decision in the case of Marco DeFunis.

1990.  DeFichy, Wendy.  AFFIRMATIVE ACTION: EQUAL OPPORTUNITY FOR WOMEN IN LIBRARY MANAGEMENT. *Coll. and Res. Lib. 1973 34(3): 194-201.* Urges the establishment of affirmative action programs to admit more women into library management. Discusses strategies for Affirmative Action Committees, including the endorsement and support of national women's organizations such as the National Organization for Women. Considers suggestions on securing full cooperation from top management personnel and the role of library schools. Hopefully, "an equal opportunity library will influence employment practices within the community at large." Based on primary and secondary sources; 21 notes.                        E. R. McKinstry

1991.  Halpern, Ben.  THE "QUOTA" ISSUE.  *Midstream 1973 19(3): 3-12.* Criticizes the use of quotas to end discrimination.    S

1992.  Hook, Sidney.  FORCE FACULTY 'QUOTAS'—HEW. *Freedom at Issue 1972 (12): 1-24.* Offers evidence to support the contention that the "numbers game" pressed upon colleges by the Health, Education and Welfare Department subordinates academic qualifications to assure affirmative action in the employment of women and minorities. Suggests this will destroy the integrity of higher education.
L. C. Crook

1993.  Hook, Sidney.  SEMANTIC EVASIONS.  *Freedom at Issue 1972 (14): 12-13.* The affirmative action program of the Department of Health, Education and Welfare (HEW) imposes quotas on colleges and universities in an effort to end past discrimination against minorities and women in higher education. To meet HEW pressure, colleges have turned to employment practices which they attempt to mask by "semantic evasions."                                    L. C. Crook

1994.  Hook, Sidney and Todorovich, Miro.  THE TYRANNY OF REVERSE DISCRIMINATION.  *Change 1975/76 7(10): 42-43.* Discusses implications of the federal government's affirmative action program in higher education designed to abolish discrimination against minorities and women, but which has resulted in discrimination against white males, 1975.

1995.  Lerner, Abba P.  THE DEFORMATION OF AFFIRMATIVE ACTION.  *Midstream 1973 19(4): 33-38.* The original goals of Affirmative Action have been distorted beyond recognition.        S

1996.  Ornstein, Allan C.  QUALITY, NOT QUOTAS.  *Society 1976 13(2): 10, 14-17.* Discusses the dangers of reverse discrimination in the 1970's, whereby women and ethnic minorities receive preferential treatment in government and academic institutions.

1997.  Seabury, Paul.  HEW & THE UNIVERSITIES.  *Commentary 1972 53(2): 38-44.* The Health, Education and Welfare Department's stand on Affirmative Action programs in an effort to end sex discrimination has subordinated merit and jeopardized quality in colleges and universities.                                      S

1998.  Silvestri, Marco J. and Kane, Paul L.  HOW AFFIRMATIVE IS THE ACTION FOR ADMINISTRATIVE POSITIONS IN HIGHER EDUCATION?  *J. of Higher Educ. 1975 46(4): 445-450.* This paper discusses a research project assessing the affirmative action commitment of postsecondary institutions. The project, using an unobtrusive technique involving fictitious position-wanted ads in the *Chronicle of Higher Education,* supplies modest empirical data suggesting reluctant institutional commitment to locate and recruit female and minority candidates for administrative positions.                        J

1999.  Sowell, Thomas.  "AFFIRMATIVE ACTION" RECONSIDERED.  *Public Interest 1976 42: 47-65.* A 1971 regulation of the Health, Education and Welfare Department introduced affirmative action to academia by requiring colleges and universities to set numerical goals and timetables for the hiring of minorities and women, in order to compensate for past discrimination against these groups. No investigation of the conditions of academic employment, pay, and promotion as of 1971 was made, and consequently a useless "affirmative action" program resulted, which in fact has negative side effects. An analysis of readily available pre-1971 data shows that when career characteristics—academic degrees, publications, specialization—are the same, there are no concrete occupational differences between black and female academics and the rest of the profession. Affirmative action has brought practically no positive change for women and minorities but rather has created the impression that achievements by these groups have been conferred rather than earned. 3 tables.                                    S. Harrow

2000.  Squires, Gregory D.  AFFIRMATIVE ACTION, QUOTAS, AND INEQUALITY.  *J. of Intergroup Relations 1974 3(4): 26-37.* Argues that affirmative action programs, without accompanying institutional changes, will effect only small changes in the present unequal distribution of income in the United States.

2001.  Sugnet, Charles J.  THE UNIVERSITY OF MINNESOTA: THE UNCERTAIN PROGRESS OF AFFIRMATIVE ACTION. *Change 1974 6(4): 37-42.* The author describes his institution's experience with compliance and wonders, now that the crash-program period is past, what the next phase will be.                        J

2002.  —.  RACE, SEX AND JOBS.  *Change 1972 4(8): 24-35.*
Pottinger, J. Stanley.  THE DRIVE FOR EQUALITY,  *pp. 24, 26-29.*
Bunzel, John H. THE POLITICS OF QUOTAS,  *pp. 25, 30-35.* The government's drive to have academic institutions hire more black and women faculty has boiled over into one of the hottest philosophic controversies of recent years. In two articles, the chief architect of the government drive explains what "affirmative action" does and does not mean, while a noted university president expresses his fears of a new quota approach that threatens academic excellence.                J

## Domestic Labor

2003.  Clemens, James W.  HOW TO BE A GOOD HOUSEKEEPER. *Missouri Hist. Soc. Bull. 1964 20(2): 146-147.*

2004.  Gerstein, Ira.  DOMESTIC WORK AND CAPITALISM. *Radical Am. 1973 7(4/5): 101-130.* A Marxist view of the role of the domestic laborer working for families in a capitalistic economic system, 1970-73.                                      S

2005.Glazer-Malbin,N.  HOUSEWORK.  *Signs 1976 1(4):905-22.*Recent scholarship on housework centers on three issues: 1) the monetary value of housework to the family and as an estimated contribution to the gross national product, 2) the social role of the housewife, and 3) the integration of housework into an analysis of capitalism. Earlier studies viewed housework as a biologically determined task of women. Ann Oakley's study of the housewife from pre-industrial times to the present finds women dissatisfied with doing housework. John K. Galbraith concludes women are exploited. The housewife works for the maintenance of capitalism rather than simply being a worker for her family. The working-class man's domination of his wife deflects his dissatisfaction with the economic system with the economic system and gives him the illusion of power. Based on secondary works; 54 notes.

　　　　　　　　　　　　　　　　　　　　　　J. Gammage

2006. Phelps, Charlotte D.　IS THE HOUSEHOLD OBSOLETE? *Am. Econ. Rev. 1972 62(2): 167-174.*

2007. —.　[THE HOUSEWIFE AS AN ECONOMIC ASSET].
Pyun, C. S.　MONETARY VALUE OF A HOUSEWIFE, 1969, *Am. J. of Econ. and Sociol. 1969 28(3): 271-284.* Discusses the replacement costs resulting from the death of a housewife.
Rosen, Harvey S.　THE MONETARY VALUE OF A HOUSEWIFE: A REPLACEMENT COST APPROACH, 1974, *Am. J. of Econ. and Sociol. 1974 33(1): 65-73.* Criticizes Pyun's article and offers an alternative methodology for measuring the value of a housewife, using a utility function and budget constraints. Secondary sources; 2 figs., 23 notes, appendix.　　　　　　　W. L. Marr and S

## Labor Relations and Reform

2008. Alutto, Joseph A. and Belasco, James A.　DETERMINANTS OF ATTITUDINAL MILITANCY AMONG NURSES AND TEACHERS.　*Industrial and Labor Relations R. 1974 27(2): 216-227.* "Although the increase in union activity among white-collar workers has been widespread, it is apparent that differences in militancy still exist among these workers. This study explores these differences by means of a questionnaire survey that measured the attitudes of approximately nine hundred nurses and teachers toward subjects such as collective bargaining and strikes by professional workers. The results demonstrate that attitudinal militancy does vary between these occupations and also within each occupation, according to the nature of the employing institution and the age, seniority, and certain personal characteristics of individual nurses and teachers."　　　　　　　　　　　　　J

2009. Carr, Shirley.　WOMEN'S YEAR—UNION ROLE.　*Can. Labour 1975 20(2): 2-6, 34.* Discusses worldwide sex discrimination and the role of labor unions in fighting it.

2010. Cole, Stephen　THE UNIONIZATION OF TEACHERS: DETERMINANTS OF RANK-AND-FILE SUPPORT.　*Sociol. of Educ. 1968 41(1): 66-87.* "Teachers have traditionally been thought of as conservative and submissive. Yet they have increasingly adopted militant tactics to achieve their goals. Using data from two surveys this paper analyzes the determinants of rank-and-file support of militancy. We show how non-teaching statuses were influential in creating either positive or negative predisposition towards the union movement. Statuses such as religion, political affiliation, and class of origin provided socialization in attitudes towards unions. Teachers with generally favorable attitudes towards unions were more likely to support a union in their own profession. Other non-teaching statuses, such as sex, influenced militancy by providing a frame of reference in which the teacher could evaluate his job. Men, comparing their jobs with those having higher prestige, were more likely than women to feel relatively deprived and to be militant. Finally, we show how changes in personnel input to the school system provided the union movement with a larger base of potential supporters and a larger pool from which leaders could be recruited."　　　　J

2011. Cook, Alice H.　WOMEN AND AMERICAN TRADE UNIONS.　*Ann. of the Am. Acad. of Pol. and Social Sci. 1968 375: 124-132.* "Four aspects of women's participation in trade-union life are examined: the attitude of unions today toward protective legislation for women; the effect which the recent federal legislation on 'equality' has had on women's opportunities in the shops and the unions' attitudes toward handling these new kinds of grievances and demands; the degree to which unions include special clauses covering women's wages and conditions in their contracts; and the participation of women in the political life of the unions. Few changes in attitudes or practice are found to characterize the unions in the 1960's as compared with those in the 1940's, when *The Annals* last carried a report on this subject."　　J

2012. Green, James.　FIGHTING ON TWO FRONTS: WORKING-CLASS MILITANCY IN THE 1940'S.　*Radical Am. 1975 9(4-5): 7-48.* Changes occurred in labor unions with the entrance of women and Negroes into the labor force.　　　　　　　　　　　S

2013. Jordan, Joan.　WORKING WOMEN AND THE EQUAL RIGHTS AMENDMENT.　*Trans-Action 1970 8(1/2): 16-23.* Recommends nonsupport for the Equal Rights Amendment unless it is amended so that existing labor standards will not be destroyed.

2014. McKelvey, Jean T.　SEX AND THE SINGLE ARBITRATOR. *Industrial and Labor Relations R. 1971 24(3): 335-354.* When conduct sanctioned by a collective bargaining agreement conflicts with the law, what course should the arbitrator take? Should he respect the terms of the agreement or be guided by the provisions of the law in making his award? The importance of this oft-debated issue has been enhanced by the ban on sex discrimination contained in Title VII of the Civil Rights Act of 1964, which conflicts not only with many collective agreements but with state labor laws as well. Arbitrators have been reluctant to deal with the conflict, preferring to stay with the doctrine of separation between contract and law and to avoid the responsibility of deciding issues of public policy. This negative attitude is criticized by the author, who argues that arbitration cannot remain relevant to economic and social needs if it shies away from the legal aspects of emerging public policies.

　　　　　　　　　　　　　　　　　　　　　　J

2015. O'Brien, David.　AMERICAN CATHOLICS AND ORGANIZED LABOR IN THE 1930'S.　*Catholic Hist. R. 1966 52(3): 323-349.* American Catholics were deeply involved in the growth of organized labor in the 1930's. Generally church spokesmen endorsed collective bargaining but many were critical of the policies and leadership of the American Federation of Labor (AFL) and welcomed the Congress of Industrial Organizations (CIO). Later, journals like *America* and the *Catholic World,* Father Charles E. Coughlin, and a number of prominent Catholic prelates became highly critical of the CIO's militancy and its association with Communists. Others such as Bishop Robert Lucey, John Ryan, and Raymond McGowan of the National Catholic Welfare Conference, Dorothy Day of the Catholic Worker Movement, and numerous labor priests gave more or less enthusiastic support to the new unionism, support centering upon the Association of Catholic Trade Unionists. Underlying this growing divergence in Catholic opinion was the ambiguity of Catholic social doctrine and the peculiar defensive position of Catholics in the United States.　　　　　　　　　A

2016. Pichler, Joseph A. and Fitch, H. Gordon.　AND WOMEN MUST WEEP: THE NLRB AS FILM CRITIC.　*Industrial and Labor Relations R. 1975 28(3): 395-410.* Discusses the use of the anti-union film *And Women Must Weep* during the 1950's-70's, and the 1974 decision by the National Labor Relations Board that this use does not constitute an unfair labor practice by employers.　　　　　　　S

2017. Reverby, Susan.　HOSPITAL ORGANIZING IN THE 1950's: AN INTERVIEW WITH LILLIAN ROBERTS.　*Signs 1976 1(4): 1053-1063.* Little unionizing of hospital personnel occurred in the United States until the late 1950's, when the racial makeup of nonprofessionals change to black, Puerto Rican, and Chicano job issues became linked to civil rights. Lillian Roberts, a black nurses' aide who became a union organizer, attempted to unionize Mt. Sinai Hospital in Chicago. A strike for union recognition ensued, but support from other unions or the public was not forthcoming. The strikers, mostly southern blacks who had migrated to Chicago, were ineffective in gaining union recognition, but they did acquire a wage increase and better working conditions. Based on oral interview; 2 notes.　　　　　　J.Gammage

2018. Rosenberg, Bernard and Weinman, Saul.　YOUNG WOMEN WHO WORK: AN INTERVIEW WITH MYRA WOLFGANG. *Dissent 1972 19(1): 29-36.*

2019. Sexton, Brendan and Sexton, Patricia Cayo.　LABOR'S DECADE: MAYBE.　*Dissent 1971 18(4): 365-374.* In the 1970's, labor will break out of several decades' stagnation and move toward greater social concern and new areas of union membership. Union leadership will begin to reflect the growing numbers of young, militant members. Union organizing will increase in the South and among women, the working

poor, and white-collar workers. Blacks will finally achieve power in the union leadership commensurate with their growing numbers. Contrary to popular myths, union membership in the South has been growing steadily in the 1960's and promises to increase during the 1970's. Unions will once again put the crusade for social legislation at the top of their priority lists.
W. L. Hogeboom

2020. Sexton, Patricia Cayo. WORKERS (FEMALE) ARISE! *Dissent 1974 21(3): 380-396.* Discusses sex discrimination and the need for women to form labor organizations in the 1970's.                       S

2021. Withorn, Ann. THE DEATH OF CLUW. *Radical Am. 1976 10(2): 47-51.* The Coalition of Labor Union Women has been divided in membership and purpose since its founding in 1973, between women in the upper levels of the trade union bureaucracy and women from various segments of the political Left. As described by a CLUW member, this division resulted in the ending of the organization as a viable group for all practical purposes at its first constitutional convention in December, 1975. The forces of conflict within the body included trade union women using the CLUW for upward mobility within union ranks, the internal divisions of the Left, the economic crisis, and the nature of American trade unionism.                       N. Lederer

## Welfare

2022. Goodwin, Leonard. ENVIRONMENT AND THE POOR: TOWARD MORE REALISTIC WELFARE POLICIES. *Current Hist. 1971 61(363): 290-296, 307.* Discusses welfare reform issues regarding the poverty of Negroes, women, and youth, emphasizing unemployment and the effectiveness of the Aid to Families with Dependent Children program, 1968-71.

2023. Kogan, Leonard S. THE USE OF FAMILY DAY CARE BY AFDC RECIPIENTS. *Public Welfare 1971 29(2): 206-208.* Research in 1967 on public welfare recipients' attitudes toward alternate forms of day care resulted in a redetermination of program objectives by the City of New York Department of Social Services.                       S

2024. Moynihan, Daniel Patrick. POVERTY AND PROGRESS. *Am. Scholar 1964 33(4): 594-606.* While the industrial democracies of Northern and Western Europe have in the past 15 years "quietly put an end to poverty in their own nations," we in the United States seem to think that industrial progress has to produce poverty. We face the danger of not having the "social creativity to make our system run properly," of "making up its shortcomings by massive programs of public assistance." Our excellent welfare system must not "become the economic system of a permanent subculture." The objects of the war on poverty are jobs and job training, education and community action in order that families may have fathers and communities independence.                       E. P. Stickney

2025. Nathan, Richard P. AN INCREMENTAL APPROACH TO WELFARE REFORM. *Public Welfare 1976 34(2): 21-22.* Proposes guidelines for welfare reform legislation in the 1970's aimed at the low-income family, emphasizing the Dole-McGovern food stamp bill, medical insurance programs, subsidized housing, and aspects of income tax.

2026. Safa, Helen Icken. THE FEMALE-BASED HOUSEHOLD IN PUBLIC HOUSING: A CASE STUDY IN PUERTO RICO. *Human Organization 1965 24(2): 135-139.* Notes a 25 percent increase in the number of families in Puerto Rico with a female head during 1950-60. Examines several of the traditional rationales for the existence of female-headed households and suggests that public housing and the fact that public welfare programs are female and child oriented have reduced the male economic role and thus encouraged the female household. Checks the hypothesis with data from a public housing project in San Juan and finds that the selection procedures were biased toward the female-based household and that welfare encouraged separation of married couples. Concludes that public housing and welfare are contributing factors toward the increase in the number of female-headed households. 5 tables, 17 notes.                       E. S. Johnson

2027. Silverman, Herbert A. A BELEAGUERED WELFARE PROGRAM: A CASE STUDY IN ORGANIZATIONAL RESPONSE. *Social Service R. 1971 45(2): 147-158.* Reviews the development of organizational theory and the impact of an external event on the level of organizational efficiency. In 1965 the Pennsylvania Public Welfare Department initiated a program of reimbursement for family planning services. By 1966 clever legislative opposition forced a compromise, denying payments to the unwed. Evaluates the impact of this compromise. The immediate and enduring decline in the use made of the program outstripped the simple limiting of those still eligible. This was in part a function of the dimmed enthusiasm of the social workers themselves and the presence of Planned Parenthood Clinics in particular localities. Based on computerized data; table, 6 notes, biblio.                       M. Hough

2028. Townsend, Alair A. REFORMING WELFARE: CRITERIA AND OBJECTIVES. *Public Welfare 1976 34(2): 18-21.* Discusses Congressional approaches to welfare and tax reform in the 1970's, emphasizing the implications of the Griffiths bill for the low-income family.

2029. Wohlenberg, Ernest H. INTERSTATE VARIATIONS IN AFDC PROGRAMS. *Econ. Geography 1976 52(3): 254-266.* Presents variability in interstate eligibility requirements, grant size, effectiveness, and restrictions for Aid to Families with Dependent Children Programs, 1972.

# Social Sphere

## General

2030. Acker, Joan. WOMEN AND SOCIAL STRATIFICATION: A CASE OF INTELLECTUAL SEXISM. *Am. J. of Sociol. 1973 78(4): 936-945.* "Although women, as aggregates, have lower social status than men in all known societies, sex-based inequalities have not been considered in most theoretical and empirical work on social stratification. Assumptions about the social position of women, found in the stratification literature, implicitly justify the exclusion of sex as a significant variable. This paper argues that these assumptions are logically contradictory and empirically unsupported. If sex is to be taken as a significant variable, the family can no longer be viewed as the unit in social stratification. Conceptual and methodological problems are generated if the family is not considered as the unit. However, a reconceptualization which includes sex-based inequalities may lead to a more accurate and more complex picture of stratification systems.                       J

2031. Ballweg, John A. HUSBAND-WIFE RESPONSE SIMILARITIES ON EVALUATIVE AND NON-EVALUATIVE SURVEY QUESTIONS. *Public Opinion Q. 1969 33(2): 249-254.* "The likelihood of husband-wife consensus in responses to survey questions is greater when the data requested can be assigned a fixed numerical value than when evaluation by the respondent is required....Responses to data requiring evaluation are likely to stress the importance of the respondent's role in the family over that of the spouse." The implication for research designed to secure information about family behavior patterns is that researchers "must recognize the limitations imposed by interviews with a single family member." Based on a survey of 179 couples regarding family income and discipline of children; table, 7 notes.
D. J. Trickey

2032. Barnett, Larry D. WOMEN'S ATTITUDES TOWARD FAMILY LIFE AND U.S. POPULATION GROWTH. *Pacific Sociol. Rev. 1969 12(2): 95-100.* Presents the results of public opinion polls regarding women's attitudes toward family structure, church attendance, and population growth in 1967.

2033. Beck, Jane C. A TRADITIONAL WITCH OF THE TWENTIETH CENTURY. *New York Folklore Q. 1974 30(2): 101-116.* Study of Dolorez Amelia Gomez of Philadelphia, Pennsylvania, who practices traditional witchcraft.                       S

2034. Bell, Inge Powell. THE DOUBLE STANDARD. *Trans-Action 1970 8(1/2): 75-80.* Examines the differences in definitions of age for women and men; points out that women lose attractiveness more quickly than men do in terms of sexuality, prestige, and economic values, concluding that value change is necessary to remedy this situation.

2035. Blood, Robert O., Jr. and Wolfe, Donald M. NEGRO-WHITE DIFFERENCES IN BLUE-COLLAR MARRIAGES IN A NORTH-ERN METROPOLIS. *Social Forces 1969 48(1): 59-64.* "Representative samples of Negro and white blue-collar marriages in the Detroit Metropolitan Area show differences in marriage patterns even when comparisons are limited to low blue-collar or high blue-collar marriages only. Negro families are more often wife-dominant at the expense of equalitarianism in making major family decisions. The division of labor in Negro homes involves less sharing and flexibility despite a slightly higher proportion of working wives. Negro wives are more self-reliant in coping with their own emotional problems and emphasize their own contributions to the family welfare, rather than the husband's occupational prospects. Negro men are less companionable to their wives and are generally evaluated less favorably as marriage partners than white husbands of the same occupational level."                                                                J

2036. Bridenthal, Renate. THE DIALECTICS OF PRODUCTION AND REPRODUCTION IN HISTORY. *Radical Am. 1976 10(2): 3-11.* Based on the major frames of reference of Marxist and functionalist thought, women's participation in production and reproduction is described as having shifted from the private to the social arena and from relatively direct to relatively mediated participation. This process has resulted in feelings of alienation, giving rise to a recent wave of organized feminism. Analysis of social classes must take into account recognition of sex differences, since women have important experiences differing from those of the men in their class. Based on secondary sources.
                                                                N. Lederer

2037. Carranco, Lynwood A MISCELLANY OF FOLK BELIEFS FROM THE REDWOOD COUNTRY. *Western Folklore 1967 26(3): 169-176.* This collection of 146 folk beliefs or superstitions obtained from students and residents of Humboldt County, California, are classified as: logger folk beliefs; folk beliefs of commercial fishermen; birth, infancy, childhood; body, folk medicine; witchcraft, ghosts; death, funeral practices; animals, animal husbandry; sports, fishing, hunting; wishes, dreams; marriage, future husband; cosmic phenomena; weather, seasons; bad luck, good luck; folk beliefs of local Indians, miscellaneous folk beliefs; and Hawaiian folk beliefs. 2 notes.          D. L. Smith

2038. Castor, Jane and Hudson, Pamela Sue. FERTILITY REGU-LATION: A PROBLEM OF TODAY. *Public Welfare 1969 27(1): 3-9.* Discusses the dissemination of birth control information by social workers in a special section entitled "Family Planning."                  S

2039. Chilman, Catherine S. PUBLIC SOCIAL POLICY AND POP-ULATION PROBLEMS IN THE UNITED STATES. *Social Service R. 1973 47(4): 511-530.* Attempts to propose the broadest context for social planning related to population limitation. Sees the current narrow governmental concern for provision of family planning information to the poor as totally insufficient, stating that the proposals of the President's Commission on Population Growth and the American Future are broader. Cites other organizations designed to foster a positive rather than negative climate for the pursuit of smaller families, in a changing society. 2 tables, 25 notes.                        M. Hough

2040. Clavan, Sylvia. CHANGING FEMALE SEXUAL BEHAV-IOR AND FUTURE FAMILY STRUCTURE. *Pacific Sociol. Rev. 1972 15(3): 295-308.* Discusses the role of women in changing sexual behavior and roles, family structure, and child care in the 1970's.

2041. Fish, Lydia. THE OLD WIFE IN THE DORMITORY: SEX-UAL FOLKLORE AND MAGICAL PRACTICES FROM STATE UNIVERSITY COLLEGE. *New York Folklore Q. 1972 28(1): 30-36.* Discusses young women's superstitions about sex in the 1960's and 70's, including attitudes toward menstruation, contraceptives, and pregnancy.

2042. Freeman, Jo. GROWING UP GIRLISH. *Trans-Action 1970 8(1/2): 36-43.* Discusses elements in socialization which differentiate women from men in their sex roles, including mothering, a practice instilled in the minds of young girls; general familial tendencies to favor

male offspring both in terms of division of labor and in economic provisions for future education; and the male dominant/female subserviant social organization followed in most American homes, 1940-70. Discusses changes in society which have effected changes in the value structure without concomitant change in the social structure. Examines needed changes in political and economic organization as well as necessary changes in family structure which can bring this evolution about.
                                                                G. A. Hewlett

2043. Gersh, Ellen. LIVING AND PARTLY LIVING: OLDER WOMEN IN AMERICA. *Internat. Socialist R. 1973 35(3): 12-15, 44-47.*

2044. Herzog, Elizabeth SOME ASSUMPTIONS ABOUT THE POOR. *Social Service R. 1963 37(4): 389-402.* Concerns three assumptions about poor people. "There is a culture of poverty. The family and sex patterns of the poor differ from those of the middle class. The family and sex patterns of poor Negroes differ from those of whites on the same socioeconomic level." The "culture" of the poor in America, while real enough in certain respects, is lacking in other important aspects. Family patterns among the poor differ from those of the middle-class or rich, but distinctions between Negroes and whites seem more solidly based on economic levels than on race. Based on 46 studies; 5 notes.
                                                                M. W. Machan

2045. Hodge, Robert W. and Treiman, Donald J. SOCIAL PARTIC-IPATION AND SOCIAL STATUS. *Am. Sociol. R. 1968 33(5): 722-740.* "The relationships between various aspects of social participation - voluntary organization memberships, church attendance, and informal association with friends - and a number of social status and social background factors are examined using data from a representative sample of residents of a suburban county adjacent to Washington, D.C. In particular, the role of direct intergenerational transmission of participation patterns in determining levels of social participation is investigated by using the technique of path analysis to derive estimates of the effects of parents' participation patterns (for which no direct measurements are available) upon those of their offspring. For both males and females, membership in voluntary organizations appears to be at least as strongly influenced by parent's level of participation in such organizations as by respondent's socioeconomic status. In the case of church attendance, however, a strong direct intergenerational effect is found only for females, and not for males. Church attendance of males appears to be strongly influenced by their spouses' attendance patterns, a result which is consistent with the role of women as expressive leaders of families."                        J

2046. Hogan, Timothy D. AN ECONOMIC ANALYSIS OF THE PUBLIC GOODS NATURE OF POPULATION CONTROL. *Rocky Mountain Social Sci. J. 1973 10(2): 11-16.* Family planning programs will be an ineffective tool for population control.      S

2047. Huber, Joan. [CHANGING WOMEN IN A CHANGING SOCIETY]. *Am. J. of Sociol. 1973 78(4): 763-766.* Editor's introduction to 21 articles on the title topic in this issue.          S

2048. Jitodai, Ted T. MIGRATION AND KINSHIP CONTACTS. *Pacific Sociol. R. 1963 6(2): 49-55.* Migrant behavior (social participation) is dependent on the type of movement (rural or urban) which is made. Migrants with rural backgrounds are less prepared for the kind of organized life experienced in the urban setting than those migrants with solely urban backgrounds. These differences apply most in formal voluntary urban associations and political institutions. Participation in informal groupings is more universal among migrants, where urban-rural differences are not important. Contact with relatives is the most frequent type of contact, followed by contact with neighbors, friends, and co-workers, in that order. Most respondents have more weekly contacts in kinship groupings than in any other informal groupings. Rural migrants have higher rates of weekly contacts with relatives than do urban migrants. In general, people in lower socioeconomic strata tend to participate in kinship groupings more than people of higher status. Two explanations for this are given: 1) there is a selective process of out-migration operating over a period of time in regard to kinship contacts; and 2) that the modern family in an industrialized, bureaucratic society does not necessarily break away from an extended family system. Based on a sample drawn from the Detroit area; 4 tables, 18 notes.
                                                                A. S. Freedman

2049. Johnson, Robbie Davis. FOLKLORE AND WOMEN: A SOCIAL INTERACTIONAL ANALYSIS OF THE FOLKLORE OF A TEXAS MADAM. *J. of Am. Folklore 1973 86(341): 211-224.* Examines the role of a brothel madam as a social controller.                    S

2050. Kando, Thomas. PASSING AND STIGMA MANAGEMENT: THE CASE OF THE TRANSSEXUAL. *Sociol. Q. 1972 13(4): 475-483.* The nature of the transsexual's stigma is such that she can pass as a natural female with little difficulty if she chooses to. At the same time, transsexuals do not once and for all become women after their conversion operation. Their ambiguous gender implies at least a double identity: some of the feminized transsexual's social circles remain associated with her former (male) gender, while some center around her new identity. Thus, it is more accurate to say that the transsexual is ongoingly passing than that she has passed. This led to the formulation of two hypotheses: (1) transsexuals compartmentalize their social circles to a greater extent than normals, and (2) transsexuals experience greater incompatibility of their social circles than normals. To operationalize social circles, the family and present friends were chosen. In terms of this operationalization, the findings support the first hypothesis but not the second. It is argued that transsexuals do not experience unusual incompatibility between family and friends because they either minimize contacts with the former, or do so with the latter, or segregate the two. In the final analysis, the transsexual's double identity is not simply a double gender identity, but also the product of participation in the radically different cultures and lifestyles of her rural background on the one hand and her present urban underworld environment on the other.                    J

2051. Kanter, Rosabeth Moss. WOMEN AND THE STRUCTURE OF ORGANIZATIONS: EXPLORATIONS IN THEORY AND BEHAVIOR. *Sociol. Inquiry 1975 45(2-3): 34-74.* Discusses the positions women hold in organizational structures, the nature of the sociology of organizations, and the direction future sociological research should take.

2052. Keller, Suzanne. THE FUTURE ROLE OF WOMEN. *Ann. of the Am. Acad. of Pol. and Social Sci. 1973 408: 1-12.* "During the next century, societies will have to plan their populations along with other national resources. The success of this objective will depend, in large part, on the reproductive ambitions of women and the availability of effective substitutes for maternity. These broad developments will necessitate a reorganization of national priorities, as well as changes in family, household and work patterns. Among the foreseeable consequences are: reduced occupational sex typing, lessened emphasis on marriage and maternity as supreme goals for women and greater participation of women in all spheres of the labor force. As a result, we must expect and prepare for both new forms of socialization and self-images by gender. Concluding the paper are suggestions for steps society might take to help ease the transition into the new era."                    J

2053. Kim, Bok-Lim C. CASEWORK WITH JAPANESE AND KOREAN WIVES OF AMERICANS. *Social Casework 1972 53(5): 273-279.* A study of the needs of Oriental wives of Americans. When a Korean or Japanese wife leaves her family, friends, and way of life to come to America, her husband becomes her sole guiding and supporting person. In the military, army privileges and local market conditions made it possible for the couples to live luxuriously. Interracial couples were considered a social aristocracy, and they experienced feelings of superiority. When they came to America, they faced inadequate income, substandard housing, need for medical care, etc., all without supportive relatives or friends. The wives face an acute sense of isolation. Husbands who once valued the submissiveness of their wives become angry when feeling overburdened by the wives' dependence. Wives continue to view husbands as omnipotent, rather than recognizing the problems faced by the husbands in returning to civilian life. The social caseworker must recognize the unique social and psychological problems faced by people in this condition, and casework should be tailored to fit their special needs. 4 notes.
                    M. A. Kaufman

2054. Lopata, Helena Znaniecki. THE EFFECT OF SCHOOLING ON SOCIAL CONTACTS OF URBAN WOMEN. *Am. J. of Sociol. 1973 79(3): 604-619.* "This paper examines two sets of data, one derived from a study of 571 housewives and married working women, the other of 301 widows, aged 50 and over, for the association between social relationships and formal schooling. All the women live in a metropolitan area in America. The conclusion is that urbanization and industrialization trends make formal education a major requirement for the social engagement of women. The less educated an urban woman, the more probable her social isolation. This variable is more important than any other in predicting the degree to which a woman is able to engage in society and her attitude toward her social world."                    J

2055. Lopata, Helen Z. THE SOCIAL INVOLVEMENT OF AMERICAN WIDOWS. *Am. Behavioral Scientist 1970 14(1): 41-58.* Discusses the social involvement of aged widows (1968-69) in an industrialized and urbanized society after the death of their spouses.

2056. Lopata, Helena Znaniecki. SOCIAL RELATIONS OF BLACK AND WHITE WIDOWED WOMEN IN A NORTHERN METROPOLIS. *Am. J. of Sociol. 1973 78(4): 1003-1010.* "Based on a modified area probability sample that included 244 white and 52 black older widowed women living in a northern metropolitan area [Chicago], this paper contrasts their social contacts with organizations, neighbors, siblings, and children. The black women had less education and lower incomes than the white women. But their level of contact with friends, kin, and organizations was about the same as that of whites. The common notion that older black widowed women are surrounded by kin applied only to about one-third of the respondents of this study." One of 21 articles in this issue on changing women in a changing society.                    J

2057. Lovett, Robert W. FRANCIS A. COUNTWAY AND "THE LEVER WAY." *Harvard Lib. Bull. 1970 18(1): 84-93.* Chronicles the business career of Francis A. Countway (1876-1955) who, as president of Lever Brothers Company during 1918-46, brought its annual turnover in soap products to $200,000,000. Countway lacked formal education but rose from salesman to president through his understanding of the psychology of the American consumer's response to advertising. Bachelor and multimillionaire, Countway lived with his sister, Sanda, who after his death arranged for most of his fortune to be donated to build the medical library at Harvard bearing his name. Based on interviews, documents in the Harvard libraries, and secondary works; 15 notes.                    L. Smith

2058. Mednick, Martha Shuch and Tangri, Sandra Schwartz. NEW SOCIAL PSYCHOLOGICAL PERSPECTIVES ON WOMEN. *J. of Social Issues 1972 28(2): 1-16.*

2059. Mitchell, Juliet. FOUR STRUCTURES IN A COMPLEX UNITY. Carroll, Berenice A., ed. Liberating Women's History (Chicago: U. of Illinois Pr., 1976): pp. 385-399. Women's condition is a complex unity made up of four elements: production, reproduction, sexuality, and socialization of children. Different combinations of these elements result in a variation of women's position. Because each of these key structures can vary at different historical periods, each element must be studied separately to note how it might be changed. The liberation of women can be achieved only if all four elements are transformed, for a change in only one structure can be offset by a reinforcement of another. 29 notes.                    B. Sussman

2060. Nag, Moni. SEX, CULTURE AND HUMAN FERTILITY: INDIA AND THE UNITED STATES. *Current Anthrop. 1972 13(2): 231-237.* "It has been suggested that a high frequency of coitus contributes to the high level of fertility in nonindustrial societies where modern contraceptive methods are not widely practiced. Two questions can be raised: Is there any correlation between the average frequency of coitus experienced by a woman and the probability of conception? Is the average frequency of coitus among women in nonindustrial societies higher than in industrial societies? A review of recent literature shows that the probability of conception increases as the average frequency of coitus per week increases from less than one to four and more. The data from India and the US provide no good evidence for an affirmative answer to the second question. Average frequency of coitus is less among Indian women than American white women of corresponding age groups. Factors in the Indian situation that may help to explain this difference are suggested. It appears that high fertility cannot be attributed to high frequency of coitus in India. The paucity of reliable data on the frequency of coitus makes it impossible to assess its possible role in explaining the variations in the fertility levels of groups and subgroups not using modern contraceptives."
                    (AIA 3:4:1937)

2061. Page, Eleanor. THE PASSAVANT COTILLION—AND OTHERS. *Chicago Hist. 1972 2(2): 68-77.* The Passavant Cotillion and Christmas Ball was established in December 1949 to raise money for the Passavant Hospital. By 1971 the debutante presentation had raised nearly $2,000,000 for the hospital. Colleen Hargrave was responsible for having the idea of the cotillion accepted by the Passavant Woman's Aid Society. Other debutante parties date back to 1939. Based on primary sources; 8 photos.                                                      N. A. Kuntz

2062. Snook, Lois. THE FUTURE OF INTIMACY: A BIBLIO-GRAPHIC REPORT. *Lutheran Q. 1974 26(4): 383-394.* A socioreligious discussion on marriage and male-female relationships, with accompanying bibliographies.                                      S

2063. Sontag, Susan. THE THIRD WORLD OF WOMEN. *Partisan R. 1973 40(2): 180-206.* Cites the now familiar differences between "masculinity" and "femininity" as expressions of cultural values. The Industrial Revolution provided the basis for female liberation in two ways. Women who are truly liberated reject the ideology of unlimited growth (the creed of all industrial nations) and the same women seek true and genuine autonomy. States that "the very conception of sexuality is an instrument of repression." Terms of complete equality must exist at all levels of civilization and culture. One means to this equality is the abolition of the nuclear family. Concludes that a woman must be true to herself and still maintain solidarity with other women.
D. K. Pickens

2064. Ulrich, Laurel Thatcher. AND WOE UNTO THEM THAT ARE WITH CHILD IN THOSE DAYS. *Dialogue: A J. of Mormon Thought 1971 6(2): 41-46.* The author, a Mormon and a mother of four, considers the population explosion, zero population growth, family planning, and Mormonism.                                      S

2065. Wilkening, Eugene A. and Bharadwaj, Lakshmi K. ASPIRATIONS AND TASK INVOLVEMENT AS RELATED TO DECISION-MAKING AMONG FARM HUSBANDS AND WIVES. *Rural Sociol. 1968 33(1): 30-45.* "Measures of the dimensions of aspirations, allocation of tasks, and in decisions of husbands and wives are developed with the use of factor analysis. Interrelations among these dimensions indicate that the involvement of husbands and wives in farm, home, and family decisions is influenced by their task involvement and aspirations. Involvement in tasks is correlated with involvement in decisions in the same area with other factors controlled. Aspirations of wife and of husband in the home area tend to affect wife's involvement in farm decisions, but other aspirations have little effect on decision-making patterns."                                                        J

2066. Zube, Margaret J. CHANGING CONCEPTS OF MORALITY: 1948-69. *Social Forces 1972 50(3): 385-392.* "Quantitative content analysis of selected issues of the *Ladies' Home Journal* revealed shifts in value orientations - most notably from *future* to *present* and from *doing* to *being*. A qualitative analysis relates these findings to behavior changes and life-style as portrayed in these same issues and places particular emphasis on concepts of morality. Several trends are noted: (1) morality as a rather permanent inflexible set of standards becomes a more fluid concept which each defines for himself; (2) the use of psychological explanation for *understanding* behaviors becomes increasingly used to *justify* behaviors; (3) the importance of mental health for the good of family and society gives way to concern with psychological adjustments to meet the needs of the individual; (4) a not altogether clear relationship appears between the housewife's need to turn outward beyond home and family responsibility and her changing attitudes toward marriage."    J

## Marriage and the Family

### General

2067. Adams, Bert N. OCCUPATIONAL POSITION, MOBILITY, AND THE KIN OF ORIENTATION. *Am. Sociol. R. 1967 32(3): 364-377.* "This paper considers the influence of the middle-class achievement motif in American society upon adult relations, objective and subjective, with the kin of orientation, i.e., parents and siblings. In a sample of 799 young married residents of Greensboro, North Carolina, relations with one's father are more likely to be subjectively close if the *father* is middle-class, relations with the mother are closer if the *respondent* is middle-class, and relations with a sibling are seldom close unless the *sibling* is middle-class. Although there are variations by sex within these patterns, socialization and achievement - defined in middle-class terms - appear to be more crucial to relations between the kin of orientation than is intergenerational occupational mobility or stability. Simple frequency of interaction is an excellent indicator of residential distances and of the differential significance of parents and siblings. However, interaction frequency does not mirror subjective variations *within* these categories, since such feelings are mitigated by obligation, combination opportunities, and/or circumstances before they can be manifested interactionally."
J

2068. Adams, Robert Lynn and Mogey, John. MARRIAGE, MEMBERSHIP AND MOBILITY IN CHURCH AND SECT. *Sociol. Analysis 1967 28(4): 205-214.* A study of marriage records between 1943 and 1964 in five congregations of the Disciples of Chirst in Nashville, Tennessee, covered four major issues concerning marriage and the family: 1) the husband's church affiliation is more influential than the wife's when deciding religious affiliation, 2) liberal church doctrine influences the decision to leave whereas a conservative belief motivates one to join a church, 3) social class is not as influential in choosing a church as is theology, and 4) if both spouses join a new religious group after marriage they prefer a sect to a church. 5 tables, 11 notes.    K. Adelfang

2069. Baker, Katharine Gratwick. MOBILITY AND FOREIGN SERVICE WIVES. *Foreign Service J. 1976 53(2): 12-14, 27-29.* Discusses the views held by the wives of Foreign Service officers primarily in 1974 on the impact of their husband's occupational mobility on themselves and their families.

2070. Becker, Gary S. ON THE RELEVANCE OF THE NEW ECONOMICS OF THE FAMILY. *Am. Econ. R. 1974 64(2): 317-319.* Discusses new work in economics on the family in order to show the increasing relevancy of economic theory for the understanding of human behavior.

2071. Berger, Peter and Kellner, Hansfried. MARRIAGE AND THE CONSTRUCTION OF REALITY; AN EXERCISE IN THE MICROSOCIOLOGY OF KNOWLEDGE. *Diogenes [France] 1964 46: 1-24.* Examines the institution of marriage in the United States "as a social arrangement that creates for the individual the sort of order in which he can experience his life as making sense." In the characteristic circumstances of American society, two individuals bring differing sets of experience to the dramatic act of marriage which then provides the context, working through the medium of continuing conversation, for the structuring - or often restructuring - of the private sphere of life. This process, largely unperceived by the principals, serves as a framework for empirical study of the family and also as a "microsociological focus" of importance in the sociology of knowledge.          L. H. Legters

2072. Bettelheim, Bruno. UNTYING THE FAMILY. *Center Mag. 1976 9(5): 5-9.* Discusses social change in middle-class family structure in the 1970's, emphasizing parent-child relations and the changing role of women.

2073. Birdwhistell, Ray L. THE IDEALIZED MODEL OF THE AMERICAN FAMILY. *Social Casework 1970 51(4): 195-198.* Due to largely unattainable ideals about romantic love and child-rearing, many people fail as parents and spouses. Many in the "silent majority" are preoccupied with faltering marriages and strained parent-child relationships. The "generation gap" is one result of difficulties with the idealized model family. Such problems cannot be solved until the family is opened up and until lawmakers, clinicians, and moralists begin to accept the impossibility of these ideals, and to operate in other terms. Note.
M. A. Kaufman

2074. Blee, Ben W. PRESTIGE AND THE NAVY FAMILY. *U.S. Naval Inst. Pro. 1964 90(11): 58-65.* Asks for increased effort within and without the navy to give the navy man and his family a greater sense of prestige. Recommendations included.          W. C. Frank

2075. Bowerman, Charles E. and Elder, Glen H., Jr. VARIATIONS IN ADOLESCENT PERCEPTION OF FAMILY POWER STRUCTURE. *Am. Sociol. R. 1964 29(4): 551-567.* "Some studies of family structure have focused on the effects of the conjugal balance of power, while others have assessed the influence of parental power in the child-rearing relationship. Results obtained from these studies differ considerably, tending to create more confusion than clarity because researchers not infrequently fail to make explicit the relational referents of their concepts of family structure. This study examines the structure of marital, parental and parent-youth relations as perceived by a large sample of adolescents. Variations in the structure of each of these relationships are examined in relation to the adolescent's age, sex and social class, and structural models based on two or more of these relationship are constructed. The effects of the different family structural patterns on adolescent scholastic motivation and college plans and on parental affect are assessed." J

2076. Bowers, Donald W. and Hastings, Donald W. CHILDSPACING AND WIFE'S EMPLOYMENT STATUS AMONG 1940-41 UNIVERSITY OF UTAH GRADUATES. *Rocky Mountain Social Sci. J. 1970 7(2): 125-136.* Examines the factors of religion and wife's employment status as related to fertility and childspacing for a contrived population of University of Utah family units. A survey of 890 Utah alumni focused on 1) the differences in family size according to wife's employment status for Mormon and non-Mormon couples, and 2) intervals between marriage and first birth and between successive children according to couples' religious preference and wife's employment status. Fertility and childspacing patterns among working wives differed from their nonworking counterparts. Mormon couples, whether the wife worked or not, had higher fertility and shorter intervals between marriage and first birth than non-Mormons. The sequential relationship between the period wives worked and childspacing was not established. 10 tables, 13 notes. A. P. Young

2077. Boyers, Robert. THE WOMAN QUESTION AND THE DEATH OF THE FAMILY. *Dissent 1973 20(1): 57-66.*

2078. Browning, Harley L. TIMING OF OUR LIVES. *Transaction 1969 6(11): 22-27.* The increasing term of man's biological life will have profound social effects. In developing countries where the nuclear family is the norm, new family organizations may develop. Marriage may be delayed and children may be more widely spaced. In the United States there is little advantage to compressing education, marriage, and child-rearing into a small period of an ever-lengthening lifetime. If society encourages marriage to be delayed, it will have to find approved ways of diverting the sexual drive or will have to devise various types of marriage. 3 photos, biblio. A. Erlebacher

2079. Catton, William R., Jr. and Smircich, R. J. A COMPARISON OF MATHEMATICAL MODELS FOR THE EFFECT OF RESIDENTIAL PROPINQUITY ON MATE SELECTION. *Am. Sociol. R. 1964 29(4): 522-529.* The extent to which mate selection is limited by residential propinquity is greater than has been apparent in the usual presentation of a mere frequency distribution, but less than it should be according to the usual theoretical interpretation. In a sample of Seattle marriages, the usual propinquity pattern holds, but the data are better fitted by Zipf's $P_1P_2/D$ model than by Stouffer's intervening opportunites model or the model implied by the Katz-Hill "norm interaction" theory. Distance gradients in marriage rates thus seem to reflect an economy of time and energy, rather than competition between near and remote courtship opportunities, or operation of normative factors. It may therefore be more accurate to say that norms are enforceable because departures from them are rare for other reasons, rather than to explain homogamy or other conforming behavior as a result of norms. J

2080. Centers, Richard; Raven, Bertram H.; and Rodrigues, Aroldo. CONJUGAL POWER STRUCTURE: A RE-EXAMINATION. *Am. Sociol. R. 1971 36(2): 264-278.* "A representative sample of 776 husbands and wives in the Los Angeles area were interviewed regarding the relative power of husbands and wives in various decision areas, following the basic procedures utilized by Blood and Wolfe in their 1959 study of wives only, in Detroit. Essentially, these results paralleled those obtained by Blood and Wolfe, extending their findings to responses from husbands and in a different area. Husband power was greatest among Oriental couples and least among Negro couples; it decreases with age,

with length of marriage, and is less where a second marriage is involved; husband power increases with occupational status and educational level. The current study questions the effects of sampling of conjugal decision areas. With a somewhat more representative sampling of decisions, the distribution of power changes dramatically. Husband dominant families tend to show high authoritarianism scores for both husbands and wives. Least marital satisfaction is associated with wife dominance. While the current investigation centers on power relationships between husbands and wives, the basic approach can be extended to analysis in other types of groups." J

2081. Chaskel, Ruth. EFFECT OF MOBILITY ON FAMILY LIFE. *Social Work 1964 9(4): 83-91.* Shifting patterns of industry and automation, both industrial and agricultural, push thousands of Americans away from home. The American economy demands and creates a work force able and willing to move while our social habits and customs give mobility a negative value. The best adjustment made by families to the stresses of mobility are those characterized by adaptability, integration, affection between family members, good marital adjustment of husband and wife, companionable parent-child relationships, and family council type of control in decisions. The empirical experience in Travelers Aid indicates that the healthier the structure of the family, the more able are its members to cope with the problems of mobility. Individualized services will continue to be needed by those individuals and families whose inner organization is disturbed. W. L. Willigan

2082. Conger, John J. A WORLD THEY NEVER KNEW: THE FAMILY AND SOCIAL CHANGE. *Daedalus 1971 100(4): 1105-1138.* Examines changes in family life, the family's relationships to society, and the effects of these upon contemporary adolescents and their parents. Offers suggestions for society to fulfill its responsibilities to adolescents. 67 notes. W. L. Willigan

2083. Connor, John W. AMERICAN-JAPANESE MARRIAGES - HOW STABLE ARE THEY? *Pacific Historian 1969 13(1): 25-36.* Reports on a study of 20 American-Japanese marriages in 1965-66 in the Sacramento area. Five Japanese women whose marriages had failed were also interviewed. Despite the gloomy prognoses of sociologists, the marriages are at least as stable and the couples as well-adjusted as are the marriages and adjustments of American Caucasian couples of comparable marital experience and social-economic backgrounds. Factors explaining this situation include a similarity in value orientations between the Japanese and American middle classes, declining anti-Oriental prejudice, the stabilizing effect for the wife in moving from the constrictive Japanese traditional family to the more permissive American conjugal family, and the strong selective factor involved in those who would enter such a marriage (i.e., only rather stubborn and independent people would enter a marriage in which initially they had to contend with official disapproval and the disapproval of their friends). 21 notes. F. I. Murphy

2084. Coser, Rose Laub. STAY HOME, LITTLE SHEBA: ON PLACEMENT, DISPLACEMENT, AND SOCIAL CHANGE. *Social Problems 1975 22(4): 470-480.* The busing of school children and federal support for child-care centers have the potential to create radical change by altering the social placement function of the American family —parents losing control of their children. Traveling away from home threatens the class structure and creates social disruption. Strong negative reactions from the public and government testify to the radical implications of the two issues. Notes, biblio. A. M. Osur

2085. Davies, James C. THE FAMILY'S ROLE IN POLITICAL SOCIALIZATION. *Ann. of the Am. Acad. of Pol. and Social Sci. 1965 361: 10-19.* In the normal family the father's role as breadwinner means that his influence is important politically. The child develops early ties to the wielders and visible symbols of public authority, represented by the president of the United States, the local policeman, and the flag. In America the process of political socialization is basically complete by the age of 13. Adolescence may bring change from political identification with parents, especially in highly politicized families where politics are available as an object of protest. Crisis (such as the foreign policy crisis in America of the 1960's) "is likely to reactivate intrafamilial tensions as the youth diverge from familial political loyalties and outlook." 23 notes. E. P. Stickney

2086.  Elder, Glen H., Jr. and Bowerman, Charles E.  FAMILY STRUCTURE AND CHILD-REARING PATTERNS: THE EFFECT OF FAMILY SIZE AND SEX COMPOSITION.  *Am. Sociol. R. 1963 28(6): 891-905.* Small group research has shown that the instrumental and emotional dimensions of group life vary considerably with the number of members in the group. Although many of the findings from these studies as well as from Bossard's investigations of child development in large and small families are highly suggestive with respect to the effects of family size on child rearing, very little research has focused on this problem. Effects of the number and sex of children on paternal involvement and behavior-control methods are investigated. It was hypothesized that paternal involvement and external behavior control would occur more often in large families than in small and more often in families composed of boys rather than girls. This hypothesis was elaborated according to known variations in child-rearing by the sex and social class of children. Data from a sample of 1261 Protestant seventh-grade students provided considerable support for the hypothesis.                    J

2087.  Elmer, M. C.  THE FAMILY AND OUR SOCIAL HERITAGE.  *Social Sci. 1965 40(1): 3-6.* Holds that the perpetuation of the social heritage is chiefly the concern of the family. The fact that the household groups have lost many economic activities has actually increased the social importance of the family, whose most distinctive and universal function has been the socialization of its members. The family gives the plan and pattern by which the tapestry of the social order is woven.                    M. Small

2088.  Erickson, Ann  CLOTHING THE URBAN AMERICAN FAMILY: HOW MUCH FOR WHOM?  *Monthly Labor R. 1968 91(1): 14-19.* Clothing expenditures for the urban American family member generally increase from infancy to late teens and early twenties and then decline. Women's clothing bills are larger than men's at all ages. The author analyzes clothing expenditures by sex, age, family income, and region. 3 tables, 12 notes.                    A. P. Young

2089.  Furstenberg, Frank F., Jr.  THE TRANSMISSION OF MOBILITY ORIENTATION IN THE FAMILY.  *Social Forces 1971 49(4): 595-603.* There is a need to test the widely accepted assumption that the child's attitudes are acquired directly from his parents. Previous research may have exaggerated the extent to which attitudes are transmitted in the family. Using a sample of 466 parent-child pairs, it was discovered that there was a low association between family members' mobility orientations. Various conditions within the family had a noticeable effect on the level of parent-child agreement. Interpretation of the results suggests general conditions that may affect the success of parental socialization.                    J

2090.  Gardiner, Harry W.; Singh, U. P.; and D'Orazio, Donald.  THE LIBERATED WOMAN IN THREE CULTURES: MARITAL-ROLE PREFERENCES IN THAILAND, INDIA AND THE UNITED STATES.  *Human Organization 1974 33(4): 413-416.*

2091.  Gaylin, Ned L.  THE FAMILY IS DEAD—LONG LIVE THE FAMILY.  *Youth & Soc. 1971 3(1): 60-79.* Due to the decline of community, the family's functions are more and more taken over by institutions. Child rearing becomes an assembly line operation, adapting people for an industrial society. The family has not failed society, but rather has conformed to society's new demands where only vertical, peer-group relationships are desired. Biblio.                    J. H. Sweetland

2092.  Goldman, Nathan.  SOCIAL BREAKDOWN.  *Ann. of the Am. Acad. of Pol. and Social Sci. 1967 373: 156-179.* "Although problems of family breakdown, drug and alcohol addiction, mental disorder, suicide, and sexual deviation appear to be increasing, the available data are either so deficient or so incomplete that accurate appraisal of the situation is impossible. However, some of these problems seem to be more than maladjustments in themselves. To achieve our goal of maximizing the social health of American society, we must consider these problems as indicators of strain, and focus our national resources on the reduction of these strains. We need to improve the collection of data on these indicators, and to devise new ones, in order to identify and locate those situations which interfere with the ideal functioning of our social system. A significant aspect of social breakdown is seen in the inability of the society to mobilize for an attack on situations which it has defined as

undesirable. Our concern should be with the identification of these processes as well as the underlying social strains of which social problems are overt indicators. We must establish standard definitions or criteria of social problems and increase the scope and accuracy of our data-collection. Information-gathering on the local or state level would need to be co-ordinated on a nationwide basis to provide a useful set of indicators of the social state of the nation."                    J

2093.  Guillory, Ferrel.  FAMILY PLANNING IN LOUISIANA.  *New South 1971 26(4): 29-34.* Reports on the success of Family Health Inc.'s statewide family planning program for the indigent of Louisiana, which was established in 1966 by its director, Joseph D. Beasley, and which will serve as a model for similar projects.

2094.  Hauser, Philip M.  DEMOGRAPHY AND ECOLOGY.  *Ann. of the Am. Acad. of Pol. and Social Sci. 1965 362: 129-138.* A survey of literature since 1959. Recent advances are: increasing emphasis on crosscultural and comparative research; regional studies; investigations of the typology of urban areas; advances in methodology; greatly enriched data provided by the U.S. 1960 Censuses of Population and Housing; the interlinking of experimental family planning programs and fertility studies; and the advance in mathematical demography including the increased use of the computer. "It has become increasingly clear that economic planning must take population factors into account if it is to be realistic and that population control would contribute materially to economic advance in the developing areas." 31 notes.                    E. P. Stickney

2095.  Jarvie, I. C.  RECENT FILMS ABOUT MARRIAGE.  *J. of Popular Film 1973 2(3): 278-299.* Discusses the development since the mid-1960's of the "comedy of sexual manners crossed with the examination of married life."                    S

2096.  Kiefert, Robert M. and Dixon, George I. J.  A PRELIMINARY STUDY OF THE CHILDLESS COUPLE.  *Rocky Mountain Social Sci. J. 1968 5(1): 119-128.* It is noted that in the literature concerning the "population explosion" and fertility limitation, little attention is given to making childless marriages socially acceptable. They surveyed a sample of childless women and women with children in a Wisconsin city. They found that the societal norm that children are an essential part of marriage did operate in decisions to have children and that some dissonance was reflected in the childless women surveyed. 9 tables, 6 notes.                    R. F. Allen

2097.  Leary, John P.  WOMAN IN AMERICAN SOCIETY TODAY.  *Thought 1967 42(164): 112-120.* Reconsiders the changing and widening role of woman in American society today manifested by her needs, her desires, and her deep and gracious potencies. "The most unchallenged monopoly of woman, however, is in the field of motherhood. This is not merely because she is biologically equipped to carry and give birth to the child but also because she is able to rear the child, especially in the important early years, with appreciation of all the nuances of character, the almost elemental dispositions that are developed before the child is six. The mother presides at and develops these shapings....The wife-mother-homemaker role scarcely wants defense." After discussing the philosophy of the double breadwinner - mother and father both working to obtain "the little extras which can be at once so unnecessary and so legitimate" - the author is convinced that "the boredom and vacancy of home, once children are off to school, must be...an appalling experience. However attractive the furniture and whatever challenges a garden or an afghan may afford, much of this can remain simply contrived occupation, busy work in the strict sense of that word."                    D. D. Cameron

2098.  Leslie, Gerald R. and Johnsen, Kathryn P.  CHANGED PERCEPTIONS OF THE MATERNAL ROLE.  *Am. Sociol. R. 1963 28(6): 919-928.* The validity of using maternal behavior in one area of childrearing to indicate general maternal orientation or change over time is questioned. Findings from this study of 265 college-educated mothers and their perceptions of their own mothers' behavior indicate that 1) the change toward more permissiveness varies with the area of childrearing studied; and 2) the change varies from role concept to different measures of role performance. The amount of change is linked both to social mobility and to grandmothers' childrearing practices. Generalization from infant care practices to childrearing generally and to the personality characteristics desired in children is especially hazardous and should not be continued.                                                                J

2099.  Liddle, Gordon P.  THE ROLE OF PARENTS AND FAMILY LIFE.  *J. of Negro Educ. 1964 33(3): 311-317.* Parental support is necessary for a successful school program for socially disadvantaged children and youth. School personnel must assume the initative in communicating with parents and securing their interest.

S. C. Pearson, Jr.

2100.  Linden, Sophie.  THE PRIVATE CONTRACT IN MARRIAGE.  *Social Service R. 1969 43(2): 155-164.* Explores the instrumental nature of disturbed marriages in which each partner tries to use the other to get something he feels is lacking in himself.                          S

2101.  Lingren, Herbert G.  PERCEPTION CHANGES OF FARM IMMIGRANTS BEFORE AND AFTER MIGRATION.  *Rural Sociol. 1969 34(2): 223-228.* Studies the perceptions of the productive young farm migrants (here defined as heads of households under 38 years of age) in regard to selected economic, personal, family, and community opportunities, and how these perceptions changed with nonfarm living. Terminal interviews were made in 1961 for the Iowa Farm and Home Development Study with 21 husband-wife pairs who had been established in farming by 1956, but who had changed their place of residence and had left farming for nonfarming employment. Eight factors were selected as being involved in the decisionmaking process about whether or not to migrate: 1) net income; 2) opportunity to get ahead; 3) freedom to make decisions; 4) amount of leisure time; 5) social standing; 6) opportunities for children; 7) religious opportunities; and 8) moral character of the community. There was a significant group change in perception in only two of these eight variables: freedom to make decisions and amount of leisure time. About the same percent of men and women changed their perceptions toward the farm as changed toward nonfarm. Based on a paper delivered at the Rural Sociological Society meeting in Miami, August 1966; 3 tables, 4 notes, biblio.               D. D. Cameron

2102.  McEaddy, Beverly Johnson.  WOMEN WHO HEAD FAMILIES: A SOCIOECONOMIC ANALYSIS.  *Monthly Labor R. 1976 99(6): 3-9.* Analyzes the results of a Special Labor Force Report (1975), detailing the increase of families headed by women since 1960, giving characteristics of age, marital status, and labor force participation.

2103.  Mead, Margaret.  FUTURE FAMILY.  *Trans-action 1971 8(11): 50-53.* Based on an address given to Barnard students and parents, 12 February 1970.                                                           S

2104.  Monahan, Thomas P.  ARE INTERRACIAL MARRIAGES REALLY LESS STABLE?  *Social Forces 1970 48(4): 461-472.* "There is an insufficiency of demographic knowledge about interracial marriage in the continental United States, and also a contradiction of facts and viewpoints. Without much statistical confirmation it has been argued that mixed-race marriages are and are not increasing, and that Negro-White marriages, in particular, are and are not more stable than homogamous ones. An analysis of a set of data on the State of Iowa covering almost 30 years, although of small size, discloses that mixed Negro marriages have increased in the last decade. The divorce rate for Negro-Negro couples is about twice as high as that for whites. But the divorce ratios of other minority couples, and their mixed marriages with whites, are higher or lower than the average, depending upon the particular minority involved. Most remarkably, the information for Iowa indicates that as regards divorce Negro-white marriages are more stable than Negro-Negro marriages, and Negro husbands with white wives have a lower divorce outcome than do white couples."                          J

2105.  Morgan, James N.  SOME PILOT STUDIES OF COMMUNICATION AND CONSENSUS IN THE FAMILY.  *Public Opinion Q. 1968 32(1): 113-121.* A study to test procedures for investigating the extent to which husband and wife communicate, accurately perceive the other person, and predict future actions. The author focuses on economic activities since these are explicit and the outcome is more easily defined. In the first study data was obtained from a survey of a small sample of married couples in Detroit in 1963, with two interviewers interviewing husband and wife separately but simultaneously, and a follow-up by a single interviewer six months later to determine what action had taken

place. The author concludes that "separate and simultaneous personal interviews with a national sample would be difficult and expensive." In the second experiment data were provided by simple paper and pencil questionnaires administered by a single interviewer who asked general questions verbally. This procedure, though it generated less revealing data than the simultaneous interviews, was recommended for its relative economy and ease of administration. 7 notes.                       D. J. Trickey

2106.  Myers, George C.  THE ELUSIVE MALE: SOME METHODOLOGICAL NOTES ON SURVEY RESEARCH DESIGN.  *Public Opinion Q. 1969 33(2): 254-259.* Discusses impact of "decisions made in a field investigation carried out in San Juan, Puerto Rico in the summer of 1966..." to interview both male and female householders. The result was that it was possible to complete interviews with both spouses in just slightly over half of the eligible households, thus casting "doubt on the feasibility of designing research in which several household members are to be interviewed, unless special efforts are made to implement the survey." The survey was designed to investigate economic, demographic, and social implications of urban housing policy, encompassing public housing, slums, lower-class areas, and lower-middle class areas. 2 tables, 2 notes.

D. J. Trickey

2107.  Neil, J. Meredith.  COMMUNES AND FAMILIES: REVIEW ESSAY.  *J. of Popular Culture 1973 6(4): 865-870.* Reviews 10 books published 1969-72 on communes, counter culture, and attempts to found an alternative society.                                                       S

2108.  Noble, Trevor.  FAMILY BREAKDOWN AND SOCIAL NETWORKS.  *British J. of Sociol. 1970 21(2): 135-150.* A study of stability of families in relation to the connectedness of their social networks, hypothesizing that family breakdown 1) will be more frequent in urban areas than rural areas, 2) will be more frequent in urban areas where social networks are more likely to be loose-knit than close-knit, 3) will be most frequent in socioeconomic status groups in which loose-knit social networks are most common. This would suppose that families of rural workers would be less prone to breakdown than those of urban workers, that in the United States breakdown will be less frequent in the higher socioeconomic status groups, but in Britain among the lower socioeconomic status groups. Examination of the data from Britain and the United States shows that 1) the hypothesis for urban-rural difference is valid for England and Wales, but instability of U.S. farm laborers' families limits the validity of the generalization for the United States, 2) divorced men and women concentrate in areas where it is likely that social networks are loose-knit, 3) in Britain the relationship between breakdown and social status is not clear and is more likely to exist between breakdown and types of work conditions and consequent residential patterns. 5 tables, 36 notes, biblio.                              D. H. Murdoch

2109.  Potvin, Raymond H. and Burch, Thomas K.  FERTILITY, IDEAL FAMILY-SIZE AND RELIGIOUS ORIENTATION AMONG U.S. CATHOLICS.  *Sociol. Analysis 1968 29(1): 29-34.* Questions the traditional values attributed to the concept "religiousness." Draws data from a nationally representative sample of 1,028 married Catholic women interviewed by the National Opinion Research Center in 1964. Methods of factor analysis reveal that little association exists between "religiousness" and actual family size. "Conformity" and "nonconformity" may be more significant than "religiousness." Scales 28 items, such as, "The world is basically a dangerous place where there is much evil and sin," and "The Church teaches that a good Christian ought to think about the next life and not worry about fighting against poverty and injustice in this life." 4 tables, 9 notes.                A. S. Freedman

2110.  Presser, Harriet B.  AGE DIFFERENCES BETWEEN SPOUSES: TRENDS, PATTERNS AND SOCIAL IMPLICATIONS.  *Am. Behavioral Scientist 1975 19(2): 190-205.* Discusses some of the effects of the fact that in most marriages in American society the man is older than the woman.

2111.  Rodgers, Roy H.  SOME FACTORS ASSOCIATED WITH HOMOGENEOUS ROLE PATTERNS IN FAMILY LIFE CYCLE CAREERS.  *Pacific Sociological R. 1964 7(1): 38-48.* Presents some of the findings which are associated with family life cycle career patterns. "By joining together the social-psychological conceptualization of the family as a unity of interacting personalities with the structure-function idea of the family as a social system, and adding the dimension of change and development over time, the view of the family as a semi-closed system of interacting personalities with changing patterns of behavior over its life history emerged." The author brings these two streams together by further specifying the conceptual formulations of family development, deriving a set of family life-cycle stages based on the conceptual framework, and utilizing these stages in the analysis of data which were gathered as part of a larger project dealing with family decisionmaking carried on by the Minnesota Family Study Center at the University of Minnesota in 1958 and 1959. Strong relationships were found between size of family and the family life-cycle careers. The relationship between spacing of children was also statistically quite strong. "In analyzing the relationship of family life cycle careers to the variables of age at marriage, historical date of marriage, and socio-economic status, the findings...fell in the direction which could be expected on the basis of the conceptual framework developed." 2 exhibits, 3 figs., 4 tables, 11 notes.

D. D. Cameron

2112. Rubin, Zick. DO AMERICAN WOMEN MARRY UP? *Am. Sociol. R. 1968 33(5): 750-760.* "It has frequently been assumed that American women tend to marry men whose socioeconomic origins are higher than their own. One rationale for this assumption is the notion that the woman's romantic orientation is more adaptive and directive than that of the man. A review of the evidence reveals that the assumption has not been adequately tested, however. The present study approached the question by applying several statistical techniques to large-sample data on husbands' and wives' fathers' occupations. No overall tendency for American women to marry up was found. If only the two highest occupational categories are considered, however, women apparently do tend to marry up. In addition, farmers' daughters are more likely than farmers' sons to marry the children of white-collar workers."    J

2113. Rushdoony, Rousas J. THE FAMILY. *Freeman 1973 23(7): 429-432.* The foundation of the social order, the family, is under attack, but there is no cause for alarm; the attack on the family is merely the last hapless charge of statism. "The approaching collapse of the age of humanism and the state will see the strong revival of familism, and the United States is already giving evidence of this." Reprinted from *Applied Christianity* (December 1972).    D. A. Yanchisin

2114. Scott, John Finley. THE AMERICAN COLLEGE SORORITY: ITS ROLE IN CLASS AND ETHNIC ENDOGAMY. *Am. Sociol. R. 1965 30(4): 515-527.* "The college sorority, though academically disesteemed, is sociologically relevant as an agent of ascriptive groups, maintaining normative controls over courtship which in simpler societies requires less specialized expression. Norms of endogamy persist in industrial societies, applying more strongly to women than to men, and being harder to maintain in higher strata. Religion- and class-specific schools provide control, but most students today attend heterogeneous public campuses. Since nubile appeal is high at collegiate ages, control by postponing marriage would disadvantage women. Ascriptive control therefore calls for an organization which simultaneously will discourage improper marriage and encourage proper marriage; further it must operate where opportunities and temptations for exogamy and hypogamy are strong and at a physical remove from those most committed to control." 35 notes.    J

2115. Smith, Elmer L. AMISH NAMES. *Names 1968 16(2): 105-110.* Amish family genealogies are almost inextricably intertwined after more than 250 years of intermarriage among members of the sect. This is due to the restriction of the selection of a mate to within the sect and to the lack of missionary and evangelical activities which would bring in converts and, therefore, new names. Discusses the problems caused by the limited number of given names for men and women. Middle names are generally the mother's maiden name. To attempt to remedy this, the father's first name is often used in conjunction with the first name of his child for identification purposes, or nicknames are adopted. 8 notes.

P. McClure

2116. Spraic, Mark A. SEXUAL SELECTION AND THE LAW. *Colorado Q. 1972 20(4): 516-529.* In the near future, prospective parents will be able to control, with certainty, the sex of their offspring. Reactions to this possibility vary. Amitai Etzioni has argued that there will be a significant surplus of males and a resultant coarsening and degradation

of society. Edward Pohlman, on the other hand, feels that families would tend to develop a one-to-one ratio of males and females. Legal control of use of sex selection will be difficult, and it will be best to wait and see what does happen. There is a great potential for the abuse of sex control, but the best legal approach at present is "hands off."    B. A. Storey

2117. Steinmetz, Suzanne K. and Straus, Murray A. THE FAMILY AS CRADLE OF VIOLENCE. *Society 1973 10(6): 50-56.*

2118. Sussman, Marvin B. FAMILY SYSTEMS IN THE 1970'S: ANALYSIS, POLICIES, AND PROGRAMS. *Ann. of the Am. Acad. of Pol. and Social Sci. 1971 (396): 40-56.* "This paper contains a brief review of some of the salient discoveries and theoretical formulations which provide the most powerful explanation of the issues and problems faced by different types of families in their dealings with institutional systems and bureaucratic organizations. Specifically covered are variant family forms; structural properties of kin family systems; family/organizational linkages; major tasks and functions of families; the kin network as a mediating-linking system; and changes in the internal role structure of the family. The second section deals with practical applications, needed policies, programs, and strategies for increasing the level of competence of human service systems to meet the expectations, capabilities, interests, and aspirations of members of variant family forms found in pluralistic societies."    J

2119. Theodorson, George A. ROMANTICISM AND MOTIVATION TO MARRY IN THE UNITED STATES, SINGAPORE, BURMA, AND INDIA. *Social Forces 1965 44(1): 17-26.* "Attitudes toward marriage of 3,847 American, Singapore Chinese, Chinese, Burmese, and Indian students are analyzed to determine whether there is evidence of acceptance of the American type romantic orientation to marriage among the most highly educated and Westernized classes in Chinese Singapore, Burma, and India. It is found that the three groups of Asian respondents while all showing a persistence of a contractual orientation to marriage may be ranked by degree of contractualism. This ranking is related to the interaction of two analytical variables - contractualism of the traditional culture and degree of cultural change. Motivation to marry in the four cultures is then analyzed, and found to follow the same rank order as degree of romanticism."    J

2120. Udry, J. Richard. SEX AND FAMILY LIFE. *Ann. of the Am. Acad. of Pol. and Social Sci. 1968 376: 25-35.* "Sex plays a fundamentally different role in the lives of women than it does in the lives of men. A partial explanation of this may be that men are sexually more conditionable by their environment. Men and women also attach different meanings to sex. Not only is sex a more important determinant in a man's decision to marry, but also it is a more important factor in his evaluation of his marriage. Sexual behavior and sexual values are derivative for women. Emotional factors are more responsible for a woman's satisfaction with her marriage. These factors are irrelevant, however, for the highly segregated marriages of the lower class. The role of parents in shaping the adult sexual behvaior of their children is not clear. The only apparent, important considerations are their provision of the socioeconomic and religious backgrounds for the development of sexual attitudes and behavior."    J

2121. Useem, Ruth Hill. THE AMERICAN FAMILY IN INDIA. *Ann. of the Am. Acad. of Pol. and Social Sci. 1966 368: 132-145.* "In India, overseas American men under government, business, missionary, and cultural-exchange sponsorship typically are married. Although their wives perform many of the same functions abroad as at home, the cultural, social, and physical contexts are quite divergent. In addition, their 'dependency' and 'representational' statuses mean that family life and work life of husbands are closely intertwined. There are three areas which are unusually productive of family stresses early in the overseas assignment which ramify into the effectiveness of the primary employee: unavailability of housing and protracted stays in hotels; difficulties in interacting with servants because of the gross cultural, social, and linguistic disparities between the American wife and household employees; and illness precipitated by high exposure to hazards for which they have not yet developed routinized health practices. Wives, the local American communities, and the organizational sponsors have developed reasonably satisfactory 'third-cultural' solutions which in time are utilized by most families to meet these stress-producing circumstances. A fourth area, inadequate educational facilities for children, because it is least subject to individual resolution or even the action of a single organization, remains a major obstacle in the retention of American fathers most qualified for work roles in Idnia, especially as their children approach the secondary school age."                                                                      J

2122. Veevers, J. E. VOLUNTARILY CHILDLESS WIVES: AN EXPLORATORY STUDY. *Sociol. and Social Res. 1973 57(3): 356-366.* "In-depth unstructured interviews with a non-random sample of 52 voluntarily childless wives suggest that most remain childless through a series of postponements of child-bearing, involving at least four separate stages. Informal sanctioning of childless couples is most intense during the fourth and fifth years of marriage. Factors related to satisfaction with childlessness are discussed in terms of the symbolic importance of adoption and of supportive ideologies."                                          J

2123. Watson, Walter B. and Barth, Ernest A. T. QUESTIONABLE ASSUMPTIONS IN THE THEORY OF SOCIAL STRATIFICATION. *Pacific Sociological R. 1964 7(1): 10-16.* A review of the literature and some recent empirical evidence concerning the adequacy of following two present-day theories of stratification: 1) that the family is a unit of equivalent evaluation on all systems of social stratification; and 2) that occupation should be used as a basis for class placement. The logical and empirical justifications for these two propositions are questioned, and the implications of what seem to be inadequacies in reasoning are investigated. "Several logical deficiencies in the assumptions that the family is a solidary unit of equivalent evaluation and that the husband's occupation is the principal index of evaluation have been noted. The patriarchal model of family organization has also been questioned. Data on women in the labor force and with occupations at levels different from those of their husbands suggest empirical weaknesses in these postulates as well. It is suggested that in urban industrial society the degree of role differentiation and sole insulation is such that here may be many situations in which the family is not a solidary unit of equivalent evaluation." 5 tables, 40 notes.                                                     D. D. Cameron

2124. Wilkening, Eugene A. and Guerrero, Sylvia. CONSENSUS IN ASPIRATIONS FOR FARM IMPROVEMENT AND ADOPTION OF FARM PRACTICES. *Rural Sociol. 1969 34(2): 182-196.* "This study tests the combined effect of farm husbands' and wives' aspirations for farm improvement on the adoption of different types of improved farm practices. The sample involved 500 Wisconsin farm couples. The results show that consensus in aspirations between husband and wife is associated with higher adoption than when only one spouse has high aspirations. This association holds for the adoption of most practices when income is controlled. The hypothesis that practice adoption is higher when the husband has high and the wife has low aspirations for farm improvement than when the opposite is true is not supported."       J

2125. —. [BENEFITS OF WOMEN'S EDUCATION WITHIN MARRIAGE]. *J. of Pol. Econ. 1974 82(2, part II): 57-75.*
Benham, Lee. BENEFITS OF WOMEN'S EDUCATION WITHIN MARRIAGE, *pp. 57-71.*
Welch, Finis. COMMENT, *pp. 72-75.*
Proceedings of a conference on marriage, family, human capital, and fertility on 4-5 June, 1973.                                             S

2126. —. [MARRIAGE IN AMERICA]. *J. of Pol. Econ. 1974 82(2, part II): 34-56.*
Freiden, Alan. THE UNITED STATES MARRIAGE MARKET, *pp. 34-53.*
Wallace, T. Dudley. COMMENT, *pp. 54-56.*
Proceedings of a conference on marriage, family, human capital, and fertility on 4-5 June, 1973.                                             S

## Fertility

2127. Beegle, J. Allan. SOCIAL STRUCTURE AND CHANGING FERTILITY OF THE FARM POPULATION. *Rural Sociol. 1966 31(4): 415-427.* "Relatively large rural-urban differences persisted in the United States in 1960 despite the well-documented narrowing of many of the usual fertility differentials. Higher rural-farm than urban fertility

levels were found for all age groups of married women in all census divisions, as measured by the number of children ever-born per 1,000 married women aged 15 to 45. Nine independent variables were successful in explaining a substantial proportion of the variation in rural-farm fertility levels of whites and nonwhites. Location of the farm population with respect to a metropolitan area was the most useful 'explanatory' variable in most of the analyses. It is suggested that rural-urban fertility differences will continue to diminish as the two sectors become even less differentiated. The apparent strength of the fertility differential in 1960, it is contended, is related to the farm family structure which is not yet obsolete in a large sector of American agriculture."                      J

2128. Blake, J. REPRODUCTIVE IDEALS AND EDUCATIONAL ATTAINMENT AMONG WHITE AMERICANS, 1943-60. *Population Studies [Great Britain] 1967 21(2): 159-174.* "Would the persistent inverse relation between educational attainment and family size in the United States be removed if actual fertility were equal to ideal? Data on ideal family size from ten national surveys among white Americans of both sexes (from 1943 to 1960) show that grade-school level respondents have higher ideals than the more educated even when age, religion affiliation, and farm residence are used as controls. Comparison of these ideals with the actual family size or ever-fertile woman in the United States indicates that, on the average, the actual family size of all major educational groups falls below the ideal, but the college-educated are farthest from their ideal. If this group lessened the gap between actual and ideal family size, the educational differential in fertility would decrease, but at the price of increasing the rate of population growth." 12 tables, 7 notes.
                                                                         J

2129. Bouvier, Leon F. THE FERTILITY OF RHODE ISLAND CATHOLICS: 1968-1969. *Sociol. Analysis 1973 34(2): 124-139.* "This is an analysis of fertility differentials between Catholics and non-Catholics in Rhode Island. Representative samples of the population were derived and interviews conducted in 1968 and 1969. Although Catholics exhibit higher fertility expectation than do non-Catholics, differences are smaller than those observed in earlier national surveys. Furthermore, Catholics indicate an increasing tendency to practice birth control, though not to the extent of non-Catholics. It is suggested that the recent emergence of American Catholics into the 'power structure' has resulted in a loss of minority-status feeling. This may partially explain the developing convergence noted between the two groups. However, a strong religious ideology, limiting birth control to the rhythm method, continues to influence many Catholics and this is preventing a complete convergence in fertility behavior."                                                      J

2130. Coombs, Lola Gene and Freedman, Ronald. USE OF TELEPHONE INTERVIEWS IN A LONGITUDINAL FERTILITY STUDY. *Public Opinion Q. 1964 28(1): 112-117.* Describes efforts and results of reinterviewing 1,300 women in a Detroit area fertility study.
                                                                  B. E. Swanson

2131. Cutright, P. and Galle, O. THE EFFECT OF ILLEGITIMACY ON U.S. GENERAL FERTILITY RATES AND POPULATION GROWTH. *Population Studies [Great Britain] 1973 27(3): 515-526.* "Following analysis of the contribution of illegitimacy rates to changes in US general fertility rates after 1940 this paper examines the likely impact of births conceived out of wedlock on completed fertility. Comparison of a proxy measure of completed fertility among ever-married mothers who differed in the timing of their first birth relatively to their date of marriage suggested that births conceived out of wedlock may inflate the completed fertility of whites and non-whites by 1.2 and 2.6% respectively. The estimate for non-whites is reduced to about zero, if the lower-than-average fertility of never-married mothers is seen as a consequence of illegitimacy. The large difference in the proportion of first births conceived out of wedlock between white and non-white mothers does not explain higher non-white fertility. Some implications of these findings are discussed."                                          J

2132. Frejka, T. REFLECTIONS ON THE DEMOGRAPHIC CONDITIONS NEEDED TO ESTABLISH A U. S. STATIONARY POPULATION GROWTH. *Population Studies [Great Britain] 1968 22(3): 379-398.* "It is assumed that in the long run U. S. population growth will have to cease, as otherwise life will become physically impossible. Various hypothetical possibilities of achieving such a type of development are investigated. Alternatives of reproduction rate trends are considered in terms of alternatives of interactions of assumed age-specific fertility and mortality trends and these are computed and evaluated. The various computations then indicate the nature of childbearing attitudes and behaviour which the 'average population' would have to adopt in order to achieve the desired stationary population growth after a certain period of time. . . . " Appendix; 15 notes.　　　J

2133.　Groat, H. Theodore and Neal, Arthur G.　SOCIAL PSYCHO-LOGICAL CORRELATES OF URBAN FERTILITY.　Am. Sociol. R. 1967 32(6): 945-959. "From a sample of women who delivered a child in the Toledo metropolitan area during 1962, measures of meaningless-ness, powerlessness, normlessness, and social isolation were related to fertility. Positive correlations between alienation variables and fertility were hypothesized within religious and educational categories. Meaning-lessness and normlessness were found to differentiate fertility significantly in the hypothesized direction, within both religious and educational cate-gories. Powerlessness was significantly related to fertility as hypothesized among Catholics, but not among Protestants. While exceptions to the high alienation-high fertility hypotheses were noted, the overall findings indicated the relevance of specific alienation variables in differentiating fertility within the broad categories of religion and socioeconomic status."　　　J

2134.　Harrison, Beverly.　WHEN FRUITFULNESS AND BLESSEDNESS DIVERGE.　Religion in Life 1972 41(4): 480-496. Speaks to the population crisis from a woman's perspective. 18 notes.　　　W. H. Mulligan

2135.　James, W. H.　THE FECUNDABILITY OF U.S. WOMEN. Population Studies [Great Britain] 1973 27(3): 493-500. "It seems likely that mean marital fecundability increases with wife's age until about age 21. Thereafter it may be supposed to decline slowly: there would seem no biological reason for positing a plateau across an appreciable range of wives' ages. Arithmetic mean fecundability at marriage of U.S. non-sterile couples is estimated at about 0.15; it is suggested that this value declines roughly linearly to the value of about 0.04 at age 40. It is suggested that the decline is due to a decline in coital rates and (possibly) to an increase in unrecognised spontaneous abortion."　　　J

2136.　Lee, Eun Sul.　TRENDS IN FERTILITY DIFFERENTIALS IN KENTUCKY.　Rural Sociol. 1972 37(3): 389-400. "Changes in fertility differentials among different segments of Kentucky's population are analyzed on the basis of the available statistics from the United States censuses of 1940, 1950, and 1960. Child-woman ratios, adjusted for un-derenumeration and mortality of children and standardized for age of woman, were used to examine the differentials and trends. Fertility differ-entials among counties have been diminishing. The rural-urban differen-tial has been decreasing. The traditional inverse relationships between fertility and socioeconomic variables have been weakening both among urban and rural populations. A new positive relationship emerges be-tween fertility and income among urban populations. Diminution of fer-tility differentials among different segments of Kentucky's population may well be a transitional phenomenon indicating that a new type of population is evolving through social and economic change in the state. The evidence of a positive relationship between fertility and income may be an indication of the future population of the state."　　　J

2137.　Lloyd, Cynthia B.　AN ECONOMIC ANALYSIS OF THE IMPACT OF GOVERNMENT ON FERTILITY: SOME EXAMPLES FROM THE DEVELOPED COUNTRIES.　Public Policy 1974 22(4): 489-512. Many governmental activities have unconsidered population implications. Child subsidies, which may take such forms as income tax deductions, cash payments, or free public education, reduce the direct costs of children. Laws which discriminate against a woman's entry into the labor market reduce the indirect costs of children. In their haste to emulate industrialized countries, developing nations have adopted or re-tained measures which have undesired effects upon their birth rates. Those aspects of the economic environment which constrain family size must be considered and investigated as part of the analysis of a policy's alternatives. Mentions the US throughout. Based on unpublished statis-tics and secondary sources; 8 tables, 51 notes, appendix.　　　S. Bruntjen

2138.　Macisco, John J., Jr.　FERTILITY OF WHITE MIGRANT WOMEN, U.S. 1960: A STREAM ANALYSIS.　Rural Sociol. 1968 33(4): 474-479. Presents a stream analysis of the fertility of three types of migrant women: 1) nonmetropolitan to metropolitan; 2) metropolitan to nonmetropolitan; and 3) metropolitan to different metropolitan. The migration data were derived from a comparison between place of resi-dence in April 1955 and place of residence in April 1960, the time of the Census of Population. This study shows that the cumulative fertility rate of white ever-married women who entered or left a Standard Metropoli-tan Statistical Area between 1955 and 1960 is lower than their nonmi-grant counterparts; that women who migrated from nonmetropolitan to metropolitan areas had the highest standardized fertility; that the metro-politan to metropolitan area migrants had the lowest; and that metropoli-tan to nonmetropolitan migrants were intermediate in their fertility. The migrants had lower fertility through age 29 when a "crossover" took place, again suggesting that a nonmetropolitan residence may have an effect on fertility. 7 notes, 3 tables.　　　D. D. Cameron

2139.　Mileti, Dennis S.　CHANGE RATIOS IN AGE-SPECIFIC PERCENT CONTRIBUTIONS TO FERTILITY.　Pacific Sociol. R. 1974 17(1): 3-26. Analyzes the effect of women in different age groups on the decline of fertility since 1957.　　　S

2140.　Neal, Arthur G. and Groat, H. Theodore.　ALIENATION CORRELATES OF CATHOLIC FERTILITY.　Am. J. of Sociol. 1970 76(3): 460-473. "Alienation profiles are used as a means of unifying a series of cognitive conditions related to motivational and control- relevant dimensions of family size among a sample of Catholic mothers. Through cumulative scaling of powerlessness, meaninglessness, and normlessness, fertility differentials by alienation profiles significantly exceed differen-tials obtained by the separate alienation measures as well as by combina-tions of religion and socioeconomic status. An exception to the high alienation-high fertility relationship is noted for social isolation, where the level of isolation is inversely related to the number of children."　　　J

2141.　Nuesse, C. Joseph.　RECENT CATHOLIC FERTILITY IN RURAL WISCONSIN.　Rural Sociol. 1963 28(4): 379-393. "Analysis of age-standardized child-woman ratios of rural townships in northeast-ern Wisconsin suggests that religious differentials in fertility were at least maintained and perhaps enhanced in importance during the period 1940-60, a period marked by a notable rise in the level of fertility of the general population. Although the controls which can be applied to economic and other factors are so limited that definitive conclusions cannot be drawn, when townships in a fifteen-county region, a five-county subregion, and two selected categories are dichotomized as either more or less than 50 percent Catholic, the ratios of the population of the townships more than 50 percent Catholic are found to be higher than those of corresponding classes of the regional population for each census year, and the ratios of the populations of the townships less than 50 percent Catholic are found to be lower. The increased divergence between the two classes of town-ships within some categories and the character of the trend observed in all categories suggest renewal of the importance of the religious factor in fertility. Comparisons of predominantly Catholic populations of Belgian, Bohemian, Dutch, German, Polish, and mixed stock show that rural Catholic fertility continues to be subculturally differentiated, however."　　　J

2142.　Perrucci, Carolyn Cummings.　SOCIAL ORIGINS, MOBIL-ITY PATTERNS AND FERTILITY.　Am. Sociol. R. 1967 32(4): 615-625. "This study is an examination of social origins, education level, and career mobility in relation to a series of events concerning fertility within marriage; namely, timing of marriage, timing of first three births within marriage, and family size. Data were analyzed for a sample of 1,029 engineering graduates from two large west coast universities. Respon-dents' educational level was positively related to the time interval between college graduation and marriage and the time interval between college graduation and birth of first child. In general, intergenerational mobility preceded marriage and initial reproductive behavior. An intercohort com-parison of graduates revealed, however, that more recent terminal bache-lor's degree recipients tended to marry and begin families prior to graduation. Social origins played a small part in fertility behavior - in the timing of the second child. The finding that career mobility was positively related to time interval between college graduation and birth of first child as well as inversely related to average birthdate of second child indicated some support for the fertility/mobility hypothesis for engineers during the early career years."

J

2143. Polgar, S. and Hiday, Virginia A. THE EFFECT OF ADDITIONAL BIRTH ON LOW-INCOME URBAN FAMILIES. *Population Studies [Great Britain] 1974 28(3): 463-472.* "The effects of the birth of an additional child to families living in poverty areas of New York City are studied in this paper. Surveys conducted by the National Opinion Research Center in 1965 and 1967 provided the data in a panel of parous or married women of childbearing age. Controlling for the number of children in the family in 1965, the non-occurrence of an additional birth in the following two years was found to have a significant effect on current income, savings, reliance on public assistance, general ability to plan and organize one's household, and wife's employment. No significant effects were found with respect to possession of consumer durables or attending a school or training course. While many claims have been made about the beneficial effects of family planning on family welfare, this study is among a very small number where such effects are empirically documented."

J

2144. Potter, R. G. and Sakoda, J. M. FAMILY PLANNING AND FECUNDITY. *Population Studies [Great Britain] 1967 20(3): 311-328.* "A computerized probability model of family-building, Fermod, is described and then utilized in an investigation of relations between family planning and fecundity as applying to white couples of the contemporary United States. Models of this type that formulate reproductive performance as a stochastic process permit one to explore relations that are not directly observable and in this manner to secure at least partial answers to questions not subject to investigation by survey research alone. Two main questions are addressed concerning the dependence of family planning success upon fecundity: (1) How quickly does spacing control deteriorate when natural fecundability is taken at progressively lower values? (2) What is the distribution of unsought births among couples of average fecundity when they practise contraception with specified effectiveness and have stipulated spacing and family size goals?" 7 tables, 26 notes.

J

2145. Ritchey, P. Neal. EFFECTS OF MARITAL STATUS ON THE FERTILITY OF RURAL-URBAN AND URBAN-RURAL MIGRANTS. *Rural Sociol. 1973 38(1): 26-35.* "Existing knowledge on the relationship between migration and fertility has been based on studies of married women. Furthermore, research has focused on the fertility of rural-urban migrants and has tended to ignore fertility among urban-rural migrants. These two factual gaps have limited the ability to assess the contribution made by the fertility of migrants to either population growth or the urban-rural differential in fertility. This paper reports on data from the 1967 Survey of Economic Opportunity. Determining the intervening effects of marital status on the relation between migration and fertility was the study's major objective. Among white, married women 20 to 44 years of age, rural-urban migrants have only slightly higher fertility than that of indigenous urban women, which slightly increases the rate of population growth in urban areas. Urban-rural migrants, on the other hand, have lower fertility than indigenous rural women and consequently serve to lower the growth rate in rural areas. The relative effect upon the growth rates at place of destination is greater for urban-rural than for rural-urban migrants. When the analysis is not restricted to married women, the impact of migration on both urban and rural fertility is considerably changed. In general, migrants were more likely than indigenous sending and receiving populations to have been ever-married and be married and living with spouse—including being in a sustained first marriage and being remarried. Proportionately more migrants and less indigenous women bear children. Therefore, when we examine fertility of all women, irrespective of marital status, the childbearing of rural-urban migrants makes a moderate contribution to increasing the population growth rate in urban areas. In rural areas, when women's marital status is ignored, the presence of urban-rural migrants sustains the rate of population growth— partially offsetting the lowering effect of the fertility of the rural indigenous women."

J

2146. Ritchey, P. Neal. THE FERTILITY OF NEGROES WITHOUT SOUTHERN RURAL EXPERIENCE: A RE-EXAMINATION OF THE 1960 GAF STUDY FINDINGS WITH 1967 SEO DATA. *Population Studies [Great Britain] 1973 27(1): 127-134.* "A major finding of the 1960 'Growth of American Families' (GAF) study was that whites and blacks without southern rural experience had similar fertility. This paper reports on a re-examination of this finding with a substantially larger black sample. Data from the 1967 Survey of Economic Opportunity demonstrated that the residence background classification utilized in the GAF study defeated, in part, the attempt to remove the effects of rural experience on fertility. Indigenous urban blacks had 25% higher fertility than indigenous urban whites. The fertility of urban black migrants out of the rural South was sharply curtailed in contrast to those remaining in the rural South. Although urban blacks of southern rural background had nominally higher fertility than indigenous urban blacks, the difference was neither statistically nor substantively significant. These results demand a re-ordering of the interpretation of the impact that migration has on urban black fertility and the white-black differential in fertility."

J

2147. Slesinger, Doris P. THE RELATIONSHIP OF FERTILITY TO MEASURES OF METROPOLITAN DOMINANCE: A NEW LOOK. *Rural Sociol. 1974 39(3): 350-361.* "Examines the relationship of fertility to three measures of metropolitan dominance: size of place, distance from central city, and the Stoeckel-Beegle size-distance index. Using data from the 1965 National Fertility Study, the number of children ever born to married women under 45 is examined. Fertility differentials exist within all three dominance measures, with rural farm areas having high fertility and central city residents low fertility. However, when duration of marriage, religion, work experience, and education are controlled in a multiple regression model, very little additional variance was explained by metropolitan dominance measures. It is suggested that fertility differentials are due to the characteristics of the women living in these areas rather than to the influence of the city on the hinterland."

J

2148. Sweetser, Frank L. and Piepponen, Paavo. POSTWAR FERTILITY TRENDS AND THEIR CONSEQUENCES IN FINLAND AND THE UNITED STATES. *J. of Social Hist. 1967 1(2): 101-118.* An effort to analyze the large age-cohorts of the postwar period in the United States and Finland in relation to changing fertility patterns and to social and economic causes and consequences. Both nations experienced a similar postwar fertility rise during the late 1940's, which was followed by: 1) a progressive decline in fertility for Finland throughout the 1950's and into the mid-1960's; and 2) a progressive rise in the U.S. fertility until the later 1950's, followed by a high plateau and then a marked decline from 1961 to 1965. The relationship of demographic variables, especially changing age structure, is emphasized. The authors conclude that, just as age structure affects fertility, so too do sustained periods of low fertility (as in the 1930's) and high fertility affect age structure. Socioeconomic conditions, such as levels of economic activity and the inception and termination of wars, are related to fertility because of the effect they have on patterns of family formation and the norms and values that determine reproductive behavior in societies where birth control is widely practiced. The author stresses the fact that periods of high fertility have far-reaching consequences in the social, economic, and political history of nations for three generations. 4 notes.

N. M. Drescher

2149. Wells, R. V. FAMILY SIZE AND FERTILITY CONTROL IN EIGHTEENTH-CENTURY AMERICA: A STUDY OF QUAKER FAMILIES. *Population Studies [Great Britain] 1971 25(1, pt. 1): 73-82.* "This is a study of 276 Quaker families of the eighteenth century, whose records of births, marriages and deaths are to be found in registers kept in the area of New York, New Jersey and Pennsylvania. The average number of children born per married couple was found to be declining by the end of the eighteenth century. This reduction in family size was caused primarily by a decline in childbearing within marriage. An analysis of age-specific marital fertility rates, the ages of mothers at the birth of their last child, and of the length of the last birth interval indicates that deliberate family limitation was responsible for much of the decline. It seems apparent, however, that the fertility rates of the Quakers studied in the late eighteenth and early nineteenth centuries were considerably lower than those found in the general American population at the same time."

J

2150. —. [POPULATION AND THE AMERICAN FUTURE: A REVIEW SYMPOSIUM]. *Social Sci. Q. 1972 53(3): 445-473.*

Browning, Harley L. and Poston, Dudley L., Jr. DISCUSSION AND INTRODUCTION, *pp. 445-451.*
Spengler, Joseph J. NUMBERS VERSUS WELFARE, *pp. 452-458.*
Dyck, Arthur J. ETHICAL ASSUMPTIONS AND IMPLICATIONS OF THE POPULATION COMMISSION'S REPORT, *pp. 459-464.*
Edwards, Ozzie. THE COMMISSION'S RECOMMENDATIONS FROM THE STANDPOINT OF MINORITIES, *pp. 465-469.*
Gustavus, Susan O. COMMISSION REPORT: IMPLICATIONS FOR WOMEN, *pp. 470-473.*
*Population and the American Future: The Report of The Commission on Population Growth and the American Future* is the subject of the symposium given the lead position in this issue. Harley L. Browning and Dudley L. Poston, Jr. . . . note how the report is a landmark in the American posture toward population change and describe President Nixon's "limited and selective" response to it.

J

## Childcare

2151. Haase, Ronald W. CHILD CARE TRAINING CENTER - RESTON, VIRGINIA. *Contemporary Educ. 1969 40(3): 159-165.* Architects plan to build a child care center whose major functions will be the "training and supervision of family care mothers, nursery and day care teachers and recreation leaders." Illus., drawings.

E. R. Beauchamp

2152. Hill, C. Russell. GUARANTEEING INCOME AND ENCOURAGING CHILD CARE. *R. of Social Econ. 1975 33(1): 15-25.*

2153. Johnson, Scott R. MODEL CITIES. *Hist. J. of Western Massachusetts 1972 1(1): 37-46.* The Model Cities program is the antithesis of welfare and uncoordinated bureaucracy. By targeting a few slum neighborhoods, giving high priorities to creating a wide range of housing, and sponsoring a variety of childcare centers, planners hope "to break the poverty-breeding cycle." Based on interviews with members of the Springfield Planning Board; 25 notes.

S. S. Sprague

2154. Mead, Margaret. WORKING MOTHERS AND THEIR CHILDREN. *Catholic World 1970 212(1268): 78-82.* Discusses the special needs of infants and children under the age of three, and how these are better handled by the family than by day nurseries.

S

2155. Mueller, Jeanne; Phillips, Michael; and Goldman, Joseph. DAY CARE—SOME UNANSWERED QUESTIONS. *Public Welfare 1971 29(2): 202-206.* Discusses questions concerning administrative capabilities, consumer preferences, and recruitment and selection methods aimed at improving child day care services.

S

2156. Steiner, Gilbert Y. DAY CARE CENTERS: HYPE OR HOPE? *Trans-action 1971 8(9/10): 50-57.* Excerpt from the author's *The State of Welfare* (Washington, D.C.: Brookings Institution, 1971).

S

2157. Stone, Michael and Kestenbaum, Clarice. MATERNAL DEPRIVATION IN CHILDREN OF THE WEALTHY: A PARADOX IN SOCIOECONOMIC VS. PSYCHOLOGICAL CLASS. *Hist. of Childhood Q. 1974 2(1): 79-106.* Examines 17 case histories involving prolonged maternal absence or a strict, aloof mother (maternal deprivation) in wealthy families. Such deprivation led to severe emotional and psychological debilities. The cases were predominantly female, probably a result of lower expectations for female offspring from upper class parents. Recent interpretations of the history of childhood may be flawed by reliance on elite sources: the elite may perpetuate maternal deprivation more than others. Based on case histories and secondary sources; biblio.

R. E. Butchart

2158. Taveggia, Thomas C. and Thomas, Ellen M. LATCHKEY CHILDREN. *Pacific Sociol. R. 1974 17(1): 27-34.* Synthesizes 24 studies comparing children of working and nonworking mothers.

S

## Divorce

2159. Day, Lincoln H. PATTERNS OF DIVORCE IN AUSTRALIA AND THE UNITED STATES. *Am. Sociol. R. 1964 29(4): 509-522.* "The incidence and patterning of divorce in Australia differs substantially from that in the United States: Australians resort to divorce less frequently than do Americans, and generally only after a much longer duration of marriage. It is suggested that this arises from differences between the two countries in 1) the availability of divorce (in both existential and normative senses), 2) the availability of alternative 'remedies' for marital disharmony, and 3) the extent of marital disharmony itself."

J

2160. Gallagher, John T. NO-FAULT DIVORCE IN DELAWARE. *Am. Bar. Assoc. J. 1973 59(8): 873-876.* "Although it is not generally known, Delaware has had a no-fault divorce statute since 1957, and incompatibility has been the main ground for divorce since 1968. Although conservatives still have doubts, a majority of Delawareans appear to believe that there is little value in laws that compel spouses to remain married to each other. The Delaware example is a good one for other states."

J

2161. Pang, Henry and Hanson, Sue Marie. HIGHEST DIVORCE RATES IN WESTERN UNITED STATES. *Sociol. and Social Res. 1968 52(2): 228-236.* "The problem of the high divorce rate in the Western United States has been evident for decades. It is believed to be associated with regional, mobility, demographic, marital, socioeconomic, and miscellaneous factors. The article is concerned with a development of a frame of reference to examine some of the possible interrelated reasons for the high divorce rate in the West. Regional differences in divorce rates are not likely to disappear in the near future."

J

2162. Wadlington, Walter. DIVORCE WITHOUT FAULT WITHOUT PERJURY. *Virginia Law R. 1966 52(1): 32-87.* The recent increase in resort to migratory divorce has prompted many states to review their divorce laws. The author conducts a broad review of the various grounds for divorce and argues that they are outmoded and unrealistic. This is the case because statutory grounds for divorce are too often based on the concept of "fault." The requirement of fault, he argues, leads to perjury, and it fails to allow that marriages can break down in fact without specific fault on the part of either spouse. The author advocates a "breakdown" proceeding to dissolve marriages when the parties cannot be reconciled. This would be accomplished through nonfault separation statutes which have already been tested in several states and which have been found to operate satisfactorily. Based on State law reports, State statutes and codes, legal journals, and newspapers; 237 notes.

G. P. Smith

## Sex Roles

### General

2163. Beuf, Ann. DOCTOR, LAWYER, HOUSEHOLD DRUDGE. *J. of Communication 1974 24(2): 142-145.* Examines sex-role perception of 63 children aged three to six in a 1973 study which seeks to determine whether children born since the beginning of the Women's Liberation Movement have different sex-role perceptions than pre-movement era children.

2164. Boles, Jacqueline and Garbin, Albeno P. THE STRIP CLUB AND STRIPPER-CUSTOMER PATTERNS OF INTERACTION. *Sociol. and Social Res. 1974 58(2): 136-144.* "The major purpose of this article is to further understanding of the social organization of the strip club by relating the effects of environmental and spatial factors on stripper-customer relationships. The data were derived from observations at nine strip clubs in a large southeastern city, and interviews with 51 strippers at these clubs. Findings illuminate and support the major thesis of the article, that the interactions between strippers and customers are characterized by a counterfeiting of intimacy based upon inauthentic relations."

J

2165. Broverman, Inge K.; Vogel, Susan Raymond; Broverman, Donald M.; Clarkson, Frank E.; and Rosenkrantz, Paul S. SEX-ROLE STEREOTYPES: A CURRENT APPRAISAL. *J. of Social Issues 1972 28(2): 59-78.* Discusses the effect of these stereotypes on women, 1960's.

2166. Cameron, Paul. PERSONALITY DIFFERENCES BETWEEN TYPICAL URBAN NEGROES AND WHITES. *J. of Negro Educ. 1971 40(1): 66-75.* Presents a detailed survey, conducted in 1968, dealing with neuroticism, extraversion, ego strength, a lie scale, religiosity, hostility, and masculinity-femininity. Concludes that Negroes and whites appear more similar psychologically than dissimilar.

2167. Cothran, Kay L. TALKING TRASH IN THE OKEFENOKEE SWAMP RIM, GEORGIA. *J. of Am. Folklore 1974 87(346): 340-356.* "Talking Trash" is a male leisure-time social activity of lower Georgia's "cracker culture." Small talk, personal experience, whoppers, tall tales, relations of practical joking, and tales of killings and lynchings evaluate human relationships and behavior and offer a character-strutting fantasy realm which sneers at middle-class values. Women enjoy hearing of foolish males, but find the wild pranks disconcerting. Based on field-work and secondary sources; 17 notes. W. D. Piersen

2168. Dean, Dwight G.; Braito, Rita; Powers, Edward A.; and Bruton, Brent. CULTURAL CONTRADICTIONS AND SEX ROLES REVISITED: A REPLICATION AND A REASSESSMENT. *Sociol. Q. 1975 16(2): 207-215.* The Komarovsky-Wallin thesis of women's pretending inferiority in dating situations was replicated (287 women) and is challenged. Questions are raised as to the appropriate collapsing of categories of responses and the incidence of pretended inferiority in relation to number of dates. Data from a comparison sample of men (318) are also presented. Evidence does not sustain the belief of women's pretensions of inferiority. J

2169. Dixon, John W., Jr. PARADIGMS OF SEXUALITY. *Anglican Theological R. 1974 56(2): 151-169.* An understanding of woman is requisite to an understanding of sexual paradigms in our cultural history. S

2170. Domenach, Jean-Marie. NOTES D'UN RETOUR EN AMERIQUE [Notes on a return to America]. *Esprit [France] 1966 34(11): 614-625.* Expresses a Frenchman's views of the United States in the summer of 1966, taking account of social customs and attitudes toward such matters as university education, the war in Vietnam, sex, and crime, especially as they differ from French attitudes. M. H. Quinlan

2171. Dorn, Dean S. IDEALIZED SEX ROLES AMONG YOUNG PEOPLE. *J. of Human Relations 1970 18(1): 789-797.* By statistical analysis of a random sampling of college men and women at a western college, the author attempts to determine attitudes toward the role of young women in contemporary society. Concludes from the evidence that there has been a decline in the "double standard" as it was known in the 1950's, that the definition of women's role is increasingly showing a trend toward establishing a career, and that there still exists much confusion and ambivalence about the behavior of the female. Based on secondary sources; 12 notes. W. A. Wiegand

2172. Doubilet, Ann. A WOMAN'S PLACE. *New Generation 1969 51(4): 3-8.* The roots of the oppression of women lie in the roles women play as wives and mothers in the family structure.

2173. Fengler, Alfred P. and Wood, Vivian. CONTINUITY BETWEEN THE GENERATIONS: DIFFERENTIAL INFLUENCE OF MOTHERS AND FATHERS. *Youth and Soc. 1973 4(3): 359-372.* Discusses sex role influences on student attitudes. S

2174. Ferber, Marianne Abeles and Huber, Joan Althaus. SEX OF STUDENT AND INSTRUCTOR: A STUDY OF STUDENT BIAS. *Am. J. of Sociol. 1975 80(4): 949-963.* Fails to substantiate the theory that women sabotage themselves by a collective antiwoman bias. S

2175. Fernández Cintrón, Celia and Rivera Quintero, Marcia. BASES DE LA SOCIEDAD SEXISTA EN PUERTO RICO [The foundations of sexist society in Puerto Rico]. *R. Interamericana [Puerto Rico] 1974 4(2): 239-245.* Puerto Rican females currently occupy a position subordinate to males. The family and schools pass on traditional values concerning women to each generation, but male-dominated economic, religious, and political institutions also play a role in perpetuating sex discrimination. Only direct action by Puerto Rican women can change this situation. J. A. Lewis

2176. Haft, Marilyn G. HUSTLING FOR RIGHTS. *Civil Liberties R. 1974 1(2): 8-26.* "The prostitutes announced they didn't want to be rehabilitated. Calling the stunned feminists hypocrites, they asked how many women could honestly say they didn't prostitute themselves in marriage." J

2177. Heilbrun, Carolyn. FURTHER NOTES TOWARD A RECOGNITION OF ANDROGYNY. *Women's Studies 1974 2(2): 143-149.* Author deals with the responses to her book, *Toward a Recognition of Androgyny,* 1973, and to her use of the word "androgyny." Discusses the significance of sexual polarization in American society, defines the concept of androgyny, suggests how this concept helps to bring a new perspective to the study of literature, and anticipates a time when an anti-androgynous world and the word "androgyny" itself disappear. A. E. Wiederrecht

2178. Hein, Hilde S. WOMEN: ON LIBERATION FROM EXPECTATIONS. *Soundings [Nashville, TN] 1974 57(3): 354-362.* Sex stereotypes unjustly cast women into predetermined roles.

2179. Henneman, Sandra. WOMEN'S IMPOSSIBLE DREAM? *Can. Dimension 1975 10(8): 11-14.* Societal and cultural conditioning which forces women into "powerless, statusless, nameless positions" is an extension of early childhood sex-typing and can be eliminated only by first eliminating the early imposition of sex roles. S

2180. Hertz, Robert N. FOREIGN STUDENTS AND THE AMERICAN COED. *Phylon 1964 25(1): 65-71.* Building a case largely upon his personal knowledge of foreign students in America, Hertz argues that the majority of such students "are mainly observers of a social world in which they do not actually participate" and that they often form faulty impressions which sometimes lead to embarrassment and bitterness. S. C. Pearson, Jr.

2181. Hunt, Janet G. and Hunt, Larry L. THE SEXUAL MYSTIQUE: A COMMON DIMENSION OF RACIAL AND SEXUAL STRATIFICATION. *Sociol. and Social Res. 1975 59(3): 231-242.* In this essay low-status black males and "high status" white females are compared, and some propositions concerning similar personal consequences of racial and sexual stratification are presented. The view formulated draws extensively on the ideas of Elliot Liebow (1967) and Betty Friedan (1963) and suggests that, while many dimensions of their circumstances and the content of their personal identities may differ radically, low-status black males and high-status white females may evidence similar responses to structural barriers to achievement on the level of identity integration and in the compensatory nature of sex-role identification. J

2182. Iglitzin, Lynne B. A CASE STUDY IN PATRIARCHAL POLITICS: WOMEN ON WELFARE. *Am. Behavioral Scientist 1974 17(4): 487-506.* Seattle study concludes that public welfare reinforces the socialization of women into feminine stereotypes. S

2183. Kinzer, Nora Scott. THE BEAUTY CULT. *Center Mag. 1974 7(6): 2-9.* Observations on the beauty cult and concern with aging among American women in the 20th century. S

2184. Knowles, Lyle and Poorkaj, Houshang. ATTITUDES AND BEHAVIOR ON VIEWING SEXUAL ACTIVITY IN PUBLIC PLACES. *Sociol. and Social Res. 1974 58(2): 130-135.* "This study examines the attitudes of adults regarding the availability for viewing of sexually explicit activities in public places of entertainment, and the relationship of these attitudes to the frequency with which the subjects reportedly attended such activities within the previous year. Although a positive association was found between permissiveness and viewing participation, inconsistent behavioral and attitudinal trends appeared with respect to more explicit activities and attendance." J

2185. Larson, Richard F. and Leslie, Gerald R. PRESTIGE INFLU-ENCES IN SERIOUS DATING RELATIONSHIPS OF UNIVER-SITY STUDENTS. *Social Forces 1968 47(2): 195-202.* "The idea of a status hierarchy governing the serious dating relationships of university students is subjected to definitive test. The data, from a state university population, support the assertion. High agreement, within and between sexes, is found on the ranking of fraternities and sororities. Drops, pinnings, and engagements all tend to occur disproportionately among persons from similar prestige levels. The findings hold both for Greek-affiliated and for independent students. The degree of status homogamy tends to increase with the seriousness of the involvement. Interpretations of the findings are offered."                    J

2186. Lee, Marcia Manning. WHY FEW WOMEN HOLD PUBLIC OFFICE: DEMOCRACY AND SEXUAL ROLES. *Pol. Sci. Q. 1976 91(2): 297-314.* Argues that the percentage of women holding elected public office is unlikely to increase by a substantial amount in the future unless radical changes occur in current sexual role assignments, particularly those related to child care.                    J

2187. Lee, Patrick H. MALE AND FEMALE TEACHERS IN ELE-MENTARY SCHOOLS: AN ECOLOGICAL ANALYSIS. *Teachers College Record 1973 75(1): 79-98.* Studies the preponderance of female teachers in elementary education, and the socializing impact on students.                    S

2188. Mason, Karen Oppenheim and Bumpass, Larry L. U.S. WOM-EN'S SEX-ROLE IDEOLOGY, 1970. *Am. J. of Sociol. 1975 80(5): 1212-1219.* Recently collected sex-role attitude data are analyzed with a view to understanding the ideological bases of specific attitudes. Correlation analysis suggests that women do not currently organize all sex-role attitudes along a single dimension, although their outlook toward the sex-based familial division of labor is supported by beliefs about the needs of children and women. Regression analysis of attitudes in relation to personal characteristics suggests that attitudes are at least partly based on group norms or values.                    J

2189. Michel, Andrée. WORKING WIVES AND FAMILY IN-TERACTION IN FRENCH AND AMERICAN FAMILIES. *Internat. J. of Comparative Sociol. [Canada] 1970 11(2): 156-165.* Family interaction patterns in France and the United States, as measured by budget management, husband's authority, household task performances, and family planning, show a greater trend toward equality when the wife works.                    P. Gustafson

2190. Phillips, Derek L. and Segal, Bernard E. SEXUAL STATUS AND PSYCHIATRIC SYMPTOMS. *Am. Sociol. R. 1969 34(1): 58-72.* "This paper is concerned with testing the hypothesis that women will report more psychiatric symptoms than will men with an equal number of physical illnesses. Our hypothesis arises from an assessment of the societal definitions of what is 'appropriate' or 'inappropriate' behavior for someone occupying the status of male or female. In our view, men are expected to be less expressive than women in their emotional behavior. Analysis of data collected from a sample of 278 adults in 1965 and 1966 provides strong support for the hypothesis. On two indices consisting of what are judged to be psychological and psychophysiological symptoms, a greater percentage of women than men have 'high' scores. Two other indices, containing physiological and ambiguous items, show a tendency for men to have slightly higher scores. Since the first two indices contain 15 items and the other two only 7, not unexpectedly women are higher than men on the over-all mental health inventory. This pattern is revealed in the analysis of data for both 1965 and 1966, and is also shown in analysis of 'turnover' during the one-year period. A further finding is that women are more likely to seek medical care than are men with the same number of physical illnesses and similar psychiatric symptoms."                    J

2191. Phillips, Derek L. and Clancy, Kevin J. SOME EFFECTS OF "SOCIAL DESIRABILITY" IN SURVEY STUDIES. *Am. J. of Sociol. 1972 77(5): 921-940.* "This paper is concerned with social desirability as a source of bias and invalidity in survey studies. Two components of social desirability—'trait desirability' and 'need for social approval'—are examined to assess the extent to which they affect people's responses to several sociological measures (e.g., happiness, religiosity). This analysis reveals that both components of a social-desirability re-

sponse set, while generally unrelated to one another, are independently related to our dependent variables, people's responses on the various measures. The more important of the two components, trait desirability, is then examined with regard to its effect on the relationship between people's sexual status and the dependent variables. This introduction to the analysis of trait desirability as a test factor tends to specify both the magnitude and the direction of the original relationships involving sexual status. Finally, the results are discussed with regard to their implications for the validity of various sociological measures and the validity of the sociological investigator's findings."                    J

2192. Powers, Edward A.; Braito, Rita; and Dean, Dwight G. CULTURAL CONTRADICTIONS AND SEX ROLES: FACT OR ARTI-FACT? *Youth and Soc. 1974 6(1): 113-120.* Re-examines traditional sociological tenets regarding conflicts in sex roles of college women.                    S

2193. Rachlin, Susan Kessler and Vogt, Glenda L. SEX ROLES AS PRESENTED TO CHILDREN BY COLORING BOOKS. *J. of Popular Culture 1974 8(3): 549-556.*

2194. Reichert, William O. WOMAN, VIOLENCE AND SOCIAL ORDER IN AMERICA. *Centennial R. 1971 15(1): 1-22.* Argues that an imbalance exists in American society which causes men to "brutalize and overpower femininity." The opposite was true in the Middle Ages, when feminine qualities under the auspices of the Church had a civilizing effect. The Church's influence was overthrown and women made their peace with men on men's terms, thus losing out to the seekers of power. "America has entered its own dark ages." Presents the views of Henry Adams, Moses Harman, Lois Waisbrooker, and Karl Stern, all of whom deplored the decline of the role of women in society. Men lack the feminine qualities of poetry and art. Instead, the advanced standing of American technology indicates an opposite trend, and even the study of political science is concerned only with power. One reason for the brutality and violence of America is that woman has allowed herself to become a sex symbol. But there is hope, since today's youths do not shun the feminine qualities of poetry and art, and do not mask themselves in the masculine qualities of their fathers. The most basic need is to eliminate the masculine element in the political realm, and to bring in the feminine qualities of "compassion and reconciliation." It is time to "cease worshipping at the shrine of masculine power."                    A. R. Stoesen

2195. Riedl, Norbert F. and Buckles, Carol K. HOUSE CUSTOMS AND BELIEFS IN EAST TENNESSEE. *Tennessee Folklore Soc. Bull. 1975 41(2): 47-56.* Poses and attempts to answer questions in four broad categories: building a house, entering and leaving a house, life crises and the house, and housecleaning.                    S

2196. Rosenfeld, Lawrence B. and Christie, Vickie R. SEX AND PERSUASIBILITY REVISITED. *Western Speech 1974 38(4): 244-253.* "It is futile to attempt to conclude that one sex is more persuasible than another based upon the present study and other available research."                    S

2197. Saario, Terry N.; Jacklin, Carol Nagy; and Tittle, Carol Kehr. SEX ROLE STEREOTYPING IN THE PUBLIC SCHOOLS. *Harvard Educ. R. 1973 43(3): 386-416.* Based on their study of elementary school basal readers, educational achievement tests, and differential curricular requirements for males and females, the authors argue that schools exert a powerful and limiting influence on the development of sex roles by defining specific attitudes, modes of acting, and opportunities as appropriate for boys and girls, which limit the choices open to each sex. Sex role research needs to better understand androgynous behavior which is representative of neither maleness nor femaleness, and, starting with that understanding, to avoid stereotypical perceptions of male and female behavior. Fairness and equity demand rejection of restrictive stereotypes and acceptance of diversity and flexibility in a definition of sex roles. 11 notes, biblio.                    J. Herbst

2198. Sennholz, Hans F. ARE WE MARXIANS NOW? *Freeman 1972 22(8): 451-460.* While Marxism represents an alien ideology for most Americans, contemporary thought in the United States is determined by principles similar to Marx's concepts about the inevitability of social conflict, business concentration, and world outlook. A variant of

Marx's exploitation theory is readily apparent in American attitudes toward the struggle of economic interests, labor relations, generation differences, and racial and sexual conflicts. Long-standing American opposition to monopoly and colonialism agrees with the views of Marx.
D. A. Yanchisin

2199.  Skipper, James K., Jr. and McCaghy, Charles H.  RESPONDENTS' INTRUSION UPON THE SITUATION: THE PROBLEM OF INTERVIEWING SUBJECTS WITH SPECIAL QUALITIES. *Sociol. Q. 1972 13(2): 237-243.* Researchers have long been aware that when they become part of the system they are investigating, their own behavior may affect the behavior they wish to study. Little data has been collected on the effect of respondents on the researcher and the consequences of this on the research process. The problem is described and analyzed in this paper. We contend that respondents who have special qualities may intrude upon the researcher's role and make it difficult for him to collect necessary data. An illustration is presented from the authors' study of stripteasers.                                                    J

2200.  Smith, Paul M., Jr.  A DESCRIPTIVE SELF-CONCEPT OF HIGH SCHOOL COUNSELORS.  *J. of Negro Educ. 1963 32(2): 179-182.* Basing his findings on a 1961 study of 31 male and 31 female high school counselors, the author observes that the self concepts of high school counselors are generally positive and that the sex role is a dominant factor in framing such concepts. While many descriptive adjectives were chosen by both male and female counselors, men emphasized fairminded and responsible while women emphasized kind and sympathetic as descriptive of themselves.                               S. C. Pearson, Jr.

2201.  Spaulding, Charles B.  THE ROMANTIC LOVE COMPLEX IN AMERICAN CULTURE.  *Sociol. and Social Research 1970 55(1): 82-100.* "Analysis of questionnaires completed by freshman college students suggests that the acceptance of the Romantic Love Complex is somewhat more strongly associated with the acceptance of traditional conservative cultural values than with personality variables. There is, however, some tendency for male romantics to be weak and disturbed and for such women to be strong and outgoing. Male romantics also tend to accept domestic values and to resist certain nonmasculine values."   J

2202.  Steinmann, Anne.  THE AMBIVALENT WOMAN.  *New Generation 1969 51(4): 29-32.* Argues for the resolution of conflicting cultural ideals which prevent human beings from accepting the double-edged aspects of their natures—both submissive and dominant—and force them into male and female roles.

2203.  Toby, Jackson.  VIOLENCE AND THE MASCULINE IDEAL: SOME QUALITATIVE DATA.  *Ann. of the Am. Acad. of Pol. and Social Sci. 1966 364: 19-27.* "Given the family structure common in urban industrial societies, it is less easy for boys to grow up confident of their fundamental masculinity than for boys in the extended families of preliterate societies. One response to doubts about masculinity is compulsive masculinity: an exaggerated insistance on characteristics differentiating males from females. Superior strength and a readiness to exhibit it obviously fill the specifications. This analysis explains why violence, though punishable by law and condemned by custom, nevertheless remains a clandestine masculine ideal in Western culture. The assumptions of this ideal are mostly explicitly formulated in certain subcultures within the larger culture - and especially among those segments of the population unable to wield symbolic power. Excerpts from a tape-recorded interview with an imprisoned armed robber illustrate these assumptions."   J

2204.  Tresemer, David and Pleck, Joseph.  SEX-ROLE BOUNDARIES AND RESISTANCE TO SEX-ROLE CHANGE.  *Women's Studies 1974 2(1): 61-78.* Discusses sex-role stereotypes as conceptual images in a culture. These images, in the form of male and female role-expectations, are necessary for an integrated self. Male and female sex roles have clear boundaries, and conformity to sex role has important social and psychological functions. The most obvious function of conformity to sex role is the avoidance of the negative results of deviance from the sex role. This is shown by studies of sex-role incongruent behavior and sex-role congruent behavior. An examination of male responses to the changing role of women shows how men are responding to women's challenging of traditional male instrumental dominance and to women becoming less expressive and socially emotional. Many men live vicari-

ously through and depend emotionally on the women's emotionality. The changing role of women frustrates this traditional dependence. Focusing on male maladaptive behavior to female role changes, the authors suggest that stereotyping and hostile resistance are two major defensive styles men use to deal with female achievement. Refs., notes.
A. E. Wiederrecht

2205.  Turner, Barbara F. and Turner, Castellano B.  THE POLITICAL IMPLICATIONS OF SOCIAL STEREOTYPING OF WOMEN AND MEN AMONG BLACK AND WHITE COLLEGE STUDENTS.  *Sociol. and Social Res. 1974 58(2): 155-162.* "Semantic differential scales rating the concepts 'Most women are . . .' and 'Most men are . . .' were administered to black female, black male, white female, and white male university freshmen. White females were the only group to rate the opposite sex significantly more positively than their own sex. Black females did *not* share white females' tendency to idealize men. Black females rated men as more unreliable than did the other groups. Further, black females were the only group to rate men as significantly more unreliable than they rated women. Otherwise, black females' evaluations of men did not differ from those of male."   J

2206.  Turow, Joseph.  ADVISING AND ORDERING: DAYTIME, PRIME TIME.  *J. of Communication 1974 24(2): 138-141.* Studies the patterns of giving and receiving advice and orders as a means of showing the underlying relationship between male and female characters in television dramas, contrasting patterns on daytime television with its predominantly female audience and on prime time television with its mixed audience.

2207.  Vanderbilt, Amy.  BAD MANNERS IN AMERICA.  *Ann. of the Am. Acad. of Pol. and Social Sci. 1968 378: 90-98.* "The widely held contention that American manners are uniformly bad is not tenable. The very mobility of American society brings into sharp focus the bad manners of the minority, thus making bad manners seem to be the norm. The sharp delineations between classes are less important as proponents of exemplary manners and mores. The changes in etiquette frequently come from other sources. Higher education does not necessarily result in culture. Education and social grace are today not necessarily synonymous. The decline of the mother's influence in the home has meant the decline of what was once known as 'ordinary' manners among America's children. Because of many economic pressures, we are living more simply, with less formality and a minimum restriction upon the family. The pattern of meal-taking has changed drastically. There is a blurring, too, of the difference between the sexes, with a resulting difference in our approach to manners between them. 'Society' has taken on many meanings and is influenced by geography. Reduction in service has been one of the most striking changes in our society, along with a great change in our attitude toward language, from which 'indelicacies' have virtually disappeared. The Negro revolution is making, and will continue to make, a great change in our manners and mores. The admission of new peoples into our social stream has made changes in our behavior. We have become increasingly forthright. Our etiquette is changing. When developing manners are deemed 'bad,' they are usually modified because bad manners make people uncomfortable."   J

2208.  Wedel, Jean.  MALE-FEMALE ROLES IN OUR SOCIETY.  *Mennonite Life 1971 26(1): 27-31.* An analysis of the relationship between the sexes in the context of modern social change. Today's woman, no longer content with her traditional place in the home, is symptomatic of the inappropriateness of the historical conceptions of the roles of males and females in society. If we are to adjust to these new circumstances, we must reduce "the traditional social-sexual differentiations between men and women." Biblio.                                              J. A. Casada

2209.  Winick, Charles.  THE BEIGE EPOCH: DEPOLARIZATION OF SEX ROLES IN AMERICA.  *Ann. of the Am. Acad. of Pol. and Social Sci. 1968 376: 18-24.* "One of the most pervasive features of our cultural landscape is the depolarization of sex roles and a noncomitant blurring of many other differences. The appearance, given names, and play of boys and girls have become less gender-specific since World War II. Young girls appear to be demonstrating the sexual precocity and aggressiveness once associated with boys. Clothing and appearance are steadily becoming increasingly ambisexual, along with recreational activites, work, and family roles. Extremes of taste in food and drink are less common. Blandness also characterizes the color and shape of home interiors and the exteriors of many buildings. Opera, theatre, musical theatre, and movies have been dominated by women in recent decades although male stars once were the major audience attractions. Our rapid industrialization and World War II are among the contributors to depolarization, and the trend may have some ominous implications for the future."

J

2210. Winthrop, Henry. SEXUAL REVOLUTION OR INNER EMPTINESS: PORTENTS OF BRAVE NEW WORLD. *J. of Human Relations 1970 18(1): 764-777.* Analyzes the social and psychological ramifications of the sexual revolution. Aldous Leonard Huxley's readers were repulsed by his treatment of sex in his 1932 *Brave New World* (New York: Harper and Row), but the new contemporary attitudes toward sex approach closely those he described. Presents summaries of those favoring and those opposed to this new impulse. Conservative views should not be shrugged off as uninformed or psychologically illiberal. Based on secondary sources; 14 notes.                    W. A. Wiegand

2211. Wolf, Charlotte. SEX ROLES AS PORTRAYED IN MARRIAGE AND THE FAMILY TEXTBOOKS: CONTRIBUTIONS TO THE STATUS QUO. *Women's Studies 1975 3(1): 45-60.* Marriage and family textbooks portray only the young, white, middle class, nuclear family in which sex roles are normative. The male instrumental role is active and occupationally dynamic. The female expressive role is passive and nurturant in the domestic sphere. The two roles are polarized, fixed, and complementary. Occasionally the texts present minor variations as sex role options but the usual emphasis is upon women and men's adjustment to and conformity with prescribed social norms. Violations of sex roles are considered destructive to the home, family, and individual personalities. Women's employment outside the home is especially subversive. Prevailing textbook opinions reenforce the status quo and envision little sex role change in the future. It is time to examine such textbook assumptions and to explore role alternatives and processes by which to escape from the dominant group's social norms. 8 notes.

A. E. Wiederrecht

2212. —. THE PASSION FOR FASHION. *Wisconsin Then and Now 1965 11(12): 1-3.* A large variety of women's costumes are in the collection of the State Historical Society of Wisconsin, having been collected from its beginning in 1846. Men's uniforms from all periods are included. More men's and children's clothes before 1890 are needed. Illus.

E. P. Stickney

## Sexual Behavior
### *(including birth control and morals)*

2213. Aron, Harry. SEX: THE IRON MAIDEN. *J. of Human Relations 1968 16(4): 475-489.* Discusses the current so-called "sexual revolution." The present sexual revolution is but a variant of the larger attempt to keep individuals from looking about, from noticing, from seeing, and from reducing fear. " 'Fright without reason' is the hope of all states, all authorities. Sexual codes provide 'fright without reason,' not without training, but without relevance - thus without reason....The universal attempt to control man has employed the idealization of man (the pure, the innocent, the proper)." Undocumented.                    D. J. Abramoske

2214. Bardis, Panos D. A PILL SCALE: A TECHNIQUE FOR THE MEASUREMENT OF ATTITUDES TOWARD ORAL CONTRACEPTION. *Social Sci. 1969 44(1): 35-42.* Discusses the use of a scientific device for the objective and quantitative measurement of attitudes toward oral contraception. The author selected the Likert scaling technique ("the technique of summated ratings") and constructed a 25-item pill scale for his measurements. Several tests have established the validity and reliability of the scale. "The pill scale may be employed to investigate the relationship between attitudes toward oral contraception and age, sex, race, religion, nationality, size of home town, order of birth, family size, marital status, marital happiness, amount and kind of education, occupation, income, and so forth." 32 notes.

D. D. Cameron

2215. Berger, Bennett M. HIPPIE MORALITY - MORE OLD THAN NEW. *Transaction 1967 5(2): 19-27.* Contends that the main characteristics of hippie morality were all pointed out by Malcolm Cowley in his *Exile's Return* (1934). Self-expression, paganism, living for the moment, full liberty, female equality, and love of the exotic were noted in the 1920's. What is new is that larger numbers are accepting such a philosophy and still greater numbers (nonhippies) have become tolerant of such Bohemian behavior. Thus, the new morality of our times is far more acceptable than that of previous generations. Based on reading underground papers such as the *Berkeley Barb,* the *East Village Other,* and the *San Francisco Oracle;* illus.                    A. Erlebacher

2216. Burton, G. and Kaplan, H. M. SEXUAL BEHAVIOR AND ADJUSTMENT OF MARRIED ALCOHOLICS. *Q. J. of Studies on Alcohol 1968 29(3): 603-609.* "A questionnaire on sexual behavior and adjustment was administered to 16 married couples of whom the husbands were alcoholics, and 16 couples without alcohol problems. Both groups were receiving counseling for marital difficulties. The mean length of marriage of the alcoholic couples was 13.1 years; the mean age of the husbands was 37.9, and of the wives, 36.4. The alcoholic husbands reported sexual intercourse 1.6 times a week, their wives 2.1 times; 7 of the husbands and 10 of the wives were satisfied by this frequency. Many wives reported withholding sexual activity in order to control their husband's drinking. The alcoholics' wives experienced sexual orgasm 'nearly always' and more frequently than did the wives of the nonalcoholics. Most of the alcoholics and their wives were able to discuss sexual matters freely; fewer of the nonalcoholic couples were able to do so. Most of the alcoholics (81 [percent] and their wives (63 [percent] reported that the husband took the initiative in sexual activity. Both alcoholics and their wives reported some disagreement over sexual adjustment, but considerably less than the nonalcoholic couples. Dissatisfaction over sex was reported by 9 of the alcoholics and their wives; the wives' dissatisfaction included the husband's drinking, his attitude toward sex and his oral sex activities; the husband's dissatisfaction included infrequency of intercourse and the wife's lack of initiative and warmth. Dissatisfaction was reported by a similar proportion of the nonalcoholic couples, but while 62 [percent] of the alcoholic couples' comments about dissatisfaction were over attitudes (e.g., frequency), 67 [percent] of the nonalcoholic couples' comments were over techniques (e.g., premature ejaculation); the difference is attributed to the alcoholic couples' greater ability to discuss sexual matters."                    J

2217. Calderone, Mary. IT'S SOCIETY THAT IS CHANGING SEXUALITY, *Center Mag. 1972 5(4): 58-69.* Discusses the sexual changes which are affecting American culture (1960's-72).

2218. Calderone, Mary S. SEX EDUCATION AND THE ROLES OF SCHOOL AND CHURCH. *Ann. of the Am. Acad. of Pol. and Social Sci. 1968 376: 53-60.* "When sex education is properly recognized for what it is, a birth to death continuum, the increase of awareness of and involvement in it as a process, on the part of society's institutions, school and church, is striking in recent years. This involvement is looked upon as complementary and supplementary to the role of the family, and is being recognized as requiring didactic and pedagogic preparation. Thus, the number of schools, public, private, and parochial, engaged in developing sex education programs is increasing daily, as are teacher-training programs in institutions of higher learning. Movement away from emphasis on details of reproduction and into the area of the dynamics of male-female roles and relationships has been spearheaded by the major religious communions, which can be expected to continue and expand their leadership roles at both national and community levels. Other professional disciplines, especially in medicine, are also studying their roles in education for sexuality."                    J

2219. Callahan, Daniel. CONTRACEPTION AND ABORTION: AMERICAN CATHOLIC RESPONSES. *Ann. of the Am. Acad. of Pol. and Social Sci. 1970 387: 109-117.* "The struggle within Roman Catholicism over contraception, and the struggle which is likely to arise over abortion, reflect a mixture of theological and social change. The challenge to papal authority inherent in the dissent from Pope Paul's encyclical on birth control is bound to have profound ramifications in the church. At the same time, however, the fact of Catholic assimilation into the mainstream of American life, a life manifesting the impact of urbanization and technology, made a conflict over contraception almost inevitable."                    J

2220. Castor, Jane and Hudson, Pamela Sue. SOCIAL WORK ATTITUDES TOWARD REFERRAL TO PLANNED PARENTHOOD. *Social Service R. 1971 45(3): 302-309.* "Can the social work profession learn to adapt or lead, or will it succumb to institutional arthritis?" This challenge stems from findings that while supporting the general notion of birth control, a substantial number of social workers are deterred from expressing it through counseling or referrals by real or imagined disapprobation from a variety of sources (community, agency, fellow workers, and client). Others yield to the notion that they lack the skills to discuss the subject. Study (1966-69) combines a number of related studies and shows no substantial improvement in the attitudes or the rate of referral. Table, 3 notes, biblio.                                                    M. Hough

2221. Damico, James. INGRID FROM LORRAINE TO STROMBOLI: ANALYZING THE PUBLIC'S PERCEPTION OF A FILM STAR. *J. of Popular Film 1975 4(1): 3-20.* Analyzes Ingrid Bergman's 1949 love affair with Roberto Rossellini and the impact it had on her film roles, her image as put forth by her studio, and public opinion.      S

2222. Davis, Keith E. and Braucht, G. Nicholas. EXPOSURE TO PORNOGRAPHY, CHARACTER, AND SEXUAL DEVIANCE: A RETROSPECTIVE SURVEY. *J. of Social Issues 1973 29(3): 183-196.* "Data from 365 subjects from seven types of social groups (jail inmates, college students of three ethnic backgrounds, members of Catholic and Protestant religious organizations) were examined. While amount of exposure was negatively related to the overall index of character, the relationship held primarily for those subjects first exposed after age 17. Amount of exposure to pornography was positively related to self-acknowledged sexual 'deviance' at all ages of first exposure. Exposure was also related to a number of life history variables indicating early significant heterosexual experience and a greater involvement in homosexual and deviant sexual practices. A number of analyses were undertaken to explore the possible causal status which exposure to pornography may have with respect to sexual deviance. The pattern of obtained results leaves open the possibility that early exposure to pornography plays some causal role in the development of sexually deviant life styles or the possibility that exposure is merely part of or a product of adopting a sexually deviant life style."      J

2223. Ellis, Albert. REASONS FOR HAVING EXTRAMARITAL RELATIONS. *J. of Human Relations 1968 16(4): 490-501.* Hypothesizes "the following healthy reasons for husbands and wives, even when they are happily married and want to continue their marital relationships, strongly wanting and doing their best to discreetly carry on extramarital affairs": sexual varietism, love enhancement, experiential drives, adventure seeking, sexual curiosity, social inducements, and sexual deprivation. The self-defeating or emotionally disturbed impulses behind adultery include: low frustration tolerance, hostility to one's spouse, self-deprecation, ego-bolstering, escapism, sexual disturbances, and excitement needs. The healthy adulterer is noncompulsive, usually manages to carry on his affairs without unduly disturbing his marriage, never condemns himself because of his extramarital desires, does not use his adulterous relationships as a means of avoiding any of his serious problems, is tolerant of himself when he makes errors, and is sexually adequate with his spouse. Based on clinical interviews and unofficial talks with scores of nonpatients; 5 notes.                                                 D. J. Abramoske

2224. Ellis, Albert. SEXUAL PROMISCUITY IN AMERICA. *Ann. of the Am. Acad. of Pol. and Social Sci. 1968 378: 58-67.* "Although true promiscuity, or highly indiscriminate sexual participation, is rare in human history, plural sexuality in a somewhat casual manner has been part of the American scene since Colonial days and is still very much with us. At the present time, nonmonogamous indulgence appears to be increasing, especially on the part of educated and middle-class females; and the pronounced feelings of anxiety, guilt, and depression that once resulted from premarital and extramarital promiscuity are being considerably reduced. A recent development has been the advocacy and practice of group love as well as group sex relations by certain segments of our population. Several important factors have encouraged American sexual promiscuity during the last decade - including technological advances, marital disillusionment, sociopolitical alienation, increasing libertarianism, and the involvement of many individuals in intensive psychotherapy. While some authorities feel that promiscuous sex is thoroughly incompatible with mental health, others take the view that it is not. There seem

to be both healthy and disturbed reasons why certain individuals freely engage in a variety of sex-love affairs. Though sexual promiscuity in America will probably not grow by leaps and bounds in the near future, there are indications that a slow advance to new levels of sane and enlightened sexual freedom is likely to occur."      J

2225. Erskine, Hazel Gaudet. THE POLLS: MORALITY. *Public Opinion Q. 1966/67 30(4): 669-680.* Surveys results from "the few items pertaining to morality that have appeared in regularly published polls since 1936." Includes questions on general morality, sexual morality, marital morality, premarital morality, and decency in women's clothing.                                                          D. J. Trickey

2226. Ferdinand, Theodore N. SEX BEHAVIOR AND THE AMERICAN CLASS STRUCTURE: A MOSAIC. *Ann. of the Am. Acad. of Pol. and Social Sci. 1968 376: 76-85.* "Close parallels in ancient Rome and present-day America suggest that the sexual revolutions in both societies were significantly influenced by the existential conditions that they confronted at the height of their powers. At the same time, each was constrained in its sociocultural responses by the nature of its social-class structure. In America we must examine the ethos of each of six broad strata to comprehend in detail the nature of the American sexual revolution. When we do, we see that many of the changes in our sexual mores and behavior can be traced to recent changes in the social-class structure. The spread of higher education among the middle class has meant that a substantial portion of American adolescents are regularly exposed to a social setting in which their sexual behavior is governed essentially by the adolescents themselves. Such a situation could not help but be more permissive than that which prevailed before the modern period. Moreover, since a substantial portion of the population is now embraced by the middle classes, a growing portion of the population is exposed to this permissive sexual environment. The sexual revolution in America, therefore, is largely a blend of existential and structural pressures impinging upon only a segment of the total population."      J

2227. Gagnon, John H. and Simon, William. SEXUAL DEVIANCE IN CONTEMPORARY AMERICA. *Ann. of the Am. Acad. of Pol. and Social Sci. 1968 376: 106-122.* "Sexual deviance was traditionally seen within the framework of a society's definition of morality and sin; today it is being viewed from the vantage point of the society's definition of mental health and emotional disturbance. A typology of categories of sex deviance is suggested, using three variables: incidence or frequency, the level of invoked sanctions, and the existence of a specialized social structure that may arise out of the deviant behavior or may be necessary to support it. It is suggested that the deviant subcultures do not attain their new adherents by recruitment, but rather by enlistment. Several shifts in the patterns of deviant behavior are noted."      J

2228. Greenberg, Andrea. DRUGGED AND SEDUCED: A CONTEMPORARY LEGEND. *New York Folklore Q. 1973 29(2): 131-158.* Folktales about the drugging and seduction of college women are a form of social control on morals.      S

2229. Hampe, Gary D. INTERFAITH DATING: RELIGION, SOCIAL CLASS AND PREMARITAL SEXUAL ATTITUDES. *Sociol. Analysis 1971 32(2): 97-106.* Numerous studies have revealed the pattern of greater interfaith dating by Catholics in comparison to Protestants. This study of a sample of college students focuses upon the effect of several social variables on the interfaith dating of Catholics, and in particular, Catholic females Interfaith dating of Catholics was found to be related to the percentage of Catholics in the population, a lower social status, and premarital sexually permissive attitudes of both Catholic males and females, not just to Catholic females as was hypothesized.                                                              J

2230. Johnson, Robert C. KINSEY VS. CHRISTIANITY: A CLASH OF "PARADIGMS" ON HUMAN NATURE. *Q. J. of Speech 1975 61(1): 59-70.* Discusses the Christian reaction to Alfred C. Kinsey's view of human nature presented in his writings about sexual behavior.      S

2231. Kanin, Eugene J. and Davidson, Karen R. SOME EVIDENCE BEARING ON THE AIM-INHIBITION HYPOTHESES OF LOVE. *Sociol. Q. 1972 13(2): 210-217.* Discusses the effects of premarital sex and the consequences of coitus on established love relationships (1960's-70's).

2232.  Kelly, Edward.  A NEW IMAGE FOR THE NAUGHTY DILDO?  *J. of Popular Culture 1974 7(4): 804-809.*  Battery-powered plastic vibrators or "facial massagers," the latest version of the age-old masturbatory device, are now widely advertised in magazines, newspapers, and mail-order catalogs with approbation and openly suggestive language.        S

2233.  McCracken, Samuel.  THE POPULATION CONTROLLERS.  *Commentary 1972 53(5): 45-52.*  Examines differences in the thinking of the proponents of birth control, including ideas on the ethics of government regulation of contraception and abortion.        S

2234.  Padgett, Jack F.  SEX AND THE SEARCH FOR MEANING.  *Liberal Educ. 1972 58(3): 381-390.*  Although new and more open sex mores have emerged, the birth control pill failed to remove sexual conflict and anxiety for either men or women. The meaning of sex is part of the wider problem of the meaning of human relationships. Secondary sources; 22 notes.        W. H. Ahern

2235.  Palley, Howard A.  COMMUNITY IN CONFLICT: FAMILY PLANNING IN METROVILLE.  *Social Service R. 1967 41(1): 55-65.*  Studies how the organization of medical services and religious and sociopolitical values within the community can prevent development of public health services.

2236.  Palson, Charles and Palson, Rebecca.  SWINGING IN WEDLOCK.  *Society 1972 9(4): 28-30, 35-37.*  Discusses mate swapping or "swinging" among middle class couples.        S

2237.  Placek, Paul J.  DIRECT MAIL AND INFORMATION DIFFUSION: FAMILY PLANNING.  *Public Opinion Q. 1974/75 38(4): 548-561.*  "The success of family planning programs partially depends upon informal diffusion within the target population. This study examines the effects of direct mailing on knowledge, opinion leadership, and diffusion. Information about local birth control clinics, the pill, the IUD [intrauterine device], and other methods of birth control was sent to a random half of a total sample of 300 welfare mothers. Subsequent interviews showed that the direct mailing improved knowledge and increased diffusion, but had no effect on self-concept as an opinion leader."        J

2238.  Polgar, Steven.  SOCIOCULTURAL RESEARCH IN FAMILY PLANNING IN THE UNITED STATES: REVIEW AND PROSPECTS.  *Human Organization 1966 25(4): 321-329.*  Reviews family planning and demographic trends in the United States. Examines contraceptive use among the poor. Proposes several areas of potentially valuable anthropological research including diffusion of contraceptive techniques and motivation in family planning. 2 tables, 56 notes.        E. S. Johnson

2239.  Reiss, Ira L.  PREMARITAL SEXUAL PERMISSIVENESS AMONG NEGROES AND WHITES.  *Am. Sociol. R. 1964 29(5): 688-698.*  "Results from a sample of 903 students and 1515 adults indicate that Negroes and whites differ considerably in the ways in which premarital sexual attitudes are produced and maintained. The white group is less permissive, and its permissiveness is inversely related to church attendance and belief in romantic love and positively related to the number of times in love. In the Negro group these associations were either absent or in the opposite direction. A similar pattern distinguished men from women within each racial group. The theory advanced to explain these findings proposes that the lower the traditional level of sexual permissiveness in a group, the greater the likelihood that social factors will alter individual levels of permissiveness."        J

2240.  Reiss, Ira L.  SOCIAL CLASS AND PREMARITAL SEXUAL PERMISSIVENESS: A RE-EXAMINATION.  *Am. Sociol. R. 1965 30(5): 747-756.*  "Data from samples of 903 students and 1515 adults were used to investigate the hypothesis that persons of higher social status are less permissive than lower-status persons regarding premarital sexual behavior. In neither sample did the expected negative relation between class and permissiveness appear, but among persons displaying conservative characteristics generally, the relationship was negative. Among those with liberal characteristics, the relationship was positive. Conversely, general liberalism enhanced sexual permissiveness more in higher than in the lower-class groups. These findings are consistent with the theory that in groups or classes where the traditional level of sexual permissiveness is low, social forces are more likely to alter individual levels of permissiveness. The evidence also supports the thesis that the more generally liberal a group, the sharper the differences in attitudes between liberals and conservatives in that group."        J

2241.  Rosenberg, Bernard and Bensman, Joseph.  SEXUAL PATTERNS IN THREE ETHNIC SUBCULTURES OF AN AMERICAN UNDERCLASS.  *Ann. of the Am. Acad. of Pol. and Social Sci. 1968 376: 61-75.*  "Three American ethnic subcultures, all consisting of transmigrated groups living in poverty, were studied and the sexual patterns of the youth described. The groups consisted of white Appalachians living in Chicago, Negroes in Washington, D.C., and Puerto Ricans in New York. Sharply differentiated patterns of sexual behavior, involving conquest, sex education, sex misinformation, attitudes toward females, responsibility, and affect were discovered, and these patterns are reflected in the language of the subcultures, particularly in their argot. The underclass sexual mores differ from those of the American middle class, but not more than they differ from each other among the three ethnic groups. Sexual practices are related to general life styles, and reflect ghettoization, subcultural isolation, and short-range hedonism in groups only recently transplanted from their rural areas of origin."        J

2242.  Sagarin, Edward.  TAKING STOCK OF STUDIES OF SEX.  *Ann. of the Am. Acad. of Pol. and Social Sci. 1968 376: 1-5.*  "Scientific studies of sexual behavior have proliferated during recent decades. One period of research was ushered in by Freud; a second, by Kinsey; and perhaps a third is being innovated by Masters and Johnson. Four major problems, that demand solutions at this stage of research, are cited. They include the ethical problem of the effect of research on the subject, the ideological one of researchers' biases, the social one of the effects of the sexual revolution on behavior and on human fulfillment, and the normative one of the establishment of guideposts for sexual activity in a world in which sex and procreation are but slightly related."        J

2243.  Scott, Joseph E. and Franklin, Jack L.  THE CHANGING NATURE OF SEX REFERENCES IN MASS CIRCULATION MAGAZINES.  *Public Opinion Q. 1972 36(1): 80-86.*  Presents the results of a study of sex references in five national magazines of general interest during the years 1950-1970. References to sex and a more sympathetic treatment of it occurred but not to a startling degree. The increase in the references has been modest and does not represent a sexual revolution. Opinions differ about whether or not the actual practice of sexual relations has increased, but there is no doubt that general interest in it has increased. Based on a survey of five national magazines; table, 9 notes.        V. L. Human

2244.  Shorter, Edward.  CAPITALISM, CULTURE, AND SEXUALITY: SOME COMPETING MODELS.  *Social Sci. Q. 1972 53(2): 338-356.*  "Presents three models of how economic change result in sexual liberalization, premarital intercourse and illegitimacy. First, the 'cultural disorganization' model predicts normlessness in the wake of dislocating social change, and therewith sex outside of marriage. The second 'bridge' model calls for the formation of subcultures with sexually liberal values in consequence of social upheaval, but spots, as an immediate consequence of such upheaval, anomie and value confusion. The third 'subculture of gratification' model hypothesizes that sexual liberalization will occur only *after* social changes have created a new working-class or adolescent sub-culture, but that exposure to such structural transformations as those brought by the free market economy causes individuals to become indifferent to community controls on sexuality as they become oriented to self-gratification . . . . Research on sexual and family history in modern Europe suggests the validity of the third model."        J

2245.  Sisk, John P.  SEX AND ARMAGEDDON.  *Commentary 1970 50(6): 83-94.*  An essay on the sexual liberation movement.        S

2246.  Smith, Wilford E.  MORALITY ON CAMPUS.  *Dialogue: A J. of Mormon Thought 1968 3(2): 161-165.*  An analysis of the sexual behavior and attitudes of Mormon college students as compared to non-Mormon college students in the West. Mormons appeared to be more chaste. One-half of non-Mormon males and one-third of Mormon males admitted having had sexual intercourse, as compared to one-fifth to one-sixth of non-Mormon females and one-seventh of Mormon females. Large numbers of youth have withstood heterosexual temptation, but the results of the survey are still shocking, and illustrate lack of rigid standards of right and wrong. Suggests an extensive campaign to teach morality.

J. L. Rasmussen

2247. Stycos, J. Mayone. SOME DIMENSIONS OF POPULATION AND FAMILY PLANNING: GOALS AND MEANS. *J. of Social Issues 1974 30(4): 1-29.* Where population planning and family planning programs converge and diverge are discussed in terms of ultimate and intermediate goals, and the means by which goals are achieved. Broad variations are found within the ranks of both groups of planning advocates. This variation is both cause and effect of differing levels of concern over the societal consequences of population growth and size and of family growth and size. When degree of concern over population problems is compared with the degree of difficulty of solution regarded as necessary or desirable, a number of instances are found in which the relation is not as expected. This is due in part to the heterogeneity of the goals and in part to ideological considerations affecting attitudes toward means as well as ends.                                                         J

2248. Varni, Charles A. AN EXPLORATORY STUDY OF SPOUSE-SWAPPING. *Pacific Sociol. Rev. 1972 15(4): 507-522.* San Diego swingers answering an underground newspaper were studied in terms of initiation into the ranks of free spirits, forms, and effects of swinging, as well as the typology of a swinger.

2249. Weaver, Herbert B. and Arkoff, Abe. MEASUREMENT OF ATTITUDES CONCERNING SEXUAL PERMISSIVENESS. *Social Sci. 1965 40(3): 163-168.* Describes the efforts of the authors to construct a scale which measures attitudes in the United States toward sexual permissiveness.                                             M. Small

2250. Webber, Robert L. MYTHS ABOUT BIRTH CONTROL. *Public Welfare 1969 27(1): 9-12.* Dispels myths concerning the usefulness of birth control information for youth and the poor in a special section entitled "Family Planning."                                               S

2251. Williamson, Nancy E. SEX PREFERENCES, SEX CONTROL, AND THE STATUS OF WOMEN. *Signs 1976 1(4): 847-862.* Since the 1930's, sex preference studies in the United States reveal a clear preference for boys, with men prefering boys more strongly than women do. Since three methods of sex control are available in America today, the quality of women's lives and the status of women could be profoundly affected. Women would bear the risk, inconvenience, and psychic costs. Preference studies indicate first borns would be male, so females as a group might suffer, as studies of first borns conclude that they are high achievers. If the population contains less women, more societal pressure to marry and have children could result. Age differences between husbands and wives would increase, thus placing women in a more dependent, less experienced situation. Based on sociological studies; 46 notes.                                       J. Gammage

## Psychology

2252. Bart, Pauline. MOTHER PORTNOY'S COMPLAINT. *Trans-Action 1970 8(1/2): 69-74.* Examines cases of depression among middle-aged women, pointing out that Jews are more apt to experience this syndrome; concludes that the women's liberation movement is part of the remedy because it can free women to choose their own careers, thus simultaneously freeing them from the necessity to judge their own worth through the accomplishments of their children and husbands and allowing them to take pride in their own accomplishments.

G. A. Hewlett

2253. Carlson, Rae. UNDERSTANDING WOMEN: IMPLICATIONS FOR PERSONALITY THEORY AND RESEARCH. *J. of Social Issues 1972 28(2): 17-32.* Discusses the psychology of women.

2254. DeLamater, John and Fidell, Linda S. ON THE STATUS OF WOMEN: AN ASSESSMENT AND INTRODUCTION. *Am. Behavioral Scientist 1971 15(2): 163-171.* Three themes are common to several

of the following papers: 1) the discrepancy between the perception of the situation by women and by men and social scientists, 2) women's negative self-image as a major barrier to status improvement, and 3) the necessity of informal attitude changes by both sexes. 3 notes.

D. G. Davis, Jr.

2255. Edwards, P.; Harvey, C.; and Whitehead, P. WIVES OF ALCOHOLICS: A CRITICAL REVIEW AND ANALYSIS. *Q. J. of Studies on Alcohol 1973 34(1A): 112-132.* "A review of the literature [40 items] on personality structure and characteristics of wives of alcoholics is presented. It is concluded that the classic clinical description of the wives of alcoholics as aggressive, domineering women is inaccurate. None of the later experimental studies (with such instruments as the MMPI, the Interpersonal Check List and the Index of Psychophysiological Disturbances) have supported it, nor have they established the existence of a personality type unique to alcoholics' wives. The decompensation hypothesis—that the wives tend to deteriorate as their husbands become abstinent—has also not been supported by recent research. Jackson's theory [Quart. J. Stud. Alc. 15: 562-586, 1954] that the wives' personalities would fluctuate in accordance with their husbands' involvement with alcohol has, however, received support from later investigations. The most recent theory—the psychosocial—therefore incorporates a stress component (from Jackson) but not a decompensation one. Wives of alcoholics appear to be women who have essentially normal personalities of different types. They may suffer personality dysfunction and react to their situations with changes in coping methods and roles within the family when their husbands are drinking to excess; but if their husbands become abstinent, they will experience progressively less dysfunction. Thus, they seem much like other women with marital problems."                 J

2256. Farber, Leslie H. HE SAID, SHE SAID. *Commentary 1972 53(3): 53-59.* Analyzes psychological difficulties in communication between men and women.                                                          S

2257. Gitter, A. George; Black, Harvey; and Mostofsky, David. RACE AND SEX IN THE PERCEPTION OF EMOTION. *J. of Social Issues 1972 28(4): 63-78.* A factorial design was utilized to investigate the effects of race of expresser (black or white), sex of expresser, race of perceiver (black or white), and sex of perceiver on the perception of emotion (POE), employing seven emotions (anger, happiness, surprise, fear, disgust, pain, and sadness). Overall results indicate significant main effects: for race of expresser (whites were more accurately perceived), for sex of expresser (females were more accurately perceived), for race of perceiver (blacks were more accurately perceived). There was no significant effect associated with sex of perceiver.                               J

2258. Gump, Janice Porter. SEX-ROLE ATTITUDES AND PSYCHOLOGICAL WELL-BEING. *J. of Social Issues 1972 28(2): 79-92.* Describes how these attitudes determine career-versus-family choices for women.

2259. Horner, Matina S. TOWARD AN UNDERSTANDING OF ACHIEVEMENT-RELATED CONFLICTS IN WOMEN. *J. of Social Issues 1972 28(2): 157-176.*

2260. Landis, Judson; Sullivan, Daryl; and Sheley, Joseph. FEMINIST ATTITUDES AS RELATED TO THE SEX OF THE INTERVIEWER. *Pacific Sociol. R. 1973 16(3): 305-314.*

2261. Laws, Judy Long. FEMINIST ANALYSIS OF RELATIVE DEPRIVATION IN ACADEMIC WOMEN. *Rev. of Radical Pol. Econ. 1972 4(3): 107-119.* Using Stouffer's concept of relative deprivation, examines the case of the female faculty member. Finding that the potential for feelings of inferiority in job gratification is present in comparisons with male colleagues, and with female students, the author examines the psychological roles they assume to avoid these comparisons. Based on secondary sources; 13 refs., 7 notes.                           C. P. de Young

2262. Levine, Adeline and Crumrine, Janice. WOMEN AND THE FEAR OF SUCCESS: A PROBLEM IN REPLICATION. *Am. J. of Sociol. 1975 80(4): 964-974.* Describes difficulties and methodology of replicating Matina Horner's findings (1970) which concluded that women are motivated to avoid success.                                              S

2263.   Newman, Lucile F.   FOLKLORE OF PREGNANCY: WIVES' TALES IN CONTRA COSTA COUNTY, CALIFORNIA.   *Western Folklore 1969 28(2): 112-135.* Examines birth folklore in both a general sense and in one California county. Beliefs and rules about pregnancy are still very prevalent; new beliefs are being introduced. The cultural meaning of wives' tales is not to impart useful instructions to the expectant mother, but to symbolize the status of pregnancy. Several differences appear in the pregnancy beliefs of Negro and white groups. Negro beliefs tend largely to magic and are mostly concerned with marking or death. White beliefs are largely signs for determining sex and avoiding pain. Discusses traditional beliefs and modern tales which talk in medical terms, but which are still presented as superstitions. Fear of the unknown keeps these beliefs alive. Lists 284 pregnancy beliefs collected in Contra Costa County. Based on secondary sources and questionnaires; 23 notes, appendix.                                                R. A. Trennert

2264.   Rothstein, Arnold.   DEPRESSION IN PREGNANCY AS IT RELATES TO FEMININE IDENTIFICATION CONFLICT AND PERCEIVED ENVIRONMENTAL SUPPORT.   *Smith Coll. Studies in Social Work 1971 42(1): 23-25.* "A non-supporting environment has the potential to aggravate a normal phase-specific crisis into a pathological reaction."                          M. A. Kaufman and S

2265.   Rudikoff, Sonya.   WOMEN AND SUCCESS.   *Commentary 1974 58(4): 49-59.* Applies Matina Horner's seminal study on women's fear of success to several prominent figures—among others, Rose Kennedy, Frieda Lawrence, Jane Addams, and Hannah Senesh.            S

# Youth

2266.   Blane, H. T., Hill, M. J., and Brown, E.   ALIENATION, SELF-ESTEEM AND ATTITUDES TOWARD DRINKING IN HIGH-SCHOOL STUDENTS.   *Q. J. of Studies on Alcohol 1968 29(2): 350-354.* "The Williams Attitudes toward Temperate and Irresponsible Use of Alcohol Scale, a modified version of the Dean Alienation Scale, and a measure of self-esteem (the Feelings of Inadequacy subscale of the Janis and Field Personality Questionnaire) were administered to all students (256 boys, 270 girls) of a rural high school located in a predominantly Protestant northern New England resort area. It was found that favorability of attitudes to irresponsible use of alcohol was positively associated with alienation [r equals] .19) but bore no association to self-esteem [r equals] .04). Two alienation subscales, powerlessness and normlessness, were related to attitudes toward irresponsible use [r equals] .20 and .25, respectively), but the third subscale, social isolation, was not. Alienation and self-esteem were negatively related [r equals] .44). There were no sex or age differences among the correlations, although boys held significantly more favorable attitudes to both temperate and irresponsible use of alcohol than girls; boys also rated themselves higher than girls on self-esteem."                                                    J

2267.   Bohlen, Joe M. and Yoesting, Dean R.   CONGRUENCY BETWEEN OCCUPATIONAL ASPIRATIONS AND ATTAINMENTS OF IOWA YOUNG PEOPLE.   *Rural Sociol. 1968 33(2): 207-213.* Presents longitudinal data about the relationship of occupational aspirations in 1948 (as indicated by a sample of 152 high school seniors from eight rural high schools in Hamilton County and the high school in the adjoining Story County community of Story City) compared with occupational attainments by 1956. The analysis shows that occupational aspirations are not good predictors of the type of occupation attained, that certain occupations have more predictive power than others, and that a significant relationship did exist between congruency and training beyond high school for the males, but not for the females. Contrary to expectations, additional training was associated with incongruency. 3 tables, 17 notes.                                                D. D. Cameron

2268.   Brackbill, Yvonne and Howell, Embry M.   RELIGIOUS DIFFERENCES IN FAMILY SIZE PREFERENCE AMONG AMERICAN TEENAGERS.   *Sociol. Analysis 1974 35(1): 35-44.* "This paper analyzes differences between Catholic and non-Catholic young people in attitudes toward family formation. A sample of 941 students in junior high schools, high schools, and colleges in the Washington, D.C. area responded to a self-administered questionnaire in 1971. Data were ob-

tained on students' background, attitudes toward family formation, girls' career aspirations, and population awareness. In general, results emphasize and reemphasize the continuing importance of a religious differential in family size preference. Religious affiliation was more predictive of preferred family size than was race, sex, age, socio-economic status, number of siblings, type of school, maternal work history, or girls' career aspirations. These results differ from those obtained in recent studies based on short term trends in religious conformity but are consistent with longer term trends."                                                J

2269.   Carey, James T.   CHANGING COURTSHIP PATTERNS IN THE POPULAR SONG.   *Am. J. of Sociol. 1969 74(6): 720-731.* "A content analysis of popular lyrics from song magazines and accepted rankings reveals a change in perspective on boy-girl relationships over the past eleven years. The new orientation prizes autonomy in personal relations and is most clearly portrayed in rock and roll lyrics. The career of the affair is traced from its inception to its final dissolution. Proportionally fewer lyrics deal with boy-girl relationships today than in the mid-1950's. A wider range of concerns are evident and raise questions about the individual's relations to the social order. The questions may reflect the preoccupations of a growing number of disaffected young people who constitute the audience for the new lyrics, or the emergence of more democratic controls in songwriting."                                    J

2270.   Carter, Barbara L.   REFORM SCHOOL FAMILIES.   *Society 1973 11(1): 36-43.* Describes the establishment of make-believe families in a girls' reform school.                                            S

2271.   Chainey, Steve.   THE HIGH SCHOOL REVOLT.   *Int. Socialist Rev. 1972 33(3): 12-17, 35-37.* Considers the youth movement and the revolt against high school bureaucracy, ethnic and sex discrimination, the tracking system, and denial of constitutional rights, 1971.

2272.   Distler, Luther S.   THE ADOLESCENT "HIPPIE" AND THE EMERGENCE OF A MATRISTIC CULTURE.   *Psychiatry 1970 33(3): 362-371.* A description of hippie culture as developed by the author in therapy group sessions with many junior and senior high school students who have used drugs. There is a radical shift in the dominant culture from patristic to matristic, and young people are most affected by the shift. In the patristic culture, a value is placed on achievement, individual responsibility, and goal-directedness. As a result of automation, population growth, and urbanization, many people feel unable to fill satisfactory roles, especially with the educational revolution which has kept large numbers of young people in extended adolescent roles. The emerging matristic culture values expressive roles, feelings, intimacy, sensory experiences, and self-exploration. In the early stages of matristic culture, the adolescent is antipatristic, being disillusioned with the faults of the patristic society. He sees his parents as unhappy in their roles but unable to do anything about it. The hippies are especially dissatisfied with the current stereotypes of adult roles, which are based on patristic values. Biblio.                                                M. A. Kaufman

2273.   Foster, Sallie.   PREGNANCY AMONG SCHOOL-AGED GIRLS: A LOCAL EVALUATION OF A NATIONAL PROBLEM.   *Public Welfare 1972 30(4): 8-13.* Discusses the extent of the problem of out-of-wedlock pregnancy among teenage girls in Los Angeles County, California, advocating the need for the federal government and the Health, Education and Welfare Department to take action on a national level, 1969-71.

2274.   Freeman, J. Leiper   PARENTS, IT'S NOT ALL YOUR FAULT, BUT....   *J. of Pol. 1969 31(3): 812-817.* A study of the background influences affecting students who participate in demonstrations. Most students who demonstrate come from "politically concerned, liberal homes." Male students are highly influenced by home discussions; females are to a lesser extent. The children of liberal parents tend to be among those most interested in politics. 4 tables, 4 notes.
                                                    A. R. Stoesen

2275.   Gustavus, Susan O. and Mommsen, Kent G.   BLACK-WHITE DIFFERENTIALS IN FAMILY SIZE PREFERENCES AMONG YOUTH.   *Pacific Sociol. R. 1973 16(1): 107-119.*

2276. Hollander, Elaine K. and Vollmer, Howard M. ATTITUDES TOWARD "OPEN MARRIAGE" AMONG COLLEGE STUDENTS AS INFLUENCED BY PLACE OF RESIDENCE. *Youth and Soc. 1974 6(1): 3-21.* Examines attitudes of college students at the American University, Washington, D.C., over a one year period.    S

2277. Jesser, Clinton J. A DIM LIGHT ON THE WAY TO DAMASCUS: SELECTIVE FEMINISM AMONG COLLEGE WOMEN. *Youth and Soc. 1974 6(1): 49-62.* Examines selected women's perceptions of issues concerning the changing of sex roles.    S

2278. Kane, R. L. and Patterson, E. DRINKING ATTITUDES AND BEHAVIOR OF HIGH-SCHOOL STUDENTS IN KENTUCKY. *Q. J. of Studies on Alcohol 1972 33(3, pt. A): 635-646.* "Of the 21,264 students in grades 7 to 12 of schools in 7 northern Kentucky counties, 19,929 completed a questionnaire. The median age of the students was 15.5; 53 [percent] were girls; 97 [percent] were White; 47 [percent] were Protestant, 31 [percent] Catholic, 2 [percent] Jewish, and 17 [percent] of other denominations (mostly Protestant); 33 [percent] lived in towns of less than 500 people. Almost half (45 [percent] ) of the students were nondrinkers; 26 [percent] drank once or twice a year (infrequent drinkers), 18 [percent] once or twice a month; 8 [percent] drank every week-end, 3 [percent] several times a week (heavy drinkers). Of the drinkers, 46 [percent] had their first drink before age 13, 42 [percent] at ages 14 and 15; 50 [percent] generally drank beer, 34 [percent] wine, 16 [percent] distilled spirits. When they drank, 46 [percent] usually drank less than 2 drinks, 20 [percent] up to 6 drinks, and 34 [percent] drank more. Of all the students, 6 [percent] had drunk nonbeverage alcohol, such as Sterno, paint thinner and hair tonic; 3 [percent] had drunk an alcoholic beverage before or instead of breakfast; 3 [percent] reported that drinking had occasionally interfered with their school work; 8 [percent] had been in a fight or destroyed property as a result of drinking, and in 4 [percent] drinking had resulted in an accident, injury or arrest, or had brought them before school officials. Restricting drinking of alcohol to adults was favored by 41 [percent] of all students; 30 [percent] opposed all drinking; 70 [percent] believed that teen-agers should have the opportunity to learn more about alcoholic beverages. Seventy-seven per cent of the heavy drinkers and 40 [percent] of the nondrinkers were boys; 41 and 16 [percent] were Catholics, 32 and 57 [percent] Protestants; 16 and 2 [percent] attended church regularly; 34 and 19 [percent] had failed 1 or more grades in school; 30 and 4 [percent] reported that almost all the students in their grade were drinkers; 50 and 3 [percent] reported that almost all their friends were drinkers. Forty-nine per cent of the heavy drinkers usually drank beer, 42 [percent] distilled spirits and 9 [percent] wine; among the infrequent drinkers the proportions were 39, 31 and 30 [percent]; 32 [percent] of the heavy drinkers and 68 [percent] of the infrequent drinkers usually obtained alcohol from their parents; 41 and 28 [percent] reported that their usual drinking companions were friends of their own age; 10 and 7 [percent] reported drinking alone; the parents of 15 and 2 [percent] approved of their drinking; drinking had frequently interfered with the school work of 13 and 2 [percent]; 45 and 4 [percent] reported fighting or destruction of property while drinking, 28 and 2 [percent] injury or arrest because of drinking; 22 and 8 [percent] had drunk nonbeverage alcohol; 17 and 9 [percent] were worried about their drinking. The results are compared with those of other studies of teen-age drinking in the United States."    J

2279. Kohak, Erazim. BEING YOUNG IN POSTINDUSTRIAL SOCIETY. *Dissent 1971 18(1): 30-40.* The campus youth revolution is not a revolution in any accepted sense of the word. It is motivated more by fantasies than by real alternatives. It is an "...amorphous, discontinuous series of outbursts, which attach themselves to anything from fads in dress and music to radical activism." It is a product of postindustrial affluence which provides the milieu in which the student is free to "drop out" and still not run the risk of cutting himself off from that affluence. This phenomenon illustrates the Marxian dictum of the connection between technology and ideology. One must look past the revolutionary rhetoric to see how technological change affects being young by prolonging the training period, while at the same time obscuring the relationship between training or education and later work. Student revolutionaries have reacted to this situation by believing that problems of technological society are something to be transcended rather than solved. Therefore problems such as racism, sexism, and imperialism are oversimplified, so that they become emotional, not rational, issues. All this is symptomatic of the fact that what the students are doing (studying) does not seem important or relevant. This is but one of the many aspects of a postindustrial society that has no real role for its young.    W. L. Hogeboom

2280. Krauss, Irving. SOURCES OF EDUCATIONAL ASPIRATIONS AMONG WORKING-CLASS YOUTH. *Am. Sociol. R. 1964 29(6): 867-879.* "Data on 387 working-class and 267 middle-class high school seniors, obtained through a pre-coded questionnaire, indicate that the following conditions affect working-class college aspirations: status discrepancies wherein the mother has married 'down,' or is presently in a white-collar job; having a grandfather who was in non-manual work; family members or friends of the family with college experience, and the father in a high status occupation. Also important were the college aspirations of the student's acquaintances, participation in extra-curricular activities, and attending a predominantly middle-class rather than working-class school."    J

2281. Miller, Walter B. THE MOLLS. *Society 1973 11(1): 32-35.* Analyzes a girls' corner gang.    S

2282. Morris, Celia; Christie, Andrew; Nobel, Jeremy; Roos, Margit; and Wasserheit, Judith. *Change 1973 5(5): 36-41. Change* conducts a panel discussion at Princeton University where four undergraduates articulate the dilemmas they face and the hopes they have at college as students of the seventies.    J

2283. Neumann, C. P. and Tamerin, J. S. THE TREATMENT OF ADULT ALCOHOLICS AND TEEN-AGE DRUG ADDICTS IN ONE HOSPITAL; A COMPARISON AND CRITICAL APPRAISAL OF FACTORS RELATED TO OUTCOME. *Q. J. of Studies on Alcohol 1971 32(1): 82-93.* "The Silver Hill Foundation, an open-type hospital located in rural Connecticut, has experienced about 50 [percent] success in treating middle- and higher-class adult alcoholics by a program of individual and group psychotherapy and physical and occupational therapy. The same program essentially failed with adolescent drug addicts (22 patients) from the same social classes. The results are analyzed in terms of the different characteristics of the patient groups: The successfully treated alcoholics are largely self-referred, recognizing the severity of their drinking problem, highly motivated to give up alcohol, often by the threat of familial or economic loss. They had experienced some success in life, had families dependent on them. Their personality structure is usually passive-dependent, passive-aggressive or obsessional. They can form meaningful therapeutic relationships, can anticipate advantages and rewards from giving up alcohol, and be compliant and cooperative in their hospital environment. In contrast, the adolescent drug addicts came under parental duress, usually when threatened with imprisonment, had not internalized the reality of their problem, had no desire to change or adapt to societal standards but were locked in sadomasochistic relationships with parents, had severe superego defects and could neither appreciate the therapeutic milieu nor form relationships with the therapists whom they regarded, along with the other patients, as members of a despicable 'establishment.' They could see no gain from giving up drug-taking and managed to obtain drugs and take them while in the hospital. The adolescent drug addicts are comparable rather to the lowest-class alcoholics and some women alcoholics in their inability to respond to the type of treatment offered in the described milieu."    J

2284. Perebinossoff, Philippe. WHAT DOES A KISS MEAN? THE LOVE COMIC FORMULA AND THE CREATION OF THE IDEAL TEEN-AGE GIRL. *J. of Popular Culture 1974 8(4): 825-835.* Discusses love comics (*Love Me Again, Young Romance, Girls' Love* as role examples for teenage girls which purport to foster the ideal, but in fact reflect traditional values and unchanging male/female roles.

2285. Rein, Martin. REMOVING THE ARTIFICIAL BOUNDARIES BETWEEN SCHOOL, WORK AND FAMILY. *New Generation 1969 51(1): 11-16.* American society is committed to the linear system of racial progress: school, work, marriage, children, retirement. The need for a "cycling conception" is now self-evident. Young people must have the opportunity to move back and forth from work to school or training to have their families when they choose to do so. Three options are suggested: postponement, cycling between work and school, and simultaneous mix of work and school. The needs of our society no longer permit us to view school, work, and family in isolation from one another. Calls for more research and new, more flexible social policies. Note.    K. E. Hendrickson

2286. Rogers, Kristine Olson. "FOR HER OWN PROTEC-TION . . .": CONDITIONS OF INCARCERATION FOR FEMALE JUVENILE OFFENDERS IN THE STATE OF CONNECTICUT. *Law and Soc. Rev. 1972 7(2): 223-246.* While male juvenile offenders in Connecticut are accorded 20th-century penal and rehabilitative treatment, female juvenile cases are subjected to 19th-century prison conditions in 1970.                                                         S

2287. Rushing, William A. ADOLESCENT-PARENT RELATIONSHIP AND MOBILITY ASPIRATIONS. *Social Forces 1964 43(2): 157-166.* "To aspire beyond one's present station in life constitutes an important American norm, but all persons do not have such aspiration. One hypothesis of differential mobility aspirations is that individuals who experience a depriving family of orientation milieux are more likely to be aspirants than are individuals who experience more satisfying milieux. Using a relative measure of mobility aspirations, it was found that the deprivation-aspirations hypothesis was supported for female adolescents, but only in reference to the father-daughter relationship. Consideration of parents' socioeconomic status revealed that father's occupation was significantly related to males' mobility aspirations but not to females' aspirations, and that it was related to the deprivation of neither sex."
                                                                         J

2288. Sadler, A.W. THE LOVE COMICS AND AMERICAN POPULAR CULTURE. *Am. Q. 1964 16(3): 486-490.* Maintains that love comics provide a sense of stability to small town girls in their late teens. In these magazines they read about and identify with lower-middle-class girls who try to escape the boredom of jobs or dull boy friends, but realize, before it is too late, that virtue is derived from frugality and honesty. The repentant heroines, now able to distinguish between the true and the false are rewarded with successful marriages.                    R. S. Pickett

2289. Sanders, Elizabeth Braly. WHAT DO YOUNG WOMEN WANT? *Youth & Soc. 1971 3(1): 36-59.* Reports attitudes of young women aged 17-19 and 22-24. Long-range goals expressed are for changes in social and economic institutional structures to allow for greater pluralism and a more humanistic society. Discrimination due to age disturbs young women. Black women's concerns are more complex than white women's, and emphasize racial rather than sexual discrimination. Based on author's discussions with young women and the literature of the women's movement; biblio.                            J. H. Sweetland

2290. Schwartz, Michael and Baden, Mary Anna. FEMALE ADOLESCENT SELF-CONCEPT: AN EXAMINATION OF THE RELATIVE INFLUENCE OF PEERS AND ADULTS. *Youth and Soc. 1973 5(1): 115-128.* Examines the pattern of significant others for adolescent females in a transactional analysis framework.         S

2291. Starr, Jerold M. THE PEACE AND LOVE GENERATION: CHANGING ATTITUDES TOWARD SEX AND VIOLENCE AMONG COLLEGE YOUTH. *J. of Social Issues 1974 30(2): 73-106.* "The period of the sixties marked the emergence of a distinctive generational ideology among a substantial segment of American youth. This 'peace and love' ideology featured a high degree of age group consciousness and unique integration of life style and political concerns, the psychological foundation for which was laid by the increased differentiation of age roles and de-differentiation of sex roles associated with advanced industrial development. The expansion of higher education, emergence of the multibillion dollar youth market, and growth of the mass media provided the means by which many such youth were able to achieve consciousness of their common interests and join active generation units with distinctive styles of expression. The war in Indochina constituted the traumatic episode which differentiated the various age groups in America and galvanized the middle class, college segment of the youth cohort into action."                                                                 J

2292. Thomas, Darwin L. and Weigert, Andrew J. SOCIALIZATION AND ADOLESCENT CONFORMITY TO SIGNIFICANT OTHERS: A CROSS-NATIONAL ANALYSIS. *Am. Sociol. R. 1971 36(5): 835-847.* "On the basis of classical urban theory and Latin and Anglo cultural differences, this paper first hypothesizes an increase in conformity to significant others (best friend, mother, father, priest) for middle-class Catholic male and female adolescents as one moves across four purposive samples: New York; St. Paul; San Juan, Puerto Rico;

Merida, Yucatan. Second, building on studies of parent-child interaction, it is hypothesized that parental (mother and/or father) control and support are positively related to conformity; and third, that a high degree of both control and support results in a high degree of conformity to significant others in each sample. The findings selectively corroborate the first two hypotheses, except for conformity to best friend, and for the relationship between control and conformity, while the third hypothesis receives limited support. The findings suggest that conformity to 'authoritative others' (parents, priest) should be distinguished from conformity to peers (best friend), and that support from parents rather than control is associated with the adolescents' tendency to conform to the expectations of authoritative others."                                              J

2293. Zucker, R. A. SEX-ROLE IDENTITY PATTERNS AND DRINKING BEHAVIOR OF ADOLESCENTS. *Q. J. of Studies on Alcohol 1968 29(4): 868-884.* "Clinical studies of heavy-drinking men and alcoholics have suggested that problem drinking is associated with a cross-sex (feminine) identity pattern and that, in this context, heavy drinking is reinforcing since it gratifies passive-dependent needs. It has also been noted that alcoholic and nonalcoholic heavier-drinking populations show evidence of hypermasculine characteristics. A multilevel theory, (1) that in terms of conscious self-representation heavier-drinking men show a more masculine sex-role identity pattern than moderate drinkers, (2) that in terms of unconscious need patterns, heavier-drinking men show a more feminine identity pattern, and (3) that heavier-drinking women show a more masculine identity pattern, was tested in 143 boys and 221 girls (mean age 15 years) using 2 measures of sex-role identity: conscious sex-role patterning in 68 boys and 76 girls assessed with the Gough Femininity scale; more subtle (and presumably unconscious) sex-role patterning in 75 boys and 145 girls assessed by means of codes for sex-typed fantasy preferences applied to books and movies that the adolescents reported liking or disliking. The first hypothesis, but not the second or third, was supported. Drinking was categorized by both a quantity and a frequency measure: on the quantity measure 40 boys and 37 girls were classed as heavy drinkers (2 to 9 drinks per drinking occasion), 61 and 53 as moderate drinkers (1 drink) and 42 and 69 as nondrinkers; and on the frequency measure (answers to 9 questions ranging from 'once a day or more' to 'I've never tasted alcoholic beverages and never will') 34 and 48 as regular, 89 and 55 as moderate and 20 and 57 as nondrinkers. On the Gough scale, the heavy-drinking boys (mean score 14.14 on the quantity and 14.56 on the frequency measure) were significantly more masculine than the moderate drinkers (17.35 and 16.80, $p$ [less than] .01 and .05). The heavy vs nondrinker comparison (nondrinker means of 16.09 and 14.60) was significant only on the quantity measure. The differences between the moderate- and nondrinkers were not significant, nor were significant differences found among the girls' drinking groups. On the fantasy-preference measure no differences were found among the drinking groups of either boys or girls. The results are interpreted as indicating that the difference between the heavier and lighter drinking boys is one of sex-role façade, the former consciously picturing themselves as more masculine."                                                    J

## Women's Organizations

2294. Demos, Vasilikie. FEMALE ROLE ORIENTATION AND PARTICIPATION IN A WOMAN'S VOLUNTARY ASSOCIATION. *Social Sci. 1975 50(3): 136-140.* This paper examines the relationship between female role orientation and volunteer participation in a local Girl Scout council. Indicators of female role orientation consist of social background characteristics and organization experiences. The indicator of volunteer participation is membership longevity. Data analysis is based upon questionnaire responses received from 336 present and former Girl Scout volunteers.                                                  J

2295. Galper, Miriam and Washburne, Carolyn Kott. A WOMEN'S SELF-HELP PROGRAM IN ACTION. *Social Policy 1976 6(5): 46-52.* Discusses women's social service programs and counseling services in child care, abortion, health care, jobs, and single parenthood, emphasizing the activities of Women in Transition, Inc.

2296. Krieger, David M. THE ANOTHER MOTHER FOR PEACE CONSUMER CAMPAIGN: A CAMPAIGN THAT FAILED.

*J. of Peace Res. [Norway] 1971 8(2): 163-166.* Analyzes the extent and effectiveness of a consumer letter-writing campaign against defense industries by the Another Mother for Peace Organization. Its membership of 130,000 produced not more than 5,000 letters and not more than 500 went to any single firm. Company policies were not altered. The leadership failed to ignite in its members a strong desire to participate in the effort. The campaign would have been more effective if a single vulnerable industry had been selected. Based on a survey of industry letters received and executive response to them.                    V. L. Human

2297. Nash, Dennison. COHESIVENESS IN AN AMERICAN COMMUNITY ABROAD. *Pacific Sociol. Rev. 1969 12(1): 40-48.* Discusses patterns of social cohesion and stranger anxiety among expatriated Americans living in Ciudad Condal, Spain, in the 1960's, emphasizing stratification of the Women's Club.

2298. Robertson, Mary Helen. THE LEAGUE OF WOMEN VOTERS' ROLE, *Natl. Civic Rev. 1971 60(8): 438-443, 480.* In 1967 the league campaigned "for passage of the referendum calling for a [constitutional] convention." The league actively lobbied for a new constitution when the constitutional convention convened. Two league publications were useful during the election campaign for the constitution. In December 1970, 59 percent of the voters accepted the new constitution.
H. S. Marks

# Political Sphere

## General

2299. Arnott, Catherine. FEMINISTS AND ANTI-FEMINISTS AS "TRUE BELIEVERS." *Sociol. and Social Res. 1973 57(3): 300-306.* "[Eric] Hoffer (1951) maintained [in *The True Believer* (New York: Harper and Row)] that proponents of opposing ideologies (radicals and reactionaries) are drawn from the same '*personality* pool.' Data drawn from a comparison of women in feminist and anti-feminist groups provided an opportunity to examine Hoffer's thesis from a *sociological* viewpoint. Findings revealed that, for this sample of married women, 20 active in feminist and 41 in anti-feminist groups, background variables and attitudes toward self, husband, children, and life-goals were as divergent as their ideology."                    J

2300. Baldwin, James and Katz, Shlomo. OF ANGELA DAVIS AND "THE JEWISH HOUSEWIFE HEADED FOR DACHAU." *Midstream 1971 17(6): 3-7.* Baldwin answers Katz, who had challenged his comparison of the aloneness of Angela Davis to that of "the Jewish housewife...headed for Dachau." Katz then gives a rejoinder to Baldwin's reply, emphasizing the amount of anti-Semitism among present Negro leaders.                    R. J. Wechman

2301. Bickel, Alexander M. [BOOK REVIEW] THE ROSENBERG AFFAIR: INVITATION TO AN INQUEST. BY WALTER AND MIRIAM SCHNEIR. *Commentary 1966 41(1): 69-76.* Review of *Invitation to An Inquest* (Garden City: Doubleday, 1965) on the case of Julius and Ethel Rosenberg, executed in 1953 for allegedly giving secrets of construction of the atom bomb to the Soviet Union. The Schneirs' book "mounts the most uncompromising argument yet for the innocence of the Rosenbergs," alleging that the entire case was set up by the government. The reviewer examines their argument in detail, concluding that it fails. However, he states that the case was "nevertheless an unforgivable disgrace to the American administration of justice," because the punishment was not nearly justified by the crime. The judge who sentenced the Rosenbergs blamed them not only for transmitting information to the Soviets but also for the Korean War and its possible results and sentenced them accordingly. Despite this and other irregularities, neither the Court of Appeals nor the Supreme Court was willing to examine the case, primarily because of the national climate of hysteria at the time.
A. K. Main

2302. Bingham, June. BEFORE THE COLORS FADE: ALICE ROOSEVELT LONGWORTH. *Am. Heritage 1969 20(2): 42-43, 73.* Anecdotes about the daughter of Theodore Roosevelt.                    S

2303. Boyd, James. FOLLOWING THE RULES WITH DITA AND DICK. *Washington Monthly 1972 4(5): 5-26.* Examines the subterfuges of the International Telephone and Telegraph Company, the Nixon administration, and the Republican Party in the wake of the revelation of political corruption and bribes involving those three parties and the lobbyist Dita Beard and exposed by the columnist Jack Anderson in 1972.                    S

2304. Burrows, E. G. AN INTERVIEW WITH DENISE LEVERTOV. *Michigan Q. R. 1968 7(4): 239-242.* The author, manager of the University of Michigan's radio station, WUOM, interviewed Denise Levertov, "one of America's leading poets," in April 1968. Levertov described her role as an active participant in the anti-Vietnam War, antidraft group, RESIST. She explained how RESIST originated, and its goals and successes. Relating her anti-Vietnam War activities to poetry, Levertov contended that her humanistic poetry led her into political action. Her poems of the late 1960's focus largely on ending the Vietnam War.                    H. R. Grant

2305. Colon, Frank T. THE ELECTED WOMAN. *Social Studies 1967 58(6): 256-261.* Analyzes the status of women with regard to public elective and appointive positions particularly at the Federal level. The author illustrates the low proportion of women holding public offices and points out factors which limit their appointments. Some of these factors are: prejudice of men office holders, the conflict of such jobs with marital and other household duties, and the location of such jobs away from home. The qualifying factors for public positions should be the ability and experience of the job seeker rather than the whimsical thinking of the prejudiced public. 8 notes.                    L. Raife

2306. Dubeck, Paula J. WOMEN AND ACCESS TO POLITICAL OFFICE: A COMPARISON OF FEMALE AND MALE STATE LEGISLATORS. *Sociol. Q. 1976 17(1): 42-52.* The status of women in state legislatures is examined in terms of representation across the United States. A sample of female state legislators and a sample of male state legislators are compared on social and political career characteristics, including marital status, education, occupation, age when one began serving, election mobility, party leadership, and tenure. Party leadership, education, age and, to a lesser extent, occupation were found to distinguish female from male legislators. But party leadership significantly differentiated only between female and male legislators with less than a college degree. Overall, access to state legislative office seems to depend on the same characteristics which define success in society as a whole; for certain groups of women, however, achievement within party ranks provides an alternative mechanism to this end.                    J

2307. Fallows, James. MARY MC CARTHY—THE BLINDERS SHE WEARS. *Washington Monthly 1974 6(3): 5-18.*

2308. Freshley, Dwight L. GUBERNATORIAL GHOST WRITERS. *Southern Speech J. 1965 31(2): 95-105.* Describes the speech writers of state governors in terms of their age, sex, educational level, academic major and minor, professional background, methods of speech writing, and criteria for evaluating speeches. 4 notes.
H. G. Stelzner

2309. Fuchs, Lawrence H. THE SENATOR AND THE LADY. *Am. Heritage 1974 25(6): 57-61, 81-83.* Recalls Eleanor Roosevelt's opposition to the presidential nomination of John F. Kennedy and their eventual reconciliation.                    S

2310. Gehlen, Frieda L. WOMEN IN CONGRESS. *Trans-action 1969 6(11): 36-40.* Women have occupied committees of lesser stature; determination of conscious bias in this is difficult. In chairmanships the criterion is seniority, not sex. Congresswomen have the greatest difficulty in establishing the informal relationships that tie males together (golf course, bar, etc.) although the women belong to more formalized structures such as study groups, State delegations, and freshmen clubs. Many Congresswomen may be more knowledgeable than Congressmen, but they find real power difficult to reach. Photo, biblio.
A. Erlebacher

2311. Glazer, Nathan. HANNAH ARENDT'S AMERICA. *Commentary 1975 60(3): 61-67.* Critically analyzes a recent article by

Hannah Arendt on the political effects of the Vietnam War, the Watergate scandal, economic conditions, and public relations techniques.   S

2312. Harris, Ted C.   JEANNETTE RANKIN IN GEORGIA. *Georgia Hist. Q. 1974 58(1): 55-78.* Jeannette Rankin (1880-1973) of Montana, the nation's first congresswoman, chose Georgia as a retreat and second home. It became her base of operations for peace and feminism activities. 3 illus., 93 notes.                    D. L. Smith

2313. Hunt, John Clark.   WESTWAYS WOMEN: MAURINE, MARGARINE AND CIGARETTES.   *Westways 1975 67(11): 46-50, 85.* Examines the accomplishments of Maurine Neuberger, one of two women elected to the US Senate, in consumer protection legislation during the 1960's.                    S

2314. Jackson, James.   LESSONS OF THE BATTLE FOR ANGELA DAVIS.   *World Marxist Rev. [Canada] 1972 15(8): 123-125.* Discusses the condemnation and trial of American Communist Party member Angela Davis in the 1970's, emphasizing her moral and political attitudes.

2315. Jensen, Joan M.   ANNETTE ABBOTT ADAMS, POLITICIAN.   *Pacific Hist. R. 1966 35(2): 185-201.* Re-creates Mrs. Adams' career in California law and politics, her campaign for the vice-presidential Democratic nomination in 1920 and her work as assistant attorney general. The author concludes that, despite gaining suffrage in California in 1911, women in California found it difficult to get elected to political office.                    J. McCutcheon

2316. Katz, Shlomo.   AN OPEN LETTER TO JAMES BALDWIN. *Midstream 1971 17(4): 3-5.* Discusses an open letter that James Baldwin wrote to Angela Davis likening her to the Jewish mother on her way to Dachau. Strongly takes exception to that comparison, enunciates differences between the two, and condemns Davis for not speaking out against her Communist supporters in Russia on behalf of the Russian Jews who are victims of Soviet tyranny.                    R. J. Wechman

2317. Kaufman, Paul J.   ALICE'S WONDERLAND.   *Appalachian J. 1975 2(3): 162-168.* Examines Alice Moore's views on modern textbooks and education and her place in the Kanawha County, West Virginia, textbook dispute of 1974.                    S

2318. Kornberg, Allan and Brehm, Mary L.   IDEOLOGY, INSTITUTIONAL IDENTIFICATION, AND CAMPUS ACTIVISM.   *Social Forces 1971 49(3): 445-459.* "The purpose of this analysis is to determine which independent variable employed, as for example, age, sex, and religion, as well as indices of institutional and ideological identification, contributed maximally to the differences between two polar groups of undergraduates and faculty within Duke University - those that held sympathetic as opposed to unsympathetic attitudes toward a protest incident and its handling. The same variables were employed to discriminate between groups engaged in active or passive opposition to the incident and those who displayed active or passive support. A multiple discriminant function analysis revealed that ideological position (whether one perceives himself as a conservative, 'middle-of-the-roader,' liberal, or radical) and attachment to and satisfaction with the University were the two variables that discriminated most strongly between the two polar attitudinal groups and also between the groups who, by their actions, either opposed or supported the incident."                    J

2319. Lachman, Seymour P.   THE CARDINAL, THE CONGRESSMEN, AND THE FIRST LADY.   *J. of Church and State 1965 7(1): 35-66.* Reviews the history of Federal aid to public education bills, but the main theme is the fate of the bills known as the Thomas-Taft bill and Barden bill, which failed to pass the 81st Congress. The differences between the more liberal Thomas bill and the conservative Barden bill are analyzed. Roman Catholic reaction to the Barden bill was bitter, because it prohibited using public funds for social services to pupils of nonpublic schools which had nothing to do with the religious affiliation of the school. As a byproduct of the debate, Mrs. Eleanor Roosevelt and Francis Cardinal Spellman got involved in a public debate, and finally the aid to education problem became so emotionally overheated that no bill was enacted in the 1949/50 session of Congress. President John F. Kennedy, then a Congressman from Massachusetts, played an important role in the negotiations of the bills. 97 notes.                    S. A. Rein

2320. Laue, James H.   THE MOVEMENT: DISCOVERING WHERE IT'S AT AND HOW TO GET IT.   *Urban and Social Change R. 1970 3(2): 6-11.* The civil rights movement of the early 1960's made some gains for blacks, such as desegregation of public accommodations and registration of black voters in the South. But it did not solve the black's fundamental socioeconomic problems. It did, however, sanction "protest as a legitimate activity for large groups of Americans who have heretofore been apolitical." Moving beyond the tactics and goals of the civil rights movement, the current "movement" demands "that significant group gains in a pluralistic society come not from the benevolence of the rulers, but from organization, negotiable power, self-advocacy, and confrontation." Its goals are more radical today, and its most important tactic is the use of the radical reform caucus within existing institutions and organizations. Also important is the new emphasis on ageism and sexism. 3 illus., 7 notes.                    R. D. Cohen

2321. Magowan, Robin.   NANCY LING: THE CALIFORNIA DREAM.   *Partisan R. 1976 43(2): 224-244.* In this selection from his autobiography, the author analyzes his relationship with Nancy Ling Perry, who later joined the Symbionese Liberation Army. Focuses on California culture.                    D. K. Pickens

2322. Marx, Leo.   SUSAN SONTAG'S "NEW LEFT" PASTORAL: NOTES ON REVOLUTIONARY PASTORALISM IN AMERICA. *TriQuarterly 1972 (23/24): 552-575.* Discusses the current mingling of pastoralism and revolution in American radicalism, emphasizing the ideas of social critic Susan Sontag.                    S

2323. McCoy, Donald R. and Ruetten, Richard T.   THE CIVIL RIGHTS MOVEMENT: 1940-1954.   *Midwest Q. 1969 11(1): 11-34.* Studies the Negro rights movement, pointing out its weakness before the 1930's and the legislation which brought about the great change between the years 1940-54. Franklin D. Roosevelt, and especially Eleanor Roosevelt, had principally a psychological effect on civil rights but the first government action was forced by A. Philip Randolph's "March on Washington Movement." To avoid the movement, Mr. Roosevelt issued Executive Order 8802 which halted discrimination on all new defense contracts. The author traces the legislation and Supreme Court decisions through 1954 when progress slackened and little more happened. After moving ahead thus far, the expectations of Negroes were not met and the result was frustration. The author concludes that continuing unemployment, segregation, and discrimination underlie the frustrations causing the unprecedented abrasive civil rights movement of the 1960's. References to specific legislation.                    G. H. G. Jones

2324. McGrath, Wilma E. and Soule, John W.   ROCKING THE CRADLE OR ROCKING THE BOAT: WOMEN AT THE 1972 DEMOCRATIC NATIONAL CONVENTION.   *Social Sci. Q. 1974 55(1): 141-150.* ". . . Women delegates were deeply influenced by the women's liberation movement, were keenly aware of sex discrimination in politics, and they were more liberal on questions of public policy than their male counterparts."                    J

2325. Mead, Margaret.   WOMEN IN NATIONAL SERVICE. *Teachers Coll. Record 1971 73(1): 59-63.* In the future there must be more thought on the role of women in the armed and civilian sectors of a national service program.                    S

2326. Miller, Laura.   1972: BIGGEST SOCIALIST ELECTION CAMPAIGN SINCE DEBS.   *Internat. Socialist Rev. 1971 32(9): 4-6.* Discusses the Socialist Workers Party's political campaign in the 1972 presidential election, emphasizing the policies and platform of candidates Linda Jenness and Andrew Pulley.

2327. Moon, Henry Lee.   THE CARSWELL DEFEAT: RACISM AGAIN REPULSED.   *Crisis 1970 77(4): 144-151.* On 8 April 1970 the United States Senate defeated the nomination of Judge G. Harrold Carswell to the US Supreme Court by a vote of 51-45. This came five months after Judge Clement F. Haynsworth was rejected by the Senate. Even though Carswell was described as more racist and less competent than Haynsworth, many observers felt that the forces which had opposed President Nixon's first choice would be too exhausted to defeat his second. But civil rights organizations, organized labor, women, and legal scholars joined together with Senators Edward W. Brooke and Birch

Bayh and refused to confirm the President's nomination of Judge Carswell.                                                                 A. G. Belles

2328. O'Riordan, Timothy   THE THIRD AMERICAN CONSERVATION MOVEMENT: NEW IMPLICATIONS FOR PUBLIC POLICY.   *J. of Am. Studies [Great Britain] 1971 5(2): 155-171.* Treats the development and philosophies of American conservationists since 1943 - the "third conservation movement" in America. This movement contains elements common to earlier movements which Theodore Roosevelt, Gifford Pinchot, John Wesley Powell, and Franklin Delano Roosevelt spearheaded. The "third conservation movement," under the guidance of John F. Kennedy, Stewart L. Udall, Rachel Louise Carson, and numerous other contemporary politicians and ecologists, differs from previous conservation movements in numerous ways. The "third" conservationists seek to change American goals and "value systems." 4 figs., 34 notes.
                                                                         H. T. Lovin

2329. Rabinowitz, Victor.   THE ROSENBERG CASE AND UNITED STATES POLICY.   *Sci. and Soc. 1967 31(1): 67-73.* Review of *Invitation to An Inquest* (Garden City: Doubleday, 1965), by Walter and Miriam Schneir. The Rosenberg-Sobell trial is an example of the establishment's use of a public trial in times of political stress to serve a political purpose. The Schneirs offer a narration of the case, to justify the accusation that the government perpetrated "a gigantic frame-up as an essential part of its campaign in the Cold War," and substantial arguments for Sobell's release.   R. S. Burns       G. H. G. Jones

2330. Schwartz, Benjamin I.   THE RELIGION OF POLITICS: REFLECTIONS ON THE THOUGHT OF HANNAH ARENDT.   *Dissent 1970 17(2): 144-161.* Examines Hannah Arendt's book *Eichmann in Jerusalem: A Report on the Banality of Evil* (New York: Viking Press, 1963) within the context of her philosophy. After reading a number of other books and essays by the same author, Schwartz concludes that *Eichmann in Jerusalem* fails to do justice to Arendt as a philosopher since the book can be understood only in terms of a "preestablished conceptual framework." Traces a number of Arendt's themes, most of which relate to the New Left, to the role of Jews in the New Left, and to certain characteristic forms of Jewish self-flagellation. Concludes that a religion of politics based on a vision of classical antiquity evolves in Arendt's writings. Her thinking is placed in a context of ancient Judaism, Hellenism, and Marxism. Concludes that her political vision is not relevant to the general "crisis of our times." Based on secondary sources; 33 notes.
                                                                         N. E. Tutorow

2331. Smith, Margaret Chase.   HOW MARGARET CHASE SMITH WOULD MONITOR THE CIA.   *Freedom at Issue 1976 35: 11-13.* Presents the author's opinions regarding Congress' role in preventing presidential abuse of the Central Intelligence Agency from the 1950's-70's.

2332. Stern, Robert N.; Gove, Walter R.; and Galle, Omer R.   EQUALITY FOR BLACKS AND WOMEN: AN ESSAY ON RELATIVE PROGRESS.   *Social Sci. Q. 1976 56(4): 664-672.* Applies the minority group perspective traditionally used in examining the position of U.S. blacks to the status of females and the movement toward equality. Their indices show gains for blacks are considerably better than for women.                                                                      J

2333. Taylor, Gordon O.   CASE A COLD "I": MARY MC CARTHY ON VIETNAM.   *J. of Am. Studies [Great Britain] 1975 9(1): 103-114.* Reviews three works by Mary McCarthy—*Vietnam* (1967), *Hanoi* (1968), and *Medina* (1972). Read in sequence, the books reflect the intellectual processes by which McCarthy evolved her social and political attitudes concerning the Vietnam War. 6 notes.
                                                                         H. T. Lovin

2334. Whiteman, Marjorie M.   MRS. FRANKLIN D. ROOSEVELT AND THE HUMAN RIGHTS COMMISSION.   *Am. J. of Internat. Law 1968 62(4): 918-921.* Describes the qualities of character, persistence, and wisdom that enabled Mrs. Roosevelt, as Chairman of the Human Rights Commission, 1947 to 1951, to lead the commission to its crowning success in drafting the Declaration of Human Rights.
                                                                         G. L. Lycan

2335. Williams, J. R.   DOROTHY DEEMER HOUGHTON: A MEMOIR.   *Palimpsest 1973 54(3): 24-30.* A grandson's memoir of Dorothy Deemer Houghton, whose political activities included serving as Director of the Office of Refugees, Migration and Voluntary Assistance under Eisenhower and as President of the Electoral College.   S

2336. Windle, Charles.   FACTORS IN THE PASSAGE OF STERILIZATION LEGISLATION: THE CASE OF VIRGINIA.   *Public Opinion Q. 1965 29(2): 306-314.* Compares the factors found to be associated with roll-call behavior on a sterilization bill with the public arguments on the bill. The highly related questions of race relations and welfare seem to have been central to the legislative process but the public discussion concerning voluntary sterilization made it seem a conflict between freedom and public morality. 4 tables, 17 notes.
                                                                         E. P. Stickney

2337. Wolff, Carole E. and Landis, Judson R.   DR. IRENE HICKMAN AND TAX REFORM IN SACRAMENTO COUNTY, CALIF.   *Am. J. of Econ. and Sociol. 1969 28(4): 409-421.*

2338. —.   CURRENT DOCUMENTS: DEMOCRATIC AND REPUBLICAN PLATFORM PLANKS.   *Current Hist. 1964 47(278): 236-248, 245.* Excerpts from the Democratic and Republican platforms of 1964. In spite of the highly partisan nature of these documents, the two parties largely agree on such issues as civil rights, liberalization of immigration laws, equal rights for women, economy in government, and higher Social Security benefits. They disagree on such issues as the relationship of the Federal government to the States (the Republicans call for a strictly limited role by Washington), and the proper rule of government in aiding the poor (the Democrats pledge a "war on poverty," while the Republicans suggest the adoption of "practical free enterprise measures" to benefit the needy). The Democrats denounce extremism in any form. The Republicans endorse the concept of public prayer. In foreign policy both parties call for containment of Communism, for arms control, and for support of the United Nations (although the Republicans advocate changes in the General Assembly which will reflect the power realities of the world).                                                         B. D. Rhodes

2339. —.   THE FIRST LADIES OF SOUTH DAKOTA.   *South Dakota Hist. 1973 3(2): 156-168.* Biographical sketches and portraits (now in the Governor's Mansion) of South Dakota's 24 first ladies. 24 illus.                                                             A. J. Larson

2340. —.   INTERVIEW WITH REPRESENTATIVE EDITH GREEN.   *Urban Rev. 1969 4(1): 3-8.* Former teacher Congresswoman Edith Green of Oregon expresses her opinions on the "crisis" of education in the 1970's. She believes that integration must be accompanied by academic excellence; federal support of education should be increased, especially in vocational education and programs for the "disadvantaged"; quality of teaching, particularly at the college level, needs improvement; and channels of communication should be opened between boards of trustees and their campuses with student participation on the boards. Thinks certain strings should be attached to the federal educational dollar, but the executive branch cut congressionally approved appropriations to 40 percent. She is discouraged by classrooms turning into battlefields, white flight from the cities and public schools, and busing unaccompanied by quality education.                                                   D. E. Washburn

## Legal Status and the Courts

2341. Abzug, Bella S.   CREDIT WHERE IT'S (OVER)DUE.   *Civil Liberties R. 1974 1(3): 137-139.* Discusses Congressional measures being taken to counter sex discrimination by bank officials, mortgage lenders, and credit card companies.

2342. Freed, Doris Jonas.   ETATS-UNIS: LES SYSTEMES DE COMMON LAW   [The United States: the systems of common law].   *R. Internat. de Droit Comparé [France] 1965 17(3): 661-668.* As part of a study of contemporary marriage law begun in 1955 by the Institute of Comparative Law at the University of Paris, recent cases and legislation dealing with the dower and courtesy are described. There is a tendency in several states to discontinue the traditional form of tenancy by entireties. In the seven community property states (not including Louisiana), legislation has attempted to clarify and develop certain aspects of the community property laws, usually to the advantage of the wife. 40 notes.

J. S. Gassner

2343. Ginsburg, Ruth Bader. THE NEED FOR THE EQUAL RIGHTS AMENDMENT. *Am. Bar Assoc. J. 1973 59(9): 1013-1019.* Unless the proposed equal rights amendment is ratified, an overhaul of laws that differentiate on the basis of sex is unlikely.     S

2344. Guillot, Ellen Elizabeth. CONGRESS AND THE FAMILY: REFLECTIONS OF SOCIAL PROCESSES AND VALUES IN BENEFITS IN OASDI. *Social Service R. 1971 45(2): 173-183.* Examines the notion that social change brings policy change and, conversely, that changes in a public program reflect changes in society. Details the changes since 1935 in the various subsystems of the family and the various kinds of entitlement. Generally speaking, Congress has been slower to recognize changes in the relationship between husband and wife in the labor force and in marriage than those between parents and children resulting from greater frequency of divorce. The most decisive legislative efforts to keep abreast of circumstances lie in the independence of grandparents and parents from children for support. Notes some areas where laws shape further social change and suggests needed research. 14 notes, biblio.     M. Hough

2345. Halvonik, Paul N. HOPE AND AFFECTION IN MILWAUKEE. *Civil Liberties R. 1974 1(4): 132-137.* Discusses issues raised at the 1974 American Civil Liberties Union Biennial Conference in Milwaukee, Wisconsin, particularly those involving victimless crimes involving sexual behavior.     S

2346. Janeway, Elizabeth. ON OTHERNESS: WOMAN'S IMAGE. *Civil Liberties R. 1974 1(2): 109-116.* Discusses recent writings and thought on women's rights issues and priorities during the 1970's.

2347. Nagel, Stuart and Weitzman, Lenore J. DOUBLE STANDARD OF AMERICAN JUSTICE. *Society 1972 9(5): 18-25, 62-63.* Describes ways women are discriminated against in courts.     S

2348. Nagel, Stuart and Weitzman, Lenore. SEX AND THE UNBIASED JURY. *Judicature 1972 56(3): 108-111.* Effects of sex discrimination in the selection of juries.     S

2349. Raymond, John M. DON'T RATIFY THE HUMAN RIGHTS CONVENTIONS. *Am. Bar Assoc. J. 1968 54(2): 141-143.* Replying to an article "A Costly Anachronism" [by Richard N. Gardner 1967 53(10)], Mr. Raymond argues that the failure of the United States to ratify two human rights treaties now before the Senate—those on forced labor and on the political rights of women—would not be anachronistic, but rather would be eminently sound. Our adherence to these treaties, he writes, would not advance these human rights in the nations that do not now accord them.     J

2350. Strum, Philippa. THE SUPREME COURT AND SEXUAL EQUALITY: A CASE STUDY OF FACTORS AFFECTING JUDICIAL POLICY-MAKING. *Policy Studies J. 1975 4(2): 146-150.* In a series of decisions during 1971-75 the Supreme Court has come close to pronouncing a new constitutional right of equality for women.

2351. Tucker, John H. ETATS-UNIS: LA LOUISIANE [The United States: Louisiana]. *R. Internat. de Droit Comparé [France] 1965 17(3): 669-670.* The Civil Code of Louisiana was amended to clarify the wife's rights in the disposition of community property, and a recent court decision ended doubt regarding her right to income from a donation later revoked. Part of a study of contemporary marriage law begun in 1955 by the Institute of Comparative Law at the University of Paris; 2 notes.

J. S. Gassner

2352. Van Dyke, Jon M. THE CASE FOR A GENERAL AMNESTY. *Center Mag. 1971 4(1): 64-68.* Discusses the need for a general amnesty to cover sexual behavior, abortion, juvenile delinquency, and conscientious objectors (1960's).

2353. Wadlington, Walter. DOMESTIC RELATIONS AND EVIDENCE. *Virginia Law R. 1967 53(7): 1620-1641.* The domestic relations cases cover the following areas: prohibition of miscegenous marriages, child support payments, the presumption of paternity, and child custody. The cases on evidence cover admissibility, weight and sufficiency, and evidence after trial. 103 notes.     G. P. Smith

# Political Behavior

2354. Abzug, Bella S. and Edgar, Cynthia. WOMEN AND POLITICS: THE STRUGGLE FOR REPRESENTATION. *Massachusetts R. 1972 13(1/2): 17-24.* Women have been neither "seen nor heard" in American politics, and the U.S. political system has a "masculine bias." Sexual bias makes Congress insensitive to the needs of women, the poor, and the blacks and Chicanos. Women should get involved in the political process, for they can help secure peace and social justice for all. Note.

G. Kurland

2355. Beck, Paul Allen and Jennings, M. Kent. LOWERING THE VOTING AGE: THE CASE OF THE RELUCTANT ELECTORATE. *Public Opinion Q. 1969 33(3): 370-379.* There was considerable variation by region - 59 percent of the students in the South and 37 percent of the students in the West - and by sex - 52 percent of the boys and 40 percent of the girls - but little overall enthusiasm for reducing the minimum voting age to 18. Based on data gathered in 1965 from a national probability sample of 1669 high school seniors; fig., 4 notes.

D. J. Trickey

2356. Beck, Paul Allen and Jennings, M. Kent. PARENTS AS "MIDDLEPERSONS" IN POLITICAL SOCIALIZATION. *J. of Pol. 1975 37(1): 83-107.* Based on a 1965 national sample of high school seniors and their parents, examines the flow of partisanship across three generations—grandparent, parent, and adolescent.... Finds that the roots of cross-generational similarities and differences lie in the pivotal "middleperson" role played by parents in the political socialization process. Parents carry moderately similar, inherited partisan traditions with them into marriage and exert a strong influence on the partisanship of their children. The greater continuity of the paternal grandparent tradition arises from the more frequent wife than husband conversions to spouse's partisanship in the parental generation. Yet the traditional primacy of the father as the purveyor of partisanship is eroding as a result of distinct changes in sex-related political behavior over time. A key element in this transmission process is the relative salience of politics. Despite strong cross-generalization similarity, within-family partisan turnover and reconstitution are vital elements in the dynamics of the party system.

J

2357. Bertelsen, Judy. POLITICAL INTEREST, INFLUENCE, AND EFFICACY: DIFFERENCES BETWEEN THE SEXES AND AMONG MARITAL STATUS GROUPS. *Am. Pol. Q. 1974 2(4): 412-426.* Analyzes the differences by sex and marital status of individual opinions on personal political interest, influence, and effectiveness (1968).

S

2358. Bourque, Susan C. and Grossholtz, Jean. POLITICS AN UNNATURAL PRACTICE: POLITICAL SCIENCE LOOKS AT FEMALE PARTICIPATION. *Pol. and Soc. 1974 4(2): 225-266.* Charges that there is an acceptance of a sex-oriented difference in politics, and that this acceptance of sexual stereotypes has "relegated most women to the status of camp follower and the rest to the status of deviants" in politics. Concludes "that there is a high level of distortion" in recent political science literature that perpetuates the stereotype of ideal political behavior as necessarily masculine in nature. 128 notes, appendix.

D. G. Nielson

2359. Brady, David W. and Tedin, Kent L. LADIES IN PINK: RELIGION AND POLITICAL IDEOLOGY IN THE ANTI-*ERA* MOVEMENT. *Social Sci. Q. 1976 56(4): 564-575.* Brady and Tedin, concerned with anti-ERA activists in 1975, seek to identify the sources of the anti-feminist orientation.     J

2360. Branch, Taylor. JOHN GARDNER AND THE ALBANY NYMPHETTES. *Washington Monthly 1975 7(5/6): 49-55.* Chronicles the case of Common Cause lobbyist Albert N. Podell, who was censured by the New York State legislature at Albany in 1975 for engaging young women in lobbying activities.

2361. Bullock, Charles S., III and Heys, Patricia Lee Findley. RECRUITMENT OF WOMEN FOR CONGRESS: A RESEARCH NOTE. *Western Pol. Q. 1972 25(3): 416-423.* Tests the assumption that regularly elected women, as opposed to widows filling their husband's vacancies, demonstrate more of an interest in a congressional career. Reelection rates and norm adherence were compared for the two groups. Congresswomen who win regular elections have background characteristics more similar to congressmen than do widows. The greater frequency with which the congresswomen sought reelection substantiated their perceptions of the office as a career. Based on secondary sources; 6 tables, 20 notes.                                           C. A. Gallacci

2362. Costantini, Edmond and Craik, Kenneth H. WOMEN AS POLITICIANS: THE SOCIAL BACKGROUND, PERSONALITY, AND POLITICAL CAREERS OF FEMALE PARTY LEADERS. *J. of Social Issues 1972 28(2): 217-236.*

2363. Feltner, Paula and Goldie, Leneen. IMPACT OF SOCIALIZATION AND PERSONALITY ON THE FEMALE VOTER: SPECULATIONS TESTED WITH 1964 PRESIDENTIAL DATA. *Western Pol. Q. 1974 27(4): 680-692.* Explains origins of distinctly female political attitudes.                                                     S

2364. Ferree, Myra Marx. A WOMAN FOR PRESIDENT? CHANGING RESPONSES: 1958-1972. *Public Opinion Q. 1974 38(3): 390-399.* An analysis of five political surveys conducted by the American Institute of Public Opinion (the Gallup Poll) from 1958-69 and by the National Opinion Research Center, in its "General Social Survey" in 1972, on the willingness to vote for "a well-qualified woman of your party" for president of the United States. "The sudden change in attitudes toward women seems first, to have come from both men and women, but from women much more dramatically than men.... Second, it comes from younger and better educated women.... Third, the change comes from those who are already tolerant of other minorities. ... In summary, we can say that despite the fact that 'voting' for a woman was harder in 1972 than voting for a black ... it was surely much easier in absolute terms than it had been earlier, and much more predictable and systematic. In general, this seems to have been due to women themselves." 7 tables, 4 notes.                                                D. D. Cameron

2365. Grahan, Mary W. MARGARET CHASE SMITH. *Q. J. of Speech 1964 50(4): 390-394.* The rhetoric of the 1964 presidential campaigns is considered in detail. Margaret Chase Smith did respectably well, considering her lack of organization, time, and money. As a speaker she was pleasant and smiling; reasoned in her answers and without invective, she campaigned on the issues. Four conclusions are drawn about the rhetoric of the Republican Convention: 1) none of the speaking appeared to have any material effect on the outcome of the nominating balloting, 2) most of the major public speeches were incongruous with reality, 3) the ideological characteristics of the "conservative" movement were synthesized in Goldwater's acceptance speech, and 4) the image of the Republicans that emerged from the convention was of a dominating negative nature. Contemporary newspaper reports and tape recordings constitute 10 chief sources, documented, 85 notes.                          M. A. Hayes

2366. Hansen, Susan B.; Franz, Linda M.; and Netemeyer-Mays, Margaret. WOMEN'S POLITICAL PARTICIPATION AND POLICY PREFERENCES. *Social Sci. Q. 1976 56(4): 576-590.* Uses sex differences in participation and the preferences of political activists to explore some policy consequences of women's increasing political participation.                                                               J

2367. Iglitzin, Lynne. POLITICAL EDUCATION AND SEXUAL LIBERATION. *Pol. and Soc. 1972 2(2): 241-254.* Since political education necessarily includes the joys and responsibilities of full civic participation, it is apparent that women have been trained, channeled, and molded into being women first, and citizens second. Deals with recent developments in political thought concerning the role of women as citizens and the provocative challenges raised by the women's liberation movement. Based on secondary sources; 33 notes.        J. G. Verner

2368. Jennings, M. Kent. THE DIVISION OF POLITICAL LABOR BETWEEN MOTHERS AND FATHERS. *Am. Pol. Sci. R. 1971 65(1): 69-82.* "This paper starts from the premise that traditional views of political roles among married couples emphasize role-differentiation, leading to masculine superiority; more recent perspectives stress role-sharing, leading to equality. The implications for individual political participation and political socialization vary according to the prevalence of and conditions surrounding the two patterns. Interview data from a national sample of middle-aged couples reveal substantial equality with respect to command over political resources, attention paid to politics, and manifest political participation. Levels of equality remain high under a variety of controls. When inequalities do exist, male dominance is more common, but the extent of that dominance varies across the range of political labor. Superiority of either parent in one arena tends to occur in others also, suggesting fixed modes of behavior. The relative advantage in education and personal efficacy which one partner holds over the other vitally affects the political advantage. These factors and mother's employment status operate more strongly among working class than middle class couples. Age of children has no appreciable impact. To achieve political parity or superiority mothers ordinarily need extraordinary resources to overcome the built-in constraints of culturally-defined sex roles."        J

2369. Jennings, M. Kent and Thomas, Norman. MEN AND WOMEN IN PARTY ELITES: SOCIAL ROLES AND POLITICAL RESOURCES. *Midwest J. of Pol. Sci. 1968 12(4): 469-492.* Using mail questionnaire data obtained from the Michigan delegates to the 1964 national party conventions, the authors attempt to determine if mass, public, sex-related differences in political behavior will be found in party elites. It was found that widespread social role differentiation accounts for the fact that "male delegates have far greater political resources in terms of social backgrounds and political careers." However, it was also discovered that, due to the process of elite socialization, there was more similarity between men and women with respect to political orientation. "Some pronounced differences emerge between housewives and career women, with the latter more often resembling males." 8 tables, 33 notes.                                              J. W. Thacker, Jr.

2370. Jennings, M. Kent and Langton, Kenneth P. MOTHERS VERSUS FATHERS: THE FORMATION OF POLITICAL ORIENTATIONS AMONG YOUNG AMERICANS. *J. of Pol. 1969 31(2): 329-358.* A study of the contributions of mothers and fathers to the political orientation of 1,669 high school seniors in 97 secondary schools. The first conclusion was that the notion of the family as a monolithic political unit is wrong. A second conclusion was that Democratic parents tended to have a greater influence on their children than did Republican parents. In general, mothers have a greater influence over their children's political inclinations than fathers. This finding should tend to reduce the central position political scientists have given to fathers as models of political identification. Although any number of variables can be placed in a study of this type, such as levels of political activity and education, the authors report that it does not change their conclusion about the political influence of mothers. Two historical facts of the 20th century can be cited for the influence of mothers: the rising political activity of women since 1919, and the rising levels of education for women, which, when combined with the greater affection children have for their mothers, tend to make them the predominant influence over the orientation of their children's attitudes. 7 tables, 27 notes, appendix.          A. R. Stoesen

2371. Karnig, Albert K. and Walter, B. Oliver. ELECTIONS OF WOMEN TO CITY COUNCILS. *Social Sci. Q. 1976 56(4): 605-613.* Examines the candidacy, candidate success and overall election rates for women in city council races.                                                     J

2372. Kruschke, Earl R. LEVEL OF OPTIMISM AS RELATED TO FEMALE POLITICAL BEHAVIOR. *Social Sci. 1966 41(2): 67-75.* Concludes that women who are optimistic about the future may be more likely to become actively involved in politics than those who are pessimistic. The author explains the procedures by which he established a "level of optimism" index and the procedures for selecting "political" and "apolitical" types. Four additional control variables were tested in the analysis: income, age, religious affiliation, and political affiliation.

his analyses the author concluded that "politicals" in the upper ranges who were under 40 years of age and Protestant tended to express significantly greater optimism than did "apoliticals" in these same variable categories. Based on the author's independent research.

M. Small

2373. Lansing, Marjorie. SEX DIFFERENCES IN VOTING AND ACTIVISM. *Michigan Academician 1972 5(2): 171-175.*

2374. Lasky, Melvin J. LADY ON THE BARRICADES. *Encounter [Great Britain] 1972 39(1): 17-31.* Discusses five examples of women involved in political activism: Margit Czenki and her trial for armed bank robbery in the cause of socialism in West Germany; Diana Oughton, who accidentally blew up herself and her Weathermen comrades in New York City in 1970; Theroigne de Mericourt, the French revolutionary of 1789; Teresa Hayter and her autobiographical reminiscences of the emergence of an English revolutionary Marxist; and Beata Sturm, the jailed German urban guerrilla. 12 notes.

D. H. Murdoch

2375. Lynn, Naomi B. and Flora, Cornelia B. MOTHERHOOD AND POLITICAL PARTICIPATION: THE CHANGING SENSE OF SELF. *J. of Pol. and Military Sociol. 1973 1(1): 91-104.* "This study focuses on women and their political activity, with special emphasis on the effect which motherhood has on their self-image and its relevance for political participation. Sociologists stress the primacy of the role of mother in the identification of the adult female. Saliency of motherhood among young women has not been systematically analyzed for its political implications. Two distinct data sources were used. First, mothers and non-mothers were compared as to political participation from the 1968 study of the American electorate by the Survey Research Center, University of Michigan. The role of mother, rather than total number of children or age of child, is important in explaining political participation among women in the population who tend to be most politically efficacious— upper middle class women with some college education. To specify the process by which motherhood affects the formation of the political self, in-depth interviews were then undertaken with a sample of new mothers. Types of interaction networks are discussed and shown to be related both to becoming a mother and being politically isolated. Child-centered social networks are particularly antithetical to development of a political self."

J

2376. Montero, Darrel. SUPPORT FOR CIVIL LIBERTIES AMONG A COHORT OF HIGH SCHOOL GRADUATES AND COLLEGE STUDENTS. *J. of Social Issues 1975 31(2): 123-136.* This study examines one facet of political attitudes, support for those civil liberties guaranteed in the Bill of Rights, employing a modified version of the Selvin-Hagstrom Libertarian Index, administered by mail questionnaire to an entire high school senior class four years after graduation. The varied educational backgrounds, combined with the original relative homogeneity of the sample, allow for a refined analysis of the impact of selected demographic variables (e.g., sex, marital status, religious affiliation, political party identification, and education). The results replicate the well established finding that education is positively and highly related to support of civil liberties. In addition, sex and religion are found to exert an impact upon support for civil liberties. Findings are discussed in reference to the role of higher education in democratic societies.

J

2377. Orum, Anthony M.; Cohen, Roberta S.; Grasmuck, Sherri; and Orum, Amy W. SEX, SOCIALIZATION AND POLITICS. *Am. Sociol. R. 1974 39(2): 197-209.* Three perspectives are usually used to explain differences in political beliefs and behavior of men and women: political socialization, structural, and situational. This paper examines evidence bearing on one of these theories, political socialization, and finds relatively minor support for it. A variety of alternative explanations flows from these results, the most radical of which would call for abandoning the political socialization perspective altogether. A more cautious reading of the findings suggests a new interpretation, one that integrates both political socialization and situational theories.

J

2378. Schuman, Howard. TWO SOURCES OF ANTIWAR SENTIMENT IN AMERICA. *Am. J. of Sociol. 1972 78(3): 513-536.* "Opposition to the Vietnam war has been manifested both in university protest actions and in cross-section public opinion surveys. But the college-related protests and the wider public disenchantment have sharply differ-

ent characteristics: they have peaked at different points in the war; they are discontinuous in educational and age basis; and a substantial part of the antiwar public is also extremely hostile toward college protesters. Together these findings suggest a distinction between moral criticisms of the goals and nature of the war and pragmatic disillusionment over failure to win it. . . . The themes emphasized by the Detroit sample as a whole, and by most sub- categories defined in terms of race, sex, age, and education, are generally consistent with the moral-pragmatic distinction. Other related factors (such as traditional isolationism) are also shown to contribute to broader public disenchantment with the war."

J

2379. Swift, David W. WHO VOTED FOR RAFFERTY?: A PROFILE OF VOTERS IN THE 1962 ELECTION FOR CALIFORNIA'S SUPERINTENDENT OF PUBLIC INSTRUCTION. *California Soc. Sci. R. 1966 5(3): 24-29.* This report concludes that "in every instance Rafferty's followers were more likely to make conservative choices"; "contrasts between the groups supporting the two candidates were decidedly more pronounced among women than among men"; "Rafferty women...were the most likely of all groups to be conservative, and they were also the most likely to vote." Based on unpublished data from three polls conducted during the campaign. Each of the polls surveyed from 1,100 to 1,500 people. Charts.

F. Rotondaro

2380. Thompson, Kenneth H. UPWARD SOCIAL MOBILITY AND POLITICAL ORIENTATION: A RE-EVALUATION OF THE EVIDENCE. *Am. Sociol. R. 1971 36(2): 223-235.* "That upward social mobility has a different effect on the political orientations of Europeans than of Americans is commonly accepted. Several scholars have concluded that upwardly mobile Europeans are less conservative than middle-class stables. The contrasting conclusion that in the United States upwardly mobile people become even more conservative than middle-class stables is based on a single study completed some years ago. Here, this relationship is re-examined by analyzing data from five nationally-representative American samples over 14 years. In these samples, the upward mobiles are consistently less likely to be conservative than the middle-class stables and more likely to be conservative than the working-class stables. However, analysis of the joint effects of sex and social mobility indicates that American upwardly mobile males are more likely to approximate the politics of the class to which they have risen than are upwardly mobile females."

J

2381. Volgy, Thomas J. and Volgy, Sandra S. WOMEN AND POLITICS: POLITICAL CORRELATES OF SEX-ROLE ACCEPTANCE. *Social Sci. Q. 1975 55(4): 967-974.* Propose an alternative method of measuring sex-role related differences in mass political behavior and attitudes, and provide data to indicate that a strong and significant relationship exists between women's acceptance or rejection of traditional sex-role values and their orientation toward politics.

J

2382. —. PERSPECTIVES AND LESSONS OF THE NEW RADICALIZATION. *Internat. Socialist Rev. 1971 32(10): 7-11, 38-50.* Presents the Socialist Workers Party's position on the political radicalization of ethnic groups, the working class, women, and labor unions in 1970.

# Women's Movement

2383. Barber, Benjamin R. MAN ON WOMEN. *Worldview 1973 16(4): 17-23, (5): 47-54.* Part I. Analyzes women's liberation. "To insist that women are not oppressed is then neither to deny their grievances nor to oppose major social change. It is to insist that the abuse of women is an attribute of their relationship with men, not intrinsic to it." The feminist movement can only "obstruct the meaningful amelioration of woman's condition." Part II. "Radical feminism as a political movement is associated with a series of unjustified claims." Analyzes the feminist position on monogamous marriage, romantic love, and sexual equality.

M. L. Frey

2384. Beal, Frances M. DOUBLE JEOPARDY: TO BE BLACK AND FEMALE. *New Generation 1969 51(4): 23-31.* Describes differences between the social and economic situations of black and white women who participate in the women's liberation movement.

2385.   Bell, Carolyn Shaw.   THE NEXT REVOLUTION.   *Social Policy 1975 6(2): 5-11.* Following the equalization of employment opportunities, women's liberation must attempt to equalize family responsibilities between the sexes.

2386.   Bernard, Jessie.   AGE, SEX AND FEMINISM.   *Ann. of the Am. Acad. of Pol. and Social Sci. 1974 415: 120-137.* "This paper attempts to delineate the relationship between age and sex as independent variables and certain issues related to feminism. Neither the dependent nor the independent variable is simple and unequivocal. Also, the relations among them cannot be precisely measured with data so far available. Only general trends can be traced and hypothetical interpretations of them offered. With these qualifications, the following conclusions seem acceptable. Although more older than younger respondents of both sexes tend—expectably—to be traditional on feminist issues, older men are more favorable than older women on such issues. Among women education seems to explain a good deal of the traditionalism associated with age. However, the historical circumstances in which the generation of women now in their forties were socialized may help to explain their anomalous positions on feminist issues today. The political implications of current trends lie in increasing acceptance of feminist positions."   J

2387.   Bernard, Jessie.   MY FOUR REVOLUTIONS: AN AUTO-BIOGRAPHICAL HISTORY OF THE ASA.   *Am. J. of Sociol. 1973 78(4): 773-791.* "There have been at least four revolutions in the American Sociological Association that I know of. In the 1920s empirical research papers were introduced in the annual programs; in the 1930s the Society declared its independence of the University of Chicago; in the 1950s, the Society for the Study of Social Problems was organized. Now in the 1970s we are having a feminist revolution. Among the contributions that this fourth revolution can make to sociology is that of filling in the deficiencies resulting from its sexist bias, helping it become a science of society instead of, as so often now, a male science of society or a science of male society. All the major paradigms call for a thorough overhauling to see to what extent they are distorted by their male bias."   J

2388.   Bird, Caroline.   WOMEN'S LIB AND THE WOMEN'S COLLEGES.   *Change 1972 4(3): 60-65.* The colleges which once led the campaign for equal status for women have been upstaged by others in the current drive for "liberation." One of the founding philosophers tells why this happened, and how the Seven Sisters and the other one-sex colleges are hurrying to catch up.   J

2389.   Buggs, John A.   GROUPS' RIGHTS STRUGGLES ARE MUTUALLY BENEFICIAL.   *J. of Intergroup Relations 1975 4(1): 38-50.* Argues that presently the complementary goals of women and minority groups make struggle between underprivileged peoples unnecessary.   S

2390.   Byrd, Sandra Lee.   FEMINISM—A JOURNAL OF EMOTION.   *Focus/Midwest 1973 9(59): 18.* The primary emotion of today's feminist is the joy of freedom. Women have never been freer and more determined to be freer.   L. H. Grothaus

2391.   Campbell, Karlyn Kohrs.   THE RHETORIC OF WOMEN'S LIBERATION: AN OXYMORON.   *Q. J. of Speech 1973 59(1): 74-86.* "The rhetoric of women's liberation merits separate critical treatment because it is a unique genre of rhetoric. Its distinctive substantive characteristics arise from the peculiarly intense moral conflict it generates so that moderate and reformist options are closed to feminist advocates. Its distinctive stylistic features include emphasis on affective proofs and personal testimony, participation and dialogue, self-disclosure and self-criticism, autonomous decision making, and 'violations of the reality structure.' "   J

2392.   Cassell, Joan.   EXTERNALITIES OF CHANGE: DEFERENCE AND DEMEANOR IN CONTEMPORARY FEMINISM.   *Human Organization 1974 33(1): 85-94.* Examines the symbolic inversion of clothing and behavior among Women's Liberation participants.   S

2393.   Chafe, William H.   FEMINISM IN THE 1970'S.   *Dissent 1974 21(4): 508-518.*

2394.   Cherniss, Cary   PERSONALITY AND IDEOLOGY: A PERSONOLOGICAL STUDY OF WOMEN'S LIBERATION.   *Psychiatry 1972 35(2): 109-125.* Investigates the psychological aspects of involvement in the women's liberation movement. The study included 12 women in the movement, and a comparison group of eight others. It was found that the life-style of those involved in the movement was active, assertive, and seeking independence. They tended to have strong mothers, and as adolescents they were isolated and lonely, without any of the conventional adolescent activities such as participation in sororities. The women's liberation movement includes participation in the "consciousness-raising group," which is of great personal significance for the members. Discussion of their problems in a supportive atmosphere helps develop a sense of trust and intimacy among members, a sense of community. Many members joined a women's liberation group following a crisis of identity. The conventional models of feminine development did not fit their needs and desires. Through participation in the movement, they resolve their quest for identity. For many women, participation can be a positive experience and can bring about constructive individual growth in less time than psychotherapy or other means of personal change. 5 notes.
M. A. Kaufman

2395.   Chisholm, Shirley.   RACE, REVOLUTION AND WOMEN.   *Black Scholar 1971 3(4): 17-21.* Discusses the Black Revolution and the Women's Liberation Movement in the United States as part of a worldwide rebellion pertinent to all aspects of human life. Racism and antifeminism affect everyone. Traditional stereotypes and roles must be rejected. Women and blacks must be revolutionaries working for total freedom and to build a worldwide humanistic society.   A. E. Wiederrecht

2396.   Croce, Arlene.   SEXISM IN THE HEAD.   *Commentary 1971 51(3): 63-68.* The feminist movement has become a farce, by equating sexism with racism.   S

2397.   Domenach,   Jean-Marie.   LA   SOCIEDAD   NORTEAMERICANA EN ESCORZO: REVOLUCION INTEGRAL? [US society seen from a distance: total revolution?].   *Rev. de Ciencias Sociales [Puerto Rico] 1972 16(2): 175-186.* Discusses the confusing crosscurrents in US society during the Vietnam war. Liberation movements of racial minorities, women, and homosexuals as well as scattered opposition to the war and the counterculture of the hippies in their various forms are mentioned. At first sight it was a society in complete disarray. On closer inspection, returns to the principles of the founding fathers were indicated. The author sees America as a Frenchman and questions the influence of these developments on Europe.
F. Pollaczek

2398.   Elshtain, Jean Bethke.   THE FEMINIST MOVEMENT & THE QUESTION OF EQUALITY.   *Polity 1975 7(4): 452-477.* Equality is a rich, difficult, contested political concept, and the choice among apparently reasonable meanings has implications for the kind of social policies one urges. Prof. Elshtain moves from exposition of equality as an essentially contested political concept to examination of Feminist versions of sex equality. The dominant view in the contemporary Feminist movement emphasizes equality of opportunity, but this actually justifies a sharply inegalitarian system. Socialist Feminists, viewing persons as social by nature, introduce a sense of equality of respect and treatment that goes beyond the privatized person, formal rights perspective, Elshtain suggests. The essay is a vigorous analysis of both Feminist literature and the concept of "equality."   J

2399.   Epstein, Cynthia Fuchs.   TEN YEARS LATER: PERSPECTIVES ON THE WOMAN'S MOVEMENT.   *Dissent 1975 22(2): 169-176.*

2400.   Evans, Sara M.   THE ORIGINS OF THE WOMEN'S LIBERATION MOVEMENT.   *Radical Am. 1975 9(2): 1-14.* Considers changes in sex roles since the 1950's as women entered the service sector of the economy and participated in the Civil Rights Movement.   S

2401.   Fairlie, Henry.   ON THE HUMANITY OF WOMEN.   *Public Interest 1971 23: 16-32.* The concept of the "humanity of women" is lacking in the literature of women's liberation. The emphasis on the negative and violent aspects of the whole radical movement tends to eliminate the importance of the relationship of "one individual to another

THE UNITED STATES SINCE 1945

individual." It is necessary to go beyond the female to the feminine, and to the enduring and essential meaning of the latter word with its contribution to the civilizing aspects of human nature. E. C. Hyslop

2402. Fargo, Sondra. THE NEW FEMINISM: MADAME BOVARY GOES PROFESSIONAL. *Tri-Q. 1965 (3): 180-182, 184, 186, 188.* Betty Friedan is a reformer who sees the American housewife as the victim of bad men who keep her chained to a biological role. Friedan's answer in *The Feminine Mystique* (Nev York: 1963) is that the non-professional life is not worth living, and that the only legitimate method of self-realization is professionalism. Fargo thinks this view defines success only in commercial terms and justifies acquisitiveness in American life. The position of the American housewife today as a creature of leisure and comfort may be the position of our entire society as we move toward labor-free lives. The author compares Friedan's view of women with Flaubert's *Madame Bovary.* 13 notes. W. H. Agee

2403. Freeman, Jo. THE ORIGINS OF THE WOMEN'S LIBERATION MOVEMENT. *Am. J. of Sociol. 1973 78(4): 792-811.* "A study of the origins of the two branches of the women's liberation movement is used to illustrate the microstructural prerequisites of movement formation. It is proposed that there must be a preexisting co-optable communications network within at least part of the social base of a potential movement in order for any 'spontaneous' activity to have more than a temporary effect. This network must be galvanized by a combination of precipitating events and specific organizing activity. It is further hypothesized that the nature of the initial core groups will largely determine the subsequent structure and strategy of the movement. J

2404. Freeman, Jo. STRUCTURE AND STRATEGY IN THE WOMEN'S LIBERATION MOVEMENT. *Urban and Social Change Rev. 1972 5(2): 71-75.* Although alike ideologically, the early 1960's "reformist" feminist groups are tightly organized and seek social reform through social change, while post-1967 "radical" groups are loosely structured and develop the reform potential through education. S

2405. Freeman, Jo. WOMEN'S LIBERATION AND ITS IMPACT ON THE CAMPUS. *Liberal Educ. 1971 57(4): 468-478.* Colleges have influenced the "liberated" attitudes of women by some courses, by providing an egalitarian community, and by overtraining women for the jobs open to them. Now colleges are being challenged on the bias of most academic studies, on sex-biased job assignments, and on the male-oriented bias of student services. One response by colleges has been the establishment of women's studies courses. Warns that segregation of these studies into individual departments could lead to a repetition of the experience of Home Economics, i.e., the degeneration of a rigorous discipline into an object of derision. E. M. Gersman

2406. Freydberg, Hargret Howe. WOMEN'S LIBERATION: WHAT WILL WE LOSE? *Am. Scholar 1972/73 42(1): 139-147.* An anthology of eight essays by women outlining the women's liberation movement. As women gain more opportunity, power, and responsibility, they also begin to change in subtle ways, and no longer fit their past image. F. F. Harling

2407. Gerassi, John. SIMONE DE BEAUVOIR: THE SECOND SEX 25 YEARS LATER. *Society 1976 13(2): 79-85.* Presents an interview with author and feminist Simone de Beauvoir (b. 1908), emphasizing the worldwide struggle for women's rights in the 1970's.

2408. Hancock, Brenda Robinson. AFFIRMATION BY NEGATION IN THE WOMEN'S LIBERATION MOVEMENT. *Q. J. of Speech 1972 58(3): 264-271.* "In the early stages of the current radical feminist movement, naming men as the enemy was an important rhetorical strategy. 'Man-hating' not only allowed women to release frustration and guilt, but led to identifying female characteristics as the antithesis of male standards. The pro-woman line that developed was instrumental in giving women a new identity and sense of political strength." J

2409. Haymes, Howard J. POSTWAR WRITING AND THE LITERATURE OF THE WOMEN'S LIBERATION MOVEMENT. *Psychiatry 1975 38(4): 328-333.* Reviews writing about and by women in the light of Freudian analysis from 1946 to the 1970's.

2410. Hunter, Allen and O'Brien, James. READING ABOUT THE NEW LEFT. *Radical Am. 1972 6(4): 73-94.* Presents a bibliography on the New Left, the women's liberation movement, and the student movement of the 1960's.

2411. Jaquith, Cindy. WHERE IS THE WOMEN'S POLITICAL CAUCUS GOING? *Internat. Socialist Rev. 1972 33(5): 4-7.* Discusses the political strategy of the National Organization for Women in 1972, emphasizing the views of caucus leaders Betty Friedan, Shirley Chisholm, and Bella Abzug.

2412. Jordan, Joan. THE ECONOMICS OF WOMEN'S LIBERATION. *New Generation 1969 51(4): 9-15.* The women's liberation movement is faced with a dual problem: direct economic exploitation and various forms of social discrimination.

2413. LaRue, Linda. THE BLACK MOVEMENT AND WOMEN'S LIBERATION. *Black Scholar 1970 1(7): 36-42.* Examines the similarities in aims between the women's liberation movement and black liberation movements, maintaining that though they share some similarities, the black movement entails all sexes while women's liberation often applies only to whites of middle and upper-middle classes.

2414. Laudicina, Eleanor V. TOWARDS NEW FORMS OF LIBERATION: A MILDLY UTOPIAN PROPOSAL. *Social Theory and Practice 1973 2(3): 275-288.* Discusses recent trends and issues in the women's liberation movement, including occupational equality, sex roles, and child-rearing responsibilities.

2415. Lessard, Suzannah. THE MS. CLICK!, THE DECTER ANGUISH, THE VILAR VULGARITY. *Washington Monthly 1973 4(11): 29-37.* Critiques three approaches to feminism. S

2416. Lewis, Mary Ellen B. THE FEMINISTS HAVE DONE IT: APPLIED FOLKLORE. *J. of Am. Folklore 1974 87(343): 85-87.* The women's liberation movement has developed negative rallying cries from traditional proverbial expressions and beliefs about women (e.g., "It's a woman's perogative to change her mind"), but has overlooked many pointed examples. Secondary sources; 9 notes. W. D. Piersen

2417. Mandle, Joan D. WOMEN'S LIBERATION: HUMANIZING RATHER THAN POLARIZING. *Ann. of Am. Acad. of Pol. and Social Sci. 1971 (397): 118-128.* "An alliance of various groups of women drawn together under the umbrella of the women's liberation movement has recently demanded full social equality. The precise content of their demand, however, remains vague due to the diversity of the groups involved. Some individuals and groups focus on problems associated with female personality development, while others concentrate on women's labor force marginality. Still other groups explore the sources of the dissatisfaction with home roles in evidence among increasing numbers of American women. This paper attempts to explore the social determinants of the inferior position of women in society, and briefly touch on the responses of the women's liberation movement to this unfavorable position. The assignment of women on the basis of sex to home-oriented and low-status adult roles is advanced as the basic source of these varied problems. The various demands for equality can therefore be seen as aspects of the more general goal - the elimination of this assigned and low-status role set." J

2418. Marieskind, Helen I. and Ehrenreich, Barbara. TOWARD SOCIALIST MEDICINE: THE WOMEN'S HEALTH MOVEMENT. *Social Policy 1975 6(2): 34-42.* Discusses, in a special section entitled "Women & Health," how women's liberation and other minority reform movements have redefined the nature of socialized medicine in the 1960's and 1970's.

2419. McDonald, Donald. THE LIBERATION OF WOMEN. *Center Mag. 1972 5(3): 25-43.* Discusses the Women's Liberation Movement in the United States and the present condition of women and attempts to explain how that condition has come about. S

2420. McDowell, Margaret B. REFLECTIONS ON THE NEW FEMINISM. *Midwest Q. 1971 12(3): 309-333.* Analyzes women's liberation. Details the ideas of Simone de Beauvoir, Mary Ellmann, Eva Figes,

WOMEN IN AMERICAN HISTORY

and Doris Lessing as compared with the more strident and attention-getting rhetoric of the current best seller, Kate Millett. Emphasizes the precedence of Virginia Woolf's feminist tracts with their reasonable tone and direct style.     G. H. G. Jones

2421. Micossi, Anita Lynn. CONVERSION TO WOMEN'S LIB. *Trans-Action 1970 8(1/2): 82-90.* Discusses the diminution of women in terms of structural and material discrimination (visible in social, legal, economic, and cultural forms) and in the subjective and psychological participation in such abuse by women themselves; discusses these societal aspects in terms of the women's liberation movement, 1960's.     G. A. Hewlett

2422. Miller, Margaret I. and Linker, Helene. EQUAL RIGHTS AMENDMENT CAMPAIGNS IN CALIFORNIA AND UTAH. *Soc. 1974 11(4): 40-53.* In California, "the forceful and organized proponents of the Equal Rights Amendment overcame the opposition." In Utah, proponents were unprepared for the "hysterial HOTDOG [Humanitarians Opposed to the Degradation of Our Girls] harangues" which quickly defeated the amendment.     S

2423. Millett, Kate. LIBBIES, SMITHIES, VASSARITES. *Change 1970 2(5): 42-50.* Describes a visit to Vassar and Smith Colleges during the weekend after the invasion of Cambodia. Discusses plans for student strikes and the development of the women's liberation movement on the two campuses. 2 illus.     F. I. Murphy

2424. Mitchell, Juliet. OUT FROM UNDER . . . *Liberation 1971 16(7): 6-13.* Examines the Women's Liberation Movement in relation to socialist ideology. The feminist movement grew out of 1) the contradictions between the woman's role in the family and her role in the work force, and 2) the emergence of separatist politics among Black Power groups, and the youth and peace movements of the 1960's. Because women are oppressed as a class and are also victims of a male-dominated society, socialist analysis of feminism must accept the existence of both an oppressed consciousness and "feminist consciousness." 5 notes.     M. P. Murphy

2425. Morris, Monica B. NEWSPAPERS AND THE NEW FEMINISTS: BLACK-OUT AS SOCIAL CONTROL? *Journalism Q. 1973 50(1): 37-42.* Examines coverage, or lack of, by newspapers in Great Britain and Los Angeles of the women's liberation movement to determine society's response to an emerging social movement (1968-70).     S

2426. Morris, Monica B. THE PUBLIC DEFINITION OF A SOCIAL MOVEMENT: WOMEN'S LIBERATION. *Sociol. and Social Res. 1973 57(4): 526-543.* "Turner and Killian show that a social movement's opposition and means of action depend upon its public definition. This study examines within a conflict theory framework the women's liberation movement in Los Angeles County at two points in time compared to the movement's image in two major, local newspapers. The movement was first ignored by the newspapers but grew despite this. Later newspaper coverage was excessive compared to changes in the movement."     J

2427. Murphy, Sara. WOMEN'S LIB IN THE SOUTH. *New South 1972 27(2): 42-46.* Women in the civil rights movement of the 1960's were treated just as oppressively in the South as their counterparts in conservative social institutions.

2428. Novack, George. THE RERADICALIZATION OF AMERICAN POLITICS. *Internat. Socialist R. 1974 35(2): 4-11.* Documents the birth of recent radical movements, concentrating primarily on feminists and minorities.     S

2429. Oltman, Ruth M. WOMEN IN THE PROFESSIONAL CAUCUSES. *Am. Behavioral Scientist 1971 15(2): 281-302.* Surveys the origins and development of groups advocating women's rights within faculty, student, and professional organizations. Specific professional associations furnish detailed examples. Summarizes activities and achievements of women's caucuses or committees. Biblio., appendix.     D. G. Davis, Jr.

2430. Parker, Franklin. WOMEN'S EDUCATION: HISTORICAL AND INTERNATIONAL VIEW. *Contemporary Educ. 1972 43(4): 198-201.* Describes the fight of women for better education and better careers during the last ten years and compares gains made in the United States with those in other countries.     S

2431. Peterson, Grethe Ballif. SOMEWHERE IN BETWEEN. *Dialogue: A J. of Mormon Thought 1971 6(2): 74-76.* One Mormon's feelings about Women's Liberation.     S

2432. Reed, Evelyn. FEMINISM AND 'THE FEMALE EUNUCH.' *Internat. Socialist Rev. 1971 32(7): 10-13, 31-36.* Discusses elements of patriarchal ideology in feminist Germaine Greer's book *The Female Eunuch,* emphasizing attitudes toward sexual frigidity in women and the relationship of feminism to Marxism, 1960's-70's.

2433. Roberts, Allyn. MEN AND WOMEN AS PARTNERS IN CHANGE. *Arts in Society 1974 11(1): 62-70.* Panel discussion on the emotional reaction of men to the Women's Liberation Movement, urging a joint effort to eradicate sexism. Part of a conference on Women and the Arts, Racine, Wisconsin, 1973.     S

2434. Romer, Karen T. and Secor, Cynthia. THE TIME IS HERE FOR WOMEN'S LIBERATION. *Ann. of the Am. Acad. of Pol. and Social Sci. 1971 (397): 129-139.* "The women's liberation movement examines the ways in which women's options and patterns of behavior are limited by the sex-role stereotypes imposed on them through socialization. In the academic community these stereotypes are reinforced by a sexual etiquette which communicates an underlying reification of women and an inability of men to accept women as equal partners in professional life. Although the action of the Department of Health, Education, and Welfare and the widespread new interest in the condition of women may result in the appointment of women to prominent positions, unless concerned men join women to overcome stereotyped patterns of interpersonal relations the oppression that constantly downgrades women and isolates them from their colleagues will continue to prevail. The problem should be viewed in historical perspective. Culture as we see it manifested in institutions of higher learning is masculine. The problem that confronts male and female academicians is whether or not they can accommodate the existing masculine ideology, institutions, and behavior patterns to the emerging feminine definition of culture as articulated and practiced by both the counter-culture and the women's liberation movement. If feminism is to be the ultimate revolution, it must establish an androgynous community in which roles will not be assigned according to gender."     J

2435. Rossi, Alice. WOMEN - TERMS OF LIBERATION. *Dissent 1970 17(6): 531-541.* Evaluates the encouraging and discouraging developments of the women's movement. The author naively embarked upon an academic career, scoffing at the warnings of male colleagues that her sex was against her. A series of pointedly discriminatory acts, however, changed that outlook. Women should begin a concerted campaign on the job issue. The goal of full equality will not be achieved by those groups which settle for publicity and demands for quick solutions.     W. L. Hogeboom

2436. Rossi, Alice S. WOMEN—TERMS OF LIBERATION. *Dissent 1974 21(2): 317-327.* Background, development, and possibilities for the Women's Liberation Movement. First published in the November-December 1970 *Dissent.*     S

2437. Ruth, Sheila. A SERIOUS LOOK AT CONSCIOUSNESS-RAISING. *Social Theory and Practice 1973 2(3): 289-300.* Discusses current attitudes toward the women's liberation movement, emphasizing the importance of the concept of consciousness-raising in establishing alternative life-styles and self-images for women.

2438. Sanger, Susan Phipps and Alker, Henry A. DIMENSIONS OF INTERNAL-EXTERNAL LOCUS OF CONTROL AND THE WOMEN'S LIBERATION MOVEMENT. *J. of Social Issues 1972 28(4): 115-130.* Fifty feminists (WL) and 50 control subjects were administered Rotter's Internal-External scale and a series of questions concerning their backgrounds and their attitudes about and involvement in the women's movement. Three dimensions emerged from a factor analysis of the I-E items: personal control, protestant ethic ideology, and feminist ideology. The WL subjects were more internal than the control subjects in their sense of personal control and more external in protestant ethic ideology (PEI) and feminist ideology. Externality on these two dimensions was shown to be related to involvement in the feminist movement. Rejection of PEI was accompanied by an increased sense of personal internality for the feminists.

                 J

2439. Segers, Mary C. THE NEW CIVIL RIGHTS: FEM LIB! *Catholic World 1970 211(1265): 203-207.* Discusses social issues of the women's liberation movement in 1970, including sexual stereotypes and occupational inequality.

2440. Stoloff, Carolyn. WHO JOINS WOMEN'S LIBERATION? *Psychiatry 1973 36(3): 325-340.* Responses to questionnaires sent to female graduate students at the University of Michigan in order to determine the differences between members of the women's liberation movement and others who remained out of the movement indicate that there were distinct differences in socioeconomic, religious, intellectual and political background, and the political attitudes of the students' parents. Those who join the movement are most typically from middle- or upper-middle-class urban or suburban families, with a Jewish or "nonformalistically religious" Protestant background, and from homes in which religion was not strongly emphasized. Parents of those who joined the movement are most likely college graduates or employed in professional or intellectual occupations, and they are more politically liberal than parents of the nonjoiners. Most of those in each group reported that they had a close relationship with their mothers, but the participants reported that their mothers were considerably more competitive than mothers of nonparticipants, and somewhat more competitive than their husbands. The women's liberationists tend to be more sexually experienced, and they tended to be participants in the earlier Civil Rights movement and the recent Peace Movement. Subjects in each group, however, subscribed to the women's liberation view of women's rights, roles, and responsibilities. 6 notes, biblio.       M. Kaufman

2441. Stone, Betsey. WOMEN AND THE '72 ELECTIONS. *Int. Socialist Rev. 1972 33(2): 14-19, 39.* Points out the lack of support for women's issues by the presidential candidates of the major political parties in 1972, and discusses the perspectives of the Socialist Workers Party and the National Women's Political Caucus.

2442. Tavris, Carol. WHO LIKES WOMEN'S LIBERATION—AND WHY: THE CASE OF THE UNLIBERATED LIBERALS. *J. of Social Issues 1973 29(4): 175-198.* "This survey explored a variety of background factors that are related to a person's support of or opposition to the women's liberation movement (WLM), including religion and political preference, perception of sex differences in personality (usually called 'stereotyping') and belief as to whether these are due to biology or culture, and style of marriage (traditional or egalitarian). Also for men, a dimension of sexual threat was related to hostility toward the WLM; for women, experiences with discrimination and to a lesser extent 'sexism' contributed to their support of the WLM. The survey found that only a small proportion of men are truly threatened by the movement, but only a small proportion are truly in favor of it; most are caught in the easy middle ground, where attitudes are liberal and behavior is traditional."       J

2443. Turock, Betty. WOMEN'S INFORMATION AND REFERRAL SERVICE ASKS COMMUNITY FOR ANSWERS. *Wilson Lib. Bull. 1975 49(8): 568-572.* Describes the success of the Women's Information and Referral Service (WIRS) in the Montclair, New Jersey, Public Library—a project recommended and funded by the New Jersey Commission on Women in 1973.       S

2444. Vogel, Lise. THE EARTHLY FAMILY. *Radical Am. 1973 7(4/5): 9-50.* A Marxist approach to providing adequate theory for the Women's Liberation Movement.       S

2445. Weil, Mildred. THE RISE AND FALL OF WOMEN'S LIBERATION: THE NEW FEMINISM EMERGES. *Social Studies 1975 66(4): 164-167.* Advances arguments for the changing roles of women based upon general changes in the social structure. Though controversial, many changes seem to benefit the women's liberation groups. 9 notes.       L. R. Raife

2446. Welch, Susan. SUPPORT AMONG WOMEN FOR THE ISSUES OF THE WOMEN'S MOVEMENT. *Sociol. Q. 1975 16(2): 216-227.* Using both data from a national and community sample, this paper explores support among women for issues relevant to the women's rights movement and the extent to which the issues of the movement are perceived as a coherent whole by women. Five distinct issue dimensions emerged. Support for or agreement with each of the issue areas was only slightly correlated with support for the others. Thus, some types of women are supportive of the variety of issues and in agreement with the basic assumptions of the movement while others are more selective in their support. In general, support for any particular issue area is greater than support for women's liberation, yet even those opposing women's liberation agree with the position of the women's movement on a majority of issues examined.       J

2447. Wohl, Lisa Cronin. WHITE GLOVES AND COMBAT BOOTS: THE FIGHT FOR ERA. *Civil Liberties R. 1974 1(4): 77-86.* The Equal Rights Amendment's (ERA) "language sounds innocuous enough, but its supporters have found themselves in the toughest fight involving a women's issue since suffrage."       J

2448. —. FIGHT AGAINST WOMEN'S OPPRESSION PARALLELS STRUGGLE AGAINST RACISM. *Progressive Labor 1973 9(3): 24-29.* Links women's liberation with trade union objectives and the struggle for racial justice. Argues that the "only chance to end women's oppression is to overthrow capitalism, but revolution doesn't guarantee an end to women's oppression."       S and J

2449. —. TOWARD A MASS FEMINIST MOVEMENT. *Internat. Socialist Rev. 1971 32(10): 19-23, 57-66.* Discusses issues in feminism in the 1970's, including sexism, the role of the family, child care, abortion, and political activism.

## Women in the Military

2450. Brewer, Margaret A. THE MARINE TEAM: MEN AND WOMEN WORKING TOGETHER. *Marine Corps Gazette 1976 60(4): 18-25.* Discusses administrative and occupational opportunities for women in the US Marines, 1974-76.

2451. Goldman, Nancy. THE CHANGING ROLE OF WOMEN IN THE ARMED FORCES. *Am. J. of Sociol. 1973 78(4): 892-911.* "During the last decade there has been an increase in the number of women in the armed forces and this can be projected to continue in the decade of the 1970s. In addition, the position women occupy in the military has broadened. Strains associated with this change in the concentration of women are investigated. Occupational equality for women in the services is not developing since women have historically been excluded from the basic combat roles and this definition is being continued. Among those women who volunteer for military service, the personal goal is not the achievement of 'complete equality' but the attainment of a wider range of assignments. A greater emphasis in the military on administration and logistics contributes to this expansion of roles. However, significant strains present are those associated with social relations betweeen the sexes and with child-rearing requirements."       J

2452. Goldman, Nancy. THE UTILIZATION OF WOMEN IN THE MILITARY. *Ann. of the Am. Acad. of Pol. and Social Sci. 1973 (406): 107-116.* "In the decade of the 1970s there will be an increase in the number and percent of women in the United States military. Trends indicate that this rise will move steadily but gradually from less than 2 percent women in the armed services to approximately 4 percent. Although the number and percent of women in uniform will remain small, their increase will assist in meeting the expected 'short fall' in manpower. The trend to expand the number of women in the military will continue in the 1980s, but it seems unlikely that a 10-percent level, which could be considered possible, will be reached. Historically in industrialized countries women have been excluded from armed combat roles and significant positions in administration. They have served as nurses, secretaries, and clerks and in routine types of communications. Each service has made plans and proposals to increase the number of women and the variety of jobs open to them and to deal with other expressed dissatisfactions, such as living quarters and regulations related to the retention of the careers of married women. Additional problems of protocol between the sexes and the integration of women in the military will have to be faced. Although it is likely that the military will continue its tradition of excluding women from direct combat positions, with an increased emphasis on deterrence there will be an increase in the number of positions in which the 'fighting spirit' is irrelevant, many of which will become available to women."

J

2453. Goldman, Nancy L. WOMEN IN NATO ARMED FORCES. *Military R. 1974 54(10): 72-82.* Examines the increased use in the 1970's of women in the armed forces of NATO countries.

2454. Kosier, Edwin J. THE STORY OF THE WAF: WOMEN IN THE AIR FORCE...YESTERDAY, TODAY AND TOMORROW. *Aerospace Historian 1968 15(2): 18-23.* Relates the growth of the Women in the Air Force (WAF) from its beginning in 1942 as "Air-WAAC's" to its present role in which women serve in many of the career fields of the Air Force. Personnel policy and career management procedures preclude discrimination, and women compete for promotion and job assignment on the same basis as men. The Women Air Service Pilots (WASPs) were a World War II civilian contract program, not military. 2 illus., 10 photos.

C. W. Ohrvall

2455. Schlitz, William P. BRIG. GEN. JEANNE HOLM, USAF. *Air Force Mag. 1971 54(9): 72-75.* Analyzes the role and opportunities available to women in the US Air Force. Special emphasis is accorded to the career of Jeanne Holm, the first female general in the USAF. Focuses on job opportunities, career options, life styles, and policy matters.

R. W. Dubay

2456. Schreiber, Mark E. CIVIL LIBERTIES IN THE GREEN MACHINE. *Civil Liberties Rev. 1976 3(2): 34-47.* Discusses civil rights issues in the military, especially discrimination against Negroes in terms of housing, jobs, and promotions, and discrimination against women, especially those who have children.

2457. —. WOMEN IN COMBAT: A TWO-PART DIALOGUE *Air U. Rev. 1970 28(5): 64-69.*
Werrell, Kenneth P. SHOULD WOMEN BE PERMITTED IN COMBAT? YES, *pp. 64-68.* Examines the progress made by women in the military services since 1948. Discusses and criticizes the arguments against women being allowed to participate in combat, advocating that the Air Force lead the way by training women for combat. 17 notes.
Cochran, Jacqueline. SHOULD WOMEN BE PERMITTED IN COMBAT? NO, *p. 69.* Opposes the use of military women in actual combat roles. No documentation.

J. W. Thacker, Jr.

# Religion and Ethnicity

## Religion

### General

2458. Alston, Jon P. RELIGIOUS MOBILITY AND SOCIOECONOMIC STATUS. *Sociol. Analysis 1971 32(3): 140-148.* Analysis of a 1955 survey of the American white adult population indicates that only fifteen percent have changed their religious membership. The Catholic, Jewish, and Baptist groups are the most stable. The higher-status Presbyterian, Congregational and Episcopalian denominations had the highest proportions of members who had changed their membership. No differences are found between the religious mobiles and non-mobiles in terms of occupation, education, and age. However, the religious mobiles were predominately (65%) females, indicating that most religious mobility involves intermarriage. Mobiles were also found to be slightly more active church-goers than were the non-mobiles.

J

2459. Bennett, John C. and Bennett, Anne M. THE CHURCH AND THE STRUGGLES FOR LIBERATION. *Foundations: A Baptist J.*

*of Hist. and Theology 1975 18(1): 53-60.* Commencement address at the Colgate Rochester-Bexley Halls-Crozer Theological Schools, 10 May 1974. Dr. John C. Bennett and his wife Anne M. Bennett discussed liberation in a theological context. Women's liberation was the focus of the discussion, but minorities and races were included as they related to women.

E. E. Eminhizer

2460. Burchard, Waldo W. DENOMINATION CORRELATES OF CHANGING RELIGIOUS BELIEFS IN COLLEGE. *Sociol. Analysis 1970 31(1): 36-45.* "This report, based on data from a study of the effects of college education on religious beliefs and behavior, analyzes the responses, by religious membership (Catholic and Protestant) of 106 women and 66 men who as freshmen and again as seniors responded to identical items in a questionnaire dealing with religious and moral beliefs. Ten items for men and eleven items for women (from a total of 73) were selected for this analysis. Responses to all items show that there has been a change toward more liberal beliefs for men and women, Catholics and Protestants, although in general Catholic responses are more conservative than Protestant. Responses for Catholic men exhibit a pattern - although vague - which appears to be related to their religious membership. No such pattern appears in the responses of Protestant men or in those of either Catholic or Protestant women. Although a religious differential is apparent in the responses, the data at hand do not reveal the nature of its influence."

J

2461. Clayton, Richard R. RELIGIOSITY AND PREMARITAL SEXUAL PERMISSIVENESS: ELABORATION OF THE RELATIONSHIP AND DEBATE. *Sociol. Analysis 1971 32(2): 81-96.* The purpose of this article was to expand and perhaps clarify the relationship of religiosity to premarital sexual permissiveness and the Reiss-Heltsley and Broderick-Ruppel debate. Religiosity was assessed by the Ritualistic, Experiential, and Ideological scales from Faulkner and DeJong and a composite scale developed for this study. The following three variables were used as test factors: (1) premarital coitus which was reported to have occurred during the year preceding the study; (2) lie propensity as measured by the Lie scale from the M.M.P.I.; and, (3) permissiveness norms perceived to be prevalent in the groups designated by the respondents as being of most importance to them (i.e., normative reference groups). In terms of its effect on the original relationship, premarital coitus consistently served as an intervening variable for females and seemed to be a specification variable for males. Lie propensity consistently specified the religiosity-permissiveness relationship for both sexes. For females N.R.G. norms of permissiveness consistently acted as an intervening variable while for males the results were not as consistent. Overall, these data seem to suggest that there are other variables which need to be considered before any final answer can be pronounced on the "traditionalism" proposition of Reiss. An alternative way of stating the proposition is offered.

J

2462. Croog, Sydney H. and Teele, James E. RELIGIOUS IDENTITY AND CHURCH ATTENDANCE OF SONS OF RELIGIOUS INTERMARRIAGES. *Am. Sociol. R. 1967 32(1): 93-103.* "Prior investigations have suggested that offspring of religious intermarriages tend to adopt the religion of the mother. However, studies of religious identity and of the religious practices of these offspring are extremely rare. The present report focuses on both the religious identity and the church attendance of sons of Protestant-Catholic intermarriages. It is based on responses to questionnaires completed by a study population of army inductees at Fort Dix, New Jersey. Data are presented suggesting that the offspring of father-Protestant, mother-Catholic marriages are more likely to be Catholic than Protestant. However, the sons of father-Catholic, mother-Protestant marriages are almost equally divided into Protestants and Catholics. When paternal education is controlled, it appears that there are equal proportions of Protestant, Catholic, and unaffiliated respondents among offspring of college-educated men in the father-Protestant, mother-Catholic marriages. With regard to church-attendance practices, Catholic offspring of intermarriages report attending approximately as often as the men from homogeneous Catholic marriages. Protestant offspring of intermarriages present a mixed picture in church-attendance pattern. Educational level of the offspring is used in the explication of the analysis of church attendance data. Various related areas for further research are suggested."

J

2463. Erskine, Hazel Gaudet. THE POLLS: ORGANIZED RELI-GION. *Public Opinion Q. 1965 29(2): 326-337.* Poll results on nation-wide U.S. attitudes toward various aspects of religion. Included are the distribution of religious groups, attitudes toward unification, religion and the public schools, Federal aid to parochial schools, church vs. state, freedom of religion, criticisms of the church, and miscellaneous topics from opinion on women as ministers to the practice of tithing.

E. P. Stickney

2464. Foster, A. Durwood. GOD AND WOMAN: SOME THESES ON THEOLOGY, ETHICS, AND WOMEN'S LIB. *Religion in Life 1973 42(1): 42-55.*

2465. Griffiss, James E. THEOLOGY AND SEXUALITY IN SOME RECENT LITERATURE. *Anglican Theological R. 1973 55(2): 225-234.*

2466. Hartnett, Rodney T. and Peterson, Richard E. RELIGIOUS PREFERENCE AS A FACTOR IN ATTITUDINAL AND BACK-GROUND DIFFERENCES AMONG COLLEGE FRESHMEN. *Sociol. of Educ. 1968 41(2): 227-237.* "Differences among four religious preference groups - Catholic, Protestant, Jewish, and those with no for-mal religion (NFR) - in a cross section of 1500 college freshmen were explored by means of the College Student Questionnaires, Part 1. Of the seven CSQ-1 scales (Family Independence, Peer Independence, Liberal-ism, Social Conscience, Cultural Sophistication, Motivation for Grades, and Family Status), variation on six was significantly associated with religious preference for both sexes. Protestant-Catholic differences were small compared to the differences between the combined Catholic and Protestant groups vs. non-Christians (Jews and NFR's). Differences among Protestant denominations were also slight." J

2467. Hudson, Lee. BELTING THE BIBLE: MADALYN MUR-RAY O'HAIR VS. FUNDAMENTALISM. *Western Speech 1972 36(4): 233-240.* Analyzes rhetorical devices and audience interaction in a debate between atheist Madalyn Murray O'Hair and nationally known anti-Communist fundamentalist Dr. Carl McIntire. O'Hair argues for a strict separation of church and state and criticizes the mixing of politics and religion in national events such as NASA arranging to have a Bible read by an astronaut in space. L. Russell and S

2468. Lazerwitz, Bernard. CONTRASTING THE EFFECTS OF GENERATION, CLASS, SEX, AND AGE ON GROUP IDENTIFI-CATION IN THE JEWISH AND PROTESTANT COMMUNITIES. *Social Forces 1970 49(1): 50-58.* "This article presents a joint set of eight religio-ethnic identification dimensions which are equally applicable to the Jewish and Protestant communities. Given such a conceptual scheme, it becomes possible to evaluate the impacts of United States generations, social status, sex, and age, upon group identification. Such an evaluation reveals the rejection by the younger, higher-status members of both groups of many of their traditional acts and beliefs but a constant, or strengthened, interest in improved religious education for their children and upon activity in religio-ethnic organizations. When upper-status Jews and Protestants are compared, the surprising thing is their fairly similar index values on the dimensions of religious behavior, pietism, and reli-gious education. However, such Jews are a lot more active in Jewish organizations than are their Protestant equivalents. Upper-status Jews and Protestants further differ in that the Jews are less traditional in beliefs, socialize to a greater degree within their ethnic community, and are more concerned about the religious education of their children." J

2469. McLaughlin, Eleanor. THE CHRISTIAN PAST: DOES IT HOLD A FUTURE FOR WOMEN? *Anglican Theological R. 1975 57(1): 36-56.* Plea for a revisionist approach to church history to reflect a feminist heritage in the Christian tradition. S

2470. Mueller, Charles W. and Johnson, Weldon T. SOCIOECO-NOMIC STATUS AND RELIGIOUS PARTICIPATION. *Am. Sociol. R. 1975 40(6): 785-800.* The relationship between socioeconomic status and frequency of religious participation is examined for a 1970 U.S. sample of males and females. Although some support is found for the frequently observed positive relationship between these two variables, the data require that such a generalization be qualified. The zero-order rela-tionship generally is stronger for males than females and is positive and weak for Protestants, but is essentially zero for Catholics and negative in sign for Jews and unaffiliated whites. Where the relationship is positive, it is not entirely explainable by the positive relationship of our measure of general social participation with both SES and religious participation. In addition, the examination of interactions with marital status and the presence of children under age 16 indicated that the SES-religious partici-pation relationship is strongest for those who are married and responsible for young children. Even with these significant variations by relevant subpopulations, we conclude that the explanatory power of socioeco-nomic status in predicting religious participation is small both in absolute terms and in comparison with other possible determinants examined.

J

2471. Spaeth, Joe L. RELIGION, FERTILITY, AND COLLEGE TYPE AMONG COLLEGE GRADUATES. *Sociol. Analysis 1968 29(3): 155-159.* "In the first three years after college graduation, gradu-ates of Catholic colleges have more children than other Catholics, who in turn tend to have more children than Protestants, Jews, or agnostics. In the first year of marriage, differences between the two groups of Catholics are not great, but they increase over the next two years. Type of college seems unrelated to the timing of the first child but is related to planning for subsequent ones." J

2472. Stupple, David. THE "I AM" SECT TODAY: AN *UN* OBITUARY. *J. of Popular Culture 1974 8(4): 897-905.* Discusses the occultist I AM sect and its founders and "Ascended Masters," Edna and Guy Ballard; traces current ritual and belief in contemporary groups, 1930's-75.

2473. Suther, Judith D. THE SPIRITUAL TRIAD OF JACQUES AND RAISSA MARITAIN AND THOMAS MERTON. *Encounter 1976 37(2): 129-151.* Discusses the influence of Jacques and Raissa Marit-ain and Thomas Merton on the intellectual and religious life of the United States since the 1940's, with special emphasis on Maritain's concept of creative innocence in the art of poetry.

2474. Wallace, Ruth A. BRINGING WOMEN IN: MARGINAL-ITY IN THE CHURCHES. *Sociol. Analysis 1975 36(4): 291-303.* Dis-cusses possible cases of sex discrimination against women clergy in the Catholic Church and Protestant Churches in the 1970's.

2475. Wilson, Charles Morrow. THE CASE OF THE MULTIPLY-ING WOMEN PREACHERS. *Modern Age 1969 13(4): 393-402.* Cites the growing trend in the number of women pastors, and shows their value and flexibility. They often are able to do what their male counterparts are unable or do not wish to do. Current resistance to women in the clergy is rooted in prejudice. Pastor selection committees are dominated by men and have to be overcome. Based on primary and secondary sources.

M. J. Barach

2476. Wingfield, Mrs. Marshall. CHURCH WOMEN UNITED IN MEMPHIS AND SHELBY COUNTY. *West Tennessee Hist. Soc. Papers 1971 (25): 135-137.* A brief vignette describing the organization and development of Church Women United in Memphis, from its small beginnings in 1937 to 1969. A decade after its organization, members of Negro churches were accepted, and in 1966 Roman Catholics joined. At the annual meeting in 1969 a black president was elected for a three-year term. Chronicles the numerous religious and community activities of the group. Note. H. M. Parker, Jr.

## Protestant

2477. Bomberger, Herbert L. THE PARSONAGE: A WAY OF CHRISTIAN FAMILY LIVING. *Lutheran Q. 1974 26(1): 58-63.* Ex-amines the myths, opportunities for growth, and avenues for strengthen-ing marriage and family life within the parsonage. S

2478. Caldwell, Wallace F. RELIGIOUS LIBERTY AND THE "BLOOD CASES." *Res. Studies 1967 35(2): 109-121.* Examines the relationship between religious freedom and the rights of children reflected by court decisions made in a 1964 case of a Jehovah's Witness woman whose refusal of forced blood transfusions threatened her life as well as that of her unborn child.

2479. Capon, Robert Farrar. THE ORDINATION OF WOMEN: A NON-BOOK. *Anglican Theological R. Supplementary Series 1973 (2): 68-78.*

2480. Christensen, Harold T. STRESS POINTS IN MORMON FAMILY CULTURE. *Dialogue: A J. of Mormon Thought 1972 7(4): 20-34.* A discussion of Mormon family culture in terms of a constructive structural analysis of its weaknesses.                                    S

2481. Durham, Christine Meaders. HAVING ONE'S CAKE AND EATING IT TOO. *Dialogue: A J. of Mormon Thought 1971 6(2): 35-40.* The conflicts in the life of a Mormon woman between education and career, and marriage and family.                                    S

2482. Edwards, Jaroldeen Asplund. FULL HOUSE. *Dialogue: A J. of Mormon Thought 1971 6(2): 9-13.* A day in the life of a Mormon mother.                                    S

2483. Elifson, Kirk W. RELIGIOUS BEHAVIOR AMONG URBAN SOUTHERN BAPTISTS: A CAUSAL INQUIRY. *Sociol. Analysis 1976 37(1): 32-44.* Separate male and female causal models of religious behavior were developed in accordance with relevant literature and were tested using a 1968 sample of 1014 urban Southern Baptists. Incorporated in the models were demographic, contextual, attitudinal and behavioral measures. The latter two measures were developed via factor analysis, and path analysis was used to assess the respective models. Women were found to be more 'predictable' than men, intergenerational transmission of religious values was minimal for both, and the factor analysis revealed that the content of the attitudinal and behavioral dimensions of religiosity varies slightly by sex.                                    J

2484. Frary, Joseph P. REPORT: A CONFERENCE ON "THE QUESTION OF WOMEN PRIESTS." *Anglican Theological R. 1973 55(3): 352-353.*

2485. Huefner, Dixie Snow. A SURVEY OF WOMEN GENERAL BOARD MEMBERS. *Dialogue: A J. of Mormon Thought 1971 6(2): 61-70.* This survey was designed to help determine the responses of Mormon women in leadership positions to contemporary concerns regarding the role of women.                                    S

2486. Hulme, William E. SECULAR SEX. *Lutheran Q. 1966 18(1): 43-48.* One of nine articles examining the validity of Harvey Cox's book *The Secular City* (New York: Macmillan, 1965) for American Lutherans. Hulme analyzes the secularization of sex.                        R. B. Lange

2487. Lynch, John E. THE ORDINATION OF WOMEN: PROTESTANT EXPERIENCE IN ECUMENICAL PERSPECTIVE. *J. of Ecumenical Studies 1975 12(2): 173-197.* Presents the issue of the ordination of women to the professional office of ministry in world Protestantism and the World Council of Churches within the past 10 years. Many churches accept women ministers, but some still hesitate. Scandinavia appears to be more progressive in this regard than either the US or England. Theological and sociological arguments favor the ordination of women, and encourage churches to keep up with social change.
                                                        J. A. Overbeck

2488. May, Cheryll Lynn. THE MORMON WOMAN AND PRIESTHOOD AUTHORITY: THE OTHER VOICE. *Dialogue: A J. of Mormon Thought 1971 6(2): 47-52.* A Mormon discusses the role of women in the Mormon church.                                    S

2489. Pitcher, B. L.; Peterson, E. T.; and Kunz, P. R. RESIDENCY DIFFERENTIALS IN MORMON FERTILITY. *Population Studies [Great Britain] 1974 28(1): 143-152.* "Although one of the most consistent findings of recent fertility studies is the convergence of the religious differentials in fertility, few data have been analysed to discover Mormon fertility trends and differentials. This paper, based on data obtained on 1,001 Mormon couples, is concerned with describing the effects that the dispersion of Mormon families from the Mormon centre in Utah to surrounding areas with various social conditions is having on the fertility

of the re-located Mormon families. Data presented clearly show that such families do, on the average, have a lower fertility than do their Mormon contemporaries residing in the homogeneous Mormon society in Utah. They probably compromise their religious obligations to have children with the contradicting demands of their new environment. Their loyalty to these religious beliefs, however, is confirmed by data which show that they tend to have larger families in their new environments than do their non-Mormon neighbours."                                    J

2490. Porter, H. Boone and Weil, Louis. WOMEN PRIESTS: SOME RECENT LITERATURE. *Anglican Theological R. Supplementary Series 1973 (2): 83-87.* Review essay discussing four works published in 1972-73.                                    S

2491. Van Beeck, Frans Josef. INVALID OR MERELY IRREGULAR—COMMENTS BY A RELUCTANT WITNESS. *J. of Ecumenical Studies 1974 11(3): 381-399.* Discusses the question of validity and regularity of the Philadelphia ordination of women into the priesthood of the Protestant Episcopal Church (1974). If the four bishops intended to do what the church does in ordaining the 11 women, then the sacrament of ordination is valid though irregular. The key word is "intended." Those who wish to prove the ordination invalid contend that no sacrament was intended. The Episcopal Church should regularize this ordination and encourage women to enter the priesthood.                        J. A. Overbeck

2492. —. [SINGLE VOICES: THE SINGLE WOMAN AND THE MORMON CHURCH]. *Dialogue: A J. of Mormon Thought 1971 6(2): 77-87.*
—. A LETTER FROM THE EAST, p. 77.
Bracy, Maryruth. A LETTER HOME, p. 77.
Higginson, Dianne. JOURNAL JOTTINGS, p. 78.
Hinman, M. Karlynn. A CANDID AND UNCENSORED INTERVIEW WITH A MORMON CAREER GIRL, p. 80.
—. A LETTER FROM THE WEST, p. 81.
Baker, Alberta. THOUGHTS ON LIVING ALONE, p. 82.

## Catholic

2493. Abramson, Harold J. INTER-ETHNIC MARRIAGE AMONG CATHOLIC AMERICANS AND CHANGES IN RELIGIOUS BEHAVIOR. *Sociol. Analysis 1971 32(1): 31-44.* The religious behavior of Catholic Americans is viewed as a composite of ethnic elements, and Catholic ethnic groups are shown to have varied levels of association within the Church. From a national sample of Catholic Americans, the religious behavior of traditionally endogamous ethnic groups is compared with that of exogamous groups. The religious involvement of endogamous nationalities reflects the historically distinctive behavior of the Irish, the Italians, and other groups studied. The change which is associated with intermarriage, as these groups assimilate within the Church, points to decline in the religious involvement of the traditionally high Irish and French-Canadians, but shows no consistent patterns for the other groups examined. These changes indicate some dimensions of the nature of ethnic religion, and give some support to the expectation that endogamy contributes to the maintenance of distinct cultural forms and that exogamy functions to alter such forms.                                    J

2494. Finn, James. THE AMERICAN CATHOLIC REVOLUTION. *Interplay 1969 2(9): 39-42.* American Catholics respond to the present disturbances in the Catholic Church in uniquely American ways. In the 1950's, American Catholics were apparently conservative, but two decades later the dominant views are undeniably progressive. The immediate cause of the ferment was the example of Pope John XXIII. The American religious pluralistic heritage was a long-range influence. Catholic progressives tend to criticize not only restrictive institutions and rules within the Church but within American society as well. Many of the various issues that now divide Catholics into opposing factions are focused on the debate over birth control. Behind the question of birth control there is the more basic issue of the relation between the Catholic communion and Papal authority. 2 photos.                        J. A. Zabel

2495. Hickey, Thomas. SOCIAL LIFE SPACE OF NUNS IN THE SEVENTIES. *Catholic World 1971 212(1272): 292-296.* Discusses the institutions, employment, and geriatric conditions of nuns in the Catholic Church in 1970.                                                                S

2496. Kaleane, Kay. A DIFFERENT ROUTE. *Catholic World 1969 208(1246): 160-163.* A young Catholic nun explains her attitudes and commitment to the religious community, 1968.                        S

2497. Leon, Joseph J. and Steinhoff, Patricia G. CATHOLICS' USE OF ABORTION. *Sociol. Analysis 1975 36(2): 125-136.* This study considers the methodological difficulties involved in studying abortion behavior and religious preference and uses the conception cohort as a way of handling problems of sampling and comparison. It was hypothesized that Catholic women would have fewer abortions than non-Catholic women according to 1) their proportion in the overall population and 2) their proportion in the pregnant population. Using demographic and medical data collected from hospital records on all abortion patients in the state of Hawaii and all maternity patients during the designated two-month period, a conception cohort was constructed. When the hypothesis was tested using the conception cohort, Catholics were found to have chosen abortion less often than non-Catholic women. Catholic women had a higher rate of pregnancies, but terminated a smaller proportion of these pregnancies by abortion. No difference was found between Catholics and non-Catholics with respect to gestation time and length of time from discovery of pregnancy to abortion.                        J

2498. Mailo, John R.; DiAntonio, William V.; and Liv, William T. SOURCES AND MANAGEMENT OF STRAIN IN A SOCIAL MOVEMENT: SOME PRELIMINARY OBSERVATIONS. *Sociol. Analysis 1968 29(2): 67-78.* Develops a theory of strain for the Christian Family Movement (CFM). Traces the history of CFM. The main purpose of CFM is to link religious ideals to the changing conditions of society. The appeal is largely to the middle-class Catholic families. Action is the key to CFM. Membership is on a married couple basis. The basic ideology is that the marriage bond will be strengthened through husbands and wives working together in the community. A group of six to eight couples forms one parish's action group. Couples observe, judge, and act; much action is problem-oriented. Relates CFM to the theory of social movements. Cites the works of Seymour Martin Lipset. Explores conflict resolution and points out that no stigma results from dropping out of CFM. Mentions the relationship between social movements and complex organizations. 20 notes.                        A. S. Freedman

2499. Michael, Sister M. THE NUN ENTERS THE NEWMAN APOSTOLATE. *Catholic World 1966 203(1,217): 293-296.* The religious sister makes a varied but professional contribution to the Newman centers on secular campuses. She acts as counsellor, teacher, organizer of intellectual programs and promoter of those activities that make possible the apostolic formation of the student. Her best form of guidance is given when she works with individuals as moderator of a committee or activity. She also provides leadership training in apostolic activities in the local community beyond the campus. Undocumented.                        M. Campion

2500. Moberg, David O. and McEnery, Jean N. CHANGES IN CHURCH-RELATED BEHAVIOR AND ATTITUDES OF CATHOLIC STUDENTS, 1961-1971. *Sociol. Analysis 1976 37(1): 53-62.* The Marquette Study of Student Values analyzes religious practices, moral values, and attitudes among Catholic college students. From 1961 to 1971 decreasing frequency of student attendance at Mass and Confession together with attitudinal changes toward religious practices are evident. Changes in attitudes about dating, decreased scrupulosity in areas of personal honesty and responsibility, looser attitudes toward selected items of personal morality, and increased consideration for others also were revealed. Most changes may be interpreted as reflecting decreased compliance with traditional Church norms, increased conformity to values of American society, and conflicting values related to both cultural pluralism and pluralism within the Catholic Church.                        J

2501. Poorman, Richard O. RELIGIOUS OBEDIENCE AND SHARED DECISION-MAKING IN CATHOLIC HIGHER EDUCATION. *Catholic Educ. R. 1964 62(6): 384-394.* The alleged conflict between administrative patterns built upon the "team" approach and those resulting from an older, more autocratic structure is found to require "a reorientation of administrative ideology" but not a "complete overhauling of administrative machinery." Notre Dame's Vice President

for Academic Affairs poses the problem: more than seven thousand religions in the United States operate 235 colleges and universities; does their vow of obedience preclude development of a democratic, "human relations" administrative structure? Is the "closed shop" a reality or are there zones of decentralization within the hierarchical structure of the religious community where lay as well as religious staff members can participate in decisionmaking? Distinction between *virtue* and *vow* of obedience seems to hold the key to desired "reorientation."                        D. Broderick

2502. Potvin, Raymond H. and Westoff, Charles F. HIGHER EDUCATION AND THE FAMILY NORMATIVE BELIEFS OF CATHOLIC WOMEN. *Sociol. Analysis 1967 28(1): 14-21.* Raises questions of family belief system of Catholic women such as size of family and statements on marriage. Comparisons are made between women in nonsectarian colleges and women in Catholic colleges, between freshmen of different secondary schools, and in different types of institutions about the question of fertility, and between freshmen and seniors in nonsectarian and Catholic colleges on the influence of college. Data were obtained from questionnaires given to fifteen thousand freshmen and senior women from 46 U.S. colleges and universities. The results showed that women with Catholic education placed a high emphasis upon large families and having children as the most important function of marriage. Women with non-sectarian education showed belief in smaller families. For all groups a college education encouraged the women to think about providing for their children and hence a trend toward lower fertility. Table, 19 notes.                        K. Adelfang

2503. Potvin, Raymond H. and Westoff, Charles F. SOCIAL FACTORS IN CATHOLIC WOMEN'S CHOICE OF A COLLEGE. *Sociol. Analysis 1967 28(4): 196-204.* Some findings from a survey of about 6,500 Catholic women in 45 colleges. Those who go to a Catholic high school choose a Catholic college and a nonsectarian college if their high school was nonsectarian. Catholic colleges tend to select students from the upper socioeconomic level. Furthermore, if the parents were very religious, the daughter would be more committed to going to a Catholic college. 6 tables, 8 notes.                        K. Adelfang

2504. Westoff, Charles F. and Potvin, Raymond H. HIGHER EDUCATION, RELIGION AND WOMEN'S FAMILY-SIZE ORIENTATIONS. *Am. Sociol. R. 1966 31(4): 489-496.* "Is the high fertility of Catholic women who have attended Catholic institutions of higher education primarily a consequence of that experience or a reflection of selectivity for other characteristics relevant to family formation? Does a non-sectarian education diminish the number of children desired by women of all religious groups? These questions are answered by a study of nearly fifteen thousand women in a probability sample of 45 colleges and universities throughout the country. Although not without qualifications, the main conclusion is that selectivity is more important than college experience in explaining differentials in family-size preference among Catholic college women. The one exception is found among women who were graduated from Catholic high schools and enrolled in a non-sectarian institution; for them a decline in family-size preference, apparently not due to selectivity, was observed. Though some decline is also observed for the other groups, the differentials are slight and could easily be due to factors other than the college experience itself."                        J

## Jewish

2505. Balswick, Jack. ARE AMERICAN-JEWISH FAMILIES CLOSELY KNIT? A REVIEW OF THE LITERATURE. *Jewish Social Studies 1966 28(3): 159-167.* In this summary of sociological surveys, the weight of evidence available offers an affirmative conclusion, i.e., the Jewish family has tended to be more closely-knit than other segments of the American population. The studies cited embraced a sampling of urban groups, as in Detroit, as well as suburban. Criteria included such factors as divorce rates and standards of obligation by parents and children. The author concludes that there is a need for further empirical data to test his hypothesis.                        J. Brandes

2506. Hofstein, Saul; Shapiro, Manheim S.; and Berman, Louis A. THE JEWISH FAMILY IN A CHANGING SOCIETY. *Dimensions 1969 4(1): 14-23.* Discusses Jewish family practices in fact and in fiction, with emphasis on the formidable figure of the Jewish mother in the 1970's.                                                                                                    S

2507.   Plotnicov, Leonard.   [AMERICAN JEWISH FAMILIES].
FIRST [AND] SECOND GENERATION AMERICAN JEWISH FAMILIES: SOURCES OF CONFLICTS AND TENSIONS. *Kroeber Anthrop. Soc. Papers 1968 38: 11-25.* Most anthropologists studying contemporary American urban conditions are concerned with stresses within the nuclear family that operate to disrupt its solidarity. The author examines stresses often encountered by first and second generation American Jews of Eastern European origin. Concentrates on the seemingly paradoxically low divorce rates and high upward social mobility achieved by these people. 7 notes, biblio.
AN AMERICAN JEWISH VACATION PATTERN: THE ACCOMMODATION OF CONJUGAL TENSIONS.   *Kroeber Anthrop. Soc. Papers 1968 39: 54-62.* Summer vacation behavior in American Jewish culture relieves the pressure of tensions and stresses of conjugal relationships, and thereby helps to explain the low divorce and separation rates of these people. 2 notes, biblio.
C. N. Warren

2508.   Sachar, Howard Morley.   OBJECTIVITY AND JEWISH SOCIAL SCIENCE.   *Am. Jewish Hist. Q. 1966 55(4): 434-450.* In this address at the 64th annual meeting of the American Jewish Historical Society, Professor Sachar of George Washington University argues for the need of Jewish social scientists to adopt objective standards for the appraisal and evaluation of modern Jewish history. The argument is supported by an examination of the *cause célèbre,* the Adolf Eichman-Hannah Arendt furor among concerned Jewish writers and apologists.
F. Rosenthal

2509.   Segal, Sheila F.   FEMINISTS FOR JUDAISM.   *Midstream 1975 21(7): 59-65.* Discusses the compatibility of Judaism and feminism (1970's).                                                                                     S

2510.   Sklare, Marshall.   INTERMARRIAGE AND THE JEWISH FUTURE.   *Commentary 1964 37(4): 46-52.* Recent statistics concerning Jewish intermarriage in the United States call into question earlier assumptions about the causes (held to be largely personal aberration or social persecution) and the rate of Jewish intermarriage. The growing rate of intermarriage exposes the contradictory nature of some American-Jewish adjustment theories, including the issues of conversion, birth control and the nature of Jewish separateness.   J. J. Appel

2511.   Spiro, Jack D.   FAMILY LIFE IN JEWISH EDUCATION. *Dimensions 1971 5(4): 38-41.* Discusses problems in the 1970's regarding the family life of American Jews, notably regarding marriage.   S

# Ethnicity

## General

2512.   Cooney, Rosemary Santana.   CHANGING LABOR FORCE PARTICIPATION OF MEXICAN AMERICAN WIVES: A COMPARISON WITH ANGLOS AND BLACKS.   *Social Sci. Q. 1975 56(2): 252-261.* Data on Mexican American married women, aged 15-54, in the Southwest in 1960 and 1970 and data on comparable Anglo and black females substantiate the importance of socioeconomic factors for explaining interethnic variations in female labor force participation, but are also consistent with the hypothesis that the importance of familism for the Mexican American population has declined.   J

2513.   Dowdall, Jean A.   WOMEN'S ATTITUDES TOWARD EMPLOYMENT AND FAMILY ROLES.   *Sociol. Analysis 1974 35(4): 251-262.* "Greeley has argued that not enough is known about American ethnic group differences but that such differences exist primarily in the 'common core of assumptions' about familial role expectations. A measure of women's attitudes toward questions of female employment and family responsibilities is taken as an index of such expectations. Using a sample of 673 white, native born, married Rhode Island women, nationality, religious affiliation and social class are explored in relation to atti-

tudes. Significant nationality-linked differences in attitudes were found. Religion was not significantly associated with attitudes, but among Catholic respondents there were significant differences associated with nationality. Taking social class into consideration, nationality group differences in attitudes were significant only among non-high school graduates and among those from non-white collar families. As Greeley predicted, there is considerable nationality-linked attitudinal variation among working class women; the reasons for it require further research."   J

2514.   Ehrlich, Clara Hilderman.   MY CHILDHOOD ON THE PRAIRIE.   *Colorado Mag. 1974 51(2): 115-140.* A descriptive autobiographical social history of the late 19th- and early 20th-century life of German-Russian immigrant farmers who settled in the South Platte Valley of northeastern Colorado. Described are sodhouses, sugar beet farming, kraut-making, butchering, hay-making, laundering, baking and shopping visits to the nearby village. Based upon reminiscences; 9 illus., 5 notes.   O. H. Zabel

2515.   Goldscheider, Calvin and Uhlenberg, Peter R.   MINORITY GROUP STATUS AND FERTILITY.   *Am. J. of Sociol. 1969 74(4): 361-372.* "Most studies of minority group fertility assume that as assimilation proceeds the fertility of minority and majority populations will converge. Differences between minority and majority fertility are usually treated as temporary phenomena and often are interpreted in terms of the social, demographic, and economic characteristics of minority group members. Empirical evidence, however, does not fully support the 'characteristics' explanation of Negro, Jewish, Japanese-American, or Catholic fertility. An alternative hypothesis is presented with respect to the independent effect of minority group status on fertility. Some parameters of the interrelationship of minority group status and fertility are discussed."   J

2516.   Greeley, Andrew M. and McCready, William C.   DOES ETHNICITY MATTER?   *Ethnicity 1974 1(1): 91-108.* Discusses the continuing impact of Old World heritages on the personalities and behavior patterns of American ethnic groups. Based on studies of Ireland and southern Italy, the authors predicted patterns of responses of Italian and Irish Americans in comparison with Anglo Americans in terms of seven personality variables, political participation, drinking habits, and sexual attitudes. Twenty-two of 45 hypotheses were validated, and the conclusions held when controlling for region, education, and generation. 6 tables, 6 notes, biblio., appendix.   E. R. Barkan

2517.   Kinloch, Graham C. and Borders, Jeffrey A.   RACIAL STEREOTYPES AND SOCIAL DISTANCE AMONG ELEMENTARY SCHOOL CHILDREN IN HAWAII.   *Sociol. and Social Res. 1972 56(3): 368-377.* "This study is concerned with racial stereotypes and social distance patterns among Japanese, Chinese, and racially-mixed elementary school children in Hawaii. A fairly high level of stereotyping and an even higher degree of social distance was discovered. Some stereotypes were fairly generally accepted while others were clearly patterned by racial origin. Social distance patterns revealed low rejection of Japanese, Chinese, and Hawaiians, in contrast to Caucasians, Filipinos, Negroes, and Samoans. Age, sex, and family size were associated with general level of stereotyping and social distance. It was concluded that racial attitudes in Hawaii, even among elementary school students, show a clear socioeconomic hierarchy, and are defined by age, sex, and family characteristics, as well as the particular social setting in which they occur."   J

2518.   Penn, Nolan.   RACIAL INFLUENCE ON VOCATIONAL CHOICE.   *J. of Negro Educ. 1966 35(1): 88-89.* Reports the findings of a study conducted among junior high school students in Compton, California. Students were asked, "Will your racial background help, hinder, neither, your getting the type of job you would like most to spend your whole life working at?" Students questioned were classified as Negro, white, Mexican, Chinese, Japanese, or Jewish. The results of the study suggest that the racial or ethnic background of boys included does have some influence on their vocational choices. This was less apparent with respect to the girls.   S. C. Pearson, Jr.

## Blacks

2519.　Arnez, Nancy Levi and Anthony, Clara B.　CONTEMPO-RARY NEGRO HUMOR AS SOCIAL SATIRE.　*Phylon 1968 29(4): 339-346.* There have been three distinct stages of Negro humor: (1) "an oral tradition in which the group pokes fun at its customs, its idioms, its folkways" - totally in-group humor; (2) a public humor perpetuated by outsiders using "minority group, Negroes, as the brunt of half-truth caricatures"; and (3) today's self-conscious humor, which is image-creating. "Now the group permits a sharing of its humor with the outside group, while continuing to perpetuate and enrich its own private in-group humor." Using the humor of Dick Gregory, Moms Mabley, Flip Wilson, and Godfrey Cambridge, the authors illustrate the third stage. The study of current black humor can be very valuable in understanding black attitudes in America. 6 notes.　　　　　　　　　R. D. Cohen

2520.　Barnes, Annie S.　THE BLACK BEAUTY PARLOR COM-PLEX IN A SOUTHERN CITY.　*Phylon 1975 36(2): 149-154.* In New-port News, Virginia, beauty parlors serve as important social centers for the lower, middle, and upper class women of the black community. Not only are the parlors used as a means of enhancing personal appearance, they also act as centers of communication. Basically, an inverse relation-ship exists between social class of customers and significance of hair grooming services, frequency of visits, disposition of customers, and infor-mality of communication. The lower class beauty parlor is the more important for its customers because of the limited number of social gath-ering places for them and because enhancing personal appearance also enhances self-esteem.　　　　　　　　　B. A. Glasrud

2521.　Beal, Frances M.　SLAVE OF A SLAVE NO MORE: BLACK WOMEN IN STRUGGLE.　*Black Scholar 1975 6(6): 2-10.* Discusses Negro women's struggle for civil rights in the 1970's, emphasizing the double obstacle of racism and sex discrimination.

2522.　Bell, Robert Roy.　LOWER CLASS NEGRO MOTHERS' AS-PIRATIONS FOR THEIR CHILDREN.　*Social Forces 1965 43(4): 493-500.* "The data given in this paper support the hypothesis that it is possible to distinguish different subgroups along the Negro lower class continuum. Given the importance of the Negro mother in the lower class Negro family, her values and aspirations for her children are very influen-tial for her children's future. Significant differences were found in the responses of low status and high status lower class mothers to questions concerning their aspirations for their children."　　　　　　　J

2523.　Bryce, Herrington J. and Warrick, Alan E.　BLACK WOMEN IN ELECTIVE OFFICES.　*Black Scholar 1974 6(2): 17-20.* Examines 1973 statistics reflecting the relatively sparse occurrence of black women in elective offices, exploring geographical, sexual, and racial comparisons. 4 tables, 7 notes.

2524.　Challenor, Herschelle.　TRANS-AFRICANISM: A NEW STRATEGY FOR BLACK AMERICANISM?　*Center Report 1972 5(5): 7-10.* Focuses on the concept of Trans-Africanism and stresses the similarities between southern Saharan and northern African rather than the differences. Black Americans should work for the improvement of conditions here and in Africa under the rubric of "unity without uniform-ity" rather than stumble over differences in short run strategy. Discusses the relationship between the feminist movement and the black struggles. Black women are the most oppressed but are not able to enjoy the luxury of the middle class white feminist enthusiasm without jeopardizing the unity of the black efforts at the moment.　　　　　　　M. Hough

2525.　Clarizio, Harvey F.　MATERNAL ATTITUDE CHANGE ASSOCIATED WITH INVOLVEMENT IN PROJECT HEAD START.　*J. of Negro Educ. 1968 37(2): 106-113.* Reports the findings of a study designed to determine differences in maternal attitude toward schools and education following participation of children in Head Start projects. In one experimental group primary parental contact was through group meetings while in a second an individual counseling rela-tionship was established. A control group was made up of mothers from similar socioeconomic circumstances whose children were not accepted for Head Start programs. Both a maternal attitude scale and a teacher rating scale were used to measure results. Differences among the groups

were not statistically significant and suggested that the school-home as-pect of Head Start programs has not modified the educational attitudes of lower-class mothers. 2 notes.　　　　　　　S. C. Pearson, Jr.

2526.　Clarke, James W.　FAMILY STRUCTURE AND POLITI-CAL SOCIALIZATION AMONG URBAN BLACK CHILDREN.　*Am. J. of Pol. Sci. 1973 17(2): 302-315.* "The results of this study of 94 urban black children suggest that father absence is an important variable in their political socialization. Father-absent children tend to be more cynical and also express much stronger preferences for a racially segre-gated environment. Beyond this, the results underscore the importance of intra-family relationships in the political socialization process."　　J

2527.　Coleman, Della.　SEARCHING FOR A DECENT PLACE TO LIVE.　*Public Welfare 1971 29(1): 27-28.* In a symposium entitled "Of Human Dignity," a Negro mother describes her search in Norfolk, Vir-ginia, in the 1960's for adequate housing and discusses how public welfare agencies can more effectively aid the poor to find housing.　　　S

2528.　Conyers, James E. and Kennedy, T. H.　REPORTED KNOWL-EDGE NEGRO AND WHITE COLLEGE STUDENTS HAVE OF NEGROES WHO HAVE PASSED AS WHITES.　*J. of Negro Educ. 1964 33(4): 454-459.* Deals with problems of gathering reliable statistics on the phenomenon of "passing" and relates the findings of a 1961 study in which 930 college students (404 Negro, 526 white) were questioned about their knowledge of Negroes who had passed as whites. One hundred and twenty Negro and 48 white respondents indicated knowledge of Negroes who had permanently passed as white, and 260 Negro and 105 white respondents indicated knowledge of Negroes who had temporarily passed as white. Negro respondents indicated that the large number of cases of which they had knowledge were females. Based on data in Con-yers' unpublished Ph.D. dissertation, "Selected Aspects of the Phenome-non of Negro Passing" (Washington State U., 1962).

S. C. Pearson, Jr.

2529.　Davies, Shane and Fowler, Gary L.　THE DISADVANTAGED URBAN MIGRANT IN INDIANAPOLIS.　*Econ. Geography 1972 48(2): 153-167.* The typical migrant to Indianapolis is a southern black woman, with several children and insufficient education to compete in the job market. She is forced to live in one of 11 central city poverty areas, and an inefficient public transportation system cuts off access to all but low paying service occupations. 7 tables, 5 figs., literature cited.

W. H. Mulligan, Jr.

2530.　Derbyshire, Robert L.　THE UNCOMPLETED NEGRO FAMILY: SUGGESTED RESEARCH UPON HIS OWN AND OTHER AMERICAN SEXUAL ATTITUDES AND BEHAVIOR.　*J. of Human Relations 1967 15(4): 458-468.* Discusses the impact of caste and class upon American Negroes and their sexual behavior. Living under a caste system with two sets of behavior expectations is disruptive to U.S. identity for Negroes. Without a pragmatic ego-identity to mini-mize anxiety during the assimilation process in American cities, the Ne-gro, "to a greater degree than other minorities, experiences personal and social disorganization, a result of the disintegrative function of identity conflict." A number of sexual patterns are noted among lower-class urban Negroes. "Both males and females have sexual contact early in adoles-cence," for example. These sexual patterns may be explained by four hypotheses: the female status and freedom from anxiety hypothesis, the cultural negativism toward contraceptive hypothesis, the potency hypoth-esis, and the male hostility hypothesis. The disorganization of the urban Negro will be alleviated by the elimination of the Negro caste system. Based on recent studies of Negroes and other minorities. 21 notes.

D. J. Abramoske

2531.　Dodd, John M. and Randall, Robert R.　A COMPARISON OF NEGRO CHILDREN'S DRAWINGS OF A MAN AND A WOMAN.　*J. of Negro Educ. 1966 35(3): 287-288.* Reports the findings of a study designed to determine whether the prekindergarten, culturally-deprived Negro children's drawings of men or women are more complete. Both boys and girls did draw more complete women than men, and, while the difference did not appear significant, the authors believe additional stud-ies should be made.　　　　　　　S. C. Pearson, Jr.

2532. Edwards, G. Franklin. MARRIAGE AND FAMILY LIFE AMONG NEGROES. *J. of Negro Educ. 1963 32(4): 451-465.*

2533. Edwards, Ozzie L. COHORT AND SEX CHANGES IN BLACK EDUCATIONAL ACHIEVEMENT. *Sociol. and Social Res. 1975 59(2): 110-120.* "Census data are used to apply the cohort approach in studying temporal changes in educational achievement for Blacks. There is a consistent increase in number and proportion of college graduates over four successively younger adult cohorts at given ages and within each cohort as it increases in age. Time is operating in favor of black males, increasing their educational advantage over black females in the North and West, and reducing their disadvantage in the South. Data on graduate training among Blacks classified by sex and region suggest the need for revision of notions of female superiority in educational achievement."                                                                            J

2534. Epstein, Cynthia Fuchs. POSITIVE EFFECTS OF THE MULTIPLE NEGATIVE: EXPLAINING THE SUCCESS OF BLACK PROFESSIONAL WOMEN. *Am. J. of Sociol. 1973 78(4): 912-935.* "To be both black and a woman in American society has most typically meant being cumulatively disadvantaged with regard to positions of power and prestige. Holding these multiple negatively evaluated statuses has meant that black women have clustered at the very bottom of most strata. This paper explores the patterns leading to success of a small minority of black women who have managed to work in occupations of high rank. It points to the special factors which have not only canceled the negative effect of holding statuses of low rank, but which have produced a positive and facilitating context for career. Among these are the models in the black community of women as 'doers'; the support of extended kin in assisting women with family responsibilities; pressure on black women to be economically productive and financially independent; and a number of other conditions leading to self-confidence and autonomy.                                                                                         J

2535. Ford, Nick Aaron. THE FIRE NEXT TIME? A CRITICAL SURVEY OF BELLES LETTRES BY AND ABOUT NEGROES PUBLISHED IN 1963. *Phylon 1964 25(2): 123-134.* Reviews briefly James Baldwin, *The Fire Next Time* (1963); Gwendolyn Brooks, *Selected Poems* (1963); Langston Hughes, *Five Plays;* and nine novels: by William Gardner Smith, *The Stone Face;* John A. Williams, *Sissie;* Charles Wright, *The Messenger;* Mary Elizabeth Vroman, *Esther;* Gordon Parks, *The Learning Tree;* Richard Wright, *Lawd Today;* and Junior Edwards, *If We Must Die;* and anthologies: edited by Arna Bontemps, *American Negro Poetry;* and Herbert Hill, *Soon One Morning.*
                                                                              S. C. Pearson, Jr.

2536. Foster, Francis S. CHANGING CONCEPTS OF THE BLACK WOMAN. *J. of Black Studies 1973 3(4): 433-454.* Black women are abandoning stereotypes about themselves and developing pride in their absexual and racial identity, while remaining separate from white women's movements. The works of black women writers reflect these new attitudes. Biblio.                                 K. Butcher

2537. Furstenberg, Frank F., Jr. PREMARITAL PREGNANCY AMONG BLACK TEEN-AGERS. *Trans-action 1970 7(7): 52-55.*

2538. Gurin, Patricia and Gaylord, Carolyn. EDUCATIONAL AND OCCUPATIONAL GOALS OF MEN AND WOMEN AT BLACK COLLEGES. *Monthly Labor R. 1976 99(6): 10-16.* Discusses the results of surveys conducted in 1964-65 and again in 1970 among students at black colleges, finding that sex-role influences inhibited the educational and career goals of black women in ways similar to findings among white women.

2539. Halisi, Imamu Clyde. MAULANA RON KARENGA: BLACK LEADER IN CAPTIVITY. *Black Scholar 1972 3(9): 27-31.* Chronicles the trial of Maulana Ron Karenga for the torture of two black women, allegedly a trial of political harassment for his attitudes toward black nationalism and liberation, 1971.

2540. Haney, C. Allen; Michielutte, Robert; Vincent, Clark E.; and Cochrane, Carl. FACTORS ASSOCIATED WITH THE POVERTY OF BLACK WOMEN. *Sociol. and Social Res. 1974 59(1): 40-49.* "Data from a group of southern, black women reveal an association between a composite index of current life situation and educational attainment, age at first conception, emotional relationship with partner for first conception, and age first learned of contraception. These findings have implications in conflict with a 'culture of poverty' or 'evil-causes-evil' explanation for their economic and other problems."               J

2541. Hare, Nathan and Hare, Julia. BLACK WOMEN 1970. *Trans-Action 1970 8(1/2): 65-69, 90.* Examines women in the black movement and their relations with both sexes, Negroes and whites; concludes that liberation must be gained for both black men and women before true black liberation is achieved, 1960's-70's.

2542. Harris, Edward E. FAMILY AND STUDENT IDENTITIES: AN EXPLORATORY STUDY IN SELF AND "WE-GROUP" ATTITUDES. *J. of Negro Educ. 1965 34(1): 17-22.* Explores the influence of race, sex, and the combined influence of race and sex on the presence and absence of family, self and "we-group" attitudes. The family self-identity appeared more often among females and whites. Family "we-group" identities were found among a relatively small proportion of the respondents. Almost all respondents identified themselves in terms of a student self-identity. Studied were students from two midwestern universities, one predominantly white and one predominantly Negro.
                                                                              S. C. Pearson, Jr.

2543. Hess, Robert D.; Shipman, Virginia; and Jackson, David. SOME NEW DIMENSIONS IN PROVIDING EQUAL EDUCATIONAL OPPORTUNITY. *J. of Negro Educ. 1965 34(3): 220-231.* A report of findings of research projects which supports the contention "first, that the behavior which leads to social, educational, and economic poverty is socialized to early childhood, that is, it is learned; and, second, that the central quality involved in the effects of cultural deprivation is a lack of cognitive meaning in the mother-child communication system."
                                                                              S. C. Pearson, Jr.

2544. Hyman, Herbert H. and Reed, John Shelton. "BLACK MATRIARCHY" RECONSIDERED: EVIDENCE FROM SECONDARY ANALYSIS OF SAMPLE SURVEYS. *Public Opinion Q. 1969 33(3): 346-354.* Finds no evidence for any pattern of matriarchy peculiar to the Negro family when viewed from the perspective of survey results for white families. Examines three surveys: a 1960 National Opinion Research Center sample of one thousand adults over 18, including 100 Negroes who were asked who made the decisions in their family; a 1951 Gallup Poll of 1,400 adults who were asked which parent had been most influential during their childhood; and a 1965 sample of 2,500 high school seniors, including 150 Negroes, whose parents had differing political loyalties, who were asked their political preferences. Table, 14 notes.
                                                                              D. J. Trickey

2545. Jackson, Jacquelyne J. BUT WHERE ARE THE MEN? *Black Scholar 1971 3(4): 30-41.* According to myth, black women have had educational, occupational, employment, and income privileges compared to black men. In reality, data for 1940-70 shows that black women are the most disadvantaged group in the United States. The black woman is not a matriarch nor has she emasculated the black man. There are fewer black males than black females and the sex ratio has increased since 1940. Without enough men to conform to the traditional, white patterns of sex, marriage, and family living, blacks have developed alternative familial forms such as female-headed households and illegitimacy. Based on primary and secondary sources; 5 tables, 11 notes.
                                                                              A. E. Wiederrecht

2546. Kandel, Denise B. RACE, MATERNAL AUTHORITY, AND ADOLESCENT ASPIRATION. *Am. J. of Sociol. 1971 76(6): 999-1020.* "The present paper tests the prevalent hypotheses that the matriarchal character of black families is associated principally with father absence from the home and that a matriarchal family structure has detrimental educational consequences for black males. Within the limitations imposed by the samples, the results lead to the tentative rejection of these hypotheses. Among blacks, the authority of mothers tends to be stronger in intact than in broken families. Furthermore, maternal authority in the household and identification with a female role model do not appear to have the negative consequences on educational aspirations and school performance for black adolescent boys which have been attributed to them. Black mothers and their children have the same or higher educational aspirations than white regardless of the fact that the black adolescents tend to identify more closely with their mothers. The lower educational attainment of blacks must be sought in other factors within and outside the family which make it difficult for black adolescents to translate educational aspirations into educational achievement."   J

2547. Karenga, Maulana Ron. IN DEFENSE OF SIS. JOANNE: FOR OURSELVES AND HISTORY. *Black Scholar 1975 6(10): 37-42.* Discusses the 1975 Joanne Little trial in Wake County, North Carolina, and its meaning for Negroes.

2548. Karenga, Maulana Ron. IN LOVE AND STRUGGLE: TOWARD A GREATER TOGETHERNESS. *Black Scholar 1975 6(6): 16-28.* Advocates unification of efforts of black men and women toward attaining equal rights in the 1970's, emphasizing the divisiveness of sexual separatism.

2549. King, A. Thomas and Mieszkowski, Peter. RACIAL DISCRIMINATION, SEGREGATION, AND THE PRICE OF HOUSING. *J. of Pol. Econ. 1973 81(3): 590-606.* "This article presents empirical estimates of racial discrimination in the New Haven, Connecticut, housing market. The results are based on over 200 rental units for which there is comprehensive information on the characteristics of the dwellings. Using multiple-regression techniques, we estimate that blacks and whites *do* pay different amounts for equivalent units. For black female-headed households the markup relative to white males is 16 percent; for black male-headed households, 7.5 percent. Also the work indicates that rents for whites in boundary (integrated) areas are about 7 percent lower than for black households in these areas."   J

2550. LaRue, Linda J. M. BLACK LIBERATION AND WOMEN'S LIB. *Trans-Action 1970 8(1/2): 59-64.* Discusses the role which women's liberation plays in the black movement; discusses the discovery of the myth of matriarchy, assumption of power positions among black women, and the deep indoctrination from the doctrine of inferiority; concludes that lessons from the women's liberation movement have shown blacks that their liberation must be for both sexes, 1960's-70's.
G. A. Hewlett

2551. Lee, Betty. BLACK WOMEN AS FEMINISTS. *Focus/-Midwest 1973 9(59): 18-23.* While sympathetic to greater freedom for the black women and to a need for greater economic benefits, the author feels her primary concern is to fight the racism which oppresses both black men and women.
L. H. Grothaus

2552. Mitchell, William S. UNCLE TOMS AND AUNT MARTHAS. *J. of Black Studies 1972 3(2): 259-263.* Argues against the indiscriminate labeling of blacks, particularly older generation blacks, as "Uncle Toms" and "Aunt Marthas."
K. Butcher

2553. Montgomery, Roger and Kaufman, David. "BEHIND GHETTO WALLS: BLACK FAMILY LIFE IN A FEDERAL SLUM" BY LEE RAINWATER. *Urban Affairs Q. 1971 7(1): 109-124.* A review symposium. *Behind Ghetto Walls* (Chicago: Aldine, 1970) is an account of family life in the Pruitt-Igoe housing project in St. Louis, Missouri. Pruitt-Igoe is the prototypic slum, a slum constructed and encouraged by slum clearance and low-cost housing programs. In a series of case studies, Rainwater sought to amplify the argument that deviant behavior in slums is a result of adaptive responses to poverty. The book is a study of the classic slum, and Rainwater points out some of the problems in American city planning. There is an attack on the American class system within Rainwater's book, and planners are seen as agents of the class system. Rainwater's basic point is that poverty programs and plans will not succeed unless planners realize that the culture of the poor renders impossible programs which are achievement-oriented and even cause more suffering to the poor. Public institutions must change in ways to allow them to serve poor people without stripping the poor of their dignity.
J. Rabin

2554. Moynihan, Daniel P. EMPLOYMENT, INCOME, AND THE ORDEAL OF THE NEGRO FAMILY. *Daedalus 1965 94(4): 745-770.* Distinguishes two phases in the Negro civil rights movement: the fight for liberty and the fight for equality. During the second phase the greatest difficulties may be anticipated since it is so little understood. Considers employment as the primary element introducing Negroes to the full range of American economic, social, and political life. Assesses current unemployment, occupational patterns, income, and the social and economic tragedies in Negro homes as a result of illegitimate births, broken homes, and unemployment. 11 tables and graphs, 12 notes.
R. V. Ritter

2555. Moynihan, Daniel P. THE PRESIDENT AND THE NEGRO: THE MOMENT LOST. *Commentary 1967 43(2): 31-45.* "It appears that the nation may be in the process of reproducing the tragic events of the Reconstruction: giving to Negroes the forms of legal equality, but withholding the economic and political resources which are the bases of social equality." In June 1965 President Johnson gave an address at Howard University which was revolutionary in its scope and new proposals to go beyond the issue of legal civil rights for Negroes to find ways of bringing them into the mainstream of American society. This new departure was influenced primarily by a report prepared by the author for the Department of Labor, entitled *The Negro Family: The Case for National Action* ("Moynihan report"). The report spoke of the paramount importance of somehow reforming Negro family life by providing "the economic stability that was clearly the basis of family stability." Unfortunately, the civil rights movement seized upon the Moynihan report rather than the initiative offered by the President, and found in its emphasis upon the poor family life of lower-class Negroes a kind of condescending racism. A tremendous furor developed, and, as a consequence, the movement was unable to take advantage of the opportunity offered; instead, the conference called by the President, "To Fulfill These Rights," was spent in ratifying old clichés which accomplished nothing. Meanwhile, the Watts riots had destroyed the image of the nonviolent, suffering, and deserving Negro, and the 1966 elections closed the doors on further progress at this time.
A. K. Main

2556. Moynihan, Daniel P. THE SCHISM IN BLACK AMERICA. *Public Interest 1972 (27): 3-24.* The racial situation is getting both worse and better, notwithstanding denials of both trends. The black experience is an "up and down" model with upward mobility closely related to social class development within the black community. Younger black husband-wife families have closed the income gap outside the south, while the poverty level has increased in the female-headed households. The income level of college-educated blacks has risen more rapidly than that of equivalent whites, but the percentages of illegitimate births and female-headed families among blacks provides a deepening schism. Both whites and blacks who find these and other statistics hard to accept ignore or deny them because they contradict their preconceived theories.
E. C. Hyslop

2557. Myers, Lena Wright. BLACK WOMEN AND SELF-ESTEEM. *Sociol. Inquiry 1975 45(2-3): 240-250.* Traditionally, social scientists assume that black women have little opportunity for a positive self image; it is time to eradicate such biases from social research and to allow for the possibility that black women have self-esteem.

2558. Nelson, Charmeynne D. MYTHS ABOUT BLACK WOMEN WORKERS IN MODERN AMERICA. *Black Scholar 1975 6(6): 11-15.* Explores myths about Negro women workers, 1969-75, emphasizing those regarding employment and heads of families.

2559. Niemi, Albert W., Jr. CHANGES IN RACIALLY STRUCTURED EMPLOYMENT PATTERNS IN THE NORTHEAST AND SOUTH, 1940-60. *Am. J. of Econ. and Sociol. 1972 31(2): 173-180.* "This paper provides an examination of Negro employment patterns for the South and the Northeast over 1940-60. . . . The first step in the examination is to review differences in occupational structure between Negroes and non-Negroes in the respective areas. Following this, interregional racial employment patterns are compared over time. The major conclusions to be demonstrated are as follows: Employment patterns in 1940 were drawn on very sharp racial lines in both the Northeast and South. In both areas the stratification of 1940 employment was much more rigid for female Negroes than for males. The shift over 1940-60 away from racial employment patterns has been occurring at a moderate rate in the Northeast and has been more or less non-existent in the South. In fact, southern male Negroes appear to be faced by increasingly more rigid racial employment patterns over time. Within the Northeast the relative gains of female Negroes in the direction of equality of occupational status have been most marked."   J

2560. North, George E. and Buchanan, O. Lee. MATERNAL ATTITUDES IN A POVERTY AREA. *J. of Negro Educ. 1968 37(4): 418-425.* A 1967 study of 4- and 5-year-old children and their mothers in a Negro poverty area of Phoenix. The authors used primarily the Parental Attitude Research Instrument and the Illinois Test of Psycholingual Ability. They found two distinct types of maternal authoritarianism: "disgruntled authoritarianism (disgusted and pushing kind of control) and self-sacrificing authoritarianism (martyred kind of control)." They found a strong relationship between authoritarian mothers and low social class or low educational level. The authors surmise that these authoritarian attitudes are a response of poor mothers to the burdens of too many children, lack of resources, and little economic or family security. Table, 19 notes. B. D. Johnson

2561. Ohlendorf, George W. and Kuvlesky, William P. RACIAL DIFFERENCES IN THE EDUCATIONAL ORIENTATIONS OF RURAL YOUTHS. *Social Sci. Q. 1968 49(2): 274-283.* A survey to ascertain whether racial differences exist in reference to the following dimensions of educational status orientations: "aspirations, expectations, anticipatory deflection, intensity of aspiration and certainty of expectation." The data were obtained from 530 students residing in three rural east central Texas counties. It is concluded that rural Negro boys and girls have higher educational aspirations and expectations than rural white youth. 5 tables, 27 notes. D. F. Henderson

2562. Paschal, Billy J. THE ROLE OF SELF CONCEPT IN ACHIEVEMENT. *J. of Negro Educ. 1968 37(4): 392-396.* A study of 152 seventh graders of a junior high school in Dade County, Florida, using the Spivack Response Form. The subjects, 80 boys and 72 girls, were from 11 to 14 years old and lived in an urban, middle-class community. The study showed a relationship between the student's self concept and his grades in all major subjects except for the nonverbal subject of mathematics. It was also found that a disproportionate number of those in the Inadequate Self Concept category were younger siblings. The author extends these findings to the hypothesis that possibly the Negro student's self concept has a relationship to his grades. 2 tables, 9 notes. B. D. Johnson

2563. Peck, Sidney M. and Rosen, Sidney. THE INFLUENCE OF THE PEER GROUP ON THE ATTITUDES OF GIRLS TOWARD COLOR DIFFERENCES. *Phylon 1965 26(1): 50-63.* Considers the extent to which their peer group influences the attitudes of six- and eight-year-old white girls toward Negro youngsters. The material is based on a study among children in Milwaukee, Wisconsin, into whose neighborhood Negroes were beginning to move. It was found that the girls "were aware of color differences; that they rigidly preferred white to Negro children; that they categorically excluded Negro youngsters from private fun clubs; and that they were influenced markedly by their peers in the acceptance and rejection of colored children." S. C. Pearson, Jr.

2564. Petrof, John V. THE EFFECT OF STUDENT BOYCOTTS UPON THE PURCHASING HABITS OF NEGRO FAMILIES IN ATLANTA, GEORGIA. *Phylon 1963 24(3): 266-270.* A survey of 594 Negro families in Atlanta, Georgia, disclosed that after a student boycott of downtown merchants many Negro families failed to return to previous shopping patterns and that their expenditures in downtown Atlanta decreased significantly. S. C. Pearson, Jr.

2565. Phillips, Romeo Eldridge. STUDENT ACTIVITIES AND SELF-CONCEPT. *J. of Negro Educ. 1969 38(1): 32-37.* Reports on the results of a study made at a high school in Marquis, Michigan, to determine if there was a significant correlation between participation in student activities and scores on a self-concept measure. The students were 80 percent Negro, and only seniors who had been at the school since the ninth grade were subjects. The Osgood Semantic Differential was used to measure self-concept. A high correlation was found between participation and self-concept for boys, but there was no apparent relationship for girls. Eighty-five percent of the nonparticipants, however, had high self-concept scores, indicating that other variables were affecting positive self-concepts. A questionnaire on the activities students found most helpful showed they preferred those which gave public exposure, such as athletics and music. Table, 8 notes. B. D. Johnson

2566. Pierce, John C.; Avery, William P.; and Addison, Carey, Jr. SEX DIFFERENCES IN BLACK POLITICAL BELIEFS AND BEHAVIOR. *Am. J. of Pol. Sci. 1973 17(2): 422-430.* Women traditionally are less interested in politics than men. Argues that black women more often head families and assume other male roles, suggesting that their political beliefs and behavior may not mimic that of women generally. Analysis of 300 black men and women living in New Orleans reveals that their political participation levels are virtually identical. Black women, like other women, believe their political efforts to be inefficacious. The sample is small and from a single city, but it serves to cast doubt on the concept of male political dominance. 4 tables, 13 notes. V. L. Human

2567. Pilling, Patricia L. SEGREGATION: COTTAGE RENTAL IN MICHIGAN. *Phylon 1964 25(2): 191-201.* Describes an attempt of two women, one Negro and one white, the latter accompanied by her three children, to find cottage accommodations for a week-long summer vacation in southwestern Michigan. Though Michigan in 1962 had an equal accommodations law, separate letters to 16 resorts produced four replies indicating only one vacancy (not for the date requested) for the Negro and ten replies indicating eight vacancies for the white. Accommodations were eventually secured near Jackson, Michigan, through inquiry among friends. S. C. Pearson, Jr.

2568. Pressman, Sonia. JOB DISCRIMINATION AND THE BLACK WOMAN. *Crisis 1970 77(3): 103-108.* Facts and statistics disprove the myth that black women easily find employment and displace black men. Black women are at the bottom of the economic totem pole in terms of numbers working, percentage working, and median annual wages. Unemployment is most severe among black women. They are trapped by discrimination, low-skilled, low-pay jobs, and separate lines of seniority and progression. The Equal Employment Opportunity Commission may now use statute and executive order to bring improvement and justice to the female labor force. A. G. Belles

2569. Radin, Norma and Kamii, Constance K. THE CHILD-REARING ATTITUDES OF DISADVANTAGED NEGRO MOTHERS AND SOME EDUCATIONAL IMPLICATIONS. *J. of Negro Educ. 1965 34(2): 138-146.* Reports a study conducted in Ypsilanti, Michigan, in which 44 culturally deprived Negro mothers and 50 middle-class Caucasian mothers of children aged three to five, were investigated. The feelings of the disadvantaged group toward childrearing "shed light on why children from this socioeconomic group have such difficulty participating in our middle-class schools and ultimately in middle-class society." Such disadvantaged mothers fail to "conceive of children's potential for developing inner control. Children are seen as objects to be carefully protected when young and helpless and then controlled, shielded, and suppressed as they grow older." S. C. Pearson, Jr.

2570. Rainwater, Lee. CRUCIBLE OF IDENTITY: THE NEGRO LOWER-CLASS FAMILY. *Daedalus 1966 95(1): 172-216.* Notes the autonomy of the slum ghetto and discusses the functional autonomy of the Negro family. The high proportion of mother-headed households is a result of the move to the city. Outlines the several stages and forms of Negro lower-class family life, with examples. Present Negro family patterns have been created as adaptations to a particular socioeconomic situation; if we change that situation we should expect the people involved to make new adaptations with the passage of time. Needed remedies are: employment income for men, income maintenance for mothers, meaningful education of the next generation, organizational participation for aggressive pursuit of Negroes' self-interest, sanctions against indifferent service to slum Negroes, and pride in group identity. Basic reform is needed, not symptom-treatment. Deals with examples from the Pruitt-Igoe housing project in St. Louis. Table, 42 notes. E. P. Stickney

2571. Rauch, Julia B. FEDERAL FAMILY PLANNING PROGRAMS: CHOICE OR COERCION? *Social Work 1970 15(4): 68-75.* Evaluates charges by blacks that "genocide" is inherent in Federal planning programs. Explicates individual and structural theories explaining poverty, as well as the argument for considering the access of the poor to family planning service as a medical, not a welfare, problem. 23 notes. W. L. Willigan

2572. Schwartz, Michael. THE NORTHERN UNITED STATES NEGRO MATRIARCH: STATUS VERSUS AUTHORITY. *Phylon 1965 26(1): 18-24.* Reports the findings of a study based on interviews and observations in the city of Detroit. The matriarchal family pattern among lower-class Negroes does not result solely from the negative effects of restricted opportunities for exploiting one's life chances in a market. Much matriarchal family organization among lower-class Negroes is "maladaptive" in the sense that status and authority inhere in different persons. Questions the matriarchal system as a preferred and valued style of life among persons of this class.       S. C. Pearson, Jr.

2573. Sly, David F. MINORITY-GROUP STATUS AND FERTILITY: AN EXTENSION OF GOLDSCHEIDER AND UHLENBERG. *Am. J. of Sociol. 1970 76(3): 443-459.* "It has been common to approach the study of differences in Negro-white fertility from an assimilationist perspective. A recent paper criticized this approach, suggesting as an alternative a social psychological argument which approaches the differential in terms of the insecurities associated with minority-group status. This explanation suggests that 1) minority-group status exercises an independent effect on fertility, and 2) minority-group status and certain structural factors interact to effect fertility. This paper attempts to test these two aspects of the "minority-group status hypothesis." The use of simple descriptive statistics early in the analysis tends to support the minority-group status hypothesis; however, the use of more rigorous inductive statistical techniques suggests that the hypothesis does not stand when applied to Negro-white fertility differences. It is suggested that the hypothesis be reformulated to take account of the extent of structural assimilation."       J

2574. Smalley, Hazel C. BLACK WOMEN LEGISLATORS ANSWER QUESTIONS. *Black Politician 1971 2(4): 4-45.* Black women officeholders hold a variety of opinions on social and political issues. Most do not believe sex is a handicap in politics, but believe the 18-year-old voter will be more tolerant of female candidates. They feel law enforcement, jobs, crime, drugs and housing are leading problems. Most are skeptical of women's liberation and feel black male liberation more important.       L. H. Grothaus

2575. Sorkin, Alan L. OCCUPATIONAL STATUS AND UNEMPLOYMENT OF NONWHITE WOMEN. *Social Forces 1971 49(3): 393-397.* "The purpose of this paper is to analyze two important dimensions of the relative economic status of nonwhite women, namely occupational position and unemployment. It is found that Negro women have made major gains in upgrading their occupational status, but that for a variety of reasons their relative unemployment rates have increased."       J

2576. Stevenson, Janet. ROSA PARKS WOULDN'T BUDGE. *Am. Heritage 1972 23(2): 56-64, 85.* Rosa Parks' refusal to give up her bus seat to a white man on 1 December 1955 was the spark which united Montgomery Alabama Negroes behind a challenge of the constitutionality of state law which decreed segregated buses. The black community, led by the newly-formed Montgomery Improvement Association and its president, Martin Luther King, Jr., organized a successful bus boycott. The buses were integrated a year later after the Supreme Court affirmed a special three-judge federal court decision declaring segregated seating on buses to be unconstitutional. 5 illus.       J. F. Paul

2577. TenHouten, Warren D. THE BLACK FAMILY: MYTH AND REALITY. *Psychiatry 1970 33(2): 145-173.* Examines Daniel Patrick Moynihan's report on the black family. There is no evidence for Moynihan's conclusions that rates of illegitimacy, female-headed families, and unemployment indicate deterioration of the black family. A detailed analysis of Los Angeles male-headed black families indicates that black fathers are no less powerful than white fathers, and that black husbands are no weaker in their marital role than white husbands. 14 notes.       M. A. Kaufman

2578. Turner, Marjorie W. LOTTIE PEARL MITCHELL. *Crisis 1974 81(10): 349-351.* Biography of this Negro woman, emphasizing her work in the National Association for the Advancement of Colored People, 1950's-74.       S

2579. Udry, J. Richard; Bauman, Karl E.; and Chase, Charles. SKIN COLOR, STATUS, AND MATE SELECTION. *Am. J. of Sociol. 1971 76(4): 722-733.* "Data from a sample of 350 Negro married couples in Washington, D.C., are analyzed to examine the changing relationship between status attributes, mate selection, and skin color, by comparison of duration-of-marriage cohorts. We find that the traditional status advantage of light-skinned women holds for all cohorts, with little indication of change. For men, on the other hand, darker-skinned men experienced better status and mate-selection opportunities in more recent cohorts than in earlier ones. The higher job-mobility orientation of dark-skinned men evidently explains their improved mobility. These findings suggest a change in the evaluation of differential skin color for men within the Negro community."       J

2580. Vermeer, Donald E. and Frate, Dennis A. GEOPHAGY IN A MISSISSIPPI COUNTY. *Ann. of the Assoc. of Am. Geographers 1975 65(3): 414-424.* Discusses the phenomenon of earth-eating by Negro women and children in Holmes County, Mississippi (1975).       S

2581. Vittenson, Lillian K. AREAS OF CONCERN TO NEGRO COLLEGE STUDENTS AS INDICATED BY THEIR RESPONSES TO THE MOONEY PROBLEM CHECK LIST. *J. of Negro Educ. 1967 36(1): 51-57.* Reports the findings of a study of 100 Negro students in Illinois Teachers Colleges in Chicago. Most students indicated concern about their adjustment to college work. The second largest area of concern centered about the area of social and recreational activities. Comparisons of responses between sexes, freshmen and seniors, and age groups are provided. The author recommends early identification, encouragement, and guidance for the academically capable Negro student with placement in a college preparatory high school curriculum. She also suggests that Negro boys be placed in contact with Negro teenagers and adults who can serve as models with whom they can identify.       S. C. Pearson, Jr.

2582. Wareham, Roger S. and Bynoe, Peter C. THE NEW STEREOTYPES ARE NO BETTER THAN THE OLD. *Urban Rev. 1972 6(2): 14-18.* Discusses racial stereotypes of Negroes in television shows in the 1960's and 70's, including *I Spy, Julia, The Flip Wilson Show,* and *Sanford and Son.*

2583. Webster, Staten W. SOME CORRELATES OF REPORTED ACADEMICALLY SUPPORTIVE BEHAVIORS OF NEGRO MOTHERS TOWARD THEIR CHILDREN. *J. of Negro Educ. 1965 34(2): 114-120.* The author studied 311 Negro adolescents in three integrated high schools of a San Francisco Bay Area high school district in an attempt to determine the role of maternal supportive behavior in the self-perceptions and levels of academic achievement of their offspring. Results indicate that academically supportive behavior encourages favorable self-perceptions, vocational aspirations, and predictions of educational attainment. However, such behavior was not found to be directly related to high school grades when the sex of the offspring was taken into consideration.       S. C. Pearson, Jr.

2584. Weiss, Carol H. VALIDITY OF WELFARE MOTHERS' INTERVIEW RESPONSES. *Public Opinion Q. 1968 32(4): 622-633.* Examines the accuracy of responses of a sample of 680 New York City Negro welfare mothers and finds this group neither more nor less accurate than middle-class groups. Interviewers too similar in status to respondents tend to get more biased answers, indicating a need for reorientation of training of these interviewers. 6 tables, 14 notes.       D. J. Trickey

2585. Whitaker, Barbara. BREAKDOWN IN THE NEGRO FAMILY: MYTH OR REALITY? *New South 1967 22(4): 37-47.* Discusses whether Negro family structure is breaking down in the United States in the 1960's, emphasizing the problems of family income and illegitimate births.       S

2586. White, Kinnard and Knight, James H. SCHOOL DESEGREGATION, SOCIOECONOMIC STATUS, SEX AND THE ASPIRATIONS OF SOUTHERN NEGRO ADOLESCENTS. *J. of Negro Educ. 1973 42(1): 71-78.*

2587. Williams, Cecil. A CONVERSATION WITH ANGELA. *Black Scholar 1972 3(7/8): 36-49.* Reprints the text of an interview between Angela Davis and Cecil Williams while the former was incarcerated in the Santa Clara County Jail, 1970-71.

2588. Willner, Milton. FAMILY DAY CARE: AN ESCAPE FROM POVERTY. *Social Work 1971 16(2): 30-35.* Analysis of a three-year research study of 203 Negro working mothers in New York City who sought child care arrangements reveals the need for sufficient day care facilities, properly supervised service, and built-in safeguards to guarantee the total development of children. 11 notes. W. L. Willigan

2589. Winslow, David J. OCCUPATIONAL SUPERSTITIONS OF NEGRO PROSTITUTES IN AN UPSTATE NEW YORK CITY. *New York Folklore Q. 1968 24(4): 294-301.* Discusses sexual superstitions of Negro prostitutes in Saratoga Springs, New York, in 1964-65.

2590. —. *BLACK SCHOLAR* INTERVIEWS KATHLEEN CLEAVER. *Black Scholar 1971 3(4): 54-59.* Interview of Kathleen Cleaver in which she discusses the nature of society and the problems of the women's liberation movement. She relates her own involvement, since 1966, in the black liberation and women's liberation movements and tells how her experiences in the Black Panther Party led to her interest in women's problems. She analyzes the relation of black and white women in the struggle to obtain liberation, the exploitation of black and white women by the American slave system, the current status of women in Western societies, and the relationship between black men and black women in liberation efforts. A. E. Wiederrecht

2591. —. ELIZABETH DUNCAN KOONTZ - PRESIDENT OF THE NAT'L EDUCATION ASSN'S DEPT. OF CLASSROOM TEACHERS. *Negro Hist. Bull. 1964 28(3): 55-56.* Describes the educational contributions of Mrs. Koontz, a Negro educator, and excerpts a newspaper article about her. L. Gara

2592. —. THREE NEGROES RECEIVE 1964 PRESIDENTIAL FREEDOM MEDAL. *Negro Hist. Bull. 1964 28(3): 58-59.* Brief profiles of the three Negro recipients of 1964 Presidential Freedom Medals: Dr. Lena F. Edwards, medical missionary, Leontyne Price, concert singer, and A. Philip Randolph, labor leader. L. Gara

## Indians

2593. Ackerman, Lillian A. MARITAL INSTABILITY AND JUVENILE DELINQUENCY AMONG THE NEZ PERCES. *Am. Anthropologist 1971 73(3): 595-603.* "This study is concerned with the causes of juvenile delinquency among the Nez Perce Indians of Idaho. Marital instability is examined in the past and present for its relationship to contemporary juvenile delinquency. Additional factors considered include the loss of aboriginal communal discipline, the loss of patrilocality, and the continuation of inappropriate aboriginal male and female roles into the present." AIA(3:1:101) J

2594. Blanchard, Kendall. CHANGING SEX ROLES AND PROTESTANTISM AMONG THE NAVAJO WOMEN IN RAMAH. *J. for the Sci. Study of Religion 1975 14(1): 43-50.* Discusses the tendency of Navajo women to join Protestant missions in Ramah, New Mexico, due to cultural changes in the 1970's which affect sex roles. S

2595. Brant, Charles S. JOE BLACKBEAR'S STORY OF THE ORIGIN OF THE PEYOTE RELIGION. *Plains Anthropologist 1963 8(21): 180-181.* The story of the origin of the peyote religion. "Long ago," when the Indians were still fighting each other, a group of Lipan Apache was camped on the other side of New Mexico when they were attacked by other bands of Indians. The tribe was scattered, leaving behind a woman and her son. The boy went out early in the morning to look for the tribe. As he walked around, a voice spoke to him from above, telling him of the peyote and that he should eat some. He ate some with his mother and they were soon full. The mother prayed to the providing spirit for rain and it rained. That night she dreamed of finding the tribe on a mountain to the east. The next morning they set out toward the mountain and found the tribe. He introduced peyote to the tribe and since then it has been used on special occasions such as Thanksgiving and Easter. C. B. Schroeder

2596. Chandonnet, Ann. SOPHIA PIETNIKOFF'S CLOTH MADE OF GRASS. *Alaska J. 1975 5(1): 55-58.* Sophia Pietnikoff is one of the last of the traditional Aleut basket weavers. Describes her life in some detail, along with the preparation of the material she uses to make baskets, dolls, and other native objects. 5 photos. E. E. Eminhizer

2597. Clinton, Lawrence; Chadwick, Bruce A.; and Bahr, Howard M. VOCATIONAL TRAINING FOR INDIAN MIGRANTS: CORRELATES OF "SUCCESS" IN A FEDERAL PROGRAM. *Human Organization 1973 32(1): 17-27.* Uses records from the Adult Vocational Training Program of the Bureau of Indian Affairs' office in Portland to determine the factors that lead to successful completion of the program. Males are more likely to complete the program than are females. Successful previous employment was the most important correlate for male completion, while off-reservation living experience was the most important for females. Abstracts in English, French, and Spanish. Tables, 2 notes, biblio. E. S. Johnson

2598. Downs, James F. THE COWBOY AND THE LADY: MODELS AS A DETERMINANT OF THE RATE OF ACCULTURATION AMONG THE PIÑON NAVAJO. *Kroeber Anthrop. Soc. Papers 1963 29: 53-67.* Many writers put forth the general assumption that conservatism is a general characteristic of all women, and that the Navajo are a good example in support of this assumption. This is based on the fact that Navajo men seem quite willing to adopt western ways in dress patterns (cowboy) and economic activities (cattle-herding is a major goal), while the women tend much more to fit into traditional Navajo patterns. It is more likely that these two patterns of behavior are traceable to the models of white society available and the possibility of emulation of those models. For the male, the model is the cowboy, as seen on television, in films, and throughout the Southwest; for the female, no one model is presented, other than perhaps the standard white middle-class mother-wife seen in television commercials. Since the model for the male is possible without total repudiation of Navajo life, he adopts it; for the female, however, it is impossible in the context of the reservation, and it is therefore rejected. Based on primary and secondary sources, as well as field investigation; 5 notes, biblio. C. N. Warren

2599. Freeman, Patricia Anne. KIOWA APACHE CONCEPTS AND ATTITUDES TOWARD THE CHILD. *Papers in Anthrop., U. of Oklahoma 1971 12(1): 90-160.* This study attempts to investigate a relatively narrow aspect of the total interaction which takes place between the Kiowa Apache child and his culture. Its focus is the body of concepts and attitudes which influence the adult in his behavior toward the child. Such concepts, and the behavior springing from them, shape only a small portion of the total environment, experience, and world of meanings of the child. AIA (3:3:1050)J

2600. Garbarine, Merwyn S. SEMINOLE GIRL. *Trans-Action 1970 7(4): 40-46.* Nellie Greene, a Seminole girl, tells her life's story. After receiving an education, she left the reservation to take a skilled job in Miami. She subsequently returned to the reservation because she thought her skills could be useful to her people. However, upon returning home, she found that she was alienated from them. They feel she should have returned because it was the right thing for her to do rather than because she had a mission to help them. Garbarine concludes that the efforts of the Bureau of Indian Affairs to stop the brain drain from the reservations may not be effective. Educated Indians are going to be disappointed if they expect to find status among their own people. Illus. A. Erlebacher

2601. Hackenberg, Robert A. and Wilson, C. Roderick. RELUCTANT EMIGRANTS: THE ROLE OF MIGRATION IN PAPAGO INDIAN ADAPTATION. *Human Organization 1972 31(2): 171-186.* Surveys the districts of the Papago reservation to measure the composition and destinations of migrants. Finds that nearly half of the residents will migrate, one-third will leave the reservation, females are more likely to migrate than males, and economic motives explain most of the migrating behavior. Also notes that migrants away from the reservation pay frequent visits to the reservation community. 13 tables, 4 notes, biblio. E. S. Johnson

2602. Hennigh, Lawrence. CONTROL OF INCEST IN ESKIMO FOLKTALES. *J. of Am. Folklore 1966 79(312): 356-369.* Recounts and analyzes four Eskimo folktales chosen from among one hundred tales collected along the Alaskan Arctic coast during the period 1961-62. At the end of the recital of each tale, the Eskimo informant was interviewed at some length about the story. "Examination of four folktales has resulted in three testable hypotheses: 1. A necessary condition for the expression of incest in folktales is the denial by the audience of at least one of these aspects: incestuous fact, incestuous motive, or identification with the incestuous person. 2. Incest may be directly expressed with pleasure to nonincestuous sources (i.e., when a means of denying identification is available). 3. No correlation exists between directness of expression of incest in folktales and conscious awareness by the audience of incest in folktales....The more interesting points are not the hypotheses but the type of data which produced them. The meaning of a folktale...exists not only in the text but also in the context in which it is told and the cultural interpretation which the audience brings to it." 8 notes.

D. D. Cameron

2603. Johnston, Thomas F. ALASKAN NATIVE SOCIAL ADJUSTMENT AND THE ROLE OF ESKIMO AND INDIAN MUSIC. J. of Ethnic Studies 1976 3(4): 21-36. Examines the cultural revival of native Alaskans who, through a diversity of musical activities, are achieving biculturality rather than totally assimilating. While analyzing the physiological effects produced by musical stimuli, especially altered states of consciousness due to the nonspecific pitch of tom-tom drumming, the author stresses the communal immersion in rhythmic kinesthetics which brings "tactile reinforcement of group identity." The social and psychological background of native music provides clues to understanding indigenous sex roles, forms of aggression, and humor, while harmonic stratification parallels social stratification, and song words reflect cultural values and environmental themes of seasonal life, stress on brightness (daylight), and the struggle for survival in a harsh land. Official efforts at developing and preserving these cultural forms, then, must be stressed in today's Alaskan educational systems, since music should not be the property of an elite. Based on field work and secondary sources; 21 notes.

G. J. Bobango

2604. Kline, J. A. and Roberts, A. C. A RESIDENTIAL ALCOHOLISM TREATMENT PROGRAM FOR AMERICAN INDIANS. Q. J. of Studies on Alcohol 1973 34(3-Part A): 860-868. "An inpatient alcoholism treatment program for American Indian alcoholics at the Mendocino (CA) State Hospital is described. The average age of 65 patients (6 women) was 32; 60% had not finished high school; 14% were married. During the year prior to admission, 57% had been employed for an average of 2.3 months, 60% had received welfare benefits, and 86% had been arrested, averaging 3.2 arrests and 8 weeks in jail. The average age at first drink was 13 years, first time drunk, 14.5 years, onset of blackouts, 25.1, onset of 'shakes,' 29.1. The preferred beverage was wine, followed by beer and spirits. Most drinking occurred in a car or out-of-doors; over 80% reported that most of their drinking was with friends. About half the patients reported drinking steadily and half reported binge drinking. The patients are admitted to a ward exclusively for Indians; the average length of stay is 2 months. The use of disulfiram is encouraged. Individual therapy is more successful than group therapy. The Intertribal Council of California's alcoholism counselors act as liaison between the Indian communities and the hospital. The particular problems of Indian alcoholics are discussed: intemperate use of alcoholic beverages is an accepted mode of social behavior; Indian personality characteristics of impassivity in new situations and reticence to discuss personal problems make them difficult to involve in treatment. The use of self-help groups is discussed in view of Indian culture." J

2605. Kunitz, Stephen J.; Levy, Jerrold E.; Odoroff, Charles L.; and Bollinger, J. THE EPIDEMIOLOGY OF ALCOHOLIC CIRRHOSIS IN TWO SOUTHWESTERN INDIAN TRIBES. Q. J. of Studies on Alcohol 1971 32(3): 706-720. "Data on liver cirrhosis among the Hopi (population, 6000) and the Navaho (over 100,000) were obtained from the 1965-67 records of the U.S. Public Health Service hospitals and clinics in Phoenix and Window Rock, Ariz. Of 25 identified Hopi cirrhotics (10 women), 10 had died (4 women); of 91 Navaho cirrhotics (36 women) 17 had died (10 women). The average age of the Hopi cirrhotic men was 42, women 38; of the Navaho, 41 and 44. Their marital status was not significantly different from that of the rest of the population. Among the Hopi fewer of the cirrhotics came from traditional villages or from on-reservation wage-work communities than from off-reservation locations;

none of the 9 on-reservation cirrhotics came from the more traditional villages that had refused to vote in the election of a tribal council. Among the Navaho fewer cases came from isolated areas and the incidence increased in areas closer to off-reservation communities. The cirrhosis mortality rate per 100,000 adults (20 years and over) was 13.0 (high-population estimate) or 17.0 (low estimate) among the Navaho and 104.0 among the Hopi, compared with the national adult rate of 19.9. It is suggested that the differences in cirrhosis rates reflect different drinking patterns. The Navaho tend to be abstainers or, as young men, heavy drinkers, many of whom stop drinking before their health is affected. The Hopi condemn drinking since it threatens the 'Hopi way' of peace and harmony. The heavy drinker is ejected from the community, continues to drink and is thus more likely to develop cirrhosis. The hypothesis that acculturation stress is the explanation of Indian problem drinking may hide many important cultural differences that exist between tribes." J

2606. Liberty, Margot. POPULATION TRENDS AMONG PRESENT-DAY OMAHA INDIANS. Plains Anthropologist 1975 20(69): 225-230. Data collected in 1972 from three communities in Nebraska, through intensive interviewing of women of childbearing age, are summarized. Rural-urban contrasts in variables related to population growth indicate that Omaha women are having many wanted children (4.5 by age 34). City residents have (and want) families at least as large as those had (and wanted) by reservation residents. Large families are not explained by (a) religious factors, (b) greater desire for children of one sex, i.e. boys, (c) ignorance or disapproval of birth control or (d) rural residence. Explanation appears to lie partly in large-family values derived from an Omaha past laced with disastrous epidemics which struck six times in the 19th century, killing from 50 to 1500 persons or from 5% to 75% of the tribe. J

2607. Marriott, Alice and Rachlin, Carol. INDIANS: 1966 - FOUR CASE HISTORIES. Southwest R. 1966 51(2): 149-160. Sketches the problems faced by rural Indian families in moving into the urban environment of a southwestern city where they must adapt to mechanization and new surroundings besides losing at least part of their tribal identity.

D. F. Henderson

2608. Mori, Joyce and Mori, John. MODERN HOPI COILED BASKETRY. Masterkey 1972 46(1): 4-17. The women of the Second Mesa in northeastern Arizona specialize in coiled basketry. Baskets are produced on a part-time basis for daily use, for ritual purposes, for gifts, and for income from the tourist trade. Describes the basketmaking process and the problems of continuing the craft. Training the younger generation is more and more difficult. Despite the relatively high retail price of a Hopi basket, the return to the basketmaker is a very low hourly wage. Tourists do not find baskets appealing and must be educated concerning the amount of work and skill required to produce one. 9 figs., 7 refs.

J. D. Falk

2609. Morris, Clyde P. YAVAPAI-APACHE FAMILY ORGANIZATION ON A RESERVATION CONTEXT. Plateau 1972 44(3): 105-110. "Existing residence patterns of the Yavapai-Apache living on the Camp and Middle Verde reservations show a persistence of traditional matrilocal residence multihousehold family clusters. This persistence has been facilitated by divorce, welfare, and marriage practices on the reservations operating in a context of varying reservation and regional economic circumstances that necessitated off-reservation employment." J

2610. Oswalt, Wendell H. TRADITIONAL STORYKNIFE TALES OF YUK GIRLS. Pro. of the Am. Phil. Soc. 1964 108(4): 310-336. An ethnographic analysis based on 41 stories told between 1956-60 by young Yuk girls at the Eskimo village of Napaskiak in Alaska. The stories, illustrated during narration by stylized drawings executed on a mud surface with a traditional "storyknife," a stick, or a table knife, usually have a grandmother and granddaughter as central characters and provide some clues to an earlier aboriginal life as well as the worldview of children in another society. The "storyknife complex" seems to be limited to the Eskimo girls of the Yuk or Yuit linguistic family in littoral southern Alaska. Illus., documented. R. G. Comegys

2611. Tyroler, H. A. and Patrick, Ralph. EPIDEMIOLOGIC STUDIES OF PAPAGO INDIAN MORTALITY. Human Organization

*1972 31(2): 163-170.* Examines and compares birth and death rate statistics. Finds rates for the Papago in general agreement with US Indian populations, but both birth and death rates higher for modern Papago settlements than traditional ones. 6 tables, 2 notes, biblio.

E. S. Johnson

2612. Uhlmann, Julie M. THE IMPACT OF MODERNIZATION ON PAPAGO INDIAN FERTILITY. *Human Organization 1972 31(2): 149-161.* Examines the fertility of the Papago Indians and finds that at present the tribe is in a stage of rapid population growth. Notes, in comparing fertility in eight communities, that the urban Papago women in Tucson have fewer children and cease to have them at an earlier age, reflecting both differential migration and modernization. 17 tables, 7 notes, biblio.

E. S. Johnson

2613. Whitaker, Kathleen. NA IH ES: AN APACHE PUBERTY CEREMONY. *Masterkey 1971 45(1): 4-12.* An eyewitness account of a contemporary (3 October 1969) San Carlos Apache puberty ceremony for girls, *Na ih es.* Through this detailed account of the rite, the author denies that today most of the intrinsic beauty and spiritual value of American Indian religious practices has been lost. 2 photos, 2 notes, biblio.

D. Anness

## Mexican Americans

2614. Arroyo, Laura E. INDUSTRIAL AND OCCUPATIONAL DISTRIBUTION OF CHICANA WORKERS. *Aztlán 1973 4(2): 343-382.*

2615. Baca Zinn, Maxine. POLITICAL FAMILIALISM: TOWARD SEX ROLE EQUALITY IN CHICANO FAMILIES. *Aztlan 1975 6(1): 13-37.* Interprets changes in the Chicano family in light of the family's self-conscious efforts to resist colonial oppression and discrimination. Political familialism is the fusion of cultural and political resistance within the family unit. The family, for Mexican Americans, has come to have a broader meaning than in the past, since it incorporates loyalty to political or cultural organizations. Chicanos have been changing their own values regarding *machismo* and women's roles. 37 notes.

R. Griswold del Castillo

2616. Bean, Frank D. COMPONENTS OF INCOME AND EXPECTED FAMILY SIZE AMONG MEXICAN AMERICANS. *Social Sci. Q. 1973 54(1): 103-116.* "Considering alternative hypotheses relevant to the income-fertility relationship, husband's income is partitioned into two components, each of which bears special salience to alternative hypotheses. The different relations of the components to expected family size among Mexican Americans underscores the notion that social processes of a reference group nature need to be better taken into account in the socioeconomic theory of family formation." J

2617. Bradshaw, Benjamin S. and Bean, Frank D. TRENDS IN THE FERTILITY OF MEXICAN AMERICANS, 1950-1970. *Social Sci. Q. 1973 53(4): 688-696.* "The data provide little evidence to support the thesis that the fertility levels of the Anglo and Mexican American populations have substantially converged during the last two decades." J

2618. Felder, Dell. THE EDUCATION OF MEXICAN-AMERICANS: FALLACIES OF THE MONOCULTURE APPROACH. *Social Educ. 1970 34(6): 639-642.* The education of Mexican-American children is a complex and difficult task in an educational system in which cultural difference are "un-American and undesirable." The author believes that the American educational system, in which curricula are devised to "mirror" and to perpetuate "anglo culture," cannot effectively educate Mexican-American students who come to school with substantially different cultural patterns. For example, even the most basic concept of role identity confuses the Spanish-speaking child. The male is expected to play a dominant and superior role in his culture; the female a more passive and subordinate one. In the classroom, the male may be forced to accept an authoritative female teacher, while the female Mexican American is pressured to "perform as an equal with her male classmates." 2 notes.

G. D. Doyle

2619. Hawes, Bess Lomax. LA LLORONA IN JUVENILE HALL. *Western Folklore 1968 27(3): 153-170.* La Llorona, the "Weeping Woman," is a ghost figure from Mexico that appears in a number of "migrant legends" on both sides of the border. Of disputed origin, she is important in Mexican legendry and folklore. Usually the tale relates some of her misfortunes while she was still alive, or it describes a confrontation with her ghostly form. The analysis made here is of a collection of 31 La Llorona items made in a girls' correctional school in Los Angeles County, California. 37 notes.

D. L. Smith

2620. Patella, Victoria and Kuvlesky, William P. SITUATIONAL VARIATION IN LANGUAGE PATTERNS OF MEXICAN AMERICAN BOYS AND GIRLS. *Social Sci. Q. 1973 53(4): 855-864.* "[The authors] report findings on the situational variation in language patterns of Mexican American boys and girls. They found that Spanish was used in almost all cases with parents and that the use of both languages was the predominant pattern for other situations. Exclusive use of Spanish decreased as the situations moved from family centered interaction to the neighborhood and to school, work, and social contexts. Girls used English more often than boys and students more often than dropouts." J

2621. Riddell, Adaljiza Sosa. CHICANAS AND EL MOVIMIENTO. *Aztlán 1974 5(1/2): 155-165.* Examines the concept of machismo, and the action of the Catholic Church in the context of American society; discusses how these affect the involvement of Chicanas in the Mexican American movement during the 1970's. S

2622. Temply-Trujillo, Rita E. CONCEPTIONS OF THE CHICANO FAMILY. *Smith Coll. Studies in Social Work 1974 45(1): 1-20.* Reviews a range of formulations about the Chicano family drawn from a sample of social science literature (1968-74), and criticizes the stereotyped conception of ideal family models used as criteria for study of Mexican Americans. S

2623. Vidal, Mirta. NEW VOICE OF LA RAZA: CHICANAS SPEAK OUT. *Internat. Socialist Rev. 1971 32(9): 7-9, 31-33.* Discusses issues in feminism for Chicano women in the 1970's, emphasizing "machismo" sexism, abortion, and child care.

## Other

2624. Arafat, Ibtihaj S. TRENDS IN FAMILY PLANNING: THE AMERICAN-EGYPTIANS' CASE. *Internat. Migration Rev. 1972 6(4): 393-402.* Studies Egyptian family size in Egypt and the United States, and compares family size of the present generation to that of their parents and grandparents. S

2625. Elam, Sophie L. POVERTY AND ACCULTURATION IN A MIGRANT PUERTO RICAN FAMILY. *Teachers Coll. Record 1969 70(7): 617-627.* Outlines the problems of acculturation confronting a Puerto Rican immigrant family living in New York City by considering Puerto Rican cultural roles and values. S

2626. Fong, Stanley L. M. ASSIMILATION AND CHANGING SOCIAL ROLES OF CHINESE AMERICANS. *J. of Social Issues 1973 29(2): 115-128.* "This article is concerned with the effects of social change on the role relationships and adjustment of Chinese Americans. The influences of cultural and social assimilation have undermined the commitment of Chinese youths to traditional cultural norms, and social disequilibrium can be seen within the family as well as outside the home. The changing sex role of females has affected their relationships with their parents and the opposite sex. Chinese vary in the extent to which they have become progressively removed from their parental culture, and the social distances between Chinese with different life styles have segregated them into a variety of disparate groups. Some of the changes in the psychological and social characteristics of the Chinese are examined from empirical studies." J

2627. Fontes, Manuel da Costa. A NEW PORTUGUESE BALLAD COLLECTION FROM CALIFORNIA. *Western Folklore 1975 34(4): 299-310.* The author describes his work and that of Joanne B. Purcell in collecting traditional ballads among Portuguese immigrants to southern

California. He urges more research in this area since the materials immigrants remember are quickly disappearing and "the oral tradition in Portugal itself is weakening." Partial texts of several ballads and a list of 56 ballad variations are included. Based on personal interviews and primary and secondary sources; 24 notes.                    S. L. Myres

2628. Glazer, Nathan. THE PUERTO RICANS. *Commentary 1963 36(1): 1-9.* Analyzes migration, assimilation, and adjustment patterns of Puerto Ricans who have settled in New York City, with emphasis on their family structure, housing, religion, voting habits, social and sexual mores, employment and business activities, organizational life, and relationships with other ethnic groups and with Puerto Rico. Though many of these newcomers live in a "veritable sea of misery" and present difficult problems for New York City's schools and welfare agencies, the migrants' experience has on the whole been "remarkably successful," following the path taken by earlier ethnic groups like the Jews and Italians rather than that of the American Negro. The Puerto Ricans' most significant contribution to New York may well turn out to be their indifference to the color bar which has marked American social behavior.
                    J. J. Appel

2629. Jaffe, A. J. and Cullen, Ruth M. FERTILITY OF THE PUERTO RICAN ORIGIN POPULATION—MAINLAND UNITED STATES AND PUERTO RICO: 1970. *Internat. Migration R. 1975 9(2): 193-209.* Demonstrates that the apparent higher fertility of Puerto Rican women, both in Puerto Rico and on the mainland, is due to age structure and socioeconomic status.

2630. Kikumura, Akemi and Kitano, Harry H. L. INTERRACIAL MARRIAGE: A PICTURE OF THE JAPANESE AMERICANS. *J. of Social Issues 1973 29(2): 67-82.* "The most outstanding fact about Japanese American marriage patterns prior to the 1960's was that Japanese tended to marry predominately within their own group. However, a review of past studies and an analysis of current rates of intermarriage indicate that this pattern is rapidly changing. Outgroup rates approaching 50 percent for Japanese American marriages occur in areas as diverse as Hawaii, Los Angeles, Fresno, and San Francisco. The varying rates and patterns of Japanese outmarriages are discussed."                    J

2631. Lewis, Oscar. I'M PROUD TO BE POOR. *Commentary 1966 42(2): 44-47.* An interview with a young Puerto Rican who arrived in New York and found a job in a finishing factory. He liked his Jewish boss and felt that his boss trusted him. He describes relationships with his wife, his sisters, and his mother. His philosophy is that destiny isn't all; "You yourself have a part in deciding what you are, and what you do. Before you can do that, you have to know yourself. And it's up to each one of us to know himself." Based on a forthcoming book.                    C. Grollman

2632. Macisco, John J., Jr. ASSIMILATION OF THE PUERTO RICANS ON THE MAINLAND: A SOCIO-DEMOGRAPHIC APPROACH. *Internat. Migration Rev. 1968 2(2): 21-39.* Examines the value of socio-demographic analysis in the study of assimilation. Using the 1960 census, studies the difference between first- and second-generation Puerto Ricans in the United States. The dimensions compared are age, education, labor force status, income, occupation, age at first marriage, and fertility. Describes why these dimensions were selected and the process of obtaining the conclusions. The data indicate that second-generation Puerto Ricans have moved closer to the characteristics of the average U.S. citizen. Based on secondary sources and the 1960 census; 8 tables, 20 notes.                    G. O. Gagnon

2633. Mook, Maurice A. BREAD BAKING IN MIFFLIN COUNTY, PENNSYLVANIA: COMMENTARY FOR THE DOCUMENTARY FILM IN THE "ENCYCLOPAEDIA CINEMATOGRAPHICA." *Pennsylvania Folklife 1971 21(1): 42-45.* Provides information on the culture and population of a Pennsylvania German community in Mifflin County, and details their old-fashioned methods (including recipes) of baking bread.                    S

2634. Rindfuss, Ronald R. FERTILITY AND MIGRATION: THE CASE OF PUERTO RICO. *Internat. Migration R. 1976 10(2): 191-203.* Discusses the relationship (1965-70) between childbirth, fertility and migration in Puerto Ricans and in Puerto Ricans who have migrated to the US mainland, using US Census statistics.

2635. Rosenswaike, Ira. TWO GENERATIONS OF ITALIANS IN AMERICA: THEIR FERTILITY EXPERIENCE. *Internat. Migration R. 1973 7(3): 271-280.*

2636. Tinker, John N. INTERMARRIAGE AND ETHNIC BOUNDARIES: THE JAPANESE AMERICAN CASE. *J. of Social Issues 1973 29(2): 49-66.* "Intermarriage is an especially sensitive indicator of the permeability of ethnic boundaries: The rate can tell us something about how rigid the boundaries are, while the patterns can suggest the forces that maintain or reduce them. A survey of the marriage records of Japanese Americans in Fresno, California indicates that both the pattern of intermarriage (that is, whether the minority group partners are male or female) and the rate of intermarriage have changed noticeably in the last decade. Explanations are suggested for these changes and implications for the boundary surrounding the Japanese Americans are discussed."                    J

2637. Yuan, D. Y. SOCIAL CONSEQUENCES OF RECENT CHANGES IN THE DEMOGRAPHIC STRUCTURE OF NEW YORK CHINATOWN. *Phylon 1974 35(2): 156-164.* The 1955 federal law permitting increased immigration of Chinese nationals has resulted in a new social structure in New York's Chinatown. Families began to arrive, replacing the aged, single men of the past. Taiwanese immigrants are usually well educated and employable; those from Hong Kong are considerably less so. Tension between the two groups, low salaries, and lack of facilities for growing numbers of teenagers are primary problems. Existing social structures are poorly equipped to deal with these new problems. Table, 27 notes.                    V. L. Human

# Social Problems

## General
### (including race relations)

2638. Berreman, Gerald D. RACE, CASTE, AND OTHER INVIDIOUS DISTINCTIONS IN SOCIAL STRATIFICATION. *Race 1972 13(4): 385-414.* "This study explores whether social ranking by race is absolutely distinctive, not significantly distinctive, or whether it is one criterion among others upon which significantly similar systems of social ranking may be based. Some models and concepts concerning nature and comparability of systems of social ranking are identified to provide a framework for the discussion: stratification; ethnicity; caste; race; race versus caste; colonialism; class; pluralism; hierarchy as symbolic interaction; hierarchy as ideology; and sexual stratification. Whether and to what extent each is relevant and applicable to all or some systems of birth ascribed social separation and inequality is analyzed with special attention to Ruanda, India, Swat, Japan and the United States. It is concluded that race, as the term is used in America, Europe, and South Africa, is not qualitatively different from other systems of stratification in its implications for human social life."                    (AIA 3:4:1582)

2639. Brathwaite, Edward. RACE AND THE DIVIDED SELF. *Frontier [Great Britain] 1971 14(4): 202-210.* An analysis of *A Rap on Race* (New York: Dell Publishing Co., 1972) between Margaret Mead and James Baldwin. Despite the dialogue between two enlightened and communicative individuals, the author perceives a mutual and profound lack of understanding between them. Attributes the difficulty to two factors: 1) Mead's membership in the "dominant" culture and Baldwin's membership in the "sub-dominant," and 2) Mead's alternating concern and condescension in relation to Baldwin's initial hesitancy and later assertiveness. Supplies excerpts from *A Rap on Race,* and the quotations stress the aforementioned problems in the relationship of the participants. Illus.                    G. Waldo

2640. Cahalan, Don and Cisin, Ira H. AMERICAN DRINKING PRACTICES: SUMMARY OF FINDINGS FROM A NATIONAL PROBABILITY SAMPLE. *Q. J. of Studies on Alcohol 1968 29(1): 130-151, (3): 642-656.* I. EXTENT OF DRINKING BY POPULATION SUBGROUPS, (1): 130-151. Data were gathered by means of a random probability sample survey of 2,746 persons (1,177 men) representative of the adult household population of the continental U.S.A. (except

Alaska, Hawaii), interviewed in late 1964 and early 1965. All interviewers were nonabstaining men. Drinking was found to be typical behavior; both total abstention and heavy drinking were atypical. Of the household population, 68 [percent] were drinkers (men 77 [percent], women 60 [percent] ): 77 [percent] of the White and 79 [percent] of the Negro men, and 61 [percent] of the White and 49 [percent] of the Negro women, were drinkers. A Quantity-Frequency-Variability Drinking Index was constructed and showed that 32 [percent] of the respondents were abstainers, 15 [percent] infrequent drinkers (less than once a month), 28 [percent] light drinkers (no more than one or two drinks per occasion at least once a month), 13 [percent] moderate drinkers (no more than three or four drinks usually several times a month), 12 [percent] heavy drinkers (five or more drinks nearly every day or at least weekly). Half of the heavy drinkers were classified as escape drinkers on the basis of the answers they gave about their reasons for drinking (e.g., 'I drink when I want to forget everything,' or 'because I need it when tense and nervous'). Groups showing below-average numbers of drinkers were: women 40 years and older (52 [percent] drinkers); men 60 years and older (65 [percent] ); respondents with family incomes below [six thousand dollars] (55 [percent] ); farm owners (42 [percent] ), service workers (61 [percent] ), laborers (57 [percent] ) and semiskilled operatives (62 [percent] ); those who had not completed high school (57 [percent] ); residents of the South Atlantic region (58 [percent] ), East South Central (35 [percent] ), West South Central (62 [percent] ), West North Central (66 [percent] ), and Mountain states (58 [percent] ); respondents living outside Standard Metropolitan Statistical Areas (51 [percent] ); Baptists (47 [percent] and members of other conservative Protestant denominations (36 [percent] ); and those identifying their national origin as U.S. (46 [percent] ), English or Scotch (60 [percent] ), Scotch-Irish (50 [percent] ), and Latin-American or Caribbean (63 [percent] ). The prevalence of drinking varied directly by social status as measured by the Hollingshead Index of Social Position; a materially higher proportion of those of upper status (76 [percent] of highest and upper-middle) were drinkers. However, among those who drank at all, those of lower status had a slightly higher proportion of heavy drinkers (18 [percent] of lower-middle and lowest status). Four out of 10 of the respondents said they had either cut down or quit drinking, while 14 [percent] said they were now drinking more than previously. Retrospective responses and evidence from past studies indicate that the proportion of drinkers among women - especially younger women - is increasing. Multivariate analysis of the interaction of various factors is required to attain adequate understanding of the complex interrelationships in drinking behavior. Thus, while higher urbanization is usually associated with a higher proportion of heavy drinkers, the relationship is much more pronounced when sociocultural status and age are held constant: the greatest difference was found among men aged 45 or older of lower status, among whom 31 [percent] of those of higher urbanization were heavy drinkers, compared with 7 [percent] of men over 45 of lower status living in areas of lower urbanization. It is concluded that common sociological variables such as sex, age, socioeconomic status, religion, region and urbanization are sufficient to explain much of the variance in whether an individual drinks at all. In addition, certain measures of individual personality were useful in explaining the variance in heavy drinking: measures of psychological involvement with alcohol, alienation, and psychoneurotic tendencies." II. MEASUREMENT OF MASSED VERSUS SPACED DRINKING, (3): 642-656. "A new Volume-Variability (V-V) index of drinking behavior consists of eight groups (ranging from abstainer to high-volume-high-maximum consumption) and two amount-per-occasion levels (five or more drinks at least occasionally vs always less than five) for each of three volume-per-month groups (high, medium and low volume). A comparison with the Quantity-Frequency-Variability index as described in Part I of this study...demonstrates the relative simplicity and freedom from arbitrary definitions offered by the V-V index, which also eliminates grouping as 'heavy drinkers' those who drink small amounts daily with those who drink large amounts sporadically. Data from the authors' 1964-1965 national survey of 2746 adults interpreted by the V-V index are tabulated in detail. When aggregate consumption was held constant, those who never drank as many as five drinks on an occasion, when compared with those who did, were older, of higher social status, better adapted to their environments and more successful and satisfied in achieving their life goals, as well as less likely to worry about their drinking or feel they would miss alcohol if forced to give it up, and less dependent upon drinking to cope with problems."                                                                     J

2641.  Carman, Jessor R. and Grossman, P. H.  EXPECTATIONS OF NEED SATISFACTION AND DRINKING PATTERNS OF COLLEGE STUDENTS.  *Q. J. of Studies on Alcohol 1968 29(1): 101-116.* "The hypothesis that alcohol use may serve as an alternative behavior for the attainment of goals otherwise unattainable or for coping with the failure to attain valued goals was studied. The subjects were 38 men 50 women (mean age 19.2 years) from sophomore-level psychology classes at the University of Colorado who volunteered to participate in a drinking study. Two areas of need satisfaction thought to be central for college students were investigated: achievement and affection. Expectations of attaining satisfaction in these areas were measured by means of a 30-item questionnaire. Test-retest reliability of the questionnaire was above .90, and significant correlations with external criteria of achievement and affection provided validity evidence. Drinking behavior was assessed by questionnaire in small groups of 20: men reported greater intake and more drunkenness and drinking-related complications. Analyses of the relationship between expectations of need satisfaction and drinking behavior lent initial support to the hypothesis that the lower the expectations of need satisfaction, the greater the recourse to alcohol and alcohol-related consequences, especially among women. Subgroup analyses considering both need areas simultaneously provided additional support; the group with low expectations in both need areas had the highest drinking behavior scores; results were more consistent among women. The functions attributed to alcohol use were then studied. A list of meanings or psychological functions of drinking was constructed comprising four separate categories: positive-social, conforming-social, psychophysiological and personality-effects functions. Significant negative relationships were obtained between expectations of need satisfaction and the degree to which personality-effects functions were attributed to the subjects' use of alcohol. Results were clearest in women. The degree to which personality-effects functions characterize alcohol use was shown to relate to amount of intake, drunkenness and complications, especially in women. The study has provided evidence linking low expectations of need satisfaction to patterns of drinking behavior among college youth. It has also shown that that link is mediated by the psychological functions attributed to alcohol use. The evidence supports the view that drinking may serve as an alternative means to goal attainment or as a way of coping with failure to attain valued goals."                                                              J

2642.  Covner, B. J.  SCREENING VOLUNTEER ALCOHOLISM COUNSELORS.  *Q. J. of Studies on Alcohol 1969 30(2): 420-425.* "On the basis of the results of an intelligence test (Personnel Classification Test), an interest inventory and a personality test (California Psychological Inventory), 26 of 56 applicants were accepted as volunteer alcoholism counselors at the Fairfield County (Conn.) Council of Alcoholism. After training, the counselors worked with alcoholics and their families for 11 months and their performance was evaluated: 11 of the 16 women and 5 of the 10 men were rated as successful counselors. Of the 11 successful women counselors, 6 were alcoholics compared with 2 of the 5 unsuccessful counselors; equal numbers of successful (4) and unsuccessful (4) men counselors were alcoholics. The successful and unsuccessful women counselors did not differ in age (average 42 vs 46 years), in years of education (14 vs 15) or in verbal intelligence (average score of 97th percentile). The successful men and women counselors had stronger profiles on the personality test. The successful men counselors were older (51 vs 42 years) and had more years of education (15 vs 13) but did not differ in intelligence. The use of volunteer counselors was viewed as successful: no significant differences in outcome were found between patients counseled exclusively by treatment staff and those counseled chiefly by volunteers."                                                                     J

2643.  Cudaback, Dorothea.  CASE-SHARING IN THE A.F.D.C. PROGRAM: THE USE OF WELFARE SERVICE AIDS.  *Social Work 1969 14(3): 93-99.* A large urban California county trained AFDC (Aid to Families with Dependent Children) mothers to assist welfare department line workers on a team basis. This study outlines how ex-clients (A.F.D.C. mothers) and professional line workers from the public welfare department were able to bridge class, race, education, and age differences when there was a job to be done and the will to do it. Such teamwork represents a new way of solving welfare problems. 2 tables, 9 notes.                                                                W. L. Willigan

2644.  Esselstyn, T. C.  PROSTITUTION IN THE UNITED STATES.  *Ann. of the Am. Acad. of Pol. and Social Sci. 1968 376:*

*123-135.* "Currently, the demand for suppressing prostitution is far less insistent than it used to be. Some cities have experienced an apparent revival in prostitution, but this appearance is due chiefly to the visibility of the young, aggressive, attractive streetwalker. The prostitute now moves freely through all layers and areas of the community. While there is no census of prostitutes in the United States, it is believed that their numbers have not changed recently. About the same proportion of men patronize prostitutes as three decades ago, but their contacts are less frequent. The slack is taken up by nonprostitutes, in keeping with the greater sexual accessibility of women of all classes. Women become prostitutes for a complex of reasons, most of them quite rational. Men seek out prostitutes from a variety of long-recognized motives. The male prostitute is a youth who has sex relations with men. Much less is known about him, but he has been sufficiently studied to permit a rough profile. Currently, he is a potent source of venereal infection. Future public policy toward the female prostitute might include her under Social Security. Policy toward the male prostitute should start with educational measures and heightened concern for youth generally." J

2645. Ford, W. Scott. INTERRACIAL PUBLIC HOUSING IN A BORDER CITY: ANOTHER LOOK AT THE CONTACT HYPOTHESIS. *Am. J. of Sociol. 1973 78(6): 1426-1447.* "The contact hypothesis is reexamined within the context of public housing in a border-state city. Black and white housewives were interviewed in racially segregated and desegregated projects to determine the extent to which engaging in equal-status interracial contacts was related to racially tolerant attitudes. Whereas the findings clearly support the contact hypothesis for lower-income white housewives, in contrast to some earlier studies, the hypothesis as it applies to black women residing in the same environment is not supported. Discussion and suggested explanations of the seemingly discrepant findings emphasize the necessity of gaining a thorough understanding of the specific conditions under which interracial contact occurs and examining the meaning such contact has for blacks in contrast to their white counterparts." J

2646. Garrett, Gerald R. and Bahr, Howard M. WOMEN ON SKID ROW. *Q. J. of Studies of Alcohol 1973 34(4): 1228-1243.* "The drinking patterns and practices of homeless women and men are compared. Homeless women alcoholics may well be the most isolated and disaffiliated residents of Skid Row." J

2647. Gibbs, Jack P. MARITAL STATUS AND SUICIDE IN THE UNITED STATES: A SPECIAL TEST OF THE STATUS INTEGRATION THEORY. *Am. J. of Sociol. 1969 74(5): 521-533.* "Data on suicide by age, sex, and marital status in the United States, 1959-61, are employed to test the theory of status integration. On the whole, the findings are consistent with the theory, but more so for males than females. Such differential results are analyzed in terms of four principles that stipulate ideal test conditions. These principles are not *ad hoc* explanations of negative findings, meaning that they can be generalized to all tests of the theory. Data are available for systematic application of three of the four principles, and that opportunity should be realized in future research." J

2648. Goodwin, D. W. ALCOHOL IN SUICIDE AND HOMICIDE. *Q. J. of Studies on Alcohol 1973 34(1A): 144-156.* "The literature [58 items] on the association between suicide and alcoholism and between homicide and drinking is reviewed. While suicide is substantially more frequent among alcoholics than in the general population, alcoholism is more common among attempters than among suicides; men outnumber women alcoholics among both suicides and attempters. Suicide rates are lower among Black than among White alcoholics, and risk of suicide declines in all alcoholics after age 50. Suicide in alcoholics seems to be a response to loss of status, occupational role and relationships and occurs relatively early. The low suicide rate among Black alcoholics may be due to the early onset of problem drinking among them which may produce enough brain damage by middle age to dull the sufferings of alcoholics, and to the fact that few Black alcoholics have had much wealth or status to lose. Suicide and alcoholism can be considered as expressions of the same self-destructive instinct or of the same predisposition to depression. Although about one-quarter of all suicide victims (alcoholics and nonalcoholics) drink immediately before death, little is known concerning the role of intoxication in suicide. In homicide, both killer and victim commonly have been drinking, often to intoxication,

immediately before the event, but few murderers are alcoholics. Most murderers apparently do not respond to drinking in a pathological way, and drinking does not seem to produce aggressive behavior except in certain social situations." J

2649. Hausman, Leonard J. POTENTIAL FOR FINANCING SELF-SUPPORT AMONG AFDC AND AFDC-UP RECIPIENTS. *Southern Econ. J. 1969 36(1): 60-66.* Most female heads of families receiving Aid to Families with Dependent Children (AFDC), and a sizeable majority of male heads of families receiving Aid to Families with Dependent Children of Unemployed Parents (AFDC-UP), do not possess the earning capacity to forego public welfare support. The basic data relate to 1965. The statistical methods are discussed in an appendix. A. W. Coats

2650. Jaworski, Suzanne W. THE EVOLUTION OF A WHITE'S BLACK CONSCIOUSNESS. *Youth and Soc. 1972 4(2): 131-153.* Relates the evolution of a white woman's attitude toward Negroes.

2651. Kallen, D. J. and Miller, D. PUBLIC ATTITUDES TOWARD WELFARE. *Social Work 1971 16(3): 83-90.* Compares the attitudes of 300 white and 300 black women in Baltimore (1964) toward welfare. A series of tables compares the mean scale scores by education, percentage of antiwelfare responses expressed by whites by item and education; the same percentage scale for blacks, and the intercorrelations of attitude items. 4 tables, 5 notes. W. L. Willigan

2652. Kolodny, Ralph L. and Reilly, Willow V. GROUP WORK WITH TODAY'S UNMARRIED MOTHER. *Social Casework 1972 53(10): 613-622.* Describes, with case illustrations, a way "to afford young women support and social insight from peers in a period when problems arise from alienating environmental qualities." The flexible group approach deserves consideration by all social workers in this field. 14 notes. E. P. Stickney

2653. Levin, Herman. THE FUTURE OF VOLUNTARY FAMILY AND CHILDREN'S SOCIAL WORK: A HISTORICAL VIEW. *Social Service R. 1964 38(2): 163-173.* After commenting on the 1961 Rockefeller Foundation report on voluntary health and welfare agencies, and the 1962 amendments to the Social Security Act, the author places in historical perspective the growing shift in responsibility for all the community's families from the traditional voluntary family and children's agencies to community organization facilities. "It is shown that voluntary social agencies evolved from an earlier need for new patterns of integrating community services and that they move toward offering direct service to people...as efforts to organize services turned up unmet needs....Modern community organization facilities...seem to be taking a familiar path of development as they move from efforts to organize community services to beginning efforts at offering direct service to individuals in need." Based partly on reports issued by the National Social Welfare Assembly and by the Family Service Association of America, from 1934 to 1962; 40 notes. D. D. Cameron

2654. Levin, Jack and Taube, Gerald. BUREAUCRACY AND THE SOCIALLY HANDICAPPED: A STUDY OF LOWER-STATUS TENANTS IN PUBLIC HOUSING. *Sociol. and Social Res. 1970 54(2): 209-219.* "Results obtained in a study of 452 female tenants from 25 public housing projects in a large northeastern city suggest that the relationship of the lower-status tenant to the public housing authority is not unlike that between socially handicapped groups and client-centered bureaucracy generally. Lower-status tenants were less knowledgable about bureaucratic power structure and less likely to obtain adequate housing-related services than other tenants." J

2655. Morrison, Joseph L. ILLEGITIMACY, STERILIZATION, AND RACISM: A NORTH CAROLINA CASE HISTORY. *Social Service R. 1965 39(1): 1-10.* A history and analysis of two bills which were presented to the General Assemblies of North Carolina: in 1957, an amendment (SB 321) to the Eugenic Sterilization Law, which made sterilization of sexually delinquent individuals permissible at State expense; and, in 1959, a still more stringent Sterilization Bill (SB 113) which provided for compulsory sterilization of grossly sexually delinquent persons. "Neither of these two bills became law, but the concerns that gave rise to such bizarre legislative 'solutions' remain latent and endemic. The illegitimacy-sterilization-racist mixture is strong medicine, which remains potentially dangerous." In North Carolina, the prevalence of illegitimacy among the lower-class Negro population created a particular difficulty for social agencies because the majority of these unmarried mothers had no means of support except through public assistance. "The Jolly-Davis Sterilization Bill was defeated not by the established welfare agencies...but by ordinary people offended in their religion and in their sense of humanity." 43 notes.                                                   D. D. Cameron

2656. Otto, Herbert A.   SEX AND VIOLENCE IN CONTEMPORARY MEDIA - THREE STUDIES.   *J. of Human Relations 1968 16(4): 571-589.* Reports the results of a content analysis of American humor magazines, television cartoons, men's magazine articles on wife swapping, and men's physique magazines. Comparing this series of studies with previous studies made in the early 1960's, there are clear indications that the use of sexual themes in the media has progressed at a rapid rate. "Film cartoon humor, offered mostly to juvenile audiences, consists essentially of endlessly repeated variations on the theme of violence (mostly killing) or impending violence....The current mounting emphasis on violence in our media is much more destructive and frightening in its implications than the emphasis on sex themes. We cannot close our eyes to the fact that...the youth of America can often be found viewing cartoons where violence is being perpetrated at about the rate of one violent incident every fifty seconds....The fact that in 1967 most United States cities reported large gains in the crime rates...seems to...reveal that the public is responding to many years of conditioning for violence by becoming increasingly violent." 24 notes.                        D. J. Abramoske

2657. Rains, Prudence M.   MORAL REINSTATEMENT: THE CHARACTERISTICS OF MATERNITY HOMES.   *Am. Behavioral Scientist 1970 14(2): 219-236.* Discusses the role of maternity homes in providing moral reprieve and reinstatement for unwed mothers (1968).

2658. Retherford, R. D.   CIGARETTE SMOKING AND WIDOWHOOD IN THE UNITED STATES.   *Population Studies [Great Britain] 1973 27(2): 193-206.* "Earlier work has shown that tobacco consumption, primarily of cigarettes, accounted for almost half of the female-male difference in life expectancy in the United States in 1962. The present paper examines a related problem, the contribution of cigarette smoking of husbands to the high probability of widowhood for older wives and to the high expectation of widowed life for wives. The analysis is based on comparison of couple-life-table parameters by level of cigarette consumption of each spouse. A salient finding is that for initially intact couples, wife aged 37 and husband aged 39, who never divorce or re-marry after death of spouse, the probability of widowhood at age 62 for wives with non-smoking husbands is 0.125 whereas for wives with husbands who smoke 40 or more cigarettes per day it is 0.285. Another is that non-smoking wives with non-smoking husbands can expect to spend 18.7% of their remaining years after age 37 in widowhood, whereas non-smoking wives with husbands who smoke 40 or more cigarettes a day can expect to spend 30.7% of their remaining years in widowhood."                                                                    J

2659. Rubin, Lillian.   THE RACIST LIBERALS - AN EPISODE IN A COUNTY JAIL.   *Trans-action 1968 5(9): 39-44.* Describes and analyzes racial relations among 70 women arrested in Alameda County, California, during an antiwar demonstration. Although a large percentage of the prison's regular inmates were black, only one of the 70 women arrested at the antiwar demonstration was black. The white demonstrators were anxious to prove their lack of racism toward black inmates by seeming to condone even their most aggressive actions, and they made demands on themselves that they would not make on blacks. The white demonstrators largely shied away from any of the physical contact that prevailed among the black prisoners. Tension increased between the one black demonstrator and a white demonstrator over the issue of a fast. There was a tendency on the part of some of the whites to explain away any antisocial behavior of the blacks. Many of the whites did not understand the subtle racial overtones of having lower expectations of blacks. There was a tendency to treat the single black demonstrator as "our nigger." The author concludes that the behavior described by Jonathan Kozol in *Death at an Early Age* prevailed here - an unawareness of one's own deep connection with the racist structure and with the attitudes of society. Photo.                                                    A. Erlebacher

2660. Rushing, W. A.   ALCOHOLISM AND SUICIDE RATES BY STATUS SET AND OCCUPATION.   *Q. J. of Studies on Alcohol 1968 29(2): 399-412.* "Although many investigations have shown that alcoholism and suicide are related, few show this to be the case for population rates. Furthermore, alcoholism-suicide investigations have usually failed to control for the effects of other variables, such as age, economic and marital status. Using the liver cirrhosis mortality rate as an index of the alcoholism rate, the relationship between alcoholism and suicide for age-sex-race status sets and occupations was analyzed, while the effects of age, economic and marital status were statistically controlled. For age-sex-race status sets, the Spearman rank correlation between liver cirrhosis and suicide was .75. When rank correlations were computed for sex-race status sets for each of 10 separate age groups, the 7 age-specific correlations from age 35 up were positive. For occupations, the zero-order Pearsonian correlation between the two rates, standardized for age, was .67, indicating that the relationship is independent of age. Partial correlational analysis, controlling for median occupational income, occupational prestige and percentage of incumbents who are unemployed, single and divorced, revealed that partial $r$'s vary between .61 and .72, suggesting that the relationship is also independent of socioeconomic and marital status. The results permit at least two interpretations. One posits that alcoholism and suicide are the product of the same variables not controlled for, such as social disorganization, urbanization or personality structure. The other is a processional interpretation, with alcoholism viewed as leading to disrupted social relations and hence to suicide. [Bibliography of 40 items]."                                               J

2661. Schenck, Mary-Low.   A SOUTHERN NEGRO GIRL IN A WHITE NORTHERN FAMILY: A CASE STUDY.   *Social Work 1969 14(3): 77-83.* Reports the case of a Southern Negro girl who used skillful dissembling, a practice upon which the Negro's survival in the South depends. In this case "such behavior seriously hampered the adjustment of a southern Negro high school student" during the two years she lived with the author's white Northern family. This experience was part of a program entitled the Southern Student Project sponsored by the American Friends' Service Committee. 5 notes.                          E. P. Stickney

2662. Siassi, I.; Crocetti, G.; and Spiro, H. R.   DRINKING PATTERNS AND ALCOHOLISM IN A BLUE COLLAR POPULATION.   *Q. J. of Studies on Alcohol 1973 34(3-Part A): 917-926.* "Interviews were conducted with 937 members (429 women) of the Baltimore United Auto Workers Union and their spouses as part of a larger survey on mental illness; 18 questions related to drinking. The average respondent was 40.2 years old, had 9.7 years of education, had been married 17.2 years and had 3.7 children, had been on the present job 13.5 years and earned $8700 a year; 97% were White; 40% Catholic and 51% Protestant; 85% were married and 6% were single; 50% were born in Baltimore and 64% had lived at the same address for more than 5 years. Of the respondents, 377 (97 women) were drinkers (average age 41.1) and of these, 67% of the men and 38% of the women were heavy drinkers (6 or more drinks of any alcoholic beverage a week), and 10% of the men and 3% of the women were heavy-escape drinkers (heavy drinkers who frequently drank for psychological reasons). The average ages of the heavy and the heavy-escape drinkers were 41.4 and 38.9. Of the drinkers, 25% and 26% drank to be sociable or when others were drinking, 32% drank as part of an important occasion, 5% drank when nervous or tense, 4% to forget troubles. Of the drinkers, 44% had less than 9 years of education and 33% more than 12 years; 48% earned less than $6000, and 51%, over $10,000; 49% were Catholic and 40% Protestants. The findings are compared with those of a national sample reported by Cahalan [*Quart. J. Stud. Alc.* 29: 130-151, 1968] [see abstract 9:1609]. With social class held constant, there were more drinkers in the national sample (64 vs 41%), fewer heavy drinkers (19 vs 67%) and the same percentage of heavy-escape drinkers (9%). The ratio of men to women heavy drinkers in the national sample was 3:1, in the present sample 2:1; of heavy-escape drinkers, 2.6:1 compared with 3.3:1. Possible reasons for the differences are discussed."                                                                    J

2663. Stringer, Patricia.   WHITE TEACHER, BLACK CAMPUS.   *Change 1974 6(9): 27-31.* A white woman teaching at a predominantly black Southern college discovers that her sex presents as many problems as her race.                                                              J

2664. Turner, R. G. and Bilodeau, Marc. RELIGIOUS PARTICI-PATION AND RACIAL PREJUDICE IN A SOUTHERN WOMEN'S COLLEGE. *Radford R. 1972 26(2): 75-83.* Restricted study confirms earlier studies showing a positive relationship between high levels of religious participation (determined by church attendance and frequency of prayer) and race prejudice. Primary and secondary sources; 3 tables, 13 notes.      C. A. Newton

2665. Willerman, Lee; Naylor, Alfred F.; and Myrianthopoulos, Ntinos G. INTELLECTUAL DEVELOPMENT OF CHILDREN FROM INTERRACIAL MATINGS. *Science 1970 170(3964): 1329-1330.* "Interracial offspring of white mothers obtained significantly higher IQ scores at four years of age than offspring of Negro mothers, suggesting that environmental factors play an important role in the lower intellectual performance of Negro children."      AIA(2:1:171) J

2666. Wingfield, Mrs. Marshall. THE MEMPHIS EYE BANK FOR SIGHT RESTORATION. *West Tennessee Hist. Soc. Papers 1970 24: 129-131.* Discusses the successful endeavor to establish an eye bank in Memphis. Beginning in 1945 as a project of the business women of the First Congregational Church, it attracted the assistance of the Lions Club as well as the ophthalmologists of the city. The eye bank was chartered in 1946. Later a new charter was given and the local eye bank affiliated with the National Eye Bank of America.      H. M. Parker, Jr.

2667. Young, Don J.; Alverson, Patricia Young; and Young, Don J., M.D. COURT-ORDERED CONTRACEPTION. *Am. Bar Assoc. J. 1969 55(March): 223-226.* Advocates court-ordered contraception through the intrauterine contraceptive device to reduce the number of second pregnancies among delinquent female juveniles. One illegitimate pregnancy often leads to another. Court-ordered contraception is legally and medically feasible, and would allow more time for social casework for the delinquent. Based on secondary sources; table, 23 notes.      W. R. Larsen

2668. —. PROGRAMS AND PROBLEMS IN CHILD WELFARE. *Ann. of the Am. Acad. of Pol. and Social Sci. 1964 355: 1-139.* Keith-Lucas, Alan. CHILD WELFARE SERVICES TODAY: AN OVERVIEW AND SOME QUESTIONS, *pp. 1-8.*
Glover, E. Elizabeth. UNMET AND FUTURE NEEDS, *pp. 9-19.*
Mech, Edmund V. CHILD WELFARE RESEARCH: A REVIEW AND CRITIQUE, *pp. 20-30.*
Lewis, Mary. FOSTER-FAMILY CARE: HAS IT FULFILLED ITS PROMISE? *pp. 31-41.*
Hollingsworth, Hansel H. THE CHILD-CARING INSTITUTION ON THE MOVE, *pp. 42-48.*
Dowling, Donald D. NEW METHODS OF CARE, *pp. 49-55.*
Hosley, Eleanor M. PART-TIME CARE: THE DAY-CARE PROB-LEM, *pp. 56-61.*
McDowell, John T. A COMMUNITY APPROACH TO THE HOME: HOMEMAKER SERVICE, *pp. 62-68.*
Schoenberg, Carl. ADOPTION: THE CREATED FAMILY, *pp. 69-74.*
Wiltse, Kermit T. AID TO FAMILIES WITH DEPENDENT CHIL-DREN: THE BASIC SERVICE, *pp. 75-81.*
Bishop, Julia Ann. HELPING NEGLECTFUL PARENTS, *pp. 82-89.*
Farrow, Richard G. HELPING THE CHILD WHO COMES INTO CONFLICTS WITH THE LAW, *pp. 90-97.*
Milner, John G. THE RESIDENTIAL TREATMENT CENTER, *pp. 98-104.*
Brieland, Donald and Booth, Norman J. CHILD GUIDANCE AS A COMMUNITY SERVICE, *pp. 105-111.*
Yankauer, Alfred. MATERNAL AND CHILD HEALTH PROB-LEMS, *pp. 112-120.*
Gardipee, Charles R. THE HANDICAPPED CHILD, *pp. 121-127.*
Corry, Claud B. THE LICENSING OF CHILD-CARE FACILITIES, *pp. 128-133.*
Weissman, Irving. GUARDIANSHIP: EVERY CHILD'S RIGHT, *pp. 134-139.*
The basic philosophy of the field of child welfare has never been clarified; trends toward both family-centered work and child-centered work are observable. A major need is the clarification at law of the rights and

responsibilities of parents, children, and agencies. In the last 15 years three new major forms of foster care have developed: family group homes, agency group foster homes, and agency-operated group homes. Another modern procedure consists of emphasis on help to parents to provide needed care as opposed to punishment of parents and removal of children. Homemaking services are found a practical community approach. There is now an increased interest in service to disadvantaged groups. A greater share of our national wealth should be directed into services for the handicapped, and a major priority in research should aim at preventive measures.      E. P. Stickney

2669. —. [RACE, SEX, AND VIOLENCE]. *Am. J. of Sociol. 1975 81(3): 629-642.*
Yee, William. COMMENT ON SCHULMAN'S ARTICLE, *pp. 629-633.*
Faris, John H. ON "RACE, SEX, and VIOLENCE," *pp. 634-635.*
Schulman, Gary I. REPLY TO YEE AND FARIS, *pp. 635-641.*
Presents three differing opinions on Gary I. Schulman's article, "Race, Sex and Violence: A Laboratory Test of the Sexual Threat of the Black Male Hypothesis," dealing with the willingness of a male subject to electrically shock a male victim having sexual relations with a cross-racial female.

# Crime
## *(by and against women)*

2670. Ball, John C.; Ross, Alan; and Simpson, Alice. INCIDENCE AND ESTIMATED PREVALENCE OF RECORDED DELIN-QUENCY IN A METROPOLITAN AREA. *Am. Soc. R. 1964 29(1): 90-93.* Juvenile court data from Fayette County, Kentucky, a metropoli-tan area, were used to compute the incidence and prevalent rates of delinquency for 1960. The incidence varies markedly with age and sex, the highest being among 17-year-old boys. The outcome of the study is a new procedure for estimating the prevalence of delinquency in a given population. 7 notes, 2 tables.      E. P. Stickney

2671. Bohmer, Carol. JUDICIAL ATTITUDES TOWARD RAPE VICTIMS. *Judicature 1974 57(7): 303-307.*

2672. Davis, Angela Y. RACISM AND CONTEMPORARY LIT-ERATURE ON RAPE. *Freedomways 1976 16(1). 25-33.* Discusses rape in the context of the black male and the negative and wholly racist images which are conjured in Susan Brownmiller's *Against Our Will: Men, Women, and Rape* (New York: Simon and Schuster, 1975).

2673. Field, Martha H. and Field, Henry F. MARITAL VIOLENCE AND THE CRIMINAL PROCESS: NEITHER JUSTICE NOR PEACE. *Social Service R. 1973 47(2): 221-240.* Marital violence is currently dealt with by the criminal justice process. Policies and services focused on deterring or limiting this behavior would make more sense than to continue to treat the maritally violent as beyond the concern of social work. Details various patterns of law enforcement and the limita-tions of criminal justice procedures. Offers alternatives to the criminal law, ranging from altered laws to improved counseling services for both police and offenders. 32 notes.      M. Hough

2674. MacNamara, Donal E. J. SEX OFFENSES AND SEX OF-FENDERS. *Ann. of the Am. Acad. of Pol. and Social Sci. 1968 376: 148-155.* "Sex and sex-related conduct is rigidly circumscribed by law in the United States, and rigorous penalties are provided for deviations from the limited forms of sexual expression (or choice of sexual partners) permitted. These laws reflect a puritanical sociosexual culture, strangled in taboos, but do not accurately depict either the incidence or modes of sexual conduct. They do, however, create a body of sexual offenders (perhaps exaggerated as to numbers and certainly exaggerated as to de-gree of social danger) who are differentially subjected to hysterical, almost sadistically punitive sanctions by public, police, courts, and corrections authorities. Little research and experimentation is supported in this field, and less treatment is provided in the nation's penal institutions. While sex acts committed by force or threat, and sexual advances to very young children, must be restrained by penal sanctions (at least in the absence of effective therapeutic techniques), many of the sex statutes punishing consensual or autoerotic conduct, or nuisance manifestations of minor sexual pathology, might well be repealed. This would permit the development of a legal code more consistent with the changing sociosexual mores and folkways of our culture."                                                                                      J

2675.  McGuirl, Marlene C.  "THE FORGOTTEN POPULATION": WOMEN IN PRISON.  *Q. J. of the Lib. of Congress 1975 32(4): 338-345.* Analysis shows that women have been convicted of crimes of a primarily economic nature, that 80% of the imprisoned females have children, that 30% of women in prison were on public welfare, and that women as a group received lighter or shorter sentences than men, although indeterminate sentences may lead to a longer period of detainment. 49 notes.                                                          E. P. Stickney

2676.  Miller, Walter B.  VIOLENT CRIMES IN CITY GANGS. *Ann. of the Am. Acad. of Pol. and Social Sci. 1966 364: 96-112.* "The urban street gang plays a central role in the imagery of violence currently being disseminated by the mass media. Testing the reality of this image requires careful empirical studies of actual gangs. A study involving 150 gangs in 'Midcity,' a slum district of an eastern metropolis, and focusing on seven gangs subject to intensive field observation, reveals marked differences between the public imagery and research-derived findings. While members of slum street gangs engaged in violent crime to a greater degree than middle-class adolescents, violence was not a central preoccupation of the gangs, and most 'violent' crimes were of the less serious variety. Cruel or sadistic violence was rare; violence was seldom 'senseless' or irrational. Property damage was relatively uncommon. Participation in violent crimes had little to do with race, but was directly related to sex, age, and social status; most active were males of lower social status during late adolescence. The control of gang violence is seen to involve techniques for altering motivations similar to those which undergird national wars."                                                                                        J

2677.  Simon, Dorothy.  FEMINISTS AND HISTORY: A NEW VIEW OF RAPE.  *Mankind 1976 5(8): 20-22, 46-49.* A discussion of Susan Brownmiller's *Against Our Will: Men, Women and Rape* was engaged in by 12 men and women, including lawyers, police officers, a historian, a rape victim, and women active in the feminist movement. Includes portions of the book as well as excerpts from an interview with Brownmiller. Seven issues were explored, including the author's method of history, the relationship of prostitution and pornography to rape, rape as a political crime, the laws on rape, jail as a deterrent, female self-defense, and women in positions of authority.                          N. Lederer

2678.  Simon, Rita J.  AMERICAN WOMEN AND CRIME. *Ann. of the Am. Acad. of Pol. and Social Sci. 1976 (423): 31-46.* The topic of women and crime is currently enjoying a vogue, because women, in general, and research related to many aspects of women's lives are now popular topics for research. This article analyzes the relationship between the contemporary woman's movement, the role of women in crime, and the changing socioeconomic and political statuses of American women. Statistics on female arrest patterns for different types of offenses going back four decades are presented. The changes in women's propensities for committing different types of crimes are discussed and explanations about why these changes have occurred are offered. Statistics describing American women are compared with female crime data available for some 25 different countries. The extent to which women are victims of various types of offenses is also discussed. In its conclusion, the article offers some prognosis for the short-run future on how American women are likely to participate in criminal activities.                                                         J

2679.  Szajkowski, Zosa.  DOUBLE JEOPARDY - THE ABRAMS CASE OF 1919.  *Am. Jewish Arch. 1971 23(1): 6-32.* Traces the prosecution of anarchists Jacob Abrams, Mollie Steiner, and other Russian Jews under the 1917 Espionage Act. The case ultimately went to the Supreme Court, which upheld the Federal Government's case despite a dissent by Justice Oliver Wendell Holmes. Efforts to win the release of the convicted succeeded in 1921 when they were deported to the Soviet Union. Mollie Steiner was sentenced there to two years of exile in Siberia, and was later deported to Germany; Abrams went to Mexico after five years. Based on primary and secondary sources; photo, 43 notes.
                                                                                        E. S. Shapiro

2680.  Toynbee, Polly.  "CLASSIFICATION" AND "ADJUSTMENT" IN A MARYLAND WOMEN'S PRISON.  *Washington Monthly 1973 5(7): 41-58.*

2681.  Yoder, R. D. and Moore, R. A.  CHARACTERISTICS OF CONVICTED DRUNKEN DRIVERS.  *Q. J. of Studies on Alcohol 1973 34(3-Part A): 927-936.* "Demographic data were obtained from 310 persons (206 first and 104 repeat offenders, 56 women) consecutively convicted in El Cajon, California, of driving while under the influence of alcohol. Ages ranged from under 20 to over 60 and 93% were between 20 and 59 years old; 86% were "Anglos," 10% Mexican Americans, 3% American Indians; 55% were married and 11% single; 65% had 12 or more years of schooling; 85% were employed; all were enrolled in a course on drinking and driving as a condition of probation. Prior to being arrested, 52% of the 140 probationers who submitted narratives had been drinking at bars or pool halls and 22% at friends' homes, parties or picnics; 46% had been drinking beer, 16% mixed drinks, 14% beer and mixed drinks, 10% other combinations. Fatigue (21%), stress (17%) and concurrent use of other drugs (5%) were also involved. No attempt had been made to prevent 92% from driving. Denial or projection of guilt were noted in 31% of the narratives. The Michigan Alcoholism Screening Test (MAST) was given to 269 of these (201 first and 68 repeat offenders, 35 and 5 women, respectively). Repeat offenders had significantly higher MAST scores (indicating likelihood of alcoholism) than first offenders (p [is less than] .01); among first offenders, men had higher mean MAST scores than women (9.4 vs. 5.9) but the proportion of men with scores indicating alcoholism (71%) was not significantly different from that of women (63%). There was no correlation between age and MAST scores. Blood alcohol concentrations (BAC) were obtained from 346 men and 78 women first offenders and from 131 men and 16 women repeat offenders. A significant difference between BACs of repeat offenders of both sexes and first offenders (mean 0.22 vs. 0.19%, p [is less than] .01) was found, but not between those of men and women."                                          J

2682.  —.  WOMEN AND CRIME.  *Social Sci. Q. 1976 56(4): 650-663.*
Noblit, George W. and Burcart, Janie M.  WOMEN AND CRIME: 1960-1970,  pp. 650-657.  Presents data which suggest both changes in crime rates among women and some changes in the patterns of their crimes.
Simon, Rita J.  WOMEN AND CRIME REVISITED,  pp. 658-663. Elaborates on—and disputes some of—Noblit and Burcart's findings and interpretations by presenting data from her recent monograph, *The Contemporary Woman and Crime*.                                     J

# Illness and Medical Treatment

## General

2683.  Garrett, Gerald R. and Bahr, Howard M.  THE FAMILY BACKGROUNDS OF SKID ROW WOMEN.  *Signs 1976 2(2): 369-381.* A sociological investigation of female alcoholism, homelessness, and family background which concludes that females end on skid row because of failures in social relationships, whereas men become disaffiliated because of occupational failures. Family instability during childhood and marriage failure, often attributed to spousal infidelity, appear as key variables in explaining "skid behavior" in women. Based on life history interviews in New York City; 2 tables, 17 notes.                     J. Gammage

2684.  Page, Joseph A.  WHAT THE FDA WON'T TELL YOU ABOUT FDS.  *Washington Monthly 1973 5(1): 19-25.* Bureaucracy and nonforcefulness in the Food and Drug Administration result in unknown dangers for users of feminine deodorant products.                             S

2685.  Seaman, Barbara.  PELVIC AUTONOMY: FOUR PROPOSALS.  *Social Policy 1975 6(2): 43-47.* Proposes feminist-oriented reforms in obstetrics and gynecology, foundation grants, law, and population conferences, in a special section entitled "Women & Health."

2686.  Winokur, G. and Clayton, P. J.  FAMILY HISTORY STUDIES. IV. COMPARISON OF MALE AND FEMALE ALCOHOLICS. *Q. J. of Studies on Alcohol 1968 29(4): 885-891.* "A systematic evaluation of family histories and clinical symptoms was made on 69 male alcoholics and 45 female alcoholics at time of admission to a private psychiatric hospital. The mean age of the men was 48, women 46 years. The 2 groups differed in age of onset of alcoholism (men 26, women 34 years) and on having a secondary diagnosis of depressive reaction (men 19 percent] ), women 31 percent] ). The women were more likely to show such symptoms as retardation (29 vs 16 percent] ), suicidal thoughts (53 vs 24 percent] ) and delusions (27 vs 7 percent] ). The parents of the women were significantly more likely to be psychiatrically ill or unknown *(p less than]* .0125) than those of the men, due in part to an increased prevalence of alcoholism in the women's mothers (12 vs 3 percent] ) and fathers (28 vs 21 percent] ). The incidence of psychiatric illness was the same in both the men's and women's siblings, but was twice as frequent in the women's female siblings (23 percent] ) as male siblings (11 percent] ). Alcoholism was more frequent in the men's second-degree relatives (21 percent] ) than the women's (10 percent] ) and affective disorder more frequent in the women's second-degree relatives (20 vs 11 percent] ). The results were interpreted as indicating that female alcoholics are not a homogeneous group, but rather have affective disorder in addition to alcoholism or alcoholism as a symptom of affective disorder in some cases; and that an X-linked gene may be implicated in alcoholism."    J

2687. —. MEDICINE AND SOCIETY. *Ann. of the Am. Acad. of Pol. and Social Sci. 1963 346: 1-148.*
Clausen, John A. and Straus, Robert. HEALTH, SOCIETY AND SOCIAL SCIENCE, *pp. 1-8.* [I] *Society and Medicine: Perspectives.*
Pellegrino, Edmund D. MEDICINE, HISTORY, AND THE IDEA OF MAN, *pp. 9-20.*
Parsons, Talcott. SOCIAL CHANGE AND MEDICAL ORGANIZATION IN THE UNITED STATES: A SOCIOLOGICAL PERSPECTIVE, *pp. 21-33.*
Paul, Benjamin D. ANTHROPOLOGICAL PERSPECTIVES ON MEDICINE AND PUBLIC HEALTH, *pp. 34-43.* [II] *The Organization of Medical Resources.*
Roemer, Milton I. CHANGING PATTERNS OF HEALTH SERVICE: THEIR DEPENDENCE ON A CHANGING WORLD, *pp. 44-56.*
Freidson, Eliot. MEDICAL CARE AND THE PUBLIC: CASE STUDY OF A MEDICAL GROUP, *pp. 57-66.*
Wilson, Robert N. THE SOCIAL STRUCTURE OF A GENERAL HOSPITAL, *pp. 67-76.* [III] *Education for the Health Professions.*
Bloom, Samuel W. THE PROCESS OF BECOMING A PHYSICIAN, *pp. 77-86.*
Mauksch, Hans O. BECOMING A NURSE: A SELECTIVE VIEW, *pp. 88-98.*
Straus, Robert. A ROLE FOR BEHAVIORAL SCIENCE IN A UNIVERSITY MEDICAL CENTER, *pp. 99-108.* [IV] *Health and Human Behavior.*
Vincent, Clark E. THE FAMILY IN HEALTH AND ILLNESS: SOME NEGLECTED AREAS, *pp. 109-116.*
Brown, Esther Lucile. MEETING PATIENTS' PSYCHOSOCIAL NEEDS IN THE GENERAL HOSPITAL, *pp. 117-125.*
Cottrell, Leonard S., Jr. and Sheldon, Eleanor Bernert. PROBLEMS OF COLLABORATION BETWEEN SOCIAL SCIENTISTS AND THE PRACTICING PROFESSIONS, *pp. 126-137.*
Clausen, John A. SOCIAL FACTORS IN DISEASE, *pp. 138-148.*    S

## Abortion

2688. Clayton, Richard R. and Tolone, William L. RELIGIOSITY AND ATTITUDES TOWARD INDUCED ABORTION: AN ELABORATION OF THE RELATIONSHIP. *Sociol. Analysis 1973 34(1): 26-39.* "This study, using a sample of 821 college students at three different universities, attempted to elaborate the relationship between religiosity (ideological commitment assessed by a five item Guttman-type scale) and attitudes toward induced abortion for seven situational conditions (woman's health endangered, rape, serious defect in child, low income, unmarried, want no more children, and incest). Controls for sex (as gender) and two Guttman-type scales designed to measure attitudes

toward other types of fertility control (one scale dealt with coercive controls on fertility while the other assessed a more traditional endorsement of the preventive and educational orientation), produced expected results on the zero-order relationship between ideological commitment and attitudes toward induced abortion."    J

2689. Djerassi, Carl. FERTILITY CONTROL THROUGH ABORTION: AN ASSESSMENT OF THE PERIOD 1950-1980. *Sci. and Public Affairs 1972 28(1): 9-14, 41-45.* Notes the necessity of population control and methods to achieve it, focusing on abortion and abortion research.    S

2690. Drinan, Robert F. REFLECTIONS ON NEW YORK'S COMMISSION ON ABORTION. *Catholic World 1968 207(1242): 261-263.* The majority report of Governor Nelson Rockefeller's Commision on New York State's Abortion Law seeks a "reasonable compromise" but not answers to the questions relating to the morals of abortion. The minority report has a certain unyielding tone. The greatest impact of the report lies in the way it highlights the erosion of conscience on crucial moral issues in American society.    M. C. Kuhn

2691. Hurlbut, Biddy. WHO OWNS YOUR BODY? *Focus/Midwest 1973 9(59): 12-13.* Supports fertility control, the Supreme Court's abortion decision, and changes in abortion laws. Male and religious groups are determined to reverse the gains.    L. H. Grothaus

2692. Jenness, Linda. WHY WE SHOULD FIGHT THE ANTIABORTION LAWS. *Internat. Socialist Rev. 1971 32(7): 6-7.* Advocates women's opposition to government abortion laws in 1971 and discusses the need for birth control and pregnancy tests.

2693. Johnson, Thomas L. ABORTION: A METAPHYSICAL APPROACH. *Freeman 1972 22(8): 498-505.* The abortion controversy is the most important issue of our times because it deals with the most fundamental of human rights, the right to life. Metaphysics is the only proper approach to the question of abortion. Reviews the biological data and applies that information to ethics. Concludes that the unborn child is entitled to the basic right to life. Note.    D. A. Yanchisin

2694. Knowles, John H. PUBLIC POLICY ON ABORTION. *Society 1974 11(5): 15-18.* The Supreme Court ruling on abortion constitutes a mandate to create a satisfactory program ensuring individual access under safe, dignified, and humane conditions.    S

2695. Lund, Caroline and Jaquith, Cindy. ABORTION ON DEMAND: A WOMAN'S RIGHT. *Internat. Socialist R. 1971 32(5): 7-9, 40-41.* The right to abortion has become the focus of the counterattack against Women's Liberation, thus demonstrating its importance.    J. S. Brown

2696. MacMullen, Sherry A. A PUBLIC AGENCY REACHES OUT TO WOMEN IN CRISIS. *Public Welfare 1972 30(2): 2-4.* Discusses the ability of public welfare agencies in Los Angeles County, California, to deal with abortion problems of women, 1970's, emphasizing the role of the Medi-Cal agency.

2697. Mears, Judith M. THE DOCTOR AS ABORTION ALLY. *Civil Liberties R. 1974 1(3): 134-136.* Discusses the Supreme Court ruling that women have a constitutionally protected right to bodily privacy and speculates on the ways doctors could support this decision.

2698. Moriarty, Claire. WOMEN'S RIGHTS VS. CATHOLIC DOGMA: WHY THE CHURCH FATHERS OPPOSE ABORTION. *Internat. Socialist R. 1973 34(3): 8-11, 44-45.*

2699. Renzi, Mario. IDEAL FAMILY SIZE AS AN INTERVENING VARIABLE BETWEEN RELIGION AND ATTITUDES TOWARDS ABORTION. *J. for the Sci. Study of Religion 1975 14(1): 23-27.* Analyzes data defining the relationships between family size preferences, religion, and attitudes on abortion.    S

2700. Richardson, James T. and Fox, Sandie Wightman. RELIGION AND VOTING ON ABORTION REFORM: A FOLLOW-UP STUDY. *J. for the Sci. Study of Religion 1975 14(2): 159-165.* Discusses the effect of religious affiliation on voting behavior of legislators in an unidentified western state on the issue of abortion.                                     S

2701. Rossi, Alice S. ABORTION AND SOCIAL CHANGE. *Dissent 1969 16(4): 338-346.*

2702. Schur, Edwin M. ABORTION. *Ann. of the Am. Acad. of Pol. and Social Sci. 1968 376: 136-147.* "As part of the increasingly open discussion of sexual matters in our society, new public attention has been focused on the abortion 'problem.' In America, induced abortion (which medically can be a simple procedure) has been subject to legal proscription and administrative control. The current narrow legal exception for 'therapeutic abortion' does not accord with accepted standards of good medical practice, and is now being challenged by medical practitioners and organizations. Instead of curbing abortion, the criminal-law ban simply diverts the demand for such services to illicit sources. The results are a thriving illegal business; subjection of abortion-seekers to the dangers of criminal abortion; a process of 'criminalization'; and - for women in the lower socio-economic strata - discriminatory treatment, according to their financial and informational resources. An important trend toward liberalization of abortion laws is related to broader currents of social change in our society - involving norms governing private sexual behavior, fertility control, and the social roles of women. The keynote of such change is the extension to women of areas of free choice hitherto not accorded them. How far this trend will be carried with respect to freedom of abortion remains to be seen."                                     J

2703. Wachtel, Dawn Day. OPTIONS OF THE SINGLE PREGNANT WOMAN. *Rev. of Radical Pol. Econ. 1972 4(3): 86-106.* Ready availability of abortion is very important to the liberation of young American women. Discusses the history of abortion in America and comments on contradictions which have arisen. Financial costs may restrict abortion even where it is legal. Adoption may become more available to minority groups as white women choose abortion. Based on statistical and secondary data; 12 tables, 30 notes.                                     C. P. de Young

2704. Wassmer, Thomas A. THE CRUCIAL QUESTION ABOUT ABORTION. *Catholic World 1967 206(1232): 57-61.* The crucial question is, "When *does* the human person begin its life?" Favors the 1959 recommendation of the American Law Institute permitting abortion in some instances.                                     M. C. Kuhn and S

2705. Welch, Delpfine. DEFENDING THE RIGHT TO ABORTION IN NEW YORK. *Internat. Socialist R. 1973 34(1): 10-13.*

## Psychiatry

2706. Breggin, Peter. LOBOTOMY—IT'S COMING BACK. *Liberation 1972 17(7): 15-16, 30-35.* Reports on the abridgment of mental patients' human rights in performing this psychosurgical operation aimed at modifying the behavior of socially aberrant individuals and its use particularly on the elderly, the poor, and women since the 1950's.                                     S

2707. Clancy, Kevin and Gove, Walter. SEX DIFFERENCES IN MENTAL ILLNESS: AN ANALYSIS OF RESPONSE BIAS IN SELF-REPORTS. *Am. J. of Sociol. 1974 80(1): 205-216.* "Phillips and Segal (1969) and Cooperstock (1971) have argued that the consistent finding that women have higher rates of mental illness than men is a product of response bias and does not reflect actual differences in rates of mental illness. In the present paper we look at the effect three forms of response bias—perceived trait desirability, need for social approval, and naysaying—have on respondents' reports of psychiatric symptoms. When these three forms of response bias are controlled for, the difference between the sexes does not diminish but instead increases."                                     J

2708. Gove, Walter R. and Tudor, Jeannette F. ADULT SEX ROLES AND MENTAL ILLNESS. *Am. J. of Sociol. 1973 78(4): 812-835.* "This paper looks at the relationship between adult sex roles and mental illness. A fairly precise definition of mental illness is used, limiting

it to functional disorders characterized by anxiety (neurosis) and/or mental disorganization (psychosis). A number of characteristics of the woman's role in modern industrial societies that might promote the development of mental illness are discussed. The rates of mental illness for men and women following World War II are then compared by looking at community surveys, first admissions to mental hospitals, psychiatric treatment in general hospitals, psychiatric outpatient clinics, private outpatient psychiatric care, and the practices of general physicians. These data uniformly indicate that adult women have higher rates of mental illness than adult men. A survey of other disorders which appear to be a response to stress also shows women to have higher rates than men. Alternatives to the role explanation of the observed relationships are shown to be inadequate.                                     J

2709. Leininger, Madeleine. WITCHCRAFT PRACTICES AND PSYCHOCULTURAL THERAPY WITH URBAN U.S. FAMILIES. *Human Organization 1973 32(1): 73-83.* The increased interest in witchcraft and the occult is an expression of social-cultural stress. Relates two case-work experiences to support the argument that the treatment of witchcraft victims in traditional mental health clinics may be detrimental. Presents a theoretical model to guide in providing understanding psychocultural therapy in treating witchcraft victims. Abstracts in English, French, and Spanish. Fig., 3 notes, biblio.                                     E. S. Johnson

2711. Phillips, Derek L. REJECTION OF THE MENTALLY ILL: THE INFLUENCE OF BEHAVIOR AND SEX. *Am. Sociol. R. 1964 29(5): 679-687.* "The effects of the behavior and the sex of four descriptions of mentally ill persons are examined to ascertain the relative importance of each in determining attitudes toward the mentally ill. The findings indicate that the visibility with which an individual deviates from socially prescribed behavior, rather than the pathology of the behavior from a mental-hygiene point of view, determines the strength of rejection. In addition, men are rejected more strongly than women exhibiting the same behavior."                                     J

2712. Schleifer, Carl; Derbyshire, Robert; and Brown, Jeffrey. SYMPTOMS AND SYMPTOM CHANGE IN HOSPITALIZED NEGRO AND WHITE MENTAL PATIENTS. *J. of Human Relations 1964 12(4): 476-485.* Reports the results of tests given to 64 patients in two of Maryland's mental institutions. The purpose of the study was "to determine their clinical pictures at the first and third day of hospitalization." Negro patients "presented a more disturbed clinical picture" than did whites. Female patients recovered "significantly faster" than did males. No difference was found between the races with regard to rate of recovery. Possible reasons for the results are discussed.

D. J. Abramoske

2713. Stevens, Barbara. THE PSYCHOTHERAPIST AND WOMEN'S LIBERATION. *Social Work 1971 16(3): 12-18.* Analysis of the problems flowing fron the modern "oppressive" division of sex roles is viewed from the viewpoint of the therapists' values and attitudes toward female patients. Presents one case study. 10 notes.

W. L. Willigan

2714. Weissman, Myrna M. and Siegel, Rise. THE DEPRESSED WOMAN AND HER REBELLIOUS ADOLESCENT. *Social Casework 1972 53(9): 563-570.* A description and analysis of the interrelationships between the depressed woman and her children, emphasizing the family dynamics of the situation. During this study of depressed women, the most impaired relationship was with their children. A great deal of deviant behavior was found in their adolescent children, and the conclusion is that an acute depressive illness "significantly affected the depressed woman's capacity as a mother." 21 notes.                                     M. Kaufman

2715. Weston, Lynda Martin et al. FEMINIST PSYCHOTHERAPY. *Social Policy 1975 6(2): 54-62.* Discusses feminist psychotherapy as practiced since 1972 by the Feminist Counseling Collective in Washington, D.C.

## Pornography

**2716.** Bonniwell, Bernard L. THE SOCIAL CONTROL OF POR-NOGRAPHY AND SEXUAL BEHAVIOR. *Ann. of the Am. Acad. of Pol. and Social Sci.* 1971 (397): 97-104. "In a normless society, such as ours, the probability of continuing deterioration is evident if the mass communications media's emotional debasing of human behavior continues unabated. The law, cognizant of the problem but unable to effectively moderate the flow of pornography and demeaning sexual behavior in areas of public communication, suggests the need to establish some form of direct social control. In order to offset their cumulative and debasing effect, it is tentatively proposed that the flexibility of the mass media be matched by an equally flexible monitoring-voting system ('monivoting'), under which public controls may be imposed within a matter of hours. The proposals are perceived as a socio-cultural necessity for the continuing vitality of the nation." J

**2717.** Douglas, Melvyn; Eldridge, Florence; March, Frederic; and Wheeler, Harvey. ON PORNO AND VIOLENCE. *Center Report* 1973 6(5): 28-30. A colloquy conducted by Harvey Wheeler in which stage and screen stars Frederic March, Florence Eldridge, and Melvyn Douglas audit the dialogue sessions. S

**2718.** Falk, Gerhard. THE *ROTH* DECISION IN THE LIGHT OF SOCIOLOGICAL KNOWLEDGE. *Am. Bar Assoc. J.* 1968 54(3): 288-292. The confusion created in pornography cases by the Roth case (*Roth* v. *United States*, 1957) can only be clarified by the application of sociological insights into the effect of obscenity on individuals, and on the nature of the "average person" and "community standards." 22 notes. J. M. McCarthy

**2719.** Hamalian, Leo. THE SECRET CAREERS OF SAMUEL ROTH. *J. of Popular Culture* 1968 1(4): 317-338. In the history of publishing Samuel Roth will appear as a pornographer, a pirate, a ghost-writer, both authorized and unauthorized, an aspiring artist who wrote under many names, and an unsung hero in the fight against censorship. He made legal history in *Roth* v. *United States* (US, 1956) in which the Supreme Court laid down the "prurient interest" test and thereby opened up the publishing of erotica. S

**2720.** Leventhal, Harold. THE 1973 ROUND OF OBSCENITY-PORNOGRAPHY DECISIONS. *Am. Bar Assoc. J.* 1973 59(11): 1261-1266. "The guidelines for dealing with obscenity and pornography laid down by the Supreme Court at the end of its last term may be convenient markers for the problems of the past, but there will be no dearth of these problems in the future. Legislatures must decide whether the system of criminal justice is the appropriate mechanism for handling the pressures involved.... Drawn ... from material ... presented at an 'impact decision' program at the American Bar Association annual meeting in Washington in 1973." J

**2721.** Misham, Edward J. MAKING THE WORLD SAFE FOR PORNOGRAPHY. *Encounter [Great Britain]* 1972 38(3): 9-30. Describes the "permissive revolution" and "the growth over the last decade of the erotic, the 'lascivious,' the 'obscure' and the 'pornographic' in literature, art, and entertainment." Discusses the problems of censorship and its appropriateness in dealing with "the trend toward increasing sexual obscenity" as part of the larger issue of whether the growth of sexual permissiveness should or should not be curbed. 22 notes. D. H. Murdoch

**2722.** Packer, Herbert L. THE PORNOGRAPHY CAPER. *Commentary* 1971 51(2): 72-77. A critical assessment of behavioral studies supporting the *President's Commission Report on Obscenity and Pornography* (New York: Random House, 1971). S

**2723.** Wilson, W. Cody and Abelson, Herbert I. EXPERIENCE WITH AND ATTITUDES TOWARD EXPLICIT SEXUAL MATE-RIALS. *J. of Social Issues* 1973 29(3): 19-40. "The data reported in this paper come from a national probability sample survey designed to provide an empirical description of the national experience with explicit sexual materials, the public's attitudes toward these types of material, and social-psychological correlates of both experience and attitudes. An overwhelm-

ing majority of adults report having been exposed at some time in their life to very explicit sexual materials that are often labeled pornography. Nevertheless, considerable variation in experience does exist. Differential exposure is related to the content of depictions, mode of depiction, and characteristics of the viewer. The data do not support a concept of a 'contemporary community standard' relating to the representation of sexual matters: There does not exist anything approaching consensus in attitudes regarding the availability of sexual materials; attitudes toward availability vary greatly according to the circumstances of availability; and attitudes vary considerably among groups formed on the basis of demographic characteristics." J

**2724.** Wilson, W. Cody. FACTS VERSUS FEARS: WHY SHOULD WE WORRY ABOUT PORNOGRAPHY? *Ann. of the Am. Acad. of Pol. and Social Sci.* 1971 (398): 105-117. "Prior to the work of the U.S. Commission on Obscenity and Pornography, the discussion of pornography necessarily had to be based on fear because there were few facts available. As a result of the Commission's work there are now data to inform the discussion. Many of our cultural myths in this area are not borne out by empirical facts. Nearly everyone in our society has been voluntarily exposed to depictions of explicit sexual activity often referred to as pornography. Initial exposure generally occurs before the end of high school; perhaps 50 percent are first exposed in junior high school. Viewing or reading sexual depictions generally produces sexual arousal but this does not necessarily eventuate in sexual activity. Sex criminals have had less experience with explicit sexual materials than have normal people. Exposure to explicit sexual materials does not produce bad moral character nor calloused sexual attitudes toward women. The gaining of information is perhaps the most common enduring consequence of exposure to sexual materials. But to many people these facts are irrelevant; and this poses a potential threat to our society." J

**2725.** Wilson, W. Cody. LAW ENFORCEMENT OFFICERS' PER-CEPTIONS OF PORNOGRAPHY AS A SOCIAL ISSUE. *J. of Social Issues* 1973 29(3): 41-52. "Data are presented from a questionnaire mailed to a random sample of District Attorneys stratified by state and by population of county, achieving a 69 percent response. Prosecuting attorneys, as a group, vary greatly among themselves in their perceptions of the degree to which obscenity and pornography constitute a problem in their communities. Concern about pornography is very highly correlated with size of community and with changes in the availability of pornography: concern is found in large urban situations and when the availability of pornography seems to be increasing (but not when it is stable). Behavioral indices of concern, such as effort expended in law enforcement and numbers of prosecutions, do not indicate as serious concern as do verbal indices. Those aspects of the distribution of pornography that are verbally reported to be the source of concern are not the aspects of distribution that are prosecuted. The citizenry in general is perceived as somewhat apathetic about pornography. A post hoc analysis attempts to make conceptual sense of these empirical data." J

## Image and Self-Image

**2726.** Birstein, Ann. AMERICAN SCHOLAR FORUM: WOMEN ON WOMEN. *Am. Scholar* 1972 41(4): 599-627. Describes interviews with five prominent women of various backgrounds, in New York City. Explores the current status of the position of women, and includes an interpretation of the scope of the interview. F. F. Harling

**2727.** Brown, Richard C. POSTAGE STAMPS AND AMERICAN WOMEN: STAMPING OUT DISCRIMINATION IN THE MAILS. *Social Educ.* 1974 38(1): 20-23.

**2728.** Courtney, Alice E. and Whipple, Thomas W. WOMEN IN TV COMMERCIALS. *J. of Communication* 1974 24(2): 110-118. Discusses four studies of women in television commercials during 1971-73, showing that while some aspects of the commercials may have changed, the image of women is still presented largely in terms of a sex object.

**2729.** Downing, Mildred. HEROINE OF THE DAYTIME SERIAL. *J. of Communication* 1974 24(2): 130-137. Examines the roles of heroines in the daytime television serials, finding that these roles give a more complete treatment of women, partly because these shows are directed toward a largely female audience.

2730. Falke, Anne. THE ART OF CONVENTION: IMAGES OF WOMEN IN THE MODERN WESTERN NOVELS OF HENRY WILSON ALLEN. *North Dakota Q. 1974 42(2): 17-27.*

2731. Gutman, Jonathan. SELF-CONCEPTS AND TELEVISION VIEWING AMONG WOMEN. *Public Opinion Q. 1973 37(3): 388-397.* "In studies of TV program preference, personality traits have been relegated to the background. This article, in which TV viewing, itself, is considered value-expressive behavior, compares the self-concepts and ideal self-concepts of light and heavy TV viewers and relates them to demographic variables."                                                                J

2732. Kane, Kathy. WOMEN AND ADVERTISING. *Focus/-Midwest 1973 9(59): 10-11.* Criticizes gender stereotypes in advertising. Women are usually treated as girls with no minds but with bodies for everyone. Reviews advertisements in St. Louis newspapers.
L. H. Grothaus

2733. Kennedy, Beth C. ON BEING A WOMAN—INDIAN AND AMERICAN: A COMPARATIVE STUDY. *Asian Survey 1973 13(9): 833-852.* Studies the differences in feelings women in the United States and India have about themselves as interpreted from their drawings and writings.                                                                                                S

2734. Kramer, Cheris. STEREOTYPES OF WOMEN'S SPEECH: THE WORD FROM CARTOONS. *J. of Popular Culture 1974 8(3): 624-630.* Covers cartoons in the *New Yorker, Playboy, Cosmopolitan,* and *Ladies' Home Journal,* 1972-73.

2735. Kramer, Cheris. WOMEN'S SPEECH: SEPARATE BUT UNEQUAL? *Q. J. of Speech 1974 60(1): 14-24.* "The stereotype concepts of the way women speak offer a rich variety of hypotheses to test. Some of these hypotheses are that women talk more than men, have a more limited vocabulary, have a more irregular sentence structure, ask more questions, and use more adjectives, adverbs, and hyperbole."         J

2736. Levinson, Richard M. FROM OLIVE OYL TO SWEET POLLY PUREBREAD: SEX ROLE STEREOTYPES AND TELEVISED CARTOONS. *J. of Popular Culture 1974 9(3): 561-572.* Examines the sex role portrayal in Saturday morning television cartoons in 1973 and the media's role in socialization. The three-to-one ratio of males to females overall increased to four-to-one in adult roles; hence there are few adult female models. Cartoons showed very little variety in careers for females and stereotyped them as passive characters providing social or emotional support to males. The television cartoons reflected not real world events but the values of traditional sex roles. 2 tables, 44 notes.
J. D. Falk

2737. Moles, Elizabeth R. and Friedman, Norman L. THE AIRLINE HOSTESS: REALITIES OF AN OCCUPATION WITH A POPULAR CULTURAL IMAGE. *J. of Popular Culture 1973 7(2): 305-313.* Discusses the popular image of airline stewardesses as cultivated by advertising and stereotypical prejudices.                                                  S

2738. Mussell, Kay J. BEAUTIFUL AND DAMNED: THE SEXUAL WOMAN IN GOTHIC FICTION. *J. of Popular Culture 1975 9(1): 84-89.* The gothic novels of Mary Stewart, Victoria Holt, Dorothy Eden, and Phyllis Whitney support the double standard for the sexes by portraying two kinds of women: traditional domestic heroines and nonconforming passionate women who are thus failures. 38 notes.
J. D. Falk

2739. Rossi, Lee D. THE WHORE VS. THE GIRL-NEXT-DOOR: STEREOTYPES OF WOMAN IN *PLAYBOY, PENTHOUSE,* AND *OUI. J. of Popular Culture 1975 9(1): 90-94.* The soft-core pornographic magazines have a new image of woman, but Hugh Hefner's Playboy philosophy in no way threatens male domination of the female, and his "liberated" woman, the girl-next-door type, is compatible with traditional sex roles. The new magazines *Penthouse* and *OUI* are hostile to the women's movement, too, but their image of women differs from *Playboy*'s. The images of women in these men's magazines are even more demeaning than the traditional images they claim to supplant.
J. D. Falk

2740. Schechter, Harold. KALI ON MAIN STREET: THE RISE OF THE TERRIBLE MOTHER IN AMERICA. *J. of Popular Culture 1973 7(2): 251-263.* Discusses the image of women as "man-eating" (both emotionally and physically) in popular culture media such as comic books, sex machines, and rock music groups.                        S

2741. Scully, Diana and Bart, Pauline. A FUNNY THING HAPPENED ON THE WAY TO THE ORIFICE: WOMEN IN GYNECOLOGY TEXTBOOKS. *Am. J. of Sociol. 1973 78(4): 1045-1050.* "An analysis of 27 gynecology texts written over the past three decades reveals a continuing tendency to present traditional views of female sexuality and personality. Women are stereotyped as primarily wives and mothers and as having a lesser capacity for sex. This study, in the tradition of other studies of sex-role stereotypes, demonstrates sexism in our society."                                                                                  J

2742. Sobchack, Vivian C. *THE LEECH WOMAN'S* REVENGE, OR A CASE FOR EQUAL MISREPRESENTATION. *J. of Popular Film 1975 4(3): 236-257.* Using a horror film, *The Leech Woman* (1960), as an example, the author probes the role of women in films during the 1960's-70's.                                                                                    S

2743. Stone, Kay. THINGS WALT DISNEY NEVER TOLD US. *J. Am. Folklore 1975 88(347): 42-50.* North American Children's literature and the films of Walt Disney (1901-66) limit fairy-tale heroines to passive princesses whose only tests require demonstration of innate beauty or pleasing temperament. However, Anglo-American oral traditions are replete with sexual symbolism and aggressive heroines proving themselves in action. Women's role-models in fairy tales could be much more than Cinderellas. Based on primary and secondary sources; 39 notes.
W. D. Piersen

2744. Streicher, Helen White. THE GIRLS IN THE CARTOONS. *J. of Communication 1974 24(2): 125-129.* Discusses the roles held by female characters in television cartoons, showing the majority of them to stress female dependency and helplessness.

# Culture, the Arts, and Recreation

## General

2745. Aldridge, A. Owen. AMERICAN BURLESQUE AT HOME AND ABROAD: TOGETHER WITH THE ETYMOLOGY OF *GO-GO GIRL. J. of Popular Culture 1971 5(3): 565-575.* Outlines the history of American burlesque, its influence in foreign countries, and its evolution into the topless dancing performed by women in discotheques.

2746. Berger, Arthur. VARIETIES OF TOPLESS EXPERIENCE. *J. of Popular Culture 1970 4(2): 419-424.* Briefly describes the topless dancing phenomenon and Carol Doda and Tara of San Francisco in particular.                                                                                   S

2747. Bostian, Lloyd R. and Ross, John E. FUNCTIONS AND MEANINGS OF MASS MEDIA FOR WISCONSIN FARM WOMEN. *Journalism Q. 1965 42(1): 69-76.* Four different types of measuring devices yield similar pictures of the functions and meaning of mass media for 540 Wisconsin farm women, but indicate that more attention should be paid to qualitative social-psychological variables.
S. E. Humphreys

2748. Burr, Elizabeth et al. WOMEN AND THE LANGUAGE OF INEQUALITY. *Social Educ. 1972 36(8): 841-845.* Analyzes how languages, with reference to English in particular, reflect outdated assumptions concerning the role and status of women in the popular mind. Illustrations demonstrate that literature is male-oriented in approach, historical presentation, and descriptive terminology. A number of changes in language usage are recommended in order to eliminate phraseology which subordinates females and contributes to their unequal status. Concludes that the role of women as whole human beings would be more accurately represented if alternative approaches to language were employed.
R. W. Dubay

2749. Defluer, Melvin. OCCUPATIONAL ROLES AS POR-TRAYED ON TELEVISION. *Public Opinion Q. 1964 28(1): 57-74.* An analysis of six months of 250 half-hour television programs in a mid-western community during children's hours. It examines the occupational roles presented, their settings and the characteristics of the workers portrayed. The author finds a heavy preoccupation with enforcement and administration of the law and an over-representation of high prestige managerial and professional roles. Television tends to "reinforce and perpetuate stereotyped ideas and incorrect generalizations about specific occupational roles." B. E. Swanson

2750. Deford, Frank. BEAUTY AND EVERLASTING FAITH AT THE LOCAL LEVEL. *Audience 1971 1(5): 56-72.* Deals with the Wilson, North Carolina, contest to choose a girl to compete in the Miss America pageant. Sponsored by the local Jaycees, the Wilson pageant is an important event in the life of the town and involves much preparation on the part of the contestants and sponsors. Up to 100 local white girls are invited to enter the contest, though no Negro has ever been asked to enter. In the 1970 contest there were 8 contestants who developed their talent, skills, etiquette, and poise, aided by professional pageant directors and producers. The contest is similar to the national pageant. Discusses the organization of the pageant and focuses on the two leading contenders. J. Coberly

2751. Gerson, Walter M. and Lund, Sander H. *PLAYBOY* MAGA-ZINE: SOPHISTICATED SMUT OR SOCIAL REVOLUTION? *J. of Popular Culture 1967 1(3): 218-227.* Analyzes the social functions of *Playboy* magazine and its impact on sexual norms.

2752. Glueck, Grace. MAKING CULTURAL INSTITUTIONS MORE RESPONSIVE TO SOCIAL NEEDS. *Arts in Society 1974 11(1): 48-54.* Paper delivered at a conference on Women and the Arts, Racine, Wisconsin, 1973. S

2753. Guenin, Zena Beth. WOMEN'S PAGES IN AMERICAN NEWSPAPERS: MISSING OUT ON CONTEMPORARY CON-TENT. *Journalism Q. 1975 52(1): 66-69.* Compares traditional women's sections and modernized, general interest newspaper sections. Traditional content is higher in traditional sections, but changing the section to cover broad interests, including entertainment, does not necessarily bring better coverage. Broad interest sections contain more pages, while consumer news is lacking in both types of sections. Based on analysis of six newspapers and primary sources; table, 6 notes. K. J. Puffer

2754. Hirsch, Robin. WIND-UP DOLLS. *Western Folklore 1964 23(2): 107-110.* Discussion of the origin and the circulation of the Wind-up Doll jokes which began to appear in September 1960. Also a list of 44 of these jokes divided into "Hollywood Dolls" and "Political Dolls." L. J. White

2755. James, Clive. MAILER'S "MARILYN." *Commentary 1973 56(4): 44-49.* Reviews Norman Mailer's biography of Marilyn Monroe, *Marilyn* (New York: Grosset & Dunlap, 1973). S

2756. Joslyn, James and Pendleton, John. THE ADVENTURES OF OZZIE AND HARRIET. *J. of Popular Culture 1973 7(1): 23-41.* Discusses the cultural influence of the *Ozzie and Harriet* television program, 1950's-66, and its demise due to cultural and social change; includes interviews with the Nelsons. S

2757. Lanham, Betty B. and Shimura, Masao. FOLKTALES COM-MONLY TOLD AMERICAN AND JAPANESE CHILDREN. *J. of Am. Folklore 1967 80(315): 33-48.* Compares types and meanings of childrens' stories in America and Japan. The authors trace certain stories to a preliterate society's need for entertainment and education. American stories are often about beautiful and virtuous, or ugly and cruel, women; the Japanese stories stress male personalities. Also, ethical points differ in the stories that are most familiar in the two countries. Japanese tales often encourage kindness and forgiveness, but American tales come out squarely against only one vice - vanity. Detailed analyses of folktales are given. 5 tables, 28 notes, appendix. M. W. Machan

2758. Magid, Nora L. THE HEART, THE MIND, THE PICKLED OKRA: WOMEN'S MAGAZINES IN THE SIXTIES. *North American Rev. 1970 7(4): 20:37.* Illustrates the cult of personality, the consumerism, and the glamour tips that pass for literature in the 1960's women's periodicals.

2759. Malko, George. PAULINE KAEL WANTS PEOPLE TO GO TO THE MOVIES: A PROFILE. *Audience 1972 2(1): 38-48.* Presents a biographical profile of movie critic Pauline Kael which includes her work methods and attitudes toward films. J. Coberly

2760. McBride, Robert M. THE HISTORICAL ENRICHMENT OF THE GOVERNOR'S RESIDENCE. *Tennessee Hist. Q. 1971 30(2): 215-219.* With the inauguration of B. W. C. Dunn as Governor of Tennessee in 1971, Mrs. Dunn, following the practice of neighboring states, began a program of collecting items of Tennessee state history to be displayed to the public in the Governor's Mansion. M. B. Lucas

2761. Michelson, Peter. THE PLEASURES OF COMMODITY OR HOW TO MAKE THE WORLD SAFE FOR PORNOGRAPHY. *Antioch R. 1969 29(1): 77-90.* Compares the evolution of the *Playboy* magazine phenomenon which "has managed to change sex from a dirty joke into "entertainment served up with humor, sophistication, and spice," to the earlier shift in attitudes toward sex as seen in 18th-century novels (Sterne and Richardson). The author indicates that *Playboy* has equated sex with profit and has evolved from the sleazy, smutty "skin" pictures to the *Playboy* "Playmate" image. *Cosmopolitan* is credited with performing a similar, although less significant transformation in the women's magazine area. Undocumented. F. Harrold

2762. Miller, James E., Jr. THE CREATION OF WOMEN: CONFESSIONS OF A SHAKEN LIBERAL. *Centennial R. 1974 18(3): 231-247.* In the past decade many Americans "have gone through strange personal transfigurations" in attitudes toward race and sex. In the process many weaknesses have been exposed in traditional liberal postures. Some liberals who experience this transfiguration have moved toward a more genuine liberalism minus the rhetoric and facade of the past. Personal change may be gauged by rereading works of literature involving women as well as contemporary biographies of women. If the change one feels in this process can be magnified to a national level, one's faith in the American future will be reinforced. 16 notes. A. R. Stoesen

2763. Miller, Susan H. THE CONTENT OF NEWS PHOTOS: WOMEN'S AND MEN'S ROLES. *Journalism Q. 1975 52(1): 70-75.* Examines roles of women in newspaper photographs in comparison with coverage of men. Men's photos outnumbered women's, the ratio varying in different newspaper sections. Life-style sections contained almost half the women's photos. Social roles of half of the women photographed were those of spouse, socialite, or entertainer; roles of 75% of the men were those of politician, professional, or sports figure. Revised from a presentation to the Association for Education in Journalism Convention, San Diego, August 1974. Based on examination of the Los Angeles *Times* and Washington *Post*; 3 tables, 8 notes. K. J. Puffer

2764. Monteiro, Lois A. NURSING-LORE. *New York Folklore Q. 1973 29(2): 97-110.* Nurses' folk beliefs and euphemisms. S

2765. Moore, J. W. E. EVANSVIEW AND OTHER MUSEUM HOUSES OF THE COLONIAL DAMES OF AMERICA. *Historic Preservation 1964 16(5): 166-171.* Traces the background and history of Evansview in Natchez, Mississippi and describes three other houses whose preservation has been assisted by the Colonial Dames. Photographs and a listing of state organizations of Colonial Dames who have assisted in the preservation of historic areas are included. J. M. Hawes

2766. Naison, Mark. SPORTS AND THE AMERICAN EMPIRE. *Radical Am. 1972 6(4): 95-120.* Discusses the role and ideology of sports since 1945, emphasizing the position of Negroes and women.

2767. Otto, Herbert A. SEX AND VIOLENCE ON THE AMERI-CAN NEWSSTAND. *Journalism Q. 1963 40(1): 19-26.* Three studies of sex and violence in mass communications - one of 55 magazines in

1961, one of 296 paperback books, one of 10 leading newspapers. Most magazines were found to be riddled with a metastasis of sex and violence. Paperback books show a significant increase in the quantity of violence and sex themes over the last 10 years. The newspaper press is not so preoccupied with these themes. S. E. Humphreys

2768. Parker, Edwin B. and Paisley, William J. PREDICTING LIBRARY CIRCULATION FROM COMMUNITY CHARACTERISTICS. *Public Opinion Q. 1965 29(1): 39-53.* "Based on data from libraries in 2,702 U.S. communities as reported in 1956 to the Office of Education." Through correlation analysis of eight variables "female education emerges as the strongest single predictor of library circulation." Size of population served predicts fiction circulation while the average income of the community predicts nonfiction circulation. This latter statement may reflect that "richer communities are better able to provide an adequate collection of non-fiction titles." The data seem to show that nonfiction collections in many libraries are inadequate to meet the needs of their communities. Further research is needed on the problem of the extent to which the book stocks of libraries are shaping the demand structure in communities rather than being shaped by this structure. 8 tables, 11 notes. E. P. Stickney

2769. Seldes, Gilbert. PUBLIC ENTERTAINMENT AND THE SUBVERSION OF ETHICAL STANDARDS. *Ann. of the Am. Acad. of Pol. and Social Sci. 1966 363: 87-94.* "The entertainments provided by the mass media are like the epic, the ancient theater, or the novel in that all present fiction which is received as truth. The new are more persuasive than the old because of the technological changes in the means of production and dissemination, because the line between the real and the fictional is blurred, and because, for economic reasons, the formation of habit, as well as a dulling of the critical faculties, has become desirable, especially in commercial broadcasting. The patron of the entertainment likes what he gets, without question, and certain of his wants are satisfied. There is, however, little effort to enlarge the range of satisfactions, and so much is given that such wants as are more difficult to satisfy and such satisfaction as can stir intelligence or criticism are generally neglected. By inducing inertia, the mass entertainments may contribute to the specific abuses of which they are often accused, such as incitement to violence or indifference to a strict sexual code. But it is their failure to serve the independence of mind of their followers, to stir the critical faculties, that is more serious." J

2770. Thompson, Lawrence S. THE BROOM IN THE OHIO VALLEY. *Kentucky Folklore Record 1963 9(4): 91-94.* A sampling of modern superstitions pertaining to the broom with special reference to courtship, marriage and folk remedies. Some similarities to European beliefs are noted. Documented. J. C. Crowe

2771. White, William. ON COLLECTING MARILYN MONROE. *Am. Book Collector 1974 24(5): 23-26.* Lists some of the better books on Marilyn Monroe. S

2772. Williams, Carol Traynor. IT'S NOT SO MUCH, "YOU'VE COME A LONG WAY, BABY"—AS "YOU'RE GONNA MAKE IT AFTER ALL." *J. of Popular Culture 1974 7(4): 981-989.* Discusses the comic and social values of the television situation comedy, *The Mary Tyler Moore Show.* S

2773. Yates, John. WHY THERE ARE NO WOMEN IN THE MOVIES. *J. of Popular Film 1975 4(3): 223-234.* Discusses the role of women in many recent films during the 1940's-70's.

2774. —. FABRICS FOR THE WHITE HOUSE. *Art in Am. 1963 51(1): 86-87.* Mrs. John F. Kennedy's refurnishing of the White House. Illus. W. K. Bottorff

## Education

2775. Atkyns, Glenn C. TRENDS IN THE RETENTION OF MARRIED AND PREGNANT STUDENTS IN AMERICAN PUBLIC SCHOOLS. *Sociol. of Educ. 1968 41(1): 57-65.* "Western nations are experiencing a lowering age of puberty. Many show a declining age of first

marriage. Technological developments have dictated an increasing age of economic maturity. The divergence between the ages of sexual maturity and economic maturity affects other social institutions. United States school practice has tended to prohibit attendance for married students, pregnant students, and student mothers. This study illustrates the decrease in restrictive practice since 1940 in large school districts, by regions, and compares it with small districts. Note is made of special programs and the scarcity of studies made by school districts regarding this subject area." J

2776. Bakke, E. Wight. GRADUATE EDUCATION FOR WOMEN AT YALE. *Ventures 1969 9(2): 11-25.* There has been no significant discrimination against women in the graduate academic programs at Yale, although there appears to have been social isolation in terms of facilities and environment for women in that academic community. A survey of graduate programs (not professional schools) indicated that higher percentages of women fail to complete their degrees, that women are often unclear about their career goals, and that the alternative career of marriage and motherhood often contributes to these factors. Furthermore, those women who complete graduate work do not often contribute research of as high a quality as men's, nor are their professional careers as academically oriented as those of men. None of these factors negates the value of graduate education for women, particularly in face of the major changes in the life-styles of American women and in the increasing professional opportunities open to them. The substance and quality of graduate education must be the same for both sexes, but the pattern and timing of graduate work for women should be selectively modified through such programs of continuing education as renewal education, opportunities for part-time study and extended time requirements for degrees, and emphasis on the Master of Philosophy degree and other innovative programs. Excerpts from a report of a committee on the Graduate Education of Women at Yale. R. J. Wurtz

2777. Barasch, Frances. HEW, THE UNIVERSITY, AND WOMEN. *Dissent 1973 20(3): 332-339.*

2778. Bayer, Alan E. THE COLLEGE DROP-OUT: FACTORS AFFECTING SENIOR COLLEGE COMPLETION. *Sociol. of Educ. 1968 41(3): 305-316.* "In this follow-up study of 8,567 Project TALENT students who had attended senior college within five years after high school graduation, the relative influence of 38 personal and background factors are examined as they relate to college completion. Aptitude measures and marriage and family variables are shown to be primary determinants of progress through college. However, inclusion of all 38 variables in a multiple regression prediction equation accounted for less than 30 percent of the variance in dropping out versus completing senior college for women, and less than 20 percent of the variance in this criterion for men. While the variables employed in this study yield results which are a considerable improvement over the results of other prediction studies, the degree of accuracy in prediction is not sufficient to be applicable in educational guidance and policy considerations. Other research strategies implied by the findings which may yield relatively high probability predictions are discussed." J

2779. Beck, Rochelle and Buter, John. AN INTERVIEW WITH MARIAN WRIGHT EDELMAN. *Harvard Educ. R. 1974 44(1): 53-73.* Explores Marian Wright Edelman's views on forms necessary to increase children's rights in education and discusses the work of the Children's Defense Fund. S

2780. Berger, Barbara. RESEARCHING DOTTORESSA MONTESSORI. *Urban R. 1967 2(3): 21-23.* The revival of interest in Montessori's teaching methodology raises a number of questions about its possible effect on developing personality traits in a child. Berger suggests the implications of this pedagogy as compared with more traditional methods and points to the research which is needed to verify her ideas. 2 notes. H. B. Powell

2781. Bunzel, John H. THE QUOTA MENTALITY. *Freedom At Issue 1973 (22): 10-14.* Critique of quotas as a method of dealing with discrimination in academics. S

2782. Burstyn, Joan N. EDUCATIONAL EXPERIENCES FOR WOMEN AT CARNEGIE-MELLON UNIVERSITY: A BRIEF HIS-

TORY. *Western Pennsylvania Hist. Mag. 1973 56(2): 141-153.* Reorganizations have limited the opportunities in professional training for women.                                                                                     S

2783.   Chalmers, E. L.   ACHIEVING EQUITY FOR WOMEN IN HIGHER EDUCATION GRADUATE ENROLLMENT AND FACULTY STATUS.  *J. of Higher Educ. 1972 43(7): 517-524.* Discusses sex discrimination toward women in faculty status and graduate enrollment in colleges and universities in the 1970's.

2784.   Cohen, Audrey C.   THE COLLEGE FOR HUMAN SERVICES.  *Teachers Coll. Record 1968 69(7): 665-682.* Colleges and universities are not geared to (and may not want to) admit to their institutions mature individuals from the ghettos who need and want higher education, but who have been deprived of sufficient preparatory education in their youth. The Women's Talent Corps is proposing a new people's college, the College for Human Services. This proposal is an outgrowth of the success of the Corps training program for careers in community service, particularly in New York City. The work-study principle will be carried over to the College, where the distinction between academic and field training is eliminated and subject matter content is integrated with on-the-job learning experience. The summer months will be utilized to encourage students to prepare for the high school equivalency examination. Immediate concentration on the social and behavioral sciences is a reversal of the ordinary college curriculum which normally requires general education in the first two years of college work. It is hoped that other colleges will accept graduates of the College for Human Services as transfer students for the bachelor's degree and will permit them to complete their liberal arts program in the junior and senior years.
C. P. McMahon

2785.   Cohen, Carl.   HONORABLE ENDS, UNSAVORY MEANS. *Civil Liberties Rev. 1975 2(2): 107-114, 115-116.* A few years ago the University of Washington Law School, one of many troubled by the small number of blacks in the legal profession, began to give preference to black applicants who had met the basic requirements for admission and were competing for places against whites who had passed that same initial hurdle. In 1971 Marco DeFunis, Jr., a white applicant who had been turned down in two successive years, sued the law school, alleging that the school had discriminated against him: while his grades and aptitude test scores were high, he said, other candidates with qualifications and credentials inferior to his had been admitted. A lower court in the state agreed with DeFunis's contention and ordered the school to admit him. The school did so. It then appealed to the Supreme Court of the State of Washington, which decided in favor of the school's right to exercise its preferential admission policy. DeFunis's attorney appealed to the U.S. Supreme Court. By the time the high court heard the case, DeFunis, who had been permitted to remain in school, was about to receive his law degree. In April 1974 the Supreme Court, by a 5-to-4 majority, declared the case to be without practical significance and rendered no decision on the issues involved. The issues raised by the DeFunis case—"reverse discrimination," quota systems, the application of the equal protection of the laws doctrine of the Constitution—aroused so much interest and concern that the Court received 30 "friend-of-the-court" briefs on both sides of the case from such diverse quarters as organized labor, business groups, educational associations, Jewish organizations, black organizations, chicano organizations, the American Bar Association, and the American Civil Liberties Union. Though Marco DeFunis's own case had to do with preference for blacks in admission to law school, its implications are broader: they concern all disadvantaged groups seeking access to better education and better jobs. How blacks, other racial minorities, and women can be enabled to catch up to the rest of a society that has discriminated against them for centuries, and to do so in a way that is fair and constitutional. In the absence of an easy answer, it is not surprising that the issue of preferential treatment is once again before the courts in a number of cases. To shed more light on the civil liberties aspects of preferential treatment, we invited two civil libertarians who took opposing positions on *DeFunis* to join in debate in our pages. Each debater states his case at length, and then each briefly rebuts the other.          J

2786.   Conway, Jill K.   COEDUCATION AND WOMEN'S STUDIES: TWO APPROACHES TO THE QUESTION OF WOMAN'S PLACE IN THE CONTEMPORARY UNIVERSITY.  *Daedalus 1974 103(4): 239-249.*                                                                 S

2787.   Cook, William D.   MISS LEESY'S MAGIC.  *Am. Educ. 1967 3(10): 8-10.* Describes the development and operation of a cultural enrichment program in 21 ghetto schools of St. Louis. Paraprofessionals who have recently traveled in a variety of countries are employed to excite the interest of culturally deprived children. The system's superintendent concluded, "The cultural enrichment program has been an unqualified success, and those working in it are rendering a service of inestimable worth to the community." Undocumented, 3 photos.
W. R. Boedecker

2788.   Cotter, Katharine C.   EXPLORATIONS AND DISCOURSE ON SCHOOL FAILURES.  *Catholic Educ. R. 1964 62(3): 169-182.* Summarizes components of the "non-achievement syndrome" as related to secondary school especially but with some reference to college youth. General nonadjustment, poor self-concept, and sex appear to be significant factors. Boys are shown to possess less of what it takes than girls. Lower social class is a negative factor related to individual performance, and also weakness in teaching. "Social promotion" is attacked as only protracting failure. The study recommends "greater knowledge" on the part of teachers and administrators "of psycho-educational effects of out-of-school causative agents" - causes currently often used as a defense rather than as a starting point for prevention and remediation.
K. V. Lottich

2789.   Cottle, Thomas J.   COLLEGE WOMAN.  *Liberal Educ. 1974 60(4): 514-520.* An encounter between the author and an academic woman.                                                                              S

2790.   Deutsch, Martin.   SOCIAL AND PSYCHOLOGICAL PERSPECTIVES ON THE DEVELOPMENT OF THE DISADVANTAGED LEARNER.  *J. of Negro Educ. 1964 33(3): 232-244.* The author presents the thesis "that the behavioral scientist and the educator can facilitate the evolution of the educational institution for preparing all children for optimal social participation as the racial, social class, and sex gatekeepers become inoperative" and argues that the curriculum "should serve both for the primary prevention of the social deviancies associated with deprivation and for the stimulation of healthy growth and utilization of individual resources."
S. C. Pearson, Jr.

2791.   Duncan, Jim.   GIRLS' BASKETBALL: 1950-68.  *Palimpsest 1968 49(4): 145-160.* Discusses girls' high school basketball in Iowa, 1950-68.                                                                               S

2792.   Dunsire, Charles.   PREP SCHOOL FOR MOM AND DAD. *Am. Educ. 1968 4(9): 20-23.* An account of a Family Life Education program in Seattle where adults are given guidance in solving a wide variety of parental problems. Most of the classes in the program are intended to promote better family relations, although some are courses to train adults to assist in the teaching of preschool children. Based on interviews with members of the program staff; undocumented, 5 photos.
W. R. Boedecker

2793.   Eisenman, M. Victoria.   IMPLICATIONS OF CLIENT-CENTERED THERAPY FOR ELEMENTARY-SCHOOL TEACHING. *Catholic Educ. R. 1963 61(7): 475-479.* Using the theme that "the implications of Rogers' theory (non-directive) for elementary teaching is a valuable and so far untapped area," arguments are advanced that the elementary teacher be herself, try to experience the child's world *as if* it were her own, and leave many questions raised by students unanswered to shock them into group action and/or group responsibility. The hiatus between counseling attitudes and the conventional teaching attitude is inspected, with the solution suggested that - while not necessarily progressive philosophies must obtain - the teacher examine her basic self projection.
K. V. Lottich

2794.   Ellmann, Mary.   ACADEMIC WOMEN.  *Commentary 1965 39(3): 67-70.* A humorous, sympathetic review of *Academic Women* (1965) by Mrs. Jessie Bernard; and a commentary on the biases against women in academic pursuits.
R. J. Moore

2795.   Farquhar, Norma and Mohlman, Carol.   LIFE COMPETENCE: A NON-SEXIST INTRODUCTION TO PRACTICAL ARTS.  *Social Educ. 1973 37(6): 516-519.* Discusses the application of the study of social sciences to career education, planning, and opportunity.
R. W. Dubay and S

2796. Feldman, Saul D. IMPEDIMENT OR STIMULANT? MARITAL STATUS AND GRADUATE EDUCATION. *Am. J. of Sociol. 1973 78(4): 982-994.* "This paper examines the effect of marriage upon the student role of men and women in American graduate education. Married women are caught between two conflicting prime roles—student and spouse. They appear to be the least successful graduate students. Married men, on the other hand, do not feel such a conflict and appear to be productive and happy. For women, divorce appears to be a liberation from the role conflict. Divorced women appear to be very productive and very involved in the student role, while divorced men have lost a source of psychological support and appear unhappy and less productive than their female counterparts. Marital status is, therefore, an important variable that must be taken into account in examining the role performance of graduate students.                                             J

2797. Fishel, Andrew. ORGANIZATIONAL POSITIONS ON TITLE IX: CONFLICTING PERSPECTIVES ON SEX DISCRIMINATION IN EDUCATION. *J. of Higher Educ. 1976 47(1): 93-105.* The comments submitted by organizations and individuals to the Department of Health, Education, and Welfare on the proposed regulations to implement Title IX of the Education Amendments of 1972 provide a unique opportunity to determine the positions of a wide variety of groups on issues relating to sex discrimination in education. A content analysis was made of the comments submitted by 50 groups and 74 college and university administrators on six key issues. The extent to which groups supported or opposed the recommendations made by the Women's Equity Action League and Representative Bella Abzug was determined. The results of this analysis demonstrate that groups representing women, teachers, students, and national civil rights commissions have a substantially different view from public school and higher education administrators; athletic groups; and elementary, secondary, and higher education groups on what constitutes sex discrimination in education and what procedures the federal government should require to eliminate it.      J

2798. Gerson, Walter M. THE COLLEGE SORORITY AS A SOCIAL SYSTEM. *Sociol. and Social Res. 1969 53(3): 385-394.* "This article constitutes a suggestive functional analysis of the social system of a college sorority. Membership recruiting is discussed in terms of pattern maintenance. It is suggested that sorority ceremony and ritual have the consequence of symbolic boundary maintenance. Some aspects of sorority in-group life are approached from a perspective of social insulation and integration."                                                        J

2799. Goodman, Elizabeth and Ferber, Ellen. SHE WON'T BE BACK. *Am. Educ. 1967 3(9): 6-8.* Describes the development and operation of Webster Girls School, the first free, fulltime, full curriculum public school for pregnant girls in the United States. Primarily intended as a means of reducing the dropout rate in the schools, it also is involved in providing for "the educational, psychological, social, and maternal needs of the students and later for their babies." Highly individualized programs are developed for each student. Followup studies indicate attendance had a significant effect on the attitude of the girls participating. Apparently based on an unpublished report made by the Bureau of Social Science Research and interviews with members and students of the school, photo.                                        W. R. Boedecker

2800. Gorman, M. Adele Francis. IN DEFENSE OF THE FOUR-YEAR CATHOLIC WOMEN'S COLLEGE. *Catholic Educ. R. 1965 63(6): 369-375.* For the past decade, the Catholic educational system has been under severe attack from the inside. Critics such as Father Neil McClusky, S.J., for example, of Gonzaga University have suggested that teachers now employed in Catholic women's colleges might be shifted to the secondary level. The arguments are stated and then answers to them are given. The place and purpose of such schools in American life are defended. Not only the continuation of Catholic women's colleges but also their expansion (including their "proliferation" which is decried by many Catholic educators) is urged. Attention is called to Richard Poorman's "The Small Catholic College: A Second Look" in the *Catholic Educational Review.*                                   D. H. Broderick

2801. Hansot, Elisabeth. A "SECOND-CHANCE" PROGRAM FOR WOMEN. *Change 1973 5(1): 49-51.* The New School's Human Relations Center has produced some highly imaginative educational services for urban and suburban women.                                   J

2802. Hoedel, M. Celestine. SEX DIFFERENCES IN ADOLESCENCE AND THEIR IMPLICATIONS FOR EDUCATION. *Catholic Educ. R. 1965 63(4): 217-228.* Pointing out through research studies that content and method in existing school programs are male-oriented whereas rewards (grades, scholarships, etc.) favor females, the author urges realistic utilization of sex differences in the learning process. Two distinct educational programs are suggested; coeducation versus separation of the sexes is not at issue.                         D. H. Broderick

2803. Hoffer, Stefan N. PRIVATE RATES OF RETURN TO HIGHER EDUCATION FOR WOMEN. *R. of Econ. and Statistics 1973 55(4): 482-486.* Examines the benefits of academic degrees for women in the United States.

2804. Jaffe, Lorna. WOMEN'S PLACE IN ACADEME. *Midwest Q. 1973 15(1): 16-30.*

2805. Katz, Joseph. THE CHALLENGE TO "BODY OF KNOWLEDGE" LEARNING FROM PERSON-CENTERED ADVOCATES. *Liberal Educ. 1972 58(2): 141-149.* Of these two approaches to education, only the one which focuses on the personal development of the learner reflects systematic research. After summarizing the findings of developmental theory, the author notes the many studies which suggest the relatively small impact of the faculty and the classroom on students. Faculty development must receive support and it must be more responsive to student needs and less dictated by professional needs. Greater flexibility must characterize the curriculum. Colleges have especially neglected the developmental needs of women students.              W. H. Ahern

2806. Kilson, Marion. THE STATUS OF WOMEN IN HIGHER EDUCATION. *Signs 1976 1(4): 935-942.* Because of demographic changes and economic constraints in academe today, the status of women in higher education promises to decline. The demise of women's colleges, the diminished number of top-level female administrators, the decline of tenured women, and the growing salary differential between men and women in university positions are indicators of this decline in status. The proportion of women degree recipients has exceeded the proportion of women faculty in academe since 1910. "Differences in men's and women's careers within academe may be attributed to factors ranging from institutional discrimination, through women's internal ambivalences . . . , to the existence of a culturally preferred academic career pattern tailored to the image of a 'family-free' man." Based on research studies and secondary works; 40 notes.            J. Gammage

2807. King, Charles E.; Mayer, Robin R.; and Borders-Patterson, Anne. DIFFERENTIAL RESPONSES TO BLACK AND WHITE MALES BY FEMALE TEACHERS IN A SOUTHERN CITY. *Sociol. and Social Res. 1973 57(4): 482-494.* "This article discusses the impact of a rather far-reaching school desegregation plan on teacher-pupil interaction at the classroom level. White males were most skillful in teacher-interaction and black males were least skillful of the four race-sex groups. All students interacted more with teachers in an integrated than in the all-black school."                                                J

2808. Kinnane, Mary. CATHOLIC STUDENTS' ATTITUDES TOWARD COLLEGE AUTHORITY. *Catholic Educ. R. 1963 61(5): 294-301.* The hypothesis of rebelliousness and rejection of college authority was tested as far as Boston College is concerned by questionnaires administered to 412 students including 354 males and 58 females. The response was generally high on the side of authority. Three hundred students answered "No" to "Students...should not be subject to regulations regarding their conduct or behavior." One hundred and eighty-one were favorable to "editors of student publications should be responsible to a student-faculty committee." There were three hundred and ten positive responses to "I believe that B.C. standards for students are part of the B.C. tradition and should be maintained." The author's final question "Do you believe B.C. administration should have the ultimate power of veto...?" answered with 293 "Yesses" appears to substantiate her conclusion that Boston College students responded "maturely and responsibly," at least for the situation tested.                       K. V. Lottich

2809. Kolesnik, Walter B. SHOULD STUDENTS BE SEPARATED BY SEX? *Catholic Educ. R. 1965 63(2): 73-81.* This analysis of opinion from 83 experienced teachers (only six men) as to educational implications of sex differences challenges current practice of coeducation in U.S. church-related schools, grades 7-12. The significance of this continuing study at the University of Detroit is apparent in the questions and responses included. (An encyclical of Pius XI describes coeducation as "false" and "harmful.")         D. H. Broderick

2810. Krueger, Cynthia. DO "BAD GIRLS" BECOME GOOD NURSES? *Trans-action 1968 5(8): 31-36.* Compares the behavior and attitudes of two categories of student nurses. The first comprises those who seem to abide by the principles posited by nursing-school administrators. The second consists of those who view their off-duty behavior as unrelated to their vocational aspirations. The author studies the behavior of each group toward the profession, medicine, and their personal goals. Although the school administrators were highly sympathetic toward the group which were apologists for the administrators' principles and critical of the "rebel" group, the results seemed surprising. The "rebels" turned out to be fine nurses. A much greater proportion of them than of the "well-adjusted" group continued their careers in hospitals. Most of those who had followed the wishes of the administration during their student days went into private practice, clinic work, or directly into marriage. Thus the author concludes that the nursing school's preferential treatment of the student-officer group needs reevaluation. Those who were "wild" did not see the relationship between their attitudes as students and their attitudes as professionals. They were willing to develop expertise as nurses but unwilling to kow-tow to rules which did not seem relevant. Illus., biblio.         A. Erlebacher

2811. LaFarge, Phyllis. REVOLUTION AT RADCLIFFE. *Interplay 1969 3(3): 10-15.* An analysis of the contemporary "Radcliffe girl." Speaks of the projected complete merger of Radcliffe College with Harvard University and the effects it will have on the two institutions and particularly on the students' relationships. Notes also the Radcliffe students' "search for sincerity," their desire to participate in all aspects of education and university life, and their interests in understanding "what they can do with what they have learned and with what they know of the system." 2 photos.         J. A. Zabel

2812. Lee, Patrick C. and Gropper, Nancy B. SEX-ROLE CULTURE AND EDUCATIONAL PRACTICE. *Harvard Educ. R. 1974 44(3): 369-410.* "The school's task is to provide children with equal access to traditionally sex-typed educational and cultural resources."    S

2813. Levy, Betty. THE SCHOOL'S ROLE IN THE SEX-ROLE STEREOTYPING OF GIRLS: A FEMINIST REVIEW OF THE LITERATURE. *Feminist Studies 1972 1(1): 5-23.* Reviews research studies, informal reports, and speculative writings. Critics have studied sex role learning but not how schools perpetuate traditional sex roles. Rather than "feminizing" or emasculating boys, women elementary teachers give them more attention, which develops their saliency, originality, and self-assertion while girls learn to behave properly. Traditional sex roles are reinforced through the authority structure of the school, segregated activities, and sex-typing in elementary reading materials and, later, of the subjects studied. The same factors occur at the secondary school level. 86 notes.         J. D. Falk

2814. Mayer, Martin. SCHOOLS, SLUMS AND MONTESSORI. *Commentary 1964 37(6): 33-39.* The Montessori spirit and some methods used by Maria Montessori in her work with genetically and environmentally crippled children can contribute toward better nursery and kindergarten instructions for "multiple-problem" slum, working-class children. Montessori's method does not prescribe teaching procedures based on learning theory but develops instructional techniques from observations in selected classrooms. Those founding new Montessori schools should be willing to reject aspects of her method which no longer fit American conditions; to make school attendance an earned privilege, not a right; to insist that the school and its personnel become part of the community they serve; and that the people served accept some responsibility for the school.         J. J. Appel

2815. Metzger, Walter P. THE CRISIS OF ACADEMIC AUTHORITY. *Daedalus 1970 99(3): 568-608.* Discusses the growing resistance to academic authority and regulations, both nonviolent and violent. Major problems alienating students from the university are the disparate relationships between academic and nonacademic persons, as well as the

exploitation of the disadvantaged by the university (e.g., the events at Columbia University in April 1968). In this connection, what students want is to be able to control decisions that affect their lives and to discontinue inequities against the poor, Negroes, women, and students. What is needed is a reordering of roles (i.e., academic roles), proper instruction, and allowing authority to be retained by the university as a resource, not as an issue. 11 notes.         A. Krichmar

2816. Morris, Celia. ON BEING A STUDENT IN THE 1950'S: LEARNING THE HARD WAY. *Change 1974 6(6): 42-47.* The author looks ambivalently at an education that partly civilized her and her friends, but that taught them too little about themselves and their culture.         J

2817. Nowak, Marion. "HOW TO BE A WOMAN": THEORIES OF FEMALE EDUCATION IN THE 1950'S. *J. of Popular Culture 1975 9(1): 77-83.* Examines the new domesticity entrenched in American life through specially geared education which severely restricted the interpretation of women's role in life and reduced the number of women pursuing higher education. 13 notes.         J. D. Falk

2818. Parr, Mary Y. WHATEVER HAPPENED TO THE CLASS OF 1962? *Coll. and Res. Lib. 1967 28(3): 208-216.* Little research has been made to discover why some students fail to graduate. To remedy the lack in one field (librarianship), this statistical study follows the school and subsequent careers of the 378 applicants accepted for admission in 1961 to the graduate library schools of Drexel Institute of Technology and Pratt Institute. Statistics are developed on the factors affecting the students' progress toward graduation or nongraduation, including background, sex, marital status, grades, and probation; on the number of inactives and dropouts; and on the present positions of the Class of 1962. The conclusion drawn from this study is that the schools need to improve selection techniques and admissions procedures to guarantee a higher graduation rate, and that graduates are not subsequently lost to other professions. 8 tables, 11 notes.         V. J. Carter

2819. Pender, Albert R. ATTENTION MEN: WOMEN ARE COMING. *Contemporary Educ. 1972 43(4): 219-223.* Describes the emotional stress on women working on graduate degrees and how it may break down potentially productive women who could be used in business and industry.         S

2820. Perel, W. M. and Vairo, Philip D. THE CATHOLIC UNIVERSITY AND COLLEGE - TODAY AND TOMORROW. *Liberal Educ. 1968 54(4): 528-532.* Catholic colleges have improved, but they still have many weaknesses. They are too small, inadequately financed, and poorly staffed. The author recommends that small Catholic colleges near one another should combine to form one larger institution and that single-sexed colleges become coeducational. The large Catholic universities do not measure up to the state universities. These Catholic universities pay their faculties less than prestigious state universities, lack the library resources of many private and state universities, and have been unable to obtain financial support from foundations or from the government. The author concludes by pointing out that America needs private colleges for educational experimentation.         C. Grollman

2821. Powers, Helen. LPN: THE GENTLE PEOPLE. *Am. Educ. 1965 1(8): 12-14.* Description of the training program and conditions of employment for licensed practical nurses. Concludes that federal programs to provide funds for practical nurse training will aid in filling the growing demand for nursing services. Illus.         W. R. Boedecker

2822. Raffel, Norma K. THE WOMEN'S MOVEMENT AND ITS IMPACT ON HIGHER EDUCATION. *Liberal Educ. 1973 59(2): 246-254.* The law and women's consciousness of existing inequities will lead to greater equality in academia. Discusses the ways in which this will improve the policies and practices of higher education. Secondary sources; 3 notes.         W. H. Ahern

2823. Real, James. IMMACULATE HEART OF HOLLYWOOD. *Change 1971 3(3): 48-53.* Discusses the problems confronted by Immaculate Heart College during its transition from a highly traditional Catholic college for women to a coeducational college run by a noncanonical community of lay women.         P. R. Byrne

2824. Ruud, Millard H. THAT BURGEONING LAW SCHOOL ENROLLMENT IS PORTIA. *Am. Bar Assoc. J. 1974 60(2): 182-184.* "The most noteworthy aspect of this academic year's enrollment figures is the dramatic increase in number of women law students." J

2825. Sadker, David; Sadker, Myra; and Simon, Sidney. CLARIFYING SEXIST VALUES. *Social Educ. 1973 37(8): 756-760.* Discusses sex role stereotyping in schools and offers ways to combat it through directed teaching. S

2826. Scates, Alice Y. WOMEN MOVING AHEAD. *Am. Educ. 1966 2(3): 1-4.* Surveys the phenomenon of women returning to schools and universities after marrying and raising families. Concludes that the trend is the product of a growing desire by women to avoid having an "educational ceiling clamped over their abilities and aspirations." Illus. W. R. Boedecker

2827. Sewell, William H. COMMUNITY OF RESIDENCE AND COLLEGE PLANS. *Am. Sociol. R. 1964 29(1): 24-38.* The relation between community of residence and college plans of Wisconsin high school seniors is examined. With each increase in community size category, the percentage of students with college plans increase....Intelligence and socioeconomic status explain most of the differences among girls in this sample, but other factors are needed to account completely for the residential differences in college plans of boys. Residential differences are most marked for boys in the high intelligence and socioeconomic status categories - the ones intellectually and economically most able to attend college. The failure of able rural boys, particularly farm boys, to plan on college contributes most to the observed differences, since the differences between the various urban size categories tend to vanish when intelligence and socioeconomic status are partialled out. 6 tables, 27 notes. J

2828. Sewell, William H. INEQUALITY OF OPPORTUNITY FOR HIGHER EDUCATION. *Am. Sociol. R. 1971 36(5): 793-809.* Reports on research based on a longitudinal study of approximately nine thousand randomly selected high school seniors in Wisconsin which was begun in 1957. "Our data provide information not only on socioeconomic origins, sex, academic ability, and post-high school educational and occupational attainments, but also on such matters as the student's performance in high school, the expectations of parents and teachers and peers, and the student's educational and occupational aspirations. With these data we have examined in detail inequalities in opportunities for higher education and have also devised explanatory models for the educational attainment process." The data "furnish solid documentation for the claim that there is substantially reduced opportunity for higher education in America for those of lower socioeconomic origins and for women, and that this inequality cannot be explained by differences in academic ability....all new subsidy programs [should] be limited to those who need the subsidy.... Most of the funds should go directly to students rather than to institutions." More attention should be given "to such psychological factors as the development of cognitive skills, academic performance, the influence of significant others, and the stimulation of educational and occupational aspirations." The Presidential Address at the 66th Annual Meeting of the American Sociological Association, 30 August 1971 in Denver, Colorado. 23 notes, biblio. D. D. Cameron

2829. Sewell, William H. and Shah, Vimal P. PARENTS' EDUCATION AND CHILDREN'S EDUCATIONAL ASPIRATIONS AND ACHIEVEMENTS. *Am. Sociol. R. 1968 33(2): 191-209.* "In this study of a large randomly selected cohort of Wisconsin high school seniors, who were followed for a seven-year period, multivariate cross-tabular and regression analyses showed that father's education has a slightly stronger effect than mother's education on perceived parental encouragement, college plans, college attendance, and college graduation for males, but that both father's and mother's education have almost equal effect for females. Mother's education has a modest effect independent of father's education, but the independent effect of mother's education is stronger for females than for males. When parents have discrepant levels of educational achievement, the answer to the question of which parent's education has more effect on educational aspiration and achievement depends on the child's sex and intelligence level as well as on each parent's level of educational achievement. In terms of the additional amount of variance explained, the interaction effect is negligible for all of the dependent variables. Discrepancy in parents' educational achievements is far less

important in motivating children to high-level aspiration and achievement than is consistently high educational achievement of both parents." J

2830. Shryock, Henry S., Jr. and Nam, Charles B. EDUCATIONAL SELECTIVITY OF INTERREGIONAL MIGRATION. *Social Forces 1965 43(3): 299-310.* "Over the last quarter of a century, the educational selectivity of interregional migration has varied somewhat among time periods, age groups, and interregional streams; but there have been a number of persistent tendencies, particularly with respect to migration to and from the South. In general, interregional migration tends to be selective of the better educated. Within age, sex, and color groups, interregional migrants tend to be better educated than nonmigrants at their origin or destination. The net effect of this selectivity upon the educational distribution of the population in the regions has been rather slight, however." J

2831. Silk, Andrew. BRYN MAWR AND HAVERFORD: COOPERATION VERSUS COEDUCATION. *Change 1974 6(3): 32.* Discusses the decision of Haverford College in early 1974 to increase its cooperation with Bryn Mawr instead of admitting women directly. S

2832. Stimpson, Catharine R. WOMEN AT BRYN MAWR. *Change 1974 6(3): 24-31, 62-63.* A college that has nurtured proud, stubborn independence is harried by forces indifferent to its passion for excellence. J

2833. Suval, Elizabeth M. and Hamilton, C. Horace. SOME NEW EVIDENCE ON EDUCATIONAL SELECTIVITY IN MIGRATION TO AND FROM THE SOUTH. *Social Forces 1965 43(4): 536-547.* "Analysis of the 1960 United States Census data on lifetime and recent migration confirms the general hypothesis that migration to and from the South is correlated with education. However, the correlation between migration and education varies by age, sex, and color. Gross migration, both to and from the South, is positively correlated with education and there is little difference between the educational level of in- and out-migrants. Adverse educational selectivity of net migration from the South is greatest among young people, among Negroes, and among males. Gross migration rates among the white population, both to and from the South, are greater than those among the nonwhite population at all educational levels; but *net* migration from the South is relatively greater in the nonwhite than in the white population because the gross movement of Negroes back to the South is relatively much less than that of white people. Regional differences in migration, in relation to education, reflect differences in industrialization and urbanization. Areas with large expanding metropolitan populations are attracting well-educated migrants, and rural areas of the South are continuing to lose more well-educated people than they gain." J

2834. Taylor, Phoebe. COEDUCATION FOR THE COLLEGES: WHY? HOW? AND WHEN? *Liberal Educ. 1966 52(3): 271-279.* Finds the most effective approach to education is through coeducational forms rather than noncoeducational forms. For a world in which the individual has a relatively free choice of association, only the coeducational model provides experience of reality. Of the three main forms of coeducation available in the United States - unified, coordinate, and cooperative - the unified is less desirable as "constant meeting of the sexes may distract from study." The opportunities for either coordinate or cooperative forms is immediate, waiting for the colleges to act. W. R. Boedecker

2835. Tidball, M. Elizabeth. WOMEN ON CAMPUS. *Liberal Educ. 1975 61(2): 285-292.* Stresses the propaganda power of wives of high officials, teachers, and administrators of colleges and universities, and suggests methods to promote women in higher education. S

2836. Tompkins, Pauline. WHAT FUTURE FOR THE WOMEN'S COLLEGE? *Liberal Educ. 1972 58(2): 298-303.* The strongest rationale for women's colleges is their ability to provide women with the same educational advantages given men in coeducational institutions. Describes the signs of decline in the popularity of women's colleges, the reasons for their low-profile in recruitment, and the ways in which coeducational institutions favor men. Concludes that women's colleges should remain and provide a challenge to discrimination in coeducational education. W. H. Ahern

2837. Vaccaro, Louis C. UNIVERSITY PARTICIPATION IN CONTINUING EDUCATION. *Catholic Educ. R. 1966 64(1): 42-45.* Adult education centers of the university fill a vital need in a technological society. The concept of terminal education is in fact outmoded as Americans must face up to the complex, changing demands of citizenship, family life, employment, etc. (Continuing education, a creative program for adults, is not the same as remedial or citizenship education.) Association of adult education centers with the university is critical, as no other institution has the freedom and the diversity to serve as "society's conscience."                                                     D. H. Broderick

2838. Walster, Elaine; Cleary, T. Anne; and Clifford, Margaret M. RESEARCH NOTE: THE EFFECT OF RACE AND SEX ON COLLEGE ADMISSION. *Sociol. of Educ. 1971 44(2): 237-244.* "Applications for admission were sent to a random sample of 240 American colleges and universities. For three different student ability levels, forms that were identical in all respects, save race and sex, were prepared. Each college was sent a single application with a randomly assigned race, sex, and ability level. Contrary to our expectations, white applicants were accepted slightly more frequently than black. In accordance with our predictions, males received preference over females. However, in both cases, the data did not reach the .05 level of significance. In addition there was an unpredicted and statistically significant sex by ability interaction; males were markedly preferred over females at the low ability level, but this difference disappeared at the higher levels. Since there are more young people, both male and female, at the lowest of our ability levels, it is clear that overall, women are discriminated against in college admissions."                                                                      J

2839. Weismann, Myrna W. et al. THE FACULTY WIFE: HER ACADEMIC INTERESTS AND QUALIFICATIONS. *AAUP Bull. 1972 58(3): 287-292.* Most faculty wives either work or study or plan to do so. The problem of interrupted careers and study is an evident theme for them. Faculty wives exhibit high academic standards and ask no special privileges, but feel they should not be penalized by nepotism rules. 2 tables, 10 notes.                                                      J. M. McCarthy

2840. Werts, Charles E. A COMPARISON OF MALE VS. FEMALE COLLEGE ATTENDANCE PROBABILITIES. *Sociol. of Educ. 1968 41(1): 103-110.* "The ratio of males to females in a sample of 127,125 college freshmen was computed for various fathers' occupations, levels of fathers' education, and academic achievement. Among low achievers, boys were much more likely than girls to enter college, while among high achievers, boys and girls were equally likely to enter college. Among low-SES students, boys were much more likely than girls to go to college. Boys and girls whose fathers were closely associated with academia had similar college attendance rates."                        J

2841. Westervelt, Esther M. A REPORT BY THE CARNEGIE COMMISSION: *OPPORTUNITIES FOR WOMEN IN HIGHER EDUCATION. Harvard Educ. R. 1974 44(2): 295-313.* Essay review of *Opportunities for Women in Higher Education: Their Current Participation, Prospects for the Future, and Recommendations for Action*, by the Carnegie Commission on Higher Education (1973).                           S

2842. Wilson, John D. THE LIBERAL ARTS COLLEGE FOR WOMEN: AN ASSESSMENT OF CURRENT PROBLEMS. *Centennial R. 1970 14(1): 108-124.* Despite the trend on the part of women's liberal arts colleges to admit male students, much can be said for those that have resisted this trend. The problems and pressures created by not admitting men are numerous, but some women's colleges will "survive and flourish" because they deserve to. Their original purpose was to provide superior education for women, and they have shown that they can do it. To survive women's colleges had to show excellence, and those that remain are stronger than ever. But the women's colleges have become "uneasy and nervous" with the contemporary trend away from single-sex institutions. The author believes, however, that they can survive. Most arguments against the women's colleges are "suspiciously thin and enervated." The women's colleges continue to represent "liberal arts education at its best." It is possible to consider them the only true liberal arts colleges, since they contain virtually no vocationally-oriented courses. The women's colleges are not divorced from the "real world" as many have charged. Women mature earlier than men, and there is a distinct advantage to letting them proceed at their own pace. If the women's

liberal arts colleges remain true to the liberal arts, and meet their challenges squarely on this basis, the "future can be met with the same confidence as in the past."                                            A. R. Stoesen

2843. Yeakel, Margaret. THE SMITH ALUMNI SURVEY. *Smith Coll. Studies in Social Work 1971 41(2): 147-171.* An analysis of the responses to the Smith Alumni Survey of 1967-68, concerning graduates from 1960 through 1967. Of all 1960-67 alumni, 80 percent responded to the questionnaire. Of those, 94 percent were women. This represents a rise in the male alumni, as all but one-fourth of one percent of the pre-1960 alumni were women. About half of the graduates were married. The survey continues to analyze the two different approaches to social work education, the 27-month Plan A, and the 15-month Plan B, in terms of the type of student attracted to each, as well as the relevance of the plans to social work practice.                           M. A. Kaufman

2844. Ziemke, Donald C. THE MARKS OF THE UNIVERSITY'S STUDENT IN HUMANITIES. *North Dakota Q. 1965 33(3/4): 72-80.* Details the results of a survey of North Dakota University graduates, 1960-65, with humanities majors. They show that, among other things, 1) social and natural sciences were predominantly male, the other fields were equally divided among men and women; 2) social science majors had the greatest elapsed time between high school and college graduations; 3) majors in natural sciences showed a single-minded devotion to their field from high school through college; 4) almost no student, even social science majors, liked their high school social science courses; 5) art and history drew their majors, disproportionately, from the lower high school class ranks, and their majors showed lowest college grade point averages. Numerous tables.                                                J. F. Mahoney

2845. —. COMPARATIVE STUDY OF CATHOLIC AND PUBLIC SCHOOL BUILDING PROJECTS; PHILOSOPHICAL STUDY OF THE NATURE AND DIVISIONS OF RIGHTS AND THEIR APPRECIATION TO EDUCATION; CAUSAL PATTERNS IN CURRICULUM CHOICE OF POTENTIAL HIGH ACHIEVERS IN A CATHOLIC HIGH SCHOOL FOR GIRLS; THE INFLUENCE OF MEDICAL CARE AND ASSISTANCE FOR CHILDREN WITH A VISUAL DEFICIENCY ON THEIR ACHIEVEMENT IN READING, SPELLING, AND ARITHMETIC AT THE SECOND-GRADE LEVEL; THE EXTENT AND USE OF ORAL VOCABULARY OF CHILDREN AT THE CLOSE OF ONE YEAR OF KINDERGARTEN EXPERIENCE; THE DEVELOPMENT AND BEHAVIORAL CHANGES IN TWENTY CEREBRAL PALSIED CHILDREN AS MEASURED DURING A PRESCHOOL TRAINING PROGRAM; A STUDY OF WHARTON MEMORIAL INSTITUTE FOR EXCEPTIONAL CHILDREN. *Catholic Educ. R. 1964 62(4): 258-260.*

2846. —. GOODBYE TO THE BIRDS AND THE BEES. *Am. Educ. 1966 2(10): 16-22.*
Ferber, Ellen and Sofokidis, Jeanette H. WHAT'S HAPPENING, *pp. 16, 19-22.* A description of programs of sex and family life education developed by public school districts across the United States. Undocumented, illus.
Calderone, Mary S. AN APPROACH, *pp. 17-18.* Proposes the development of a program of sex education beginning in kindergarten and continuing into college. "We have not developed the know-how or the courage to convey to each rising generation even the little that science has learned about human sexuality." Undocumented, illus.                                                      W. R. Boedecker

2847. —. IS COLLEGE NECESSARY? CAROLINE BIRD TALKS WITH ERNEST BOYER. *Change 1975 7(1): 32-37.* A noted author and feminist and a prominent educator talk about the good and the bad aspects of mass education.                                             J

2848. —. SPECIAL REPORT. *Am. Educ. 1968 4(4): 5-6, 10-12, 20-24, 28-30.* This issue is devoted to an appraisal of Federal aid to education. The human side of the story, rather than statistics, was chosen to be emphasized. Most of the vignettes are based on interviews with people who have experienced the impact of the new role played by the Federal Government.
Stocker, Joseph. I HAVE A PROBLEM, MISS ENGEL, p. 5. Tells how a graduate program funded by the National Defense Education Act permitted the development of new educational leadership.

Gish, Thomas. THE HAPPY SOUND OF LEARNING, p. 10. Examines the way in which the health services sponsored by Federal programs influenced the education of a handicapped girl.

Harry, Margaret M. SHE TURNS A NEW LEAF - LITERALLY, p. 11. Reviews the effect of use of funds for materials for a reading workshop on a girl who had been labeled a discipline problem.

Horn, William A. SMILE, MARY ANN, pp. 20-21. Tells how the dramatic ambition of a college student was furthered through the financial assistance of the College Work-Study Program and a National Defense Education Act student loan.

Levine, Richard H. MARTHA'S WORLD, pp. 22-23. Describes the effects of an experimental program developed by the Institute for Behavioral Research on a teen-age girl of computer-assisted instruction.

Dunsire, Charles. HOMEWORK FOR THE HAGEN GIRLS, p. 28. Description of the retraining of a middle-aged, unemployable woman on welfare through a Manpower Development course.

Kraus, Carroll J. HEAD START AND A FRESH START, pp. 29-30. Considers how a variety of federally-sponsored programs have influenced the life of a 33-year-old woman with two children living on child support payments and an Aid to Dependent Children allowance. The programs included Head Start, Follow Through, VISTA, and Work Experience.

W. R. Boedecker

# Literature

## (including journalism)

2849. Bailey, Margaret. THE WOMAN'S MAGAZINE SHORT-STORY HEROINE IN 1957 AND 1967. *Journalism Q. 1969 46(2): 364-366.* In Betty Friedan's *Feminine Mystique* (New York: W. W. Norton, 1963), a study of woman's magazine heroines showed that in 1939 most were career women. By 1949 this situation was slipping; in 1958-59 the happy housewife heroine was dominant. In 1949, Ann Griffith deplored this change and asserted that few of the stories concerned genuine problems with believable people or settings. To determine whether woman's magazine short-story heroines had changed, 1957-67, *McCalls, Ladies' Home Journal,* and *Good Housekeeping* were studied. Preliminary interviews with fiction editors indicated that they felt that more adventuresome fiction would be too great a risk, that more changes would be found in nonfiction, and that responsibility for bringing change rested with the writers. The study of the short stories showed that the typical heroine was still a housewife with love-oriented goals. Problems in 1967 were psychological rather than romantic, but not deeply serious. Characters with careers decreased and were unsympathetic. Based on primary sources; 5 notes.
K. J. Puffer

2850. Baron, Nancy. CHILDREN'S LITERATURE, SEX ROLES AND MENTAL HEALTH. *Focus/Midwest 1973 9(59): 7-8.* Criticizes children's books that teach girls a passive and service oriented role in life. Urges a children's literature that will eliminate stereotypes and emphasize mentally healthy, nonsexist roles. Secondary sources; 21 notes.
L. H. Grothaus

2851. Boyers, Robert. ATTITUDES TOWARD SEX IN AMERICAN "HIGH CULTURE." *Ann. of the Am. Acad. of Pol. and Social Sci. 1968 376: 36-52.* "An analysis is presented of particular themes and attitudes in several works of fiction published in the United States in the last decade. There is a special emphasis on varieties of apocalyptic sexuality, with an attempt to relate this focus to broader questions of a political and social nature. Problems of literary style and characterization connected with the presentation of sexual styles and orientations are also discussed, and there is comparison of typical American and European literary customs with regard to the presentation of sex."
J

2852. Burger, Nash K. ELIZABETH SPENCER'S THREE MISSISSIPPI NOVELS. *South Atlantic Q. 1964 63(3): 351-362.* A synopsis-analysis of *Fire in the Morning* (1948), *This Crooked Way* (1952), and *The Voice at the Back Door* (1956).
J. Frazier

2853. Burke, Michael. THE BEST ARM IN BASEBALL. *Wilson Lib. Bull. 1969 43(7): 622-623.* Presents an appreciation of Marianne Moore, the poet and baseball fan. Illus.
M. J. Kroeger

2854. Burns, Stuart L. O'CONNOR AND THE CRITICS: AN OVERVIEW. *Mississippi Q. 1974 27(4): 483-496.*

2855. Clark, Laverne Harrell. "THE INDIAN WRITINGS OF MARI SANDOZ: A LONE ONE LEFT FROM THE OLD TIMES." *Am. Indian Q. 1974 1(4): 269-280.* Mari Sandoz reconstructed for her readers the very spirit of the language and the essence of the thinking of many Indian people and cultures. Her most forceful contribution to an understanding of the American Indian includes sketches of the nature of Indian philosophy and lifeways, characterizations of various Plains Indians, and a style of writing which deliberately reflects Indian idioms. Based on primary sources; 19 notes.
G. L. Olson

2856. Cline, C. L. A VISIT TO FRIEDA. *Lib. Chronicle of the U. of Texas 1974 7: 37-41.* Describes a visit in 1956 to Frieda Lawrence in Taos, New Mexico, shortly before her death and the author's attempt to purchase her D. H. Lawrence collection, the majority of which was purchased by the University of California, Berkeley.
S

2857. Coffey, Warren FLANNERY O'CONNOR. *Commentary 1965 40(5): 93-99.* Analyzes two collections of short stories by Flannery O'Connor (1925-64), *A Good Man Is Hard to Find* (New York: Harcourt Brace, 1955) and *Everything that Rises Must Converge* (New York: Farrar, Straus and Giroux, 1965); and analyzes her novels, *Wise Blood* (New York: Farrar, Straus and Giroux, 1962) and *The Violent Bear It Away* (New York: Farrar, Straus and Giroux, 1960). Flannery O'Connor greatly admired and was indebted to William Faulkner, Ring Lardner, and Nathaniel West. "She found the human heart a pretty dark place... but she was not a hater, and she never trafficked in despair. She did much of her writing with death more or less in the next room but went on until she had sent into the world the tough and brilliant comic stories of which all readers now become...the heirs and assigns forever."
D. D. Cameron

2858. Curley, Thomas F. CATHOLIC NOVELS AND AMERICAN CULTURE. *Commentary 1963 36(1): 34-42.* Considers James T. Farrell as the "most representative of the American 'Catholic' novelists" because he has been trying to deal with an American Catholic experience or ethos which is "more than personal and less than national." Catholics like O'Neill, Hemingway, and Fitzgerald grew up when Catholicism in the USA was "only a religion" and have therefore only a "peripheral interest" for critics of the American novelist who is trying to cope with his Catholic ethics as an American. The younger writers among American Catholics, chief among them Edwin O'Connor, J. F. Powers, and Flannery O'Connor, by entering imaginatively into the parochial American experience, may be able to provide for American Catholics in general "that bridge between living as Americans and thinking as Americans which they have for so long been afraid to build."
J. J. Appel

2859. Denne, Constance Ayers and Rogers, Katherine M. WOMEN NOVELISTS: A DISTINCT GROUP? *Women's Studies 1975 3(1): 5-28.* Transcript of a panel discussion on "Women Novelists: A Distinct Group?" held at the Modern Language Association convention in New York City. The panelists were Erica Jong, Nancy Milford, Elaine Showalter, and Elizabeth Hardwick. They discussed many topics including: feminist consciousness, women's literary tradition, the male writer's appropriation of female consciousness, and why women write.
A. E. Wiederrecht

2860. Donaldson, Scott. FAMILY CRISES IN THE POPULAR NOVEL OF NIXON'S ADMINISTRATION. *J. of Popular Culture 1972 6(2): 374-382.* Analyzes the crisis in the American family as depicted in the popular novels, Philip Roth's *Portnoy's Complaint* (New York, 1970), Jacqueline Susan's *The Love Machine* (New York, 1970), Mario Puzo's *Godfather* (New York, 1970), and Erich Segal's *Love Story* (New York, 1970).

2861. Fallows, James. MAKING IT WITH MAILER, MILLETT, AND CAPOTE. *Washington Monthly 1974 6(4): 57-61.* The celebrity of Norman Mailer, Kate Millett, and Truman Capote.
S

2862. Gershator, David. POETRY OF THE VIRGIN ISLANDS: PAST AND PRESENT. *Rev. Interamericana Rev. [Puerto Rico] 1972 2(3): 408-414.* The poetry of the Virgin Islands did not begin until the

20th century, but it has thrived since then. The pioneering work of J. Antonio Jarvis and J. P. Giménez, characterized by a sharp historical consciousness, has been equaled by the present generation of island poets, most notably Althea Romeo and Bertica Hodge. Note.                    J. Lewis

2863. Gower, Herschel. MILDRED HAUN: THE PERSISTENCE OF THE SUPERNATURAL. *Louisiana Studies 1968 7(1): 65-71.* Analyzes the stories of Mildred Haun showing the persistence of the supernatural in ballads and customs of those folk isolated from mass media. Fiction depicting these people of the southern Appalachians takes note of environment and the reaction of the people to the environment and to the behavior of each other. Supernatural powers are attributed to phenomena not readily understood. 4 notes.                    G. W. McGinty

2864. Harris, Janice. D. H. LAWRENCE AND KATE MILLETT. *Mass. R. 1974 15(3): 522-529.* Evaluates Kate Millett's criticism of D. H. Lawrence and presents the aims of feminist criticism.                    S

2865. Hertil, Hans. MYTEN OM FITZGERALD [The myth about Fitzgerald]. *Samtiden [Norway] 1964 73(8): 505-516.* A review article of a biography on F. Scott Fitzgerald by Andrew Turnbull [ *Letters of F. Scott Fitzgerald* (New York: Charles Scribner's Sons, 1963) ], which is also compared with Arthur Mizener's *The Far Side of Paradise* (1951). Hertil contends that Turnbull failed to produce any significant new sources on Fitzgerald except for a few letters and some interviews, and that his work was lacking in scholarly criticism and displayed an excessive emphasis on anecdotes. Turnbull also relied in part on Mizener's "material and organization." Fitzgerald's relationship with Zelda is described, and Turnbull analyzes his literary work of the 1930's (especially the *Pat Hobby Stories* written for *Esquire* magazine) as well as his career in Hollywood, California, as a script writer. Hertil discusses Fitzgerald's literary production and characteristics relative to his personality and life, agreeing with the following quotation from Fitzgerald: "my characters are all Scott Fitzgerald. Even my feminine characters are feminine Scott Fitzgeralds." Undocumented.                    P. O. Jonsson

2866. Holland, Robert B. DIALOGUE AS A REFLECTION OF PLACE IN "THE PONDER HEART." *Am. Literature 1963 35(3): 352-358.* In Eudora Welty's *The Ponder Heart* (1954), the characters' patterned sentence structures reflect the highly patterned culture in which they live. 18 notes.                    R. S. Burns

2867. Howell, Elmo. EUDORA WELTY'S COMEDY OF MANNERS. *South Atlantic Q. 1970 69(4): 469-479.* An analysis of Eudora Welty's novel, *Delta Wedding* (1946), in terms of the family relationships which underlie and structure the work.

2868. Jordan, Rene. A SOUTHERN DRAWL FROM BEYOND THE GRAVE. *British Assoc. for Am. Studies Bull. [Great Britain] 1966 (12/13): 99-101.* A critique of Flannery O'Connor's posthumous collection of short stories, *Everything that Rises Must Converge,* "a book conceived by a dying woman who is not afraid of going to hell....brutal themes turn on a cruel spit and get roasted to a char." Miss O'Connor "is less a writer in search of an audience than a seeress in need of a cult. Her temple will always be visited, with passion and awe, by the few who suspect she may be right, and that the ultimate joke is that being *is* nothingness."                    D. J. Abramoske

2869. Kohak, Erazim V. TURNING ON FOR FREEDOM. *Dissent 1969 16(5): 437-443.* The relation of sex and socialism in literature.                    S

2870. Lauretis, Teresa de. REBIRTH IN *THE BELL JAR.* *Women's Studies 1976 3(2): 173-183.* Sylvia Plath's autobiographical novel, *The Bell Jar,* has become a feminist manifesto. The novel's protagonist is a woman, Esther Greenwood, whose experiences document the female condition in contemporary society. Themes of birth, disintegration, and rebirth underlie the narrative as Esther's ultimate attainment of self-unity and self-determination make her a cultural heroine. The novel's central symbolic incident involves a mercury ball which, like the self, can break into numerous pieces and then again become a whole. Esther is an image of womanhood viewed from a woman's perspective. She is a heroine who reaches for freedom and self-development and who refuses to accept the culturally defined roles open to her. 4 notes.                    A. E. Wiederrecht

2871. Long, Margaret. THE SENSE OF HER PRESENCE: A MEMORIAL FOR LILLIAN SMITH. *New South 1966 21(4): 71-77.* Discusses the life and career of 20th-century Southern novelist Lillian Smith.                    S

2872. Lubbers, Klaus. THE NECESSARY ORDER: A STUDY OF THEME AND STRUCTURE IN CARSON MCCULLERS' FICTION. *Jahrbuch für Amerikastudien [West Germany] 1963 8: 187-204.* Based on her novels: *The Heart is a Lonely Hunter* (1940); *Reflections in a Golden Eye* (1941); *The Member of the Wedding* (1946); *The Ballad of the Sad Café* (1951); *Clock Without Hands* (1961).                    G. Bassler

2873. Martin, Wendy. "GOD'S LIONESS": SYLVIA PLATH, HER PROSE AND POETRY. *Women's Studies 1973 1(2): 191-198.* Examines the life and writings of Sylvia Plath (1932-1963). Her autobiographical novel, *The Bell Jar,* chronicles and explores a woman's life during the passage from girlhood to womanhood. The books deals with sexual initiation, childbirth, femininity, and woman's isolation, despair, depression, anxiety, intellectual development, and creativity. Plath's poetry frequently expresses anger, bitterness, and aggression. These are feelings which women writers traditionally are not supposed to articulate. While critics often note Plath's love/hate for her father, they overlook the loss-of-mother-love theme which her poetry also reveals. Both Plath and Virginia Woolf experience Oedipal and sibling conflicts, confronted depression and suicidal impulses, and had to deal with the demands of domestic responsibilities. Unwilling to hide or disguise her honest emotions, Plath challenged the traditional literary privatization of female experience by voicing her hostility, aggression, and despair. Based on primary materials; 10 notes.                    A. E. Wiederrecht

2874. McMurtry, Larry. FROM MICKEY SPILLANE TO ERICA JONG. *Washington Monthly 1975 7(3): 12-20.* Examines the sexual climate promoted by pornographic fiction, 1947-75.

2875. Montgomery, Marion. SOUTHERN REFLECTIONS ON SOLZHENITSYN. *Modern Age 1975 19(2): 190-198.* " 'What has given the South her identity,' says [southern novelist Flannery] O'Connor, 'are those beliefs and qualities which she has absorbed from the scriptures and from her own history of defeat and violation: a distrust of the abstract, a sense of human dependence on the grace of God, and a knowledge that evil is not simply a problem to be solved, but a mystery to be endured." When the "Southern writer" recognizes the point, one of the things he may write is the *Gulag Archipelago*. . . . Solzhenitsyn, like Flannery O'Connor, is a reactionary . . . He wants to turn the clock back. . . . All the way back to Bethlehem."                    S

2876. Murr, Judy Smith. HISTORY IN *BARREN GROUND* AND *VEIN OF IRON:* THEORY, STRUCTURE, AND SYMBOL. *Southern Literary J. 1975 8(1): 39-54.* Discusses the literary symbolism and levels of history used in the novels of Ellen Glasgow during the 1950's.

2877. Phillips, Robert S. SHIRLEY JACKSON: A CHRONOLOGY AND A SUPPLEMENTARY CHECKLIST. *Papers of the Biblio. Soc. of Am. 1966 60(2): 203-213.* Supplement to the 1962 checklist. The list, complete as of January 1966, includes in addition to writings both by and about Miss Jackson (1919-65) a chronology of highlights in her literary career.                    C. A. Newton

2878. Reuben, Elaine. FEMINIST CRITICISM IN THE CLASSROOM, OR, "WHAT DO YOU MEAN *WE,* WHITE MAN?" *Women's Studies 1973 1(3): 315-325.* Examines the class nature of literary tradition which is predominantly a white male tradition. A woman who teaches from a feminist perspective can show the limitations of the tradition. Author discusses her own classroom example using *Lady Chatterley's Lover* which particularly lends itself to feminist analysis. It is also important that each student bring her or his own intellect, emotions, and experiences to bear when making a judgment about a book. 17 notes.                    A. E. Wiederrecht

2879. Root, Robert and Root, Christine V. MAGAZINES IN THE UNITED STATES: DYING OR THRIVING? *Journalism Q. 1964 41(1): 15-22.* Between 1938 and 1963 circulations of many magazines grew faster than the rate of population increase. General magazines gained an average of 61 percent, news magazines 131.3, home magazines 150.1, women's magazines 135.8, business magazines 210.2, "serious" magazines, 148.2, "idea" magazines 244.2, leisure magazines, 336.5, outdoor magazines 393:9.                                        S. E. Humphreys

2880. Ruoff, James. KATHERINE ANNE PORTER COMES TO KANSAS. *Midwest Q. 1963 4(4): 305-314.* Taped group interview with Porter (b. 1890) on her trip to the University of Wichita in 1961, in which she discusses *Ship of Fools.*                                        S

2881. Russ, Joanna. SOMEBODY'S TRYING TO KILL ME AND I THINK IT'S MY HUSBAND: THE MODERN GOTHIC. *J. of Popular Culture 1973 6(4): 666-691.* Modern gothic fiction, which does not resemble traditional, literary gothics, is a "direct expression of the traditional feminine situation (at least a middle-class feminine situation)," and provides the "escape reading a middle-class believer in the feminine mystique needs." Based on five of Ace Books' best sellers.     S

2882. Showalter, Elaine and Smith, Carol. A NURTURING RELATIONSHIP: A CONVERSATION WITH ANNE SEXTON AND MAXINE KUMIN, APRIL 15, 1974. *Women's Studies 1976 4(1): 115-135.* A brief introduction discussing the work and friendship of Anne Sexton and Maxine Kumin, two poets, precedes the transcript of a conversation recorded on 15 April 1974. The conversation primarily is between Sexton and Kumin but also contains questions from Elaine Showalter and Carol Smith. The conversation reveals how Sexton and Kumin work, their friendship, poetry, poetry readings and classes, mutual supportiveness, lives as poets, wives and mothers, and their relation to the feminist movement.                                        A. E. Wiederrecht

2883. Sonenschein, David. LOVE AND SEX IN THE ROMANCE MAGAZINES. *J. of Popular Culture 1970 4(2): 398-409.* Analyzes the content of fiction in eight magazines and shows that the explicit treatment of sex argues for the continuity of the American way of life.     S

2884. Stephan, John J. RUTH STEPHAN (1910-74): A TRIBUTE. *Yale U. Lib. Gazette 1976 50(4): 225-233.* Contains a biographical sketch and brief comments on the literary career of Ruth Stephan (Ruth Walgreen Franklin), the only daughter of the entrepreneur Charles R. Walgreen. She was a poet of the second rank and world traveler partly in revolt against her father and her first husband, Justin Dart. Her papers bequeathed to Yale University are to be the subject of an article in the *Gazette.*                                        D. A. Yanchisin

2885. Thorburn, Neil. "STRANGE FRUIT" AND SOUTHERN TRADITION. *Midwest Q. 1971 12(2): 157-171.* Discusses Lillian Smith's 1944 novel *Strange Fruit* (New York: New American Library, 1954) and her 1949 nonfiction *Killers of Dream* (New York: Doubleday and Co., 1963). Points out Smith's importance as a pioneer analyst of racism. This gracious and aristocratic Southern lady posed basic questions for Southern whites and shed light on the pervasiveness of Southern racial tradition. Smith (1897-1966) questioned whether segregation was an outmoded custom that could be gradually eliminated. She reasoned that change must begin in the heart and that white Southerners must first admit the existence of their racial feelings. In her books she pointed out the need for the more sophisticated of them to drop their complacent tendency to blame everything anti-Negro on the poor whites, and to begin to improve race relations themselves. Biblio.     G. H. G. Jones

2886. Whittier, Gayle. THE DIVIDED WOMAN AND GENERIC DOUBLENESS IN *THE BELL JAR. Women's Studies 1976 3(2): 127-146.* Examines the duality and ambiguity in Sylvia Plath's novel, *The Bell Jar.* Insanity and sanity, life and death, male and female, schizophrenia and personal wholeness, conformity and deviance, illness and cure are some of the themes discussed. Esther Greenwood, the protagonist, is an intellectual woman who is divided by society into incompatible halves. Her entrance into madness and her return to normality are chronicled. The price she pays to be normal is the conventional means of maternity. In the process of returning to normality, Esther loses her passion, clarity of vision, and keen awareness and becomes a passive, dispassionate reporter of her life. 11 notes.                                        A. E. Wiederrecht

2887.  —. [FLANNERY O'CONNOR]. *Miss. Q. 1968 21(4): 235-251.*

Montgomery, Marion   FLANNERY O'CONNOR AND THE NATURAL MAN, *pp. 235-242.* Interpreting Flannery O'Connor's symbols in her fiction is not any easy matter. She was concerned with the separation of the supernatural from the natural by the intellect, which (through its illusion of reality) led one to the devil's work. She attacked the natural, self-made man as an object of worship. For the natural man, in O'Connor's vision, a shocking revelation of the Hell he inhabits may set his soul ready in its desires for the terrors of mercy. Her characters, Asbury and Tarwater, can warn of the "terrible speed of Mercy" since they have confronted dragon of death - not death of body, but of soul. Her vision of Hell is that of the modern heresy of the natural man with his fear of natural rather than spiritual death. Ultimately, what O'Connor does is affirm human nature transformed by the blessing of the incarnation. Based mainly on published material; 13 notes.

Byrd, Turner F.   IRONIC DIMENSION IN FLANNERY O'CONNOR'S "THE ARTIFICIAL NIGGER," *pp. 243-251.* Carefully constructed, O'Connor's story "The Artificial Nigger" shows consummate artistry in the blending of classic literary allegory and theology, although the story is often misread at its most crucial point. Failure to detect the ironic mode as the basis of her technique has caused many to accept Mr. Head's judgment of his condition in the denouement as a true moment of grace, rather than as an extension of his stubborn, misguided omniscience. It is important for the reader to see the character Mr. Head not merely as O'Connor sees him but also as he sees himself; the reader must also interpret the action of the story and Mr. Head's conception of his grandson through the grandfather's distorted vision. The reader can then accept the author's artistic irony. Based mainly on published material; 5 notes.                                        R. V. Calvert

## Arts and Music
### (including Folk Art)

2888. Bush, Joseph Bevans. DEATH OF LIZZIE MILES ENDS GREAT ERA OF BLUES SHOUTERS. *Negro Hist. Bull. 1963 27(3): 69.*

2889. Chandonnet, Ann. THE GOODALES: PAINTERS OF ALASKA FOR 32 YEARS. *Alaska J. 1975 5(4): 217-223.* Explores the painting careers of Harvey and Ellen Goodale, 1943-75, whose paintings portray the life, landscape, and native inhabitants of Alaska.

2890. Crouch, Voula B. SCULPTRESS IN SOAPSTONE. *Alaska J. 1972 2(1): 38-40.* Description of the work of Mary Annis of Anchorage, Alaska.                                        S

2891. Doherty, Mary Austin. THE ETHICS OF POWER. *Arts in Society 1974 11(1): 76-79.* Panel of women artists analyze their uses of and attitudes toward power. Part of a conference on Women and the Arts, Racine, Wisconsin, 1973.                                        S

2892. Evett, Robert. MRS. SHOUSE'S NEW PLEASURE DOME. *Smithsonian 1971 2(6): 32-35.* Summarizes the foundation and operation of Wolf Trap in Virginia as the United States' first national park for culture. Catherine Filene Shouse donated 117 acres and some buildings to the US government, which placed the complex in the custody of the National Park Service. Filene Center accommodates 3,500 people, and the park accommodates 15,000. Through affiliation with the American University, the Center offers educational programs for singers, dancers, theater people, and orchestral performers who appear at the Center. The Wolf Trap Foundation Board of Directors has responsibility for engaging performers.                                        K. A. Harvey

2893. Ewing, Robert A. THE SANTA FE ART SCENE TODAY. *Western R. 1972 9(1): 31-49.* Santa Fe, New Mexico, has been an important art center throughout the 20th century. There are various dynamic movements thriving today. The "New Indian Art" is an important recent development and there are also non-Indian artists inspired by Indian themes. Some young artists called "magic realists" are developing a "regional surrealism." Numerous art exhibitions and other cultural attractions are available to those who visit Santa Fe. Photographs taken by David Lee Guss feature the work of the following artists: Dennis Culver, Fremont Ellis, Boris Gilbertson, Una Hanburg, Paul Kinslow, Janet Lippincott, Bernique Longley, James McGrath, Fritz Scholder, Sam Scott, Mike Selig, Eugenie Shonnard, Storm Townsend, Seymour Tubis, John Wagner, and Mike Zolpe. 18 photos.　　　　　W. J. Furdell

2894. Farb, Joanne. PIECIN' AND QUILTIN': TWO QUILTERS IN SOUTHWEST ARKANSAS. *Southern Folklore Q. 1975 39(4): 363-375.* Discusses the craft of quilt making by two women in southwest Arkansas in the 1970's, emphasizing appliqué designs and types of fabrics.

2895. Foote, Nancy. WHO WAS SONIA SEKULA? *Art in Am. 1971 59(5): 73-80.* Sonia Sekula was a tormented painter in New York City in the 1950's who eventually committed suicide in 1963.　S

2896. Fosburgh, James W. COLLECTOR: THE WHITE HOUSE. *Art in Am. 1963 51(3): 62-69.* Interim report by the chairman of Mrs. John F. Kennedy's Committee on Paintings for the White House reveals what has been done, the rationale, and what it is hoped will be done to beautify the president's residence. Illus.　　　W. K. Bottorff

2897. Fox, William S. and Wince, Michael H. MUSICAL TASTE CULTURES AND TASTE PUBLICS. *Youth & Soc. 1975 7(2): 198-224.* There are at least five musical taste publics: jazz-blues, popular hits, folk, rock-protest, and country western. These are related to religion, hometown size, father's education and occupation, sex, and age, with religion the most important background factor. Social class is of little importance. Based on the work of Herbert J. Gans, a survey of University of Iowa students in 1973, other primary and secondary sources; 2 tables, 14 notes, biblio.　　　　　　　J. H. Sweetland

2898. French, Michael R. SEX IN THE CURRENT CINEMA. *Kansas Q. 1972 4(2): 39-46.* Discusses pornographic films. Legitimate commercial films "have conspicuously less to do with idle nudity" than pornographic ones and their "sex is seldom in drooling quantity or offered simply for its own sake . . . . They find in sex a subject as profoundly disturbing as what pornographic movies find to be mindlessly pleasurable, which constitutes the most trustworthy distinction between the genres." *Carnal Knowledge, Husbands, Five Easy Pieces, Diary of a Mad Housewife, Klute, McCabe and Mrs. Miller, The Devils, Taking Off, Making It,* and *Alice's Restaurant* are discussed as filmmakers' attempts to appraise the sexual revolution of the sixties.　　　B. A. Storey

2899. Gans, Herbert J. AMERICA'S NEW SEXUAL IDOLS. *Twentieth Cent. [Great Britain] 1964 173(1023): 86-92.* The people of a country make domestic fantasies out of foreign images. America uses British erotic performers in the fields of sex and satire to supply its hidden and forbidden needs.　　　　　　　　L. Knafla

2900. Gold, Barbara. PORTRAIT OF MARISOL. *Interplay 1968 1(6): 52-55.* Intersperses Marisol's personality and life history with comments on her art pieces and place in the art history of the 1950's and 1960's.　　　　　　　　　　　W. L. Marr

2901. Hatcher, Mildred. FOLK SONGS MY MOTHER SANG. *Kentucky Folklore Record 1971 17(4): 78-82.* The author presents four ballads which her mother sang to her and a sister in their childhood.
　　　　　　　　　　　　　　　　　　J. C. Crowe

2902. Hayden, Dolores and Wright, Gwendolyn. ARCHITECTURE AND URBAN PLANNING. *Signs 1976 1(4): 923-933.* Research concerning women in architecture and city planning is scant and provides a field ripe for feminist study. A few works focus on women as designers, but most examine the impact of environmental design on women's lives and work. Advances in technology and standardized housing raised the standards expected of women, as well as increased the kinds of tasks assigned to them. Contemporary housing studies emphasize and idealize the mother-child relationship instead of contributing to shared parenting. Utopian communities were an attempt to find an alternative to the nuclear family. Some attention has been given to women's working conditions, especially offices and factory sweatshops. Based on manuscripts, research studies, and secondary works; 48 notes.　　J. Gammage

2903. Innes, Jacqueline Simone. BELMONT STATUARY: FOUR PIECES. *Tennessee Hist. Q. 1971 30(4): 369-379.* Describes the three pieces of statuary in the ballroom of Belmont, the estate of Adelicia Acklen, located two miles south of Nasville. The pieces are Randolph Rogers' "Ruth," a version of W. T. Rinehart's "Sleeping Children," and C. B. Ives' "Rebecca at the Well." There also is a piece in the Acklen Mausoleum at Mount Olivet Cemetery, Nashville, by Randolph Rogers, the "Peri." All four pieces were carved in Rome. 5 notes.
　　　　　　　　　　　　　　　　　　R. V. Ritter

2904. Mainardi, Patricia. [QUILTS: THE GREAT AMERICAN ART]. *Radical Am. 1973 7(1): 36-68.*
QUILTS: THE GREAT AMERICAN ART, *pp. 36-42.*
QUILTS BY AMERICAN WOMEN: A PORTFOLIO OF PHOTO-
　　GRAPHS, *pp. 43-68.*　　　　　　　　　　　S

2905. McBride, Joseph. ROUGH SLEDDING WITH PAULINE KAEL. *Film Heritage 1971 7(1): 13-16, 32.* Criticizes Kael's account of the dispute between Orson Welles and Herman J. Mankiewicz over the credit for the script of *Citizen Kane.* Claims that Kael ignored facts in the material at her disposal and was inaccurate about other points in her discussions of *Kane* in *The New Yorker* and in her edition of the script entitled *The Citizen Kane Book* (Atlantic, Little Brown, 1971).
　　　　　　　　　　　　　　　　　　J. D. Falk

2906. McCollom, Pat. JOAN KIMURA: CONTEMPORARY ARTIST OF ANCHORAGE. *Alaska J. 1973 3(4): 226-231.* Discusses impressionistic art works of contemporary Alaskan artist Joan Kimura.

2907. McMahon, Hilarie. TOWARDS A FEMINIST ART. *Focus/Midwest 1973 9(59): 17.* Rejects use of Freudian symbols in analyzing feminist art and urges a more subtle form of symbolism. Feminist art must be "first person" art that is assertive and diverse.
　　　　　　　　　　　　　　　　　　L. H. Grothaus

2908. Morgan, Lael. JO GORDON: PAINTING AND PRIVACY. *Alaska J. 1975 5(4): 228-230.* Discusses the painting 1956-75 (primarily Alaskan scenes) of Jo Gordon, highlighting the inspirations which first started her painting and her philosophy, privacy, which she applies to her life and her art.

2909. Munoz, Rie. DIANA TILLION. *Alaska J. 1975 5(3): 153-159.* Discusses the paintings depicting Alaskan landscape and Eskimo life done by Diana Tillion, 1939-75, which are particularly unique because of her use of octopus ink as a medium. 6 photos, 7 reproductions.

2910. Pflager, Dorothy H. WATER-COLOR SKETCHES OF THE MILL CREEK VALLEY BY DOROTHY HOLLOWAY PFLAGER. *Missouri Hist. Soc. Bull. 1964 20(3): 192-193.* Presented to the Missouri Historical Society in 1962. Illus.　　　　　　　　S

2911. Poulson, Anabel. NANCY STONINGTON: WATERCOLORIST. *Alaska J. 1975 5(1): 32-40.* Describes Nancy Stonington's background and achievements. She is well known for her watercolors of southeastern Alaska. Reproduces 12 of her paintings in color. 2 photos.
　　　　　　　　　　　　　　　　　　E. E. Eminhizer

2912. Rosenstone, Robert A. "THE TIMES THEY ARE A-CHANGIN'": THE MUSIC OF PROTEST. *Ann. of the Am. Acad. of Pol. and Social Sci. 1969 382: 131-144.* "Once a medium of vapid love lyrics, popular music in the 1960's has taken on a new seriousness. In the words of popular songs, young musicians have begun to express their alienation from and disdain for American institutions and mores. Part of this has taken the form of traditional attacks on war and intolerance. More significant, however, have been criticisms of the quality of life in an affluent society. In their music, youth have worried about such things as the impact of technology on man, the confused state of American sexual practices, and the repressive nature of supposedly democratic institutions. Affirming a strong faith in the freedom of the individual, song writers have turned their backs on pragmatic reality and have sought freedom in a transcendental exploration of man's internal reality. Part of this has been done with 'mind-expanding drugs,' and many songs have urged listeners on to the use of hallucinogens. For youth, music has come to serve the function of helping to define and codify the standards of their own subculture. And it has also put them in touch with more serious critiques of American life made by the intellectual community." J

2913. Samuel, Aliza. A LISTEN AGAIN TO JOAN BAEZ: RE-FLECTIONS OF A NEW ISRAELI. *Midstream 1975 21(5): 33-43.* A concert in Israel in which Joan Baez expressed sentiments of pacifism becomes the springboard for the author to ponder her own transition from American liberal to Israeli citizen.

2914. Siegel, Joel. *THE PIRATE. Film Heritage 1971 7(1): 21-32.* Screen musicals have declined in artistic vitality and popular appeal, but musical revivals are flourishing. One of the best is *The Pirate,* starring Judy Garland and Gene Kelly with a score by Cole Porter, directed by Vincente Minnelli. It is a parody of operetta conventions and a satire of theatrical and literary conventions. It is derived from Ludwig Fulda's play *Der Seeräuber* (1911) and S. N. Behrman's play *The Pirate,* and obviously influenced Jean Renoir's 1952 comedy *The Golden Coach.* The film was not a success. Garland appeared as a beautiful, polished come-dienne rather than "dear little Judy" and Minnelli's appeal to the senses through striking decor and expressive color cinematography did not save it from neglect. 2 illus. J. D. Falk

2915. Smith, Barbara Herrnstein. WOMEN ARTISTS: SOME MUTED TONES. *J. of Communication 1974 24(2): 146-149.* Discusses the concepts of "masculinity" and "femininity," showing the strong cultural hold that these concepts have on women, especially women artists.

2916. Stewart, Karen. MAKING APPLE CIDER IN WESTERN KENTUCKY. *Kentucky Folklore Record 1972 18(4): 93-95.* Describes cider making from the art and mill of Randall and Daisy Lytle of Wood-burn, Kentucky. J. C. Crowe

2917. Sutherland, David. TRADITIONAL BASKETMAKING IN KENTUCKY. *Kentucky Folklore Record 1972 18(4): 89-92.* Describes the art of basketmaking displayed by Francine Alvey, one of the few remaining traditional basketmakers, and the only one in Wax, Kentucky. J. C. Crowe

2918. Thomas, Cheryl Irwin. "LOOK WHAT THEY'VE DONE TO MY SONG, MA": THE PERSUASIVENESS OF SONG. *Southern Speech Communication J. 1974 39(3): 260-268.* Discusses the use of song as a tool for social reform as used by singer Joan Baez. S

2919. Walton, David A. *DIANA ROSS AND THE SUPREMES' GREATEST HITS. J. of Popular Culture 1967 1(3): 291-295.* Reviews *Diana Ross and The Supremes' Greatest Hits* (Motown Record Corporation, MS 2-663, 1967) and the changes in popular music from the 1950's to 1967.

2920. Willard, Charlotte. PORTRAIT: GEORGIA O'KEEFE. *Art in America 1963 51(5): 92-96.* Word and picture portrait, review of the life and paintings of Georgia O'Keeffe. Undocumented, illus. W. K. Bottorff

2921. Wilmeth, Don B. THE MARGO JONES THEATRE. *Southern Speech J. 1967 32(3): 188-195.* Led by Margo Jones, Dallas, Texas, spearheaded the movement to decentralize the American theater. A brief history of the movement is included, the central position of the playwright is analyzed, and the choice of arena staging as the sole method of production is discussed. 12 notes. H. G. Stelzner

2922. —. NEW TALENT USA: FIFTY-SIX PAINTERS AND SCULPTORS. *Art in America 1964 52(4): 22-79.* Presents brief biographical sketches and pictures of the works of a cross section of some 200 painters and sculptors recognized as new talent during the past decade, including Larry Rivers, José Guerrero, Grace Hartigan, William Kienbusch, Sam Francis, Jane Wilson, Constantino Nivola, Richard Lytle, Helen Frankenthaler, and Elmer Bischoff. Illus. W. K. Bottorff

2923. —. TO JOHN F. KENNEDY - HOMAGE BY ARTISTS. *Art in America 1964 52(5): 90-95.* Works honoring the late President Kennedy by such artists as Hans Hofmann, Robert Rauschenberg, and Elaine De Kooning. The works are in a variety of media and are of great intensity. Illus. W. K. Bottorff

# 7. United States: Regional

*(Includes memoirs, eyewitness accounts, biographies of individual women, travel
descriptions, demographics. Abstracts have been categorized by topic whenever possible.
A memoir of the Civil War in Georgia, for example, appears under Civil War.)*

## General

2924. Blair, John L., ed. MRS. MARY DEWEES'S JOURNAL FROM PHILADELPHIA TO KENTUCKY. *Register of the Kentucky Hist. Soc. 1965 63(3): 195-218.* Presents a rather obscure diary which describes the scenes visited and the difficulties encountered on a pioneer family's trip across the Alleghenies. The diary has appeared in print twice previously, but this is the first time it has been published from the original manuscript with lengthy explanatory notes. Documented.
J. F. Cook

2925. Hazard, Sarah Congdon. AROUND THE HORN: JOURNAL OF THE CAPTAIN'S WIFE. *Newport Hist. 1965 38(4): 131-149.* Diary of a trip on the ship *Lancashire* from New York to San Francisco, July to December 1863, describing life on shipboard and a storm off Cape Horn. The captain was Lewis Ludlam Hazard, brother of Oliver Perry Hazard. Illus.
E. P. Stickney

2926. Leadingham, Grace. JULIET WELLS BRIER: HEROINE OF DEATH VALLEY. *Pacific Historian 1964 8(1): 13-20.* Attempts to depict the early life of Juliet W. Brier, "a member of the most unfortunate overland emigrant party of 1849." She was born in 1814 in Bennington, Vermont. As depressed conditions worsened in the 1820's the family moved to Michigan. Their early life was influenced by revivalism and Horace Greeley's temperance speeches. While still poverty-stricken in Michigan, she married a Pennsylvania circuit rider, James Brier, and in 1841 began a life of "wayfaring." No sources cited save for one letter: Julia Brier to "My dear brother," 25 February 1849 and a brief reference to the St. Joseph Company, Michigan "vital statistics."
T. R. Cripps

2927. Lowry, W. McNeil. ADRIENNE KOCH KEGAN. *Maryland Hist. 1972 3(1): 15-16.* A eulogy for Adrienne Koch.
G. O. Gagnon

2928. Reed, Merl E., ed. JOURNAL OF A TRIP FROM PHILADELPHIA TO SALISBURY, N.C., IN 1848. *Mississippi Q. 1968 21(1): 71-77.* Returning to her native State in the summer of 1848 from Philadelphia, 22-year-old Susan Burns kept a record of her trip in the form of a long letter to her brother. She went by steamship, railroad, and stagecoach over rugged roads to Salisbury, North Carolina. The editor considers particularly noteworthy her description of the relationship between the Piedmont area class structure and the type of dwelling each class occupied. The grades of civilization, according to Miss Burns, were as follows: first, log-cabins with a hole in the roof to let smoke out; then, cabins with daubed chimneys; next, weatherboarded houses without window sashes; still higher, frame tenements with glass windows; and, finally, painted dwellings. Those of the last class were so scarce that the young lady did not see a single one on a 38-mile, all-day trip. Based on a privately owned manuscript, microfilm in Emory University Library; 14 notes.
R. V. Calvert

2929. Souchy, Augustin. "DER REBELL IM PARADIES" [Rebel in paradise]. *Geist und Tat [West Germany] 1964 19(5): 148-150.* This is a highly favorable review of Richard Drinnon's *Rebel in Paradise: A Biography of Emma Goldman* (Chicago: U. of Chicago Press, 1961) affording the reviewer an opportunity to sum up the story of Emma Goldman's life with some personal comment.
E. W. Hathaway

2930. Stroup, Russell. ADRIENNE KOCH KEGAN. *Maryland Hist. 1972 3(1): 17.* A eulogy for Adrienne Koch. G. O. Gagnon

2931. —. [KATE STEINITZ: LIBRARIAN, ARTIST, SCHOLAR]. *Wilson Lib. Bull. 1970 44(5): 512-537.*
Belt, Elmer. THE JOY OF KATE STEINITZ, *pp. 514-517.*
Bier, Justus. FOND RECOLLECTIONS OF KATE STEINITZ, *pp. 518-519.*
Zeitlin, Jacob. EVICTED NOVA—THE UNIQUE KATE STEINITZ, *pp. 519-520.*
Lowry, Bates. KATE'S WORLD: AN AWESOME COLLAGE, *pp. 520-522.*
Selz, Peter. A DADA SALON AND A RENAISSANCE LIBRARY, *pp. 522-523.*
Boggs, Jean Sutherland. KATE, A VERY SPECIAL LIBRARIAN, *pp. 523-524.*
Reti, Ladislao. THE RENAISSANCE OF A WOMAN, *pp. 524-525.*
Schmeid, Wieland. NOT ONE BUT MANY, *p. 527.*
Hopps, Walter. KS & KS, *p. 528.*
Edelstein, J. M. KATE'S WRITINGS: A SELECTED BIBLIOGRAPHY, *pp. 529-534.*
Emboden, William A., Jr. TWO PORTRAITS, A BOUQUET, AND TWO VALENTINES, *pp. 535-537.*

## Northeast

2932. Adler, Della Rubenstein. IMMIGRANTS IN BUFFALO. *Am. Jewish Arch. 1966 18(1): 20-28.* The author, mother of historian Selig Adler, was born in Buffalo, New York in 1876. She recalls the experiences and hardships of her parents, who were among the earlier East European Jewish immigrants to that city. The author describes the economic, communal and religious activities of the Jewish peddlers, artisans, and small shopkeepers of Buffalo. Attention is given to the early role of religious and philanthropic institutions within the community. Includes anecdotes and personality sketches.
J. Brandes

2933. Alexander, Mrs. Robert R. QUAKER MEETING RECORDS OF MARRIAGES, BIRTHS, AND DEATHS IN LYCOMING, NORTHUMBERLAND, AND COLUMBIA COUNTIES, 1796-1860. *Now and Then 1969 16(3): 133-151.*

2934. Allen, Eleanor W. BOSTON'S WOMEN'S EDUCATIONAL AND INDUSTRIAL UNION. *New-England Galaxy 1965 6(4): 30-39.* The Women's Educational and Industrial Union, incorporated in 1880, has had a long history of service to generations of Bostonians. From the beginning a nonprofit social service agency, it has always stressed cooperation. It has cooperated with the Red Cross, Travelers' Aid, the Family Society, the Adult Education Council, the City Board of Public Welfare, the Federal Works Progress Administration, and many others. Illus.
Edith P. Stickney

2935. Anderson, Maizie B. LIGHTHOUSE WOMAN. *New-England Galaxy 1973 15(1): 34-40.* A biography (1903-42) of the author's mother, the wife of a lighthouse keeper in Frenchman's Bay, Maine.
S

2936. Anderson, Robert C. A NOTE ON THE GAY-BORDEN FAMILIES IN EARLY NEW ENGLAND. *New England Hist. and Geneal. Register 1976 130: 35-39.* Traces the relationship between the Borden and Gay families of early Massachusetts and Connecticut. The immigrant John Borden (d. 1635) arrived in New England with his family (a wife and two children) in the summer of 1635. By 1638 his widow, Joanna (d. 1691), had married John Gay (d. 1688). They had 10 children. The author establishes the various locales in which the two Borden children lived. Based on primary and secondary sources; 27 notes.
S. L. Patterson

2937. Baldwin, Abigail Pollard. SELECTIONS FROM THE PLYMOUTH DIARY OF ABIGAIL BALDWIN, 1853-4. *Vermont Hist. 1972 40(3): 218-223.* After visiting her daughter in San Antonio, where Mrs. Baldwin's husband served as a minister in the Presbyterian Church, October 1851-June 1853, Mrs. Baldwin preferred her hometown of Plymouth, Vermont, to Texas. She records visits to the sick, funerals, weddings, church services, town elections and holidays, raising a new house that the wind blew down, household chores, and her religious feelings.
T. D. S. Bassett

2938. Bassett, Preston R. CARLOTTA, THE LADY AERONAUT OF THE MOHAWK VALLEY. *New York Hist. 1963 44(2): 145-172.* The story of Mary H. Myers (Carlotta) and her pioneer flights in balloons invented and manufactured by her husband, Carl E. Myers. The author covers their flights from 1880 until her retirement in 1891, and the activities of their "Balloon Farm" at Frankfort, New York, where the vehicles were manufactured.
A. B. Rollins

2939. Bixler, Miriam Eyde. AUNT MAME. *J. of the Lancaster County Hist. Soc. 1971 75(3): 101-106.* The patriotic activities of Gertrude Diller who in 1920 instigated Memorial Day services at Penn Square monument.
S

2940. Bourgo, Fanya del and Botkin, B. A., ed. LOVE IN THE CITY. *New York Folklore Q. 1965 21(3): 165-178.* Discusses the experiences of youth in New York City's East Side in the 1920's, including the attractions of Coney Island, Greenwich Village, and Brooklyn.

2941. Carroll, Gladys Hasty. EVER WAS AND ALWAYS SHALL BE. *New-England Galaxy 1971 12(3): 16-26.* Remeniscences on the author's family and house in Maine (ca. 1860-1930).
S

2942. Chute, William J., ed. REMINISCENCES OF WINCHESTER, C. 1825 FROM THE DIARY OF MRS. HARRIETTE SMITH KIDDER. *Connecticut Hist. Soc. Bull. 1964 29(1): 9-16.* Harriette Smith (1816-1916) was born in Litchfield County, Connecticut, of parents who had been converted to Methodism. She was educated in a seminary, tutoring children of local families to support herself. She then taught briefly at a Methodist female seminary at Worthington, Ohio, where she soon married the minister. Her reminiscences tell of weaving and knitting, gathering wild berries, fireplaces and cooking arrangements, and entertaining circuit riders and attending "Quarterly Meetings."
E. P. Stickney

2943. Cohn, Henry S. CONNECTICUT'S DIVORCE MECHANISM, 1636-1969. *Amer. J. of Legal Hist. 1970 14(1): 35-54.* Traces the development of Connecticut's divorce procedures, with particular reference to the means employed by parties to obtain divorce. The four historical periods are 1636-67, 1667-1790, 1790-1880, and 1880-1963. Examples are cited from the legislative records and court documents of the state of Connecticut. 85 notes.
L. A. Knafla

2944. Crombie, John Newell, ed. ACCOUNT OF THE PENNSYLVANIA RAILROAD RIOTS FROM A YOUNG GIRL'S DIARY. *Western Pennsylvania Hist. Mag. 1971 54(4): 385-389.*

2945. Dana, Nathalie. FARM TO CITY - A NEW YORK ROMANCE. *New York Hist. Soc. Q. 1965 49(3): 217-255.* An account of the life of David Everett Wheeler and his wife, Elizabeth Jarvis. Wheeler was a man of some prominence in New York City during 1833-48. Although much of the article concerns family relations, it contains some information concerning social and cultural history of the period. Based on family letters in possession of the author.
C. L. Grant

2946. Davis, Allen F., ed. THE GIRL HE LEFT BEHIND: THE LETTERS OF HARRIET HUTCHINSON SALISBURY. *Vermont Hist. 1965 33(1): 274-282.* Selections from Harriet Salisbury's reports from East Braintree to her fiancé in Illinois and Missouri, gossip and details of trips to Stowe and Fort Ticonderoga, "more interesting...than important."
T. D. S. Bassett

2947. Davis, Sharon Carbonti. VERMONT'S ADOPTED SONS AND DAUGHTERS. *Vermont Hist. 1963 31(2): 122-127.* Third prize in state essay contest, on seven notable Negro residents and natives. One

of these, the Reverend Lemuel Hayes, was a Congregational minister; another, Sister St. Mary Magdalen, of the Congregation of Notre Dame, had been born on a Georgia plantation of a mulatto slave mother.
T. D. S. Bassett

2948. Fant, H. B., ed. LEVI WOODBURY'S WEEK IN VERMONT. *Vermont Hist. 1966 34(1): 36-62.* Diary of a trip by Levi Woodbury, a Republican judge, in a one-horse chaise through western Vermont between sessions of the New Hampshire Superior Court at Charlestown and Lancaster, 11-17 May 1819, written for his fiancée, Elizabeth Clapp of Portland, Maines. Since his purpose is to amuse, Baedeker facts and wayfarer weariness are interspersed with pungencies of social significance ("Mistress wiped the inside of the tumbler with her hand," p. 56). Found in the Blair Family Papers, Manuscripts Division, Library of Congress.
T. D. S. Bassett

2949. Foster, Abram J. THE FORTY-THIRD ANNUAL MEETING. *Pennsylvania Hist. 1975 42(1): 70-76.* The 43d annual meeting of the Pennsylvania Historical Association was held at Westminster College in New Wilmington on 25-26 October 1975. Sessions were devoted to Pennsylvania in the American Revolution, women in the commonwealth, the battle of Gettysburg, and higher education. Caroline Robbins, the principal speaker, discussed "Rights and Grievances at Carpenters' Hall, the First Continental Congress, 1774."
D. C. Swift

2950. Franz, Eleanor. ADIRONDACK LADY. *New York Folklore Q. 1968 24(3): 194-202.* Discusses the life of Bea Holliday in the Adirondack Mountains of New York from the 1920's to 60's, emphasizing her cooking recipes.

2951. Frederick, Peter J. VIDA DUTTON SCUDDER: THE PROFESSOR AS SOCIAL ACTIVIST. *New England Q. 1970 43(3): 407-433.* Scudder was a popular teacher of English literature at Wellesley College from 1887 to 1927, a founder of settlement houses in New York, Boston, and Philadelphia, an ardent Christian Socialist, and an active member of a number of reform organizations. Born of a Congregational missionary family, she received a superior education in Boston and abroad, reading widely in Ruskin, Carlyle, Arnold, and Tolstoy. She came to share their concern for improving the material and spiritual lot of the masses of men impoverished by an unjust social order and for bringing beauty into their lives. Later she became more critical of their idealism and, under the influence of Marx, Bakunin, and "realistic" socialists, became more militant. She lived long enough to feel a lively sense of disappointment in the defeat of her ideals, and came to feel that, as an academic, she had not been sufficiently engaged in the struggle. 102 notes.
K. B. West

2952. Green, Frances. WICKFORD, MY VILLAGE OF DREAMS. *New-England Galaxy 1975 17(1): 14-24.* Recounts life in the colonial town of Wickford, Rhode Island, 1890-1974. The 1937 hurricane and the establishment of the Quonset Air Station left this village and its sturdy inhabitants outwardly unaffected. 7 illus.
P. C. Marshall

2953. Hall, Kathryn Hulbert. COHASSET'S CENTENARIAN. *New-England Galaxy 1967 8(3): 13-19.* Frances Osgood Collier (1862-1965) spent most of her 102 years in Cohasset.
S

2954. Himelhoch, Myra. THE SUICIDE OF SALLY PERRY. *Vermont Hist. 1965 33(1): 283-289.* Reconstructs circumstances (setting, motivation, deterrents) of the death of Sally Perry, a seamstress, whose grave was subsequently robbed. From local records.
T. D. S. Bassett

2955. Hinckley, Anita W. WICKFORD TALES. *Am. Heritage 1965 16(4): 80-90.* A lifelong resident of Wickford, Rhode Island (population 2,437), reminisces about some of the more colorful events in that community's history - unsolved murders, fires, unrequited love - as well as about her family and some incidents she fondly recalls.
J. D. Filipiak

2956. Johnson, Margaret L. FLORA BELLE LUDINGTON: A BIOGRAPHY AND BIBLIOGRAPHY. *Coll. and Res. Lib. 1964 25(5): 375-379.* An account of the library career of Flora Belle Ludington. She served as a librarian at Mount Holyoke College from 1926 until her retirement in 1964. In 1951 she was instrumental in establishing the Hampshire Inter-Library Center. In 1953 Mills College granted her an honorary LL.D. In 1957 she received from the American Library Association the Joseph W. Lippincott Award for high achievement. Note, biblio.

D. D. Cameron

2957. Kenney, Alice P. KATE GANSEVOORT'S GRAND TOUR. *New York Hist. 1966 47(4): 343-361.* For 15 months during the period 1859-60, Kate Gansevoort toured Europe with her socially prominent Albany, New York, family. The article chronicles the 21-year-old woman's reactions to Europe and the comparisons made to her native New York. Based on the diary kept by Miss Gansevoort; 4 illus., 32 notes.

G. Kurland

2958. Kitsen, Mary Louise. THE MIRACLE OF SOPHIA. *New-England Galaxy 1974 15(3): 33-39.* Discusses the meeting, marriage, and lives of Sophia Peabody and Nathaniel Hawthorne (1804-64).

S

2959. Knight, Lee. A REMEMBRANCE OF MARJORIE LANSING PORTER. *New York Folklore Q. 1974 30(1): 77-80.*

2960. Krebs, Albert. RÉGIS DE TROBRIAND ET "LE COURRIER DES ÉTATS-UNIS", JOURNAL FRANÇAIS DE NEW YORK (1841-1865) [Régis de Trobriand and *Le Courrier des États-Unis*, a French newspaper in New York (1841-1865)]. *Rev. d'Hist. Moderne et Contemporaine [France] 1971 18(4): 574-588.* Recalls the journalistic career of French-born noble Régis de Trobriand (1816-82) with the French newspaper *Le Courrier des États-Unis* in New York. Ushered into New York's high society by *Courrier* owner Félix Gaillardet, de Trobriand married Chemical Bank heiress Mary Jones, became a US citizen, supported American democracy, and served as an officer in the Union Army in the American Civil War. Based on de Trobriand's works, newspapers, and secondary souces; 16 notes.

C. Collon

2961. Lacy, Harriet S., ed. REMINISCENCES OF THE WHITE MOUNTAINS. *Hist. New Hampshire 1973 28(1): 37-52.* Mary Jane Thomas (1806-97) reminisces about a tour in the summer of 1831 through Crawford Notch to Lancaster, New Hampshire. Her husband, Moses G. Thomas (1805-80), first pastor of the Concord Unitarian Church, borrowed his father-in-law's "one-horse shay" and they took a steamer from Laconia to Center Harbor. They climbed Red Hill, slept at North Conway, and waited a week at Abel Crowford's for clear weather to climb Mt. Washington. 5 illus.

T. D. S. Bassett

2962. Legge, Christopher. IN SEARCH OF PHEBE. *Am. Neptune 1965 25(4): 274-277.* Recounts, from a journal published in 1851 by Mrs. Benjamin Wallis *(Life in Feejee),* two voyages aboard the bark *Zotoff* with her husband, the captain, between the Fiji Islands and Salem, Massachusetts. Along with the ports of call, cargoes carried, comments on the natives, etc., Mrs. Wallis referred several times to a Fiji girl, Phebe, given her by a chief. After sailing with the Wallises on the second voyage and returning to Salem, all reference to her disappears. Illus.

J. G. Lydon

2963. Madden, Sheila. MRS. ABBA ALCOTT: BULWARK OF A FAMOUS FAMILY. *New-England Galaxy 1973 15(2): 15-25.* A biography of Abigail May Alcott.

S

2964. Magnusson, Margaret L. "YOUR AFFECTIONATE MARY": A VERMONT GIRL AT MOUNT HOLYOKE. *Vermont Hist. 1963 31(3): 181-192.* Based on letters from Mary O. Nutting, at school in Massachusetts, to her father, William, describing the trip from Randolph, Vermont, living conditions, studies, routines, and most of all, "religious privileges." Miss Nutting taught school, wrote religious juvenilia, and became the first librarian of Mt. Holyoke College.

T. D. S. Bassett

2965. Margolies, Alan. THE EDITING AND PUBLICATION OF "THE JOURNAL OF MADAM KNIGHT." *Papers of the Biblio. Soc. of America 1964 58(1): 25-32.* Summarizes attempts to authenticate Sarah Kemble Knight's diary of her journey to New York in 1704-05, first published in 1825 and edited by Theodore Dwight, Jr. Initially presumed by many to be the work of Samuel Lorenzo Knapp, correct authorship

was established by Charles Deane in 1858 and William Law Learned in 1865. The text of the diary, however, must be accepted as it appeared at the time of the first printing, since most of the manuscript was destroyed prior to 1846. Sources are printed letters, articles and books.

C. A. Newton

2966. McCauley, Elfreida B. THE MANUFACTURERS' AND VILLAGE LIBRARY OF SOMERSWORTH, NEW HAMPSHIRE. *Hist. New Hampshire 1972 27(2): 89-107.* The Great Falls Manufacturing Company, of Somersworth, hired 1,500 women for its six cotton mills on the Salmon Falls River and ran one of the largest operations of its kind in New England in the 1850's. Converting from woolens to cottons in 1826, the mills failed to make money until after 1840. Managers, trained in Lowell mills, rearranged and rebuilt plant and equipment; and, in 1841, started a library, primarily for the factory girls. Organized in the local Baptist church, over three-quarters of whose 300 members were women, the library raised a book fund through transferable proprietorships, smaller dues from mill girls, and an annual donation from the company. One thousand volumes were acquired within two months, 1,627 volumes by 1847, and six thousand by 1880. The books were kept in company buildings which were open two or three evenings a week for circulation. All librarians were men until the town acquired the collection in 1899; the proprietors incorporated in 1849 and were chartered by the State in 1855. Fiction and Sunday School juvenile titles were lacking from the collection and use declined. Lecture series competed with fortune tellers and music teachers, each dispelling provincialism from the backcountry mill town. Magazines aimed at a mill girl audience and published operatives' pieces. 40 notes.

T. D. S. Bassett

2967. Morcom, Richmond. THEY ALL LOVED LUCY. *Am. Heritage 1970 21(6): 12-15.* Lucy Lambert Hale, daughter of a New Hampshire senator, charmed Oliver Wendell Holmes, Jr., Robert Lincoln, John Wilkes Booth, and John Hay, all of whom wrote her love letters which are reproduced here.

S

2968. Moreton, Dorothy. EMERALD VELOUR IN THE KITCHEN. *New-England Galaxy 1969 10(3): 19-24.* Anecdotes about Jane Welton and her daughter, two unconventional ladies in 19th-century Waterbury.

S

2969. Murray, Donald M. and Rodney, Robert M. SYLVIA DRAKE, 1784-1868: THE SELF PORTRAIT OF A SEAMSTRESS OF WEYBRIDGE. *Vermont Hist. 1966 34(2): 125-135.* Excerpts and summaries from a diary in the Sheldon Museum, Middlebury, Vermont, reveal that Sylvia Drake, companion and sewing partner of Charity Bryant, aunt of William Cullen Bryant, was concerned with conventional Congregationalism, illness, daily chores, and visits. Included is a pious 1829 letter and sample entries on a month's trip to Bridgewater and Cummington, Massachusetts.

T. D. S. Bassett

2970. Myerson, Joel. "A TRUE & HIGH MINDED PERSON": TRANSCENDENTALIST SARAH CLARKE. *Southwest R. 1974 59(2): 163-172.* Sarah Freeman Clarke's letters help illuminate the activities of the New England Transcendentalists, many of whom she knew personally.

S

2971. Petrikin, Dorothy H. THE MRS. FANNIE PETRIKIN HOUSE. *Now and Then 1970 16(6): 313-317.* Identifies the three Petrikin houses in Muncy, Pennsylvania, and provides a biographical sketch of Mrs. Fannie Petrikin, who lived in one of them for over half a century (1850-1902). Mention is made of other occupants. 2 photos.

C. A. Newton

2972. Pike, Robert E. THE FEMALE HERMIT. *New York Folklore Q. 1967 23(2): 133-135.* Discusses the life of female hermit Sarah Bishop in Salem from 1800-23.

2973. Potter, Gail M. THE CAPTIVITY OF JEMIMA HOWE. *New-England Galaxy 1966 8(1): 10-15.* Jemima Howe (1723-1805) was captured by the St. Francis Indians at Vernon, Vermont, in 1755. She remained a captive of the Indians and the French until 1760 when she returned to Vermont.

T. J. Farnham

2974. Reese, Dora J. AN ENGLISH GIRL COMES TO CONNECT-ICUT. *New-England Galaxy 1974 15(4): 42-47.* An authentic account of Jane Hill, who immigrated to New England.          S

2975. Reninger, Marion Wallace. SUSAN CARPENTER FRAZER. *J. of the Lancaster County Hist. Soc. 1972 76(2): 53-57.* Biography of Susan Carpenter Frazer, a community leader, member of patriotic societies and other clubs, and an acknowledged "great lady" of her day.                                                                S

2976. Riegel, Lewis Edgar. REMINISCENCES OF CENTERPORT, 1876-1885. *Pennsylvania Folklife 1964 14(2): 34-47.* An autobiographical account of the author's childhood in Berks County, Pennsylvania, 1876-85. Relates the personal family life of the author and gives a feeling for the daily life of the area during this period. Notes what men and women wore, Christmas and New Year's celebrations, the town of Centerport, some of the customs of the day, entertainment, and outdoor recreation. 5 illus.                          M. J. McBaine

2977. Riegel, Robert E. CAROLINE HEALY DALL. *New-England Galaxy 1967 9(1): 27-31.* Dall (1822-1912), a 19th-century feminist, advocated suffrage, education, and adequate employment for women.                                                                S

2978. Riegel, Robert E., ed. "WOMAN'S RIGHTS AND OTHER 'REFORMS' IN SENECA FALLS:" A CONTEMPORARY VIEW. *New York Hist. 1965 46(1): 41-59.* Contemporary description by Mary Sherwood Bull (1835-1881) of activities in Seneca Falls, New York, by abolitionists, Millerites, the temperance Washingtonians (both the Washingtonian Society and the Martha Washington Society), feminists and other reformers.                                          A. B. Rollins

2979. Rosa, Alfred F. THE NOVELS OF MARI TOMASI. *Italian Americana 1975 2(1): 66-78.* Traces the life and works of Vermont novelist Mari Tomasi (1909-65), who wrote of Italian immigrant stonecutters.

2980. Rosenberger, Homer T. HARRIET LANE JOHNSTON: PIONEER ADVOCATE OF SPECIAL CARE FOR CHILDREN WITH CHRONIC DISEASES. *J. of the Lancaster County Hist. Soc. 1972 76(1): 1-28.* Presents a history of the Harriet Lane Home for Invalid Children of Baltimore City. The home is named after Harriet Lane Johnston, an early advocate of specialized care for handicapped children.

2981. Rosenberger, Homer T. HARRIET LANE JOHNSTON: FOUNDER OF ST. ALBANS SCHOOL FOR BOYS. *J. of the Lancaster County Hist. Soc. 1972 76(3): 136-153.* Discusses the career of Harriet Lane Johnston and her role in establishing St. Albans School for Boys in Washington, D.C.

2982. Rosenberger, Homer T. THE PASSING OF A GREAT LADY: MRS. HARRIET LANE JOHNSTON. *J. of the Lancaster County Hist. Soc. 1971 75(1): 1-18.* Harriet Lane Johnston, niece of President James Buchanan, presided over the White House during her uncle's term and died in 1903.                                    S

2983. Schuchmann, Heinz and Weiser, Frederick S., trans. SIBYLLA CHARLOTTA WINCHENBACH, THE WIFE OF JOSHUA KOCHERTHAL. *Concordia Hist. Inst. Q. 1971 44(3): 136-140.* Tracing the ancestry of Joshua Kocherthal-Harrsch (d. 1719) leads to a tentative identification of his wife of 17 years, Sibylla Charlotta Winchenbach (1676-1713), and further illuminates the background of the Palatine Lutherans who came to America in the early 18th century. Concludes with an ancestry list from the parsonage at Gerichstetten as an additional aid in establishing the identity of Kocherthal's wife. Based on primary and secondary sources; 8 notes.                                      A. M. Brescia

2984. Search, Robert M. and Search, Helen C. THE SECOND WIFE OF ICHABOD HINCKLEY OF TOLLAND. *Connecticut Hist. Soc. Bull. 1963 28(1): 30-32.* Discusses the mysteries in attempting to determine the maiden name of the second wife of Ichabod Hinckley and the place and date of her death. Some of her descendants went to Marietta, Ohio, in 1788, part of the first permanent settlement in the Northwest Territory. Documented.                                        E. P. Stickney

2985. Strong, Kate W. MADAM MARTHA SMITH "THE PERFECT WOMAN." *Long Island Forum 1973 36(11): 218-220.* Chronicles the life of Martha Tunstall Smith, a pioneer woman.          S

2986. Stryker-Rodda, Harriet Mott. ARLINGTON REMEMBERED. *Pro. of the New Jersey Hist. Soc. 1966 84(1): 30-43.* Describes in detail, from girlhood memories, the schools of Arlington, New Jersey, from 1910 to 1924, including ways in which they were affected by World War I. Retail stores of the town are also minutely recalled.
                                                                E. P. Stickney

2987. Taylor, Lloyd C., Jr. JOSEPHINE SHAW LOWELL AND AMERICAN PHILANTHROPY. *New York Hist. 1963 44(4): 336-364.* Describes the broad and influential activities of Mrs. Lowell (1843-1905) in social and charity work in the state and city of New York.
                                                                A. B. Rollins

2988. Taylor, W. Bronson. THE DEATH OF MRS. POWELL. *New York Folklore Q. 1964 20(1): 37-41.* Discusses the mystery surrounding the murder of a Mrs. Powell during the berry picking season near Barker, New York, at the turn of the 20th century.

2989. Thorp, Margaret Farrand. SOME LADIES ADMITTED TO PRINCETON. *New Jersey Hist. Soc. Pro. 1963 81(2): 85-102.* Sketches briefly the wives of the presidents of Princeton University. "The reason we have such tantalizingly vague impressions of so many of our former presidents' wives is that so few of their contemporaries had any historical sense. They did not realize...what kind of details about a period and about persons it is important to preserve." Illus.             E. P. Stickney

2990. Wainright, Nicholas B. LOIS GIVEN BOBB. *Pennsylvania Mag. of Hist. and Biog. 1965 89(2): 145-146.* A tribute to Lois Given Bobb, who left the staff of *The Pennsylvania Magazine of History and Biography* in February 1965. She had served the publication in various capacities since July 1948.                                      D. P. Gallagher

2991. Warren, Dale. AS IT WAS YEARS AGO IN PLAINFIELD. *Pro. of the New Jersey Hist. Soc. 1965 83(2): 107-117.* A description of family life in Plainfield, New Jersey, from about 1912 to 1935. "We were probably the last family east of the Mississippi to relinquish horses in favor of the automobile." Sports interests centered in tennis. Authors and singers associated with Plainfield included Van Wyck Brooks and Anna Case, a Metropolitan Opera star, now Mrs. Clarence Mackay. The account includes vacations out of town. Illus.              E. P. Stickney

2992. Watson, Hildegarde Lasell. OUR TOWN. *New-England Galaxy 1969 11(1): 36-43.* Author's reminiscences of her childhood in Whitinsville, Massachusetts.                                          S

2993. Whipkey, Harry E. THE 1972 RESEARCH CONFERENCE AT HARRISBURG: THE ANTHRACITE REGION, ETHNIC STUDIES, AND WOMEN IN PENNSYLVANIA HISTORY. *Pennsylvania Hist. 1972 39(4): 485-517.* The 7th annual research conference of the Pennsylvania Historical and Museum Commission and the Pennsylvania Historical Association was held in Harrisburg on 28-29 April 1972. Sessions centered upon three topics: 1) life and industry in the anthracite region, 2) ethnic groups in Pennsylvania, and 3) the role of women in Pennsylvania history. Particular emphasis was placed upon sources and avenues for further research.                       D. C. Swift

2994. White, Margaret E. ANTIQUER'S ATTIC: "WEAVERS OF NEW JERSEY." *New Jersey Hist. Soc. Pro. 1964 82(4): 283-288.* Discusses weaving in the 17th and 18th centuries when it was a major activity in New Jersey. Woven coverlets and pieced quilts, largely from the early 19th century, are described. Illus.                               E. P. Stickney

2995. White, Philip L., ed. AN IRISH IMMIGRANT HOUSEWIFE ON THE NEW YORK FRONTIER. *New York Hist. 1967 48(2): 182-188.* Minerva Padden came to the United States from Ireland in 1834 with the ambition of owning her own farm. Lacking the funds to settle in the interior, she became a domestic servant in the Beekman household in New York City. Four years later, she married Timothy Donovan and settled at Hannibal Township, Oswego, New York. In 1846 when her family was almost destitute, she wrote her former employers requesting financial assistance which was generously granted. In her letters to James W. Beekman, Mrs. Donovan described the hardships of farm life on the New York frontier. Three of the letters are preserved in the Beekman Family Papers at the New-York Historical Society. 4 notes.

G. Kurland

2996. Whitehall, Walter Muir. PEREZ MORTON'S DAUGHTER REVISITS BOSTON IN 1825. *Massachusetts Hist. Soc. Pro. 1970 82: 21-47.* Provides insights into the social life of Boston by Sarah Apthorp Morton Cunningham, wife of Richard Cunningham and daughter of Perez Morton, a Boston lawyer and supporter of the Revolutionary cause. These letters are largely limited to social happenings, although they contain occasional glimpses of historical figures (e.g., Daniel Webster). Based on the correspondence of Mrs. Cunningham to her daughter; 38 notes.

J. B. Duff

2997. Wiggins, Florence Roe. HESTER MAHIEU COOKE: THE FRENCH FLOWER THAT BLOOMED AT PLYMOUTH. *Daughters of the Am. Revolution Mag. 1973 107(2): 120-121, 168.*

2998. Wiggins, Florence Roe. MARTHA PITKIN WOLCOTT, A FOUNDING MOTHER. *New-England Galaxy 1974 15(4): 53-58.*

2999. Wilson, Marion Ball. MENNONITE MAIDS. *Pennsylvania Folklife 1966 15(3): 38-39.* Description of two rag dolls made for Mennonites Lizzie and Ellen Carper in the 19th century.

S

3000. Winey, Fay McAfee. BELSNICKLING IN PAXTONVILLE. *Pennsylvania Folklife 1969 19(2): 10-13.* The author reminisces about New Year's Day celebrations in her childhood when adults dressed up in masks and costumes, went to the railroad station, and delighted in scaring passengers, school children, and passersby. The children, also dressed up, would go from house to house seeking treats. The adults represented "Bel-Schnickel," who traditionally punished the naughty. Later "Belsnickling" gave way to the traditional Halloween. Previously, Halloween had not been a costume affair, but an occasion for rather nasty tricks.

F. L. Harrold

3001. —. MUNCY WOMEN TO REMEMBER. *Now and Then 1966 15(2): 63-65.*

3002. —. THE SIMPLE ART OF STITCHERY: A PHOTOGRAPHIC RESUME. *Hist. New Hampshire 1963 18(3): 42-49.* Eight illustrations of needlework exhibited at the New Hampshire Historical Society's museum.

T. D. S. Bassett

# Northcentral

3003. Baker, Donald E., ed. THE CONINE FAMILY LETTERS, 1849-1851: EMPLOYED IN HONEST BUSINESS AND DOING THE BEST WE CAN. *Indiana Mag. of Hist. 1973 69(4): 320-365.* Twelve letters, most of which were written to Mrs. Mary Ann Conine Seymour by her father, Derrick Conine, and her sister Jane in New York and by her sisters Emily and Catharine and her brother Horace in northern Indiana. The letters are all intimate, unpolished notes dealing with family affairs and domestic life. They demonstrate considerable privation, loneliness, and hard labor in converting a wilderness tract into a farm and home. Concludes that Conines were representative of those who settled in the Old Northwest during the Forties and Fifties and that their letters are the rare exception to the rule that one generation's treasures are another's trash. Based on primary sources; 10 photos, 105 notes.

N. E. Tutorow

3004. Baker, Donald E., ed. THE CONINE FAMILY LETTERS, 1852-1863: "JUST THINK HOW WE ARE SCATTERED." *Indiana Mag. of Hist. 1974 70(2): 122-178.* Continued from a previous article. Publishes a series of letters from various members of the Conine family to Mary Ann Conine Seymour during the years 1852-63. The letters ignore the burning sociopolitical questions of the day, instead being concerned with matters of farm, home, school, and church, and are thus excellent accounts of pioneer life in the midwestern states. Based on letters in the possession of Ruth Seymour Burmester; 2 photos, 120 notes.

V. L. Human

3005. Brunger, Ronald A. THE LADIES AID SOCIETIES IN MICHIGAN METHODISM. *Methodist Hist. 1967 5(2): 31-48.* The women of the Methodist Church began to organize in Michigan in the mid-19th century. The development of these sewing groups and other organizations which grew into the Ladies Aid Society is shown by illustrations from many localities. Their activities were social as well as religious in nature. They provided financial and other assistance to the local church as a substitute for stewardship in many cases. Their internal organization, structural changes, and gradual lessening in importance are discussed. 55 notes.

H. L. Calkin

3006. Brush, Jane D. FATHER WAS A PREACHER: REMINISCENCES OF EARLY CADILLAC. *Michigan Hist. 1963 47(2): 97-126, and (3): 226-242.* Part I. A young girl's recollections of life in a lumbering town between 1875 and 1883. During this period Mrs. Brush's father, Augustus Marsh, served as minister of the Presbyterian church of what first was called Clam Lake and later Cadillac. There is an account of Cadillac's incorporation as a city in 1877 and its designation as the seat of Wexford county five years later. Part II. Describes Cadillac as an emerging metropolitan area. There are interesting glimpses of the local literary club, a women's temperance movement, and problems of public sanitation in Michigan's pine region.

J. K. Flack

3007. Burd, Van Akin. A LOUISIANA ESTIMATE OF AN "AMERICAN ROUSSEAU": SARAH ANNE DORSEY ON HENRY DAVID THOREAU. *Louisiana Hist. 1964 5(3): 296-309.* Analyzes the appraisal of Henry David Thoreau written by Mrs. Sarah Anne Ellis Dorsey in a letter to Edward Lyulph Stanley, 28 December 1871. Mrs. Dorsey was the wife of a Louisiana judge and was a novelist of some repute; Stanley was a close friend in England. Mrs. Dorsey, after reading *The Maine Woods* (1863), praised Thoreau as "our 'American Rousseau'...with all the love of nature and of man, of the Frenchman, without his impurities or egotisms." The author calls this a "startling estimate" since it "records a much more generous view of the Concord writer than other Americans were expressing at the time." The original letter is in the Dorsey-Stanley Correspondence, John Rylands Library, Manchester, England.

D. C. James

3008. Donovan, Ruth G. THE NEBRASKA LEAGUE OF WOMEN VOTERS. *Nebraska Hist. 1971 52(3): 311-328.* Surveys the history of the Nebraska league from its creation in June 1920 to the present, stressing its concern with issues pertaining to the welfare of women and children.

R. Lowitt

3009. Ekman, Ernst. FREDERIKA BREMER IN CHICAGO IN 1850. *Swedish Pioneer Hist. Q. 1968 19(4): 234-244.* The author has translated and edited sections of several letters written from Chicago by the Swedish writer Frederika Bremer during the latter half of September 1850. The letters give the writer's impressions of Chicago and of Illinois, formed during her brief travels in the area. Also included is a short biography of Bremer. 2 notes.

E. P. Costello

3010. Erickson, Gary. THE GRAVES OF ANN RUTLEDGE AND THE OLD CONCORD BURIAL GROUND. *Lincoln Herald 1969 71(3): 90-107.* Describes and analyzes the circumstances under which Ann Rutledge's remains were moved in 1890 from the Old Concord Burial Ground in New Salem, Illinois, to Oakland Cemetery in Petersburg, Illinois.

S. L. Jones

3011. Flak, Florence. DISTRICT HISTORY. *Palimpsest 1971 52(3): 143-145.* Describes the history of the organization of the Iowa State Federation of Business and Professional Women's Clubs into districts since 1927. No documentation; illus.

J. C. German

3012. Greene, Elizabeth Venilea Trowbridge. A JOURNEY TO ILLINOIS IN 1835. *Vermont Hist. 1973 41(2): 95-100.* Elizabeth Greene's (1814-85) account of her journey from Ogden, New York to Lisle, Illinois. She, her husband, and another family traveled 31 days across Ontario to Detroit, along Lake Michigan, and west of Chicago. They carried provisions and household goods in covered lumber wagons. Written in 1884; reprinted from a genealogy compiled by William B. Greene, *The Greenes on the East Branch of the DuPage* (Aurora, Illinois: privately printed, 1966). Illus.

T. D. S. Bassett

3013. Haselmayer, Louis A.   JESSIE HARLAN LINCOLN IN IOWA.   *Ann. of Iowa 1968 39(6): 414-424.* Jessie Harlan Lincoln, granddaughter of President Abraham Lincoln, spent part of her childhood in her mother's home state of Iowa where she was born in 1875. She attended Iowa Wesleyan University of which her maternal grandfather had been president. Miss Lincoln married into an Iowa family and had frequent associations with the State until about 1911. 46 notes, 7 illus.
D. L. Smith

3014. Hopkins, Vivian C., ed.   DIARY OF AN IOWA FARM GIRL: JOSEPHINE EDITH BROWN, 1892-1901.   *Ann. of Iowa 1973 42(2): 126-146.* A 14-year-old girl's records of daily life in a small Iowa community at the turn of the 20th century. Supplemented with information from *A History of the Shelby, Iowa Community from Early Times until its Centennial Year of 1970;* 4 photos.
C. W. Olson

3015. Hopkins, Vivian C., ed.   SOLDIER OF THE 92ND ILLINOIS: LETTERS OF WILLIAM H. BROWN AND HIS FIANCEE, EMMA JANE FRAZEY.   *Bull. of the N. Y. Public Lib. 1969 73(2): 114-136.* Twelve letters from William H. Brown of the 92nd Illinois Volunteers and 10 from his sweetheart Emma Jane Frazey of Lanark, Illinois, covering the period from September 1862 to May 1867. The editor, a granddaughter of William and Emma Jane who were married on 26 March 1867, provides biographical data on the two correspondents. An appendix contains three additional items: a letter to Emma Jane from J. R. Callahan; another from Henry Frazey, a cousin; and a manuscript in Emma Jane's handwriting entitled "Evils of War." 3 illus., 35 notes.
W. L. Bowers

3016. Jones, Daryl E. and Pickering, James W., eds.   A YOUNG WOMAN IN THE MIDWEST: THE JOURNAL OF MARY SEARS 1859-1860.   *Ohio Hist. 1973 82(3/4): 215-234.* Extracts from a 119-page journal written by a 20-year-old girl mention politics, everyday life, deaths, and a tornado. 3 illus., 29 notes.
S. S. Sprague

3017. Lentz, Lula Gillespie.   ILLINOIS COMMENTARY: THE REMINISCENCES OF LULA GILLESPIE LENTZ.   *J. of the Illinois State Hist. Soc. 1975 68(3): 267-288, (4): 353-367.* Part I. The author describes life on an Illinois farm in the late 19th century and mentions the farm homestead and furnishings, work routine and daily chores, food preparation, home manufacture of clothing, and sports and games, especially hunting. Discusses the family's practice of its Baptist faith and provides a first-hand account of rural education. Part II. The author describes her experiences of farm life and later town residency, rural education, marriage, and early married life with Eli G. Lentz, a school superintendent and later professor at Southern Illinois Normal University. Covers 1890 to 1929.
N. Lederer

3018. Lykins-Bingham, Mattie.   RECOLLECTIONS OF OLD TIMES.   *Westport Hist. Q. 1971 7(2): 15-24.* A young woman's life in Kansas City, Missouri, 1851-52.
S

3019. Mitchell, Bonnie.   WADE HOUSE SERVES AS LASTING MEMORIAL TO HISTORY-MINDED WISCONSIN WOMAN.   *Wisconsin Then and Now 1968 15(6): 1-4.* Traces the active career of Ruth de Young Kohler. Miss De Young began her distinguished career as a newspaperwoman on the Chicago Tribune in 1929. Eventually she became the woman's editor and conducted its annual Woman Congress featuring speakers of national and international fame. In 1937 she married Herbert V. Kohler, a brother of the former governor of Wisconsin, and moved to Wisconsin where she became involved in numerous local history projects. She served as vice president and curator of the State Historical Society in the 1940's, and launched the Women's Auxiliary in 1950. Her two most visible historical monuments are the restored Wade House and the Butternut House in Greenbush.
D. P. Peltier

3020. Mitchell, Clara.   "IN SOCIETY."   *Missouri Hist. Soc. Bull. 1965 22(2): 115-132.* Unannotated extract from the diary of the author (1867-1903) from February to November 1887. Published "merely as a reflection of the pattern of social life enjoyed by an earlier generation of St. Louisans," it refers to evenings out, visits to various entertainments, and remarks about various escorts. The diarist mentions cycling, tennis, musical events, and her abhorrence of alcohol.
T. M. Condon

3021. Murray, Margaret E. Archer.   MEMOIR OF THE WILLIAM ARCHER FAMILY.   *Ann. of Iowa 1968 39(5): 357-371.* These memoirs begin with the author's parents' journey to Iowa in 1846 and details her childhood reminiscences. Illus.
D. C. Swift

3022. Naumann, G. H.   SEARCH FOR THREE SISTERS.   *Concordia Hist. Inst. Q. 1966 39(1): 20-32.* Translates several letters, stories, and an autobiographical sketch written by Juliana Steinmeyer, a poor German-Lutheran immigrant who lived in Missouri from the 1840's through the 1860's. Her writings reveal "pietistic and sentimental overtones but are full of deeply sincere religious feeling and of doctrinal content."
D. J. Abramoske

3023. Norton, Henry L., ed.   THE TRAVELS OF THE MARSTONS.   *J. of the Illinois State Hist. Soc. 1965 58(3): 279-300.* Edited by her grandnephew, Mrs. Margaret Marston Lawrence recounts in her memoirs principally the story of the 1849 migration of the Marston family to the United States. She was the eldest of the eight children of a comfortable middle-class family in England. Her father was a clothing manufacturer and shopkeeper. A Boonville, Missouri newspaper editor who was in England on business convinced the Marstons and another family that his home was a veritable Eden. The realities of a frontier community in a slave state were too much for the English families to tolerate. After several months they moved to Quincy, Illinois, and soon settled down with comfortable satisfaction. Illus.
D. L. Smith

3024. Olson, Helene Dean.   THE FLU—1918.   *Kansas Q. 1976 8(2): 35-40.* Reminisces on the terrifying Spanish Influenza epidemic resulting in numerous deaths of friends and loved ones; discusses early methods of treatment and prevention in Ames, Iowa, and the impact on this small town of the signing of the Armistice.

3025. Olson, Helene Dean.   MY FIRST AUTO TRIP.   *Kansas Q. 1976 8(2): 21-24.* Describes a 400-mile automobile trip from northwestern Iowa to Janesville, Wisconsin, in August 1914—a three-day adventure involving problems such as bad roads, river crossings, and car trouble.

3026. Ostendorf, Lloyd.   A MONUMENT FOR ONE OF THE LINCOLN MAIDS.   *Lincoln Herald 1964 66(4): 184-186.* Includes biographical information about Mariah Vance (1819-1904) who served as a maid to the Lincoln family longer than anyone else and describes the efforts which led to the erection of a headstone at her grave in special ceremonies at Danville, Illinois, on 12 August 1964.
S. L. Jones

3027. Ostendorf, Lloyd.   THE PHOTOGRAPHS OF MARY TODD LINCOLN.   *J. of the Illinois State Hist. Soc. 1968 61(3): 269-332.* Contains copies of all the known photographs of Mrs. Lincoln. The author has provided an introductory description of the state of the photographic art in Springfield during the period of residence of the Lincoln family and an analysis of the family's attitude toward photography. Background information is supplied for each of the photographs. A selection of seven photographs of Mr. and Mrs. Lincoln together and information about these is supplied at the end of the article.
S. L. Jones

3028. Pearson, Norman Holmes.   A "GOOD THING" FOR HAWTHORNE.   *Essex Inst. Hist. Collections 1964 100(4): 300-305.* Hawthorne's sister-in-law, Elizabeth Peabody, provided him not only with personal encouragement but with assistance in obtaining his post at the Boston Custom House. Documented with excerpts from their correspondence.
J. M. Bumsted

3029. Peterson, Walter F.   MARY MORTIMER: A STUDY IN NINETEENTH CENTURY CONVERSION.   *J. of Presbyterian Hist. 1963 41(2): 80-88.* Mary Mortimer (1816-77) was a founder and first principal of the Normal Institute and High School of Milwaukee, later named the Milwaukee Female College. Her conversion to Christianity, described in some detail, occurred in December 1837, at Madam Ricord's Seminary in Geneva, New York and was unusual in that it was intellectually based and occurred in the atmosphere of an intellectual institution. During her 15 years at Milwaukee Female College, teaching courses in religion, she insisted on a rigorous, skeptical search for truth as the only sound pathway to Christian belief.
W. D. Metz

3030.   Pryor, Helen B.   GIRLHOOD IN WATERLOO.   *Palimpsest 1971 52(7): 353-363.* Discusses Lou Henry's childhood in Waterloo, Iowa, 1874-84.

3031.   Reed, Doris.   THE IOWA BUSINESS WOMAN.   *Palimpsest 1971 52(3): 151-154.* Describes the history of the official publication of the Iowa Federation of Business and Professional Women's Clubs, *The Iowa Business Woman,* since its inception in 1921.
                                                                J. C. German

3032.   Simon, John Y., ed.   HANNAH FANCHER'S NOTES ON OHIO SPEECH IN 1824.   *Ohio Hist. 1964 73(1): 34-38.* A speech on United States speech characteristics.                                S

3033.   Soderbergh, Peter A.   "OLD SCHOOL DAYS" ON THE MIDDLE BORDER, 1849-1859: THE MARY PAYNE BEARD LETTERS.   *Hist. of Educ. Q. 1968 8(4): 497-504.* Two letters in the archives of De Pauw University from Mary Payne Beard to her son Charles A. Beard, the historian, describe mid-19th century school life in Indiana. The letters are here reprinted. They document the transition of the common school from a monitorial, two-family enterprise to that of the fixed-seat, multigrade, heterogeneous, racially mixed, and teacher-centered classroom. The author speculates that Charles A. Beard's interest in and activities for public education were due, in part, to his family background.
                                                                J. Herbst

3034.   Solberg, Winton U.   MARTHA G. RIPLEY: PIONEER DOCTOR AND SOCIAL REFORMER.   *Minnesota Hist. 1964 39(1): 1-17.* This article traces the life of Martha G. Ripley, born on the frontier in Minnesota, who later became a leader in the woman suffrage movement in the East and who still later returned to Minnesota as a doctor and continued her campaign to improve the rights of women. An advocate of "modern" progress both in attitudes and medical practice, she opened one of the first hospitals in the United States for unwed mothers and gave it a fine reputation for high medical standards.              P. L. Simon

3035.   Thompson, Dorothy Brown.   A YOUNG GIRL IN THE MISSOURI BORDER WAR.   *Missouri Hist. R. 1963 58(1): 55-69.* To demonstrate the thesis that warfare on the Missouri border was an intensely personal disaster, the author presents a collection of letters that was found in her grandfather's attic. The writer of the letters, Laura Brown, was a teenager during the 1850's. Her letters deal primarily with family and personal matters, but there are occasional references to political and military matters in Missouri and the United States.
                                                                W. F. Zornow

3036.   Vanderburg, Helen.   THE THREAD OF LEGISLATION.   *Palimpsest 1971 52(3): 146-150.* Describes the lobbying activities of the Iowa Business and Professional Women's Clubs from its initial demand in 1919 for good-looking shoes for business wear, through its activities in the 1960's working for legislation affording equal rights to men and women. Subjects lobbied for included the Sheppard-Towner Maternity bill, opposition against wages and hours laws applying only to women, eligibility of women to serve in the Iowa General Assembly, sex discrimination of any kind, aid to dependent children and support of premarital examinations, support of the Equal Rights Amendment during World War II, interest in probation and adoption laws, school reorganization, four-year terms for county officials, legislative reapportionment, development of technical and vocational schools, regional jails, revision of divorce and child labor laws, equalization of salaries, support of local law enforcement, and environmental concern.              J. C. German

3037.   Yzenbaard, John H. and Hoffmann, John, eds.   "BETWEEN HOPE AND FEAR": THE LIFE OF LETTIE TEEPLE.   *Michigan Hist. 1974 58(3): 219-278, (4): 291-352.* Part I. The first chapter of the uncompleted autobiography of Aletta Teeple Rellingston Pennoyer, written in 1885. Emphasizing detail but sensitively written, this chapter covers 1829-50: her childhood, adolescence, and first marriage. Born on a farm in Wayne County, she moved with her family at age seven to a homestead near Grand Rapids, where she became a keen observer of nature and of agricultural pursuits on the sparsely settled western Michigan frontier. The chapter concludes with a description of her brief career as a teacher and her seven-month marriage to William Rellingston. 3 illus., 2 maps, 5 photos, 52 notes. Part II. This second and final chapter

covers 1850-68: the early years of her marriage to Henry Pennoyer, an innkeeper, farmer, and leader in the civic affairs of Grand Haven. Pennoyer was a typical frontier entrepreneur, optimistic despite repeated failure. As Pennoyer's wife, Lettie assumed much managerial work at the hotel of which he was proprietor, and was burdened even more when he gave up the hotel business to become a farmer. The narrative ends unexplainably in 1868. 4 illus., 11 photos, 61 notes.              D. W. Johnson

3038.   Zagel, Henrietta.   BPW IN RETROSPECT.   *Palimpsest 1971 52(3): 155-158.* Mentions some of the service activities of the Business and Professional Women's Clubs in Iowa, such as scholarship programs, support of the Red Cross and bloodmobiles, and historical preservation.
                                                                J. C. German

3039.   Zagel, Henrietta.   THE IOWA BPW—1919-1970.   *Palimpsest 1971 52(3): 129-142.* Describes the founding of the Iowa Federation of Business and Professional Women's Clubs, highlights of national conventions, descriptions of the federation's changing interests, and achievements of some of its officers.                                J. C. German

3040.   —.   THE GAY NINETIES IN CHICAGO, A FRENCH VIEW.   *Chicago Hist. 1966 7(11): 341-348.* Describes some of the experiences of Madame Léon Grandin, who visited Chicago from July 1892 to May 1893 and recorded her impressions in a book, *Impressions d'une Parisienne à Chicago,* published in 1894. Such topics as life in boardinghouses, the position of women, and the "servant problem" are touched upon. Madame Grandin had some difficulty adjusting to Chicago but she eventually became unhappy over the prospect of returning to France. "I left profoundly sad at leaving. I left the country where I felt free, with liberty of thought, with allurements that would never be allowed under our sun where narrow prejudices, ridiculous etiquette, and absurd conventions flourish."                                D. J. Abramoske

3041.   —.   "KATE! THE BARN IS AFIRE!"   *Chicago Hist. 1971 1(4): 216-219.* A selection from the testimony of Mrs. Catherine O'Leary and Catherine McLaughlin, Mrs. O'Leary's tenant, taken in November 1871. Mrs. O'Leary was more interested in her personal losses than in the origin of the fire. Transcript from the Official Fire Department Inquiry, 1871. 2 photos.                                N. A. Kuntz

# South

3042.   Curran, Charles.   THE THREE LIVES OF JUDAH P. BENJAMIN.   *Hist. Today [Great Britain] 1967 17(9): 583-592.* Judah P. Benjamin was a well-known 19th century Southern lawyer who was, respectively, a U.S. Senator, a cabinet minister of the Confederacy, and a prosperous English lawyer. A significant point made by the author is that Benjamin's incentive for achieving high office and wealth was his extravagant wife, Natalie.                                L. A. Knafla

3043.   Donaldson, Scott.   SCOTT FITZGERALD'S ROMANCE WITH THE SOUTH.   *Southern Literary J. 1973 5(2): 3-18.* F. Scott Fitzgerald's attitudes toward the American South were shaped by the two most important relationships of his life: those with his wife, Zelda Sayre of Alabama, and those with his father, Edward Fitzgerald of Maryland. From his father he inherited a tendency to glamorize the South. His spiritual home remained Maryland all his life. His fascination with Zelda and with the southern belle as a type culminated in the symbolic marriage of his brilliant northern success with her golden southern beauty. That fascination steadily waned, however, as evidenced by his fiction, until his eventual realization that he and Zelda were locked in a struggle for survival. 36 notes.                                J. L. Colwell

3044.   Foster, Virginia.   THE EMANCIPATION OF PURE, WHITE, SOUTHERN WOMANHOOD.   *New South 1971 26(1): 46-54.* Reminisces about being raised as an example of white southern womanhood and being confronted by racial equality at a New England college in the 1920's.

3045.   Massey, Mary Elizabeth.   THE MAKING OF A FEMINIST.   *J. of Southern Hist. 1973 39(1): 3-22.* Ella Gertrude Clanton Thomas's journal of 41 years, 1848-89, is "among the most revealing records to come from the Civil War generation." It is "especially valuable for showing how and why a southern lady, reared in the tradition of the Old South, came to question its teachings and eventually to play a part in overturning many of its time-honored concepts." 81 notes.                     I. M. Leonard

3046. Mayo, Selz Cabot and Hamilton, C. Horace. CURRENT POPULATION TRENDS IN THE SOUTH. *Social Forces 1963 42(1): 77-88.* "Important patterns in the changing population of the South in the last decade show a growing heterogeneity of the southern population. The southern population is increasing slower than the national population, but it is converging with the national patterns in many respects. Migration caused a redistribution of the South's population between states and between residence groups. General increases occurred in the urban and rural nonfarm populations in number of females working, in number of professional people, in urban fringe population, in school enrollment, and in educational levels achieved. Net out migration was the major factor in the decline in the South's total population. If the age-sex-color specific rates of migration and natural increase of the 1950's continue, the population of the South will increase 14.8 percent during the 1960's as compared with an expected national increase of 17.4 percent."
J

3047. Snell, David. THE GREEN WORLD OF CARRIE DORMON. *Smithsonian 1972 2(11): 28-33.* Discusses Carrie Dormon, Louisiana naturalist and artist—"perhaps the foremost authority on wild flowers of the southern United States." Mentions Dormon's work late in life and reproduces some of her paintings of southern wild flowers. Illus., photos.                     J. M. Hawes

# Southeast

3048. Anderson, Sterling P., Jr. "QUEEN MOLLY" AND "THE VIRGINIA HOUSEWIFE." *Virginia Cavalcade 1971 20(4): 29-35.* An account of the life of Mary Randolph (1768-1828), author of the first book of recipes and household hints published in the South. Mrs. Randolph, known as "Queen Molly," opened a boarding house in Richmond in 1808 after her husband, David Meade Randolph, suffered financial reverses. Among the friends and acquaintances of Mary and David Randolph were William Ellery Channing (who came to Virginia from New England to tutor their four sons), Aaron Burr, the John Marshalls, the John Wickhams, and George Washington Parke Custis. Mary Randolph died in Washington, D.C., and was buried on a hillside just west of the Custis mansion, Arlington. She was the first person buried in the now-famous Arlington Cemetery. 10 illus.                     N. L. Peterson

3049. Blackshear, Helen F. MAMA SAYRE, SCOTT FITZGERALD'S MOTHER-IN-LAW. *Georgia R. 1965 19(4): 465-470.* Born before the Civil War, Minerva Sayre lived into the 20th century and despite numerous tragedies radiated a glow of charm and friendship that was admired by her friends. The author provides no information on Scott Fitzgerald. Most of the material was gathered during "parlor visits" by the author.                     H. G. Earnhart

3050. Buckner, Gladys. WOMAN'S LIB—1853. *Daughters of the Am. Revolution Mag. 1976 110(2): 192-195.* Discusses the life of Ann Pamela Cunningham (1816-1875), founder of the Mount Vernon Ladies' Association which in 1858 acquired George Washington's home, Mount Vernon, in Virginia, and has operated it since as a national shrine.

3051. Buni, Andrew, ed. "RAMBLES AMONG THE VIRGINIA MOUNTAINS" - THE JOURNAL OF MARY JANE BOGGS, JUNE 1851. *Virginia Mag. of Hist. and Biog. 1969 77(1): 78-111.* Reprints, with introduction and notes, Miss Boggs's account of her trip through the Shenandoah Valley 10-30 June 1851. 34 notes.                     K. J. Bauer

3052. Carpenter, Charles, ed. HENRY DANA WARD: EARLY DIARIST OF THE KANAWHA VALLEY. *West Virginia Hist. 1975 37(1): 34-48.* Excerpts from the diary of Henry Dana Ward, Yankee Episcopal minister in Charleston, (West) Virginia, 1845-47, discuss the importance of the salt industry in the Kanawha Valley, the operation of his wife's private school in Charleston, and the river traffic on the Ohio. 2 illus., 18 notes.                     J. H. Broussard

3053. Coddington, John Insley. ANCESTORS AND DESCENDANTS OF LADY CHRISTINA STUART (1741-1807) WIFE OF THE HON. CYRUS GRIFFIN OF VIRGINIA. *Natl. Geneal. Soc. Q. 1964 52(1): 25-36.* A genealogical account of the ancestors and descendants of Lady Christina Stuart, who was born at Traquair House, Peebles County, Scotland, in 1741. Lady Christina eloped with Cyrus Griffin (1748-1810), a young Virginian who was studying law in Edinburgh. They were married in Edinburgh on 29 April 1770. A few months later they moved to London, where Griffin became a law student at the Middle Temple. The couple settled in Virginia late in 1773. "During much of his later life, Cyrus Griffin and his family lived in 'Griffin House,' on the corner of Queen and Nicholson Streets, Williamsburg, Va., and there Lady Christina Griffin presumably died, 8 Oct. 1807." 127 notes.
D. D. Cameron

3054. Coffin, Annie Roulhac. AUDUBON'S FRIEND - MARIA MARTIN. *New York Hist. Soc. Q. 1965 49(1): 29-51.* One of the collaborators with John James Audubon was Maria Martin of South Carolina. An artist in her own right, she painted many of the backgrounds for the well-known Audubon paintings. Her association with Audubon is described and several watercolors reproduced, some for the first time.
C. L. Grant

3055. Craven, Martha Jacquelyn. A PORTRAIT OF EMILY TUBMAN. *Richmond County Hist. 1974 6(1): 4-10.* Presents a short biography of Emily Tubman, 1818-85, following her life as it coincided with events in Georgia and the South, and examines her efforts to aid in the establishment of Liberia. Reproduction, 27 notes.

3056. Craven, Martha Jacquelyn. A PORTRAIT OF OCTAVIA. *Richmond County Hist. 1972 4(2): 5-11.* Sketches the life of Octavia Walton LeVert (1810-77), a socially prominent native of Augusta. Known for her great beauty, poise, and social position, Miss Walton made her debut in Washington, D.C., in 1833. Three years later she married Dr. Henry Stephen LeVert, a Mobile, Alabama, physician. Mrs. LeVert reached the zenith of her social career during an 1853-55 tour of Europe when she met many crowned heads, including England's Queen Victoria. Although she supported the Confederacy, her alleged friendship toward Union officers during Reconstruction forced her from her Mobile home. Mrs. LeVert's remaining years were spent mostly in Augusta. Based on published materials and LeVert manuscripts; illus., 44 notes.
H. R. Grant

3057. Davis, Mollie C. THE COUNTESS OF HUNTINGDON AND WHITEFIELD'S BETHESDA. *Georgia Hist. Q. 1972 56(1): 72-82.* Argues that Selina Hastings, the Countess of Huntingdon, was "a product of the 18th century in her spirit of viewing red and black men as infidel children of nature; she promoted humanitarianism and stressed the individual. The very factors operating on her affected the Georgia frontier differently and promoted independence and individualism of another sort. The new Georgia threw out many utopian aspirations in order to accomplish materialistic and nationalistic purposes." Both Georgians and the Countess were receptive to a movement to establish an orphanage and college at Bethesda on the Whitefield model, demonstrating that materialistic and utopian interests might not be incompatible. Although the orphanage and college plan failed, the idea remained alive. Based on published primary sources; 16 notes.                     R. M. Miller

3058. DeNoya, Mary Musselwhite. MASSACRE AT THE MEADOWS. *Daughters of the Am. Revolution Mag. 1972 106(2): 132-136, 230.* The stories (1755-61) of Mary Draper Ingles and Elizabeth ("Bettie") Draper, pioneer women of Draper's Meadow, Virginia, who were captured by, and later escaped from, a Shawnee tribe.                     S

3059. Edmonds, Katharine Spicer. IN THE REALM OF HOSPITALITY: COOKBOOKS OF THE EASTERN SHORE. *Virginia Cavalcade 1974 24(4): 9-17.* Surveys a spate of cookbooks produced on the eastern shore of Virginia during the 19th and 20th centuries and probably inspired by the first eastern shore cookbook, Bessie Gunter's *Housekeeper's Companion* (1889).                     S

3060. Flory, Clause R. ANNIE OAKLEY IN THE SOUTH. *North Carolina Hist. R. 1966 43(3): 333-343.* Despite Annie Oakley's association with the Wild West, she was born Phoebe Ann Oakley Moses in Ohio, of Pennsylvania Quaker stock, and some of the most important incidents of her life occurred in North Carolina and Florida. Although she worked all her life with firearms, her only injuries came in a North Carolina trainwreck in 1901 and a Florida automobile accident in 1922, the latter contributing to her death in 1926. 33 notes.

J. M. Bumsted

3061. Foulk, Virginia. WOMEN AUTHORS OF WEST VIRGINIA. *West Virginia Hist.* 1964 25(3): 206-210. An account of some West Virginia women who have made contributions in the field of literature. Mentions Margaret Blennerhassett, wife of the man implicated in the Burr conspiracy. Also calls attention to Anne Royall, authoress of the 10-volume *Travels in the United States* (1826-31) and Rebecca Harding Davis, mother of Richard, as representatives of the 19th century. Modern authors noted are Elizabeth and Mary Ferrell, Pearl Buck, Margaret Montague, and Louise McNeill. This undocumented paper was read at the annual meeting of the West Virginia Historical Society in 1963.

D. N. Brown

3062. Gass, W. Conrad. A FELICITOUS LIFE: LUCY MARTIN BATTLE, 1805-1874. *North Carolina Hist. R.* 1975 52(4): 367-393. During the long and distinguished career of her lawyer-judge husband, William Horn Battle, Lucy Martin Battle assumed much of the responsibility for managing his private affairs. Mrs. Battle served briefly as his amanuensis, and then ran the large household of children and slaves, first in Raleigh, then in Chapel Hill, during her husband's frequent and lengthy absences. Her success at these tasks permitted William Battle to participate fully in public life in antebellum North Carolina. Based primarily on the Battle Family Papers, as well as other manuscript collections, newspaper accounts, public documents, and secondary sources; 7 illus., 94 notes.

T. L. Savitt

3063. Groene, Bertram H., ed. LIZZIE BROWN'S TALLAHASSEE. *Florida Hist. Q.* 1969 48(2): 155-175. Virginia planter Thomas Brown, later governor of Florida (1849-53), brought his family to Leon County, Florida, in the winter of 1827-28, when his daughter Francis Elizabeth was 10 years old. Her memoirs, recorded in 1894, have been edited, deleting personal material and revealing a picture of Tallahassee's early years. She recalls early prominent neighbors, Indian friends, strolling players coming into town, a duel fought in the Capitol Square, her father's trips to New Orleans to buy provisions and clothing, and being sent to Virginia by her father when Indian hostilities broke out in 1836. Based on a manuscript in private possession; 2 illus, 39 notes.

R. V. Calvert

3064. Groover, Robert L. PROTECTOR OF GEORGIA HERITAGE: THE STORY OF MARY GIVENS BRYAN. *Georgia Hist. Q.* 1967 51(1): 1-14. A biography of Mary Givens Bryan, longtime Georgia archivist and director of the Georgia Department of Archives and History from 1951 until her death in 1964. During her service with the archives, beginning in 1934, Mrs. Bryan was instrumental in searching out large bodies of local and county records for preservation through lamination and microfilming. Her career was capped with the completion of a new state archives building in Atlanta in 1964. Undocumented.

R. A. Mohl

3065. Henry, Bessie M. A YANKEE SCHOOLMISTRESS DISCOVERS VIRGINIA. *Essex Inst. Hist. Collections* 1965 101(2): 121-132. Biographical sketch of Abigail Mason of Salem, Massachusetts, as an introduction to the reprinting of a series of letters she wrote to relatives in the 1830's while serving as a schoolmistress on the plantations of the upper James River. The letters describe their author's views on dining customs (including Thanksgiving Virginia style), slavery, religious revivalism, and Christmas.

J. M. Bumsted

3066. Hower, Charles C. THE EUROPEAN ANCESTORS OF BARBARA FRITCHIE, BORN HAUER. *Maryland Hist. Mag.* 1973 68(1): 94-103. Traces the ancestry of Barbara Fritchie of Maryland, focusing on the Hauer family, German immigrants from Lorraine. Based on primary and secondary sources; list, illus., 25 notes.

G. J. Bobango and S

3067. Laurens, Caroline Olivia and King, Louise C., ed. JOURNAL OF A VISIT TO GREENVILLE FROM CHARLESTON IN THE

SUMMER OF 1825. *South Carolina Hist. Mag.* 1971 72(3): 164-173; 72(4): 220-233. Part I. Reprints Laurens' journal 23 May-7 July 1825 in which she writes her impressions of Greenville. Part II. Reprints Laurens' diary and her impressions of Greenville, 8 July-11 November 1825.

3068. Marszalek, John F. THE CHARLESTON FIRE OF 1861 AS DESCRIBED IN THE EMMA E. HOLMES DIARY. *South Carolina Hist. Mag.* 1975 76(2): 60-67. Immediately after the Charleston fire of 1861, Emma E. Holmes, daughter of a prominent physician who died in 1854, began keeping a diary. Entries reveal the panic as well as heroic actions taken in futile attempts to stop the blaze, which destroyed many businesses and homes, including that of Holmes. Primary sources; note.

R. H. Tomlinson

3069. Meaders, Margaret Inman. APPALACHIA, OF THEE I SING...REMEMBERING. *Georgia R.* 1968 22(2): 170-179. Reminisces about Appalachia in the early 20th century. The author's childhood days vanished with the changes in society and social values during the past half-century. Laments the loss of open land, the old swimming hole, and human companionship.

J. S. Pula

3070. Montague, Ludwell Lee, ed. CORNELIA LEE'S WEDDING AS REPORTED IN A LETTER FROM ANN CALVERT STUART TO MRS. ELIZABETH LEE, OCTOBER 19, 1806. *Virginia Mag. of Hist. and Biog.* 1972 80(4): 453-460. Biographical sketch prefaces the letter describing the wedding of Cornelia Lee to John Hopkins. Published and unpublished sources; 50 notes.

C. A. Newton

3071. Moore, John H. JUDITH RIVES OF CASTLE HILL. *Virginia Cavalcade* 1964 13(4): 30-35. An account of the life of Judith Walker Rives, wife of William Cabell Rives, American minister to France and senator and congressman from Virginia. Descriptions of her life in Virginia and Paris are taken from her unpublished autobiography which was written in 1861.

Roberta B. Lange

3072. Moore, Ray Nichols. MOLLY HUSTON LEE: A PROFILE. *Wilson Lib. Bull.* 1975 46(6): 432-439. Biographical portrait of librarian Molly Huston Lee, guiding light of the Richard B. Harrison Library for Negroes, founded in 1935 in Raleigh, North Carolina.

S

3073. Murray, Irene J. HENRIETTA LISTON IN AMERICA. *Virginia Cavalcade* 1964 14(1): 28-33. Tells of the impressions of Federalist America received by Henrietta Liston, wife of the British Minister to the United States and recorded in her journal. She describes diplomatic life during Washington's second administration and tells of her travels through Virginia and Maryland. The unpublished journals are preserved in the National Library of Scotland. Illus.

R. B. Lange

3074. Murray, Irene J. MRS. LISTON RETURNS TO VIRGINIA. *Virginia Cavalcade* 1965 15(1): 40-46. The Virginia travels in 1800 of Robert Liston, the British minister, and his wife Henrietta are described. Their meals, accommodations, and mode of travel are recounted as well as visits to the Natural Bridge and the homes of Jefferson, Madison, and Washington. Drawn from the journals of Mrs. Liston.

R. B. Lange

3075. Nesbitt, Martha C. TO FAIRFIELD WITH LOVE: A RURAL MARYLAND HOUSE AND HOUSEHOLD. *Maryland Hist. Mag.* 1975 70(1): 68-89. Emphasizes the "almost human attributes of character and personality" represented by certain old homes of Montgomery County and chronicles the building and family history of *Fairfield*, home of the Pierce-Iddings-Willson Family for 115 years, and located in present-day Brighton community. Built by Edward Pierce for his father and sister Ann in 1856, the house also became his home after his marriage to Sophia Kummer from the Moravian Female Seminary of Bethlehem, Pennsylvania. The strong Quaker heritage of the area was enriched by Sophie's musical enthusiasm. The Pierces' daughter Fanny married William Iddings in 1894 and they inaugurated a carpet, rug, and mat-weaving business into the family homestead, which continued through the 1960's. Deborah Alice Iddings (1896- ) lived at Fairfield until its sale in 1968. A re-roofing job in the 1950's uncovered a cache of letters and an 1817 diary of one of the Kummer sisters which shed new light on the early Moravian community and its personnel. The author knew Fanny Pierce Iddings personally and much of this article consists of her personal reminiscences and writings. Longevity seems inherent in the Fairfield clan, for all the principals lived into their late eighties and nineties. Based on family Day Books, diaries, letters, interviews by the author, and secondary sources; 5 illus., 28 notes. G. J. Bobango

3076. O'Hara, Constance. MRS. MARMADUKE FLOYD: A TRIUMPHANT LIFE. *Georgia Hist. Q. 1968 52(3): 293-304.* A tribute to the late Mrs. Marmaduke Floyd, researcher in the history of Georgia, librarian of the Georgia Historical Society, and a leading spirit in the movement for the preservation of historical sites in Savannah. Undocumented. R. A. Mohl

3077. Peterson, Helen Stone. THE PRESIDENT'S DAUGHTERS. *Virginia Cavalcade 1963 13(2): 18-22.* Discusses Thomas Jefferson's affection for his daughters, Martha Jefferson Randolph and Maria Jefferson Eppes. Undocumented. R. B. Lange

3078. Ravenel, Virginia. "FLORENCE, FLORENCE." *South Carolina Hist. Illus. 1970 1(1): 40-42, 62-65.* Traces the life of Florence Henning Harllee (1848-1927) for whom Florence, South Carolina, was named. Her father was active in South Carolina politics, but she died nearly penniless in 1927. Undocumented; 5 photos. J. W. Flynt

3079. Reagon, Bernice. THE LADYSTREETSINGER. *Southern Exposure 1974 2(1): 38-41.* Portrays the life of Flora Molton, a black woman, who has sung her folk songs on the streets of the District of Columbia since the 1930's. S

3080. Stickley, Julia Ward. CATHOLIC CEREMONIES IN THE WHITE HOUSE, 1832-1833. ANDREW JACKSON'S FORGOTTEN WARD, MARY LEWIS. *Catholic Hist. R. 1965 51(2): 192-198.* Mary Anne Lewis, daughter of Major William Berkeley Lewis, the quartermaster for General Andrew Jackson and treasury official during Jackson's presidency, became engaged to French diplomat Alphonse Joseph Yves Pageot while visiting at the White House. At the president's wish, they were married at the White House, 29 November 1832. The Catholic ceremony was performed by Father Matthews of St. Patrick's Church, Washington. A year later, at the White House, Father Matthews christened their son, Andrew Jackson Pageot, the president being the godfather. Pageot became French minister to the United States under King Louis Philippe. Mme. Pageot died at Avignon, 26 November 1866. A

3081. Trotter, Margaret G. A GLIMPSE OF CHARLESTON IN THE 1890S: FROM A CONTEMPORARY DIARY. *West Virginia Hist. 1974 35(2): 131-144.* Charleston, West Virginia, in the 1890's had 10,000 people but maintained its rural heritage. Houses were gas-lit but heated by fireplaces, window-screens had just arrived, and there was no telephone service. Air pollution was created by the coal industry and a local welfare problem was beginning. Based on the diary of Elizabeth Ruffner Wilson; 138 notes. J. H. Broussard

3082. Turman, Nora Miller and Lewis, Mark C., eds. THE WILL OF ANN LITTLETON OF NORTHAMPTON COUNTY, VIRGINIA, 1656. *Virginia Mag. of Hist. and Biog. 1967 75(1): 11-21.* Reprints with extensive introduction a will dated 28 October 1656. The introduction is chiefly based on legal records. 44 notes. K. J. Bauer

3083. Vossler, Kathryn Babb. WOMEN AND EDUCATION IN WEST VIRGINIA, 1810-1909. *West Virginia Hist. 1975 36(4): 271-290.* West Virginia schools in the 19th century educated women only in their traditional roles as homemakers, mothers, and moral guardians of society. Several private academies took women students before the Civil War, and the public school system also served females, but not with the same variety of courses open to males. Industrialization improved the position of women, and by the 1890's schools offered new opportunities, especially in the prosperous coal counties. Based on local records and secondary sources; 6 tables, 69 notes. J. H. Broussard

3084. Weaver, Bettie Woodson. MARY JEFFERSON AND EPPINGTON. *Virginia Cavalcade 1969 19(2): 30-35.* A biographical sketch of Thomas Jefferson's younger daughter Mary (1778-1804), who upon the death of her mother in 1782, was placed under the care of Elizabeth and Francis Eppes at their plantation, Eppington, in Chester-

field County. She remained there until 1787 when her father, then in France as minister plenipotentiary, sent for her. In 1797 Mary Jefferson married John Wayles Eppes, son of Elizabeth and Francis, and spent much of her brief married life at Eppington. Her great affection for the plantation is stressed. The article includes information on the architecture of Eppington. Undocumented, illus. N. L. Peterson

3085. Wiles, William G. THE PARENTS OF SUSANNAH WILES (WEILLS) RINEHART. *West Virginia Hist. 1970 31(3): 185-188.* Cites family histories and additional genealogical sources to disclose that Susannah Wiles Rinehart (fl. 1791) was the daughter of neither A. D. nor William Wiles (as claimed in published histories) but of George Wiles (d. 1811), whose will is quoted in its entirety. C. A. Newton

3086. Williams, Walter L. A SOUTHERNER IN THE PHILIPPINES, 1901-1903. *Res. Studies 1971 39(2): 156-165.* Reviews the letters exchanged between Lieutenant George D. Jarrett and his mother, Elizabeth Lucas Jarrett, of Tugalo, Georgia, during the time that George Jarrett was stationed in the Philippines; the letters describe the thoughts and feelings of someone caught up in the imperialist American policy of the time.

3087. Wilson, W. Emerson, ed. PHOEBE GEORGE BRADFORD DIARIES. *Delaware Hist. 1975 16(3): 244-267, 16(4): 337-357.* Continued from a previous article. Part III. This installment publishes excerpts from the diaries for the period 1835-38. Mrs. Bradford recounts her difficulties with domestic help, black and white; her travel to New Jersey; visits to Bristol College in Pennsylvania and to Delaware College in Newark; a lecture on electricity, life in New Castle and Wilmington; local preachers and politicians; and family concerns. 42 notes. Part IV. The final installment covers the period from February 1838 to April 1839. The diary describes local church life, particularly the move of the Rev. John W. McCullough to Wilmington's Trinity Episcopal church and his feuds with Rev. John V. E. Thorn of St. Andrews Church. Entries also describe the graduation ceremonies at Delaware College, reactions to a Catholic service, the purchase and furnishing of the Bradford's new home in Wilmington, relations with artisans, local personalities, and customs. Illus., 26 notes. R. M. Miller

3088. Wilson, W. Emerson, ed. PHOEBE GEORGE BRADFORD DIARIES. *Delaware Hist. 1974 16(2): 132-151.* Continued from a previous article. This installment publishes Phoebe Bradford's diaries for the period January 1833 to March 1835. Discusses local social events and town gossip, her visit to her birthplace, Mt. Harmon, in Cecil County, Maryland, Bristol College in Pennsylvania, a circus in Wilmington, and her involvement in various local social groups and reform societies as well as the Episcopal church. Illus., 39 notes. Article to be continued. R. M. Miller

3089. Wilson, W. Emerson, ed. PHOEBE GEORGE BRADFORD DIARIES. *Delaware Hist. 1974 16(1): 1-21.* Part I. Selections (1832-33) from the diary of Phoebe George Bradford, daughter of Sidney George, Jr., of Cecil County and wife of Whig editor Moses Bradford, relating to her Mt. Harmon plantation in Maryland, life in Wilmington, family, Wilmington religious fare and ministers, gardening interests, the Female Colonization Society, and prominent or obscure state and national political figures including Henry Clay and the McLane family. 48 notes. Article to be continued. R. M. Miller

3090. Wright, Louis B. ANTIDOTE TO ROMANTIC CONCEPTS OF COLONIAL VIRGINIA. *Virginia Q. R. 1966 42(1): 137-141.* A review essay of *The Diary of Colonel Landon Carter of Sabine Hall, 1752-1778,* edited by Jack P. Greene (Charlottesville: U. Press of Virginia, 1964). A detailed social history of the daily life of a prominent Virginia aristocrat, it presents a remarkably complete picture of 18th-century Virginia agriculture and describes intimate details of family life, slavery, and treatment of illnesses. While this 1,150-page diary is gloomy and pessimistic, it provides an antidote to romantic notions of ease, luxury, and comfort surrounding 18th-century Virginia aristocrats. O. H. Zabel

3091. —. [WILTON MANSION]. *Virginia Calvacade 1966 15(4): 9-29.*

—.  THE LADIES MOVE A MANSION,  *pp. 9-17.* A history of Wilton, an 18th-century house in Virginia. Originally built by William Randolph III, Wilton fell into neglect and disuse in the late 18th and early 19th centuries. In 1933 the title to the estate was acquired by the National Society of the Colonial Dames of America, who moved and restored the house and now operate it as a museum. Undocumented, illus.

Rice, A. Bransford, Jr.  A PORTFOLIO OF WILTON, *pp. 18-29.* A pictoral tour of Wilton with 10 pages of photographs follows a short description of the restoration of the mansion.

R. B. Lange

# Southcentral

3092.  Alexander, Charles C.  WHITE-ROBED REFORMERS: THE KU KLUX KLAN COMES TO ARKANSAS, 1921-22. *Arkansas Hist. Q. 1963 22(1): 8-23.* Based on unpublished doctoral dissertation, University of Texas, 1962. In 1920 Edward Young Clarke and Elizabeth Tyler entered into a business partnership with William Joseph Simmons, founder of the Ku Klux Klan. "Partly because of Clarke's propagandizing, but largely because of the passions of the people who joined it," the Klan became the primary outlet for hatred of Catholics, Jews, Negroes, foreigners, radicals, as well as bootleggers, adulterers, and other "objectionable" types. Eventually anti-Catholicism obscured all other prejudices. In Klan history in Arkansas it is surprising that, considering the social acceptability of violence against Negroes, only a few were assaulted. 34 notes.

E. P. Stickney

3093.  Bennett, Marj D.  COUNTRY KITCHEN. *Chronicles of Oklahoma 1973 51(3): 305-308.* Personal account of life in a country kitchen in early 20th-century Oklahoma.                                S

3094.  Berry, Becky.  GRANDMA BERRY'S NINETY YEARS IN OKLAHOMA. *Chronicles of Oklahoma 1967 45(1): 58-67.* Mrs. H. H. Berry of Norman, Oklahoma, was born in Boggy Depot, Indian Territory, in 1875. Some of her ancestors were fullblooded Choctaw Indians who lived in Mississippi and Alabama 150 years ago. In this article by her granddaughter, Grandma Berry reminisces about life in early Oklahoma. She attended the Baptist school at Atoka, Indian Territory, in 1888 and graduated from Kidd-Key College in Sherman, Texas, in 1894. She married Houston Henry Berry in 1903. Three sons and two daughters attended the University of Oklahoma. 21 notes, biblio.

K. P. Davis

3095.  Blum, Eleanor.  MEMORIES OF A MISSISSIPPI CHILDHOOD. *Antioch R. 1965 25(2): 248-266.* An account of the author's life in Mississippi in the 1920's and early 1930's. She discusses the mores, education, culture, economics, and the Negro question as she experienced them.

D. F. Rossi

3096.  Bush, Robert.  CHARLES GAYARRÉ AND GRACE KING: LETTERS OF A LOUISIANA FRIENDSHIP. *Southern Literary J. 1974 7(1): 100-131.* Reprints 14 letters of Charles Gayarré, a Creole, and Grace King who learned a love of Louisiana history from him, and wrote several historical works on the subject.                                S

3097.  Campbell, Mrs. Paul M.  NORTH LOUISIANA HISTORICAL ASSOCIATION'S OLDEST MEMBER: "MISS LUCILE." *North Louisiana Hist. Assoc. J. 1975 6(3): 123-130.* "Miss Lucile" is 99-year-old Mrs. Robert Augustus Perryman (*nee* Melvill Lucile Martin) of Minden, Louisiana. She was born on Roslyn Plantation in the Flat Lick area of Claiborne Parish, one of several plantations owned by the Martin family. Describes her early years, her marriage on 16 August 1900 to Robert Augustus Perryman (1868-1930) of Coushatta, her son Robert Shelley Perryman, and her later years. Photo, 17 notes.

A. N. Garland

3098.  Cannon, Myrtle H. and Cloud, Bessie, eds.  BLIZZARD ON ONION CREEK, BY ROSE ANN HARPER. *Texana 1972 10(1): 45-50.* Rose Ann Harper reminisces about a central Texas blizzard in the mid-1860's as told to her granddaughters. Repeats actual conversations and tells about life on a sheep ranch during the storm. Fourteen-hundred sheep froze to death and were able to be shorn before they thawed.

J. E. Findling

3099.  Carson, W. G. B.  ANNE EWING LANE. *Missouri Hist. Soc. Bull. 1965 21(2): 87-99.* Life of Anne Ewing Lane, daughter of Dr. William Lane, first mayor of St. Louis. After being cured of spine trouble in 1830, Anne, with her sister Sarah, was educated in Philadelphia. After Sarah married in 1840, Anne traveled in Pennsylvania, New York, and New England. In 1852 her father was appointed Governor of New Mexico, and she visited Washington with him in 1853. A Southern sympathizer, she cared for sick sister's children from 1858. Describes the problems of Civil War St. Louis, and Anne's particular problem of a Unionist brother-in-law, William Glasgow. Mentions the years of travel and reconciliation during and after the war. Based on letters in the Missouri Historical Society's archives; 16 notes.    T. M. Condon

3100.  Carter, Deane G.  A PLACE IN HISTORY FOR ANN JAMES. *Arkansas Hist. Q. 1969 28(4): 309-323.* Recounts the work of Ann James (1813-1910), pioneer teacher, missionary worker, and founder of her own female seminary in northwest Arkansas in the 1840's. Photos, 18 notes.

B. A. Drummond

3101.  Clark, J. Stanley.  CAROLYN THOMAS FOREMAN. *Chronicles of Oklahoma 1968 45(4): 368-375.* Carolyn Thomas Foreman (1872-1967) was a historian of Oklahoma as well as an assistant to the career of her husband Grant as a historian. Author and coauthor of numerous books and articles, her principal contributions were a history of prestatehood printing and a study of Indians abroad. Mrs. Foreman also inspired the Indian-Pioneer History project that resulted in the compilation of some 90 bound volumes. Illus., biblio., note.

D. L. Smith

3102.  Darst, W. Maury, ed.  SEPTEMBER 8, 1900: AN ACCOUNT BY A MOTHER TO HER DAUGHTERS. *Southwestern Hist. Q. 1969 73(1): 56-82.* Reprints two letters which give an account of the confusion in Galveston after the destructive hurricane and 14-foot tidal wave of 8 September 1900. The two letters give news of the friends and acquaintances of the John Focke family. The hurricane was a major disaster in which about six thousand people lost their lives and most of Galveston was wrecked, with property damage estimated at more than 25 million dollars. Following the two letters are some photos of the destruction and of members of the John Focke family of Galveston.

R. W. Delaney

3103.  Debo, Angie.  A DEDICATION TO THE MEMORY OF CAROLYN THOMAS FOREMAN, 1872-1967. *Arizona and the West 1974 16(3): 214-218.* Carolyn Thomas was raised in the home of an Illinois congressman who became a federal judge in Indian Territory. She married Grant Foreman, a young law partner of her father. By the 1920's Foreman was well enough established to give up law. The Foremans devoted the rest of their lives to historical scholarship—collecting, research, and writing on Oklahoma and the Southwest. They produced more on the early history of Oklahoma, especially Indians, than all other scholars combined. Mrs. Foreman contributed articles to several journals, 87 to the *Chronicles of Oklahoma* alone, and wrote several books. Illus., biblio.

D. L. Smith

3104.  Everett, Mark R.  IN MEMORY OF ANNA LESS BROSIUS KORN. *Chronicles of Oklahoma 1966 44(2): 144-146.* Anna B. Korn died 12 October 1965 at the age of 96 and was buried in Hamilton, Missouri, where she was born. She wrote the state song for Missouri. She published a number of poems and wrote a state song for Oklahoma. An active clubwoman, she authored legislation establishing 16 November as Oklahoma Day. She was a director of the Oklahoma Historical Society and established the Oklahoma Memorial Association and Hall of Fame. Photo.

I. W. Van Noppen

3105.  Fischer, LeRoy H.  MURIEL H. WRIGHT, HISTORIAN OF OKLAHOMA. *Chronicles of Oklahoma 1974 52(1): 3-29.* A biographical account of Muriel Hazel Wright, Oklahoma teacher, historian, and editor, who is an active member of Choctaw tribal affairs. In her writings and lectures, she has emphasized the role of the Indian in Oklahoma and American history and culture. Wright also served as editor of *The Chronicles of Oklahoma*, 1955-73. Includes a bibliography of her works. Based on autobiographical notes and secondary sources; 6 photos, 27 notes.

N. J. Street

3106. Graham, Philip, ed. TEXAS MEMOIRS OF AMELIA E. BARR. *Southwestern Hist. Q. 1966 69(4): 473-498.* The Robert Barr family lived in Texas, 1857-67. Except for the last year in Galveston, their home was in Austin. Mrs. Amelia Edith Huddleston Barr (1831-1919) was later to become one of America's most prolific novelists. After her mother's death, daughter Lillie Barr Munroe (b. 1853) wrote a memoir, included here, describing their Texas years. Note.                    D. L. Smith

3107. Griffith, Lucille. ANNE ROYALL IN ALABAMA. *Alabama R. 1968 21(1): 53-63.* An account of author Anne Royall, born Anne Newport, who published several travel accounts during the first third of the 19th century, including *A Southern Tour* (1830-31), and *Letters from Alabama* (Washington, 1830). 24 notes.               D. F. Henderson

3108. Harris, Clyta Foster, ed. MEMORIES OF A PIONEER WIDOW. *Red River Valley Hist. R. 1975 2(2): 287-293.* An autobiographical sketch of Rebecca A. Foster, a pioneer in Johnson County, Arkansas, 1840's-60's.                    S

3109. Hartshorn, Merrill F. NOTES AND NEWS. *Social Educ. 1968 32(6): 583-588.* Presents an obituary of Myrtle Roberts, 1893-1968, a leader of social studies teachers in Texas, and news of the National Council for the Social Studies, 1967.                    S

3110. Hartwell, Joan M. MARGARET LEA OF ALABAMA, MRS. SAM HOUSTON. *Alabama R. 1964 17(4): 271-279.* Brief biographical sketch of Margaret Moffette Lea (1819-67), daughter of Temple and Nancy Lea of Marion, Alabama, wife of Sam Houston, president of the Republic and governor of the State of Texas.        D. F. Henderson

3111. Holding, Vera. A HERITAGE TO SHARE. *Chronicles of Oklahoma 1964 42(1): 2-6.* An epic account of the moving of the Cooke family to Custer County, Oklahoma, following the "run" into the Cheyenne-Arapaho country 19 April 1892. The narrative is told of Ida Cooke who traveled by covered wagon to cook for her father and brothers on the 14-day trip to their 160 acres and their 16 x 18-foot dugout with a sod roof. She attended school in a dugout house, but soon Mt. Olive Church was built of hewn logs. There Ida married Del Fancher and moved to his half-dugout of split logs chinked with mud. The earth floor was covered with braided rugs and Indian blankets. A photograph shows Ida Fancher with four generations of her descendants.
                    I. W. Van Noppen

3112. Holway, Hope. LUCIA LOOMIS FERGUSON (MRS. WALTER FERGUSON) 1886-1962. *Chronicles of Oklahoma 1963 41(4): 365-369.* A memorial tribute to Lucia Loomis Ferguson, editor of the weekly *Cherokee Republican* and author of the "Woman's View" and "Lucia Loomis" columns for the Scripps-Howard newspapers. Tribute is also paid to Mrs. Ferguson as a public-spirited citizen.
                    I. W. Van Noppen

3113. Houchens, Mariam S. CORDIA GREER-PETRIE AND "ANGELINE AT THE SEELBACH." *Southern Folklore Q. 1965 29(2): 164-168.* Cordia Greer-Petrie died in Louisville in 1964 at the age of 92. She lived in several communities of eastern Kentucky in the early 1900's; her first book, *Angeline at the Seelbach,* published in 1921, has gone through 26 editions. It captures the manners, speech and folklore of that area and era.                    H. Aptheker

3114. Jensen, Mrs. Dana O. THE JOURNAL OF SALLIE D. SMITH. *Missouri Hist. Soc. Bull. 1964 20(2): 124-145.* Extracts from the diary of a 19-year-old young lady describing her trip from Missouri to visit in Kentucky between June and October 1868. Included are descriptions of steamboat travel and general domestic life.
                    R. J. Hanks

3115. Johnson, Mary Tabb. "PAGES FROM A NINETEENTH-CENTURY ALBUM." *Alabama Hist. Q. 1972 34(3/4): 228-233.* Reproduces two poems from an autograph album of Sarah Gayle, daughter of Alabama Governor John Gayle. The first is a depressing poem by Albert A. Muller, minister of the Tuscaloosa, Alabama, Episcopal Church, probably written in 1834-35. The second is a reply to the first by A. B. Meek, dated 1835. Meek was editor of the short-lived magazine, *The Southern.* 12 notes.                    E. E. Eminhizer

3116. Jones, Virginia K., ed. THE JOURNAL OF SARAH G. FOLLANSBEE. *Alabama Hist. Q. 1965 27(34): 213-258.* The journal, which begins in 1859 when Miss Follansbee moved to Alabama as a teacher and continues to 1871, contains descriptions of people, cost of goods, and conditions during the Civil War and after.
                    E. E. Eminhizer

3117. King, C. Richard. MARGARET BORLAND. *Texana 1972 10(4): 321-327.* Discusses Margaret Borland's life, which spanned the middle of the 19th century and which was chiefly notable for Mrs. Borland's success as a horse trader.

3118. Lawlor, Virginia G. "I, MARY MORRISS SMITH, DO.... " *Tennessee Hist. Q. 1970 29(1): 79-87.* The Tennessee State Library and Archives recently acquired the manuscript recollections of early Tennessee life by Mary Morriss Smith, who arrived in Wilson County in 1812. The manuscripts, several pages of which are reproduced, were written in the 1890's, and contain descriptions of terrain, camp meetings, schools, life-styles, and crops. Mentions numerous names of interest to genealogists. 6 notes.                    M. B. Lucas

3119. Lawrence, Stephen S. TULIP GROVE: NEIGHBOR TO THE HERMITAGE. *Tennessee Hist. Q. 1967 26(1): 3-22.* A history of the original and last owners of the building traces the acquisition of the land and the conditions of its inheritance by Andrew Jackson Donelson. The services of Donelson and his wife to his uncle Andrew Jackson and the strife over Peggy Eaton are discussed. The building of Tulip Grove (1834-36), the death of Donelson's first wife and his second marriage, his diplomatic experiences in Texas and Prussia, and his unsuccessful campaign for the vice presidency are surveyed. The author concludes with a history of the later owners of Tulip Grove and its restoration and maintenance by the Ladies' Hermitage Association. Based mostly on secondary sources; illus., 15 notes.                    C. F. Ogilvie

3120. Leeper, Kate D. A MINOR PLANET,.... *Tennessee Hist. Q. 1973 32(4): 355-359.* Sketches the story of a Tennessee astronomer's wife, Rhoda Calvert Barnard, and the planetoid that was named after her in 1921.                    S

3121. Lehman, Leola. LIFE IN THE TERRITORIES. *Chronicles of Oklahoma 1963 41(4): 370-381.* A graphic account of the life of the author's mother in the Oklahoma and Indian Territories, and in the Oklahoma Panhandle where, at Nabisco, the family lived in a dugout. The neighbors were friendly and cooperative. A farmers' union was organized and a flour mill built. 4 illus.                    I. W. Van Noppen

3122. Lewis, Willard M. FROM BUTTERMILK TO GUM LOG.... *Am. Educ. 1967 3(6): 8-11.* Discusses the services provided by the Arkansas River Valley Regional Library for residents of seven counties located in the remote Ozark foothills. Books were supplied to Head Start, Work-Study, Day Care Centers, VISTA, and Home Management Aides programs sponsored by the Office of Economic Opportunity. After meeting with initial reticence, the project eventually gained enthusiastic approval. "Along with prodding the deprived families to read, the aides offered practical advice and help in how to alter clothing, and how to preserve foods, and how to prepare meals with surplus commodities." 6 photos.
                    W. R. Boedecker

3123. Liggin, Edna. BERTHA PORTER BURNS—FROM THE NORTH CORNER OF SHILOH. *North Louisiana Hist. Assoc. J. 1975 6(2):81-84.* Bertha Porter Burns was born north of Shiloh on 24 October 1884. In 1974, she was the "living widow of the late M. V. Burns, country preacher . . . mother to six children" with "the courage to live alone in her house in Bernice." She taught school at Mt. Sterling, Salem, and Mt. Patrick, all Baptist church-schoolhouses, and married the Reverend Marion Van Burns on 5 December 1905. They lived first in Oakland (Louisiana) and then in Shiloh, before moving to Bernice in 1922. "Generously and courageously, Bertha Burns shared with countless people the life of her husband." He died on 7 August 1965. 2 photos.
                    A. N. Garland

3124. Liggin, Edna. CATHERINE COOK MABRY: MOTHER OF TWELVE, FROM THE WEST CORNER OF SHILOH. *North Louisiana Hist. Assoc. J. 1975 7(1): 23-25.* William Pierce Mabry and Catherine Cook were married in Alabama and lived for a time at Muscle Shoals, across the Dog River. They moved to Louisiana with two children and settled first at Patton Town, near present-day Lisbon. Later they moved to a farm about a mile northwest of the present town of Bernice and 10 more children were born to them; in all, they had 10 boys and 2 girls. In 1885, William Mabry was killed by bullets fired by four concealed gunmen. The four were captured and brought to trial, during which they claimed they had shot the wrong man. Catherine Cook Mabry continued to operate the farm and remained active until she was quite old. All except one of her children lived to be over 80 years of age. She eventually sold the farm and spent her remaining years with her children and grandchildren. Photo.                                        A. N. Garland

3125. Liggin, Edna. MARGARET FULLER ELAM, SOLDIER'S DAUGHTER: FROM THE SOUTH CORNER OF SHILOH. *North Louisiana Assoc. J. 1975 6(4): 175-177.* Margaret Fuller Elam, now 100 years old, blind, and living in a nursing home in Bernice, was born 3 February 1874 "across Middlefork Creek, south of Shiloh." As a young girl she worked on her father's farm and during the summer went to Fellowship Church School. She married Henry Clay Elam, of Missouri, and bore four children, two of whom died at early ages. Her father, Alf Fuller, became famous as a Civil War veteran and was the last surviving veteran of the Civil War in Lincoln Parish. Margaret Fuller Elam has been a member of the Fellowship Baptist Church for 87 years. Photo.                                        A. N. Garland

3126. Liggin, Edna. MARGIE HEARD LAURENCE, LIVING LINK WITH TWO GOVERNORS. *North Louisiana Hist. Assoc. J. 1974 5(2): 58-66.* Mrs. Margie Heard Laurence is related to two former Louisiana governors, William Wright Heard (1900-04) and Ruffin G. Pleasant (1916-20), both born near the Union Parish town of Shiloh. Although it has been decades since Mrs. Laurence left Shiloh, she has many pictures, mementoes, and clippings of the family history. Based on a personal interview and primary sources; 2 photos.

A. N. Garland

3127. Liggin, Edna. MARY EDMUNDS TABOR LEE—FROM THE EAST CORNER OF SHILOH. *North Louisiana Hist. Assoc. J. 1975 6(3): 133-135.* Mary Edmunds Tabor Lee was born in Georgia but moved with her family to settle in Union Parish, west of Farmerville, in the 1840's. On 4 December 1852, 15-year-old Mary married George Tabor, and they lived in a house on property given them by her father some three miles east of Shiloh. They had five children during 1852-61, when George went off to war. He died, apparently in 1863, in Holly Springs, Mississippi. Mary married Dan Lee, about whom little is known, in 1866; he disappeared in 1871, after having fathered three children. From time to time thereafter Mary was "involved in litigation that complicated her life." She never married again and eventually "gained a reputation as a 'medicine woman,' and was sent for wherever there was sickness." Mary died 22 January 1926 and was buried at Shiloh.

A. N. Garland

3128. Lucas, Robert C. and Gilstrap, Lucille. HOMESTEADING THE STRIP. *Chronicles of Oklahoma 1973 51(3): 285-308.* Personal account of a homesteading family from 1889 to 1903 in the Cherokee Outlet in Indian Territory.                                        S

3129. McGinty, Garnie W. THE HEARTACHES OF A SLAVE OWNER'S WIFE. *North Louisiana Hist. Assoc. J. 1973 5(1): 14-18.* Dempsey Hall died in 1854. Lists the inventory and appraisal of the Hall slaves and property made in February 1861; "a partition in kind could be made of the slaves." Only one of the five Hall boys survived the Civil War; previously, four Hall children had died at early ages. The only survivor among the nine children, Henry Johniken Hall, lived until 1915. The widowed Mariah M. Hall lived until a month before her 78th birthday, in 1891. "During her last twenty-six years she was alone except for one son . . . and had to experience the adjustment to widowhood, the war, along with the memory of four sons sacrificed in the conflict." Photo, 11 notes.                                        A. N. Garland

3130. McGinty, Garnie W. MARY JANE CONLY LESHE: PIONEER WOMAN OF BIENVILLE PARISH (1849-1932). *North Louisiana Hist. Assoc. J. 1976 7(2): 61-63.* Mary Jane Conly was the third child of Cullen Thomas Conly, of Savannah, Georgia. When she was

about 20 she married Usir Leshe (1839-1934) and moved with him to Bienville Parish. She bore 14 children; one died in infancy, 13 reached adulthood. "The Leshe family were fervent patriots" and Mary Jane Leshe promoted "education and patriotism, instilling frugality, thrift, and industry in her descendants." She was a "deeply religious woman" and "a loyal and devoted member of the Baptist Church." Photo, 4 notes.

A. N. Garland

3131. Nielsen, George R., ed. LYDIA ANN MC HENRY AND REVOLUTIONARY TEXAS. *Southwestern Hist. Q. 1971 74(3): 393-408.* Miss McHenry migrated to Texas in 1833 with her sister and brother-in-law who was an itinerant Methodist preacher. She is known for nurturing Methodism in Mexican Texas and, with her sister, opening the first school. Five of her letters (part of a larger collection) to her brother, John Hardin McHenry, in Kentucky, dating from 1835 to 1836, here published for the first time, reveal conditions in Austin's colony and Texas during the period of the Texas Revolution. 33 notes.

R. V. Ritter

3132. Oneal, Marion S. GROWING UP IN NEW ORLEANS: MEMORIES OF THE 1890'S. *Louisiana Hist. 1964 5(1): 75-86.* Gives first-hand impressions of various everyday incidents in New Orleans which she witnessed as a young woman in the 1890's. She describes Sunday afternoon activities, a tour of Frenchtown, construction of a church, river-front activities, and domestic chores.            D. C. James

3133. Oneal, Marion S. A SCHOOL MA'AM IN LOUISIANA'S PINEY WOODS, 1902-1903. *Louisiana Hist. 1964 5(2): 135-142.* Reminisces on several aspects of everyday life at Hill Switch in 1902-03. Mrs. Oneal was teaching at the time near this small sawmill town in the piney-woods region of Louisiana above Lake Pontchartrain. Emphasis is on the local "hard-shell Baptist" church which she attended.

D. C. James

3134. Patty, James S. A WOMAN JOURNALIST IN RECONSTRUCTION LOUISIANA: MRS. MARY E. BRYAN. *Louisiana Studies 1964 3(1): 77-104.* A survey of the writings of Mrs. Mary E. Bryan (1842-1913) who was born in Florida, spent her childhood in Georgia, but lived in Louisiana for the greater part of two decades (1854-74). The multivarious subjects she wrote about; her observations and attitudes are stimulating and enlightening. A reading of her writings opens up new avenues for study even though it would be most difficult to draw any general conclusions regarding her philosophy, attitudes, and rank as a literary figure.                                        G. W. McGinty

3135. Powell, Lawrence Clark. LETTER FROM THE SOUTHWEST. *Westways 1975 67(3): 18-21.* Notes several citizens—librarian Maud Sullivan, humanist C. L. Sonnichsen, writer Tom Lea, printer Carl Hertzog, and illustrator Jose Cisneros—who have helped make El Paso a center of Southwest culture.                                        S

3136. Ragland, H. D. THE DIARY OF MRS. ANNA S. WOOD: TRIP TO THE OPENING OF THE CHEROKEE OUTLET IN 1893. *Chronicles of Oklahoma 1972 50(3): 307-325.* Tells of pioneer life in Oklahoma.                                        S

3137. Rothrock, Mary U., ed. FAMILY LETTERS: HOME LIFE IN CARROLL AND GIBSON COUNTIES, TENNESSEE, 1868. *West Tennessee Hist. Soc. Papers 1971 (25): 107-134.* Presents letters written during June 1-December 31, 1868, by members of the William Woods Herron family to Utopia Herron, a student and then an instructor at Synodical Female College, Florence, Alabama. The letters discuss the response of the family to the election of Ulysses S. Grant as President and the closeness of the Herron family. During this time the family moved from its home in South Carroll to near Trenton, Tennessee. The letters provide insights into southern family life and attitudes in the immediate postbellum era. 3 notes.                                        H. M. Parker, Jr.

3138. Rothrock, Mary U., ed. FAMILY LETTERS: HOME LIFE IN GIBSON COUNTY, TENNESSEE, JANUARY-JUNE, 1869. *West Tennessee Hist. Soc. Papers 1972 (26): 94-130.* Presents letters written to Utopia Herron, a teacher at the Synodical Female College, Florence, Alabama, by members of her family. Give insights into the Presbyterian views, social life, and school life of brother John Herron.

Letters also reveal the dearness of family life in this post-War period. 5 notes.
H. M. Parker, Jr.

3139. Rothrock, Mary U., ed. FAMILY LETTERS: HOME LIFE IN MADISON AND CARROLL COUNTIES, TENNESSEE, 1868. *West Tennessee Hist. Soc. Papers 1970 24: 106-129.* Presents the Herron family letters. Most of the letters center around nineteen-year-old Utopia Herron who was attending the Florence Synodical Female College at Florence, Alabama, January to May, 1868. Reveals the life and mind of a female college student in this period as well as the close relationship between the family and Utopia. 2 notes.
H. M. Parker, Jr.

3140. Rothrock, Mary U., ed. FAMILY LETTERS: HOME LIFE IN MADISON AND CARROLL COUNTIES, TENNESSEE, 1864-1867. *West Tennessee Hist. Soc. Papers 1969 23: 110-129.* Presents letters of the children of the W. W. Herron family of West Tennessee written to a daughter, Utopia, who was a student at the Memphis Conference Female Institute and the Florence Synodical Female college. Gives glimpses into the home life and social conditions in rural West Tennessee immediately after the Civil War and provides insights into female college life, particularly the curriculum and boarding facilities. Reveals a close, warm relationship between the eight children of the Herron family. Most letters were written during November and December, 1867. 5 notes.
H. M. Parker, Jr.

3141. Shirk, Lucyl A. MURIEL H. WRIGHT: A LEGEND. *Chronicles of Oklahoma 1975 53(3): 397-399.* Obituary of Muriel Hazel Wright, 1889-1975, member of the Board of Directors of the Oklahoma Historical Society.

3142. Smith, Goldie C. GEORGIA'S GIFT TO TEXAS: THE LONE STAR FLAG. *Georgia R. 1965 19(1): 60-67.* The Lone Star Flag was made by Joanna Troutman, an 18-year-old Georgia girl, in 1835. Gives some military history connected with the history of the flag. Undocumented.
H. G. Earnhart

3143. Smith, James M. THOMAS HUXLEY IN NASHVILLE. *Tennessee Hist. Q. 1974 33(2): 191-203; (3): 322-341.* Part I. In September of 1876, Thomas Huxley arrived in Nashville for a visit with his sister, Lizzie Huxley Scott, who was living in the city. Though an attempt was made to make the visit a quiet one, news of Huxley's visit was voiced around Nashville, creating great interest. The Nashville Huxley visited was one in which the intellectual community still looked to England and Europe for cultural leadership. Secondary sources; 3 notes. Part II. Thomas Huxley's trip to Tennessee in 1876, originally intended as a vacation with his sister, Lizzie Huxley Scott, virtually became an official visit to Nashville. A meeting with the governor was followed by meetings with the Superintendent of Instruction and the Commissioner of Agriculture, as well as visits to the State Library, Fisk University, and Vanderbilt University. Leading citizens then called upon Huxley, and he agreed to deliver his first public lecture in America. Secondary sources; 36 notes.
M. B. Lucas

3144. Thompson, Lawrence S. MARRIAGE AND COURTSHIP CUSTOMS IN THE OHIO VALLEY. *Kentucky Folklore Record 1963 9(3): 47-50.* A list of regional marriage customs and beliefs supplementing those published in Daniel and Lucy Thomas, *Kentucky Superstitions* (Princeton: Princeton U. Press, 1920). 10 notes.
J. C. Crowe

3145. Voorhies, Edward. PASSENGER ON HISTORY-MAKING EXCURSION TRAIN OF EIGHTY-THREE YEARS AGO RETROSPECTS. *Louisiana Hist. 1965 6(3): 307-311.* Reminiscences of Mary Mamie Murphy, last survivor of a history-making (Southern Pacific) train excursion from New Orleans to St. Martinville, Louisiana, in May 1882. This was the first, long-awaited train. A year later, the little girl came to St. Martinville to live. She recalls in letters to Mr. Voorhies aspects of social life including a shocking double murder, balls and theatrical performances, the first horse-drawn fire wagon, children's amusements, and neighborliness. 2 notes.
E. P. Stickney

3146. Webb, Allie Bayne. EARLY DAYS IN LOUISIANA: SKETCHES OF THE LAND AND THE PEOPLE. *North Louisiana Hist. Assoc. J. 1972 3(2): 35-38.* Discusses the writings of several individ-

uals who worked and traveled in north Louisiana from the early 1600's to the mid-1800's. The individuals include Father du Poisson, an early French Jesuit; Dr. John Sibley, (1757-1837) an Indian agent to the Caddo Indians; Charles Caesar Robin, a French scientist who "came to North Louisiana in 1802;" Amelia Murray; Frederick Law Olmstead; and William Dunbar (1749-1810). While many "persons recorded impressions of Indians and slaves, only a few described the free Negroes, that colony of 'Redbones' living at Isle Brevel near Natchitoches." Map, 26 notes.
A. N. Garland

3147. Welsh, Jack. THE BELL WITCH. *Kentucky Folklore Record 1973 19(4): 112-116.* Stories of Kate Bell, a witch in 19th-century Tennessee.
S

3148. Woodson, Mary Willis. MY RECOLLECTIONS OF FRANKFORT. *Register of the Kentucky Hist. Soc. 1963 61(3): 193-213.* Born Mary Willis Rennick, "Aunt Willie" wrote her reminiscences, published here from the manuscript in the Archives of the Kentucky Historical Society.
E. P. Stickney

# West

3149. Adams, Donald K., ed. THE JOURNAL OF ADA A. VOGDES, 1868-1871. *Montana: Mag. of Hist. 1963 13(3): 2-17.* A young army wife relates the experiences and sensations encountered during residence at Fort Laramie and Fort Fetterman, deep in the country of hostile Indians. The observations of this sensitive white woman on such matters as Indian dress and behavior, and primitive social life at these remote posts, are stressed in these selections from the original diary which is held in the Henry H. Huntington Library.
L. G. Nelson

3150. Allison, Elsie North. A ONE-ROOM SCHOOL IN LABETTE COUNTY. *Kansas Q. 1976 8(2): 5-10.* Reflections of a retired schoolteacher on the contrast between large city classrooms and her own rural education in a one-room, country schoolhouse in Kansas during the 1880's-90's.

3151. Barnes, Lela, ed. NORTH CENTRAL KANSAS IN 1887-1889. FROM THE LETTERS OF LESLIE AND SUSAN SNOW OF JUNCTION CITY - CONCLUDED. *Kansas Hist. Q. 1963 29(4): 372-428.* Continued from 1963 29(3): 267-323. The concluding section contains letters written between 24 June 1888 and 27 May 1889. The first group consists of letters written by Leslie Snow to his sweetheart from such towns as Mankato, Hastings, Salem, Concordia, Glenn Elder, Council Grove, Cawker City, Abilene, and from his principal base of operations in Junction City. The letters are filled with descriptions of his own feelings, local news, and general observations on his job with the U.S. Bureau of Pensions. On 4 December Susan Currier Snow wrote her first letter to her parents from her new home in Junction City. Her letters are filled with general comments on life in the West and careful descriptions of her own daily experiences.
W. F. Zornow

3152. Beebe, Lucius. THE INDESTRUCTIBLE MRS. BROWN. *Am. West 1966 3(2): 48-53, 93-95.* "The Unsinkable Mrs. Brown," heroine of the *Titanic*, was Margaret Tobin Brown, wife of James J. Brown, a hard-rock miner whose employer gave him a substantial share in a Colorado mining venture that struck it rich. With the looks, charm, and culture of "an Irish washerwoman," Mrs. Brown was unable to buy her way into Denver's formal society. Her preposterous taste for furs, for example, earned her the name of "Colorado's unique fur-bearing animal." Her return on the *Titanic* from a tour abroad to seek recognition in Europe's less exclusive spas catapulted her into the limelight. She was, on that occasion, a veritable "heroine of a disaster." Her insatiable desire for attention after that "personified the essence of corn" and gained her no greater fame than that of an international eccentric. Appended with an autobiographical assessment of Lucius Beebe from the San Francisco *Chronicle,* 13 February 1966, and a Beebe vita; illus.
D. L. Smith

3153. Bern, Enid. THE ENCHANTED YEARS ON THE PRAIRIES. *North Dakota Hist. 1973 40(4): 5-19.* The author gives personal reminiscences of her childhood as a homesteader in Hettinger County,

North Dakota, 1907-12. Describes daily life, schooling, the personalities of other settlers, and the hazards and insecurities of life on the prairie from a child's point of view. 13 photos.

3154. Bowie, Nancy. CLOUD CITY CAMEO. *Westways 1976 68(5): 18-21, 79.* Horace A. W. Tabor, an investor in silver mining in Leadville, Colorado, 1877-93, used his wealth to develop the town, build its opera house, divorce his wife, and marry Elizabeth McCourt "Baby Doe"; both died in poverty.

3155. Brown, Mabel E. LADY FROM LEBANON: THE STORY OF MARY FARAH. *Bits and Pieces 1972 8(4): 1-7.* Biography of Mary Farah of Newcastle, Wyoming.                                    S

3156. Cannon, Helen. FIRST LADIES OF COLORADO. REBECCA HILL EATON. *Colorado Mag. 1965 42(1): 37-45.* Biographical sketch of Mrs. Benjamin Harrison Eaton whose husband was governor of Colorado, 1885-87.                          I. W. Van Noppen

3157. Cannon, Helen. FIRST LADIES OF COLORADO: JANE OLIVIA BARNES COOPER. *Colorado Mag. 1967 44(2): 129-138.* One of a series of biographical sketches of Colorado's first ladies, this one deals with the wife of the sixth Governor, 1889-1891. Of New England parentage (her father was a Congregational minister and an abolitionist), Jane Olivia was born in Ohio, graduated from Rockford Seminary, and married a lawyer, Job Adams Cooper. The family moved to Colorado and prospered. Mrs. Cooper was active in charitable and philanthropic organizations all of her life, an energetic and tireless woman. Mr. Cooper gave the land for the campus of Colorado Woman's College. The Craig Rehabilitation Hospital, a sanitarium for the treatment of tuberculosis, was Mrs. Cooper's crowning achievement. 4 illus., 37 notes.
                                                        I. W. Van Noppen

3158. Cannon, Helen. FIRST LADIES OF COLORADO: ELLA NYE ADAMS. *Colorado Mag. 1966 43(2): 121-131.* Of English ancestry, born in Bangor, Maine, Ella Charlotte Nye married Alva Adams, governor of Colorado for three terms during the period 1887-1905. Ella continued to be socially active until her death in 1931.
                                                        I. W. Van Noppen

3159. Cannon, Helen. FIRST LADIES OF COLORADO: NELLIE MARTIN ORMAN. *Colorado Mag. 1973 50(1): 57-65.* Biography of Mrs. Orman (1858-1918), the wife of James Bradley Orman, governor of Colorado 1901-03. Married to Orman in 1876, she lived most of her life in Pueblo. She was a kind, philanthropic activist who loved to entertain.
                                                        O. H. Zabel

3160. Chapman, B. B. THE LAND RUN OF 1893, AS SEEN AT KIOWA. *Kansas Hist. Q. 1965 31(1): 67-75.* Cordelia Rumsey was at Kiowa on 16 September 1893 and witnessed the land run into the Cherokee Outlet. On 18 September she wrote a letter to her son in which she described the events from 10 September, when men began to assemble along the line until the rush began. She insisted the signal for the rush was premature and suggested that her husband was prepared to give testimony to that effect, if action were taken against the soldiers.
                                                        W. F. Zornow

3161. Clark, Edith K. O. THE DIARY OF EDITH K. O. CLARK. *Ann. of Wyoming 1967 39(2): 217-244.* Presents a verbatim printing of the diary kept by Miss Edith K. O. Clark during the summers of 1933 and 1934. A former teacher and Wyoming State Superintendent of Public Instruction, she recorded her impressions while building a log cabin near Buffalo, Wyoming. Her diary includes descriptions of logging, scenery, weather, wild life, and forest fire. Illus.           R. L. Nichols

3162. Dalziel, Hazel Webb. THE WAY IT WAS. *Colorado Mag. 1968 45(2): 101-119.* A nostalgic but perceptive reminiscence about farm life in the last decade of the 19th century in Weld County, Colorado. The author describes the daily tasks, joys, and sorrows of an age now gone forever. Her descriptions of rural home life - sans plumbing, electricity, central heating, and other conveniences now taken for granted - present a valuable commentary on "the way it was." 2 notes.
                                                        O. H. Zabel

3163. DeLapp, Mary. PIONEER WOMAN NATURALIST. *Colorado Q. 1964 13(1): 91-96.* The story of Martha Maxwell (1831-81), Colorado naturalist of the 1860's, who is credited with being the first taxidermist to place animals and birds in their natural settings.
                                                        A. Zilversmit

3164. Ellis, Bruce T. LINCOLN COUNTY POSTSCRIPT: NOTES ON ROBERT A. WIDENMANN BY HIS DAUGHTER, ELSIE WIDENMAN. *New Mexico Hist. R. 1975 50(3): 213-230.* Material relating to New Mexico's "Lincoln County War" is scanty and often controversial. The exact role of Robert Adolph Widenmann in the war is obscure, even though there are many letters, reports, and court depositions available. There has been much speculation concerning the relations of Widenmann and John Henry Tunstall, who were associated in business for some time. Tunstall was killed at the beginning of what is known as the Lincoln County War, and in his letters stated that Widenmann was obstinate and contrary. 37 notes.                          J. H. Krenkel

3165. Ellsworth, S. George. UTAH'S STRUGGLE FOR STATEHOOD. *Utah Hist. Q. 1963 31(3): 60-69.* In this address, delivered at the statehood celebration, 4 January 1963, at Salt Lake City, Utah, the author reviewed "the trials and persecutions and troublous times" of the half century antecedent to Utah's attainment of statehood. Chief subjects of the address were the struggles between the Mormons and settlers of other religious beliefs, the acts of Congress intended to suppress polygamy, and the capitulation by the Mormons beginning in 1890 to the demands that they end polygamy, with the result that Utah was admitted to statehood in 1896. The address concluded that "Accommodation by the people of Utah to the norms of American society yielded enormous dividends..."                                    S. L. Jones

3166. Fierman, Floyd S. and West, James O. BILLY THE KID, THE COWBOY OUTLAW: AN INCIDENT RECALLED BY FLORA SPIEGELBERG. *Am. Jewish Hist. Q. 1965 65(1): 98-106.* An incident, recalled by Mrs. Flora Spiegelberg in her old age, involving Billy the Kid's ambush of a stagecoach and his duping by one of the women passengers. The story is analyzed as to the common folkloristic elements present which would lead one to wonder about the veracity of the details remembered by the elderly woman. Both story and analysis are documented.
                                                        F. Rosenthal

3167. Fleckenstein, Opal. FIRST YEARS IN KANSAS. *Organon 1970 2(1): 11-18.* Describes life on the Kansas plains during the 1880's. Details life in the family home, the simple fare, the dangers of prairie fires, the incidence of blizzards, and the search for fuel. Money was scarce among these simple but proud people. The sod house school was a focal point in local affairs. Classes were held irregularly, but the school building served as a gathering place for social functions and other meetings. Undocumented.                                    P. W. Kennedy

3168. Gambone, Joseph G., ed. THE FORGOTTEN FEMINIST OF KANSAS: THE PAPERS OF CLARINA I. H. NICHOLS, 1854-1885. *Kansas Hist. Q. 1973 39(3): 392-444, 39(4): 515-563, 1974 40(1): 72-135, (2): 241-292, (3): 410-459, (4): 503-562.* Continued from a previous article. Part III. After returning to Kansas from the East in 1857, Mrs. Nichols became associate editor of the *Quindaro Chindowan,* a weekly Free-State journal. Her editorials are reprinted here. Giving up this position, Mrs. Nichols resumed her voluminous correspondence with prominent persons about the territorial strife in Kansas. In numerous letters to Susan B. Anthony she continued her discussion of antifeminism both in Kansas and in the nation as a whole. 142 notes. Part IV. Covers letters written during the late 1860's to the editors of the *Vermont Phoenix,* Wyandotte *Commerical Gazette,* and *Western Home Journal,* in which Mrs. Nichols discusses the status of women in Kansas and what might be done to improve their lot. She wrote at great length against the views of Rev. Eben Blachly, mustering an array of scriptural proof against his assertion that God had intended women to be inferior beings. 6 illus., 110 notes. Part V. In letters written from Wyandotte to the editors of the Topeka *Weekly Leader,* the *Kansas Daily Commonwealth,* and the *Vermont Phoenix,* Mrs. Nichols offers evidence to show that the women of Kansas did not enjoy their constitutional rights, contrary to a misconception apparently widely held in Kansas and other states at the time. She reviews scriptural evidence of the inferiority of women and again concludes that the Bible has been misinterpreted by men. She also elaborates on the ways in which homestead legislation worked to married women's disadvantage. Based on primary and secondary sources; illus., 77 notes. Part VI. Reproduces 1870-72 letters by Mrs. Nichols. From Potter Valley, California, in 1872 she described the daily life of immigrants around San Francisco. 71 notes. Part VII. Reprints more letters, 1873-80. Part VIII. Reprints letters from Mrs. Nichols' correspondence, 1881-85.

W. F. Zornow and S

3169. Hargreaves, Mary W. M. HOMESTEADING AND HOME-MAKING ON THE PLAINS: A REVIEW. *Agric. Hist. 1973 47(2): 156-163.* Reviews three books about 20th-century homesteading on the northern Great Plains: Faye Cashatt Lewis' *Nothing to Make a Shadow* (Ames: Iowa State U. Press, 1972), Sarah Ellen Roberts' *Alberta Homestead: Chronicle of a Pioneer Family,* ed. Lanthrop E. Roberts (Austin: U. of Texas Press, 1971), and Walker D. Wyman's *Frontier Woman: the Life of a Woman Homesteader on the Dakota Frontier, Retold from the Original Notes and Letters of Grace Fairchild* (1972). 12 notes.

D. E. Brewster

3170. Hargreaves, Mary W. M. WOMEN IN THE AGRICULTURAL SETTLEMENT OF THE NORTHERN PLAINS. *Agric. Hist. 1976 50(1): 179-189.* The few women on the plains in the early days enjoyed a relatively high status. Their hardships included loneliness, fear, illness, and rude surroundings. Modern conveniences came later to the plains than elsewhere, but women who did not mind hardship could adapt to western life. 39 notes. D. E. Bowers

3171. Johnson, Dorothy M. CAREFREE YOUTH AND DUDES IN GLACIER. *Montana: Mag. of Western Hist. 1975 25(3): 48-59.* Reminiscences of Glacier National Park since 1916 as recalled by a girl from the vicinity. She met some noted personalities, including Irvin S. Cobb, Mary Roberts Rinehart, and Charles M. Russell. Illus.

S. R. Davison

3172. Johnson, Dorothy M. THE FOREIGNERS. *Montana: Mag. of Western Hist. 1976 26(3): 62-67.* Recollections of childhood experiences with non-English speaking neighbors in Montana towns in the era before World War I. Human warmth overcame difficulties in communication and differences in life-styles. S. R. Davison

3173. Johnson, Dorothy M. THE SAFE AND EASY WAY TO ADVENTURE. *Montana: Mag. of Western Hist. 1974 24(3): 81-86.* Reminisces about childhood and early interest in writing. Even when she was employed elsewhere, the author's interest in the West prevailed. She wrote many short stories and books with themes related to Indians, cowboys, and other frontier types. S. R. Davison

3174. Johnson, Dorothy M. THE SMALL-TOWN WORLD BEFORE RADIO. *Montana: Mag. of Western Hist. 1974 24(2): 44-53.* Personal reminiscences of juvenile life in Whitefish, Montana, after World War I. S. R. Davison

3175. Johnson, Dorothy M. WHEN THE PREACHER KEPT A COW. *Montana: Mag. of Western Hist. 1976 26(2): 32-41.* The author reminiscences about her childhood in Whitefish, Montana in 1915, detailing small-town interest in gardens, cows, and chickens. Nostalgic reflections mingle with contrasting descriptions of modern conditions. One of a series of personal recollections. S. R. Davison

3176. Judge, Frances. CARRIE AND THE GRAND TETONS. *Montana: Mag. of Western Hist. 1968 18(3): 44-57.* Presents the reminiscences of a woman who had witnessed homesteading in the Jackson Hole area of Wyoming in the late 1890's, when she was about 10 years old. Included is biographical material about three generations of women—Carrie Nesbitt Dunn (the principal narrator), her mother, and her daughter who writes the supporting account. Illustrations are family photographs and portraits. S. R. Davison

3177. Keleher, W. A. ERNA MARY FERGUSSON, 1888-1964. *New Mexico Hist. R. 1964 39(4): 345-350.* Address delivered 1 August 1964 at the memorial services for Miss Fergusson, author of *Dancing Gods* (1931), *Fiesta in Mexico* (1934), *New Mexico, A Pageant of Three Peoples* (1951), and several other books on the Southwest and Latin America. D. F. Henderson

3178. King, James T., ed. FORT MC PHERSON IN 1870: A NOTE BY AN ARMY WIFE. *Nebraska Hist. 1964 45(1): 99-107.* Reminiscences written in 1910 by Mary Magwire Carr, wife of Brevet Major General Eugene A. Carr, of the two years she spent at Fort McPherson, Nebraska from October 1869 to November 1871. R. Lowitt

3179. Lamb, Helen Keithley. THE FLOOD OF 1951. *Kansas Q. 1976 8(2): 65-70.* A letter, written following the great flood of July 1951 in Manhattan, Kansas, describing the danger and hardship of the evacuation of 6,000 people, the extensive water damage, and the difficulties in cleanup after the water receded.

3180. Larson, T. A. WOMEN'S ROLE IN THE AMERICAN WEST. *Montana: Mag. of Western Hist. 1974 24(3): 2-11.* Analyzes women's part in settling the West, showing that their contribution was greater than is usually indicated in textbooks and general histories. Census figures and other statistics provide data on presence and distribution of females in the West of the 19th century. Illus., 40 notes.

S. R. Davison

3181. Lassila, Jean, ed. LIFE IN NATRONA COUNTY, 1899 TO 1900—RECOLLECTIONS OF MYRTLE CHALFANT GREGG. *Ann. of Wyoming 1974 46(1): 113-122.* Personal recollections tracing the three-week journey of the Chalfant family from Howard County, Nebraska, to relatives' homesteads near Casper, Wyoming. The family turned the 600-mile trip into a tourist outing. Their memories of Casper and its surrounding area during 1899 are included. One daughter, Myrtle Chalfant, remained in Casper and married a local rancher in January 1901. She recounts the stories of friends, ranch life, and a visit to the 1903 State Industrial Convention. M. L. Tate

3182. Mahoney, Donald, ed. END OF AN ERA: THE TRAVEL JOURNAL OF MARY MAHONEY. *Nebraska Hist. 1966 47(3): 329-338.* A day-by-day report of a 1901 covered wagon journey by seven farm families from western Nebraska to Colorado looking for better land, written by Mary Mahoney, the wife of one of the leaders of the expedition. R. Lowitt

3183. McDonough, Marian M. QUEST FOR HEALTH, NOT WEALTH, 1871. *Montana: Mag. of Western Hist. 1964 14(1): 25-37.* Account of a family's migration from Chicago to Colorado, and settlement in the Colorado Springs area. Based on the diary of Mary Eliza Willard Young, whose illness occasioned the trip. L. G. Nelson

3184. Potter, James E., ed. THE RANCH LETTERS OF EMMA ROBERTSON, 1891-1892. *Nebraska Hist. 1975 56(2): 221-229.* Four letters written by the wife of a ranch manager to her aunt in Iowa describing her experiences on the Hershey Stock Ranch in North Bend, Nebraska. R. Lowitt

3185. Reid, Russell. SAKAKAWEA. *North Dakota Hist. 1963 30(2/3): 101-113.* North Dakota claimed that Sakakawea, the bird woman, young Indian wife of Charbonneau and member of the Lewis and Clark expedition, was the Snake squaw who died in 1811 at the age of 25 in South Dakota. This claim is based on the journal of John Luttig, a clerk of Manuel Lisa's Missouri Fur Company. Wyoming accepts the claim of Dr. Grace Raymond Hebard in her book *Sacajawea* (1933) (the accepted spelling in Wyoming), that the Indian woman was a Shoshone who lived to the age of 100 years and died in Wyoming in 1884. Map and illus.

I. W. Van Noppen

3186. Riley, Paul D., ed. NEIGHBOR TO THE MORTONS. *Nebraska Hist. 1972 53(1): 15-34.* Reminiscences of Kate Winslow Davis, writing in the 1920's, who in the 1860's became acquainted with the Julius Sterling Morton (1832-1902) family in Nebraska City. Her father managed Morton's farm for two years before moving in 1865 to a farm of his own. R. Lowitt

3187. Rose, Forest. THE DIARY OF FOREST ROSE. *High Country 1972 (21): 24-30.* Presents Forest Rose's travel account covering 17-19 November 1887, noting vistas and people seen from a train east of Dodge City to her final destination in San Diego. Describes the plains and mountains of Colorado, fields of grains, Indians in Raton, New Mexico, western Arizona, and eastern California. First glimpses of plains and Pacific Ocean outside San Diego are carefully noted.

K. E. Gilmont

3188. Salmans, Mary Blake. MRS. BLAKE'S SUNDAY SCHOOL. *New Mexico Hist. R. 1963 38(4): 312-322.* Reflections on the establishment of a Sunday school in Deming, New Mexico, in 1882, including a visit from the toughest cowboy in town.                D. F. Henderson

3189. Schenck, Annie B. CAMPING VACATION, 1871. *Colorado Mag. 1965 42(3): 185-215.* An account by an eastern lady of a camping trip through the Colorado Rockies, 4-29 August 1871. Her daily journal entries present an unusual picture of the mountain wilderness of frontier Colorado. She includes accounts of visits to ghost and near-ghost mining towns in the higher elevations.                R. Sexauer

3190. Schmidt, William F. THE LETTERS OF CHARLES AND HELEN WOOSTER: THE PROBLEMS OF SETTLEMENT. *Nebraska Hist. 1965 46(2): 121-137.* Letters deal with Wooster's experiences during the year 1872 when he settled in Nebraska, and his wife remained in Michigan while he prepared a home for her.
                R. Lowitt

3191. Scrimsher, Lila Gravatt, ed. THE DIARY OF ANNA WEBBER: EARLY DAY TEACHER OF MITCHELL COUNTY. *Kansas Hist. Q. 1972 38(3): 320-337.* Anna Webber (1860-1948) was hired in 1881 to teach a three-month term at the district school near Blue Hill, Center Township, Mitchell County. Her diary, which consists of entries varying in length from one sentence to a lengthy paragraph for most of the days between 9 May 1881 and 27 July 1881, contains information about Anna Webber's personal life and reaction to the Kansas scene. Anna Webber's papers are in the possession of her daughter, Mrs. Lila Gravatt Scrimsher. Photo, 20 notes.                W. F. Zornow

3192. Snedecor, Marie, ed. THE HOMESTEADERS: THEIR DREAMS HELD NO SHADOWS. *Montana: Mag. of Western Hist. 1969 19(2): 10-27.* The letters of Lillie Klein written to her parents from a homestead in Blaine County, Montana, in 1913. There are details of housebuilding and other phases of pioneering in the dry-land wheat area of Montana's "High Line." Illus.                S. R. Davison

3193. Snell, Joseph W., ed. BY WAGON FROM KANSAS TO ARIZONA - THE TRAVEL DIARY OF LYDIA E. ENGLISH. *Kansas Hist. Q. 1970 36(4): 369-389.* Lydia E. English was one of 13 adults and an unspecified number of children who traveled from Concordia, Kansas, to Prescott, Arizona, between 20 September and 6 December 1875. Her diary ran in the 18 and 25 February and the 3 and 10 March 1876 issues of the Concordia *Empire,* the source for the present edition of the diary. English described the countryside, towns, and inhabitants she encountered. The diary interests because it was written when most settlers were moving to central Kansas rather than from it, and because it blends contemporary situations into a background provided by the earlier history of the Southwest. This happened because the party followed both the Santa Fe Trail and parts of the older trails established by Spanish priests. Based on articles, local histories, and manuscripts in the Kansas State Historical Society; illus., 44 notes.
                W. F. Zornow

3194. Snell, Joseph W., ed. ROUGHING IT ON HER KANSAS CLAIM: THE DIARY OF ABBIE BRIGHT, 1870-1871. *Kansas Hist. Q. 1971 37(3): 233-268, (4): 394-428.* Part I. This portion of the diary contains the entries from 2 September 1870 to 30 June 1871. Abbie Bright (1848-1926) was from Pennsylvania. After visiting her brother Hiram in Indiana, she visited her brother Philip who was homesteading in Kansas. Abbie's account of her teaching in Indiana, her trip from Kansas City to Wichita, the daily routine of homesteaders, and her own experience as a homesteader in Kansas, provides illuminating if not entirely new glimpses of life on the frontier. Two copies of the diary are owned by the diarist's grandson, Donald G. Fairchild of Gladbrook, Iowa. Based primarily on the second and fuller version of the diary, although some material from the first version is incorporated when it provides supplementary information; illus., map, 26 notes. Part II. Covers entries for 2 July to 20 December 1871. Abbie Bright wrote about her brothers, neighbors, cooking, sewing, gardening, letter writing, illness, buffalo hunting, and other personal experiences and housekeeping chores. Illus., 44 notes.
                W. F. Zornow

3195. Socolofsky, Homer E., ed. THE PRIVATE JOURNALS OF FLORENCE CRAWFORD AND ARTHUR CAPPER, 1891-1892. *Kansas Hist. Q. 1964 30(1): 15-61; (2): 163-208.* Florence Crawford, the daughter of Samuel Crawford a former Kansas governor, and Arthur Capper, a rising young newspaper man and future U.S. senator from Topeka, Kansas, were to be married. The young man went to New York, Boston and Washington for journalistic experience. His fiancée suggested that both of them keep a daily record of their experiences. The author has paired their entries for each day. Capper's entries are short and to the point, but Miss Crawford introduced much local information of interest. The persons mentioned in the journals are identified in footnotes. The journals are now the property of the Kansas State Historical Society.
                W. F. Zornow

3196. Sprague, Marshall. LOVE IN THE PARK. *Am. Heritage 1967 18(2): 8-13, 80-85.* Love affair in 1873 between travel writer Isabella Lucy Bird and fur trapper Jim Nugent in Estes Park, Colorado. From Sprague's *A Gallery of Dudes* (Boston: Little, Brown, 1967).        S

3197. Stokes, Elsie Carlson. A HISTORY OF THE AU7. *Bits and Pieces 1971 7(1): 21-28.* Elsie Carlson Stokes, partly of Swedish ancestry, grew up on the AU7 ranch in Hot Springs, South Dakota, where the boredom of frontier life was broken by the activities of Swedish servant girls, blizzards, prairie fires, the annual hog-butchering, and an old Indian who asked for the cow to eat when it died. In spite of these interruptions, the family raised cows, hogs, and sheep, and farmed vegetables.

3198. Thorpe, Elizabeth J. 'NONI'. *Bits and Pieces 1971 7(1): 10-16.* Minnie Grosso Zanoni came to Newcastle, Wyoming, from Montelange, Italy, at age 15. She met and married Ben Zanoni, a coalminer and later a barkeeper. They raised two boys, both of whom died without heirs. Minnie Zanoni loved children, babysat for her entire neighborhood, and became beloved by all for her fine spirit and prize angelfood cakes.
                N. Gamer

3199. Trenholm, Virginia Cole. AMANDA MARY AND THE DOG SOLDIERS. *Ann. of Wyoming 1974 46(1): 5-46.* Tells the story of two girls captured in 1865 by Cheyennes and Arapahoes at Rock Creek Crossing, Wyoming. Amanda Mary Fletcher was ransomed nine months later, but her sister Lizzie remained with the Indians and subsequently married an Arapaho man, John Broken Horn. The article recounts the girls' capture, attempts by the army to rescue them, and Amanda's continuing efforts to locate her sister. In 1902 they were briefly reunited, but Lizzie Broken Horn denied her white ancestry and refused to return to Iowa with her family. 5 photos, 43 notes.                M. L. Tate

3200. White, Victor. FRIEDA AND THE LAWRENCE LEGEND. *Southwest R. 1965 50(4): 388-397.* Based on an acquaintanceship of a quarter of a century with Frieda Lawrence in Taos, New Mexico. Frieda, wife of D. H. Lawrence, did much to enlarge and perpetrate the Lawrence legend. She did this for two reasons: first, the legend reflected "more and more glory on Frieda," and second, it brought in "more and more cash."
                D. F. Henderson

3201. Wishart, David J. AGE AND SEX COMPOSITION OF THE POPULATION ON THE NEBRASKA FRONTIER, 1860-1880. *Nebraska Hist. 1973 54(1): 107-119.* Careful analysis reveals that the initial phase of settlement in Nebraska was characterized by the family unit of young adults with children. As the frontier society matured, young immigrants ceased to constitute such a high proportion of the total population. While males were more numerous than females on the frontier, the numerical difference was often small and often increased with longer settlement.                R. Lowitt

3202. —. EARLY DAYS: THE STORY OF SARAH THAL. *Am. Jewish Arch. 1971 23(1): 47-62.* Memoirs of Sarah Thal, who left Germany in the 1880's for Nelson County, North Dakota. Hardship and privation marked her years in the Dakota Territory. Schools, growing population, and the introduction of luxuries gradually made life on the plains more comfortable. Undocumented; photo.                E. S. Shapiro

3203. —. WOMEN IN THE WEST: A PICTORIAL VIEW. *Montana: Mag. of Western Hist. 1974 24(3): 39-57.* Some 60 photos of women in varied activities, from early gold-rush days to the present. A brief essay stresses the impossibility of a reliable stereotype of frontier women.                                                                    S. R. Davison

# Far West

3204.   Alkire, Frank T.   THE LITTLE LADY OF THE [TRIANGLE BAR].   *J. of Arizona Hist. 1974 15(2): 107-118.* City-born Asenath Phelps Alkire (1865-1950) lived on the Triangle Bar Ranch near Phoenix, 1889-95. This 1942 memoir by her husband describes ranch life in the 1890's and her adjustment to it. Illus.                               D. L. Smith

3205.   Arrington, Leonard J.   WOMEN AS A FORCE IN THE HISTORY OF UTAH.   *Utah Hist. Q. 1970 38(1): 3-6.* A brief introduction to an issue devoted entirely to the subject of women in Utah. Special attention is given to the achievements of Susan Young Gates.
                                                                            S. L. Jones

3206.   Bayless, June E., ed.   MY STORY AT MOLINO VIEJO.   *California Hist. Soc. Q. 1969 48(2): 171-175.* The manuscript of Rebecca Humphreys Turner's *My Story: a Pioneer* and a letter to her from her fiancé William F. Turner have been deposited with the San Marino Public Library. Mrs. Turner's family lived at El Molino Viejo, now the southern California quarters of the California Historical Society. Bayless relates the circumstances by which the letter came to be written. A series of misunderstandings in 1871 caused the engaged couple to be estranged for a time. The problem was solved after Turner's letter made a tardy arrival.
                                                                            A. Hoffman

3207.   Bitton, Davis and Ursenbach, Maureen.   RIDING HERD: A CONVERSATION WITH JUANITA BROOKS.   *Dialogue: A J. of Mormon Thought 1974 9(1): 11-33.* An interview with Juanita Brooks about her childhood and teaching and writing careers in Utah. Discusses her history of the Mountain Meadows massacre (1857), her major work, for which she was persecuted by the Mormons. 5 illus., biblio.
                                                                            D. L. Rowe

3208.   Choynski, Isidor N. and Eckman, Julius.   TWO LETTERS TO HARRIET CHOYNSKI.   *Western States Jewish Hist. Q. 1974 7(1): 44-48.* Two letters addressed to Harriet Choynski written in 1863 and 1872 give a glimpse of life in the West at that time. Mrs. Choynski had five children, taught at a religious school in San Francisco for many years, and marched in San Francisco's first May Day parade. 19 notes.
                                                                            R. A. Garfinkle

3209.   Clarke, Jessie and Bifford, Florence.   NOTES ON PINOLE, CALIFORNIA AND SOME EARLY RESIDENTS.   *Pacific Historian 1972 16(2): 65-71.* Discusses the family of Bernardo Fernandez, who established Rancho El Pinole on the San Pablo Bay, and some subsequent inhabitants of the town, 1823-1902.

3210.   Colliver, Iva Cooley.   YOSEMITE HONEYMOON.   *Pacific Historian 1971 15(2): 75-82.* Recounts the events of the author's 1915 camping honeymoon in Yosemite National Park.

3211.   Dixson, Elizabeth I., ed.   EARLY SAN FERNANDO: MEMOIRS OF CATHERINE HUBBARD DACE.   *Southern California Q. 1962 44(3): 219-267.* An oral history account of the development of the San Fernando Valley from a pastoral-rural setting to the present commercial-urban life. Charles Maclay was the founder of the City of San Fernando; he was a member of the California State Assembly and Senate from 1861 until 1873. Senator George K. Porter and his brother Benjamin F. Porter bought land in the valley and, in partnership with Maclay, developed the settlement of the entire valley of over one hundred thousand acres. The San Fernando Mission was occupied by Andres Pico's family from 1846 until purchased by the San Fernando Farm Homestead Association in 1869. The narrative is very rich in family accounts of prominent people in 19th-century southern California. 62 notes.
                                                                            D. H. Swift

3212.   Doan, May Cargill.   I WOULDN'T TRADE THESE YESTERDAYS: THE REMINISCENCE OF MAY CARGILL DOAN.   *J. of Arizona Hist. 1965 6(3): 116-131.* The first part of the memoirs of

a daughter of Andrew Hays Cargill, an Arizona pioneer, are frank regarding her father and provide a description of life in Yuma, Arizona, after she arrived there in 1902. Editorial and corrective notes have been added. Illus. To be continued.                                        J. D. Filipiak

3213.   Doan, May Cargill.   I WOULDN'T TRADE THESE YESTERDAYS: THE REMINISCENCES OF MAY CARGILL DOAN.   *J. of Arizona Hist. 1965 6(4): 188-203.* Conclusion of the author's reminiscences of early 20th-century life in the Arizona Territory, particularly the communities of Yuma and Silverbell. Illus., map, notes.

3214.   Ellis, Anna B. Lincoln.   THE LINCOLN HOUSE.   *Noticias 1972 8(1): 18-21.* In 1869 Amasa Lincoln and his wife Abbie arrived in Santa Barbara. Noting the need for a boarding house, Abbie Lincoln purchased lots from J. E. Goux. In November 1871, Mr. Lincoln began building the Lincoln House, now known as the Hotel Upham, at Sola and De La Vina Streets. In the following years Abbie Lincoln bought the adjoining lots where the Hotel Upham annex now stands. In 1898 Cyrus Upham bought the entire land. He sold a portion of it to Ira Goodridge in 1911. His daughter, Elizabeth Goodridge Hall managed it until her death, in 1969.                                              K. Butcher

3215.   Faulk, Odie B.   LIFE IN TOMBSTONE.   *J. of the West 1972 11(3): 495-512.* Reproduces a chapter of the author's new book, *Tombstone: Myth and Reality,* which describes daily life in a frontier mining community. Despite primitive living conditions, the citizens were quick to establish churches, schools, theaters, and other civic improvements which competed with saloons and gambling halls for the miners' participation. Based on memoirs and secondary works; 31 notes.
                                                                            B. S. Porter

3216.   Hosmer, Helen.   ARRIVEDERCI, VENICE.   *Am. West 1968 5(2): 43-48.* A reminiscence by the author of her childhood experiences while on summer holidays with her family at the seaside resort of Venice, California, a few miles from Los Angeles. 6 illus.            D. L. Smith

3217.   Jackson, Sheldon G., ed.   AN ENGLISH QUAKER TOURS CALIFORNIA; THE JOURNAL OF SARAH LINDSEY, 1859-1860, PARTS I AND II.   *Southern California Q. 1969 51(1): 1-33, and (2): 153-175.* Entries from the journal of an English Quaker minister, Sarah Lindsey, who accompanied her husband to California in 1859-60. Sarah was the wife of Robert Lindsey, wealthy industrialist and Quaker minister who devoted much of his life to a worldwide ministry. The Lindseys ministered to California gold miners, and visited the giant redwoods and San Francisco. Besides relating the religious aspects of their journey, Mrs. Lindsey gives a description of the countryside and some glimpses of the life of the people living there. Based on a manuscript in the Devonshire House Library, London, and a number of secondary works; 31 notes.
                                                                            W. L. Bowers

3218.   Kizer, Benjamin H.   MAY ARKWRIGHT HUTTON.   *Pacific Northwest Q. 1966 57(2): 49-56.* Biographical sketch of orphan May Arkwright Hutton through early years of privation in mining towns of Idaho, the successful investment of her small wages in a mine which became a bonanza; then middle-aged years in Spokane as a philanthropist, establishing and supporting homes for orphans. Included are incidents of her roles in union labor activities and politics.          C. C. Gorchels

3219.   Kroll, Frances Cooper.   SANTA BARBARA YOUTH IN THE NINETIES.   *Noticias 1963 9(2): 4-17.* Reminiscences of the author about daily life in Santa Barbara during the 1890's.

3220.   Larn, Hubert.   "FANTASTIC HILDA" - PIONEER HISTORY PERSONIFIED.   *Swedish Pioneer Hist. Q. 1964 15(2): 63-76.* An interview with Swedish-born American pioneer Mrs. Hilda Erickson who, in 1963, celebrated her 104th birthday. Her story begins when she, her mother, and two of her brothers left Sweden in 1866 (the rest of the family followed later), sailed the Atlantic, rode from New York to Saint Joseph by rail, journeyed up the Missouri River to Omaha, and then joined a wagon train traveling to Grantsville, Utah. In Grantsville, Hilda later married John August Erickson and began a career which included roles as wife, mother, grocer, midwife, farmer, dentist, doctor to the Indians, and seamstress. Photo.                                     K. Chappell

3221.   Lee, Ellen K.   THE CATHOLIC MODJESKA.   *Polish Am. Studies 1974 31(1): 20-27.* Describes the great Shakesperean actress, Helena Modrzejewska [or Modjeska, as she anglicized the name]. She came to San Francisco in 1876, at the age of 36, with her husband, son, and a small group of friends hoping to establish a Polish colony near Los Angeles. Though she was recognized in Russian Poland through her association with the Imperial Theater of Warsaw, the language barrier delayed her rise to fame in the United States. Deals mostly with services rendered for the small Catholic churches which she attended. Includes an account of a confrontation in Santa Ana, California in 1897 between Madame Modjeska and the American Protective Association. 23 notes.
S. R. Pliska

3222.   Lee, Ellen K.   HELENA MODJESKA AND THE FRANCISCO TORRES AFFAIR, SUMMER, 1892.   *Southern California Q. 1969 51(1): 35-56.* Polish Actress Helena Modjeska spent part of her life on an Orange County ranch which she acquired in 1888. This is primarily an account of the murder of her ranch foreman William McKelvey during the summer of 1892 and the subsequent lynching of Francisco Torres, a Modjeska ranch hand who was accused of the crime. Near the end of July 1892, McKelvey deducted two-and-a-half dollars from Torres' weekly earnings to pay his road poll tax and Torres, who spoke little English, apparently did not understand but thought he was being cheated. He claimed later that he killed McKelvey in self-defense, but before he could be given a trial a mob of armed and masked men took him out of the Santa Ana jail where he was being held and hanged him from a telephone pole. What impact these events had on Madame Modjeska is not known, but the author suggests that she probably never forgot the horror of the summer of 1892. Based on personal letters, newspaper articles, and secondary works; 51 notes.
W. L. Bowers

3223.   Lincoln, Anna Blake.   LINCOLN LETTERS.   *Noticias 1964 10(4): 1-23.* Reprints letters from Abbie Smith Patrick Lincoln to her Eastern relatives, describing daily life in Santa Barbara, California, in 1869.

3224.   Lowney, Barbara.   LADY BOUNTIFUL: MARGARET CROCKER OF SACRAMENTO.   *California Hist. Soc. Q. 1968 47(2): 99-112.* Mrs. Crocker (1821-1901) was born Margaret Ellen Rhodes, the 13th child in the family. Her youth was that of a pioneer woman in northern Ohio. At the age of 26 she met Edwin Bryant Crocker, a lawyer and widower, in South Bend, Indiana. After marriage they moved to Sacramento, where he set up a successful law practice and was later appointed to the Supreme Court of California. The Crockers were noted for their hospitality and charity, and for founding an outstanding art gallery. On 6 May 1885 Sacramento held a floral festival in her honor. Illus., 38 notes.
W. A. Buckman

3225.   MacPhail, Elizabeth C.   EARLY DAYS IN SAN DIEGO: THE MEMOIRS OF AUGUSTA BARRETT SHERMAN.   *J. San Diego Hist. 1972 18(4): 28-34.* San Diego's second Old Town "school marm" dictated these memoirs in 1890. They relate primarily to conditions there in the 1860's. 8 notes.
S. S. Sprague

3226.   Miller, David E., ed.   A GREAT ADVENTURE ON GREAT SALT LAKE: A TRUE STORY OF KATE Y. NOBLE.   *Utah Hist. Q. 1965 33(3): 218-236.* An account written by Mrs. Noble of how she with her first husband Uriah J. Wenner and their three children lived on Frémont Island in Great Salt Lake in the years 1886-91. The editor has provided additional information about the island, its history, and the Wenners in an introduction and footnotes. The text of a statement written by John E. Jones after a visit to the island in 1942 and letters to him from Mrs. Noble and her daughter, Blanche H. Wenner, concerning the burial ground on the island are provided also. Illus., 36 notes.
S. L. Jones

3227.   Morrill, Allen C. and Morrill, Eleanor D.   THE MEASURING WOMAN AND THE COOK.   *Idaho Yesterdays 1963 7(3): 2-15.* Tells of the work of anthropologist Alice Cunningham Fletcher and her companion Jane Gay among the Nez Perce Indians of North Idaho from May 1889 to September 1892. Sent by the U.S. government to measure and allocate land to the Indians under the provisions of the Dawes Act of 1887, the two women worked to overcome the hostility of the remnants of Chief Joseph's band. The authors depend largely on the letters of Jane Gay in the Women's Archives at Radcliffe College and on the published works of missionary Kate McBeth.
M. Small

3228.   Murphy, Miriam B.   SARAH ELIZABETH CARMICHAEL: POETIC GENIUS OF PIONEER UTAH.   *Utah Hist. Q. 1975 43(1): 52-66.* Pioneer Utah poet Sarah Elizabeth Carmichael (1838-1901) was the daughter of William and Mary Ann Carmichael, whose double cousinship tragically flawed her heredity. She married Jonathan M. Williamson in 1866. After displaying a poetic brilliance that brought her national recognition at an early age, she suffered more than 30 years of mental instability until her death. Handicapped by lack of training, she produced poems of genuine literary merit which have been obscured in the general eclipse of pioneer poetry. Primary and secondary sources; 2 illus., 38 notes.
J. L. Hazelton

3229.   Newmark, Helen.   A NINETEENTH CENTURY MEMOIR.   *Western States Jewish Hist. Q. 1974 6(3): 204-218.* Autobiography of Helen Newmark (1840-1911), written in 1900. Immigrating in 1855 from Posen, Poland, Newmark gives a good account of life in San Francisco in the latter half of the 19th century. 3 photos, 15 notes.
R. A. Garfinkle

3230.   Pace, Josephine.   KIMBERLY AS I REMEMBER HER.   *Utah Hist. Q. 1967 35(2): 112-120.* Contains the author's reminiscences of her girlhood, when her father operated a hotel at the Kimberly gold mine, owned by the Annie Laurie Consolidated Gold Mining Company.
S. L. Jones

3231.   Painter, Margaret.   THE INDOMITABLE YANCEY SPIRIT.   *Pacific Historian 1976 20(2): 132-139.* Frances Mary Hines' recollections of her father, Bud Yancey, and his move to Tuolumne County timber country in the 1890's and life there until 1907.
G. L. Olson

3232.   Posner, Russel M.   CALIFORNIA THROUGH ENGLISH EYES, 1858-1861.   *J. of the West 1972 11(4): 663-669.* Harvey Tower (1831-1870), a British Army veteran, visited California in 1858 and saw the usual tourist spots: gold mines, the Calaveras Grove of Big Trees, and the New Almaden Quicksilver Mine. He greatly enjoyed the night life in San Francisco. Sophia Cracroft (1816-1892) accompanied her aunt, Lady Jane Franklin (1792-1875), on a trip around the world. They visited California's gold mines, Mammoth Grove, and Warm Springs in the summer of 1861. Tower and Cracroft praised the scenery and crops of California but were critical of the towns and Yankee manners. Based on privately owned diary and correspondence.
B. S. Porter

3233.   Pryor, Helen B.   A NEW LIFE IN CALIFORNIA.   *Palimpsest 1971 52(7): 364-368.* Discusses Lou Henry Hoover's life in California from the age of 10 until she graduated from Stanford University in 1898.

3234.   Reinhardt, Richard, ed.   ON THE BRINK OF THE BOOM: SOUTHERN CALIFORNIA IN 1877 AS WITNESSED BY MRS. FRANK LESLIE.   *California Hist. Q. 1973 52(1): 64-79.* In 1877 the British-born publisher Frank Leslie (1821-80) and his wife, Miriam Florence Follin Leslie (1836?-1914), took a train across the United States. Mrs. Leslie recorded her impressions, generally favorable, of Chinatown, Mission San Gabriel, the Santa Monica resort area, the salubrious climate, the incipient tourist and citrus enterprises, and California society. Contrasts the California she described to the southern California that underwent a real estate boom less than 10 years later. Excerpted from Miriam Leslie's book about the trip. Illus., photos, 12 notes.
A. Hoffman

3235.   Ridgeway, Rick.   AT HOME IN MALIBU.   *Westways 1976 68(6): 20-21.* Discusses the life of Rhoda Rindge Adamson and the building of the family home at Vaquero Point on Rancho Malibu, 1928.

3236.   Romer, Margaret.   THE STORY OF LOS ANGELES.   *J. of the West 1964 3(1): 1-39, (2): 199-220, and (4): 459-488.* Los Angeles grew from a relatively small city in 1900 to a large metropolis in 1930. Contributing factors to this expansion were the advent of the automobile, the development of the motion picture industry, extension of the railroads, and the completion of the Owens River Aqueduct which brought water to the thirsty city. The author details all of this and shows the effect upon government, education, society, and the economic bases of the entire area. Emphasis is placed upon the increasing importance of motion pictures and upon the struggle to secure an adequate supply of water, but the author does not slight social and cultural achievements or the individuals responsible for them. During the years of World War I and the 1920's, not only did the city and the county expand rapidly in population but many notable events occurred. The harbor of Los Angeles became an important port, the people of the city made outstanding contributions to the war effort, Henry Huntington established a renowned library, the Hollywood Bowl and the Coliseum had their inception, the City Hall was constructed, and the meetings of Aimee Semple McPherson became a tourist attraction of almost as great importance as the homes of the movie stars in Beverly Hills. The history of the city from the 1930's to 1960 presents such diverse events as the establishment of the Farmer's Market, labor-management difficulties, construction of the Colorado River aqueduct, and the effects of World War II on the city. The coming of television and major league baseball, political developments, freeway construction, building of the new civic Center, and natural disasters are detailed. Undocumented, illus., biblio. D. N. Brown

3237. Sandberg, Lucille. A RADIANT SPIRIT. *Pacific Hist. 1972 16(4): 25-28.* Short biographical sketch of Ellen Loraine Deering, an early resident of Chico, California, 1900-20.

3238. Sargent, Shirley. SIDE-SADDLE TOURISTS AT YOSEMITE. *Pacific Historian 1968 12(1): 6-13.* Discusses women tourists to California's Yosemite Valley in the 1870's. S

3239. Sayre, Florence. MY VALLEY. *Idaho Yesterdays 1964 8(3): 18-25.* A nostalgic memoir of a little girl's life in Long Valley (near Council, Idaho) at the turn of the century. The author moved to Idaho from Ohio, lived there briefly, then returned to Ohio. M. Small

3240. Singer, Eleanor. IN MEMORIAM: HAZEL ERSKINE, 1908-1975. *Public Opinion Q. 1975/76 39(4): 571-579.* When Hazel Erskine died, on July 10, 1975, it became clear that no one person could write a memorial tribute that would do justice to the many extraordinary qualities and achievements of her life. We therefore invited several of her colleagues to write about her from the perspective from which they knew her best: Herbert Hyman, who knew her as a social researcher and editor of the *Public Opinion Quarterly*'s "Polls"; George Rudiak and Ralph Denton, who worked with her in many Nevada political campaigns; Elmer Rusco and Richard Siegel, her co-workers in the Nevada chapter of the American Civil Liberties Union; and John Aberasturi, who, as superintendent of the Northern Nevada Children's Home, worked with Hazel in her capacity as a member of the Nevada state welfare board. They, and we at the Public Opinion Quarterly, will miss her sorely in the years to come. J

3241. Spearman, Walter. THE BARON AND THE SEÑORITA. *Am. Hist. Illus. 1966 1(4): 40-46.* The Russian Baron Nikolai Rezanov dreamed of making the entire areas of Alaska, California, and Hawaii part of the Russian Empire. In 1805 he sailed to Alaska and found the Sitka colony suffering from starvation. He continued on to the Spanish settlement of San Francisco hoping to sell his cargo for food to take back to the Alaskan colony. He was welcomed by the Spanish commandant José Arguello. It is only speculation as to whether Rezanov actually fell in love with Arguello's 15-year-old daughter Concepción or whether he merely pretended in order to gain his needed supplies. Whatever his reasons, it is certain that he did view this marriage alliance as a beginning link toward his goal of a Russian colony in California. While returning to gain the czar's permission for the marriage he died. Concepción joined a convent at the news of his death. Even though the dream was never realized, a small colony (Fort Ross) was established. However, the Russian American Company did not prosper there, and in 1841 John Augustus Sutter purchased Fort Ross from the Russians. 5 illus. M. J. McBaine

3242. Steunenberg, Bess. EARLY DAYS IN CALDWELL. *Idaho Yesterdays 1966 10(4): 12-17.* "Recollections of what Caldwell was like, at least in the eyes of a child, at the turn of the century." The author describes her home town at the turn of the century, including the physical setting and prominent landmarks of the community. The College of Idaho was a factor in community growth and helped produce leaders in business, civic, and cultural endeavors. Caldwell was the central market for a large farming area. It also developed as a railroad shipping point for miners, wool growers, and cattlemen in Owyhee County. 5 illus. D. H. Swift

3243. Winkels, George. QUEEN OF THE MALIBU. *High Country 1972 (21): 4-10.* Malibu, California's heritage of protecting the land against encroaching superhighways and advancing housing developments is due largely to the efforts of May Knight Rindge, who came to California in 1887 from Marblehead, Massachusetts. She loved the natural area and fought to have it preserved. She fought long, bitter, and costly legal battles against the Southern Pacific Railroad, the City of Los Angeles, and state and federal forces. They cost her her fortune and portions of her ranch lands. Ultimately her estate was liquidated. Today the Serra Retreat, a Franciscan Order, is the only remnant of her dream house. Her spirit of preservation has restricted the building of superhighways and housing developments and has kept the natural beauty intact. K. E. Gilmont

3244. Wood, Raymund F. MARIANA ANDRADA IN CALIFORNIA. *Pacific Historian 1972 16(3): 77-81.* Andrada claimed to be the widow of Joaquin Murrieta, but was actually only an immigrant from Mexico who enhanced her mystique as a fandango dancer by perpetuating this rumor.

# Atlantic and Pacific Dependencies

3245. Bryce-Laporte, Roy Simon. FAMILY ADAPTATION OF RELOCATED SLUM DWELLERS IN PUERTO RICO: IMPLICATIONS FOR URBAN RESEARCH AND DEVELOPMENT. *J. of Developing Areas 1968 2(4): 533-539.* The imposition of relocation on slum dwellers to relieve congestion can lead to latent adaptations which are overlooked by researchers and planners. The author observed a family form in relocated Puerto Ricans, not nuclear and not the classical extended, but a modified extended: a series of families joined for mutual aid without geographical propinquity or occupational similarity. The problem of urban planning is how to eliminate congestion and its negative effects without destroying the extended family and its benefits. Misconceptions about lower-class families (e.g., illegitimacy, consensual unions) are not problems but slum dwellers' solutions to problems. It is recommended that urban planners develop more humanistic reforms and spend less time correcting distasteful behavior. 10 notes. R. F. Allen

3246. Neggers, Gladys. CLARA LAIR Y JULIA DE BURGOS: REMINISCENCIAS DE EVARISTO RIBERA CHEVREMONT Y JORGE FONT SALDAÑA [Clara Lair and Julia de Burgos: Reminiscences of Evaristo Ribera Chevremont and Jorge Font Saldaña]. *R. Interamericana [Puerto Rico] 1974 4(2): 258-263.* The lives and personalities of Puerto Rico's most prominent poetesses of the 20th century, Clara Lair (1895-1973) and Julia de Burgos (1914-53), are explored through the memories of friends. Based on personal interviews; 4 notes, biblio. J. A. Lewis

# 8. Canada

## Discovery Period to 1867

**3247.** Bennet, C. L. AN UNPUBLISHED MANUSCRIPT OF THE FIRST CANADIAN NOVELIST. *Dalhousie R. [Canada] 1963 43(3): 317-332.* The author of the first novel published in Canada, *St. Ursula's Convent,* 1824, Julia Catherine Hart, also wrote a second novel of intricate plot, adventure, 19th century sentiment, and "Gothic mystery," *Edith* or *The Doom,* here described in detail from the unpublished manuscript. M. B. Rex

**3248.** Bibeau, Hector. LE CLIMAT MARIAL EN NOUVELLE-FRANCE A L'ARRIVÉE DE MGR DE SAINT-VALLIER [The Marian atmosphere in New France on the arrival of Mgr. Saint-Vallier]. *Rev. d'Hist. de l'Amérique Française [Canada] 1968 22(3): 415-428.* Describes the devotion to the Virgin Mary in the first half of the 17th century, the prevailing cult of the Immaculate Conception, the role of the Jesuits and pious organizations, the emphasis on religious festivities, and the growth of parishes and religious orders including Ursulines, Sulpicians, Hospitalers. Notes satisfaction and support of Mgr. Saint-Vallier. Based on scholarly texts and archives; 50 notes. C. Bates

**3249.** Chaput, Donald. FROM INDIAN TO FRENCH: A FEMALE NAME CURIOSITY. *Names 1966 14(3): 143-149.* An examination of French names bestowed on Indian women who married Frenchmen in North America. The French made no attempt to translate the Indian name. Rather the Indian woman was simply given a saint's name for her first name. Her surname was usually entered in the records as "Sauvage," "Sauvagesse," or "Panis(e)" (the last stemming from Pawnee originally but having assumed the meaning of any person captured from another tribe), or with a tribal name such as "Huronne." Based on French-Canadian histories and genealogical works; 19 notes. D. Lindsey

**3250.** Douville, Raymond. QUELQUES NOTES INEDITES SUR NICOLAS PERROT ET SA FAMILLE [Some unpublished notes on Nicholas Perrot and his family]. *Cahiers des Dix [Canada] 1963 28: 43-62.* Attempts to identify the birthplace of Nicolas Perrot (ca. 1643-1717), *coureur de bois* and Indian agent. It was most probably in the parish of Darcy, diocese of Autun, France. His 11 children are identified with notes on their lives. There were numerous legal actions involving Perrot in his later years. After his death, his wife Magdeleine Reclos, (d. 1724) became more mentally depressed than ever before and her children made numerous complex arrangements for her welfare. L. F. S. Upton

**3251.** Mathews, Robin. SUSANNA MOODIE, PINK TORYISM, AND NINETEENTH CENTURY IDEAS OF CANADIAN IDENTITY. *J. of Can. Studies 1975 10(3): 3-15.* Discusses the social stratification theory of Canadian writer Susanna Moodie *(Roughing It in the Bush, Life in the Clearings),* 1832-53, including her conception of Canada's national self-image.

**3252.** Oury, Dom Guy. UN NOUVEAU MANUSCRIT DES LETTRES DE MARIE DE L'INCARNATION [A new manuscript of letters of Marie de l'Incarnation]. *R. d'Hist. de l'Amérique Française 1967 21(1): 51-63.* The Archives of Canada has recently acquired a manuscript entitled "Letters Moral and Edifying of Marie de l'Incarnation, Mother Superior of the Ursulines in Canada (America)." The manuscript is purportedly a 17th century transcription containing 183 letters. It is composed of 17 quarto letter books containing in all 415 pages. Most of the letters were published by Dom Claude Martin in 1681. A collation of the manuscript and the Martin edition indicates that while the manuscript and the edition are substantially identical, the manuscript departs even further from the originals than the Martin edition. The manuscript contains a number of inventions of the copyist, and internal evidence indicates that it postdates the French Revolution. Although useless for a critical edition of the writings of Marie de l'Incarnation, it shows the interest maintained in France in the letters of the great Ursuline. J. M. Bumsted

**3253.** Prentice, Alison. THE FEMINIZATION OF TEACHING IN BRITISH NORTH AMERICA AND CANADA 1845-1875. *Social Hist. [Canada] 1975 8(15): 5-20.* Entry of women into Canadian public school teaching was facilitated in the second half of the 19th century when school administrators wanted to divide schools into grade levels and promote the pay and status of the male teaching profession. Women were brought in at lower grade levels and at lower pay and status while the pay and status of men at higher levels was increased. Women were attracted to teaching because even low salaries provided an avenue for respectable independence not otherwise available. They may also have been attracted by the ideology that women were especially suited to early childhood education. Based on documents in the Public Archives of Nova Scotia and Ontario, published school reports, and secondary sources; 4 tables, 40 notes. W. K. Hobson

**3254.** Séguin, Jacques. LE COMITE DES FONDATEURS DE L'EGLISE CANADIENNE [The Founders Committee of the (Catholic) Church of Canada]. *Sessions d'Étude: Soc. Can. d'Hist. de l'Eglise Catholique. Rapport [Canada] 1964 31: 23-29.* The committee calls for a campaign of prayer and publicity to make known the works and merits of the founders of the Catholic Church in Canada, three hundred years ago, for the purpose of securing their canonization. These "Pioneers of the Faith" were Msgr. de Laval, Marie de l'Incarnation, Catherine de Saint-Augustin, Marguerite Bourgenoys, and also Jeanne Mance and Marguerite d'Youville. The vigorous publicizing of their lives, by every medium, and especially in the schools, should lead not only to their canonization but also to increased reverence for these "spiritual ancestors" as examples and as intercessors at the Throne of Grace. Undocumented. S

**3255.** Shipley, Nan. ANNE AND ALEXANDER MURRAY. *Beaver [Canada] 1967 298(Winter): 22-26.* Anne Campbell (1831-1907) met Alexander Hunter Murray (1819-74) in 1846 as she was returning home from Miss Davis' school at Lockport. They were married and sent to the Hudson's Bay Company's isolated new post of Fort Yukon in what is now Alaska. Murray kept a notebook with sketches of life in the wilderness. By 1856 he had won promotion to chief trader and in 1862 was in charge of Lower Fort Garry. He retired in 1865. Illus. L. F. S. Upton

## Since 1867

### General

**3256.** Cuneo, Carl J. and Curtis, James E. SOCIAL ASCRIPTION IN THE EDUCATIONAL AND OCCUPATIONAL STATUS ATTAINMENT OF URBAN CANADIANS. *Can. R. of Sociol. and Anthrop. 1975 12(1): 6-24.* This paper reports on a replication and extension of the Blau-Duncan model of the process of social stratification—an extension to urban Canadian samples and additional independent variables. We focus on the nature and extent of social ascription—the effect of family background, language, and gender on the educational and occupational status attainment of respondents. The analysis is comparative for four subsamples of urban Canadians: francophone men and women and anglophone men and women. The findings show that social ascription is strong in this country in that family background has rather strong and different effects on occupational attainment, through its influence on respondent's education, among women and men and among francophones and anglophones. Some parallel findings from a comparable subgroup of Blau and Duncan's American respondents are also briefly reported on. Among our Canadian findings are the following: mother's education has, of all family background variables, the strongest effect on respondent's education among French males; family size has a greater negative impact on education among anglophones than among francophones; respondent's education has greater effects on occupation among francophones than among anglophones, and among men than among women. Interpretations of these patterns are given and a set of considerations requiring future investigations are presented. In particular, argues that previous American and Canadian data on social mobility have often shown strong ascriptive effects in stratification in contrast to the achievement interpretation which has been placed on them. J

3257. DeValk, Alphonse A. M. THE ABORTION ISSUE IN CONTEMPORARY CANADIAN HISTORY: THE UNFINISHED DEBATE. *Study Sessions [Canada] 1974 41: 81-100.* Presents Canadian press and public opinion surrounding the abortion issue. A paper read at the 1974 annual meeting of the Canadian Catholic Historical Association. S

3258. Handfield, Marthe. LES EVEQUES CANADIENS FACE A LA POLITIQUE D'OTTAWA SUR LE "BIRTH CONTROL." [The Canadian bishops as regards Ottawa's actions concerning birth control]. *Action Nationale [Canada] 1967 56(5): 453-461.* A decision not to interfere with the government's proposed modification of article 150 of the Criminal Code (dealing with sale of contraceptives and diffusion of birth control information) was recently taken by the Roman Catholic bishops of Canada. The bishops, at the same time, made it clear that in accepting modifications they were not attributing to the House of Commons primacy in the realm of moral order. In part, their action resulted from the realization that the law had become a dead letter, and that under actual circumstances this would probably lead to an attitude of indifference that would weaken the government's right to legislate. This action by the Canadian clergy means that the government must assume its new responsibilities. 5 notes. A. E. LeBlanc

3259. Hutcheson, Amy M. ELIZABETH HOMER MORTON, CLA-ACB EXECUTIVE DIRECTOR 1946-1968. *Can. Lib. J. 1968 25(1): 8-17.* Remarks at dinner in tribute to Elizabeth Homer Morton, Executive Director of the Canadian Library Association for 22 years. S

3260. LaTerreur, Marc. CORRESPONDENCE LAURIER-MME. JOSEPH LAVERGNE, 1891-1893 [The letters of Laurier to Madame Joseph Lavergne, 1891-93]. *Canadian Hist. Assoc. Annual Report 1964: 37-51.* Examines the relationship of Laurier and Mme. Lavergne in the light of his letters to her during this two-year period. These letters were given to the author by the nephew of Mme. Lavergne who received them from her. J. J. McCusker

3261. Marchak, Patricia. A CRITICAL REVIEW OF THE STATUS OF WOMEN *REPORT. Can. R. of Sociol. and Anthrop. 1972 9(1): 72-85.* A critical analysis of the *Report* of the Royal Commission on the Status of Women in Canada (Ottawa: Information Canada, 1970). The Commission issued 11 additional commissioned studies listed with full bibliographic information, and commissioned 23 studies as yet unpublished. The report proposes "the conscious removal of sex prejudice in the socialization process, and the provision of equal opportunities and rewards.... Recommendations on legal protection, educational opportunities, economic rights, and political opportunities for women are all aimed at reducing inequalities." Covers both the general report and the commissioned studies. 25 bibliographic references. R. V. Ritter

3262. Morton, Elizabeth Homer. RAISING THE STATUS OF CANADIAN WOMEN. *Queen's Q. [Canada] 1971 78(2): 304-308.* Discusses the *Report of the Royal Commission on the Status of Women in Canada* and Kathleen Archibald's *Sex and the Public Service: A Report to the Public Service Commission of Canada.* Both works stress the need for equalizing opportunities for women as well as recognizing that everyone in Canada, regardless of sex, is entitled to the same basic rights and freedoms. Until such equality is achieved, a vital human resource is not being fully utilized. J. A. Casada

## Economic Sphere

3263. Belzile, Bertrand and Larouche, Viateur. MOTIVATION AU TRAVAIL DES PARENTS DE FAMILLES À FAIBLE REVENU: MODÈLE CONCEPTUEL [Motivation to work of parents of low-income families: Conceptual framework]. *Industrial Relations [Canada] 1974 29(4): 643-670.* "The authors attempt to discover the factors that motivate parents of low-income families to find jobs (to work), or not to find them (to not work)." Presents a motivation model relying on a literary magazine and interviews with key informants. In addition, "the authors formulate a hypothesis on the relation between motivation and the rate of participation in manpower."

3264. David-McNeil, Jeannine. DISPARITÉ DES SALAIRES MASCULINS ET FÉMININS AU CANADA [Disparity between male and female salaries in Canada]. *Actualité Econ. [Canada] 1964 40(3): 469-.* Purely sexually related factors are not responsible for differences in male and female salaries for the same job. Notes that it is impossible to isolate such factors in any case. Suggests that regional variations, type of employment, and salary disparities within specific industries are relevant factors. 5 tables, 2 graphs, 14 notes. W. B. Whitham

3265. Gelber, Sylva. WOMEN AND WORK: THE LEGISLATIVE BASE. *Can. Labour 1975 20(2): 7-10.* Presents Canada's labor laws as they pertain to women since 1951. S

3266. Harvey, Edward and Harvey, Lorna R. ADOLESCENCE, SOCIAL CLASS, AND OCCUPATIONAL EXPECTATIONS. *Can. R. of Sociol. and Anthrop. 1970 7(2): 138-147.* A questionnaire survey of 345 tenth-grade students in a socioeconomically heterogeneous, multi-program urban high school was conducted to measure the amount of congruence in three areas of the students' conceptions of their future work lives: (1) congruence between a student's occupational values and occupational choice; (2) congruence between a student's financial expectations of his work and his actual likely earnings; and (3) congruence between a student's occupational choice and his parents' occupational choice for him. Findings showed that students from higher socioeconomic backgrounds experienced more congruence in all three dimensions than students from lower socioeconomic backgrounds. Sex differences were important only among students of lower socioeconomic background. Some implications for the future work life of these students are drawn. J

3267. Klement, Susan. FEMINISM AND PROFESSIONALISM IN LIBRARIANSHIP: AN INTERVIEW WITH SHERRILL CHEDA. *Can. Lib. J. 1974 31(6): 520-528.* Sherrill Cheda, campus librarian at Seneca College, Willowdale, Ontario, discusses the current feminist movement, unions, community involvement of librarians, and the Canadian Library Association Committee on the Status of Women. S

3268. Marchak, Patricia. WOMEN WORKERS AND WHITE-COLLAR UNIONS. *Can. R. of Sociol. and Anthrop. 1973 10(2): 134-147.* "A survey of white-collar workers in British Columbia revealed that union potential is higher among women than among men and is directly related to income and levels of job control. Union members provided an opposite response pattern to that of non-union workers in similar jobs. Men were more supportive of their union than were women, and their support was greater as their control and income levels increased. The descriptive data show that women have low incomes regardless of job control, education, or union status, that most have low job control regardless of education or union status, and that their hopes for promotion are small compared to those of men. The income and control allocations strongly suggest that existing white-collar unions do not benefit women workers." J

3269. Martin, Anita Shilton. WOMEN AND IMPERIALISM. *Can. Dimension 1975 10(8): 19-25.* Socialist women in Canada systematically analyze how women have been affected by the operation of capitalism on a world scale, from the late 19th century to the present.

3270. Ruggeri, Giuseppe C. HIDDEN UNEMPLOYMENT BY AGE AND SEX IN CANADA: 1957-1970. *Industrial Relations [Canada] 1975 30(2): 181-196.* This study presents yearly estimates of hidden unemployment and job requirements for full employment in Canada by age and sex for the period 1957 to 1970. The method employed in deriving these estimates involved the calculation of the potential labour force, total and by specific age-sex groups, and the formulation of a relationship relating group employment to total employment. J

3271. Smith, Janet. EQUAL OPPORTUNITY IN THE PUBLIC SERVICE. *Can. Labour 1975 20(2): 13-15, 24.* Notes sex discrimination in Canada's public service since 1870. S

3272. Tracy, R. J. THEY WEAR THEIR WINGS WITH PRIDE. *Can. Forces Sentinel 1970 6(7): 24-27.* Women in the Canadian Air Force. **S**

3273. —. CUPE PROGRAMME FOR WOMEN'S YEAR. *Can. Labour 1975 20(2): 16-18.* Notes the efforts of the Canadian Union of Public Employees to fight sex discrimination in 1975. **S**

3274. —. ILGWU WOMEN'S YEAR SEMINAR. *Can. Labour 1975 20(2): 26-27, 36.* Reviews the International Ladies' Garment Workers' Union's efforts on behalf of the International Women's Year at their 1975 Montreal seminar. **S**

3275. —. [WOMEN AND EMPLOYMENT]. *Can. Labour [Canada] 1972 17(5): 2-8, 16.*
—. WOMEN WORKERS, *pp. 2-3.*
Gelber, Sylva M. 'WHICH SIDE ARE YOU ON?', *pp, 4-6, 16.*
Kehoe, Mary. MARRIED WOMEN IN THE JOB MARKET, *pp. 7-8.* Discusses the participation of married and single women in the labor force and labor organizations in Canada in the 1960's and 70's, including possible sex discrimination in women's wages and pensions.

## Social Sphere

3276. Bliss, Michael. "PURE BOOKS ON AVOIDED SUBJECTS": PRE-FREUDIAN SEXUAL IDEAS IN CANADA. *Can. Hist. Assoc. Hist. Papers 1970: 90-108.* Discusses sex manuals and attitudes toward sex in Canada, 1900-15. **S**

3277. Driedger, Otto H. MENNONITE FAMILY STRESSES IN THE CITY. *Mennonite Life 1968 23(4): 176-178.* Rapid change and the assimilation of ethnic groups into the larger Canadian culture mean that children grow up in a different milieu than did their parents. Conflict thus frequently arises between parents and teen-agers. Disintegrating families do not make use of community services. "The Mennonite work ethic on the farm was acquired by the children through the socialization process....The parent-child relationship, 'Mennonite discipleship,' and the work ethic were frequently transmitted non-verbally while working together. In the urban setting, this socialization requires a triple shift: 1) verbalizing discipleship, 2) developing parent-child relationships, and 3) transmitting the work ethic or its alternate in other ways." Mennonite families appear to be aided in their adaptability to the city by their religious faith. Based on published and unpublished sources; 6 notes.
D. J. Abramoske

3278. Furney, Shirley. A WIFE GOES OUT ON AN ARGUS PATROL. *Can. Forces Sentinel 1968 4(9): 12-14.* A military wife describes her experiences on a routine aerial patrol with her husband. Undocumented, illus.
J. H. Scrivner, Jr.

3279. Henripin, Jacques and Légaré, Jacques. RECENT TRENDS IN CANADIAN FERTILITY. *Can. R. of Sociol. and Anthrop. 1971 8(2): 106-118.* Observers have witnessed important changes in the level of fertility in Canada since 1941. The trend is often illustrated by variations in the birth rate. To understand these variations better, the main components of the birth rate will be analysed: age distribution of total and married female population, and age-specific fertility rates for all women and married women. The decline of marital fertility is mostly responsible for the fall of the birth rate observed since 1959. In a further analysis, period and cohort marital fertility are compared: from 1946 to 1960, period measures were much higher than cohort measures; in contrast to what happened during those years we now observe a spread in birth intervals, so that, since 1960, period measures are much lower than cohort marital fertility measures. **J**

3280. Henshel, Anne-Marie. SWINGING: A STUDY OF DECISION MAKING IN MARRIAGE. *Am. J. of Sociol. 1973 78(4): 885-891.* "This article examines decision making patterns in marriage with regard to involvement in group sex or swinging. Twenty-five Toronto wives constitute the sample studied. It is found that husbands have an advantage on the three indicators of decision making used in this study:

they more frequently are the first of the two spouses to learn of swinging, they tend to be the first to suggest swinging as an alternative for them, and they are more frequently the ones to reach the final decision leading to involvement in group sex. The results are discussed within the framework of power and exchange as well as in relation to studies on marital involvement and adjustment. **J**

3281. Jarvis, Julia. THE FOUNDING OF THE GIRL GUIDE MOVEMENT IN CANADA, 1910. *Ontario Hist. [Canada] 1970 62(4): 213- .* The author disputes standard accounts and claims that her sister was the moving spirit in the founding of the Girl Guides in Canada. The Jarvis sisters founded the first such troop in Toronto in 1909, prompted by their brother's enjoyment of Boy Scouting. 14 notes.
W. B. Whitham and S

3282. Labovitz, Sanford. SOME EVIDENCE OF CANADIAN ETHNIC, RACIAL, AND SEXUAL ANTAGONISM. *Can. R. of Sociol. and Anthrop. 1974 11(3): 247-254.* "Two studies designed to tap the nature of ethnic, racial, and sexual antagonism in mid-western Canada were carried out in 1972 and 1973. A definite pattern of such antagonism was discovered by using the evaluation of name types that represented selected ethnic groups. Respondents differentially evaluated the names of Edward Blake (English-Canadian male), Edith Blake (English-Canadian female), Joseph Walking Bear (Canadian Indian male), and Marcel Fournier (French-Canadian male). The rank ordering of names on an evaluational scale ranging from highly favourable to highly unfavourable was: (1) Edward Blake, (2) Edith Blake, (3) Joseph Walking Bear, (4) Marcel Fournier. The Indian and the French names were ranked well below the two names representing English Canadians." **J**

3283. Légaré, Jacques. DEMOGRAPHIC HIGHLIGHTS ON FERTILITY DECLINE IN CANADIAN MARRIAGE COHORTS. *Can. R. of Sociol. and Anthrop. 1974 11(4): 287-307.* "The purpose of this study is to examine the family-formation behaviour of marriage cohorts in Canada, using data from the 1961 census. Some comparisons are made with similar data from the 1960 United States census. Since the mean age of women at first marriage was fairly constant for the cohorts involved, fertility trends are then independent of the average nuptiality behaviour. Levels and trends in average family size are different for each country. In Canada, the average family size has gone down to 2.9 children per family for couples married between 1945 and 1950, while in the United States, the level has been rather constant—around 2.5 children per family—for couples married between 1920 and 1950. When age at marriage is taken into account, the comparisons of average family size and of the proportion of childless marriages in Canada and the United States become more interesting. The analysis for Canada of the distribution of families by size and of the parity progression ratios indicates the part played in the past by age at marriage: the younger the bride the larger the family. These differences are much less important for the latest cohorts, however. Unfortunately, childspacing could be estimated in only a crude way, and it appears that in Canada birth intervals are rather long. Finally, for Canadian couples married after 1950, recent trends in birth statistics suggest that the average family size will not remain at the level of 2.9 children per family but rather will decline to a level equivalent to that attained in the United States." **J**

3284. Pike, Robert. LEGAL ACCESS AND THE INCIDENCE OF DIVORCE IN CANADA: A SOCIOHISTORICAL ANALYSIS. *Can. R. of Sociol. and Anthrop. 1975 12(2): 115-133.* Long-term trends in divorce rates in Canada are examined within the framework of Canadian divorce law and of changes in social attitudes and family structure. It is suggested, in particular, that an essential concept in an analysis of the changing incidence of divorce is that of 'legal access,' by which is meant the impact on divorce rates of the nature of the legal grounds for divorce, as well as the impact of the provision, or lack of provision, of divorce court facilities. More specifically, Canadian divorce rates prior to the divorce law reforms of 1968 are shown to have provided a very poor indication of the actual rate of marriage breakdown owing to the stringent nature of the legal grounds of divorce and the lack of divorce court facilities in some provinces. Furthermore, the existence of major legal barriers to divorce fostered patterns of institutionalized evasion amongst those seeking divorces including migratory divorces and fraudulent divorce actions. However, the continued existence of large, and long-term, variations in divorce rates between the Canadian provinces highlights the need for further analysis of a wide variety of social, cultural, and demographic variables which appear to be associated with the differential regional incidence of divorce in this country.                                                J

3285.   Pool, D. I. and Bracher, M. D.   ASPECTS OF FAMILY FORMATION IN CANADA. *Can. R. of Sociol. and Anthrop. 1974 11(4): 308-323.* "Fertility is declining in Canada. We attempt to account for this change and to suggest policy implications. We review recent Canadian studies fitting them into an adaptation of the Davis-Blake framework. This permits the formulation of hypotheses at two levels implicit in the framework: 1) social structural (independent variables); 2) proximate ("intermediate" variables). Hypotheses were tested against available data, but a problem remained: does the decline result from deferring or averting of births?"                                                      J

3286.   Ryan, M. T.   CANADA'S FAMILY ALLOWANCE PROGRAM. *R. de l'U. d'Ottawa 1964 34(4): 427-438.* After a description of the nature of the family allowance in Canada, first supported by Father Lebel, Director of the Catholic Farmers Union, in 1927 and made law in 1944, five possible philosophies leading to it and three possible objections to it are considered. The conclusion drawn is that the allowance represents the fulfillment of a duty of social justice.                    M. Petrie

3287.   Schlesinger, Benjamin.   THE SINGLE WOMAN IN SECOND MARRIAGES. *Social Sci. 1974 49(2): 104-109.* "The topic of remarriage has been neglected in the field of family sociology in North America. With more and more persons deciding to marry again, we need to examine the adjustment problems in these unions. The few available studies have focused on the person who marries for the second time. This paper examines some of the selected findings of a Canadian study which included 28 single women, who married men who had been married previously. Their feelings, attitudes, and problems in this type of union give us direction for further research in this important and growing area of family life."                                                               J

3288.   Tepperman, Lorne.   ETHNIC VARIATIONS IN MARRIAGE AND FERTILITY: CANADA, 1871. *Can. R. of Sociol. and Anthrop. 1974 11(4): 324-343.* "The Canadian census of 1871 provided data for the estimation of ethnic variations in marriage and fertility. These variations largely account for the observed provincial variations in mean age at marriage, marital fertility, and birth rate, in 1871. Ethnic identity exercised an extremely strong influence on nuptiality and fertility, both directly and indirectly through the impact of ethnic custom on land distribution. Customs of inheritance and land partibility affected land inequality and mean size of landholdings, which in turn increased or decreased the feasibility of high levels of nuptiality and fertility. However, nuptiality was less influenced by land distribution than was fertility, implying that ethnic customs of nuptiality continued to predominate in the direct determination of marriage levels. It is concluded that regional and provincial variations in nuptiality and fertility can be satisfactorily accounted for by variations in ethnic composition and, perhaps secondarily, by historical patterns of land settlement. Ethnic reproductive practices were part of the cultural heritage brought to Canada by its immigrants, and they continued largely unaffected by the changed environment. Their continuity signified and maintained ethnic distinctiveness in Canadian society, but may also have had implications for the development of the Canadian 'vertical mosaic.' "                         J

3289.   Wakil, Parvez A.   ON THE QUESTION OF DEVELOPING A SOCIOLOGY OF THE CANADIAN FAMILY: A METHODOLOGICAL STATEMENT. *Can. R. of Sociol. and Anthrop. 1970 7(2): 154-157.* Discusses the findings presented at the 11th annual meeting of the Western Association of Sociology and Anthropology, held in Banff, Alberta, December 1969. Opposes the notion that, in view of the interdisciplinary nature of the field and the current lack of theory, there is no need for developing a sociology of the family in Canada. Seeks to clarify the methodological and substantive issues involved in this notion. There are today no fields of methodological study absolutely unique and having "real" boundaries. The degree of overlap may vary, but that there is overlap is indisputable. Moreover, the prior existence of a "process theory" unique to sociology is not essential to the development of a sociology of the family. Such a sociology will cover types, structural and organizational variations, degree of change and stresses involved, and success in adjustment to new structures. 4 notes.              R. V. Ritter

## Political Sphere

3290.   Dubois, Maria.   THE FEMINISTS, THE FUZZ AND THE COMMUNISTS. *Communist Viewpoint [Canada] 1971 3(2): 38-43.* The Women's Liberation Movement can learn from the Communist Party the true source of their exploitation. From a symposium on 50 years of the Canadian Communist Party's thought and action.              S

3291.   Farid, Z. and Kuyek, Joan.   WHO SPEAKS FOR WORKING-CLASS WOMEN? *Can. Dimension 1975 10(8): 80-82.* The Women's Liberation Movement in Canada, dominated by middle-class women, ought to turn its attention to working-class women and such goals as equal access to jobs and promotions, state-supported day nurseries, and equality before the law.              S

3292.   Gorham, Deborah.   "SINGING UP THE HILL." *Can. Dimension 1975 10(8): 26-38.* Discusses the significance of the British North America Act of 1929 by which Canadian women were declared to be legally "persons," and traces the suffragist movement and equal rights advocates in Canada from the late 19th through the early 20th century.              S

3293.   MacPherson, Kay.   THE SEEDS OF THE 70'S. *Can. Dimension 1975 10(8): 39-42.* Surveys the Canadian Women's Liberation Movement's progress during the last 20 years.              S

3294.   Maghami, Farhat Ghaem.   POLITICAL KNOWLEDGE AMONG YOUTH: SOME NOTES ON PUBLIC OPINION FORMATION. *Can. J. of Pol. Sci. 1974 7(2): 334-340.* Devised a political knowledge scale to test a sampling of Canadian college and university students. Relates findings to socio-economic background, religion, sex, and education. 5 tables, 8 notes, 2 appendices.              R. V. Kubicek

3295.   Matheson, Gwen.   NELLIE MC CLUNG. *Can. Dimension 1975 10(8): 42-48.* Provides a biographical sketch of early 20th century feminist Nellie McClung and reviews her book *In Times Like These*, first published in 1915 and recently edited by Veronica Strong-Boag (Toronto: U. of Toronto Pr., 1972).              S

3296.   Trofimenkoff, Susan Mann.   HENRI BOURASSA AND "THE WOMAN QUESTION." *J. of Can. Studies 1975 10(4): 3-11.* Discusses the opposition of writer Henry Bourassa to feminism, woman suffrage and divorce in Canada, 1913-25.

3297.   Yanovsky, Avrom and Fairley, Margaret.   MARGARET FAIRLEY. A REMEMBRANCE. THE CULTURAL WORKER'S RESPONSIBILITY TO THE PEOPLE. *Horizons: The Marxist Q. [Canada] 1968 25: 1-6.* Three short articles, the first two in remembrance of Margaret Fairley (1885-1968), and the third her last written work. The first article, unsigned, highlights her life, including her role in founding the journals *Canadian Forum, Frontiers,* and *Horizons.* In "A Remembrance," Avrom Yanovsky stresses her great love for Canada, her determined spirit when fighting for a principle of cause she believed in, and her habit of carrying out her fight in a form that was popular. He concludes: "Like Dr. Norman Bethune, Margaret Fairley was an outstanding example of the Communist intellectual who combines the search for deeper cultural values, with the daily struggles to improve the ordinary conditions of the people as part of the overall movement for socialism." In her article, Margaret Fairley decries the fashionable and widespread "flight of artists from responsibility," and their concentration on "painting and poetry which say nothing of importance about anything, and nothing at all about the outer world." Artists should strive to "enlarge the experience of the people, giving them through thought and feeling a widening and deepening of their whole personalities."              W. E. Ratliff

## Religion and Ethnicity

3298.   Chimbos, Peter D.   IMMIGRANTS' ATTITUDES TOWARD THEIR CHILDREN'S INTERETHNIC MARRIAGES IN A CANADIAN COMMUNITY. *Internat. Migration R. 1971 5(1): 5-17.* Inaugurates sociological study of the family life of immigrants. Compares parental attitudes toward exogamous marriages in the Dutch, Greek, and Slovak communities. Sampling was done in Ontario City. Dutch immigrant parents expressed least opposition to exogamous marriage; Greek immigrant parents expressed most. Other controlling factors were the respondent's sex, education, and size of natal community. Resumé in English, French, Spanish, and German. 10 notes.          G. O. Gagnon

3299. Damas, David. SOCIAL ANTHROPOLOGY OF THE CENTRAL ESKIMO. *Can. R. of Sociol. and Anthrop. 1975 12(3): 252-266.* Current and recent literature on the anthropology of Central Eskimos deals mainly with family and local social organization, authority structure, alliance mechanisms, and cultural ecology.

3300. DeMoissac, R. Élizabeth. LES SOEURS GRISES ET LES ÉVENEMENTS DE 1869-1870 [The Grey Sisters and the events of 1869-1870]. *Sessions d'Étude: Soc. Can. d'Hist. de l'Église Catholique [Canada] 1970 (37): 215-228.* Recounts the charitable exploits of the "Grey Sisters," a Catholic religious order, during a period of great civil strife in the history of western Canada.

3301. Grisdale, Alex and Shipley, Nan. BLACK STONE'S WIFE: A SAULTEAUX INDIAN TALE. *Queen's Q. [Canada] 1968 75(4): 592-595.* Presents a folktale of the Saulteaux Indians of Canada in the 20th century, emphasizing the theme of marriage.

3302. Légaré, Jacques. LES RELIGIEUSES DU CANADA: LEUR EVOLUTION NUMERIQUE ENTRE 1965 ET 1980 [Nuns of Canada: their numerical evolution between 1965 and 1980]. *Recherches Sociographiques [Canada] 1969 10(1): 7-21.* Due to such social factors as advanced education and greater career opportunities, the number of young girls entering into religous communities of nuns has declined to rock-bottom level. This, accompanied by the aging process of those already within these communities, indicates that by 1975, or at the latest 1980, a state of crisis will exist. This situation will inevitably bring about fundamental changes in the role played by religious communities in Canadian society and it will force a reorientation of the organizational thinking of these same communities. Based on questionnaires answered by 65,248 Canadian nuns and on earlier studies of religious communities both in and out of Canada.          A. E. LeBlanc

3303. Lessard, Marc-André and Montminy, Jean-Paul. LES RELIGIEUSES DU CANADA: AGE, RECRUTEMENT, ET PERSERVERANCE [Canadian Nuns: age, recruitment, and perserverance]. *Recherches Sociographiques [Canada] 1967 8(1): 15-48.* Studies the ages of Canadian nuns and the relation of age to the various duties and positions of the nuns, with a look at the interaction of perserverance and recruitment in their formation and training. 26 tables.          C. P. LeBris

3304. Loranger, T. R. Madeleine. HISTORIQUE DE LA CONGRÉGATION DES MISSIONNAIRES DE L'IMMACULÉE-CONCEPTION ET DES ORIGINES DE LA SOCIÉTÉ DES MISSIONS-ETRANGÈRES DE QUÉBEC [An account of the Congregation of Missionaries of the Immaculate Conception and the origins of the Society of Foreign Missions of Quebec]. *Sessions d'Étude: Soc. Can. d'Hist. de l'Église Catholique [Canada] 1971 (38): 71-84.* Surveys the apostolic accomplishments, especially in China and Taiwan, of the Sister Missionaries of the Immaculate Conception since its founding in 1902 and in concert with the Society of Foreign Missions of Quebec.

3305. Pouliot, Leon. MGR. BOURGET ET LES INSTITUTS CONTEMPLATIFS [Msgr. Bourget and the contemplative institutes]. *R. d'Hist. de l'Amérique Française [Canada] 1963 17(1): 12-18.* The writings and deeds of Msgr. Bourget concerning the contemplative orders. In the 36 years of his bishopric (1840-75) he introduced to Canada the Oblates of Mary-Immaculate (1841), the Jesuits and the religious of the Sacred Heart (1842), the religious of the Good Shepherd (1844), the clergy of St. Viateur, the fathers, brothers, and sisters of the Holy Cross (1847), and the brothers of Mercy (1865). He founded the order of Sisters of Providence (1843), the Sisters of the Holy Names of Jesus and Mary (1844), the Sisters of Compassion (1848), and the Sisters of St. Anne (1850).          L. F. S. Upton

3306. Romaniuk, A. MODERNIZATION AND FERTILITY: THE CASE OF THE JAMES BAY INDIANS. *Can. R. of Sociol. and Anthrop. 1974 11(4): 344-359.* "The theory that modernization at its initial stage may result in an increase in fertility through the relaxation of restrictive customs governing procreative behaviours of premodern societies has often been postulated, but little empirical evidence has been provided to support it. Data collected on fertility for Indians living in the James Bay area of Canada tend to confirm the validity of this theory. They reveal, for this population, that intervals between successive births tend to become shorter among younger as compared to older generations of mothers, and this is attributed to three factors related to modernization: 1) changes in lactation habits whereby an increasingly larger proportion of mothers either do not breast-feed at all, or do so for shorter periods of time than did the older generations; 2) reduction in the level of pregnancy wastage resulting both from medical progress and from the fact that hardship and pregnancy accidents to which the pregnant mothers were formerly exposed probably have diminished as James Bay Indians have shifted from a nomadic to a sedentary society; and 3) reduction in the incidence of prolonged temporary separation of spouses as the communication between home villages of spouses has improved and as Indian families have given up their nomadic mode of life."          J

3307. Romaniuk, A. and Piché, V. NATALITY ESTIMATES FOR THE CANADIAN INDIANS BY STABLE POPULATION MODELS, 1900-1969. *Can. R. of Sociol. and Anthrop. 1972 9(1): 1-20.* After having shown that official series of birth rates for the Indian population prior to 1960 suffer from considerable deficiencies, two indirect methods are applied to arrive at some trustworthy estimates of these rates. Use is made, in the one case, of the age distribution data available since 1900, and, in the other case, of 1961 census data on children ever-born to women by age. In both instances stable population models are used for analyzing the underlying data and for deriving the estimates. According to the best obtained estimates, the birth-rate for the Indian population seems to have remained relatively stable in the past, at a level close to 50 per 1000 persons. A gradual decline in fertility has been taking place since about 1960. Thus the birth-rate has dropped from 46.0 in 1961 to 36.8 in 1969, the latest available figure. This trend may be regarded as a major development in the demography of this ethnic group which is, in many respects, unique in the Canadian context.          J

3308. Whyte, John D. THE LAVELL CASE AND EQUALITY IN CANADA. *Queen's Q. [Canada] 1974 81(1): 28-41.* Analyzes the controversial 1973 verdict by the Supreme Court of Canada in the Lavell case. The central issues in the case were "the legitimacy of administration of native peoples in Canada" and "the constitutional value of equality" of sexes. Feels the Supreme Court failed to resolve key points at issue and as a result "cast doubt on the Court's adequacy to perform this duty." 8 notes.          J. A. Casada

3309. Wilkinson, Paul. THE DOMESTICATION OF THE MUSK-OX. *Polar Record [Great Britain] 1971 15(98): 683-690.* Domestication of the musk-ox was begun in 1953 by John J. Teal, Jr., in an effort to improve the native economic base by using a species native to the Arctic. Calves were quickly and permanently tamed and later bred successfully under farm conditions. The wool (qiviut) is superior to cashmere and has a large potential market. Full-scale breeding began at College, Alaska, in 1966, supported by the W. K. Kellogg Foundation. Breeding stations were established at Old Fort Chimo, Quebec, in 1967; and at Bardu, Norway, in 1969. In Alaska, musk-oxen will be lent to villages, with production and marketing of the qiviut controlled by a cooperative. Each village will produce distinctively patterned garments. At present prices and pay-rates a woman can earn $400-500 a year knitting qiviut garments. Primary and secondary sources; illus.          L. L. Hubbard

## Culture, the Arts, and Recreation

3310. Blissett, W. F., ed. LETTERS FROM EMILY CARR. *U. of Toronto Q. [Canada] 1972 41(2): 93-150.* Publishes 44 letters written by Emily Carr (1871-1945), Canadian painter and writer, to Miss Ruth Humphrey, Professor of English at Victoria College, between 1937 and 1944. Miss Carr suffered from infirmities associated with advanced age during the period of the correspondence, but this did not keep her "courage, humor, curiosity, and friendly concern" from shining through her comments on illness, frustration, and restriction of activity. The letters also contain reference to a number of the Canadian literary and art personalities of the day. 57 notes. W. L. Bowers

3311. Boyle, Richard P. COMMUNITY INFLUENCE ON COLLEGE ASPIRATIONS: AN EMPIRICAL EVALUATION OF EXPLANATORY FACTORS. *Rural Sociol. 1966 31(3): 277-292.* "The fact that adolescent residents of smaller communities have lower aspirations than adolescent residents of larger communities is well documented. A number of possible explanations have been suggested: (1) financial resources and needs, (2) educational opportunities, (3) the sociocultural context of community life, and (4) special consequences of farming. However, no previous researcher has attempted a direct empirical evaluation of the relative importance of these explanations. In this paper data from a survey of Canadian high school girls were used to evaluate the first three, since the fourth appears to apply only to boys. This analysis indicates that educational opportunity explains most of the relationship; and when both educational opportunity and community context are controlled, all relationship between community size and college aspiration disappears. Previous research allows tentative generalization of these findings to high school boys." J

3312. Chalmers, John W. FRANCES ANN HOPKINS: THE LADY WHO PAINTED CANOES. *Can. Geographical J. 1971 83(1): 18-27.* The artist Frances Ann Hopkins painted scenes of Canada's fur trade. S

3313. Chalmers, John W. KLEE WYCK. *Alaska J. 1975 5(4): 231-238.* Discusses the life and paintings of Emily Carr, 1888-1972, a Canadian whose nickname, Klee Wyck, was an Indian name meaning Laughing One, and who spent most of her life painting and drawing the Indians of Western Canada.

3314. Dudek, Louis. NATIONALISM IN CANADIAN POETRY. *Queen's Q. [Canada] 1968 75(4): 557-567.* Discusses elements of nationalism in Canadian poetry during 1864-1946, including the works of Helen Johnson and W. D. Lighthall.

3315. Johnson, Alice M. EDWARD AND FRANCES HOPKINS OF MONTREAL. *Beaver [Canada] 1971 302(2): 4-17.* Edward Hopkins traveled for the Hudson's Bay Company, and his wife Frances painted scenes of their travels. S

3316. Martin, Mary F. THE SHORT LIFE OF ISABELLA VALANCY CRAWFORD. *Dalhousie Rev. 1972 52(3): 390-400.* Presents a biographical and critical study of the life and literary activities of Isabella Valancy Crawford, who spent most of her life in various towns, and ultimately, in Toronto, Ontario, Canada. There is considerable disagreement about most of her life. She was "Canada's first considerable woman poet." 14 notes. R. V. Ritter

3317. New, William H. THE 'GENIUS' OF PLACE AND TIME: THE FICTION OF ETHEL WILSON. *J. of Can. Studies 1968 3(4): 39-48.* Discusses the fiction of Canadian novelist Ethel Wilson (*Hetty Dorval, The Equations of Love, Swamp Angel*), 1947-61.

3318. Struthers, J. R. ALICE MUNRO AND THE AMERICAN SOUTH. *Can. R. of Am. Studies 1975 6(2): 196-204.* Analyzes the works of Alice Munro, a Canadian writer of fiction. She was most influenced by early 20th century literary and historical suppositions about the nature and character of white society in the American South. She believed that many of the values, biases, and cultural peculiarities of the American South flourished in the rural sections of Ontario. Based on Munro's writings and secondary sources; 42 notes. H. T. Lovin

3319. Tippett, Maria. EMILY CARR'S FOREST. *J. of Forest Hist. 1974 18(4): 133-137.* Emily Carr's paintings of British Columbia forests and Indian villages placed her among Canada's finest artists. 20 notes. L. F. Johnson

# Regional

## General

3320. Easton, Carol. HISTORY AT PEACE. *Westways 1976 68(6): 32-35, 62-63.* Discusses the North Peace Country of Western Canada, focusing on homesteaders and the stories of pioneers, 1914-76.

3321. Tremblay, Marc-Adelard. EVOLUTION DE LA STRUCTURE FAMILIALE A L'ANSE-DES-LAVALLEE [Evolution of family structure at Anse-des-Lavallée]. *Recherches Sociographiques [Canada] 1963 4(3): 351-357.* General sociological study of family relations in a small village. Sources from observations, 7 notes. C. P. LeBris

3322. Van Kirk, Sylvia. WOMEN AND THE FUR TRADE. *Beaver [Canada] 1972 303(3): 4-21.* The coming of white women into Indian country upset the social order of common law marriage between fur traders and Indian women. S

## Atlantic Provinces

3323. Barclay, C. N. BENEDICT ARNOLD: TURN-COAT AND INTERNATIONAL ADVENTURER. *Army Q. and Defence J. [Great Britain] 1975 105(2): 208-213.* Emphasizes the activities of Benedict Arnold and his wife Peggy Arnold in Great Britain, the West Indies, and New Brunswick, 1781-1801.

3324. Campbell, G. G. SUSAN DUNLAP: HER DIARY. *Dalhousie R. [Canada] 1966 46(2): 215-222.* Susan Dunlap (1850-1916) of Stewiacke, Nova Scotia, kept a diary from January 1866 to 1912. Day by day she covered every inch of every page with fine crowded writing, and in hundreds of terse entries presented an intimate picture of the home and community she knew. Excerpts from the first two years of the diary are included. L. F. S. Upton

3325. Dunlop, Allan C. PHARMACIST AND ENTREPRENEUR PICTOU'S J. D. B. FRASER. *Nova Scotia Hist. Q. [Canada] 1974 4(1): 1-21.* James Daniel Bain Fraser (1807-69), pioneer pharmacist of Pictou, Nova Scotia, served the community as Justice of the Peace, dentist, Commissioner of Streets, and inventor. He is best remembered, however, for the first use of chloroform in childbirth. Based on documents in the Public Archives of Nova Scotia (W721) and secondary sources; 69 notes. H. M. Evans

3326. Grant, Dorothy Metie. "WE SHALL CONQUER YET!" *Nova Scotia Hist. Q. [Canada] 1972 2(3): 243-251.* Recounts the persistent efforts of Hugh Bell of Halifax, Nova Scotia, who helped found the Provincial Hospital for the Insane. Support from Dorothea Dix, who visited Nova Scotia in the 1840's, contributed to Bell's success by attracting attention and prompting public action. The hospital opened in the 1850's at a location near Dartmouth, Nova Scotia. Based on primary and secondary sources; biblio. C. K. Piehl

3327. Grant, Francis W. A DAUGHTER OF MAITLAND. *Nova Scotia Hist. Q. [Canada] 1972 2(2): 153-162.* Bibliographical sketch of Helen Smith Grant, daughter of a Maitland, Nova Scotia, shipbuilder and wife of William Grant, ship captain and owner. After her marriage in 1873, she spent 13 years at sea with her husband, raising two sons in the process. Describes illness and storms at sea. In the 1880's the Grants moved to Victoria, British Columbia, where her husband was involved in sealing and Mrs. Grant devoted her efforts to charity, temperance, and women's organizations. C. K. Piehl

3328. Mauro, R. G. DILLON WALLACE OF LABRADOR. *Beaver [Canada] 1975 301(1): 50-57.* In 1903 Leonidas Hubbard and Dillon Wallace set out to explore the northeast section of Labrador. Accompanied only by one guide, the party suffered from weather and lack of food. Hubbard froze to death. In 1905 Wallace, feeling a debt to Hubbard, decided to complete the expedition. However, he was competing with Hubbard's widow, who set out with her own party. She won the race, and both explorers published results of their trips. She suspected that Wallace knew more about her husband's death than he had revealed. Critics praised both works, pointing out the professional maps and diagrams in the widow's book, while granting to Wallace the better interpretation of the expedition trials. 22 illus., 2 maps.                    D. Chaput

3329. Pocius, Gerald L. "THE FIRST DAY THAT I THOUGHT OF IT SINCE I GOT WED": ROLE EXPECTATIONS AND SINGER STATUS IN A NEWFOUNDLAND OUTPOST. *Western Folklore* 1976 35(2): 109-122. Explores the importance of social status and male-female roles among recognized singers in Calvert, Newfoundland, an outport village. The author believes social recognition and sex roles often lead to neglect of some "areas of the singing tradition." Based on primary and secondary sources; 17 notes.                    S. L. Myres

## Quebec

3330. Barbe, Raoul. CANADA: LA PROVINCE DE QUEBEC [Canada: the Province of Quebec]. *R. Internat. de Droit Comparé [France] 1965 17(3): 640-642.* As part of a study of contemporary marriage law begun by the Institute of Comparative Law of the University of Paris in 1966, the latest changes in the laws of Quebec are described. These have increased the wife's control over her property, her voice in regard to community property, and her power to act for her husband. Documented, 5 notes.                    J. S. Gassner

3331. Bélanger, Anna R. UNE ÉDUCATRICE D'HIER POUR AUJOURD'HUI: MARIE GUYART DE L'INCARNATION [An educator of yesterday for today: Marie Guyart de l'Incarnation]. *Sessions d'Étude: Soc. Can. d'Hist. de l'Église Catholique [Canada] 1972: 55-64.* Marie Guyart de l'Incarnation, a French nun who came to Canada in 1639 to teach, had a very modern conception of education, emphasizing love and parental concern for students, who in this case were Indian.

3332. Breton, Yvan. MORPHOLOGIE SOCIALE ET MARIAGE A ST. PAUL RIVER [Social morphology and marriage at St. Paul River]. *Recherches Sociographiques [Canada] 1970 11(1/2): 117-149.* The village of St. Paul River is much more economically underdeveloped than others in the Quebec Northeast. One is immediately struck by the overall youth of the population and the high density of male inhabitants. Most of the families are large and family attachments are strong. Approximately three-fourths of the population is Protestant, the remaining quarter Roman Catholic. All of these factors play an important role in the marriage customs and expectations of the village, due primarily to the restricted female population, which in turn causes St. Paul River to possess anthropological norms that do not follow the regular pattern. 6 tables, 5 graphs, 35 notes.                    A. E. LeBlanc

3333. Brière, Germain. LA REFORME DE LA CAPACITE DE LA FEMME MARIEE DANS LA PROVINCE DE QUEBEC [Reform of the legal status of married women in the province of Quebec]. *R. Internat. de Droit Comparé [France] 1966 18(1): 83-88.* On 1 July 1964 a new law on the legal status of married women went into effect in Quebec. Provisions covering the personal relationship of husband and wife did not go to the extent of making the wife full equal of the husband. Those concerned with financial relationship give the wife more freedom in her own financial and property transactions and a greater voice in the management of family affairs. Documented.                    J. S. Gassner

3334. Chabot, Marie Emmanuel. LES URSULINES DE QUÉBEC EN 1850 [The Ursulines of Quebec in 1850]. *Sessions d'Étude: Soc. Can. d'Hist. de l'Église Catholique [Canada] 1969 (36): 75-92.* Retraces the history of the Ursulines of Quebec, focusing on those individuals in the order who contributed most to its development and reputation up to 1850.

3335. Charland, Thomas. LES NEVEUX DE MADAME DE BEAUBASSIN [The nephews of Madame de Beaubassin]. *Rev. d'Hist. de l'Amérique Française [Canada] 1969 23(1): 68-91.* Describes the lives of the six Hertel brothers. They were soldiers, well liked by Montcalm, who was on friendly terms with their aunt, Madame de Beaubassin. Details their families, their battles in the campaign against the British, and their deaths. Based on archives; 91 notes.                    C. Bates

3336. Chartier, Roger. LA RÉPARATION DES ACCIDENTS DU TRAVAIL ET LA COMMISSION DU SALAIRE MINIMUM DES FEMMES (1925-1931) [Workmen's compensation and the Commission on the minimum wage for women (1925-31)]. *Industrial Relations [Canada] 1963 18(1): 44-58.* Fifth in a series of texts on the history of Quebec labor law and the services of the Ministry of Labor, 1885-1963.

3337. Côté, Andre and McComber, Marie. SOURCES DE L'HISTOIRE DU SAGUENAY-LAC-SAINT-JEAN: INVENTAIRE DU FONDS DUBUC [Historical resources of Saguenay-Lac-Saint-Jean: inventory of the Dubuc Estate]. *Protée [Canada] 1976 4(1): 129-153.* Gives an inventory of the Dubuc family papers of three generations, 1892-ca. 1963, dealing with some 50 pulp and paper companies founded and directed by J.-E. Alfred Dubuc of Chicoutimi and by his son Antoine Dubuc, with personal correspondence of his wife and family.

3338. Côte, Imelda. LES SOEURS DU BON PASTEUR AU SAGUENAY [The Sisters of the Good Shepherd in the Saguenay]. *Sessions d'Étude: Soc. Can. d'Hist. l'Eglise Catholique, Rapport [Canada] 1965: 21-27.* The Order of the Good Shepherd, founded in 1850, opened the first girls' boarding school in Chicoutimi in 1864 and organized the first regional normal school in 1907. The Saguenay region became a province for the order in 1933. Today, the Sisters of the Good Shepherd supervise 20 schools, 278 classrooms and 8,600 students in the Saguenay area. Undocumented.                    C. Thibault

3339. D'Allaire, Micheline. ORIGINE SOCIALE DES RELIGIEUSES DE L'HÔSPITAL-GÉNÉRAL DE QUÉBEC [The social origins of the nuns of the General Hospital of Quebec]. *Rev. d'Hist. de l'Amérique Française [Canada] 1970 23(4): 559-582.* Presents a sociological study of the nuns of the General Hospital, comparing similar religious groups, the nuns of the Hôtel-Dieu Hospital and the Ursuline Convent. Separation of these previously interdependent houses tended to isolate social types. Compares the backgrounds of the nuns and the dowries offered by their families to their order as an indication of their economic status. Concludes that most nuns of the General Hospital were from an elite social milieu. Based on official published records, secondary sources; 5 tables, 14 notes.                    S. Sevilla

3340. Demers, George-Edouard. DE TOURS A QUEBEC [From Tours to Quebec]. *R. de l'U. Laval [Canada] 1964 19(2): 99-104.* Relates the vision and the events leading to her journey to Canada of Mother Mary of the Incarnation who founded the first mission in French Canada, and who was accompanied by one nun from Tours and two from Paris and by Mme. de la Peltrie, a rich widow, who had vowed to devote her fortune to endow a seminary for Indian girls.                    M. Petrie

3341. Dorais, Louis-Jacques. LA VIE TRADITIONELLE SUR LA CÔTE DE BEAUPRE, AU DEBUT XXE SIECLE [The traditional life on the coast of Beaupré at the beginning of the 20th century]. *R. d'Hist. de l'Amérique Française [Canada] 1966 19(4): 535-550.* In certain rural areas of Quebec, the way of life introduced during the French regime was preserved in an integrated manner into the 20th century. Such is the case with the coast of Beaupré. The author discusses the "material culture" (houses and interior decoration, the rural outbuildings); the daily life (which continued to be agricultural, broken by simple distractions like folk singing); social relations (in a society basically homogeneous and free from class structure, the basic unit being the family); and folklore (customs, beliefs, and the feast-days which had spiritual significance but also broke the monotony of daily life). Despite a belief in legend and superstition, the people of this society were extremely realistic and practical, concerned with daily existence and the concrete. Undocumented.
                    J. M. Bumsted

3342. Dupont, Antonin. LOUIS-ALEXANDRE TASCHEREAU ET LA LÉGISLATION SOCIALE AU QUÉBEC, 1920-1936 [Louis Alexandre Taschereau and social laws in Quebec province 1920-1936]. *Rev. d'Hist. de l'Amérique Française [Canada] 1972 26(3): 397-426.* Laws passed by the liberal Premier of Quebec province, Louis-Alexandre Taschereau, led to the hostility of the Catholic clergy who considered social welfare its domain and violently opposed progressive laws concerning women's suffrage, observance of the Sabbath, adoption of children, and sale of alcohol. Taschereau's government, though moderate, threatened the power of the Catholic clergy by assuming responsibility in social matters. Based on Quebec archives, personal letters, newspapers, and secondary sources; 82 notes.                                          C. Collon

3343. Frégault, Guy. LA NOUVELLE FRANCE A L'EPOQUE DE MARIE DE L'INCARNATION [New France in the time of Marie de l'Incarnation]. *R. d'Hist. de l'Amérique Française [Canada] 1964 18(2): 167-175.* Developments in New France from the arrival of Marie de l'Incarnation in 1639 to her death in 1672, especially those reflected by her letters which, in part, deal with the foundation of Montreal, and the conflict between religious and commercial (missionary and colonial) interests, with the latter gradually prevailing.                    E. W. Hathaway

3344. Giovanni, M. THE ROLE OF RELIGIOUS IN PHARMACY UNDER CANADA'S "ANCIEN REGIME." *Culture [Canada] 1963 24(1): 13-32 and (2): 138-151.* From the arrival of the Recollet Friars in 1615, the religious played an important role in the dissemination and accumulation of pharmaceutical knowledge. Making use of French pharmaceutical know-how and native Indian remedies, the religious ministered to the needs of the colony. Poultices and purgatives were used to combat the ills created by epidemics and warfare. The nuns of the Hôtel Dieu at Quebec were especially helpful and hard-working in this regard. Several remedies used during the period are included and a good deal is said about the endeavors of Michael Sarrazin. References are made to the variety of things to be found in the Archives of the Hôtel Dieu. Based on printed collections of primary materials; several works of a secondary nature are used.                                                    A. E. LeBlanc

3345. Heroux, Liliane. DES FEMMES EN GRIS [Women in grey]. *Sessions d'Étude: Soc. Can. d'Hist. de l'Église Catholique [Canada] 1969 (36): 49-56* Sketches the history of the Grey Sisters, a religious order devoted to the care of the sick and indigent, and discusses their activities in Montreal and Quebec during the second half of the 19th century.

3346. Jutras, Rene. VIABILITE DE LA FAMILLE QUEBECOISE [Viability of the Quebec family]. *Action Natl. [Canada] 1972 61(5): 357-383.* Defines the family and its importance to a nation, and traces the pattern of family growth in Quebec. During 1608-1760, phenomenal growth occurred. Then, until the early 1960's, fecundity maintained itself, especially when compared to growth patterns of the remainder of the Western world. The clear decline since the early 1960's is a clear reflection of the social climate that reigns in Quebec. It is time for the state to examine this crisis and to present the necessary solutions that take into account the crucial importance of the family. 15 tables, biblio.
                                                                        A. E. LeBlanc

3347. Langis, Jean. LES DEBUTS DE SAINT-SULPICE A MONTREAL (1657-1688) [The beginnings of Saint-Sulpice at Montreal (1657-88) ]. *Sessions d'Étude: Soc. Can. d'Hist. de l'Eglise Catholique. Rapport [Canada] 1964 31: 15-22.* Gives an abridged history of the first French priests sent by Father Jean Jacques Olier de Verneuil, founder of Saint-Sulpice, from 1657 to 1688. Outstanding figures in this period are Gabriel Souart (1611-91), first missionary priest of Ville Marie; Marguerite Bourgeoys (1620-1700); Gabriel de Thubière de Lévy de Queylus (1612-77), first superior of the seminary; and François Dollier de Casson (1636-1701), his successor.                                        E. P. Stickney

3348. Lavigne, Marie et al. LA FÉDÉRATION NATIONALE SAINT-JEAN-BAPTISTE ET LES REVENDICATIONS FÉMINISTES AU DÉBUT DU XXᵉ SIÈCLE [The Saint John the Baptist National Federation and feminist demands at the start of the 20th century]. *R. d'hist. de l'Amérique française [Canada] 1975 29(3): 353-373.* Surveys the history of the Fédération Nationale Saint-Jean-Baptiste from 1907-33, and discusses the role of its founder, Marie Gérin-Lajoie (1867-1945). In order to develop in French-Canadian society, the Fédération, a feminist group, had to make alliances with the Catholic clergy and compromises with the prevailing ideology. While calling for increased political rights for women, it supported the integrity of the family and the traditional female familial role. The organization did not succeed in synthesizing these paradoxical interests, and its influence declined after 1933. Based on documents in the Archives de la Fédération Nationale Saint-Jean-Baptiste (Montréal), Archives de la Communauté des Soeurs de Notre-Dame-du-Bon Conseil (Montréal), and secondary sources; 31 notes.                                                              L. B. Chan

3349. Maurault, Olivier. DEUX PRECIEUX MANUSCRITS [Two valuable manuscripts]. *Cahiers des Dix [Canada] 1963 28: 33-42.* Describes two manuscripts in the Marguerite Bourgeoys Room of the Congregation of Notre Dame, Montreal. The first is a biography of Mademoiselle Jeanne Le Ber (d. 1714) by M. Vachon de Belmont (d. 1732). This was part of a work entitled "Eloges de quelques personnes mortes en odeur de sainteté à Montreal en Canada" [Eulogies on some persons who died in the odor of sanctity at Montreal, Canada]. It was presented to the Abbé of Saint Aubin in 1722, but he decided not to publish it. Mademoiselle Le Ber was a recluse who shut herself in her room in 1680. More active was the life of Sister Marguerite Bourgeoys (d. 1700) narrated in the second manuscript, "Vie de la Soeur Marguerite Bourgeoys...la conduite et les actions de cette Vénérable Souer" [Life of Sister Marguerite Bourgeoys...the conduct and actions of this venerable sister]. The circumstances are described in which Monsieur Charles Glandelet of the Seminary of Quebec wrote this still unpublished account shortly after Sister Bourgeoys' death.                          L. F. S. Upton

3350. Mère Marie-de-la-Nativité. L'ECOLE MENAGERE DE ROBERVAL, OEUVRE DE MERE SAINT-RAPHAEL [The school of home economics, the foundation of Mother Saint Raphael]. *Sessions d'Étude: Soc. Can. d'Hist. l'Eglise Catholique, Rapport [Canada] 1965: 91-100.* Relates the foundation and growth of a school for the teaching of home economics in a forested region of the Saguenay. Undocumented.
                                                                        C. Thibault

3351. Nish, Cameron. LA BOURGEOISIE ET LES MARIAGES 1729-1748 [The middle class and the institution of marriage 1729-48]. *R. d'Hist. de l'Amérique Française [Canada] 1966 19(4): 585-605.* In New France, matrimonial lines were established on the same pattern as in the English colonies. There was a striking degree of social mobility. It was not a vertical mobility; a habitant could not climb the social ladder. It was a horizontal mobility in which class lines were erased among a group of people who in their economic functions could be labeled "bourgeoisie," and the nobility and aristocracy. The important families of the colony intermarried to such an extent that it is impossible to consider its class structure in classical terms. In New France, the "estates" were not clearly separated, but blurred. An appendix lists some of the more prevalent marriage lines. Documented.                                        J. M. Bumsted

3352. Provost, Honorius. LA DEVOTION A LA SAINTE FAMILLE EN CANADA [The devotion to the Holy Family in Canada]. *R. de l'U. Laval [Canada] 1964 18(5): 395-405, and (6): 543-552.* Part I. Recounts yet another of the many influences left on Quebec by Msgr. de Laval. During three centuries since he initiated the devotion of the Holy Family, the sisterhood among the women of Quebec has been maintained practically without interruption. The organizations of children, men, and savages had a briefer history. Part II. The cult of the Holy Family has lasted nearly 300 years as a women's organization. The various dates upon which the festival was held, annually, from 1665 to the last change of date in 1921, are examined. The appendix discusses the determination of these dates as a case in historical criticism.                          G. H. Kelsey

3353. Robert, Bernard. CONSEQUENCES DE L'EXODE RURAL SUR LA COMPOSITION PAR SEXE DES POPULATIONS DES CAMPAGNES [Consequence of rural exodus on sex structure of rural population]. *Industrial Relations [Canada] 1968 23(1): 123-142.* Discusses the population growth in the province of Quebec revealing the existence of powerful migratory currents which radically modify the demographic structures in the regions of exodus and the regions of settlement. Internal migrations of population, affecting selectively the groups inhabiting the regions of depopulation, contribute to the creation of serious imbalances in the proportion of males to females. In particular, it appears that the demographic distribution is characterized by the numerical superiority of the male group in rural areas, while the female group is dominant in the urban regions.                              P. Rabineau

3354. Saint-Laurent, Jacques. STRUCTURE ET ÉVOLUTION DES TAUX DE RÉMUNÉRATION DES INFIRMIÈRES DU DIOCÈSE DU QUÉBEC, 1944-1962 [Structure and evolution of nurses' salaries in the Diocese of Quebec, 1944-62]. *Industrial Relations [Canada] 1963 18(2): 149-161.* Examines wages of nurses in the Diocese of Quebec, with regards to the evolution of the variables taken into consideration in the determination of salaries. The analysis is incomplete and pretends only to be a starting point for further investigation.            P. Rabineau

3355. Séguin, Robert-Lionel. LES DIVERTISSEMENTS AU QUÉBEC AUX XVII<sup>e</sup> ET XVIII<sup>e</sup> SIÈCLES [Amusements in Quebec during the 17th and 18th centuries]. *Rev. Française d'Hist. d'Outre-Mer [France] 1974 61(222): 5-17.* The social and cultural conditions in New France did not favor parties and amusements. War with the Indians was a real danger. The Church did not approve of balls, dancing, or the theater. Despite the attitudes of secular and ecclesiastical authorities, the people of New France knew how to amuse themselves by dancing, laughing, and singing. Based on notarial registries in the Archives nationales du Québec and secondary works; biblio. L. B. Chan

3356. Tremblay, Marc-Adélard. MODELES D'AUTORITE DANS LA FAMILLE CANADIENNE-FRANÇAISE [The model of authority in the French-Canadian family]. *Recherches Sociographiques [Canada] 1966 7(1/2): 215-230.* Studies the pattern of authority in the structure of the family in French Canada and notes the change as society evolved from traditional to industrial. 34 notes from secondary sources. C. P. LeBris

3357. —. ANALYSIS OF FACTORS CAPABLE OF AFFECTING LABOUR SUPPLY: THE CASE OF PARENTS OF LOW-INCOME FAMILIES. *Industrial Relations [Canada] 1975 30(2): 162-165.* The present article presents in part a progress report of research which tries to estimate the impact of public programs of economic security in Quebec on the work effort of parents of low-income families. Our interest in such research comes from the recent but increasing effort of our society to fight poverty, and more particularly from the passing of the Social Aid Act by the Quebec Government in 1969. The question of incentive to work takes on particular importance, since, according to this Act, benefits to families are calculated as the difference between income and needs, whatever the labor force participation of their members. J

## Ontario

3358. Begnal, Calista. THE SISTERS OF THE CONGREGATION OF NOTRE DAME, NINETEENTH-CENTURY KINGSTON. *Study Sessions: Can. Catholic Hist. Assoc. 1973 40: 27-34.* Examines the efforts of religious women during 1841-48, important years in the history of religious education. S

3359. Bolus, Malvina. THE SON OF I. GUNN. *Beaver [Canada] 1971 302(3): 23-26.* Hudson's Bay Company employee John Fubbister turned out to be a woman, Isabel Gunn, who gave birth to a son at Albany factory on 29 December 1807. S

3360. Davey, Ian E. TRENDS IN FEMALE SCHOOL ATTENDANCE IN MID-NINETEENTH CENTURY ONTARIO. *Social Hist. [Canada] 1975 8(16): 238-254.* Although there was a steady increase in female attendance at schools in Ontario in the 1850's-60's, it was more spectacular in cities than in rural areas. The increase seems directly attributable to the greater availability of public schools. Despite these trends, the long-standing class and sex biases in school attendance persisted. Girls were more likely than their brothers to be withdrawn from school in times of economic hardship. Middle-class girls were far more likely to attend school than were children of the working class. Based on superintendents' annual reports, Hamilton school records, and the Hamilton manuscript census. 10 tables, 20 notes. W. K. Hobson

3361. Denton, Frank T. and George Peter J. SOCIO-ECONOMIC CHARACTERISTICS OF FAMILIES IN WENTWORTH COUNTY, 1871: SOME FURTHER RESULTS. *Social Hist. [Canada] 1974 7(13): 103-110.* Study of 429 urban and 671 rural families in Wentworth County, Ontario in 1871 reveals that most occupational, religious, birthplace, and ethnic origin variables were not significantly related to number of children; only the wife's birthplace was. The observed urban-rural difference in family size was not due to the differences in socio-economic characteristics of rural and urban families. School attendance was significantly related to father's occupation, parental birthplace, and to basic urban-rural differences, but not to religion or ethnic origin. Based on manuscript census; 2 tables, 6 notes. W. K. Hobson

3362. Dreyer, Fred. THREE YEARS IN THE TORONTO GARRISON. *Ontario Hist. 1965 57(1): 29-38.* The experiences of Gilbert Elliot, a younger son of the Earl of Minto, as a subaltern doing garrison duty in Toronto. Included are Gilbert's impressions of Toronto society, of Canadian weather, of Indians, and of desertion in the army. Also mentioned is Gilbert's engagement, broken by his parents because his Toronto fiancée was too colonial and without dowry. Based on Gilbert's letters to his family. G. Emery

3363. Fowler, Marian E. PORTRAIT OF SUSAN SIBBALD: WRITER AND PIONEER. *Ontario Hist. [Canada] 1974 66(1): 50-.* Describes the life of Susan Sibbald, based on her *Memoirs* (1926) and other sources. Photo, 62 notes. W. B. Whitham and S

3364. Hancock, Harold B. MARY ANN SHADD: NEGRO EDITOR, EDUCATOR, AND LAWYER. *Delaware Hist. 1973 15(3): 187-194.* Mary Ann Shadd (d. 1893) was the daughter of Abraham D. Shadd, a Delaware Negro abolitionist prominent in the Negro convention movement. She was nursed on Quaker teachings and antislavery witness. The family moved to Ontario, Canada, in 1851, but the Shadd family maintained contacts with Wilmington (Delaware) and West Chester (Pennsylvania) friends. Mary Ann Shadd first earned her antislavery reputation by investigating the possibilities of Negro settlement in Canada to escape the baneful effects of the invigorated Fugitive Slave Act of 1850. In a pamphlet in 1852 she called attention to opportunities for Negroes in Canada, and lectured widely on the subject. Her most significant contribution was her leading role as editor, 1854-59, in the publication of the weekly *Provincial Freeman*, the first antislavery newspaper in Ontario. From its inception in 1854 the *Freeman* attacked the mismanagement of experimental Negro communities, opposed segregation, and assaulted slavery in the United States. She lectured in the United States in 1855. She also taught school, initially through the American Missionary Association, participated in women's rights reform, and published articles encouraging Negroes to patronize Negro businesses. Based on newspapers and unpublished letters; 27 notes. R. M. Miller

3365. Ingram, George. THE STORY OF LAURA SECORD REVISITED. *Ontario Hist. 1965 57(2): 85-97.* Critics have gone too far in attacking the myth of Laura who contributed to the British victory at Beaver Dams by warning James Fitzgibbon, the British commander, of the impending American attack. Though neither Laura's warning nor Fitzgibbon were important in the victory, which was largely won by Britain's Indian allies, Fitzgibbon had acted on Laura's warning and had relaxed his ambush preparations previous to the battle only because the Americans did not arrive as forecast but 24 hours later. Laura's heroism remains. G. Emery

3366. Lapp, Eula C. WHEN ONTARIO GIRLS WERE GOING WEST. *Ontario Hist. [Canada] 1968 60(2): 71-79.* Examines the diary of Mary Bell "Molly" Bond for a key to the concerns and characteristics of women immigrating from Ontario to the North-West Territories. 12 notes. S

3367. Moir, John S. FOUR POEMS ON THE REBELLION OF 1837 BY SUSANNAH MOODIE. *Ontario Hist. [Canada] 1965 57(1): 47-52.* Suggests that, of all the poems inspired by the 1837 rebellions, only those of Susannah Moodie possess literary merit. Of the four poems considered, three are loyal and patriotic, as might have been expected from the wife of a loyalist militia officer who was also a Tory. Yet the fourth poem shows sympathy for a convict's wife. Mrs. Moddie's poems won her national fame in the 1840's preceding her international fame of the 1850's which came from her two autobiographical volumes, *Roughing It in the Bush* (London, 1852) and *Life in the Clearings* (London, 1853). G. Emery

3368. Wollock, Jeffrey. DID STINSON JARVIS HYPNOTIZE "KIT OF THE MAIL?" *Ontario Hist. [Canada] 1975 67(4): 241-245.* Suggests a relationship between Kathleen Watkins ("Kit of the Mail"), the newspaperwoman, and Stinson Jarvis, the novelist. Argues that this relationship grew from a mutual interest, typical of the time and place, in psychic phenomena and especially hypnotic ones. From this, speculates on the extent and nature of the link between them. Based on primary sources; 20 notes. W. B. Whitham

# Prairie Provinces

## Alberta

3369.  Bailey, Mary C.   THE BEGINNING OF LESLIEVILLE. *Alberta Hist. R. [Canada] 1965 13(4): 21-23.* A description of the settlement of Leslieville, Alberta by one of the original settlers.
H. M. Burns

3370.  Bailey, Mary C.   REMINISCENCES OF A PIONEER. *Alberta Hist. R. 1967 15(4): 17-25.* An account of pioneer life in the Red Deer area of Alberta by Mary C. Bailey, an original settler.
H. M. Burns

3371.  Dempsey, Hugh A.   DOROTHY AND THE BACHELORS. *Alberta Hist. [Canada] 1976 24(1): 12-14.* Although males greatly outnumbered females on the frontier, such a ratio did not necessarily lead to quick marriages for females. In 1895 "Dorothy" wrote to the Calgary *Herald* complaining that the men of the city resisted marriage for a strange variety of bad reasons. She challenged them, and in a series of exchanges in the *Herald*, was challenged by the bachelors. A promising courtship between "Dorothy" and a correspondent named "P. Kaboo" never materialized, as a few crimes and scandals shifted the readers' interest away from the question. Illus., 9 notes.
D. Chaput

3372.  Holmes, Mrs. Robert.   EXPERIENCES OF A MISSIONARY'S WIFE. *Alberta Hist. R. [Canada] 1964 12(2): 18-25.* With her husband, an Anglican missionary, the author arrived in Edmonton from Liverpool in 1902. Their life in the Athabaska country, where he served 1902-04, and in the Peace River country, where he served until 1915, is described. Her husband died in 1916 in Saskatchewan.
G. Emery

3373.  Inderwick, Mary E.   A LADY AND HER RANCH. *Alberta Hist. R. 1967 15(4): 1-9.* Extracts from letters written by a cattle rancher's bride describing life in the Pincher Creek area of Alberta. Details are given of visits to the Indian reservations and to Fort McLeod.
H. M. Burns

3374.  Jameson, Sheilagh S.   GIVE YOUR OTHER VOTE TO THE SISTER. *Alberta Hist. R. 1967 15(4): 10-16.* Account of a campaign on behalf of Roberta Catherine MacAdams, a nursing sister and one of the first two women representatives to serve in the Alberta Legislature. Details regarding her background, her decision to stand for election as an armed services representative in 1917, and of her later life are given.
H. M. Burns

3375.  Kinsey, B. A. and Phillips, L.   EVALUATION OF ANOMY AS A PREDISPOSING OR DEVELOPMENTAL FACTOR IN ALCOHOL ADDICTION. *Q. J. of Studies on Alcohol 1968 29(4): 892-898.* "Sociocultural information and ratings on an alcoholism-phase scale and the McCloskey-Schaar Anomy Scale were obtained from 93 outpatients (12 women) at an alcoholism clinic in Edmonton, Alberta. Most of the patients were aged less than 45, about 50 [percent] were married and employed. The 10 early-stage alcoholics were rated as nonanomic (agreed with from 0 to 2 items on the 9-item anomy scale), the 25 middle-stage alcoholics as moderately anomic (3 to 5 items) and the 58 late-stage alcoholics as severely anomic (6 to 9 items). The degree of association between stage of alcoholism and degree of anomy was statistically significant (rho [equals] .544). Religion, sex, age, marital status, years of drinking, and years drinking had been a problem were not significantly related to anomy when the stage of alcoholism was controlled. It is suggested that anomy develops concomitantly with alcoholism and that it is a factor in the alcoholic's loss of control over drinking."
J

3376.  Woywitka, Anne B.   HOMESTEADER'S WOMAN. *Alberta Hist. [Canada] 1976 24(2): 20-24.* Dominka Roshko, born in 1893 in the Ukraine, came to Manitoba with her family in 1900. In 1912 she married Monoly Zahara, and they went to homestead in the Peace River country. Examines frontier living, such as clearing the land, farming, lack of medical facilities, and education. 2 illus.
D. Chaput

## Manitoba

3377.  Cooper, Joy.   RED LIGHTS OF WINNIPEG. *Tr. of the Hist. and Sci. Soc. of Manitoba 1970-71 Series 3(27): 61-74.* Discusses a condensed version of a paper on prostitution in Winnipeg during its formative years. Males far outnumbered the female population, and by tacit public consent bordellos were tolerated so long as they were confined to one district of the city. The problem was a crucial one in the first decade of the 20th century, and it created both moral and political furor. Ultimately a Royal Commission was established in the aftermath of charges that Winnipeg's moral corruption was the worst in Canada. The Commission exonerated the city from the charge, and Mayor Sanford Evans utilized the situation and shrewd political moves to good advantage. Prostitution itself, however, continued to exist for many years after his reelection in 1910.
J. A. Casada

3378.  Hildebrand, Menno.   THE SOMMERFELD MENNONITES OF MANITOBA. *Mennonite Life 1970 25(3): 99-107.* Describes the religious and social life of the Sommerfeld Mennonite Church, Manitoba, which was founded in 1890. Worship and communion services, church membership and baptism, holidays, the use of Low and High German, and courtship and wedding customs are among the topics discussed. No matter how hard the Sommerfeld Mennonites have tried to keep the status quo, things have changed. In 1935, for example, a group broke away over the issues of evening services, music in the church, Sunday school, and a mission outreach. In 1958 another split occurred over the question of the use of electricity in the church. In 1948 many of the more conservative members migrated to South America. Based on the author's personal observations and secondary sources; illus.
D. J. Abramoske

3379.  Peters, Victor.   THE HUTTERIANS - HISTORY AND COMMUNAL ORGANIZATION OF A RURAL GROUP IN MANITOBA. *Hist. and Sci. Soc. of Manitoba Papers, [Canada] 1960-61 1964 Series 3(17): 6-14.* This group of descendants of the Anabaptists, whose cardinal article of faith is the common ownership of all their property, left the Ukraine in 1874 to settle in Manitoba, South Dakota, Alberta, Saskatchewan, and Montana. Most of the American colonies transferred to Canada in 1918 on the same terms as had been extended to the Mennonites: exemption from military service. Since World War II the Hutterian colonies have become targets for public criticism. Alberta and Manitoba restrict Hutterian expansion. An account follows of life in their cluster-type villages, with their democratic government, highly diversified agriculture, and emphasis on religion and family life. Illus., 11 notes.
E. P. Stickney

3380.  Thompson, Arthur N.   THE WIFE OF THE MISSIONARY. *J. of the Can. Church Hist. Soc. [Canada] 1973 15(2): 35-44.* A study of the wives of early Anglican missionaries in the Canadian Red River settlement from 1820 to 1840. Born and reared in England, some complained bitterly about their new deprivations. Yet the wives vigorously supported their husbands' work. They bore many children, managed households, taught Sunday school classes, and taught in the missionary boarding schools and cared for the students who lived with them. Although some of the women were hostile to the Indians, most missionary wives treated Indians with warmth and visited them in their homes. In short, the missionaries' wives deserve much credit for their part in maintaining the influence of education and religion in the Red River area. Based on primary and secondary sources; 50 notes.
J. A. Kicklighter

## Saskatchewan

3381.  Bailey, Mrs. A. W.   THE YEAR WE MOVED. *Saskatchewan Hist. 1967 20(1): 19-31.* The story of one family that was forced by drought conditions in southern Saskatchewan in the 1930's to establish a new home in the north. Illus.
A. H. Lawrance

3382.  Buck, Ruth Matheson, ed.   DOCUMENTS OF WESTERN HISTORY: THE JOURNAL OF ELEANOR SHEPPHIRD MATHESON, 1920. *Saskatchewan Hist. [Canada] 1969 22(2): 66-72, (3): 109-117.* Part I. A daily journal of a canoe trip from the Pas to Lac La Ronge, a distance of 700 miles, in the summer of 1920. Eleanor Matheson was accompanied by her husband, the Reverend Canon Matheson, Archdeacon John Alexander Mackay, and Miss K. Halson. Indian missions were the destination of the canoe journey. 14 notes. Part II. More daily details of events on the trip by canoe with missionaries from the Pas to Lac La Ronge and back in 1920. Photos, 13 notes.                    C. A. Bishop

3383. Crone, Ray H. AVIATION PIONEERS IN SASKATCHE-WAN. *Saskatchewan Hist. [Canada] 1975 28(1): 9-28.* Discusses aviation in Saskatchewan from the first flight, by balloon, in 1908 by an unknown aeronaut, to the appearance of Katharine Stinson in Regina in the summer of 1918. Mentions W. W. Gibson, Don and Jim Brown, George and Ace Pepper, Bob St. Henry, Glenn L. Martin, Jimmy Ward, and Alfred Blakley. 7 photos, 47 notes.                    C. Held

3384. Denny, C. D. IN MEMORY OF MARY ROSE (PRITCH-ARD) SAYERS: THE LAST WITNESS. *Saskatchewan Hist. [Canada] 1971 24(2): 63-72.* On 2 April 1885, Wandering Spirit and his band perpetrated the Frog Lake Massacre. On 27 December 1970, Mary Rose Pritchard, the last witness to the event, died. She was eleven years old at the time of the massacre. Only one white man, William B. Cameron, lived to write of the event in a book entitled *Blood Red the Sun.* The trials of Mary Rose's father, John Pritchard, in attempting to save the lives of the widows of the men murdered at Frog Lake and his attempts to reestablish the family following collapse of the Rebellion are described. Photo, 38 notes.                    C. Held

3385. Goodwin, Theresa. RECOLLECTIONS AND REMINIS-CENCES OF AN ENGLISH SCHOOL MARM IN SASKATCHE-WAN. *Saskatchewan Hist. [Canada] 1974 27(2): 103-107.* The author writes of her teaching experiences in Chaplin and Duval, 1912-13. Photo.                    C. Held

3386. Hoffman, George. THE SASKATCHEWAN FARMER-LABOR PARTY, 1932-1934: HOW RADICAL WAS IT AT ITS ORIGIN? *Saskatchewan Hist. [Canada] 1975 28(2): 52-64.* While socialist and radical to some degree, in its early years the Farmer-Labor Party was moderated by the leadership of such persons as Tom Johnson, Mrs. A. Hollis of Shaunavon, Violet McNaughton, and M. J. Coldwell. There was considerable rank and file support for the social credit ideas of Major C. H. Douglas as well. "The generally held theory that the radical fathers of the party substantially moderated and compromised their ideas after 1934 needs to be seriously reassessed." 77 notes.                    C. Held

3387. O'Neill, P. B. REGINA'S GOLDEN AGE OF THEATER: HER PLAYHOUSES AND PLAYERS. *Saskatchewan Hist. [Canada] 1975 28(1): 29-37.* The "Golden Age" of theater in North America, including Regina, was 1900-14. Mentions nearly a dozen theaters and several well-known performers, including Melba, Madame Albani, Minnie Maddern Fiske, Sophie Tucker, Lewis Waller, and Sir Johnston Forbes-Robertson. 3 photos, 35 notes.                    C. Held

## British Columbia

3388. Brothers, Ryan. COWICHAN KNITTERS. *Beaver [Canada] 1965 296(Summer): 42-46.* Describes the cottage industry of the Cowichan Indians near Duncan, 40 miles north of Victoria, British Columbia. They learned the art of knitting from Scottish immigrants to Vancouver Island in the mid-19th century. Illus.                    L. F. S. Upton

3389. Langan, Joy. BCFL WOMEN'S RIGHTS COMMITTEE. *Can. Labour 1975 20(2): 11-12, 34.* Discusses the British Columbia Federation of Labour's Committee for Women's Rights since 1970.                    S

3390. Sawer, Barbara J. PREDICTORS OF THE FARM WIFE'S INVOLVEMENT IN GENERAL MANAGEMENT AND ADOPTION DECISIONS. *Rural Sociol. 1973 38(4): 412-426.* "Examined are predictor variables hypothesized to be associated with the extent of the wife's involvement in decisions concerning the general management and decisions leading to the adoption of agricultural innovations. Tests of directional hypotheses suggest that involvement in both

types of decisions is related to the wife's farm information-seeking activity, her involvement in farm tasks, and situational variables including family size, income, and farm size. Interrelationships among variables are explored through factor analysis, with a factor emerging as *wife's business partner role* found to account for the largest percentage of common factor variance. The discussion focuses on behaviors associated with the wife's decision-making activity and how family resources may affect her emphasis on a business partner role. Implications for educational program planning are discussed by considering existing family decision-making patterns as frameworks useful for the diffusion of decision-making information." [Data for the study were obtained in British Columbia in 1970.]
J

## Northwest Territories and Yukon

3391. Boyd, Josephine W. ON SOME WHITE WOMEN IN THE WILDS OF NORTHERN NORTH AMERICA. *Arctic [Canada] 1974 27(3): 167-174.* Describes the activities of the first white women in the northern Arctic, their role and lives there from the late 19th century to the present. Special emphasis is placed on Mollie Ward Greist, a pioneering nurse. Illus., biblio.                    J. A. Casada

3392. Flyger, Vagn. HUNTERS OF WHITE WHALES. *Beaver [Canada] 1965 296(Winter): 32-37.* Every summer thousands of beluga whales pass between the outer islands of the Mackenzie Delta. The whales are from 12 to 16 feet in length and weigh between 1,500 and 4,000 pounds. A hunting camp is formed early in July at Kendall Island by people from Aklavik, Inuvik, and Reindeer Station; it breaks up in mid-August. The whales are harpooned, shot, and hauled ashore to be cut up by the womenfolk. As other foods become increasingly available to the Eskimos, the importance of the whale hunt is rapidly diminishing. Illus.
L. F. S. Upton

3393. Freeman, Milton M. R. A SOCIAL AND ECOLOGIC ANALYSIS OF SYSTEMATIC FEMALE INFANTICIDE AMONG THE NETSILIK ESKIMO. *Am. Anthropologist 1971 73(5): 1011-1018.* "Systematic female infanticide among the Pelly Bay [Northwest Territories] Eskimos is subjected to functional analysis wherein the adaptive rather than purposive nature of the behavior is stressed. The trait is seen to be ecologically adaptive insofar as it increases population, and in turn ecosystem, stability. It is argued that the explanation for the uniquely systematic infanticide practiced by this group is to be sought within the social dynamic of the individual household, and is not satisfactorily explained by recourse to environmental-demographic explanations."
(AIA 3:2:526) J

3394. Lubart, Joseph M. FIELD STUDY OF THE PROBLEMS OF ADAPTATION OF MACKENZIE DELTA ESKIMOS TO SOCIAL AND ECONOMIC CHANGE. *Psychiatry 1969 32(4): 447-458.* Disappearance of the food supply forced the Mackenzie Delta Eskimos to move into Canadian settlements. The culture that bound them together in cooperative survival groups was no longer viable. The Eskimos tried to adapt to a radically different culture, with profound effects on their personality. The Eskimo male, who once did the hunting, now is an unskilled failure in Western society. He has lost his sense of usefulness and as a result is radically depressed. Most males turn to alcohol as a means of regaining control of the situation. The Eskimo female has lost her respect for the male, as she compares him to the more successful white man. She tries to find acceptance through sexual activity with whites. She has an intense wish to be white, trying to imitate dress styles, hair styles, and even manners of the white woman. Whereas the male Eskimo dreams of returning to the Land territory of the past, the Eskimo female repudiates her parents' values, looking for assimilation into white society. The situation is a classical description of denying possibilities of equality to a group with radically different cultural values, and then considering the psychological breakdown as evidence of inferiority. 7 notes, biblio.
M. A. Kaufman

3395. Soper, Carolyn K. A NURSE GOES TO BAFFIN ISLAND. *Beaver [Canada] 1964 295(Winter): 30-38.* Reminiscences of Carolyn K. Soper's life at Lake Harbour, Baffin Island. Illus.
L. F. S. Upton

# SUBJECT INDEX

Subject Profile Index (SPIndex) carries both generic and specific index terms. Begin a search at the general term but also look under more specific or related terms. Cross-references are included.

Each string of index descriptors is intended to present a profile of a given article; however, no particular relationship between any two terms in the profile is implied. Terms within the profile are listed alphabetically after the leading term. The variety of punctuation and capitalization reflects production methods and has no intrinsic meaning; e.g., there is no difference in meaning between "History, study of" and "History (study of)."

Cities, towns, and counties are listed following their respective states or provinces; e.g., "Ohio (Columbus)." Terms beginning with an arabic numeral are listed after the letter Z. The chronology of the bibliographic entry follows the index descriptors. In the chronology, "c" stands for "century"; e.g., "19c" means "19th century."

Note that "United States" is not used as a leading index term; if no country is mentioned, the index entry refers to the United States alone. When an entry refers to both Canada and the United States, both "Canada" and "USA" appear in the string of index descriptors, but "USA" is not a leading term. When an entry refers to any other country and the United States, only the other country is indexed.

The last number in the index string, in italics, refers to the bibliographic entry number.

## A

Abbie Putnam (fictional character). Morality. O'Neill, Eugene (*Desire Under the Elms,* 1925). Sexual behavior. 1925. *1672*

Abbott, Grace. Child welfare. Kelley, Florence. Lathrop, Julia. Legislation. Politics. Sheppard-Towner Act. Social reform. Wald, Lillian. 1900-35. *1236*

—. Children's Bureau. Nebraska. 1878-1939. *1214*

Abel-Henderson, Annie Heloise. Indians (historiography). Scholarship. 1900-47. *1886*

Abolition Movement *See also* Emancipation.

—. Authors. Farrar, Eliza. Follen, Eliza. Harvard University. Literature (children's). Massachusetts (Cambridge). 19c. *1022*

—. Butler, Pierce. Kemble, Frances Anne. Marriage. Theater. 1809-93. *125*

—. Chandler, Elizabeth Margaret. Friends, Society of (Hicksites). Michigan. 1830's-60. *871*

—. Chapman, Maria Weston. Child, Lydia Maria. Foster, Abby Kelly. Holley, Sallie. 1820-60. *851*

—. Civil War. Feminist movement. Negroes. Social Reform. Tubman, Harriet. Underground railroad. 1820-1913. *379*

—. Connecticut (Canterbury). Crandall, Prudence. Feminism. Massachusetts. May, Samuel J. 1832-61. *840*

—. Connecticut (Canterbury). Crandall, Prudence. Garrison, William Lloyd. Racism. Sexism. 1830-40. *847*

—. Connecticut (Torringford). Hudson, Martha Turner. 1833-77. *853*

—. Constitutional Amendment (19th). Feminism. Marriage. New York (Seneca Falls). Strikes. Suffrage. 1848-1920. *299*

—. Family. Feminism. Grimké, Angelina. Grimké, Sarah. ca 1830's-40's. *757*

—. Female Anti-Slavery Society. Grimké, Angelina. Grimké, Sarah. 1829-70. *854*

—. Feminism. Grimké, Angelina. Grimké, Sarah. Massachusetts. 1837-38. *839*

—. Feminism. Grimké, Angelina. Grimké, Sarah. Northeastern or North Atlantic States. Religion. South Carolina (Charleston). ca 1825-70. *857*

—. Feminism. Sculpture. Social Reform. Socialism. Whitney, Anne. ca 1850-1915. *1770*

—. Feminism. Truth, Sojourner. 1820-78. *899*

—. Foster, Abby Kelley. Foster, Stephen Symonds. New England. 1830's-50's. *852*

—. Friends, Society of. Grimké, Angelina. Grimké, Sarah. 19c. *881*

—. Fuller, Margaret. 1830's-40's. *849*

—. Grimké, Angelina. Grimké, Sarah. 1830's-60. *850*

—. Literature. Painting. Stowe, Harriet Beecher. 1832-96. *113*

—. Women's history. 19c-20c. *24*

Abolitionism. Kentucky. Stowe, Harriet Beecher (influence). Webster, Delia. 1810-61. *855*

—. Middle Classes. Sexuality. Social Reform. 1830-65. *856*

Abolitionists. Negroes. Politics. Suffrage. 1865-69. *1358*

Abortion. Adoption. Children. Economic Conditions. Minorities. Whites. 1972. *2703*

—. American Law Institute. Law and Society. 1959-67. *2704*

—. Amnesty, general. Sexual behavior. 1960's. *2352*

—. Attitudes. Birth Control. Religiosity. Students, college. 1960-71. *2688*

—. Attitudes. Family size preferences. Religion. 1972. *2699*

—. Birth Control. Catholic Church. 1960's. *2219*

—. Birth control. Ethics. Federal Regulation. Population control. 1960-72. *2233*

—. Birth control. Government. Law. Pregnancy tests. 1971. *2692*

—. Birth Control. Law. 1970's. *2691*

—. California (Los Angeles County). Medi-Cal. Public welfare agencies. 1970's. *2696*

—. Canada. Press. Public opinion. Social Change. 1960's-74. *3257*

—. Catholic Church. Feminism. 1960's-73. *2698*

—. Child care. Family. Feminist movement. Political activism. Sexism. 1970's. *2449*

—. Child care. Feminism. Machismo. Mexican Americans. 1970's. *2623*

—. Criminal Law. Medicine and State. Sex roles. Social Classes. 1960's. *2702*

—. Feminist movement. 1971. *2695*

—. Fertility. Population control. 1950-80. *2689*

—. Law Reform. Public Opinion. 1800-1973. *236*

—. Law Reform. Social change. 1969. *2701*

—. Legislators. Religion. Voting and Voting Behavior. Western States. 1975. *2700*

—. Morality. New York State's Abortion Law, Commission on. 1968. *2690*

—. New York. Women's National Abortion Action Coalition. 1968-74. *2705*

—. Physicians. Privacy, right to. Supreme Court. 1970's. *2697*

—. Public policy. Supreme Court decisions. 1971-74. *2694*

Abortion behavior. Catholic Church. Hawaii. 1965-74. *2497*

Abortion controversy. Ethics. Metaphysics. 1965-72. *2693*

Abzug, Bella. Chisholm, Shirley. Friedan, Betty. National Organization for Women. Political strategy. 1972. *2411*

—. Education Amendments (1972, Title IX). Sex discrimination. Women's Equity Action League. 1972-74. *2797*

Academic achievement. Adolescents. Behavior (supportive). California (San Francisco Bay area). Mothers. Negroes. Self concepts. 1960's. *2583*

—. Colleges and Universities (attendance). Students. 1960's. *2840*

—. Secondary Education. Sex. Social Classes. 1960's. *2788*

Academic careers. Archivists. Discrimination. Rossi, Alice. 1915-72. *1952*

Academic Freedom. Colleges and Universities. Fingerprinting. Mitford, Jessica. San Jose State University. 1973. *1858*

Acculturation. Catholic Church. Family. Italian Americans (review article). Social Organization. 1880's-20c. *373*

—. Chinese. Family. Immigrants. Marriage. 1850-1960. *218*

—. Eskimos. Food Supply. Northwest Territories (Mackenzie Delta). Sexual behavior. Social Change. 1960's. *3394*

—. Family structure. Federal Policy. Indians. 1776-1965. *372*

—. Family structure. Idaho. Marriage. Nez Percé Indians. 19c-20c. *362*

—. Immigrants. Indiana (Gary). Public welfare programs. Settlement houses. 1906-40. *1410*

—. Immigrants. Swedes. 1850-90. *1490*

—. New York City. Poverty. Puerto Ricans. 1950-69. *2625*

Achievement. Psychological Conflicts. 1972. *2259*

Achievement values. Anomie. Education. Family. Poor. Religion. 1960's. *1803*

Acklen, Adelicia. Architecture. Belmont Estate. Tennessee (Nashville). ca 1825-1970. *423*

—. Belmont Estate. Sculpture. Tennessee (Nashville). 1971. *2903*

Activism. Employment. Labor Unions and Organizations. Working class. 1940's. *2012*

Actors and Actresses. American Company of Comedians. Cheer, Margaret. Marriage. South Carolina (Charles-Town). 1764-68. *606*

—. American Protective Association. California (Los Angeles area). Catholic churches. Modjeska, Helena. Polish Americans. 1876-1909. *3221*

—. Bernhardt, Sarah. Georgia (Savannah). Theater. 1892. 1906. *1769*

—. California (Hollywood). Films. Lanchester, Elsa. Laughton, Charles. Marriage. 1929-62. *415*

—. Dwyer, Ada. Lowell, Amy. Poetry. ca 1880-1925. *1774*

—. Films. Mailer, Norman (review article). Monroe, Marilyn. 1950's. *2755*

—. Films. Negri, Pola. Valentino, Rudolph. 1926. *1767*

—. Georgia. Kemble, Frances Anne (diary). Slavery. 1832-64. *953*

—. Langtry, Lillie. West. 1884-1913. *1761*

Adams, Abigail. Adams, John. Attitudes. Letters. Sex roles. 1776-1804. *760*

—. Adams, John. Friendship. Marriage. Presidents. 1764-77. *500*

—. Adams, John. Great Britain (London). Marriage. Smith, Abigail Adams. Smith, William Stephens. 1780's. *667*

—. American Revolution. Feminism. Letters. Warren, Mercy Otis. Washington, Martha. 18c. *542*

—. Childrearing. Education. Family. Jefferson, Thomas. Morality. Politics. Values. 1774-1804. *756*

—. Coolidge, Anna Goddhue. Harding, Florence Kling. Letters. Pierce, Jane Means Appleton. Roosevelt, Eleanor. 18c-20c. *292*

—. First Ladies. Portraits. Presidents. Roosevelt, Eleanor. 18c-20c. *277*

Adams, Abigail (diary). Butterfield, L. H. (review article). 1755-1804. *737*

Adams, Abigail (letters). Friendship. Jefferson, Thomas (letters). Politics. 1790's-1826. *764*

Adams, Alva. Adams, Ella Nye. Colorado. Governors. Social Conditions. 1887-1931. *3158*

## C

Camp Dodge. Army (88th Division). Iowa. Journalism. Pownall, Dorothy Ashby (reminiscences). Schumann-Heink, Madame. World War I. 1917-19. *1295*

Camp followers. Courts Martial and Courts of Inquiry. Military. Prostitution. World War I. 1917-18. *1293*

Camp Grant Massacre. Indians (massacre of). Press. 1871. *906*

Campaigns, Political. *See* Political Campaigns.

Campbell, Elizabeth W. Crozer. Archaeology. California (Lake Mojave). 1930's-40's. *1109*

Camping. California. Colliver, Iva Cooley. Yosemite National Park. 1915. *3210*

—. Colorado. Mining towns. Rocky Mountains. Schenck, Annie B. (journal). 1871. *3189*

—. Moore, Alice (diary). Wyoming. 1912. *1797*

Canada *See also* individual provinces; British North America.

—. Abortion. Press. Public opinion. Social Change. 1960's-74. *3257*

—. Age. Birth rate. Fertility rates. Marriage. 1941-71. *3279*

—. Age. Sex differences. Unemployment. 1957-70. *3270*

—. Air Forces. 1970. *3272*

—. Archibald, Kathleen *(Sex and the Public Service)*. Royal Commission on the Status of Women in Canada (report, 1970). 1960's-71. *3262*

—. Argus Patrol. Military. Wives. 1960's. *3278*

—. Art and Society. Communism. Fairley, Margaret. Periodicals. 1885-1968. *3297*

—. Artists. Carr, Emily. Humphrey, Ruth. Letters. 1937-44. *3310*

—. Artists. Fur Trade. Hopkins, Edward. Hopkins, Frances Ann. Hudson's Bay Company. ca 1857-1918. *3315*

—. Attitudes. Courtship. Interpersonal Relations. Sex roles. Students. USA. 1969. *217*

—. Attitudes. Family. Marriage. 1974. *3287*

—. Attitudes. Sex manuals. 1900-15. *3276*

—. *Attorney General of Canada* v. *Lavell* (1973). Lavell, Jeannette. Sex Discrimination. Supreme Court. Wikwemikong Indians. 1973-74. *3308*

—. Authority structure. Eskimos. Family. Social organization. 1970's. *3299*

—. Birth Control. Catholic Church. Legislation. 1960's. *3258*

—. Birth rate. Ethnic Groups. Fertility. Immigrants. Marriage. 1871. *3288*

—. Birth rate. Indians. 1900-69. *3307*

—. Birth Rate (decline). Demography. Family size. Marriage. USA. 1945-61. *3283*

—. Bourassa, Henry. Divorce. Feminism. Suffrage. 1913-25. *3296*

—. Bourgeoys, Marguerite. Catherine de Saint-Augustin. Catholic Church (founders of). Mance, Jeanne. Marie de l'Incarnation. Youville, Marguerite dé. 17c. *3254*

—. British North America. Public schools. Social Status. Teaching. Wages. 1845-75. *3253*

—. British North America Act of 1929. Feminism. Legal status. Suffrage. 1870's-1940's. *3292*

—. California. Immigrants. Modjeska, Helena. Polish. USA. 19c. *425*

—. Capitalism. Imperialism. Socialism. ca 1870-1975. *3269*

—. Catholic Church. Letters. Marie de l'Incarnation. Religious Orders. Ursulines. 17c. *3252*

—. Children. Mental Illness. Perrot, Nicholas (family of). Reclos, Magdeleine. 1660's-1724. *3250*

—. Church Schools. Daughters of Saint Ann. Social services. Sureau, Marie Esther. USA. 1848-20c. *381*

—. Cities. Education. Family. Occupations. Sex differences. Social mobility. 1972. *3256*

—. Colleges and Universities. Educational opportunity. Rural-Urban Studies. 1960's. *3311*

—. Colleges and Universities. Political knowledge scale. Public opinion formation. Students. 1974. *3294*

—. Communist Party. Feminist movement. 1921-71. *3290*

—. Day Nurseries. Employment opportunities. Feminist movement. Legal status. Social Classes. 1975. *3291*

—. Demography. Family. Fertility (decline). 1961-71. *3285*

—. Demography. Organizations (joining). Sex roles. USA. 1960's. *190*

—. Divorce. Legal access (concept of). Social Change. 1867-1973. *3284*

—. Economic Conditions. Marriage trends. Sex ratios. USA. 1830-1970. *197*

—. Employment. Labor Unions and Organizations. Marriage. Pensions. Sex discrimination. Wages. 1960's-70's. *3275*

—. Employment. Sex Discrimination. Wages. 1960-64. *3264*

—. Employment (motivation). Family (low-income). Methodology. Models. 1974. *3263*

—. Family. Mennonites. Rural-Urban Studies. 1960's. *3277*

—. Family. Methodology. Sociology. Western Association of Sociology and Anthropology (annual meeting). 1969. *3289*

—. Family allowance program. 1927-60's. *3286*

—. Family (single parent). USA. Widows. 1960's. *237*

—. Feminism. Ideology. Middle Classes. Political Leadership. USA. 1960-75. *270*

—. Feminism. McClung, Nellie *(In Times Like These,* 1915). 1902-15. *3295*

—. Feminist movement. Social Reform. 1955-75. *3293*

—. Fertility. Marriage. Rural-Urban Studies. USA. 1940-60's. *219*

—. Fiction. Wilson, Ethel. 1947-61. *3317*

—. Folktales. Marriage. Saulteaux Indians. 20c. *3301*

—. French. Indians. Names. 17c-18c. *3249*

—. Fur trade. Hopkins, Frances Ann. Painting. 1860-79. *3312*

—. Fur trade. Indian-White Relations. Marriage, common law. 18c-1932. *3322*

—. Girl Guides (founding of). Jarvis sisters. 1900-25. *3281*

—. Hart, Julia Catherine. Novels. 19c. *3247*

—. Horticulture. Indian-White Relations. Oneida Indians. USA. 17c-1860. *376*

—. Immigrants. Jews. Rosenbaum, Bella W. (reminiscences). Social Conditions. USA. 1880's-1910's. *120*

—. Immigrants. Occupations. Statistics. USA. 1964-71. *136*

—. International organizations. Sex Discrimination. USA. 1960's-70's. *116*

—. Johnson, Helen. Nationalism. Poetry. 1864-1946. *3314*

—. Labor law. 1951-71. *3265*

—. Laurier, Wilfrid. Lavergne, Mme. Joseph. Letters. 1891-93. *3260*

—. Literature. Moodie, Susanna. National self-image. Social Classes. 1832-53. *3251*

—. Occupational expectations. Social classes. Students, 10th-grade. 1970. *3266*

—. Political Participation. Public office. USA. Voting and Voting Behavior. 1920-60's. *266*

—. Public service. Sex discrimination. 1870-1975. *3271*

—. Religious Orders. 1960's. *3303*

—. Religious Orders. 1840-75. *3305*

—. Religious Orders. Social Conditions. 1965-80. *3302*

—. Royal Commission on the Status of Women in Canada (Report, 1970). Sex Discrimination. 1972. *3261*

Canada (Anse-des-Lavallée). Family structure. 1960's. *3321*

Canada (James Bay area). Cree Indians. Fertility. Modernization. Mothers. 1968. *3306*

Canada, mid-western. Ethnic groups. Sex Discrimination. 1972-73. *3282*

Canada, western. Carr, Emily. Indians. Painting. 1888-1972. *3313*

—. Catholic Church. Charities. Grey Sisters. Religious Orders. 1869-70. *3300*

—. Peace River country, north. Pioneers. 1914-76. *3320*

Canadian Library Association. Morton, Elizabeth Homer. 1946-68. *3259*

Canadian Library Association Committee on the Status of Women. Cheda, Sherrill (interview). Feminism. Labor Unions and Organizations. Librarians. 1973-74. *3267*

Canadian Union of Public Employees. Public Employees. Sex discrimination. 1975. *3273*

Canals. *See* names of canals, e.g. Panama Canal, etc.

Canibas Indians (murder of). King Philip's War. Massachusetts (Marblehead). Roules, Robert (court deposition). 1677. *595*

Cannibalism, fantasies of. Image. Kali (goddess). Mother. Popular culture. 1960's. *2740*

Cannon, Ida M. Massachusetts General Hospital. Medicine (practice of). Social work. 1877-1960. *1053*

Canon Law. Episcopal Church, Protestant. Marriage. Sex. 1909-73. *329*

—. Episcopal Church, Protestant. Ordination. Sex Discrimination. 1966-74. *2491*

Capital. *See* Banking; Capitalism; Labor; Monopoly Power.

Capital Punishment. Adultery. Connecticut (Hartford). Johnson, Elizabeth. Newton, Thomas. Trials. Witchcraft (supposed). 1648-92. *600*

—. Murder. New York (Cortland County; Truxton). O'Donough, Patrick. 1852-53. *920*

Capitalism *See also* Socialism.

—. Androgyny. Patriarchy. Sex roles. Symbolism. Prehistory-1974. *173*

—. Canada. Imperialism. Socialism. ca 1870-1975. *3269*

—. Domestic Labor. 1970-73. *2004*

—. Economic change. Models. Sexual behavior. Social Change. 1972. *2244*

—. Employment. Feminism. Wages. 1950's-60's. *1829*

—. Employment. Housework. 1690-1976. *167*

—. Employment. Racism. Sex Discrimination. 1960's-70's. *1984*

—. Family consumption. Housewives. Inflation. Labor force. 20c. *164*

—. Feminism. Marxism. 1100-1974. *284*

—. Feminism. Racism. Revolution. 1973. *2448*

—. Galbraith, John K. Housework. Oakley, Ann. Sex roles. 1950-70's. *2005*

—. Housework. 19c-20c. *175*

—. James, Selma *(Women, the Unions and Work, or What is Not to be Done)*. Labor Unions and Organizations. Social Conditions. 1972-73. *1834*

Capitol Commission. Mears, Helen Farnsworth. Sculpture. Wisconsin (Madison). 1911. *1789*

Capper, Arthur. Crawford, Florence. Daily Life. Diaries. Kansas. 1891-92. *3195*

Cardome (home). Catholic Church. Education. Kentucky (Scott County; Georgetown). Mount Admirabilis (academy). Religious Orders. Sisters of the Visitation. 1875-1975. *308*

Career aspirations *See also* Occupational aspirations.

—. Desegregation. Negroes. Schools. Sex. Social Status. Youth. 1969. *2586*

—. Economists. Education. 1970's. *1913*

—. Family size preferences. Religion. Youth. 1971-74. *2268*

—. Mothers. Teachers. 1960's. *1925*

Career characteristics. Political Parties. State legislators. 1950's-70's. *2306*

Career counselors. Employment. Sex Discrimination. 1960's. *1974*

Career fulfillment. Work (expectations, realities). 1970's. *1814*

Career patterns. Discrimination, Employment. Higher education. 1970's. *2806*

Careers. Attitudes. Family. Psychology. Sex roles. 1960's-72. *2258*

—. Birth control, oral. Social Change. Values. 1930-70. *193*

—. Family. Feminist movement. Psychological depression. Psychology. 1970. *2252*

Careers, interrupted. Colleges and Universities. Nepotism rules. Students. Wives, faculty. 1972. *2839*

Cargill, Andrew Hays. Arizona (Yuma). Doan, May Cargill (reminiscences). Social Conditions. 1900's. *3212*

Caricatures. *See* Cartoons and Caricatures.

Carman, William Bliss. Guiney, Louise Imogen. Letters. Poets. 1887-98. *1651*

Carmelites. Indian Territory. Missions and Missionaries. Newchurch, Mary Agnes (recollections). Oklahoma (Tulsa). Social Customs. 1902-03. *1439*

Carmichael, Mary Ann. Carmichael, Sarah Elizabeth. Mental Illness. Poetry. Utah. 1838-1901. *3228*

Carmichael, Sarah Elizabeth. Carmichael, Mary Ann. Mental Illness. Poetry. Utah. 1838-1901. *3228*

Carnegie Commission on Higher Education. Higher Education (opportunities; review essay). 1973. *2841*

Carnegie-Mellon University. Professional Education. 1920-71. *2782*

Carolinas. Frontier and Pioneer Life. Hutchins, Ann White. Mississippi (Natchez). 1768-1811. *702*

Carpenter, Mary. Benton, Harriet. Georgia. Gladdy, Mary. Hawkins, Ella. Kimbrough, Frances. Negroes. Slavery. Young, Dink Walton ("Mammy Dink"). 1830's-60. *945*

Carper, Ellen. Carper, Lizzie. Dolls, rag. Mennonites. Pennsylvania (Lititz). 19c. *2999*

Carper, Lizzie. Carper, Ellen. Dolls, rag. Mennonites. Pennsylvania (Lititz). 19c. *2999*

Carr, Emily. Artists. Canada. Humphrey, Ruth. Letters. 1937-44. *3310*

—. British Columbia. Forests. Indian villages. Painting. 1904-45. *3319*

—. Canada, western. Indians. Painting. 1888-1972. *3313*

Carr, Eugene A. Army. Carr, Mary Magwire (reminiscences). Fort McPherson. Nebraska. 1869-71. *3178*

Carr, Mary Magwire (reminiscences). Army. Carr, Eugene A. Fort McPherson. Nebraska. 1869-71. *3178*

Carroll, Anna Ella. Civil War (biography). Historiography. 1815-93. *802*

Carroll, Anna Ella (letters). Civil War (strategy). Feminism. Fillmore, Millard. Politics. 1852-73. *817*

Carroll, Gladys Hasty (*As the Earth Turns*). Assimilation. Family. Immigrants. Novels. Polish Americans. 1944. *1503*

Carroll, Gladys Hasty (memoirs). Family. Maine (Newichewannock River). ca 1860-1930. *2941*

Carson, Christopher (Kit). Frémont, Jessie Benton (letter). ca 1863. *708*

Carson, Rachel Louise. Conservation movement. Public Policy. 1943-70. *2328*

Carswell, G. Harrold. Organizations. Political behavior. Supreme Court nominations. 1970. *2327*

Carter, Langden (diary). Family life. Slavery. Social Conditions. Upper Classes. Virginia. 1752-78. *3090*

Cartoons. Periodicals. Speech. Stereotypes. 1972-73. *2734*

—. Sex roles. Stereotypes. Television. 1973. *2736*

Cartoons and Caricatures. Catholic Church. Convent (burning of). Johnston, David Claypool. Massachusetts (Charlestown). 1834. *880*

—. Fictional characters. Morality. Politics. Stowe, Harriet Beecher (*Uncle Tom's Cabin*, 1852). 1888-1960. *478*

—. Image. Sex roles. Television. 1974. *2744*

Caruthers, William Alexander. Georgia. Griffin, Sara Lawrence Drew. Letters. Literature. Periodicals. 1841. *1000*

Cary, Alice. Cary, Phoebe. Poetry. 1820-71. *1019*

Cary, Phoebe. Cary, Alice. Poetry. 1820-71. *1019*

Case, Anna. Family life. New Jersey (Plainfield). Recreation. 1912-35. *2991*

Case, Luella J. B. Edgarton, Sarah. Family. Literature. Marriage. New England. Sisterhood. ca 1839-46. *650*

Cashman, Nellie. Jackson (Dawson). Arizona (Tombstone). Business. Mining experts. 1851-1925. *1098*

Cassatt, Mary. Painting. Pennsylvania (Allegheny City). 1844-1926. *1768*

Castes. *See* Social Classes.

Cather, Charles (and family). Cather, Willa. Nebraska. 19c-20c. *1602*

Cather, Willa. Cather, Charles (and family). Nebraska. 19c-20c. *1602*

—. Davenport, Marcia. Deland, Margaret. Literature. Long, Haniel. Pennsylvania (Pittsburgh). Rinehart, Mary Roberts. Schmitt, Gladys. 18c-20c. *430*

—. Fiction. Folklore. 1900-47. *1604*

—. Fiction. Humanism. Western States. 1890's-1940's. *1734*

—. Fiction. Journalism. Literary criticism. Pennsylvania (Pittsburgh). 1896-1906. *1612*

—. Fiction. Land. Symbolism in Literature. ca 1890's-1930's. *1709*

—. Fiction. Nebraska. Regionalism. ca 1880's-1930's. *1716*

—. Frontier and Pioneer Life. Myths and Symbols (use of). Novels. 19c-20c. *1658*

—. Image. Literature, western. Sandoz, Mari. Sex roles. Western States. 1890-1954. *1548*

—. Literary criticism. 1893-96. *1615*

—. Literature. Nebraska. Regionalism. 1890-1923. *1598*

—. Literature. Nebraska (Webster County). Prairie (influence of). Regionalism. 1974-75. *1603*

Cather, Willa (*Death Comes for the Archbishop,* 1927). Aesthetics. Chavannes, Pierre Puvis de. 1927. *1664*

—. Antonio Jose Martinez (fictional character). Fiction. New Mexico (Taos). 1830's. 1927. *1733*

—. Fiction. Kentucky girl (fictional type). South or Southern States. 1905-26. *1724*

—. Music. Symbolism in Literature. 1927. *1641*

Cather, Willa (*Shadows on the Rock,* 1931). Quebec. Symbolism in Literature. 1931. *1611*

Catherine de Saint-Augustin. Bourgeoys, Marguerite. Canada. Catholic Church (founders of). Mance, Jeanne. Marie de l'Incarnation. Youville, Marguerite dé. 17c. *3254*

Catherwood, Mary Hartwell. Fiction. Ohio (Cincinnati). 1847-1902. *1702*

Catholic Church *See also* religious orders by name, e.g. Franciscans, Jesuits, etc.

—. Abortion. Birth Control. 1960's. *2219*

—. Abortion. Feminism. 1960's-73. *2698*

—. Abortion behavior. Hawaii. 1965-74. *2497*

—. Acculturation. Family. Italian Americans (review article). Social Organization. 1880's-20c. *373*

—. Adoption. Children. Clergy. Law. Public Welfare. Quebec. Suffrage. 1920-36. *3342*

—. Antifeminism. Brownson, Orestes A. Suffrage. 1844-70's. *845*

—. Arguello, Maria de la Concepcion. California. Orthodox Eastern Church, Russian. Rezanov, Nikolai. 1806. *887*

—. Arkansas (Jonesboro). Missions and Missionaries. Olivetan Benedictine Sisters, American. Renggli, Rose (Mother Mary Beatrice). 1847-1942. *1448*

—. Attitudes. Behavior. Morality. Religion. Students (college). 1961-71. *2500*

—. Attitudes. Colleges and Universities (effects of). Protestantism. 1960's. *2460*

—. Attitudes. Dating, interfaith. Sex, premarital. Social status. 1971. *2229*

—. Attitudes. Nuns. 1968. *2496*

—. Authority. Birth Control. 1960's. *2494*

—. Authority. Colleges and Universities. Decisionmaking. 1960's. *2501*

—. Authority. Conformity. Family. Youth. 1960's. *2292*

—. Avery, Martha Moore. Massachusetts (Boston). Social Reform. ca 1880's-1929. *1210*

—. Birth Control. Canada. Legislation. 1960's. *3258*

—. Bourgeoys, Marguerite. LeBer, Jeanne. Quebec. 17c. *3349*

—. Bourgeoys, Marguerite. Quebec (Montreal). 1620-1700. *3347*

—. California (Hollywood). Coeducation. Colleges and Universities. Educational Reform. Immaculate Heart College. Religious Orders. 1960's-70's. *2823*

—. Canada. Letters. Marie de l'Incarnation. Religious Orders. Ursulines. 17c. *3252*

—. Canada, western. Charities. Grey Sisters. Religious Orders. 1869-70. *3300*

—. Cardome (home). Education. Kentucky (Scott County; Georgetown). Mount Admirabilis (academy). Religious Orders. Sisters of the Visitation. 1875-1975. *308*

—. Cartoons and Caricatures. Convent (burning of). Johnston, David Claypool. Massachusetts (Charlestown). 1834. *880*

—. Children. Colleges and Universities. Family. Fertility. 1960's. *2502*

—. Christian Family Movement. Marriage. Social Change. 1960's. *2498*

—. Church Schools. Congregation of Notre Dame. Ontario (Kingston). Religious Orders. 1841-48. *3358*

—. Church Schools. Congregation of Sisters of Mercy. Mount St. Vincent Academy. Pennsylvania. Religious Orders. Warde, Frances. 1843-51. *876*

—. Church Schools. Felicians. Polish Americans. Social Mobility. Social Work. 1855-1975. *374*

—. Church Schools. Quebec (Saguenay). Sisters of the Good Shepherd. 1850-1960's. *3338*

—. Church Schools. Secondary Education. Segregation. Sex. 1960's. *2809*

—. Church Schools. Seton, Elizabeth Ann. 1774-1821. *873*

—. Church Schools. Sister Formation Conference. Students. Teachers. 19c-20c. *322*

—. Clergy. Episcopal Church, Protestant. Ordination. Theology. 44-1974. *305*

—. Clergy. Protestant Churches. Sex discrimination. 1970's. *2474*

—. Coeducation. Colleges and Universities. Economic Conditions. 1960's. *2820*

—. Colleges and Universities. Family size. Fertility. 1960's. *2504*

—. Colleges and Universities. Newman centers. Nuns. 1960's. *2499*

—. Colleges and Universities. Social Conditions. 1960's. *2503*

—. Colleges and Universities. Teachers. 1955-65. *2800*

—. Congress. Federal Aid to Education. Roosevelt, Eleanor. 1949-50. *2319*

—. Curricula. High Schools. 1960's. *2845*

—. Day, Dorothy. Labor Unions and Organizations. 1930's. *2015*

—. Day, Dorothy. Social work. 1917-67. *97*

—. Dorsey, Ann Hanson McKenney. Novels. Sadlier, Mary Anne Madden. 1829-65. *885*

—. Economic Conditions. Family size. Income. 1936-66. *98*

—. Education. Family size preferences. 1964-74. *1441*

—. Employment. Geriatric conditions. Institutions. Nuns. 1970. *2495*

—. Ethnic Groups. Fertility. Rural Settlements. Wisconsin. 1940-60. *2141*

—. Ethnic groups. Marriage. Religion. 1971. *2493*

—. Family. Labor force. 1972. *132*

—. Family size. Fertility. 1964. *2109*

—. Fédération Nationale Saint-Jean-Baptiste. Feminism. Gérin-Lajoie, Marie. Quebec. 1907-33. *3348*

—. Home Economics. Quebec (Saguenay). Schools. 1870-1965. *3350*

—. Immigrants. Nativism. Sex roles. Social Change. 1830's-1920's. *307*

—. Indians. Marie de l'Incarnation. Quebec. Religious Orders. Teachers. 17c. *3331*

—. Infant mortality. New Jersey (Jersey City). Progressivism. Protestantism. Settlement houses. Social reform. Whittier House. 1890-1917. *1391*

—. Jews. Protestantism. Religion. Social Status. 1970. *2470*

—. Machismo. Mexican American movement. Social Customs. 1970's. *2621*

—. Marriage. Mothers. New Jersey (Fort Dix). Protestantism. 1960's. *2462*

—. Massachusetts. Suffrage. ca 1870-1920. *1340*

—. Missionaries of the Immaculate Conception. Quebec. Religious Orders. Society of Foreign Missions of Quebec. 1902-70. *3304*

—. Novels. O'Connor, Flannery. 20c. *2858*

—. Pennsylvania (Danville). St. Cyril Academy. Sisters of SS. Cyril and Methodius. Slovak culture. 1909-73. *388*

—. Quebec. Religious Orders. Ursulines. 1850. *3334*

—. Religious Orders. Sisters of Notre Dame de Namur. Sisters of Sainte-Marie de Namur. 17c-20c. *357*

Catholic Church (ceremonies). District of Columbia. Jackson, Andrew. Lewis, Mary Anne. White House. 1832-33. *3080*

Catholic Church (founders of). Bourgeoys, Marguerite. Canada. Catherine de Saint-Augustin. Mance, Jeanne. Marie de l'Incarnation. Youville, Marguerite dé. 17c. *3254*

Catholic churches. Actors and Actresses. American Protective Association. California (Los Angeles area). Modjeska, Helena. Polish Americans. 1876-1909. *3221*

Catholics. Alienation profiles. Fertility. Mothers. 1970. *2140*

Caton, Elizabeth. Caton, Louisa Catherine. Caton, Mary. Caton, Mary Ann. Historical Sites and Parks. Maryland (Baltimore). 19c-20c. *422*

Caton, Louisa Catherine. Caton, Elizabeth. Caton, Mary. Caton, Mary Ann. Historical Sites and Parks. Maryland (Baltimore). 19c-20c. *422*

Caton, Mary. Caton, Elizabeth. Caton, Louisa Catherine. Caton, Mary Ann. Historical Sites and Parks. Maryland (Baltimore). 19c-20c. *422*

Caton, Mary Ann. Caton, Elizabeth. Caton, Louisa Catherine. Caton, Mary. Historical Sites and Parks. Maryland (Baltimore). 19c-20c. *422*

Catt, Carrie Chapman. Ames, Marie. Gellhorn, Edna. League of Women Voters. Missouri (St. Louis). Organizations. 1919-29. *1277*

—. Duniway, Abigail Scott. Idaho. National American Woman Suffrage Association. Suffrage. Woman's Christian Temperance Union. 1870-96. *1350*

—. Feminism. Gilman, Charlotte Perkins. Louisiana (New Orleans). Shaw, Anna Howard. Social Conditions. 1890's-1903. *1318*

—. *Frank Leslie's Illustrated Newspaper* (periodical). Leslie, Miriam F. F. Publishers and Publishing. Suffrage. ca 1914-1914. *1617*

—. Hooper, Jessie Jack. League of Women Voters. Legislation. Wisconsin. 1921-60's. *286*

Cattle Raising. Alberta (Pincher Creek). Daily Life. Fort McLeod. Indians (reservations). Letters. 1884. *3373*

Caulkins, Frances Manwaring. Connecticut. Historians. Larned, Ellen Douglas. ca 1850-1912. *1050*

Cayuse Indians. Missions and Missionaries. Oregon Territory. Waiilatpu Mission. Whitman, Narcissa. 1836-47. *728*

—. Missions and Missionaries. Oregon Territory. Whitman, Marcus. Whitman, Narcissa. 1836-47. *882*

Celibacy. Communes. Lee, Ann. Northeastern or North Atlantic States. Sex life. Shakers. 1774-1968. *378*

Cemeteries. Illinois (New Salem, Petersburg). Rutledge, Ann. 1890. *3010*

Cendoya, Manuel de (death of). Florida. Inheritance. Law Reform. Olazarraga y Aramburu, Sebastiana. Widows. 1670-85. *548*

Censorship See also Freedom of Speech.

—. Authors. Child, Lydia Maria. Law. Sanger, Margaret. ca 1833-1950's. *285*

—. Channing, William Henry. Clarke, James Freeman. Emerson, Ralph Waldo. Fuller, Margaret (papers). ca 1842-1969. *632*

—. Pornography. Publishers and Publishing. *Roth* v. *United States* (US, 1957). 1914-67. *2719*

—. Pornography. Sexual permissiveness. 1963-72. *2721*

Census See also Statistics.

—. Bureau of Indian Affairs. Demography. Kansa Indians (number of). 1843. *905*

—. Prostitution. Tennessee (Nashville). 1860. *923*

Census statistics. Childbirth. Fertility. Migration. Puerto Ricans. 1965-70. *2634*

Centennial Celebrations. American Revolution. Elliott, Susannah. Flags, regimental. South Carolina Regiment, 2nd. 1776-79. 1970. *564*

—. Feminism. Housework, professionalization of. Pennsylvania (Philadelphia). Technology. Woman's Building. 1830-76. *168*

Centennial Exposition. Exhibits and Expositions. Missouri. 1876. *1554*

Central Intelligence Agency. Congress. Executive Power. Smith, Margaret Chase. 1950's-70's. *2331*

Central Normal School (Canterbury College). Indiana. Teacher Training. 1900-51. *1563*

Cesarean operation. California. Franciscans. Medicine (practice of). Missions and Missionaries. 1769-1833. *934*

Chancellor, Sue M. (reminiscences). Chancellorville (battle). Civil War. Family. Hospitals. Virginia. 1863. *782*

Chancellorville (battle). Chancellor, Sue M. (reminiscences). Civil War. Family. Hospitals. Virginia. 1863. *782*

Chandler, Elizabeth Margaret. Abolition Movement. Friends, Society of (Hicksites). Michigan. 1830's-60. *871*

Channing, William Henry. Censorship. Clarke, James Freeman. Emerson, Ralph Waldo. Fuller, Margaret (papers). ca 1842-1969. *632*

—. Feminism. Letters. Massachusetts (Worcester). Wells, Charlotte Fowler. Woman's Rights Convention (2nd national). 1851. *844*

Chapman, Maria Weston. Abolition Movement. Child, Lydia Maria. Foster, Abby Kelly. Holley, Sallie. 1820-60. *851*

Charities See also Philanthropy; Public Welfare.

—. Asher, Meta. Brandt, Mrs. Noah. California (San Francisco). Frank, Ray. Jaffa, Adele Solomons. Jews. Levinson, Amelia. Organizations. Prag, Mary. Selling, Natalie. Wolf, Alice. Wolf, Emma. 1896. *1429*

—. California (San Francisco). Economic Aid. Immigration. Ladies' Protection and Relief Society. Voluntary Associations. ca 1850-60. *625*

—. Canada, western. Catholic Church. Grey Sisters. Religious Orders. 1869-70. *3300*

—. Debutante parties. Hargrave, Colleen. Hospitals. Illinois (Chicago). Passavant Woman's Aid Society. 1939-71. *2061*

—. Pennsylvania (Philadelphia). Social work. Society for Organizing Charitable Relief and Repressing Mendicancy. 1864-1909. *1196*

—. Social Work. Volunteerism. ca 1850-20c. *1505*

Charities (fundraising). Cookbooks. New Jersey. Social Customs. 1879-1915. *1137*

Charity organization movement. Illinois (Chicago). Public Welfare. Rural-Urban Studies. Social Classes. 1880-1930. *1512*

—. Social Classes. 1874-1900. *1509*

Chase, Kate. Chase, Salmon P. Civil War. Politics. ca 1860-65. *784*

Chase, Mary Mehitabel. Albany Female Academy. Education. New York. Poetry. Teaching. 19c. *998*

Chase, Salmon P. Chase, Kate. Civil War. Politics. ca 1860-65. *784*

Chastity myth. Images. National Characteristics. Theater, musical. 1943-45. *1545*

Chautauqua circuit. Day, Louise (reminiscences). Social Customs. 1919-20. *1557*

—. Gravitz, Maybelle (reminiscences). 1874-1920's. *1558*

—. Lectures. Social Reform. Tarbell, Ida M. 1916-32. *1601*

Chavannes, Pierre Puvis de. Aesthetics. Cather, Willa (*Death Comes for the Archbishop*, 1927). 1927. *1664*

Cheda, Sherrill (interview). Canadian Library Association Committee on the Status of Women. Feminism. Labor Unions and Organizations. Librarians. 1973-74. *3267*

Cheer, Margaret. Actors and Actresses. American Company of Comedians. Marriage. South Carolina (Charles-Town). 1764-68. *606*

Chemistry history. Armstrong, Eva Vivian (obituary). Historians. Pennsylvania, University of (Edgar Fahs Smith Memorial Collection). 1877-1962. *1859*

Chenoweth, Peggy. Chenoweth, Richard. Frontier and Pioneer Life. Indian Wars. Kentucky (Louisville). 1750-1802. *700*

Chenoweth, Richard. Chenoweth, Peggy. Frontier and Pioneer Life. Indian Wars. Kentucky (Louisville). 1750-1802. *700*

Cherokee Indians. Agriculture. American Revolution. Indian removal. Ward, Nancy. ca 1755-1800. *387*

—. American Revolution. Tennessee. Ward, Nancy. 1738-1822. *588*

—. Boudinot, Elias. Connecticut (Cornwall). Gold, Harriet. Indian-White Relations. Marriage. 1824-39. *922*

Cherokee Outlet. Kansas (Kiowa). Landrush. Rumsey, Cordelia (letter). 1893. *3160*

*Cherokee Republican* (newspaper). Ferguson, Lucia Loomis. Journalism. Oklahoma. 1886-1962. *3112*

Chestnut Street Female Seminary. *See* Ogontz School for Young Ladies.

Cheyenne Indians. Arapaho Indians. Broken Horn, Lizzie Fletcher. Fletcher, Amanda Mary. Indians (captivities). Wyoming (Rock Creek Crossing). 1865-1930. *3199*

—. Dougherty, John. Pawnee Indians (Skidi). Religion. Rites and Ceremonies (sacrificial). 1827. *910*

Chicago *Daily Tribune* (newspaper). Child Welfare. Divorce. Domestic servants. Illinois. Marks, Nora (pseud. of Eleanora Stackhouse). Reporters and Reporting. Social Problems. 1888-90. *1673*

Chicanos. *See* Mexican Americans.

Chief Justices. *See* Judges; Supreme Court.

Chiefs of State. *See* types of chiefs of state, e.g. kings, presidents, etc.; and names of individual chiefs of state.

Child care. Abortion. Family. Feminist movement. Political activism. Sexism. 1970's. *2449*

—. Abortion. Feminism. Machismo. Mexican Americans. 1970's. *2623*

—. Behavioral science. Parent education. 1897-1929. *1167*

—. Collective ventures. Feminist Alliance. Housing. New York (Greenwich Village, Washington Square). Rodman, Henrietta. 1914-17. *1324*

—. Family structure. Sexual behavior. Social Change. 1970's. *2040*

—. Income, guaranteed. Poor. 1975. *2152*

—. Politics. Public Welfare. 1940-45. *1221*

—. Public office. Sex roles. Social Change. 1976. *2186*

Child development. Behavior modification. Education, Experimental Methods. Olerich, Henry. Olerich, Viola. 1897-1902. *980*

—. Montessori, Maria. Teaching methods. 1960's-. *2780*

Child labor. Barnard, Kate. Law Reform. Oklahoma. Southern Conference on Woman and Child Labor. 1904-24. *1202*

Child Labor Law. Gordon, Jean. Louisiana (New Orleans). Theatrical Syndicate. 1908-12. *1230*

Child, Lydia Maria. Abolition Movement. Chapman, Maria Weston. Foster, Abby Kelly. Holley, Sallie. 1820-60. *851*

—. Authors. Censorship. Law. Sanger, Margaret. ca 1833-1950's. *285*

—. Femininity (concept of). Fiction. Marriage. 1828-74. *210*

Child Lydia Maria (letters). Antislavery Sentiments. Secession. South or Southern States. Underwood, John Curtiss. 1860. *848*

Child, Lydia Marie (*The American Frugal Housewife*, 1833). Frugality. Housewives. 1830's. *676*

Child mortality. Economic Conditions. Fertility. 1800-1965. *208*

Child Study. *See* Adolescence; Kindergarten.

Child Welfare See also Child Labor; Children; Day Nurseries; Juvenile Delinquency.

—. Abbott, Grace. Kelley, Florence. Lathrop, Julia. Legislation. Politics. Sheppard-Towner Act. Social reform. Wald, Lillian. 1900-35. *1236*

—. Chicago *Daily Tribune* (newspaper). Divorce. Domestic servants. Illinois. Marks, Nora (pseud. of Eleanora Stackhouse). Reporters and Reporting. Social Problems. 1888-90. *1673*

—. Children's Code Commission. Missouri. Organizations. Social Reform. Suffrage. Woman's Christian Temperance Union. 1915-19. *1284*

—. Consumers. Day Nurseries. 1971. *2155*

—. Day Nurseries. Family. Social service agencies. 1940's-60's. *2668*

—. Day Nurseries. Health, Education and Welfare Department (policies). 1961-71. *2156*

—. Jones, Mary Harris. Labor Reform. United Mine Workers of America. Working Conditions. 1903-12. *1132*

Child Welfare Commission. Children's Codes. Hospitals (maternity). Minnesota. 1913-19. *1530*

Child Welfare (infants). Day nurseries. Family. 1969. *2154*

Childbearing. Attitudes. Gynecologists, male. Medicine (practice of). Social roles. 19c. *231*

Childbearing patterns. Family structure. Modernization. Papago Indians. Social Conditions. 1875-1970. *382*

Childbirth. Adultery. Marriage. New England. Prostitution. Puritans. Satire. Ward, Nathaniel (*The Simple Cobler of Aggawam in America*). 1647. *495*

—. Census statistics. Fertility. Migration. Puerto Ricans. 1965-70. *2634*

—. Death and Dying. Family. Marriage. Norris, Isacc, II. Norris, Sarah Elizabeth Logan. Pennsylvania. 1739-44. *514*

—. Discrimination. Family breakdown. Illegitimacy. Negroes. Sex roles. Social Problems. 18c-1972. *371*

—. Family structure. Illegitimacy. Income. Negroes. 1960's. *2585*

—. Fertility rates. Illegitimacy. Population growth. 1940-73. *2131*

Childcare. Genetics. Marriage. New York. Noyes, John Humphrey. Oneida community. Stirpiculture experiment. 1848-86. *867*

Childcare Centers. *See* Day Nurseries.

Childhood. Bern, Enid (reminiscences). Daily Life. Homesteading and Homesteaders. North Dakota (Hettinger County). 1907-12. *3153*

—. Brooks, Juanita (interview). Mormons. Mountain Meadows massacre. Teaching. Utah. ca 1909-74. *3207*

—. Duck, Edward Walker (reminiscences). Family life. Farms. Social Conditions. Tennessee (Cedar Grove). 1890-1910. *1153*

—. Fiction. Harvard University (Houghton Library; Lennox Collection). Lennox, Charlotte (letters). New York. ca 1729-1804. *611*

—. Hoover, Lou Henry. Iowa (Waterloo). 1874-84. *3030*

—. Indians. Literature. Nebraska (Sheridan County). Plains Indians. Sandoz, Mari. 1870's-1931. *1619*

—. Johnson, Dorothy M. (reminiscences). Montana (Whitefish). 1915. *3175*

—. Massachusetts (Whitinsville). Social Customs. Watson, Hildegarde Lasell (reminiscences). 19c. *2992*

—. Sex roles. Social Status. 1973-75. *2179*

Childlessness. Negroes. Whites. 1906-70. *248*

Childlessness (voluntary). Wives. 1973. *2122*

Childrearing. Adams, Abigail. Education. Family. Jefferson, Thomas. Morality. Politics. Values. 1774-1804. *756*

—. Attitudes. Letters. Roosevelt, Eleanor. Spain. 1930's. *1224*

—. Bixby, Widow. Lincoln, Abraham. Wheelwright, Sarah Cabot. 1861-65. *814*

—. Boyd, Belle. Compton, William Boyd. Kerr, Kate. 1860-65. *815*

—. Brown, William H. Frazey, Emma Jane. Illinois. Letters. 1862-67. *3015*

—. Buchanan, Sophia. Letters. Michigan. 1862-65. *773*

—. Chancellor, Sue M. (reminiscences). Chancellorville (battle). Family. Hospitals. Virginia. 1863. *782*

—. Chase, Kate. Chase, Salmon P. Politics. ca 1860-65. *784*

—. Clothing. New York (Syracuse). Painting. Redfield, Amy. 1860-65. *781*

—. Confederate Army. Danville Female Academy. Missouri. Robinson, Mary (reminiscences). 1864. *795*

—. Confederate Army. Hospitals. Tompkins, Sally. Virginia (Richmond). 1860-65. *811*

—. Confederate Army. Military Intelligence. Sheridan, Philip H. Virginia (Shenandoah Valley; Winchester). Wright, Rebecca. 1864. *786*

—. Confederate States of America. Espionage. Goldsborough, Effie. 1860-65. *788*

—. Confederate States of America. Espionage. Nurses and Nursing. Social Conditions. 1861-65. *827*

—. Confederate States of America. Polish Americans. Sosnowski, Sophie. Tochman, Apolonia Jagiello. 1860-65. *830*

—. Courtship. Illinois Volunteer Infantry (12th). Marriage. 1860-65. *776*

—. Cox, Nancy (letter). Reconstruction. Tennessee (Readyville). 1866. *774*

—. Cushman, Pauline. Espionage. Theater. 1863-93. *809*

—. Cushman, W. H. W. Lincoln, Abraham. Lincoln, Mary Todd. Wives. 1860's. *820*

—. Daily Life. Family. Illinois (Fayette County). Letters. Phifer, Louisa Jane. 1864-1904. *808*

—. Dix, Dorothea. 1860-65. *806*

—. Duncan, Mrs. Henry. Letters. Middleton, Harriott. Middleton, Susan. Social Conditions. South or Southern States. 1863-65. *800*

—. Economic Conditions. Groves, Avline (letters). Politics. Reconstruction. 1860-67. *791*

—. Economic Conditions. Letters. McCalla, Margaret. South or Southern States. 1863-65. *807*

—. Edmonds, Sarah Emma. Michigan Infantry Regiment, 2nd. 1860-65. *790*

—. Education. Lane, Anne Ewing. Reconstruction. Travel. ca 1830-70's. *3099*

—. Employment. Federal government. Wages. 1860-70. *789*

—. Family. Louisiana. Negroes. Refugees. 1860-65. *898*

—. Farmer, Alice (autobiography). Louisiana. South or Southern States. 1850-72. *803*

—. Feminism. Great Northwestern Fair. Illinois (Chicago). Livermore, Mary. Sanitary Commission. 1861-69. *813*

—. Food Supply. Georgia (Milledgeville). Poverty. South or Southern States. Widows. 1865. *796*

—. Georgia. Resettlement. Roswell Factory. Sherman, William T. Textile workers. 1864. *779*

—. Georgia (northwest). McClatchey, Minerva Leah Rowles (diary). Social Conditions. 1864-65. *777*

—. Glasgow, Sarah Lane. Lane, Anne Ewing. Letters. Missouri (St. Louis). 1861-63. *780*

—. Hall, Mariah M. Louisiana. Slaveowners. Widowhood. 1854-91. *3129*

—. Harrison, Constance Cary. Novels. Plantation life. South or Southern States. 1863-1911. *1710*

—. Hunter, Kate. Recreation. Rhode Island (Newport). Social Conditions. 1863-64. *794*

—. Image. Novels, romantic. 1866. *1695*

—. Iowa. Orphanages. Wittenmyer, Annie. 1864-1949. *1507*

—. Jackson, Eleanor Hardin. Letters. Social Conditions. Tennessee (Rutherford County). 1860-65. *818*

—. Labadie, Cecilia (diary). Texas (Galveston). 1863. *828*

—. Letters. Middleton, Harriott. Middleton, Susan. Social Conditions. South or Southern States. 1861-65. *799*

—. Letters. Middleton, Harriott. Middleton, Susan. South or Southern States. 1861-65. *801*

—. Letters. Nurses and Nursing. Sanitary Commission. Whetten, Harriet Douglas. 1862. *792*

—. Letters. Rawlings, Clarissa Lawrence. Rawlings, Hannah Garlick. Virginia (Orange County). 1865. *778*

—. Letters. Social Conditions. 1860-65. *810*

—. Letters. Tompkins, Ellen Wilkins. West Virginia (Fayette County). 1861. *822*

—. Marchmann, Anna. Marchmann, Mrs. George (diary). Transportation problems. Travel accounts. 1861. *787*

—. Nurses and Nursing. Peninsular campaign. Sanitary Commission. Whetten, Harriet Douglas (diary). 1862. *793*

—. Salt works. Tynes, Mollie. Virginia. 1860-65. *812*

Civil War (biography). Carroll, Anna Ella. Historiography. 1815-93. *802*

Civil War (diaries). Louisiana. 1860-65. *829*

Civil War (effects). Protestantism. South. Widows. 1861-65. *785*

Civil War (intelligence). Van Lew, Elizabeth. Virginia (Richmond). 1818-1900. *823*

Civil War (medical and sanitary affairs). Barton, Clara. Bickerdyke, Mary Ann. Dix, Dorothea. Nurses and Nursing. Wittenmyer, Annie. 1861-65. *831*

Civil War (outcome). Attitudes. Confederate States of America. 1865. *797*

Civil War (personal narratives). Clemson, Floride (letters). Pennsylvania. Social Customs. 1863. *798*

—. Family life. Letters. Levy, Richard. Levy, Rosena Hutzler. South or Southern States. 1860-65. 1907. *824*

—. Genealogy. McGuire, Judith W. (diary). Virginia. 1861-65. *825*

—. Hospitals. Nurses and Nursing. Ricketts, Frances L. (diary). Virginia (Manassas, Richmond). 1861-63. *805*

—. Smith, Maria MacGregor. 1864. *816*

—. South Carolina. Thomas, Anna Hasell (diary). 1864-65. *821*

Civil War (strategy). Carroll, Anna Ella (letters). Feminism. Fillmore, Millard. Politics. 1852-73. *817*

Clanton, Gertrude T. Chopin, Kate. Clay, Laura. Felton, Rebecca L. Feminism. Glasgow, Ellen. Gordon, Kate M. Kearney, Belle. South. 1830-1945. *1310*

Clapp, Elizabeth. Social Conditions. Travel. Vermont (western). Woodbury, Levi (diary). 1819. *2948*

Clapp, Elsie Ripley. Depressions. Education, community. Federal Programs. New Deal. Resettlement. Roosevelt, Eleanor. Rural Development. West Virginia (Arthurdale). 1933-44. *1204*

Clark, Edith K. O. (diary). Wyoming (Buffalo). 1933-34. *3161*

Clark, Judith (Julia). Clark, William (journal). Costume. ca 1805-16. *683*

Clark, Lemuel (daughter of). Fox, Katie. Fox, Margaretta. Seances. Spiritualism. 1848. *883*

Clark, William (journal). Clark, Judith (Julia). Costume. ca 1805-16. *683*

Clarke, James Freeman. Censorship. Channing, William Henry. Emerson, Ralph Waldo. Fuller, Margaret (papers). ca 1842-1969. *632*

Clarke, Sarah F. (letters). New England. Transcendentalists. 1832-40. *2970*

Class consciousness. Cohn, Fannia. International Ladies' Garment Workers' Union. Jews. Labor Unions and Organizations. Newman, Pauline. Pesotta, Rose. 1900-35. *1126*

—. Feminism. International Federation of Working Women. Organizations. Suffrage. Women's Trade Union League. 1890-1925. *1280*

Classroom structure. Sociology of education. Teachers. 1970's. *59*

Clay, Henry (tribute). Levert, Octavia Walton (speech). 1856. *739*

Clay, Laura. Breckinridge, Madeline McDowell. Constitutional amendment (19th). Federation of Women's Clubs. Kentucky Equal Rights Association. Suffrage. 1908-20. *1362*

—. Chopin, Kate. Clanton, Gertrude T. Felton, Rebecca L. Feminism. Glasgow, Ellen. Gordon, Kate M. Kearney, Belle. South. 1830-1945. *1310*

Cleaver, Kathleen (interview). Black Panther Party. Feminism. Negroes. 19c-20c. 1966-71. *2590*

Clemenceau, George. Family. Marriage. Plummer, Mary. 1849-1923. *1240*

Clemens, Samuel Langhorne. *See* Twain, Mark.

Clemm, Maria (letters). Longfellow, Henry Wadsworth. Poe, Edgar Allan. 1850-66. *993*

Clemson, Floride (letters). Civil War (personal narratives). Pennsylvania. Social Customs. 1863. *798*

Clergy *See also* specific denominations by name.

—. Adoption. Catholic Church. Children. Law. Public Welfare. Quebec. Suffrage. 1920-36. *3342*

—. Anglican Communion. Sex Discrimination (review article). 1973. *2490*

—. Antinomian Controversy. Cotton, John. Hutchinson, Anne. Massachusetts (Boston). Puritans. Theology. 1636. *581*

—. Baldwin, Abigail Pollard (diary). Daily Life. Presbyterian Church. Texas (San Antonio). Vermont (Plymouth). 1853-54. *2937*

—. Baptists. Burns, Bertha Porter. Burns, Marion Van. Louisiana (Shiloh). Teachers. 1884-1975. *3123*

—. Biographical dictionary. Helvie, Clara Cook. Sex Discrimination. Unitarian Church. Universalist Church of America. 1860-1976. *349*

—. Breckenridge, Juanita (letters). Congregational Church. Education. Employment (professional). Family. New York (Brookton, Ithaca). 1872-93. *1084*

—. Brown, Antoinette Louisa. Brown, Olympia. Friends, Society of. Hanaford, Phebe. Jones, Sybil. Mott, Lucretia. Oliver, Anne. Protestant Churches. Smiley, Sarah Frances. Van Cott, Maggie Newton. 19c. *345*

—. Catholic Church. Episcopal Church, Protestant. Ordination. Theology. 44-1974. *305*

—. Catholic Church. Protestant Churches. Sex discrimination. 1970's. *2474*

—. Christian Science (influence of). Churches. Eddy, Mary Baker. 1880-1910. *1423*

—. Divorce. Feminism. Public Opinion. Sociologists. 1906-20's. *1165*

—. Episcopal Church, Protestant. Ordination. Sex Discrimination. 1973. *2484*

—. Friends, Society of. Sex roles. 19c. *320*

—. Historiography. New England. Puritans. Sexual equality. 1668-1735. *498*

—. Ordination. Protestantism. Social change. World Council of Churches. 1945-75. *2487*

—. Public Opinion. Religion. 1960's. *2463*

—. Sex Discrimination. 1969. *2475*

Clerical work force. Employment. Sex Discrimination. 1974. *1939*

Client centered therapy. Elementary Education. Students. Teachers. 1960's-. *2793*

Clothing *See also* Costume; Fashions.

—. Age. Consumers. Family (urban). Sex. 1960's. *2088*

—. Behavior. Feminists. Symbolism. 1973. *2392*

—. Behavior. Popular Culture. Sex roles. Social Conditions. 1945-60's. *2209*

—. Civil War. New York (Syracuse). Painting. Redfield, Amy. 1860-65. *781*

—. Department stores. Merchandising. Neiman, Carrie. Neiman-Marcus Co. Texas (Dallas). 1900-17. *1044*

—. Fashions. 1860's. *685*

—. Flappers. Morality. Sex. Social Change. 1920's. *1189*

—. Historical Societies. Wisconsin. 1846-20c. *2212*

—. Industrial Revolution. Social Customs. 18c-20c. *212*

—. Marriage. Morality. Public Opinion. Sex. Social Customs. 1936-65. *2225*

—. Mennonites. Sex roles. 16c-20c. *338*

—. Sex. Social Change. 19c-20c. *191*

—. Shakers. 19c. *300*

Coal Mines and Mining. Jones, Mary Harris. Labor Unions and Organizations. United Mine Workers of America. West Virginia. 1901. *1133*

Coal mines, anthracite. Employment opportunities. Family incomes (supplementary). Pennsylvania. 1880-1900. *1051*

Coalition of Labor Union Women. Labor Unions and Organizations. Leftism. 1973-75. *2021*

Cobb, Mary Ann. Confederate States of America. Georgia (Athens). Plantation life. 1860-65. *783*

Cody, Margaret E. Gould, Helen. Gould, Jay. Trials. Wills. 1880-98. *1239*

Cody, William F. (Buffalo Bill). Oakley, Annie. Wild West Show. 1882-93. *1561*

—. Politics. Suffrage. Waite, Celia O. Crane. Waite, Davis Hanson. 1890's-1937. *1208*
—. Politics. Thomas, Charles S. Thomas, Emma Fletcher. 1853-1940. *1209*
—. Suffrage. 1893. *1337*
—. Suffrage. Waite, Davis Hanson. 1890's. *1359*
Colorado (Colorado Springs). Travel. Westward Movement. Young, Mary Eliza Willard (diary). 1871. *3183*
Colorado (Denver). Brown, Margaret Tobin. Europe. Social Conditions. *Titanic* (vessel). 19c-1912. *3152*
—. Family. Immigration. Jews. Shwayder, Rachel. 1865-1916. *1418*
Colorado (Estes Park). Bishop, Isabella Lucy Bird. Nugent, Jim. Travel. 1873. *3196*
Colorado (Lavender). Frontier and Pioneer Life. Robinson, Nellie Carnahan (memoirs). Social Customs. Teachers. 1897-1907. *1081*
Colorado (Leadville). Silver mining. Tabor, Elizabeth "Baby Doe". Tabor, Horace A. W. 1877-1935. *3154*
Colorado (Pueblo). Orman, Nellie Martin. Philanthropy. 1876-1918. *3159*
Colorado (South Platte Valley). Daily Life. Farmers. Frontier and Pioneer Life. German Russians. Immigration. Social Conditions. 1890-ca 1907. *2514*
Colorado (southern). Boardinghouses. Mining camps. Piedmontese. 1890's. *1112*
Colorado (Uncompahgre Plateau). Daily life. Matlock, Mary Jane (reminiscences). Pioneers. 1870's-80's. *701*
Colorado (Weld County). Daily Life. Dalziel, Hazel Webb (reminiscences). Farms. 1890's. *3162*
Colorado Woman's College. Cooper, Jane Olivia Barnes. Philanthropy. Social Reform. 19c. *3157*
Coloring books. Children. Sex roles. 1970-72. *2193*
Columbia Female Academy. Education. Missouri. 1833-55. *977*
Comanche Indians. Polygamy. Social Conditions. 19c. *1480*
Comedy. Films. Marriage. Sex. 1965-71. *2095*
Comic books. Sex roles. Stereotypes. Youth. 1969-72. *2284*
Comics, love. Adolescence. Popular Culture. Social Classes. Values. 20c. *2288*
Commerce. *See* Banking; Business; Monopoly Power; Prices; Statistics; Transportation.
Commercials. Image. Sex roles. Television. 1971-73. *2728*
Commission on Obscenity and Pornography. Attitudes. Pornography. Sexual behavior. 1960's. *2724*
Commission on the Minimun Wage for Women. Labor law. Quebec. Wages. 1925-31. *3336*
Commission on the Status and Role of Women in the United Methodist Church. Feminism. Methodism. Missions and Missionaries. Organizations. 1869-1974. *368*
Commission on the Status of Women. Civil Service. Employment. 1962. *1872*
Committee for Women's Rights. British Columbia Federation of Labour. Labor Unions and Organizations. 1970-75. *3389*
Committee on Paintings. District of Columbia. Onassis, Jacqueline Kennedy. White House. 1963. *2896*
Committee on the Status of Women in the Archival Profession. Archivists. Employment. Sex discrimination. Wages. 1972-74. *1941*
Common Cause. Citizen Lobbies. New York. Podell, Albert N. State legislature. 1975. *2360*
Communalism. *See* Communes.
Communes *See also* names of individual communes; Utopias.
—. Celibacy. Lee, Ann. Northeastern or North Atlantic States. Sex life. Shakers. 1774-1968. *378*
—. Economic Conditions. McWhirter, Martha White. Sanctified Sisters. Texas (Belton). 1866-99. *1432*
—. Family. Hutterites. Manitoba. 1874-1960's. *3379*
—. Harmony Society. Indiana. Politics. Sunwoman prophecy. 1814-24. *858*
Communes (review article). Families. Societies (alternative). 1960's-70's. *2107*
Communication networks. American Public Health Association. Employment. Professionals. Sex Discrimination. 1975. *1986*

Communications. *See* Language; Mass Media; Newspapers.
Communism *See also* Anarchism and Anarchists; Leftism; Marxism; Socialism.
—. Art and Society. Canada. Fairley, Margaret. Periodicals. 1885-1968. *3297*
—. Baldwin, James (open letter). Davis, Angela. Jews. 1960's-71. *2316*
—. China. Journalism. Strong, Anna Louise. 1917-70. *261*
—. China. Journalism. Strong, Anna Louise. USSR. 20c. *276*
—. Feminism. Flynn, Elizabeth Gurley. ca 1890-1920. *1203*
Communist Party. Alabama (Scottsboro). NAACP. Negroes. Rape. 1931-32. *1524*
—. Canada. Feminist movement. 1921-71. *3290*
—. Davis, Angela. Morality. Political attitudes. Trials. 1970's. *2314*
Community leadership. Editors and Editing. Florida. Panama City *Pilot* (newspaper). West, Lillian Carlisle. 1916-37. *1678*
Community services. Children. Family. Social Work. 1934-62. *2653*
Community studies. Anthropology. Appalachia, southern. Demography. Fertility decline. Methodology. 1973. *53*
Community work. Negroes. Organizations. Racial pride. 1892-1932. *1465*
Composers. Kansas (Kansas City). Woodbury, Mrs. Frank. 1895-97. *1775*
—. Korn, Anna Less Brosius (tribute). Legislation. Oklahoma. Poetry. 19c-1965. *3104*
Compton, William Boyd. Boyd, Belle. Civil War. Kerr, Kate. 1860-65. *815*
Compulsory Education. *See* Child Labor; Schools.
Computers. *See* names of specific computers, e.g. IBM 370 (computer).
Comstock, Anthony. Birth control. Morality. Pornography. Social Reform. 1871-1915. *1504*
Comstock, Joseph. Hazard, Nancy. Hysteria. Medicine (practice of). Music therapy. Tarantism. Witchcraft, suspicion of. 1801. *929*
Cone, Claribel. Art collectors. Cone, Etta. Stein, Gertrude. 1900-51. *1750*
Cone, Etta. Art collectors. Cone, Claribel. Stein, Gertrude. 1900-51. *1750*
Confederate Army *See also* Confederate States of America.
—. Civil War. Danville Female Academy. Missouri. Robinson, Mary (reminiscences). 1864. *795*
—. Civil War. Hospitals. Tompkins, Sally. Virginia (Richmond). 1860-65. *811*
—. Civil War. Military Intelligence. Sheridan, Philip H. Virginia (Shenandoah Valley; Winchester). Wright, Rebecca. 1864. *786*
Confederate States of America *See also* names of individual states; Confederate Army; Reconstruction.
—. Attitudes. Civil War (outcome). 1865. *797*
—. Civil War. Espionage. Goldsborough, Effie. 1860-65. *788*
—. Civil War. Espionage. Nurses and Nursing. Social Conditions. 1861-65. *827*
—. Civil War. Polish Americans. Sosnowski, Sophie. Tochman, Apolonia Jagiello. 1860-65. *830*
—. Cobb, Mary Ann. Georgia (Athens). Plantation life. 1860-65. *783*
Conformity. Authority. Catholic Church. Family. Youth. 1960's. *2292*
Conger, Sarah J. Pike. China. Christianity. 1898-1905. *1420*
Congregation of Notre Dame. Catholic Church. Church Schools. Ontario (Kingston). Religious Orders. 1841-48. *3358*
Congregation of Sisters of Mercy. Catholic Church. Church Schools. Mount St. Vincent Academy. Pennsylvania. Religious Orders. Warde, Frances. 1843-51. *876*
Congregational Church. Breckenridge, Juanita (letters). Clergy. Education. Employment (professional). Family. New York (Brookton, Ithaca). 1872-93. *1084*
Congregational Church, First. Eye bank. Tennessee (Memphis). 1940-65. *2666*
Congregationalism *See also* Friends, Society of; Puritans; Unitarianism.
—. Bryant, Charity. Daily Life. Drake, Sylvia (diary). Sewing. Vermont (Weybridge). 1784-1868. *2969*
—. Choctaw Indians. Harkins, Mrs. Richard. Harkins, Richard (death of). Missions and Missionaries. Murder. Slavery. 1858-59. *911*

Congress *See also* House of Representatives; Legislation; Senate.
—. Army. Civil War. Physicians. Walker, Mary. 1861-1917. *826*
—. Banking. Credit card companies. Mortgage lenders. Sex discrimination. 1972-74. *2341*
—. Catholic Church. Federal Aid to Education. Roosevelt, Eleanor. 1949-50. *2319*
—. Central Intelligence Agency. Executive Power. Smith, Margaret Chase. 1950's-70's. *2331*
—. Conservation groups. Federal government. Forests and Forestry. Legislation. Minnesota Federation of Women's Clubs. Minnesota National Forest. Organizations. 1898-1908. *1286*
—. Constitutional amendment (19th). Lobbying. Organizations. Women's Joint Congressional Committee. 1920-29. *1281*
—. Constitutions, State. Mormons. Polygamy. Utah. Woodruff Manifesto (1890). 1890. *1449*
—. Education. Marriage. Political Parties. State Legislatures. 1916-64. *297*
—. Educational Reform. Green, Edith (interview). 1970's. *2340*
—. Elections. Robertson, Alice M. Veterans' benefits. 1920-24. *1248*
—. Equal employment opportunity. Executive Power. 1964-69. *1907*
—. Family. Law. Old-Age, Survivors', and Disability Insurance. Public Welfare. Social change. 1935-71. *2344*
—. Family. Public Welfare. Reform. Taxation. 1970's. *2028*
—. Geography (effects of). Political Leadership. Social Conditions. State Legislatures. 1920-64. *298*
—. Montana. Politics. Rankin, Jeannette. Suffrage. 1913-18. *1263*
—. Mormons. Polygamy. Religious Liberty. Utah (statehood). 1840's-96. *3165*
—. Oklahoma. Political Campaigns. Robertson, Alice M. 1898-1923. *1273*
—. Politics. Sex Discrimination. 1970's. *2354*
—. Rankin, Jeannette. Suffrage. Unemployment. World War I. 20c. *265*
Congressional Union for Woman Suffrage. Arizona. Democratic Party. Political Campaigns. Suffrage. 1914. 1916. *1370*
Congresswomen. Elections. Political Leadership. Widows. 1970's. *2361*
—. Human Relations. Social Organizations. 1960's. *2310*
Conine, Catharine. Conine, Emily. Conine, Jane. Daily Life. Indiana. Letters. Pioneers. Seymour, Mary Ann Conine. 1849-51. *3003*
Conine, Emily. Conine, Catharine. Conine, Jane. Daily Life. Indiana. Letters. Pioneers. Seymour, Mary Ann Conine. 1849-51. *3003*
Conine family. Daily Life. Letters. North Central States. Pioneers. Seymour, Mary Ann Conine. 1852-63. *3004*
Conine, Jane. Conine, Catharine. Conine, Emily. Daily Life. Indiana. Letters. Pioneers. Seymour, Mary Ann Conine. 1849-51. *3003*
Conley, James. Frank, Leo (trial). Georgia (Atlanta). Jews. Murder. Negroes. Press. 1913-15. *1522*
Connecticut *See also* New England; Northeastern or North Atlantic States.
—. Alcoholism. Drug Abuse. Silver Hill Foundation. Youth. 1960's. *2283*
—. Birth Control. Civil Rights. Law. Massachusetts. 19c. *1205*
—. Borden family. Gay, Joanna Bordon (and family). Massachusetts. 1635-91. *2936*
—. Bradstreet, Anne. Poetry. Wolcott, Roger (journal). ca 1650-1758. *609*
—. Caulkins, Frances Manwaring. Historians. Larned, Ellen Douglas. ca 1850-1912. *1050*
—. Divorce. Law. 1636-1963. *2943*
—. Education. Litchfield Female Seminary. Pierce, Sarah. 1784-1852. *972*
—. Foote, Lucinda. Students. Yale University. 1783. *610*
—. Juvenile offenders. Prisons. Sex Discrimination. 1970's. *2286*
Connecticut (Canterbury). Abolition Movement. Crandall, Prudence. Feminism. Massachusetts. May, Samuel J. 1832-61. *840*
—. Abolition Movement. Crandall, Prudence. Garrison, William Lloyd. Racism. Sexism. 1830-40. *847*
—. Crandall, Prudence. Law. Negroes. Schools. 1830's. *892*
Connecticut (Cornwall). Boudinot, Elias. Cherokee Indians. Gold, Harriet. Indian-White Relations. Marriage. 1824-39. *922*

Counseling *See also* Social Work.
—. Social service programs. Women in Transition, Inc. (agency). 1970's. *2295*
Counseling (volunteer). Alcoholism. Connecticut (Fairfield County). Council of Alcoholism. 1960's. *2642*
Counselors. High Schools. Self concepts. Sex roles. 1961. *2200*
Counter Culture. *See* Communes.
*Country Gentleman* (periodical). Farm life. Jones, Nellie Kedzie (letters). Wisconsin. 1912-16. *1066*
Country Life *See also* Rural Settlements.
—. Allison, Elsie North (recollections). Kansas (Labette County). Schools. 1880's-90's. *3150*
—. Blake, John Laurus (*The Farmer's Everyday Book*, 1850). Farmers. Housework. Social Customs. Wives. 1850's-60's. *649*
—. California (Tuolumne County). Hines, Frances Mary (recollections). Yancey, Bud. 1890-1907. *3231*
—. Cooking recipes. Holliday, Bea. New York (Adirondack Mountains). 1920's-60's. *2950*
—. Fairfield (family home). Iddings, Deborah Alice. Iddings, Fanny Pierce (reminiscences). Maryland (Montgomery County). Moravian Female Seminary. Pierce, Ann. Pierce, Sophia Kummer. 1728-1968. *3075*
—. Farms. Illinois (southern). Lentz, Lula Gillespie (reminiscences). Marriage. 1883-1929. *3017*
—. Foreman, Susan E. (diary). Oklahoma (Webber's Falls). Teachers. 1862-63. *621*
—. Frontier and Pioneer Life. Great Plains (northern). Technology. 1870-1970. *3170*
—. Kitchens. Oklahoma. ca 1900-20's. *3093*
—. Paintings. Texas (Iredell). Williamson, Clara McDonald. 1890's-1930's. *1759*
Countway, Sanda. Francis A. Countway Medical Library (Harvard University). Lever Brothers Company. Philanthropy. ca 1955. *2057*
County Government. *See* Local Government; State Government.
County Library Law (1919). Gunter, Lillian. Libraries. Politics. Texas. 1914-19. *1249*
Court records. North Carolina. Patients. Physicians. 1732-78. *602*
Courts *See also* Judges; Juries; Supreme Court.
—. Baptism. Christianity. Key, Elizabeth. Law. Negroes. Slavery. Virginia. 1607-90. *584*
—. Birth Control. Juvenile Delinquency. Pregnancy (extramarital). 1960's-. *2667*
—. California (Malibu). Environmental protection. Government. Rindge, May Knight. Southern Pacific Railroad. ca 1900-72. *3243*
—. Children. Human Rights. Jehovah's Witnesses. Religious Liberty. 1964. *2478*
—. Divorce. Lawyers. Oklahoma Territory. 1890-1906. *1161*
—. Domestic relations. Law. Virginia. 1960's. *2353*
—. Employment. Law. Sex Discrimination. 1964-72. *1960*
—. Sex Discrimination. 1873-1973. *289*
—. Sex Discrimination. 1962-72. *2347*
Courts Martial and Courts of Inquiry. Camp followers. Military. Prostitution. World War I. 1917-18. *1293*
Courts (reforms). Juries, selection of. Sex discrimination. 1972. *2348*
Courtship *See also* Dating.
—. Ambler, Polly. Marriage. Marshall, John (letters). 1780-1835. *631*
—. Appleton, Fanny. Longfellow, Henry Wadsworth. Massachusetts (Boston, Cambridge). 1841-43. *1001*
—. Attitudes. Canada. Interpersonal Relations. Sex roles. Students. USA. 1969. *217*
—. Automobiles. Morality. Youth. ca 1920's. *1184*
—. Brooms. Folklore. Marriage. Ohio River Valley. 1960's. *2770*
—. California. Dame Shirley (pseud. of Louise A. K. S. Clappe). Gold Rushes. Letters. Marriage. 1838-1906. *711*
—. Civil War. Illinois Volunteer Infantry (12th). Marriage. 1860-65. *776*
—. Colleges and Universities. Marriage. Sororities. 1960's. *2114*
—. Davis, Richard Harding (letters). Fox, John. Scheff, Fritzi. 1908. *1762*
—. Economic Conditions. Marriage. Social conditions. Urbanization. 1871-1911. *1158*
—. Family. Maine. Marriage. Penobscot Indians. Social Customs. 1492-1900. *370*
—. Frontier and Pioneer Life. Humor. Louisiana. Marriage. 1840's. *965*

—. Hayes, Lucy Webb. Hayes, Rutherford B. Marriage. Politics. 1850's-80's. *1227*
—. Kentucky. Marriage. Ohio River Valley. Social Customs. 19c-20c. *3144*
—. Manitoba. Marriage (customs). Mennonites. Sommerfield Mennonite Church. 1890-1960's. *3378*
—. Marriage. New England. Sexual behavior. Social Customs. 1632-1783. *510*
—. Marriage. Pershing, John J. Warren, Frances. 1903-15. *1170*
—. Songs, popular. Youth. 1950's-69. *2269*
Cowboys. Cities. Culture. Kansas. Morality. Prostitution. 19c. *1139*
—. Daily Life. Gregg, Myrtle Chalfant (reminiscences). Nebraska (Howard County). Travel. Wyoming (Casper). 1899-1909. *3181*
Cowan, Bertha Muzzy Bower Sinclair. *See* Bower, B. M.
Cowichan Indians. British Columbia. Industry (cottage). Needlework (knitting). 1850's-1960's. *3388*
Cox, Minnie M. Mississippi (Indianola). Negroes. Politics. Roosevelt, Theodore. 1903-04. *1463*
Cox, Nancy (letter). Civil War. Reconstruction. Tennessee (Readyville). 1866. *774*
Cracroft, Sophia. California. Franklin, Jane. Social Conditions. Travel accounts. 1858-61. *3232*
Crafts. *See* Arts and Crafts; Home Economics.
Cragin, Mary. Marriage. Noyes, John Humphrey. Psychology. Sex. Utopias. 1830's-40's. *865*
Crandall, Prudence. Abolition Movement. Connecticut (Canterbury). Feminism. Massachusetts. May, Samuel J. 1832-61. *840*
—. Abolition Movement. Connecticut (Canterbury). Garrison, William Lloyd. Racism. Sexism. 1830-40. *847*
—. Connecticut (Canterbury). Law. Negroes. Schools. 1830's. *892*
—. Connecticut (Kingston). Harris, Sarah (biography). Negroes. Social Reform. 1781-1902. *902*
Crane, Caroline Bartlett. Cities. Michigan (Kalamazoo). Progressivism. Reform. Sanitation (municipal). 1858-1935. *1383*
Craton, Ann Washington. Amalgamated Clothing Workers Union. Labor Unions and Organizations. Social Reform. 1915-44. *1125*
Crawford, Florence. Capper, Arthur. Daily Life. Diaries. Kansas. 1891-92. *3195*
Crawford, Isabella Valancy. Ontario (Toronto). Poetry. ca 1850-87. *3316*
Creative innocence, concept of. Intellectuals. Maritain, Jacques. Maritain, Raissa. Poetry. Religion. 1940's-75. *2473*
Credit. *See* Banking.
Credit card companies. Banking. Congress. Mortgage lenders. Sex discrimination. 1972-74. *2341*
Cree Indians. Canada (James Bay area). Fertility. Modernization. Mothers. 1968. *3306*
Creek Indians. Family. Lewis, Kendall. Marriage. Settlement. Texas (Titus County). 1781-1917. *913*
Crime and Criminals *See also* names of crimes, e.g. Murder, etc.; Criminal Law; Juvenile Delinquency; Outlaws; Police; Prisons; Riots; Trials; Violence.
—. 1960-70. *2682*
—. American Civil Liberties Union Biennial Conference. Law Reform. Sexual behavior. Wisconsin (Milwaukee). 1974. *2345*
—. Barrow, Clyde. Darby, H. Dillard. Louisiana (Ruston). Parker, Bonnie. Stone, Sophia. 1933. *1517*
—. Barrow, Clyde. Death and Dying. Folk heroes. Louisiana. Thornton, Bonnie Parker. 1934. *1525*
—. Economic Conditions. Prisons. 1975. *2675*
—. Feminism. Social Change. 1932-72. *2678*
—. Law. Sex. Social Change. 1960's. *2674*
—. Law and Society. Morality. Public opinion. Sex. Social problems. 1619-1776. *598*
Criminal Law *See also* Juries; Trials.
—. Abortion. Medicine and State. Sex roles. Social Classes. 1960's. *2702*
—. Behavioral studies. Constitutional Law. Pornography. President's Commission on Obscenity and Pornography. 1970-71. *2722*
—. Marriage. Social Work. Violence. 1970-73. *2673*
—. Obscenity. Pornography. State Legislatures. Supreme Court. 1973. *2720*
Criminal prosecution. New York City. 1691-1776. *599*

*Crisis* (periodical). DuBois, W. E. B. Negroes. Suffrage. 1910-34. *1380*
Crocker, Edwin Bryant. California (Sacramento). Crocker, Margaret Ellen Rhodes. Marriage. Philanthropy. 1821-1901. *3224*
Crocker, Margaret Ellen Rhodes. California (Sacramento). Crocker, Edwin Bryant. Marriage. Philanthropy. 1821-1901. *3224*
Croly, Jane Cunningham (Jennie June). General Federation of Women's Clubs. Journalism. Organizations. Press clubs. Sorosis. 19c. *1717*
Crombie, Helen Elizabeth (diary). Labor Disputes. Pennsylvania (Pittsburgh). Railroads. Riots. 1877. *2944*
Cromwinshield, Louise du Pont. Bullock, Helen Duprey (interview). Historic Preservation. National Trust for Historic Preservation. 1974. *1878*
Crops. *See* names of crops and farm products, e.g. Hay, Corn, etc.
Crowds. *See* Demonstrations; Riots; Social Psychology.
Crozier, Alice (review article). Novels. Parker, Gail Thain (review article). Stowe, Harriet Beecher. Womanhood (concept of). Women's Studies. 1820-1920. 1972-73. *2*
Cultism concepts. Hero, concepts of. Historians (male). 1873-1974. *27*
Cultural center. Libraries. Sullivan, Maud. Texas (El Paso). 1920's-75. *3135*
Cultural change. Art history. Feminism. Painting (genre, narrative). 19c. *450*
Cultural debate. Image. Literature. Passion. Reason. Sex roles. 1775-1850. *959*
Cultural deprivation. Childrearing. Educational opportunity. Mothers. Negroes. 1960's. *2543*
Cultural differences. Domestic adjustment. Family (American). India. Wives. 1960's. *2121*
Cultural enrichment program. Leesy, Miss. Missouri (St. Louis). Public Schools. 1960's. *2787*
Cultural History. Domestic culture. Methodology. 1960's. *67*
—. Sexuality. Social Organization. 1974. *2169*
Cultural ideals (conflicting). Sex roles. 1969. *2202*
Cultural influence. Nelson, Harriet (interview). *Ozzie and Harriet* (program). Social change. Television. 1950's-66. *2756*
Culture *See also* Education; Popular Culture; Scholarship.
—. Alcoholic cirrhosis. Arizona. Hopi Indians. Navajo Indians. 1965-67. *2605*
—. Authors. Hurston, Zora Neale. Migration, Internal. Negroes. Toomer, Jean. 1860-1960. *336*
—. Birth Control. Fertility. Sexual intercourse. 1960's-70's. *2060*
—. Cities. Cowboys. Kansas. Morality. Prostitution. 19c. *1139*
—. Connecticut, eastern. Family. Tombstone carvings. Wheeler, Obadiah. 1702-49. *517*
—. Fiction. Munro, Alice. Ontario. South. 1940's-70's. *3318*
—. Folklore. Hurston, Zora Neale. Negroes. Novels. 1930's-60. *449*
—. Language. Welty, Eudora (*The Ponder Heart*, 1954). 1954. *2866*
—. National Parks and Reserves. Shouse, Catherine Filene. Virginia (Wolf Trap). 1960. *2892*
Culture, creation of. 17c-20c. *471*
Cunningham, Ann Pamela. Historical Sites and Parks. Mount Vernon Ladies' Association. Virginia. 1816-75. *3050*
Cunningham, Sarah Apthorp Morton. Letters. Massachusetts (Boston). Politics. Social Conditions. 1825. *2996*
Curricula. Barham, Jane. Secondary Education. South Carolina Female Collegiate Institute (Barhamville). Warne, Julia. 1826-69. *987*
—. Barnes, Mary Sheldon. History teaching. Methodology. 1880's. 1960's. *1106*
—. Bibliographies. California (San Diego). High schools. Women's Studies. 1975. *23*
—. Bibliographies. Colleges and Universities. Economics. Syllabi. Women's Studies. 1972. *35*
—. Catholic Church. High Schools. 1960's. *2845*
—. Colleges and Universities. Sex Discrimination. Women's Studies. 1972. *3*
—. Colleges and Universities. Women's Studies. 1969. *45*
—. Developmental theory. Higher Education. Teaching. 1972. *2805*

—. Educational Reform. Feminism. Women's Studies. 1960's-73. *43*

—. Employment. Secondary Education. Sex discrimination. Social Status. Teachers. 1969. *1980*

—. Family life. Public Schools. Sex Education. 1960's. *2846*

—. Feminism. Higher Education. Historians. Teaching. Women's Studies. 1940-73. *14*

—. History Teaching (Western American). Westward movement. Yale University. 1973. *707*

—. New York, State University of, at Buffalo. Women's Studies College. 1971-73. *19*

—. Schools. Sex roles. Stereotypes. Teachers. 1939-72. *2813*

Curry, John Steuart. Curry, Mrs. John Steuart (interview). Painting. Schuster, Mrs. Daniel Curry (interview). 1897-1946. *1786*

Curry, Mrs. John Steuart (interview). Curry, John Steuart. Painting. Schuster, Mrs. Daniel Curry (interview). 1897-1946. *1786*

Curtis, Natalie. Austin, Mary Hunter. Corbin, Alice. Densmore, Frances. Fletcher, Alice Cunningham. Folk Songs. Indian culture. Literature. Translating and Interpreting. Underhill, Ruth Murray. Walton, Eda Lou. West. 1880-1965. *433*

Curwen, Alice (letter). Antislavery Sentiments. Friends, Society of. Tavernor, Martha. 1675-76. *571*

Cushman, Charlotte Saunders. Bankhead, Tallulah. Cornell, Katharine. Duncan, Isadora. Farrar, Geraldine. Hallam, Nancy. Hayes, Helen. Lind, Jenny. National Portrait Gallery. Patti, Adelina. Portraits. Theater. 1971. *418*

—. Bowery Theater. New York City. Public Opinion. Theater. 1836. *1036*

—. New York (Albany). Theater. 1836-37. *1034*

—. New York City. Theater. 1837. *1035*

Cushman, Pauline. Civil War. Espionage. Theater. 1863-93. *809*

Cushman, W. H. W. Civil War. Lincoln, Abraham. Lincoln, Mary Todd. Wives. 1860's. *820*

Custer, Elizabeth Bacon. Christmas. Frontier and Pioneer Life. Great Plains. 19c. *717*

—. Economic Conditions. Family. Widows. 7th Cavalry, US. 1876. *1172*

Custer, Elizabeth Bacon (letter). Daily Life. Fort Riley. Kansas. Richmond, Rebecca. Travel. 1866. *710*

Custis family. Custis, Frances Parke. Marriage. Virginia. Washington, Martha. ca 1670's-1750's. *501*

Custis, Frances Parke. Custis family. Marriage. Virginia. Washington, Martha. ca 1670's-1750's. *501*

Customer-stripper relationships. Behavior. Strip clubs. ca 1970-74. *2164*

# D

Dace, Catherine Hubbard (memoirs). California (San Fernando Valley). Settlement. ca 1840's-90's. *3211*

*Daily Alta California* (newspaper). California (San Francisco). Journalism. Stoddard, Elizabeth Barstow. 1854-57. *1013*

Daily Life *See also* Popular Culture.

—. Adams, Henry Brooks. Tone, Aileen. 1913-18. *1200*

—. Alberta (Pincher Creek). Cattle Raising. Fort McLeod. Indians (reservations). Letters. 1884. *3373*

—. Army forts. Family. Frontier and Pioneer Life. Social Conditions. Western States. 1860's. *689*

—. AU7 Ranch. South Dakota (Hot Springs). Stokes, Elsie Carlson. Swedish Americans. ca 1910-30. *3197*

—. Baldwin, Abigail Pollard (diary). Clergy. Presbyterian Church. Texas (San Antonio). Vermont (Plymouth). 1853-54. *2937*

—. Baptists. Louisiana (Hill Switch). Oneal, Marion S. (reminiscences). 1902-03. *3133*

—. Battle, Lucy Martin. Battle, William Horn. North Carolina. Plantations. 1805-74. *3062*

—. Bentley, Anna Briggs (letter). Friends, Society of. Frontier and Pioneer Life. Ohio (Columbiana County). 1826. *709*

—. Bern, Enid (reminiscences). Childhood. Homesteading and Homesteaders. North Dakota (Hettinger County). 1907-12. *3153*

—. Berry, Mrs. H. H. (reminiscences). Education. Family. Oklahoma. 1875-20c. *3094*

—. Bradford, Phoebe George (diary). Delaware. Female Colonization Society. 1832-33. *3089*

—. Bradford, Phoebe George (diary). Delaware (Wilmington). 1835-39. *3087*

—. Bradford, Phoebe George (diary). Delaware (Wilmington). Social Conditions. 1833-35. *3088*

—. Bright, Abbie (diary). Homesteading and Homesteaders. Kansas. 1870-71. *3194*

—. Brown, Josephine Edith (diary). Iowa (Shelby). 1892-1901. *3014*

—. Bryant, Charity. Congregationalism. Drake, Sylvia (diary). Sewing. Vermont (Weybridge). 1784-1868. *2969*

—. California (Santa Barbara). Kroll, Frances Cooper (reminiscences). 1890's. *3219*

—. California (Santa Barbara). Letters. Lincoln, Abbie Smith Patrick. 1869. *3223*

—. Capper, Arthur. Crawford, Florence. Diaries. Kansas. 1891-92. *3195*

—. Children. Dakota Territory. Fort Randall. Photographs. Sioux Indians. Sitting Bull Collection. Wives. 1869-83. *1489*

—. Civil War. Family. Illinois (Fayette County). Letters. Phifer, Louisa Jane. 1864-1904. *808*

—. Colorado (South Platte Valley). Farmers. Frontier and Pioneer Life. German Russians. Immigration. Social Conditions. 1890-ca 1907. *2514*

—. Colorado (Uncompahgre Plateau). Matlock, Mary Jane (reminiscences). Pioneers. 1870's-80's. *701*

—. Colorado (Weld County). Dalziel, Hazel Webb (reminiscences). Farms. 1890's. *3162*

—. Conine, Catharine. Conine, Emily. Conine, Jane. Indiana. Letters. Pioneers. Seymour, Mary Ann Conine. 1849-51. *3003*

—. Conine family. Letters. North Central States. Pioneers. Seymour, Mary Ann Conine. 1852-63. *3004*

—. Connecticut (Winchester). Education. Kidder, Harriette Smith (diary). Methodism. 1825. *2942*

—. Cowboys. Gregg, Myrtle Chalfant (reminiscences). Nebraska (Howard County). Travel. Wyoming (Casper). 1899-1909. *3181*

—. Custer, Elizabeth Bacon (letter). Fort Riley. Kansas. Richmond, Rebecca. Travel. 1866. *710*

—. Dean, Teresa. Reporters and Reporting. Sioux Indians. South Dakota (Wounded Knee). 1891. *1661*

—. District of Columbia. Family. Jones, Anne Neville (letters). Jones, Roland (letters). Louisiana (Shreveport). Politics. 1853-54. *745*

—. Divorce. Family. Feminism (review article). Historiography. 1967-70. *15*

—. Dunlap, Susan. Nova Scotia (Stewiacke). Social Conditions. 1866-1912. *3324*

—. Ethnic Groups. Johnson, Dorothy M. (reminiscences). Montana. ca 1915. *3172*

—. Eubank, Mary James (travel diary). Frontier and Pioneer Life. Kentucky. Migration, Internal. Texas. 1853. *715*

—. Family. Homesteading and Homesteaders. Kansas. Warner, Luna E. (diary). 1871-74. *688*

—. Family. Noble, Katey. Utah (Frémont Island). Wenner, Uriah J. 1886-91. *3226*

—. Family. Pennsylvania (Pine Creek Valley). Pioneers. 1772-1825. *719*

—. Family. Quebec (Beaupré). Rural Settlements. Social Conditions. ca 1900. *3341*

—. Folklore. Food Consumption. Homesteading and Homesteaders. Social Conditions. 19c. *733*

—. Folklore. Houses. Social Customs. Tennessee (east). 1974. *2195*

—. Frontier and Pioneer Life. Marriage. 1770's-80's. *694*

—. Housekeepers. Immigration. Oregon (Carlton, Yamhill River Valley). Social Customs. Swedish Americans. 19c. *1501*

—. Immigrants. Norwegians. Social Conditions. Texas. Waerenskjold, Elise (letter). 1841-51. *696*

—. Kansas. Pioneers. Schools. 1880's. *3167*

—. Kansas (Junction City). Letters. Snow, Leslie. Snow, Susan Currier. 1888-89. *3151*

—. Kentucky (Pleasant Hill). Lee, Ann. Sexes (segregation of). Shakers. 1774-1916. *353*

—. Lindner, Anna. Painting. ca 1863-1914. *1788*

—. Louisiana (New Orleans). Oneal, Marion S. (reminiscences). Social Conditions. 1890's. *3132*

—. Lykins-Bingham, Mattie (reminiscences). Missouri (Kansas City). 1851-52. *3018*

—. Missouri (St. Louis). Mitchell, Clara (diary). Recreation. Social Conditions. 1887. *3020*

—. North Central States. Politics. Sears, Mary (journal). 1859-60. *3016*

—. Novels. Phelps, Elizabeth Stuart. 1868-1900. *1723*

—. Ohio (Cincinnati). Social Conditions. Travel. Trollope, Frances (*Domestic Manners of the Americans,* 1832). 1820's-30's. *638*

—. Pennsylvania (Berks County). Riegel, Lewis Edgar (reminiscences). Social Customs. 1876-85. *2976*

Dakota Indians. *See* Sioux Indians.

Dakota Territory. Children. Daily life. Fort Randall. Photographs. Sioux Indians. Sitting Bull Collection. Wives. 1869-83. *1489*

Dall, Caroline Healy (biography). Feminism. Massachusetts. 1822-1912. *2977*

Dall, Caroline Healy (journal). Fuller, Margaret. Greek Mythology, Conversations on. Intellectuals. Peabody, Elizabeth Palmer. Transcendentalism. 1841. *969*

Dalziel, Hazel Webb (reminiscences). Colorado (Weld County). Daily Life. Farms. 1890's. *3162*

Dame Shirley (pseud. of Louise A. K. S. Clappe). California. Courtship. Gold Rushes. Letters. Marriage. 1838-1906. *711*

—. California. Gold Rushes. Letters. 1851-1906. *716*

Dams *See also* names of dams, e.g. Hoover Dam, etc.

—. California (Yosemite; Hetch Hetchy Valley). Conservation of Natural Resources. Duryea, Robert. Stillman, Dorothy. 1914. *3016*

Dance. Arts. Duncan, Isadora. Transcendental renaissance. 1890-1920. *1754*

—. Colleges and Universities. H'Doubler, Margaret N. Physical education. Wisconsin, University of. 1910-26. *1773*

Dance halls. Cities. Music. ca 1910-29. *1798*

—. Frontier and Pioneer Life. Mining towns. Montana. Prostitution. Social Reform. ca 1870's-1910's. *1537*

—. Saloons. Wright, Nettie. Wyoming (Buffalo). 1864-65. *1078*

Dance troupe. Negroes. Theater. Whitman Sisters. 1903-43. *1781*

Dances. Cilley, Florence L. Vermont (Plymouth). 1926. *1799*

—. Jamaica Masonic Lodge. New York (Long Island). Soldiers. World War I. 1917-18. *1296*

Danville Female Academy. Civil War. Confederate Army. Missouri. Robinson, Mary (reminiscences). 1864. *795*

Darby, H. Dillard. Barrow, Clyde. Crime and Criminals. Louisiana (Ruston). Parker, Bonnie. Stone, Sophia. 1933. *1517*

Darrow, Clarence. Addams, Jane. Altgeld, Emma. Friendship. Illinois (Chicago). Intellectuals. ca 1880-1938. *1223*

Dating *See also* Courtship.

—. Behavior. Inferiority (pretensions to). Sex roles. 1950-72. *2168*

—. Colleges and Universities. Social Status. Students. 1960's. *2185*

Dating, interfaith. Attitudes. Catholic Church. Sex, premarital. Social status. 1971. *2229*

Daughters of Saint Ann. Canada. Church Schools. Social services. Sureau, Marie Esther. USA. 1848-20c. *381*

Daughters of the American Revolution. Children (care of). Federal Government. League of Women Voters. Maternal care. Organizations. Sheppard-Towner Act. 1920's. *1282*

—. Flags (State). Fluke, Mrs. George. Oklahoma. Organizations. 1911-41. *1279*

Daughters of the American Revolution museum. First ladies, exhibits. Museums. Texas (Denton). Texas Women's University. 1940-73. *78*

Daughters of the Cross. Church Schools. Louisiana (Shreveport, Fairfield Hill). St. Vincent's Academy. 1866-1971. *1576*

Daughters of the Republic of Texas. Alamo (custody dispute). De Zavala, Adina. Driscoll, Clara. Texas. 1903-13. *1193*

Davenport, Marcia. Cather, Willa. Deland, Margaret. Literature. Long, Haniel. Pennsylvania (Pittsburgh). Rinehart, Mary Roberts. Schmitt, Gladys. 18c-20c. *430*

Davis, Allen F. (review article). Addams, Jane. Social reform. 1880's-1930's. *1256*

Davis, Angela. Baldwin, James. Jews. Negroes. 1960's-71. *2300*

—. Baldwin, James (open letter). Communism. Jews. 1960's-71. *2316*

—. Bell, Hugh. Nova Scotia (Halifax, Dartmouth). Provincial Hospital for the Insane. ca 1832-60. *3326*

—. Civil War. 1860-65. *806*

—. Hospitals. Medicine (practice of). Mental Illness. Psychiatry. Social reform. 19c. *933*

Doan, May Cargill (reminiscences). Arizona Territory (Silverbell, Yuma). ca 1900-14. *3213*

—. Arizona (Yuma). Cargill, Andrew Hays. Social Conditions. 1900's. *3212*

Doane, Emily Greenhow (reminiscences). Frontier and Pioneer Life. Nebraska. Social Conditions. 19c. *732*

Doche, Marie Louise Combs. Farms (silk). Mississippi (Corinth). 1880's. *1048*

Dock, Mira Lloyd. City beautification. Civic Club of Harrisburg. Pennsylvania (Harrisburg). 1900-03. *1262*

Documents *See also* Manuscripts.

—. Editors and Editing. National Historical Publications Committee. 1975. *85*

Doda, Carol. California (San Francisco). Popular Culture. Tara. Topless dancing. 1965-66. *2746*

Dodge, Mary Abigail. Authors. Feminism. Journalism. Massachusetts (Hamilton). 1833-96. *457*

Dodge, Mary Elizabeth Mapes. Alcott, Louisa May. Fiction. Negroes. Pierson, Helen W. Stereotypes. 1860's. *1620*

Dolls, rag. Carper, Ellen. Carper, Lizzie. Mennonites. Pennsylvania (Lititz). 19c. *2999*

Dolls (wind-up). Humor. Politics. 1960's. *2754*

Domestic adjustment. Cultural differences. Family (American). India. Wives. 1960's. *2121*

Domestic arts. Keckley, Elizabeth. Lincoln, Abraham (relics). Lincoln, Mary Todd. Seamstresses. Teaching. Wilberforce University. 1865-68. *1093*

Domestic culture. Cultural History. Methodology. 1960's. *67*

Domestic education. Image. Industrialization. Morality. Motherhood. Protestantism. 1830-70. *956*

Domestic Labor. Capitalism. 1970-73. *2004*

—. Donovan, Minerva Padden. Economic Conditions. Farms. Irish Americans. New York. 1834-46. *2995*

—. Grandin, Mme. Léon. Illinois (Chicago). Sex roles. Social Conditions. 1892-93. *3040*

—. Households. *2006*

—. Housewives. Image. Periodicals. Social change. Technology. 1920-40. *1113*

Domestic life. Cookbooks. Social Customs. 19c. *214*

Domestic Policy. *See* Federal Policy.

Domestic relations. Courts. Law. Virginia. 1960's. *2353*

Domestic responsibilities. Farmers. Negroes. Plantation system. 1600-1975. *317*

Domestic roles. Beecher, Catharine E. Education. 19c. *975*

—. Massachusetts (Salem). Social Change. Wills. 1660-1770. *496*

Domestic servants. Chicago *Daily Tribune* (newspaper). Child Welfare. Divorce. Illinois. Marks, Nora (pseud. of Eleanora Stackhouse). Reporters and Reporting. Social Problems. 1888-90. *1673*

—. German Americans. Household structure. Irish Americans. Life cycles. New York (Buffalo). Whites (native born). 1855. *636*

—. Northeastern or North Atlantic States. Rice, Sally (letters). Textile workers. 1821-47. *623*

Domestic skills. Arkansas River Valley Regional Library. Family. Federal Programs. 1960's. *3122*

Domestic workers. Industrial Workers of the World. Labor Unions and Organizations. Street, Jane (letter). 1917. *1121*

Domesticity. Higher education. Sex roles. 1950's. *2817*

Donan, Peter. Armory. Broom brigades. Fund raising. Missouri (St. Louis). Organizations. 1880's. *1198*

Donelson, Andrew Jackson (family). Eaton, Margaret (Peggy) O'Neale. Jackson, Andrew. Ladies Hermitage Association. Restorations. Tennessee (Tulip Grove). 1829-20c. *3119*

Donelson, Emily. District of Columbia. Eastin, Mary. Eaton, Margaret (Peggy) O'Neale. Jackson, Andrew (letter). Politics. ca 1828-32. *746*

Donner party. California. Overland Journeys to the Pacific. Reed, Virginia Elizabeth. 1846. *691*

Donovan, Minerva Padden. Domestic labor. Economic Conditions. Farms. Irish Americans. New York. 1834-46. *2995*

Dorman, Carrie. Natural History. Painting. South or Southern States. 1920's-50's. *3047*

Dorsey, Ann Hanson McKenney. Catholic Church. Novels. Sadlier, Mary Anne Madden. 1829-65. *885*

Dorsey, Sarah Anne. Novels. South or Southern States. 1863-77. *1592*

Dorsey, Sarah Anne (letter). Literature. Thoreau, Henry David. 1871. *3007*

Doub, Peter. Education. Methodist Episcopal Church. North Carolina. 1796-1869. *982*

Dougherty, John. Cheyenne Indians. Pawnee Indians (Skidi). Religion. Rites and Ceremonies (sacrificial). 1827. *910*

Douglass, Anna Murry. District of Columbia. Fisher, Ruth Anna. Negroes. Terrell, Mary Church. 1830's-1975. *375*

Dower rights. Aged. Connecticut (Wethersfield). Economic conditions. Marriage patterns. Sex roles. Widows. 1640-1700. *489*

Dowries. Family. Land. Marriage. Massachusetts (Barnstable County). Peasants. Values. 1620's-1720's. *520*

—. Ontario (Toronto). Social Conditions. 1847-50. *3362*

Drake, James A. (family). Children. Family life. Photographs. 1880-1900. *1169*

Drake, Sylvia (diary). Bryant, Charity. Congregationalism. Daily Life. Sewing. Vermont (Weybridge). 1784-1868. *2969*

Drama *See also* Dramatists; Films; Theater.

—. American Revolution. Blockheadism. Political propaganda. Warren, Mercy Otis. 1775. *566*

—. Anderson, Maxwell. 1929-48. *1782*

—. Family structure. Jefferson, Joseph. "Rip Van Winkle" (play). 1865. ca 1900-70's. *672*

—. Feminism. Fitch, Clyde. Moody, William Vaughn. Walter Eugene. 1908-10. *1757*

—. Feminism. Social Classes. Stereotypes. 1906-07. *1756*

—. Films. Parker, Charlotte Blair. "Way Down East" (play). ca 1900-37. *1747*

—. Films. Stowe, Harriet Beecher (*Uncle Tom's Cabin*, 1852). ca 1850-1973. *465*

Dramatists. Hellman, Lillian. Manuscripts. Texas, University of (Lillian Hellman Collection). 1934-63. *90*

—. Massachusetts (Boston). Murray, Judith Sargent Stevens (*The Medium, or Happy Tea Party*). Theater. Tyler, Royall. 1795. *1038*

Draper, Elizabeth ("Bettie"). Indians (captivities). Ingles, Mary Draper. Shawnee Indians. Virginia (Draper's Meadow). 1755-61. *3058*

Dress. *See* Clothing; Costume.

Dress reform. Anti-Crinoline League. Texas (Brenham). 1893. *1187*

—. Bicycles, popularity of. Technology. 1890's. *1183*

—. Bloomer, Amelia. Godwin, William. Oakeshott, Michael. 1798-1966. *221*

—. Flappers. Sexual behavior. Social Change. 1920's. *1138*

Dress reform movement. Feminism. 1870's-1920's. *1320*

Driggs, Nevada W. (memoir). Nevada (Panaca). Polygamy. Utah. 1890-93. *1152*

Drinnon, Richard (review article). Goldman, Emma. 1961. *2929*

Driscoll, Clara. Alamo (custody dispute). Daughters of the Republic of Texas. De Zavala, Adina. Texas. 1903-13. *1193*

Droughts. Family. Geographic Mobility. Saskatchewan. 1930's. *3381*

Drug Abuse *See also* Crime and Criminals; Juvenile Delinquency.

—. Adolescence. Hippies. Matriarchal culture. Social Change. 1960's. *2272*

—. Alcoholism. Connecticut. Silver Hill Foundation. Youth. 1960's. *2283*

Drugging. Folktales. Seduction. Sexual behavior. Social control. 1970-73. *2228*

Drunken drivers. Alcoholism (surveys). Sex differences. 1973. *2681*

Druse, Roxalana. Folk songs. Murder. New York (Herkimer County). 1880's. *1518*

Du Bois, W. E. B. Feminism. Human rights. Negroes. 1910-20. *1454*

DuBois, W. E. B. *Crisis* (periodical). Negroes. Suffrage. 1910-34. *1380*

Dubuc family papers. Paper Industry. Quebec (Saguenay River, Lake St. John). 1892-1963. *3337*

Duck, Edward Walker (reminiscences). Childhood. Family life. Farms. Social Conditions. Tennessee (Cedar Grove). 1890-1910. *1153*

Dughton, Diana. New York City. Political activism. Weathermen. 1972. *2374*

Duke University. Ideology. Sexes. 1960's-70. *2318*

Duncan, Isadora. Arts. Dance. Transcendental renaissance. 1890-1920. *1754*

—. Bankhead, Tallulah. Cornell, Katharine. Cushman, Charlotte Saunders. Farrar, Geraldine. Hallam, Nancy. Hayes, Helen. Lind, Jenny. National Portrait Gallery. Patti, Adelina. Portraits. Theater. 1971. *418*

Duncan, Mrs. Henry. Civil War. Letters. Middleton, Harriet. Middleton, Susan. Social Conditions. South or Southern States. 1863-65. *800*

Duniway, Abigail Scott. Catt, Carrie Chapman. Idaho. National American Woman Suffrage Association. Suffrage. Woman's Christian Temperance Union. 1870-96. *1350*

—. Constitutions, State. Oregon. Suffrage. 1860's-1912. *1331*

—. Pacific Northwest. Suffrage. 1870's-1915. *1365*

—. Prohibition movement. Suffrage. 1870's-1914. *1355*

Dunlap, Susan. Daily Life. Nova Scotia (Stewiacke). Social Conditions. 1866-1912. *3324*

Dunn, Carrie Nesbitt (reminiscences). Homesteading and Homesteaders. Wyoming (Jackson Hole). 1890's. *3176*

Dunn, Mrs. B. W. C. Governor's Residence (historical collection). Tennessee (Nashville). 1971. *2760*

Dunne, Edward F. Addams, Jane. Educational Reform. Illinois (Chicago). Progressivism. Young, Ella Flagg. 1905-10. *1384*

DuPont, Josephine. Costume. Letters. Manigault, Margaret Izard. New York City. South Carolina (Charleston). 1795-1824. *684*

Durant, Ariel. Durant, William. Historians. 1910's-70's. *99*

Durant, William. Durant, Ariel. Historians. 1910's-70's. *99*

Duryea, Etta. Cameron, Lucille. Johnson, Jack. Nebraska (Omaha). Press. Race Relations. Values. 1908-15. *1513*

Duryea, Robert. California (Yosemite; Hetch Hetchy Valley). Conservation of Natural Resources. Dams. Stillman, Dorothy. 1914. *1225*

Dustin, Hannah. Frontier. Indians (captivities). Iroquois Indians. Massachusetts (Haverhill). Neff, Mary. 1697. *597*

—. Indians (captivities). Massachusetts (Haverhill). Murder. 1697. *601*

—. Indians (captivities). Massachusetts (Haverhill). Murder. Neff, Mary. New Hampshire (Penacook Island). 1697. *596*

—. Indians (captivities). Massachusetts (Haverhill). 1697. *603*

Dutch. Arbitration, mercantile. Law. New Netherland. 1662. *545*

—. Family. Germans. Government (concepts of). 17c-18c. *508*

—. Family. Marriage. New York (Albany). Politics. 1683-1809. *507*

—. Irving, Washington. Katrina Van Tassel (fictional character). New York (Kinderhook). Pioneers. Van Alen House. 17c-18c. *612*

Dutch traditions. Ferris, Mary L. D. Literature. 1855-1932. *1665*

Dwyer, Ada. Actors and Actresses. Lowell, Amy. Poetry. ca 1880-1925. *1774*

Dyer, Mary. Friends, Society of. Massachusetts (Boston). Persecution. Puritans. Religious Liberty. 1635-57. *580*

—. Hutchinson, Anne. Massachusetts Bay Colony. Politics. Sex roles. Theology. Trials. 1636-43. *540*

—. Hutchinson, Anne. Massachusetts (Boston). Persecution. Puritans. Religious Liberty. 1635-51. *579*

# E

Earhart, Amelia. Airplanes. 1937. *1080*

Earth. *See* Geography.

East Greenwich Neighborhood Cottage. Negroes. Rhode Island (Scolloptown). Settlement house movement. 1902-14. *1406*

East Indians. *See* Asians.

—. Ballou, Adin Augustus. Hopedale Community. Massachusetts (Milford). Utopias. 1824-56. *861*

—. Bashford, James W. China. Methodist Episcopal Church. Missions and Missionaries. Social gospel. 1889-1919. *1316*

—. Beard, Mary R. (*Woman as Force in History,* 1946). Historiography. Women's history. 1946-60's. *8*

—. Beard, Mary R. (*Woman as Force in History,* 1946). Historiography. Women's history. 1946-73. *10*

—. Behavior. Social deviance. Sociology. Stereotypes. 1970's. *63*

—. Bennett, Anne M. Bennett, John C. Theology. 1974. *2459*

—. Bibliographies. Satire. 1700-1800. *72*

—. Birth control. Eugenics movement. Politics. 1915-74. *202*

—. Black liberation. Negroes. 1960's-70's. *2541*

—. Black Nationalism. Negroes. Trans-Africanism, concept of. 1970's. *2524*

—. Black Panther Party. Cleaver, Kathleen (interview). Negroes. 19c-20c. 1966-71. *2590*

—. Bloomer, Amelia. Lecture tours. Ohio (Mt. Vernon). 1853-54. *841*

—. Books (review article). Sociology. 1970-71. *12*

—. Bourassa, Henry. Canada. Divorce. Suffrage. 1913-25. *3296*

—. Bradwell, Myra. Illinois (Chicago). Law reform. 1855-92. *1241*

—. British North America Act of 1929. Canada. Legal status. Suffrage. 1870's-1940's. *3292*

—. Bryn Mawr College. Palmer, Alice Freeman. Sex roles. Thomas, M. Carey. Wellesley College. 1875-1918. *1585*

—. Bull, Mary Sherwood. New York (Seneca Falls). Social Reform. 1830's-80's. *2978*

—. California (Los Angeles). Friday Morning Club. Severance, Caroline M. 1891-1960's. *209*

—. Canada. Ideology. Middle Classes. Political Leadership. USA. 1960-75. *270*

—. Canada. McClung, Nellie (*In Times Like These,* 1915). 1902-15. *3295*

—. Canadian Library Association Committee on the Status of Women. Cheda, Sherrill (interview). Labor Unions and Organizations. Librarians. 1973-74. *3267*

—. Capitalism. Employment. Wages. 1950's-60's. *1829*

—. Capitalism. Marxism. 1100-1974. *284*

—. Capitalism. Racism. Revolution. 1973. *2448*

—. Carroll, Anna Ella (letters). Civil War (strategy). Fillmore, Millard. Politics. 1852-73. *817*

—. Catholic Church. Fédération Nationale Saint-Jean-Baptiste. Gérin-Lajoie, Marie. Quebec. 1907-33. *3348*

—. Catt, Carrie Chapman. Gilman, Charlotte Perkins. Louisiana (New Orleans). Shaw, Anna Howard. Social Conditions. 1890's-1903. *1318*

—. Centennial Celebrations. Housework, professionalization of. Pennsylvania (Philadelphia). Technology. Woman's Building. 1830-76. *168*

—. Channing, William Henry. Letters. Massachusetts (Worcester). Wells, Charlotte Fowler. Woman's Rights Convention (2nd national). 1851. *844*

—. Childrearing. Reproduction. Sexuality. Social Conditions. 1960's. *2059*

—. Children. Day Nurseries. Social reform. 1854-1973. *234*

—. Children. Industrial Revolution. Marriage. 19c-20c. *267*

—. Chopin, Kate. Clanton, Gertrude T. Clay, Laura. Felton, Rebecca L. Glasgow, Ellen. Gordon, Kate M. Kearney, Belle. South. 1830-1945. *1310*

—. Christianity. Church history. 1975. *2469*

—. Christianity. Davis, Elizabeth Gould (review article). Historiography. Matriarchy. Prehistory-1970. *21*

—. Civic participation. Political education. 1966-71. *2367*

—. Civil Rights. 1940-75. *2389*

—. Civil Rights Movement. Employment. Sex roles. 1950's-75. *2400*

—. Civil rights movement. Sex Discrimination. South. 1960's. *2427*

—. Civil War. Great Northwestern Fair. Illinois (Chicago). Livermore, Mary. Sanitary Commission. 1861-69. *813*

—. Class consciousness. International Federation of Working Women. Organizations. Suffrage. Women's Trade Union League. 1890-1925. *1280*

—. Clergy. Divorce. Public Opinion. Sociologists. 1906-20's. *1165*

—. Coeducation. Dewey, John (letters). Suffrage. 1915-31. *1308*

—. Colleges and Universities. Organizations. Professions. 1960's-70. *2429*

—. Colleges and Universities. Scholarship. 1837-1974. *293*

—. Colleges and Universities. Sex Discrimination. Women's studies. 1960's. *2405*

—. Colleges and Universities. Sex roles. Stereotypes. 1960's. *2434*

—. Colleges and Universities (women's). 1972. *2388*

—. Commission on the Status and Role of Women in the United Methodist Church. Methodism. Missions and Missionaries. Organizations. 1869-1974. *368*

—. Communism. Flynn, Elizabeth Gurley. ca 1890-1920. *1203*

—. Consciousness-raising groups. Psychology. 1960's-70's. *2394*

—. Crime and Criminals. Social Change. 1932-72. *2678*

—. Curricula. Educational Reform. Women's Studies. 1960's-73. *43*

—. Curricula. Higher Education. Historians. Teaching. Women's Studies. 1940-73. *14*

—. Dall, Caroline Healy (biography). Massachusetts. 1822-1912. *2977*

—. Decter, Midge. Steinem, Gloria. Vilar, Esther. 1973. *2415*

—. Democratic Party. Political Conventions. Sex Discrimination. 1972. *2324*

—. *Dial* (periodical). Fuller, Margaret. Journalism. New York *Tribune* (newspaper). 1810-50. *833*

—. Drama. Fitch, Clyde. Moody, William Vaughn. Walter Eugene. 1908-10. *1757*

—. Drama. Social Classes. Stereotypes. 1906-07. *1756*

—. Dress reform movement. 1870's-1920's. *1320*

—. Du Bois, W. E. B. Human rights. Negroes. 1910-20. *1454*

—. Economic Conditions. Negroes. Politics. 19c-20c. *330*

—. Economic Conditions. Sex Discrimination. 1969-70. *1822*

—. Education. Employment. Gage, Frances Dana. *Ohio Cultivator* (newspaper). Suffrage. Tracy-Cutler, Hannah Maria. 1845-55. *836*

—. Education. Employment. Sex Discrimination. 1960-70. *2430*

—. Education. Marriage. Social Status. Values. 1925-65. *100*

—. Elections (presidential). National Women's Political Caucus. Political parties. Socialist Workers Party. 1972. *2441*

—. Emerson, Ralph Waldo. Fuller, Margaret. Fuller, Timothy. Politics. Sex roles. 1826-50. *834*

—. Employment. Historiography. Libraries (public). Working Conditions. 1850-1975. *166*

—. Employment. Organizations. Sex roles. Social Conditions. 1960's. *2417*

—. Employment. Sex Discrimination. 1960's. *2435*

—. Employment. Wages. 1972. *1881*

—. Employment opportunities. Family responsibilities. 1975. *2385*

—. Employment (professional). Friedan, Betty. Housewives. 1960's. *2402*

—. Equal Rights Amendment. National Organization for Women. 1923-74. *2447*

—. Esther Greenwood (fictional character). Image. Novels. Plath, Sylvia. Sex roles. Symbolism in Literature. 1960's-70's. *2870*

—. Ethics. Theology. 1973. *2464*

—. Family. 1973. *2077*

—. Family, nuclear (abolition of). Industrial Revolution. Sex roles. 19c-1960's. *2063*

—. Family structure. Sex roles. 1969. *2172*

—. Folklore, applied. Language. Popular Culture. 1970-75. *2416*

—. Fuller, Margaret. Jefferson, Thomas (influence). Journalism. Politics. Social criticism. 1840-50. *832*

—. Functionalism. Marxism. Production and reproduction (dialectics of). Social classes. 1976. *2036*

—. Georgia. Peace Movements. Rankin, Jeannette. 1924-73. *2312*

—. *Godey's Lady's Book* (periodical). Hale, Sarah Josepha. Journalism. Social Reform. 1788-1878. *1021*

—. Hardwick, Elizabeth. Jong, Erica. Literature. Milford, Nancy. Showalter, Elaine. 1975. *2859*

—. Hawthorne, Nathaniel *The Scarlet Letter.* Hutchinson, Anne. Puritans. Sex Discrimination. Theology. Winthrop, John. 1634-38. 1850. *534*

—. Higher education. Letters. Lowry, Morrow B. Pennsylvania. 1868. *1312*

—. Higher Education Act of 1972. Law. 1970. *2822*

—. Historiography. Methodology. Sexism. Women's history. 1970's. *51*

—. Historiography. Organizations. Urbanization. 19c-1973. *30*

—. Holiness Movement. Palmer, Phoebe. Wesley, Susanna. 1732-1973. *327*

—. Holley, Marietta (writings). Humor. Literature. 1870-1926. *1623*

—. Humanism. Ideology. 1960's. *2401*

—. Hydropathy. Medicine. 1843-1900. *1323*

—. Image. Novels. Social Conditions. 1752-1911. *468*

—. Intellectuals. Social Change. Values. Victorianism. 1920's. *1136*

—. International Ladies' Garment Workers' Union. International Women's Year. Labor Unions and Organizations. Quebec (Montreal). 1975. *3274*

—. Interpersonal Relations. Political movements. 1960's-73. *2383*

—. Judaism. BC-1970's. *339*

—. Judaism. 1970's. *2509*

—. Kansas. Nichols, Clarina I. H. (papers). Social Reform. 1839-56. *835*

—. Labor Unions and Organizations. New York City. Social reform. Women's Trade Union League. 1903-14. *1278*

—. Lawrence, D. H. Literary Criticism. Millett, Kate. 20c. *2864*

—. Librarians. Mann, Margaret. Sharp, Katharine Lucinda. ca 1900. *1073*

—. Literary criticism. Teaching. 1968-73. *2878*

—. Literature. Negroes. Stowe, Harriet Beecher. Truth, Sojourner. 1850's-90's. *280*

—. Marxism. 1848-1970's. *295*

—. Medicine, socialized. Reform movements. 1960's-70's. *2418*

—. Methodology. Social Conditions. Women's history. 1775-1973. *57*

—. Methodology. Women's history. 1970's. *64*

—. Morality. Mother-child relationship. Social Organization. 1972. *287*

—. Mormons. 1971. *2431*

—. Negroes. 1973. *2551*

—. Negroes. Newspapers. Police. Suffrage. 19c-20c. *283*

—. Northeastern or North Atlantic States. Organizations (benevolent societies). Social Reform. 1800-30's. *648*

—. Novels. Plath, Sylvia. Poetry. Sex roles. 1932-63. *2873*

—. Organizations. Protestant Churches. Social Reform. South. Young Women's Christian Association. 1920's. *1307*

—. Paine, Thomas. Sex roles. Social Theory. Wollstonecraft, Mary. 18c. *538*

—. Politics. Slavery. Socialism. Wright, Frances. 1795-1852. *838*

—. Press. Social Reform. Woodhull, Victoria. 1873. *1311*

—. Prison reform. Sex roles. 1870-1900. *1519*

—. Protestantism. ca 16c-1973. *367*

—. Racism. Revolutionary Movements. Stereotypes. 1970. *2395*

—. Racism. Sexism. 1960-71. *2396*

—. Radicals and Radicalism. Settlement houses. Suffrage. Women's Trade Union League. ca 1890's-1920's. *1314*

—. Rhetoric. 1960's-73. *2391*

—. Scholarship. *Women's Studies* (periodical). 1972. *31*

—. Sex Discrimination. Social Work. Wages. 1960's-70's. *1978*

—. Sex roles. Ward, Lester Frank. ca 1870's-1900. *1321*

—. Sex roles. Women's history. 1960's-70. *28*

—. Social Change. 1970-75. *2445*

—. Social reform. Spiritualism. Temperance Movements. 1847-1900. *269*

—. Sociology. 1970's. *9*

—. Sociology. 1973. *42*

—. South. Thomas, Ella Gertrude Clanton. 1848-89. *3045*

—. Speeches, Addresses, etc.. Wright, Frances. 1828-30. *837*
—. Students. Teaching. Women's history. 1974. *33*
—. Working Class. 1940's-73. *1882*
Feminism, cultural. Education. Japan. Tsuda, Ume. USA. 1900-30. *1322*
Feminism, domestic. Birth Control. Family. Social Status. ca 1870's-1900. *1168*
Feminism (review article). Antislavery sentiments. Grimké, Angelina. Josephson, Hannah. Lumpkin, Katharine Du Pre. Political Reform. Psychohistory. Rankin, Jeannette. 19c-20c. 1974. *262*
—. Daily Life. Divorce. Family. Historiography. 1967-70. *15*
—. Ideology. Politics. Suffrage. 1830-1920. 1969-70. *216*
Feminism, social. Labor. Legislation. Organizations. Progressivism. 1919-33. *1128*
Feminist Alliance. Child care. Collective ventures. Housing. New York (Greenwich Village, Washington Square). Rodman, Henrietta. 1914-17. *1324*
Feminist Counseling Collective. District of Columbia. Psychotherapy. 1972-75. *2715*
Feminist criticism. Methodology. Women's Studies. 1972-74. *61*
Feminist culture. Colleges and Universities. Patriarchy. Violence. Women's Studies. 1974. *34*
Feminist groups. Birth control. Motherhood. Sex roles. 1870's-80's. *1181*
Feminist issues. Aged. Attitudes. Politics. Sexes. 1968-74. *2386*
Feminist movement. 1960's-73. *2442*
—. Abolition Movement. Civil War. Negroes. Social Reform. Tubman, Harriet. Underground railroad. 1820-1913. *379*
—. Abortion. 1971. *2695*
—. Abortion. Child care. Family. Political activism. Sexism. 1970's. *2449*
—. Androgyny. Fuller, Margaret. Sexual categories. 1840-1974. *290*
—. Androgyny. Image. Novels. 19c-20c. 1972. *393*
—. Androgyny. *Women's Studies* (periodical). 1973-74. *39*
—. Anthony, Susan B. (personal library). Books. Library of Congress. Manuscripts. ca 1840's-1903. *77*
—. Attitudes. Brownmiller, Susan (review article). Rape. 1976. *2677*
—. Attitudes. Consciousness-raising, concept of. Life-styles, alternative. Self concepts. 1973. *2437*
—. Attitudes. Control, locus of. Ideology. Protestant ethic. 1972. *2438*
—. Attitudes. Social Surveys. 1972-75. *2446*
—. Beauvoir, Simone de (interview). 1970's. *2407*
—. Bibliographies. 1848-1975. *75*
—. Bibliographies. 1960's. *2410*
—. Black liberation movement. Discrimination. Negroes. Social Classes. 1970. *2413*
—. California (Los Angeles). Newspapers. Social control. 1968-70. *2425*
—. California (Los Angeles County). Newspapers. 1973. *2426*
—. Cambodia, invasion of. Smith College. Student strikes. Vassar College. 1970. *2423*
—. Canada. Communist Party. 1921-71. *3290*
—. Canada. Day Nurseries. Employment opportunities. Legal status. Social Classes. 1975. *3291*
—. Canada. Social Reform. 1955-75. *3293*
—. Careers. Family. Psychological depression. Psychology. 1970. *2252*
—. Childrearing. Occupational equality. Sex roles. 1970's. *2414*
—. Children. Family. Patriarchy. Politics. Social organization. Prehistory-1971. *109*
—. Children. Sex roles. 1973. *2163*
—. Civil Rights. Inferiority, doctrine of. Matriarchy, myth of. Negroes. 1960's-70's. *2550*
—. District of Columbia. Gillett, Emma M. Higher Education. Law schools. Mussey, Ellen Spencer. Temperance Movements. Washington College of Law. 1869-1949. *1580*
—. Economic Conditions. Negroes. Social Conditions. Whites. 1969. *2384*
—. Economic exploitation. Sex discrimination. 1940's-60's. *2412*
—. Emerson, Ralph Waldo. Individualism. ca 1836-65. *842*
—. Employment. Family. Socialism. 1960-71. *2424*

—. Employment. Political change. Suffrage. 19c-1970's. *279*
—. Equality. Social policies. 1950-75. *2398*
—. Family. Friendship. Kumin, Maxine. Poetry. Sexton, Anne. Showalter, Elaine. Smith, Carol. 1950-74. *2882*
—. Filene, Peter Gabriel (review article). Middle classes. Sex roles. 1890's-1970's. 1974. *215*
—. Freudian analysis. Literature. 1946-70's. *2409*
—. Image. Social Change. 1972-73. *2406*
—. Man-hating. Politics. Rhetorical strategy. 1972. *2408*
— National Organization for Women. Organizations. Politics. Racism. Suffrage. 20c. *294*
—. Occupational inequality. Social problems. Stereotypes. 1970. *2439*
—. Organizations (structures). Political strategy. Reform. Social Change. 1961-72. *2404*
—. Political Theory. Radicals and Radicalism. 1960-72. *2444*
—. Sex Discrimination. 1960's. *2421*
—. Sex Discrimination. 1950-74. *2436*
—. Social Change. 1960's-70's. *2397*
—. Social Organization. 1972. *2419*
Feminist movement (origins). Social Organizations. 1960-71. *2403*
Feminist movement (review essay). Historiography. Politics. Sexual revolution. Social Conditions. 1920's. *1313*
Feminists. Antifeminism. Hoffer, Eric. Ideology. Personality. 1951-73. *2299*
—. Behavior. Clothing. Symbolism. 1973. *2392*
—. Constitutional amendment (19th). Pennsylvania. Suffrage. 1837-1920. *1319*
—. Death date (disputed). Indians. Sacagawea (Shoshoni). 1804-12. ca 1890-1910. *904*
—. Family. Political Attitudes. Religion. Social Classes. ca 1970-73. *2440*
—. Politics. Radicals and Radicalism. 1955-73. *2428*
—. Prostitution. Rehabilitation (rejection of). ca 1900-73. *2176*
Fenollosa, Mary McNeil. Alabama. Literature. ca 1870's-1915. *1627*
Ferber, Edna. Novels. 20c. *427*
Ferguson, Catherine. Negroes. New York City. Religious Education (Sunday school). Slavery. 1779-1854. *894*
Ferguson, Lucia Loomis. *Cherokee Republican* (newspaper). Journalism. Oklahoma. 1886-1962. *3112*
Fergusson, Edna Mary. Southwest. 1888-1964. *3177*
Fernandez, Bernardo. California (San Pablo Bay). Family. Rancho El Pinole. 1823-1902. *3209*
Ferris, Mary L. D. Dutch traditions. Literature. 1855-1932. *1665*
Fertility. Abortion. Population control. 1950-80. *2689*
—. Age. Birth Rate. Sexual intercourse. 1973. *2135*
—. Age. Birth Rate (decline). 1940-68. *2139*
—. Age structure. Birth Rate. Population trends. Rural-Urban Studies. 20c. *126*
—. Age structure. Economic Conditions. Puerto Ricans. Puerto Rico. Social Status. USA. 1970. *2629*
—. Alienation profiles. Catholics. Mothers. 1970. *2140*
—. Assimilation. Demography. Marriage. Puerto Ricans. 1960. *2632*
—. Assimilation. Minority group status. Negroes. Social Status. 1970. *2573*
—. Attitudes. Birth Rate. Population growth. 1960's-. *2132*
—. Attitudes. Economic Conditions. Social Classes. 1830-1960's. *249*
—. Birth Control. Culture. Sexual intercourse. 1960's-70's. *2060*
—. Birth Control. Family planning. Models. 1960's. *2144*
—. Birth rate. Canada. Ethnic Groups. Immigrants. Marriage. 1871. *3288*
—. Birth Rate. Childrearing. Family life cycles. Marriage. 18c-20c. *254*
—. Birth Rate. Mortality. Negroes. Whites. 1850-1960's. *326*
—. Canada. Marriage. Rural-Urban Studies. USA. 1940-60's. *219*
—. Canada (James Bay area). Cree Indians. Modernization. Mothers. 1968. *3306*
—. Catholic Church. Children. Colleges and Universities. Family. 1960's. *2502*
—. Catholic Church. Colleges and Universities. Family size. 1960's. *2504*

—. Catholic Church. Ethnic Groups. Rural Settlements. Wisconsin. 1940-60. *2141*
—. Catholic Church. Family size. 1964. *2109*
—. Census statistics. Childbirth. Migration. Puerto Ricans. 1965-70. *2634*
—. Child mortality. Economic Conditions. 1800-1965. *208*
—. Childspacing patterns. Employment. Mormons and non-Mormons. Utah. 1940-60's. *2076*
—. Cities. Ohio (Toledo). Psychology. Religion. Social Conditions. 1962. *2133*
—. Connecticut (Ipswich). Family. Mortality rates. Population growth. 1633-1790. *513*
—. Day Nurseries. Employment. Family. Wages. 1971-72. *1927*
—. Demography. Economic Conditions. Migration, Internal. Social Conditions. 20c. *127*
—. Demography. Slavery (review article). ca 1800-61. *952*
—. Economic Conditions. Farm settlement. Population trends. 1700-20c. *259*
—. Economic Conditions. Marriage. Rhode Island (Warren). Sex ratios. Social Conditions. ca 1840-60. *670*
—. Education. Engineering graduates. Marriage. Occupational mobility. 1960's. *2142*
—. Education. Family size. Values. 1943-60. *2128*
—. Education. Religion. 1960's. *2471*
—. Ethnicity. Marriage. Massachusetts (Boston; South, South End). Occupations. 1880. *1452*
—. Family size. Friends, Society of. 18c. *2149*
—. Family structure. Frontier. Indiana. Population growth. Rural-Urban Studies. 1820. *669*
—. Family structure. Rural-Urban Studies. 1960. *2127*
—. Growth of American Families study. Negroes. Rural-Urban Studies. South. Survey of Economic Opportunity. Whites. 1960. 1967. *2146*
—. Immigration. Walker, Francis A. (thesis). Whites (native born). 1800-60. *673*
—. Income. Kentucky. Rural-Urban Studies. Social Classes. 1940-60. *2136*
—. Italian Americans. 1940-60. *2635*
—. Louisiana. Northwestern State College (graduates of). 1920-50. *1174*
—. Marital status. Migration, Internal. Rural-Urban Studies. 1967. *2145*
—. Michigan (Detroit). Public Opinion. 1960's. *2130*
—. Migration, Internal. Mormon families. Social Conditions. ca 1960-74. *2489*
—. Migration, Internal. Whites. 1955-60. *2138*
—. Minorities. Social Status. 1969. *2515*
—. Modernization (impact of). Papago Indians. Rural-Urban Studies. 1960's-70's. *2612*
—. Negroes. 1830-50. *903*
—. Ohio. Population pressure. Sex ratios. Whites. 1810-60. *666*
—. Population crisis. 1970's. *2134*
—. Rural-Urban Studies. 1965. *2147*
Fertility decline. Anthropology. Appalachia, southern. Community studies. Demography. Methodology. 1973. *53*
—. Canada. Demography. Family. 1961-71. *3285*
Fertility differences. Birth Control. Religion. Rhode Island. 1968-69. *2129*
Fertility rates. Age. Birth Control. Demography. Economic Conditions. 1945-65. *2148*
—. Age. Birth rate. Canada. Marriage. 1941-71. *3279*
—. Childbirth. Illegitimacy. Population growth. 1940-73. *2131*
—. Mexican Americans. 1950-70. *2617*
Fertility regulation. Birth control information. Family Planning. Social workers. 1960's. *2038*
Fertility studies. Birth Control. Demography. Economic Planning. Family planning programs. 1959-65. *2094*
Few, Frances (diary). District of Columbia. Gallatin, Hannah Nicholson. Madison, Dolley Payne. Presidents. 1808-09. *748*
Fiction *See also* Novels.
—. Aggressive acts (depiction). Periodicals (popular). Sex. Social Classes. 1925-65. *395*
—. Alcott, Louisa May. Dodge, Mary Elizabeth Mapes. Negroes. Pierson, Helen W. Stereotypes. 1860's. *1620*
—. Aldrich, Bess Streeter. Nebraska. Rural Settlements. 1881-1954. *1685*
—. American dream (theme). Porter, Katherine Anne. South. 1930's-60's. *447*

# G

Georgia (Augusta). Alabama (Mobile). Civil War. District of Columbia. Europe. LeVert, Octavia Walton. Reconstruction. Social career. ca 1830-80. *3056*

Georgia (Bethesda). Hastings, Selina (Countess of Huntingdon). Humanitarianism. Social Reform. 1770-1807. *3057*

Georgia (Cartersville). Baptists. Moon, Lottie. Secondary Education. 1870-1903. *1419*

Georgia Female College. Higher Education. Wesleyan Female College. 1835-40. *981*

Georgia (Macon). Bernd, Florence. Teaching. ca 1890's-1940's. *1092*

—. Higher Education. Letters. Wesleyan Female College. 1861. *976*

—. Higher Education. Wesleyan College. 1836-60's. *475*

Georgia (Milledgeville). Civil War. Food Supply. Poverty. South or Southern States. Widows. 1865. *796*

Georgia (northwest). Civil War. McClatchey, Minerva Leah Rowles (diary). Social Conditions. 1864-65. *777*

Georgia (Okefenokee Swamp Rim). Folklore. Men. Social Customs. Talking Trash (idiom). 1966-72. *2167*

Georgia (Savannah). Actors and Actresses. Bernhardt, Sarah. Theater. 1892. 1906. *1769*

Georgia (Tugalo). Attitudes. Imperialism. Jarrett, Elizabeth Lucas. Jarrett, George D. Letters. Philippines. 1901-03. *3086*

Georgian Clinic. Alcoholism (treatment). Family. Georgia (Atlanta). 1956-60's. *1527*

Gerard, Anne. Genealogy. Gerard, Jane. Gerard, Judith. Gerard, Thomas (daughters). Marriage. Maryland (St. Mary's County). 1650-76. *519*

Gerard, Jane. Genealogy. Gerard, Anne. Gerard, Judith. Gerard, Thomas (daughters). Marriage. Maryland (St. Mary's County). 1650-76. *519*

Gerard, Judith. Genealogy. Gerard, Anne. Gerard, Jane. Gerard, Thomas (daughters). Marriage. Maryland (St. Mary's County). 1650-76. *519*

Gerard, Thomas (daughters). Genealogy. Gerard, Anne. Gerard, Jane. Gerard, Judith. Marriage. Maryland (St. Mary's County). 1650-76. *519*

Geriatric conditions. Catholic Church. Employment. Institutions. Nuns. 1970. *2495*

Geriatrics. *See* Death and Dying; Aged.

Gérin-Lajoie, Marie. Catholic Church. Fédération Nationale Saint-Jean-Baptiste. Feminism. Quebec. 1907-33. *3348*

German Americans. Christmas. Cookie making. Pennsylvania. Social Customs. ca 18c-20c. *352*

—. Domestic servants. Household structure. Irish Americans. Life cycles. New York (Buffalo). Whites (native born). 1855. *636*

—. Family. Jews. Social Organizations. ca 1870-1920's. *1428*

—. Farms. Frontier and Pioneer Life. Immigrants. Lutheran Church. Texas. Wiederaenders family. 1850's. *736*

—. Immigrants. Missouri. Religion. Steinmeyer, Juliana (writings). 1840's-60's. *3022*

German philosophers (influence of). Language. Massachusetts (Boston). Peabody, Elizabeth Palmer. Philosophy. ca 1830's-40's. *971*

German Russians. Colorado (South Platte Valley). Daily Life. Farmers. Frontier and Pioneer Life. Immigration. Social Conditions. 1890-ca 1907. *2514*

Germans. Dutch. Family. Government (concepts of). 17c-18c. *508*

—. Fritchie, Barbara. Genealogy. Hauer family. Immigration. Maryland (Frederick). 1733-1834. *3066*

—. Genealogy. Lutheran Church. Winchenbach, Sibylla Charlotta. ca 1700-13. *2983*

—. Immigration. Jews. Organizations. Russians. 1880-1924. *1447*

Gibson, Charles Dana. American Girl (idealization of). Image. ca 1890's-1910. *1547*

—. Gibson Girls. Images. Pin-ups. 1890's-1900's. *1552*

Gibson Girls. Gibson, Charles Dana. Images. Pin-ups. 1890's-1900's. *1552*

Gilbert, Lydia. Behavior. Connecticut (Windsor). Religion. Witchcraft. 1654. *529*

Gillett, Emma M. District of Columbia. Feminist movement. Higher Education. Law schools. Mussey, Ellen Spencer. Temperance Movements. Washington College of Law. 1869-1949. *1580*

Gilman, Charlotte Perkins. Anthony, Lucy. Anthony, Susan B. Feminism. National American Woman Suffrage Association. Sanger, Margaret. Shaw, Anna Howard. Suffrage. 1847-1919. *1317*

—. Catt, Carrie Chapman. Feminism. Louisiana (New Orleans). Shaw, Anna Howard. Social Conditions. 1890's-1903. *1318*

Girl Guides (founding of). Canada. Jarvis sisters. 1900-25. *3281*

Girl Scouts of America. California. Finnish Relief Fund. Hoover, Lou Henry. Stanford University, Hoover War Library. 1933-44. *1253*

—. Sex role orientation. Voluntary Associations. ca 1965-75. *2294*

Girls' Training School. Hall, Emma. Michigan (Adrian). Prison reform. 1881-84. *1506*

Gish, Lillian (papers). Library of Congress, Manuscript Division. Manuscripts. Meyer, Agnes E. (papers). 1974. *92*

Glacier National Park. Johnson, Dorothy M. (reminiscences). Montana. National Parks and Reserves. Rinehart, Mary Roberts. 1916-1970's. *3171*

Gladdy, Mary. Benton, Harriet. Carpenter, Mary. Georgia. Hawkins, Ella. Kimbrough, Frances. Negroes. Slavery. Young, Dink Walton ("Mammy Dink"). 1830's-60. *945*

Glasgow, Ellen. Cabell, James Branch. Letters. Literature. Virginia (Richmond). ca 1900-40's. *1681*

—. Chopin, Kate. Clanton, Gertrude T. Clay, Laura. Felton, Rebecca L. Feminism. Gordon, Kate M. Kearney, Belle. South. 1830-1945. *1310*

—. Chopin, Kate (*The Awakening*, 1899). Fiction. South or Southern States. 1890's-1920. *1745*

—. Fiction. Letters. 1925-37. *1626*

—. Fiction. Reconstruction. South. 1895-1905. *1643*

—. Fictional characters. 1900-29. *1656*

—. History (literary use of). Novels. Symbolism in Literature. 1950's. *2876*

Glasgow, Ellen (*The Descendant*). Alcott, Louisa May (*Jo's Boys*). Barr, Amelia Edith Huddleston (*Between Two Loves*). Chopin, Kate (*The Awakening*). Harrison, Constance Cary (*A Bachelor Maid*). Image. Jewitt, Sarah Orne (*A Country Doctor*). Novels. Sex roles. Social Change. 1880-1900. *1639*

Glasgow, Sarah Lane. Civil War. Lane, Anne Ewing. Letters. Missouri (St. Louis). 1861-63. *780*

Glasse, Hannah. Cookbooks. Food Consumption. New England. 1758. *486*

Goddard, Sarah Updike. Journalism. *Providence Gazette and Country Journal* (newspaper). Rhode Island. 1762-70. *605*

*Godey's Lady's Book* (periodical). Art. Hale, Sarah Josepha. Sex roles. Womanhood (image of). 1830-60. *960*

—. Education. Hale, Sarah Josepha. *Ladies' Magazine* (periodical). Motherhood. 1830's-40's. *988*

—. Feminism. Hale, Sarah Josepha. Journalism. Social Reform. 1788-1878. *1021*

—. Literature. New York. Social criticism. Whitcher, Frances Berry (*Widow Bedott Papers*). 1847-55. *1017*

Godwin, William. Bloomer, Amelia. Dress reform. Oakeshott, Michael. 1798-1966. *221*

Gold, Harriet. Boudinot, Elias. Cherokee Indians. Connecticut (Cornwall). Indian-White Relations. Marriage. 1824-39. *922*

Gold Rushes. California. Courtship. Dame Shirley (pseud. of Louise A. K. S. Clappe). Letters. Marriage. 1838-1906. *711*

—. California. Dame Shirley (pseud. of Louise A. K. S. Clappe). Letters. 1851-1906. *716*

—. Edgerton, Mary Wright (letters). Frontier and Pioneer Life. Montana (Bannack). 1863-65. *727*

Goldman, Emma. Drinnon, Richard (review article). 1961. *2929*

Goldsborough, Effie. Civil War. Confederate States of America. Espionage. 1860-65. *788*

Goldstücker, Eduard (reminiscences). Youth. 1930's. 1960's. *103*

Gomez, Dolorez Amelia. Folklore. Pennsylvania (Philadelphia). Witchcraft. 1974. *2033*

Goodale, Ellen. Alaska. Paintings. 1943-75. *2889*

Goodwin, Theresa (reminiscences). Saskatchewan (Chaplin, Duval). Teaching. 1912-13. *3385*

Goranson, Greta K. (personal account). Genealogy. Immigration. Sweden. USA. 1832-1973. *340*

Gordon, Caroline. Fiction. Heroines. Sex roles. South or Southern States. 1918-60's. *420*

Gordon, Jean. Child Labor Law. Louisiana (New Orleans). Theatrical Syndicate. 1908-12. *1230*

Gordon, Jo. Alaska. Painting. 1956-75. *2908*

Gordon, Kate M. Chopin, Kate. Clanton, Gertrude T. Clay, Laura. Felton, Rebecca L. Feminism. Glasgow, Ellen. Kearney, Belle. South. 1830-1945. *1310*

—. Racism. South or Southern States. States' rights. Suffrage. 1913-20. *1339*

Gordon, Linda. Medical practice (review essay). Rosenberg, Charles E. Sex Discrimination. Smith-Rosenberg, Carroll. Wood, Ann D. 19c. *253*

Gottschalk, Stephen (review article). Christian Science. Eddy, Mary Baker. 1885-1910. *1435*

Gould, Helen. Cody, Margaret E. Gould, Jay. Trials. Wills. 1880-98. *1239*

Gould, Jay. Cody, Margaret E. Gould, Helen. Trials. Wills. 1880-98. *1239*

Government *See also* Cabinet; City Government; Civil Service; Federal Government; Legislative Bodies; Local Government; Political Science; Politics; Public Employees; State Government.

—. Abortion. Birth control. Law. Pregnancy tests. 1971. *2692*

—. Addams, Jane. Romanticism. Social Reform. 1889-1912. *1268*

—. California (Malibu). Courts. Environmental protection. Rindge, May Knight. Southern Pacific Railroad. ca 1900-72. *3243*

—. Discrimination, reverse. Higher Education. 1970's. *1996*

Government (concepts of). Dutch. Family. Germans. 17c-18c. *508*

Government (county, state). California (Topanga Canyon). Rancho Topanga Malibu Sequit. Rindge, May Knight. Roads. 1905-25. *1243*

Government Employees. *See* Civil Service; Public Employees; and the various levels of government with the subdivisions (officials and employees).

Government expenditures. Labor. Taxation. 1970's. *1848*

Government (tribal). Iroquois Indians. Social Customs. 18c. *589*

Government, Resistance to. *See* Revolution.

Governors. Adams, Alva. Adams, Ella Nye. Colorado. Social Conditions. 1887-1931. *3158*

—. Family history. Laurence, Margie Heard. Louisiana (Union Parish). 1850's-1920. 1974. *3126*

—. Sexes. Speechwriters. 1960's. *2308*

Governor's Residence (historical collection). Dunn, Mrs. B. W. C. Tennessee (Nashville). 1971. *2760*

Graduate degree programs. Colleges and Universities. Emotional stress. 1970's. *2819*

—. Connecticut (New Haven). Higher Education. Yale University. 1960's. *2776*

Graduate education. Divorce. Marriage. Student roles. 1969-72. *2796*

Graduate enrollments. Colleges and universities. Employment. Sex discrimination. 1970's. *2783*

Grandin, Mme. Léon. Domestic labor. Illinois (Chicago). Sex roles. Social Conditions. 1892-93. *3040*

Grandmothers (role of). Family. Negroes. Social Status. 19c-20c. *359*

Grant, Helen Smith. British Columbia (Victoria). Family. Maritime History. Nova Scotia (Maitland). Social Reform. 1850-1910. *3327*

Grant, James Benton. Colorado. Grant, Mary Matteson Goodell. Politics. 1857-1941. *1207*

Grant, Mary Matteson Goodell. Colorado. Grant, James Benton. Politics. 1857-1941. *1207*

Gravitz, Maybelle (reminiscences). Chautauqua circuit. 1874-1920's. *1558*

Great Awakening. Religion. Sex. 1740's. *574*

Great Britain. Antislavery lecturer. Massachusetts (Salem). Negroes. Remond, Sara Parker. 1856-87. *890*

—. Armstrong, Aeneas R. Armstrong, Henriette Vickers. Brontë, Charlotte. Georgia. Reading habits. 1861. *968*

—. Arnold, Benedict. Arnold, Peggy. New Brunswick. West Indies. 1781-1801. *3323*

—. Buchanan, James. Lane, Harriet. Presidency. Social Work. USA. 19c. *128*

Great Britain (London). Adams, Abigail. Adams, John. Marriage. Smith, Abigail Adams. Smith, William Stephens. 1780's. *667*

# H

Harrison, Constance Cary (*A Bachelor Maid*). Alcott, Louisa May (*Jo's Boys*). Barr, Amelia Edith Huddleston (*Between Two Loves*). Chopin, Kate (*The Awakening*, 1899). Glasgow, Ellen (*The Descendant*). Image. Jewitt, Sarah Orne (*A Country Doctor*). Novels. Sex roles. Social Change. 1880-1900. *1639*

Harrison, Lucy H. Church of England. Genealogy. Maryland (Somerset Parish). Parish records. 1692-1805. *304*

Hart, Julia Catherine. Canada. Novels. 19c. *3247*

Hartigan, Grace. Frankenthaler, Helen. Painting. Sculpture. Wilson, Jane. 1950's-60's. *2922*

Harvard University. Abolition Movement. Authors. Farrar, Eliza. Follen, Eliza. Literature (children's). Massachusetts (Cambridge). 19c. *1022*

—. Coeducation. Massachusetts (Cambridge). Radcliffe College. 1960's. *2811*

Harvard University (Houghton Library; Lennox Collection). Childhood. Fiction. Lennox, Charlotte (letters). New York. ca 1729-1804. *611*

Harvey, Frederick Henry. Employment. Santa Fe Railroad. Waitresses. 1859-20c. *147*

Hastings, Selina (Countess of Huntingdon). Georgia (Bethesda). Humanitarianism. Social Reform. 1770-1807. *3057*

Hauer family. Fritchie, Barbara. Genealogy. Germans. Immigration. Maryland (Frederick). 1733-1834. *3066*

Haun, Mildred. Appalachia. Fiction. Folklore. 1930-66. *2863*

Haverford College. Bryn Mawr College. Coeducation. Colleges and Universities. Pennsylvania. 1969-74. *2831*

Hawaii *See also* Far Western States.

—. Abortion behavior. Catholic Church. 1965-74. *2497*

—. Children. Racism. Social distance. Stereotypes. ca 1960's-70's. *2517*

—. Emigration. Russians. Zaharoff, Evdokia Gregovna (travel account). ca 1900-17. *1502*

—. Kaahumanu, Queen. Keopuolani. Political Participation. 1778-1823. *768*

—. Missions and Missionaries. Negroes. Presbyterian Church. Stockton, Betsey. 1822-65. *888*

Hawaii (Cadillac). Brush, Jane D. (reminiscences). Presbyterian Church. Social Conditions. Temperance Movements. 1875-83. *3006*

Hawaii (Iwilei district, Honolulu). Prostitution. Social Reform. 1835-1917. *204*

Hawaii (Oahu). Journalism. Massie, Mrs. Thomas. Police. Race Relations. Rape. 1931. *1520*

Hawkins, Ella. Benton, Harriet. Carpenter, Mary. Georgia. Gladdy, Mary. Kimbrough, Frances. Negroes. Slavery. Young, Dink Walton ("Mammy Dink"). 1830's-60. *945*

Hawthorne, Nathaniel. Beecher, Catharine E. Holmes, Oliver Wendell. Sexual spheres, concept of. Sigourney, Lydia Howard. 1868-91. *1694*

—. Dickinson, Emily ("Further in Summer than the Birds," 1866). Literature. 1866. *1676*

—. Fuller, Margaret. Hester Prynne (fictional character). 1850. *1010*

—. Hawthorne, Sophia Peabody. Marriage. ca 1825-50. *2958*

—. Peabody, Elizabeth Palmer. 19c. *3028*

Hawthorne, Nathaniel (*The House of the Seven Gables*, 1851). Hepzibah Pyncheon (fictional character). Language (theory of). Peabody, Elizabeth Palmer. Teaching. 1840's. *986*

Hawthorne, Nathaniel (*The House of the Seven Gables*). Folklore. New England. Witchcraft, theme of. 1851. *1015*

Hawthorne, Nathaniel (*The Scarlet Letter*). Adultery. Hester Prynne (fictional character). Symbolism in Literature. 1850. *1660*

—. Attitudes. Sex. 1850. *958*

—. Feminism. Hutchinson, Anne. Puritans. Sex Discrimination. Theology. Winthrop, John. 1634-38. 1850. *534*

Hawthorne, Sophia Peabody. Hawthorne, Nathaniel. Marriage. ca 1825-50. *2958*

Hayes, Helen. Bankhead, Tallulah. Cornell, Katharine. Cushman, Charlotte Saunders. Duncan, Isadora. Farrar, Geraldine. Hallam, Nancy. Lind, Jenny. National Portrait Gallery. Patti, Adelina. Portraits. Theater. 1971. *418*

Hayes, Lucy Webb. Courtship. Hayes, Rutherford B. Marriage. Politics. 1850's-80's. *1227*

Hayes, Rutherford B. Courtship. Hayes, Lucy Webb. Marriage. Politics. 1850's-80's. *1227*

Hayes, Rutherford B. (administration). Federal Policy. Indians. Jackson, Helen Hunt (*A Century of Dishonor*). 1877-81. *1219*

Hazard, Nancy. Comstock, Joseph. Hysteria. Medicine (practice of). Music therapy. Tarantism. Witchcraft, suspicion of. 1801. *929*

Hazard, Sarah Congdon (diary). California (San Francisco). *Lancashire* (vessel). New York City. Voyages. 1863. *2925*

Hazen, Lillian W. Journalism. Montana (Gilt Edge). Poetry. Weston, Edward Payson. 1899-1949. *1677*

H'Doubler, Margaret N. Colleges and Universities. Dance. Physical education. Wisconsin, University of. 1910-26. *1773*

Head Start programs. Attitudes. Children. Education. Mothers. Negroes. 1960's. *2525*

Healey, Caroline. Fuller, Margaret. Massachusetts (Boston). Sex roles. Social Reform. 19c. *654*

Health. Higher education. Science and Society. Sex Discrimination. ca 1870's-1900's. *1583*

Health care. Historiography. Mitchell, S. Weir. Physicians. Sex roles. 19c. *222*

Health dangers. Advertising. Consumers. Deodorant products, feminine. Food and Drug Administration. 1970-73. *2684*

Health, Education and Welfare Department. Adolescence. California (Los Angeles County). Federal Policy. Pregnancy, extramarital. 1969-71. *2273*

—. Affirmative action. Colleges and universities. 1971-76. *1999*

—. Affirmative action. Colleges and Universities (faculty). Employment. 1970's. *1992*

—. Affirmative Action. Discrimination (reverse). 1965-73. *1995*

—. Affirmative Action programs. Civil Rights Act (Title VII, 1964). Colleges and universities. Sex discrimination. 1960's-72. *1997*

—. Affirmative Action (quotas). Discrimination. 1973. *1991*

—. Colleges and Universities. Employment. Nepotism rules. Sex discrimination. Wives (faculty). 1973. *1979*

—. Colleges and Universities. Equal opportunity. Sex Discrimination. 1967-73. *2777*

Health, Education and Welfare, Department of. Affirmative action (evasion of). Colleges and universities. Employment. Sex Discrimination. 1970's. *1993*

Health, Education and Welfare Department (policies). Child Welfare. Day Nurseries. 1961-71. *2156*

Health insurance, national. Insurance companies. Sex discrimination. 1975. *1819*

Hearst, Phoebe Apperson. Anthropology. California, University of. Philanthropy. 1890-1908. *1107*

Heath, Susanna (Sukey). Manuscript tune collections. Massachusetts. Music. 1782. *607*

Heck, Barbara. Dickey, Sarah. Leadership. Methodist Church. Parker, Lois Stiles. Shaw, Anna Howard. Stereotypes. Willard, Frances. 19c. *315*

Heilbrun, Carolyn. Androgyny. Literature. Sexual polarization. Social Conditions. 1973-74. *2177*

Heinz, Elizabeth Granger Rust. Ogontz School for Young Ladies. Pennsylvania (Philadelphia). Private Schools. Secondary Education. 1883-1900. *1586*

Heller, Elizabeth Wright (autobiography). Employment. Iowa. Social Customs. 1880-81. *1077*

Heller, Ernestine. Heller, Louise. Illinois (Chicago). Jews. Steiner, Ruth Heller (memoirs). 20c. *124*

Heller, Louise. Heller, Ernestine. Illinois (Chicago). Jews. Steiner, Ruth Heller (memoirs). 20c. *124*

Heller, Mary Bell Stahr (memoirs). Family. Franklin and Marshall College. Pennsylvania (Lancaster). 1878-1909. *1157*

Hellman, Lillian. Dramatists. Manuscripts. Texas, University of (Lillian Hellman Collection). 1934-63. *90*

Helvie, Clara Cook. Biographical dictionary. Clergy. Sex Discrimination. Unitarian Church. Universalist Church of America. 1860-1976. *349*

Hemings, Sally. Brodie, Fawn M. (*Thomas Jefferson, An Intimate History*). Historiography. Jefferson, Thomas (review article). 1743-1826. 1963-74. *742*

—. Coolidge, Ellen Randolph (letter). Jefferson, Thomas (personal life). 1802-26. 1858. *759*

Henderson, Lucy Ann. Oregon Trail (Applegate Cutoff). Overland Journeys to the Pacific. 1846. *726*

Hentz, Caroline Lee. Authors. Family. Feminism. Hale, Sarah Josepha. Morality. Sex roles. Sigourney, Lydia Howard. Southworth, E. D. E. N. Womanhood (image of). 19c. *961*

Hepzibah Pyncheon (fictional character). Hawthorne, Nathaniel (*The House of the Seven Gables*, 1851). Language (theory of). Peabody, Elizabeth Palmer. Teaching. 1840's. *986*

Hermits. Bishop, Sarah. Northeastern or North Atlantic States. ca 1800-23. *2972*

Hero, concepts of. Cultism concepts. Historians (male). 1873-1974. *27*

Heroines. Disney, Walt. Fairy tales. Films. Literature, children's. Oral traditions. Sex role models. 1930-75. *2743*

—. Fiction. Gordon, Caroline. Sex roles. South or Southern States. 1918-60's. *420*

—. Fiction. King, Grace Elizabeth. South or Southern States. 1850's-1900. *1636*

—. Fiction, juvenile. Florida, image of. Image. 1909-14. *1719*

—. Political Campaigns. Sacagawea (Shoshoni). Suffrage. Western States. 1902-21. *1371*

Heroines (fictional). Atherton, Gertrude. Feminism. Novels. Public Opinion. 1890's. *1736*

—. Atherton, Gertrude. Novels. Social Customs. 1880-1948. *1704*

Heroines (image of). Fiction. Periodicals. 1957-67. *2849*

Heroines, roles of. Image. Television. 1974. *2729*

Herron, Utopia. Alabama (Florence). Family. Florence Synodical Female College. Letters. Students. Tennessee (Carroll and Madison Counties). 1868. *3139*

—. Alabama (Florence). Family life. Letters. Presbyterian Church. Synodical Female College. Teachers. Tennessee (Trenton). 1869. *3138*

—. Attitudes. Family life. Letters. Politics. Synodical Female College. Tennessee (South Carroll, Trenton). 1868. *3137*

—. Family. Florence Synodical Female College. Letters. Memphis Conference Female Institute. Social conditions. Tennessee (West). 1864-67. *3140*

Hertel brothers. Beaubassin, Catherine de. Friendship. Montcalm, Louis Joseph de. Quebec. 1732-81. *3335*

Hester Prynne (fictional character). Adultery. Hawthorne, Nathaniel (*The Scarlet Letter*). Symbolism in Literature. 1850. *1660*

—. Fuller, Margaret. Hawthorne, Nathaniel. 1850. *1010*

Hewitt, Catherine. Marriage plans (alleged). Reynolds, John (family). 1863-70. *646*

Heywood, Martha Spence. Frontier and Pioneer Life. Intellectuals. King, Hannah Tapfield. Mormons. Snow, Eliza Roxcy. Utah. 1850-70. *729*

Hickman, Irene. California (Sacramento County). Tax reform. 1966-69. *2337*

High School of Fashion Industry. Discrimination, Employment. Negroes. New York City. Puerto Ricans. Vocational Education. Whites. 1975. *1930*

High Schools *See also* Junior High Schools; Secondary Education.

—. Bibliographies. California (San Diego). Curricula. Women's Studies. 1975. *23*

—. Catholic Church. Curricula. 1960's. *2845*

—. Counselors. Self concepts. Sex roles. 1961. *2200*

—. Michigan (Marquis). Negroes. Self concepts. Students. 1960's. *2565*

—. Political Protest. Sex discrimination. Youth movements. 1971. *2271*

—. Stereotypes. Textbooks (history). 1960's. *46*

Higher Education *See also* Adult Education; Colleges and Universities; Professional Education.

—. Affirmative action. Discrimination, reverse. Federal government. 1975. *1994*

—. Affirmative action. Employment. Sex Discrimination. 1974. *1998*

—. Agassiz, Elizabeth. Colleges and Universities (women's, founders). Lyon, Mary. Meyer, Annie Nathan. Northeastern or North Atlantic States. Smith, Sophia. 1830-1900. *438*

—. Career patterns. Discrimination, Employment. 1970's. *2806*

Holt, Victoria. Eden, Dorothy. Image. Novels, gothic. Stewart, Mary. Whitney, Phyllis. 1955-73. *2738*

Holy Family (cult of). Quebec. 1665-1960's. *3352*

Home Economics *See also* Arts and Crafts; Consumers; Folk Art; Food Consumption; Sewing.

—. Catholic Church. Quebec (Saguenay). Schools. 1870-1965. *3350*

Home economics movement. American Home Economics Association. Beecher, Catharine E. New York (Lake Placid). 1898-1908. *1116*

Home, image of. Architecture. Boardinghouses. Factory girls. Massachusetts (Lowell). 1820-70. *643*

Home life. Parlors. Pianos. 1771-1932. *186*

Home Service. American Red Cross. Family. Social Work. World War I. 1918-19. *1298*

Homesteading and Homesteaders. Alberta. Peace River country. Ukrainians. Zahara, Dominka Roshko. 1900-30. *3376*

—. Bern, Enid (reminiscences). Childhood. Daily Life. North Dakota (Hettinger County). 1907-12. *3153*

—. Bright, Abbie (diary). Daily Life. Kansas. 1870-71. *3194*

—. Daily Life. Family. Kansas. Warner, Luna E. (diary). 1871-74. *688*

—. Daily Life. Folklore. Food Consumption. Social Conditions. 19c. *733*

—. Dunn, Carrie Nesbitt (reminiscences). Wyoming (Jackson Hole). 1890's. *3176*

—. Indian Territory (Cherokee Outlet). Oklahoma. 1889-1903. *3128*

—. Klein, Lillie. Letters. Montana (Blaine County). 1913. *3192*

—. Oklahoma Territory. 1889-1901. *1049*

Homicide. *See* Murder.

Homosexuality. Androgyny. Social change. 1800-1974. *247*

—. Kutenai Indians. Sex roles. 19c. *914*

—. Masturbation. Medicine (practice of). 19c. *180*

Honorary Degrees. *See* Degrees, Academic.

Hooker, Isabella Beecher. Anthony, Susan B. Connecticut (Hartford). Stanton, Elizabeth Cady. Suffrage. Woodhull, Victoria. 1861-1907. *1373*

Hooper, Jessie Jack. Catt, Carrie Chapman. League of Women Voters. Legislation. Wisconsin. 1921-60's. *286*

Hoover, Herbert C. Family. Hoover, Lou Henry. Marriage. Politics. Travel. 1899-1928. *1251*

—. Hoover, Lou Henry. Presidency. 1929-32. *1252*

Hoover, Lou Henry. California. Finnish Relief Fund. Girl Scouts of America. Stanford University, Hoover War Library. 1933-44. *1253*

—. California. Stanford University. 1884-98. *3233*

—. Childhood. Iowa (Waterloo). 1874-84. *3030*

—. Family. Hoover, Herbert C. Marriage. Politics. Travel. 1899-1928. *1251*

—. Hoover, Herbert C. Presidency. 1929-32. *1252*

Hope, Lugenia Burns (papers). Editors and Editing. Negroes. ca 1890's-1930's. 1975. *1464*

Hopedale Community. Ballou, Adin Augustus. Feminism. Massachusetts (Milford). Utopias. 1824-56. *861*

Hopi Indians. Alcoholic cirrhosis. Arizona. Culture. Navajo Indians. 1965-67. *2605*

—. Arizona (Second Mesa). Basketry, coiled. Income. Tourism. 1972. *2608*

Hopkins, Edward. Artists. Canada. Fur Trade. Hopkins, Frances Ann. Hudson's Bay Company. ca 1857-1918. *3315*

Hopkins, Frances Ann. Artists. Canada. Fur Trade. Hopkins, Edward. Hudson's Bay Company. ca 1857-1918. *3315*

—. Canada. Fur trade. Painting. 1860-79. *3312*

Hopkins, Pauline Elizabeth. Negroes. Poets. 1859-1930. *1471*

Horne, Alice Merrill. Adams, Maude. Arts. Babcock, Maud May. Bowen, Emma Lucy Gates. Teasdel, Mary. Utah. 1860-1950. *1771*

Horner, Matina. Addams, Jane. Kennedy, Rose. Lawrence, Frieda. Psychology. Senesh, Hannah. Success, fear of. 20c. *2265*

—. Methodology. Motivation. Psychology. Success, fear of. 1970-74. *2262*

Horney, Karen. Deutsch, Helene. Psychology. Sex roles. ca 1890's-1970's. *176*

Horse traders. Borland, Margaret. Texas. 19c. *3117*

Horticulture. Canada. Indian-White Relations. Oneida Indians. USA. 17c-1860. *376*

Hosmer, Helen (reminiscences). California (Venice). Resorts. ca 1900-17. *3216*

Hospitals. Chancellor, Sue M. (reminiscences). Chancellorville (battle). Civil War. Family. Virginia. 1863. *782*

—. Charities. Debutante parties. Hargrave, Colleen. Illinois (Chicago). Passavant Woman's Aid Society. 1939-71. *2061*

—. Children. Harriet Lane Home for Invalid Children. Johnston, Harriet Lane. 1895-1972. *2980*

—. Civil War. Confederate Army. Tompkins, Sally. Virginia (Richmond). 1860-65. *811*

—. Civil War (personal narratives). Nurses and Nursing. Ricketts, Frances L. (diary). Virginia (Manassas, Richmond). 1861-63. *805*

—. Dix, Dorothea. Medicine (practice of). Mental Illness. Psychiatry. Social reform. 19c. *933*

—. Medicine (practice of). Nurses and Nursing. Physicians. Social stratification. 1970's. *1889*

Hospitals (maternity). Child Welfare Commission. Children's Codes. Minnesota. 1913-19. *1530*

Hotel, Motel, and Restaurant Employees' Union, Local 705. Labor. Michigan (Detroit). Wolfgang, Myra (interview). 1972. *2018*

Hotel Upham. California (Santa Barbara). Hall, Elizabeth Goodridge. Lincoln, Abbie Smith Patrick. Lincoln House. 1869-1969. *3214*

Houghton, Dorothy Deemer. Electoral College. Iowa (Red Oak). Office of Refugees, Migration and Voluntary Assistance. Political Participation. 1935-72. *2335*

House of Representatives *See also* Legislation; Senate.

—. Alabama. Hobson, Richmond Pearson. Progressivism. Suffrage. 1900-20. *1368*

Household structure. Domestic servants. German Americans. Irish Americans. Life cycles. New York (Buffalo). Whites (native born). 1855. *636*

Households. Discrimination. Economic equality. Labor market. 20c. *159*

—. Domestic labor. 2006

—. Family. New York (Kingston, Marborough, Troy). Rural-Urban Studies. 1800-60. *655*

Housekeepers. Daily Life. Immigration. Oregon (Carlton, Yamhill River Valley). Social Customs. Swedish Americans. 19c. *1501*

—. District of Columbia. Jaffray, Elizabeth (reminiscences). White House. 1910-20's. *1114*

Houses. Architecture (Victorian). Kentucky (Louisville). Landward House. Wheeler, Mrs. Blakemore. 1871-1970. *443*

—. Colonial Dames of America. Evansview (house). Mississippi (Natchez). Preservation. 20c. *2765*

—. Daily Life. Folklore. Social Customs. Tennessee (east). 1974. *2195*

—. Pennsylvania (Muncy). Petrikin, Fannie. 1850-1902. *2971*

Housewives. Capitalism. Family consumption. Inflation. Labor force. 20c. *164*

—. Child, Lydia Marie (*The American Frugal Housewife*, 1833). Frugality. 1830's. *676*

—. Childrearing. Consumers. Family. Feminine mystique. Friedan, Betty. Image. Marriage. Periodicals (women's). Technology. 1920's-30's. *1544*

—. Cookbooks. Medical remedies. ca 1600-1800. *487*

—. Domestic labor. Image. Periodicals. Social change. Technology. 1920-40. *1113*

—. Economic values. Methodology. 1969-74. *2007*

—. Employment. Professions. Schools. Social Change. 1970's. *1912*

—. Employment opportunities. Industrial Revolution. Labor-saving devices. Social change. 18c-1974. *140*

—. Employment (professional). Feminism. Friedan, Betty. 1960's. *2402*

Housework. 1963. *2003*

—. Blake, John Laurus (*The Farmer's Everyday Book*, 1850). Country Life. Farmers. Social Customs. Wives. 1850's-60's. *649*

—. Capitalism. 19c-20c. *175*

—. Capitalism. Employment. 1690-1976. *167*

—. Capitalism. Galbraith, John K. Oakley, Ann. Sex roles. 1950-70's. *2005*

—. Employment. Industrialization. Negroes. Sex discrimination. Wages. Whites. 1970. *1936*

—. Pennsylvania (Pittsburgh). Sex roles. Social Conditions. Technology. Working class. 1870-1900. *1115*

Housework, professionalization of. Centennial Celebrations. Feminism. Pennsylvania (Philadelphia). Technology. Woman's Building. 1830-76. *168*

Housing *See also* City Planning; Public Housing; Urban Renewal.

—. Architecture. City planning. Environmental design. Working conditions. 1960's-70's. *2902*

—. Architecture. Polygamy. Utah. 1850's-60's. *657*

—. Child care. Collective ventures. Feminist Alliance. New York (Greenwich Village, Washington Square). Rodman, Henrietta. 1914-17. *1324*

—. City Planning. Day Nurseries. Massachusetts (Springfield). Model Cities program. Poverty. 1965-72. *2153*

—. Family (female headed). Married couples, separation of. Public welfare. Puerto Rico. 1950-60. *2026*

—. Negroes. Poor. Public Welfare. Virginia (Norfolk). 1950's-60's. *2527*

Housing market. Connecticut (New Haven). Racism. Segregation. 1973. *2549*

Houston, Sam. Alabama. Lea, Margaret Moffette. Texas. 1819-67. *3110*

Howard, Laura. California. Edward-Dean Museum of Decorative Arts. Folk Art. Mays, Carrie. Postley, Theresa. Quiltmaking. ca 1600-1970's. *421*

Howard, Mary K. Local Government. Politics. Utah (Kanab). 1912-14. *1234*

Howard, Peggy (obituary). Economists. Radicals and Radicalism. 1944-72. *1928*

Howe, Jemima. French. Indians (captivities). Vermont. 1755-60. *2973*

Howells, William Dean. Illinois (Chicago). Novels. Wyatt, Edith Franklin. 1900's. *1666*

Hoxie, Vinnie Ream. Lincoln, Abraham (statue of). Sculpture. 1865-71. *1780*

Hubbard, Leonidas. Explorers. Hubbard, Mrs. Leonidas. Labrador (northeast). Wallace, Dillon. 1903-05. *3328*

Hubbard, Mrs. Leonidas. Explorers. Hubbard, Leonidas. Labrador (northeast). Wallace, Dillon. 1903-05. *3328*

Hudson, Martha Turner. Abolition Movement. Connecticut (Torringford). 1833-77. *853*

Hudson's Bay Company. Artists. Canada. Fur Trade. Hopkins, Edward. Hopkins, Frances Ann. ca 1857-1918. *3315*

—. Employment. Gunn, Isabel (alias John Fubbister). Ontario (Albany factory). 1806-09. *3359*

—. Fort Yukon. Marriage. Murray, Alexander Hunter. Murray, Anne Cambell. 1846-65. *3255*

Hull House. Addams, Jane. Education. Ideology. Illinois (Chicago). Sex roles. Social Reform. 1875-1930. *1411*

—. Addams, Jane. Illinois (Chicago). Letters. Starr, Ellen Gates. 1889-90. *1409*

Hull, Millie. New York City (Bowery). Tattoo artists. 1939. *1056*

Human nature. Christianity. Kinsey, Alfred C. (writings). Sexual behavior. 1948-54. *2230*

Human Relations *See also* Discrimination; Family; Labor; Marriage; Race Relations.

—. Cities. Education. Industrialization. Social Conditions. 1956-72. *2054*

—. City Life. Family. Illinois (Chicago). Negroes. Social Conditions. Whites. Widows. 1968-72. *2056*

—. Congresswomen. Social Organizations. 1960's. *2310*

Human rights. Behavior (modification). Lobotomy. Mental Illness. Sex Discrimination. Social control. 1950's-71. *2706*

—. Children. Courts. Jehovah's Witnesses. Religious Liberty. 1964. *2478*

—. Du Bois, W. E. B. Feminism. Negroes. 1910-20. *1454*

Human Rights Commission. Roosevelt, Eleanor. 1947-51. *2334*

Humanism. Cather, Willa. Fiction. Western States. 1890's-1940's. *1734*

—. Feminism. Ideology. 1960's. *2401*

Humanitarianism. Georgia (Bethesda). Hastings, Selina (Countess of Huntingdon). Social Reform. 1770-1807. *3057*

Humanities *See also* such subjects as Art, Literature, Music, Philosophy, etc.

Humanities (majors in). North Dakota University. Students. 1960-65. *2844*

Hume, Mrs. Samuel. Journalism. *Marion Star* (newspaper). Ohio. Politics. 1877-88. *1067*
Humor *See also* Satire.
—. Benchley, Robert. literary criticism. Parker, Dorothy. Sex. Social criticism. 1919-26. *1713*
—. Courtship. Frontier and Pioneer Life. Louisiana. Marriage. 1840's. *965*
—. Dolls (wind-up). Politics. 1960's. *2754*
—. Feminism. Holley, Marietta (writings). Literature. 1870-1926. *1623*
—. Folklore. Literary tradition. National Characteristics. Rourke, Constance (review article). 1931. *1608*
—. Mabley, Moms. Negroes. Satire. 1960's. *2519*
—. Sex. 19c-20c. *464*
Humorists. Literature. ca 1825-1907. *459*
Humphrey, Ruth. Artists. Canada. Carr, Emily. Letters. 1937-44. *3310*
Hunt, Harriot Kezia. Attitudes. Blackwell, Elizabeth. Diseases. Medicine (practice of). Ward, Elizabeth Stuart Phelps. 1840-1900. *1534*
—. Blackwell, Elizabeth. Blackwell, Emily. Medical Education. Zakrewska, Marie E. 1849-61. *973*
Hunter, Kate. Civil War. Recreation. Rhode Island (Newport). Social Conditions. 1863-64. *794*
Huntington, Arabella. Art Collecting. California (San Marino). Huntington Library and Art Gallery. 1910-20's. *1783*
Huntington, Arria. Episcopal Church, Protestant. Huntington, Frederick. Huntington, Ruth. New York. Sex roles. 1869-1904. *1440*
Huntington, Frederick. Episcopal Church, Protestant. Huntington, Arria. Huntington, Ruth. New York. Sex roles. 1869-1904. *1440*
Huntington Library and Art Gallery. Art Collecting. California (San Marino). Huntington, Arabella. 1910-20's. *1783*
Huntington, Ruth. Episcopal Church, Protestant. Huntington, Arria. Huntington, Frederick. New York. Sex roles. 1869-1904. *1440*
Hurricanes *See also* names of particular hurricanes, e.g. New England Hurricane, 1938, etc.
—. Focke, John (family). Letters. Texas (Galveston). 1900. *3102*
—. Green, Frances (reminiscences). Quonset Air Station. Rhode Island (Wickford). Social Conditions. 1890-1974. *2952*
Hurst, Lulu (career). Georgia. Occult Sciences. Theater. 1883-85. *1556*
Hurston, Zora Neale. Anthropology. Authors. Florida. Folklore. Negroes. 1901-60. *1457*
—. Authors. Culture. Migration, Internal. Negroes. Toomer, Jean. 1860-1960. *336*
—. Culture. Folklore. Negroes. Novels. 1930's-60. *449*
Husbands. Family (communication in). Wives. 1963. *2105*
Hutchins, Ann White. Carolinas. Frontier and Pioneer Life. Mississippi (Natchez). 1768-1811. *702*
Hutchinson, Anne. Antinomian Controversy. Clergy. Cotton, John. Massachusetts (Boston). Puritans. Theology. 1636. *581*
—. Antinomian controversy. Massachusetts Bay Colony. Political Protest. 1630-43. *541*
—. Antinomian controversy. Massachusetts (Boston). Puritans. Trials. 1634-38. *543*
—. Antinomians. Cotton, John. Massachusetts Bay Colony. Politics. Puritans. Theology. 1630's. *537*
—. Dyer, Mary. Massachusetts Bay Colony. Politics. Sex roles. Theology. Trials. 1636-43. *540*
—. Dyer, Mary. Massachusetts (Boston). Persecution. Puritans. Religious Liberty. 1635-51. *579*
—. Feminism. Hawthorne, Nathaniel *The Scarlet Letter*. Puritans. Sex Discrimination. Theology. Winthrop, John. 1634-38. 1850. *534*
Hutterites. Communes. Family. Manitoba. 1874-1969. *3379*
Hutton, May Arkwright. Idaho. Mining towns. Philanthropy. Politics. Washington (Spokane). ca 1870's-1920. *3218*
Huxley, Thomas. Scott, Lizzie Huxley. Tennessee (Nashville). 1876. *3143*
Hydropathy. Feminism. Medicine. 1843-1900. *1323*
—. Medicine. 1799-1850. *932*

Hyland, Mary McLaughlin. Montana. Rural schools. Social Conditions. Teachers. 1914-39. *1064*
Hyslop, Beatrice Fry (tribute). Books. French history. Historians. Society for French Historical Studies. 1899-1972. *1103*
Hysteria. Comstock, Joseph. Hazard, Nancy. Medicine (practice of). Music therapy. Tarantism. Witchcraft, suspicion of. 1801. *929*

# I

I AM sect. Ballard, Edna. Ballard, Guy. Occult Sciences. 1930's-75. *2472*
Ibsen, Henrik. LeGallienne, Eva. Literary criticism. 1889-1957. *1655*
Idaho *See also* Far Western States.
—. Acculturation. Family structure. Marriage. Nez Percé Indians. 19c-20c. *362*
—. Catt, Carrie Chapman. Duniway, Abigail Scott. National American Woman Suffrage Association. Suffrage. Woman's Christian Temperance Union. 1870-96. *1350*
—. Hutton, May Arkwright. Mining towns. Philanthropy. Politics. Washington (Spokane). ca 1870's-1920. *3218*
—. Juvenile Delinquency. Marriage (instability of). Nez Percé Indians. Sex roles. Social Change. 1960's. *2593*
—. National American Woman Suffrage Association. Suffrage. 1896-1920. *1346*
Idaho (Caldwell). Economic Conditions. Social Conditions. Steunenberg, Bess (reminiscences). ca 1900. *3242*
Idaho (Kamiah). Fletcher, Alice Cunningham. Gay, Jane. McBeth, Kate. McBeth, Sue L. Nez Percé Indian Reservation. Presbyterian Church. Thaw, Mary Copley. 1890-1915. *1438*
—. Indian-White Relations. McBeth, Kate. McBeth, Sue L. Missions and Missionaries. Nez Percé Indians. Presbyterian Church. 1885. *1437*
Idaho (Long Valley). Sayre, Florence (reminiscences). ca 1890's-1910. *3239*
Idaho (northern). Fletcher, Alice Cunningham. Gay, Jane. Nez Percé Indians. 1889-92. *3227*
Iddings, Deborah Alice. Country Life. Fairfield (family home). Iddings, Fanny Pierce (reminiscences). Maryland (Montgomery County). Moravian Female Seminary. Pierce, Ann. Pierce, Sophia Kummer. 1728-1968. *3075*
Iddings, Fanny Pierce (reminiscences). Country Life. Fairfield (family home). Iddings, Deborah Alice. Maryland (Montgomery County). Moravian Female Seminary. Pierce, Ann. Pierce, Sophia Kummer. 1728-1968. *3075*
Ideal States. See Utopias.
Ideas, History of. *See* Intellectuals.
Ideology. Addams, Jane. Education. Hull House. Illinois (Chicago). Sex roles. Social Reform. 1875-1930. *1411*
—. Anthropology. Biology. Family structure. Labor, sexual division of. Patriarchy. Stereotypes. 20c. *119*
—. Antifeminism. Feminists. Hoffer, Eric. Personality. 1951-73. *2299*
—. Attitudes. Control, locus of. Feminist movement. Protestant ethic. 1972. *2438*
—. Attitudes. Marxism. Political Theory. Sexual conflict. 1970's. *2198*
—. Attitudes. Sex roles. Values. 1963-75. *2188*
—. Canada. Feminism. Middle Classes. Political Leadership. USA. 1960-75. *270*
—. Cities. Family. Historiography. New England. Social Change. 17c-18c. 1940's-70. *506*
—. Duke University. Sexes. 1960's-70. *2318*
—. Feminism. Humanism. 1960's. *2401*
—. Feminism (review article). Politics. Suffrage. 1830-1920. 1969-70. *216*
—. Greer, Germaine (*The Female Eunuch*). Marxism. Patriarchy. Sex (frigidity). 1960's-70's. *2432*
—. Higher education. 19c-20c. *463*
—. Historiography. Sex roles. Social change. 19c-20c. *178*
—. Sports. 1945-72. *2766*
Illegitimacy. Childbirth. Discrimination. Family breakdown. Negroes. Sex roles. Social Problems. 18c-1972. *371*
—. Childbirth. Family structure. Income. Negroes. 1960's. *2585*
—. Childbirth. Fertility rates. Population growth. 1940-73. *2131*

—. Children. Eugenics. Mothers. Public Policy. Sterilization laws. 1907-66. *224*
Illinois *See also* North Central States.
—. Attitudes. Negroes. Sex differences. Students. 1960's. *2581*
—. Bradwell, Myra. Lawyers. Sex Discrimination. Supreme Court (decisions). 1873-1894. *1101*
—. Brown, William H. Civil War. Frazey, Emma Jane. Letters. 1862-67. *3015*
—. Chicago *Daily Tribune* (newspaper). Child Welfare. Divorce. Domestic servants. Marks, Nora (pseud. of Eleanora Stackhouse). Reporters and Reporting. Social Problems. 1888-90. *1673*
—. Constitutions, State (revision of). League of Women Voters. Organizations. 1967-70. *2298*
—. Erix-dotter, Christina Louisa (letter). Immigrants. Pioneers. Swedish Americans. 1854. *705*
—. Frontier and Pioneer Life. Stebbins, Sara Ames (letter). 1839. *695*
—. Greene, Elizabeth (family). Travel accounts. 1834-35. *3012*
—. Immigrants' Protective League. Social Reform. 1908-26. *1206*
Illinois (Chicago). Addams, Jane. Altgeld, Emma. Darrow, Clarence. Friendship. Intellectuals. ca 1880-1938. *1223*
—. Addams, Jane. Art. Politics. Reform. 1889-1916. *1233*
—. Addams, Jane. Cities. Family. Politics. Social Reform. ca 1889-1935. *1413*
—. Addams, Jane. Dunne, Edward F. Educational Reform. Progressivism. Young, Ella Flagg. 1905-10. *1384*
—. Addams, Jane. Education. Hull House. Ideology. Sex roles. Social Reform. 1875-1930. *1411*
—. Addams, Jane. Hull House. Letters. Starr, Ellen Gates. 1889-90. *1409*
—. Addams, Jane. Immigrants' Protective League. Social Reform. 1908-21. *1408*
—. Bradwell, Myra. Feminism. Law reform. 1855-92. *1241*
—. Bradwell, Myra. Lawyers. 1872. *1111*
—. Bremer, Frederika. Letters. Social Conditions. 1850. *3009*
—. Charities. Debutante parties. Hargrave, Colleen. Hospitals. Passavant Woman's Aid Society. 1939-71. *2061*
—. Charity organization movement. Public Welfare. Rural-Urban Studies. Social Classes. 1880-1930. *1512*
—. City Life. Family. Human Relations. Negroes. Social Conditions. Whites. Widows. 1968-72. *2056*
—. Civil War. Feminism. Great Northwestern Fair. Livermore, Mary. Sanitary Commission. 1861-69. *813*
—. Domestic labor. Grandin, Mme. Léon. Sex roles. Social Conditions. 1892-93. *3040*
—. Family (nuclear). Middle Classes. Violence. 1900-70. *241*
—. Fire. McLaughlin, Catherine. O'Leary, Catherine. 1871. *3041*
—. Garden, Mary. Opera. 1887-1960's. *1753*
—. Garment industry. Jews. Prostitution. State Legislatures (Senate Vice Committee). Working Conditions. 1913. *1120*
—. Garment workers. O'Reilly, Mary. Socialists. Strikes. Zeh, Nellie M. 1910. *1118*
—. Heller, Ernestine. Heller, Louise. Jews. Steiner, Ruth Heller (memoirs). 20c. *124*
—. Howells, William Dean. Novels. Wyatt, Edith Franklin. 1900's. *1666*
—. Illinois Women's Alliance. Labor reform. Ladies' Federal Labor Union. Morgan, Elizabeth Chambers. 1874-97. *1131*
—. Labor Unions and Organizations. Minorities. Mt. Sinai Hospital. Roberts, Lillian (interview). 1950's. *2017*
—. Literature. Monroe, Harriet. *Poetry* (periodical). 1870's-1910's. *1741*
—. Negroes. Organizations. World's Columbian Exposition (1893). 1893. *1466*
—. Progressivism. Prostitution. Social justice. 1910-15. *1535*
—. Prostitution. Social Conditions. 1860's-71. *1539*
—. Social Reform. Stereotypes. 1833-37. *697*
Illinois (Chicago, Pullman). Family. Marriage. Pullman, George Mortimer (letters). Pullman, Harriet Amelia Sanger (diary). 1867-90's. *1163*
Illinois (Cook County). Aid to Families with Dependent Children. Mothers' pensions. Public Welfare. 1911-75. *251*

—. Economic Conditions. Family structure. New York (Buffalo). Occupational patterns. 1900-30. *1497*

—. Fertility. 1940-60. *2635*

Italian Americans (review article). Acculturation. Catholic Church. Family. Social Organization. 1880's-20c. *373*

Italians. Immigration. Novels. Stonecutters. Tomasi, Mari. Vermont. 1909-65. *2979*

Italy See also Tuscany, Venetian Republic, etc.

—. Fuller, Margaret. New England. 19c. *970*

—. Novels. Stowe, Harriet Beecher (*Uncle Tom's Cabin*, 1852). 1852-1940's. *1743*

Italy (Florence). Alexander, Lucia Gray Swett. Friendship. Lowell, James Russell (letter). Poetry. 1873-74. *1744*

# J

Jackson, Andrew. Cabinet. Eaton, Margaret (Peggy) O'Neale. Politics. 1829. *747*

—. Catholic Church (ceremonies). District of Columbia. Lewis, Mary Anne. White House. 1832-33. *3080*

—. Democratic Party. Eaton, Margaret (Peggy) O'Neale. Ely, Ezra Stiles. Politics. 1829-30. *749*

—. Donelson, Andrew Jackson (family). Eaton, Margaret (Peggy) O'Neale. Ladies Hermitage Association. Restorations. Tennessee (Tulip Grove). 1829-20c. *3119*

Jackson, Andrew (letter). District of Columbia. Donelson, Emily. Eastin, Mary. Eaton, Margaret (Peggy) O'Neale. Politics. ca 1828-32. *746*

Jackson, Eleanor Hardin. Civil War. Letters. Social Conditions. Tennessee (Rutherford County). 1860-65. *818*

Jackson, Helen Hunt (*A Century of Dishonor*). Federal Policy. Hayes, Rutherford B. (administration). Indians. 1877-81. *1219*

—. Indian-White Relations. 1881. *1514*

Jackson, Sheldon. Alaska (Sitka). Indians. Kellogg, Fannie. Missions and Missionaries. Schools. ca 1878. *1079*

Jackson, Shirley. Bibliographies. Literature. 1919-65. *2877*

Jacobi, Mary Putnam. Archives. Arthur M. Schlesinger, Sr. Beard, Mary R. League of Women Voters. Park, Maud Wood. Radcliffe College (Arthur and Elizabeth Schlesinger Library). ca 1916-70. *81*

Jaffa, Adele Solomons. Asher, Meta. Brandt, Mrs. Noah. California (San Francisco). Charities. Frank, Ray. Jews. Levinson, Amelia. Organizations. Prag, Mary. Selling, Natalie. Wolf, Alice. Wolf, Emma. 1896. *1429*

Jaffray, Elizabeth (reminiscences). District of Columbia. Housekeepers. White House. 1910-20's. *1114*

Jamaica Masonic Lodge. Dances. New York (Long Island). Soldiers. World War I. 1917-18. *1296*

James, Ann. Arkansas. Missions and Missionaries. Private Schools. Teaching. 1813-1910. *3100*

James, Henry. Novels. Sex roles. Values. 1861-1914. 1960-72. *1649*

James, Henry (*The Bostonians*, 1886). Mary Prance (fictional character). Suffrage. Walker, Mary. 1886. *1679*

James, Selma (*Women, the Unions and Work, or What is Not to be Done*). Capitalism. Labor Unions and Organizations. Social Conditions. 1972-73. *1834*

Japan. Education. Feminism, cultural. Tsuda, Ume. USA. 1900-30. *1322*

Japanese Americans. California (Fresno). Ethnic boundaries. Marriage (interracial). 1960-73. *2636*

—. Marriage, interracial. 1960-73. *2630*

Jarrett, Elizabeth Lucas. Attitudes. Georgia (Tugalo). Imperialism. Jarrett, George D. Letters. Philippines. 1901-03. *3086*

Jarrett, George D. Attitudes. Georgia (Tugalo). Imperialism. Jarrett, Elizabeth Lucas. Letters. Philippines. 1901-03. *3086*

Jarvis, Elizabeth. Family. New York City. Social Conditions. Wheeler, David Everett. 1833-48. *2945*

Jarvis sisters. Canada. Girl Guides (founding of). 1900-25. *3281*

Jarvis, Stinson. Ontario. Psychic phenomena. Watkins, Kathleen ("Kit of the Mail"). 1885-95. *3368*

Jefferson, Joseph. Drama. Family structure. "Rip Van Winkle" (play). 1865. ca 1900-70's. *672*

Jefferson, Mary. Eppes, Elizabeth. Eppington (plantation). Marriage. Virginia (Chesterfield County). 1778-1804. *3084*

Jefferson, Thomas. Adams, Abigail. Childrearing. Education. Family. Morality. Politics. Values. 1774-1804. *756*

—. Eppes, Maria Jefferson. Randolph, Martha Jefferson. Virginia. 18c-19c. *3077*

—. Inheritance. Wayland, Mrs. Widows. 1782. *547*

Jefferson, Thomas (influence). Feminism. Fuller, Margaret. Journalism. Politics. Social criticism. 1840-50. *832*

Jefferson, Thomas (letters). Adams, Abigail (letters). Friendship. Politics. 1790's-1826. *764*

Jefferson, Thomas (personal life). Coolidge, Ellen Randolph (letter). Hemings, Sally. 1802-26. 1858. *759*

Jefferson, Thomas (review article). Brodie, Fawn M. (*Thomas Jefferson, An Intimate History*). Hemings, Sally. Historiography. 1743-1826. 1963-74. *742*

Jehovah's Witnesses. Children. Courts. Human Rights. Religious Liberty. 1964. *2478*

Jenness, Linda. Elections (presidential). Political campaigns. Socialist Workers Party. 1972. *2326*

Jenny (fictional character). Dickens, Charles (*The Old Curiosity Shop*). Images. Literature. Little Nell (fictional character). Segal, Erich (*Love Story*). 19c-20c. *401*

Jewett, Sarah Orne. Fiction. Maine (South Berwick). 1868-1909. *1587*

—. Letters. Literature. Whittier, John Greenleaf. 1877-90. *1614*

Jewett, Sarah Orne (*The Country of the Pointed Firs*, 1896). Fiction. New England. 1896. *1629*

Jewitt, Sarah Orne (*A Country Doctor*). Alcott, Louisa May (*Jo's Boys*). Barr, Amelia Edith Huddleston (*Between Two Loves*). Chopin, Kate (*The Awakening*, 1899). Glasgow, Ellen (*The Descendant*). Harrison, Constance Cary (*A Bachelor Maid*). Image. Novels. Sex roles. Social Change. 1880-1900. *1639*

Jews See also Judaism; Zionism.

—. Adler, Della Rubenstein (reminiscences). Immigrants. New York (Buffalo). 19c. *2932*

—. Arendt, Hannah. Historiography. 1966. *2508*

—. Arendt, Hannah (*Eichmann in Jerusalem*, 1963). New Left. Philosophy. Politics. 1963. *2330*

—. Asher, Meta. Brandt, Mrs. Noah. California (San Francisco). Charities. Frank, Ray. Jaffa, Adele Solomons. Levinson, Amelia. Organizations. Prag, Mary. Selling, Natalie. Wolf, Alice. Wolf, Emma. 1896. *1429*

—. Attitudes. Civil War. Social Conditions. 1861-65. *775*

—. Baldwin, James. Davis, Angela. Negroes. 1960's-71. *2300*

—. Baldwin, James (open letter). Communism. Davis, Angela. 1960's-71. *2316*

—. Barlow, Cornelia D. California. Marks, Bernhard. Marriage. Pioneers. Teachers. 1852-1913. *714*

—. Benevolent societies. Immigrants. New York City. Social Conditions. Widows. 1848-60. *879*

—. Benevolent societies. Rhode Island. ca 1877-1975. *351*

—. Birth Control. Marriage. 1960's. *2510*

—. Breshkovsky, Catherine. Revolutionary Movements. Russians. Sex. 1904-06. *1258*

—. California (Los Angeles). Consumers. Food (kosher). 1969. *1810*

—. California (Los Angeles). Films. Myers, Carmel (reminiscences). 1902-30. *1560*

—. California (Los Angeles). Marriage. Meyer, Harriet Newmark. Newmark, Rosa Levy (letter). Social customs. 1867. *1164*

—. California (San Francisco). Choynski, Harriet. Letters. 1850-72. *3208*

—. Canada. Immigrants. Rosenbaum, Bella W. (reminiscences). Social Conditions. USA. 1880's-1910's. *120*

—. Catholic Church. Protestantism. Religion. Social Status. 1970. *2470*

—. Cities. Family. 1960's. *2505*

—. Cities. Family. Marriage. Vacations. 1960's. *2507*

—. Class consciousness. Cohn, Fannia. International Ladies' Garment Workers' Union. Labor Unions and Organizations. Newman, Pauline. Pesotta, Rose. 1900-35. *1126*

—. Colorado (Denver). Family. Immigration. Shwayder, Rachel. 1865-1916. *1418*

—. Conley, James. Frank, Leo (trial). Georgia (Atlanta). Murder. Negroes. Press. 1913-15. *1522*

—. Education. Family life. Marriage. 1970's. *2511*

—. Family. German Americans. Social Organizations. ca 1870-1920's. *1428*

—. Family. Motherhood. Social Customs. 1970's. *2506*

—. Garment industry. Illinois (Chicago). Prostitution. State Legislatures (Senate Vice Committee). Working Conditions. 1913. *1120*

—. Germans. Immigration. Organizations. Russians. 1880-1924. *1447*

—. Heller, Ernestine. Heller, Louise. Illinois (Chicago). Steiner, Ruth Heller (memoirs). 20c. *124*

Johnson, Anna (recollections). Iowa. Rural Schools. Teachers. 1925-40's. *1083*

Johnson, Dorothy M. Montana (Whitefish). Telephone operators. 1922. *1883*

Johnson, Dorothy M. (reminiscences). Authors. Montana. Westward Movement. 1920-74. *3173*

—. Childhood. Montana (Whitefish). 1915. *3175*

—. Daily Life. Ethnic Groups. Montana. ca 1915. *3172*

—. Glacier National Park. Montana. National Parks and Reserves. Rinehart, Mary Roberts. 1916-1970's. *3171*

—. Juvenile life. Montana (Whitefish). Youth. 1918-25. *3174*

Johnson, Elizabeth. Adultery. Capital Punishment. Connecticut (Hartford). Newton, Thomas. Trials. Witchcraft (supposed). 1648-92. *600*

Johnson, Georgia Douglas. Harlem Renaissance. Imes, Nella Larsen. Literature. Negroes. 1920's. *1460*

Johnson, Helen. Canada. Nationalism. Poetry. 1864-1946. *3314*

Johnson, Jack. Cameron, Lucille. Duryea, Etta. Nebraska (Omaha). Press. Race Relations. Values. 1908-15. *1513*

Johnson, Jack (popularity). Boxing. Racism. Sexual attitudes. White women. 1912-13. *1510*

Johnson, Lyndon B. Family. Negroes. Politics. 1960's. *2555*

—. Negroes. Roosevelt, Eleanor. 1930's-70's. *296*

Johnson, Mary Elizabeth (*Indian Legends of the Wyomaca Mountains*, 1914). Alto, Mary. California (San Diego). Indian legends. 1914. *1483*

Johnson, Thomas Scott. College for Girls. Higher Education. Wisconsin (Fox Lake). ca 1860's-1900. *1579*

Johnson, William. American Revolution. Brant, Molly. Iroquois Indians. 1759-96. *587*

Johnston, David Claypool. Cartoons and Caricatures. Catholic Church. Convent (burning of). Massachusetts (Charlestown). 1834. *880*

Johnston, Harriet Lane. Buchanan, James. District of Columbia. Pennsylvania (Lancaster). Politics. Presidents. 1849-1903. *765*

—. Children. Harriet Lane Home for Invalid Children. Hospitals. 1895-1972. *2980*

—. District of Columbia. St. Albans School for Boys. 1909-72. *2981*

—. Pennsylvania (Lancaster). 1903. *2982*

Jones, Anne Neville (letters). Daily Life. District of Columbia. Family. Jones, Roland (letters). Louisiana (Shreveport). Politics. 1853-54. *745*

Jones, Hannah. Needlework (samplers). New Jersey. 1807-37. *608*

Jones, Margo. Texas (Dallas). Theater. 20c. *2921*

Jones, Mary. Marriage. New York City. Newspapers. Trobriand, Régis de (career). 1840-65. *2960*

Jones, Mary Harris. Child Welfare. Labor Reform. United Mine Workers of America. Working Conditions. 1903-12. *1132*

—. Children. Demonstrations. Labor Unions and Organizations. Textile Industry. 1903. *1129*

—. Coal Mines and Mining. Labor Unions and Organizations. United Mine Workers of America. West Virginia. 1901. *1133*

—. Illinois (Mount Olive). Mines. Union Miners Cemetary. ca 1890's-1936. *1123*

—. Labor Unions and Organizations. 1910. *1122*

# K

# L

—. Negroes. Organizations. Racial attitudes. Suffrage. 19c. *1342*

League of Nations. Decisionmaking. Presidency. Wilson, Edith Bolling. Wilson, Woodrow. 1919-20. *1250*

League of Nations Library. Library Science. Switzerland (Geneva). Wilson, Florence. 1919-26. *1065*

League of Women Voters. Ames, Marie. Catt, Carrie Chapman. Gellhorn, Edna. Missouri (St. Louis). Organizations. 1919-29. *1277*

—. Archives. Arthur M. Schlesinger, Sr. Beard, Mary R. Jacobi, Mary Putnam. Park, Maud Wood. Radcliffe College (Arthur and Elizabeth Schlesinger Library). ca 1916-70. *81*

—. Catt, Carrie Chapman. Hooper, Jessie Jack. Legislation. Wisconsin. 1921-60's. *286*

—. Children (care of). Daughters of the American Revolution. Federal Government. Maternal care. Organizations. Sheppard-Towner Act. 1920's. *1282*

—. Constitutions, State (revision of). Illinois. Organizations. 1967-70. *2298*

—. Nebraska. Social Reform. 1920-70. *3008*

—. Organizations. Politics. Reform. South or Southern States. Young Women's Christian Association. 1920's. *1285*

—. Politics. Suffrage. 1920-70. *264*

Lease, Mary Ellen. Democratic Party. Populism. 1890-94. *1212*

LeBer, Jeanne. Bourgeoys, Marguerite. Catholic Church. Quebec. 17c. *3349*

Lecture tours. Bloomer, Amelia. Feminism. Ohio (Mt. Vernon). 1853-54. *841*

Lectures *See also* Speeches, Addresses, etc.

—. Chautauqua Circuit. Social Reform. Tarbell, Ida M. 1916-32. *1601*

—. Cookery. Pennsylvania. Philadelphia Cooking School. Rorer, Sarah Tyson. 1870-1901. *1110*

—. Dickinson, Anna E. Pennsylvania (Lancaster). 1870. *1076*

Ledbetter, Huddie "Leadbelly". Folk Songs. Louisiana. Love, Blanche (reminiscences). Negroes. 1880's-1949. 1976. *1475*

LeDoux, Emma. California (Stockton). McVicar, A. N. Murder. Trials. 1906-41. *1516*

Lee, Ann. Celibacy. Communes. Northeastern or North Atlantic States. Sex life. Shakers. 1774-1968. *378*

—. Daily life. Kentucky (Pleasant Hill). Sexes (segregation of). Shakers. 1774-1916. *353*

Lee, Cornelia. Letters. Stuart, Ann Calvert. Virginia (northern). Wedding. 1780-1807. *3070*

Lee, Mary Edmunds Tabor. Family. Folk Medicine. Louisiana (Shiloh). Marriage. 1840's-1926. *3127*

Lee, Molly Huston. Librarians. Negroes. North Carolina (Raleigh). Richard B. Harrison Library. 1930-75. *3072*

Leesy, Miss. Cultural enrichment program. Missouri (St. Louis). Public Schools. 1960's. *2787*

Leftism *See also* Communism; New Left; Radicals and Radicalism; Socialism.

—. Coalition of Labor Union Women. Labor Unions and Organizations. 1973-75. *2021*

Legal access (concept of). Canada. Divorce. Social Change. 1867-1973. *3284*

Legal profession. Lawyers. Sex discrimination. 1945-69. *1943*

Legal status. British North America Act of 1929. Canada. Feminism. Suffrage. 1870's-1940's. *3292*

—. Canada. Day Nurseries. Employment opportunities. Feminist movement. Social Classes. 1975. *3291*

—. Democracy. Political Participation. 1776. *546*

—. Family structure. Sexual behavior. Social Change. Suffrage. 1700-1976. *117*

LeGallienne, Eva. Ibsen, Henrik. Literary criticism. 1889-1957. *1655*

Legislation *See also* Congress; Law; Legislative Bodies.

—. Abbott, Grace. Child welfare. Kelley, Florence. Lathrop, Julia. Politics. Sheppard-Towner Act. Social reform. Wald, Lillian. 1900-35. *1236*

—. Attitudes. Labor Unions and Organizations. Political Participation. Wages. Working Conditions. 1940's-80's. *2011*

—. Birth Control. Canada. Catholic Church. 1960's. *3258*

—. Catt, Carrie Chapman. Hooper, Jessie Jack. League of Women Voters. Wisconsin. 1921-60's. *286*

—. Composers. Korn, Anna Less Brosius (tribute). Oklahoma. Poetry. 19c-1965. *3104*

—. Congress. Conservation groups. Federal government. Forests and Forestry. Minnesota Federation of Women's Clubs. Minnesota National Forest. Organizations. 1898-1908. *1286*

—. Consumer protection. Neuberger, Maurine. Senate. 1960's. *2313*

—. Consumers. National Consumers' League. Organizations. 1900-23. *1288*

—. Employment. Liquor licences. North Carolina. Saloons (ordinaries). 17c-18c. *484*

—. Family. Poor. Public Welfare reform. 1970's. *2025*

—. Feminism, social. Labor. Organizations. Progressivism. 1919-33. *1128*

—. Minimum wage movement. New York State Factory Investigating Commission. Triangle Shirtwaist Company. 1911-38. *1045*

—. Oklahoma. Temperance Movements. Woman's Christian Temperance Union. 1907-11. *1396*

Legislative Bodies *See also* Congress; House of Representatives; Senate; State Legislatures.

—. Alberta. MacAdams, Roberta Catherine. Political Campaigns. ca 1880's-20c. *3374*

Legislators. Abortion. Religion. Voting and Voting Behavior. Western States. 1975. *2700*

—. Attitudes. Feminism. Negroes. Politics. Social Problems. 1971. *2574*

—. Utah. ca 1870's-1920's. *1260*

Leisure *See also* Recreation.

—. Labor market. Working class. 1948-75. *1824*

Lennox, Charlotte (letters). Childhood. Fiction. Harvard University (Houghton Library; Lennox Collection). New York. ca 1729-1804. *611*

Lentz, Lula Gillespie (reminiscences). Country Life. Farms. Illinois (southern). Marriage. 1883-1929. *3017*

Leshe, Mary Jane Conly. Baptists. Family. Louisiana (Bienville Parish). 1849-1932. *3130*

Leslie, Frank. *Frank Leslie's Illustrated Newspaper* (periodical). Leslie, Miriam F. F. New York City. Newspapers. 1855-1914. *1721*

Leslie, Miriam F. F. California (southern). Travel accounts. 1877. *3234*

—. Catt, Carrie Chapman. *Frank Leslie's Illustrated Newspaper* (periodical). Publishers and Publishing. Suffrage. ca 1860-1914. *1617*

—. *Frank Leslie's Illustrated Newspaper* (periodical). Leslie, Frank. New York City. Newspapers. 1855-1914. *1721*

Letters *See also* names of individuals with the subdivision letters, e.g. Jefferson, Thomas (letters).

—. Adams, Abigail. Adams, John. Attitudes. Sex roles. 1776-1804. *760*

—. Adams, Abigail. American Revolution. Feminism. Warren, Mercy Otis. Washington, Martha. 18c. *542*

—. Adams, Abigail. Coolidge, Anna Goddhue. Harding, Florence Kling. Pierce, Jane Means Appleton. Roosevelt, Eleanor. 18c-20c. *292*

—. Addams, Jane. Hull House. Illinois (Chicago). Starr, Ellen Gates. 1889-90. *1409*

—. Alabama (Florence). Family. Florence Synodical Female College. Herron, Utopia. Students. Tennessee (Carroll and Madison Counties). 1868. *3139*

—. Alabama (Florence). Family life. Herron, Utopia. Presbyterian Church. Synodical Female College. Teachers. Tennessee (Trenton). 1869. *3138*

—. Alberta (Pincher Creek). Cattle Raising. Daily Life. Fort McLeod. Indians (reservations). 1884. *3373*

—. Allen, Hope Emily. Literature. Undset, Sigrid. 1941-48. *1618*

—. American Red Cross. Barton, Clara. Solomons, Adolphus S. 1881-93. *1511*

—. American Revolution. Loyalists. Social Conditions. VanCortlandt, Mrs. Philip. 1776-77. *568*

—. American Revolution (personal narratives). Family. Pinckney, Eliza Lucas. South Carolina. 1768-82. *559*

—. Artists. Canada. Carr, Emily. Humphrey, Ruth. 1937-44. *3310*

—. Attitudes. Civil War. Roosevelt, Eleanor. Spain. 1930's. *1224*

—. Attitudes. Family life. Herron, Utopia. Politics. Synodical Female College. Tennessee (South Carroll, Trenton). 1868. *3137*

—. Attitudes. Georgia (Tugalo). Imperialism. Jarrett, Elizabeth Lucas. Jarrett, George D. Philippines. 1901-03. *3086*

—. Beard, Charles A. Beard, Mary Payne. Indiana. Schools. 1849-59. *3033*

—. Bremer, Frederika. Illinois (Chicago). Social Conditions. 1850. *3009*

—. Brown, Annie. Ohio (Ada, Cincinnati). Prostitution. 1881. *1541*

—. Brown, Laura. Family. Missouri (border). Politics. War. 1850's. *3035*

—. Brown, William H. Civil War. Frazey, Emma Jane. Illinois. 1862-67. *3015*

—. Buchanan, Sophia. Civil War. Michigan. 1862-65. *773*

—. Cabell, James Branch. Glasgow, Ellen. Literature. Virginia (Richmond). ca 1900-40's. *1681*

—. California. Courtship. Dame Shirley (pseud. of Louise A. K. S. Clappe). Gold Rushes. Marriage. 1838-1906. *711*

—. California. Dame Shirley (pseud. of Louise A. K. S. Clappe). Gold Rushes. 1851-1906. *716*

—. California (San Francisco). Choynski, Harriet. Jews. 1850-72. *3208*

—. California (Santa Barbara). Daily life. Lincoln, Abbie Smith Patrick. 1869. *3223*

—. Canada. Catholic Church. Marie de l'Incarnation. Religious Orders. Ursulines. 17c. *3252*

—. Canada. Laurier, Wilfrid. Lavergne, Mme. Joseph. 1891-93. *3260*

—. Carman, William Bliss. Guiney, Louise Imogen. Poets. 1887-98. *1651*

—. Caruthers, William Alexander. Georgia. Griffin, Sara Lawrence Drew. Literature. Periodicals. 1841. *1000*

—. Channing, William Henry. Feminism. Massachusetts (Worcester). Wells, Charlotte Fowler. Woman's Rights Convention (2nd national). 1851. *844*

—. Civil War. Daily Life. Family. Illinois (Fayette County). Phifer, Louisa Jane. 1864-1904. *808*

—. Civil War. Duncan, Mrs. Henry. Middleton, Harriott. Middleton, Susan. Social Conditions. South or Southern States. 1863-65. *800*

—. Civil War. Economic Conditions. McCalla, Margaret. South or Southern States. 1863-65. *807*

—. Civil War. Glasgow, Sarah Lane. Lane, Anne Ewing. Missouri (St. Louis). 1861-63. *780*

—. Civil War. Jackson, Eleanor Hardin. Social Conditions. Tennessee (Rutherford County). 1860-65. *818*

—. Civil War. Middleton, Harriott. Middleton, Susan. Social Conditions. South or Southern States. 1861-65. *799*

—. Civil War. Middleton, Harriott. Middleton, Susan. South or Southern States. 1861-65. *801*

—. Civil War. Nurses and Nursing. Sanitary Commission. Whetten, Harriet Douglas. 1862. *792*

—. Civil War. Rawlings, Clarissa Lawrence. Rawlings, Hannah Garlick. Virginia (Orange County). 1865. *778*

—. Civil War. Social Conditions. 1860-65. *810*

—. Civil War. Tompkins, Ellen Wilkins. West Virginia (Fayette County). 1861. *822*

—. Civil War (personal narratives). Family life. Levy, Richard. Levy, Rosena Hutzler. South or Southern States. 1860-65. 1907. *824*

—. Color (use of). Dickinson, Emily. Poetry. Symbolism in Literature. 19c. *1696*

—. Conine, Catharine. Conine, Emily. Conine, Jane. Daily Life. Indiana. Pioneers. Seymour, Mary Ann Conine. 1849-51. *3003*

—. Conine family. Daily Life. North Central States. Pioneers. Seymour, Mary Ann Conine. 1852-63. *3004*

—. Cooke, Rose Terry. Literature. Whittier, John Greenleaf. 19c. *1002*

—. Costume. DuPont, Josephine. Manigault, Margaret Izard. New York City. South Carolina (Charleston). 1795-1824. *684*

—. Cunningham, Sarah Apthorp Morton. Massachusetts (Boston). Politics. Social Conditions. 1825. *2996*

—. Daily Life. Kansas (Junction City). Snow, Leslie. Snow, Susan Currier. 1888-89. *3151*

—. Davis, Varina Anne. Davis, Varina Howell. Literature. Warner, Charles Dudley. ca 1880's. *1722*

—. DeWitt, Simeon. Irving, Washington. Sexuality. 1776. 1804. *681*

—. Diaries. Immigrants. Kansas. Lindgren, Ida Nibelius. Pioneers. Religion. Social Conditions. Swedish Americans. 1870-81. *1496*

—. District of Columbia. Hale, Lucy Lambert. 1858-70. *2967*

Lind, Jenny. Bankhead, Tallulah. Cornell, Katharine. Cushman, Charlotte Saunders. Duncan, Isadora. Farrar, Geraldine. Hallam, Nancy. Hayes, Helen. National Portrait Gallery. Patti, Adelina. Portraits. Theater. 1971. *418*

—. Marriage. Opera. Tours (national). 1850-52. *1029*

Lind, Jenny (tour). Barnum, P. T. Performing arts. Public Opinion. 1850-52. *1030*

Lindgren, Ida Nibelius. Diaries. Immigrants. Kansas. Letters. Pioneers. Religion. Social Conditions. Swedish Americans. 1870-81. *1496*

Lindner, Anna. Daily life. Painting. ca 1863-1914. *1788*

Lindsey, Robert. California. Friends, Society of. Lindsey, Sarah (journal). Travel. 1859-60. *3217*

Lindsey, Sarah (journal). California. Friends, Society of. Lindsey, Robert. Travel. 1859-60. *3217*

—. California. Friends, Society of. Social Conditions. Travel. 1859-60. *703*

Linguistics *See also* Language; Speech.

—. Bryant, Margaret M. Scholars. 1930-74. *1906*

Lippincott, Janet. Artists. Hanburg, Una. Indian themes. Longley, Bernique. New Mexico (Santa Fe). Shonnard, Eugenie. Surrealism, regional. 1972. *2893*

*Lippincott's Magazine.* Fiction. *Harper's New Monthly Magazine.* McDowell, Katharine Sherwood Bonner. South or Southern States. 1870's-80's. *1690*

Liquor industry. Advertising. 1958-60's. *1805*

Liquor licences. Employment. Legislation. North Carolina. Saloons (ordinaries). 17c-18c. *484*

Liston, Henrietta. Diplomacy. Southeastern States. Travel. 1790's. *3073*

—. Travel. Virginia. 1800. *3074*

Litchfield Female Seminary. Connecticut. Education. Pierce, Sarah. 1784-1852. *972*

Literary careers. *Atlantic Monthly* (periodical). Byron, George Gordon. Stowe, Harriet Beecher. 1869. *1674*

—. Fiction. Mexico (influence of). Porter, Katherine Anne. 1930's-60's. *446*

—. Fitzgerald, Zelda Sayre. Mencken, Sara Haardt. 20c. *1644*

Literary criticism. Benchley, Robert. Humor. Parker, Dorothy. Sex. Social criticism. 1919-26. *1713*

—. Bibliographies. Dickinson, Emily. 1930-66. *1640*

—. Bibliographies. King, Grace Elizabeth. 1888-1972. *407*

—. Bibliographies. Murfree, Mary Noailles (pseud. Charles Egbert Craddock). Tennessee. 1878-1922. *1613*

—. Cather, Willa. 1893-96. *1615*

—. Cather, Willa. Fiction. Journalism. Pennsylvania (Pittsburgh). 1896-1906. *1612*

—. Feminism. Lawrence, D. H. Millett, Kate. 20c. *2864*

—. Feminism. Teaching. 1968-73. *2878*

—. Fiction. Harris, Corra. 20c. *1631*

—. Fiction. Harris, Corra. 1903. *1714*

—. Fuller, Margaret. Transcendentalism. 1830-50. *994*

—. Harris, Corra. South. ca 1877-1904. *1715*

—. Ibsen, Henrik. LeGallienne, Eva. 1889-1957. *1655*

—. Negroes. Vroman, Mary Elizabeth. 1963. *2535*

—. Novels. Societies. Wharton, Edith. World War I. 1914-18. *1700*

Literary criticism (review article). O'Connor, Flannery. 1970's. *2854*

Literary Symbolism. *See* Symbolism in Literature.

Literary tradition. Fictional characters. South or Southern States. Stowe, Harriet Beecher. 1851-20c. *1624*

—. Folklore. Humor. National Characteristics. Rourke, Constance (review article). 1931. *1608*

Literature *See also* Authors; Autobiography and Memoirs; Biography; Books; Drama; Fiction; Humor; Journalism; Language; Novels; Poetry; Satire; Symbolism in Literature.

—. Abolition Movement. Painting. Stowe, Harriet Beecher. 1832-96. *113*

—. Alabama. Fenollosa, Mary McNeil. ca 1870's-1915. *1627*

—. Allen, Hope Emily. Letters. Undset, Sigrid. 1941-48. *1618*

—. Androgyny. Heilbrun, Carolyn. Sexual polarization. Social Conditions. 1973-74. *2177*

—. Arizona. Hall, Sharlot Mabridth. Lummis, Charles F. *Out West* (periodical). 1870-1943. *1738*

—. Art. Austin, Mary Hunter. Baumann, Gustave (recollections). New Mexico (Santa Fe). 20c. *1599*

—. Art. Stein, Gertrude (review essay). Toklas, Alice B. ca 1900-46. *1634*

—. Attitudes. Connecticut (Hartford). Sex roles. Sigourney, Lydia Howard. 1830-55. *1007*

—. Austin, Mary Hunter. Cabot, Alice. Curtis, Natalie. Densmore, Frances. Fletcher, Alice Cunningham. Folk Songs. Indian culture. Translating and Interpreting. Underhill, Ruth Murray. Walton, Eda Lou. West. 1880-1965. *433*

—. Austin, Mary Hunter. Feminism. Southwest. 1868-1934. *1701*

—. Authors. Reality (inner vs. outer). 1930-73. *428*

—. Authors. Sex. 19c-1973. *462*

—. Behavior. Powell, Dawn. Social Change. 1920-60. *1663*

—. Bibliographies. Jackson, Shirley. 1919-65. *2877*

—. Bloom, Ellen F. (reminiscence). Stein, Gertrude. 1874-1946. *1607*

—. Bower, B. M. (pseud. of Bertha Muzzy). 1904-40. *1625*

—. Cabell, James Branch. Glasgow, Ellen. Letters. Virginia (Richmond). ca 1900-40's. *1681*

—. Canada. Moodie, Susanna. National self-image. Social Classes. 1832-53. *3251*

—. Caruthers, William Alexander. Georgia. Griffin, Sara Lawrence Drew. Letters. Periodicals. 1841. *1000*

—. Case, Luella J. B. Edgarton, Sarah. Family. Marriage. New England. Sisterhood. ca 1839-46. *650*

—. Cather, Willa. Davenport, Marcia. Deland, Margaret. Long, Haniel. Pennsylvania (Pittsburgh). Rinehart, Mary Roberts. Schmitt, Gladys. 18c-20c. *430*

—. Cather, Willa. Nebraska. Regionalism. 1890-1923. *1598*

—. Cather, Willa. Nebraska (Webster County). Prairie (influence of). Regionalism. 1974-75. *1603*

—. Childhood. Indians. Nebraska (Sheridan County). Plains Indians. Sandoz, Mari. 1870's-1931. *1619*

—. Chopin, Kate. Regionalism. Social Conditions. 19c-20c. *1616*

—. Christianity. O'Connor, Flannery. South. 1940's-75. *2875*

—. Cooke, Rose Terry. Letters. Whittier, John Greenleaf. 19c. *1002*

—. Cultural tradition. Image. Passion. Reason. Sex roles. 1775-1850. *959*

—. Davis, Varina Anne. Davis, Varina Howell. Letters. Warner, Charles Dudley. ca 1880's. *1722*

—. Dickens, Charles (*The Old Curiosity Shop*). Images. Jenny (fictional character). Little Nell (fictional character). Segal, Erich (*Love Story*). 19c-20c. *401*

—. Dickinson, Emily ("Further in Summer than the Birds," 1866). Hawthorne, Nathaniel. 1866. *1676*

—. Dorsey, Sarah Anne (letter). Thoreau, Henry David. 1871. *3007*

—. Dutch traditions. Ferris, Mary L. D. 1855-1932. *1665*

—. Europe (impressions of). Fuller, Margaret. National Self-image. 1783-1860. *996*

—. Feminism. Hardwick, Elizabeth. Jong, Erica. Milford, Nancy. Showalter, Elaine. 1975. *2859*

—. Feminism. Holley, Marietta (writings). Humor. 1870-1926. *1623*

—. Feminism. Negroes. Stowe, Harriet Beecher. Truth, Sojourner. 1850's-90's. *280*

—. Feminist movement. Freudian analysis. 1946-70's. *2409*

—. Fitzgerald, F. Scott. Fitzgerald, Zelda Sayre. Pictorial essay. 1906-20. *1652*

—. Fitzgerald, F. Scott. Fitzgerald, Zelda Sayre. Southern belle (image of). 1917-45. *3043*

—. *Godey's Lady's Book* (periodical). New York. Social criticism. Whitcher, Frances Berry (*Widow Bedott Papers*). 1847-55. *1017*

—. Harlem Renaissance. Imes, Nella Larsen. Johnson, Georgia Douglas. Negroes. 1920's. *1460*

—. Humorists. ca 1825-1907. *459*

—. Illinois (Chicago). Monroe, Harriet. *Poetry* (periodical). 1870's-1910's. *1741*

—. Image. Lawrence, D. H. Marriage. Suckow, Ruth. 1920's-30's. *1667*

—. Jewett, Sarah Orne. Letters. Whittier, John Greenleaf. 1877-90. *1614*

—. Kemble, Frances Anne (*Journal*, 1835). Travel. 1832-40. *997*

—. Language. Sex Discrimination. 1972. *2748*

—. Marriage. Phelps, Elizabeth Stuart. Religion. Sex roles. ca 1820's-90's. *466*

—. McCullers, Carson. South. 1917-69. *456*

—. Metropolitan Areas. Popular Culture (underground). Prostitution. 1840-70. *925*

—. Nevada. Strobridge, Idah Meacham. 1860's-1909. *1589*

—. Ohio (Cincinnati). Semi-Colon Club. Stowe, Harriet Beecher. 1829-46. *1025*

—. Plains Indians. Sandoz, Mari. 1930's-60's. *2855*

—. Porter, Katherine Anne (interview; *Ship of Fools*). 1961. *2880*

—. Race Relations. Smith, Lillian. Social Change. South or Southern States. 1940's. *2885*

—. Racial attitudes. Slavery. Stowe, Harriet Beecher (*Uncle Tom's Cabin*, 1852). 1851-52. *942*

—. Sex. Socialism. 1969. *2869*

—. Slavery. Stowe, Harriet Beecher (*Uncle Tom's Cabin*, 1852). Thorpe, Thomas B. (*The Master's House*, 1853). 1852-54. *944*

Literature (children's). Abolition Movement. Authors. Farrar, Eliza. Follen, Eliza. Harvard University. Massachusetts (Cambridge). 19c. *1022*

—. Adams, William T. ("Oliver Optic"). Alcott, Louisa May (*Eight Cousins*). Alger, Horatio, Jr. Massachusetts (Boston). Morality. 1867-99. *1642*

—. Artists. Book illustration. Gág, Wanda (*Millions of Cats*). 1908-38. *1751*

—. Disney, Walt. Fairy tales. Films. Heroines. Oral traditions. Sex role models. 1930-75. *2743*

—. Nancy Drew (fictional character). New Deal. Stereotypes. 1930's. 1960's-70's. *399*

Literature, western. Cather, Willa. Image. Sandoz, Mari. Sex roles. Western States. 1898-1954. *1548*

Lithography, stone. Images. Postcards. 1907-17. *1549*

Little, Joanne. Negroes. North Carolina (Wake County). Trials. 1975. *2547*

Little Nell (fictional character). Dickens, Charles (*The Old Curiosity Shop*). Images. Jenny (fictional character). Literature. Segal, Erich (*Love Story*). 19c-20c. *401*

*Little Review* (periodical). Anderson, Margaret. Periodicals. 1910's-60's. *455*

Littleton, Ann. Virginia (Northampton County). Wills. 1656. *3082*

Live Oak Female Seminary. Secondary Education. Stuart Female Seminary. Texas. 1840's-1955. *458*

Livermore, Mary. Civil War. Feminism. Great Northwestern Fair. Illinois (Chicago). Sanitary Commission. 1861-69. *813*

Livestock. *See* Cattle Raising; Sheep Raising.

Lloyd, Elizabeth. Friends, Society of. Letters. Poetry. Whittier, John Greenleaf. 1840. *1006*

Lobbying *See also* Citizen Lobbies.

—. Congress. Constitutional amendment (19th). Organizations. Women's Joint Congressional Committee. 1920-29. *1281*

—. Consumers League of New York. New York (Albany). Perkins, Frances. State Legislatures. 1911. *1247*

—. Divorce. Equal Rights Amendment. Federation of Business and Professional Women's Clubs. Iowa. Sex discrimination. Sheppard-Towner Act. Social Reform. Wages. 1919-70. *3036*

Lobotomy. Behavior (modification). Human rights. Mental Illness. Sex Discrimination. Social control. 1950's-71. *2706*

Local Government *See also* Local Politics.

—. Employment. State Government. 1967-72. *1911*

—. Howard, Mary K. Politics. Utah (Kanab). 1912-14. *1234*

—. Law. Nevada. Prostitution. ca 1850-1974. *250*

Local History. Pennsylvania. 1972. *2993*

Local Politics *See also* Local Government.

—. Pennsylvania (Reading). Socialist Party. Voting and Voting Behavior. ca 1927-38. *1272*

Lockouts. *See* Arbitration, Industrial; Collective Bargaining; Labor Unions and Organizations; Strikes.

Logan, Martha Daniell. Farquher, Jane Colden. Medicine (practice of). Pinckney, Eliza Lucas. Ramsay, Martha Laurens. Scientists. 18c. *485*

Logging camps. Employment. Lind, Anna M. (reminiscences). Pacific Northwest. 1920-40. *1087*

London, Jack *(The Sea Wolf,* 1904). Browning, Elizabeth Barrett. Maud Brewster (fictional character). Strunsky, Anna. 1899-1904. *1699*

Long, Haniel. Cather, Willa. Davenport, Marcia. Deland, Margaret. Literature. Pennsylvania (Pittsburgh). Rinehart, Mary Roberts. Schmitt, Gladys. 18c-20c. *430*

Long Island (battle). American Revolution. Washington, George. 1776. *557*

Longfellow, Henry Wadsworth. Appleton, Fanny. Courtship. Massachusetts (Boston, Cambridge). 1841-43. *1001*

—. Clemm, Maria (letters). Poe, Edgar Allan. 1850-66. *993*

Longfellow, Henry Wadsworth (letters). Marshall, Emma. 1851-76. *1023*

Longley, Bernique. Artists. Hanburg, Una. Indian themes. Lippincott, Janet. New Mexico (Santa Fe). Shonnard, Eugenie. Surrealism, regional. 1972. *2893*

Longworth, Alice Roosevelt (anecdotes). 1933-69. *2302*

Loos, Anita *(Gentlemen Prefer Blondes).* Image. Middle Classes. Satire. Sex roles. Values. 1925. *1606*

Los Angeles *Times* (newspaper). News photos, content of. Sex Discrimination. Social roles. Washington *Post* (newspaper). 1974. *2763*

Louisiana *See also* South or Southern States.

—. Alexander, Elizabeth. Civil War. Cottonbales (capture of). Supreme Court. 1860-65. *804*

—. Barrow, Clyde. Crime and Criminals. Death and Dying. Folk heroes. Thornton, Bonnie Parker. 1934. *1525*

—. Bryan, Mary E. Journalism. 1854-74. *3134*

—. Civil War. Family. Negroes. Refugees. 1860-65. *898*

—. Civil War. Farmer, Alice (autobiography). South or Southern States. 1850-72. *803*

—. Civil War. Hall, Mariah M. Slaveowners. Widowhood. 1854-91. *3129*

—. Civil War (diaries). 1860-65. *829*

—. Courtship. Frontier and Pioneer Life. Humor. Marriage. 1840's. *965*

—. Family Health Inc. Family planning. Poor. 1966-70. *2093*

—. Fertility. Northwestern State College (graduates of). 1920-50. *1174*

—. Folk Songs. Ledbetter, Huddie "Leadbelly". Love, Blanche (reminiscences). Negroes. 1880's-1949. 1976. *1475*

—. Gayarré, Charles (letters). King, Grace Elizabeth (letters). 1867-95. *3096*

—. Law. Property rights. Wives. 1950's-60's. *2351*

—. Marriage notices. *New Orleans Christian Advocate* (weekly). Obituaries. 1854-55. *640*

—. Marriage notices. *New Orleans Christian Advocate* (weekly). Obituaries. 1851-55. *641*

—. Marriage notices. *New Orleans Christian Advocate* (weekly). Obituaries. 1855. *642*

—. Murray, Amelia. Travel accounts. 1600's-1850's. *3146*

Louisiana (Bernice). Baptists. Elam, Margaret Fuller. Family. 1874-1975. *3125*

—. Family. Farms. Mabry, Catherine Cook. 1885-1913. *3124*

Louisiana (Bienville Parish). Baptists. Family. Leshe, Mary Jane Conly. 1849-1932. *3130*

Louisiana (Hill Switch). Baptists. Daily Life. Oneal, Marion S. (reminiscences). 1902-03. *3133*

Louisiana (Mansfield). College reunion. Mansfield Female College. 1844-1930. 1974. *441*

Louisiana (Metoyer). Coincoin (former slave). Family. Negroes. Plantations. 1742-1850. *895*

Louisiana (Minden). Family. Marriage. Perryman, Melvill Lucile Martin. Plantation life. 1876-1975. *3097*

Louisiana (New Orleans). Black magic cults. Music (jazz). Negroes. Voodoo. 19c. *409*

—. Catt, Carrie Chapman. Feminism. Gilman, Charlotte Perkins. Shaw, Anna Howard. Social Conditions. 1890's-1903. *1318*

—. Child Labor Law. Gordon, Jean. Theatrical Syndicate. 1908-12. *1230*

—. Daily Life. Oneal, Marion S. (reminiscences). Social Conditions. 1890's. *3132*

—. Economic Conditions. Land. Negroes (free). 1850-60. *897*

—. Modjeska, Helena. Theater. 1879-1901. *1748*

—. Negroes. Political participation. Sex roles. 1969-70. *2566*

Louisiana (New Orleans, St. Martinville). Murphy, Mary Mamie (reminiscences). Social Conditions. Southern Pacific Railroad. 1882. *3145*

Louisiana (Ruston). Barrow, Clyde. Crime and Criminals. Darby, H. Dillard. Parker, Bonnie. Stone, Sophia. 1933. *1517*

Louisiana (Shiloh). Baptists. Burns, Bertha Porter. Burns, Marion Van. Clergy. Teachers. 1884-1975. *3123*

—. Family. Folk Medicine. Lee, Mary Edmunds Tabor. Marriage. 1840's-1926. *3127*

Louisiana (Shreveport). Daily Life. District of Columbia. Family. Jones, Anne Neville (letters). Jones, Roland (letters). Politics. 1853-54. *745*

Louisiana (Shreveport, Fairfield Hill). Church Schools. Daughters of the Cross. St. Vincent's Academy. 1866-1971. *1576*

Louisiana (Union Parish). Family history. Governors. Laurence, Margie Heard. 1850's-1920. 1974. *3126*

Louisiana (Vernon). Elementary Education. Mindan Female College. Smith, Anna Calhoun. Teachers. 1885-1901. *1089*

Love, attitude toward. Emerson, Ralph Waldo. Fuller, Margaret. Greeley, Horace. Transcendentalism. ca 1845. *1004*

Love, Blanche (reminiscences). Folk Songs. Ledbetter, Huddie "Leadbelly". Louisiana. Negroes. 1880's-1949. 1976. *1475*

Love relationships. Aim-inhibition hypotheses. Sex, premarital. 1960's-70's. *2231*

Lovejoy, Esther Clayson Pohl. Medical education. Oregon, University of, Medical School. 1890-94. *1575*

Lowell, Amy. Actors and Actresses. Dwyer, Ada. Poetry. ca 1880-1925. *1774*

—. Imagist movement. Poetry. Pound, Ezra. 1913-22. *1657*

—. Letters. Poetry. Wendell, Barrett. 1915-19. *1711*

Lowell, James Russell (letter). Alexander, Lucia Gray Swett. Friendship. Italy (Florence). Poetry. 1873-74. *1744*

Lowell, Josephine Shaw. New York. Social Work. 1843-1905. *2987*

Lowry, Morrow B. Feminism. Higher education. Letters. Pennsylvania. 1868. *1312*

Loyalists. American Revolution. Economic Conditions. Family. 1775-89. *558*

—. American Revolution. Frankland, Charles Henry. Marriage. Massachusetts (Boston, Marblehead). Social Customs. Surriage, Agnes. 1742-83. *494*

—. American Revolution. Letters. Social Conditions. VanCortlandt, Mrs. Philip. 1776-77. *568*

—. American Revolution. Massachusetts. Oliver, Anne. Oliver family. Political Leadership. 1632-1860. *536*

—. American Revolution. Mississippi (West Florida, Old Natchez District). Occupations. Truly, Sarah. 1773-92. *556*

—. American Revolution. Nevil, Nancy. New Jersey (Sussex County). 1779. *549*

Loyalty. *See* Patriotism.

*Lucifer's Lantern* (periodical). Mormons. Polygamy. Schroeder, Theodore. Utah. 1889-1900. *1421*

Lucy Brewer (fictional character). Morality. Novels. Patriotism. Prostitution. 1789-1818. *1014*

Ludington, Flora Belle. Bibliographies. Librarians. Mount Holyoke College. 1920-64. *2956*

Lummis, Charles F. Arizona. Hall, Sharlot Mabridth. Literature. *Out West* (periodical). 1870-1943. *1738*

Lumpkin, Katharine Du Pre. Antislavery sentiments. Feminism (review article). Grimké, Angelina. Josephson, Hannah. Political Reform. Psychohistory. Rankin, Jeannette. 19c-20c. 1974. *262*

*Lusitania* (vessel). Disasters. Pope, Theodore (letter). World War I (antecedents). 1915. *1294*

Lutheran Church. Cities. Rural-Urban Studies. Sex. 1960's. *2486*

—. Family. Marriage. Parsonage. 1974. *2477*

—. Farms. Frontier and Pioneer Life. German Americans. Immigrants. Texas. Wiederaenders family. 1850's. *736*

—. Genealogy. Germans. Winchenbach, Sibylla Charlotta. ca 1700-13. *2983*

Lutheran Church (Missouri Synod). Attitudes. Birth control. Social Change. 19c-1960's. *203*

—. Employment. Private Schools. Teachers. 1870's-1970's. *343*

—. Social service. 20c. *313*

Lykins-Bingham, Mattie (reminiscences). Daily Life. Missouri (Kansas City). 1851-52. *3018*

Lynam, John. Friends, Society of. Lynam, Margaret Ridge. Maryland. Pennsylvania. Persecution. 1660's-90's. *572*

Lynam, Margaret Ridge. Friends, Society of. Lynam, John. Maryland. Pennsylvania. Persecution. 1660's-90's. *572*

Lynching. Ames, Jessie Daniel (interview). Civil Rights. Feminism. Negroes. South. ca 1900-72. *273*

—. Association of Southern Women for the Prevention of Lynching. Negroes. Organizations. South. 1930-42. *1276*

—. Journalism. Negroes. Tennessee (Memphis). Wells, Ida B. 1884-94. *1473*

Lyon, Mary. Agassiz, Elizabeth. Colleges and Universities (women's, founders). Higher Education. Meyer, Annie Nathan. Northeastern or North Atlantic States. Smith, Sophia. 1830-1900. *438*

Lytle, Daisy. Cider making. Kentucky (Woodburn). Lytle, Randall. 1972. *2916*

Lytle, Randall. Cider making. Kentucky (Woodburn). Lytle, Daisy. 1972. *2916*

# M

Mabley, Moms. Humor. Negroes. Satire. 1960's. *2519*

Mabry, Catherine Cook. Family. Farms. Louisiana (Bernice). 1885-1913. *3124*

MacAdams, Roberta Catherine. Alberta. Legislative Bodies. Political Campaigns. ca 1880's-20c. *3374*

Machinery. *See* Inventions.

Machismo. Abortion. Child care. Feminism. Mexican Americans. 1970's. *2623*

—. Catholic Church. Mexican American movement. Social Customs. 1970's. *2621*

Maclure, William. Education. Indiana (New Harmony). Social Reform. Utopias. 19c. *868*

Madame Albini. Fiske, Minnie Maddern. Melba (actress). Saskatchewan (Regina). Theater. Tucker, Sophie. 1900-14. *3387*

Madison, Dolley Payne. District of Columbia. Few, Frances (diary). Gallatin, Hannah Nicholson. Presidents. 1808-09. *748*

—. Inheritance. 1793-95. *767*

—. Presidency. 1809-17. *741*

Magazines. *See* Periodicals.

Mageras, Georgia Lathouris. Greeks. Immigration. Midwives. Utah (Magna area). 1902-50. *1095*

Magowan, Robin (autobiography). California. Perry, Nancy Ling. Popular Culture. Symbionese Liberation Army. 1970's. *2321*

Mahoney, Mary (journal). Colorado. Farmers. Nebraska. Travel. 1901. *3182*

Mail, direct. Birth control information. Information diffusion. Public Welfare. 1972. *2237*

Mailer, Norman (review article). Actors and Actresses. Films. Monroe, Marilyn. 1950's. *2755*

Maine *See also* New England; Northeastern or North Atlantic States.

—. Bibliographies. Working Class. 1975. *74*

—. Courtship. Family. Marriage. Penobscot Indians. Social Customs. 1492-1900. *370*

Maine (Appledore Island). Poets. Thaxter, Celia. ca 1840's-60's. *1024*

Maine (Kittery). Keene, Sarah. Spinney, John. Witchcraft (supposed). 1725-26. *524*

Maine (New Sweden). Family. Immigration. Letters. Swedish Americans. Widows. 1873-88. *1498*

Maine (Newichewannock River). Carroll, Gladys Hasty (memoirs). Family. ca 1860-1930. *2941*

Maine (Petit Manan, Frenchman's Bay). Lighthouses (keepers). 1903-42. *2935*

Maine (South Berwick). Fiction. Jewett, Sarah Orne. 1868-1909. *1587*

—. Childrearing. Family (changes in). Industrialization. Sex roles. ca 1800-1960's. *199*

—. Childrearing. Family (idealized). Romanticism. 1960's. *2073*

—. Children. Family. Plymouth Colony. Social Conditions. 17c. *503*

—. Children. Feminism. Industrial Revolution. 19c-20c. *267*

—. Children. Indians (captivities). Massachusetts (Deerfield). Quebec (Caughnawaga). Williams, Eunice. 1704-80's. *366*

—. Church of England. Maryland. Morals, regulation of. Sexual behavior. 1690-1775. *490*

—. Cities. Family. Jews. Vacations. 1960's. *2507*

—. Civil War. Courtship. Illinois Volunteer Infantry (12th). 1860-65. *776*

—. Clemenceau, George. Family. Plummer, Mary. 1849-1923. *1240*

—. Clothing. Morality. Public Opinion. Sex. Social Customs. 1936-65. *2225*

—. Colleges and Universities. Courtship. Sororities. 1960's. *2114*

—. Colleges and Universities. Family. Students (drop out). 1960's. *2778*

—. Colleges and Universities. Family. Students (re-entry). 1960's. *2826*

—. Collins, June McCormick (review article). Family structure. Indians. Skagit Indians. Washington, western. Prehistory-20c. *392*

—. Comedy. Films. Sex. 1965-71. *2095*

—. Congress. Education. Political Parties. State Legislatures. 1916-64. *297*

—. Country Life. Farms. Illinois (southern). Lentz, Lula Gillespie (reminiscences). 1883-1929. *3017*

—. Courtship. Economic Conditions. Social conditions. Urbanization. 1871-1911. *1158*

—. Courtship. Family. Maine. Penobscot Indians. Social Customs. 1492-1900. *370*

—. Courtship. Frontier and Pioneer Life. Humor. Louisiana. 1840's. *965*

—. Courtship. Hayes, Lucy Webb. Hayes, Rutherford B. Politics. 1850's-80's. *1227*

—. Courtship. Kentucky. Ohio River Valley. Social Customs. 19c-20c. *3144*

—. Courtship. New England. Sexual behavior. Social Customs. 1632-1783. *510*

—. Courtship. Pershing, John J. Warren, Frances. 1903-15. *1170*

—. Cragin, Mary. Noyes, John Humphrey. Psychology. Sex. Utopias. 1830's-40's. *865*

—. Creek Indians. Family. Lewis, Kendall. Settlement. Texas (Titus County). 1781-1917. *913*

—. Criminal law. Social Work. Violence. 1970-73. *2673*

—. Custis family. Custis, Frances Parke. Virginia. Washington, Martha. ca 1670's-1750's. *501*

—. Daily Life. Frontier and Pioneer Life. 1770's-80's. *694*

—. Decisionmaking. Ontario (Toronto). Sex, group. Wives. 1967-72. *3280*

—. Demography. Divorce. Pregnancy. Utah (Salt Lake County, Utah County). 1939-51. *188*

—. Demography. Employment. Occupational dissatisfaction. Social change. 1945-72. *1898*

—. DeMun, Isabelle. DeMun, Jules. Family. Missouri. ca 1800-30's. *665*

—. Disciples of Christ. Family. Religion. Social Classes. Tennessee (Nashville). 1943-64. *2068*

—. Discrimination. Elections. Federal Government. Public office. 1960's. *2305*

—. Discrimination, Employment. Sex roles. 1972. *1826*

—. Divorce. Graduate education. Student roles. 1969-72. *2796*

—. Dowries. Family. Land. Massachusetts (Barnstable County). Peasants. Values. 1620's-1720's. *520*

—. Dutch. Family. New York (Albany). Politics. 1683-1809. *507*

—. Econometrics. Employment (participation rates). 1966-67. *1853*

—. Economic Conditions. Education. 1968. *1823*

—. Economic Conditions. Fertility. Rhode Island (Warren). Sex ratios. Social Conditions. ca 1840-60. *670*

—. Economic Conditions. Lincoln, Joseph C. (writings). Massachusetts (Cape Cod). 1880-1900. *1159*

—. Economic Conditions. Lincoln, Mary Todd. Travel. 1818-82. *94*

—. Education. Employment. Family. Mormons. 1968-71. *2481*

—. Education. Engineering graduates. Fertility. Occupational mobility. 1960's. *2142*

—. Education. Family life. Jews. 1970's. *2511*

—. Education. Feminism. Social Status. Values. 1925-65. *100*

—. Education. Nurses and Nursing. Occupations. Social Status. Wisconsin. 1957-64. *225*

—. Education. Physical appearance. Social Classes. 1920's-60's. *1140*

—. Education. Social Organization. 1960-67. *2125*

—. Employment. Income. 1960-70. *1874*

—. Employment. Labor supply. Negroes. Wages. 1947-67. *1902*

—. Employment. Maternity. Population planning. Socialization. 1973-. *2052*

—. Employment. Mothers. 1960-70. *1857*

—. Employment. Randolph, Mary. Virginia. 1768-1828. *3048*

—. Employment. Social work. 1967-72. *1851*

—. Employment. Wives. 1969. *1899*

—. Eppes, Elizabeth. Eppington (plantation). Jefferson, Mary. Virginia (Chesterfield County). 1778-1804. *3084*

—. Ethnicity. Fertility. Massachusetts (Boston; South, South End). Occupations. 1880. *1452*

—. Eugenics (Stirpiculture). New York. Oneida community. Utopias. 1848-1940's. *282*

—. Family. Folk Medicine. Tabor, Mary Edmunds Tabor. Louisiana (Shiloh). 1840's-1926. *3127*

—. Family. Geographic Mobility. Occupations (choice of). 1960's. *1905*

—. Family. Hoover, Herbert C. Hoover, Lou Henry. Politics. Travel. 1899-1928. *1251*

—. Family. Illinois (Chicago, Pullman). Pullman, George Mortimer (letters). Pullman, Harriet Amelia Sanger (diary). 1867-90's. *1163*

—. Family. Lewis and Clark expedition. Sacagawea (Shoshoni). 1803-84. *907*

—. Family. Louisiana (Minden). Perryman, Melvill Lucile Martin. Plantation life. 1876-1975. *3097*

—. Family. Lutheran Church. Parsonage. 1974. *2477*

—. Family. Middle Classes. Sex education. Values. ca 1850-1900. *1141*

—. Family. Negroes. 1960's. *2532*

—. Family. *Pennsylvania Magazine* (periodical). Witherspoon, John. 1775-76. *504*

—. Family. Rhode Island (Bristol). Social Customs. Vital Statistics. 17c-18c. *502*

—. Family life. Negroes. Pennsylvania. 18c. *585*

—. Family life. Slavery. 1800-60. *946*

—. Family size. Friends, Society of. 18c. *523*

—. Family structure. Mormons. Sex. 1940-72. *2480*

—. Family structure. Periodicals (content analysis). Sexual behavior. Values. 18c. *511*

—. Family structure. Social Conditions. 1960's-. *2078*

—. Fiction. Mormons (images of). Sex. Stereotypes. 19c. *302*

—. Fort Yukon. Hudson's Bay Company. Murray, Alexander Hunter. Murray, Anne Cambell. 1846-65. *3255*

—. Friends, Society of. Pennsylvania (Lycoming, Northumberland, and Columbia Counties). Vital Statistics. 1796-1860. *2933*

—. Frontier. Michigan (Grand Rapids, Grand Haven). Pennoyer, Aletta Teeple Rellington (autobiography). 1829-68. *3037*

—. Genealogy. Gerard, Anne. Gerard, Jane. Gerard, Judith. Gerard, Thomas (daughters). Maryland (St. Mary's County). 1650-76. *519*

—. Griffin, Cyrus. Stuart, Lady Christina. Virginia. 1741-1807. *3053*

—. Hawthorne, Nathaniel. Hawthorne, Sophia Peabody. ca 1825-50. *2958*

—. Image. Lawrence, D. H. Literature. Suckow, Ruth. 1920's-30's. *1667*

—. Images. Novels. Wharton, Edith. 1905-37. *1591*

—. Immigrants. Nagorka, Felicia Pawlowski. New York (Schenectady). Polish Americans. Religion. ca 1902-18. *1499*

—. Iowa. Iowa Wesleyan University. Lincoln, Jessie Harlan. 1875-1911. *3013*

—. Iowa. Newspapers. 1830-70. *671*

—. Jones, Mary. New York City. Newspapers. Trobriand, Régis de (career). 1840-65. *2960*

—. Law. Property. Quebec. Wives. 1960's. *3330*

—. Law. Property. Wives. 1950's-60's. *2342*

—. Law. Property rights. Quebec. Wives. 1964. *3333*

—. Lincoln, Abraham (administration). Lincoln, Mary Todd. Todd family (influence). 1842-60's. *769*

—. Lind, Jenny. Opera. Tours (national). 1850-52. *1029*

—. Literature. Phelps, Elizabeth Stuart. Religion. Sex roles. ca 1820's-90's. *466*

—. Massachusetts (Woburn). Widowhood. 1701-10. *509*

—. Mencken, Adah Isaacs. Pennsylvania (Pittsburgh). Theater. 1859-62. *1031*

—. Michigan (Detroit). Negroes. Sex roles. Whites. Working Class. 1960's. *2035*

—. Middle Classes. Spouse swapping. 1960's-72. *2236*

—. Moravians. North Carolina (Salem). Sexual behavior. Social Customs. Theocracy. 1772-1860. *884*

—. New France. Social Classes. 1729-48. *3351*

—. Owen, Robert Dale. Social Organization. Utopias. Wright, Frances. 1826-32. *863*

—. Plantations. Religion. Slaves. South. ca 1750's-1860. *950*

—. Pregnancy. Public Schools. 1940-60's. *2775*

—. Radicals and Radicalism. Sex. 19c. *240*

—. Religious mobility. 1955. *2458*

—. Sex (extramarital). 1960's. *2223*

—. Sex role preferences. 1966-68. *2090*

—. Social Classes. 1960's. *2112*

—. Social Customs. Prehistory-20c. *189*

Marriage age. Models (Hernes'). 1891-1945. *1155*

Marriage, common law. Canada. Fur trade. Indian-White Relations. 18c-1932. *3322*

—. North Carolina. 17c-19c. *291*

Marriage (customs). Courtship. Manitoba. Mennonites. Sommerfield Mennonite Church. 1890-1960's. *3378*

—. Family. Quebec (St. Paul River). Religion. Sex distribution. 1960's. *3332*

Marriage (instability of). Idaho. Juvenile Delinquency. Nez Percé Indians. Sex roles. Social Change. 1960's. *2593*

Marriage (interethnic). Ethnic Groups. Immigrants. Ontario (Ontario City). 1968-69. *3298*

Marriage (interracial). Asians. Social Classes. 1965-66. *2083*

—. California (Fresno). Ethnic boundaries. Japanese Americans. 1960-73. *2636*

—. Children. Intelligence. Mothers. 1960's. *2665*

—. Divorce. Iowa. 1940-70. *2104*

—. Japanese Americans. 1960-73. *2630*

—. Race relations. South. Travel accounts (British). ca 1865-1914. *1515*

Marriage, motivations for. Family (changes in). Periodicals (content analysis). Power patterns. Romantic love. Sexual behavior. 1825-50. *662*

Marriage notices. Louisiana. *New Orleans Christian Advocate* (weekly). Obituaries. 1854-55. *640*

—. Louisiana. *New Orleans Christian Advocate* (weekly). Obituaries. 1851-55. *641*

—. Louisiana. *New Orleans Christian Advocate* (weekly). Obituaries. 1855. *642*

—. Obituaries. *Pioneer and Yorkville Weekly Advertiser* (newspaper). South Carolina. 1823-24. *651*

—. Obituaries. South Carolina. *Yorkville Compiler* (newspaper). 1840-41. *653*

—. Obituaries. South Carolina. *Yorkville Encyclopedia* (newspaper). 1825-26. *652*

—. Obituaries. South Carolina (Charleston). 1827. *637*

Marriage, open. American University. Attitudes. District of Columbia. Students. 1945-73. *2276*

Marriage partners, selection of. Children. Parents. Virginia. 17c-18c. *516*

—. Models. Residential propinquity. Washington (Seattle). 1960's. *2079*

—. Negroes. Occupational mobility. Skin color. Social Status. 1971. *2579*

Marriage patterns. Aged. Connecticut (Wethersfield). Dower rights. Economic conditions. Sex roles. Widows. 1640-1700. *489*

—. Indians. Social organization. Prehistory-1971. *356*

Marriage plans (alleged). Hewitt, Catherine. Reynolds, John (family). 1863-70. *646*

Marriage records. Baptists. Maryland (Baltimore). Richards, Lewis. 1784-89. *668*

Marriage registers. Family. Freedmen. Reconstruction. 1865-68. *1462*

Marriage (review article). Fitzgerald, Zelda Sayre. Roosevelt, Eleanor. ca 1910's-45. *1156*

Marriage trends. Canada. Economic Conditions. Sex ratios. USA. 1830-1970. *197*

Married couples, separation of. Family (female headed). Housing. Public welfare. Puerto Rico. 1950-60. *2026*

Marshall, Emma. Longfellow, Henry Wadsworth (letters). 1851-76. *1023*

Marshall, John (letters). Ambler, Polly. Courtship. Marriage. 1780-1835. *631*

Marshall University. Teacher Training. West Virginia (Huntington). 1867-1900. *1582*

Martin, Maria. Audubon, John James. Painting (watercolors). South Carolina. 19c. *3054*

Martineau, Harriet. Economic philosophies. Fiction. Rand, Ayn. 1832-1973. *144*

Marxism *See also* Anarchism and Anarchists; Communism; Socialism.

—. Attitudes. Ideology. Political Theory. Sexual conflict. 1970's. *2198*

—. Capitalism. Feminism. 1100-1974. *284*

—. Feminism. 1848-1970's. *295*

—. Feminism. Functionalism. Production and reproduction (dialectics of). Social classes. 1976. *2036*

—. Greer, Germaine *(The Female Eunuch)*. Ideology. Patriarchy. Sex (frigidity). 1960's-70's. *2432*

Mary Prance (fictional character). James, Henry *(The Bostonians, 1886)*. Suffrage. Walker, Mary. 1886. *1679*

*Mary Tyler Moore Show.* Situation comedy. Television. Values. 1970-74. *2772*

Maryland *See also* Southeastern States.

—. Adultery. Divorce. Sewell, Eve. State Legislatures. 1638-1851. *252*

—. Church of England. Marriage. Morals, regulation of. Sexual behavior. 1690-1775. *490*

—. Friends, Society of. Harris, Elizabeth. Missions and Missionaries. 1656-62. *573*

—. Friends, Society of. Lynam, John. Lynam, Margaret Ridge. Pennsylvania. Persecution. 1660's-90's. *572*

—. Mental Illness. Negroes. Sex differences. Whites. 1960's. *2712*

—. Prisons. 1973. *2680*

—. Slaves, fugitive. Tubman, Harriet. Underground railroad. ca 1830-60. *938*

Maryland (Baltimore). Alcoholism. Working Class. 1973. *2662*

—. Attitudes. Negroes. Public Welfare. Whites. 1964. *2651*

—. Baptists. Marriage records. Richards, Lewis. 1784-89. *668*

—. Caton, Elizabeth. Caton, Louisa Catherine. Caton, Mary. Caton, Mary Ann. Historical Sites and Parks. 19c-20c. *422*

Maryland (Frederick). Fritchie, Barbara. Genealogy. Germans. Hauer family. Immigration. 1733-1834. *3066*

Maryland (Montgomery County). Country Life. Fairfield (family home). Iddings, Deborah Alice. Iddings, Fanny Pierce (reminiscences). Moravian Female Seminary. Pierce, Ann. Pierce, Sophia Kummer. 1728-1968. *3075*

Maryland (Somerset Parish). Church of England. Genealogy. Harrison, Lucy H. Parish records. 1692-1805. *304*

Maryland (St. Mary's County). Genealogy. Gerard, Anne. Gerard, Jane. Gerard, Judith. Gerard, Thomas (daughters). Marriage. 1650-76. *519*

Masculinity (concept of). Artists. Femininity (concept of). 1974. *2915*

Masculinity (ideal of). Family structure. Sex roles. Violence. 1960's. *2203*

Mason, Abigail. Letters. Plantations. Slavery. Social Conditions. Virginia. 1830's. *3065*

Mass Media *See also* Films; Newspapers; Television.

—. Employment. Library science. Sex Discrimination. Stereotypes. 1950-75. *1967*

—. Farms. Wisconsin. 1960's. *2747*

—. Pornography. Sexual behavior. Social control. 1960's-70's. *2716*

—. Sex. 1960's. *2769*

—. Sex. Violence. Youth. 1960's. *2656*

Massachusetts *See also* New England; Northeastern or North Atlantic States.

—. Abolition Movement. Connecticut (Canterbury). Crandall, Prudence. Feminism. May, Samuel J. 1832-61. *840*

—. Abolition Movement. Feminism. Grimké, Angelina. Grimké, Sarah. 1837-38. *839*

—. Age. Children. Family life cycles. Marriage. 1830-1920. *130*

—. Alcott, Bronson. Family structure. Fruitlands community. Lane, Charles. Social reform. Utopias. 1840-50. *862*

—. American Revolution. Loyalists. Oliver, Anne. Oliver family. Political Leadership. 1632-1860. *536*

—. Birth Control. Civil Rights. Connecticut. Law. 19c. *1205*

—. Borden family. Connecticut. Gay, Joanna Bordon (and family). 1635-91. *2936*

—. Catholic Church. Suffrage. ca 1870-1920. *1340*

—. Coeducation. Marblehead Academy. 1788-1865. *978*

—. Cooke, Hester Mahieu. Pilgrims. Plymouth Colony. 1623-75. *2997*

—. Dall, Caroline Healy (biography). Feminism. 1822-1912. *2977*

—. Divorce. Law. Puritans. Social conditions. 1639-92. *521*

—. Heath, Susanna (Sukey). Manuscript tune collections. Music. 1782. *607*

—. Letters. Salisbury, Harriet Hutchinson. Travel. Vermont. 1843-46. *2946*

—. Suffrage. 1895. *1341*

Massachusetts (Andover). Economic Conditions. Family. Greven, Philip J., Jr. (review article). Social Change. 17c-18c. *518*

—. Family structure. Social Conditions. 17c. *505*

Massachusetts (Barnstable County). Dowries. Family. Land. Marriage. Peasants. Values. 1620's-1720's. *520*

Massachusetts Bay Colony. Antinomian controversy. Hutchinson, Anne. Political Protest. 1630-43. *541*

—. Antinomians. Cotton, John. Hutchinson, Anne. Politics. Puritans. Theology. 1630's. *537*

—. Bradstreet, Anne. Poetry. Puritans. Sex roles. 17c. *613*

—. Dyer, Mary. Hutchinson, Anne. Politics. Sex roles. Theology. Trials. 1636-43. *540*

—. Friends, Society of. Persecution (religious). Southwick family. 1639-61. *575*

Massachusetts (Boston). Adams, William T. ("Oliver Optic"). Alcott, Louisa May *(Eight Cousins)*. Alger, Horatio, Jr. Literature (children's). Morality. 1867-99. *1642*

—. Antinomian Controversy. Clergy. Cotton, John. Hutchinson, Anne. Puritans. Theology. 1636. *581*

—. Antinomian controversy. Hutchinson, Anne. Puritans. Trials. 1634-38. *543*

—. Avery, Martha Moore. Catholic Church. Social Reform. ca 1880's-1929. *1210*

—. Business. Knight, Sarah Kemble. Teachers. Travel. 1704-27. *482*

—. Christian Science. Eddy, Mary Baker. Quimby, Phineas Parkhurst. 1821-1910. *1417*

—. Cunningham, Sarah Apthorp Morton. Letters. Politics. Social Conditions. 1825. *2996*

—. Dramatists. Murray, Judith Sargent Stevens *(The Medium, or Happy Tea Party)*. Theater. Tyler, Royall. 1795. *1038*

—. Dyer, Mary. Friends, Society of. Persecution. Puritans. Religious Liberty. 1635-57. *580*

—. Dyer, Mary. Hutchinson, Anne. Persecution. Puritans. Religious Liberty. 1635-51. *579*

—. Economic Conditions. Elites. Family. Social Change. Values. 1800-60. *658*

—. Family structure. Historiography. 19c. *205*

—. Fuller, Margaret. Healey, Caroline. Sex roles. Social Reform. 19c. *654*

—. German philosophers (influence of). Language. Peabody, Elizabeth Palmer. Philosophy. ca 1830's-40's. *971*

—. Kindergarten. Peabody, Elizabeth Palmer. Shaw, Pauline Agassiz. Social Reform. 1870-1915. *1574*

—. Museum of Fine Arts (acquisitions). Needlework (embroidery). New England. 17c-18c. 1960's. *614*

—. Negroes. Poets. Race consciousness. Wheatley, Phillis. 1753-84. *590*

—. Social services. Women's Educational and Industrial Union. 1880-1960's. *2934*

Massachusetts (Boston, Cambridge). Appleton, Fanny. Courtship. Longfellow, Henry Wadsworth. 1841-43. *1001*

Massachusetts (Boston, Marblehead). American Revolution. Frankland, Charles Henry. Loyalists. Marriage. Social Customs. Surriage, Agnes. 1742-83. *494*

Massachusetts (Boston; South, South End). Ethnicity. Fertility. Marriage. Occupations. 1880. *1452*

Massachusetts (Cambridge). Abolition Movement. Authors. Farrar, Eliza. Follen, Eliza. Harvard University. Literature (children's). 19c. *1022*

—. Coeducation. Harvard University. Radcliffe College. 1960's. *2811*

Massachusetts (Cape Cod). Economic Conditions. Lincoln, Joseph C. (writings). Marriage. 1880-1900. *1159*

Massachusetts (Charlestown). Cartoons and Caricatures. Catholic Church. Convent (burning of). Johnston, David Claypool. 1834. *880*

Massachusetts (Clinton). Textile workers. Vermont. Working Conditions. 1851. *617*

Massachusetts (Cohasset). Collier, Frances Osgood. 1862-1965. *2953*

Massachusetts (Concord). Alcott, Abigail May (biography). 1800-77. *2963*

—. Emerson, Ralph Waldo. Fuller, Margaret (journal). 1836-42. *1016*

Massachusetts (Deerfield). Children. Indians (captivities). Marriage. Quebec (Caughnawaga). Williams, Eunice. 1704-80's. *366*

Massachusetts (Essex County). Folklore. Newspapers. Witchcraft, legends of. 1812-60. *966*

Massachusetts General Hospital. Cannon, Ida M. Medicine (practice of). Social work. 1877-1960. *1053*

Massachusetts (Hamilton). Authors. Dodge, Mary Abigail. Feminism. Journalism. 1833-96. *457*

Massachusetts (Haverhill). Dustin, Hannah. Frontier. Indians (captivities). Iroquois Indians. Neff, Mary. 1697. *597*

—. Dustin, Hannah. Indians (captivities). 1697. *603*

—. Dustin, Hannah. Indians (captivities). Murder. 1697. *601*

—. Dustin, Hannah. Indians (captivities). Murder. Neff, Mary. New Hampshire (Penacook Island). 1697. *596*

Massachusetts (Lowell). Architecture. Boardinghouses. Factory girls. Home, image of. 1820-70. *643*

—. Attitudes. Robinson, Harriet Hanson (letters). Textile workers. Working Class. 1845-46. *629*

—. Boston Manufacturing Company. Textile workers. Working Conditions. 1813-50. *630*

—. Economic Conditions. Immigrants. Social Change. Textile workers. Westward movement. Working Conditions. 1834-98. *1040*

—. Ethnic Groups. Social Conditions. Textile Industry. Working Conditions. 1833-57. *628*

—. Folk songs. Textile Industry. Working Conditions. 1840's. *1037*

Massachusetts (Lynn). Family. Poverty. Working Class. 1915-40. *1151*

Massachusetts (Marblehead). Canibas Indians (murder of). King Philip's War. Roules, Robert (court deposition). 1677. *595*

—. Church and State. Saloons (grogshop). Wives. 1640-73. *492*

Massachusetts (Milford). Ballou, Adin Augustus. Feminism. Hopedale Community. Utopias. 1824-56. *861*

Massachusetts Regiment, 4th. American Revolution (biography). Military Service. Sampson, Deborah. 1775-1800. *560*

Massachusetts (Salem). Antislavery lecturer. Great Britain. Negroes. Remond, Sara Parker. 1856-87. *890*

—. Behavior. Historiography. Psychology. Puritanism. Witchcraft (review article). 1692. *532*

—. Behavior. Historiography. Psychology. Witchcraft. 1691-92. *526*

—. Behavior. Tituba (Carib Indian). Trials. Witchcraft. 1692. *531*

—. Bibliographies. Witchcraft. 1692. *530*

—. Demography. Family. Statistics. 1620-1849. *244*

—. Domestic roles. Social Change. Wills. 1660-1770. *496*

—. Fiji. Voyages. Wallis, Mrs. Benjamin. 19c. *2962*

—. Historians. Racism. Tituba (Carib Indian). Witchcraft trials. 1648-1971. *344*

—. Historiography. Mather, Cotton. Theology. Witchcraft. 1692. *533*

—. Indians. Negroes (supposed). Petry, Ann *(Tituba of Salem Village)*. Tituba (Carib Indian). Witchcraft. 1692. 1974. *369*

—. Psychology. Witchcraft. 1691. *528*

Massachusetts (South Hadley). Letters. Mount Holyoke College. Nutting, Mary O. 1850-51. *2964*

—. Hotel, Motel, and Restaurant Employees' Union, Local 705. Labor. Wolfgang, Myra (interview). 1972. *2018*

—. Marriage. Negroes. Sex roles. Whites. Working Class. 1960's. *2035*

—. Mormons. Polygamy. Prisoners. 1880's. *1154*

Michigan (Grand Rapids, Grand Haven). Frontier. Marriage. Pennoyer, Aletta Teeple Rellingston (autobiography). 1829-68. *3037*

Michigan Infantry Regiment, 2nd. Civil War. Edmonds, Sarah Emma. 1860-65. *790*

Michigan (Kalamazoo). Cities. Crane, Caroline Bartlett. Progressivism. Reform. Sanitation (municipal). 1858-1935. *1383*

Michigan (Mackinac Island). American Fur Company. Fur Trade. LaFramboise, Madeline. 1806-46. *626*

Michigan (Marquis). High Schools. Negroes. Self concepts. Students. 1960's. *2565*

Michigan (southern). Children. Family structure. Immigrants. Migration, Internal. Social Change. Urbanization. 1850-80. *1149*

Michigan (southwestern). Resorts. Segregation. 1962. *2567*

Michigan (Ypsilanti). Childrearing. Mothers (disadvantaged). Negroes. Social Classes. 1960's. *2569*

Middle Classes. Abolitionism. Sexuality. Social Reform. 1830-65. *856*

—. Addams, Jane. Sex roles. Social Reform. Stereotypes. Wald, Lillian. 1870-1930. *1275*

—. Architecture. Family. Prairie house. Wright, Frank Lloyd. 1900-09. *1173*

—. Attitudes. Image. Novels. Social Conditions. Women's history. 19c. *6*

—. Canada. Feminism. Ideology. Political Leadership. USA. 1960-75. *270*

—. Children (naming of). Family structure. 20c. *233*

—. Family. Marriage. Sex education. Values. ca 1850-1900. *1141*

—. Family (nuclear). Illinois (Chicago). Violence. 1900-70. *241*

—. Family relationships. North Carolina (Greensboro). Occupational mobility. 1960's. *2067*

—. Family structure. Parent-child relations. Sex roles. Social change. 1970's. *2072*

—. Feminist movement. Filene, Peter Gabriel (review article). Sex roles. 1890's-1970's. 1974. *215*

—. Fiction, gothic. Sex roles. Social Conditions. 1953-70. *2881*

—. Image. Loos, Anita *(Gentlemen Prefer Blondes)*. Satire. Sex roles. Values. 1925. *1606*

—. Marriage. Spouse swapping. 1960's-72. *2236*

—. Sex roles. Social norms. Textbooks, Marriage and family. 1960's-70's. *2211*

Middle East. Missions and Missionaries. Protestantism. Schools. 1810-1970's. *328*

Middleton, Harriott. Civil War. Duncan, Mrs. Henry. Letters. Middleton, Susan. Social Conditions. South or Southern States. 1863-65. *800*

—. Civil War. Letters. Middleton, Susan. Social Conditions. South or Southern States. 1861-65. *799*

—. Civil War. Letters. Middleton, Susan. South or Southern States. 1861-65. *801*

Middleton, Susan. Civil War. Duncan, Mrs. Henry. Letters. Middleton, Harriott. Social Conditions. South or Southern States. 1863-65. *800*

—. Civil War. Letters. Middleton, Harriott. Social Conditions. South or Southern States. 1861-65. *799*

—. Civil War. Letters. Middleton, Harriott. South or Southern States. 1861-65. *801*

Midwives. Arkansas. Medicine (practice of). ca 1930-74. *198*

—. Greeks. Immigration. Mageras, Georgia Lathouris. Utah (Magna area). 1902-50. *1095*

—. Gynecology. Obstetrics. Physicians. Sex Discrimination. 1760-1860. *930*

—. Halvorsen, Helen Olson (reminiscences). Motherhood. 19c. *1528*

—. Medicine. Obstetricians. 1910-19. *1086*

—. Northeastern or North Atlantic States. Whitmore, Elizabeth. 1727-1814. *488*

Migrant Labor. California. Lange, Dorothea. Photography. Rural rehabilitation. 1930's. *1257*

Migration *See also* Emigration; Immigration; Refugees.

—. Census statistics. Childbirth. Fertility. Puerto Ricans. 1965-70. *2634*

Migration, Internal *See also* Geographic Mobility.

—. Authors. Culture. Hurston, Zora Neale. Negroes. Toomer, Jean. 1860-1960. *336*

—. Bond, Mary Bell "Molly". Diaries. Northwest Territories. Ontario. 1904. *3366*

—. Children. Family structure. Immigrants. Michigan (southern). Social Change. Urbanization. 1850-80. *1149*

—. Daily Life. Eubank, Mary James (travel diary). Frontier and Pioneer Life. Kentucky. Texas. 1853. *715*

—. Demography. Economic Conditions. Fertility. Social Conditions. 20c. *127*

—. Discrimination. Indiana (Indianapolis). Negroes. Occupations. 1960-70. *2529*

—. Economic Conditions. Indians (reservations). Papago Indians. *2601*

—. Education. Regionalism. Sex differences. 1940-65. *2830*

—. Employment. Family. Farmers. Social Conditions. 1956-61. *2101*

—. Employment. Population trends. South or Southern States. 1950's-60's. *3046*

—. Family (kinship groupings). Rural-Urban Studies. Social Classes. Voluntary Associations. 1960's. *2048*

—. Fertility. Marital status. Rural-Urban Studies. 1967. *2145*

—. Fertility. Mormon families. Social Conditions. ca 1960-74. *2489*

—. Fertility. Whites. 1955-60. *2138*

—. Freedmen. Kansas. Politics. Race Relations. Rape. 1878-80. *1467*

—. Population distribution. Quebec. Rural-Urban Studies. Sex ratios. 1951-61. *3353*

Milanés, Federico (letters). America (impressions of). Milanés, José Jacinto (letters). Social Conditions. Travel. 1848-49. *644*

Milanés, José Jacinto (letters). America (impressions of). Milanés, Federico (letters). Social Conditions. Travel. 1848-49. *644*

Miles, Emma Bell. Art. Marriage. Poverty. Tennessee. 1880-1919. *1777*

Miles, Lizzie. Music (blues). Negroes. 20c. *2888*

Milford, Nancy. Feminism. Hardwick, Elizabeth. Jong, Erica. Literature. Showalter, Elaine. 1975. *2859*

Militancy, attitudinal. Labor Unions and Organizations. Nurses and Nursing. Teachers. ca 1970-74. *2008*

Military *See also* headings beginning with the words military and paramilitary; War.

—. 1970's-80's. *2452*

—. Argus Patrol. Canada. Wives. 1960's. *3278*

—. Camp followers. Courts Martial and Courts of Inquiry. Prostitution. World War I. 1917-18. *1293*

—. Civil rights. Sex Discrimination. 1976. *2456*

Military affairs. ca 10c-1964. *274*

Military Bases. *See* names of military bases, e.g. Travis Air Force Base.

Military Camps and Forts. *See* names of military camps and forts, e.g. Fort Apache.

Military Education. *See* names of service academies, e.g. US Military Academy, West Point, etc.

Military Intelligence. American Revolution. Frontier and Pioneer Life. 1770's. *567*

—. Civil War. Confederate Army. Sheridan, Philip H. Virginia (Shenandoah Valley; Winchester). Wright, Rebecca. 1864. *786*

Military Medicine. California (San Francisco Bay area). Music. Voluntary Associations. World War II. 1943-45. *1302*

Military service. 1900-73. *133*

—. 1775-1975. *275*

—. Air Forces. Women in the Air Force. 1942-60's. *2454*

—. American Revolution. Marriage. Sampson, Deborah. 1781-1827. *565*

—. American Revolution (biography). Corbin, Margaret ("Molly"). ca 1776-1800. *561*

—. American Revolution (biography). Massachusetts Regiment, 4th. Sampson, Deborah. 1775-1800. *560*

—. National service program (proposed). 1971. *2325*

—. NATO. 1970's. *2453*

—. Sex Discrimination. 1960's-70's. *2451*

Military Service (combat). Air Forces. 1948-77. *2457*

Military Service (noncombat). Air Forces. Women's Air Force Service Pilots. World War II. 1941-44. *1299*

Millay, Edna St. Vincent (papers). Library of Congress, Manuscript Division. Manuscripts. 1960's. *93*

Millett, Kate. 1960's-74. *2861*

—. Authors. Ellman, Mary. Feminism. ca 1950's-70. *2420*

—. Feminism. Lawrence, D. H. Literary Criticism. 20c. *2864*

Milwaukee Female College. Christianity. Conversion. Mortimer, Mary. Wisconsin. 1837-77. *3029*

Milwaukee-Downer Seminary and College. Education. Friend, Neita Oviatt (reminiscences). Sabin, Ellen. Wisconsin. 1905-09. *1569*

Mindan Female College. Elementary Education. Louisiana (Vernon). Smith, Anna Calhoun. Teachers. 1885-1901. *1089*

Miner, Myrtilla. District of Columbia. Education. Miner School for Negro Girls. Negroes. Spiritualism. 1851-64. *893*

Miner School for Negro Girls. District of Columbia. Education. Miner, Myrtilla. Negroes. Spiritualism. 1851-64. *893*

Miners (resettlement of). National Industrial Recovery Act (1933). New Deal. Roosevelt, Eleanor. Subsistence Homesteads Program. West Virginia (Arthurdale). 1930-46. *1213*

Mines. Illinois (Mount Olive). Jones, Mary Harris. Labor Unions and Organizations. Union Miners Cemetary. ca 1890's-1936. *1123*

Mini-Aku (Sioux). Fort Laramie. Indian legends. Sioux Indians. Spotted Tail (Sioux). Wyoming. 1866. *1477*

Minimum wage. Employment. Income distribution. Poverty. 1972-73. *1871*

Minimum wage movement. Dewson, Mary Williams. Labor Law. Social Reform. 1897-1962. *1047*

—. Legislation. New York State Factory Investigating Commission. Triangle Shirtwaist Company. 1911-38. *1045*

Mining camps. Boardinghouses. Colorado (southern). Piedmontese. 1890's. *1112*

Mining experts. Alaska (Dawson). Arizona (Tombstone). Business. Cashman, Nellie. 1851-1925. *1098*

Mining towns. Camping. Colorado. Rocky Mountains. Schenck, Annie B. (journal). 1871. *3189*

—. Dance halls. Frontier and Pioneer Life. Montana. Prostitution. Social Reform. ca 1870's-1910's. *1537*

—. Europe. Nevada, Emma. Opera. 19c-20c. *1779*

—. Hutton, May Arkwright. Idaho. Philanthropy. Politics. Washington (Spokane). ca 1870's-1920. *3218*

Ministers. *See* Clergy.

Minnesota *See also* North Central States.

—. Child Welfare Commission. Children's Codes. Hospitals (maternity). 1913-19. *1530*

—. Finnish Americans. Maternity care. Savusauna. 1867-1937. *1495*

—. Medical Reform. Ripley, Martha G. Social Reform. 19c. *3034*

—. National Woman Suffrage Association. New York (Seneca Falls convention). Suffrage. 1848-1920. *1382*

Minnesota Federation of Women's Clubs. Congress. Conservation groups. Federal government. Forests and Forestry. Legislation. Minnesota National Forest. Organizations. 1898-1908. *1286*

Minnesota (Minirara Falls; Minneapolis). Folklore. Indians. 17c-1971. *426*

Minnesota National Forest. Congress. Conservation groups. Federal government. Forests and Forestry. Legislation. Minnesota Federation of Women's Clubs. Organizations. 1898-1908. *1286*

Minnesota, University of. Affirmative action. Colleges and Universities. 1968-74. *2001*

Minorities *See also* Discrimination; Ethnic Groups; Nationalism; Racism; Segregation.

—. Abortion. Adoption. Children. Economic Conditions. Whites. 1972. *2703*

—. Discrimination. Wages. 1949-60. *1951*

—. Fertility. Social Status. 1969. *2515*

—. Illinois (Chicago). Labor Unions and Organizations. Mt. Sinai Hospital. Roberts, Lillian (interview). 1950's. *2017*

Minority group status. Assimilation. Fertility. Negroes. Social Status. 1970. *2573*

Miss America pageant. Beauty contests. North Carolina (Wilson). Racism. 1970. *2750*

Miss Porter's School. Architecture. Connecticut (Farmington). Porter, Sarah. ca 1750-1850. *1033*

Missionaries of the Immaculate Conception. Catholic Church. Quebec. Religious Orders. Society of Foreign Missions of Quebec. 1902-70. *3304*

—. Birth Rate. Fertility. Mortality. Whites. 1850-1960's. *326*
—. Black liberation. Feminism. 1960's-70's. *2541*
—. Black liberation movement. Discrimination. Feminist movement. Social Classes. 1970. *2413*
—. Black magic cults. Louisiana (New Orleans). Music (jazz). Voodoo. 19c. *409*
—. Black Nationalism. Feminism. Trans-Africanism, concept of. 1970's. *2524*
—. Black Panther Party. Cleaver, Kathleen (interview). Feminism. 19c-20c. 1966-71. *2590*
—. Brooks, Gwendolyn. Poetry. 1930's-72. *440*
—. Brownmiller, Susan (review article). Men. Racism. Rape. 1975. *2672*
—. California (Contra Costa County). Folklore. Pregnancy. Whites. Wives tales. 1960's. *2263*
—. California (San Diego). Racism. Teachers. Walker, Mary Chase. 1866. *1470*
—. Career aspirations. Desegregation. Schools. Sex. Social Status. Youth. 1969. *2586*
—. Childbirth. Discrimination. Family breakdown. Illegitimacy. Sex roles. Social Problems. 18c-1972. *371*
—. Childbirth. Family structure. Illegitimacy. Income. 1960's. *2585*
—. Childlessness. Whites. 1906-70. *248*
—. Childrearing. Cultural deprivation. Educational opportunity. Mothers. 1960's. *2543*
—. Childrearing. Michigan (Ypsilanti). Mothers (disadvantaged). Social Classes. 1960's. *2569*
—. Children. Family structure. Political Socialization. 1973. *2526*
—. Children. Food consumption. Geophagy. Mississippi (Holmes County). Poverty. 1975. *2580*
—. Children (aspirations for). Mothers. Social Classes. 1960's. *2522*
—. Cities. Economic Conditions. Family. Mothers. 1960's. *2570*
—. Cities. Sexual identity. Social Psychology. Whites. 1968. *2166*
—. Cities (inner). Colleges and universities, white. Vocational Education. 1915-73. *1801*
—. City Life. Family. Human Relations. Illinois (Chicago). Social Conditions. Whites. Widows. 1968-72. *2056*
—. Civil Rights. Feminist movement. Inferiority, doctrine of. Matriarchy, myth of. 1960's-70's. *2550*
—. Civil rights. Truth, Sojourner. 1825-60. *900*
—. Civil rights laws. Employment. Income structure. Whites. 1960-70. *1821*
—. Civil rights movement. Employment. Family. Income. 1965. *2554*
—. Civil War. Family. Louisiana. Refugees. 1860-65. *898*
—. Coincoin (former slave). Family. Louisiana (Metoyer). Plantations. 1742-1850. *895*
—. Community work. Organizations. Racial pride. 1892-1932. *1465*
—. Conley, James. Frank, Leo (trial). Georgia (Atlanta). Jews. Murder. Press. 1913-15. *1522*
—. Connecticut (Canterbury). Crandall, Prudence. Law. Schools. 1830's. *892*
—. Connecticut (Kingston). Crandall, Prudence. Harris, Sarah (biography). Social Reform. 1781-1902. *902*
—. Consumers. Family. Student boycotts (effects). 1960's. *2564*
—. Cooley, Rossa B. Penn School. Social Conditions. South Carolina (St. Helena Island). 1901-30. *1468*
—. Cox, Minnie M. Mississippi (Indianola). Politics. Roosevelt, Theodore. 1903-04. *1463*
—. *Crisis* (periodical). DuBois, W. E. B. Suffrage. 1910-34. *1380*
—. Culture. Folklore. Hurston, Zora Neale. Novels. 1930's-60. *449*
—. Dance troupe. Theater. Whitman Sisters. 1903-43. *1781*
—. Davis, Angela (interview). 1970-71. *2587*
—. Day Nurseries. Mothers (working). New York City. 1960's. *2588*
—. Discrimination. Employment. Equal Employment Opportunity Commission. 1970. *2568*
—. Discrimination. Indiana (Indianapolis). Migration, Internal. Occupations. 1960-70. *2529*

—. Discrimination, Employment. High School of Fashion Industry. New York City. Puerto Ricans. Vocational Education. Whites. 1975. *1930*
—. Discrimination, Employment. Northeastern or North Atlantic States. Occupational structures. South or Southern States. 1940-60. *2559*
—. District of Columbia. Douglass, Anna Murry. Fisher, Ruth Anna. Terrell, Mary Church. 1830's-1975. *375*
—. District of Columbia. Education. Miner, Myrtilla. Miner School for Negro Girls. Spiritualism. 1851-64. *893*
—. District of Columbia. Folk songs. Molton, Flora. 1930's-70's. *3079*
—. Domestic responsibilities. Farmers. Plantation system. 1600-1975. *317*
—. Du Bois, W. E. B. Feminism. Human rights. 1910-20. *1454*
—. East Greenwich Neighborhood Cottage. Rhode Island (Scolloptown). Settlement house movement. 1902-14. *1406*
—. Economic Conditions. Family. Matriarchy, myth of. Prisons. Slavery. 17c-20c. *384*
—. Economic Conditions. Family life. Historiography. Slavery (review article). Social Conditions. 1850's-1970's. *389*
—. Economic Conditions. Feminism. Politics. 19c-20c. *330*
—. Economic Conditions. Feminist movement. Social Conditions. Whites. 1969. *2384*
—. Editors and Editing. Hope, Lugenia Burns (papers). ca 1890's-1930's. 1975. *1464*
—. Education. Koontz, Elizabeth Duncan. National Education Association. 20c. *2591*
—. Education. Occupational aspirations. Sex roles. Students (college). 1964-70. *2538*
—. Educational achievement. Sexes. 1940-70. *2533*
—. Educational aspirations. Rural Settlements. Texas (east central). Youth. 1960's. *2561*
—. Edwards, Lena F. Presidential Freedom Medal. Price, Leontyne. 1964. *2592*
—. Elections. Mississippi Woman Suffrage Association. National American Woman Suffrage Association. State Legislatures. Suffrage. 1890-1920. *1372*
—. Elective offices. 1973. *2523*
—. Emotion, perception of. Sexes. Whites. 1972. *2257*
—. Employment. Families, heads of. 1969-75. *2558*
—. Employment. Family. Mexican Americans. Southwest. Whites. Wives. 1950-70. *2512*
—. Employment. Housework. Industrialization. Sex discrimination. Wages. Whites. 1970. *1936*
—. Employment. Labor supply. Marriage. Wages. 1947-67. *1902*
—. Employment. Montana. Nevins, Tish. 1860's-20c. *1458*
—. Employment bureau. Ohio (Cincinnati). Vocational Education. Young Women's Christian Association. 1868-1968. *1195*
—. Employment (professional). Family. Social Status. 1967-72. *2534*
—. Equal rights. Sexual separatism. 1970's. *2548*
—. Family. 1960's. *2577*
—. Family. Grandmothers (role of). Social Status. 19c-20c. *359*
—. Family. Historiography. Methodology. 17c-20c. *360*
—. Family. Johnson, Lyndon B. Politics. 1960's. *2555*
—. Family. Marriage. 1960's. *2532*
—. Family. Matriarchy. Michigan (Detroit). Social Classes. 1960's. *2572*
—. Family. Missouri (St. Louis). Pruitt-Igoe housing project. Public Housing. 1960's. *2553*
—. Family. Poor. Sex. Social Classes. Whites. 1960's. *2044*
—. Family life. Marriage. Pennsylvania. 18c. *585*
—. Family (male-, female-headed). Poverty. Social Conditions. 1972. *2556*
—. Family planning. Federal Government. Poverty. 1960's. *2571*
—. Family size preferences. Florida. Georgia. Whites. Youth. 1969. *2275*
—. Family stability. 17c-20c. *309*
—. Family stability. Whites. 1890's-1970's. *195*
—. Family structure. Sex ratios. 1940-70. *2545*
—. Female Protective Society. Organizations (mutual aid). 18c-1960's. *331*
—. Feminism. 1973. *2551*

—. Feminism. Literature. Stowe, Harriet Beecher. Truth, Sojourner. 1850's-90's. *280*
—. Feminism. Newspapers. Police. Suffrage. 19c-20c. *283*
—. Ferguson, Catherine. New York City. Religious Education (Sunday school). Slavery. 1779-1854. *894*
—. Fertility. 1830-50. *903*
—. Fertility. Growth of American Families study. Rural-Urban Studies. South. Survey of Economic Opportunity. Whites. 1960. 1967. *2146*
—. Fiction. Peterkin, Julia Mood. South or Southern States. 1920's. *1628*
—. Fiction. Reconstruction. Stowe, Harriet Beecher (*Uncle Tom's Cabin*, 1852). 1850-1900. *1705*
—. Fiction. Slavery. Stereotypes. Stowe, Harriet Beecher (*Uncle Tom's Cabin*, 1852). 1830's-50's. *954*
—. Florida (Dade County). Junior High Schools. Students (self-concepts). 1960's. *2562*
—. Folk Songs. Ledbetter, Huddie "Leadbelly". Louisiana. Love, Blanche (reminiscences). 1880's-1949. 1976. *1475*
—. Harlem Renaissance. Imes, Nella Larsen. Johnson, Georgia Douglas. Literature. 1920's. *1460*
—. Hawaii. Missions and Missionaries. Presbyterian Church. Stockton, Betsey. 1822-65. *888*
—. High Schools. Michigan (Marquis). Self concepts. Students. 1960's. *2565*
—. Higher Education. 1854-1960. *467*
—. Hopkins, Pauline Elizabeth. Poets. 1859-1930. *1471*
—. Housing. Poor. Public Welfare. Virginia (Norfolk). 1950's-60's. *2527*
—. Humor. Mabley, Moms. Satire. 1960's. *2519*
—. Illinois (Chicago). Organizations. World's Columbian Exposition (1893). 1893. *1466*
—. Income. Whites. 1949-59. *458*
—. Johnson, Lyndon B. Roosevelt, Eleanor. 1930's-70's. *296*
—. Journalism. Lynching. Tennessee (Memphis). Wells, Ida B. 1884-94. *1473*
—. Journalists. 1870's-20c. *1461*
—. *Julia* (program). Stereotypes. Television. 1960's-70's. *2582*
—. Karenga, Maulana Ron. Trials. 1971. *2539*
—. Kelley, Florence. NAACP. Social Reform. ca 1900-30. *1455*
—. Kellor, Francis A. Matthews, Victoria Earle. New York City. Ovington, Mary White. Progressivism. Social Reform. 1900-15. *1389*
—. Labor market. Occupations (diversification of). Stereotypes. 1890-1970. *346*
—. Leadership. Organizations. Racial attitudes. Suffrage. 19c. *1342*
—. Lee, Molly Huston. Librarians. North Carolina (Raleigh). Richard B. Harrison Library. 1930-75. *3072*
—. Literary Criticism. Vroman, Mary Elizabeth. 1963. *2535*
—. Little, Joanne. North Carolina (Wake County). Trials. 1975. *2547*
—. Louisiana (New Orleans). Political participation. Sex roles. 1969-70. *2566*
—. Marriage. Michigan (Detroit). Sex roles. Whites. Working Class. 1960's. *2035*
—. Marriage partners (selection of). Occupational mobility. Skin color. Social Status. 1971. *2579*
—. Maryland. Mental Illness. Sex differences. Whites. 1960's. *2712*
—. Massachusetts (Boston). Poets. Race consciousness. Wheatley, Phillis. 1753-84. *590*
—. Matriarchy (concept of). 1951-65. *2544*
—. Miles, Lizzie. Music (blues). 20c. *2888*
—. Mitchell, Lottie Pearl. National Association for the Advancement of Colored People. 1950's-74. *2578*
—. Mothers. New York City. Public Opinion (survey accuracy). Social Classes. 1960's. *2584*
—. National Association of Colored Women. Reform. Suffrage. Terrell, Mary Church. 1892-1954. *1459*
—. New York (Saratoga Springs). Prostitution. Sexual superstitions. 1964-65. *2589*
—. Occupational status. Unemployment. 1960's-70. *2575*
—. Poetry. Prince, Lucy Terry. Supreme Court. Vermont (Guilford). Williams College. 18c. *594*

Organizational structuring. New York City. Sex discrimination. Travel agency industry. 1974. *1893*

Organizations *See also* specific organizations by name and subjects subdivided by the word organizations; Societies.

—. Air Pollution. Missouri (St. Louis). Smoke abatement crusades. Wednesday Club. 1891-1924. *1194*

—. Ames, Marie. Catt, Carrie Chapman. Gellhorn, Edna. League of Women Voters. Missouri (St. Louis). 1919-29. *1277*

—. Another Mother for Peace Organization. Consumers. Defense industries. Letter-writing campaign. Pacifism. 1970. *2296*

—. Armory. Broom brigades. Donan, Peter. Fund raising. Missouri (St. Louis). 1880's. *1198*

—. Asher, Meta. Brandt, Mrs. Noah. California (San Francisco). Charities. Frank, Ray. Jaffa, Adele Solomons. Jews. Levinson, Amelia. Prag, Mary. Selling, Natalie. Wolf, Alice. Wolf, Emma. 1896. *1429*

—. Association of Southern Women for the Prevention of Lynching. Lynching. Negroes. South. 1930-42. *1276*

—. Behavior. Sociology. 1970's. *2051*

—. Carswell, G. Harrold. Political behavior. Supreme Court nominations. 1970. *2327*

—. Child Welfare. Children's Code Commission. Missouri. Social Reform. Suffrage. Woman's Christian Temperance Union. 1915-19. *1284*

—. Children (care of). Daughters of the American Revolution. Federal Government. League of Women Voters. Maternal care. Sheppard-Towner Act. 1920's. *1282*

—. Class consciousness. Feminism. International Federation of Working Women. Suffrage. Women's Trade Union League. 1890-1925. *1280*

—. Colleges and Universities. Feminism. Professions. 1960's-70. *2429*

—. Commission on the Status and Role of Women in the United Methodist Church. Feminism. Methodism. Missions and Missionaries. 1869-1974. *368*

—. Community work. Negroes. Racial pride. 1892-1932. *1465*

—. Congress. Conservation groups. Federal government. Forests and Forestry. Legislation. Minnesota Federation of Women's Clubs. Minnesota National Forest. 1898-1908. *1286*

—. Congress. Constitutional amendment (19th). Lobbying. Women's Joint Congressional Committee. 1920-29. *1281*

—. Constitutions, State (revision of). Illinois. League of Women Voters. 1967-70. *2298*

—. Consumers. Legislation. National Consumers' League. 1900-23. *1288*

—. Croly, Jane Cunningham (Jennie June). General Federation of Women's Clubs. Journalism. Press clubs. Sorosis. 19c. *1717*

—. Daughters of the American Revolution. Flags (State). Fluke, Mrs. George. Oklahoma. 1911-41. *1279*

—. Democracy. Political Speeches. Prohibition. 1920-34. *1393*

—. Education. Medicine. Missionary movement, overseas. 19c. *361*

—. Employment. Feminism. Sex roles. Social Conditions. 1960's. *2417*

—. Feminism. Historiography. Urbanization. 19c-1973. *30*

—. Feminism. Protestant Churches. Social Reform. South. Young Women's Christian Association. 1920's. *1307*

—. Feminism, social. Labor. Legislation. Progressivism. 1919-33. *1128*

—. Feminist movement. National Organization for Women. Politics. Racism. Suffrage. 20c. *294*

—. Germans. Immigration. Jews. Russians. 1880-1924. *1447*

—. Illinois (Chicago). Negroes. World's Columbian Exposition (1893). 1893. *1466*

—. Leadership. Negroes. Racial attitudes. Suffrage. 19c. *1342*

—. League of Women Voters. Politics. Reform. South or Southern States. Young Women's Christian Association. 1920's. *1285*

—. Pennsylvania (Philadelphia). Religion. Social Reform. 1870-1900. *1283*

—. Twentieth Century Club. Wyoming (Newcastle). ca 1890's-1909. *1287*

Organizations (benevolent societies). Feminism. Northeastern or North Atlantic States. Social Reform. 1800-30's. *648*

Organizations (identification with). Ethnic Groups. Religion. Sex. Social Classes. 1960's. *2468*

Organizations (joining). Canada. Demography. Sex roles. USA. 1960's. *190*

Organizations (memberships in). Frazer, Susan Carpenter. Patriotism. Pennsylvania (Lancaster County). 1852-1930. *2975*

Organizations (mutual aid). Female Protective Society. Negroes. 18c-1960's. *331*

Organizations (structures). Feminist movement. Political strategy. Reform. Social Change. 1961-72. *2404*

Orman, Nellie Martin. Colorado (Pueblo). Philanthropy. 1876-1918. *3159*

Orphanages. Civil War. Iowa. Wittenmyer, Annie. 1864-1949. *1507*

Orthodox Eastern Church, Russian. Arguello, Maria de la Concepcion. California. Catholic Church. Rezanov, Nikolai. 1806. *887*

Osborn, Sarah. Fish, Josiah. Political Leadership. Revivals. Rhode Island (Newport). 1714-67. *544*

Osgood, Frances Sargent. *Broadway Journal* (periodical). Poe, Edgar Allan. Poetry. 1840's. *1020*

*Out West* (periodical). Arizona. Hall, Sharlot Mabridth. Literature. Lummis, Charles F. 1870-1943. *1718*

Outdoor Life. *See* Camping; Country Life; Sports.

Outerbridge, Mary Ewing. Tennis. 1874-1971. *1791*

Outlaws. Billy the Kid. Folklore. Spiegelberg, Flora (recollections). 19c. *3166*

Overland Journeys to the Pacific. Brier, Juliet Wells. California (Death Valley). Family. Geographic Mobility. 1814-49. *2926*

—. California. Donner party. Reed, Virginia Elizabeth. 1846. *691*

—. California. Iowa (Howard County). Wagon train. Walker, Juliette Fish (travel account). 1862-71. *731*

—. Far Western States. Sex roles. Work roles. 1842-67. *699*

—. Henderson, Lucy Ann. Oregon Trail (Applegate Cutoff). 1846. *726*

—. Pioneers. Westward Movement. 19c. *712*

Ovington, Mary White. Kellor, Francis A. Matthews, Victoria Earle. Negroes. New York City. Progressivism. Social Reform. 1900-15. *1389*

Owen, Robert Dale. Birth control information. Foote, Edward Bliss. Hollick, Frederick. Medical profession. 19c. *256*

—. Marriage. Social Organization. Utopias. Wright, Frances. 1826-32. *863*

*Ozzie and Harriet* (program). Cultural influence. Nelson, Harriet (interview). Social change. Television. 1950's-66. *2756*

# P

Pace, Josephine (reminiscences). Utah (Kimberly). ca 1895-1908. *3230*

Pacific Mills. Employment. New Hampshire (Dover). Textile Industry. 1921. *1061*

Pacific Northwest. Duniway, Abigail Scott. Suffrage. 1870's-1915. *1365*

—. Employment. Lind, Anna M. (reminiscences). Logging camps. 1920-40. *1087*

—. Indians. Matriliny (origins of). Sex roles. Prehistory. *355*

—. Pioneers. West. 1803-1912. *693*

Pacifism *See also* Conscientious Objectors; Peace Movements.

—. Another Mother for Peace Organization. Consumers. Defense industries. Letter-writing campaign. Organizations. 1970. *2296*

—. Baez, Joan. Israel. Liberalism. 1975. *2913*

—. Conscientious objectors. Espionage Act (1917). North Dakota. O'Hare, Kate Richards. World War I. 1900-25. *1289*

Paine, Thomas. Feminism. Sex roles. Social Theory. Wollstonecraft, Mary. 18c. *538*

Painting. Abolition Movement. Literature. Stowe, Harriet Beecher. 1832-96. *113*

—. Alaska. Gordon, Jo. 1956-75. *2908*

—. British Columbia. Carr, Emily. Forests. Indian villages. 1904-45. *3319*

—. Canada. Fur trade. Hopkins, Frances Ann. 1860-79. *3312*

—. Canada, western. Carr, Emily. Indians. 1888-1972. *3313*

—. Cassatt, Mary. Pennsylvania (Allegheny City). 1844-1926. *1768*

—. Civil War. Clothing. New York (Syracuse). Redfield, Amy. 1860-65. *781*

—. Curry, John Steuart. Curry, Mrs. John Steuart (interview). Schuster, Mrs. Daniel Curry (interview). 1897-1946. *1786*

—. Daily life. Lindner, Anna. ca 1863-1914. *1788*

—. Dorman, Carrie. Natural History. South or Southern States. 1920's-50's. *3047*

—. Frankenthaler, Helen. Hartigan, Grace. Sculpture. Wilson, Jane. 1950's-60's. *2922*

—. New England. Woodbury, Marcia Oakes. 1878-1913. *1785*

—. New Mexico. O'Keefe, Georgia. 20c. *413*

—. New York City. Sekula, Sonia. 1950's-1963. *2895*

—. O'Keefe, Georgia. 1920's-70's. *2920*

—. Onderdonk, Eleanor Rogers. Texas. ca 1879-1964. *1787*

Painting (genre, narrative). Art history. Cultural change. Feminism. 19c. *450*

Painting (octopus ink). Alaska. Eskimo life. Tillion, Diana. 1939-75. *2909*

Painting (watercolors). Alaska, southeastern. Stonington, Nancy. 1965-75. *2911*

—. Audubon, John James. Martin, Maria. South Carolina. 19c. *3054*

—. Bridges, Fidelia. 1835-1923. *1778*

—. Missouri (Mill Creek Valley). Pflager, Dorothy Holloway. 1962. *2910*

Paintings. Alaska. Goodale, Ellen. 1943-75. *2889*

—. Country Life. Texas (Iredell). Williamson, Clara McDonald. 1890's-1930's. *1759*

—. Economic organization. Family. Sioux Indians (North Teton, Yankton). Social Customs. Tipi. 1864. *912*

—. Images. Summer School. 1885-1920. *1546*

Paiute Indians. California. Education. Indian-White Relations. Marriage. Social Reform. Winnemucca, Sarah (Paiute). 1840's-91. *1487*

—. Federal Government. Indian-White Relations. Winnemucca, Sarah (Paiute). 19c. *1488*

Palmer, Alice Freeman. Bryn Mawr College. Feminism. Sex roles. Thomas, M. Carey. Wellesley College. 1875-1918. *1585*

Palmer, Mamie. Anderson, Sherwood. Kit Brandon (fictional character). Novels. 1920's-30's. *1740*

Palmer, Phoebe. Feminism. Holiness Movement. Wesley, Susanna. 1732-1973. *327*

Panama City *Pilot* (newspaper). Community leadership. Editors and Editing. Florida. West, Lillian Carlisle. 1916-37. *1678*

Panama Pacific International Exposition. Field, Sara Bard. Suffrage. Tours (cross country). Wilson, Woodrow. 1915. *1333*

Pankhurst, Emmeline. Cities. Speeches, Addresses, etc. Suffrage. 1909-13. *1381*

Papago Indians. Birth Rate. Mortality. ca 1950's-70's. *2611*

—. Childbearing patterns. Family structure. Modernization. Social Conditions. 1875-1970. *382*

—. Economic Conditions. Indians (reservations). Migration, Internal. *2601*

—. Fertility. Modernization (impact of). Rural-Urban Studies. 1960's-70's. *2612*

Paper Industry. Dubuc family papers. Quebec (Saguenay River, Lake St. John). 1892-1963. *3337*

Parent education. Behavioral science. Child care. 1897-1929. *1167*

Parent-child relations. Family structure. Middle Classes. Sex roles. Social change. 1970's. *2072*

Parents. Adolescents. Family structure. Sex. Social Classes. 1960's. *2075*

—. Attitudes. Children. Family. Social Mobility aspirations. 1971. *2089*

—. Children. Family. Sex selection. 1970's-. *2116*

—. Children. Marriage partners, selection of. Virginia. 17c-18c. *516*

—. Children. Partisanship. Political socialization. Wives. 1965. *2356*

Parents (role of). Children (disadvantaged). Family life. Schools. 1960's. *2099*

Parish records. Church of England. Genealogy. Harrison, Lucy H. Maryland (Somerset Parish). 1692-1805. *304*

Park, Maud Wood. Archives. Arthur M. Schlesinger, Sr. Beard, Mary R. Jacobi, Mary Putnam. League of Women Voters. Radcliffe College (Arthur and Elizabeth Schlesinger Library). ca 1916-70. *81*

Parker, Bonnie. Barrow, Clyde. Crime and Criminals. Darby, H. Dillard. Louisiana (Ruston). Stone, Sophia. 1933. *1517*

—. Barrow, Clyde. Gangster myth. 1934-67. *258*

Parker, Charlotte Blair. Drama. Films. "Way Down East" (play). ca 1900-37. *1747*

Parker, Dorothy. Benchley, Robert. Humor. literary criticism. Sex. Social criticism. 1919-26. *1713*

Parker, Eliza Ann. Education. Family. Lincoln, Mary Todd. ca 1818-37. *754*

Parker, Gail Thain (review article). Crozier, Alice (review article). Novels. Stowe, Harriet Beecher. Womanhood (concept of). Women's Studies. 1820-1920. 1972-73. *2*

Parker, Lois Stiles. Dickey, Sarah. Heck, Barbara. Leadership. Methodist Church. Shaw, Anna Howard. Stereotypes. Willard, Frances. 19c. *315*

Parks, Rosa. Alabama (Montgomery). Civil Rights. Desegregation (buses). 1955. *2576*

Parlors. Home life. Pianos. 1771-1932. *186*

Parochial Schools. *See* Church Schools; Religious Education.

Parot, Adele. California (San Francisco). Gymnastics. Lewis, Dioclesius. Teachers colleges. Teaching. 1860's-70's. *1052*

Parsonage. Family. Lutheran Church. Marriage. 1974. *2477*

Parties, Political. *See* Political Parties.

Partisanship. Children. Parents. Political socialization. Wives. 1965. *2356*

Partridge, Caspar. Indians (alleged captivities). Menominee Indians. Nahkom (Menominee). Partridge, Lucia. Wisconsin (Winnebago County). 1840's-1916. *1482*

Partridge, Lucia. Indians (alleged captivities). Menominee Indians. Nahkom (Menominee). Partridge, Caspar. Wisconsin (Winnebago County). 1840's-1916. *1482*

*Parushim*. Kallen, Horace M. Secret Societies. Szold, Henrietta. Zionism. 1913-1920. *1443*

Passavant Woman's Aid Society. Charities. Debutante parties. Hargrave, Colleen. Hospitals. Illinois (Chicago). 1939-71. *2061*

Passion. Cultural debate. Image. Literature. Reason. Sex roles. 1775-1850. *959*

Pastoralism. Radicals and Radicalism. Social criticism. Sontag, Susan. 1968-70. *2322*

Patent medicines. Pinkham, Lydia Estes. Vegetable Compound. 1876-1910. *1042*

Patents. *See* Copyright; Inventions.

Patients. Court records. North Carolina. Physicians. 1732-78. *602*

—. Nurses and Nursing. Research. Sex Discrimination. Sociology, medical. 1970's. *60*

Patriarchy. Androgyny. Capitalism. Sex roles. Symbolism. Prehistory-1974. *173*

—. Anthropology. Biology. Family structure. Ideology. Labor, sexual division of. Stereotypes. 20c. *119*

—. Attitudes. Romanticism. Slavery. South or Southern States. 19c. *951*

—. Attitudes. Sex roles. Slavery. Social conditions. South. 1848-60. *686*

—. Children. Family. Feminist movement. Politics. Social organization. Prehistory-1971. *109*

—. Colleges and Universities. Feminist culture. Violence. Women's Studies. 1974. *34*

—. Fitzhugh, George (writings). Social Theory. South or Southern States. ca 1800-60. *633*

—. Greer, Germaine (*The Female Eunuch*). Ideology. Marxism. Sex (frigidity). 1960's-70's. *2432*

—. Historians. Methodology. Sexism. Women's history. 1970's. *58*

Patriliny. Indians. Matriliny. Southeastern States. 18c. *593*

Patriot War. Ashley, Jean. Florida (East). Property rights. Settlement. Spain. 1795-96. *743*

Patriotism. Diller, Gertrude. Memorial Day services. Pennsylvania (Lancaster, Penn Square). 1874-1956. *2939*

—. Frazer, Susan Carpenter. Organizations (memberships in). Pennsylvania (Lancaster County). 1852-1930. *2975*

—. Lucy Brewer (fictional character). Morality. Novels. Prostitution. 1789-1818. *1014*

Patterson, Rachel (journal). Friends, Society of. 19c. *870*

Patti, Adelina. Bankhead, Tallulah. Cornell, Katharine. Cushman, Charlotte Saunders. Duncan, Isadora. Farrar, Geraldine. Hallam, Nancy. Hayes, Helen. Lind, Jenny. National Portrait Gallery. Portraits. Theater. 1971. *418*

Paul, Alice. Constitutional Amendment (21st). Equal Rights Amendment. Suffrage. 1907-72. *272*

—. Suffrage. 1914-23. *1329*

Pawnee Indians (Skidi). Cheyenne Indians. Dougherty, John. Religion. Rites and Ceremonies (sacrificial). 1827. *910*

Peabody, Elizabeth Palmer. Dall, Caroline Healy (journal). Fuller, Margaret. Greek Mythology, Conversations on. Intellectuals. Transcendentalism. 1841. *969*

—. German philosophers (influence of). Language. Massachusetts (Boston). Philosophy. ca 1830's-40's. *971*

—. Hawthorne, Nathaniel. 19c. *3028*

—. Hawthorne, Nathaniel (*The House of Seven Gables*, 1851). Hepzibah Pyncheon (fictional character). Language (theory of). Teaching. 1840's. *986*

—. History (study of). Transcendentalism. 1830's-80's. *476*

—. Kindergarten. Massachusetts (Boston). Shaw, Pauline Agassiz. Social Reform. 1870-1915. *1574*

Peace. *See* Pacifism; War.

Peace Movements *See also* Antiwar Sentiment.

—. Feminism. Georgia. Rankin, Jeannette. 1924-73. *2312*

—. Foreign Policy. Politics. Women's Strike for Peace. 19c-20c. *271*

—. Wisconsin (Madison). Women's International League for Peace and Freedom. 1915-65. *263*

Peace River country. Alberta. Homesteading and Homesteaders. Ukrainians. Zahara, Dominka Roshko. 1900-30. *3376*

Peace River country, north. Canada, western. Pioneers. 1914-76. *3320*

Peasants *See also* Farmers; Working Class.

—. Dowries. Family. Land. Marriage. Massachusetts (Barnstable County). Values. 1620's-1720's. *520*

Peck, Ellen. Schools. Teachers. Vermont (East Montpelier). 19c. *620*

Peck, Mary Hulbert (letters). Galt, Edith Bolling. Political Campaigns. Presidents. Wilson, Woodrow (letters). 1907-19. *1215*

Pedagogy. *See* Teaching.

Peer group influence. Attitudes. Children. Negroes. Whites. Wisconsin (Milwaukee). 1960's. *2563*

Peninsular campaign. Civil War. Nurses and Nursing. Sanitary Commission. Whetten, Harriet Douglas (diary). 1862. *793*

Penn School. Cooley, Rossa B. Negroes. Social Conditions. South Carolina (St. Helena Island). 1901-30. *1468*

Pennoyer, Aletta Teeple Rellington (autobiography). Frontier. Marriage. Michigan (Grand Rapids, Grand Haven). 1829-68. *3037*

Pennsylvania *See also* Northeastern or North Atlantic States.

—. American Revolution. Genealogy. Novels (historical). Scully, Margaret Townsend. 18c-20c. *444*

—. American Woman Suffrage Association. Feminism. Mott, Lucretia. National Woman Suffrage Association. 1848-73. *1309*

—. Birth Control. Family planning services. Public Welfare. State Legislatures. 1965-67. *2027*

—. Bryn Mawr College. 1886-1974. *2832*

—. Bryn Mawr College. Coeducation. Colleges and Universities. Haverford College. 1969-74. *2831*

—. Catholic Church. Church Schools. Congregation of Sisters of Mercy. Mount St. Vincent Academy. Religious Orders. Warde, Frances. 1843-51. *876*

—. Childbirth. Death and Dying. Family. Marriage. Norris, Isacc, II. Norris, Sarah Elizabeth Logan. 1739-44. *514*

—. Christmas. Cookie making. German Americans. Social Customs. ca 18c-20c. *352*

—. Civil War (personal narratives). Clemson, Floride (letters). Social Customs. 1863. *798*

—. Coal mines, anthracite. Employment opportunities. Family incomes (supplementary). 1880-1900. *1051*

—. Constitutional amendment (19th). Feminists. Suffrage. 1837-1920. *1319*

—. Cookery. Lectures. Philadelphia Cooking School. Rorer, Sarah Tyson. 1870-1901. *1110*

—. Divorce. Law. ca 1660-1797. *512*

—. Family life. Folklife studies. Social Customs. West Grove Housekeepers Association. 1860-69. *1197*

—. Family life. Marriage. Negroes. 18c. *585*

—. Feminism. Higher education. Letters. Lowry, Morrow B. 1868. *1312*

—. Friends, Society of. Lynam, John. Lynam, Margaret Ridge. Maryland. Persecution. 1660's-90's. *572*

—. Local History. 1972. *2993*

—. Needlework (wallhangings). 19c. *460*

Pennsylvania (Allegheny City). Cassatt, Mary. Painting. 1844-1926. *1768*

Pennsylvania (Berks County). Daily life. Riegel, Lewis Edgar (reminiscences). Social Customs. 1876-85. *2976*

Pennsylvania (Carlisle). Artists. DeCora, Angel. Educators. Indians. 1871-1919. *1485*

Pennsylvania (Chester County). Property. Widows. Wills. 1714-1800. *480*

Pennsylvania (Chester [now Delaware] County). American Revolution. Brandywine (battle). Frazer, Mary. Philadelphia campaign (1777-78). 1777-78. *562*

Pennsylvania (Danville). Catholic Church. St. Cyril Academy. Sisters of SS. Cyril and Methodius. Slovak culture. 1909-73. *388*

Pennsylvania (East Penn Valley). Family life. Mennonites, Old Order. Social Customs. 1974. *1433*

Pennsylvania (Economy). Christian communists. Harmony Society. Pittman, Clara. 1878-79. *1265*

Pennsylvania Germans. Breadmaking. Pennsylvania (Mifflin County). Social Customs. 1969. *2633*

Pennsylvania (Harrisburg). City beautification. Civic Club of Harrisburg. Dock, Mira Lloyd. 1900-03. *1262*

Pennsylvania Historical Association (43rd annual meeting). Robbins, Caroline. 1975. *2949*

Pennsylvania (Lancaster). Buchanan, James. District of Columbia. Johnston, Harriet Lane. Politics. Presidents. 1849-1903. *765*

—. Churches. City Government. Prostitution. Social Reform. 1914-64. *1402*

—. Dickinson, Anna E. Lectures. 1870. *1076*

—. Family. Franklin and Marshall College. Heller, Mary Bell Stahr (memoirs). 1878-1909. *1157*

—. Johnston, Harriet Lane. 1903. *2982*

Pennsylvania (Lancaster County). Brubaker, Ellen A. Free Kindergarten Association. Kindergarten. Teachers. 1890-1920. *1057*

—. Frazer, Susan Carpenter. Organizations (memberships in). Patriotism. 1852-1930. *2975*

Pennsylvania (Lancaster, Penn Square). Diller, Gertrude. Memorial Day services. Patriotism. 1874-1956. *2939*

Pennsylvania (Lititz). Carper, Ellen. Carper, Lizzie. Dolls, rag. Mennonites. 19c. *2999*

Pennsylvania (Lycoming, Northumberland, and Columbia Counties). Friends, Society of. Marriage. Vital Statistics. 1796-1860. *2933*

*Pennsylvania Magazine of History and Biography*. Bobb, Lois Given. 1948-65. *2990*

*Pennsylvania Magazine* (periodical). Family. Marriage. Witherspoon, John. 1775-76. *504*

Pennsylvania (Mifflin County). Breadmaking. Pennsylvania Germans. Social Customs. 1969. *2633*

Pennsylvania (Montoursville). Indians (British-Indian relations). Interpreters. Montour, Madame. 1711-53. *583*

Pennsylvania (Muncy). ca 1800-1950. *3001*

—. Houses. Petrikin, Fannie. 1850-1902. *2971*

Pennsylvania (Paxtonville). Children. Folklore. New Years Day. Social Customs. Winey, Fay McAfee (reminiscences). 20c. *3000*

Pennsylvania (Philadelphia). Centennial Celebrations. Feminism. Housework, professionalization of. Technology. Woman's Building. 1830-76. *168*

—. Charities. Social work. Society for Organizing Charitable Relief and Repressing Mendicancy. 1864-1909. *1196*

—. Employment. Ethnic Groups. Family. Working Class. 1910-30. *1453*

—. Folklore. Gomez, Dolorez Amelia. Witchcraft. 1974. *2033*

—. Heinz, Elizabeth Granger Rust. Ogontz School for Young Ladies. Private Schools. Secondary Education. 1883-1900. *1586*

—. Octavia Hill Association. Public Welfare. Social reform. ca 1890-1909. *1199*

—. Organizations. Religion. Social Reform. 1870-1900. *1283*

Pietnikoff, Sophia. Alaska. Aleut Indians. Basketmaking. 1908-74. *2596*

Pike, Mary Hayden Green *(Ida May)*. Advertising. Antislavery Sentiments. Novels. Publishers and publishing. 1850's. *947*

Pilgrims. Cooke, Hester Mahieu. Massachusetts. Plymouth Colony. 1623-75. *2997*

Pillows. Mother, image of. Popular Culture. War. 1812-1970. *396*

Pinckney, Eliza Lucas. American Revolution (personal narratives). Family. Letters. South Carolina. 1768-82. *559*

—. Farquher, Jane Colden. Logan, Martha Daniell. Medicine (practice of). Ramsay, Martha Laurens. Scientists. 18c. *485*

—. Indigo culture. South Carolina. ca 1740's. *481*

—. Letters. Politics. ca 1742-93. *535*

Pinkham Company. Advertising. Pinkham, Lydia Estes. Vegetable Compound. 19c. *1043*

Pinkham, Lydia Estes. Advertising. Pinkham Company. Vegetable Compound. 19c. *1043*

—. Patent medicines. Vegetable Compound. 1876-1910. *1042*

Pin-ups. Army. Civil War. *Frank Leslie's Family Magazine.* 1860-65. *819*

—. Gibson, Charles Dana. Gibson Girls. Images. 1890's-1900's. *1552*

*Pioneer and Yorkville Weekly Advertiser* (newspaper). Marriage notices. Obituaries. South Carolina. 1823-24. *651*

Pioneers *See also* Frontier and Pioneer Life; Homesteading and Homesteaders; Voyages.

—. Alberta (Red Deer). Bailey, Mary C. (reminiscences). 1904-22. *3370*

—. Aldrich, Bess Streeter *(A Lantern in Her Hand)*. Family history. Nebraska. Novels. 19c. *1588*

—. Allegheny Mountains. Dewee, Mary (diary). Travel. 1788-89. *2924*

—. Arctic, northern. Greist, Mollie Ward. Nurses and Nursing. ca 1850-1970's. *3391*

—. Arkansas (Johnson County). Foster, Rebecca A. (memoirs). 1840's-60's. *3108*

—. Authors. California (Yosemite Valley). 1860's-70's. *1707*

—. Authors. Ontario. Sibbald, Susan *(Memoirs)*. 1783-1866. *3363*

—. Barlow, Cornelia D. California. Jews. Marks, Bernhard. Marriage. Teachers. 1852-1913. *714*

—. Canada, western. Peace River country, north. 1914-76. *3320*

—. Colorado (Uncompahgre Plateau). Daily life. Matlock, Mary Jane (reminiscences). 1870's-80's. *701*

—. Conine, Catharine. Conine, Emily. Conine, Jane. Daily Life. Indiana. Letters. Seymour, Mary Ann Conine. 1849-51. *3003*

—. Conine family. Daily Life. Letters. North Central States. Seymour, Mary Ann Conine. 1852-63. *3004*

—. Daily Life. Family. Pennsylvania (Pine Creek Valley). 1772-1825. *719*

—. Daily Life. Kansas. Schools. 1880's. *3167*

—. Demography. Nebraska. Sex ratios. 1860-80. *3201*

—. Diaries. Immigrants. Kansas. Letters. Lindgren, Ida Nibelius. Religion. Social Conditions. Swedish Americans. 1870-81. *1496*

—. Dutch. Irving, Washington. Katrina Van Tassel (fictional character). New York (Kinderhook). Van Alen House. 17c-18c. *612*

—. Erickson, Hilda (interview). Family. Swedish Americans. Utah (Grantsville). 1866-20c. *3220*

—. Erix-dotter, Christina Louisa (letter). Illinois. Immigrants. Swedish Americans. 1854. *705*

—. Family. Fancher, Ida Cooke. Oklahoma (Custer County). 1892. *3111*

—. Family. Farmers. Oklahoma Territory. 19c. *3121*

—. Family. New England. Wolcott, Martha Pitkin. 1639-ca 1700. *2998*

—. Lincoln, Abraham. Lincoln, Nancy Hanks. Motherhood. 1780's-1818. *687*

—. New York (Long Island). Smith, Martha Tunstall. 1675-1709. *2985*

—. North Dakota (Nelson County). Social Conditions. Thal, Sarah (memoirs). 1880's. *3202*

—. Oklahoma (Cherokee Outlet). Wood, Anna S. (diary). 1893. *3136*

—. Overland Journeys to the Pacific. Westward Movement. 19c. *712*

—. Pacific Northwest. West. 1803-1912. *693*

—. Smith, Mary Morriss (recollections). Social Conditions. Tennessee (Wilson County). 1812-30. *3118*

—. Trans-Mississippi West. Wives. 1850-1900. *698*

—. Western States. 19c. *730*

Piper, Leonora E. Spiritualism. 1884-1911. *1445*

Pittman, Clara. Christian communists. Harmony Society. Pennsylvania (Economy). 1878-79. *1265*

Plains Indians. Childhood. Indians. Literature. Nebraska (Sheridan County). Sandoz, Mari. 1870's-1931. *1619*

—. Literature. Sandoz, Mari. 1930's-60's. *2855*

Planning *See also* City Planning; Economic Planning; Urbanization.

—. Family structure. Puerto Rico. Social Classes. Urban Renewal. 1960's. *3245*

Plantation life. Civil War. Harrison, Constance Cary. Novels. South or Southern States. 1863-1911. *1710*

—. Cobb, Mary Ann. Confederate States of America. Georgia (Athens). 1860-65. *783*

—. Family. Louisiana (Minden). Marriage. Perryman, Melvill Lucile Martin. 1876-1975. *3097*

Plantation system. Domestic responsibilities. Farmers. Negroes. 1600-1975. *317*

Plantations. Army (confiscatory activity). Civil War. Mississippi (Raymond). Russell, Mrs. J. W. (letter). Slavery. 1863. *772*

—. Battle, Lucy Martin. Battle, William Horn. Daily Life. North Carolina. 1805-74. *3062*

—. Coincoin (former slave). Family. Louisiana (Metoyer). Negroes. 1742-1850. *895*

—. Griffis, Margaret Clark. Slavery. Teachers. Tennessee, West. 1850-58. *619*

—. Letters. Mason, Abigail. Slavery. Social Conditions. Virginia. 1830's. *3065*

—. Marriage. Religion. Slaves. South. ca 1750's-1860. *950*

Plath, Sylvia. Esther Greenwood (fictional character). Feminism. Image. Novels. Sex roles. Symbolism in Literature. 1960's-70's. *2870*

—. Esther Greenwood (fictional character). Maternity. Mental Illness. Novels. Sex roles. Symbolism in Literature. 1960's-70's. *2886*

—. Feminism. Novels. Poetry. Sex roles. 1932-63. *2873*

*Playboy* (periodical). Periodicals. Sexual norms. Social function. 1950's-67. *2751*

Playwrights. *See* Dramatists.

Plummer, Mary. Clemenceau, George. Family. Marriage. 1849-1923. *1240*

Pluralism. Bureaucracies. Family structure. Public Policy. Social services. 1970's. *2118*

Plymouth Colony. Children. Family. Marriage. Social Conditions. 17c. *503*

—. Cooke, Hester Mahieu. Massachusetts. Pilgrims. 1623-75. *2997*

Podell, Albert N. Citizen Lobbies. Common Cause. New York. State legislature. 1975. *2360*

Poe, Edgar Allan. *Broadway Journal* (periodical). Osgood, Frances Sargent. Poetry. 1840's. *1020*

—. Clemm, Maria (letters). Longfellow, Henry Wadsworth. 1850-66. *993*

Poems. Alabama. Gayle, Sarah (autograph album). 1835. *3115*

Poetry. Actors and Actresses. Dwyer, Ada. Lowell, Amy. ca 1880-1925. *1774*

—. Albany Female Academy. Chase, Mary Mehitabel. Education. New York. Teaching. 19c. *998*

—. Alexander, Lucia Gray Swett. Friendship. Italy (Florence). Lowell, James Russell (letter). 1873-74. *1744*

—. Antiwar Sentiment. Levertov, Denise (interview). RESIS. Vietnam War. 1960's. *2304*

—. Art. Borein, Edward. Borein, Lucile. Christmas cards. Western States. 20c. *1562*

—. Attitudes. Romantic symbology. Social Conditions. South. 1829-60. *1026*

—. Baseball fans. Moore, Marianne. 1969. *2853*

—. Bradstreet, Anne. Connecticut. Wolcott, Roger (journal). ca 1650-1758. *609*

—. Bradstreet, Anne. Massachusetts Bay Colony. Puritans. Sex roles. 17c. *613*

—. *Broadway Journal* (periodical). Osgood, Frances Sargent. Poe, Edgar Allan. 1840's. *1020*

—. Brooks, Gwendolyn. Negroes. 1930's-72. *440*

—. Burgos, Julia de. Font Saldaña, Jorge (reminiscences). Lair, Clara. Puerto Rico. Ribera Chevremont, Evaristo (reminiscences). 20c. *3246*

—. California. Coolbrith, Ina. 1841-1928. *1725*

—. California. Coolbrith, Ina. Family relationships. 1841-1928. *1646*

—. Canada. Johnson, Helen. Nationalism. 1864-1946. *3314*

—. Carmichael, Mary Ann. Carmichael, Sarah Elizabeth. Mental Illness. Utah. 1838-1901. *3228*

—. Cary, Alice. Cary, Phoebe. 1820-71. *1019*

—. Color (use of). Dickinson, Emily. Letters. Symbolism in Literature. 19c. *1696*

—. Color (use of). Dickinson, Emily. Symbolism in Literature. 1860's-80's. *1697*

—. Composers. Korn, Anna Less Brosius (tribute). Legislation. Oklahoma. 19c-1965. *3104*

—. Crawford, Isabella Valancy. Ontario (Toronto). ca 1850-87. *3316*

—. Creative innocence, concept of. Intellectuals. Maritain, Jacques. Maritain, Raissa. Religion. 1940's-75. *2473*

—. *Dial* (periodical). Moore, Marianne. ca 1914-20's. *1662*

—. Dickinson, Edward. Dickinson, Emily. 1860's-80's. *1726*

—. Dickinson, Emily. 19c. 1955. *1659*

—. Dickinson, Emily. 1861-86. *1688*

—. Dickinson, Emily. Imagery. 19c. *1742*

—. Dickinson, Emily. Manuscripts. Pershing, Mrs. John. Princeton University Library (Emily Dickinson Collection). ca 1860-1930's. 1969. *83*

—. Dickinson, Emily. Science. ca 1860's-80's. *1596*

—. Dickinson, Emily. Social criticism. Values. 19c. *1686*

—. Dickinson, Emily ("I Taste a Liquor Never Brewed"). 19c. *1630*

—. Family. Feminist movement. Friendship. Kumin, Maxine. Sexton, Anne. Showalter, Elaine. Smith, Carol. 1950-74. *2882*

—. Faugeres, Margaretta V. New York, image of. 1783-1812. *1008*

—. Feminism. Novels. Plath, Sylvia. Sex roles. 1932-63. *2873*

—. Friends, Society of. Letters. Lloyd, Elizabeth. Whittier, John Greenleaf. 1840. *1006*

—. Hazen, Lillian W. Journalism. Montana (Gilt Edge). Weston, Edward Payson. 1899-1949. *1677*

—. Hodge, Bertica. Romeo, Althea. Virgin Islands. 1900-72. *2862*

—. Imagist movement. Lowell, Amy. Pound, Ezra. 1913-22. *1657*

—. Krause, Louise Antoinette. Stein, Gertrude. 1939. *1730*

—. Letters. Lowell, Amy. Wendell, Barrett. 1915-19. *1711*

—. Moodie, Susanna. Ontario. Rebellion of 1837. 1837-50's. *3367*

—. Mother (image of). Social Customs. Symbolism in Literature. Values. 19c. *406*

—. Negroes. Prince, Lucy Terry. Supreme Court. Vermont (Guilford). Williams College. 18c. *594*

—. Novels. Wylie, Elinor Hoyt. 1885-1928. *1645*

—. Proctor, Edna. 19c. *416*

*Poetry* (periodical). Illinois (Chicago). Literature. Monroe, Harriet. 1870's-1910's. *1741*

Poets. American Revolution. Integration. Negroes. Wheatley, Phillis. 1770-1800. *592*

—. Bradstreet, Anne. New England. 16c-17c. *615*

—. California (San Francisco). Coolbrith, Ina. Librarians. 1841-1928. *1669*

—. Carman, William Bliss. Guiney, Louise Imogen. Letters. 1887-98. *1651*

—. Dickinson, Emily. Symbolism in Literature. 1858-66. *1018*

—. Hopkins, Pauline Elizabeth. Negroes. 1859-1930. *1471*

—. Maine (Appledore Island). Thaxter, Celia. ca 1840's-60's. *1024*

—. Massachusetts (Boston). Negroes. Race consciousness. Wheatley, Phillis. 1753-84. *590*

—. Sex roles. Sigourney, Lydia Howard. 1811-65. *1028*

—. Stephan, Ruth. 1910-74. *2884*

Poisoning. Langston, John Mercer. Lewis, Edmonia. Oberlin College. Trials. 1862. *921*

Poles. America (image of). Travel accounts. 1783-1870's. *106*

Price, Leontyne. Edwards, Lena F. Negroes. Presidential Freedom Medal. 1964. *2592*
Prices *See also* Wages.
—. Automobile Industry and Trade. Consumers. Discrimination. Ohio (Dayton). Salesmen and Salesmanship. 1970. *1835*
Priesthood authority. Mormons. Sex roles. Social Status. 1971. *2488*
Primaries. *See* Elections; Voting and Voting Behavior.
Primary Education. *See* Elementary Education.
Prince, Lucy Terry. Negroes. Poetry. Supreme Court. Vermont (Guilford). Williams College. 18c. *594*
Princeton University. Attitudes. Feminism. Hodge, Charles. New Jersey (Princeton). Womanhood (ornamental). 1825-55. *659*
—. Colleges and Universities (presidents). New Jersey. Wives. 18c-20c. *2989*
—. Morris, Celia. New Jersey. Roos, Margit. Students. Wasserheit, Judith. 1973. *2282*
Princeton University Library (Emily Dickinson Collection). Dickinson, Emily. Manuscripts. Pershing, Mrs. John. Poetry. ca 1860-1930's. 1969. *83*
Princeton University Library (Sylvia Beach Collection). Authors. Beach, Sylvia. Shakespeare and Company Bookshop. 1920's-30's. *1703*
Printing. *See* Books.
Prison reform. Feminism. Sex roles. 1870-1900. *1519*
—. Girls' Training School. Hall, Emma. Michigan (Adrian). 1881-84. *1506*
Prisoners. California (Alameda County). Liberalism. Racism. 1960's. *2659*
—. Michigan (Detroit). Mormons. Polygamy. 1880's. *1154*
Prisons *See also* Crime and Criminals; Criminal Law; Police.
—. Connecticut. Juvenile offenders. Sex Discrimination. 1970's. *2286*
—. Crime and Criminals. Economic Conditions. 1975. *2675*
—. District of Columbia. Suffrage. Wilson, Woodrow (administration). 1917. *1374*
—. Economic Conditions. Family. Matriarchy, myth of. Negroes. Slavery. 17c-20c. *384*
—. Maryland. 1973. *2680*
Privacy, right to. Abortion. Physicians. Supreme Court. 1970's. *2697*
Private Schools *See also* Church Schools.
—. Arkansas. James, Ann. Missions and Missionaries. Teaching. 1813-1910. *3100*
—. Belmont Estate. Students. Tennessee (Nashville). Ward-Belmont school. 1912-35. *1564*
—. Educators. Georgia. Sosnowski, Sophie. South Carolina. 1840's-70's. *992*
—. Employment. Lutheran Church (Missouri Synod). Teachers. 1870's-1970's. *343*
—. Heinz, Elizabeth Granger Rust. Ogontz School for Young Ladies. Pennsylvania (Philadelphia). Secondary Education. 1883-1900. *1586*
—. Occupational values. Public Schools. Students. 1960's. *1860*
—. Ward, Henry Dana (diary). Ward, Mrs. Henry Dana. West Virginia (Charleston). 1845-47. *3052*
Proctor, Edna. Poetry. 19c. *416*
Production and reproduction (dialectics of). Feminism. Functionalism. Marxism. Social classes. 1976. *2036*
Products (standardized). Business History. Consumers. Fashions. Marketing. 19c-20c. *157*
Professional Education *See also* Medical Education; Vocational Education.
—. Carnegie-Mellon University. 1920-71. *2782*
—. Illinois, University of, Library School. Library science. Sharp, Katharine Lucinda. Simpson, Frances. 1893-1942. *1572*
Professional Women's Caucus. Employment. Lawyers. 1869-1970's. *160*
Professionalism. Economic Conditions. Sex. Social mobility. Spiritualists. 19c. *153*
Professionalization. Discrimination. Employment. Librarians. Sex roles. 1880-1975. *137*
Professionals. American Public Health Association. Communication networks. Employment. Sex Discrimination. 1975. *1986*
—. Employment. Industry. Sex discrimination. 1960-63. *1972*
—. Employment. Managers. 1917-70. *135*
—. Industrialization. Metropolitan Areas. Sex roles. Southwest. ca 1950's-60's. *1903*
Professions. Attitudes. Behavior. Occupational status. Self concepts. 1960's-70. *1904*

—. Attitudes. Self concepts. Social Status. 1971. *2254*
—. Colleges and Universities. Feminism. Organizations. 1960's-70. *2429*
—. Economic development. Employment. 1950-67. *1845*
—. Employment. Housewives. Schools. Social Change. 1970's. *1912*
Professions (nonacademic). Political Science. Sex Discrimination. 1960's-70. *1918*
Professions (participation). Employment. Social status. 1890's-1969. *143*
Progressive Party. Social workers. 1912-16. *1386*
Progressivism. Addams, Jane. Dunne, Edward F. Educational Reform. Illinois (Chicago). Young, Ella Flagg. 1905-10. *1384*
—. Alabama. Hobson, Richmond Pearson. House of Representatives. Suffrage. 1900-20. *1368*
—. Barnard, Kate. Labor Unions and Organizations. Oklahoma. Social Reform. ca 1900-10's. *1267*
—. Catholic Church. Infant mortality. New Jersey (Jersey City). Protestantism. Settlement houses. Social reform. Whittier House. 1890-1917. *1391*
—. Cities. Crane, Caroline Bartlett. Michigan (Kalamazoo). Reform. Sanitation (municipal). 1858-1935. *1383*
—. Cities. Immigrants. Prostitution. Social reformers. 1910-15. *1387*
—. Feminism, social. Labor. Legislation. Organizations. 1919-33. *1128*
—. Fiction. Waller, Mary. Wilderness. ca 1900-20. *1708*
—. Illinois (Chicago). Prostitution. Social justice. 1910-15. *1535*
—. Industrial Relations Commission (federal). Social workers. World War I. 1911-13. *1385*
—. Kellor, Francis A. Matthews, Victoria Earle. Negroes. New York City. Ovington, Mary White. Social Reform. 1900-15. *1389*
—. Mothers' pensions. Public Welfare. Social Reform. 1911-30's. *1046*
—. Phillips, David Graham. Sex roles. Social Change. ca 1900-14. *1388*
—. Public welfare legislation. Social Reform. Wilson, Woodrow (administration). Women's Bureau. World War I. 1914-20. *1217*
Prohibition. Alaska. Woman's Christian Temperance Union. 1842-1917. *1400*
—. Democracy. Organizations. Political Speeches. 1920-34. *1393*
—. Nation, Carry. 1900's. *1399*
—. Oklahoma. Woman's Christian Temperance Union. 1888-1907. *1395*
—. Politics. Populism. Reform. Suffrage. 1891-92. *1326*
—. Referendum. Virginia. Woman's Christian Temperance Union. 1898. *1398*
Prohibition amendment campaign. Ohio. Woman's Christian Temperance Union. 1874-85. *1401*
Prohibition movement. Duniway, Abigail Scott. Suffrage. 1870's-1914. *1355*
Proletariat. *See* Working classes.
Propaganda *See also* Advertising; Public Opinion.
Propaganda power. Colleges and universities. Educators. Wives. 1970's. *2835*
Property *See also* Income.
—. Law. Marriage. Quebec. Wives. 1960's. *3330*
—. Law. Marriage. Wives. 1950's-60's. *2342*
—. Pennsylvania (Chester County). Widows. Wills. 1714-1800. *480*
Property rights. Adoption. Alimony. Children. Divorce. Family. Law. 19c-20c. *260*
—. Ashley, Jean. Florida (East). Patriot War. Settlement. Spain. 1795-96. *743*
—. Law. Louisiana. Wives. 1950's-60's. *2351*
—. Law. Marriage. Quebec. Wives. 1964. *3333*
Prostitution. Adultery. Childbirth. Marriage. New England. Puritans. Satire. Ward, Nathaniel (*The Simple Cobler of Aggawam in America*). 1647. *495*
—. Antimale sentiments. Moral reform. New York Moral Reform Society. Sex roles. ca 1830-60. *926*
—. Attitudes. Social Change. 1800-1920. *229*
—. Brothel madams. Folklore. Social control. Texas. 1973. *2049*
—. Brown, Annie. Letters. Ohio (Ada, Cincinnati). 1881. *1541*
—. Bulette, Julia. Murder. Nevada (Virginia City). 1862-64. *924*
—. California (San Diego Stingaree, Redlight district). Reform. 1870's-1917. *1540*

—. Camp followers. Courts Martial and Courts of Inquiry. Military. World War I. 1917-18. *1293*
—. Census. Tennessee (Nashville). 1860. *923*
—. Chinese Americans. Family life. Immigration. Social Organization. Tong societies. 1850-1972. *321*
—. Churches. City Government. Pennsylvania (Lancaster). Social Reform. 1914-64. *1402*
—. Cities. Cowboys. Culture. Kansas. Morality. 19c. *1139*
—. Cities. Immigrants. Progressivism. Social reformers. 1910-15. *1387*
—. Cities. Public Policy. 1930's-60's. *2644*
—. City Government. Florida (Pensacola). Social Change. 1900-40. *1542*
—. City Government. Missouri (St. Louis). State Legislatures. 1870-74. *1404*
—. Dance halls. Frontier and Pioneer Life. Mining towns. Montana. Social Reform. ca 1870's-1910's. *1537*
—. Divorce. Historiography. Reform. Sex. Social History. 17c-1972. *7*
—. Employment. Folklore. New Mexico. 1960's. *1825*
—. Feminists. Rehabilitation (rejection of). ca 1900-73. *2176*
—. Folk Songs. Stereotypes. Western States. 19c-20c. *394*
—. Garment industry. Illinois (Chicago). Jews. State Legislatures (Senate Vice Committee). Working Conditions. 1913. *1120*
—. Hawaii (Iwilei district, Honolulu). Social Reform. 1835-1917. *204*
—. Illinois (Chicago). Progressivism. Social justice. 1910-15. *1535*
—. Illinois (Chicago). Social Conditions. 1860's-71. *1539*
—. Indiana (Gary, Valparaiso). Ku Klux Klan. Nativism. 1920's. *1536*
—. Law. Local Government. Nevada. ca 1850-1974. *250*
—. Literature. Metropolitan Areas. Popular Culture (underground). 1840-70. *925*
—. Lucy Brewer (fictional character). Morality. Novels. Patriotism. 1789-1818. *1014*
—. Manitoba (Winnipeg). Moral corruption (alleged). Politics. 1900-10. *3377*
—. Morality. Nevada (Virginia City). Social Classes. 1860-88. *1538*
—. Negroes. New York (Saratoga Springs). Sexual superstitions. 1964-65. *2589*
—. Theaters. 19c. *211*
Protest Marches. *See* Demonstrations.
Protestant Churches *See also* names of churches, e.g. Methodist Church, etc.; Protestantism.
—. Brown, Antoinette Louisa. Brown, Olympia. Clergy. Friends, Society of. Hanaford, Phebe. Jones, Sybil. Mott, Lucretia. Oliver, Anne. Smiley, Sarah Frances. Van Cott, Maggie Newton. 19c. *345*
—. Catholic Church. Clergy. Sex discrimination. 1970's. *2474*
—. Feminism. Organizations. Social Reform. South. Young Women's Christian Association. 1920's. *1307*
—. Indian-White Relations. Missions and Missionaries. Spokane Indians. Walker, Elkanah. Walker, Mary. Washington (Tshimakain). 1838-48. *872*
Protestant ethic. Attitudes. Control, locus of. Feminist movement. Ideology. 1972. *2438*
Protestantism *See also* Evangelism; Fundamentalism.
—. Attitudes. Catholic Church. Colleges and Universities (effects of). 1960's. *2460*
—. Catholic Church. Infant mortality. New Jersey (Jersey City). Progressivism. Settlement houses. Social reform. Whittier House. 1890-1917. *1391*
—. Catholic Church. Jews. Religion. Social Status. 1970. *2470*
—. Catholic Church. Marriage. Mothers. New Jersey (Fort Dix). 1960's. *2462*
—. Civil War (effects). South. Widows. 1861-65. *785*
—. Clergy. Ordination. Social change. World Council of Churches. 1945-75. *2487*
—. Dickinson, Emily. Religion, philosophy of. 1860's-80's. *1689*
—. Domestic education. Image. Industrialization. Morality. Motherhood. 1830-70. *956*
—. Feminism. ca 16c-1973. *367*
—. Middle East. Missions and Missionaries. Schools. 1810-1970's. *328*
—. Navajo Indians. New Mexico (Ramah). Sex roles. 1970's. *2594*

*Providence Gazette and Country Journal*
(newspaper). Goddard, Sarah Updike.
Journalism. Rhode Island. 1762-70. *605*

*Provincial Freeman* (newspaper). Antislavery
Sentiments. Negroes. Newspapers. Ontario.
Shadd, Mary Ann. 1852-93. *3364*

Provincial Hospital for the Insane. Bell, Hugh.
Dix, Dorothea. Nova Scotia (Halifax,
Dartmouth). ca 1832-60. *3326*

Pruitt-Igoe housing project. Family. Missouri (St.
Louis). Negroes. Public Housing. 1960's.
*2553*

Psychiatry *See also* Mental Illness; Psychology.
—. Attitudes. Sex roles. Values. 1960's. *2713*
—. Dix, Dorothea. Hospitals. Medicine (practice
of). Mental Illness. Social reform. 19c. *933*

Psychic phenomena. Jarvis, Stinson. Ontario.
Watkins, Kathleen ("Kit of the Mail").
1885-95. *3368*

Psychoanalysis *See also* Psychology.
—. Foote, Mary. Jung, Carl G. Yale University
Library (Mary Foote Papers). 1872-1968.
*80*

Psychocultural therapy. Witchcraft victims. 1968-73.
*2709*

Psychohistory. Antislavery sentiments. Feminism
(review article). Grimké, Angelina. Josephson,
Hannah. Lumpkin, Katharine Du Pre. Political
Reform. Rankin, Jeannette. 19c-20c. 1974.
*262*

Psychological Conflicts. Achievement. 1972.
*2259*

Psychological depression. Careers. Family.
Feminist movement. Psychology. 1970. *2252*

Psychological Warfare. *See* Propaganda.

Psychology *See also* Psychiatry; Psychoanalysis;
Social Psychology.
—. Addams, Jane. Horner, Matina. Kennedy,
Rose. Lawrence, Frieda. Senesh, Hannah.
Success, fear of. 20c. *2265*
—. Age. Behavior (deviant). Family life. New
England. Social Conditions. Witchcraft. 17c.
*525*
—. Alcoholism (male). Marital problems. Wives.
-1973. *2255*
—. Asians. Social Problems. Wives. 1950's-70's.
*2053*
—. Attitudes. Careers. Family. Sex roles.
1960's-72. *2258*
—. Attitudes. Sex. 1960's. *2210*
—. Behavior. Historiography. Massachusetts
(Salem). Puritanism. Witchcraft (review
article). 1692. *532*
—. Behavior. Historiography. Massachusetts
(Salem). Witchcraft. 1691-92. *526*
—. Behavior. Sex roles. Stereotypes. 1949-71.
*2204*
—. Calkins, Mary Whiton. 1900-30. *1105*
—. Calkins, Mary Whiton. Scholarship. ca
1890's-1930. *1075*
—. Careers. Family. Feminist movement.
Psychological depression. 1970. *2252*
—. Childrearing. Race Relations. Sexual behavior.
Slavery. South. Stereotypes. 1800-1972.
*172*
—. Children. Maternal deprivation. Upper Classes.
1950-74. *2157*
—. Cities. Fertility. Ohio (Toledo). Religion.
Social Conditions. 1962. *2133*
—. Colleges and Universities (faculty). Deprivation,
Relative. Occupational gratification. 1972.
*2261*
—. Consciousness-raising groups. Feminism.
1960's-70's. *2394*
—. Cragin, Mary. Marriage. Noyes, John
Humphrey. Sex. Utopias. 1830's-40's. *865*
—. Democracy. Gynecology, development of.
Masturbation phobias. Men. Sexual anxieties.
Todd, John. 19c. *170*
—. Deutsch, Helene. Horney, Karen. Sex roles.
ca 1890's-1970's. *176*
—. Hollingsworth, Leta. 1886-1938. *1055*
—. Horner, Matina. Methodology. Motivation.
Success, fear of. 1970-74. *2262*
—. Interpersonal Relations. 1972. *2256*
—. Kent, Grace Helen. 1875-1973. *121*
—. Massachusetts (Salem). Witchcraft. 1691.
*528*
—. Mental illness (rates). Response bias. Sex
differences. 1970. *2707*
—. Personality theory. 1972. *2253*
—. Pregnancy. 1960's. *2264*

Psychology, Applied. *See* Counseling.

Psychotherapy. District of Columbia. Feminist
Counseling Collective. 1972-75. *2715*

Puberty. Apache Indians (San Carlos). Rites and
Ceremonies. 1969. *2613*

—. Attitudes. Femininity. Menopause. Physicians,
male. Social roles. 19c. *243*

Public Administration. *See* Bureaucracies; Civil
Service; Government.

Public Employees *See also* Civil Service.
—. Canadian Union of Public Employees. Sex
discrimination. 1975. *3273*
—. Equal employment opportunity. Federal
government. Sex discrimination. 1970's. *1953*

Public Health *See also* Cemeteries; Diseases; Drug
Abuse; Hospitals; Medicine; Sanitation.
—. Family. Medicine. Nurses and Nursing.
Social Sciences. 1960's. *2687*
—. Family planning. Values. 1960's. *2235*
—. Missouri. Nurses and Nursing. Rural
Settlements. 1960's. *1873*
—. Nurses and Nursing. Time allocation. 1960's.
*1914*

Public Housing. Bureaucracies. Cities. Social
Classes. 1960's. *2654*
—. Contact hypothesis. Race Relations. 1973.
*2645*
—. Family. Missouri (St. Louis). Negroes.
Pruitt-Igoe housing project. 1960's. *2553*

Public office. Canada. Political Participation.
USA. Voting and Voting Behavior. 1920-60's.
*266*
—. Child care. Sex roles. Social Change. 1976.
*2186*
—. Discrimination. Elections. Federal
Government. Marriage. 1960's. *2305*

Public Opinion *See also* Political Surveys;
Propaganda; Public Relations.
—. Abortion. Canada. Press. Social Change.
1960's-74. *3257*
—. Abortion. Law Reform. 1800-1973. *236*
—. Atherton, Gertrude. Feminism. Heroines
(fictional). Novels. 1890's. *1736*
—. Barnum, P. T. Lind, Jenny (tour). Performing
arts. 1850-52. *1030*
—. Bergman, Ingrid. Films. Rossellini, Roberto.
Sexual behavior. 1949. *2221*
—. Bowery Theater. Cushman, Charlotte Saunders.
New York City. Theater. 1836. *1036*
—. Clergy. Divorce. Feminism. Sociologists.
1906-20's. *1165*
—. Clergy. Religion. 1960's. *2463*
—. Clothing. Marriage. Morality. Sex. Social
Customs. 1936-65. *2225*
—. Colorado. Constitutional convention (1876).
Newspapers. Suffrage. 1870's. *1336*
—. Crime and Criminals. Law and Society.
Morality. Sex. Social problems. 1619-1776.
*598*
—. Employment. 1950's-70's. *1876*
—. Fertility. Michigan (Detroit). 1960's. *2130*
—. Morality. Mormons. Polygamy (criticisms of).
Sex. ca 1860-1900. *1176*
—. Periodicals. Sex (references to). 1950-70.
*2243*
—. Pornography. 1973. *2723*
—. Race Relations. State Legislatures. Sterilization
bill. Virginia. 1960's. *2336*

Public opinion formation. Canada. Colleges and
Universities. Political knowledge scale.
Students. 1974. *3294*

*Public Opinion Quarterly*. Erskine, Hazel (tribute).
Nevada. Politics. Public Welfare. Social
scientists. 1908-75. *3240*

Public Opinion (survey accuracy). Mothers.
Negroes. New York City. Social Classes.
1960's. *2584*

Public opinion surveys. Antiwar sentiment.
Colleges and Universities. Vietnam War.
1960's-72. *2378*
—. Behavior patterns. Family. Sex roles. Wives.
1960's. *2031*
—. Family. Methodology. Puerto Rico (San Juan).
1966. *2106*

Public places. Attitudes. Behavior. Sexual activity,
viewing. ca 1970-74. *2184*

Public policy. Abortion. Supreme Court decisions.
1971-74. *2694*
—. Birth rate. Economic Conditions. ca 1970.
*2137*
—. Buchanan, James. Lane, Harriet. Presidency.
Slavery. 1850's. *766*
—. Bureaucracies. Family structure. Pluralism.
Social services. 1970's. *2118*
—. Carson, Rachel Louise. Conservation
movement. 1943-70. *2328*
—. Children. Eugenics. Illegitimacy. Mothers.
Sterilization laws. 1907-66. *224*
—. Cities. Prostitution. 1930's-60's. *2644*
—. Civil Rights Act (Title VII, 1964). Collective
bargaining. Labor laws. Sex discrimination.
1964-71. *2014*

—. Economic Conditions. Employment. Higher
Education. Social Status. 1975. *1862*
—. Economic theory. Inflation. Unemployment.
ca 1945-72. *1808*
—. Employment. Federal programs. World War
II. 1941-45. *1303*
—. Ethics. Nixon, Richard M. Population
planning. President's Commission on Population
Growth and the American Future (report).
1972. *2150*
—. Family planning. Population. President's
Commission on Population Growth and the
American Future. 1968-72. *2039*
—. Occupations. Research. Sociology. Working
Class. Working Conditions. 1970's. *1828*
—. Political participation. 1968-72. *2366*

Public Records. *See* Archives.

Public Relations *See also* Advertising; Public
Opinion.

Public relations techniques. Arendt, Hannah (review
article). Economic conditions. Politics.
Vietnam War. Watergate scandal. 1960's-75.
*2311*

Public Schools *See also* High Schools; Junior High
Schools; Rural Schools; Schools.
—. Attitudes. Pregnancy. Webster Girls School.
1960's. *2799*
—. Behavior. Sex roles. Stereotypes. 1971-72.
*2197*
—. British North America. Canada. Social Status.
Teaching. Wages. 1845-75. *3253*
—. Cultural enrichment program. Leesy, Miss.
Missouri (St. Louis). 1960's. *2787*
—. Curricula. Family life. Sex Education. 1960's.
*2846*
—. Employment. Income. Maternity policies.
Sex discrimination. Teacher organizations.
1956-72. *1948*
—. Marriage. Pregnancy. 1940-60's. *2775*
—. Occupational values. Private Schools. Students.
1960's. *1860*
—. Teachers. Vermont. Wages. 19c. *403*

Public service. Canada. Sex discrimination.
1870-1975. *3271*

Public Welfare *See also* Charities; Child Welfare;
Children; Day Nurseries; Hospitals; Social
Work.
—. Adoption. Catholic Church. Children. Clergy.
Law. Quebec. Suffrage. 1920-36. *3342*
—. Aid to Families with Dependent Children.
1965. *2649*
—. Aid to Families with Dependent Children.
Attitudes. Day Nurseries. New York City
(Department of Social Services). 1967-71.
*2023*
—. Aid to Families with Dependent Children.
Eligibility requirements, interstate. 1972.
*2029*
—. Aid to Families with Dependent Children.
Federal Policy. Poor. Reform. Unemployment.
1968-71. *2022*
—. Aid to Families with Dependent Children.
Illinois (Cook County). Mothers' pensions.
1911-75. *251*
—. Attitudes. Maryland (Baltimore). Negroes.
Whites. 1964. *2651*
—. Birth Control. Family planning services.
Pennsylvania. State Legislatures. 1965-67.
*2027*
—. Birth control information. Information
diffusion. Mail, direct. 1972. *2237*
—. Birth Rate. Economic Conditions. Family
planning. New York City. Poverty areas.
1965-67. *2143*
—. Charity organization movement. Illinois
(Chicago). Rural-Urban Studies. Social Classes.
1880-1930. *1512*
—. Child care. Politics. 1940-45. *1221*
—. Congress. Family. Law. Old-Age, Survivors',
and Disability Insurance. Social change.
1935-71. *2344*
—. Congress. Family. Reform. Taxation. 1970's.
*2028*
—. Economic security. Employment. Families,
low-income. Quebec. Social Aid Act (1969).
1969-75. *3357*
—. Employment. Family support. 1975. *1840*
—. Erskine, Hazel (tribute). Nevada. Politics.
*Public Opinion Quarterly*. Social scientists.
1908-75. *3240*
—. Family. Social Organization. 1960's. *2024*
—. Family (female headed). Housing. Married
couples, separation of. Puerto Rico. 1950-60.
*2026*
—. Family planning programs. Population control.
1969-73. *2046*
—. Housing. Negroes. Poor. Virginia (Norfolk).
1950's-60's. *2527*

—. Children. Hawaii. Social distance. Stereotypes. ca 1960's-70's. *2517*

—. Children (illegitimate). North Carolina. State Legislatures. Sterilization. 1957-59. *2655*

—. Colleges and Universities. Religion. South. 1972. *2664*

—. Connecticut (New Haven). Housing market. Segregation. 1973. *2549*

—. Family. Slavery. South. Stowe, Harriet Beecher (*Uncle Tom's Cabin,* 1852). ca 1852-70. *941*

—. Feminism. Revolutionary Movements. Stereotypes. 1970. *2395*

—. Feminism. Sexism. 1960-71. *2396*

—. Feminist movement. National Organization for Women. Organizations. Politics. Suffrage. 20c. *294*

—. Gordon, Kate M. South or Southern States. States' rights. Suffrage. 1913-20. *1339*

—. Historians. Massachusetts (Salem). Tituba (Carib Indian). Witchcraft trials. 1648-1971. *344*

—. Negroes. Sex discrimination. 1970's. *2521*

—. Occupations. Sex Discrimination. 1960's-70's. *1966*

—. Sex. Social Psychology. Violence. 1974. *2669*

—. Sex Discrimination. Social Conditions. 1960's-70's. *2638*

Radcliffe College. Coeducation. Harvard University. Massachusetts (Cambridge). 1960's. *2811*

Radcliffe College (Arthur and Elizabeth Schlesinger Library). Archives. 1922-72. *87*

—. Archives. Arthur M. Schlesinger, Sr. Beard, Mary R. Jacobi, Mary Putnam. League of Women Voters. Park, Maud Wood. ca 1916-70. *81*

Radicals and Radicalism *See also* Leftism; Political Reform; Revolution; Social Reform.

—. Ageism. Political Protest. Sex Discrimination. 1960's. *2320*

—. Colleges and universities. Sex Discrimination. Teachers. 1974. *1934*

—. Colleges and Universities. Sex Discrimination. Technology. Youth. 1960's. *2279*

—. Economists. Howard, Peggy (obituary). 1944-72. *1928*

—. Farmer-Labor Party. Hollis, Mrs. A. McNaughton, Violet. Political Leadership. Saskatchewan. Socialism. 1932-34. *3386*

—. Feminism. Settlement houses. Suffrage. Women's Trade Union League. ca 1890's-1920's. *1314*

—. Feminist movement. Political Theory. 1960-72. *2444*

—. Feminists. Politics. 1955-73. *2428*

—. Marriage. Sex. 19c. *240*

—. Pastoralism. Social criticism. Sontag, Susan. 1968-70. *2322*

—. Politics. Socialist Workers Party. 1970. *2382*

Rafferty, Max. California. Elections. Voting and Voting Behavior. 1962. *2379*

Railroad expansion. Industrialization, impact of. Sex roles. 1890's. *1175*

Railroads. Crombie, Helen Elizabeth (diary). Labor Disputes. Pennsylvania (Pittsburgh). Riots. 1877. *2944*

—. Employment. World War I. 1917-30. *1291*

Ramsay, Martha Laurens. Farquher, Jane Colden. Logan, Martha Daniell. Medicine (practice of). Pinckney, Eliza Lucas. Scientists. 18c. *485*

Ranch life. Alkire, Asenath Phelps. Arizona. Triangle Bar Ranch. 1889-95. *3204*

—. Letters. Nebraska (North Bend). Robertson, Emma. 1891-92. *3184*

Ranching. Historians. Nevada (Las Vegas). Stewart, Helen J. 1879-1926. *1108*

Rancho El Pinole. California (San Pablo Bay). Family. Fernandez, Bernardo. 1823-1902. *3209*

Rancho Topanga Malibu Sequit. Adamson, Rhoda Rindge. California (Vaquero Point). 1928. *3235*

—. California (Topanga Canyon). Government (county, state). Rindge, May Knight. Roads. 1905-25. *1243*

Rand, Ayn. Economic philosophies. Fiction. Martineau, Harriet. 1832-1973. *144*

—. Economics. Liberals. 1975. *1811*

Randolph, Edward Brett. Religion. Slavery. Thilman, Elisa (letter). 1848. *935*

Randolph, Judith. Infanticide (alleged). Morris, Nancy Randolph. Pregnancy (premarital). Randolph, Richard. Virginia. 1792-1815. *919*

Randolph, Martha Jefferson. Eppes, Maria Jefferson. Jefferson, Thomas. Virginia. 18c-19c. *3077*

Randolph, Mary. Employment. Marriage. Virginia. 1768-1828. *3048*

Randolph, Richard. Infanticide (alleged). Morris, Nancy Randolph. Pregnancy (premarital). Randolph, Judith. Virginia. 1792-1815. *919*

Rankin, Jeannette. Antislavery sentiments. Feminism (review article). Grimké, Angelina. Josephson, Hannah. Lumpkin, Katharine Du Pre. Political Reform. Psychohistory. 19c-20c. 1974. *262*

—. Congress. Montana. Politics. Suffrage. 1913-18. *1263*

—. Congress. Suffrage. Unemployment. World War I. 20c. *265*

—. Constitutions, State. Montana. Suffrage. 1889-1914. *1347*

—. Feminism. Georgia. Peace Movements. 1924-73. *2312*

—. Montana. Suffrage. 1911-14. *1367*

Rankin, Melinda. Mexican Americans. Missions and Missionaries. Presbyterian Church. Schools. Texas. 1830-1908. *311*

Rape. Alabama (Scottsboro). Communist Party. NAACP. Negroes. 1931-32. *1524*

—. Alcalá, Tomasa. Philippines (Mindoro; Calapan). Quezon, Manuel. 1898-1910. *1521*

—. Attitudes. Brownmiller, Susan (review article). Feminist movement. 1976. *2677*

—. Attitudes. Judges. 1974. *2671*

—. Brownmiller, Susan (review article). Men. Negroes. Racism. 1975. *2672*

—. Freedmen. Kansas. Migration, Internal. Politics. Race Relations. 1878-80. *1467*

—. Hawaii (Oahu). Journalism. Massie, Mrs. Thomas. Police. Race Relations. 1931. *1520*

Rawlings, Clarissa Lawrence. Civil War. Letters. Rawlings, Hannah Garlick. Virginia (Orange County). 1865. *778*

Rawlings, Hannah Garlick. Civil War. Letters. Rawlings, Clarissa Lawrence. Virginia (Orange County). 1865. *778*

Rawlings, Marjorie Kinnan. Fiction. Florida. Regionalism. 1896-1953. *1600*

Reading. Books. Edmonston, Catherine Anne (diary). North Carolina (Halifax County). 1860-65. *985*

Reading habits. Adolescence. Alcott, Louisa May. Religion. 19c. *405*

—. Adolescence. Periodicals. Wisconsin (Madison). 1960's. *1720*

—. Armstrong, Aeneas R. Armstrong, Henriette Vickers. Brontë, Charlotte. Georgia. Great Britain. 1861. *968*

Reading texts. Elementary Education. Sex role models. 1600-1966. *257*

Readings, Public. New England. New York City. Stowe, Harriet Beecher. 1872. *1729*

Reality (inner vs. outer). Authors. Literature. 1930-73. *428*

Reason. Cultural debate. Image. Literature. Passion. Sex roles. 1775-1850. *959*

Rebellion of 1837. Moodie, Susanna. Ontario. Poetry. 1837-50's. *3367*

Rebow, Isaac Martin. Letters. Manuscripts. Rebow, Mary Martin. Washington State University Library (Mary Martin Rebow Letters). 1778-79. *86*

Rebow, Mary Martin. Letters. Manuscripts. Rebow, Isaac Martin. Washington State University Library (Mary Martin Rebow Letters). 1778-79. *86*

Recessions. *See* Business Cycles; Depressions.

Reclos, Magdeleine. Canada. Children. Mental Illness. Perrot, Nicholas (family of). 1660's-1724. *3250*

Reconstruction *See also* Confederate States of America; Emancipation; Freedmen; Ku Klux Klan; Negroes.

—. Alabama. Education. Negroes. Teachers. Violence. 1865-67. *1091*

—. Alabama (Mobile). Civil War. District of Columbia. Europe. Georgia (Augusta). LeVert, Octavia Walton. Social career. ca 1830-80. *3056*

—. Civil War. Cox, Nancy (letter). Tennessee (Readyville). 1866. *774*

—. Civil War. Economic Conditions. Groves, Avline (letters). Politics. 1860-67. *791*

—. Civil War. Education. Lane, Anne Ewing. Travel. ca 1830-70's. *3099*

—. Family. Freedmen. Marriage registers. 1865-68. *1462*

—. Fiction. Glasgow, Ellen. South. 1895-1905. *1643*

—. Fiction. Negroes. Stowe, Harriet Beecher (*Uncle Tom's Cabin,* 1852). 1850-1900. *1705*

Recreation *See also* Games; Leisure; Physical Education; Resorts; Sports; Vacations.

—. Case, Anna. Family life. New Jersey (Plainfield). 1912-35. *2991*

—. Civil War. Hunter, Kate. Rhode Island (Newport). Social Conditions. 1863-64. *794*

—. Daily Life. Missouri (St. Louis). Mitchell, Clara (diary). Social Conditions. 1887. *3020*

—. Quebec. Social Conditions. 1606-1771. *3355*

Recreation, community. Arts. Day, Ann (interview). Iowa (Waterloo). 1970's. *1854*

Red Moon Boarding School. Hammon, Ida. Oklahoma (Hammon). Secondary Education. 1892-1965. *429*

Redfield, Amy. Civil War. Clothing. New York (Syracuse). Painting. 1860-65. *781*

Reed, Daniel. Alabama (Tombigbee River, west bank). Cajuns. Demography. Reed, Rose. Settlement. Social topography. 1820-1970. *342*

Reed, Rose. Alabama (Tombigbee River, west bank). Cajuns. Demography. Reed, Daniel. Settlement. Social topography. 1820-1970. *342*

Reed, Virginia Elizabeth. California. Donner party. Overland Journeys to the Pacific. 1846. *691*

Reeder, Dorothy. American Library in Paris. Libraries. World War II. 1941-45. *1304*

Referendum. Prohibition. Virginia. Woman's Christian Temperance Union. 1914. *1398*

Reform *See also* types of reform, e.g. Economic Reform, Political Reform, etc.; reform movements, e.g. Abolition Movements, Temperance Movements, etc.; Social Conditions; Social Problems; Utopias.

—. Addams, Jane. Art. Illinois (Chicago). Politics. 1889-1916. *1233*

—. Aid to Families with Dependent Children. Federal Policy. Poor. Public Welfare. Unemployment. 1968-71. *2022*

—. *American Magazine* (periodical). Tarbell, Ida M. 1906-15. *1390*

—. California (Los Angeles). Kindergarten. Severance, Caroline M. Unitarianism. 1870's-1914. *1235*

—. California (San Diego Stingaree, Redlight district). Prostitution. 1870's-1917. *1540*

—. Cities. Crane, Caroline Bartlett. Michigan (Kalamazoo). Progressivism. Sanitation (municipal). 1858-1935. *1383*

—. Congress. Family. Public Welfare. Taxation. 1970's. *2028*

—. Divorce. Historiography. Prostitution. Sex. Social History. 17c-1972. *7*

—. Evangelism. Suffrage. Wright, Henry Clarke. 1820-60. *843*

—. Feminist movement. Organizations (structures). Political strategy. Social Change. 1961-72. *2404*

—. Foundation grants. Gynecology. Law. Obstetrics. Population conferences. 1969-75. *2685*

—. Labor Unions and Organizations. Women's Trade Union League. 1930's. *1119*

—. League of Women Voters. Organizations. Politics. South or Southern States. Young Women's Christian Association. 1920's. *1285*

—. National Association of Colored Women. Negroes. Suffrage. Terrell, Mary Church. 1892-1954. *1459*

—. Politics. Populism. Prohibition. Suffrage. 1891-92. *1326*

Reform movements. Feminism. Medicine, socialized. 1960's-70's. *2418*

Reform school, girls'. Adolescence. Families, make-believe. 1973. *2270*

Refugees. Civil War. Family. Louisiana. Negroes. 1860-65. *898*

Regionalism. Austin, Mary Hunter. Cooking. Southwest. 1868-1934. *1605*

—. Cather, Willa. Fiction. Nebraska. ca 1880's-1930's. *1716*

—. Cather, Willa. Literature. Nebraska. 1890-1923. *1598*

—. Cather, Willa. Literature. Nebraska (Webster County). Prairie (influence of). 1974-75. *1603*

—. Chopin, Kate. Literature. Social Conditions. 19c-20c. *1616*

—. Divorce. Western States. 1960's. *2161*

—. Education. Migration, Internal. Sex differences. 1940-65. *2830*

—. Fiction. Florida. Rawlings, Marjorie Kinnan. 1896-1953. *1600*

—. Friends, Society of. Mysticism. Wilkinson, Jemima. 1752-1819. *390*

—. Goddard, Sarah Updike. Journalism. *Providence Gazette and Country Journal* (newspaper). 1762-70. *605*

Rhode Island (Bristol). Family. Marriage. Social Customs. Vital Statistics. 17c-18c. *502*

Rhode Island (Lime Rock Lighthouse, Newport). Lewis, Ida. Lighthouses (keepers). 1858-1911. *1100*

Rhode Island (Newport). Civil War. Hunter, Kate. Recreation. Social Conditions. 1863-64. *794*

—. Fish, Josiah. Osborn, Sarah. Political Leadership. Revivals. 1714-67. *544*

Rhode Island (Scolloptown). East Greenwich Neighborhood Cottage. Negroes. Settlement house movement. 1902-14. *1406*

Rhode Island (Warren). Economic Conditions. Fertility. Marriage. Sex ratios. Social Conditions. ca 1840-60. *670*

Rhode Island (Wickford). Family. Hinckley, Anita W. (reminiscences). Social Conditions. 20c. *2955*

—. Green, Frances (reminiscences). Hurricanes. Quonset Air Station. Social Conditions. 1890-1974. *2952*

Ribera Chevremont, Evaristo (reminiscences). Burgos, Julia de. Font Saldaña, Jorge (reminiscences). Lair, Clara. Poetry. Puerto Rico. 20c. *3246*

Rice, Gertrude Stevens. Elections. Letters. Roosevelt, Theodore. Social workers. 1912. *1274*

Rice, Sally (letters). Domestic servants. Northeastern or North Atlantic States. Textile workers. 1821-47. *623*

Rich, Emeline Grover. Medical College of Utah. Utah (Morgan). 1880-83. *1567*

Richard B. Harrison Library. Lee, Molly Huston. Librarians. Negroes. North Carolina (Raleigh). 1930-75. *3072*

Richards, Lewis. Baptists. Marriage records. Maryland (Baltimore). 1784-89. *668*

Richardson, Frances (interview). Films. Library Science. Twentieth Century Fox Studios. ca 1940-67. *1863*

Richmond, John Lambert. Medicine (practice of). Obstetrics. Ohio. 1827. *931*

Richmond, Mary. Social Work. 20c. *228*

Richmond, Rebecca. Custer, Elizabeth Bacon (letter). Daily Life. Fort Riley. Kansas. Travel. 1866. *710*

Ricker, Marilla Marks. Diplomacy. McKinley, William. 1896-97. *1220*

Ricketts, Frances L. (diary). Civil War (personal narratives). Hospitals. Nurses and Nursing. Virginia (Manassas, Richmond). 1861-63. *805*

Riedesel, Frederich von. American Revolution. Riedesel, Frederika, Baroness von. 1776-83. *555*

Riedesel, Frederika, Baroness von. American Revolution. Riedesel, Frederich von. 1776-83. *555*

Riegel, Lewis Edgar (reminiscences). Daily life. Pennsylvania (Berks County). Social Customs. 1876-85. *2976*

Rindge, May Knight. California (Malibu). Courts. Environmental protection. Government. Southern Pacific Railroad. ca 1900-72. *3243*

—. California (Topanga Canyon). Government (county, state). Rancho Topanga Malibu Sequit. Roads. 1905-25. *1243*

Rinehart, Mary Roberts. Cather, Willa. Davenport, Marcia. Deland, Margaret. Literature. Long, Haniel. Pennsylvania (Pittsburgh). Schmitt, Gladys. 18c-20c. *430*

—. Glacier National Park. Johnson, Dorothy M. (reminiscences). Montana. National Parks and Reserves. 1916-1970's. *3171*

Rinehart, Susannah Wiles. Genealogy. West Virginia. ca 1790-1811. *3085*

*Rios* v. *Reynolds Metals Company* (1972). Arbitration, Industrial. Discrimination, Employment. *Griggs* v. *Duke Power Company* (1971). 1964-73. *1932*

Riots *See also* Demonstrations; Strikes.

—. Crombie, Helen Elizabeth (diary). Labor Disputes. Pennsylvania (Pittsburgh). Railroads. 1877. *2944*

"Rip Van Winkle" (play). Drama. Family structure. Jefferson, Joseph. 1865. ca 1900-70's. *672*

Ripley, Martha G. Medical Reform. Minnesota. Social Reform. 19c. *3034*

Rites and Ceremonies. Apache Indians (San Carlos). Puberty. 1969. *2613*

—. Colleges and Universities. Sororities (membership recruiting). 1960's. *2798*

—. Family structure. Great Plains. Indians. Sexual intercourse. 19c. *1484*

Rites and Ceremonies (sacrificial). Cheyenne Indians. Dougherty, John. Pawnee Indians (Skidi). Religion. 1827. *910*

Rites of passage. *Women's Studies* (periodical). 1976. *102*

Rivers. See Dams; Floods.

Rives, Judith Walker. France (Paris). Virginia. 19c. *3071*

Roads. California (Topanga Canyon). Government (county, state). Rancho Topanga Malibu Sequit. Rindge, May Knight. 1905-25. *1243*

Robbins, Caroline. Pennsylvania Historical Association (43rd annual meeting). 1975. *2949*

Roberts, Albert H. Elections (gubernatorial). Republican Party. Suffrage. Tennessee. 1920. *1364*

Roberts, Elizabeth Madox. Novels. 1926-30. *1691*

—. South or Southern States. Symbolism in Literature. 1930. *1718*

Roberts, Lillian (interview). Illinois (Chicago). Labor Unions and Organizations. Minorities. Mt. Sinai Hospital. 1950's. *2017*

Roberts, Myrtle (obituary). Social Studies. Teachers. Texas. 1968. *3109*

Roberts, Sarah Ellen. Frontier and Pioneer Life. Great Plains. Lewis, Faye Cashatt. Wyman, Walker D. 1900-70's. *3169*

Robertson, Alice M. Congress. Elections. Veterans' benefits. 1920-24. *1248*

—. Congress. Oklahoma. Political Campaigns. 1898-1923. *1273*

Robertson, Emma. Letters. Nebraska (North Bend). Ranch life. 1891-92. *3184*

Robinson, Harriet Hanson (letters). Attitudes. Massachusetts (Lowell). Textile workers. Working Class. 1845-46. *629*

Robinson, Mary (reminiscences). Civil War. Confederate Army. Danville Female Academy. Missouri. 1864. *795*

Robinson, Nellie Carnahan (memoirs). Colorado (Lavender). Frontier and Pioneer Life. Social Customs. Teachers. 1897-1907. *1081*

Rockefeller, John D. *McClure's Magazine.* Muckrakers. Standard Oil trust. Tarbell, Ida M. 1892-1911. *1654*

Rocky Mountains. Camping. Colorado. Mining towns. Schenck, Annie B. (journal). 1871. *3189*

Rodman, Henrietta. Child care. Collective ventures. Feminist Alliance. Housing. New York (Greenwich Village, Washington Square). 1914-17. *1324*

Roe, Mary Feake. American Revolution (intelligence). Roe, William. 1777-86. *569*

Roe, William. American Revolution (intelligence). Roe, Mary Feake. 1777-86. *569*

Roman Catholic Church. *See* Catholic Church.

Romance. Fairfax, Sally Cary. Washington, George. 1750's-99. *171*

Romance (advice on). Attitudes. Iowa. Newspapers. 19c. *226*

Romantic love. Family (changes in). Marriage, motivations for. Periodicals (content analysis). Power patterns. Sexual behavior. 1825-50. *662*

Romantic Love Complex. Colleges and Universities. Personality Traits. Students. Values. 1960's. *2201*

Romantic symbology. Attitudes. Poetry. Social Conditions. South. 1829-60. *1026*

Romanticism. Addams, Jane. Government. Social Reform. 1889-1912. *1268*

—. Attitudes. Fiction. Marriage. Norris, Kathleen. 1911-57. *1650*

—. Attitudes. Marriage. 1960's. *2119*

—. Attitudes. Patriarchy. Slavery. South or Southern States. 19c. *951*

—. Childrearing. Family (idealized). Marriage. 1960's. *2073*

—. Family. Periodicals (content analysis). Power patterns. Sex roles. 1794-1825. *663*

Romeo, Althea. Hodge, Bertica. Poetry. Virgin Islands. 1900-72. *2862*

Roos, Margit. Morris, Celia. New Jersey. Princeton University. Students. Wasserheit, Judith. 1973. *2282*

Roosevelt, Eleanor. 1886-1905. *1218*

—. Adams, Abigail. Coolidge, Anna Goddhue. Harding, Florence Kling. Letters. Pierce, Jane Means Appleton. 18c-20c. *292*

—. Adams, Abigail. First Ladies. Portraits. Presidents. 18c-20c. *277*

—. Attitudes. Civil War. Letters. Spain. 1930's. *1224*

—. Catholic Church. Congress. Federal Aid to Education. 1949-50. *2319*

—. Civil Rights Movement. 1940-54. *2323*

—. Clapp, Elsie Ripley. Depressions. Education, community. Federal Programs. New Deal. Resettlement. Rural Development. West Virginia (Arthurdale). 1933-44. *1204*

—. Democratic National Convention. Kennedy, John F. Presidential nomination. 1958-61. *2309*

—. Depressions. Federal Government. Manufactures. Social planning. West Virginia (Arthurdale). 1934-47. *1228*

—. Fitzgerald, Zelda Sayre. Marriage (review article). ca 1910's-45. *1156*

—. Human Rights Commission. 1947-51. *2334*

—. Johnson, Lyndon B. Negroes. 1930's-70's. *296*

—. Miners (resettlement of). National Industrial Recovery Act (1933). New Deal. Subsistence Homesteads Program. West Virginia (Arthurdale). 1930-46. *1213*

—. New Deal. Politics. Rural resettlement. West Virginia (Arthurdale). 1930's-40's. *1242*

Roosevelt, Theodore. Cox, Minnie M. Mississippi (Indianola). Negroes. Politics. 1903-04. *1463*

—. Elections. Letters. Rice, Gertrude Stevens. Social workers. 1912. *1274*

—. Morris, Laura Hill. Politics. 1906. *1226*

Rorer, Sarah Tyson. Cookery. Lectures. Pennsylvania. Philadelphia Cooking School. 1870-1901. *1110*

Rose, Forest. California. Diaries. Kansas. Travel. 1887. *3187*

Rosenbaum, Bella W. (reminiscences). Canada. Immigrants. Jews. Social Conditions. USA. 1880's-1910's. *120*

Rosenberg, Charles E. Gordon, Linda. Medical practice (review essay). Sex Discrimination. Smith-Rosenberg, Carroll. Wood, Ann D. 19c. *253*

Rosenberg, Ethel. Politics. Rosenberg, Julius. Schneir, Miriam (review article). Schneir, Walter (review article). Trials. 1950's-60's. *2301*

—. Politics. Rosenberg, Julius. Schneir, Miriam (review article). Schneir, Walter (review article). Trials. 1950's-60's. *2329*

Rosenberg, Julius. Politics. Rosenberg, Ethel. Schneir, Miriam (review article). Schneir, Walter (review article). Trials. 1950's-60's. *2301*

—. Politics. Rosenberg, Ethel. Schneir, Miriam (review article). Schneir, Walter (review article). Trials. 1950's-60's. *2329*

Ross, Diana (review article). Music, popular. Supremes (singing group). 1950's-67. *2919*

Rossellini, Roberto. Bergman, Ingrid. Films. Public Opinion. Sexual behavior. 1949. *2221*

Rossi, Alice. Academic careers. Archivists. Discrimination. 1915-72. *1952*

Roswell Factory. Civil War. Georgia. Resettlement. Sherman, William T. Textile workers. 1864. *779*

*Roth* v. *United States* (US, 1957). Censorship. Pornography. Publishers and Publishing. 1914-67. *2719*

—. Law and Society. Pornography. 1968. *2718*

Roules, Robert (court deposition). Canibas Indians (murder of). King Philip's War. Massachusetts (Marblehead). 1677. *595*

Rourke, Constance (review article). Folklore. Humor. Literary tradition. National Characteristics. 1931. *1608*

Rover, Ruth (pseud. of Margaret Jewett Bailey). Methodist Church. Missions and Missionaries. Oregon. 1854. *1003*

Rowson, Susanna Haswell. Morality. Novels. Sex roles. Stereotypes. 1762-1824. *1012*

Royal Commission on the Status of Women in Canada (report, 1970). Archibald, Kathleen (*Sex and the Public Service*). Canada. 1960's-71. *3262*

—. Canada. Sex Discrimination. 1972. *3261*

Royall, Anne. Alabama. Travel. 1830's. *3107*

Rumsey, Cordelia (letter). Cherokee Outlet. Kansas (Kiowa). Landrush. 1893. *3160*

Rural Development. Clapp, Elsie Ripley. Depressions. Education, community. Federal Programs. New Deal. Resettlement. Roosevelt, Eleanor. West Virginia (Arthurdale). 1933-44. *1204*

Rural Life. See Country Life.

Rural rehabilitation. California. Lange, Dorothea. Migrant Labor. Photography. 1930's. *1257*

Rural resettlement. New Deal. Politics. Roosevelt, Eleanor. West Virginia (Arthurdale). 1930's-40's. *1242*

Rural Schools. Florida. Fry, Alice (recollections). Teachers. 1909-10. *1068*

—. Hyland, Mary McLaughlin. Montana. Social Conditions. Teachers. 1914-39. *1064*

—. Illinois (southern). Stroud, Jessie Ruth (reminiscences). Teaching. 1918-19. *1104*

—. Iowa. Johnson, Anna (recollections). Teachers. 1925-40's. *1083*

—. Kansas. Nebraska. Teachers. 1870's-1910's. *1069*

Rural Settlements *See also* Settlement.

—. Aldrich, Bess Streeter. Fiction. Nebraska. 1881-1954. *1685*

—. Catholic Church. Ethnic Groups. Fertility. Wisconsin. 1940-60. *2141*

—. Daily Life. Family. Quebec (Beaupré). Social Conditions. ca 1900. *3341*

—. Educational aspirations. Negroes. Texas (east central). Youth. 1960's. *2561*

—. Iowa. Occupations (aspirations). Youth. 1948-56. *2267*

—. Missouri. Nurses and Nursing. Public Health. 1960's. *1873*

Rural Sociological Society. Employment. Sex Discrimination. Sociology. Students. 1940-70. *1950*

Rural-Urban Studies. Age structure. Birth Rate. Fertility. Population trends. 20c. *126*

—. Canada. Colleges and Universities. Educational opportunity. 1960's. *3311*

—. Canada. Family. Mennonites. 1960's. *3277*

—. Canada. Fertility. Marriage. USA. 1940-60's. *219*

—. Charity organization movement. Illinois (Chicago). Public Welfare. Social Classes. 1880-1930. *1512*

—. Cities. Lutheran Church. Sex. 1960's. *2486*

—. Colleges and Universities (plans to attend). Social Classes. Wisconsin. 1960's. *2827*

—. District Attorneys. Law enforcement. Pornography. 1965-71. *2725*

—. Employment trends. Farms. Income. Wives. 1959-72. *1916*

—. Family. Households. New York (Kingston, Marborough, Troy). 1800-60. *655*

—. Family (kinship groupings). Migration, Internal. Social Classes. Voluntary Associations. 1960's. *2048*

—. Family size. Ontario (Wentworth County). Wives. 1871. *3361*

—. Family stability. Social networks. 1960's. *2108*

—. Family structure. Fertility. 1960. *2127*

—. Family structure. Fertility. Frontier. Indiana. Population growth. 1820. *669*

—. Fertility. 1965. *2147*

—. Fertility. Growth of American Families study. Negroes. South. Survey of Economic Opportunity. Whites. 1960. 1967. *2146*

—. Fertility. Income. Kentucky. Social Classes. 1940-60. *2136*

—. Fertility. Marital status. Migration, Internal. 1967. *2145*

—. Fertility. Modernization (impact of). Papago Indians. 1960's-70's. *2612*

—. Migration, Internal. Population distribution. Quebec. Sex ratios. 1951-61. *3353*

Rural-urban tensions. Cities. Flappers. 1920's. *1186*

Rush, Benjamin. Education. 1780's-90's. *991*

Russell, Mrs. J. W. (letter). Army (confiscatory activity). Civil War. Mississippi (Raymond). Plantations. Slavery. 1863. *772*

Russell Sage Foundation. Sexism. Social research. 1907-70. *177*

Russian culture *See also* USSR.

—. Alaska (Aleutian Islands). Aleut Indians. Fur hunters. Wives. 1755-1867. *586*

Russians. Breshkovsky, Catherine. Jews. Revolutionary Movements. Sex. 1904-06. *1258*

—. Emigration. Hawaii. Zaharoff, Evdokia Gregovna (travel account). ca 1900-17. *1502*

—. Germans. Immigration. Jews. Organizations. 1880-1924. *1447*

Rutledge, Ann. Cemeteries. Illinois (New Salem, Petersburg). 1890. *3010*

# S

Sabin, Ellen. Education. Friend, Neita Oviatt (reminiscences). Milwaukee-Downer Seminary and College. Wisconsin. 1905-09. *1569*

Sacagawea (Shoshoni). Death date (disputed). Feminists. Indians. 1804-12. ca 1890-1910. *904*

—. Death (date of). 1811. 1884. *3185*

—. Death (date of). Historiography. Lewis and Clark Expedition. 1805. *909*

—. Discovery and Exploration. Indian-White Relations. Lewis and Clark Expedition. 1805-06. *908*

—. Family. Lewis and Clark expedition. Marriage. 1803-84. *907*

—. Heroines. Political Campaigns. Suffrage. Western States. 1902-21. *1371*

—. Indian-White Relations. Lewis and Clark Expedition. 1803-12. *915*

Saddle blankets. Navajo Indians. Weaving. 17c-20c. *323*

Sadlier, Mary Anne Madden. Catholic Church. Dorsey, Ann Hanson McKenney. Novels. 1829-65. *885*

Safier, Gwendolyn. Budd, Karen. Hoffman, Alice. Methodology. Nurses and Nursing. Oral History Association Colloquium (9th annual meeting). Politics. Women's Studies. 1974. *48*

Sailors. Funnemark, Brigitte. Funnemark, Christine. Washington (Tacoma). Waterfront missions. 1897-1903. *1135*

St. Albans School for Boys. District of Columbia. Johnston, Harriet Lane. 1909-72. *2981*

St. Cyril Academy. Catholic Church. Pennsylvania (Danville). Sisters of SS. Cyril and Methodius. Slovak culture. 1909-73. *388*

St. Luke's Penny Savings Bank. Banking. Black Capitalism. United Order of St. Luke. Virginia (Richmond). Walker, Maggie Lena. 1903-30. *1472*

St. Mary's Episcopal School for Indian Girls. Episcopal Church, Protestant. Indians (education). South Dakota (Springfield). 1873-1973. *363*

St. Vincent's Academy. Church Schools. Daughters of the Cross. Louisiana (Shreveport, Fairfield Hill). 1866-1971. *1576*

Saint-Gaudens, Annetta. Architecture. Historical Sites and Parks. Meetinghouses. New Hampshire (Enfield, Cornish). Shakers. 1793-1889. 1902. *1752*

Salaries. *See* Wages.

Salem Female Academy. Kaufman, Anna. Nashville Female Academy. Secondary Education. South or Southern States. 1850's. *979*

Salesmen and Salesmanship *See also* Advertising; Business.

—. Automobile Industry and Trade. Consumers. Discrimination. Ohio (Dayton). Prices. 1970. *1835*

Salisbury, Harriet Hutchinson. Letters. Massachusetts. Travel. Vermont. 1843-46. *2946*

Saloons. Dance halls. Wright, Nettie. Wyoming (Buffalo). 1864-65. *1078*

Saloons (grogshop). Church and State. Massachusetts (Marblehead). Wives. 1640-73. *492*

Saloons (ordinaries). Employment. Legislation. Liquor licences. North Carolina. 17c-18c. *484*

Salt works. Civil War. Tynes, Mollie. Virginia. 1860-65. *812*

Sampson, Deborah. American Revolution. Marriage. Military Service. 1781-1827. *565*

—. American Revolution (biography). Massachusetts Regiment, 4th. Military Service. 1775-1800. *560*

San Jose State University. Academic Freedom. Colleges and Universities. Fingerprinting. Mitford, Jessica. 1973. *1858*

Sanctified Sisters. Communes. Economic Conditions. McWhirter, Martha White. Texas (Belton). 1866-99. *1432*

Sand, Julia (letters). Arthur, Chester A. Politics. 1881-83. *1255*

Sandoz, Mari. Cather, Willa. Image. Literature, western. Sex roles. Western States. 1898-1954. *1548*

—. Childhood. Indians. Literature. Nebraska (Sheridan County). Plains Indians. 1870's-1931. *1619*

—. Fiction. 1908-35. *1647*

—. Literature. Plains Indians. 1930's-60's. *2855*

Sanger, Margaret. Anthony, Lucy. Anthony, Susan B. Feminism. Gilman, Charlotte Perkins. National American Woman Suffrage Association. Shaw, Anna Howard. Suffrage. 1847-1919. *1317*

—. Authors. Censorship. Child, Lydia Maria. Law. ca 1833-1950's. *285*

Sanitary Commission. Civil War. Feminism. Great Northwestern Fair. Illinois (Chicago). Livermore, Mary. 1861-69. *813*

—. Civil War. Letters. Nurses and Nursing. Whetten, Harriet Douglas. 1862. *792*

—. Civil War. Nurses and Nursing. Peninsular campaign. Whetten, Harriet Douglas (diary). 1862. *793*

Sanitation *See also* Cemeteries; Public Health.

Sanitation (municipal). Cities. Crane, Caroline Bartlett. Michigan (Kalamazoo). Progressivism. Reform. 1858-1935. *1383*

Santa Fe Railroad. Employment. Harvey, Frederick Henry. Waitresses. 1859-20c. *147*

Saskatchewan. Aeronautics. Stinson, Katharine. 1908-18. *3383*

—. Droughts. Family. Geographic Mobility. 1930's. *3381*

—. Farmer-Labor Party. Hollis, Mrs. A. McNaughton, Violet. Political Leadership. Radicals and Radicalism. Socialism. 1932-34. *3386*

—. Frog Lake Massacre. Indian Wars. Sayers, Mary Rose (Pritchard). Widows. ca 1885-90. *3384*

—. Indians. Matheson, Eleanor Shepphird (journal). Missions and Missionaries. Travel (canoe). 1920. *3382*

Saskatchewan (Chaplin, Duval). Goodwin, Theresa (reminiscences). Teaching. 1912-13. *3385*

Saskatchewan (Regina). Fiske, Minnie Maddern. Madame Albini. Melba (actress). Theater. Tucker, Sophie. 1900-14. *3387*

Satire. Adultery. Childbirth. Marriage. New England. Prostitution. Puritans. Ward, Nathaniel (*The Simple Cobler of Aggawam in America*). 1647. *495*

—. Bibliographies. Feminism. 1700-1800. *72*

—. British. Popular Culture. Sex. 1960's. *2899*

—. Films (musicals). Garland, Judy. *The Pirate* (film). 1948-71. *2914*

—. Humor. Mabley, Moms. Negroes. 1960's. *2519*

—. Image. Loos, Anita (*Gentlemen Prefer Blondes*). Middle Classes. Sex roles. Values. 1925. *1606*

—. New York (Elmira). Whitcher, Frances Berry. 1847-49. *1027*

*Saturday Evening Post.* Harris, Corra. Journalism. World War I. 1917-18. *1297*

Saulteaux Indians. Canada. Folktales. Marriage. 20c. *3301*

Savusauna. Finnish Americans. Maternity care. Minnesota. 1867-1937. *1495*

Sayers, Mary Rose (Pritchard). Frog Lake Massacre. Indian Wars. Saskatchewan. Widows. ca 1885-90. *3384*

Sayre, Florence (reminiscences). Idaho (Long Valley). ca 1890's-1910. *3239*

Sayre, Minerva. Fitzgerald, F. Scott. Georgia. 19c-20c. *3049*

Scheff, Fritzi. Courtship. Davis, Richard Harding (letters). Fox, John. 1908. *1762*

Schenck, Annie B. (journal). Camping. Colorado. Mining towns. Rocky Mountains. 1871. *3189*

Schlesinger, Arthur M., Sr. Beard, Mary R. Jacobi, Mary Putnam. League of Women Voters. Park, Maud Wood. Radcliffe College (Arthur and Elizabeth Schlesinger Library). ca 1916-70. *81*

Schmitt, Gladys. Cather, Willa. Davenport, Marcia. Deland, Margaret. Literature. Long, Haniel. Pennsylvania (Pittsburgh). Rinehart, Mary Roberts. 18c-20c. *430*

Schneir, Miriam (review article). Politics. Rosenberg, Ethel. Rosenberg, Julius. Schneir, Walter (review article). Trials. 1950's-60's. *2301*

—. Politics. Rosenberg, Ethel. Rosenberg, Julius. Schneir, Walter (review article). Trials. 1950's-60's. *2329*

Schneir, Walter (review article). Politics. Rosenberg, Ethel. Rosenberg, Julius. Schneir, Miriam (review article). Trials. 1950's-60's. *2301*

—. Politics. Rosenberg, Ethel. Rosenberg, Julius. Schneir, Miriam (review article). Trials. 1950's-60's. *2329*

Scholars *See also* Degrees, Academic.

—. Bryant, Margaret M. Linguistics. 1930-74. *1906*

Scholarship. Abel-Henderson, Annie Heloise. Indians (historiography). 1900-47. *1886*

—. Armes, Ethel (*The Story of Coal and Iron in Alabama*, 1910). 1910. *1041*

—. Authors. Books (review article). 1971-72. *11*

—. Calkins, Mary Whiton. Psychology. ca 1890's-1930. *1075*

—. Colleges and Universities (black). Race Relations. South or Southern States. Teaching. 1972-74. *2663*

—. Colleges and Universities (faculty). Employment. 1970's. *1942*

—. Colleges and Universities (faculty). Employment. Illinois, University of, Urbana-Champaign. Social Status. 1970-72. *1947*

—. Congress. Politics. 1970's. *2354*

—. Connecticut. Juvenile offenders. Prisons. 1970's. *2286*

—. Courts. 1873-1973. *289*

—. Courts. 1962-72. *2347*

—. Courts. Employment. Law. 1964-72. *1960*

—. Courts (reforms). Juries, selection of. 1972. *2348*

—. Curricula. Employment. Secondary Education. Social Status. Teachers. 1969. *1980*

—. Democratic Party. Feminism. Political Conventions. 1972. *2324*

—. Divorce. Equal Rights Amendment. Federation of Business and Professional Women's Clubs. Iowa. Lobbying. Sheppard-Towner Act. Social Reform. Wages. 1919-70. *3036*

—. Economic analysis. Political policy. 1970-74. *1800*

—. Economic Conditions. Feminism. 1969-70. *1822*

—. Economic exploitation. Feminist movement. 1940's-60's. *2412*

—. Economic Theory. Monopoly power. 1974. *1940*

—. Editors and Editing. Employment. Newspapers. Women's pages. 1973. *1852*

—. Education. Employment. Feminism. 1960-70. *2430*

—. Education. School boards. 1920-74. *419*

—. Education. Social Status. 18c-1976. *452*

—. Employment. 1970's. *1945*

—. Employment. Feminism. 1960's. *2435*

—. Employment. Higher education. Students. Wages. 1970. *1957*

—. Employment. Housework. Industrialization. Negroes. Wages. Whites. 1970. *1936*

—. Employment. Income. Maternity policies. Public schools. Teacher organizations. 1956-72. *1948*

—. Employment. Industry. Professionals. 1960-63. *1972*

—. Employment. Labor force. 1930-70. *1915*

—. Employment. Library science. Mass Media. Stereotypes. 1950-75. *1967*

—. Employment. Personnel departments. ca 1970-73. *1949*

—. Employment. Rural Sociological Society. Sociology. Students. 1940-70. *1950*

—. Employment. Social Status. Wages. 1960's-70. *1963*

—. Employment (inquiries). Georgia (Atlanta). Stereotypes. 1975. *1962*

—. Employment, professional. Wage differentials. 1966-71. *1965*

—. Episcopal Church, Protestant. Ordination. 1973. *2479*

—. Equal employment opportunity. Federal government. Public Employees. 1970's. *1953*

—. Equal employment opportunity. Labor Department. Women's Bureau. 1920-70. *278*

—. Equal Pay Act, 1963 (enforcement of). Labor. 1963-70. *1969*

—. Equal Rights Amendment. Law. 1921-73. *2343*

—. Femininity. Georgia. Schools. Smith, Lillian. Teaching. 1920-60. *469*

—. Feminism. Hawthorne, Nathaniel *The Scarlet Letter*. Hutchinson, Anne. Puritans. Theology. Winthrop, John. 1634-38. 1850. *534*

—. Feminism. Social Work. Wages. 1960's-70's. *1978*

—. Feminist movement. 1960's. *2421*

—. Feminist movement. 1950-74. *2436*

—. Gordon, Linda. Medical practice (review essay). Rosenberg, Charles E. Smith-Rosenberg, Carroll. Wood, Ann D. 19c. *253*

—. Gynecology. Midwives. Obstetrics. Physicians. 1760-1860. *930*

—. Health. Higher education. Science and Society. ca 1870's-1900's. *1583*

—. Health insurance, national. Insurance companies. 1975. *1819*

—. High Schools. Political Protest. Youth movements. 1971. *2271*

—. Higher Education. Social Classes. 1957-70. *2828*

—. Income differences. Labor market. ca 1950-73. *1955*

—. India (New Delhi). State Department (Foreign Service). 1971. *1954*

—. International Women's Year. Labor Unions and Organizations. 1970's. *2009*

—. Journalism. Newspapers. 1971. *1964*

—. Labor organizations (need for). 1970's. *2020*

—. Labor Reform. Working Conditions. 1830-1910. *165*

—. Language. Literature. 1972. *2748*

—. Law Reform. Lawyers. 1869-1969. *268*

—. Lawyers. 1968-72. *1982*

—. Lawyers. Legal profession. 1945-69. *1943*

—. Liberalism. Periodicals. 1971. *1938*

—. Los Angeles *Times* (newspaper). News photos, content of. Social roles. Washington *Post* (newspaper). 1974. *2763*

—. Medical profession. Nurses and Nursing. 19c-1973. *142*

—. Medicine, industrial. Nurses and Nursing. Physicians. 1848-1975. *141*

—. Methodology. Social status. Sociology. 1961-72. *2030*

—. Military Service. 1960's-70's. *2451*

—. Models. Occupational choice theories. Social Status attainment. 1954-75. *1867*

—. Negroes. Racism. 1970's. *2521*

—. New York City. Organizational structuring. Travel agency industry. 1974. *1893*

—. Nurses and Nursing. 1941-75. *1977*

—. Nurses and Nursing. Patients. Research. Sociology, medical. 1970's. *60*

—. Occupations. Racism. 1960's-70's. *1966*

—. Occupations. Wages. 1945-73. *1983*

—. Political Participation. Stereotypes. 1960's-70's. *2358*

—. Political Science. Professions (nonacademic). 1960's-70. *1918*

—. Postage Stamps. 1940-71. *2727*

—. Puerto Rico. Values. 1974. *2175*

—. Racism. Social Conditions. 1960's-70's. *2638*

—. Unemployment rate. Wages. 1947-73. *1971*

Sex Discrimination (review article). Anglican Communion. Clergy. 1973. *2490*

Sex distribution. Family. Marriage customs. Quebec (St. Paul River). Religion. 1960's. *3332*

Sex education. Attitudes. Morality. 1890-1920. *1188*

—. Children. Morality. 1833-1906. *184*

—. Churches. Family. Schools. Teacher Training. 1960's. *2218*

—. Curricula. Family life. Public Schools. 1960's. *2846*

—. Family. Marriage. Middle Classes. Values. ca 1850-1900. *1141*

Sex (extramarital). Marriage. 1960's. *2223*

Sex (frigidity). Greer, Germaine (*The Female Eunuch*). Ideology. Marxism. Patriarchy. 1960's-70's. *2432*

Sex, group. Decisionmaking. Marriage. Ontario (Toronto). Wives. 1967-72. *3280*

Sex life. Celibacy. Communes. Lee, Ann. Northeastern or North Atlantic States. Shakers. 1774-1968. *378*

Sex manuals. Attitudes. Canada. 1900-15. *3276*

—. Folk Medicine. 1700-1850. *179*

Sex, premarital. Aim-inhibition hypotheses. Love relationships. 1960's-70's. *2231*

—. Attitudes. Catholic Church. Dating, interfaith. Social status. 1971. *2229*

—. Attitudes. Negroes. Social Conditions. Whites. 1960's. *2239*

Sex ratios. Canada. Economic Conditions. Marriage trends. USA. 1830-1970. *197*

—. Cities. Employment. Industrialization. 1960's. *1880*

—. Demography. Nebraska. Pioneers. 1860-80. *3201*

—. Economic Conditions. Fertility. Marriage. Rhode Island (Warren). Social Conditions. ca 1840-60. *670*

—. Family structure. Negroes. 1940-70. *2545*

—. Fertility. Ohio. Population pressure. Whites. 1810-60. *666*

—. Leadership. Library associations. Societies. 1876-1923. *1063*

—. Migration, Internal. Population distribution. Quebec. Rural-Urban Studies. 1951-61. *3353*

Sex (references to). Periodicals. Public Opinion. 1950-70. *2243*

Sex role conflicts. Colleges and Universities. Sociology. 1946-71. *2192*

Sex role culture. Civil Rights. Educational practice. 1970's. *2812*

Sex role models. Disney, Walt. Fairy tales. Films. Heroines. Literature, children's. Oral traditions. 1930-75. *2743*

—. Elementary Education. Reading texts. 1600-1966. *257*

Sex role orientation. Girl Scouts of America. Voluntary Associations. ca 1965-75. *2294*

Sex role preferences. Marriage. 1966-68. *2090*

Sex role socialization. Family structure. Social Change. Values. 1940-70. *2042*

—. Public welfare. Stereotypes. Washington (Seattle). 1972. *2182*

Sex roles. Abortion. Criminal Law. Medicine and State. Social Classes. 1960's. *2702*

—. Adams, Abigail. Adams, John. Attitudes. Letters. 1776-1804. *760*

—. Adams, Henry Brooks. Adams, Marian (suicide). Family. 1892-1918. *1178*

—. Adams, Henry Brooks. Harman, Moses. Politics. Stern, Karl. Violence. Waisbrooker, Lois. 1960's. *2194*

—. Addams, Jane. Education. Hull House. Ideology. Illinois (Chicago). Social Reform. 1875-1930. *1411*

—. Addams, Jane. Middle Classes. Social Reform. Stereotypes. Wald, Lillian. 1870-1930. *1275*

—. Age. Marriage. Vital Statistics. 1850-1950. *1148*

—. Age roles. Attitudes. Violence. Youth Movements. 1964-73. *2291*

—. Aged. Connecticut (Wethersfield). Dower rights. Economic conditions. Marriage patterns. Widows. 1640-1700. *489*

—. Alaska. Assimilation. Biculturalism. Eskimos. Music. 1944-74. *2603*

—. Alcott, Louisa May (*Jo's Boys*). Barr, Amelia Edith Huddleston (*Between Two Loves*). Chopin, Kate (*The Awakening*, 1899). Glasgow, Ellen (*The Descendant*). Harrison, Constance Cary (*A Bachelor Maid*). Image. Jewitt, Sarah Orne (*A Country Doctor*). Novels. Social Change. 1880-1900. *1639*

—. Androgyny. Capitalism. Patriarchy. Symbolism. Prehistory-1974. *173*

—. Androgyny. Social Theory. BC-1973. *200*

—. Antimale sentiments. Moral reform. New York Moral Reform Society. Prostitution. ca 1830-60. *926*

—. Art. *Godey's Lady's Book* (periodical). Hale, Sarah Josepha. Womanhood (image of). 1830-60. *960*

—. Assimilation. Chinese Americans. Family. 1973. *2626*

—. Attitudes. Canada. Courtship. Interpersonal Relations. Students. USA. 1969. *217*

—. Attitudes. Careers. Family. Psychology. 1960's-72. *2258*

—. Attitudes. Childrearing. Friends, Society of. Theology. 17c-19c. *334*

—. Attitudes. Colleges and Universities. Students. 1950's-60's. *2171*

—. Attitudes. Connecticut (Hartford). Literature. Sigourney, Lydia Howard. 1830-55. *1007*

—. Attitudes. Ideology. Values. 1963-75. *2188*

—. Attitudes. Management. Men. New York (Rochester). 1960's-70. *1839*

—. Attitudes. Mothers. Social Psychology. Students. 1969. *2173*

—. Attitudes. Patriarchy. Slavery. Social conditions. South. 1848-60. *686*

—. Attitudes. Psychiatry. Values. 1960's. *2713*

—. Attitudes. Social Change. Students (college). 1966-72. *2277*

—. Authors. Education. Religion. Womanhood (definitions of). 1820-60. *964*

—. Authors. Family. Feminism. Hale, Sarah Josepha. Hentz, Caroline Lee. Morality. Sigourney, Lydia Howard. Southworth, E. D. E. N. Womanhood (image of). 19c. *961*

—. Authors. Fiction. Image. 1800-1914. *477*

—. Authors. Social Work. 1960's. *1909*

—. Behavior. Clothing. Popular Culture. Social Conditions. 1945-60's. *2209*

—. Behavior. Dating. Inferiority (pretensions to). 1950-72. *2168*

—. Behavior. Masturbation. Medical literature. Social classes. 1830-1900. *232*

—. Behavior. Psychology. Stereotypes. 1949-71. *2204*

—. Behavior. Public schools. Stereotypes. 1971-72. *2197*

—. Behavior models. Navajo Indians. 20c. *2598*

—. Behavior patterns. Family. Public opinion surveys. Wives. 1960's. *2031*

—. Birth control. Feminist groups. Motherhood. 1870's-80's. *1181*

—. Bradstreet, Anne. Massachusetts Bay Colony. Poetry. Puritans. 17c. *613*

—. Cooking utensils. Folklore. Food preparation. 18c-19c. *230*

—. Courtship. Family. Maine. Marriage. Penobscot Indians. 1492-1900. *370*

—. Courtship. Kentucky. Marriage. Ohio River Valley. 19c-20c. *3144*

—. Courtship. Marriage. New England. Sexual behavior. 1632-1783. *510*

—. Daily Life. Folklore. Houses. Tennessee (east). 1974. *2195*

—. Daily Life. Housekeepers. Immigration. Oregon (Carlton, Yamhill River Valley). Swedish Americans. 19c. *1501*

—. Daily life. Pennsylvania (Berks County). Riegel, Lewis Edgar (reminiscences). 1876-85. *2976*

—. Economic organization. Family. Paintings. Sioux Indians (North Teton, Yankton). Tipi. 1864. *912*

—. Employment. Heller, Elizabeth Wright (autobiography). Iowa. 1880-81. *1077*

—. Family. Jews. Motherhood. 1970's. *2506*

—. Family. Marriage. Rhode Island (Bristol). Vital Statistics. 17c-18c. *502*

—. Family life. Folklife studies. Pennsylvania. West Grove Housekeepers Association. 1860-69. *1197*

—. Family life. Mennonites, Old Order. Pennsylvania (East Penn Valley). 1974. *1433*

—. Folk Art. Handkerchiefs, historic. 19c. *470*

—. Folklore. Georgia (Okefenokee Swamp Rim). Men. Talking Trash (idiom). 1966-72. *2167*

—. Government (tribal). Iroquois Indians. 18c. *589*

—. Interpersonal Relations. Television. 1974. *2206*

—. Marriage. Prehistory-20c. *189*

—. Marriage. Moravians. North Carolina (Salem). Sexual behavior. Theocracy. 1772-1860. *884*

—. Mother (image of). Poetry. Symbolism in Literature. Values. 19c. *406*

—. Sex. 1966. *2170*

Social Customs (manners). Family relationships. Welty, Eudora (*Delta Wedding*, 1946). 1946. *2867*

Social desirability (concept of). Methodology. Sexual status. 1972. *2191*

Social deviance. Behavior. Feminism. Sociology. Stereotypes. 1970's. *63*

Social distance. Children. Hawaii. Racism. Stereotypes. ca 1960's-70's. *2517*

Social function. Periodicals. *Playboy* (periodical). Sexual norms. 1950's-67. *2751*

Social gospel. Bashford, James W. China. Feminism. Methodist Episcopal Church. Missions and Missionaries. 1889-1919. *1316*

Social Gospel Movement. Methodist Protestant Church. Shaw, Anna Howard. Suffrage. 1880-1919. *1446*

Social History. Cities. Family. Population trends. 1750-1975. *206*

—. Divorce. Historiography. Prostitution. Reform. Sex. 17c-1972. *7*

—. Family economics. Manuscripts. New England. Pierce, John. 1800-50. *647*

Social Indicators. Gans, Herbert J. Music. 1960-73. *2897*

Social Insurance. *See* Health Insurance; Pensions.

Social involvement. Aged. Industrialization. Urbanization. Widows. 1968-69. *2055*

Social justice. Illinois (Chicago). Progressivism. Prostitution. 1910-15. *1535*

Social life. Beale, Marie. Beale, Truxtun. Decatur House. District of Columbia. ca 1910-40's. *1264*

Social mobility. Canada. Cities. Education. Family. Occupations. Sex differences. 1972. *3256*

—. Catholic Church. Church Schools. Felicians. Polish Americans. Social Work. 1855-1975. *374*

—. Economic Conditions. Professionalism. Sex. Spiritualists. 19c. *153*

—. Family life. French Americans. Irish Americans. New York (Cohoes). Strikes. Textile Industry. Violence. Working Class. 1870's-80's. *1134*

—. Family structure. Immigrants. Irish Americans. Pennsylvania (Scranton). Welsh Americans. 1880-90. *1491*

—. Income distribution. Poverty. Wealth. 1945-70. *1802*

—. Occupations. 1969-73. *1888*

—. Political Attitudes. Sexes. 1950's-70. *2380*

Social Mobility aspirations. Adolescents. Family relationships. 1960's. *2287*

—. Attitudes. Children. Family. Parents. 1971. *2089*

Social movements. Cities. Suffrage. Violence. 1960-68. *1332*

Social networks. Family stability. Rural-Urban Studies. 1960's. *2108*

Social norms. Middle Classes. Sex roles. Textbooks, Marriage and family. 1960's-70's. *2211*

Social order. Employment. Family structure. Labor market. 1600-1970's. *111*

—. Family. 1960's. *2087*

—. Family. Statism. ca 1945-72. *2113*

Social Organization. Acculturation. Catholic Church. Family. Italian Americans (review article). 1880's-20c. *373*

—. Age differences. Marriage. 1974. *2110*

—. Attitudes. Behavior (adult). Children. Kiowa Apache Indians. 1971. *2599*

—. Authority structure. Canada. Eskimos. Family. 1970's. *3299*

—. Childrearing. Family. Industrialization. ca 1940-70. *2091*

—. Children. Family. Feminist movement. Patriarchy. Politics. Prehistory-1971. *109*

—. Chinese Americans. Family life. Immigration. Prostitution. Tong societies. 1850-1972. *321*

—. Colleges and Universities. Employment. Wives (faculty). Working Conditions. 1944-62. *1879*

—. Cultural history. Sexuality. 1974. *2169*

—. Demography. West. ca 1860-1900. *3180*

—. Discrimination, Employment. Education. Occupational achievement (vicarious). Sex roles. Wives. 1970-72. *1900*

—. Economic structure. Higher education. Income. 18c-1972. *461*

—. Education. Marriage. 1960-67. *2125*

—. Employment (part-time). 1967. *1896*

—. Eskimos (Netsilik). Infanticide, female. Northwest Territories (Pelly Bay). 1870's-1970's. *3393*

—. Ethnographic literature. Indians. Iroquois Indians. Lafitau, Joseph François. 1724-1970. *364*

—. Exogamy. Natchez Indians. Prehistory. *386*

—. Family. Public Welfare. 1960's. *2024*

—. Family, future. 1970. *2103*

—. Feminism. Morality. Mother-child relationship. 1972. *287*

—. Feminist movement. 1972. *2419*

—. Indians. Marriage patterns. Prehistory-1971. *356*

—. Marriage. Owen, Robert Dale. Utopias. Wright, Frances. 1826-32. *863*

—. Matriliny. Natchez Indians. Prehistory-18c. *312*

—. Mental health. Morality. Sexual deviance. 1960's. *2227*

Social Organizations. Congresswomen. Human Relations. 1960's. *2310*

—. Family. German Americans. Jews. ca 1870-1920's. *1428*

—. Feminist movement (origins). 1960-71. *2403*

Social planning. Depressions. Federal Government. Manufactures. Roosevelt, Eleanor. West Virginia (Arthurdale). 1934-47. *1228*

Social policies. Equality. Feminist movement. 1950-75. *2398*

Social Problems *See also* Aged; Alcoholism; Charities; Child Labor; Crime and Criminals; Divorce; Drug Abuse; Emigration; Housing; Immigration; Juvenile Delinquency; Migrant Labor; Prostitution; Public Welfare; Race Relations; Skid Rows; Unemployment.

—. Alcoholism. Skid Rows. 1968-71. *2646*

—. Asians. Psychology. Wives. 1950's-70's. *2053*

—. Attitudes. Feminism. Legislators. Negroes. Politics. 1971. *2574*

—. Chicago *Daily Tribune* (newspaper). Child Welfare. Divorce. Domestic servants. Illinois. Marks, Nora (pseud. of Eleanora Stackhouse). Reporters and Reporting. 1888-90. *1673*

—. Childbirth. Discrimination. Family breakdown. Illegitimacy. Negroes. Sex roles. 18c-1972. *371*

—. Crime and Criminals. Law and Society. Morality. Public opinion. Sex. 1619-1776. *598*

—. Family. 1960's. *2092*

—. Feminist movement. Occupational inequality. Stereotypes. 1972. *2439*

—. Maternity homes, role of. Moral reinstatement. Mothers, unwed. 1968. *2657*

Social Psychology *See also* Human Relations; Violence.

—. 1972. *2058*

—. Attitudes. Mothers. Sex roles. Students. 1969. *2173*

—. Cities. Negroes. Sexual identity. Whites. 1968. *2166*

—. Higher Education. Occupational role innovation. 1960's. *1917*

—. Racism. Sex. Violence. 1974. *2669*

Social Reform *See also* names of reform movements, e.g. Temperance Movements; Social Problems.

—. Abbott, Grace. Child welfare. Kelley, Florence. Lathrop, Julia. Legislation. Politics. Sheppard-Towner Act. Wald, Lillian. 1900-35. *1236*

—. Abolition Movement. Civil War. Feminist movement. Negroes. Tubman, Harriet. Underground railroad. 1820-1913. *379*

—. Abolition Movement. Feminism. Sculpture. Socialism. Whitney, Anne. ca 1850-1915. *1770*

—. Abolitionism. Middle Classes. Sexuality. 1830-65. *856*

—. Addams, Jane. Cities. Family. Illinois (Chicago). Politics. ca 1889-1935. *1413*

—. Addams, Jane. Davis, Allen F. (review article). 1880's-1930's. *1256*

—. Addams, Jane. Education. Hull House. Ideology. Illinois (Chicago). Sex roles. 1875-1930. *1411*

—. Addams, Jane. Government. Romanticism. 1889-1912. *1268*

—. Addams, Jane. Illinois (Chicago). Immigrants' Protective League. 1908-21. *1408*

—. Addams, Jane. Middle Classes. Sex roles. Stereotypes. Wald, Lillian. 1870-1930. *1275*

—. Alcott, Bronson. Family structure. Fruitlands community. Lane, Charles. Massachusetts. Utopias. 1840-50. *862*

—. Amalgamated Clothing Workers Union. Craton, Ann Washington. Labor Unions and Organizations. 1915-44. *1125*

—. American Antislavery Society. Anthony, Susan B. Constitutional Amendment (19th). Feminism. Suffrage. 1840's-1920. *1366*

—. Avery, Martha Moore. Catholic Church. Massachusetts (Boston). ca 1880's-1929. *1210*

—. Baez, Joan. Music (vocal). 1960's-74. *2918*

—. Barnard, Kate. Labor Unions and Organizations. Oklahoma. Progressivism. ca 1900-10's. *1267*

—. Birth control. Comstock, Anthony. Morality. Pornography. 1871-1915. *1504*

—. British Columbia (Victoria). Family. Grant, Helen Smith. Maritime History. Nova Scotia (Maitland). 1850-1910. *3327*

—. Bull, Mary Sherwood. Feminism. New York (Seneca Falls). 1830's-80's. *2978*

—. California. Education. Indian-White Relations. Marriage. Paiute Indians. Winnemucca, Sarah (Paiute). 1840's-91. *1487*

—. Canada. Feminist movement. 1955-75. *3293*

—. Catholic Church. Infant mortality. New Jersey (Jersey City). Progressivism. Protestantism. Settlement houses. Whittier House. 1890-1917. *1391*

—. Chautauqua Circuit. Lectures. Tarbell, Ida M. 1916-32. *1601*

—. Child Welfare. Children's Code Commission. Missouri. Organizations. Suffrage. Woman's Christian Temperance Union. 1915-19. *1284*

—. Children. Day Nurseries. Feminism. 1854-1973. *234*

—. Child-saving movement. Juvenile Delinquency. ca 1870-1900. *1271*

—. Churches. City Government. Pennsylvania (Lancaster). Prostitution. 1914-64. *1402*

—. College Settlement Association. Settlement houses. 1889-94. *1412*

—. Colorado Woman's College. Cooper, Jane Olivia Barnes. Philanthropy. 19c. *3157*

—. Connecticut (Kingston). Crandall, Prudence. Harris, Sarah (biography). Negroes. 1781-1902. *902*

—. Dance halls. Frontier and Pioneer Life. Mining towns. Montana. Prostitution. ca 1870's-1910's. *1537*

—. Dewson, Mary Williams. Labor Law. Minimum wage movement. 1897-1962. *1047*

—. Dike, Samuel W. Divorce. New England Divorce Reform League. Vermont. 1860's-1912. *1166*

—. Divorce. Equal Rights Amendment. Federation of Business and Professional Women's Clubs. Iowa. Lobbying. Sex discrimination. Sheppard-Towner Act. Wages. 1919-70. *1168*

—. Dix, Dorothea. Hospitals. Medicine (practice of). Mental Illness. Psychiatry. 19c. *933*

Steamboats. Kentucky. Missouri. Smith, Sallie D. (diary). Travel accounts. 1868. *3114*

Stebbins, Sara Ames (letter). Frontier and Pioneer Life. Illinois. 1839. *695*

Stein, Gertrude. Art collectors. Cone, Claribel. Cone, Etta. 1900-51. *1750*

—. Autobiography and Memoirs. ca 1900-40's. *1622*

—. Bloom, Ellen F. (reminiscence). Literature. 1874-1946. *1607*

—. Krause, Louise Antoinette. Poetry. 1939. *1730*

—. Nationalism. Novels. Wharton, Edith. 19c-20c. *1668*

Stein, Gertrude (review essay). Art. Literature. Toklas, Alice B. ca 1900-46. *1634*

Steinem, Gloria. Decter, Midge. Feminism. Vilar, Esther. 1973. *2415*

Steiner, Mollie. Anarchism and Anarchists. Espionage Act (1917). Supreme Court. Trials. 1917-21. *2679*

Steiner, Ruth Heller (memoirs). Heller, Ernestine. Heller, Louise. Illinois (Chicago). Jews. 20c. *124*

Steinitz, Kate (tribute). Artists. Bibliographies. Librarians. 1889-1969. *2931*

Steinmeyer, Juliana (writings). German Americans. Immigrants. Missouri. Religion. 1840's-60's. *3022*

Stephan, Ruth. Poets. 1910-74. *2884*

Stereotypes. Addams, Jane. Middle Classes. Sex roles. Social Reform. Wald, Lillian. 1870-1930. *1275*

—. Advertising. 1970's. *2732*

—. Advertising. Airline stewardesses. 1960's-70's. *2737*

—. Age. Negroes. 1972. *2552*

—. Alcott, Louisa May. Dodge, Mary Elizabeth Mapes. Fiction. Negroes. Pierson, Helen W. 1860's. *1620*

—. Alessandro, Antonietta Pisanelli. Immigrants. Pesotta, Rose. Zeman, Josephine Humpel. 1880-1924. *1550*

—. Anthropology. Biology. Family structure. Ideology. Labor, sexual division of. Patriarchy. 20c. *119*

—. Authors. Negroes. Self concepts. 1970's. *2536*

—. Behavior. Feminism. Social deviance. Sociology. 1970's. *63*

—. Behavior. Psychology. Sex roles. 1949-71. *2204*

—. Behavior. Public schools. Sex roles. 1971-72. *2197*

—. Cartoons. Periodicals. Speech. 1972-73. *2734*

—. Cartoons. Sex roles. Television. 1973. *2736*

—. Childrearing. Family patterns. Historiography. Socialization. Values. 1825-75. *656*

—. Childrearing. Psychology. Race Relations. Sexual behavior. Slavery. South. 1800-1972. *172*

—. Children. Folklore. 1960's. *2757*

—. Children. Hawaii. Racism. Social distance. ca 1960's-70's. *2517*

—. Children. Law Enforcement. Occupational roles. Television. 1960's. *2749*

—. Colleges and Universities. Feminism. Sex roles. 1960's. *2434*

—. Colleges and Universities. Textbooks, history. 1940's-70's. *38*

—. Comic books. Sex roles. Youth. 1969-72. *2284*

—. Curricula. Schools. Sex roles. Teachers. 1939-72. *2813*

—. Dickey, Sarah. Heck, Barbara. Leadership. Methodist Church. Parker, Lois Stiles. Shaw, Anna Howard. Willard, Frances. 19c. *315*

—. Drama. Feminism. Social Classes. 1906-07. *1756*

—. Elites, professional. Employment. Sex roles. 1970's. *1866*

—. Employment. Library science. Mass Media. Sex Discrimination. 1950-75. *1967*

—. Employment (inquiries). Georgia (Atlanta). Sex discrimination. 1975. *1962*

—. Family backgrounds. Femininity. Occupational aspirations. 1973. *1887*

—. Family models. Mexican Americans. 1968-74. *2622*

—. Feminism. Racism. Revolutionary Movements. 1970. *2395*

—. Feminist movement. Occupational inequality. Social problems. 1970. *2439*

—. Fiction. Marriage. Mormons (images of). Sex. 19c. *302*

—. Fiction. Negroes. Slavery. Stowe, Harriet Beecher (*Uncle Tom's Cabin,* 1852). 1830's-50's. *954*

—. Folk Songs. Prostitution. Western States. 19c-20c. *394*

—. Frontier and Pioneer Life. West. ca 1870-1974. *3203*

—. Gynecology. Sex roles. Textbooks. 1943-72. *2741*

—. High Schools. Textbooks (history). 1960's. *46*

—. Illinois (Chicago). Social Reform. 1833-37. *697*

—. Indians. 15c-20c. *341*

—. *Julia* (program). Negroes. Television. 1960's-70's. *2582*

—. Labor market. Negroes. Occupations (diversification of). 1890-1970. *346*

—. Literature (children's). Nancy Drew (fictional character). New Deal. 1930's. 1960's-70's. *399*

—. Morality. Novels. Rowson, Susanna Haswell. Sex roles. 1762-1824. *1012*

—. Negroes. Sex differences. Students, college. Whites. ca 1970-74. *2205*

—. Nurses and Nursing. Sex roles. 20c. *1924*

—. Political Participation. Sex Discrimination. 1960's-70's. *2358*

—. Public welfare. Sex role socialization. Washington (Seattle). 1972. *2182*

—. Schools. Sex roles. Teaching. 1973. *2825*

—. Sex roles. 1960's. *2165*

—. Sex roles. 1973. *2178*

—. Speech. ca 1970-74. *2735*

Sterilization. Children (illegitimate). North Carolina. Racism. State Legislatures. 1957-59. *2655*

Sterilization bill. Public Opinion. Race Relations. State Legislatures. Virginia. 1960's. *2336*

Sterilization laws. Children. Eugenics. Illegitimacy. Mothers. Public Policy. 1907-66. *224*

Sterilization movement. Birth Control. Eugenics. State Legislatures. Supreme Court. 20c. *227*

Stern, Karl. Adams, Henry Brooks. Harman, Moses. Politics. Sex roles. Violence. Waisbrooker, Lois. 1960's. *2194*

Steunenberg, Bess (reminiscences). Economic Conditions. Idaho (Caldwell). Social Conditions. ca 1900. *3242*

Stevens, Harriet F. (journal). *Continental* (steamship). Mercer, Asa Shinn. Voyages. Washington Territory. Westward Movement. 1866. *764*

Stewart, Cora Wilson. Educational Reform. Illiteracy. Kentucky Illiteracy Commission. Kentucky (Rowan County). 1910-20. *1578*

Stewart, Helen J. Historians. Nevada (Las Vegas). Ranching. 1879-1926. *1108*

Stewart, Mary. Eden, Dorothy. Holt, Victoria. Image. Novels, gothic. Whitney, Phyllis. 1955-73. *2738*

Stillman, Dorothy. California (Yosemite; Hetch Hetchy Valley). Conservation of Natural Resources. Dams. Duryea, Robert. 1914. *1225*

Stinson, Katharine. Aeronautics. Saskatchewan. 1908-18. *3383*

Stirpiculture experiment. Childcare. Genetics. Marriage. New York. Noyes, John Humphrey. Oneida community. 1848-86. *2162*

Stockton, Betsey. Hawaii. Missions and Missionaries. Negroes. Presbyterian Church. 1822-65. *888*

Stoddard, Elizabeth Barstow. California (San Francisco). *Daily Alta California* (newspaper). Journalism. 1854-57. *1013*

Stoicism. Christianity. Stowe, Harriet Beecher (*Uncle Tom's Cabin,* 1852). Uncle Tom (fictional character). 1854. *1009*

Stokes, Elsie Carlson. AU7 Ranch. Daily Life. South Dakota (Hot Springs). Swedish Americans. ca 1910-30. *3197*

Stone, Sophia. Barrow, Clyde. Crime and Criminals. Darby, H. Dillard. Louisiana (Ruston). Parker, Bonnie. 1933. *1517*

Stonecutters. Immigration. Italians. Novels. Tomasi, Mari. Vermont. 1909-65. *2979*

Stonington, Nancy. Alaska, southeastern. Painting (watercolors). 1965-75. *2911*

Storms. *See* Hurricanes.

Storms, Jane McManus. Beach, Moses Y. Diplomacy (secret). Journalism. Mexican War. Polk, James K. 1846-48. *762*

Stowe, Harriet Beecher. Abolition Movement. Literature. Painting. 1832-96. *113*

—. *Atlantic Monthly* (periodical). Byron, George Gordon. Literary careers. 1869. *1674*

—. Crozier, Alice (review article). Novels. Parker, Gail Thain (review article). Womanhood (concept of). Women's Studies. 1820-1920. 1972-73. *2*

—. Feminism. Literature. Negroes. Truth, Sojourner. 1850's-90's. *280*

—. Fiction. Folklore. 1852-72. *436*

—. Fictional characters. Literary tradition. South or Southern States. 1851-20c. *1624*

—. Literature. Ohio (Cincinnati). Semi-Colon Club. 1829-46. *1025*

—. New England. New York City. Readings, Public. 1872. *1729*

Stowe, Harriet Beecher (*Dred,* 1856). Slavery. 1856. *949*

Stowe, Harriet Beecher (influence). Abolitionism. Kentucky. Webster, Delia. 1810-61. *855*

Stowe, Harriet Beecher (*Uncle Tom's Cabin,* 1852). Antislavery Sentiments. Hildreth, Richard (*The Slave or Memoirs of Archy Moore*). Novels. 1836-50's. *999*

—. Cartoons and Caricatures. Fictional characters. Morality. Politics. 1888-1960. *478*

—. Christianity. Stoicism. Uncle Tom (fictional character). 1854. *1009*

—. Cities. Novels. Slavery. South or Southern States. 1850's. *940*

—. Drama. Films. ca 1850-1973. *465*

—. Emancipation. Race Relations. 19c. *288*

—. Family. Racism. Slavery. South. ca 1852-70. *941*

—. Fiction. Negroes. Reconstruction. 1850-1900. *1705*

—. Fiction. Negroes. Slavery. Stereotypes. 1830's-50's. *954*

—. Italy. Novels. 1852-1940's. *1743*

—. Literature. Racial attitudes. Slavery. 1851-52. *942*

—. Literature. Slavery. Thorpe, Thomas B. (*The Master's House,* 1853). 1852-54. *944*

—. Pennsylvania (Philadelphia). Periodicals. Peterson, Charles Jacobs. Womanhood (image of). ca 1840-65. *957*

—. Publishers and Publishing. ca 1852-1900. *1011*

—. Theater. 1870's. *1760*

Stratification, sexual. Friedan, Betty. Sexual identity. Social Status. 1960's. *2181*

Street, Jane (letter). Domestic workers. Industrial Workers of the World. Labor Unions and Organizations. 1917. *1121*

Strikes *See also* Arbitration, Industrial; Collective Bargaining; Labor Unions and Organizations.

—. Abolition movement. Constitutional Amendment (19th). Feminism. Marriage. New York (Seneca Falls). Suffrage. 1848-1920. *299*

—. Family life. French Americans. Irish Americans. New York (Cohoes). Social mobility. Textile Industry. Violence. Working Class. 1870's-80's. *1134*

—. Garment workers. Illinois (Chicago). O'Reilly, Mary. Socialists. Zeh, Nellie M. 1910. *1118*

—. Labor Unions and Organizations. New York (Rochester). Women's Protection Union. 1800's-1914. *152*

Strikes and Lockouts. Jones, Mary Harris. Nativism. Utah (Carbon County). Utah Fuel Company. 1902-04. *1130*

Strip clubs. Behavior. Customer-stripper relationships. ca 1970-74. *2164*

Stripteasers. Behavior. Researchers. Sociology. 1959-72. *2199*

Strobridge, Idah Meacham. Literature. Nevada. 1860's-1909. *1589*

Strong, Anna Louise. China. Communism. Journalism. 1917-70. *261*

—. China. Communism. Journalism. USSR. 20c. *276*

Stroud, Jessie Ruth (reminiscences). Illinois (southern). Rural Schools. Teaching. 1918-19. *1104*

Strunsky, Anna. Browning, Elizabeth Barrett. London, Jack (*The Sea Wolf,* 1904). Maud Brewster (fictional character). 1899-1904. *1699*

Stryker-Rodda, Harriet Mott (reminiscences). New Jersey (Arlington). Schools. World War I. 1910-24. *2986*

Stuart, Ann Calvert. Lee, Cornelia. Letters. Virginia (northern). Wedding. 1780-1807. *3070*

Stuart Female Seminary. Live Oak Female Seminary. Secondary Education. Texas. 1840's-1955. *458*

Stuart Hall. *See* Virginia Female Institute.

Stuart, Lady Christina. Griffin, Cyrus. Marriage. Virginia. 1741-1807. *3053*

Stuart, Mrs. J. E. B. Church Schools. Virginia Female Institute. Virginia (Staunton). 19c. *1570*

Student boycotts (effects). Consumers. Family. Negroes. 1960's. *2564*

Student demonstrators. Family. Liberalism. Politics. 1960's. *2274*

Student roles. Divorce. Graduate education. Marriage. 1969-72. *2796*

Student strikes. Cambodia, invasion of. Feminist movement. Smith College. Vassar College. 1970. *2423*

Students *See also* Colleges and Universities; Schools.

—. Academic achievement. Colleges and Universities (attendance). 1960's. *2840*

—. Alabama (Florence). Family. Florence Synodical Female College. Herron, Utopia. Letters. Tennessee (Carroll and Madison Counties). 1868. *3139*

—. Alcohol (use of). Colorado, University of. Sex differences. 1960's. *2641*

—. American University. Attitudes. District of Columbia. Marriage, open. 1945-73. *2276*

—. Attitudes. Authority. Boston College. 1960's. *2808*

—. Attitudes. Canada. Courtship. Interpersonal Relations. Sex roles. USA. 1969. *217*

—. Attitudes. Colleges and Universities. Religion. 1960's. *2466*

—. Attitudes. Colleges and Universities. Sex roles. 1950's-60's. *2171*

—. Attitudes. Family. Negroes. Self identity. Sex. 1960's. *2542*

—. Attitudes. Illinois. Negroes. Sex differences. 1960's. *2581*

—. Attitudes. Males, superiority of. Occupations. Sexual bias. 1960's. *1813*

—. Attitudes. Mothers. Sex roles. Social Psychology. 1969. *2173*

—. Authority. Colleges and Universities. Sex Discrimination. 1960's. *2815*

—. Belmont Estate. Private Schools. Tennessee (Nashville). Ward-Belmont school. 1912-35. *1564*

—. Canada. Colleges and Universities. Political knowledge scale. Public opinion formation. 1974. *3294*

—. Careers, interrupted. Colleges and Universities. Nepotism rules. Wives, faculty. 1972. *2839*

—. Catholic Church. Church Schools. Sister Formation Conference. Teachers. 19c-20c. *322*

—. Client centered therapy. Elementary Education. Teachers. 1960's-. *2793*

—. Colleges and Universities. Dating. Social Status. 1960's. *2185*

—. Colleges and Universities. Employment. Sex Discrimination. 1960-73. *2804*

—. Colleges and Universities. Personality Traits. Romantic Love Complex. Values. 1960's. *2201*

—. Colleges and Universities (graduate schools). Demography. Library Science. Sex. 1962. *2818*

—. Connecticut. Foote, Lucinda. Yale University. 1783. *610*

—. Education. Mothers. Political Attitudes. 1960's. *2370*

—. Education. Smith College. Social Work. 1960's. *2843*

—. Elementary education. Sex roles. Socialization. Teachers. 1959-71. *2187*

—. Employment. Higher education. Sex Discrimination. Wages. 1970. *1957*

—. Employment. Rural Sociological Society. Sex Discrimination. Sociology. 1940-70. *1950*

—. Feminism. Teaching. Women's history. 1974. *33*

—. High Schools. Michigan (Marquis). Negroes. Self concepts. 1960's. *2565*

—. Higher Education. 1950's. *2816*

—. Humanities (majors in). North Dakota University. 1960-65. *2844*

—. Morris, Celia. New Jersey. Princeton University. Roos, Margit. Wasserheit, Judith. 1973. *2282*

—. Negroes. White (passing as). 1961. *2528*

—. Occupational values. Private Schools. Public Schools. 1960's. *1860*

Students (bias of). Behavior. Sex Discrimination. Teachers. 1968-72. *2174*

Students, college. Abortion. Attitudes. Birth Control. Religiosity. 1960-71. *2688*

—. Attitudes. Behavior. Catholic Church. Morality. Religion. 1961-71. *2500*

—. Attitudes. Birth Control. Folklore. Menstruation. Pregnancy. Sex. ca 1960's-70's. *2041*

—. Attitudes. Mormons and non-Mormons. Sexual behavior. 1960's. *2246*

—. Attitudes. Sex roles. Social Change. 1966-72. *2277*

—. Education. Negroes. Occupational aspirations. Sex roles. 1964-70. *2538*

—. Negroes. Sex differences. Stereotypes. Whites. ca 1970-74. *2205*

Students (disadvantaged). Educators. Sex roles. Social Classes. 1960's-. *2790*

Students (drop out). Colleges and Universities. Family. Marriage. 1960's. *2778*

Students (foreign). Coeds. Colleges and Universities. Social Customs. 1960's. *2180*

Students (graduate). Colleges and Universities. Employment. Political Science (programs). 1960's-70. *1894*

Students (high school). Educational aspirations. Mothers. Sex. Wisconsin. 1960's. *2829*

Students (junior high school). Attitudes. California (Compton). Employment opportunities. Ethnic Groups. Sexes. 1960's. *2518*

Students (re-entry). Colleges and Universities. Family. Marriage. 1960's. *2826*

Students (self-concepts). Florida (Dade County). Junior High Schools. Negroes. 1960's. *2562*

Students, 10th-grade. Canada. Occupational expectations. Social classes. 1970. *3266*

Stutzman, Barbara. Amish. Kaufman, John D. Theology. 1830's-1913. *1431*

Subsistence Homesteads Program. Miners (resettlement of). National Industrial Recovery Act (1933). New Deal. Roosevelt, Eleanor. West Virginia (Arthurdale). 1930-46. *1213*

Suburban Life. *See* Cities; Housing.

Subversive Activities. *See* Espionage.

Success, fear of. Addams, Jane. Horner, Matina. Kennedy, Rose. Lawrence, Frieda. Psychology. Senesh, Hannah. 20c. *2265*

—. Horner, Matina. Methodology. Motivation. Psychology. 1970-74. *2262*

Suckow, Ruth. Image. Lawrence, D. H. Literature. Marriage. 1920's-30's. *1667*

Suffrage *See also* Voting and Voting Behavior.

—. Abolition movement. Constitutional Amendment (19th). Feminism. Marriage. New York (Seneca Falls). Strikes. 1848-1920. *299*

—. Abolitionists. Negroes. Politics. 1865-69. *1358*

—. Adoption. Catholic Church. Children. Clergy. Law. Public Welfare. Quebec. 1920-36. *3342*

—. Alabama. Burton, Pierce. 1867-70. *1376*

—. Alabama. Hobson, Richmond Pearson. House of Representatives. Progressivism. 1900-20. *1368*

—. American Antislavery Society. Anthony, Susan B. Constitutional Amendment (19th). Feminism. Social Reform. 1840's-1920. *1366*

—. American Revolution. Anthony, Susan B. Ellet, Elizabeth F. Historiography. Stanton, Elizabeth Cady. Women's history. 1770's-1970's. *25*

—. American Woman Suffrage Association. Constitutional Amendment (19th). National Woman's Party. Tennessee. White, Sue Shelton. 1913-20. *1353*

—. Anthony, Lucy. Anthony, Susan B. Feminism. Gilman, Charlotte Perkins. National American Woman Suffrage Association. Sanger, Margaret. Shaw, Anna Howard. 1847-1919. *1317*

—. Anthony, Susan B. Connecticut (Hartford). Hooker, Isabella Beecher. Stanton, Elizabeth Cady. Woodhull, Victoria. 1861-1907. *1373*

—. Antifeminism. Brownson, Orestes A. Catholic Church. 1844-70's. *845*

—. Arizona. Congressional Union for Woman Suffrage. Democratic Party. Political Campaigns. 1914. 1916. *1370*

—. Attitudes. Politics. Utah. Wyoming. 1869. *1345*

—. Bloomer, Amelia. Nebraska League of Woman Voters. Nebraska Woman Suffrage Association. 1855-1920. *1377*

—. Boissevain, Inez Milholland. Politics. Vassar College. ca 1900-16. *1335*

—. Bourassa, Henry. Canada. Divorce. Feminism. 1913-25. *3296*

—. Breckinridge, Madeline McDowell. Clay, Laura. Constitutional amendment (19th). Federation of Women's Clubs. Kentucky Equal Rights Association. 1908-20. *1362*

—. British North America Act of 1929. Canada. Feminism. Legal status. 1870's-1940's. *3292*

—. Brown, Olympia. Religion. Wisconsin Woman Suffrage Association. 1835-1926. *1378*

—. California. Edson, Katherine Philips. Politics. State Industrial Welfare Commission. 1911-31. *1352*

—. Catholic Church. Massachusetts. ca 1870-1920. *1340*

—. Catt, Carrie Chapman. Duniway, Abigail Scott. Idaho. National American Woman Suffrage Association. Woman's Christian Temperance Union. 1870-96. *1350*

—. Catt, Carrie Chapman. *Frank Leslie's Illustrated Newspaper* (periodical). Leslie, Miriam F. F. Publishers and Publishing. ca 1860-1914. *1617*

—. Child Welfare. Children's Code Commission. Missouri. Organizations. Social Reform. Woman's Christian Temperance Union. 1915-19. *1284*

—. Cities. Northeastern or North Atlantic States. Politics. ca 1890-1920. *1328*

—. Cities. Pankhurst, Emmeline. Speeches, Addresses, etc.. 1909-13. *1381*

—. Cities. Social movements. Violence. 1960-68. *1332*

—. Class consciousness. Feminism. International Federation of Working Women. Organizations. Women's Trade Union League. 1890-1925. *1280*

—. Coeducation. Dewey, John (letters). Feminism. 1915-31. *1308*

—. Colorado. 1893. *1337*

—. Colorado. Constitutional convention (1876). Newspapers. Public opinion. 1870's. *1336*

—. Colorado. Politics. Waite, Celia O. Crane. Waite, Davis Hanson. 1890's-1937. *1208*

—. Colorado. Waite, Davis Hanson. 1890's. *1359*

—. Congress. Montana. Politics. Rankin, Jeannette. 1913-18. *1263*

—. Congress. Rankin, Jeannette. Unemployment. World War I. 20c. *265*

—. Constitutional amendment (19th). Feminists. Pennsylvania. 1837-1920. *1319*

—. Constitutional Amendment (19th). Florida Equal Franchise League. Florida Equal Suffrage Association. 1912-20. *1338*

—. Constitutional Amendment (19th). Meriwether, Elizabeth Avery. Tennessee (Memphis). 1870's-1920. *1363*

—. Constitutional Amendment (21st). Equal Rights Amendment. Paul, Alice. 1907-72. *272*

—. Constitutional convention. Wyoming. 1880's. *1351*

—. Constitutions, state. Democrats, Southern. Oklahoma Territory. 1870-1907. *1379*

—. Constitutions, State. Duniway, Abigail Scott. Oregon. 1860's-1912. *1331*

—. Constitutions, State. Montana. Rankin, Jeannette. 1889-1914. *1347*

—. *Crisis* (periodical). DuBois, W. E. B. Negroes. 1910-34. *1380*

—. District of Columbia. Prisons. Wilson, Woodrow (administration). 1917. *1374*

—. Duniway, Abigail Scott. Pacific Northwest. 1870's-1915. *1365*

—. Duniway, Abigail Scott. Prohibition movement. 1870's-1914. *1355*

—. Edmunds-Tucker Act (1887). Mormons. Polygamy. Senate. Teller, Henry M. Utah. 1885-90. *660*

—. Edmunds-Tucker Act (1887). Polygamy (attitudes toward). Utah Territory. 1870-87. *1325*

—. Education. Employment. Feminism. Gage, Frances Dana. *Ohio Cultivator* (newspaper). Tracy-Cutler, Hannah Maria. 1845-55. *836*

—. Elections. Mississippi Woman Suffrage Association. National American Woman Suffrage Association. Negroes. State Legislatures. 1890-1920. *1372*

—. Elections (gubernatorial). Republican Party. Roberts, Albert H. Tennessee. 1920. *1364*

—. Employment. Feminist movement. Political change. 19c-1970's. *279*

—. Evangelism. Reform. Wright, Henry Clarke. 1820-60. *843*

—. Family structure. Legal status. Sexual behavior. Social Change. 1700-1976. *117*

—. Feminism. Negroes. Newspapers. Police. 19c-20c. *283*

—. Feminism. Radicals and Radicalism. Settlement houses. Women's Trade Union League. ca 1890's-1920's. *1314*

—. Feminism (review article). Ideology. Politics. 1830-1920. 1969-70. *216*

Thomas, Anna Hasell (diary). Civil War (personal narratives). South Carolina. 1864-65. *821*

Thomas, Charles S. Colorado. Politics. Thomas, Emma Fletcher. 1853-1940. *1209*

Thomas, Ella Gertrude Clanton. Feminism. South. 1848-89. *3045*

Thomas, Emma Fletcher. Colorado. Politics. Thomas, Charles S. 1853-1940. *1209*

Thomas, M. Carey. Bryn Mawr College. Feminism. Palmer, Alice Freeman. Sex roles. Wellesley College. 1875-1918. *1585*

Thomas, Mary Jane. New Hampshire. Travel accounts. 1831. *2961*

Thomas-Rapier family. Family. Slavery. South. 1790-1872. *948*

Thoreau, Henry David. Brady, Kate. 19c. *1005*
—. Dorsey, Sarah Anne (letter). Literature. 1871. *3007*

Thornton, Bonnie Parker. Barrow, Clyde. Crime and Criminals. Death and Dying. Folk heroes. Louisiana. 1934. *1525*

Thorpe, Thomas B. (*The Master's House*, 1853). Literature. Slavery. Stowe, Harriet Beecher (*Uncle Tom's Cabin*, 1852). 1852-54. *944*

Tillion, Diana. Alaska. Eskimo life. Painting (octopus ink). 1939-75. *2909*

Time allocation. Nurses and Nursing. Public Health. 1960's. *1914*

Tingley, Katherine Augusta. California (San Diego, Point Loma). Church Schools. Theosophical Institute. 1897-1940. *1416*

Tipi. Economic organization. Family. Paintings. Sioux Indians (North Teton, Yankton). Social Customs. 1864. *912*

*Titanic* (vessel). Brown, Margaret Tobin. Colorado (Denver). Europe. Social Conditions. 19c-1912. *3152*

Tituba (Carib Indian). Behavior. Massachusetts (Salem). Trials. Witchcraft. 1692. *531*
—. Historians. Massachusetts (Salem). Racism. Witchcraft trials. 1648-1971. *344*
—. Indians. Massachusetts (Salem). Negroes (supposed). Petry, Ann (*Tituba of Salem Village*). Witchcraft. 1692. 1974. *369*

Tobacco. *See* Smoking.

Tochman, Apolonia Jagiello. Civil War. Confederate States of America. Polish Americans. Sosnowski, Sophie. 1860-65. *830*

Todd family (influence). Lincoln, Abraham (administration). Lincoln, Mary Todd. Marriage. 1842-60's. *769*

Todd, John. Democracy. Gynecology, development of. Masturbation phobias. Men. Psychology. Sexual anxieties. 19c. *170*

Toklas, Alice B. Art. Literature. Stein, Gertrude (review essay). ca 1900-46. *1634*

Tomasi, Mari. Immigration. Italians. Novels. Stonecutters. Vermont. 1909-65. *2979*

Tombstone carvings. Connecticut, eastern. Culture. Family. Wheeler, Obadiah. 1702-49. *517*

Tombstones. Illinois (Danville). Lincoln, Abraham (family). Vance, Mariah. 1819-1904. 1964. *3026*

Tompkins, Ellen Wilkins. Civil War. Letters. West Virginia (Fayette County). 1861. *822*

Tompkins, Sally. Civil War. Confederate Army. Hospitals. Virginia (Richmond). 1860-65. *811*

Tone, Aileen. Adams, Henry Brooks. Daily Life. 1913-18. *1200*

Tone, Alice Walsh. Audubon, Maria (letter). 1904. *95*

Tong societies. Chinese Americans. Family life. Immigration. Prostitution. Social Organization. 1850-1972. *321*

Tool kits. Animal skin processing. Archaeology. South Dakota (Fay Tolton site). Prehistory. 1973. *319*

Tools (chopping). Shoshoni Indians. Teshoa (stone tool). Prehistory. *332*

Toomer, Jean. Authors. Culture. Hurston, Zora Neale. Migration, Internal. Negroes. 1860-1960. *336*

Topless dancing. Burlesque. Discotheques. 1920's-71. *2745*
—. California (San Francisco). Doda, Carol. Popular Culture. Tara. 1965-66. *2746*

Torres, Francisco. California (Orange County). McKelvey, William. Modjeska, Helena. Murder. 1892. *3222*

Totalitarianism. *See* Communism.

Tourism *See also* Resorts; Voyages.
—. Arizona (Second Mesa). Basketry, coiled. Hopi Indians. Income. 1972. *2608*
—. California (Yosemite Valley). 1870's. *3238*

Tours (cross country). Field, Sara Bard. Panama Pacific International Exposition. Suffrage. Wilson, Woodrow. 1915. *1333*

Tours (national). Lind, Jenny. Marriage. Opera. 1850-52. *1029*

Towne, Elizabeth. New Thought movement. Philosophy, oriental. Quimby, Phineas Parkhurst. 1850's-1917. *1559*

Toys. Barbie Doll. Business. Image. Mattel Toy Corporation. 1972. *1827*

Tracy-Cutler, Hannah Maria. Education. Employment. Feminism. Gage, Frances Dana. *Ohio Cultivator* (newspaper). Suffrage. 1845-55. *836*

Trade Unions. *See* Labor Unions and Organizations.

Transactional analysis. Adolescence. Self concepts. 1971. *2290*

Trans-Africanism, concept of. Black Nationalism. Feminism. Negroes. 1970's. *2524*

Transcendental renaissance. Arts. Dance. Duncan, Isadora. 1890-1920. *1754*

Transcendentalism. Alcott, Abigail May. Alcott, Bronson. Alcott, Louisa May. Childrearing. Family. Social Change. 1830-60. *677*
—. Children. Fiction. Wiggin, Kate Douglas. 1879-1910. *1632*
—. Dall, Caroline Healy (journal). Fuller, Margaret. Greek Mythology, Conversations on. Intellectuals. Peabody, Elizabeth Palmer. 1841. *969*
—. Emerson, Ralph Waldo. Fuller, Margaret. Greeley, Horace. Love, attitude toward. ca 1845. *1004*
—. Fuller, Margaret. Literary Criticism. 1830-50. *994*
—. History (study of). Peabody, Elizabeth Palmer. 1830's-80's. *476*

Transcendentalists. Clarke, Sarah F. (letters). New England. 1832-40. *2970*

Translating and Interpreting. Austin, Mary Hunter. Corbin, Alice. Curtis, Natalie. Densmore, Frances. Fletcher, Alice Cunningham. Folk Songs. Indian culture. Literature. Underhill, Ruth Murray. Walton, Eda Lou. West. 1880-1965. *433*

Trans-Mississippi West *See also* individual states.
—. Pioneers. Wives. 1850-1900. *698*

Transportation *See also* names of transportation vehicles, e.g. Automobiles, Ships, Buses, Trucks, Railroads, etc.; Aeronautics; Roads.
—. Metropolitan Areas. Occupations (choice of). 1968-69. *1892*

Transportation problems. Civil War. Marchmann, Anna. Marchmann, Mrs. George (diary). Travel accounts. 1861. *787*

Transsexuality. Sexual identity. Social Status. 1972. *2050*

Trapping. *See* Fur Trade.

Travel *See also* Voyages.
—. Alabama. Royall, Anne. 1830's. *3107*
—. Allegheny Mountains. Dewee, Mary (diary). Pioneers. 1788-89. *2924*
—. America (impressions of). Milanés, Federico (letters). Milanés, José Jacinto (letters). Social Conditions. 1848-49. *644*
—. Arizona (Prescott). Diaries. English, Lydia E. Kansas (Concordia). Social Conditions. 1875. *3193*
—. Benjamin, Anna Northend. Journalism. War. 1890's-1902. *1609*
—. Bishop, Isabella Lucy Bird. Colorado (Estes Park). Nugent, Jim. 1873. *3196*
—. Boggs, Mary Jane (journal). Virginia (Shenandoah Valley). 1851. *3051*
—. Burns, Susan (journal). New York. North Carolina (Salisbury). Social Classes. 1848. *2928*
—. Business. Knight, Sarah Kemble. Massachusetts (Boston). Teachers. 1704-27. *482*
—. California. Diaries. Kansas. Rose, Forest. 1887. *3187*
—. California. Friends, Society of. Lindsey, Robert. Lindsey, Sarah (journal). 1859-60. *3217*
—. California. Friends, Society of. Lindsey, Sarah (journal). Social Conditions. 1859-60. *703*
—. Civil War. Education. Lane, Anne Ewing. Reconstruction. ca 1830-70's. *3099*
—. Clapp, Elizabeth. Social Conditions. Vermont (western). Woodbury, Levi (diary). 1819. *2948*
—. Colorado. Farmers. Mahoney, Mary (journal). Nebraska. 1901. *3182*
—. Colorado (Colorado Springs). Westward Movement. Young, Mary Eliza Willard (diary). 1871. *3183*

—. Cowboys. Daily Life. Gregg, Myrtle Chalfant (reminiscences). Nebraska (Howard County). Wyoming (Casper). 1899-1909. *3181*
—. Custer, Elizabeth Bacon (letter). Daily Life. Fort Riley. Kansas. Richmond, Rebecca. 1866. *710*
—. Daily Life. Ohio (Cincinnati). Social Conditions. Trollope, Frances (*Domestic Manners of the Americans*, 1832). 1820's-30's. *638*
—. Diplomacy. Liston, Henrietta. Southeastern States. 1790's. *3073*
—. Economic Conditions. Lincoln, Mary Todd. Marriage. 1818-82. *94*
—. Editors and Editing. Knight, Sarah Kemble (diary). New York. 1704-05. 1825-65. *2965*
—. Europe (tour of). Gansevoort, Kate. New York (Albany). 1859-60. *2957*
—. Family. Hoover, Herbert C. Hoover, Lou Henry. Marriage. Politics. 1899-1928. *1251*
—. Kemble, Frances Anne (*Journal*, 1835). Literature. 1832-40. *997*
—. LaRochefoucauld-Liancourt, François Alexandre de. Social Conditions. 1794-95. *645*
—. Letters. Massachusetts. Salisbury, Harriet Hutchinson. Vermont. 1843-46. *2946*
—. Liston, Henrietta. Virginia. 1800. *3074*
—. Social Conditions. Trollope, Frances (*Domestic Manners of the Americans*, 1832). 1820's-30's. *634*

Travel accounts. America (image of). Poles. 1783-1870's. *106*
—. Ashbee, Charles Robert (*Memoirs*). Ashbee, Janet. British Arts and Crafts movement. 1900-16. *1784*
—. California. Cracroft, Sophia. Franklin, Jane. Social Conditions. 1858-61. *3232*
—. California (southern). Leslie, Miriam F. F. 1877. *3234*
—. Civil War. Marchmann, Anna. Marchmann, Mrs. George (diary). Transportation problems. 1861. *787*
—. Greene, Elizabeth (family). Illinois. 1834-35. *3012*
—. Kentucky. Missouri. Smith, Sallie D. (diary). Steamboats. 1868. *3114*
—. Louisiana. Murray, Amelia. 1600's-1850's. *3146*
—. New Hampshire. Thomas, Mary Jane. 1831. *2961*

Travel accounts (British). Marriage (interracial). Race relations. South. ca 1865-1914. *1515*

Travel agency industry. New York City. Organizational structuring. Sex discrimination. 1974. *1893*

Travel (canoe). Indians. Matheson, Eleanor Shepphird (journal). Missions and Missionaries. Saskatchewan. 1920. *3382*

Travelers' Aid Society. Immigration. New York City. Polish Americans. 1907-39. *1500*

Treaties (ratification). Political rights. 1967-68. *2349*

Trials *See also* Crime and Criminals.
—. Adultery. Capital Punishment. Connecticut (Hartford). Johnson, Elizabeth. Newton, Thomas. Witchcraft (supposed). 1648-92. *600*
—. Anarchism and Anarchists. Espionage Act (1917). Steiner, Mollie. Supreme Court. 1917-21. *2679*
—. Antinomian controversy. Hutchinson, Anne. Massachusetts (Boston). Puritans. 1634-38. *543*
—. Bagby, Sara Lucy. Fugitive Slave Act. Ohio (Cleveland). Republican Party. Slavery. 1850's. *901*
—. Behavior. Massachusetts (Salem). Tituba (Carib Indian). Witchcraft. 1692. *531*
—. California (San Francisco). Divorce. Hill, Sarah Althea. Sharon, William. 1884-89. *1162*
—. California (Stockton). LeDoux, Emma. McVicar, A. N. Murder. 1906-41. *1516*
—. Cody, Margaret E. Gould, Helen. Gould, Jay. Wills. 1880-98. *1239*
—. Communist Party. Davis, Angela. Morality. Political attitudes. 1970's. *2539*
—. Dyer, Mary. Hutchinson, Anne. Massachusetts Bay Colony. Politics. Sex roles. Theology. 1636-43. *540*
—. Karenga, Maulana Ron. Negroes. 1971. *2539*
—. Langston, John Mercer. Lewis, Edmonia. Oberlin College. Poisoning. 1862. *921*
—. Little, Joanne. Negroes. North Carolina (Wake County). 1975. *2547*

# U

Virginia (northern). Lee, Cornelia. Letters. Stuart, Ann Calvert. Wedding. 1780-1807. *3070*

Virginia (Orange County). Civil War. Letters. Rawlings, Clarissa Lawrence. Rawlings, Hannah Garlick. 1865. *778*

Virginia (Reston). Day Nurseries. Mothers. Teacher Training. 1969-. *2151*

Virginia (Richmond). Banking. Black Capitalism. St. Luke's Penny Savings Bank. United Order of St. Luke. Walker, Maggie Lena. 1903-30. *1472*

—. Cabell, James Branch. Glasgow, Ellen. Letters. Literature. ca 1900-40's. *1681*

—. Civil War. Confederate Army. Hospitals. Tompkins, Sally. 1860-65. *811*

—. Civil War (intelligence). Van Lew, Elizabeth. 1818-1900. *823*

—. Constitutional conventions (state). Green, Mrs. Thomas. Green, Thomas (diary). Politics. Social Conditions. 1829-30. *752*

Virginia (Shenandoah Valley). Boggs, Mary Jane (journal). Travel. 1851. *3051*

Virginia (Shenandoah Valley; Winchester). Civil War. Confederate Army. Military Intelligence. Sheridan, Philip H. Wright, Rebecca. 1864. *786*

Virginia (Staunton). Church Schools. Stuart, Mrs. J. E. B. Virginia Female Institute. 19c. *1570*

Virginia (Wolf Trap). Culture. National Parks and Reserves. Shouse, Catherine Filene. 1960. *2892*

Vital Statistics *See also* Birth Rate; Census; Mortality.

—. Age. Marriage. Sex roles. 1850-1950. *1148*

—. Family. Marriage. Rhode Island (Bristol). Social Customs. 17c-18c. *502*

—. Friends, Society of. Marriage. Pennsylvania (Lycoming, Northumberland, and Columbia Counties). 1796-1860. *2933*

Vocabulary. *See* Language.

Vocational Education *See also* Professional Education.

—. Art (practical). Schools. Social studies. 1970-73. *2795*

—. Bureau of Indian Affairs (Adult Vocational Training Program). Indians. Oregon (Portland). 1964-66. *2597*

—. Cities (inner). Colleges and universities. white. Negroes. 1915-73. *1801*

—. Discrimination, Employment. High School of Fashion Industry. Negroes. New York City. Puerto Ricans. Whites. 1975. *1930*

—. Employment. Federal Programs. Nurses and Nursing. 1960's. *2821*

—. Employment bureau. Negroes. Ohio (Cincinnati). Young Women's Christian Association. 1868-1968. *1195*

—. Nurses and Nursing. Wages. 1960's. *1844*

Vocational Guidance. *See* Counseling.

Vodges, Ada A. (journal). Fort Fetterman. Fort Laramie. Indians. Social Conditions. 1868-71. *3149*

Voluntary Associations. California (San Francisco). Charities. Economic Aid. Immigration. Ladies' Protection and Relief Society. ca 1850-60. *625*

—. California (San Francisco Bay area). Military Medicine. Music. World War II. 1943-45. *1302*

—. Church attendance. Sex. Social Status. 1960's. *2045*

—. Family (kinship groupings). Migration, Internal. Rural-Urban Studies. Social Classes. 1960's. *2048*

—. Girl Scouts of America. Sex role orientation. ca 1965-75. *2294*

—. Missions and Missionaries. Religion (feminization of). 1800-60. *886*

Volunteer Armies. *See* Military Service.

Volunteerism. Charities. Social Work. ca 1850-20c. *1505*

Voodoo. Black magic cults. Louisiana (New Orleans). Music (jazz). Negroes. 19c. *409*

Voting age (lowering of). Attitudes. Youth. 1965. *2355*

Voting and Voting Behavior *See also* Elections; Suffrage.

—. Abortion. Legislators. Religion. Western States. 1975. *2700*

—. California. Elections. Rafferty, Max. 1962. *2379*

—. Canada. Political Participation. Public office. USA. 1920-60's. *266*

—. Local Politics. Pennsylvania (Reading). Socialist Party. ca 1927-38. *1272*

—. Political Activism. Sex differences. 1964-72. *2373*

—. Political attitudes. Socialization. 1964. *2363*

—. Political surveys. Presidents (women as). Social Change. 1958-72. *2364*

Voyages *See also* Aeronautics; Explorers; Travel.

—. California (San Francisco). Hazard, Sarah Congdon (diary). *Lancashire* (vessel). New York City. 1863. *2925*

—. *Continental* (steamship). Mercer, Asa Shinn. Stevens, Harriet F. (journal). Washington Territory. Westward Movement. 1866. *724*

—. Fiji. Massachusetts (Salem). Wallis, Mrs. Benjamin. 19c. *2962*

Vroman, Mary Elizabeth. Literary Criticism. Negroes. 1963. *2535*

# W

Waerenskjold, Elise (letter). Daily Life. Immigrants. Norwegians. Social Conditions. Texas. 1841-51. *696*

Wage differentials. Employment, professional. Sex Discrimination. 1966-71. *1965*

Wages *See also* Minimum Wage; Prices.

—. Archivists. Committee on the Status of Women in the Archival Profession. Employment. Sex discrimination. 1972-74. *1941*

—. Attitudes. Labor Unions and Organizations. Legislation. Political Participation. Working Conditions. 1940's-60's. *2011*

—. British North America. Canada. Public schools. Social Status. Teaching. 1845-75. *3253*

—. Canada. Employment. Labor Unions and Organizations. Marriage. Pensions. Sex discrimination. 1960's-70's. *3275*

—. Canada. Employment. Sex Discrimination. 1960-64. *3264*

—. Capitalism. Employment. Feminism. 1950's-60's. *1829*

—. Civil War. Employment. Federal government. 1860-70. *789*

—. Colleges and Universities. Sex Discrimination. Teachers. 1950's-68. *1961*

—. Colleges and Universities (faculty). 1975. *1842*

—. Commission on the Minimun Wage for Women. Labor law. Quebec. 1925-31. *3336*

—. Day Nurseries. Employment. Family. Fertility. 1971-72. *1927*

—. Discrimination. Minorities. 1949-60. *1951*

—. Divorce. Equal Rights Amendment. Federation of Business and Professional Women's Clubs. Iowa. Lobbying. Sex discrimination. Sheppard-Towner Act. Social Reform. 1919-70. *3036*

—. Education. Librarians. 1967. *1910*

—. Educational reform. Teachers. 1830-60. *627*

—. Employment. Feminism. 1972. *1881*

—. Employment. Higher education. Sex Discrimination. Students. 1970. *1957*

—. Employment. Housework. Industrialization. Negroes. Sex discrimination. Whites. 1970. *1936*

—. Employment. Labor supply. Marriage. Negroes. 1947-67. *1902*

—. Employment. Sex Discrimination. Social Status. 1960's-70. *1963*

—. Employment rates (changes in). Labor force. 1920-70. *1920*

—. Family. 1967. *1836*

—. Family. Income tax, progressive. Labor force. 1970's. *1820*

—. Feminism. Sex Discrimination. Social Work. 1960's-70's. *1978*

—. Labor. Technology. Textile industry. Working Conditions. 1947-67. *1926*

—. Labor market. Models. Nurses and Nursing. 1950-60. *1841*

—. Negroes. Whites. 1950-74. *1806*

—. Nurses and Nursing. Quebec. 1944-62. *3354*

—. Nurses and Nursing. Vocational Education. 1960's. *1844*

—. Occupational status. 1870-1970. *162*

—. Occupations. Sex discrimination. 1945-73. *1983*

—. Occupations. Sexual segregation. *1987*

—. Public Schools. Teachers. Vermont. 19c. *403*

—. Sex Discrimination. Unemployment rate. 1947-73. *1971*

Wagner, Louis. Christensen, Anethe. Christensen, Karen. Isles of Shoals. Murder. New England. 1873-75. *1523*

Wagon train. California. Iowa (Howard County). Overland Journeys to the Pacific. Walker, Juliette Fish (travel account). 1862-71. *731*

Waheenee-wea ("Buffalo Bird Woman"). Great Plains. Sioux Indians (Hidatsa). Social Conditions. Wilson, Gilbert L. (*Waheenee,* 1921). 19c. 1921. *917*

Waiilatpu Mission. Cayuse Indians. Missions and Missionaries. Oregon Territory. Whitman, Narcissa. 1836-47. *728*

Waisbrooker, Lois. Adams, Henry Brooks. Harman, Moses. Politics. Sex roles. Stern, Karl. Violence. 1960's. *2194*

Waite, Celia O. Crane. Colorado. Politics. Suffrage. Waite, Davis Hanson. 1890's-1937. *1208*

Waite, Davis Hanson. Colorado. Politics. Suffrage. Waite, Celia O. Crane. 1890's-1937. *1208*

—. Colorado. Suffrage. 1890's. *1359*

Waitresses. Employment. Harvey, Frederick Henry. Santa Fe Railroad. 1859-20c. *147*

Wald, Lillian. Abbott, Grace. Child welfare. Kelley, Florence. Lathrop, Julia. Legislation. Politics. Sheppard-Towner Act. Social reform. 1900-35. *1236*

—. Addams, Jane. Middle Classes. Sex roles. Social Reform. Stereotypes. 1870-1930. *1275*

Walker, Elkanah. Indian-White Relations. Missions and Missionaries. Protestant Churches. Spokane Indians. Walker, Mary. Washington (Tshimakain). 1838-48. *872*

Walker, Francis A. (thesis). Fertility. Immigration. Whites (native born). 1800-60. *673*

Walker, Juliette Fish (travel account). California. Iowa (Howard County). Overland Journeys to the Pacific. Wagon train. 1862-71. *731*

Walker, Maggie Lena. Banking. Black Capitalism. St. Luke's Penny Savings Bank. United Order of St. Luke. Virginia (Richmond). 1903-30. *1472*

Walker, Mary. Army. Civil War. Congress. Physicians. 1861-1917. *826*

—. Indian-White Relations. Missions and Missionaries. Protestant Churches. Spokane Indians. Walker, Elkanah. Washington (Tshimakain). 1838-48. *872*

—. James, Henry (*The Bostonians,* 1886). Mary Prance (fictional character). Suffrage. 1886. *1679*

Walker, Mary Chase. California (San Diego). Negroes. Racism. Teachers. 1866. *1470*

Wallace, Dillon. Explorers. Hubbard, Leonidas. Hubbard, Mrs. Leonidas. Labrador (northeast). 1903-05. *3328*

Waller, Mary. Fiction. Progressivism. Wilderness. ca 1900-20. *1708*

Wallis, Mrs. Benjamin. Fiji. Massachusetts (Salem). Voyages. 19c. *2962*

Walter Eugene. Drama. Feminism. Fitch, Clyde. Moody, William Vaughn. 1908-10. *1757*

Walton, Eda Lou. Austin, Mary Hunter. Corbin, Alice. Curtis, Natalie. Densmore, Frances. Fletcher, Alice Cunningham. Folk Songs. Indian culture. Literature. Translating and Interpreting. Underhill, Ruth Murray. West. 1880-1965. *433*

War *See also* names of wars, battles, etc., e.g. American Revolution, Gettysburg (battle), etc.; Antiwar Sentiment; Civil War; Military; Refugees.

—. Benjamin, Anna Northend. Journalism. Travel. 1890's-1902. *1609*

—. Brown, Laura. Family. Letters. Missouri (border). Politics. 1850's. *3035*

—. Indians. 19c. *1479*

—. Mother, image of. Pillows. Popular Culture. 1812-1970. *396*

War of 1812. Beaver Dams (battle of). Ontario. Secord, Laura. 1813. *3365*

War Victims. *See* Refugees.

Ward, Elizabeth Stuart Phelps. Attitudes. Blackwell, Elizabeth. Diseases. Hunt, Harriot Kezia. Medicine (practice of). 1840-1900. *1534*

Ward, Henry Dana (diary). Private Schools. Ward, Mrs. Henry Dana. West Virginia (Charleston). 1845-47. *3052*

Ward, Lester Frank. Feminism. Sex roles. ca 1870's-1900. *1321*

Ward, Mrs. Henry Dana. Private Schools. Ward, Henry Dana (diary). West Virginia (Charleston). 1845-47. *3052*

Ward, Nancy. Agriculture. American Revolution. Cherokee Indians. Indian removal. ca 1755-1800. *387*

—. American Revolution. Cherokee Indians. Tennessee. 1738-1822. *588*

Ward, Nathaniel (*The Simple Cobler of Aggawam in America*). Adultery. Childbirth. Marriage. New England. Prostitution. Puritans. Satire. 1647. *495*

—. Educational aspirations. Family. Mothers. Working Class. 1960's. *2280*
—. Educational aspirations. Negroes. Rural Settlements. Texas (east central). 1960's. *2561*
—. Ethnic Groups. Language. Sexual behavior. Social Classes. 1960's. *2241*
—. Family size preferences. Florida. Georgia. Negroes. Whites. 1969. *2275*
—. Goldstücker, Eduard (reminiscences). 1930's. 1960's. *103*
—. Iowa. Occupations (aspirations). Rural Settlements. 1948-56. *2267*
—. Johnson, Dorothy M. (reminiscences). Juvenile life. Montana (Whitefish). 1918-25. *3174*
—. Mass Media. Sex. Violence. 1960's. *2656*
—. Sexual behavior. Social Classes. 1960's. *2226*
Youth Movements *See also* Demonstrations.
—. Age roles. Attitudes. Sex roles. Violence. 1964-73. *2291*

—. High Schools. Political Protest. Sex discrimination. 1971. *2271*
Youville, Marguerite dé. Bourgeoys, Marguerite. Canada. Catherine de Saint-Augustin. Catholic Church (founders of). Mance, Jeanne. Marie de l'Incarnation. 17c. *3254*
Yukon Territory. *See* Northwest Territories.

# Z

Zahara, Dominka Roshko. Alberta. Homesteading and Homesteaders. Peace River country. Ukrainians. 1900-30. *3376*
Zaharoff, Evdokia Gregovna (travel account). Emigration. Hawaii. Russians. ca 1900-17. *1502*
Zakrewska, Marie E. Blackwell, Elizabeth. Blackwell, Emily. Hunt, Harriot Kezia. Medical Education. 1849-61. *973*

Zanoni, Minnie Grosso. Children. Wyoming (Newcastle). 1896-1971. *3198*
Zeh, Nellie M. Garment workers. Illinois (Chicago). O'Reilly, Mary. Socialists. Strikes. 1910. *1118*
Zeman, Josephine Humpel. Alessandro, Antonietta Pisanelli. Immigrants. Pesotta, Rose. Stereotypes. 1880-1924. *1550*
Zionism *See also* Jews.
—. Kallen, Horace M. *Parushim*. Secret Societies. Szold, Henrietta. 1913-1920. *1443*
Zoology. *See* Natural History.

# 7

7th Cavalry, US. Custer, Elizabeth Bacon. Economic Conditions. Family. Widows. 1876. *1172*

Van Kirk, Sylvia 3322
Van Ness, James S. 252
Vance, W. Silas 1584
Vanderbilt, Amy 2207
Vanderburg, Helen 3036
Varni, Charles A. 2248
Vatter, Ethel L. 158
Vaughan, Alma F. 1732
Veevers, J. E. 2122
Velarde, Albert J. 1832
Venn, George W. 1259
Verbrugge, Martha H. 253
Vermeer, Donald E. 2580
Vernon-Jackson, H. O. 568
Vidal, Mirta 2623
Viener, Saul 824
Vigil, Ralph H. 1733
Vincent, Clark E. 2540 2687
Vinovskis, Maris A. 518 952
  1452
Vittenson, Lillian K. 2581
Vogel, Lise 2444
Vogel, Susan Raymond 2165
Voght, Martha 180 181
Vogt, Glenda L. 2193
Volgy, Sandra S. 2381
Volgy, Thomas J. 2381
Vollmer, Howard M. 2276
Voorhies, Edward 3145
Vossler, Kathryn Babb 3083
Voth, M. Agnes 1448

# W

Wachtel, Dawn Day 2703
Wadlington, Walter 2162
  2353
Wagner, William 388
Wainright, Nicholas B. 2990
Waite, Linda J. 1919
Wakil, Parvez A. 3289
Waldman, Elizabeth 1833
  1920
Walker, Don D. 1734
Walker, Juliette Fish 731
Walkowitz, Daniel J. 1134
Wallace, Ruth A. 2474
Wallace, T. Dudley 2126
Waller, Bret 1786
Waller, Jennifer R. 615
Walling, William 1474
Walsh, Peggy M. 1026
Walster, Elaine 2838
Walter, B. Oliver 2371
Walters, Ronald G. 675 856
Walton, David A. 2919
Walton, John 519
Walzer, John 677
Wardle, Ralph M. 732
Wareham, Roger S. 2582

Wark, Robert R. 1783
Warlick, Mark 1832
Warner, Robert M. 1149
Warner, Sam Bass, Jr. 1149
Warren, Claude N. 1109
Warren, Dale 1146 2991
Warrick, Alan E. 2523
Washburne, Carolyn Kott
  2295
Wasserheit, Judith 2282
Wassmer, Thomas A. 2704
Waters, John J. 520
Waters, Mary-Alice 295
Watson, Barbara 2585
Watson, Hildegarde Lasell
  2992
Watson, Ora V. 1174
Watson, Helen 1739
Watson, Walter B. 2123
Watts, Phyllis Atwood 1298
Weathers, Willie T. 825
Weaver, Bettie Woodson 3084
Weaver, Herbert B. 2249
Weaver, Robert C. 296
Webb, Allie Bayne 3146
Webber, Robert L. 2250
Webster, Staten W. 2583
Wedel, Jean 2208
Wegelin, Christof 1735
Weigert, Andrew J. 2292
Weigley, Emma 1110 1116
Weil, Louis 2490
Weil, Mildred 2445
Wein, Roberta 1585
Weinman, Saul 2018
Weinstein, Allen 47
Weir, Angela 1834
Weir, Sybil 1736
Weisberg, D. Kelly 521
Weiser, Frederick S. 2983
Weismann, Myrna W. 2839
Weiss, Carol H. 2584
Weissbrodt, Sylvia 1921
Weisskoff, Francine Blau 1922
Weissman, Irving 2668
Weissman, Myrna M. 2714
Weitzman, Lenore 2347 2348
Welch, Delpfine 2705
Welch, Finis 2125
Welch, Susan 2446
Wells, Laurence K. 651 652
  653
Wells, R. V. 2149
Wells, Robert V. 254 522 523
Welsch, Roger L. 733
Welsh, Jack 3147
Welter, Barbara 654 886 963
  964
Werking, Richard H. 533
Werlich, Robert 826
Werner, Emmy E. 297 298
Wernick, Robert 953

Werrell, Kenneth P. 2457
Werts, Charles E. 2840
West, James O. 3166
West, John Foster 1737
Westervelt, Esther M. 2841
Westoff, Charles F. 2502 2503
  2504
Weston, James J. 1738
Weston, Lynda Martin 2715
Wetzler, James 1802
Wheeler, Harvey 2717
Whipkey, Harry E. 2993
Whipple, Thomas W. 2728
Whitaker, Barbara 2585
Whitaker, F. M. 1401
Whitaker, Kathleen 2613
White, Helen 1739
White, Jean Bickmore 1260
  1375
White, John 389
White, Kinnard 2586
White, Lonnie J. 734
White, Margaret E. 616 2994
White, Mary 1261
White, Mary H. 992
White, Philip L. 2995
White, Ray Lewis 1740
White, Victor 3200
White, William 473 2771
Whitehall, Walter Muir 2996
Whitehead, P. C. 2255
Whiteman, Marjorie M. 2334
Whitford, Kathryn 603
Whitman, Clifford Dale 735
Whittier, Gayle 2886
Whyte, J. Bruce 390
Whyte, John D. 3308
Wiederaenders, Roland P. 736
Wiggins, Florence Roe 569
  2997 2998
Wiggins, Sarah W. 1376
Wildavsky, Aaron 131
Wiles, William G. 3085
Wiley, Bell I. 827
Wilhite, Ann L. Wiegman
  1377
Wilke, Phyllis Kay 1795
Wilkening, Eugene A. 2065
  2124
Wilkinson, Paul 3309
Willacy, Hazel M. 1923
Willard, Charlotte 2920
Willerman, Lee 2665
Williams, Carol Traynor 2772
Williams, Cecil 2587
Williams, Ellen 1741
Williams, Gregory 1985
Williams, J. R. 2335
Williams, Marjorie Logan 828
Williams, Ora G. 829
Williams, Roger 474

Williams, Walter L. 3086
Williamson, Nancy E. 2251
Williman, William H. 857
Willis, Gwendolen B. 1378
Willis, William S., Jr. 593
Willner, Milton 2588
Wilmeth, Don B. 2921
Wilson, C. Roderick 2601
Wilson, Charles Morrow 2475
Wilson, Elisabeth 1834
Wilson, Gilbert L. 917
Wilson, Harold 475
Wilson, Joan Hoff 485
Wilson, John B. 476 971
Wilson, John D. 2842
Wilson, Marion Ball 2999
Wilson, Robert N. 2687
Wilson, Suzanne M. 1742
Wilson, Victoria 1924
Wilson, W. Cody 2723 2724
  2725
Wilson, W. Emerson 3087
  3088 3089
Wilson, William E. 918
Wilson, William H. 1262
Wiltse, Kermit T. 2668
Wince, Michael H. 2897
Windham, Wyolene 1475
Windle, Charles 2336
Winestine, Belle Fligelman
  1263
Winey, Fay McAfee 3000
Wingfield, Mrs. Marshall
  2476 2666
Winick, Charles 2209
Winkels, George 3243
Winokur, G. 2686
Winslow, David J. 2589
Winter, Robert W. 1784
Winthrop, Henry 2210
Wisbey, Herbert A., Jr. 391
  1027
Wise, Gordon L. 1835
Wishart, David J. 3201
Withorn, Ann 2021
Wohl, Lisa Cronin 2447
Wohlenberg, Ernest H. 2029
Wolf, Charlotte 2211
Wolfe, Allis Rosenberg 629
  1288
Wolfe, Donald M. 2035
Wolff, Carole E. 2337
Wolfinger, Henry J. 1449
Wollheim, Peter 258
Wollock, Jeffrey 3368
Wong, Celia 830
Wood, Ann Douglas 477 831
  1028 1534
Wood, Elizabeth B. 67
Wood, Raymund F. 887 3244

Wood, Vivian 2173
Woodbury, David O. 1785
Woodress, James 1743
Woodroofe, Debby 299
Woodson, Mary Willis 3148
Woodward, Carl R. 902
Word, S. Buford 255
Wortham, Thomas 1744
Woywitka, Anne B. 3376
Wreede, Estella H. 676
Wright, Benjamin D. 1925
Wright, Eugene Patrick 91
Wright, Gwendolyn 2902
Wright, Helena 630
Wright, James R., Jr. 1379
Wright, Louis B. 3090
Wright, Martha R. 594
Wyatt, Philip R. 867
Wyllie, John C. 547
Wynes, Charles E. 1515

# Y

Yankauer, Alfred 2668
Yanovsky, Avrom 3297
Yates, John 2773
Yates, Wilson 256
Yeager, Edna H. 570
Yeakel, Margaret 2843
Yee, William 2669
Yellin, Jean Fagan 1380
Yellis, Kenneth A. 1189
Yezer, Anthony M. J. 1820
Yoder, R. D. 2681
Yoesting, Dean R. 2267
Yokopenic, Patricia A. 1986
Young, Don J. 2667
Young, Don J., M.D 2667
Yuan, D. Y. 2637
Yzenbaard, John H. 3037

# Z

Zacharis, John C. 1381
Zagel, Henrietta 3038 3039
Zanger, Jules 954
Zangrando, Joanna Schneider
  68
Zebrowski, Walter 1503
Zeisel, Rose N. 1926
Zeitlin, Jacob 2931
Zellner, Harriet 1987
Zelnik, M. 903
Ziebarth, Marilyn 1382
Ziemke, Donald C. 2844
Zimbalist, Andrew 1802
Zimet, Sara Goodman 257
Zimmerman, Bonnie 19
Zube, Margaret J. 2066
Zucker, R. A. 2293

# LIST OF PERIODICALS

## A

AAUP Bulletin
Action Nationale   Canada
Actualité Économique   Canada
Adirondack Life
Administrative Science Quarterly
Aerospace Historian
Agricultural History
Air Force Magazine
Air University Review
Alabama Historical Quarterly
Alabama Journal of Medical Sciences
Alabama Review
Alaska Journal
Alberta Historical Review (old title, see Alberta History)   Canada
Alberta History   Canada
American Anthropologist (AIA)
American Archivist
American Bar Association Journal
American Behavioral Scientist
American Benedictine Review
American Book Collector
American Economic Review
American Education
American Heritage
American Historical Review
American History Illustrated
American Indian Quarterly: A Journal of Anthropology, History and Literature
American Jewish Archives
American Jewish Historical Quarterly (old title, see American Jewish History)
American Journal of Economics and Sociology
American Journal of International Law
American Journal of Legal History
American Journal of Political Science
American Journal of Sociology
American Literary Realism, 1870-1910
American Literature
American Neptune
American Political Science Review
American Politics Quarterly
American Quarterly
American Scholar
American Sociological Review
American Studies in Scandinavia   Norway
American Studies (Lawrence, KS)
American West
Anglican Theological Review
Annals of Iowa
Annals of the American Academy of Political and Social Science
Annals of the Association of American Geographers
Annals of Wyoming
Antioch Review
Anuario Indigenista   Mexico
Appalachian Journal
Arbitration Journal
Arctic   Canada
Arizona and the West
Arizona Quarterly
Arkansas Historical Quarterly
Army Quarterly and Defence Journal   Great Britain
Art in America
Arts in Society (ceased pub 1976)
Asian Profile   Hong Kong
Asian Survey
Audience (ceased pub 1973)
Australian Economic History Review   Australia
Aztlán

## B

Baptist History and Heritage
Beaver   Canada
Bits and Pieces
Black Politician (ceased pub)
Black Scholar
British Association for American Studies Bulletin (old title, see Journal of American Studies)   Great Britain
British Journal of Sociology   Great Britain
Bulletin des Séances de l'Académie Royale des Sciences d'Outre-Mer   Belgium
Bulletin of Bibliography and Magazine Notes
Bulletin of the History of Medicine
Bulletin of the New York Public Library (superseded by Bulletin of Research in the Humanities)
Bulletin of the Society for the Study of Labour History   Great Britain
Business History Review

## C

Cahiers des Dix Canada
Cahiers d'Histoire Mondiale (superseded by Cultures)   France
California Historian
California Historical Quarterly (old title, see California History)
California Historical Society Quarterly (old title, see California Historical Quarterly)
California Librarian
California Social Science Review (old title, see California Council for the Social Studies Review)
Canadian Catholic Historical Association Annual Report
Canadian Dimension   Canada
Canadian Forces Sentinel   Canada
Canadian Geographical Journal (old title, see Canadian Geographic)   Canada
Canadian Historical Association Annual Report (old title, see Canadian Historical Association Historical Papers)   Canada
Canadian Historical Association Historical Papers   Canada
Canadian Journal of History of Sport and Physical Education   Canada
Canadian Journal of Political Science   Canada
Canadian Labour   Canada
Canadian Library Journal   Canada
Canadian Review of American Studies   Canada
Canadian Review of Sociology and Anthropology   Canada
Capitol Studies
Catholic Educational Review (suspended pub 1969)
Catholic Historical Review
Catholic World (old title, see New Catholic World)
Centennial Review
Center Magazine
Center Report
Change
Chicago History
Chronicles of Oklahoma
Church History
Cincinnati Historical Society Bulletin
Civil Liberties Review
Civil War History
Civil War Times Illustrated
College and Research Libraries
Colorado Magazine
Colorado Quarterly
Commentary
Communist Viewpoint   Canada
Concordia Historical Institute Quarterly
Connecticut Historical Society Bulletin
Contemporary Education
Contemporary Review   Great Britain
Cornell Library Journal (ceased pub 1972)
Crisis
Culture (ceased pub 1970)   Canada
Current Anthropology (AIA)
Current History

## D

Daedalus
Dalhousie Review   Canada
Daughters of the American Revolution Magazine
Delaware History
Dialogue: A Journal of Mormon Thought
Dimensions (ceased pub 1971)
Diogenes   Italy
Dissent
Duquesne Review (ceased pub 1973)

## E

Early American Literature
Eastern Horizon   Hong Kong
Economic Geography
Eighteenth Century Life
Encounter   Great Britain
Encounter
Escribano
Esprit   France
Essex Institute Historical Collections
Ethnicity
Ethnohistory

Ethnology (AIA)
Études   France

## F

Feminist Studies
Film and History
Film Heritage
Filson Club History Quarterly
Florida Historical Quarterly
Focus/Midwest
Foreign Service Journal
Foundations: A Baptist Journal of History and Theology
Frankfurter Hefte   German Federal Republic
Freedom at Issue
Freedomways
Freeman
French Historical Studies
Frontier   Great Britain

## G

Geist und Tat (ceased pub 1971)   German Federal Republic
Georgia Historical Quarterly
Georgia Review

## H

Hacettepe Bulletin of Social Sciences and Humanities   Turkey
Halve Maen
Harvard Educational Review
Harvard Library Bulletin
Hawaiian Journal of History
High Country
Historian
Historic Preservation
Historical and Scientific Society of Manitoba Papers (old title, see Transactions of the Historical and Scientific Society of Manitoba)   Canada
Historical Journal of Western Massachusetts
Historical Magazine of the Protestant Episcopal Church
Historical Methods Newsletter
Historical New Hampshire
Historical Reflections   Canada
Historical Review of Berks County
History of Childhood Quarterly: The Journal of Psychohistory (old title, see Journal of Psychohistory)
History of Education Quarterly
History Teacher
History Today   Great Britain
Horizon
Horizons: The Marxist Quarterly (ceased pub 1969)   Canada
Human Organization
Huntington Library Quarterly

## I

Idaho Yesterdays
Indian Historian
Indian Journal of American Studies   India
Indian Sociological Bulletin (old title, see International Journal of Contemporary Sociology)   India
Indiana Magazine of History
Indiana Social Studies Quarterly
Industrial and Labor Relations Review
Industrial Relations   Canada
Information Historique   France
Inland Seas
International Journal of Comparative Sociology   Canada
International Migration Review
International Social Science Journal   France
International Socialist Review
Interplay (ceased pub 1971)
Isis
Italian Americana

## J

Jahrbuch für Amerikastudien (old title, see Amerikastudien/American Studies)   German Federal Republic
Jewish Social Studies

Journal for the Scientific Study of Religion
Journal of American Folklore
Journal of American History
Journal of American Studies   Great Britain
Journal of Arizona History
Journal of Asian Studies
Journal of Black Studies
Journal of Business
Journal of Canadian Studies   Canada
Journal of Church and State
Journal of Communication
Journal of Developing Areas
Journal of Economic History
Journal of Economic Literature
Journal of Ecumenical Studies
Journal of Ethnic Studies
Journal of Forest History
Journal of Higher Education
Journal of Historical Studies (ceased pub 1970)
Journal of Human Relations (suspended pub 1973)
Journal of Interdisciplinary History
Journal of Intergroup Relations
Journal of Jazz Studies
Journal of Library History, Philosophy, and
   Comparative Librarianship
Journal of Long Island History
Journal of Marriage and the Family (AIA)
Journal of Mississippi History
Journal of Negro Education
Journal of Negro History
Journal of Peace Research   Norway
Journal of Political and Military Sociology
Journal of Political Economy
Journal of Politics
Journal of Popular Culture
Journal of Popular Film (old title, see Journal of
   Popular Film and Television)
Journal of Presbyterian History
Journal of San Diego History
Journal of Social History
Journal of Social Issues
Journal of Southern History
Journal of Sport History
Journal of the Canadian Church Historical Society
   Canada
Journal of the History of Ideas
Journal of the History of Medicine and Allied
   Sciences
Journal of the History of the Behavioral Sciences
Journal of the Illinois State Historical Society
Journal of the Lancaster County Historical Society
Journal of the Rutgers University Library
Journal of the Society of Architectural Historians
Journal of the Universalist Historical Society
Journal of the West
Journal of Urban History
Journalism Quarterly
Judicature

### K

Kansas Historical Quarterly (superseded by Kansas
   History)
Kansas Quarterly
Kentucky Folklore Record
Kiva
Kroeber Anthropological Society Papers

### L

Labor History
Law and Society Review
Liberal Education
Liberation
Library Chronicle of the University of Texas
Library Quarterly
Lincoln Herald
Long Island Forum
Louisiana History
Louisiana Studies (old title, see Southern Studies: An
   Interdisciplinary Journal of the South)
Lutheran Quarterly (ceased pub 1977)

### M

Mankind
Manuscripts
Marine Corps Gazette
Maryland Historian
Maryland Historical Magazine
Massachusetts Historical Society Proceedings
Massachusetts Review
Masterkey
Medicinhistorisk Årsbok (old title, see Nordisk
   Medicinhistorisk Årsbok)   Sweden

Mennonite Life
Mennonite Quarterly Review
Methodist History
Michigan Academician
Michigan History
Michigan Quarterly Review
Mid-America
MidContinent American Studies Journal (old title,
   see American Studies)
Midstream
Midwest Journal of Political Science (old title, see
   American Journal of Political Science)
Midwest Quarterly
Military Review
Minnesota History
Mississippi Quarterly
Missouri Historical Review
Missouri Historical Society Bulletin
Modern Age
Montana Magazine of History (old title, see
   Montana: Magazine of Western History)
Montana: Magazine of Western History
Montclair Journal of Social Sciences and Humanities
   (ceased
Monthly Labor Review
Monthly Review
Museum of Fine Arts, Boston.

### N

Names
National Civic Review
National Genealogical Society Quarterly
Nebraska History
Negro History Bulletin
Nevada Historical Society Quarterly
New England Historical and Genealogical Register
New England Quarterly
New Generation
New Jersey History
New Mexico Historical Review
New Scholar
New South (superseded by Southern Voices)
New York Affairs
New York Folklore Quarterly (superseded by New
   York Folklore)
New York Historical Society Quarterly
New York History
New Zealand Journal of History   New Zealand
Newberry Library Bulletin
New-England Galaxy
Newport History
New-York Historical Society Quarterly
Nineteenth-Century Fiction
North American Review
North Carolina Folklore (old title, see North
   Carolina Folklore Journal)
North Carolina Historical Review
North Dakota History
North Dakota Quarterly
North Jersey Highlander
North Louisiana Historical Association Journal
Northwest Ohio Quarterly: a Journal of History and
   Civilization
Northwestern Report
Norwegian-American Studies and Records (old title,
   see Norwegian-American Studies)
Noticias
Nouvelle Revue des Deux Mondes   France
Nova Scotia Historical Quarterly   Canada
Now and Then
Nuova Antologia   Italy

### O

Ohio History
Old-Time New England
Ontario History   Canada
Oral History Review
Oregon Historical Quarterly
Organon (ceased pub 1972)

### P

Pacific Historian
Pacific Historical Review
Pacific Northwest Quarterly
Pacific Sociological Review
Palacio
Palimpsest
Pan-African Journal   Kenya
Papers in Anthropology, University of Oklahoma
Papers of the Bibliographical Society of America
Partisan Review
Pennsylvania Folklife

Pennsylvania History
Pennsylvania Magazine of History and Biography
Perspectives in American History
Phylon
Plains Anthropologist
Plateau
Polar Record   Great Britain
Policy Studies Journal
Polish American Studies
Political Science   New Zealand
Political Science Quarterly
Politics and Society
Polity
Population Studies   Great Britain
Princeton University Library Chronicle
Problemi di Ulisse   Italy
Proceedings of the Academy of Political Science
Proceedings of the American Antiquarian Society
Proceedings of the American Philosophical Society
Proceedings of the New Jersey Historical Society
   (old title, see New Jersey History)
Progressive Labor
Prologue: the Journal of the National Archives
Protée   Canada
Psychiatry: Journal for the Study of Interpersonal
   Processes
Public Administration Review
Public Interest
Public Opinion Quarterly
Public Policy
Public Welfare

### Q

Quaker History
Quarterly Journal of Economics
Quarterly Journal of Speech
Quarterly Journal of Studies on Alcohol (old title,
   see Journal of Studies on Alcohol)
Quarterly Journal of the Library of Congress
Queen's Quarterly   Canada

### R

Race
Radford Review (ceased pub 1972)
Radical America
Recherches Sociographiques   Canada
Record
Records of the American Catholic Historical Society
   of Philadelphia
Red River Valley Historical Review
Register of the Kentucky Historical Association
Religion in Life
Rendezvous
Research Studies
Review of Economics and Statistics
Review of Politics
Review of Radical Political Economics
Review of Social Economy
Reviews in American History
Revista de Ciencias Sociales  [Puerto Rico]
Revista/Review Interamericana   Puerto Rico
Revue de l'Université d'Ottawa   Canada
Revue de l'Université Laval (ceased pub 1966)
   Canada
Revue d'Histoire de l'Amérique Française  [Canada]
Revue d'Histoire Moderne et Contemporaine
   France
Revue Française d'Histoire d'Outre-Mer   France
Revue Internationale de Droit Comparé   France
Rhode Island History
Rhode Island Jewish Historical Notes
Richmond County History
Rochester History
Rocky Mountain Social Science Journal (old title,
   see Social Science Journal)
Rural Sociology

### S

Samtiden   Norway
San José Studies
Saskatchewan History   Canada
Science
Science and Public Affairs (see Bulletin of the
   Atomic Scientists)
Science and Society
Sessions d'Étude: Société Canadienne d'Histoire de
   l'Église Catholique (published simultaneously in
   one volume with Study Sessions: Canadian
   Catholic Historical Association)   Canada
Signs: Journal of Women in Culture and Society
Slovakia
Smith College Studies in Social Work

Smithsonian
Social Casework
Social Education
Social Forces
Social History   Canada
Social Policy
Social Problems
Social Science
Social Science Quarterly
Social Science Research Council Items
Social Service Review
Social Studies
Social Theory and Practice
Social Work
Societas
Society
Sociological Analysis
Sociological Inquiry   Canada
Sociological Quarterly
Sociology and Social Research
Sociology of Education
Soundings (Nashville, TN)
South Atlantic Quarterly
South Carolina Historical Magazine
South Carolina History Illustrated (ceased pub 1970)
South Carolina Review
South Dakota History
Southeast Asia
Southern California Quarterly
Southern Economic Journal
Southern Exposure
Southern Folklore Quarterly
Southern Humanities Review
Southern Literary Journal
Southern Quarterly
Southern Review
Southern Speech Communication Journal
Southern Speech Journal (old title, see Southern Speech Communication Journal)
Southwest Review
Southwestern Art
Southwestern Historical Quarterly
Southwestern Social Science Quarterly (old title, see Social Science Quarterly)
Sovetskaia Etnografiia   Union of Soviet Socialist Republic
Speech Monographs (old title, see Communication Monographs)
Staten Island Historian
Studies in History and Society
Study Sessions: Canadian Catholic Historical Association (published simultaneously in one volume with Sessions d'Étude: Société Canadienne d'Histoire de l'Église Catholique) Canada

Survey   Great Britain
Swedish Pioneer Historical Quarterly
Synthesis

## T

Teachers College Record
Technology and Culture
Tennessee Folklore Society Bulletin
Tennessee Historical Quarterly
Tequesta
Texana (ceased pub 1974)
Texas Quarterly
Thought
Trans-Action: Social Science and Modern Society (old title, see Society)
Transactions of the Historical and Scientific Society of Manitoba   Canada
TriQuarterly
Twentieth Century   Great Britain

## U

United States Naval Institute Proceedings
Universalist Historical Society Journal
University of Toronto Quarterly   Canada
University of Wyoming Publications
Urban Affairs Quarterly
Urban and Social Change Review
Urban Review
Utah Historical Quarterly

## V

Ventures (ceased pub 1971)
Vermont History
Viewpoints: Georgia Baptist History
Virginia Cavalcade
Virginia Law Review
Virginia Magazine of History and Biography
Virginia Quarterly Review

## W

Washington Monthly
West Tennessee Historical Society Papers

West Virginia History
Western American Literature
Western Explorer (ceased pub 1968)
Western Folklore
Western Historical Quarterly
Western Humanities Review
Western Pennsylvania Historical Magazine
Western Political Quarterly
Western Review (ceased pub 1973)
Western Speech (old title, see Western Speech Communication)
Western States Jewish Historical Quarterly
Westport Historical Quarterly
Westways
William and Mary Quarterly
Wilson Library Bulletin
Winterthur Portfolio
Wisconsin Magazine of History
Wisconsin Then and Now
Women's Studies
Working Papers for a New Society
World Affairs
World Marxist Review   Canada
Worldview
Wyoming Archaeologist (AIA)

## Y

Yale Alumni Magazine (AIA)
Yale University Library Gazette
York State Tradition (ceased pub 1974)
Youth and Society

# FESTSCHRIFTEN

Clio's Consciousness Raised: New Perspectives on the History of Women (New York: Harper Torchbooks, 1974).

Essays on American Literature in Honor of Jay B. Hubbell (Durham: Duke U. Pr., 1967).

Liberating Women's History: Theoretical and Critical Essays (Chicago: U. of Illinois Pr., 1976).

Remember the Ladies: New Perspectives on Women in American History—Essays in Honor of Nelson Manfred Blake (Syracuse: Syracuse U. Pr., 1975).

Women in the World: A Comparative Study (Santa Barbara: Clio Books, 1976).

# LIST OF ABSTRACTERS

## A

Abramoske, D. J.
Adams, G. R.
Adams, R. K.
Adelfang, K.
Agee, W. H.
Ahern, W. H.
Aimone, A. C.
Allen, C. R.
Allen, R. F.
Alvis, R. N.
Andrew, J.
Anness, D.
Appel, J. J.
Aptheker, H.
Athey, L. L.

## B

Banks, S. L.
Barach, M. J.
Bardsley, V. O.
Barkan, E. R.
Bassett, T. D. S.
Bassler, G.
Bates, C.
Bauer, K. J.
Baylen, J. O.
Beaber, P. A.
Beauchamp, E. R.
Beauregard, E. E.
Bedford, H. F.
Bedford, W. B.
Belles, A. G.
Benson, J. A.
Benthuysen, R. Van
Berman, M.
Bishop, C. A.
Bobango, G. J.
Boedecker, W. R.
Boehm, A.
Bolton, G. A.
Born, J. D.
Bottorff, W. K.
Bowers, D. E.
Bowers, W. L.
Brandes, J.
Brescia, A. M.
Brewster, D. E.
Brinley, J. E.
Brockman, N.
Brockway, D.
Broderick, D.
Broussard, J. H.
Brown, D. N.
Brown, J. S.
Bruntjen, S.
Buckman, W. A.
Bumsted, J. M.
Burckel, N. C.
Burke, R. S.
Burns, H. M.
Burns, R. S.
Butchart, R. E.
Butcher, K.
Byrne, P. R.

## C

Calkin, H. L.
Calvert, R. V.
Cameron, D. D.
Campion, M.
Carp, E. W.
Carter, V. J.
Casada, J. A.
Castillo, R. Griswold del
Chan, L. B.
Chappell, K.
Chaput, D.
Chard, D. F.
Coates, W. H.
Coats, A. W.
Coberly, J.
Cohen, R. D.
Coleman, P. J.
Collon, C.
Colwell, J. L.
Comegys, R. G.
Condon, T. M.
Cook, J. F.

Costello, E. P.
Cripps, T. R.
Crook, L. C.
Crossley, W. H.
Crowe, J. C.
Curl, D. W.

## D

Davis, D. G.
Davis, K. P.
Davison, S. R.
Delaney, R. W.
Detrick, R. H.
Dewees, A. C.
Dibert, M. D.
Dodd, D. B.
Doyle, G. D.
Drescher, N. M.
Drummond, B. A.
Dubay, R. W.
Duff, J. B.
Duguid, S. R.
Duniway, D. C.

## E

Eads, O. W.
Earnhart, H. G.
Eichelberger, C. L.
Eid, L.
Eiel, C. G.
Emery, G.
Eminhizer, E. E.
Engler, D. J.
Erlebacher, A.
Evans, H. M.

## F

Falk, J. D.
Farnham, T. J.
Fenske, B. L.
Filipiak, J. D.
Filler, L.
Findlay, J.
Findling, J. E.
Fishman, G. M.
Flack, J. K.
Flynt, A. W.
Flynt, J. W.
Fox, W. L.
Frame, R. M., III.
Frank, S. H.
Frank, W. C.
Franz, D. A.
Frazier, J.
Freedman, A. S.
Frey, M. L.
Fulton, R. T.
Furdell, W. J.

## G

Gagnon, G. O.
Gallacci, C. A.
Gallagher, D. P.
Gamer, N.
Gammage, J.
Gara, L.
Garfinkle, R. A.
Garland, A. N.
Gassner, J. S.
Genung, M.
German, J. C.
Gersman, E. M.
Gillam, M. R.
Gilmont, K. E.
Glasrud, B. A.
Glen, R.
Goldstein, K.
Gorchels, C. C.
Graham, H. J.
Grant, C. L.
Grant, H. R.
Grollman, C.
Grothaus, L. H.
Groves, J. V.
Gustafson, P.

## H

Hamilton, A. J.
Hamilton, C. G.
Hanks, R. J.
Harahan, J. P.
Harling, F. F.
Harrold, F.
Harrow, S.
Harvey, K. A.
Hathaway, E. W.
Hawes, J. M.
Hayes, M. A.
Hazelton, J. L.
Hedrick, D. M.
Held, C.
Henderson, D. F.
Hendrickson, K. E.
Herbst, J.
Herman, P. T.
Herman, T. Z.
Hewlett, G. A.
Hillje, J. W.
Hobson, W. K.
Hočevar, T.
Hofeling, L. P.
Hoffman, A.
Hogeboom, W. L.
Holzinger, J.
Horn, D. E.
Hough, M.
Howell, R.
Hubbard, L. L.
Huff, A. V.
Human, V. L.
Humphreys, S. E.
Hundert, E. J.
Hyslop, E. C.

## J

James, D. C.
Jamieson, D. R.
Jensen, J.
Johnson, B. D.
Johnson, D. W.
Johnson, E. D.
Johnson, E. S.
Johnson, L. F.
Jones, G. H. G.
Jones, S. L.
Jonsson, P. O.
Jordan, H. D.
Judd, J.

## K

Kaufman, M.
Keiser, J. H.
Kellogg, M. K.
Kelsey, G. H.
Kelsey, H.
Kennedy, P. W.
Kicklighter, J. A.
Klutts, W. A.
Knafla, L. A.
Krenkel, J. H.
Krichmar, A.
Kroeger, M.
Kroeger, M. J.
Kubicek, R. V.
Kuhn, M. C.
Kuntz, N. A.
Kurland, G.

## L

Lampe, A. B.
Lange, R. B.
Larsen, W. R.
Larson, A. J.
Lawrance, A. H.
LeBlanc, A. E.
LeBris, C. P.
Lederer, N.
Legters, L. H.
Leonard, I. M.
Lewis, J.
Lewis, J. A.
Lindsey, D.
Lohof, B. A.

Lokken, R. N.
Loose, J. W. W.
Lottich, K. V.
Lovin, H. T.
Lowitt, R.
Lucas, M. B.
Lycan, G. L.
Lydon, J. G.

## M

Machan, M. W.
Mahoney, J. F.
Main, A. K.
Malyon, H.
Marks, H. S.
Marr, W. L.
Marshall, P. C.
Marti, D. B.
McAuley, Sr. M.
McBaine, M. J.
McBaine, R. V.
McCarthy, E.
McCarthy, J. M.
McClure, P.
McCusker, J. J.
McCutcheon, J.
McGinty, G. W.
McKinney, G. B.
McKinstry, E. R.
McMahon, C. P.
McNeel, S. L.
McNiff, W. J.
Melamed, R. S.
Metz, W. D.
Miller, O. L.
Miller, R. M.
Miller, W. B.
Mitchell, R. G.
Moen, N. W.
Mohl, R. A.
Moore, R. J.
Morgan, W. G.
Morrison, B. M.
Mulligan, W. H.
Murdoch, D. H.
Murdock, E. C.
Murphy, F. I.
Murphy, M. P.
Myres, S. L.

## N

Negaard, H. A.
Nelson, L. G.
Newman, B.
Newton, C. A.
Nichols, R. L.
Nielson, D. G.
Noppen, I. W. Van

## O

Oaks, R. F.
O'Brien, E. J.
Ogilvie, C. F.
Ohl, J. K.
Ohrvall, C. W.
Olbrich, W. L.
Olson, C. W.
Olson, G. L.
Orr, R. B.
Osur, A. M.
Overbeck, J. A.
Owen, G. L.

## P

Panting, G. E.
Parker, H. M.
Patterson, S. L.
Paul, B. J.
Paul, J. F.
Pearson, S. C.
Peltier, D. P.
Peterson, N. L.
Petrie, M.
Picht, D. R.
Pickens, D. K.
Pickett, R. S.
Piehl, C. K.

Piersen, W. D.
Pliska, S. R.
Pollaczek, F.
Porter, B. S.
Pouncey, L.
Powell, H. B.
Pragman, J. H.
Proschansky, H.
Puffer, K. J.
Pula, J. S.

## Q

Quinlan, M. H.
Quinlan, S. J.
Quinten, B. T.

## R

Rabin, J.
Rabineau, P.
Raife, L.
Ramirez, N. E.
Rasmussen, J. L.
Ratliff, W. E.
Reid, W. S.
Rein, S. A.
Rex, M. B.
Rhodes, B. D.
Richardson, D. R.
Ritter, R. V.
Rollins, A. B.
Rollins, R. M.
Rosen, H. M.
Rosenthal, F.
Roske, R. J.
Rossi, D. F.
Rotondaro, F.
Rowe, D. L.
Russell, L.

## S

Sapper, N. G.
Savitt, T. L.
Schalck, H.
Schoonover, T. D.
Schroeder, C. B.
Scrivner, J. H.
Selleck, R. G.
Sevilla, S.
Sexauer, R.
Shapiro, E. S.
Shapiro, V.
Sharrer, G. T.
Silveri, L. D.
Simmerman, T.
Simon, P. L.
Skau, G. H.
Sloan, D. A.
Small, M.
Smith, C. O.
Smith, D. L.
Smith, G. P.
Smith, J. D.
Smith, L.
Smith, L. C.
Smith, L. D.
Smith, R. A.
Smith, T. W.
Snow, G. E.
Soff, H. G.
Sprague, S. S.
Stelzner, H. G.
Stickney, E. P.
Stockstill, M.
Stoesen, A. R.
Storey, K. S.
Stout, L. J.
Strain, R.
Street, J. B.
Street, N. J.
Susskind, J. L.
Sussman, L.
Swanson, B. E.
Sweetland, J. H.
Swift, B. B.
Swift, D. C.
Swift, D. H.

## T

Tate, M. L.
Taylorson, P.
Thacker, J. W.
Tharaud, B. C.
Thibault, C.
Thomas, P. D.
Tissing, R. W.
Tomlinson, R. H.
Trauth, M. P.
Trennert, R. A.
Trickey, D. J.
Turner, A.

Tutorow, N. E.

## U

Upton, L. F. S.
Utt, R. L.

## V

Verner, J. G.

Vivian, J. F.

## W

Waldo, G.
Ward, H. M.
Warren, C. N.
Washburn, D. E.
Wechman, R. J.
Wentworth, M. J.

West, K. B.
Wharton, D. P.
White, L. J.
Whitham, W. B.
Wiederrecht, A. E.
Wiegand, W. A.
Wilkins, B.
Will, L. G.
Williams, D. G.
Williams, J. W.
Williamson, M. M.
Willigan, W. L.
Wilson, M. T.
Woodward, R. L.
Wurtz, R. J.

## Y

Yanchisin, D. A.
Young, A. P.
Young, C. P. de

## Z

Zabel, J. A.
Zabel, O. H.
Ziewacz, L. E.
Zilversmit, A.
Zornow, W. F.